THE MOTHER
OF ALL
WINDOWS™
BOOKS

Being a compendium of incantations,
imprecations, supplications, and mollifications
known to appease the daemons within Windows.

Woody Leonhard & Barry Simon

Addison-Wesley Publishing Company
Reading, Massachusetts Menlo Park, California New York
Don Mills, Ontario Wokingham, England Amsterdam Bonn
Sydney Singapore Tokyo Madrid San Juan
Paris Seoul Milan Mexico City Taipei

ISBN 0-201 62475-3
ISBN 0-201-62708-6

Cover design by: Barbara T. Atkinson

Set in 11-point Garamond by Benchmark Productions, Inc.

1 2 3 4 5 6 7 8 9-BAH-9796959493

First printing, October 1993

Addison-Wesley books are available for bulk purchases by corporations, institutions, and other organizations. For more information please contact the Corporate, Government, and Special Sales Department at (617) 944-3700 x2915.

Part of the proceeds from this book will be used to help Tibetan refugees and their families, most of whom live in relocation camps in India.

If you're curious about the plight of these horribly oppressed people and their rapidly vanishing way of life — or if you can find it in your heart to aid their children — please contact:

Tibetan Children's Fund
637 South Broadway
#B125
Boulder, CO 80303

CompuServe: GO TIBET

Dedicated to our Moms,
Rubye and Minnie;
and our kids' Moms,
Martha and Linda.

Contents

SECTION 1: HACKER'S GUIDE TO THE UNIVERS

CHAPTER 1

GUI, Phooey, Kablooey..1

CHAPTER 2

Windows Concepts 17

CHAPTER 12
Mom's Utilities 807

Do You Need This Book?

Somehow you managed to get Windows working. You played around with icons long enough to get mondo-bored. You figured out how to double-click on an icon, to make a program spring to life; and you figured out that the little up-arrow makes a window bigger, the down-arrow makes it smaller. *Rocket science, eh?*

You aren't a dummy. Good. I'm not either. What you want is a bit of advice, a touch of help, maybe a nudge in the right direction, a little enlightenment ... not a put-down. Oh. And it wouldn't hurt if the ludicrous computer jargon were kept to a minimum.

So you threw away some money on an "Intro to" Windows book. It showed you how to double-click on icons, how to type numbers into the calculator, and how to click on the up-arrow and the down-arrow. It's probably sitting on your bookshelf right now.

You bought an "Advanced" Windows book, but couldn't really care less about the settings for Miss Daisywheel drivers, or the key combinations that turn your Electric Pencil text green. It's probably on your bookshelf, too, gathering dust right next to the "Intro" book.

You have a few Windows applications — probably the biggies, like Excel or Word or Quattro Pro or WordPerfect — and you (or your company) spent major league bucks for 'em. You've tried and tried, crashed Windows a few times, pulled your hair out, and wondered how something that looks so simple can be so damn hard.

Most of all, you have a pile of work to be done, and you're starting to wonder how in the blue blazes Windows is going to help you do it.

Guess what?

You're in the right place.

The Mother of All Windows Books — *MOM* for short — won't concentrate on explaining how to move an icon, or show you ten different key combinations that will rearrange File Manager's windows. If you don't know that stuff already, and really want to know, you can always hit F1 and find the answer in a split-second. No need to disturb the dust on those books.

MOM won't waste your time going over the details of the Windows clock, calculator, or calendar. Instead of telling you how to use Windows Write, for example, Mom will tell you why and when Write may be the right solution to a real-live problem. If it's the right tool, you can spend three minutes working with it — instead of twenty minutes reading about it — and get the job done. Just like that. You get the idea.

MOM won't stun you with the intricacies of programming Windows. While taming Windows with custom programs is much, much simpler than you might think — if you know Basic or any macro language, you're ready to start — there's already a book on that topic, *Windows 3.1 Programming for Mere Mortals* (Addison-Wesley, 1992).

Nope. *MOM* shoots for the middle ground. *MOM*'s going to show you how to really *use* Windows, how all sorts of folks use Windows, every day. How to beat the beast into submission. How to get some work out of those fancy-schmancy applications. And you won't need a degree in Computer Science to follow along. Promise.

MOM delves deep into important topics, ferreting out information buried deep in boring technical references, presenting it to you in ways you can use. Take fonts for example. *MOM* doesn't merely list common TrueType fonts or expound on plotter fonts (which you don't — and shouldn't! — care about anyway). Instead, *MOM* takes you behind the scenes. Shows you the differences that matter. Explains it all in plain English. Tells you when and if you need TrueType or PostScript Type 1 fonts. Shows you which font packages might be worth buying. Steps you through some of the tools that turn fonts every which way but loose. And solves real problems you hit every day — one favorite is entering those funny characters that aren't on your keyboard, like ¢ or • or " or ". It's easy when you know how. *MOM* tells all.

MOM also shows you how to do Windows better. What hardware works, what doesn't. How to tweak and kick and cajole Windows into being all it can be. How to use Windows applications together to get stuff out the door, get home earlier at night. Important things.

More than that, *MOM*'s CD (we call it CD-Mom) is the most useful collection of Windows software ever assembled.

Ever wondered what it's really like using Ami Pro, on your machine, with your work? Can't tell from the reviews if Quark will do what you want? CD-Mom includes an enormous selection of working models from the major software vendors: simply copy the files to your hard disk, install the model, and you can go for a test drive, right there on your own machine.

But wait! There's more! CD-Mom is chock full of software you need. Updated video and printer drivers. Shareware. Freeware. Fonts. Icons. Sound files. Wallpaper. Utilities. Games. Applications. Add-ons. Replacements. Improvements. Use just a few of those files and you'll pay for the CD over and over again. It's a first; MOM's heart is pounding with pride at being able to bring it to you.

MOM will take you where no book has gone before.

We'll have a bit of fun along the way. It won't hurt one little bit. You'll see.

Castigat Ridendo Mores[†]

Woody Leonhard
Coal Creek Canyon, Colorado

Barry Simon
Los Angeles, California

[†] Figuratively, *a laugh will work when a lecture won't.*

What You Should Have

If this were a software package, it would say **Requires Windows 3.1 running in 386 Enhanced mode; mouse highly recommended**. Oh, you can learn a lot about Windows here, even if you are running Windows 3.0 in Standard mode. However, we aren't going to normally tell you what is 3.1 specific and we won't cover the places where Standard and Enhanced modes differ. For example, we'll only talk about Enhanced mode **PIF**s. Let's take the requirements one at a time and see why they are there.

First Windows 3.1. The upgrade is a no brainer. If you use Windows enough to even think about buying a book on it, you should have upgraded to Windows 3.1. The stability of the product is enough improved over 3.0, that that alone is cause to run out and get it. But there is much, much more from TrueType and Sound to a vastly improved File Manager. If your, er, Mom only gave you enough money to buy this book or the upgrade, the choice is clear — get the upgrade. But come back next week and buy the book.

Oh, a hint about books, a kind of, er, Windows 3.1 Books Secrets. The ones that still have Windows 3.1 marked in the margin are usually the ones that were written based on the Windows 3.1 beta and are basically Windows 3.0 retreads.

Next, Enhanced mode. There are a few good reasons to be in Standard rather than Enhanced mode. The legitimate one, first — if you have a 286-based computer, you are stuck with Standard mode. We won't be glib about going out and getting an upgrade, but it is something to consider.

Other reasons that people give are less valid. They'll tell you that Enhanced mode is unstable on their systems. Windows 3.0 Enhanced mode was flaky for many but that's gone for most with Windows 3.1. If you have problems with Enhanced mode, read the readme files for tips, get a new video driver, ask questions on CompuServe — you'll be up in running in no time. And the statement that Windows using only Winapps runs faster in Standard mode is true but the difference is so small as to be insignificant.

On the other hand, there are a significant number of programs and even hardware coming out which require Enhanced mode. If you use any DOS programs,

Enhanced mode lets you run them in a Window and provides services that gives you significantly more memory for DOS programs than you'd get in Standard mode.

What about Windows NT and Windows for Workgroups? Even the Windows NT product manager has said that 90% of desktops have no reason for running NT. The *raison d'etre* for NT is to capture the enterprise wide operations as it moves down from mainframes. If Microsoft can make noise about power users and thereby kick some sand in OS/2's eyes while doing this, it figures that it may as well. But the upgrade path to 32 bit nirvana for Windows users will be 4.0. The NT desktop pioneers will have a lot of arrows in their backs. This book is not for them.

As for Windows for Workgroups, if you are running that, this book is for you because you are running Windows 3.1 but with a network – in many way, your Windows needs are not much different from Netware or Lantastic or ... users. A few of the applets have changed slightly, notably FileMan and we'll talk about the non-workgroups versions, but on the whole this is the book for you if you are running Windows for Workgroups and what to know general things about Windows.

Finally, the mouse. We'll have a lot to say about when to use a mouse and more importantly, when not to. But we'll skip the keyboard when a program provides access to some function with a click or two with a mouse and has a keyboard route that is clearly an afterthought added when someone in marketing said "But what if they don't have a mouse?" Since we feel that the keyboard is often more efficient than the mouse, you'll see lots about keyboard here – the **mouse recommended** is more to say, we don't feel forced to always talk about the keyboard equivalent and won't, for example, ever mention Program Manager's **Move** menu command since dragging with the mouse is clearly the way to go to move icons from one group to another.

Conventions

Most of *MOM* is in plain English. Sometimes, though, *MOM* has to lapse into computer-speak — as infrequently as possible, I promise! — and when computer terminology comes to the forefront, conventions can't be far behind.

I'll put file names in a different font, just to warn you that a computer thing is coming. Like this: `autoexec.bat`. Stuff on the menus will receive similar treatment; I might say: Click `File` then `Exit`. Rarely I'll talk about pushing keys (ach! so *pedestrian!*), but if I want you to hold down two or more keys at once I'll use a `+` plus sign, e.g.: `Ctrl+Alt+Del`.

So much for the technical gobbledygook.

Let me introduce you to the cast and crew, the folks who carry this little soapless opera to its muddied conclusion. *Look, Harry! It's a computer book. No, it's a novel. No, it's a floor wax. Wait! It's all three!*

You'll find a few odd people populating these pages. Each has a special role in life, a *MOM raison d'etre*, as it were; each should draw your attention to important points.

 First is Mom herself. Mom will start talking whenever there's a bit of motherly advice floating around. "Whattsamattah, you? It's raining outside. Wear your rubbers." That kind of thing.

Like your Mom — or at least *my* Mom — this Mom is a mixture of emotion, silliness, and gems of wisdom. She knows a mouse from a molehill. She doesn't take any backtalk. These multi-billion-dollar computer companies and publishing conglomerates don't faze her. And she doesn't refrain from the lectures, no sireeeeee. . .

 Second is my long-time sidekick Igor. He says his name is pronounced "Eeeee-eeeegore," not "Eye-gore," and he gets mad when folks get it wrong. *Believe me, you don't want to get Igor mad.* His purpose on these pages is to point out the stuff that could prove detrimental to your health. Gaps in Windows. Problems with applications. Even the "B" word. . .Bugs.

xxii   •   Conventions

Igor's full name: Igor Guido Salvatorre. He's the product of a proud Rumanian mother and a strict San Marinese father. San Marino, the smallest and oldest republic in Europe, is a tiny enclave carved out of Northern Italy. But then you knew that, didn't you? *Hey, you were smart enough to get this book... no dummies here...*

Igor learned the English phrase "yes, master," at his mother's knee; that helped convince Mom to bring him in as part of the team. He speaks Italian, Rumanian, English, and Brooklyn, more or less fluently, and sometimes all at once. Mom finally decided on Igor when she overheard someone saying, "He's a real hit, man." For Igor was trained by his father's ... er ... family.

 Finally, please greet CTO Mao, Mom's major-domo. *Minor, too.* Once upon a time he was Chairman, master of all he surveyed, but like so many other technoids who made it to the top, he decided to step aside and let things go to hell at the hands of marketing slime.

As Mom's Chief Technical Officer, CTO Mao is the tips man, the one who doles out words of wisdom — whether you want 'em or not — straight from his little red book.

That's the *MOM* pantheon, the celestial celebrities, the icons incarnate. Do pay attention please. Especially when Igor gets his dander up. You never know how he'll react....

Dander, huh? Lemme tell ya something. I'm suspicious of the Microsoft crowd. They're my type, but they ain't my family, ya know. I don't turn my back on 'em.

I'm convinced the 'Softies put out Windows as some kinda plot to make folks buy more hardware. Heard a rumor that Gates bought up rights on all the silicon in Saudi Arabia; they're going to re-name that big desert "Rub al-Billi." And a cousin of mine says Gates is trying to trademark the name "Chip."

Don't discount that hardware theory out of hand, oh enforcer. The view is shared by many in the computer industry who think of Microsoft as the Dark Side of the Force. Certainly, no-one named Ruth works there.

Microsoft *did* sell a few hundred million dollars' worth of mice, but I don't think hardware was the controlling factor in His Gatesness' vision of Windows Everywhere.

Consider, grasshopper: before Windows, *Microsoft Word* ran a very distant second in the word processing market, and Microsoft's spreadsheet — *Multiplan* — might've garnered a 27th place, on a good day with a strong tail wind. Windows has changed all that. Oh, yes, indeed. *Many that are first shall be last; and the last shall be first....*

I admire the Microsoft take-no-prisoners, keep-at-it-'til-you-get-it-right attitude. Reminds me of what I tried to do myself before shifting to the technical side. I'm a student of Chairman Bill and *his* revolution.

 I'm sure that nice Mr. Gates means nobody any harm. Just look at him, that boyish face, those glasses slipping down his nose. Cuddly enough to hug and spank, simultaneously. Surely Microsoft can do no wrong, with a fine boy like that at the helm. But I must say this talk of a divorce with IBM has caused me some sleepless nights. Who's going to take care of the kids?

As for Borland, Igor shies away from them because (he claims) Philippe Kahn looks like a San Marino Inspector of Police. Mao figures anyone with the name Kahn has to be a terror. Mom refuses to listen to anything about Borland because she misunderstood when someone told her Philippe is a sax maniac.

Barry and Woody wrote this book, but they've gone to great pains to fade into the background. Think of them as the crew: invisible and wholly dispensable. Mom, Igor, and Mao are far more interesting than the authors anyway. They kind of moved into the manuscript and took over, evolving a life of their own. Besides, without a doubt, given a choice, you'd much rather meet the three talking heads than the two authors.

At least *I* would.

The CD

Quick. Flip to the back of this book. Go ahead. Do it. There. That plastic thingy inside the back jacket? Look inside.

If you see a CD, you've hit the jackpot. Congratulations. You have chosen well. This must be the CD-ROM edition of *The Mother of All Windows Books.*

If you see two diskettes, but no CD, there should be a coupon in the back that will let you order a CD for ten bucks shipping and handling. Tear it out and send it in. Right away. By the time you get the CD back in the mail, you'll be ready for it.

EVEN IF YOU DON'T OWN A CD-ROM DRIVE!

As long as you can beg, borrow, or steal a CD-ROM drive — and you'll only need it for a few minutes — you'll want that CD. In Chapter 11, we'll show you how to grab stuff off the CD and shove it onto your own diskettes, a bit at a time. It's easy.

Yeah, using the CD is easier and faster if you have a CD-ROM drive on your computer. But the stuff on that CD is so important, you'll want it *even if you have to scale Kachejunga to find a drive.*

CD MOM has so much on it, no serious Windows user should be without it. Dozens of working models, of many top Windows applications, that you can take for a test drive on your own computer. The latest Windows drivers for printers, video cards, sound boards, and much more. A full, commercial copy of WinCIM —for Windows access to CompuServe, plus a free CompuServe sign-up and your first month of basic services free. A hundred shareware and freeware fonts — good ones, not throw-away junk. Video clips. Movie trailers. Thousands of icons. The best electronic newsletters. Concert-quality audio recordings. Fun "system event" sounds. Latest versions of the top 100 Windows shareware and freeware programs — utilities, add-ins, replacements, games, and more — in short, the most useful Windows software collection ever assembled.

You'd spend dozens of hours and hundreds of dollars downloading *just the major parts* of CD MOM from bulletin boards or on-line services — assuming you could find it all. Or you can just pop the CD into your drive (or one at work, at the office, even at a friendly computer store), copy the files you want, and be on your merry way.

Why are there two versions of this book, one with and one without the CD? Glad you asked. The whole concept of CDs in books is new, experimental, something nobody has ever tried before (at least not in a general PC book). Nobody knows if the experiment will work, if Windows users will *insist* on getting the CD.

Matter of fact, some folks are afraid you'll pick up this book, see the CD, then put it back on the shelves right away, assuming that the CD won't do you any good if you don't have a CD-ROM drive on your machine. Nothing could be farther from the truth.

You'll see.

The diskette-only version of *The Mother of All Windows Books* is ten bucks cheaper than the CD version; you end up paying the same amount no matter how you get the CD. It's a hell of a deal, no matter how you cut it.

So order the CD — *now!* — if it isn't in that plastic thingy.

Mom says so.

Igor's Road Map

 This book is. . . well, it is a Mother of a book. I figured that I'd better give you a once over — a sort of preliminary softening up, just as I learned to do in school.

You should think of *MOM* as being in six parts. I guess we have twice as much gall as Caesar.

- Chapters 1 and 2 are conceptual.

- Chapters 3, 4 and 5 are on software utility tools; things that make Windows sing.

- Chapter 6 is a guide to keeping up with Windows — magazines, online services, users groups, stuff like that.

- Chapter 7 is a hardware guide, specifically for Windows. Skim through it to pick up the basics. Memorize it before spending hard bucks on a Windows computer.

- Chapters 8, 9 and 10 are an encyclopedia of initialization files. It's a reference. Don't even think about reading them from beginning to end, unless you have already absorbed the *Encyclopedia Brittanica* the same way.

- Chapters 11 and 12 talk about what's on CD MOM and on the diskettes.

- Chapters 13, 14, and the appendices are a pot pourri of references for icons, fonts, and other goodies. Truly, "all other."

Here's a little more detail.

Chapter 1 sets the stage. You'll likely read it once and never go back to it.

 Chapter 2 is *Windows for Idiots* - NOT! It's for folks who have progressed beyond the quick-fix tips and shortcuts stage. Sure it's nice to see how a Ctrl+F12 in the WhatsIts Manager can cut out a few mouse clicks, or how the Snidely Whiplash App lets you put 4,000 icons at your fingertips. But it's far more important to understand, fundamentally, *what the hell is going on.* That's where Chapter 2 comes in.

Chapter 2 talks about concepts — first for the Windows interface, the foundation of Windows, and then for Windows' parts: images, fonts, sound, color. Chapter 2 is not the sort of place you'll go to figure out exactly how to copy files in File Manager with a minimum number of keystrokes. It's much more important than that.

If you take my advice, you'll reread Chapter 2 every few months. I bet that you will find that each time you read it, you will come away understanding Windows better, simply because of the deeper understanding that you'll be bringing to it.

Chapter 3 starts looking more like a garden-variety kind of Windows book - tips and hints and all that. *Well, it's a little bizarre in places, but still...* Chapter 3 covers the big stuff that comes with Windows, like Program Manager. Chapter 4 continues in the same vein, covering the small stuff, like the sound applets.

 Hey, sonny (or sonnette). Listen up! This is really important. You may figure if the authors say that something is small stuff, you can skip it with impunity. But if you skip Chapter 4, you'll miss the fascinating story of mystery and intrigue that begins in the section called *Le Scandale du Wave Mapper.* It's sort of a Shlock Holmes story, replete with three-dimensional characters, pacing, denouement, and even a happy ending. Igor stands in for LeStrade. Check it out!

Often there are other, add-in products that run rings around Windows, or perform functions that you can't even get with Windows. Chapter 5 contains mini-reviews of the best of these utility products. There *are* some great Windows products that don't come from Redmond.

Chapter 6 discusses sources of more information — from a thorough introduction of CompuServe, the Mother of All Information Services, to how to read a magazine review. Windows is changing so fast that keeping up is an art. It's the kind of thing you won't find in other books simply because, quite frankly, nobody has mastered it. Still, *MOM* gives it the ol' college try.

Chapter 7 is a discussion of hardware, from the (un?)importance of benchmarks, to how a cache can screw up, to why you might want to shell out extra bucks for a wave table sound card. It also introduces a new PC performance benchmark, the ToastedBunnyMark, and a new PC performance *benchamarker's* benchmark, the MhomStone. You'll see.

Chapters 1 through 7 were written so you could read through from start to finish, hopefully without falling asleep, maybe with a chuckle here and there. Even Windows novices — anyone who has taken the Windows on-line tutorial — should be able to pick up quite a bit of information from those chapters.

Not so chapters 8 through 10, which could be subtitled *Everything you wanted to know about ini files but were afraid to ask.* This is the hard-core stuff, the driving force behind Windows. Chapter 8 is on **WIN.INI**, 9 on **SYSTEM.INI** and 10 on the other Windows **INI** files. Only a masochist on a binge would even *consider* reading those end to end. It's bad enough they had to be written that way.

 I tried to make those chapters as readable as I could, considering the *<yawwwwwn!>* subject matter. In fact, I hope Chapters 8, 9 and 10 are more readable than the *non*-technical stuff in the other Windows books. But I don't expect you to read *them* straight through either.

By the way, there's a difference between what I say about **INI** file settings and what the other books say about **INI** file settings. You see, I prodded and poked and tried every bloody setting — almost 300 pages' worth — one by one by one by one. Then I wrote down what I found: the unvarnished, naked, often horrible truth. *I tore out Windows' heart and stomped on it....* Ahem....

There will undoubtedly be mistakes in what I said but they are *my* mistakes. All too often the other references you'll find on **INI** files just copied from the *Windows Resource Kit*, the official Microsoft technical Windows reference. That's why you'll see the same mistakes — the same bum advice — repeated over and over, in book after book after book.

Lemme give you an example, if you know a bit about **INI** files. (If you don't, not to worry; I'll explain it all in Chapter 8.)

Take the **[ports]** section of **win.ini**... please. The *Windows Resource Kit* says **[ports]** is limited to 10 items, ten lines that can be listed after the **[ports]** entry. *WRONG!* Now go to your favorite secret bible of Windows information. Just pluck one off the shelf, or drop by your local bookstore. I bet that book also tells you there's a limit of 10 items, maybe even warning of dire consequences if you should slip and go above ten.

Hey, it says so in the official docs, right? Microsoft never makes mistakes.

Now take a look at *your* **WIN.INI** and count the number of items in the **[ports]** section. I'll bet you dollars to donuts it has more than 10 items. How can I tell? Because if you install a fresh copy of Windows 3.1, it installs with 11 items right then and there, straight out of the box! *Those other books didn't even count the number of ports in their own lousy win.ini.* If you can't trust those books on such simple stuff, how can you trust them on the tricky ones?

I spent months testing every setting in the **INI** files I could get my hands on. What *MOM* says is how it really is, or at least how I *think* it really is — not how the official docs say it should be.

Chapters 11 and 12 explain what is on CD MOM, how to get it off the CD (even if you have to borrow a CD-ROM drive), and how to install what is there. Chapter 12 covers shareware; Chapter 11 goes through everything else. You should break into these chapters when you have some spare time. You'll be rewarded by some truly outstanding extensions to Windows — stuff that can really save you time and money, day after day.

The last chapters and appendices catalog nearly 5,000 icons from CD MOM, and about a thousand fonts. It also includes a list of useful phone numbers/email addresses. Have you misplaced Bill's email address? We'll remind you of it there — and, considering what's good to get goosed has got to get gandered (say *that* ten times real fast), you'll find the authors' CompuServe i.d.s there also.

We don't pull any punches; you'll get the straight, unvarnished truth, as best we can deliver it. Matter of fact, you'll probably find we knock ourselves at least as many times as we knock the big manufacturers. Fair 'nuff. *Quid pro quo* and all that.

In the end, the authors say they hope you have as much fun reading this book as they had writing it. But what the hell do they know. . .

Acknowledgments

Thanks to Justin, Rivka, Sanford, Benny, Zvi, Ari, and Chana, who make it all worthwhile. You lost yet another summer to this particular form of insanity. But, *Oy!* Was it fun.

MOM owes much to Andrew Schulman, who started it all; Claudette Moore, who kept it rolling; and Chris Williams, Amy Pedersen, and Andrew Williams, who did the hard work.

Special thanks to Mom's beta testers, the folks who told us right from wrong, left from right — even when we weren't quite sure which end was up:

Yitzhak Adlerstein, Vince Chen, Paul Friedman, Mike Maurice, Edward Mendelson, Ellen Nagler, Sally Neuman, Robert Norton, Earle Robinson, Monty Schmidt, Andrew Schulman, Steve Shaiman, Sanford and Rivka Weinberg, and others who must (regrettably!) remain nameless..

While we know *MOM* may offend folks in just about every segment of the computer community, we hope that the fire has been evenly applied and that Mom's criticisms are received in the manner in which they were intended: not as condemnation, but as an exhortation to create better products, for more attention to the consumer, easier access for the novice, and above all honesty — *even when it hurts*.

It's inevitable that some folks will come to the conclusion that we don't like Windows, that our railings against the WinDiety amount to condemnation, fear and/or loathing. Not true! Not true! We use Windows all day, every day, and strongly recommend that our friends and family do, too. Microsoft has built a truly magnificent, rich, incredibly robust foundation.

While it has become fashionable to knock Windows and its (significant!) shortcomings, remember that Windows has delivered computing power to millions and millions of people. Because of that fact, Windows — Prometheus in modern, digital clothing — may well be the single most important advance in computer history.

SECTION 1
Hacker's Guide to the Univers

There is nothing uncultivated, nothing sterile, nothing dead in the universe;
there is no chaos, no confusion except in appearance.

— G.W. Leibnitz, *The Monadology*, 1714

 Section 1 introduces the *real* Windows, an odd universe of routines that interact with you and with each other in often strange ways. We'll take you on a quick guided tour, point out the major landmarks, then dive into the belly of the beast. By the time you're done with Section 1, you'll be able to take advantage of many of the manifest wonders within Windows.

Chapter 1 — What Makes Windows Tick (In Five Minutes or Less)

Chapter 2 — Windows Concepts

Chapter 3 — Windows Components

Chapter 4 — Windows Applets

Chapter 5 — Windows Utilities

Chapter 6 — Staying Current

CHAPTER 1

What Makes Windows Tick
(In Five Minutes or Less)

 I don't care *who* this Billy friend of yours is. It don't matter a bit if his family *is* rich — them rich people is different from us anyway. That's the last straw. If people say blasphemous stuff about Billy, I don't want you playing with him or his toys. Ever. *You hear me?*

Our father who art in Redmond

Hallowed be thy DOS. Thy OS/2 come

Thy version 3 be done

on RISC as it was on CISC.

Give us this day our daily update

As we give to them who report all the bugs.

Lead us not into closed systems,

But deliver us from UNIX

As we deliver those who buy our products.

For thine is the platform,

The language and the application

For ever and ever.

Amen.

— From the electronic underground, late 1980s

GUI, Phooey, Kablooey

> You know more than you think you do.
>
> — Dr. Spock, *Baby and Child Care*, 1946

Dr. Spock began his 1946 classic with those words. Almost fifty years later, and in a somewhat different context, it remains true. Why? Because in many cases Windows behaves the way you think it should. And in those trying times, when Windows seems dumber than a horse's ass, once you see how to perform whatever it is you're trying to do, you'll probably remember how to do it.

That's an amazing accomplishment for something as foreign as a computer. Much of the credit goes to Windows' interface, the way Windows presents itself.

What's a GUI?

When OS/2 2.0 hit the streets, war broke out in the online services. Windows and OS/2 factions quickly formed and started firing salvos at each other. Global thermonuclear war had nothing on this raging debate: indeed, if the *real* bomb had dropped, neither side would've stopped for more time than it took to switch on CNN.

During the OS/2 wars, you could instigate a debate by merely calling Windows an "operating system." Windows baiters pointed out that DOS, which operates below Windows, was The True Operating System, like the True Grail or the True Footprint of the Buddha. (As so often happens, operating system Truth lies in the eye of the Beleaguered Beholder, with more to be gained in the pursuit than the possession.)

 This splitting of semantic hairs misses the point of course. To the computer user — you, me, all of us afflicted with this particular obsession — Windows is not merely an operating system, *it's a way of life.*

The user level Windows gestalt, with its roots in Xerox's Palo Alto Research Center and Apple's Macintosh and parallels in Unix's XWindows and NeXT's systems, is called a Graphical User Interface or GUI (pronounced "gooey").

A lot fits under the GUI umbrella:

- conventions for dialogs and mouse actions

- an interface that has common elements across applications

- a sincere attempt to have documents look the same on printer and on screen

- a multi-windowed environment with quick access to many applications

- good inter-connections between applications

Let's take 'em one at a time.

The GUI Interface: Icons, Pointers, and Dialogs

 GUI Interface is a redundancy, isn't it?

 Like saying the hoi polloi?

If you've been in the computer industry for a while, you probably harbor fond memories of older, slightly less capable user interfaces. Twenty five years ago, the computer's maw was stuffed with punched cards.

 Want to add a name to the database? Easy, kid. Here. This is an IBM 029. Don't forget the "0" — that's part of its name. See this stack of cards? Yeah, it has funny little numbers from 1 to 80 going across the top. This 029 is the latest. You can type in 80 alphanumeric characters on a single card. "Alphanumeric" means alphabetic or numbers. You gotta learn the lingo, kiddo. This here 029 cost us ten thousand smackers, but man is it fast. Lesseee. . . Stick the card in here, on the left, see, and push Feed. There. You got it. Ooops. Damn! I forgot to take the program card out of the drum. Wait a second. Errrghh Blrrrffff. . . Heh heh heh. . . Sorry, kid. One cardinal rule of 029 etiquette — never punch with a tie on.

Back then, you prepared your input on punch cards and submitted them as a batch to the operator. If you made a mistake it often took 12 to 24 hours before you learned about it and could correct it. To this day, the term "batch file" survives in Windows, just to remind us of the good old times when card punches and card hole dust presented very real fire hazards.

Then came dumb terminals — initially Teletype terminals, later TV-like screens and keyboards — that let you type in simple commands. Communication back and forth between human and computer proceeded a line at a time. Depending on your perspective, the experience was either leisurely or abominably slow. Commands had carefully defined syntax that you *had* to get right. . . or else.

DOS' command line was built on this model. If you learned the syntax well enough, you could communicate with your beast fairly efficiently. To this day, you occasionally see some old time DOSaholic being dragged to Windows screaming

```
dir *.* /s |find expletive*.* |del
```

complaining about the loss of their beloved command line. (Expletives deleted, of course.)

 The wizened and grizzled old timers, our venerable intellectual elders, are not entirely wrong: No matter how you slice it, some things *are* harder in Windows than they need to be, and there are times I dearly wish I had a command line. But it isn't all that bad. Actually, Windows has a pretty good command line built in — it's called a DOS window. I'll talk more about it later.

The next stage in WinEvolution began with arrival of the menu. "Menu driven" became the rage. The menu is a simple list on the screen with a request for the user to pick a number. DOS menus could drag on forever if the command was complex. Mutations appeared. The bouncing bar menu. Its functional equivalent — the Lotus-style two-lines-at-the-top menu. These made the initial stages of selecting actions easier, but still demanded a lot of the user.

We entered modern pre-history with something that's at the core of many every-day functions of Windows: the dialog box. A dialog box provides a focal point, a single place where you can easily cram a lot of information into the programs you are working with. Or against. That's the thing to remember about dialogs: they're the place where you make your wishes known, where you give Aladdin's Genie his orders.

The flip side of the coin is how to *find* stuff: how to reach the dialogs and get to the programs you want. It gets harder and harder as programs take on more functions. And at this point we broach Windows Recorded History.

Enter the mouse and the icon, stage left.

In addition to text menus, icons — little bits of fluff made up of barely over a thousand dots — have taken over the screen. Often they are inscrutable. It's remarkable what some vendors concoct to put on their buttons and expect us to understand.

And the mouse? Ah, you already know all about *genus Mus*. It's the navigator, natch. We'll have much to say about the nasty little rodent — even if he has become a Microsoft cash cow.

All is not well in Recorded History. *The geese aren't yet honking; Rome may yet burn.*

It's unfortunate, for example, that the Windows programming guidelines don't provide a set of guidelines for button bars ("button bars" is a handy, untrademarked, generic term for collections of icons). A reasonable developer might wonder which icon should be used for FileNew and which for FileSave? And it is unfortunate that it hasn't become standard to have a status bar that tells you what a button does when the mouse pointer is over it. But in spite of these lacks, button bars have become remarkably popular with most users: They're a quick way to get things done. And that's what a good interface is all about.

But what if you hate button bars?

Turn 'em off!

There are two themes that run throughout this book. First, the "P" in PC stands for Personal. It's *your* machine and you should be able to drive it the way you see fit. Windows often has enough flexibility so that one size need not fit all. That's the genius of this particular GUI: it was built so you can take your destiny into your own hands.

Sometimes Windows lacks this flexibility — which leads to the second theme. There are often remarkable third-party software tools available that let you customize Windows to suit *your* needs. We'll tell you all about the best of these tools in Chapter 5, and we'll tell you how to fully utilize the tools that come with Windows, specifically in Chapters 3 and 4.

And that is the future of the GUI interface. Customization. Tweaks. Personality. Originality. *Anarchy. . . sorta. . .*

The Common Interface

> You can't step twice into the same river.
>
> — Heraclitus, *On the Universe*, ca 500 B.C.

The greatest benefit of the GUI has nothing to do with the "graphical" part — it's really something called a CUI. (Pretend you're Jed Clampett and say, "koooo-eeee! doggies!")

CUI, the Common User Interface, refers to the fact that well-written Windows programs look and behave very similarly. That's a revolutionary improvement, a fundamentally important development for computer users everywhere, though it hardly originated with Windows.

Under DOS, the function of any key was a guessing game. In many programs **Esc** might back out (Escape!), but it was the menu key in DOS Microsoft Word. Depending on the program, the key to call up the menus could be **Esc**, **F7**, **F10**, **Alt**, **Backslash**, or . . . As a result, it became difficult to use multiple programs. If you did use multiple programs, there was a temptation to get them from the same vendor in the hope they used the same basic keys.

Windows encourages — but doesn't force — developers to use a common interface. You can be 99% sure that if a program can open any files, you'll get to the dialog that does so by hitting **Alt+F**, then **O**. Alas, too often the promise of a common interface is honored in the breach and for two reasons.

First, the elements that are specified in the Windows programming documentation are. . . ahem. . . pretty thin. For example, there are no guidelines for right mouse clicks or button bars so you really have just the general mishmash on how those aspects of the interface operate.

Second, and most significantly, CUI works for *your* benefit, not the software vendors', so the incentives can be all higgledy-piggledy. Competition among vendors is fierce (as you'd expect in a growing multi-billion-buck market with low per unit costs). Vendors seek product differentiation, something that will make their shining face stand out in an increasingly overwhelming crowd. User interface bells and whistles is an obvious place to be different. Commonality often suffers.

There is a fine line here. While the right buttons and button bars and other non-standard "standards" are confusing, they are also useful. They have entered the mainstream because some vendors have pushed the interface envelope. Much of this experimentation hasn't interfered with CUI because it involves previously undefined interface elements. It could be worse. What if Software Megalomania's new *WurdPluPerfect* suddenly decided the **Alt** key would repaginate a document?

 Consider the dialog that is invoked by the File/Open menu command. Windows 3.1 has a "Common" dialog for file open: programmers of all stripes are encouraged to use it. I am a big fan of the File Open common dialog, not because it's great, or even good, but because it's *common*.

Nonetheless, I've sympathy for programs that use a modified version of this common dialog just because they want to add an extra feature — like, say, thumbnails (little preview pictures) in a graphics program. I'm especially sympathetic if some care is taken to keep as many elements as possible of the official common dialog, including look and position of controls.

I've much less sympathy for programs that change the dialog merely to give it a 3-D look. . . and, oh, by the way, while they're at it change the fonts, the way the tree looks, and the position of the buttons. Some day the Windows common dialogs may have a 3-D look, and that'll be great. But until then, change for the sake of change rings hollow.

WYSIWYG and All That

Paradoxically, the most significant graphical part of the GUI model involves words, not pictures, and how letters can now have different widths.

Fixed pitch fonts — typewriter style fonts, where the "i" and "M" have the same width — are a recent development in the history of humanity and the written word. Imagine a page of ancient illuminated text, culled from some musty urn in the Negev, tenderly spread crinkled and cracked on a squat and rough-hewn table, the archaeologist's magnifying glass trembling as he holds it to his eye: and all the characters on the page line up top-to-bottom, all the lines end flush right.

B-o-r-i-n-g!

Fixed pitch fonts are an artifice of the past century: The first usable typewriter appeared in the 1860s, just after the American Civil War. There's nothing sacred — or even mildly interesting — going on here. It's just a throwback to the days of the typewriter. . . days that are rapidly drawing to a close.

Early dot matrix printers fumbled and groped around the edges of proportionally spaced fonts (ones where the space taken up by a letter can depend on its visual width; the way Jupiter intended, when he invented the Roman alphabet). With the advent of Laser Printers, proportionally spaced fonts came into their own.

To see how two fonts might look together in a document, to place drop caps and other special elements, or to adjust column widths in a table, you need to see on screen a good approximation of how things will look on paper. The term WYSIWYG ("whizz-ee-wig," short for "What You See Is What You Get") was introduced to describe this theoretical confluence of what you see on screen and what you get on the printed page.

I like the term WYSIWYGSO ("SO" = Sort Of) because all too often there's a gulf between screen and paper. In the early days of Windows there were huge gaps in the similarities. Many were caused by juggling different types of fonts on screen and printer. Robust font technology represented originally by Adobe Type Manager and later by Windows 3.1's TrueType changed that and has produced effortless, efficient, close to true WYSIWYG. Usually.

All the World's a TSR

I take the world to be but as a stage,
Where net-maskt men do play their personage.

— Du Bartas, *Heraclitus and Democritus*, ca 1580
(Shakespeare's *As You Like It* dates to 1598)

One reason that DOS computing has persisted is the extensibility produced by "Terminate and Stay Resident" programs (TSRs). You might not be able to run multiple programs at once but you could load, say, a Rolodex program as a TSR. Then, when you needed it, you hit the magic key combination, suspended the current program, and popped up that Rolodex.

The TSRs had to be specially written — you would often run out of memory for them and sometimes two of them conflicted — but they were immensely popular.

WinTerminator, Too

The neat thing about Windows is that in a real sense, every Windows application is a TSR. Windows itself is a TSR.

Think of Windows as this big, primeval ooze, in which programs — called "dynamic link libraries" — bounce around, bumping into each other, talking to each other, occasionally killing each other. Accidentally, of course. Zap!

When you start a Windows program, it isn't as much *executed*, in the DOS sense of the word, as it is tossed into the primeval WinOoze. Once in the soup, it must sink or swim, along with all the other denizens of the bog. If your Windows program needs something — such as a file on your disk or a piece of real estate on the screen — it communicates with the other globs in the ooze.

If they're properly dispatched, the globs will go out and fetch whatever the Windows program requires. If they *aren't* properly dispatched, they'll croak. When an improperly dispatched glob in the WinOoze croaks, the epitaph reads "General Protection Fault." If the glob takes out the whole bog, Windows freezes tighter than an outhouse door in a Colorado snowstorm.

Now here's the bizarre part. When you interact with your computer, everything you do is intercepted by a glob in the WinOoze. You may think you're typing in your word processor, or clicking an icon in your spreadsheet, but noooooooooo. . .

Anything you do feeds one of these globs, one of these Windows dynamic link libraries. The glob is responsible for finding the appropriate program, tapping it on the shoulder, and passing along your actions. You have no direct contact with your program. And it has no direct contact with you. Everything — typing at the keyboard, clicking a mouse, updating the screen, reading from a disk, printing on the printer — *every bloody thing* has to go through a Windows glob. And all of these globs are running, more or less, at the same time.

That's the essence of the "event-driven model" you may have heard about. It's the conceptual underpinning of Windows, the rules globs use to keep chugging in the WinOoze. (You might have heard it called "Object Oriented," but it isn't, not by a long shot.) Remain ever mindful of the globs and the WinOoze, and you'll stand a fighting chance at understanding all the myriad things that can — and do — go wrong.

It's a jungle, er, bog out there.

Information at Your Fingertips

"Information at your fingertips" is the Microsoft anthem for the 1990s. They mean it as a mantra for the information bazaar, but the Windows desktop is an even better metaphor.

 Wasn't their motto for the 80's a chicken in every pot, a car in every garage?

 Not quite, Igor — "a computer on every desktop and in every home."

Preemptive multitasking — where programs jockey around, trying to get control of the computer, isn't all it's cracked up to be. It *can* be useful if you are online, downloading a file in the background, but most of the time it doesn't mean much, especially if you have a way to print while getting some other work done.

What's really important, though, is task switching — having several programs loaded and waiting for you, so you can pick and choose which program you want to run. Say you get a phone call, you can minimize that spreadsheet you were working on, click on your phone book to record the call, and then return to the spreadsheet. Major productivity comes from setting things carefully so Windows starts with the programs you need, and then having those tools at your disposal throughout the day.

 Alas, there is one rub in this lovely task switching stew and that's what Windows calls Free Resources. You may think that when you purchased a machine with 8 MB, you were in memory hog heaven. NOT!

If you develop a taste for lots of programs, your Windows life will be plagued by three specific areas in memory, three bins, each a measly 65,536 bytes (64K) in size. Their size is pre-ordained: you can't change it, no way, no how. Your humongo 8 MB machine is limited by a part of it that comprises a mere 3/4 of one percent of memory.

When a program wants some more memory to store data it says "Yo, Windows baby, lay another meg on me." Windows dutifully finds that meg of memory from your 8 MB or whatever of RAM, possibly using virtual memory on disk in your swap file. Big chunks of regular memory come fast and easy.

When that same program wants to draw a little button on screen, though, it passes the button off to Windows. As Windows does the actual drawing, it zaps out a piece of that itty-bitty 64K bin to store the button. Little chunks of memory in these bins is dear.

There are other system objects like menus and icons, bits of stuff handled by Windows that are called "resources." For performance reasons, Windows crams all of your "resources" into three 64K bins. Menus go into one bin, buttons another — the details of what goes where are technical and unimportant. What is important is that if any bin fills up, Windows decides to go south for the holidays — your system slows to a crawl if you are lucky and goes belly up if you are not. So what matters is how much space is left in the bin with the least free space.

Available memory in each of these bins is expressed as a percentage of the original 64K. If Windows is currently using 16K of a 64K bin, it reports that 75% of the bin is free. If you look at all three bins and take the smallest percentage of the three, that number is called **free system resources** or just **free resources.** If one area has 6.4K free, say, another 20K and the third 35K, your free resources is 10%. You can see your current free system resources by clicking on Help/About in Program Manager.

If free resources get below about 15%, you'll likely experience programming difficulties. If it dips below 25%, say, you may get strange "Insufficient Memory" messages that have absolutely nothing to do with how much memory you have installed on your machine. Watch out!

64K is 2 to the sixteenth power and the 64K bin size is connected to the fact that the Windows core is written in 16-bit code, a holdover from the limitations of the original chips (8086 and 80286) used in PCs. When Windows shifts over to 32-bit code, possibly in the next major version, the free resources headache should become history. We can always hope so.

Serious Windows users like me tend to use a program that will display the percentage of free resources in an icon (Mao will discuss some later) and keep an eye on it. As programs get loaded and unloaded, that number drops. And drops. And drops. Some users have to exit and reenter Windows several times a day. I do.

In any event, the free resources limitation does put a crimp on keeping too much immediately at hand. Information at your fingertips, at least in the current incarnation of Windows, is doled out in teensy-tiny 64K chunks.

Interprocess Communication

> Public telephones in Europe are like our pinball machines.
> They are primarily a form of entertainment and a test of skill
> rather than a means of communication.
>
> — Miss Piggy, *Guide to Life*, 1981

Windows goes way beyond mere task switching. It sets up pathways for you to use programs *together*, telephone lines that let applications communicate with each other in ways that keep getting better and better. The original intercommunication device was the clipboard, an area in memory managed by Windows where you could copy information from one application and paste it into another.

In 1989–90, DDE ("dee-dee-ee," short for Dynamic Data Exchange) descended on Windows, allowing programs to request information from one another. With the right macros, you can highlight a name in a word processor, hit a key, have the name looked up in your PIM, get the address from there, and have it pasted into the word processor.

The OLE ("olé!," short for Object Linking and Embedding) 1.0 spec was introduced in 1991–92. Its most dramatic ability is to embed an "object" created in one program into another — e.g., to put a piece of an Excel spreadsheet in an Ami Pro document — and let you edit the object in its original creating program by doubling clicking on the object in the host. Like the clicks of Dorothy's magic shoes, a simple tap or two propels you back whence you came.

The OLE 2.0 spec was introduced in 1993. It allows in-place editing — the ability for the creating application to take over the menus of the host program giving the user the feel of working on a single integrated document. Instead of the magic shoes whisking you back home, in-place editing brings home to *you*. OLE 2.0 also provides a replacement interprogram communication method to DDE that promises greater flexibility and power, and with a spot o' luck, fewer crashes.

Windows. The great communicator.

Little Windows' Report Card

O vain futile frivolous boy. Smirking. I won't have it. I won't have it. I won't have it.
Go find the headmaster and ask him to beat you within an inch of your life.
And say please.

— Alan Bennett, *Forty Years On*, 1968

Here's a chance for the students to grade the teacher; the inmates to rate the asylum.
It's also a chance for you to see what our three icons really think of Windows. Perhaps
you'll hear your voice in their plaintive cries.

 I got together with Mao and Igor to make Windows' GUI report card to
send home to Windows' pop, Mr. Bill. I gave out two grades in each area:
one for the overriding concepts behind Windows treatment of the five GUI
elements; and one for how well the concept is actually carried out.

This is the report card that Mom sent to Mr. Bill.

New Technologies/Dear Ole School		
	Concept	Implementation
GUI Dialogs & All That	B	B
Common Interface	A–	C+
WYSIWYG	B+	A
Multiple Programs	A	C–
Interprocess communications	A+	I
Dear Mr. Gates: Little Windows has become a very popular kid in class. She has been a lot less unruly since she passed her 3.1st birthday. By the way, that Macintosh boy did much better in these grades but he has his own problems.		

GUI Dialogs and All That: The basic interface is good but has some shortcomings like
multiple letter scroll to, better use of drag and drop,. . . a solid B but no better.

Common Interface: Windows could use more thorough guidelines but what it has is
excellent so I gave out A– for the concept. The implementation grade here hinges on
how well the industry respects — and obeys! — the idea of a common interface that is

more than skin deep. I figured that half the industry got a B+ for that and half the industry an F. I'm an easy grader, so I averaged that out as a C+.

WYSIWYG: I decided that the basic concept wasn't that central to many users so I only gave a B+ for the concept. The TrueType implementation is so good, that I gave an A for implementation. Good show, Winnie.

Multiple Programs: The basic idea — lots of programs available as icons on the bottom row which you can even call with hotkeys — makes my heart leap for joy. So the concept got an A. But the resource limitations are so severe that I only gave a (generous) C– for implementation. Igor thinks it shoulda been an F.

Interprocess Communications: As Microsoft marketers would say, OLE 2.0 is so hot it's cool. *I mean, way cool, you know. Neat.* A+. Alas at the time I sent home the report card, no major applications implementing OLE 2 were available so I couldn't judge how well it worked in practice. That's an Incomplete.

As you might expect this report card caused a lot of discussion at Mom's place.

 I wonder what Mr. Bill will think about Windows' grades – not exactly something to brag to *his* Mom about.

 Igor, I think what Mr. Bill most cares about is that Windows is popular with the other kids.

How come Windows is a she?

Elementary; it is MS Windows after all.

But then why is the Macintosh a he?

Mac is a boy's name you know.

Why do you suppose Mom added that stuff at the end about Mac?

She had visions of Apple using her report card in ads and this might stop them.

What are Mac's problems?

Most of all price. Similar Mac setups cost 1.5 to 2 times what it costs on a PC, especially at the high end where Apple and the third-party add-in makers think they can soak the users. But also the momentum of new products is very much running in Windows favor.

Well, wasn't Mom worried about IBM using her report in one of their ads as brilliant mass marketing savvy.

Ouch! Just bit the oxymoron on my tongue. The base problem behind OS/2 is that it serves no compelling purpose for IBM's business to have an open operating system. At this point it is being driven by corporate pride.

Mao! You realize after saying that I'm going to have to hire bodyguards for you if you step onto certain parts of CompuServe.

Go ahead.

Make my day.

Will the Real Windows Please Stand Up?

> The real problem is not whether machines think
> but whether men do.
>
> — B.F. Skinner, *Contingencies of Reinforcement*, 1969

So there you have it. Windows on the half-shell. An insider's peek at what really happens inside the stew you call Windows. A quick chance to wallow around in the WinOoze, and rub up against several of the most offensive parts of the Windows milieu.

I hope you leave this chapter with the impression that Windows sits atop a rather flimsy foundation; that the internal workings of Windows can be mysterious, even to the most savvy. . . uh. . . savant; and that pieces of Windows must work together carefully to avoid the catastrophic.

I also hope you leave this chapter with the impression that Windows offers huge, uncharted territories; enormous power and flexibility; a logical starting point for the creation of mind-boggling applications; and a chance for you to leverage your knowledge of one application to come up to speed on another.

Finally, I know you'll leave this chapter articulating what an entire multi-billion-dollar industry feels.

Like it or not, the best stuff is on Windows.

The *Hitchhiker's Guide to the Galaxy* has, in what we laughingly call the past, had a great deal to say on the subject of parallel universes. Very little of this is, however, at all comprehensible to anyone below the level of advanced god. . .

One encouraging thing the *Guide* does have to say on the subject of parallel universes is that you don't stand the remotest chance of understanding it. You can therefore say "What?" and "Eh?" and even go cross-eyed and start to blither if you like without any fear of making a fool of yourself.

The first thing to realize about parallel universes, the *Guide* says, is that they are not parallel.

It is also important to realize that they are not, strictly speaking, universes either, but it is easiest if you don't try to realize that until a little later, after you've realized that everything you've realized up to that moment is not true.

The reason they are not universes is that any given universe is not actually a thing as such, but is just a way of looking at what is technically known as the WSOGMM, or Whole Sort of General Mish Mash. The Whole Sort of General Mish Mash doesn't actually exist either, but is just the sum total of all the different ways there would be of looking at it if it did. . .

Please feel free to blither now.

— Douglas Adams, *Mostly Harmless*

Of Mice and Menus — The Windows Interface

> But Mice and Rats and such small deer
> Have been Tom's food for seven long year.

— Shakespeare, King Lear, 1605

Windows, windows, and Those Funny Thingies

There's a dumb user joke from the DOS days where the tech support lady told the user to "put the diskette in the drive and close the door" so the user put the diskette in, got up, walked to the door, and closed it. The Windows update of that joke would have the tech support lady say "hit the third radio button" and have the user change to a news station. No doubt about it — you gotta learn the lingo or you'll find yourself saying "now which thingee do you want me to push, darn it?" So I'll begin with an anatomy lesson — but while we're at it you'll pick up some tips that you might not know like what happens when you double click on a title bar.

 I (leer) always loved anatomy lessons, especially the parts about the special little buttons.

It's called Windows (with a cap W and a ™) because it has a lot of windows (with a small w and no ™). From a programmer's point of view there are windows all over the place. Each button is actually a window but I'll talk about windows as the user sees them. Take a look at Figure 2-1, a window with all the trimmings.

There's the basic window border stuff, the menu bar, the MDI stuff, and a dialog with its controls. Let's take 'em one at a time.

Most application windows can be in three different states — normal, minimized, and maximized. Normal, is, well, normal. In this state, the window can be moved and resized. A minimized window is also called iconized — it gives you one of those funny pictures on the bottom row of your screen. A maximized window fills the whole screen, so, it can't be moved or resized.

Don't be fooled by the tiny iconized state of a minimized application — to think that means it stops running. It will run just as much as if it were a normal window other than the currently active one. That can be good if you want it to do stuff in the background; it's bad if you just want the program to be handy even though it isn't doing anything because it will still be using some system resources. To complicate things, some Windows shells — notably Norton Desktop and PC Tools — let you keep nonrunning programs on the desktop as icons, albeit icons that they attempt to distinguish from the standard icons by raising the background behind the icon.

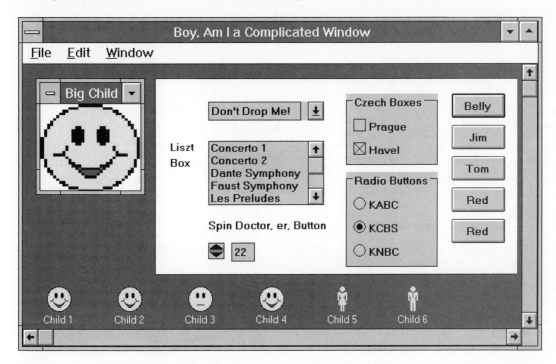

Figure 2-1: A whimsical window

The window in Figure 2-2 shows only the border stuff.

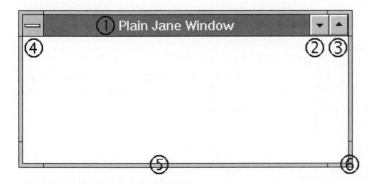

Figure 2-2: A simple window

The bar at the top (label ①) is called the **title bar**. It's an incredibly handy part of the window. Place the mouse pointer over it, press the left button and drag, and you can easily move the window! Double click on the title bar and the window will maximize. If a window is already maximized, double clicking the title bar will restore it to normal state with the position and size it had when it was last normal.

No doubt, you've run off to check out this double click stuff — welcome back. Some of you may have found it didn't work! I need to warn you that much of what I'll say about the basics only holds true most of the time. Load Windows Write and double click on the title bar and boom, maximo real estate. But load Windows Calculator and double click the title bar and it's "boy, he doesn't know what he's talking about!". Windows provides a very flexible framework to its applications. An application writer can choose to disable the maximize state as did the writer of Calculator (and hey, notice that one of the arrows is missing on Calculator's window). So remember, that while what I tell you is the truth and nothing but the truth, it ain't the whole truth. The authors of Calculator probably had a good reason to disable maximize — alas, too often programs fail to support the Windows' standards merely to assert their individuality and not for any reason important to you. All we can do is rail against those programmers who fail to remember whose machine it is after all.

But I digress. The words on the title bar are sometimes called the **title** — I bet you guessed that. They are also more often called the **window caption** or just **caption**. That's because the title is placed under the icon when a program is minimized so it's just like the caption in a cartoon.

Again, this is only what's usually true — a program can ask Windows to inform it when the user asks to minimize it and it can change the caption to something different from the title. In fact, in the Wild West that Windows really is, one program can hijack another program's icon and/or caption and change it. For example, hDC's Power Launcher (see Chapter 5) lets you change the icon and/or caption of a program when you load it so you could change Solitaire to use the Excel icon and have the caption read **Microsoft Excel–JONES.XLS** and have the ultimate Boss Screen.

 Psst, CTO, what's a boss screen?

 In some DOS games, you could hit a key and bring up a screen from a spreadsheet to fool your boss if she came in while you were playing. Called a Boss Screen.

Most often, programs put their name in the title and will add the name of the document that is currently active. Boy do I hate it when they also insist on putting the full path name there because, when you iconize, the caption is so long it tends to sprawl over neighboring captions. Jeez, talk about inconsiderate.

To the right of the title bar in Figure 2-2 are two buttons — label ② is called the minimize button because it minimizes the application; the down arrow is hint of what it does. Label ③is called the maximize button. Since you can double click the title bar, the maximize button is redundant but you're likely to forget the title bar trick and use the button instead.

When you maximize a window, what was the maximize button changes from

 to

which is called a restore button because it restores the window to normal state. If you remember to use it, double clicking the title bar is usually a quicker way to restore a window. If you are a klutz, like I sometimes am, and if you use the restore button (see Figure 2-3) instead of double clicking the title bar, you risk hitting the minimize button in error.

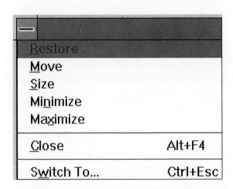

Figure 2-3: The System Menu

Then there's label ④, which you can only describe to someone as that thingee in the corner unless you learn its name. It's called the **system menu button** or the **control menu button**. The funny line on it is *not* a hyphen or a minus — it's a spacebar and supposed to remind you of the keyboard shortcut which is **Alt+spacebar**.

Clicking once on the system menu button or hitting the keyboard shortcut brings down the system (also called control) menu which has three sections by default — including a five item section to Restore, Maximize, or Minimize and to Move or Size the window. Depending on the state, some of these choices are grayed out (so not active). These are intended partially for keyboard users but there are times even the mouse fan will want to use them as I'll explain real soon.

The system menu button is not available when an application is minimized since it then only shows an icon and caption. Single clicking an iconized application will bring up the system menu; double clicking will restore it to its last state (which could be normal or maximized).

Since virtually all applications have a system menu, it's an attractive place for utilities to add their own stuff. For example, the WinJet drivers from LaserMaster, add direct access to the Printer Page settings from an system menu. And many popular Windows program launchers, including Norton Desktop, PC Tools, and Power Launcher add entire user-defined launch menus to the system menu.

 This empowers the user and is a good thing although sometimes it seems as if the system menu is going to fill the whole screen. But what is decidedly not a good thing is that some vendors feel they have a right to announce their presence by placing their logo in the system menu box so that the familiar button:

is replaced. May as well name the guilty parties — hDC does it with Power Launcher and Central Point with PC Tools for Windows. This is an extreme of developer/corporate hubris — whose machine is it, anyway?

The final part of the standard Windows window is the border around it — the thick line — called the **border** (isn't this technical jargon just awful). If you look closely, you'll notice its actually broken into eight separate pieces by thin lines. There are four straight bits like the piece we labeled number ⑤ and four corners like number 6. When you pass the cursor over a border area its changes from a normal pointer like

to a double headed cursor like

At the sides, the double pointed arrow is left right and at the corners it's diagonal. If you depress the mouse button at the point where the cursor changed, and drag, you resize the window. The edges size in one direction and the corners let you resize two directions at once.

There are times when it's a pain and a half to grab that darned border. Maybe there's another window just nearby or some child window but you find yourself trying to move the mouse just the slightest bit, failing and mumbling about how great DOS was.

That's the time to take a deep breath and remember that Windows usually gives you more than one way to skin a cat. Select the window you want, hit **Alt+spacebar** and choose Size (hitting the S is the fastest way to do that but you can use the mouse or the arrow keys). Suddenly, a strange four headed jobbie appears:

You then hit an arrow key to determine which edge you get to move — there is no way to access the equivalent of a corner — and the arrow keys let you move it in or out. The moving part isn't as much fun but getting there can sure beat mousing around some of the time!

 You'd better talk about "skinning the cockroach" instead of "skinning the cat." The non-IBM author of an IBM-approved book about Micro Channel Architecture talked about an argument in quantum mechanics called "the paradox of Schrödinger's cat" where Schrödinger imagined a cat in box with a vile of poison gas and. . . The IBM committee that had to approve the book worried about the reaction of the cat lovers of America and changed all the references to "Schrödinger's cockroach." Don't we want cat lovers to read this book? Better change what we say.

 What about the cockroach lovers?

For the most part, when Windows is running, there is a currently active application — the one that will get any keys that you hit. There are times there is no active application (in a sense the desktop is the active application) but there is never more than one active application. Windows uses colors to give you a visual clue as to what's the active application; the built-in color schemes use different colors for active and inactive Windows. It's strange that Windows doesn't make title bars 3-D and use depth as a second visual clue — *Makeover*, discussed in Chapter 5, will let you do that and more.

Waiter — Menu, Please

While our Plain Jane Window doesn't have one, most application windows have a menu underneath the title bar. The menu usually has the names of submenus. Hitting the **Alt** key with nothing else will move you to the menu bar where you can use the arrow keys and enter. If a menu item has an underlined letter like File or Edit or

Mi<u>d</u>dle, hitting **Alt+F** or **Alt+E** or **Alt+D** (no, you don't need to shift the F to get **Alt+F**) will pull down the menu. It is often easier to use the keyboard accelerator when you've been typing then to grab the mouse and drag it to the menus.

A combo like **Alt+F** is called an *accelerator key*. You'll sometimes see someone write &File or Mi&ddle because that's what Windows programmers do to tell Windows about accelerator keys. You need to know about this funny & convention because it carries over to quite a few programs that let you buils your own menus or customize the ones the program already has.

Select a submenu name with the mouse or accelerator and down pops a submenu. There are many conventions about what symbols in a submenu mean

- no special symbol means that an immediate action is taken. Since top menu choices normally invoke submenus — in those rare programs that take immediate actions from the top menu bar an exclamation point is used to signify this immediate action. So if a menu item says **Format!** rather than **Forma<u>t</u>**, you'd better be sure you know what's about to be formatted with no questions asked!

- If the choice is going to just invoke a further submenu, then the symbol ▶ appears to the right of the menu choice. The sub-submenu is called a cascading submenu.

- If the menu choice is going to invoke a dialog box (I'll talk about them later), the choice is followed by an ellipsis (. . .).

- If a submenu choice isn't available, it will often still appear but in a lighter gray color (said to be "grayed out").

- Some menu items act as a toggle, for example determining whether a toolbar is displayed or not. If the option is toggled on, they'll appear with a ✓ to their left (not the right as for other symbols).

- If there is an accelerator key for a menu option giving you a shortcut to invoke the item without traversing the menus, then the accelerator key is shown to the right of the menu choice; it is right justified. Not all programs are thoughtful enough to provide this great educational tool into their shortcuts — kudos to those that do. Major kudos to those programs that let you assign menu items to your *own* choices of accelerator keys and then display those choices for you on the menus.

The Windows SDK — the Software Development Kit that Windows developers often get from Microsoft includes a little booklet called *The Windows Interface: An Application Design Guide*. (Let's call it the *Interface Guide*.) It should be required reading for Windows developers because it sets up some standards so that applications will act the same. If anything, it doesn't set up enough conventions and too many developer's don't follow the ones that are there. Don't get me wrong — innovations in interface design are very important; button bars, right mouse properties menus, and other good things that have entered the mainstream wouldn't be there if developers were forced to tow a Redmond line on all interface issues (although it has now gotten to the point that the button bars and right buttons working differently in different programs has become a problem;–I wish there were at least more completely recognized de facto standards). But these innovations were in addition to the standards — there is no excuse (at least in most cases) for a program to fail to implement the *Interface Guide* standards or even worse to implement a functionality in the guide but in a nonstandard way.

 Gee, I have ways to make those recalcitrant developers listen.

 We all do Igor. Complain loudly to any company that decides its individuality takes precedence over your productivity and, if need be, vote with your wallet.

The *Interface Guide* includes three "standard" menus that it recommends all applications have and two "common" optional ones. The three standard menus are File, Edit and Help. The first two are supposed to be the first two menu bar choices and Help is supposed to the last.

The File menu is supposed to have the following entries:

New or New...   Should always be the first item; should create a new document with a standard name like Untitled; the ... is for programs that let you set document size.

Open...   Should lead to the Windows Common Dialog included with Windows 3.1. These standard dialogs for Open and Save are elegant and convenient. It would be great if everyone used them. Too often, vendors insist on rolling their own. Sometimes there is a good reason like the desire to include a file preview but usually, its just to distinguish themselves in a place where nothing is gained by doing that.

Close

Optional item for systems using the multiple document interface (MDI) which I'll discuss next. Closes the active MDI child. Note that the Close command on the system menu closes the application so it is like an Exit command on the File menu rather than like the Close command. A certain logic but confusing nonetheless.

Save

Also should use the Windows Common Dialog. If the document has never been saved, this entry should invoke Save As...

Save As

Allows renaming of document before saving as well as change of format when appropriate

Print or Print...

Should use the current printer. If it is appropriate to allow the user to specify a page range or. . ., a dialog should popup. To avoid, confusion, this dialog should not allow change of printer but it should list the current printer

Print Setup

Again should invoke a Windows Common Dialog, the one that lets you change among printers. Setup for a specific printer can be called from that dialog.

Exit

This should be the last command on the File menu

It is sad that the *Interface Guide* has no standard accelerator keys for the File Menu items. In particular, I often weep that **Ctrl+S** isn't quite a standard for Save although it is frequently used as such. There are standard accelerator keys for some of the Edit Menu. The Edit Menu largely refers to clipboard-related commands — we'll discuss the clipboard later; for now, we note it's a place that programs can use to exchange data both within the application and between distinct applications. The *Interface Guide* lists some OLE/DDE commands (Paste Link and Links. . .) that we'll defer until our discussion of those subjects. Here's what is supposed to be on the Edit Menu:

Undo **Ctrl+Z**

Not appropriate for all programs but implementing it separates the most user-friendly program from the pack. Those few programs with a multilevel undo are especially blessed. The *Interface Guide* specifies that the action to be undone is listed as in *Undo Formatting* or *Undo Paste*. If the last action can't be undone, this command should be grayed and optionally changed to *Can't Undo*.

Cut   **Ctrl+X**   Copies selected data to the Clipboard and deletes
             (Shift+Del)   it from the application. "Selected" data has a
                                 special meaning in Windows which I'll explain
                                 when we talk about *For the Select Few*. This
                                 command should be grayed out if there is
                                 currently no selected data.

Copy   **Ctrl+C**   Copies the selected data to the clipboard without
             (Ctrl+Ins)   deleting it from the application. Like Cut, should
                                 be grayed out if nothing is selected.

Paste   **Ctrl+V**   Copies data from the clipboard to the current
             (Shift+Ins)   insertion point (for text, where typing would
                                 enter text) in your document. If there is selected
                                 data, it should replace that data. This item should
                                 be grayed out if the clipboard has no data or
                                 does not have data in a form appropriate for the
                                 current insertion point.

The key combination in parentheses are the ones that were standard in Windows 2.x
and 3.0. Microsoft, in what I think was a terrible blunder in interface consistency,
changed them to something close to the Mac keystrokes (the Macintosh doesn't have a
Ctrl–key but it has one called **Command** — Paste on a Mac is **Command+V**). I guess
they figured they'd rather be like the Mac than like OS/2! The *Interface Guide* clearly
states that while the new keystrokes should be implemented and appear on the Edit
Menu, the old style keystrokes should be also be implemented but undocumented.
Alas, too many vendors don't pay attention so we have a mishmash — some programs
that use only the old keystrokes, some that use only the new, and some that allow
both. As usual, we poor users take it on the chin. The moral is that if you are used to
one key combination and it doesn't work in some application, try the other or go to
the menus rather than assume something is broken. Cheer up — in about five years, it
should be cleared up and the new **Ctrl+X**, etc. will be in place.

 Hey, I've a great idea. Why doesn't Apple run a bunch of radio commercials touting the
advantage of the Mac over Windows in terms of consistency and simplicity? Gotta find
some reason to convince folks to fork over the extra bucks for a Mac.

The View Menu, often the third menu, should give us ways to change the view of our
data and turn on/off special panels like a toolbox in a paint program. The Window
Menu, often the next to last is an MDI feature (to be discussed momentarily).

The standardization of the user interface, both via the *Interface Guide* and the Common Dialogs is one of the great promises/advantages of Windows. Too bad the industry has done such a half-baked job of implementing this consistency.

Honor Thy Parent

Some programs implement an optional Windows spec called MDI for "multiple document interface." The main program window (called the MDI parent window) then becomes a model of the Windows desktop. Each document you open (and "documents" can mean pictures if the program is an image editor!) is in a separate window inside the parent. These windows are called MDI children. Like an application window, an MDI child can be in three states — normal, minimized, and maximized. In normal mode, MDI children look and act a lot like an application window with a title bar, minimize/maximize button, a sizing border, and one of those thingees in the left corner. But if you look closely the system menu button of the application window,

has changed to a

You'll notice the bar looks a lot more like a hyphen or minus sign. The accelerator key for this system menu is **Alt+minus** so you have access (at the same time) to both system menus from the keyboard.

But a maximized MDI child is different from a maximized application window because its title bar has disappeared. You can't use the trick of double clicking the title bar on the child window to restore it because there is no title bar! Without the title bar, where have the **Alt+minus** control menu and restore/minimize buttons gone? The **Alt+minus** and Restore buttons migrate to the extreme left and extreme right of the menu bar in the parent application. The minimize button disappears — you can only minimize a maximized MDI child by going through the normal state or by using the **Alt+minus** menu.

MDI applications should have a Window menu which most importantly should list the titles of the open MDI children. If appropriate, it should also have Cascade and Tile items and an Arrange Icons. Cascade (see Figure 2-4) makes each Window a convenient size and overlays them, one on top the other offset slightly to the right and down. Tile places them in non-overlapping windows (see Figure 2-5). Since a picture is worth a thousand words, here is Sysedit with cascaded windows and tiled windows.

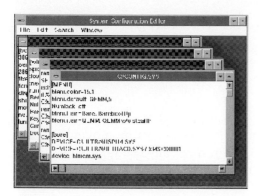

Figure 2-4: A cascaded window

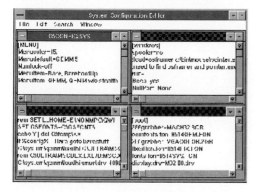

Figure 2-5: A tiled window

Arrange Icons lines up any minimized MDI children at the bottom of the parent window. MDI is far from universal. Some programs only have a bastardized version of the spec, Word for Windows, whose multiple document code goes back to Windows 2.11, is a notorious example. Others don't handle multiple documents at all — Notepad is a significant example of that. Since Sysedit has the code needed to make an MDI Notepad, it's crazy that Windows 3.1 kept a single file Notepad.

Windows are cascaded in the order of last access. That is, the bottom of the pile is the one accessed longest ago and the top is the currently active child or one last active. Access here can be a single click on the window. So, for example, to cascade some open windows in ProgMan, just click on the windows in the inverse order that you want them stacked and then choose **Cascade** from the **Window** menu.

A few programs prefer to handle multiple documents by asking you to launch multiple instances (that is launch the program more than once). For example, PC Tool's File Manager launches multiple instances rather than have an MDI interface to show multiple drives. But it keeps them talking to each other in the background so this is really just another way of skinning the cockroach.

Scrollin' on Down

When a window has data that is hidden from view, it's supposed to let you know that by showing one or more scroll bars. If there is data to be uncovered by moving up or down, the bar, like the one shown in Figure 2-6, appears vertically on the right of the data window and if there is data to the left or right, there should be a horizontal scrollbar on the bottom.

Figure 2-6: A scrollbar

The scroll bar has four parts — the scroll arrows on the top and bottom, the scroll shaft (that's really what the *Interface Guide* calls it) which is the long strip between the arrows, and the thingee in the middle. Most folks call that thingee the slider; some call it the elevator, while it mentions those names, the *Interface Guide* calls it the scroll box — no kidding. I'll call it the slider.

While the action is pretty intuitive, there are a few points you may not realize. I'll describe how the *Interface Guide* says it should work. As is so often the case, some programs pay no attention so they really give you the shaft.

Clicking on the top or bottom arrows is supposed to move the contents of the window up or down by a single line, or single unit if there is one. For a bitmap, there isn't a natural unit (other than a single line of dots which is much too small), so the program is supposed to choose its own unit.

 Clicking the top scrolls a line above what was visible into view so really it moves the viewport up and the contents actually move down. It's the natural thing to do although if you state as "clicking the up arrow moves the contents down" you'll get a headache which goes to prove that it sometimes doesn't pay to think something through. The boys'll continue to talk about the contents moving up when they really should say viewpoint moving up.

Clicking an empty part of the shaft is supposed to move the content up by a screenful if you click above the slider and down a screenful if you click below. Actually as the *Interface Guide* explains, not quite a full screen — a single line of overlap should be preserved (so it moves by a screen minus one line) to keep your bearings.

Finally, you can drag the slider. Dragging to the top of the shaft, should take you to the top of the document and dragging to the bottom of the shaft should take you to the end of the document. For something like a spreadsheet which has empty rows at its bottom, dragging to the bottom of the shaft should take you to the end of the data, not the last empty row of the spreadsheet.

If you drag the slider 30% of the way down, the document should scroll to the 30% mark. As you scroll with the keyboard by using **PgUp**/**PgDn**, the slider should move to give you a visual clue of where you are.

That's it. That's how the *Interface Guide* describes it. No special action of double click other than effecting two single clicks and moving you by two screenfuls. But some programs insist that a double click above the slider takes you to the top of the document and a double click below to the end.

That's certainly a lot more convenient than dragging all the way *but* it's a bad idea! If you only ran one Winapp, such an extension would be great, but if you run seven apps, why should you have to keep track of the two that do things differently.

So, Mr. or Ms. Software Vendor — donna do me no favors. Make standard stuff woik the way dey's supposed to woik. If you want to extend it in non-standard ways, add something nonstandard! You wanna give me a click way to go to the top of the document add an extra thingee above the scroll bar. Ok, Mr. or Ms. Vendor?

When Igor lapses into Patois Bronx, he's really angry and thinking over what he learned at his family's feet. And you don't want to get Igor angry. Actually, there is some logic in the *Interface Guide* deciding *not* to have double clicks go to the top/bottom of the document. If you double click by mistake with the correct implementation, it is easy to go back where you were — just double click on the other side of the side of the scroll bar. But if you are in the middle of your 700-page novel and you find an accidental double click takes you to the top of the document, you'll have a devil of a time getting back to where you were.

Time for a Dialog

> He who has been earnest in the love of knowledge and of true wisdom,
> and has exercised his intellect more than any other part of him,
> must have thoughts immortal and divine.
>
> — Plato, *Timaeus* Dialogue, ca 475 B.C.

Menu items that end with a . . . and a variety of buttons and other actions while you run Windows, produce dialog boxes — panels, sometimes without borders, that allow you to communicate with the program. The elements of the dialog are called controls. Programs can implement their own custom controls. Some programming languages have their own set of custom controls so you'll often see the same custom controls or nonstandard look in several programs from different vendors because they used the same compiler. In particular, dialog boxes in applications made with Borland compilers have their own chiseled grey look. The clincher is if the buttons look like this:

Figure 2-7 shows a typical dialog box with lots of trimings:

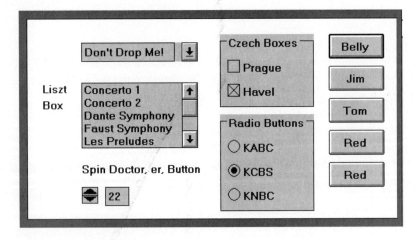

Figure 2-7: A dialog box

At the right side of Figure 2-7 are **command buttons** or just **buttons.** Most often, you'll execute a button by clicking it. If you look closely, one of the buttons sometimes has a highlight around it. That's the one that will get executed if you hit the **Enter** key. If an non-button control is highlighted — say you are typing in a string, and there is a button labelled OK, then **Enter** is supposed to execute it. If there is a button marked Cancel, then the **Esc** key should enter it.

Psst, CTO, I get the Belly and the pair of Reds but what's with Jim and Tom?

 Jim Button is the author of PC File and one of the fathers of shareware. Tom Button is an obscure Microsoft executive in the Visual Basic Group — at least, he used to be obscure.

If the dialog has some places you need to type in a word, moving your hand from the keyboard to mouse and back can be a pain so it pays to learn the keyboard methods.

Often a button will have an underlined character like menus have. Like a menu, they are indications of accelerator keys. A button called T̲om with an underlined T can be executed from anywhere by hitting **Alt+T**. But there is one difference with a menu. If you have a menu called Forma̲t, you can pull it down with either **Alt+T** or first hitting **Alt** and then **T**. With a button called Forma̲t, you can only use **Alt+T** and not the two separate keystrokes.

Several controls in a dialog can be grouped together by surrounding them with a big box called a frame. It's especially common to group together several check boxes and/or radio buttons.

One control consists of some text written to the right of a box □, which sometimes appears with an x, like so ☒.

It is called a check box and when the cross is there the box is "checked." Check boxes are for options that are on or off — checked means on. Sometimes when you call up a dialog, it refers to several options at once; for example, you might select some text in a word processor and call up a character formatting dialog which includes a check box for *Italic*. If all the selected text is italic, the box is checked and if none is, it is unchecked. But what if some of the text is italic and some is not? In that case, the box is grey. Clicking once will check it and turn on the option for all selected items and clicking again would turn it off for all.

The keyboard way to toggle a checkbox is to use the **space bar**.

A dialog can have any number of check boxes, grouped or not, and each box can be checked/unchecked independently of the others, even others in the same group.

Check boxes are used for True/False questions and radio buttons for multiple choice questions. (Windows programmers hate grading essay questions, so you won't find many of those). A radio button is a control with some text written to the right of a circle O. This can be seen in Figure 2-8. Sometimes the circle is filled in like so ⦿. The name comes from the fact that these are supposed to look like the on/off switches on an old radio — talk about obscure! Normally several radio buttons are grouped together inside a single group. A typical example is the simple dialog that pops up from the File/New... menu in ProgMan. Notice that since there are only two choices, it could have been set up as a *single* check box, but it is much clearer as a radio button group.

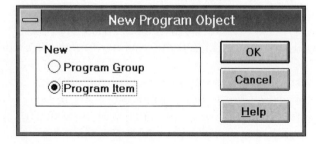

Figure 2-8: A dialog from Program Manager

 The *Interface Guide* calls them *option buttons*, but the rest of the world refers to them as *radio buttons*.

Radio buttons are intended for mutually exclusive choices. That means that only a single radio button can be clicked in a each group. A dialog can have several groups of radio buttons each in its own frame. If there is a set of related choices to be made which are not mutually exclusive, they'll appear as several check boxes in a single frame.

As you click around a dialog box, the control that the keyboard is addressing changes. This control is said to have focus. Windows tries to show what control has focus by highlighting it. It will use a dotted line around check box or radio button text and a solid line around the button with focus. Windows uses highlighting for *both* the control with focus and the default button — the one that will get executed if you hit **Enter**. In the ProgMan dialog you see in Figure 2-8, the OK button is highlighted but there is a dotted line around Program Item. That means that Program Item has the focus and OK is the default. If you wanted to move the focus to Cancel, you'd need to hit **Tab** twice — once to move the focus to OK and once to move it to Cancel.

Each dialog box has a Tab Order, an order that the focus changes if you hit **Tab**. Some programs have a random Tab Order because unless the programmer takes the trouble to fix it, Windows will set the Tab Order to be the order in which the programmer put the controls on the dialog — so if a programmer puts in an extra control late in development and doesn't both to fix the Tab Order, that last minute control will wind up last in the order.

Tab does not move from one of several radio buttons to the next but will only move from another control to the chosen radio button. To change which radio button is chosen from the keyboard, you use the arrow keys.

Often, dialogs want to let you choose from a list of items. Among the Windows standard controls are four that display lists: list boxes, drop down list boxes, straight combo boxes, and drop down combo boxes. A list box is a panel with a set of choices; if there are more choices than fit in the box, a standard scroll bar appears. An example of a list box is the directory listing in the standard FileOpen dialog shown in Figure 2-9. It has an item which is highlighted. In this dialog, the number of items shown fits exactly and the scroll bars are greyed out. Depending on the application, some list boxes only show scroll bars if they are required and show no scroll bars rather than grey ones.

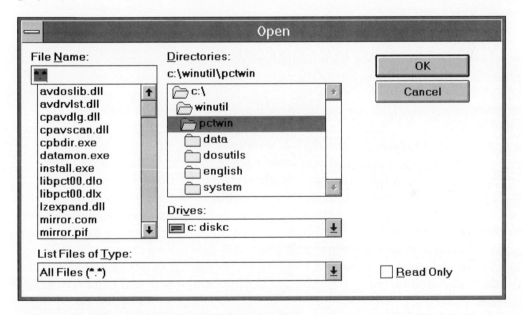

Figure 2-9: The Common Dialog Open Box

A drop down list is like a list, except as the name implies it is dropped down. It has a down pointing arrow next to it and you drop the list down by clicking the arrow. You can drop it down with the keyboard by tabbing to it and hitting **Alt+Down Arrow**. Once it is dropped down, you can make a choice with the arrow keys.

List boxes only let you choose from the items that the program decides to list for you — you cannot type in your own choice. A combo list displays a list but also lets you type in your own choice. An example is the Filename list in the Common File Dialog shown in Figure 2-9. There is also a combo drop down. It displays the area you type your choice in and allows you to type in a personal choice with or without dropping down the fixed list.

Drop down lists and combo drop downs are distinguished by a subtly different look — plain drop downs appear with the arrow right next to the current value:

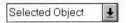

while combo drop downs have a space between the value and the arrow:

A final standard control is the spin button:

which appears next to an edit box with a number. You can type in a new value or increase/decrease the value by pressing the buttons.

If a list consists of alphabetized names, hitting a letter key is supposed to take you to the first item that starts with that letter, hitting the letter a second time, will take you to the next item, etc. That means that the default Windows behavior won't let you easily get to the first item starting with "St" if you have a lot of "S" items. For combo boxes where you'll start entering a full name "St" should scroll to the first "St" item. This conflicting behavior is doubly unfortunate — it means two controls with a similar look behave differently and it prevents an attractive behavior for list boxes of multi-letter searches. Norton Desktop and PCTools implement multiple letter scrolling in lists when you type. While I am normally unhappy with programs that violate the standards, this behavior is so intuitive and valuable that I applaud it. Besides it is implemented in a way that makes its difference from the standard obvious and it acts like combo boxes.

 The two programs use the same interface for this multiple letter search, making a kind of de facto standard. Wouldn't it be grand if others emulated it. Even better, wouldn't it be neat if the next version of the *Interface Guide* adopted it.

What's a Poor Fella to Do When Enter Won't Enter?

Tab is very convenient for, er, tabbing around a dialog and when you want to quickly execute a default button **Enter** is great, but it took some getting used to to find that **Enter** didn't just take you to the next field but exited the darned dialog, didn't it? But what if the dialog box has a multiple line edit field. How do you change lines if **Enter** is reserved for a default button. How do you enter a **Tab** character?

Alas, there is no standard. In some programs, when in a multiple line edit field, `Enter` and `Tab` don't have their default dialog box meaning but have the standard editor meaning (so Enter goes to a new line instead of picking a default button). In others, `Ctrl+Enter` and `Ctrl+Tab` are used instead. The lessons? First, do try `Ctrl+Enter` and `Ctrl+Tab` if desperate. Second, the *Interface Guide* really does need to address minutiae (and it does not in this case)!

While I'm on the subject of `Tab` and special keys, don't forget about `Alt+Tab`. I hear lots of folks don't use it because they never learned or forgot. I'll talk about it in the *Keys to the Kingdom* section later in this chapter, but go ahead, try it now — make my day.

Come on, Dialogs!

It's comforting to know that almost every Windows application will have a File menu and an Open item as a choice on that menu. Wouldn't it be great if making that choice always led to a dialog with a common feel. As it stands, you have to squint at the dialog and try to figure out if this is one of the jobbies where you change drives in a separate drop down or if you have to scroll through an interminably long list of directories to find the drives listed there.

 Microsoft bears some of the blame for this confusion of where the drives appear in file choice dialogs. Windows 3.0 used the combined directory/drive list while Windows 3.1 shifted. But, they not only got it right (separate lists) in Windows 3.1 — they also provided the dialogs directly to applications for the first time then.

Windows 3.1 introduced a collection of five "common dialogs" to access five standard operations — file open, file save, color choice, font choice and print. They felt so strongly about the importance of this common look that the program that implements these dialogs (called commdlg.dll) was made available to developers before Windows 3.1 shipped and they had permission to ship it with their applications. These dialogs are fairly intelligent and flexible. You'd think with the end user benefit of a common interface that there would be a big push for everyone to use these common dialogs, wouldn't you? Don't you believe it!

I'd estimate a third of the major applications that shipped since Windows 3.1 have used common dialogs and a few others have used their own dialogs that at least have the feel of the common dialogs (same elements in the same position but a possibly different look). It's just too tempting for developers to either use their old code (despite its Windows 3.0 feel) or to show their incredible inventiveness, intelligence, and charm by designing their own dialogs. Fooey!

The FileOpen is shown in Figure 2-9 and the FileSave dialog has a similar look. They are marked by separate drive and directory controls and a drop down list from which to choose file type (extension). Especially appreciated are programs that remember your choice of file type from one running to the text, and which provide you with a list of recently used files, for example in the File pulldown.

The color and font dialogs are quite sophisticated. The color dialog pops up with a direct choice of basic and custom colors. You can expand the dialog to pick you custom colors using the HSV (Hue/Saturation/Value) model. I'll talk about the color dialog in detail later in this chapter in the section *Some of My Friends Are Pals and Some Are Palettes*. The font dialog shows you samples. The Print dialog lets you specify what page range to print and can call a standard Print Setup command to change printers.

The dialogs are shown in Figures 2-10 to 2-14. Look at them carefully because their use shows you a vendor who is interested in helping you out with a standard interface.

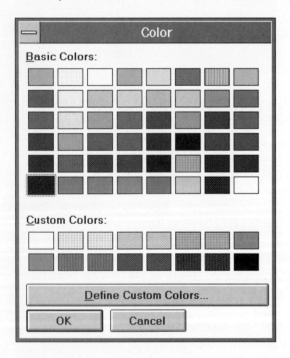

Figure 2-10: The Color picker in the Common Color dialog

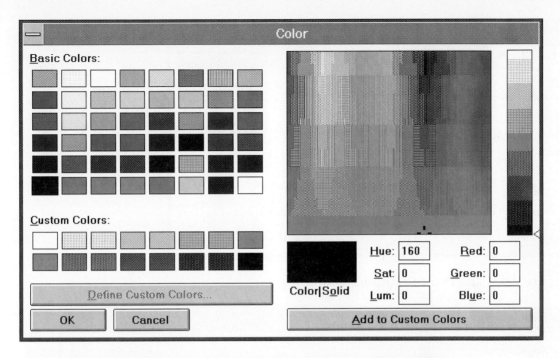

Figure 2-11: The Color Picker Expanded Common Color Dialog

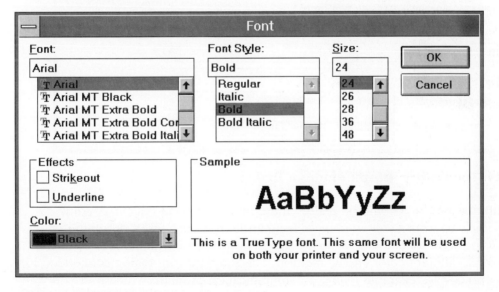

Figure 2-12: The Common Font Dialog

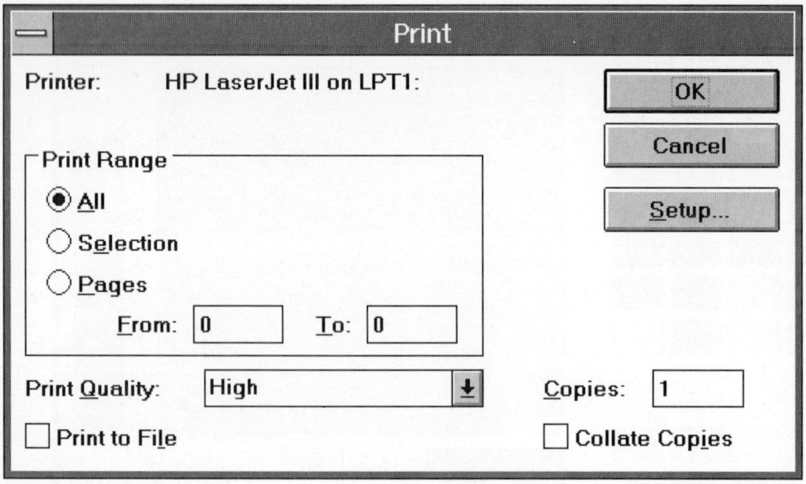

Figure 2-13: The Print Common Dialog

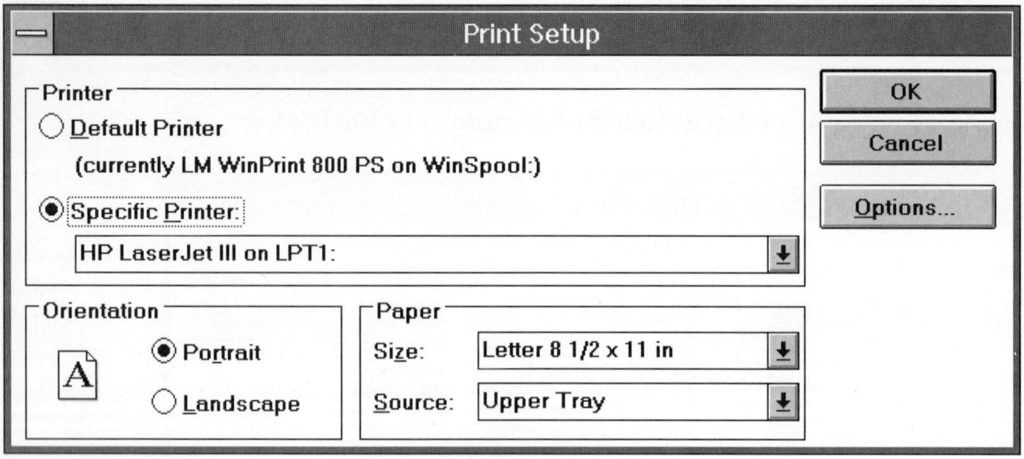

Figure 2-14: The Printer SetUp Commom Dialog

If a program doesn't use a common dialog, there may be a good reason. A paint program is likely to want to allow choices from an RGB model and a program that manipulates the color palette (see *Some of My Friends Are Pals and Some Are Palettes*) will also need a different color choice method. The standard font dialog is intended for global font choices, for example telling a communication program which font you want it to use in terminal mode. Programs that need frequent font choices, like a word processor, have good reason for a specialized method like the ribbon in Word for Windows. If there isn't any obvious reason, get mad at the programmers — at least yell at the screen.

For the Select Few

> War er nicht Held schon in dir, O Mutter, begann nicht
> dort schon, in dir, seine herrische Auswahl?[†]
>
> — Rilke, *Duineser Elegien*, 1924

Many lists in Windows dialogs are single choice lists — that is lists that only allow you to make a single choice just as if there were a radio button next to each item. A few lists are multiple choice lists — you can choose more than one item. There's a convention on using a mouse to select multiple items which is specified in the *Interface Guide*. When there are chosen items, there is one called the **anchor** which can be the same as or different from the item with focus. The anchor is usually, but not always, a selected item. If there are no selected items, the anchor can be regarded as being identical to the item with focus.

 I don't understand what the *Interface Guide* is saying about how `Shift+Click` is supposed to behave when the anchor is not selected, but I'm not alone. There are two programs included with Windows that have multiple selection lists — File Manager and the Fonts applet in Control panel. Their behavior under `Shift+Click` when the anchor is unselected is different. If the Windows group can't even get it consistent, how can anyone else? Fortunately, this is an unusual situation. The boys will use File Manager to define the "correct" behavior in this case.

- Clicking an item deselects any items already selected, selects the clicked item, and moves both the anchor and focus to the clicked item

- **Shift+Clicking**, that is clicking while holding down either **Shift** key moves the focus to the clicked item. If the anchor is currently selected, all items between the anchor and the clicked item are selected; any other items, even those selected before the **Shift+Click** are not selected; the anchor doesn't move. If the anchor is currently not selected, all items are removed from the selection list.

- **Ctrl+Clicking** moves both the focus and the anchor to the clicked item. It toggles the selection state of the clicked item to the opposite of what it was. If you **Ctrl+Click** a selected item, the new item becomes an unselected anchor.

- **Shift+Ctrl+Clicking** (you only like this if you can wiggle your nose and twiddle your thumbs at the same time). If the anchor is currently selected, all items between the anchor and the clicked item are added to the selection list. Items outside that range remain selected if they were previously selected. The anchor is not moved. If the anchor is currently not selected, all items between the anchor and the click item are taken off the selected list and the anchor doesn't move.

[†] *Wasn't he already a hero inside you, Mother? Didn't his imperious choice begin there, in you?*

As an example, suppose you have items 1,. . .,10 in order and you do the following: **Click** 2, **Shift+Click** 9, **Ctrl+Click** 4, and finally **Shift+Ctrl+Click** 6. Here's the state after each mouse action:

After Action	Selected items	Focus	Anchor
Click 2	2	2	2
Shift+Click 9	2,3,4,5,6,7,8,9	9	2
Ctrl+Click 4	2,3,5,6,7,8,9	4	4
Shift+Ctrl+Click 6	2,3,7,8,9	6	4

Click and drag will select contiguously; that is, act as if you clicked the item where you start the drag and then shift click the item where you stopped the drag.

With the keyboard, normally moving the cursor with the arrow keys changes a single selected item. Shift arrows produce a contiguous block that starts where you began the shift arrows and extends to the item you've moved to. To produce a non-contiguous block you need to enter Add Mode by hitting **Shift+F8**. In add mode, the cursor moves without changing the selection. You can change the selection with the spacebar which acts as a toggle. Hitting **Shift+F8** or clicking while in Add Mode toggles you out of Add Mode. Even if you normally prefer the mouse, Add Mode can be easier to make noncontiguous selections than **Ctrl+clicking** all over the place.

Alas, not all programs fully implement the *Interface Guide* recommendations — for example, **Shift+F8** Add Mode does not work in PC Tools File Manager (although it *does* work in the File Manager that ships with Windows itself and in the fonts applet that ships with Windows).

Many of these methods also work when selecting inside an application like your word processor. Don't always make selections by dragging; it may be easier to click at one end and shift click at the other. This is especially true if lots of scrolling is involved and your application will scroll without moving the position of the anchor. A very few applications have something like Add Mode — Word for Windows comes to mind although its mode works on **F8**, not Shift+F8.

Here's a useful selection trick — double clicking will normally select a complete object, like a word in a word processor. So what? Do you shudder at the thought of changing the font in Winword from Arial to Windsor because your font list is a mile long and scrolling through it the pits? You tried clicking on the font name and typing **W**, hoping it would scroll to the W fonts but instead go a font named WArial. You finally figured out you could drag the cursor across the font name, type **W** and hit the arrow, and you get the W fonts. But that drag is a drag. Remember the double click. Go up to the font name in Winword, double click, type **W,** and hit the down arrow. Voilà.

Here's a convention that seems not to be in the *Interface Guide* (alas) although it is implemented in both the multiple list boxes that come with Windows and in some but not all applications (sigh): `Ctrl+/` selects all items in a list and `Ctrl+\` deselects all items but the one with current focus.

 He says "seems not to be in.." because the index in the *Interface Guide* is not very extensive and there is no simple way to find all (or even any) references to a given keystroke. Oh, well, maybe Microsoft doesn't really want anyone to use it after all!

Paragraph Lost

> The girl who can't dance says the orchestra can't keep time.
>
> — Old Proverb

While talking about selections, I should mention a Windows convention that is sometimes useful but often dangerous — it's called "typing replaces selection". If you select some text and start typing, the typed material is supposed to replace what you selected — that is, the selected material is deleted.

On balance, I wish this wasn't the ways things worked. Sure, it saves you from having to explicitly, hit the **Del** key and that is convenient. I'm not someone who thinks that single keystroke savings don't count. They add up, and not having to move your fingers from the keyboard can be useful if you select with the keyboard (but I'll bet you use the mouse don't ya). But, and there is a but for the klutzes of the world — suppose you select a paragraph in Winword intending to hit the bold button on its ribbon. After selecting, you notice the mouse is in a bad place so you lift it up to move it and accidentally brush the extra **Enter** key on the side of the keyboard. Whoops, there goes the paragraph! Serves you right — you really shouldn't boldface whole paragraphs, ya know.

You may rightly point out that if you immediately choose **Undo** from the **Edit** menu, you'll get that paragraph back. But try the following experiment — select some text in Winword, hit the **Enter** key and then press the B button on the ribbon. Then look and see what the **Undo** item in the **Edit** menu says. Ulp — **Can't Undo**! Better be careful to notice this kind of error right away.

One of life's hardest lessons is to learn we have to live with our mistakes. But, listen up. I've another lesson for you. You have to learn to live with Microsoft's mistakes too. This convention isn't Microsoft's — they got it from the Mac. Microsoft's mistake was following the Mac.

But it's now a fact of Windows' being. Couldn't it be changed without having applications act differently. In fact, I think consistency among applications is so important that my advice is not to change the convention in those few programs, like Winword, that let you turn off "typing replaces selection." (But, hey, it's your machine — ignore this advice without any compunction.)

So when you are selecting a large part of a document, *be careful.* Keep your powder dry and save your work often.

The Thoroughly Modren Interface

When Windows 3.0 came out, interaction with Windows applications was mainly through menus and dialog boxes but there has been a subtle shift since then. Three interface devices have become more and more popular and more and more common — the button bar, drag 'n drop, and right mouse menus, aka property inspectors.

Alas, there are almost no official standards for these devices which means how they act can be confusing. I'll talk about the last two when CTO Mao gets around to musing on mice (see *Smell the Rodent-dentra* later in this chapter). Button bars belong here. One can understand why they are popular; they give single click access to items that previously required several clicks and more importantly they specify which item on that menu you want. The down side — some of the weirdest, most obscure icons you've ever seen. The solution? Icons bars should be linked to status bars at the bottom of a window. The best are those few applications that have the status bar say what the button does as the mouse passes over the buttons. Not as great, but still acceptable, are programs that tell you in the status bar what the button does at the time you press it but let you back out if you pull the cursor off the button before releasing it.

Interface, Not in Yer Face

A man after fourteen years' penance in a solitary forest obtained at last the power of walking on water. Overjoyed at this, he went to his guru and said, "Master, master, I have acquired the power of walking on water." The master rebukingly replied, "Fie, O child! Is this the result of thy fourteen years' labours? Verily thou hast obtained only that which is worth a penny; for what thou hast accomplished after fourteen years' arduous labour ordinary men do by paying a penny to the boatman."

— Sri Ramakrishna, ca 1860

Some final thoughts on interfaces and consistency.

It's a fine line to decide when a programmer is justified in departing from interface standards. The key issue is what and who gains. If a program fails to adopt the Windows 3.1 common dialogs because it was easier not to upgrade the code, it's clear who has gained and who has lost. The lame excuse that it was done to be compatible with the old version is just that lame because users will be adapting to the common interface in other programs. If the reason is "to give our program suite a common feel," that can be done in places other than how dialogs work. If it's because the vendor thinks their nonstandard dialogs look pretty, well, I think that's also limping along. If *you* get more functionality, why, that's a good reason.

 Wouldn't it be grand if users started calling up vendors and saying, "I'm mad and I'm not going to take it any more."

 Don't get mad, get even.

Ironically, an especially good reason for programs to use common dialogs is that it allows users to customize their common dialogs. Huh? There could be a thriving cottage industry in replacement `commdlg.dll`'s! I've seen a replacement that took Microsoft's version and just edited the FileOpen and FileSave dialogs to make the file and directory lists longer. Someone could make dialogs with a lovely 3-D effect. If the user (the *user*, not the *programmer*!) decides to switch, that's the user's choice and if the dialogs were universally used, it's a change the user would get everywhere and so they would still be the advantage of common interfaces.

Of course, if you did change your `commdlg.dll`, some bozo installation program would come along and copy Microsoft's version over yours! But bozo installation programs are a different symptom of the same problem and one I'll discuss later.

Smell the Rodent-dentra

> Parturient montes, nascetur ridiculus mus.[†]
>
> — Horace, *Ars Poetica*, ca 20 B.C.

CTO Mao has strong feelings about the use of mice, so much so that he's codified three rules about them into the official wisdom of CTO Mao:

 Mao's first rule on mousing around in Windows: **Get and use a mouse**. I don't care if you hate the beasts. Continue to hate 'em but still use one. There's just too much that you can't do or can't do easily without a mouse. And "mouse" here includes trackballs or other alternate pointing devices — personally, I find a trackball

---

[†] Loosely, sheesh — all that work, nothing to show for it. Lit, *mountains will be in labor, and an absurd mouse will be born.*

ungainly, but use whichever variant feels best to you.

To anyone that has used a mouse in Windows, this dictum is so evident that it may seem crazy to pontificate about it. But there are users who think mice are silly — often the same users who are dragged kicking and screaming into Windows. Mice *are* silly. They look like bars of soap and getting double clicking or dragging down pat can be the pits. They turn computing into a video game, darn it. But once you learn a little, the beasts sure are handy.

The *Interface Guide* says that applications should provide keyboard access to all interface elements. That is desirable but it isn't always possible and is often ignored by programs even when it is possible. Windows games are notorious for requiring a mouse. I don't think it unreasonable for programmers to expect users to have a mouse.

The exception, of course, is a laptop — airplane trays are not the best place to try to roll a mouse even if you have one along with you. The solution is to look into a program that lets you simulate a mouse from the keyboard. For example, *NoMouse* (Abacus Software, voice: 616-698-0330).

 Mao's second rule on mousing around in Windows: **Don't always use the mouse.** The keyboard is often the best way to input choices.

The people who avoided using a mouse in Windows now find themselves using the mouse for everything. If you are in the middle of typing and want to save your work, having your hand find the mouse, dragging the pointer to the File menu, locating the Save entry and hitting it can be disconcernting. But if you train your fingers to do `Alt+F` followed by `S`, you've found a quick way to save. Selection is often done more easily from the keyboard.

 Mao's third rule on mousing around in Windows: **Don't be afraid to experiment by clicking around.** Consider double clicking around your applications and hitting the right mouse button. Who knows what interesting features you'll discover .

 Hey, maybe they could find out those things by reading the manuals. But, no, the vendors don't bother to write decent manuals because users don't read 'em and users don't read 'em because they aren't decent. What a vicious cycle. Hehe, you know I like vicious stuff.

 Barry once made "Click all around" as a tip in *PC Magazine* and a corporate support person wrote a strong letter to the editor calling the magazine irresponsible for advising stuff that causes all sorts of unexpected things to happen (which was the point after all!) and confuses his dumb users. So listen up, kids, don't do this at home unless you are prepared for the consequences.

 You know, there are a lot of jokes about dumb users and a lot of support people who belittle users but I don't think many users are Dummies and the three who are don't read *PC Magazine* or this book.

There isn't much to say about mouse technique. There's left click and right click — the trick is to press and release quickly. Double clicking means to click twice, quickly in succession. When there is no qualifier, double click means left double click (or is it double left click).

Double clicking is normally supposed to cause an action if one is possible. For example, double clicking on a check box or radio button in a dialog should check the box and execute the default button. Be aware that double clicking anywhere in certain dialogs will execute the default button, but alas other dialogs behave differently.

Drag 'til You Drop

There are two identical mouse actions, given different names depending on the behavior on the screen — "click and drag" and "drag and drop." Either means to press the button and not let go but to move the mouse. An example of "click and drag" is to fire up Notepad, type and select the text by clicking and dragging. When you let go of the button, no action happens — rather the selection stops.

"Drag and drop" has the same `press the mouse button and move while the button is depressed' defining motion but the feedback and action are different. You have the feedback of something moving and you drop the moving object onto a target. For example, if you single click on an icon in a Program Manager group window and move the mouse, you see an outline of the icon move. You can then drop it in another window and so move an item from one window to another. All very intuitive.

The problem comes in trying to figure out what "the expected behavior" of a drop should be. The *Interface Guide* is not much help here. It describes a complex mishmash of possible behaviors.

 It's almost as if the Windows guys went and looked at how every different Microsoft product reacted to drag and drop and then made sure that each such behavior was allowed within the guidelines.

And the real world is a mishmash. Drag a filename from File Manager to Notepad and Notepad will open it, closing what was there. If you'd changed what was there, Notepad will ask if you want to save it. Pretty neat! Take an editor like the one in Norton Desktop (called Deskedit) which supports MDI and it will just open another window with the file dropped in; it'll even let you select several files in FileMan, drag and drop 'em on Deskedit and have all of them opened. I could get to like this.

Now drag and drop a native Windows Write file (a *.wri file) onto Windows Write and it acts screwy. The file does not open. Instead it gets embedded as an OLE client. I'll talk about OLE later but it hardly matters. Winword acts the same way.

It's neat that Write can embed its own files as OLE objects, something that you might use once in ten years — if you were bored and had nothing better to do. But still, it's kinda neat. But no way could that be what you desire in 99.999999999999% of the cases when you drop a *.wri file on Write. OLE, OY VEY — when you drop a native file on Write, you want it opened in Write — don't ya? But the bases are covered — Write isn't violating the *Interface Guide*. Sigh. Maybe I should get a Mac. Well, most of the time, drag and drop is great.

Keys to the Kingdom

It pays to remember the reserved keystrokes that Windows uses and that are common to most Winapps, both to avoid inadvertently assigning them to macros and as shortcut keys you get into the habit of using. If one of your DOS programs use some of these special keys, you may be able to tell Windows not to use them for that program; look at the discussion of the PIF editor in Chapter 3.

Below are some global keystrokes. These keys even work in full-screen DOS sessions; however, if some DOS application uses one of them, say your favorite word processor, *foowrite*, uses **Ctrl+Esc** to access its menus, you can reserve their use for that DOS session in the advanced section of the PIF file.

Ctrl+Esc   This brings up the Windows Task Manager that allows you to switch between applications via a menu. Double clicking on a blank area of the desktop also invokes TaskMan. I'll discuss TaskMan in Chapter 3.

`Alt+Tab`	This invokes a feature that Microsoft calls "Cool Switch" which means they think it must be pretty neat. It is one of the most underused neat things in Windows. Hitting `Alt+Tab` cycles through your applications without actually cycling through them! Instead it displays their names and lets you stop when you reach the one you want. The trick is to hold the `Alt` key down and hit the `Tab` key multiple times. It tends to cycle in the order last used so, if you go to a DOS session from a Winapp, a single `Alt+Tab` will normally bring you back to that last used Winapp. You can turn off `Alt+Tab` in the Desktop dialog that you invoke from Control Panel but you wouldn't be so silly would you? If you start `Alt+Tab` and change your mind, hitting `Esc` while `Alt` is still down will get you out!
`Alt+Shift+Tab`	Like `Alt+Tab`, only it cycles in the opposite direction. It's unlikely you'd want to start moving with `Alt+Shift+Tab` (how could you remember which of the currently open applications you used the longest time ago!), but if you start `Alt+Tab`bing and overshoot then `Alt+Shift+Tab` (remembering to keep the `Alt` down) will let you backup
`Alt+Esc`	This is like `Alt+Tab`, except rather than showing you just the name of the application, it shifts to it, redrawing the screen and. . . It's there for compatibility with Windows 3.0. It's hard to imagine you'd want to use it instead of `Alt+Tab`. Well, maybe if you were 100% sure you wanted to go to the last program you used. Bear in mind that if you click on a window to move it out of the way, Windows thinks you used it and will put it into the `Alt+Tab`/`Alt+Esc` cycle as the last used application!
`Alt+Shift+Esc`	Like `Alt+Esc`, except it cycles in the opposite direction.
`PrintScreen`	Here's another underused goodie. Did you know that Windows comes with its own Screen Capture utility — you know the kind of thing you pay $39 to get all by itself? Hit `PrintScreen` (`Shift+PrtScr` on some keyboards) and Windows copies the current screen to the clipboard (as a bitmap). In the Windows desktop, it's copied as a graphic (and you can paste it into Paintbrush but see the discussion of Paintbrush in Chapter 4).

In DOS text mode, it is copied as text. If you are in 386 enhanced mode running a full screen DOS session in a standard graphics mode, it'll even copy that as a graphic! You do lose the convenience of DOS PrintScreen going to the printer although by pasting from the clipboard into Write, shifting to Courier font and printing, you can duplicate what DOS PrintScreen does, albeit awkwardly.

Alt+PrintScreen   In DOS mode, this does what **PrintScreen** does but on the Windows desktop, it copies the current window only to the clipboard (as a bitmap).

Alt+Spacebar   This invokes the system menu. it even works in full screen DOS sessions run in 386 enhanced mode — shifting to a windowed DOS session and pulling down the system menu!

Other common keystrokes that you need to know about, although they are application dependent, are the Cut/Copy/Paste commands (discussed previously in *Waiter — Menu Please,* the keystrokes are either **Ctrl+X/Ctrl+C/Ctrl+V** or **Shift+Del/Ctrl+Ins/Shift+Ins** depending on the application), the DOS session **Alt+Enter** (which toggles between full screen and windowed DOS), and **Alt+F4** (which closes most applications).

Dialog à la Modal

Program designers can designate a dialog to be modal or modeless. **Modal** dialogs must be filled out and dispatched (or **Cancel**led) before you can access the rest of the program. **Modeless** dialogs continue to allow you to access the underlying program, its menus, and data.

There is not any simple way to tell if a dialog is modal by just looking at it, although as a general rule dialogs with a title bar but no system menu on it are modal and those with a system menu are modeless. Of course there are exceptions to this rule. If a dialog is up and you try to access the program and get beeped, you'll know the dialog is modal.

Some dialogs need to be modal because they provide information that the program designer wants to be sure you acknowledge before going on. Others may need to be modal because of possible confusion as to what they refer to if you return to your document. For example, the paragraph format dialog in Winword is modal, presumably on the assumption that it wouldn't be clear what paragraph you were referring to if you moved the cursor while the dialog was up.

But generally, modal dialogs are a bad thing since they give you lack of flexiblity.

 Sometimes modal dialogs down right destroy functionality. The worst example that I can think of was the initial release of PackRat 5.0. The phone conversation dialog which is suppposed to time a call and allow you to take notes was modal so you were helpless if you needed to consult your schedule or address book during your call.

While modal dialogs will prevent access to the underlying program, they do not normally prevent access to other programs. If the application is running full screen, you may need an `Alt+Tab` or `Ctrl+Esc` to get to the other programs but you can't. The exception is a dialog called a **system modal** dialog. When one of those appears, you can't access anything in Windows until you dispatch it. There are reasons for Windows itself to issue such dialogs but I can't think of any reason for an individual program to do so.

The Path to True Enlightenment

> Direct us in the right path.
>
> — The Koran 1:2

You should know where Windows looks for files. You may recall that you can set a DOS search path where DOS looks for programs. Windows first uses the home directory for Windows, then its System subdirectory and then it searches down the DOS path.

This means that you need not have Windows in your DOS path, at least not once Windows loads. If you run Windows in your autoexec.bat it is best to explicitly switch to the Windows directory than to reply on a path anyways.

It also means that if you want to slim down your Windows and/or System directories, you can generally move drv, ttf or other files to a convenient subdirectory so long as it is in your DOS path.

I'll have more to say about what to do about long paths in Chapter 3 in the section entitled *You Mean This Thing Runs on 88 Octane DOS?*

Who's Driving this Thing Anyway?

> KERMIT: Where did you learn to drive?
> FOZZIE: I took a correspondence course.
>
> — *The Muppet Movie*

To understand Windows, it sometimes pays to look at the real world, but a somewhat skewed real world. The plumbing industry has settled on standard pipe size and connectors but suppose it didn't and you wanted a new sink connected to the city lines. The poor plumber would have to ask you exactly what brand and model sink you had and what kind of incoming pipe you have and make sure that he had the right connection to join them. If there were 40 kinds of sinks and 30 kinds of pipes, the plumber would need 1200 (40 times 30, ya see) connectors to cover all the possibilities.

Pretty heavy toolkit to carry around. If the plumber were really clever, she might figure out the following. Develop a special standard intermediate piping. Then all she'd need is 40 connectors to connect the sink to the special intermediate piping and 30 connectors for the other side. Only 70 (the sum) rather than 1200. Big improvement.

If the plumber really had clout in the industry, she'd convince the sink makers that *they* should supply the 40 connectors for the sinks to the standard. True, with the extra connectors, there would be more chance of leaks but if handled right, this would simplify every thing.

The same idea is central to much in the world of computing. Rather than have every thing connect directly to each other and require products of connections, we use a protocol (like the standard pipe) and only need the sum of the possibilities, not the product. We'll see this several times (for example when I talk about SCSI and ASPI) but it comes up first in understanding the Windows API and the role of drivers.

Take printing. Please. The confused world of 1200 connectors is the DOS world. Each printer had its own quirks and command set. Each application had to provide its own connector for each printer out there — called printer drivers. Lots of duplicated effort, lots of application programmer time wasted writing drivers and the people who knew the quirks of individual printers best — the printer manufacturers — were not those who wrote the drivers.

Windows is like the smart plumber. It provides a standard intermediate connector, the Windows API for printing. The applications talk to the API. The printers connect to the API by providing drivers that are loaded as part of Windows. Not only is this paradigm used for printers, but for monitor adapters (screen drivers), sound cards, and more.

Microsoft includes some generic drivers with Windows itself but hardware that wants to go beyond generic needs to provide its own drivers. An advantage of this scheme is that the hardware manufacturers who presumably know their products best are responsible for the drivers. Another advantage is that a manufacturer can provide a fancy new piece of hardware and have its features work with most Windows software just by writing the driver. For example, HP could up the printer resolution from 300 dpi to 600 dpi without waiting for application software to catch up; they supplied a new printer driver and the software automatically caught up!

If you got the impression that drivers are pretty important parts of your system, you'd be right on. Probably no third party component of Windows is used more than your screen driver.

Ah, you say. Screen drivers are the critical component of a new adapter card. Must be that the driver writers are treated as gods by the hardware makers. And the magazines must test out those drivers thoroughly to make sure that they correctly implement each and every API call.

NOT!

Hardware makers are enamored of hardware. Their driver writers, who are after all only writing software, are undervalued and often less experienced programmers. And because the drivers are especially tricky programming, drivers have lots of bugs. Some drivers have so many bugs that they swarm.

Magazines do test drivers, but generally for speed, not for working correctly. So cruise the bulletin boards and you'll hear about lots of driver problems.

 What to do? First, do try to check out other people's impression of the quality of drivers by consulting friends or looking on CompuServe (WINADV and IBMHW are two forums to ask on). Secondly, be VERY careful when upgrading a driver. Back up the old version because you may find that the fancy new upgraded driver that you got from the vendor causes some program you need to stop working. So you'll want to be able to go back.

Unless you are sure your drivers are ultrasolid, keep your eyes open for upgraded drivers. Most vendors supply new drivers for no cost if your download from CompuServe or the vendor's BBS.

T'aint Necessarily So (that Printer Drivers Print)

They're called printer drivers so they must print. Right? Well, no. "Printing" is just a way of outputting a document from an application, usually as a set of dots. If you want to send that document over the phone lines to someone's FAX machine, it's just like printing so the natural way to implement FAXing from Windows is via a printer driver that doesn't print! Instead, the driver pops up a box asking who you want to send the FAX to and then it sends the bit pattern out the serial port to your FAX modem instead of out a parallel port to your printer!

Similarly, the portable document idea I'll discuss at the end of the Section *Putting Up a Good Font* later in this chapter depends on "printing" a document to a file. The moral is to keep in mind that "printer drivers" are really "output drivers" and may not actually print!

Communication is the Key to a Good Relationship

What distinguishes Windows from DOS? You may be tempted to give the WIMP answer–no, I'm not insulting you — WIMP stands for Windows, Icons, Mice, and Pointers. No doubt, the GUI is the most evident difference. But at a much deeper level, what makes Windows so different and what to me is its greatest virtue over DOS is the built in interprogram communication.

From Windows 2.03 onwards, a central component of the interprocess strategy has been the clipboard, a common storage area. DDE and OLE, protocols for higher level communication where introduced in Windows 2.x and 3.x.

The Delivery Van — Clipboard

The clipboard is an area of memory that Windows sets aside to store data to facilitate data transfer between applications and even within an application. In its simplest form, you select data in an application, copy or cut it to the clipboard, and paste it into an application which can be the same or different type of application.

We'll give both the Windows 3.0 and 3.1 hotkeys for these operations–they changed from one version to the other. Both will work in applications written after Windows 3.1 which follows the *Interface Guide*. Alas, you need to know both sets of keys because there are applications in which only one of the two sets works; if all else fails, you can use the Edit menu.

Copy (hotkey is **Ctrl+Ins** or **Ctrl+C**) leaves the source document alone but places the data on the clipboard. Cut (hotkey is **Shift+Del** or **Ctrl+X**) copies to the clipboard and deletes the material from the source. Paste (hotkey is `Shift+Ins` or `Ctrl+V`) copies the data from the clipboard to target application.

That's the simple idea, but the question comes up — in what format does the clipboard transfer data? Does it include font information if you copy from one word processor to another. How about spreadsheet formula if you copy between spreadsheets? The answer is, that depends on the source and the target. Figure 2-15 shows some clipboard formats.

Display

Auto

Picture
√ Bitmap
Biff4
Biff3
Biff
Sylk
Wk1
DIF
Text
Csv
Rich Text Format
Native
OwnerLink
Link
ObjectLink
Display Text
OEM Text

Figure 2-15: A host of clipboard formats

The clipboard itself is very flexible. If you have Excel, open it, load a spreadsheet, mark some data and copy it to the clipboard. Then run Windows clipboard viewer discussed in the section of Chapter 4 entitled *Clip Joint*. One of the menu item in that view is "Display." Pull it down and it gives you a list of 17 formats — five are black and 12 are grey. What does that mean? The five black formats are actually placed on the clipboard by Excel. For the other 12, it only places a promise on the clipboard. Essentially, it tells target applications — "if you have a need for the data in a promised format, let the clipboard know and it will get that format from me to give to you." By only promising data, not as much memory is taken and the copy is faster.

The downside of promised rather than actual data is that you have to keep the source application open to fulfill the promise. If you close an application before pasting, the clipboard removes the promised formats from the list it offers to transfer. So if you are trying to transfer anything more complex than straight text, be sure to keep the source application open until after you paste.

The clipboard uses terms that may differ from those that applications use. It will say **`Picture`** for what many applications call **`Windows Metafile`** or **`WMF`** and it will say **`Bitmap`** for what applications may call **`BMP`**. If you never look at the viewer, this terminology is irrelevant because the applications and clipboard can talk about these standard formats but it may confuse you if you do look and aren't aware of the terms.

When you paste into an application, *it* will pick the format to use. The **`Edit`** menu sometimes has a **`Paste Special`** command — *you* then get to pick the format used from the ones that are both on the clipboard and understood by the target application.

How well does transfer with formatting actually do? About the simplest formatting information you could imagine transferring is text with some of the words in bold. Windows Write and Word for Windows both come from Microsoft — surely you must be able to transfer bold text from one to the other. Ha! Don't you believe it. Copy "this is **bold**" in Write and Paste into Winword and it pastes unformatted text. If you try **`Paste Special`**, the only format listed is Unformatted Text. In the other direction, it is worse! Copy text in Winword and try to paste into Write and it's Oy vey OLE. It imbeds a Winword icon in Write — double click in Write and it will launch Winword with text, admittedly with proper formatting. By using **`Paste Special`** in Write, you can get at the actual text but without formatting.

What's the simplest piece of spreadsheet data that you can think of more complicated than a set of numbers? A column of numbers with an @SUM formula at the end. Try copying and pasting that from Quattro Pro for Windows to Excel and the sum is pasted as a number, not as the formula. Try **`Paste Special`** in Excel; one of the choices is WK1–that sure seems promising but it doesn't work. No format copies the formula as opposed to the number. In the other direction is no better (although Quattro Pro, proving it can use its own conventions to keep you on your toes, greys out **`Paste Special`** and offers a **`Paste Format`** command).

The moral is to use straight Clipboard copy and paste for unformatted data–ASCII text, tables of numbers, bitmaps and pictures — but not to rely on it for transferring formatting *between* applications. That doesn't mean that you shouldn't try the format transfer, especially in a situation where you might be able to use it in the future if it works. But be pleasantly surprised if it works rather than disappointed if it doesn't. Using the clipboard within an application to transfer from one part of a document to another or between documents is an entirely different story. You should expect formatting to translate perfectly in that case.

For some users, the biggest disappointment in the clipboard is that there is no **`append`** command. **`Copy`** or **`Cut`** anything to the clipboard and whatever was there is gone, vaporized, moved to the great electron graveyard. What was there is replaced by the new cut. It's unfortunate that Windows doesn't have an append command built in for the special case where the clipboard has text and what you try to append is also text. But it does not. A few applications do implement append themselves (e.g., the shareware batch language Winbatch, which you'll find on CD MOM) but it is rare.

The *ahem* Bill of Lading — DDE

DDE stands for Dynamic Data Exchange. It's a built-in part of the Windows architecture that is of special importance for programmers. It was added to the Windows spec in 1989–90 at the request of Aldus and Microsoft's Power Point groups. It impacts end users mainly through a command called **Paste Link**. If you write really fancy macros, you need to know about DDE at the level beyond **Paste Link** and we recommend that you look at Woody's *Windows Programming for Mere Mortals* (Addison-Wesley, 1992). If you aren't going to do programming (including macro programming), don't worry your pretty head about anything but **Paste Link**.

Aren't I a little old for you to be hitting me up with this "pretty head" stuff. And isn't it a bit sexist.

I think he was talking to Igor.

Paste Link extends the idea of promised data to the idea of future promises. Not only does the source provide data now but it promises to provide data again in the future. Why would you want to do that? Suppose that you are preparing a daily report for your boss in Winword and part of it is a table of data that needs to be computed in Excel. If you link the data rather than just paste it, that data can be updated automatically so that the most current data is used without you having to do an explicit copy and paste again.

For example, if you have an Excel sheet called **daily.xls** and position **R6:C2** is a piece of data that you want to link into an Ami document called **report.sam**, you select the cell in Excel, pick copy from the **Edit** menu, go to Ami and pick **Paste Link** from its **Edit** menu. Ami not only stores and displays the current value of the number in that cell, it also stores the application it is linked to (Excel), the filename (**daily.xls**) and the topic — the identifying tag it needs to send Excel to get that number back in future (**R6:C2** in this case).

Links come in two main varieties: hot and cold. There is a third kind called warm, but it's unlikely you'll run into it. A cold link is only updated when you explicitly request an update; you need to use a command in the target file to do the updating. Hot links are updated whenever you open the file with the target link (the Ami file in the example). With hot links, the target application also asks the source application to inform it whenever the source of the link is changed; it's impressive to make a link like the Excel/Ami link we described and type in changes in Excel while you have the Ami window visible on the screen. You see the numbers updated in real time.

If the link is hot and the source of the DDE link isn't open when the target application loads the file with the target link (for example, if Excel isn't open when Ami loads `report.sam`), then the target will offer to open the source and update the links. Either way, Ami begins a DDE conversation with Excel that begins "Hey, Excel, ole buddy, how ya been?" Quite literally, the first step in a DDE exchange is initialization. It continues with asking for and getting the linked data. The line is kept open for Excel to inform Ami of further changes in real time. Often, users don't get to determine which kind of link it is — that's set by the target application — but it is important that you understand which kind of link it is so you know if and when to ask for an explicit update.

Winword's Links dialog is shown in Figure 2-16.

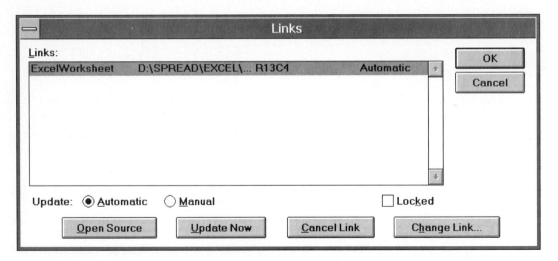

Figure 2-16: Winword's Links Dialog

Civilized applications give you control over the links through a **Links...** command in the **Edit** menu. For example, Winword will popup the dialog shown below. Notice the radio button that will change the link from **Automatic** to **Manual**. That's a change from hot to cold in our language.

While as a non-programmer you needn't worry about understanding DDE beyond **Paste Link,** you should be concerned about whether your applications support DDE because of the potential third-party add-in possibilities that come with DDE. For example, both PackRat and Winword support DDE. PackRat is a PIM which can contain your name and address database. With the proper DDE links you can have an

Insert Address command on a Winword menu that will let you highlight a name in Winword, pick the command, and have the address filled in automagically. Indeed, PackRat ships with macros that do precisely that and there is a set of souped up third-party linking macros (Prime; voice: 818-716-6783) that also do that. This magic is only possible because both applications support DDE.

OLÉ, José

HP's New Wave has not been a commercial success but it has an important legacy. It introduced the idea of compound document to the PC world. DOS is a program-centric universe. At any given time you basically have one program running and each document is firmly associated with a single application. New Wave uses a document-centric paradigm.

If you have an Ami word processing file with a piece of an Excel spreadsheet, a photo touched with PhotoFinish, and a Corel Draw graphic in it, Windows 3.0 thinks of that as a file made with Ami that happens to have pieces pasted in from other applications. Most likely, the files from PhotoFinish and Corel Draw were saved to disk and just copied into the Ami document, although the Excel spreadsheet fragment might have been **Paste Link**ed.

The New Wave paradigm would view such a document as one that was a single piece whose parts you would edit and act on with four separate tools — the four programs that make up the pieces. If there were New Wave versions of the four programs (of the four, only Ami had a New Wave specific version), you could have treated the file as a compound document with the menus changing as you moved through the pieces of the document. Alas, New Wave didn't control the operating environment, so it's view of compound documents never took off.

New Wave and related ideas in the academic literature and other platforms captured the imagination of Microsoft and the industry enough so that Windows is moving towards this document-centric view. According to Microsoft's version of the history, OLE came out of a proposal of Lotus and the OLE 1.0 spec was formulated by a committee of programmers from Lotus, WordPerfect, Aldus, and Microsoft's application programming group with input from Micrografx, Samna, Borland, Metaphor, and Iris. About six months before Windows 3.1 shipped, Microsoft released OLE DLLs that third parties could distribute and these OLE 1.0 spec libraries where included with Windows 3.1. In the middle of 1993, Microsoft released libraries implementing the OLE 2.0 spec based on input from many ISV (ISV=Independent Software Vendors).

While there is no doubt that Microsoft has listened to other vendors, it is clearly first among equals and it is a remarkable coincidence that Microsoft's applications and languages seem to be the first ones to have the various versions of OLE implemented.

OLE is not automatically built in to all applications — they have to have code to support it. So you likely have a hybrid collection of applications with no OLE support, with OLE 1.0 support and with OLE 2.0 support.

OLE stands for "Object Linking and Embedding" although "Object Linking or Embedding" might be clearer. It is pronounced to rhyme with FritoLay. The bitmap that you'd edited with PhotoFinish would be embedded in your Ami document as a picture before OLE. If you didn't like the way it looked, you'd launch PhotoFinish from Program Manager or your favorite launcher, load the on disk file, edit it, save it to disk, and tell Ami to update it. Not hard but tedious.

The OLE 1.0 spec presented a better way. If the photo is an on-disk file placed inside the Ami doc, it is linked as a PCX file to PhotoFinish. A database is kept by Windows that OLE PCX objects are to be edited by PhotoFinish (if that happens to be your photo editor). Double click on the picture in the Ami document and PhotoFinish is loaded with the picture already opened. Edit it and close PhotoFinish and you are asked if you want to update the linked object. The tedium above is somewhat reduced and you have much more of a feel that you are working on a single document.

It isn't even necessary to have an on-disk file. You can instead "embed" the object in the target document, that is save the data that PhotoFinish needs to describe a bitmap as part of the Ami document. This is done when you create the object while in Ami and tell it you want to embed an object and have it load PhotoFinish for you.

At a technical level, the difference between linking and embedding is that Linking only stores display data in the document and to edit it a file needs to be loaded from disk. Embedding also stores the native data that an editor needs. At the user level, linking is the way to go if you have a file, such as a company logo, that you want to share among several documents where editing it once effects all documents using it. Embedding is the best thing to use if you want to send the document to someone else without worrying about sending the right files or problems with the directory structure being different on the new machine.

While the OLE 1.0 spec started us down the document-centric road, there is still a feel of separate programs, because you double click when you want to edit and editing takes place in a separate window that feels (and is) a separate program. OLE 2.0 introduced the idea of "in-place editing." Click on a photo inside a word processor doc, and, if the word processor and photo editor both supports OLE 2.0, the menus change to those of your OLE 2.0 photo editor. You now have the feel of a single application acting on a single document with menus changing appropriately to the part of the document you are editing.

A second important element of the OLE 2.0 is a protocol for programs to drive each other that goes way beyond the DDE spec and allows the potential of universal macro languages. As applications supporting OLE 2.0 become available, the importance of this feature will become clearer.

Microsoft says that with the release of OLE 2.0, the correct terms are not client and server but controller and object.

 Controller? Into the SM scene, are we?

 I think I'll scream is anything else is called an object. I assume some purist at Microsoft thinking of an object heirarchy thought themselves really clever to use the word object to refer to the controlled program in an OLE 2 conversation. But that's a big mistake. Oy. I think I'll shoot the next thing that is called an object!

 What if I said that Mom was the object of your affection?

And Dots Not All

> I could never make out what those damned dots meant.
>
> — Winston Churchill (speaking of decimal points)

Well, Blast My Raster

Run your finger along a piece of glass. GET YOUR FINGER AWAY FROM THAT MONITOR!!! It's a little known fact that computer monitor screens are treated with special chemicals that draw the grease out of your fingertips. Some advanced models have the ability to draw it out from across the room. So use a window. NO, NOT THAT KIND OF WINDOW.

Is the piece of glass a smooth surface or is it a bunch of tiny bead-like atoms spread out in two dimensions? It's really a set of atoms, but it's useful to think of it both ways.

If you want to understand the sounds made when you hit a glass with a spoon, the smooth surface model may be better; but to understand how the kind of sand used to make the glass effects its strength, the atomic model may be better.

In the same way, what you see on a screen or what is printed out on a piece of paper is really a bunch of dots. And the computer or printer thinks of it that way. Before the display on your screen reaches the monitor it is put into the language of pixels–the color of each and every dot on your screen needs to be specified. (Pixel is short for "picture element.") In 1024x768 mode, there are 786,432 pixels on the screen. With that kind of job to do, it's no wonder Windows can be slow! Similarly, when printing a graphics on a 300 dpi Laser Printer on 11"x8.5" paper, the computer needs to send 8,415,000 dots per page to the printer!

With those kinds of numbers involved, it is often better to think on an abstract level in terms of lines and suitable curves. Windows accelerated display cards work on that principle; in detail

this is the line that Windows wants to draw

this is the driver that got passed the line that Windows wants to draw

this is the accelerator chip that understands lines that got one from the driver that got passed the line that Windows wants to draw

this is the adapter RAM where bits were placed by the accelerator chip that understands lines that got one from the driver that got passed the line that Windows wants to draw

this is the monitor that turns the on the pixels sent to it by the adapter RAM where bits were placed by the accelerator chip that understands lines that got one from the driver that got passed the line that Windows wants to draw

all without your CPU worrying its pretty head.

Similarly, if a file can describe a graphic in terms of lines and other objects — for example, solid rectangles and text, it can be a lot smaller than if it has to describe every color. Twenty-four bit color is so-called because it takes 3 bytes (24 bits) to describe the color of each pixel. So a 24-bit color, 1024x768 file describing bits would require 2,359,296 bytes(1024x768x3) — that's over 2 megabytes on disk!

Alas, lines and shapes do have their limits. If you have a large, solid blue rectangular shape, you can hope to use a description in terms of lines; but if you have a photo of the sky, the various shades of blue can't be captured in terms of higher-order graphics but only via "this here dot is royal blue, that one over there is kinda cyan,. . .".

So both descriptions via dots and descriptions with graphics objects have their place. If you ever want to manipulate either, you'd better know which is which so you should to learn some names and file types.

Files that describe graphics in terms of dots (or pixels) are called bit-mapped files, bitmapped files or just plain bitmaps. They are also called raster based. Windows has a native bitmapped file format distinguished by the file extention BMP. Wallpaper has to be a *.BMP file and Windows ships with a whole bunch of them which it probably installed on your disk. Other bitmapped formats are PC Paintbrush (*.PCX), TIFF (short for Tagged Image File Format — *.TIF), CompuServe's Graphics Image Format (*.GIF) and the Joint Photographic Expert Group compressed file format (called JPEG with name *.JPG).

Programs that manipulate bitmaps are sometimes called Paint programs although the higher class name is Image Editor. Occasionally, the Paint name is for programs that focus on creating bitmaps (Factal Painter is the best example) and the Image Editor for programs that focus more on Editing a photo you've gotten (by purchase or scanning). There are some superb low priced but still powerful Image Editors (PhotoFinish and PhotoMagic) as well as some wonderful high end packages (PhotoShop, PhotoStyler and Picture Publisher). Windows itself comes with Paintbrush which is a bitmap manipulation program.

Files that describe graphics in terms of higher order objects are called vector graphics or object graphics. Different formats will support different kinds of objects but almost all support lines, some kinds of curves, and text. Many allow a special kind of complicated curve called a Bezier. Alas, there isn't really anything like a common standard in vector graphics. The closest things are Windows built-in formats called Windows Metafile (or *.wmf) and Encapsulated Postscript. WMF doesn't allow Bezier curves so it isn't suitable for use with programs that use them. EPS is intended for use with PostScript Printer's only and reading an EPS file requires a program to have a full-scale PostScript interpreter built in. A third common format is a holdover from DOS called Computer Graphics Metafile (*.CGM). Many of the high end vector graphics editors have their own file formats making the area much more confused than the bitmapped arena. Even worse, many programs that use EPS or CGM files support only some of the files which have that designation!

Programs that manipulate vector graphics are called draw programs, drawing programs or illustration programs. The leading products are Adobe Illustrator, Corel Draw, and

Micrografx Designer. A draw program with less power but a unique, easy-to-use interface is Visio. The idea is to provide a large library of building blocks out of which you make your drawings.

In addition to solid colors, many vector formats allow gradient fills — I discuss that later in the section called *Which One is Burnt Umber?*.

For special effects, most vector formats allow a bitmap to be an object as part of their graphic. And several recently released bitmapped edit programs (Image Wizard, Picture Publisher 4.0, and Altimira Composer) allow an object layer in their files, so that, for example, they can leave text as separate letters rather than embedding it as a bunch of pixels.

Generally photographs that you get from third parties, and items that you scan in are bitmaps. Most clipart is vector.

The Scales of Just Us

Vector graphics has a special advantage because it is scalable. Consider a capital A.

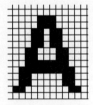

In a font like Arial, it consists of three straight lines — two forming a tent and one crossbar. TrueType stores it as a vector graphic. Of course, when you type an A on the screen, it has to be shown as bits so the TrueType engine makes the translation. The process of changing from vector to raster is called rasterization. Here is a blow up of a bold face 10-point Arial A shown on a pixel-sized grid to see the rasterization. Suppose we take the bitmap and blindly blow it up to double size. Thus every black pixel becomes a 2x2 grid of pixels and you get the blown up A shown on the left in Figure 2-17a. Figure 2-17b shows a blowup of the TrueType rasterized 20-point bold cap A in Arial font. Basically, it has rasterized the line. Notice that the straight blowup is blocky and ugly compared to the A made directly from the vector rasterized at the larger size. The blockiness is even evident in Figure 2-18 where the letters are shown in the same orientation without the blowup.

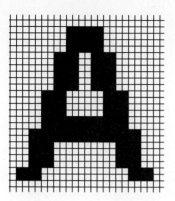
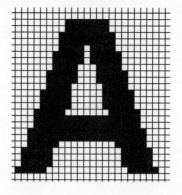

Figure 2-17a: Small A scaled up

Figure 2-17b: A rasterized at the larger size

Actually, this particular example involves more than just rasterization of lines — in the 20-point A, the rather delicate (and effective) single pixel black rows at the bottom and single white row just above the cross bar are a consequence of hinting. We'll see what that means when I discuss *Could You Gimme a Hint?* soon.

The moral of this is that vector graphics are scalable. Bitmaps are not. If you scan in line art and want to blow it up, try to convert it to a vector graphic, blow that up, and convert back (I'll talk about conversion in a bit). Blowing up a full color picture without blockiness is a different story and one of real importance to those with 640x480 Windows wallpaper that they want to move to 800x600 or 1024x768. I'll give you the secret of that when I talk about *Wallpaper on the Rack*.

That's a Cockroach of a Different Color

Another wrinkle in rasterization concerns the use of colors, a process known as antialiasing. Allow me to explain.

If you were computing in the ancient days when VGAs were first introduced, you may recall that it had two "spectacular" new graphics modes. (The modern equivalent of telling your kid about trudging through the snow to school may be recalling the CGA — "Gee, I remember when graphics modes had only four colors"; "Was that before or after the end of the Civil War, Dad?". But I digress.) There was 640x400 in 16 colors and 320x200 in 256 colors. The remarkable thing was that the lower resolution but higher color mode looked more life-like and seemed to actually be higher resolution than the 16-color mode.

This is an example of the phenomenon that, as far as perception is concerned, you can often trade color depth for resolution. This can place a monitor which is low resolution

(640x480 on a 15-inch monitor works out to about 55 dpi=dots per inch) but lots of colors on a closer footing to the latest popular Laser Printers which are high resolution (600 dpi) but only two colors (black and white!).

In one direction, consider how a Laser Printer handles grey scale printing. The printer has no grey ink. It mimics grey by putting down black dots in differing densities. A light grey will print as few dots among the white background while darker shades have more dots for the same area. If the resolution is high enough, you don't see the dots but perceive shades of grey. What is effectively a "grey dot" is a mix of several black dots amid white space resulting in less resolution when printing in greys. The printer has traded resolution for extra colors.

 Hewlett-Packard III and IV printers use variable sized dots to help mimic grey scales, a procedure the called RET — resolution enhancement technology — but the idea is the same.

The precise way that greys are translated depends on an algorithm which has to be carefully chosen to avoid banding and other artifacts. Usually your applications and the printer handle this for you, but if you read or hear about halftone frequency and angle, or error diffusion, someone is talking about this grey to dot pattern translation.

On screen, when translating from a vector object like a line at some angle to dots, the problem is that rasterization occurs in block size units — the ideal rasterization might be to only take a third of some block but pixels don't come in thirds. Or do they? When the object suggests that one take only a third of pixel, why not use a shade of light grey, roughly one third of the way from white to black. That's what antialiasing does.

To illustrate this, I looked at a 20 point Arial cap A as entered in the paint program PhotoMagic with and without antialiasing, an option which it supports. Figure 2-20 shows the two A's normal size with the antialiased version on the right. If you look closely, you'll see that the normal A (Figure 2-19a) has a more noticeable staircase effect. The antialiased letter (Figure 2-19b) is smoother, although a little fuzzy. The other two parts of the figure show blowups of the two letters. There are several different grey scale levels used to produce the effect.

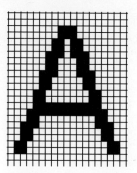

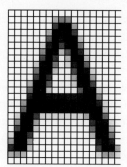

A A

Figure 2-20

Figure 2-19a: A in black and white

Figure 2-19b: Antialiased A

So what does antialiasing mean to you? Antialiasing should be available to make screen fonts look better. Ideally, Microsoft will add it to the TrueType rasterizer when Windows 4.0 is released. Until then, the main place to find it for screen fonts is the optional Crystal Fonts feature of ATI drivers (which work only with ATI cards). Be warned that many users have found numerous problems with Crystal Fonts and they have turned off this option.

In addition, some bitmap editing programs give you antialiased fonts and curves as an option. If you plan to print out a bitmap, it is preferable to keep the font as a vector object (for example in programs with a vector layer). Rather than turn on grey scale and then have the printer turn those to thinned out black areas, it is better to have the rasterization done at the higher resolution by the printer. If you are sending a presentation out to a service bureau to make slides, the same considerations are true — try to keep anything that can be a vector object as one. But if your goal is to display fonts in an on-screen presentation, it will pay to use antialiasing when you prepare the final screens.

Ain't Just Missionaries that Do Conversions

> Domini, domini, domini
> You're all converted now
>
> — Firesign Theater

Graphics files are a Tower of Babel. Not only are there bitmaps and vector graphics, but there are oodles of formats for each. You really need a translation utility to transfer between formats.

I'll talk about my favorite third-party utilities in Chapter 5 but I'd like to tell you some general things now. You have to realize that there are four kinds of translations and each faces a different set of problems:

- **Raster to Raster** — This is the most straight forward. The different formats have slightly different headers (the start of bitmapped files contains information like the dimensions, color depth, etc; it is called a header because it comes at the beginning of the file) and use different compression schemes (some formats use data compression schemes that allow you to take less space without loosing any information), but basically, they list each and ever pixel color one after the other. So translation is relatively straight forward. If you have a decent bitmapped editor, you can usually convert between formats by loading in one and saving in another without the need of a special utility. Most of the time you'll want to keep your files in PCX or TIF format which are accepted by virtually any program that supports bitmaps at all.

- **Vector to Raster** — This is the second easiest conversion — it is what we called rasterization and has all the issues of antialiasing. Still, you can expect a decent conversion program (like Hijaak) to handle this without surprises.

- **Vector to Vector** — This is tricky and fraught with peril. The biggest problem is that different formats support different objects. If a program tries to translate from a format that understands Bezier curves to one that doesn't, the best it can do is use a polyline — something that looks like a curve but is really a bunch of short lines strung together. So the file swells in size and complexity. Avoid such conversions if at all possible.

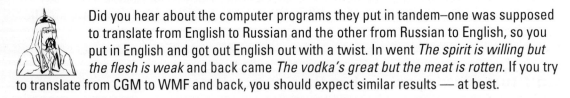

Did you hear about the computer programs they put in tandem–one was supposed to translate from English to Russian and the other from Russian to English, so you put in English and got out English out with a twist. In went *The spirit is willing but the flesh is weak* and back came *The vodka's great but the meat is rotten*. If you try to translate from CGM to WMF and back, you should expect similar results — at best.

- **Raster to Vector** — This is really an art rather than a conversion! In fact, you won't normally find it in a conversion utility except in special programs called autotrace programs. The best known one is Adobe Streamline which is bundled with Adobe Illustrator. Corel Draw also comes with an autotrace utility. If you have a complicated bitmap with subtle colors, successful autotracing is close to impossible. If you want to scan in line art or a logo in a fancy font and blow it up, you can hope to successfully use autotrace but be prepared to do some correcting of the trace by hand in a drawing program — most likely, the trace will put too many nodes on a polyline and you'll want to smooth that out.

To be clear about blowing up a line art logo you have on paper, you

- Scan in the line art. This will produce a TIFF file in bitmapped format. If you can set the scanner for line art or two color rather than grey scale, do so.

- Run the bitmap through an autotrace program. This will change the file to some vector format, for example, AI (a variant of EPS) in Adobe Streamline.

- Look at the vector file in a draw program that uses that file as its native format — presumably you'd use Illustrator with Streamline and Corel Draw for Corel Trace. See if you need to clean it up.

- Ideally, you'll use the logo in a program that understands your vector format so that blowing up is as simple as setting dimensions in a dialog or dragging on some handles. If you really need a bitmap, blow up the vector image in a draw program and use a conversion program for vector to bitmap. Your draw program may allow you to save as a bitmap or you may need to use a program like Hijaak.

Putting Up a Good Font

As soon has he learned that I was writing a Windows book, Igor, who has been taking font lessons from Mao, starting bugging me to be sure that when I talked about fonts, he could get a chance to tell you about 'em. So, here's Eeeeegor:

 To explain fonts to folks, you print out samples of the good fonts and the bad fonts. Then you hold the page of good fonts up to the light and twirl it. You give a knowing look and remark "1984 was an exquisite year for Caslons." Then you bring the page of good fonts carefully up to your nose and say "Quelle arôme, quel bouquet."

Whoops; it appears that Igor mixed up the wine lessons he's been getting from Mao with the font lessons. That's the point. You've probably learned to ignore the wine snobs. That doesn't mean you have to drink rotgut. You can enjoy a good wine and learn some basics, like when to serve a white wine without becoming a wine snob yourself and without paying any real attention to the wine snobs.

But the same folks who don't let the wine snobs and the hifi snobs faze 'em turn to jell-o in the face of font snobs. Funny thing is that while we know a very few sensible font experts, most font snobs are pompous fools. If you don't believe me, just ask the other font snobs. So *illigitimus non carborundum*.

Both to cope with the font snobs and to understand the simple do's and don'ts, you need to learn some of the basic language so, forthwith, I'll present a beginner course in fonts and then an intermediate course later. If you want to know more, say enough to know what it means when you tell a font snob to go kern himself, you'll want the advanced course in a later section. I'll then let Mao tell you some of what his little red book says about fonts and I'll talk about fonts technology in Windows and present some of my favorite fonts.

In understanding the language of fonts, you need to remember you are dealing with an art that goes back over 500 years. The terms more closely reflect the technology of 100 years ago than the changes of the past fifteen years. Most of all, they deal with movable metal type.

 The terminology enters in places you may not realize. Before the advent of computerized typesetting, a printer set type by grabbing the letters from two boxes, each with compartments for the individual letters. The boxes were typically laid out with one over the other. The capital letters were in the box on top (because they were used less often) and the other letters were in the bottom box. These boxes were called cases and the two of them were the Upper-case and the Lower-case. I kid you not.

Fonts 101

Here are the basic terms. The first thing that you have to realize is that what you think is a font, you know, something like Arial or Times or Courier, isn't a font (nor is it a parallel universe). It's a type family! A **font** is a set of letter forms (fancy pants name for shapes of letters), at a given size, weight, style, and type family. The **type family** is the family of similar looking fonts. **Size** is a measure of the vertical height of the font (normally the widths scale as the height does, so an 11 point font is not only 10% taller than a 10 point font, but also 10% wider. **Weight** refers to a measure of how heavy the strokes in the font are — the most common weights are **normal** and **bold** but you can have an **extra bold** or a **light** at the heavier and lighter ends of the spectrum. **Style** is an expression of orientation — the most common are **Roman** and **italic**.

Fonts are also called **typefaces** and, as the irreducible typographical unit, go back to those cases of type which contained letters from a single font. A set of fonts where only size is varied should have a convenient, simple name given current practice in computer typesetting, but not so. I'll call it a **scalable typeface**.

You can also have fonts with the same type family name and weight that are distinguished by how wide the letters are. If the font is made less wide for a given height, it is called **condensed** or **narrow**. If it is made wider, it called **expanded.** Condensed fonts are useful in situations where you want to squeeze a lot of text into a headline.

Here are typical examples for the Arial font:

Normal:	ABCDEFGHIJKLMnopqrstuvwxyz
Bold:	**ABCDEFGHIJKLMnopqrstuvwxyz**
Extra Bold:	**ABCDEFGHIJKLMnopqrstuvwxyz**
Black (Extra, Extra bold!):	**ABCDEFGHIJKLMnopqrstuvwxyz**
Extra Bold Condensed:	**ABCDEFGHIJKLMnopqrstuvwxyz**
Narrow:	ABCDEFGHIJKLMnopqrstuvwxyz
Italic:	*ABCDEFGHIJKLMnopqrstuvwxyz*
Bold Italic:	***ABCDEFGHIJKLMnopqrstuvwxyz***

Bear in mind that a well-made italic font is not merely a font with the slant added, nor is a condensed font made by blindly scaling the widths. There are subtle design changes that a skillful type designer will make when italicizing or condensing. Of course, if the font is a schlock font made by scanning and autotracing, it is likely that the italic is made by simple skewing the outlines!

Interestingly enough, while a good font design is a work of art, fonts cannot be copyrighted in the United States or directly protected. Some bozo in the copyright office decided years ago that the alphabet is the alphabet so what's to copyright. That doesn't mean that you can buy a font pack and give all the files on it to all your friends. Those files are computer programs and, as such, *are* protected. What it does mean is that if you are a font producer, you can try to make a perfect copy of a fancy new font you see; you can even print out that font, scan it in, autotrace it, and sell that as your own. However, font names can be trademarked so you have the phenomenon that Helvetica has called Aristocrat, Claro, Corvus, Europa Grotesk, Geneva, Hamilton, Helios, Holsatia, Megaron, Newton, Spectra, Swiss, Vega, and Video Spectra among other names.

Hehe, Europa Grotesk. I like that. I'll have to remember that name when I next have a run in with the Swiss gendarmes.

Monotype's Arial is not a copy of Helvetica, as some might think, but a separate font with some similar characteristics and arranged to have identical widths to the Adobe Helvetica font. But enough of culture! Let's return to our list of font terminology.

How are sizes measured? Fonts define a number of horizontal lines, all shown in Figure 2-21.

Figure 2-21: The definition of Point Size for a font

The letters E and x are especially regular. The line at their bottoms, which also lies on the bottom of most letters, is called the **baseline**. An imaginary line at the top of the cap E is called the **Cap height**. Most caps go up to the same line but some like cap S often extend slightly above. (The height of the letter x, called the **x–height** — another one of those obscure technical terms — is the typical height of many lower-case letters). Any lower-case letter which extends above the x-height is said to have an **ascender**. Typical examples are the letters t, h, and f (note that the t does not extend above the cap height but is still considered to have an ascender). Lower-case letters that fall below the base line are said to have a **descender**. Typical are g, j, and y.

The point size of metal type was easy to define; it was the height of the slug of metal that the letter floated on. The type designer would include an extra space below the lowest descender to avoid a cramped look. If more space was desired between lines, a strip of lead was inserted. This practice was called leading.

So **Point Size** is the distance between base lines of two successive lines of text. It is the distance from the top of the highest ascender and the bottom of the longest descender plus the default spacing designated by the designer.

The space taken by a line of type on a page is determined not only by the point size because the blank space between the bottom of the descenders of one row and the top of the ascenders of the next can be adjusted. This is called **leading** after the lead that printers once used to change that space! The term is pronounced to rhyme with "bedding," not with "seeding." With computer type unlike the metal version, one can even have negative leading!

One often talks of the sum of the extra space and the point size. So a 10-point font with an extra one point leading between lines is called a 10-point font with an 11-point spacing or just "10 on 11."

As the name *point size* suggests, the height is usually measured in a unit called **points**. A point was once approximately 1/72 inch but since the United States is the hand that rocks the computer cradle, it is now considered to be exactly 1/72 inch. The rest of the world may be metric but we continue to impose our weird measurements on them. So an 8-point font is 1/9 of an inch and a 11-point font with 12-point spacing fits six lines to the inch.

Having told you that a font isn't a font but is a scalable typeface, I'll misuse the terms and talk about fonts unless there is a need for clarity. What do vendors do? Why, of course, they use the terms in a way that will let them blazon the largest number of "fonts" in their packages. When fonts were sold in bitmapped form so that size mattered, a vendor could sell you two type families but in the standard four weight/styles (normal, bold, italic, and bold italic) and in seven point sizes (say 6, 8, 10, 11, 12, 14, 18) and yell about having 56 fonts! The two type families blossomed to 56 by multiplying 2x4x7.

Now that most fonts are outlines, vendors aren't able to multiply by the number of font sizes but you can bet they still count different weights/styles as separate "fonts." So, for example, the Monotype Value Pack says it has "57 typefaces." In fact it has seven type families in the standard four weight/styles, 21 display/symbol/script type families in 25 combinations, four Arial fonts and one Times New Roman at weights that supplement the ones in Windows. I'm not sure how they count 57, since by their rules I count 58, but its only a 2% error and no doubt it makes Heinz happy so why complain? However, by what a naive user would think fonts means, this package has 30 "fonts."

Monotype isn't to be singled out. Every vendor counts the same way and every naïve user misunderstands! In the naive terms, it is not atypical for a package that claims N fonts to have N/2 or N/2.5 type families. Indeed the celebrated 35 Postscript fonts are actually eight families of the standard four weight/styles and three specialized fonts for only 11 type families.

Type families are often grouped together in various ways. The simplest is fixed pitch vs. proportional spacing. **Fixed pitch** fonts have a common width for all letters so that M takes the same space as i while **proportional fonts** have variable letter widths within the single font. Here is the effect seen with Courier — a fixed pitch font, versus Arial — a proportional one:

Courier: MMMMMMMMMM   Arial: MMMMMMMMMM
               iiiiiiiiii   iiiiiiiiii

$$1234567890 \qquad \mathbf{1234567890}$$
$$1111144444 \qquad \mathbf{1111144444}$$

To have numbers line up, all numbers have a common width in either fixed pitch or proportional fonts.

Fonts 201

A more complex but useful breakdown is: serif, sans serif, script, display, and symbol. The first two sets are the work horses of typography — the ones you'd normally use for body text. A serif is the funny hook that some fonts have at their edges. Look at the four letters shown in Figure 2-22. The letters on the left are in a Sans Serif font (Arial) and the ones in the right in a Serif font (Times New Roman). Serif fonts are more common and include Baskerville, **Century Schoolbook**, Garamond, **Palatino**, and Times. Sans serif fonts include Avant Garde, **Futura**, and Helvetica.

I I T T

Figure 2-22: Sans Serif vs. Serif

Script fonts are ones you might use for invitations like **_Brush Script_**, _Zapf Chancery,_ and 𝔒𝔩𝔡 𝔈𝔫𝔤𝔩𝔦𝔰𝔥. Display fonts are usually used only in small amounts, mainly in headlines or letterheads. Among the more famous ones are **Cooper Black**, **Broadway**, **Bodoni**, and Pᴇɪɢɴᴏᴛ. Symbol fonts include foreign alphabets — notably Greek (αβχδεφγηιφκλμνοπ), math symbols (∫, ⊗ , Σ, ∉) and dingbats, those little pieces of fluff that make bulleted lists more exciting (☎, ✆, ➜, ✍, ☺).

It turns out that making dingbat fonts is fraught with peril! If you take the letters NYC, highlight them and change the font to Wingdings, you get:

A New York-based consultant discovered this shortly after Windows 3.1 shipped and suddenly the _New York Post_ blazoned on its front page

Software Company Vows Death to New York Jews

I kid you not — it really happened. Isn't technology grand?

 If you're really into Microsoft conspiracy theories, there's a better one. This story was short-lived because the Los Angeles riots broke out the next day and moved this story off the front page even in the Post.

 It's an interesting sidelight to the story, that six high ranking Microsoft executives met the next day to decide how to react to the story. Of the six, four are Jewish, including the managers of the font and Windows units.

 Personally, I think what the message really means is "if you take poison, see a Jewish doctor and you'll feel better." It's also interesting that they didn't complain about Mr. Zapf. In *his* dingbats, $A4 becomes ✄ ✡ ✔.Surely, the *Post* could have made something of that.

Windows also groups fonts into families but marches to its own drummer. This classification isn't used much but every font tells Windows (via its header) which of these groupings it falls into and you may see the names peeking out. Here are translations of Windows names:

- Modern — Fixed stroke-width fonts. This includes all fixed pitch fonts but is also supposed to include proportional fonts which have fixed width lines making them up. Of hundreds of fonts that I've seen the only proportional font that I've ever seen assigned to this family is one of the plotter fonts that ships with Windows called Modern. These are only modern in the sense that the printers before 1880 had enough sense not to think of them!

- Roman — what we'd call Serif fonts with a variable stroke weight, for example, Times New Roman

- Swiss — what we'd call Sans Serif fonts variable stroke weight, for example, Arial

- Script — at last, a standard name; this means script fonts

- Decorative — what the Windows SDK calls "a novelty font." Ransom in the second Microsoft Font Pack is an example

- Don't Care — A font whose maker doesn't care to put it into one of Windows weird groupings, a sensible attitude

To illustrate how little Microsoft cares about this way of classifying, the SDK gives Old English as an example of a Decorative font but the Old English Font in the second Microsoft Font Pack is assigned to Roman (at least according to the header in Fontographer). And you might think that Ransom was a novely font but it too is declared to be Roman. If any font should be Swiss, it would be Arial but it is assigned to Roman. So it seems that our favorite category Don't Care is a fitting closing thought for this classification.

Fonts 378

Herewith, a primer of some of the more esoteric font terminology:

- **Tracking** — This refers to letter spacing in a font as a whole or in a chunk of text as a whole. Useful only for special situations. Here's an example that should make it clear.

How big did you say that the fish was? It was a real WOPR, sir.	How big did you say that the fish was? It was a real WOPR, sir.	How big did you say that the fish was? It was a real WOPR, sir.
Default tracking	Tracked (too) tight	Tracked (too) loose

- **Kerning** — This refers to spacing between pairs of letters. Without kerning each letter has a fixed width — different width for different letters but, in the absence of kerning, all occurrences of one letter have the same width as all other occurrences . The space next to a **T** is the same for **Th** as for **To**. There is room to slightly tuck the o under the T which makes for a more attractive possibility at large point size. Look at the three following examples; the one where the o is nudged under the T is more attractive. High class fonts come with kerning information — tables to tell programs how to kern if they want to kern automatically. There are two types of kerning — automatic (for fonts that include kerning information) and manual. For headlines at large point sizes, you may want to do this manual adjustment.

To	To	To
No kerning	Kerned Condensed	Kerned Expanded

Here's how you hand kern in each of the three major Windows word processors:

- In Microsoft Word for Windows, only manual kerning is supported. The `Character...` item on the `Format` menu brings up a dialog that includes a spacing item. This is used to adjust kerning. Select the text you want and go to that dialog.

- In Word Perfect for Windows, manual and automatic kerning are both available from the `Typesetting...` dialog in the `Layout` menu.

- In Ami Pro, you can tell the program to kern automatically by using the `Options...` button in the `Tools/User Setup...` menu choice.

- **Hanging Indent** – This is the name given to a paragraph where the first line starts to the left of the rest of the paragraph, like the example below:

  > This text has a hanging indent. You'll notice that the second and subsequent lines start indented. Hanging indents are most naturally used when discussing a list of items. The indentation makes it easy for the eye to see when a new item has begun. Often with such a list, the first line has a bullet or dingbat so the text on line one is actually aligned with the lower lines. Typographers still regard that as having a hanging indent, since the bullet is included in line one.

- **Dropped Caps** and **Raised Caps**

This is a dropped cap, determined by making the initial letter large and having it dropped down into the text. A few programs allow you to pick dropped caps from a menu but otherwise you need to fool around with frames. Dropped caps should be arranged so that they lie on the base line of a lower line of type.

This is a raised cap. It is made by picking a large point size for the initial letter. It isn't as effective as a drop cap.

This is a fancy dropped cap made by changing the initial cap to a display font, in this case Augsberger Initial from the Microsoft Font Pack 2. It can be very effective unless you over use it in which case it can be a real drag. There are even fancier even fancier initial cap fonts available but only at specialty font prices.

- **Rules** is Rules; actually, rules are fancy names for lines.

> The most famous kind of rules are ones that are used for **pull quotes**, quotes from your text that you pull out and then make stand out by placing lines, I mean rules, above and below

- **En** and **Em** — font dependent measures of horizontal space. At one time, the em was the width of the letter M and the en was half an em. Now, an em is a horizontal space exactly equal to the point size and an en is half an em. Most important for referring to dashes of that width, specifically – and —.

- **Small Caps** — If you want an effect like Small Caps, you can try to use a smaller point size for the letters mall but the proportions aren't quite what a typographic purist would want. Some typefaces have special small caps fonts in their family. These are available in a few PostScript fonts but not in TrueType.

- **Lower-case** or **old style numerals** — The numerals included with modern fonts are called **lining numerals** because they are fixed width and will line up under one another. For a spreadsheet, you want to use these kinds of numerals but they do not look right is you are typing the time where 1:11 should have very different letter widths than 6:00. Again old style numerals are available in some PostScript fonts but not in TrueType.

- **Justification** — Your word processor probably supports four varieties as shown below:

There is text squeezed against the left side of the page but without any lining up on the right side. It is often called **ragged right** or sometimes **left justified**.

Text which is set to line up on both sides is called justified. Your word processor adds extra spaces between words to arrange for the text to line up

Text made to line up on the right side is called **right justified**. It is useful only in special circumstances like entering the date in a letter.

Centered text is also only useful in very special circumstances. Use it sparingly.

- **Widows** and **Orphans** — Yeah, I know, you gave at the office. To adequately tell you about these terms, I need to talk about my poor friend Sylvia from Boston, who married John from London. One day John and Sylvia's parents were in a terrible car accident and they were all killed. So Sylvia is a widow in England but

an orphan in the United States. In the same way, at one point, a paragraph with a
few words straggling onto the next page was called a widow in England and an
orphan in the United States. Since then an array of books on desktop publishing
has so muddied the waters that it is not clear what exactly is a widow and what an
orphan. The thing to avoid is either a paragraph with a single line at the bottom of
one page and its bulk on the next, or one with a single line at the end of a
paragraph carried to the next page. When you see either, flip a coin and then
knowingly say "Oh my, an orphan" or "Oh my, a widow" depending on whether
the coin is heads or tails. This terminology is also sometimes used to refer to single
words on the last line of a paragraph. Desktop publishers need to worry about this.
You can safely ignore it for correspondence or standards memos.

- **Ligatures** — Certain combinations, namely fi, fl, ffi, and ffl should be spaced so
  close together that they really should be treated as a single character (and the i's
  dot is wrong if you just kern the letters). In some specialized fonts they are treated
  as single characters. These characters are called ligatures.

Good Writing Needs Character Development

> Simplicity of character is no hindrance to subtlety of intellect.
>
> — John Morely, *Life of Gladstone*, 1903

In addition to the physical characteristics of size, weight, and style, the font you use has
a character set, the actual mapping of computer codes to symbols. Not only letters like
A or **x** but special symbols like ™ or ½. The initial starting point for PC character sets is
the ASCII code, a 7-bit assignment of a specific symbol to each number from 0 to 127
(ASCII is short for American Standard Codes for Information Interchange). This starts
with 32 control characters (holdovers from the days of Teletypes!) with codes 0 to 31.
It is followed by 32 symbols starting with space at code 32, punctuation like !. and ,
and the ten numerals. At code 64 is the character @ followed by the 26 cap letters in
ABC.. order and then five more symbols to round out the third set of 32. The final 32
start with ` and then have the 26 lower-case letters, each exactly 32 codes beyond the
corresponding caps. The basic ASCII set is rounded out by 5 final symbols (see Figures
2-23 and 2-24 — the codes from 32 to 127).

When IBM introduced the PC, the architecture of the system CPU made it natural to use
8-bit characters so IBM extended the ASCII set in two ways. It gave symbols to the
codes below 32, strange one like the playing card suits and the closest that the original
PC had to dingbats. In the area above 128, it placed accented letters like ê or á, line
drawing characters to allow the placement of frames, and a pitifully small selection of

Greek letters and mathematical symbols. Figures 2-23 and 2-24 show two views of the IBM character set (also called extended ASCII):

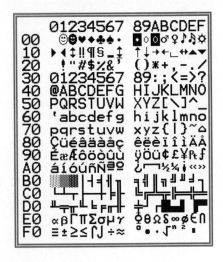

Figure 2-23: ASCII codes in
hexadecimal

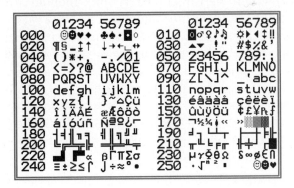

Figure 2-24: ASCII codes in decimal

Figure 2-24 is a decimal labeled table so that cap **A** is in the 060 row and the 5 column so its ASCII code is 65 decimal. In Figure 2-23 is a hexadecimal (base 16 labeled) table. Here A is in row 40 and column 1 so its code is 41H (which is of course 65 decimal).

These character sets are mainly of historical interest. Occasionally, users brought up in DOS desperately look for fixed pitch TrueType fonts with line draw characters but are unable to use them. Windows has one fixed pitch font that uses this character set which it installs automatically. It has a name like EGAOEM.FON or VGAOEM.FOM or 8514OEM.FON. It's a bitmapped font and is needed to display text copied from a DOS session on the clipboard viewer. Windows also ships with fonts using this character set for use in windowed DOS sessions but they are not normally installed for using in Windows applications.

I'm hoping that the next version of Windows has a TrueType OEM fixed pitch font and we can scale our DOS windows with automatic font adjustment. This is a feature in DesqView/X.

It's interesting that while everyone else calls this the IBM character set, Microsoft insists on calling it the OEM font. OEM is short for Original Equipment Manufacturer and could be IBM or Compaq or. . .

For other Windows fonts, a different character set is normally used — it is called the Windows ANSI character set. ANSI is short for American National Standards Institute and you'll see their name pop up all the time as you learn about computers. Microsoft has modified the set and makes some refinements as time goes on. In particular, some of the codes in the 140–160 range were not in Windows 3.0 but were added in Windows 3.1. A few of these "new" codes only codified what you could call black market codes — for example, ones for fancy quotes that the main desktop publisher's had set up. Figure 2-25 shows the Windows ANSI set:

	!	"	#	$	%	&	'	(	)	*	+	,	-	.	/	0	1	2	3	4	5	6	7	8	9	:	;	<	=	>	?
@	A	B	C	D	E	F	G	H	I	J	K	L	M	N	O	P	Q	R	S	T	U	V	W	X	Y	Z	[	\	]	^	_
`	a	b	c	d	e	f	g	h	i	j	k	l	m	n	o	p	q	r	s	t	u	v	w	x	y	z	{	|	}	~	□
□	□	‚	ƒ	„	…	†	‡	ˆ	‰	Š	‹	Œ	□	□	□	□	‘	’	“	”	•	–	—	˜	™	š	›	œ	□	□	Ÿ
	¡	¢	£	¤	¥	¦	§	¨	©	ª	«	¬	-	®	¯	°	±	²	³	´	µ	¶	·	¸	¹	º	»	¼	½	¾	¿
À	Á	Â	Ã	Ä	Å	Æ	Ç	È	É	Ê	Ë	Ì	Í	Î	Ï	Ð	Ñ	Ò	Ó	Ô	Õ	Ö	×	Ø	Ù	Ú	Û	Ü	Ý	Þ	ß
à	á	â	ã	ä	å	æ	ç	è	é	ê	ë	ì	í	î	ï	ð	ñ	ò	ó	ô	õ	ö	÷	ø	ù	ú	û	ü	ý	þ	ÿ

Figure 2-25: Windows ANSI characters

It's displayed with 32 characters in each row and starts with character 32, the space. Unassigned codes are shown with a box. The first three rows are the standard ASCII characters from code 32 to 126. The 0 in row one is at position 16 which is a useful marking point so, for example, the box below the 0 in row 4 is at position 128+16=144 and the quotes are at 145–148.

As I'll explain in Chapter 5 if you use the right utility (Compose), you can enter all these funny characters easily without worrying about the numbers (although you may need the numbers one time if you want to customize Compose) but if you don't get Compose you'll occasionally need to know the numbers so we note especially:

Types of Characters	Examples	Codes
Publisher's Quotes	‘ ’ “ ”	145–148
En and Em Dash	– —	150, 151
Trademark, etc	™ ® ©	153, 169, 174
Fractions	¼ ½ ¾	188–190
Currency	¢ £ ¥	162, 163, 165
Dots and Daggers	† ‡ •	134, 135, 149
typographic symbols	§ ¶	167, 182
Accented letters	ä Ø ç ñ	192–256

How do you enter these funny ANSI characters? There are three ways:

- the best way is to use Compose

- you can use the Windows applet Character Map which I'll discuss in Chapter 4

- you can enter a character with code 192, by holding down the **Alt** key and hitting

$$0 \quad 1 \quad 9 \quad 2$$

on the keypad

IBM (whoops, OEM) and Windows ANSI aren't the whole story for the forward looking Windows mayven. Extended ASCII and Windows ANSI are one byte character codes which means only 256 codes. This is stretched already but if one thinks of the ideographs of Japan and China, it is clearly too restricted. Unicode is a proposed two byte scheme which therefore allows 65,536 possible characters. Quite a bit of homework for you to learn them all, isn't it? The codes are described in two 600+ page volumes, the second of which is devoted solely to East Asian ideographs. Volume One starts with ASCII and then includes the Greek, Cyrillic, Armenian, Hebrew, Arabic, Devanagari, Bengali, Gurmukhi, Gujarti, Oriya, Tamil, Telugu, Kannada, Malayalam, Thai, Lao, Tibetan, and Georgian alphabets as well as assorted dingbats, math symbols, arrows and currency symbols.

Microsoft has announced its intention to move to Unicode in a future version of Windows. Think of all the symbols you'll have and think of all the programs that could break! Progress is rarely cheap.

Actually, grasshopper, Windows already supports Unicode. The fonts that ship with the Hebrew and Arabic versions of Windows are encoded in Unicode and those versions seem to have at least some degree of real Unicode support. What's even more interesting is that you can install them in the U. S. version of Windows without the system totally croaking. Character Map shows some of the font and you can enter its characters in Word for Windows (using a character remapping that you can read off from Character Map). It displays properly in Winword even after saving and reloading. But it doesn't print properly or paste properly into Write. Mind you, there is not supposed to be Unicode support in the U.S. version so what's notable is that anything works, not that it doesn't work completely! It shows that Windows transition to Unicode has already begun!

The Font of All Wisdom

CTO Mao has a whole chapter in his little red book on use and misuse of fonts. He's authorized me to quote liberally from it.

Avoid ransom note typography. It is the biggest type-based sin in a world with hundreds of fonts.

Ransom note typography is the name given to material that uses too many fonts–sort of like the imfamous ransom notes that are cut out of magazine ads with each letter in a different **font**. There are rules of thumb you'll see noted but they may be too generous to the fontoholic. The advice is somewhat different for **heading text**, the words used as section titles, and **body text**, the bulk of what you are saying.

Never use multiple fonts for body text on a single page. Indeed, consider using a single body text font in each document. Some of the font etiquette books suggest using a Serif font for body text and a Sans Serif font for headings. That's O.K., but it is often more elegant to use the same font for heading and body with the heading in bold and at a larger point size. Normally, you'd want to use the same typeface for heading and for page header/footer but, as this book shows, there can be special reasons to violate that `rule`.

Boy, the authors of this book should hang their heads in shame. They complain about ransom note typography and just look at the pages where we icons are all talking to each other. They complain about Windows Clock manuals and, what do they do but give you a windows clock manual. They rant and rave about benchmarks and give you benchmark numbers. Geez!

Well, Igor, you know that Emerson said that a foolish consistency is the hobgoblin of small minds.

Oh, yeah, that must be it. They don't want to look foolish. Geez!

Consider 11-point text for correspondence.

Ten-point text is more ordinary but it looks small. Some users jump to 12 point. Before scalable text, many font collections only had 10 and 12 point and skipped 11 but if you are using scalable fonts, 11 is easy. And it's a good compromise.

Throw out your fixed pitch fonts.

Well, don't exactly throw them out. Fixed pitch fonts are a holdover from obsolete technology. Typewriters couldn't handle proportional spacing so fixed pitch was introduced. The two fonts used in IBM typewriters — Courier and Elite — became the standard for business correspondence and even now law offices and some other businesses still tend to use them. But they are ugly. Avoid their use except for special purposes like our use of a fixed pitch font for keyboard keys.

Don't think that to get numbers to line up in a column, you need fixed pitch — all fonts used a fixed pitch for their numerals. Proper use of tabs, especially of right as well as left tabs is a more effective way to align columns with text.

Neither a borrower nor a lender be.

Igor, you cut that one out from the wrong part of the book! Besides, isn't that Tobias, not Mao?

Well, from someone guilty of Polonius assault.

As a general rule, set body text in a font with serifs.

The general wisdom is that for large chunks of text a font with serifs is easier to read because the serifs sweep the eyes along. The exception to this rule is the next rule!

Use sans serif fonts for smaller point sizes.

Eight point type and certainly anything smaller is more legible without the clutter of serifs. So if you are typing up a legal contract, use Arial for the fine print. This rule is an artifact of computer generated fonts. Hot metal fonts compensated for smaller sizes by thickening strokes and increasing x-heights. With such fonts, serif fonts were more legible at smaller sizes. This is not true for computer generated fonts.

 Think about your audience when using fonts.

This may be obvious but users caught up in the excitement of the great new font forget it. Fonts are important because, in unseen ways, they really can set the tone of a document. You should use the template/style sheet feature of your word processors to pick the fonts for different kinds of documents and stick with it. You can make exceptions for the announcement of the company picnic.

 So he's saying to thine own self be true.

 Igor, your fixation on the bard is too much with us.

 Avoid using dingbats and other doo-hickeys too much. Similarly avoid using too many rules.

Remember that the point of using fonts is to make your point — to get a message across. You risk having the messenger get in the way if you overload the text with stuff that distracts rather than complements. Again you can make exceptions for the announcement of the company picnic.

 Yo, Mom. Did ya see what he said about avoiding too many rules. Kids would sure like that!

 He meant publisher's rules. The lines that make up boxes or can break text.

 For long documents, use ragged right text. For short business correspondence and memos of less than a page, consider using justified text.

This advice is somewhat controversial. Justified text is definitely harder to read (which is why you want to avoid it in long documents), less elegant to my taste, and enough to make the font snobs wince. But it looks more business like.

 Use publisher's quotes like "…" and '…' and the real apostrophe ' rather than the lower ASCII characters ", ' and `. Also use the en dash – and em dash — rather than a hyphen -

It is a pain to enter these characters from the keyboard so you'll need some method to help. Use the Compose utility I'll discuss in Chapter 5. Use macros for your word processor that go through documents and fix up the quotes from " to " and ".

 Be consistent. A good rule in dealing with children, employees, and type. Use the same font including weight and point size for heading throughout a document.

 Avoid too much dense text. If you want people to read and understand what you write, don't have long paragraphs. Be sure to place some white space between paragraphs. Remember that the concentration span of the MTV generation for written text is about three words.

 AVOID USING ALL CAPS. They are actually harder to read because the eye prefers variation and they don't even produce the desired emphasis. Besides needing to use all caps for emphasis is the sign of a limited typographic environment as you'd find with a typewriter or in online messages. Use **bold** for emphasis.

 Use real **bold** and *italic*. If you use a font that doesn't have a bold or an italic, Windows will try to fake it and the results are not as fine as you get with a font that has the extra weights/styles. Alas, the only way to know if the bold/italic is real is to remember from the ad for the font or to look at the font list in Write (or if you are dealing with TrueType fonts, in the fonts applet of Control Panel).

 Don't be cowed by this advice or the advice of others. Do experiment and do consider breaking rules (the rules that get pontificated, not the rules that are really straight lines!). If you've understood the reason for a rule and have reason to break it, you're almost sure to do the right thing.

Could You Gimme a Hint?

That faculty of beholding at a hint the face of his desire and the shape of his dream,
without which the earth would know no lover and no adventurer.

— Joseph Conrad, *Lord Jim*, 1900

You want a hint sonny, I'll give you a hint! You go to New York and
don't call your Aunt Sally, I'll... Lemme give ya a hint. It's spelled E–G–
O–R–E.

I guess Mom had a bad day. But when you hear about how good Microsoft's hinting is,
most likely, the speaker is not referring to how well their press agency seeds rumors
but to the care put into their TrueType fonts.

If you print a 72-point letter on a 2200 dpi Linotronic, the letter will be at least a
thousand dots high and a few dots won't matter. But consider a 15 inch monitor
running at 800x600. A 15-inch diagonal at a 4x3 aspect ratio, means a 9-inch height or
fewer than 72 dots per inch so on screen an 8-point letter could have five or six dots
in it.

Hey, CTO, how comes
he didn't say 2200 dots
for the Linotronic and 8
dots for the 8 point?

Remember that point size is measured from the
top of the tallest letter to the bottom of the
letter that drops down the most plus a default
line spacing. So no letter has a height equal to
the point size!

The best fonts in Windows are scalable fonts which are stored as outlines which are
rasterized before being displayed on your screen or printer. In case you skipped it, I
discussed rasterization earlier in *And dots not all.*

The two main outline formats in terms of usage are TrueType and PostScript Type 1.
TrueType is included in Windows 3.1. To rasterize Post Script fonts on screen, you
need a copy of Adobe Type Manager (ATM). You can purchase ATM separately or find
it bundled with a variety of word processors, graphics and other applications and I'll
tell you about whether I think you need it in the next section.

The dumb algorithm for rasterizing an outline font is to pretend to draw the objects at
a much higher resolution on top of a grid representing the available resolution. If a box
is more than 50% covered, fill in the corresponding dot as black. Otherwise leave it
blank. This algorithm could do violence to a letter form. In many fonts, W is left —
right symmetric. But if the grid is not aligned to the exact character width, using the
dumb algorithm could destroy that symmetry. So an intelligent font rasterization

scheme allows for information about symmetry. **Hints** are the name given to all information beyond the pure outlines that are included with a font.

Hints include information to be sure serifs aren't dropped, that essential type elements like a cross bar on the t aren't dropped and are uniform from left to right when they need to be. Both TrueType and PostScript Type 1 have hinting engines built into them so that font vendors can supply this extra information.

Hinting has three levels of sophistication. Some fonts in these formats have no hinting because the vendor didn't bother. Some are autohinted. That means that an automated program was used to make the hints. A few have hand-tuned hints — hints added by a professional type designer usually after autohinting is first done.

Both ATM and TrueType include font caches. They save in memory the raster patterns for recently rasterized letters and don't have to do it again and again. On slower machines you may note a pause the first time you use a font in a session compared to later usage — that's the effect of the font not being in the cache the first time around.

The biggest font vendors have their own programs for internal use. And they will also hand-tune afterwards. Microsoft did all the right things when it added TrueType to Windows. First they started with a good specification. Indeed, TrueType hinting is a superset of what is in PostScript. Second, they introduced new printing technology that substantially sped up printing on HP Laser (and related) printers compared to ATM 1.0. That version of ATM rasterized a page of text as dots and sent it to the printer as a graphic. Suppose a page had the letter **A** 200 times on the page, all in the precisely identical font. Because of the font cache, ATM would rasterize it only once and get it the other times from the cache. Because the dot pattern is sent as a graphic, the dot pattern for that **A** would get sent to the printer 200 times on that page. Since the parallel port is one of the slowest links on computer, that's a lengthy process.

Windows TrueType engine used the ability of laser printers to understand downloadable fonts. It would send the characters needed for that page to the printer as a soft font sending each dot pattern only once. Then those 200 could be sent as characters requiring only 1 byte each. ATM added that feature in version 2.0 but the speed boost was a welcome addition for which Microsoft deserves the bulk of the credit.

Third, Microsoft provided 14 TrueType fonts with Windows — not just mediocre fonts but great ones. There were four weights each of three basic typefaces, Times New Roman, Arial, and Courier New. All were licensed from Monotype and all had hand-tuned hints. Times New Roman is certainly my favorite variant of Times and one of the best fonts period. These 12 fonts were supplemented by a symbol font and the Wingdings font.

Finally, Microsoft broke the back of high font prices with its first TrueType font pack but more of that in the section after the next.

Love Me True (Type)

The $64,000 question for fonts is "Do I need PostScript and ATM if I already have TrueType under Windows 3.1?" There's a simple answer and a complicated answer.

The simple answer is: TrueType is a superb engine. There are lots of inexpensive, well-done TrueType fonts available, and it's built into Windows. And you can be sure that any application will support it. Au contraire, ATM's font cache will take a significant chunk of memory and will be supported by most but not all applications. So no, you don't need ATM.

The complex answer is: TrueType is a superb engine, there are lots of inexpensive, well-done TrueType fonts available, and it's built into Windows. And you can be sure that any application will support it. Au contraire, ATM's font cache will take a significant chunk of memory and will be supported by most but not all applications. So no, you don't need ATM. . . *except* under special circumstances.

Let's consider some possible special circumstances in Q/A format.

Q: I do desktop publishing and my service bureau insists on using Type 1 fonts. Do I need ATM?

A: This is a serious reason to use ATM but many service bureaus see the handwriting on the wall (it's in Lucida Handwriting font of course) and are shifting to support TrueType also. Perhaps yours is. Or maybe you were looking for an excuse to change service bureaus? But this is certainly a case where you may want to install ATM.

Q: I've a PostScript printer with the standard 35 resident fonts in printer. Shouldn't I use those resident fonts? And, if I use the resident fonts, don't I need ATM to get the right fonts on screen.

A: No and No! Printing with the resident is faster but because of the laser printer strategy used by TrueType, the speed penalty in not using the resident fonts is not large at all. Thus, the question of whether to use the resident fonts or not is partly dependent on taste. Times New Roman is superior to Adobe Times and to my eye the others are at least comparable.

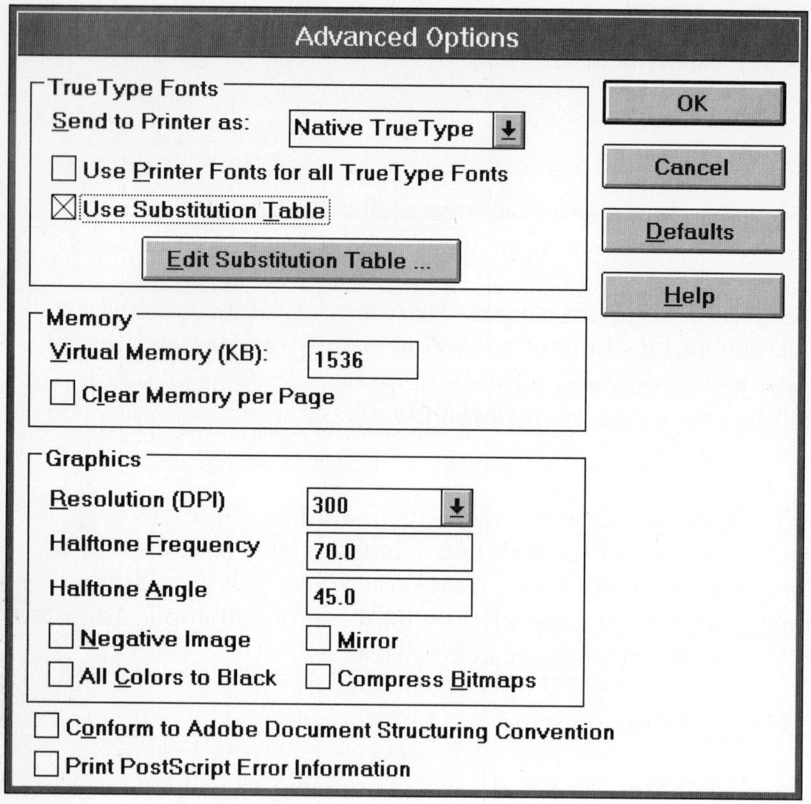

Figure 2-26: The PostScript Driver Advanced Options dialog

Even if you decide to use the printer's resident fonts, you still don't need ATM if you get the Microsoft Font Pack 1. Here's what you do. Call up the Printers applet from Control Panel and call up the setup for your PostScript printer. Hit the Options button and then the Advanced button in the Options dialog. Make sure the dialog that then pops up has the check box next to **Use Substitution Table** checked (see Figure 2-26). It's as simple as that. The substitution table tells the printer driver, for example, to not print Book Antiqua by rasterizing but to instead use the printer font called Palatino. Since the two fonts are arranged to have the same width tables the substitution will work. If you only want some of the fonts translated, say you want to use the resident Palatino but want to use Times New Roman you can use the **Edit Substitution Table** dialog. In addition, the Font Pack installation adds the line

Palatino=Book Antiqua

to the [FontSubstitutes] section of your win.ini file. This means that any program that asks for a Palatino font will get Book Antiqua on screen (and if you've checked **Use Substitution Table** it will get Palatino again on the printer!).

Q: I bought a program that ships with ATM. Won't it expect ATM to be there?

A: Probably not. Even Adobe PhotoShop (but not Adobe Illustrator whose native format is EPS) works as well with TrueType fonts as with PostScript and ATM.

Q: I brought a program that ships with some PostScript fonts or I have this neat PostScript font I bought three years ago. Won't I need ATM to use them?

A: Well, yes. But you could consider a conversion program like FontMonger which I'll tell you about in Chapter 5 although if the fonts are really well hinted, you'll lose most of that in translation.

Q: I'm in love with old fashioned numerals and small caps and the Adobe expert sets. Can I get those with TrueType?

A: Adobe has resisted TrueType. I guess pride is more important than money. So you can't get their expert sets. So far, I'm not aware of TrueType fonts with small caps and old fashioned numerals. But you could consider a conversion program.

Q: I've heard that there is more variety of fonts with better hinting available with PostScript. Is that true?

A: Yes. Not all of the foundries have moved all their fonts to TrueType and those fonts that have moved are often not as well hinted. At current font prices and the current level of sophistication of most font purchasers, there is a tremendous temptation for font makers to not invest the considerable time in hinting as well as Monotype hinted the TrueType fonts that ship with Windows.

(Well) Bred and Better

There are a few fonts suitable for body text that you'll use most of the time — your bread and butter fonts. I want to tell you how I chose those. The main font foundries really do have better fonts and the advice I'd give you is to go with a top foundry — most notably Monotype. Here's the advice in more detail.

The fonts that come with Windows are so good that you'd be happy using just them. They are so common though that if you want to show some individuality, you may decide to buy some more fonts. You won't be alone. Igor's limited market research suggests that fonts are over a $100 million a year business.

I, Igor, figured out this sales figure from two numbers I did know. Bitstream's 1990–92 sales were over $20 million each year. In 1992, Microsoft offered its font pack as an option for direct mail Windows 3.1 upgrades and about 1 million upgraders got the pack at about $40. So counting Adobe (whose 1992 sales including not only fonts but also PostScript licenses and their software programs was over $250 million), I figure it most be over $100 million.

Fonts are the potato chips of the Windows world. You can't eat only one. A few years ago, a better analogy would be nicotine. The font companies had their few samples to hook you — their Joey camels. All sorts of programs were bundled with Bitstream Dutch and Swiss which vendors got for very little. But if they hooked you, boy, did you have to raid the cookie jar. A single typeface (in four outlines for the standard weight/styles) beyond the basics went for $200–$300. That's $50 or more per font.

 The boys'll count fonts the way the foundries do. If a font pack has the wonderful new Foorific™ font as Foorific™ Roman, Foorific™ Bold, Foorific™ Italic and Foorific™ Italic Bold, they call it four fonts even though you and I know it is really only one type family. This counting isn't so bad. Decorative typefaces usually come in one weight/style. You'll use the four weight/style typefaces at least four times as much as the decorative one.

But then Microsoft went and spoiled the party! Their Font Pack I gave you 44 fonts for a street price of under $50. Fonts were suddenly only a buck each. At that price, you can afford to nibble quite a few potato chips. The major font foundries gritted their teeth and, gasp, competed. They kept some of their fonts at the old rate to catch the pathetic guys huddled in the corner shooting up every new font that shows up but they also produced font packs at the buck-a-font street price. And, surprise, they did quite well because the volumes were enormous compared to what it was for the $50/font market.

The schlock font vendors competed. They blazon **250 fonts for $49.99**. Those fonts tend to run 20–25 cents each. I'd go with the higher priced buck apiece fonts. Even if there doesn't seem to be huge differences, there are subtle differences. The $30–$50 fonts pack price is similar — it's a choice between 50 or 200 fonts at that price. I ask you: are you even gonna want to install those two hundred fonts?

You are likely to regret installing more than about 150 fonts. Every time a program gives you a font choice via the fonts common dialog, you'll be able to get a cup of coffee while the dialog loads. Some apps literally become demented if you install more than about 250 fonts. I tried it in Word for Windows 2.0 (where the limit is 255) and Word refused to list some of the fonts and started listing others multiple times. It was a very unhappy application.

If you insist on having so many fonts, you'll need a font organizer like Microsoft Font Assistant (discussed in Chapter 5).

So who are the good font vendors? Before TrueType, they were Adobe, Monotype, and Bitstream. In the TrueType world, Adobe has dropped out, and Microsoft has replaced it at the level of offering excellent font packs. My advice is to stick with these three for your bread and butter fonts, but if you can't resist getting more than an 100 fonts in one package for pennies a font, the best of the second tier font vendors is Casady & Greene.

Chapter 13 shows samples of bread and butter fonts from the three big vendors and from Casady & Greene. I wanted to give you a complete catalog so I've shown every font from their broad based collections of bread and butter fonts. In a few cases, there may not be bold italic or some other variant but the basic fonts are there at a large point size and for the body text fonts at a medium point size.

The street price of the Casady & Greene collection is about 35 cents per font. The other collections are closer to a dollar a font.

I tried to separate into body text vs. other families fonts (script or decorative), usually using the division that the vendor supplies but in some cases deciding myself. Some of the doo-hickey fonts I'll showcase in the next section come in packages which include some bread and butter fonts and there are a few doo-hickey fonts in these collections.

My favorite among the font packs is the Monotype TrueType Value Pack with 58 fonts. Monotype is an honored name in font design going back to the last century. Their font Times New Roman is called that because it was commissioned by The Times when it wanted to have a new body font. That was in the 1920's so the "new" isn't so new! And The Times is "of London" — did you have another one in mind? When Microsoft wanted to be sure the fonts bundled with Windows 3.1 were really first rate, they went to Monotype and licensed their Times New Roman and Arial.

Times New Roman and Arial are equivalents to two of the fonts included in the "standard 35 PostScript" fonts, the ones included on most high end PostScript printers. Equivalent means more than that they sorta look the same. It means that they have identical width tables so you can use an equivalent font on screen to represent a printer font. If you take my advice about using TrueType for printing, that won't be important, but if you are dealing with a PostScript-only service bureau, it will be. The full list and their Monotype equivalents are:

@ PostScript Name	Number	Monotype Name
Courier	4	Courier New
Helvetica	4	Arial
Symbol	1	Symbol
Times Roman	4	Times New Roman
Avant Garde	4	Century Gothic
Bookman	4	Bookman Old Style
Helvetica Condensed	4	Arial Narrow
New Century Schoolbook	4	Century Schoolbook
Palatino	4	Book Antiqua
Zapf Chancery	1	Monotype Corsiva
Zapf Dingbats	1	Monotype Sorts

The thirteen fonts above the line are included with Windows 3.1 (which includes a fourteenth TrueType font — Wingdings). The 22 afterwards are among those available in the Monotype Value Pack. Monotype also leverages its ownership of the rights to Arial and Times New Roman by including five additional weights of these fonts: a Times New Roman Extra Bold and Arial Extra Bold, Arial Extra Bold Italic, Arial Extra Bold Condensed, and Arial Black (even bolder than Extra Bold).

There are two families of serif fonts provided in the four standard weight/styles: Baskerville and Chalets. Both are light and legible. Finally there are eight script fonts and twelve headline faces. Most of these are Monotype originals rather than the war-horses of the font world so you won't find a Broadway, Exotic, Cooper Black, or Embassy type script. About the only fonts in the collection you're likely to be familiar with are Bodoni and Rockwell.

This lack of famous fonts has both positives and negatives — you may have a favorite which is missing, but, if your goal is to use fonts to make your output stand out, using well-made but uncommon fonts will help. About the only real downsides of the Monotype Value Pack is that you won't want it if you already have the Microsoft Font Pack 1 (as I'll explain in a moment) and it is going to be harder to find at a street price than the other products I'll be discussing. But it is worth looking or even (horrors!) paying retail for Monotype!

Surely the most popular font collection ever (measured in sales!) must be the 44 font Microsoft Font Pack 1 which was offered in a special deal at the time of the Windows 3.1 upgrade. Microsoft first licensed the 22 fonts that Monotype uses in its own Value Pack to complete the PostScript 35 (that is the fonts under the line in the above table).

Microsoft added an additional 22 fonts in a single family called Lucida, licensed from Bigelow & Holmes: basic Serif and Sans Serif fonts plus fonts called FAX and Typewriter in four weights, three script fonts, and three mathematical fonts. The idea of fonts with similar shapes in a variety of formats, a kind of extended type family is an interesting one and the math fonts are useful if you are into that sort of thing. Indeed Bigelow & Holmes invented the Lucida family as a font set to be used with TeX a mathematical markup language. On the whole, the Lucida fonts aren't as well-done as the other fonts in the packs from the big three.

Because of the overlap of the 22 Monotype PostScript Equivalent fonts, you will not want both this collection and the Monotype Value Pack. If you have neither yet, I urge you to get the Monotype offering; if you have the Microsoft Pack 1, enjoy it!

Microsoft's Font Pack 2 is another 44 font collection, all of them well made. Four of them are called Ransom because they look like ransom notes, not exactly something you'd use in business or, for that matter anywhere else except for a conversation piece.

I've some friends who could sure use that ransom note font. But other than that, seems like a waste of 10% of the pack, doesn't it.

Futura is a war-horse but a nice alternative to the ubiquitous Arial/Helvetica for sans serif. Contemporary Brush, Playbill and Mistral are also common fonts in good variants. All in all, this package is a good mix of the usual and the unusual, body and headline. There are even two more Wingding fonts for the doo-hickey lover. Add to the fonts, the useful Font Assistant utility and you have my second favorite of the collections.

Bitstream also has a long history of dedication to the typographer's trade. They own the largest collection of fonts. Bitstream has two bread and butter collections, the 40 font Bitstream TrueType Font Pack and the 20 font Bitstream TrueType Font Pack 2. The company has a love for obscure names. The font file themselves have names like tt0051m_.ttf (Zapf Elliptical if you care) and even the fonts have numbers in their names, e.g. Humanist 521. As we were going to press, Bitstream announced that its typeface library of almost 1,100 fonts is now available in TrueType format. Fonts start at $32.

Zapf Chancery, Zapf Dingbats, Zapf Elliptical,. . . Hermann Zapf is one of the world's great type designers still going strong at age 75! A deserved legend who awes even the font snobs.

The first pack has a Vineta font that actually pulls off a 3-D effect. The Imperial and Humanist fonts present an attractive alternative to using Times and Helvetica. For the war-horse font lover, the second pack has classic Cooper Black, Embassy, Exotic and Hobo.

One note: because stores don't like to sell products for much under $20, even though the first font pack has twice as many fonts as the second, the street prices are similar. But you should buy on the basis of what fonts appeal to you, not on mere font count.

Casady & Greene's Fluent Laser Fonts 2 is a superset of their Fluent Laser Fonts 1 which is no longer available. Their Button and Checkbox fonts shows their heritage as a Mac font vendor but you should forgive them for that! A few of their speciality fonts are interesting — the Collegiate series and Michelle come to mind. There are so many fonts that in any category, you'll find something to your liking.

Fontasy

Besides, the bread and butter fonts, Mom's font catalog has a large selection of doo-hickey fonts.

 Igor's Computer dictionary defines a doo-hickey font as one that the fonts snobs call silly.

The snobs have a point. A lot of them are silly but they are fun and can make a special point if used sparingly and in the right place. As always, when dealing with fonts, ask the key question — is this use adding to the impact of what I want to communicate or is it likely to be a distraction?

Doo-hickey fonts are mainly dingbat and other pictograph fonts – purely symbolic but there are some text faces (the Looney Tunes fonts come to mind) which clearly fall into this category. Basically, a doo-hickey text font is one that you wouldn't consider using in business correspondence or memos, like the Ransom font.

I dunno. Some of my colleagues would use Ransom in their business correspondence.

Mom's divided her catalog into complete packages since that's what you have to buy. So the bread and butter font packs have some doo-hickey fonts (not many) and the doo-hickey font packs have some bread and butter fonts thrown in (quite common).

Once again Montoype tops Mom's pantheon of font packs. Montoype Fun Fonts has 25 fonts in all — one family (Amasis) in the standard four weights/styles, 10 decorative fonts and 11 of what it calls art fonts that are symbols of various types. The centerpiece, of course are the symbol fonts. Four of them are "dull" — numbers and the alphabet in inside a circle or square with the inside filled or not. Only the upper-case letters are used but the lower-case keyboard has twenty left and right half circle/square with a number so you can also have two digit numbers. These are ideal for special effects.

For the doohickey lover, the center of the Fun Fonts are the seven true symbol fonts: Almanac (signs of the Zodiac, moon, sun, etc), Flowers, Arrows, two Sports symbols, transport and vacation. For these seven fonts, only the 52 upper- and lower-case letters have symbols. That's the one disappointment — there is an advantage to using the keyboard but the ten numbers and eleven punctuation keys could have allowed another 42 symbols in each font.

Agfa's Discovery Font Pack is for the doo-hickey lover willing to trade fonts somewhat below the very top quality for quantity. Besides the fifteen clip art fonts, there are seventeen text fonts in four families and fourteen headline fonts including such war horses as Cooper Black, Broadway, and Don Casual. Again the centerpieces are the clipart fonts in seven groupings: Borders&Ornaments, Communications, Games&Sports, Holidays, Industry&Engineering, and Transportation. Some fonts have close to the 94 symbol maximum that you can get by using the central keys in shifted and unshifted states but others do not. Indeed, while there are three separate Sports fonts, they only total 163 symbols and could have fit in two. A nice touch is a help file that shows the keyboard layouts for the symbol fonts.

For the kids in your life, if they are into fonts, Bitstream offers six separate Li'l Bits collections: Star Trek in new and old generation, Winter Holiday, Looney Tunes, Jetson, and Flintstones. Each includes five or six fonts, typically half standard Bitstream fonts and half speciality. Definitely novelty items but that's what this side of the font business has become.

Finally, we mention Davka Bats (Davka Software, Voice:800-621-8227) is a dingbat font with Judaic themes. It's pricey for a single font but it is in a niche area.

The Mother of All Font catalogs (Chapter 13) has samples of all these fonts.

Not with My System Directory, You Don't

This section is kinda tech. Feel free to skip it. I'm gonna tell you about the places that Windows stores font information. Why should you care?

Oh, Mao, I love it when you talk techie to me. Gives me goose bumps.

Perhaps you have the same hangup I have that there is too much stuff that every Tom, Dick, and Harry places in the System subdirectory of my Windows directory. I'm gonna first give you Igor's simple method for moving font files out of your system directory. I like to keep the TrueType font files that are supplied by different vendors each in a vendor specific directory and for that I'll need a more involved method. So I'm going to tell you how to do that and that will involve some understanding of this stuff. Along the way, I'll tell you how to change the font Windows uses for icon captions

Moreover, there are some error situations where knowing this can come in handy. Just the other day, Mom's Word for Windows wouldn't recognize some font she knew she had and which Windows claimed were loaded. Igor tried the Printer Setup shuffle but that didn't solve the problem. Mao fixed it using what he knew about font files.

The Printer Setup Shuffle concerns the fact that Winword keeps its own font database which may get out of synch from what is actually installed in Windows. Just choosing `Printer Setup` from the `File Menu`, choosing the Setup button in the resulting dialog and clicking OK twice to get out will update this internal font information.

Windows keeps font information in both **win.ini** and **system.ini**. It also stores information in two kinds of Windows specific files with extensions **FON** and **FOT**. The actual TrueType fonts are contained in files supplied by the font vendor with an extension of **TTF**. If you use PostScript and *ATM*, there are even more kinds of font files to worry about.

I just make a `fonts` subdirectory of my Windows directory, add it to my path, move all the `fon`, `fot`, and `ttf` files to it and be done with it. Windows looks down the path for all these things if it can't find the files where the path names say they can be so it has no trouble locating my fonts. It probably takes a few more milliseconds to load but I'm off checking the mail then so I don't care. Mao wants to use so many directories to store his fonts that he can't put them all in his path and needs to to all the complicated stuff he'll tell you about. Some people just can't take the easy way, can they?

The **FON** files are bitmapped fonts. Windows normally requires some of those to display menus and icon captions. System.ini contains information on what **FON** file is used for DOS to be displayed in a window. It has to be a **FON** bitmapped fonts although I hope that in a future version of Windows they'll let us use TrueType fonts. Even better, I hope they let you pick the font as part of the PIF file! I'll tell you a lot more about how Windows picks fonts for windowed DOS sessions in the section called *DOS Fonts* in Chapter 3.

You can change the font that Windows uses to display Icon Captions and that Progman Uses to display its icon captions. The key is several entries in the `[desktop]` section of `win.ini`. For example you might have:

> IconTitleFaceName=Times New Roman
>
> IconTitleSize=10
>
> IconTitleStyle=1

The first entry tells Windows what font to use. It must be one of the font names that appears in [fonts] section of win.ini that the boys'll tell you about in a moment. The second is the size. You'll want 7, 8, 9, or 10. The last says to use boldface. You can have none of these lines or only one or two and Windows only makes the change you have lines for.

Windows knows what fonts are installed because of the **[fonts]** section of **win.ini**. Entries have the form:

fontname=name of FOT or FON file

for example

Arial (TrueType)=C:\WINDOWS\SYSTEM\ARIAL.FOT

or

MS Serif 8,10,12,14,18,24 (VGA res)=SERIFE.FON

The pathname (the part that says C:\WINDOWS\SYSTEM\ in the Arial entry) is not needed — Windows assumes it but it will let you move your FOT and FON files out of the system directory. That I don't do because the Fonts applet in Control Panel insists on writing the FOT files in the system directory and it's just too complicate to fight city hall like that.

You will not normally change this section of **win.ini** by hand although you may need to consult it (I'll explain one reason below but it can also give you a quick count of just how many fonts you have — just call **win.ini** into an editor with a line count function and count the lines). You control the FOT and FON files entries as well as FOT files with the Fonts applet.

The FOT files are really Windows DLLs. If you look at them in a Hex viewer, you'll see they contain the complete path name of the TTF file. That's part of the key to moving out the TTF — no don't use a Hex editor to change it! See below.

If you want to install a font from a font package into a directory other than the system, the easiest way is not to use the Install program (unless there are other programs as part of the package like the Font Assistant in the Microsoft Font Pack 2). Here's what you do:

1. Copy the TTF files on the install disks into the directory you want. If you can't find any TTF files but only TT_ files, those are compressed and you'll need to follow step 1a instead.

1a. To handle compressed TT_ files, you need the expand program which is a DOS (horrors!) program in the Windows directory. If the font files are in A and your windows directory is C:\windows, open a DOS session, go to the directory you want to put the files in and enter

```
C:\windows\expand A:*.tt_ .
```

(note the period (dot) at the end of the line; be sure to type it in). This will expand them but they'll still be named tt_ so then enter

```
ren *.tt_ *.ttf
```

2. Now run the Fonts applet and choose Add. In the dialog that pops up (see Figure 2-27) be sure that the check box labelled **Copy Fonts to Windows Directory** is **not** checked. Now click OK and you are done. Windows makes the **FOT** files but points 'em in the right place.

But what if you already have lots of TTF files in your system directory? Then the process is a little more complicated. Hold on to your seat — here goes:

1. If you have ALL your TrueType fonts in the system directory and want to move them wholesale to a single directory, you can skip this one. Otherwise, you'll need to print out the **[Fonts]** section of win.ini and a directory listing of the TTF fonts in your system directory (for example with

```
dir *.ttf >prn
```

at a DOS prompt in the system directory. An entry (with Bistream's crazy names) might be

```
Cooper Black BT (TrueType)=C:\WINDOWS\SYSTEM\TT0630M_.FOT
```

That tells you that the name of the Copper Black font file is **TT0630M_.TTF** which may or may not actually be in the system directory (the **FOT** file is there but the **TTF** may not be). From that figure out what the names are of the **TTF** files you want to move. Fortunately, they will be grouped in the order you installed them so, for example, all the fonts in the Monotype Pack will likely be together in the **[Fonts]** section.

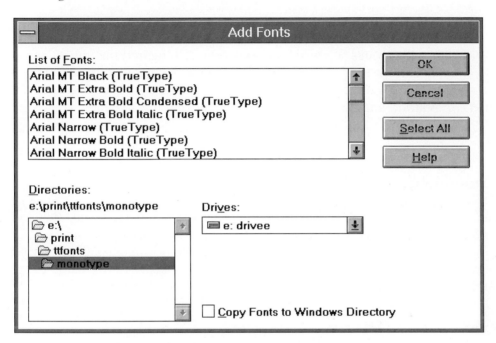

Figure 2-27: The Add Fonts dialog in the Fonts Applet

2.   Now copy (**not** move) the TTF from their current place to where you want them to be, for example from C:\system\windows to C:\ttfonts\monotype. You can move different **TTF**s to different directories.

3.   Call up the Fonts applet, **Ctrl+Click** to select all the fonts that you want moved. Make sure you don't **Shift+Click** by mistake and that you really have copied the **TTF**s since you are about to delete those **TTF** files. Scroll through you selection list to make sure that you got it right. The applet will use the names on the right of the = sign in the **[Fonts]** sections. The file names are on the left. (The names on the left are actually taken by Windows from the inside of the **TTF** file!). Now click the **Remove** button and check the box labelled **Delete font file from disk**. If you are feeling brave, click on **Yes to All**, otherwise go through **Yes** one at a time. What you have just done is remove the FOT files for

those fonts (that happens whether that box is checked or not), remove the TTF files in the old location (because you checked the box) and updated win.ini.

4. Now click the Add button in the Fonts applet, go to the directory where you copied the TTFs, be sure to uncheck the **Copy Fonts to Windows Directory** box and hit OK.

That's it; too bad that Windows has made it so hard, isn't it.

Finally, how did Mao solve Mom's Winword font problem? He figured that the problem was probably corrupt FOT files. So he called up the Font applet, removed the fonts that Winword couldn't see (being careful to NOT check the **Delete font file from disk** button), and then added them back picking the TTF files. Voilà — Mom was back in business.

Portable Documents

The only universal format for exchange of textual information is ASCII, a format that has been in place for many years. Clearly, we need a format that supports font information, pictures, and all that so we can transmit "portable documents." There are the beginnings of proposals for such a format at least in the context of proprietary file structures. At this time, only one set of products has shipped but there are rumors of competing proposals/prodcuts and it is not clear what will win the hearts and minds of the marketplace.

The one set of products are from Adobe involving a format they call PDF (portable document format) and a set of products under the name Acrobat — specificaly Acrobat Reader, Acrobat Exchange, and Acrobat Distiller. The Reader is included in the other products and will view Acrobat documents created with the other products. The PDF includes general information on the fonts used in the document and the reader has technology to produce an approximation of the font on your screen and printer even if you don't own the actual font. The output won't make a font lover do cartwheels but it will look a lot like the true original.

Acrobat Exchange for Windows includes a "printer driver" that lets you "print" a document to a PDF file. The Distiller allows full postscript output to the pseudo printer including support for EPS files. With either product, there is a PDF editor that lets you add hyperlinks, annotations and more to a PDF file.

By using compression technology and settling for approximations of the actual document, PDF files can be much smaller than the original document. In one sample that Adobe talks about, an 80 MB PageMaker document (with lots of big bitmaps) produces a PDF under 2 MB. Impresssive technology, well worth watching.

 With Adobe's name behind it and such technology, one might expect that Adobe's format will win the day but I think Adobe isn't serious about wanting to become a universal standard. If they were, they'd provide a public domain reader. Frankly, it should be the whole shebang, but even one without support for hyperlinks and annotation might carry the day. If they did that, doc files, BBS manifestos and whatnot would start appearing in the format and folks would feel they had to get the reader. Then to make the files, many people would buy the programs that produce PDF files. But under their current scheme, it is going to be a niche product and one that most Windows users can ignore.

 My advice is to keep an eye on the portable document scene but you can probably stay on the sidelines. If Adobe releases a public domain reader, you should probably think seriously about buying the writer! Until then, relax and wait and see when Microsoft adds something to Windows.

Winning on the First Palette

The next few sections are gonna be colorful, that's for sure. Well, at least color full.

Which One is Burnt Umber?

> But soft! what light through yonder window breaks
>
> — William Shakespeare, *Romeo and Julliet,* Act II, Scene II

Remember when Mom got you your first 64 crayon Crayola set? Your friend said "gimme that brown" but you couldn't figure out which crayon she meant since the one you had was called burnt umber. Well, you have to pick colors a lot in Winapps if you get at all graphical and so you'd better learn the way colors are named.

Alas, it ain't as simple as remembering which one is burnt umber. Colors are labelled by numbers and there are at least four different color numbering standards that are in common use: RGB, CYMK, HSB, and HLS.

RGB stands for Red, Green, Blue. Each can have a level from 0 to 255. It is a model of light, where RGB are the primary colors. As the numbers get higher, the color gets brighter so that (R=0,G=0,B=0) is black and (R=255,G=255,B=255) is white. The color space is a cube. This is the most common color model used in Windows.

 You may have heard that light has a continuous parameter called frequency representing variation in space and time. Light of wave length midway between red and green is yellow but then how can that also be a mixture of 50% red light and 50% green light. Physically, the two wave trains are very different. The answer is in our eyes. Color is percieved in terms of three types of cones in the retina. Roughly speaking the cones are sentsitive to light frequencies near pure red, near pure green, and near pure blue. True yellow light, that is light whose frequency is midway between red and green light will stimulate both the red and green sensitive cones in roughly the same way that a combination of red and green light will so they are percieved similarly even though the physical light waves are different.

CYM (we'll get to K soon) stand for Cyan, Yellow, and Magenta, the complementary colors to Red (Cyan is Green/Blue), Blue and Green. It is a model of ink, indeed color printers normally have ink in those exact colors blended to make the rainbow. As an ink model, higher numbers are darker so that (C=0,Y=0,M=0) is white and theoretically, (C=255,Y=255,M=255) is black. In fact, if you mix together those inks in high concentration, you don't get black but instead a kind of muddy dark ooze.

Muddy dark ooze. Sorta sounds like Mom's coffee. Have to remember that — CYM crouches in wait.

Hey Sonny, listen up. You are in big trouble if you knock my coffee.

Because mixing colored inks makes a lousy black, high class color printers use a fourth ink, namely blacK. Well, Black but then it would be CYMB, so it must be blacK after all. Programs that prepare pictures for actual color printing will often use the CYMB but most users will hardly see it.

HSB stands for Hue, Saturation, and Brightness. It uses a color cone model. Think of the cone as upright like an ice cream cone with the apex at the bottom and an axis running through the middle. The colors along that axis are greys. Black is at the apex and white at the center of the circle that lies at the top of the cone. The B parameter measures the distance along the axis from the apex (brightness 0) towards the brighter colors.

Hue is a discriminator of the pure color. It is connected to the color wheel. Imagine a wheel with pure red (R=255) at 3 o'clock, yellow (R=G=255) at 5 o'clock, green at 7 o'clock (G=255), cyan (R=G=255) at 9 o'clock, with blue(B=255) and magenta

(R=G=255) at 11 and 1. As you move around, the red value is 255 from 1 to 5 and 0 from 7 to 11 and changes linearly in the transition areas. Many programs measure H in degrees from 0 to 360. Windows measures from 0 to 240 so that red is H=0, yellow is H=40, green is H=80 etc.

In the HSB model, shown in Figure 2-28, the color wheel is put on the circle at the top of the cone and H measure the angle around the axis.

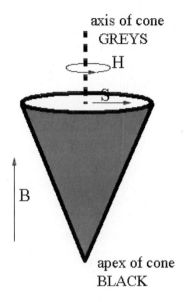

Figure 2-28:The HSB color model

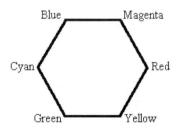

Figure 2-29: The color hexagon

The color wheel in Figure 2-29 is more naturally a hexagon with the colors at the vertices so the cone should be a hexagonal pyramid.

Finally saturation measures the distance from the axis towards the edge. S=0 is a grey. As saturation increases the color gets purer.

HLS stands for Hue, Saturation, and Luminosity. It's model is a double cone, two cones shaped like the one in HSB with one turned off and put on top of the other so there are points at the top and bottom. L=0 is black while L=240 (in Windows units) is white at the points of the double cone. The pure color wheel is in the middle at L=120. If you fix S=0, you still go through the greys. If you fix S=240 and H=0 (red) and move from L=1 down to 0, you move from white through pink, through red, then dark red to black.

Many color theorists regard the HSB/HLS models as more intuitive. In RGB, pink which is a mixture of white and red has values RGB values (255,127,127) which says red and half green and half blue which sure isn't what one thinks of as pink while HSL is pure red hue of luminosity 3/4 of the way from black to white. Moreover, the color wheel is in line with the actual physical wave length of color light.

Windows standard color dialog (which you'll find in the Color applet in Control Panel but also in any program using the Common Dialog that Windows provides) uses the HLS model. But it doesn't use cones or circles, only squares (see Figure 2-11). The slider on the right changes the L values. Slide it all the way to the top or bottom and you'll only get white or black no matter what color you pick in the middle area. In that middle area, the top is the pure color wheel if L is 120 (mid way). The bottom is a shade of grey no matter how you shift from left to right. That's because the top of the square is really a circle and the bottom is really a single point representing the center of the circle. Leave it to Microsoft to square the circle!

Color gradients are an attractive use of color you'll see in Windows and which some graphics programs let you set up. The RGB values are linearly interpolated between a starting and ending value in some direction which can be horizontal, vertical, diagonal, or radial depening on the type of gradiant.

Some of My Friends Are Pals and Some Are Palettes

If you are going to fool around with color schemes (and you may as well confess that you already have!), you should understand how Windows controls what colors you can access. I'll discuss 256 color drivers because that's what I recommend for most users (see Chapter 7). If you have only 16 colors, those are normally hard coded although a very few programs will manipulate them (if you use any program that does, you really should shift to 256 colors even if it requires a new video card!). Twenty-four-bit color doesn't use this palette and dither stuff but represents everything as a pure color. For now, 24-bit color exacts enough of a performance and cost premium that you don't need it unless you are editing color images much of the day but within a few years, 24-bit color should be standard!

Drivers that display 256 colors are capable of picking those 256 colors from among either 262,144 colors (2 to the power 18) or 16,777,216 colors (2 to the power 24). VGA cards and older SuperVGA cards have the smaller number while higher end adapters and card that has a 24 bit mode have the larger number.

 "Oh, boy," you must be thinking, "I get to pick what color my title bar is from hundreds of thousands of colors." Not so; read on.

Windows keeps track of which 256 colors of those 262,144 or 16,777,216 are to be displayed and such an assignment is called a **palette**. If a program asks for a color not in the current palette, Windows fakes it — it uses a **dithered** color that is nearby dots of two different colors which when blended sorta give the desired colors. Pure colors look great; dithered colors often look awful. For example, call up the color applet in Control Panel, hit the `Color Palette` button. I'm sure several of the 48 colors shown don't look like colors but like polka dots. I can't tell you precisely which box to look at since exactly what colors are displayed where is screen driver dependent but many drivers follow the scheme used by the 8514 driver supplied with Windows and it has the worst polka dots in row 5, column 6 and row 1, column 7.

Programs can also attempt to manipulate the palette and tell Windows to change what colors are used. If colors can be manipulated by programs, how does Windows deal with the fact that you want you title bar color to be consistent across applications. It makes a compromise. Twenty colors of the 256 are **reserved**, for all 256 color drivers that we are aware of (technically the driver writer gets to decide this but the sample drivers in the Driver Development Kit reserve 20 colors so that's what everyone else does). The other 236 colors can be freely changed by applications that need to. (Actually, programs that really need to are allowed to change 254 of the colors leaving only black and white alone but that is very rare — indeed, I know of no program that takes advantage of this.)

As you switch from one program to another, Windows changes the palette to the one that the active program has set. Since most programs don't change the default palette, you may not see any changes but image editors and some other graphics programs will change the palette and then you'll often see funny flashes as you switch and perhaps fouled up colors on your wallpaper when you are in certain programs.

Some image editors, when displaying several images, will adjust the palette to be ideal for the one you are working on; others adjust it so that all the image display in a not too bad way but still save most of the 236 colors for the foreground image.

Because Windows is worried about what other programs may do to their 236 colors, it will only let you use the 20 reserved colors for title bars, menu barss and the like. Moreover, you cannot change those 20 colors, in part because applications assume they haven't changed. It would have been nice if Windows had reserved an additional 4 or so slots for user mixed custom pure colors, but it didn't.

I'll use x/y/z below to indicate R/G/B values so 123/235/68 means RGB values R=123, G=235, B=68. You can ignore them but they will tell you something about the colors if you think in the right way.

The 20 colors include the 16 which have been standard on the PC since the CGA's text mode. Those 16 colors are the six primary color wheel colors in dark and light (e.g. red is 255/0/0 and dark red is 128/0/0; magenta is 255/0/255 and dark magenta is 128/0/128) plus white (255/255/255), black (0/0/0), dark grey (128/128/128) and light grey (192/192/192).

 How come dark red is R=128 with a smaller value than red at R=255.

 Remember that RGB is a model of light so that R=255 means more intense red light which appears brighter!

Besides the 16 standard colors, there are an extra four colors that must have been picked by Bill Gates' interior decorator: a medium grey (R/G/B values 160/160/164), an eggshell white (255/251/240), an army olive (192/220/192) and a powder blue (164/200/240). Actually, the R value of the standard power blue is not 100% clear. All the drivers I looked, at including the ones that Microsoft supplies, have the R=164 value I just gave but the Windows DDK (Device Development Kit) printed documentation says 166 (a typo no doubt and developers have decided to do as Microsoft does, not as it says).

 I've a theory that the medium grey should really be 160/160/160, a true grey. Both the DDK and the sample drivers have B=164 though. But my theory has a basis that will become clear soon.

The color selection box in the Colors applet has a set of built-in color choices — 48 in most 256 color drivers. How can it have 48 colors if there are only 20 reserved? Simple — many of them are dithered. In the 8514 driver, mimicked in most other drivers (the source comes in the DDK so it is starting point of most third-party 256-color drivers), the table can be represented as follows:

—	+	eggshell*				—	
red	+	+	army olive*	cyan	powder blue*	—	magenta
	yellow	green	dark cyan		—	+	+
dark red	—	dark green		blue		dark magenta	
				dark blue	BUG 1 —	BUG 2	
black	brown		dark grey		light grey	BUG 2	white

The 19 (yes 19, not 20) slots that have lower case text in them are reserved colors and are not dithered. The others are all dithered. Some dithered colors look bad; the worst to my eyes (on the ATI board/driver on Mao's machine) have a — on the boxes. The ones with + look particularly good.

Indeed, they look so good, you may not believe me when I say they are dithered! Here are two ways to tell a color is dithered. If you have the Microsoft 9.0 mouse driver, turn on the magnify feature and magnify the colors in the box and you'll see which ones are dithered quite clearly. Or call up the `Define Custom Color...` dialog with a built-in color selected and it will show you the value for that color. In particular, there is a box in that dialog marked color/solid. Pure color show the same for the two parts–dithered colors do not.

So we come to the entries labeled bug. The box marked BUG 1 is one of the worst polka dot boxes. It has R/G/B values 160/160/160 awfully close to the 160/160/164 of the one reserved color not included in the dialog. It's got to be a bug.

Elementary, my dear Igor. Why would anyone in their right mind pick a color that is almost a true grey (one with R=G=B) and not pick the true grey? I think the bug is not in the color chart whose author got the 160/160/160 right, but in the people who wrote the DDK docs and the skeleton driver which changed from a 160 to a 164-bit bug. One moral is that if the pure medium grey appeals to you, be sure to add a color to your custom colors with R/G/B values 160/160/164.

Bug 2 concerns the fact that both those entries are the same color. Call up the **Define Custom Color...** dialog with each of them selected and you'll see the same 64/0/64 very dark magenta R/G/B values.

These bugs and problems are minor but I find it most disturbing that on something that is so fundamental, Microsoft has inconsistencies and errors among the DDK documentation, the sample driver reserved colors and the color box settings that the driver uses. If they couldn't get that right, it is no wonder that the third-party drivers which have less manpower behind them are often as buggy as a swamp.

Wallpaper on the Rack

 Isn't it supposed to be wallpaper **off** the rack?

 If we were talking about buying wallpaper in Kmart; yes. But we are talking about stretching it. It's a medieval rack, not one at Kmart.

It's a common problem. You have a really wonderful wallpaper you are using at 640x480, you upgrade your system to 800x600 or 1024x768 and you load your wallpaper and it only takes up part of the screen so it looks silly. So how do you stretch wallpaper?

The simplest method is to resize in a bitmap editor that supports that. Windows Paintbrush does not but most stand alone image editors do. The wonderful shareware PaintShop Pro (JASC Software, Voice: 612-930-9171; it is on CD MOM) that you'll want in your toolkit has a resize command. The problem with that is the blockiness I described in *The Scales of Just Us* earlier in this chapter. There's a better way. Figure 2-30 shows an original Yoda, part of a wallpaper, on the top and the straight resize in the middle. The better way is on the bottom. It's more noticeable in color than in the grey scale translation we had to use to print it! (We have taken the liberty of brightening the grey scale translation to make the pictures clearer).

Figure 2-30: A tale of three Yodas

So what's this better way? The idea is based on something akin to antialiasing. Resizing basically doubles most pixels. That is a single pixel of a given color is replaced by four pixels in a two-by-two square. When you strech the size factors are not a precise double; all the pixels aren't doubled and that adds to the blockiness. PaintShop Pro provides another method called resampling which uses color interpolation to do the resizing. Basically, a grid of the new size is put over the original. If a grid piece overlaps two pixels in the original, an in-between color is used. For resampling to work, you need to have lots of colors, so PaintShop will only resample 24-bit color pictures. Thus you start by translating the wallpaper to 24 bit, resample, and then have PaintShop reduce the colors. The final stage is computer intensive and can take a few minutes on a slower machine but it is worth it! In detail, here are the steps:

1. Load your bmp into PaintShop using the **File/Open...** command.

2. Pull down the **Colors** menu, choose the **Increase Color Depth** submenu and choose **16 million colors (24 bit)**.

3. Choose the **Image/Resample** command and in the resulting dialog pick the size you want the new wallpaper to be.

4. Choose **Decrease Color Depth** from the **Colors** submenu and choose **256 colors (8 bit)**. In the resulting dialog, don't change the two sets of radio buttons (you want the program to use the standard Windows palette and to use error diffusion) although you may want to check off **Reduce Color Bleeding**.

5. Finally pick **File/SaveAs...** and be sure to change the name. You can pick of RLE encoded BMP (RLE is a compressed format which will save disk space although on complex bitmap, not much space).

Voilà — putting Wallpaper on the rack is that simple!

 Many books will tell you not to use Wallpaper because of the resource hit and make you feel guilty if you do. That's Windows 3.0 advice and may not be correct under Windows 3.1!

The Free Resource number is actually measuring the smallest of several numbers. Under 3.0, the smaller of the free GDI heap and the free User heap. The GDI heap stores graphics objects and the User heap menus and other mainly non-graphics objects. It's the smaller that matters because once either runs low, you are in trouble! Windows 3.1 added a third heap and had ProgMan do some stuff internally that had taken resources in Windows 3.0.

Using wallpaper can take 5-10% of the GDI heap but only 1% or so of User heap. With Windows 3.0, the heap that ran out for most users was GDI and the Wallpaper hit mattered. With the restructuring of resources for Windows 3.1 is more often the User heap that runs out so that loading Wallpaper may result in NO decrease or only a percent or so. So, if you are worried about the resource hit, shift from No Wallpaper to the one you want pulling down the ProgMan **Help/About** box to look at Free Resources both before and after.

Putting Windows on a Sound Basis

Wav and MIDI

IBM included a kludgy speaker in the original PC and, in the interest of compatibility, that's what virtually all PCs have used for sound — if you can call it that. Early on, Macs had real sound allowing both voice and music as did Amigas, Ataris, Suns, and NeXT. Until recently, PC sound solutions going beyond the speaker were largely driven by the needs of games with successive standards set by Ad Lib and then Sound Blaster cards. But sound has even entered the business mainstream with sound annotation, multimedia presentations (whatever that means) and most especially Windows support for sound in version 3.1.

There are two types of sounds you can record and play under Windows. It's rasters and vectors all over again but at the sound level. One kind of sound is **digital**, the analog of a bitmap — the actual sampling or playing of sound levels. Just as the standard Windows bitmap file is the **bmp**, the Windows digital sound file standard is called a

wave file with the extension **wav**. A **wav** file literally give directions to a speaker to oscillate in a certain way.

The sound analog of vector graphics is the **synthesized sound** file, under Windows a **MIDI file** with extension **mid**. Instead of telling the sound card to oscillate in a given way, a MIDI file has commands like "play a middle C for so much time and do it as if you were playing it on a piano."

Just as it pays to keep in mind whether a graphic is raster or vector, you'll want to bear in mind the difference between digitized and synthesized sounds. Here are more details on the two types.

Riding the Perfect Wav

Bitmaps files are characterized by the number of colors and sometimes by their intended resolution. In the same way, **wav** files have some basic parameters that describe the native format of the data. Of course, just as Windows can display a 16 million color file on a 256 color screen by doing its best, it can play a stereo wav file on a mono sound card by merging the two channels. The point of a stereo file is that it can play stereo on appropriate hardware.

Wav files have three basic parameters:

- First, look at whether the sound is **mono** or **stereo**. You know the difference. Most presentations don't need stereo. Some games do. Stereo sound files run twice the size of mono, for rather obvious reasons.

- Second is something called **sample size**, a measure of how much information about a single sound sample is kept around. Four-bit sampling suffices for low fidelity voice recordings; 8-bit does a good job of reproducing speech; but 16-bit — the sample size used in CD audio — is necessary for high quality sound. Basically sample size measures the number of different sound levels that are distinguished – 4-bit has 16 levels (2 to the power 4), 8-bit has 256 levels (2 to the power 8) and 16-bit has 65536 levels (2 to the power 16). Windows 3.1 as it comes out of the box can play 8-bit **wav** files on a 16-bit card but cannot play 16-bit **wav** files on an 8-bit card so programs tend to use the lowest common denominator. I'll discuss further when I talk about the WaveMapper later in Chapter 4.

- The third measurement is the **sample rate**, a measurement of how often the computer looks at the incoming sound and translates it into numbers. Sample rate has to do with how high a frequency can be distinguished and how much one can hear differing amounts of harmonic overtones. Eleven kHz sampling (sampled

11,000 times per second, natch) sounds like AM radio. Twenty-two kHz sampling sounds like FM radio. And 44kHz sampling sounds like CD audio — because it *is* CD audio.

Most sound boards can record 8-bit mono sound at 22 kHz. Few can record at CD audio rates, i.e., 16-bit stereo 44 kHz. Even if they could, you probably wouldn't want them to: one minute of 8-bit mono 22 kHz sound generates 1.3 MB of data, hefty by any standard; one minute of 16-bit stereo 44 kHz sound would produce a 10.6 MB file. Fidelity hath its price!

 You get 1.3 MB by multiplying 22,000 by 60 seconds (since 8 bits is a byte) and 10.6 MB by multiplying 44,000 by 60 seconds, then by 2 (16 bits is 2 bytes) and then by 2 again for the stereo.

There are other digital sound file types but they are less common than alternate bitmap types because sound has less of a pre–Windows history. The ones you may see are **voc** (the Sound Blaster standard — PC digitized sound at games player prices started on the Sound Blaster), **au** (used on NeXT and Sun), **snd** (used on the Mac and Amiga and the most common pre-wav type), and **vox** (Dialogic phone answering system voice files). Just as bitmap to bitmap conversion is straight forward, so is conversion from one digitized sound format to another. One program that will do such conversions for you as well as edit is Sonic Foundry's Sound Forge (Voice: 608–256–3133). You'll find a working model of it on CD MOM.

 There is another source of digitized sound on some systems with both a sound card and CR ROM — so called **Red Book audio**. No, not my Red Book, but the standards document used to define audio CDs. Red book audio is essentially audio CD tracks embedded in the middle of a CD ROM. Multimedia CDs will sometimes have sound in that format. One way that you can hear such sounds is if you connect the output jack on your CD (assuming it has one!) to a pair of speakers. If you use that route, you'll need a mixer to use the same speakers on your sound card output. A better solution is to connect the CD output to your sound card and have the sound card send out to the speakers.

Ideally, you should use internal connections on CD and sound card assuming that the CD is internal. But be warned the internal connectors are anything but standard. After a year of trying I gave up on finding an internal connector to send the Red Book Audio from my Toshiba CD ROM to my Sound Blaster Pro. Fortunately, the external connectors are standard so a modular audio cable I picked up at Radio Shack did the trick. But it sure is silly to have a cable snaking out from the front of my CD around to the external audio input on the back of the Sound Blaster.

'mid the MIDI

MIDI is short for Musical Instrument Digital Interface. It's a standard invented to drive high-end musical devices as might be used in a recording studio but was already fairly common in non-IBM compatible computer systems (e.g. the Mac) before its adaptation by Windows in version 3.1. Microsoft is to be complemented for using an external standard rather than rolling its own, although there are Windows specific modifications in the implementation.

There is considerable confusion surrounding MIDI under Windows. To start with, there are really three separate MIDI devices relevant to a sound setup — the device used to play **mid** files, a MIDI in port and a MIDI out port.

As a preliminary, you should know there are basically two routes to synthesis on sound cards. One is called FM synthesis, usually based on a Yamaha chip. The chip understands that the general features that make something sound like a piano, or an organ, or a flute, and given a command to play a middle C as a piano would, the chip makes it up (synthesizes) the sound on the spot.

The second is wave table lookup. The sound card has actual recorded samples of a piano playing various notes and uses the lookup to do the synthesis. Typically, the wave table information is stored in ROM with 2 or even 4 MB of wave tables possible. Some cards are available with wave tables stored on your hard disk and a buffer on card.

The difference between these two sources are dramatic. FM synthesis sounds tinny and wave table lookup sounds rich. It's the same kind of dramatic difference as between a dot matrix and laser printer. Whatever you do, if your budget can't afford a wave table card, don't listen to one or you'll have a unrequited yearning. The good news is that wave table sound is coming down in price. In mid-1992 a single card had a street price over $800 but by mid-1993 you could find wave table cards as low as $250. Soon wave table will be in all but the very lowest end sound solutions.

Technology marches on. MediaVision, makers of some of the best sound boards has developed a third method called WaveGuide, which is a synthesized sound that it claims is better than wave table lookup. The physics behind it (emulating the nonlinear parts of the instruments) is intruiging. It remains to be seen if it captures the market.

Any sound card that includes a synthesizer will allow you to play **mid** files directly from the card. Some may even have multiple ways to play — for example, the Sound Blaster ASP 16 with Wave Blaster daughter card will let you play **mid** files though its Yamaha FM synthesizer or through the wave table on the Wave Blaster (you'd normally choose the Wave Blaster of course!).

If you have a MIDI out port, there is usually a choice between the internal card or the external out port as the place that **mid** files are played. You choose where **mid** files are played in the Midi Mapper applet in Control Panel.

While MIDI in and out ports are part of the MPC spec, for many users they are not so important and they tend to be an extra cost item that you can happily skip. For example, Sound Blaster cards have a box that attaches to their joy stick ports with MIDI in, MIDI out, and pass through joy stick ports on the box).

MIDI is used to attached a MIDI keyboard or other MIDI instrument. If you want to make your own music, you'll want a MIDI in port. MIDI out ports are for attaching high-end MIDI synthesizers like the Roland Sound Canvas. They present one way of adding a wave table output device to a sound card which just has an FM synthesizer although a pricey one.

Mid files have an enormous size advantage over **wav** files. Windows itself ships with one **mid** file and 4 **wav** files. The **canyon.mid** file is 33K in size and provides 2.02 minutes of sound. The largest **wav** file (**tada.wav**, the default Windows start sound) is 27K in size and provides 1.3 seconds of sound. That's right — the ratio is about 100 to 1! Another advantage of MIDI concerns the potential for editing with the ability to add orchestral effects!

Other synthesized sound file types include **rol** (the Ad Lib standard, quite popular on BBS at one time), **cmf** (the Sound Blaster attempt to replace **rol**; because **rol**'s worked on Sound Blaster, **cmf**, a subset of **mid** never really took off) and **mod** (an Amiga spec that includes the instrument data as part of the file).

So far, MIDI has played a minor role to most Windows users compared to **wav** files. One reason is that only **wav** files can be assigned to system events and that's what has most captured the public's attention. Secondly, until wave table sound becomes common, **mid** files just don't sound as rich as what you can get with Red Book Audio or with **wav** files. Finally, the cost of a decent MIDI editor is 2–3 times what a wav editor costs and requires a lot more knowledge to use.

You will need a sound card to play MIDI music. The speaker driver will let you play digitized sound (**wav** files) with only the PC speaker but not MIDI.

Wasn't General MIDI in the Battle of the Choral C?

This section gets into the guts of MIDI and may be more than you want to know. You can skip it, but remember it's here if you are ever forced into the guts of the `midi-mapper applet` or get a `mid` file that won't play on your system.

MIDI used to be a tower of Babel. MIDI instructions refer to instruments by number and exactly which instrument referred to which number was determined by the MIDI device manufacturer and/or software company. In 1991, a consortium of the leading MIDI suppliers — the MIDI Manufacturers Association (phone to get the detailed spec: (213) 649-6434) — produced a standard called **General MIDI Level 1** (sometimes called GM and sometimes just MIDI level 1). Interestingly, the original call for a spec came from a publisher of multimedia titles (Warner New Media) and the key to adopting it was a hardware manufacturer (Roland whose Sound Canvas was the first GM device).

An important part of the spec is an assignment of instruments to instrument numbers (called a **patch map**) and an assignment of percussion sounds to drum numbers (called a **key map**). I'll list these maps, more to show the breadth of MIDI (from grand piano to gunshots) than because you need to know them. By the way, you can see these lists in Windows. Just call up the **midi-mapper applet** and choose **Edit...** with the **Patch Maps** or **Key Maps** radio button picked and you'll see the GM options listed in the left.

There are 128 instruments lumped into 16 groups of 8 (with MIDI patch numbers shown):

GENERAL MIDI INSTRUMENT PATCH MAP					
	PIANO		CHROMATIC PERCUSSION		ORGAN
1	Acoustic Grand	9	Celesta	17	Hammond Organ
2	Bright Acoustic	10	Glockenspiel	18	Percussive Organ
3	Electric Grand	11	Music Box	19	Rock Organ
4	Honky-Tonk	12	Vibraphone	20	Church Organ
5	Elect. Piano 1 (Rhodes)	13	Marimba	21	Reed Organ
6	Elect. Piano2(Chorused)	14	Xylophone	22	Accordion
7	Harpsichord	15	Tubular Bells	23	Harmonica
8	Clav	16	Dulcimer	24	Tango Accordion

GUITAR		BASS		STRINGS	
25	Acoustic Guitar(nylon)	33	Acoustic Bass	41	Violin
26	Acoustic Guitar(steel)	34	Electric Bass(fingered)	42	Viola
27	Electric Guitar(jazz)	35	Electric Bass(picked)	43	Cello
28	Electric Guitar(clean)	36	Fretless Bass	44	Contrabass
29	Electric Guitar(muted)	37	Slap Bass 1	45	Tremolo Strings
30	Overdriven Guitar	38	Slap Bass 2	46	Pizzicato Strings
31	Distortion Guitar	39	Synth Bass 1	47	Orchestral Harp
32	Guitar Harmonics	40	Synth Bass 2	48	Timpani
	ENSEMBLE		**BRASS**		**REED**
49	String Ensemble 1	57	Trumpet	65	Soprano Sax
50	String Ensemble 2	58	Trombone	66	Alto Sax
51	SynthStrings 1	59	Tuba	67	Tenor Sax
52	SynthStrings 2	60	Muted Trumpet	68	Baritone Sax
53	Choir Aahs	61	French Horn	69	Oboe
54	Voice Oohs	62	Brass Section	70	English Horn
55	Synth Voice	63	SynthBrass 1	71	Bassoon
56	Orchestra Hit	64	SynthBrass 2	72	Clarinet
	PIPE		**SYNTH LEAD**		**SYNTH PAD**
73	Piccolo	81	Lead 1 (square)	89	Pad 1 (new age)
74	Flute	82	Lead 2 (sawtooth)	90	Pad 2 (warm)
75	Recorder	83	Lead 3 (calliope)	91	Pad 3 (polysynth)
76	Pan Flute	84	Lead 4 (chiff)	92	Pad 4 (choir)
77	Blown Bottle	85	Lead 5 (charang)	93	Pad 5 (bowed)
78	Skakuhachi	86	Lead 6 (voice)	94	Pad 6 (metallic)
79	Whistle	87	Lead 7 (fifths)	95	Pad 7 (halo)
80	Ocarina	88	Lead 8 (bass+lead)	96	Pad 8 (sweep)
	SYNTH EFFECTS		**ETHNIC**		
97	FX 1 (rain)	105	Sitar		
98	FX 2 (soundtrack)	106	Banjo		
99	FX 3 (crystal)	107	Shamisen		
100	FX 4 (atmosphere)	108	Koto		
101	FX 5 (brightness)	109	Kalimba		

102	FX 6 (goblins)	110	Bagpipe
103	FX 7 (echoes)	111	Fiddle
104	FX 8 (sci-fi)	112	Shanai
	PERCUSSIVE		SOUND EFFECTS
113	Tinkle Bell	121	Guitar Fret Noise
114	Agogo	122	Breath Noise
115	Steel Drums	123	Seashore
116	Woodblock	124	Bird Tweet
117	Taiko Drum	125	Telephone Ring
118	Melodic Tom	126	Helicopter
119	Synth Drum	127	Applause
120	Reverse Cymbal	128	Gunshot

There are 47 drum sounds (their key numbers start at 35):

GENERAL MIDI PERCUSSION KEY MAP

35	Acoustic Bass Drum	51	Ride Cymbal 1	67	High Agogo
36	Bass Drum 1	52	Chinese Cymbal	68	Low Agogo
37	Side Stick	53	Ride Bell	69	Cabasa
38	Acoustic Snare	54	Tambourine	70	Maracas
39	Hand Clap	55	Splash Cymbal	71	Short Whistle
40	Electric Snare	56	Cowbell	72	Long Whistle
41	Low Floor Tom	57	Crash Cymbal 2	73	Short Guiro
42	Closed Hi-Hat	58	Vibraslap	74	Long Guiro
43	High Floor Tom	59	Ride Cymbal 2	75	Claves
44	Pedal Hi-Hat	60	Hi Bongo	76	Hi Wood Block
45	Low Tom	61	Low Bongo	77	Low Wood Block
46	Open Hi-Hat	62	Mute Hi Conga	78	Mute Cuica
47	Low-Mid Tom	63	Open Hi Conga	79	Open Cuica
48	Hi-Mid Tom	64	Low Conga	80	Mute Triangle
49	Crash Cymbal 1	65	High Timbale	81	Open Triangle
50	High Tom	66	Low Timbale		

MIDI supports polyphony, that is multiple notes. These notes can be played on multiple instruments which are assigned to distinct channels. General MIDI devices are supposed to allow 32-note polyphony and to respond to 16 channels with the first 9 set for instruments and the tenth for percussion. A GM file can do whatever it wants with channels 11–16 although usually they aren't used.

In steps Windows. The designers of Windows had a big problem to cope with — not all sound devices are capable of supporting 10 channels, let alone the full 16 allowed in principle. So Windows defines two kinds of MIDI playing devices — Basic and Extended. The original Sound Blaster, early Sound Blaster Pros and AdLib cards are Basic devices. Most sound cards that are more recent are extended in the Windows parlance. If a card advertises itself as supporting general MIDI, that probably means that it is Extended (and then some).Basic devices are supposed to support four channels — three instrument channels allowing up to six notes polyphony and one drum channel allowing up to five note polyphony. Extended devices are supposed to support nine instrument channels and one drum channels with up to sixteen note polyphony on each channel.

 Here comes the kicker so pay attention!

To allow a single **mid** file to play on both basic and extended devices, Microsoft presented authoring guidelines. The piece is supposed to use channels 1–10 for extended devices and channels 13–16 for basic devices with the top channel for percussion. You'll note that the extended channels are exactly those suggested by the General MIDI spec but the basic are not.

So there are four kinds of MIDI files:

- Ones written to the Microsoft guidelines with the basic device version in channels 13–16

- Ones written to the General spec following the normal pattern of only using channels 1–10. These will be silent on basic devices since they have nothing on channels 13–16.

- Ones written to the General spec that use channels 11–16. These won't play properly on either extended or basic devices!

- Ones written before the General spec and which need a custom patch map. The Voyetra/Roland patch map will sometimes work and is available from some sound card makers.

When you install a sound card that supports General MIDI, it will load three types of midi-mappings into the midi-mapper lists. One set will be labeled **Basic**, one set will be labeled **Extended** and the third **All**. I say sets because there will generally be **Extended,** with one of the terms **Internal** or **FM** and one labeled **External** or just **MIDI**. There may also be **FM** vs. **Wave Table**. So for example, the Sound Blaster Pro has five setups: **SBP All FM**, **SBP All MIDI**, **SBP Basic FM**, **SBP Ext FM** and **SBP Ext MIDI**.

It's hard to imagine that you'd want to use the basic setup so make sure it isn't picked. If you have a Microsoft standard MIDI file, you want to pick the extended map since picking all will play both the extended and basic instruments and not sound so good. If you have a General MIDI file which uses the upper channels for its own use, you'll need to run **All** though.

 It's all a bit of a muddle isn't it! The only bright spot is that Windows may have enough clout to force the Microsoft variant on the world. Or at least get people to avoid the use of channels above 10, which for those with Extended devices is almost as good. But since the music industry is involved and not just the computer industry, I wouldn't count on it. In fact, there is some indicaton that Microsoft may back pedal and hope that users shift to sound cards supporting 16 channels and just adopt general MIDI.

 There is also an important missing gap in the API related to MIDI. Wouldn't it be great if a midi player were intelligent enough to look at a MIDI file and take an intelligent guess about what mapping it needed, for example switching to the Voyetra patch map when their copyright was found! Guess what? The only documented way to change MIDI setups or patch maps is via the MIDI Mapper applet in Contorl Panel. No way for programs to do it directly? Sigh. Maybe Microsoft will address this some time.

So, if you have a basic device, where can you find **mid** files. Check out MIDI Made Music (Llerrah, Voice: 214-422-1122). Another source for **mid** files and for discussions of MIDI in general is CompuServe's MIDI/Sound furm (GO MIDIFOR). You'll find some wonderful **mid** files on CD MOM.

Trip the Light Fantastic: Video

Video has come to Windows!! What should you do about it? My advice is to do nothing very special and don't go out and buy Microsoft Video for Windows or a video card unless you in such a special situation that you know that you need those things despite what I say (for example, you are authoring multimedia CDs!).

First, hardware isn't up to video quite yet. Even a 486/66 can't play a full screen video at video speed (30 frames a second) so most video you'll find to play in Windows will play at 15 frames a second and in a small windows. If your CPU is powerful enough, it's better than you might expect given these limitations, but nothing to turn on the MTV generation.

Secondly, the space required by video is staggering. Even at the limitation of small window and 15 frames per second, the 120 MB of video included with the Compton's Multimedia Encyclopedia plays for only about 10 minutes total.

Third and most importantly, you do *not* need special hardware or Video for Windows to play videos under Windows. The special boards are needed to capture video from a video cam or a cable and so are only needed for authoring. You *do* need some of the drivers that ship with Video for Windows to see video, but any multimedia title you buy that has video will include a runtime version of Video for Windows which it will install for you. D MOM includes some sample video files and includes this Video for Windows runime. See Chapter 11 for directions on install the video drivers if you have CD MOM.

 If sound is any guideline to what will happen with video, the Video for Windows stuff will be included in the next major rev of Windows. Just as the Multimedia Media Extensions for Windows 3.0 were a particularly poor investment because they were supplanted by components of Windows 3.1, it seems likely that Video for Windows will be a poor investment for anyone but authors.

One last note — Video for Windows has spawned a new file format for files of viedo with an audio sound track — the name is *.**avi** with **avi** short for Audio–Video–Interleaved. CD MOM has some sample AVI files for you to look at.

Media Control Interface — Do You Mean David Gergen?

Windows' support for Multimedia is extensible; drivers written to what Microsoft calls MCI, for Media Control Interface, can be plugged into any program that uses the MCI API. If you get a new multimedia device, say a video disc player, the Media Player applet can play files from it, if the vendor supplies a driver that supports MCI.

MCI defines the following standard device types:

animation	animation device like an Autodesk **fli** player
cdaudio	redbook audio from a CD
dat	digital audio tape player
digitalvideo	digital video in a window
other	undefined **MCI** type
overlay	analog video in a window
scanner	image scanner

sequencer	MIDI sequencer to play **mid** files
vcr	Video recorder or player
videodisc	Videodisc player
waveaudio	Audio device that plays digitized **wav** files

An **MCI** driver has to respond to two types of commands — a **command message interface** and a **command string interface**. The command message interface uses the Windows API call **mciSendCommand** and is intended for C programmers and is much like any other parts of the Windows API. The command string interface uses what appears to be English language. Here's a little program written in the command string interface (with comments on each line in {...}):

open tada.wav type waveaudio	{gets control of the **wav** player; gives it a file to open}
play waveaudio	{tells the driver to play the sound}
close waveaudio	{returns control of the **wav** player to Windows}

The presence of a command string interface is an indication that Microsoft expects sophisticated users to try to use **MCI** in macro languages. As a first step, Visual Basic 2.0/3.0 has an **MCI** custom control that uses a variant of the command string interface but I suspect you'll see it in your word processor's macro language before long!

To give you an idea of the power of the command string interface, I note that the commands include: open, close, play, record, pause, resume, seek, stop, status and for appropriate types, freeze (for Video) and set tempo (for MIDI).

Information on **MCI** is spread between the two basic **ini** files (see Chapters 8 and 9 for the syntax of **ini** files and a discussion of these two files in particular). **System.ini** includes an **[mci]** section that by default reads

```
WaveAudio=mciwave.drv
Sequencer=mciseq.drv
```

On a system with a CD-ROM drive, Windows also installs the following (if you add a CD ROM after installing Windows, you'll need to be sure to use the **Drivers applet** of Control Panel to add the CD Audio driver; see below)

```
CDAudio=mcicda.drv
```

Installing a CD that adds the Video for Windows runtime would add

```
MMMovie=mcimmp.drv
```

```
AVIVideo=mciavi.drv
```

This tells Windows what drivers to call to implement given devices.

To add the CDAudio driver, run the **Drivers applet**, choose the **Add..** button and pick **[MCI] CD Audio**. It will ask for the proper disk. After installing, be sure to choose **Setup...** so that the driver can determine what CDs you have. It sould tell you that it has detected one CD (unless you have more than one!). If you add the CDAudio driver, be sure to read the section *Playing the Field — Media Player* in Chapter 4.

Win.ini includes a section called **[mci extensions]** which by default reads:

```
wav=waveaudio
mid=sequencer
rmi=sequencer
```

Installing the Video for Windows runtime adds:

```
MMM=MMMovie
avi=AVIVideo
```

This extension section is not used for associations — that has to be done separately but as I'll explain later, it is used by Media Player.

A Child's Garden of File Types

I ordered Igor to put together for you as complete a listing as he could of file extensions so when you ran accross a file you'd at least have a guess of where it might have come from. Of course, some extensions do double duty, for example, DB is used by Paradox 4.0 and Managing Your Money for very different files. And doc or cfg are used by many, many programs with different formats. Igor, you did me proud producing what is truly the mother of all file extension lists. How did you do it?

When Mao was away, I snuck up on his machine and got a complete file listing and figured out all the distinct file extensions that he had. Almost a thousand! I then pared out those that were his personal quirks, uncommon files and was left with about 200. I then checked PC Tools for Windows and Hijaak for the files they supported and picked up a couple that were missing. Finally, I checked out some font programs to get the missing font formats.

Types by Type

Executable Files and other "programs"

BAT	batch file
COM	Executable Program in small format
EXE	Executable program
OVL	Overlay — used by DOS exes for storing code on disk to swap in as needed
PIF	Windows Program Information File
SYS	System file; used for config.sys and some device drivers

Windows Executable and Resource formats (DLLs and Drivers)

2GR	286 Grabber File (used by Windows in standard mode DOS sessions)
386	386 Enhanced Mode Driver for Windows
3GR	386 Grabber File (used by Windows in enhanced mode DOS sessions)
ACM	Audio Compression Module addon to MSACM.DRV Windows driver
AOL	America Online for Windows DLL
CPL	Control Panel Applet file
CUR	Windows Cursor File
DLL	Windows Dynamic Link Library (executable functions callable by programs)
DRV	Windows driver (usually a DLL in DRV clothing)
DS	TWAIN (Scanner spec) data source DLL
DSP	Norton viewer DLL
MOD	Module — used by Windows for DLL which implement DOS support
PRS	Norton Viewer DLL file
RC	Resource script used by Windows programs
RES	Compiled resource file

Misc Windows File Formats (including Icon Libraries)

CAL	Windows Calendar file
CLP	Clipboard viewer data file
GRP	Windows Progman group file
HLP	Windows Help file
ICO	Icon file
IL	hDC Designer Icon Library (in DLL format)

INI	Ini file for a Windows program
LGO	Windows Logo file shown during startup
NIL	Norton Desktop Icon Library
NSS	Norton Screen Saver module
REC	Windows Recorder Macro File
REG	File used by programs to add material to the Windows registration database using Regedit
SCR	Windows Screen Saver module; also used by WinCIM for Scripts
TRM	Windows Terminal data file
WMP	Windows Magic Icon Palette

Spreadsheet Formats

DIF	Data Interchange Format (used by Visicalc)
MU	Quattro Pro for DOS Menu definition file
SKY	SYLK Spreadsheet file (used by Multiplan)
WB1	Quattro Pro for Windows Spreadsheet Notebook
WK1	Lotus 123 2.x spreadsheet
WK3	Lotus 123 3.x spreadsheet
WK4	Lotus 123 4.x spreadsheet
WKQ	Quattro spreadsheet
WKS	Lotus 123 1.x spreadsheet
WQ1	Quattro Pro for DOS spreadsheet
WRI	Windows Write file
WRK	Lotus Symphony Spreadsheet
XLA	Excel Addin
XLB	Excel Toolbar
XLC	Excel Chart
XLL	Excel Addin
XLM	Excel Macro file
XLS	Excel spreadsheet file
XLT	Excel Template
XLW	Excel Wookbook

Database Formats

ARK	Managing Your Money Archive file
CRD	Windows cardfile data file
DB	Paradox 4.0 database; extension also used by Managing your money
DBF	Basic dBase database
DBS	Data file used by Managing Your Money
CSV	Comma Separated Variables (crude data interchange format)

MDB	Microsoft Access database
NDX	dBase index file
NFO	Filioview database
PX	Paradox 3.0
R2D	Reflex 2 datafile
RXD	Reflex 1 data file

Word Processor Formats

BMT	Ami Pro Button
BST	BiblioTex file (BiblioTex=bibliography file for TeX)
CBS	MasterWord button bar configuration file
CHP	Ventura Publisher Chapter Files
CNV	Winword DLL used as part of an import operation (CNV=convertor)
DCT	Dictionary: used by many programs with program dependent format
DIC	Dictionary: used by many programs with program dependent format
DOC	Winword native file; also used by some other programs and as ASCII doc file in many shareware programs
DOT	Winword template file
FLT	Filter; DLL used by Aldus and Winword for import; used in other contexts by many other programs with program dependent format
GLY	Winword Glossary
GV	GrandView outline file
KEX	Kedit Macro file
KML	Kedit Macro Library
LEX	short for lexigographic; dictionaries and other files; used by several programs with program dependent format
PDF	Adobe's Portable Document Format
PM3	PageMaker 3.0 data file
RTF	Rich Text Format file
SAM	Ami Pro data file (short for Samna, the name of the company before Lotus bought them)
SDW	Ami Draw Symbol file
SMM	Ami Pro Macro File
STY	Ami Pro Template (Style); used by other programs for "styles"
TEX	TeX source file
TXT	Common name for ASCII text file
WCM	WordPerfect Macro File
WP	WordPerfect format

Fonts

CHR	Borland language stroke font file
FF	Intellifont FIAS format
FNT	Font file; used by many programs for propertiary format files (including Nibus Q)
FON	Windows bitmapped font file
FOT	TrueType font resource file
LIB	Intellifont old style format
PFA	PostScript Font File
PFB	PostScript Font File
PFM	PostScript Font Metric file
SFB	HP Soft font (obsolete under Windows)
SFO	Bitstream font file — fontware format
SPD	Bitstream font file — speedo format
TDF	Speedo font metric
TFM	TeX font file
TTF	TrueType Font file
WNF	Corel Draw Font File

Bitmap Formats

!JG	Thumbnails for Photofinish change JPG to !JG, PCX to !PC, etc
BMP	BitMaP; Windows graphics format
CUT	Dr. Halo bitmmapped graphics
DIB	Device Independent Bitmap; rarely used Windows 3.0 bitmap format
FAX	Fax bitmaps in CCITT format
GIF	Compuserve's Graphics Interchange Format (bitmapped graphics)
IFF	Amiga bitmap format
IMG	GEM bitmapped graphics file
JPG	JPEG compressed bitmapped graphics format
MAC	MacPaint bitmap format; also used by many programs for macro files with program dependent format
MSP	Microsoft Paint format (from Windows 2.x)
PCD	Kodak PhotoCD file
PCX	PC Paintbrush bitmap format
PDG	Print Shop Deluxe data file
PSD	PhotoShop bitmap file
RAS	Sun Raster format
RIF	Fractal Painter bitmapped file
RLE	Run Length Encoded compressed BMP file

TGA	Targa True Color bitmapped format
THM	Picture Publisher or PhotoMagic Thumbnail
TIF	TIFF (tagged image format file) bitmapped file

Image Editor Support Files

ABM	Image PALS album file
ABR	Adobe Brush file for PhotoShop
ACF	Adobe Custom Filter for PhotoShop
ACO	Adobe Color Palette
AMS	Adobe Monitor Setup calibration file for PhotoShop
API	Adobe Printer Ink file for PhotoShop
CMP	PhotoFinish Calibration Map
AST	Adobe Color Separation Table for PhotoShop
DFX	Micrografx Effects DLL used in their bitmap editors
FIO	ImagePALS viewer DLL

Vector Graphics

AI	Adobe Illustrator EPS file
CDR	Corel Draw file
CGM	Computer Graphics Metafile; object graphics format
CH3	Harvard Graphics file format
DRW	Designer vector graphics file
DXF	AutoCAD vector graphics format
EPS	Encapulated PostScript file
GEM	Gem Vector Graphics format
GFX	Instant Artist graphics files
GRF	Stanford Graphics files; also used by Charisma
PGL	HP Plotter vector graphics format
PIC	123 Vector Graphics format
SCD	SCODOL film recorder
SY3	Harvard Graphics file format
VSD	Visio Drawing
VSS	Visio Template
VST	Visio Template
WMF	Windows MetaFile vector graphics format
WPG	Word Perfect Graphic (vector graphics)

Multimedia Formats

AU	NeXT/Sun digital audio format
AVI	Audio Visual Interleaved multimedia format
BNK	AdLib Instrument ID file

CMF	Sound Blaster Synthesized Sound File
MID	MIDI music file
MMM	MultiMedia Movie file
MOD	Amiga synthesized Sound format
RMI	Windows alternate synthesized sound format
ROL	Adlib format syntesized music file
SND	Mac/Amiga digitized sound file
VOC	Sound Blaster digitized sound format
WAV	Windows digital sound file

Language Files

APL	Support module used by Manugraphics APL products
ASM	Assembly Language source code
BAS	BASIC source code
BGI	Borland Graphics Interface; drivers for Pascal and some other Borland languages
BI	BASIC include file (Visual Basic for DOS)
C	C source code
DLG	Windows SDK dialog editor data file
FI	Fortran Include file
FOR	Fortran Source code
FRM	Visual Basic form
FRX	Visual Basic binary program file
GBL	Global module in Basic programs (gbl, glb, and glo are all used)
GLB	Global module in Basic programs (gbl, glb, and glo are all used)
GLO	Global module in Basic programs (gbl, glb, and glo are all used)
H	C header file
LIB	short for library; collection of binary routines that are bound with executable programs in some languages
MAK	Make file — list of source files for a project in some languages together with compiler directives
MAP	File with debug infomration produced by some languages
OBJ	Compiled machine language code
REX	Rexx language source file
RTS	Realizer executabel file
RUN	PC Tools for Windows batch file
TPU	Turbo Pascal Unit (precompiled turbo pascal module)
TRU	True Basic source file
VBR	Visual Basic Custom Control file
VBX	Visual Basic Custom Control file

WBT	Wilsonware Batch file used by Winbatch and Norton Desktop
WS	APL Worksheet
XCL	Xtree for Windows Script file

Compressed File Formats

ARC	Archive file for ARC, once the compression standard
ARJ	Compressed file for ARJ compression utility
LHA	File made by compression program LHA
LZH	File made by the compression program LHARC
PAK	PAK compressed format
ZIP	PKZIP compressed file format
ZOO	Zoo compressed file format

Scientific Program Files

HBK	MathCAD Handbook
M	Source file for MatLab and Mathematica (different languages using the same extention)
MA	Used by Mathematica for its notebooks and by hDC products for MicroApp executable files
MCD	MathCAD file

Misc

*_	Microsoft Setup uses _ for the final letter of compressed files
AD	After Dark Module (DLL)
ADL	MicroChannel Adapter Description Library file
ADM	After Dark support file
ADR	After Dark support file
ALO	Almanac support file
BAK	Backup File made by notepad or other programs
BIN	Binary file; used by many programs with program dependent format
BTN	Makeover Button file
CAP	ProComm Capture file
CAT	CPS Backup Catalog
CFG	Configuration file — used by many programs for configuration data with program dependent format
CMB	Xtree for Windows Button Bar file
CNF	Configuration file — used by many programs for configuration data with program dependent format
DAT	Data file — used by many applications

DEF	Definition file — used by many programs with program dependent format
DIR	CPS Backup directory file
DIZ	file_id.diz=special file placed in zips to describe shareware that some BBS can read automatically
DVI	Device Independent file made by TeX
ENV	Envelope or Environments: used by many programs with program dependent format
FAS	Macsyma compiled program
FIL	Mirror.fil is the name given to the saved FAT by the mirror program included in some versions of DOS and in PCTools
HST	History file; used by various programs, especially games, with program dependent format
INF	Information file; used by various programs, including Windows, with program dependent format
LIC	license file used by some programs to put their license on disk
MNU	Microsoft Mouse menu file (for DOS apps)
MSG	Message - used by several different Compuserve access programs to store messages with program dependent format
MXL	PackRat 5.0 support DLLs
NCD	treeinfo.ncd is a file where Norton's products store the trees of hard drives
OPT	Options; name used by many programs for configuration information
PAL	Palette file; used by many programs, each with their own format
PDB	Packrat 5.0 data file
PR1	PackRat 4.x data file
PR2	PackRat 4.x data file
PRN	Spreadsheet output (printer) file
PRO	Profile; used by many programs to store configuration data
PS	PostScript output file
QAG	Norton Destop Group file
REP	Report file used by many applications
RPB	data report file used by CP Backup
RPT	Report file used by many applications
RSL	Resource Library used by PCTools for Windows
SET	Extension used by Norton Backup and CPS Backup for setup info
SYD	Sysedit backup file
TBL	Short for Table; used by many programs
TMP	Temporary file

WAS	ProComm Script File (source code)
WAX	Procomm compiled script
WD	InfoSelect data file

An Alphabetic Listing

*_	Microsoft Setup uses _ for the final letter of compressed files
!JG	Thumbnails for Photofinish change JPG to !JG, PCX to !PC, etc
2GR	286 Grabber File (used by Windows in standard mode DOS sessions)
386	386 Enhanced Mode Driver for Windows
3GR	386 Grabber File (used by Windows in enhanced mode DOS sessions)
ABM	Image PALS album file
ABR	Adobe Brush file for PhotoShop
ACF	Adobe Custom Filter for PhotoShop
ACM	Audio Compression Module addon to MSACM.DRV Windows driver
ACO	Adobe Color Palette
AD	After Dark Module (DLL)
ADL	MicroChannel Adapter Description Library file
ADM	After Dark support file
ADR	After Dark support file
AI	Adobe Illustrator EPS file
ALO	Almanac support file
AMS	Adobe Monitor Setup calibration file for PhotoShop
AOL	America Online for Windows DLL
API	Adobe Printer Ink file for PhotoShop
APL	Support module used by Manugraphics APL products
ARC	Archive file for ARC, once the compression standard
ARJ	Compressed file for ARJ compression utility
ARK	Managing Your Money Archive file
ASM	Assembly Language source code
AST	Adobe Color Separation Table for PhotoShop
AU	NeXT/Sun digital audio format
AVI	Audio Visual Interleaved multimedia format
BAK	Backup File made by notepad or other programs
BAS	BASIC source code
BAT	batch file
BGI	Borland Graphics Interface; drivers for Pascal and some other Borland languages
BI	BASIC include file (Visual Basic for DOS)

BIN	Binary file; used by many programs with program dependent format
BMP	BitMaP; Windows graphics format
BMT	Ami Pro Button
BNK	AdLib Instrument ID file
BST	BiblioTex file (BiblioTex=bibliography file for TeX)
BTN	Makeover Button file
C	C source code
CAL	Windows Calendar file
CAP	ProComm Capture file
CAT	CPS Backup Catalog
CBS	MasterWord button bar configuration file
CDR	Corel Draw file
CFG	Configuration file — used by many programs for configuration data with program dependent format
CGM	Computer Graphics Metafile; object graphics format
CH3	Harvard Graphics file format
CHP	Ventura Publisher Chapter Files
CHR	Borland language stroke font file
CLP	Clipboard viewer data file
CMB	Xtree for Windows Button Bar file
CMF	Sound Blaster Synthesized Sound File
CMP	PhotoFinish Calibration Map
CNF	Configuration file — used by many programs for configuration data with program dependent format
CNV	Winword DLL used as part of an import operation (CNV=convertor)
COM	Executable Program in small format
CPL	Control Panel Applet file
CRD	Windows cardfile data file
CSV	Comma Separated Variables (crude data interchange format)
CUR	Windows Cursor File
CUT	Dr. Halo bitmmapped graphics
DAT	Data file — used by many applications
DB	Paradox 4.0 database; extension also used by Managing your money
DBF	Basic dBase database
DBS	Data file used by Managing Your Money
DCT	Dictionary: used by many programs with program dependent format
DEF	Definition file: used by many programs with program dependent format

DFX	Micrografx Effects DLL used in their bitmap editors
DIB	Device Independent Bitmap; rarely used Windows 3.0 bitmap format
DIC	Dictionary: used by many programs with program dependent format
DIF	Data Interchange Format (used by Visicalc)
DIR	CPS Backup directory file
DIZ	file_id.diz=special file placed in zips to describe shareware that some BBS can read automatically
DLG	Windows SDK dialog editor data file
DLL	Windows Dynamic Link Library (executable functions callable by programs)
DOC	Winword native file; also used by some other programs and as ASCII doc file in many shareware programs
DOT	Winword template file
DRV	Windows driver (usually a DLL in DRV clothing)
DRW	Designer vector graphics file
DS	TWAIN (Scanner spec) data source DLL
DSP	Norton viewer DLL
DVI	Device Independent file made by TeX
DXF	AutoCAD vector graphics format
ENV	Envelope or Environments: used by many programs with program dependent format
EPS	Encapulated PostScript file
EXE	Executable program
FAS	Macsyma compiled program
FAX	Fax bitmaps in CCITT format
FF	Intellifont FIAS format
FI	Fortran Include file
FIL	Mirror.fil is the name given to the saved FAT by the mirror program included in some versions of DOS and in PCTools
FIO	ImagePALS viewer DLL
FLT	Filter; DLL used by Aldus and Winword for import; used in other contexts by many other programs with program dependent format
FNT	Font file; used by many programs for propertiary format files (including Nibus Q)
FON	Windows bitmapped font file
FOR	Fortran Source code
FOT	TrueType font resource file
FRM	Visual Basic form

FRX	Visual Basic binary program file
GBL	Global module in Basic programs (gbl, glb and glo are all used)
GEM	Gem Vector Graphics format
GFX	Instant Artist graphics files
GIF	Compuserve's Graphics Interchange Format (bitmapped graphics)
GLB	Global module in Basic programs (gbl, glb, and glo are all used)
GLO	Global module in Basic programs (gbl, glb, and glo are all used)
GLY	Winword Glossary
GRF	Stanford Graphics files; also used by Charisma
GRP	Windows Progman group file
GV	GrandView outline file
H	C header file
HBK	MathCAD Handbook
HLP	Windows Help file
HST	History file; used by various programs, especially games, with program dependent format
ICO	Icon file
IFF	Amiga bitmap format
IL	hDC Designer Icon Library (in DLL format)
IMG	GEM bitmapped graphics file
INF	Information file; used by various programs, including Windows, with program dependent format
INI	Ini file for a Windows program
JPG	JPEG compressed bitmapped graphics format
KEX	Kedit Macro file
KML	Kedit Macro Library
LEX	short for lexigographic; dictionaries and other files; used by several programs with program dependent format
LGO	Windows Logo file shown during startup
LHA	File made by compression program LHA
LIB	Intellifont old style format
LIB	short for library; collection of binary routines that are bound with executable programs in some languages
LIC	license file used by some programs to put their license on disk
LZH	File made by the compression program LHARC
M	Source file for MatLab and Mathematica (different languages using the same extention)
MA	Used by Mathematica for its notebooks and by hDC products for MicroApp executable files
MAC	MacPaint bitmap format; also used by many programs for macro files with program dependent format

MAK	Make file — list of source files for a project in some languages together with compiler directives
MAP	File with debug infomration produced by some languages
MCD	MathCAD file
MDB	Microsoft Access database
MID	MIDI music file
MMM	MultiMedia Movie file
MNU	Microsoft Mouse menu file (for DOS apps)
MOD	Module — used by Windows for DLL which implement DOS support
MOD	Amiga synthesized Sound format
MSG	Message — used by several different Compuserve access programs to store messages with program dependent format
MSP	Microsoft Paint format (from Windows 2.x)
MU	Quattro Pro for DOS Menu definition file
MXL	PackRat 5.0 support DLLs
NCD	treeinfo.ncd is a file where Norton's products store the trees of hard drives
NDX	dBase index file
NFO	Filioview database
NIL	Norton Desktop Icon Library
NSS	Norton Screen Saver module
OBJ	Compiled machine language code
OPT	Options; name used by many programs for configuration information
OVL	Overlay — used by DOS exes for storing code on disk to swap in as needed
PAK	PAK compressed format
PAL	Palette file; used by many programs, each with their own format
PCD	Kodak PhotoCD file
PCX	PC Paintbrush bitmap format
PDB	Packrat 5.0 data file
PDF	Adobe's Portable Document Format
PDG	Print Shop Deluxe data file
PFA	PostScript Font File
PFB	PostScript Font File
PFM	PostScript Font Metric file
PGL	HP Plotter vector graphics format
PIC	123 Vector Graphics format
PIF	Windows Program Information File
PM3	PageMaker 3.0 data file

PR1	PackRat 4.x data file
PR2	PackRat 4.x data file
PRN	Spreadsheet output (printer) file
PRO	Profile; used by many programs to store configuration data
PRS	Norton Viewer DLL file
PS	PostScript output file
PSD	PhotoShop bitmap file
PX	Paradox 3.0
QAG	Norton Destop Group file
R2D	Reflex 2 datafile
RAS	Sun Raster format
RC	Resource script used by Windows programs
REC	Windows Recorder Macro File
REG	File used by programs to add material to the Windows registration database using Regedit
REP	Report file used by many applications
RES	Compiled resource file
REX	Rexx language source file
RIF	Fractal Painter bitmapped file
RLE	Run Length Encoded compressed BMP file
RMI	Windows alternate synthesized sound format
ROL	Adlib format syntesized music file
RPB	data report file used by CP Backup
RPT	Report file used by many applications
RSL	Resource Library used by PCTools for Windows
RTF	Rich Text Format file
RTS	Realizer executabel file
RUN	PC Tools for Windows batch file
RXD	Reflex 1 data file
SAM	Ami Pro data file (short for Samna, the name of the company before Lotus bought them)
SCD	SCODOL film recorder
SCR	Windows Screen Saver module; also used by WinCIM for Scripts
SDW	Ami Draw Symbol file
SET	Extension used by Norton Backup and CPS Backup for setup info
SFB	HP Soft font (obsolete under Windows)
SFO	Bitstream font file — fontware format
SKY	SYLK Spreadsheet file (used by Multiplan)
SMM	Ami Pro Macro File
SND	Mac/Amiga digitized sound file
SPD	Bitstream font file — speedo format

STY	Ami Pro Template (Style); used by other programs for "styles"
SY3	Harvard Graphics file format
SYD	Sysedit backup file
SYS	System file; used for config.sys and some device drivers
TBL	Short for Table; used by many programs
TDF	Speedo font metric
TEX	TeX source file
TFM	TeX font file
TGA	Targa True Color bitmapped format
THM	Picture Publisher or PhotoMagic Thumbnail
TIF	TIFF (tagged image format file) bitmapped file
TMP	Temporary file
TPU	Turbo Pascal Unit (precompiled turbo pascal module)
TRM	Windows Terminal data file
TRU	True Basic source file
TTF	TrueType Font file
TXT	Common name for ASCII text file
VBR	Visual Basic Custom Control file
VBX	Visual Basic Custom Control file
VOC	Sound Blaster digitized sound format
VSD	Visio Drawing
VSS	Visio Template
VST	Visio Template
WAS	ProComm Script File (source code)
WAV	Windows digital sound file
WAX	Procomm compiled script
WB1	Quattro Pro for Windows Spreadsheet Notebook
WBT	Wilsonware Batch file used by Winbatch and Norton Desktop
WCM	Word Perfect Macro File
WD	InfoSelect data file
WK1	Lotus 123 2.x spreadsheet
WK3	Lotus 123 3.x spreadsheet
WK4	Lotus 123 4.x spreadsheet
WKQ	Quattro spreadsheet
WKS	Lotus 123 1.x spreadsheet
WMF	Windows MetaFile vector graphics format
WMP	Windows Magic Icon Palette
WNF	Corel Draw Font File
WP	WordPerfect format
WPG	WordPerfect Graphic (vector graphics)
WQ1	Quattro Pro for DOS spreadsheet
WRI	Windows Write file

WRK	Lotus Symphony Spreadsheet
WS	APL Worksheet
XCL	Xtree for Windows Script file
XLA	Excel Addin
XLB	Excel Toolbar
XLC	Excel Chart
XLL	Excel Addin
XLM	Excel Macro file
XLS	Excel spreadsheet file
XLT	Excel Template
XLW	Excel Wookbook
ZIP	PKZIP compressed file format
ZOO	Zoo compressed file format

CHAPTER 3

Windows Components

"How many hours a day did you do lessons?' said Alice. . .

"Ten hours the first day," said the Mock Turtle: "nine the next, and so on."

"What a curious plan!" exclaimed Alice.

"That's the reason they're called lessons," the Gryphon remarked: "because they lessen from day to day."

That was quite a new idea to Alice, and she thought it over a little before she made her next remark. "Then the eleventh day must have been a holiday?"

"Of course it was," said the Mock Turtle.

"And how did you manage on the twelfth?" Alice went on eagerly.

"That's enough about lessons," the Gryphon interrupted in a very decided tone.

— Charles Lutwidge Dodgson, *Alice's Adventures in Wonderland*, 1865

You may not realize this, but the real reason you buy Windows is because of the services it provides to programs — the Windows API (=Application Programming Interface). The traditional attitude of MS/IBM during the DOS 1–4 days was that if the OS also included a bunch of useful programs, that's nice, but treat them as the thrown — in freebies that they were. The result, of course, was Edlin and a Backup program that until DOS 6 (when Microsoft licensed one from Norton!) was a bad joke.

My own attitude is schizophrenic. True applications like Paint, Write, and Terminal are thrown in freebies — nice to have but hardly something to go running to Mom about if they aren't so great. But some functions are the natural job of an operating system and need to be handled right. So I've divided my words about the Windows executables into two parts — the big OS type stuff in this chapter and the non OS type stuff in the next.

The division isn't always so clear cut so some OS maintenance stuff like Regedit is in the next chapter because it isn't quite so central.

Bear in mind that Windows is like a giant erector set. The various pieces that provide the API functions are crucial but virtually anything else can be replaced by a third-party component. For almost everything else there is such a third party component available. I'm of the opinion that as a serious computer user, you need to look hard at third party replacements and will have a lot more to say about them in Chapter 5.

Microsoft supports the erector set theory of utilities making it easy to make the changes (even for the two pieces that Windows treats specially). One is called the shell — it is the first program that Windows starts and its the program that will cause Windows to shut down when you exit it. Obviously, this program must be able to launch other programs but other than that it can be just any program. Certainly, it can be File Manager if you prefer. But it could be Word for Windows if you felt like using a macro to launch programs — I'm not recommending this, mind you, just showing how flexible the architecture is. But don't try a Visual Basic program as shell — it won't work. Indeed, if you do try out a new program for a shell that doesn't explicitly tell you it is made to run as one, be prepared to reboot if Windows won't come up properly and edit `system.ini` outside of Windows.

The shell is determined by a line in the **[boot]** section of **system.ini** that says

```
shell=progman.exe
```

by default. If your replacement shell is not on your path or in your Windows directory, you can place a full path name after the **=** sign. Remember to include the **.exe** at the end of the program name.

 Most programs that are intended as a shell replacement handle this change in `system.ini` for you without any editing on your part. Indeed, many make the change for you when you install them without asking — rude behavior and I don't like rude behavior. But too often, they are so egocentric that they assume you won't want to go back to your old shell and provide no automation for that. So you need to know what to change if you do want to change back to, say, ProgMan!

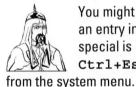 You might think that *File Manager* is the other program that is so central it has an entry in your system files, but it is just another program to Windows. What is special is *Task Manager* because its the program that Windows loads if you hit `Ctrl+Esc`, `Double Click` on the desktop or choose `Switch To...` from the system menu.

Like the shell statement, the taskman statement goes in the **[boot]** section of **system.ini**. But there is one difference: **system.ini** will have a shell statement, even if the shell is **progman.exe** but it does not need a taskman statement if **taskman.exe** is the task switcher. The syntax for a third party task switcher taken from Mao's machine (I'll discuss Metz Task Manager in Chapter 5) is:

```
taskman.exe=C:\winutil\metz\metztask.exe
```

The Big Three

I have three treasures.
Guard and keep them:
The first is deep love,
The second is frugality,
And the third is not to dare to be ahead of the world.
Because of deep love, one is courageous.
Because of frugality, one is generous.
Because of not daring to be ahead of the world, one becomes the leader of the world.

— The Way of Lao-tzu

I'll start out with the three programs that most define your interaction with the system — the file launcher (Program Manager, aka `progman.exe`, aka ProgMan), the file manipulator (File Manager, aka `winfile.exe`, aka FileMan) and the program switcher (Task Manager, aka `taskman.exe`, aka TaskMan). No, I'm not going to tell you how you need to double click on an icon to start a program or the other obvious stuff, but I will give you a collection of pointers and tips that you may not be so familiar with.

Out to Launch — ProgMan

> No! I am not Prince Hamlet, nor was meant to be;
> Am an attendant lord, one that will do
> To swell a progress, start a scene or two,
> Advise the prince; no doubt, an easy tool,
>
> — T. S. Elliot, *The Love Song of J. Alfred Prufrock*

Nothing is so familiar a symbol of Windows than the dull icons used by closed groups in ProgMan's window and the colorful icons inside the-group windows. The icons move as you nudge them by accident so one of the most important commands for you is the **Window/Arrange Icons** menu command which will line them up. To keep the icons in your ProgMan group windows nice and tidy, I recommend that you pull down the **Options** menu and make sure that the **Auto Arrange** option is checked. This keeps the program item icons in each group window lined up.

It is pretty strange that Microsoft doesn't allow you to choose which icons are used for closed groups but instead uses the same boring icon for them all. It's as if they are saying "icons are an attractive, fun way to distinguish program items with the eye but groups don't need to be distinguished!" Fortunately, third parties rush in where Redmonds fear to tred and there are many programs you can run that let you assign icons to ProgMan groups. Two — Plug-In for Progam Manager and WinMagic will be discussed in Chapter 5.

You can drag group windows around before choosing **Window/Arrange Icons** but you may find that when you restart Windows all is for naught — your carefully arranged setup has been forgotten. The standard recommendation is to be sure to check **Save Setting on Exit** on the **Options** menu. That will work most of the time but not if you turn off your machine while still inside Windows (against my recommendation) and not if some program crashes your system. Besides, why pay the time price of saving lots of group files every time you exit if you only makes changes once in blue moon? There is a better way, one of Igor's favorite tricks:

If you `Shift Double Click` on the ProgMan's system menu, that is, hold down the `Shift` Key and double click on the funny

icon, ProgMan saves its current state without thinking of exiting (which is what happens if you just double click without the `Shift`). Just remember to do that after a rearrangement session and you are all set.

Here are some tips on managing your groups:

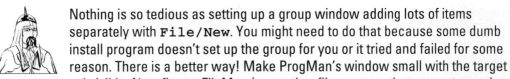

Nothing is so tedious as setting up a group window adding lots of items separately with `File/New`. You might need to do that because some dumb install program doesn't set up the group for you or it tried and failed for some reason. There is a better way! Make ProgMan's window small with the target group open and visible. Now fire up FileMan (or another file program that can act as a drag and drop source, for example, PCTool's File Manager), go to the directory containing the programs that you want to add, sort them on extension (pick `Sort by Type` from the `View` menu) so that all the **exe** files are together and select the **exe** files you want to make items for (by using `Ctrl+Click` and `Shift+Click`). Now just drag all the chosen files to the ProgMan group and voilà, instant multiple items!

Remember that you can either move *or* copy an item from one group to another. Dragging moves but hold down the `Ctrl` key while you drag and you get a copy of the icon. Why would you want to copy an icon? Well the next time you open the wrong group because you forgot where you stored an item, consider keeping the item in both places. It may be wisest to copy rather than move to your startup group.

Deleting a group is not the most intuitive action, so I'll mention the details. You have to iconize the group in question and then select it. A menu will popup —

essentially a system menu for the child window. The **Del** key does not work while that menu is up. So click on a blank spot in the ProgMan window which will get the menu to pop down and then hit **Del** or go to the **File** menu and choose **Delete**. Going to the **File** manu also makes the pop up menu pop down.

I'll discuss **grp** files in detail in a moment, but you should know that deleting a group deletes the **grp** file from the disk. If there is any chance that you may want to restore the group sometime, be sure to make a copy of the **grp** file before deleting the group. You can find the **grp** file name by hitting **Alt+Enter** or choosing **File/Properties** while the group is iconized with its caption selected.

You should copy it to a file which still has the extension **grp**. If you later want to restore the group, pick **File/New** and ask for a New Group but fill in the existing **grp** file in the second entry in the resulting dialog (Figure 3-1). When you hit **OK** in the resulting dialog, the group is restored; you don't even need to fill in the description. That is recalled from inside the **grp** file. Plug-In for Program Manager, a shareware program on CD MOM (and described in Chapter 5), has a group file manager that lets you easily remove groups and later restore them.

Program Group Properties		
Description:		OK
Group File:	oldgroup.grp	Cancel
		Help

Figure 3-1: Restoring an old group

If you possibly can avoid it, I'd urge you to avoid scroll bars in the main ProgMan window. It's too easy for a group to get lost. Consider enlarging the window or combining groups if scroll bars appear and can't be eliminated with a simple **Arrange Icons** command.

 It doesn't seem to be documented anywhere but there seems to be a limit of 40 groups in ProgMan. Don't believe me? Make 40 groups and try to add a 41st and you'll get a box that says **You have created the maximum number of groups possible in Program Manager. To create a new**

`group you must first delete a group to make room.` Sure smells like an arbitrary limitation with no special reason to me.

You can change the font used for the captions below iconized group and for program icons. It's the same font as is used for icons on the desktop and I explained how to change it in Chapter 2 (in the section *Not with My System Directory You Don't*).

✄   ✄   ✄   ✄   ✄

In an ideal world, you wouldn't care where Windows stores the information about your program items and groups, but to recover from disasters you do need to know.

 This is a good place to give you the lecture on backing up. Yeah, yeah, I know, you intend to do it every day but fess up, you forget more often than not. It's ironic that as hardware improves, software glitches replace it as a threat. It used to be that when I gave the backup lecture, I could say, "it isn't *if* your hard disk fails but *when*". But disks have gotten much better so that it is more than likely that your hard disk will not fail over the five year life you might hope to squeeze out of a machine. But with the potential danger of caches, a program going wild and crashing, and other fun events in the World of Windows computing, you can also expect that in the five year period you'll have one or more occurrences of serious file corruption due to *je ne sais quoi* (and *tu ne sais quoi* either). Make your life easy and back up regularly.

It's especially important to back up your critical files. Consider adding the following lines to your autoexec.bat as cheap insurance assuming that `C:\windows` is your windows directory and you have previously made a directory called `C:\backup`:

```
copy C:\autoexec.bat C:\backup
copy C:\config.sys C:\backup
copy C:\windows\*.ini C:\backup
copy C:\windows\*.grp C:\backup
```

Of course, if you have crash problem, those commands may copy over good files with corrupted ones so if you can afford the space, make a second directory called `backup1` and proceed the above by

```
copy C:\backup C:\backup1
```

and/or find a program that helps you run chosen autoexec commands once a day and have the backup only done that often.

But I digress. ProgMan stores its information in two sets of files — a single text file called **progman.ini** and a collection of binary **grp** files, one for each group. The structure of the grp files is described in the Windows SDK but are really of no concern to end users except to note that they store the information in the **Properties** dialog for each item and the positions of the items themselves. The icons for the items are stored there as well as the name of the original file where the icon came from. So if you have been mystified to remove a program from your disk, have its icon remain in ProgMan despite that removal and later have the icon disappear when you hit **Alt+Enter**, the explanation is that the icon is stored in the **grp** file but ProgMan tries to reread it from the original file when you call up the **Properties** dialog.

Progman.ini is a text file. You might try loading it into Notepad and seeing how it looks. The first section has information on the location and size of the ProgMan window and the status of your option choices, information that you can easily recreate if disaster strikes. But the second part contains the list of **grp** files installed into ProgMan (the captions of the groups and their location within the ProgMan window are stored in the **grp** files). The syntax is

```
Group9=C:\WINDOWS\SOUND.GRP
```

So what might you need to know about these files? Well, first of all, if some install program complains about your progman.ini, it is likely that it was written assuming that the groups are all neatly numbered **Group1=**, ProgMan is quite happy to have the lines in a funny order and even to have numbers missing. That can happen if you delete and add groups a lot but some install program are downright snitty about such a progman.ini. Don't pay 'em no mind.

The **grp** files need not be in your Windows directory but that's where ProgMan will place them by default. Some installation program will place their **grp** files in their home directories which isn't such a good idea if you like to keep stuff together, say for backup or disaster recovery purposes. The best way to move the **grp** file to the Windows directory is not to move the actual file but to do the following:

1.   Hit **Alt+Enter** with the group minimized and selected or choose **Properties** from the **File** menu.

2. The full path name of the **grp** file will appear in the result dialog; change it to your Windows Directory.

3. **Shift+Double Click** on ProgMan's system menu to save the current settings. This will save the information on the group in a newly made **grp** file in the Windows directory.

4. Now feel free to delete the original **grp** file (after confirming that the proper grp file is indeed in your Windows directory).

So disaster strikes your ProgMan. Some errant program has clobbered **progman.ini**. Of course you have a recent backup, so its no problem. What's that you say? You don't have a backup? Well, if your **grp** files are intact, the process is simple. Print out a directory of all the **grp** files in your windows directory (assuming you keep all your **grp** files there). Then call up **File/New/Group** and type in the name of the **grp** file and — surprise — the group itself including the name will load perfectly. Do that for each group. Now save setting (Step 3) and a perfectly fine progman.ini with all your groups will be constructed by ProgMan.

✄ ✄ ✄ ✄ ✄

When you add a Windows application as a new item in Program Manager, it looks in the executable file and uses the first icon it finds. For DOS products, it uses a standard dull MS-DOS icon but you can do better than that. There are thousands of free icons out on the BBS circuit many of which we've put together for you on CD MOM and cataloged in Chapter 14.

The procedure is easy. Call up the item properties dialog and pick **Change Icon...**. Then pick **Browse...** in the resulting dialog (see Figure 3-2). That will let you choose a file containing icons to use. It can be a ***.ico** file (one with a single icon), a ***.exe** (which can have zero, one or many icons) or an icon library (which can have the extension **dll**, **icl**, **nil**, or whatever the supplier of icons wants it to have!). The dialog then shows the icons with a slider (if the file has more than 5 icons) and you get to pick the one you want.

 Don't forget to use the well-made icons that Microsoft includes in **progman.exe**. There are particularly well-done mailboxes and options for painting. Think of ProgMan when you need to look at a library of icons just to see what it is in it. The scrolling viewer is a handy way to look at the library contents and if you hit `Cancel` a few times, you can back out without making any changes.

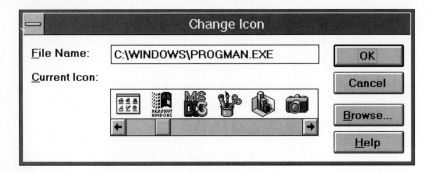

Figure 3-2: The Change Icon dialog

 Not only are there a collection of icons in `progman.exe` but there is an extra library of icons in a file called `moricons.dll` including some for third-party apps like Word Perfect. The Mother of All Icon Catalogs in Chapter 13 has all the icons in both files.

 I knew a con named Mori. Is it named after him?

If you have a tool that will extract icons from libraries, you should consider taking the icons that you need and put them in `*.ico` files in a convenient directory (I use `C:\windows\icons`). That way they are handy in one place, and if you use an icon from one **exe** program for an item not involving that program, you don't have to worry if you later remove the original **exe**. If disk space is tight and you have the utility to do so, you might put these icons into a library file. The icons are *not* compressed in the library so you might not think you saved any space but you do because of the way DOS does it's bookkeeping. Every file takes a minimum space, normally 2K (but it is 4K if your partitions are more than 128 MB and 8K if they are more than 256 MB). Icon files take 766 bytes, so for example, 10 icons in a library will use only 8K of disk space while as separate `*.ico` files, they'd take at least 20K.

Actually, not all icon files take 766 bytes. The ones that are 32x32 pixels in 16 colors are that size but there are 64x64 icons and there are monochrome icons. That said, almost any icon file that you run across will be 766 bytes. When you think about it, it is remarkable how subtle a piece of art a picture with a mere 1024 points in it can be!

For Winapps, Windows does not usually use either the caption or the icon you specify in ProgMan after the program is loaded and minimized on the desktop. It leaves them up to the program itself. But it will use both the icon and caption for minimized DOS sessions. There are third party applications, notably *hDC's Power Launcher* which do let you change the caption and icon used by a running Winapp.

✖ ✖ ✖ ✖ ✖

Surprisingly, many users don't use one of ProgMan's neatest features — it's hotkeys. It is easy to set them up. Call up the **Properties** dialog for an item (see Figure 3-3). You get this when you initially invoke **File/New/Item** or you can select the item (by single clicking rather than double clicking) and hit **Alt+Enter**. The hotkey is in the field labeled **Shortcut Key**.

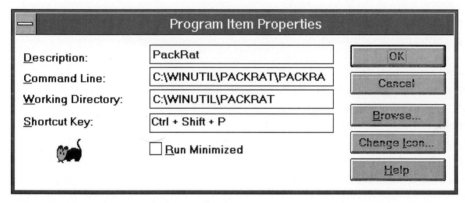

Figure 3-3: ProgMan's Hotkey Setup

ProgMan only accepts three shift combinations:

- **Ctrl+Alt+*other***
- **Ctrl+Shift+*other***
- **Ctrl+Shift+Alt+*other***

where *other* can be any alphabetic key (e.g. **Ctrl+Alt+A**), top row number
(e.g. **Ctrl+Alt+1**, even **Ctrl+Alt+=**), numeric pad key (e.g.
Ctrl+Alt+Num5), cursor key (e.g. **Ctrl+Alt+Right**), or function key
(**Ctrl+Alt+F2** but not involving **F1**).

 The *Windows User's Guide* — ya know, the manual that ships in the box
— says there are four valid shift combinations, listing **Ctrl+Shift+Alt**
and **Ctrl+Alt+Shift** as if they were separate combinations. They
aren't. Bizarre manual glitch.

You don't even need to hit all the shifts — if you type **a** when **Shortcut Key** is
the field, it will say **Ctrl+Alt+A**; type **Shift+a** and it will say
Ctrl+Shift+Alt+A. You do need to hit **Ctrl+Shift** to get that particular
combination. If you want to blank a previously assigned key use backspace while
your cursor is in that field.

Once you've assigned a hotkey, it works in two situations:

- You have started a program from a ProgMan icon; then the hotkey will switch
  to it.

- ProgMan is the active application and you hit an assigned hotkey whose
  program is not already running. Then ProgMan will launch it as if you started it
  from the icon.

Be warned that you really truly have to have started from a ProgMan icon or
hotkey. WinMagic (discused in Chapter 5) is a ProgMan add-on. It lets you right
click on a closed group icon and get a popup list of item names which you can
choose to launch from. When you do that, you'll feel that you've used ProgMan to
launch that program but you haven't — you've used WinMagic and the hotkeys will
not work.

A special feature of ProgMan hotkeys, that doesn't apply to hotkeys associated by
most other Windows shells, is that ProgMan hotkeys work from and in DOS
sessions (three other shells whose hotkeys work in DOS sessions are Dashboard,
Norton Desktop, and PCTools). This means that you may want to keep ProgMan
loaded even if you are using another program as your shell (I'll say more about this
in a moment).

While ProgMan has to be active for the hotkeys to launch an application, it can be minimized. **Single Click** on a minimized ProgMan icon and then **Single Click** on the desktop (to get rid of the control menu) and a hotkey will launch an application for you.

 Listen up sonny. Hotkeys sure beat groping around in a bunch of large Windows for the one you want, squinting at icons for-the one you want, or using TaskMan. Moreover, you can make them mnemonic so they are easy to remember, so use them. Hear?

You might think that Microsoft screwed up on two aspects of how hotkeys work:

- You have to make ProgMan active and can't use hotkeys to launch programs from anywhere else.
- You can't assign a hotkey to ProgMan itself.

Microsoft did screw up in not allowing hotkeys to launch from anywhere else.

But you can assign a hotkey to ProgMan! Here's how!

```
┌────────────────────────────────────────────────────────────┐
│ ─                  Program Item Properties                   │
├────────────────────────────────────────────────────────────┤
│                                                              │
│  Description:       ┌──────────────────────┐   ┌──────────┐ │
│                     │ ProgMan              │   │    OK    │ │
│  Command Line:      ┌──────────────────────┐   └──────────┘ │
│                     │ C:\WINDOWS\PROGMAN.EXE│   ┌──────────┐ │
│  Working Directory: ┌──────────────────────┐   │  Cancel  │ │
│                     │ C:\WINDOWS           │   └──────────┘ │
│  Shortcut Key:      ┌──────────────────────┐   ┌──────────┐ │
│                     │ Ctrl + Shift + N     │   │  Browse… │ │
│                                               └──────────┘ │
│        [icon]       ┌─┐                        ┌──────────┐ │
│                     └─┘ Run Minimized          │Change Icon…│ │
│                                               └──────────┘ │
│                                                ┌──────────┐ │
│                                                │   Help   │ │
│                                                └──────────┘ │
└────────────────────────────────────────────────────────────┘
```

Figure 3-4: ProgMan as a ProgMan item.

That's right, you can launch ProgMan from ProgMan (autoerotism at its best!). When ProgMan tries to load and sees that it is already loaded, it doesn't load a second time but three items you can set in the Properties dialog are set — the caption, the icon, and the hotkey!!! So make an item just like the one in Figure 3-4 and put it in your StartUp Group. Of course you can change the caption (the **Description**) and the Icon using **Change Icon...**. Notice here I've changed the icon to the Windows logo.

 Didn't it just say that Windows doesn't use the caption and icon from a ProgMan item that is a Winapp but leaves them up to the Winapp. Isn't ProgMan a Winapp?

 Precisely, grasshopper. Windows does leave the icon and caption to the Winapp but that is ProgMan itself and it knows enough to use the information that you gave it in the ProgMan item!

✺   ✺   ✺   ✺   ✺

If you hold down the **Shift** key when you double click on an icon in ProgMan, two special things happen:

- Independently of whether you have the **Run Minimized** box checked in the item's properties dialog, it launches minimized

- The **Minimize on Use Option** (which would minimize ProgMan on launch if checked) is ignored

This allows for quick launching of several applications at once.

✺   ✺   ✺   ✺   ✺

When Windows installs, it automatically sets up a group called StartUp. You've probably already figured out that the items you place there are automatically started up whenever Windows begins. If you want some of them to start up iconized, call up their **Properties** dialog and check the box that says **Run Minimized**. As a holdover from earlier versions of Windows, you can also startup programs with **run=** and **load=** lines in your win.ini. I urge you to put all your eggs in the StartUp Group basket and not have any **run=** or **load=** line (and if a program adds such lines, consider removing them and adding the programs to the StartUp group).

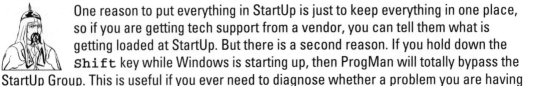 One reason to put everything in StartUp is just to keep everything in one place, so if you are getting tech support from a vendor, you can tell them what is getting loaded at StartUp. But there is a second reason. If you hold down the **Shift** key while Windows is starting up, then ProgMan will totally bypass the StartUp Group. This is useful if you ever need to diagnose whether a problem you are having

is due to a conflict with a program that you load automatically at startup. There isn't such a simple way to bypass programs in `run=` and `load=` lines. When I say hold down the `Shift` I mean it. Don't just give it a quick push but hold it down from the time you hit `Enter` after typing `win` (or from the time your batch file starts to load Windows) until ProgMan appears. There is a critical stage in the middle there where you need to have `Shift` down and, in my experience, its hard to catch it if you don't hold it down the whole time!

⌘   ⌘   ⌘   ⌘   ⌘

ProgMan has two big advantages that are so significant that I suggest you use it as your shell even if you prefer another shell. You can then run the other shell in your StartUp group and pretend it is your shell but still have the advantages of ProgMan.

 Under Windows 3.0, the idea of running both ProgMan and another shell was a no go. ProgMan had real problems as a shell by itself with each open group taking up about 5% of free resources so running two shells was out of the question. But Windows 3.1 resource handling was restructured so that ProgMan's resource hit is modest and it becomes reasonable to run both it and another launcher.

What are the two big advantages? First, installation programs expect ProgMan to be your shell and will attempt to make a new group (using DDE commands to ProgMan!). A well constructed alternate shell will include DDE commands to emulate ProgMan and a well constructed installation program will be written to support such alternates but how often can you rely on two programs being well constructed? So to keep installation programs happy, you may want to have ProgMan as the official shell loaded by Windows.

The second plus involves DOS programs — when launched from ProgMan, the desktop icons, captions, and hotkeys all work the way you'd expect and that is a real advantage. If you configure ProgMan with a group of your DOS programs open, assign it to a hotkey and check off the option that says Minimize on Use, you'll find ProgMan to be a great DOS program loader even if you prefer an alternate Windows program loader.

⌘   ⌘   ⌘   ⌘   ⌘

One final note about ProgMan; don't forget that the About command , shown in Figure 3-5, in ProgMan has some useful additional information. It tells you what mode (standard or enhanced) you are running in, it gives free memory and Free Resources. The free memory number is the sum of the virtual on-disk memory and physical RAM. You should check the **386 Enhanced applet** in Control panel to find out how much virtual memory you have. If possible, you want to keep the free memory number above the amount of virtual memory so that Windows doesn't swap to disk. That can't always be avoided but its something to strive for since disk swapping can kill decent performance. And you want to keep Free Resources above 20%.

It is inconvenient to have to keep checking the About box — I'll discuss better ways in Chapter 5 which use third-party utilities.

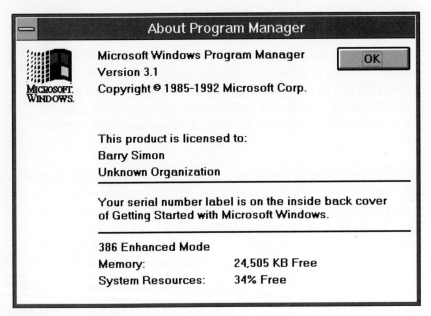

Figure 3-5: ProgMan's About box

Rank (and) File Manager

> And leave the world no copy.
>
> — William Shakespeare, *Twelfth-Night*, Act: I, Scene: v

If you are an old Windows hand, you probably got Windows 3.0, ripped off the shrinkwrap, installed it and exclaimed at how wonderful File Manager was in comparison to the MS-DOS Executive (the quaint name for the combined launcher/file manager in Windows 2.x) but you quickly realized that it was a dog, just not as big a wowser as the *Executive*. No doubt, you invested in Prompt (which wasn't that much better) or used a DOS program for file management. If you started with Windows 3.0, you probably realized that FileMan was worth the pass and stuck with Magellan or Xtree.

But a funny thing happened on the way to Windows 3.1. FileMan became a decent program! True, it had its lacks — most notably, the lack of file viewers (and I'll name more later) but it's a more than usable program, better than almost all the third party alternatives (about the only file managers that I like better are Norton Desktop, Xtree/Win and PC Tools). Be sure to take a close look if you gave up on it in an earlier incarnation.

Unlike the Windows 3.0 FileMan, this one allows multiple directory trees to be open in a full fledged MDI implementation. And it provides wondrous support of Ðdrag and Ðdrop between windows within FileMan. Want to copy a bunch of files from one directory to another drive? Select the files with the mouse (using the **Shift/Ctrl+Click** multiple list choice methods) and drag them to a second window which displays the target directory and voilà — the files are copied.

There is one convention which is not unreasonable, but is potentially confusing. If you select a group of files and drag them to a new directory what happens is dependent on whether the new directory is on the same drive or a different one. If the same drive, the file(s) is moved; if a different drive, the file(s) is copied. If you want to force a move, hold down **Shift** while dragging; to force a copy hold down **Ctrl**.

Each FileMan window will display one of three possibilities: a combined tree and directory, a tree only or a directory only. You can drag files either to the directory portion of a window or to the tree part. If you drag to a directory portion, try to drop on an empty part of the directory window and if to a tree portion, drop on the actual target directory.

 Normally, if you drag one file onto another, FileMan will treat it as copy or move to the directory with the target file. But if the target is an executable file (one with the extension **exe**, **com**, **bat** or **pif**), then FileMan will not copy/move but instead it will run that executable, passing it the name of the first of the

selected files (kids, do try this at home with Notepad.) So be careful if you drag to a directory window not to drop on an executable file unless launching is your intention.

There is a second aspect of FileMan drag and drop. It works from FileMan to other programs. When you drag a file from one program to another, the one you drag from is called the source and the one you drag to is called the target. Windows 3.0 allowed drag and drop with FileMan as source and ProgMan as target (implementing the functionality that I discussed in the last section). The idea as so attractive that the Windows SDK provide documentation for one half of the equation. Programs were told how they could become drag and drop targets for filenames dragged from FileMan.

Alas, there is no standard for what drag and drop does as I discussed in *Drag 'til You Drop* — Chapter 2. It is a mish mash at best.

The SDK did not explain how to make a program a drag and drop source, but some vendors have figured it out and a number of products besides FileMan are drag and drop sources (for example, PC Tools and Image Pals come to mind — both of them will be discussed in Chapter 5).

⌘ ⌘ ⌘ ⌘ ⌘

There is a **`Properties`** dialog for files and directories with the same access methods (**`File/Properties...`** from the menus or **`Alt+Enter`**) as for the ProgMan Properties dialog.

As seen in Figure 3-6 it includes a set of boxes called **attributes** — these refer to DOS arcanities that you may need to adjust (you could set in DOS with the **`Attrib`** command).

A file is called **Read Only** if DOS services cannot overwrite or change the file. Occasionally, a program will install its files as Read Only and you won't be able to delete them with a Del command at the DOS line. You can change that property in FileMan or just use FileMan to delete the file (it will warn you that it is Read Only — if you ask FileMan to delete it, it changes the attribute and deletes it in one fell swoop).

```
┌──────────────────────────────────────────────────────────────────┐
│ ─  │            Properties for WIN.INI                            │
├──────────────────────────────────────────────────────────────────┤
│  File Name:     WIN.INI                       ┌──────────────┐     │
│  Size:          26,722 bytes                  │     OK       │     │
│  Last Change:   6/3/93  10:10:32AM            └──────────────┘     │
│  Path:          C:\WINDOWS                    ┌──────────────┐     │
│                                               │   Cancel     │     │
│  ┌─Attributes──────────────────────────┐     └──────────────┘     │
│  │  ☐ Read Only      ☐ Hidden          │     ┌──────────────┐     │
│  │  ☐ Archive        ☐ System          │     │    Help      │     │
│  └──────────────────────────────────────┘     └──────────────┘     │
└──────────────────────────────────────────────────────────────────┘
```

Figure 3-6: The FileMan properties dialog

The **Archive** attribute is one that DOS keeps to help backup programs. Every time a file is changed or copied, DOS turns the Archive bit on. Backup programs, when asked to "backup changed files", look for files with the Archive bit on, back them up and then turn the archive bit off. If you have a file that you want included in an incremental backup even though it hasn't been changed, use the Properties dialog to turn the Archive bit on (make sure that the box is checked). Conversely, if there is a huge file that you don't need backed up in an incremental backup, you can turn the archive bit off.

The **System** and **Hidden** attributes are special. Hidden files are not displayed by the DOS directory command, so at one time, naive users didn't know they were there. Most other programs won't display them either. But you can see them with FileMan if you check off the **Show Hidden/System Files** check box in the dialog invoked with the **View/By File Type...** menu choice. So they aren't very hidden.

Generally, there is a good reason that a file is hidden (for example, Windows makes its swap file hidden so you won't accidentally delete it) so you should only change that attribute if you know why it was hidden in the first place. The idea behind the system attribute was to make it for special operating system files but it is rarely used independently of the hidden attribute. It is unlikely that you'll ever need to change it.

⌘ ⌘ ⌘ ⌘ ⌘

In its window FileMan shows one of five tiny pictures next to each file or directory:

	This is used for subdirectories of a directory. In a file window, **`double click`** on it to change to that directory
	This used for an executable file. By default that means **`exe`**, **`com`**, **`bat`** or **`pif`** files. **`Double click`** on one to launch it.
	This is used for a file with an extension in the list of associated extensions (more on that in "Meet My Associate" below) or files with an extension that is listed in the **`documents=`** line in win.ini. Such files are called **documents**.
	This is used for a file that is hidden and/or system (even if it is also a document)
	None of the above, so Windows has no idea what the file's purpose is.

`Double click` on a file whose extension has an associated program and the associated program is launched with the document you clicked on passed to the program. That normally means the program loads with the document opened in it. If your **`documents=`** line in **`win.ini`** has nothing after the equal, that means that a program will be launched when you double click in FileMan if and only if the icon is a program or doc icon.

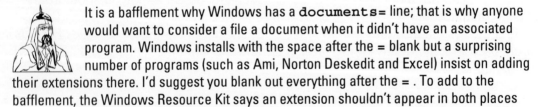

It is a bafflement why Windows has a **`documents=`** line; that is why anyone would want to consider a file a document when it didn't have an associated program. Windows installs with the space after the = blank but a surprising number of programs (such as Ami, Norton Deskedit and Excel) insist on adding their extensions there. I'd suggest you blank out everything after the = . To add to the bafflement, the Windows Resource Kit says an extension shouldn't appear in both places even though Excel puts its types in both places and there seems to be no problem with it.

❋ ❋ ❋ ❋ ❋

An oft overlooked goody in FileMan is the **File/Search...** menu command. It presents a dialog (see Figure 3-7) that lets you search for file(s) across a whole drive (just check the **Search All Subdirectories** checkbox). You can use wildcards in the name following the DOS rules: * replaces one of more characters and ? replaces single characters. The above dialog box would look for all files with the extension **ini** on all of drive C.

▬	Search	
<u>S</u>earch For:	*.INI	OK
Start <u>F</u>rom:	C:\	Cancel
	☒ <u>S</u>earch All Subdirectories	Help

Figure 3-7: The FileMan Search Dialog

You might be fooled by the large size of the entry boxes into thinking that there was a way to enter multiple file spaces (e.g. ***.com+*.exe**) but there isn't, nor is there a way to enter multiple drives. The large **Start From** is presumably to allow huge directory names and the large **Search For** is just a tease.

What's neat is what happens when files are found. Their names appear in a window and you can copy, move, delete, launch or drag and drop from that list.

❋ ❋ ❋ ❋ ❋

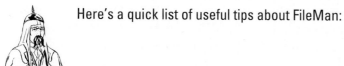

Here's a quick list of useful tips about FileMan:

- **Ctrl+/** will select all files in a file window and **Ctrl+** will deselect all files. **Ctrl+*,** when in the tree part of a window, will expand the entire tree (show all directories).

- You can copy to a disk drive by dragging to the disk icon just below the child window title bars. This is useful for floppies but less useful for hard drives since you probably don't know what directory will get used.

- **Single Click** a drive icon and it changes what drive is displayed in the **File/Directory** window. **Double click** and you open a new window with that drive displayed there. **Shift+Single Click** will change to that drive and expand its entire tree. You might guess that **Shift+Double Click** would combine the two (i.e. open a new window and display the chosen drive with tree expanded) but you'd be wrong — it does the same as plain **Double Click**.

- **Shift+Double Click** a directory in a tree or in a directory window and FileMan will open a new window with only that directory (and no tree) in it.

- The **File/Print** menu item will only work for files with an associated extension and if the associated program is in the OLE registration database. If properly registered, FileMan starts the application by using the command given for printing in the registration database. Normally that indicates printing with a command line switch or a DDE command. Depending on the associated application, this may print with no questions asked or bring up a dialog box. I'll explain how to add a program you want to print to the registration database when I discuss Regedit in the next chapter.

- There are three possible views in each FileMan window based on a choice on the top of the **View** menu: directory tree only, file list only, or both. But you can also change this with the mouse in the window by pulling on the slider. In a dual window, you'll see a thin line next to the slider to the right of the tree. Move your mouse to that line and the cursor changes. Press down and you can adjust the amount used for tree vs. file list. Move to the extreme right or left and you switch to a directory only or file list only view. File only views, have the line at their extreme left. Tree only views also have the line on the left — its not the logical place but it works.

- If you change files outside FileMan, you'll probably want to Refresh your file windows. Use **F5** or the **Window/Refresh** menu item. Alas, you will also need to refresh FileMan windows after a delete.

- Don't forget that, unlike DOS, FileMan's **Rename** command works on directories.

• The **Copy** command on the **File** menu has an option called **Copy to Clipboard**. That copies the file name to the clipboard but not as text so, alas, you can't, for example, paste it into an Open dialog. It's once more OY, VEY OLE time. The filename can only be pasted into an OLE client where it will be embedded as an OLE object. And not all OLE clients will accept it — for example Windows Write does, but Word for Windows 2.0 does not.

✂   ✂   ✂   ✂   ✂

FileMan has an extra aspect that can overcome some of its weaknesses — it can be extended in two different ways with third party products. First, the **[Settings]** section of **winfile.ini** (ini file structure is discussed in Chapter 8) can have an entry such as:

UNDELETE.DLL=C:\SYSTEM\DOS\MSTOOLS.DLL

If it does, an **Undelete...** menu item is added to FileMan's **File** menu. Second, FileMan can have extra menu items added between the Option and Window menus. Again this is done through entries in **winfile.ini**, this time in a special section called **[Addons]** and this time a typical entry might read

MS-DOS Tools Extentions=C:\SYSTEM\DOS\MSTOOLS.DLL

Figure 3-8 shows how FileMan looked with **Undelete** added to the **File** menu and with two new submenus added — named **Tools** and **Norton**.

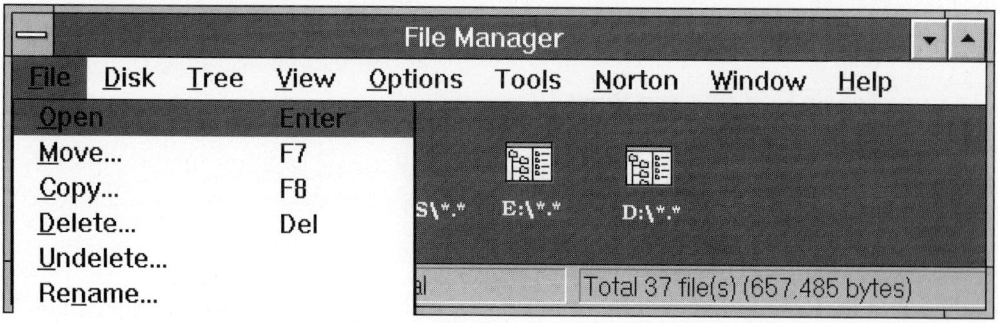

Figure 3-8: FileMan Extended

End users can't directly add their own extensions. Third parties can and when you install them, they will normally make the necessary changes to **winfile.ini**. But if you want to remove an extension, you'll need to remove the proper lines from **winfile.ini**; I recommend you comment them out by putting a semi-colon in front.

There seems to be a limit of four items in the add-on section in that if you have five or more, those after the fourth will act strangely.

If you installed MS-DOS 6.0 after Windows 3.1 and told it to install the Windows version of Undelete, BackUp, and Antivirus, it will add the two lines referring to MSTOOLS.DLL referenced above. Other programs that will add their own extensions to File Manager are Norton Desktop, Wiz Manager, OutsideIn and Metz TaskMan, all of which I'll discuss in Chapter 5. The Metz extensions allow you to add a customizable launch menu to FileMan. WizManager is on CD MOM and on the diskettes that accompany the diskette version of this book.

To allow yourself comprehensive customizability, take a look at File Commander (Wilson Windoware, Voice: 800-762-8383; 206-938-1740). It let's you run WinBatch batch files from FileMan menu entries. Both File Commander and WinBatch are shareware offerings on CD MOM.

✄   ✄   ✄   ✄   ✄

So what's missing from FileMan?

- No doubt that the biggest lack is file viewers. Heck, even the kludgy DOS Shell file manager has an ASCII file viewer. Norton and OutsideIn provide file viewing via the addon mechanism. The shareware Drag and View (Canyon Software, Voice: 415-453-9779), which you'll find on CD MOM, lets you drag files to a Viewer icon on the screen.

- Second on the list is some kind of support for pkzip — looking inside zips for example. My favorite solution for this is PCTools FileMan replacement but there are several shareware solutions on CD MOM.

- While FileMan can search on filenames, it cannot search on the contents of files. So, for example, you can't ask it to locate all files in your word processing director with the phrase Mr. Smith inside them.

- There is no way to see files on several drives in one list nor to search for filenames across multiple drives.

- There is no way to view all files on a drive other than by using global search.

- There is no way to select multiple directories for deleting, copying, or moving.

- It should be possible to paste a filename to the clipboard.

- It should be possible to print a directory listing on the printer and also to print out a directory tree. Wiz Manager adds this feature to FileMan.

- FileMan should automatically refresh its own windows when it does a file operation. It is crazy to delete a file in FileMan and have it still appear on the file list!

- The list of drives, which can be especially long on a network should appear once, on the main FileMan window rather than on each child window.

- There is no button bar on the Windows FileMan although there is in Windows for Workgroups FileMan. Again Wiz Manager adds a button bar.

Meet My Associate

> An associate producer is the only guy in Hollywood
> who will associate with a producer
>
> — Fred Allen

As I just mentioned, special treatment is given to files that have associated extensions. Windows keeps a list (inside **win.ini**) of extensions associated to some program. It is kept in a section called **[Extensions]** with the form

```
wri=write.exe ^.wri
```

(Chapter 7 discusses the format of your **ini** files in detail; I'll explain the syntax of this example in a moment). Normally programs set up these entries for you but there are many reasons you may need to change them. In FileMan, you can adjust your associations with the **File/Associate** command. I normally recommend that when there are tools to make changes in your ini files you use them rather than hand edit. As I'll explain in Chapter 8, *you should only change associations with FileMan* (or another program that also adjusts your registration database). This is not something the other books will tell you, but adjusting an existing line in your win.ini, say to replace

```
ini=notepad.exe ^.ini
```

by

```
ini=hotedit.exe ^.ini
```

will not cause clicking a an ini file in FileMan to load hotedit! Film at 11, er, more in Chapter 7.

[Extensions] associate a program to a file with a specified extension. Say the file is **name.ext**. It's entry in **win.ini** might read

```
ext=path\prog.exe /s/d  ^.ext
```

This tells FileMan or another program which uses this part of **win.ini**, that when you **Double Click** on **name.ext**, FileMan should launch the program **path\prog.exe** with the command line parameter

```
/s/d name.ext
```

That is, it replaces all occurrences of ^ by the file name. Note that the **exe** must be explicitly included.

So in the **wri** example at the start of my discussion, *Write* is launched with the ***.wri** file. The Windows installation program sets up ten associations to start with: for Cardfile (**crd**), Calendar (**cal**), Write (**wri**), Terminal (**trm**), Recorder (**rec**), Notepad (**txt** and **ini**), Paintbrush (**pcx** and **bmp**) and Help (**hlp**). In particular, the quickest way to edit an **ini** file, say **progman.ini** is to just call up **File/Run** in ProgMan and type in the file name, i.e. **progman.ini**. **File/Run** will use associations when it launches. And the easiest way to consult help for a program without launching it is to double click on the **hlp** file in a FileMan list.

Many other programs, as part of their install, add their own file extensions to your associations list. Associations also work in ProgMan, that is, you can put down the name of a file with association as the **Command Line** in a ProgMan item and have the launch work the way you'd expect. ProgMan even uses the icon in the associated program by default.

When might you need to change an association yourself?

1. Say you use Suprimo Paint to edit your bmp files. But it doesn't handle **jpg** so you pick up Picture Beautician to handle them. Picture Beautician also edits **bmp** files, so without asking it changes

    ```
    bmp=C:\suprimo\suppaint.exe ^.bmp
    ```

    to

    ```
    bmp=C:\beauty\picbeaut.exe ^.bmp
    ```

    during its installation and you'll need to change back. You might hope that such rude behavior was the exception rather than the rule but alas, I've never seen a program popup during installation, warn you that an extension is currently assigned to another program, and ask for permission to make the change. In fact, the Windows API is structured in a way that it is likely that programs making the change don't even realize that you had a conflicting assignment. Be sure to adjust this through FileMan's File/Associate menu.

    You need to watch for this problem especially if you install a kitchen sink program like Norton Desktop which literally changes dozens of extensions. Mao, who swears by PC Tools backup installed Norton for some of its other components, went to backup by clicking on an icon. He got an invalid backup file error box and decided the **set** file that PC Tools used must have gotten corrupted. After a half hour of fooling around he discovered that the problem was that *Norton* had changed the association for **set** files to it's backup, that the ProgMan entry launched a **set** file and that the unmarked error message was coming from *Norton*. He almost sent Igor out after Mr. Norton.

2. You want to add an extension to a program or one for a DOS program. For example, if you are still using DOS WordPerfect, you should add

    ```
    doc=path\wp.exe ^.doc
    ```

3. You do some directory rearranging. You may need to change the paths listed in some of your associations.

4. You use a program which allows lots of command line switches and you decide to change them.

Figure 3-9 shows what FileMan's association dialog looks like. It is a little confusing because the scrolling list uses the OLE registration database without explanation! Forget about that scrolling list for a while — most of the time you'll want to ignore it anyhow.

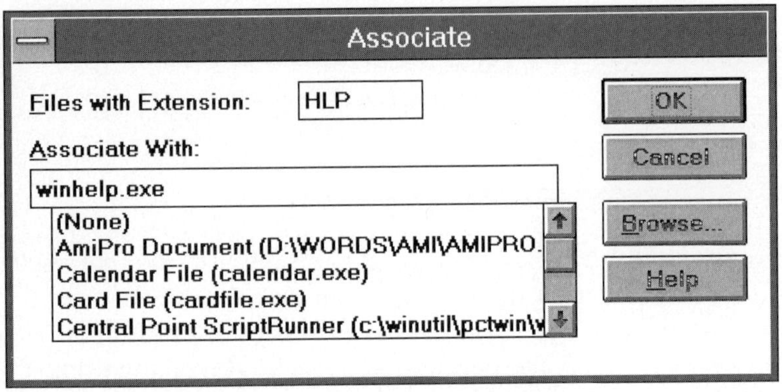

Figure 3-9: FileMan's Association dialog

When you invoke **File/Associate**, the dialog opens with the extension of the currently selected file type in the **Files with Extension** box. If you wish, you can type in another extension there. Under **Associate With** will appear either **(None)** or the name of the program that the extension is associated to if there is one. Sometimes the scrolling list will come into play and something else will appear, of which more in a moment.

Normally, you'll want to change or add a program by using the **Browse...** dialog and locating the program by browsing. That will place the full program's pathname into **win.ini** which is all to the good.

In the scroll box below **Associate With** is a list of all programs in your registration database. This allows English names to be associated to extensions which would seem to be a positive sign. But alas, OLE registration is in a sorry state so there are pitfalls! For example, if you use Winword 2.0, but previously used Winword 1.0, there is probably an entry in your **win.ini [extensions]** that says:

```
doc=C:\WINWORD\WINWORD.EXE ^.DOC
```

although the path may be different. It was put there by the Winword installation program. If you happen to scroll down the scrolling list in FileMan's File/Associate, you will notice an entry called **Word Document**. It was installed in the Registration database by Winword. "Oh," you might think, "how neat, I'll just associate my Word documents to **Word Document**". Guess what happens if you do? You wind up with **doc=** in **win.ini** with a blank after the **=** and **double clicking** on a **doc** file no longer launches Winword! (You can recover by doing a **Browse...** on **File/Associate** and choosing the actual **winword.exe** file.) The problem is that program can choose to put an open command into the registration database or not and Winword did not. It installs to use the database only for OLE stuff and not associations.

 If you install Winword 2.0 fresh, then its OLE registration does include the proper registration of open and print commands but apparently not if you install over Winword 1.0. This is typical of the confusion surrounding the registration database.

The moral is that you should ignore that scrolling list. If you choose not to ignore it, be sure that any item on the list you assign to an extension has a filename in parentheses after it.

Taking Windows to Task

> Thou thy worldly task hast done,
> Home art gone, and ta'en thy wages.
>
> — William Shakespeare, *Cymbeline*, Act: IV, Scene: ii

Ain't much to say about TaskMan (Figure 3-10). It does its job and little more. You can invoke it by hitting **Ctrl+Esc** (including from a DOS session), choosing **Switch To...** from any program's Control Menu or **double clicking** on a blank piece of desktop. Once up you get a scrolling list of all currently running programs. Actually, a list of all programs that are running and not hidden, a notion I'll discuss in Chapter 5 as part of my discussion of *The Virtual Desktop Shtick*. By double clicking, you can switch to the program you want or you can use the **Switch To** button. Remember though that you can use hotkeys instead, especially **Alt+Tab** and the ProgMan hotkeys. I predict if you get into the habit of using them, you'll hardly ever use TaskMan to switch.

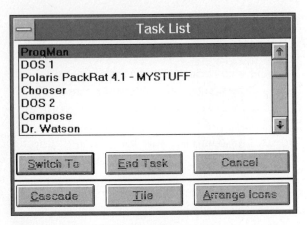

Figure 3-10: Task Manager

End Task will attempt to close the program in question. Very occasionally it will get you out of a problem where a program pops up a dialog that because of a bug won't close and which won't let you access the original program. **End Task** may get that program to end.

Arrange Icons arranges all iconized programs into a neat row at the bottom of the screen. Cascade and Tile work on the programs currently in normal state.

Mom's toolbox has a TaskMan replacement (*Metz Task Manager* discussed in Chapter 5) which does all that Windows TaskMan does and a whole lot more!

Taking Control

Windows installs a program called **control.exe** in your Windows directory and includes an icon to launch it in ProgMan's **Main** group. The name under the icon is **Control Panel**. Running this application does nothing more than open yet another window with icons inside. It looks like what you see in Figure 3-11, taken from Mao's machine. Yours will probably look very similar except that you may have a Network icon between Date/Time and MIDI Mapper, you probably don't have the ODBC icon and your mouse icon may look like a Dove Bar mouse rather than the new Microsoft Mouse 2. Also, since it is possible for third-party programs to add items to Control Panel, it is possible you have extra icons; in particular some screen drivers (notably the Orchid Fahrenheit) add an icon to Control Panel.

Beam Me Up, Scotty — Control Panel

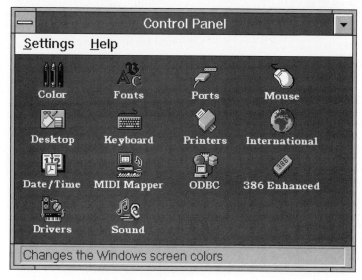

Figure 3-11: Control Panel

Double clicking on an icon in Control Panel will launch a small program called an **applet**. Normally it is a simple dialog that changes some settings in win.ini or system.ini. In case you are curious where the applets are located, the first eight (nine counting Network) are in a file called **main.cpl** which is located in the **System** subdirectory of Windows (somehow, the mouse 9.0 driver sneaks in and places its icon and applet in the mouse position. Use ProgMan to look at the icons in **main.cpl** and you'll see the Dove Bar mouse). After loading the applets in **main.cpl**, Control Panel apparently loads the applets that are contained in those drivers that Windows has previously loaded that have a built in function called CPLAPPLET. (I'd guess that Windows stores up what drivers have this property as it loads them). On most systems, there are no such drivers or just **midimap.drv** in the **System** directory. It then looks in **control.ini** for a section called **[MMCPL]** for keys other than NumApps, X, Y, W and H. For example, Mao's machine has

```
ODBC=C:\WINDOWS\SYSTEM\ODBCINST.DLL
```

to produce the **ODBC** applet placed there by Visual BASIC 3.0. Finally, Control Panel looks for files with the extension **cpl** in the **System** directory.

It says apparently about loading applets from drivers because while this clearly happens for midimap and some other drivers we know, it is not documented in the SDK which clearly states where applets are found without mentioning drivers. The SDK also says that `cpl` files are searched for in the directory where control.exe is found but that's not true. Move **snd.cpl** to the Windows directory and launch control from there and the sound applet won't appear! This is one of the few places where a search directory is hard wired in rather than following the standard search through the Windows directory, the System directory and then down your path.

 It's remarkable that the Windows Resource Kit describes the [MMCPL] section as "Specifies values related to the multimedia items in Control Panel". Sounds good, given the name, doesn't it? But, in fact, what is stored there are an entry called NumApps (that is usually the number of icons in Control Panel but it is ignored if it is wrong), the position and size of the Control Panel window and the names/locations of third party applets that may or may not have anything to do with multimedia. It's the care that the documentation writers give to this small stuff that gives me faith in how well Windows holds together. Sigh.

So third-party additions are either in **cpl** files in the **System** directory or in **dll**'s loaded because of a line in **control.ini**. If a third-party applet doesn't appear, take a look at **control.ini** and for **cpl** files — something may have gotten moved to the wrong directory.

Have you ever wished you could directly load a Control Panel applet from a ProgMan icon without having to click on an icon in Control Panel? You can! Suppose that you want to access the fonts applet directly. Here's how:

Make a New item called **Font Applet**. The command line should be

CONTROL.EXE fonts

as shown in Figure 3-12. While you are at it, pick **Change Icon** and then by typing the file name in or browsing, pick the filename **C:\windows\ system\main.cpl** for the icon file and choose the icon used for fonts. Save with a bunch of **OK**s. Clicking on this item will start Control Panel and launch the font applet. When you close the applet, Control Panel will also close (unless it was open at the point you clicked on the item). The point here is that putting down the caption of any applet after **control.exe** will launch that applet.

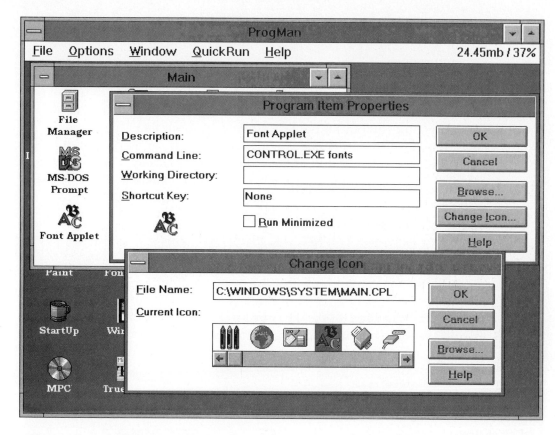

Figure 3-12: Adding a Font Applet Item

The Color applet is where you change the colors used for title bars and the like. The International applet is where you pick whether you prefer dates as 2/2/93 or 02/02/93 and the Date/Time applet lets you set the time. I'll discuss the Fonts, Printer, MidiMapper, Drivers, Sound and some parts of the 386 Enhanced applets later in this chapter. The rest of 386 Enhanced and the Mouse, Desktop, Keyboard, International, Date/Time and Printers applets will appear in Chapter 8. Yeah, Printers are so important, I'll talk about them twice.

All the Gnus That's Fit — Controlling Printing

Books are fatal: they are the curse of the human race. Nine-tenths of existing books are nonsense, and the clever books are the refutation of that nonsense. The greatest misfortune that ever befell man was the invention of printing.

— Benjamin Disraeli

Disraeli must have read a lot of Windows books.

You may attach an LCD panel to your PC or use slides for presentations and no doubt send stuff by modem, but I'll bet that most of your output comes from the printer so how Windows and printers get along has got to be an important part of your life with Windows. Much of the printer interaction, especially if things are working right will be in your application's **File/Print** command. Windows itself provides two components that deal with printing — a print spooler called Print Manager, aka PrintMan, and a **Printers Applet** in Control Panel.

PrintMan captures print output from your applications and saves it in a spool file on disk. Since sending to disk is a lot faster than sending to a printer, your application finishes a lot faster so you can go on with your business. PrintMan then sends stuff to the Printer in the background. You turn PrintMan on by checking the box labeled **Use Print Manager** in the **Printers Applet** of Control Panel (see Figure 3-13) and that's the only simple way to control this. Windows will do that by default so you only need to know about the check box if you want to turn PrintMan off.

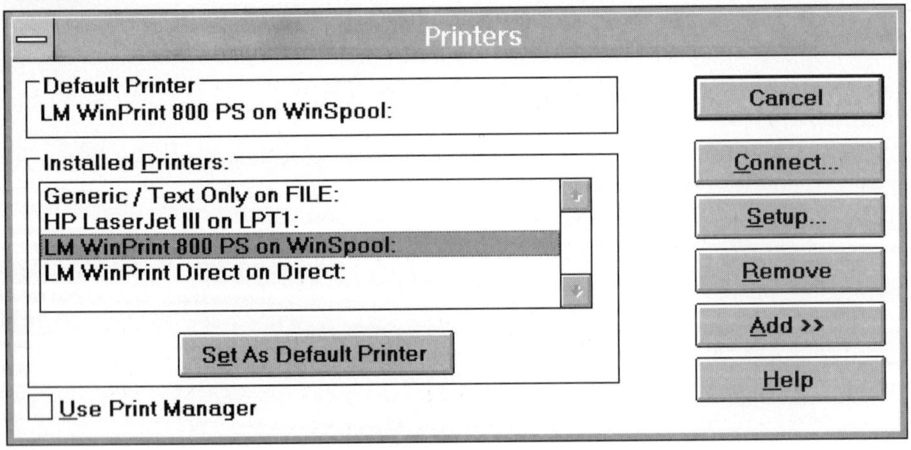

Printers	
Default Printer	Cancel
LM WinPrint 800 PS on WinSpool:	Connect...
Installed Printers:	Setup...
Generic / Text Only on FILE:	Remove
HP LaserJet III on LPT1:	Add >>
LM WinPrint 800 PS on WinSpool:	Help
LM WinPrint Direct on Direct:	
Set As Default Printer	
☐ Use Print Manager	

Figure 3-13: The Printers Applet

PrintMan places spool files in the temporary directory. By default Windows uses `C:\` for spool files but if you set a `temp` environmental variable (it may have been done for you by an installation program!), Windows will instead use the directory in that variable. I strongly advice you to make a `C:\temp` directory and add

```
set temp=C:\temp
```

to your `autoexec.bat` file. Please note that this directory is used by a lot of other programs besides PrintMan, so it is wise to set up such a temporary directory.

 The books all tell you to consider putting your `temp` directory on a RAM disk. Horse puckey, er, cockroach puckey. If your choice is a network drive or a RAM disk, then maybe its right but otherwise, cockroach puckey. I'll say more about this in Chapter 7.

 One warning and one piece of advice on the `temp` variable. The warning is that while programs cope with no `temp` variable (usually by using `C:\` as PrintMan does), most do not cope well with an invalid `temp` variable, that is one whose value is not a valid directory so exercise care. Secondly, while most programs do clean up their temp files, you'll find that some leave them in error or you have a crash or turn off your machine with some temp files active or. . . You should not delete files from the temp directory while in Windows. But since you should only have temporary files there, you can clean them out. I have a line that reads

```
echo Y | del C:\temp\*.*
```

in my `autoexec.bat`. The funny `echo Y` in front is to send a `Y` to the `Are you sure?` that gets asked.

Going back to Windows 2.x, PrintMan had a deserved reputation of being so bad you should probably turn it off. With Windows 3.1, it has gotten to the point where it is at least a positive influence on your system. Printing measured as the time it takes to get the output is slower but the time it takes for an application to get through with a print job is usually shorter.

When might you want to turn PrintMan off? If you have a huge print job, say printing the Great American Novel overnight or the Great American Short Story over lunch, where total time is more important than getting the machine back, by all means turn it off. Otherwise, unless you have an alternate spooler, be sure to leave it on.

Alternate spooler? Sure. The print enhancement hardware (Windows Printing System and WinJet) that we discuss in Chapter 7 comes with its own spooler (The WPS calls its replacement Print Manager but it is a much fancier beast than plain vanilla PrintMan.). And, there are third party spoolers that are better than what Windows offers. The best of these is Print Cache (Laser Tools, Voice 800-767-8004; 510-420-8777). Zenographics (Voice: 800-366-7494; 714-851-6352 FAX: 714-851-1314) has ZScript, an interesting PostScript print driver for non-PostScript printers that includes Super Queue, their enhanced spooler.

Driving Miss PrintMan is pretty straightforward, except for one gotcha. If your printing stops because of an error, for example, if you run out of paper, you have to explicitly restart the spooler after you correct the error. Click on the PrintMan icon and hit the Resume button.

There are two choices you need to make on PrintMan's **Option** menu. One is Priority which can be Low, Medium, or High. The lower the priority, the longer it takes to print but the less noticeable is the background printing. Medium priority is the default and will be fine for most machines. With a 486/66 screamer, you might try setting priority to high — if you don't notice any sluggishness while printing keep it that way. Contrariwise, if you have a 386/16 that seems to be molasses while you are printing, consider dropping priority to low.

The other option is what PrintMan should do if there is a Printer Error while printing and another application is active. You can set it to keep its mouth shut (**Ignore if Inactive**), discretely try to get your attention (**Flash if Inactive** which is the default) or pound you over the head (**Alert Always**). I run with **Alert Always**, figuring I want to know if the printer is out of paper.

PrintMan doesn't need to be loaded explicitly. It loads whenever you print and unloads afterwards if you never access it. If you do access it to check status or to restart it, it will not exit by itself and when printing is done, you'll want to unload it if memory is at all tight. There is one circumstance where you might want to keep it loaded, perhaps even load it in your startup group. If PrintMan is iconized and you drag a file from FileMan to PrintMan that file will print if it would have printed under FileMan's **File/Print** command, i.e. if the proper print command is registered in your OLE registration database. Since I can do this with **File/Print**, I don't bother to keep PrintMan loaded just to be able to drag and drop, but hey, if drag and drop is your thing, go ahead, make your day.

The **Printers Applet** is used to change printer drivers which you may need to do if you have a FAX driver or several printers or . . . You can also change via the **Print Setup...** command found in the **File** menu of many applications. PrintMan doesn't have a **File** Menu so its hidden **Print Setup...** in its **Options** menu. Go figure.

If you have to change printers a lot, take a look at the shareware Chooser (which you'll find on CD MOM). It installs as an icon (Figure 3-14) at the bottom of the screen and its caption shows the current printer and if the orientation is portrait or landscape — the **(P)** in the caption in Figure 3-14 shows that the orientation is Portrait. When in landscape the orientation of the big **A** coming out of the printer changes. Click on the icon and up pops a dialog that lets you change printer drivers, orientation and even call up the detailed options for the printer. Terribly handy utility. If you only need to change orientation a lot, look into Flipper, one of the Barry Press Utilities (also on CD MOM) — it installs as an icon only and clicking changes orientation.

**LM WinPrint
800 PS (P)**

Figure 3-14 : The Chooser Icon

When you get a new printer, you go to the **Printers Applet** to add its driver — the directions on screen are pretty clear. But one thing we should probably address here is using **Generic/Text on File**. The very first driver you'll see on the list of print drivers if you every choose to add a printer is called **Generic/Text Only**. Many books suggest that you install this printer and assign it to the port **File**. If a "printer" is on the port **File**, when you print to that printer a dialog will popup allowing you to specify which file to use.

The idea of Generic/Text on File is attractive — if you want to get the contents of a document in straight ASCII, just print it to that printer. I thought it sounded good when I read about it — in fact you'll see I still have that printer on my list (Figure 3-13). Alas, it doesn't work. If you don't believe me, try printing a Winword file to that printer. Weird formatting, huh? So don't try it unless you are really stuck. And you shouldn't ever be stuck. Wanna shift contents to ASCII? I'll bet your word processor has a Save As Text option and if not, try copying to the clipboard and pasting into Notepad.

Font S&M

> Print is the sharpest and the strongest weapon of our party.
>
> — Iosif Vissarionovich Dzhugashvili (aka Joseph Stalin)

Control Panel contains a handy **Font Applet**. Its primary purpose is to add or remove True Type, Screen, or Plotter fonts (I'll bet its mainly True Type fonts you need to add by hand!) I've already discussed adding fonts in Chapter 2 in the section *Not with My System Directory You Don't*. I'll note that when you remove fonts, be sure to use the feature of being able to select multiple fonts before clicking **Remove** and think hard before you check **Delete Font File from Disk**.

On the **Font Applet** dialog is a button that says **True Type...**. Clicking it sets up the two options shown in Figure. 3-15. You probably want to set them the way they are shown with TrueType fonts enabled (why not exploit one of Windows best features?). You probably don't want to **Show Only True Type Fonts in Applications**. Certainly you don't if you have ATM installed but why hamstring yourself in a communications program that may want to use a fixed pitch font and offer you the bitmapped fixed pitch fonts that ship with Windows?

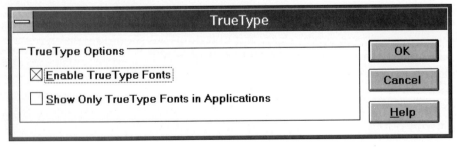

Figure 3-15: The True Type Options Dialog

The Engine Room

The Trumpets Shall Sound

> it is a tale
> Told by an idiot,
> full of sound and fury,
> Signifying nothing.

> — William Shakespeare, *Macbeth* , Act: V, Scene: v

The **Drivers Applet** of Control Panel is for installing and configuring system drivers which include sound and video drivers. At this point in time, installation of the various Video for Windows drivers is handled automatically. But there are often problems with sound drivers which I'll address with a series of tips:

- **Be sure to install the right driver.** This is not as trivial as it seems. Windows itself ships with a very limited set of sound drivers. Just because your board is Sound Blaster compatible, even if it is a Sound Blaster compatible card from Creative Labs, the makers of the original Sound Blaster, doesn't mean that the Sound Blaster driver is the right one for the card! It'll probably work but you could be forgoing the fancy features of your card. The Sound Blaster is a Basic MIDI device, not an Extended MIDI device so you could be limiting yourself unnecessarily when it comes to MIDI if you use the Sound Blaster driver. (Basic and Extended MIDI devices are described in Chapter 2 in the section *Wasn't General MIDI in the Battle of the Chorale C.*) It's analogous to using the standard VGA driver even though you purchased a Super VGA card. Look at the package the sound card came in — it almost surely has a diskette with drivers.

- **Consider updating your driver.** Most sound card manufacturers have their own BBS and often you can also get the drivers on Compuserve. In fact, before purchasing a sound card, it might be wise to check out the music related forums on Compuserve (Multimedia and MidiForum are especially recommended) for reactions to the driver situation for the card you are thinking of getting.

- **Have your hardware information handy**. Windows will ask for hardware settings: I/O port address, IRQ and perhaps DMA channel for your board. (I'll explain what IRQs are soon, but for now think of them as funny number you set with dip switches until you find a setting that works. Some installation programs will try to tell you where to set the dip switches but they won't always work. If you are lucky, the default dip switch settings work out of the box.) You should have set these when you installed the card by flipping dip switches. The default values should be listed in the manual and are no doubt what you'll try first. If you have the right driver and find **wav** files don't play at all, the most likely culprit is an incorrect hardware setting.

- **Get rid of old drivers.** If you are installing a sound driver for the first time, you can ignore this one. If you are upgrading your drivers the installation software will handle this. If you are changing sound cards or using a sound card for the first time, but had the speaker driver installed, be sure to delete the old drivers. You do this in the **Drivers Applet** by highlighting the driver and hitting Remove. Most likely the sound installation software also installed a VxD into the **[386Enh]** section of **system.ini**. Try to figure out which **device=** lines they are (they are *not* lines where the driver name starts with a *) and comment them out. For example, the Sound Blaster Pro installs:

      device=vsbpd.386

      device=vadlibd.386

- **Test out wav and midi as soon as possible after installing the driver and rebooting your system.** Call up the **Sound Applet** in Control Panel and test a sound assigned to a **wav** file. If that doesn't work, check out the IRQ and I/O port. If it does work, check MIDI next by loading the Media Player applet (installed into the **Accessories** group of ProgMan) and choosing **File/Open** and loading **canyon.mid** which should be in your Windows directory.

- Even if **canyon.mid** plays, consider reading up in the section *Wasn't General MIDI in the Battle of the Choral C* in the last chapter and making sure that the setup you pick in the **Media Mapper Applet** is the optimal one for your system and the MIDI files that you are likely to play.

- If you own a DOS program that is supposed to work on your sound card (probably a game!), first check that it works outside of Windows. Then check it in a DOS session over Windows to see if the virtual 386 mode drivers are working properly. If it doesn't check out possible work arounds with the card maker's tech support and/or ask on Compuserve.

The Sounds Shall Trumpet

> With the sense of sight, the idea communicates the emotion, whereas,
> with sound, the emotion communicates the idea,
> which is more direct and therefore more powerful.
>
> — Alfred North Whitehead, *Dialogues of Alfred North Whitehead*

Once you've installed your sound driver (including the Speaker Driver that I'll discuss in the section of Chapter 4 entitled *The Sound Driver Microsoft Left Out on Purpose*), one of the first things that you'll want to do is call up the **Sound Applet** in Control Panel, and **Enable System Sounds**. With the default you can enable the seven shown in Figure 3-16. Windows Start and Windows Exit are obvious and the default beep is exactly what it says — it sure is a pleasant replacement for the speaker beep if you have a sound card. The **Enable System Sounds** checkbox only effects the first five sounds; Exit and Start are always enabled unless you assign **<none>** to them.

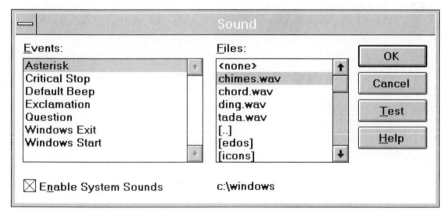

Figure 3-16: The Sound Applet

Sounds are popular with kids. My nephew's machine has Dorothy saying "We're not in Kansas anymore, Toto" at startup and Scotty saying "We're losing power on the warp engines, sir" when Windows exits. At one point his exit sound was a toilet flushing but his mother put a stop to that. Mothers know best.

Ideally, the other four sounds should be associated with the four icons one can have in message boxes:

Critical Stop

Exclamation

Question

Information

But somebody at Microsoft, when setting up standard sounds, decided to drop **Information** and add an **Asterisk** although the difference between **Asterisk** and **Exclamation** escapes me. Oh, well, three out a four ain't bad.

Alas, programmers have to take special action (note to Programmers: use the **sndPlaySound** API call which can take a **win.ini [sounds]** entry as a parameter) to support such sounds and you'll find that not many programs do (for example, FileMan does not support sounds in its message boxes) and that those that do often don't use the sound you expect.

What if your appetite is whetted and you want more sounds? There are programs that will let your windows whoosh when you minimize them, creak when you stretch a window and sound a Big Ben clock on the hour. Microsoft sells three collections of Sound Bits and each comes with a replacement sound applet allowing you to set sounds for 34 events involving opening, closing and minimizing different applications (the collections differ in the sounds offered: Classic Hollywood Movies, Cartoon Classics or Musical Instruments). The sounds in these packages are first class. But the replacement sound applet is pretty poor in comparison with other sound event handlers which have clocks and window stretches. Take a look at, er, take a hear at, EZSound FX, (Future Trends Software, Voice: (214)224-3288; FAX (214)224-3328), Wired for Sound (Aristosoft, Voice: (800) 426-8288) and Icon Hear It (Moon Valley Software, Voice: (800) 473-5509).

It is kinda neat to have a window go thunk when you close it — the first time or two — but it gets old very fast. And if it doesn't get old for you, it is likely to annoy your significant other (if on a home machine) or your co-workers (if on an office machine), so my advice is to pass on this one.

But, hey, the P in PC stands for personal. So, go ahead and get one of those packages if you want. See if I care. But, sonny, if you waste your money on that, don't try coming around and crying to me when you tire of it.

You guys are spoil sports. I like 'em and so do lots of other users. In the same *fun stuff that tires for many but others love* category are the animated icons in Moon Valley's Icon Do-It and Delta Point's Animated Desktop (voice: 408-648-4000)

Where can you get more **wav** file then the 4 that ship with Windows? All the packages mentioned above have **wav**s. Sound Source (voice:805-494-9996) sells collections of sounds from Star Trek and Star Wars in **wav** format. You'll find some free **wav** files on CD MOM. If you are really a sound freak, New Eden (Voice: 612-561-2557) sells a collection of 10 MB of **wav** files.

Port-Annoy's Complaint

> Still bent to make some port he knows not where,
> Still standing for some false impossible shore

— Mathew Arnold

We are the prisoners of our past and of our diversity. Nope, this is not the beginning of a philosophical discourse on the differences between the United States and Switzerland but of the Windows universe vs. the Mac. The Mac had it easy. Apple's attitude was that if you had an Apple II, well it would make a good door stop or charitable deduction, but it wasn't going to be Mac compatible. Clean break; the heck with the past and the heck with customers already committed to your company.

IBM, for all its faults, has been committed to protecting its customers' investments in the past (all the more to sell them more in the future). Throughout the history of the PC, there has been an often too slavish respect for the past. That is often useful, but we pay for it.

How many different video cards, scanner, printers, CD ROMs, sound cards, network cards, slide readers, slide makers, cameras, hard disks, floptical disks, magneto-optical disks, worm drives, QIC tape backup and DAT tape backups can you buy? Lost count, eh? Me too. It's nice to have the sometimes bewildering array of choices we have in the PC world but we pay for that too!

How do we pay? Listen to the Apple ads reading from Windows manual about IRQs, ports, and conflicts. Did you wryly shake your head because it sounded familiar? Do you think it is because the Mac is competent and Microsoft incompetent? You may, but that isn't the cause. Part of the IRQ/port conflict has to do with the limitations on the kind of hardware available to IBM in 1981 in its quest to put together a machine under $5000 in price. Those limitations could easily be avoided today if one were building a machine from scratch but one isn't. IBM-compatible personal computers are built so they can run DOS 2 and DOS 6 is built so it can run on an XT.

 Listen up sonny. Bottom line on the port stuff is that its complicated and will likely involve flipping dip switches on lots of boards, pulling them in and out and even risking shorting out your motherboard. Not something for a civilian. If you have a problem that sounds like a port conflict, better get some guru help. Time to make that local PC emporium that sold you the new board that doesn't work put some service behind its promises or to convince the mail order firm that the problem with your new card is due to their machine still under warranty. Or convince your teen aged child to date a young hardware hotshot. But, kids, don't do this at home. Unless, of course, you are a hardware guru yourself.

I'm gonna tell you some stories and facts about IRQs; more to satisfy your morbid curiosity and give you some real ammo in your cocktail conversations then because I expect you to actually fix this sort of thing yourself! If you are tempted to skip, at least read the end on TurboComm and KingComm.

There are ini file settings connected with comm ports and dialogs in the **386 Enhanced Applet** of Control Panel. I'll discuss them in Chapter 9.

 Mom sent me out on a house call to help out her cousin who had upgraded to a 486 from an AT, gotten Windows, installed it and found that the mouse didn't work. First thing that I did was run SetUp to confirm that there was a mouse driver installed. There was — "Microsoft or IBM PS/2". It occurred to me the driver could be wrong one for coz' mouse, but that seemed the least likely scenario so I tried something else first.

I exited Windows and typed `win /s` at the DOS prompt. "Ah, so", I thought, "the mouse runs in standard mode but not in enhanced mode. Must have something to do with the fact that comm ports are virtualized in enhanced mode. Ah, so, it could be an IRQ conflict."

So I asked coz about modems. "Oh, yeah, I moved the internal modem on my old machine to the new one." I fired up Windows Terminal while still in standard mode and by trying the possibilities, I ascertained that the internal modem was on COM3. The mouse was on COM1. Bingo — IRQ conflict. We searched and luckily found the docs for the internal modem and figured out how to set it to COM2. Now the mouse worked. End of story. Mom gave me a lollipop.

✂ ✂ ✂ ✂ ✂

"What the heck is an IRQ?" you ask. Consider a secretary, the kingpin of an office. Sits there typing away with sheets to type which rest on one of those tablets with a marker to show the place. But the office manager has something urgent to do so she goes and taps her secretary on the shoulder. He stops what he's doing, uses a paper clip to mark his place and does the special job that his boss just gave him. Then he goes back to where he'd marked with the clip and continues with his typing.

Sometimes as the officer manager is about to tap the secretary on the shoulder, he turns to the manager and says, "I'm in the middle of something very important, don't interrupt me for a moment" so the office manager waits and gives the urgent task to her secretary when he says, "OK, you can interrupt me now." This office manager is a firm believer in lines of command. The only way anyone can get to the secretary to get some work squeezed in ahead of his list is by calling the office manager and putting the request through her. She has a phone on her desk with 8 incoming lines, each one hard wired to a different employee that might need to get some work squeezed in to the secretary's schedule.

The secretary is your computer's CPU — the **central processing unit** that is more than likely made by Intel and has a number 80286, 80386 or i486. It has a set of instructions that it processes sequentially. The office manager is a chip called a PIC, short for Programmable Interrupt Controller. When something external to the CPU happens, say you hit a key, the PIC taps the CPU on the shoulder, the CPU notes where he was and processes the external event, called an **Interrupt**.

The PIC has to be there to store up interrupts in case the CPU has sent out a message that he can't be interrupted for a while. Mind you, the CPU isn't smart enough to figure out what is important and what isn't — rather the instruction to turn off interrupts is one that can be on the list of instructions the CPU processes because the author of the program being processed felt that the next set of instructions shouldn't be interrupted. Because the PIC and/or peripheral hardware that stores up the information that needs to go to the CPU (like the chip inside your keyboard that stores up exactly what key you hit) has a finite capacity to store up multiple events, the CPU can't wait too long with interrupts turned off and good programming practice turns interrupts back on as soon as possible.

Like the office run by that manager, all interrupts have to get routed through the PIC. The incoming lines are called **IRQ**'s, short for **Interrupt ReQuests**. The original PC had one PIC and 8 IRQs. The AT added a second PIC for 16 IRQs — well, not quite, the second PIC acted as a kind of deputy office manager which didn't talk directly to the CPU so it needed a phone line to contact the first PIC which then only had 7 lines for others. So modern machines have 15 IRQs available.

Fifteen sounds like a lot but it isn't for several reasons. First, quite a few are taken by the computer internals itself. The computer keeps time by using a clock chip which needs its own IRQ and the numeric coprocessor uses an IRQ. Second, some boards only support the IRQs associated to the original PIC so ther same board can be used in an 8-bit slot. So, installing boards can be a real headache trying to find an available IRQ.

 While fidelity to the past is great, there is no decent reason why hardware and software companies couldn't get together and promulgate a spec that would take the hassles out of installing boards. Have each board report to a central program what IRQs, I/O ports and DMA channels it is using and allow that program to change them to avoid conflicts. Shoulda been done in 1985 but it wasn't. Finally, in 1993, Intel and Microsoft introduced a `Plug 'n Play` spec that is supposed to do all that. It remains to be seen if the spec is successful but the signs are promising. I sure hope it succeeds.

In the original PC where each serial port required a hundred buck add in card and there weren't many serial devices, the two serial ports and IRQs assigned to them seemed like a lot. (In the current market, the wholesale price on an add-in card with two serial ports, parallel port, floppy and IDE controllers and a game port is under $20; things sure do change.) Support was added to DOS to handle COM3 and COM4 but still with only 2 IRQs. COM1 and COM3 share one as do COM2 and COM4. Sometimes, devices can manage to share an IRQ because of how drivers get loaded and unloaded, but Windows adds a new level of complexity.

Back to the secretary who is so busy that he has several desks. He does some work at one desk, then on cue, saves his place with that trusty paper clip, wheels his chair around and starts at the next desk. When the office manager comes in with a job, that job has to be placed on the appropriate desk which may not be the one that the secretary is currently sitting at. So someone might be hired to keep track of which requests go to which desk and take the requests and make sure they get put on the right desk. The office manager no longer talks directly to the secretary but only through the new hire.

Windows is the same way. Several applications are multitasking which really means that the CPU is time slicing, doing one job for a fraction of a second, then switching to the next, round and round he goes. To be sure that IRQs are properly serviced, placed on the right desk as it were, Windows does something called **virtualizing the IRQs**. Basically, it sets up a virtual IRQ processing center for each desk and it, Windows tracks which IRQ should get handled where.

 It's not the greatest of analogies because the CPU is involved at every stage. The PIC knows from nothing about Windows and only talks to the CPU. Its as if the office manager still gave stuff to the secretary who instead of putting it on his desk immediately passed it off to the desk monitor who put it on the right desk. And even that is stretching the analogy.

Windows virtualized IRQs just aren't made to share a single IRQ between the mouse and a modem so you can't, at least on most machines.

✄   ✄   ✄   ✄   ✄

In the single tasking DOS world, an external hardware interrupt could come in and get delayed because interrupts had been turned off but unless there was bad programming, that didn't happen for long, at most a few hundred CPU cycles (the ones that are measure in chip speed so a 66 MHz chip has 66 million clock cycles per second). But, with multitasking it can take a long time before the CPU actually gets around to finding out exactly which key got struck or what character has come in through the serial port. A long time means as much as a tenth of a second–peanuts for you and me but an eternity for a CPU doing which measures out its life in 66 million coffee spoons per second.

So it is important to have a serial port capable of storing up more than one incoming character while waiting its turn for the CPU's affections. Serial ports are driven by a chip called a UART — short for Universal Asynchronous

Receiver/Transmitter. The original serial ports used a chip called the 8250 UART (the AT used a UART called 16450 but since it doesn't do much more than the 8250, I'll talk about the 8250 when I really mean "8250 or 16450". Any machine you purchase these days will have either the advanced 16550 I'm about to discuss or a 16450.). Some more recent machines have a more sophisticated 16550 UART which includes a 16-byte buffer which can store up incoming characters waiting for the CPU to get around to asking for them. That 16 bytes is almost always enough at any port speed you are likely to use but with an 8250, you are likely to have problems even with 9600 baud and certainly with 19200 or more.

The 16550 isn't a really expensive part; wholesale under $10. But given that the public doesn't know to ask for them, and that there are usually two serial ports, it is tempting when putting together a computer to skimp and save those few bucks. Savvy users know enough to *always* ask if their new machine's serial ports have them and to look elsewhere if the answer is no.

But how can you tell if the machine you have has 16550 or 8250 UARTs? Exit Windows and type in `MSD` at the DOS prompt. Microsoft includes a diagnostics program (the `D` in `MSD`!) with Windows and recent versions of DOS. It is intended for their tech support but you can use it. It's no CheckIt Pro (TouchStone Software, Voice: 714- 969-7746; FAX: 714-960-1886), Winsleuth or Skylight (see Chapter 5) but it's not half bad and it will tell you about what kind of UARTs you have if you click on `COM Ports...` and look at the last line.

✳   ✳   ✳   ✳   ✳

It's time for the bad news! Windows doesn't fully support the 16550 UART!! Because of the virtualization of ports and IRQs that Windows does, explicit support for the 16550 is needed or else it will act as an 8250 (which it does very well but without exploiting the advantages it has). The Windows 3.0 comm port driver had no support for the 16550. The 3.1 driver does but only for Windows communication programs. DOS programs need not apply — I mean, DOS communications programs running under DOS sessions in Windows will not use the features of the 16550. Sigh!

What to do? Why pull out your wallet and let it bleed a little–not that much but probably close to what you paid for Windows itself. TurboComm (Bio-Engineering Research Laboratories, Voice: 503-482-2744) and KingCom (OTC Corp, Voice: 714-

832-4833, FAX: 714-832-4563) are replacement comm drivers for Windows that do support the 16550 in DOS programs and are better in many, many other respects.

 Even if you don't have a 16550, you should consider getting TurboComm or KingCom, especially if you use DOS comm programs at 9600 baud or above. Before I upgraded my system, it had an 8250 (well actually a 16450). I often ran a Compuserve access program in DOS at 9600 baud. More often than not, if I shifted the session to the background, or even hit **Alt-Enter** to change to a windowed DOS session, I'd get disconnected from CompuServe. Then I switched to TurboComm and the DOS/Compuserve session ran in the background like a champ.

There's another problem with Windows and comm ports, or more specifically with too many Windows programs that use comm ports. Windows has a built-in mechanism to handle comm port conflicts among DOS programs. Shown in Figure 3-17 is part of the **386 Enhanced applet** in Control Panel. It controls how Windows reacts if programs in more than one DOS session try to access the comm port. For example, you might have TAPCIS loaded in one session and a FAX TSR in another. **Always Warn** means that if one program tries to access the comm port while another has it in use, you are switched to Windows and given the option of terminating the first to allow access to the second. **Never Warn** means the second is told that the attempt to access the comm port failed. **Idle**, which I normally recommend, lets the second program access the comm port even if Windows thinks the first has it reserved so long as there hasn't been a recent direct access.

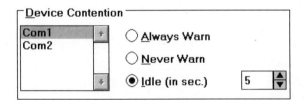

Figure 3-17: Windows DOS port contention control

Windows can provide this service for DOS apps because it virtualizes the ports and sits between the programs and the actual hardware. However, it does not virtualize the ports so far as Windows programs are concerned. It is assumed that Winapps, which, after all know they are running in a multitasking environment, can fend for themselves without getting in your way.

In my opinion, a well-behaved Windows comm program would only attempt to access the comm port at the time you asked to dial and it would give up the port when you disconnected. At a minimum, this should be an option. Instead, some comm programs insist on grabbing the port when you load them. For example, load ProComm for Windows and do nothing but minimize it, and then load WinCIM and try to run it and it will complain it can't get the comm port. That's because ProComm grabs it when it starts up.

FAX programs are notorious for grabbing the comm port. If they are in receive mode, they have no choice but to do that. But if you only want to send FAXes, it makes no sense for your comm port to be taken out of circulation.

So what's the solution if you find your Windows programs are in conflict. One is to complain to the program makers for not dealing with this problem for you. There is really no excuse for their not. But that doesn't solve the problem, does it? For many the solution was a lot of juggling, loading and unloading programs to avoid the conflicts. The most elegant solution is KingCom (see Figure 3-18). It provides virtual ports and allows you to assign any port from 1 to 9 to an actual hardware port. You can assign multiple numbers to the same physical port. By assigning comm programs/FAX drivers to distinct virtual ports, they are happy as clams and the comm driver handles conflicts.

You can configure the ports to determine which one "gets" auto answer modem calls and to indicate how you want device contention handled.

In the late beta of KingCom 2.0 Mao looked at, there were a few minor glitches that he expects will get fixed: he got no contention warning on his system when programs tried to access distinct virtual ports that mapped to the same physical port and hitting **Alt+Enter** in a full screen DOS session running a DOS program which was online but not set to have Background on caused a crash. But that's what beta tests are for.

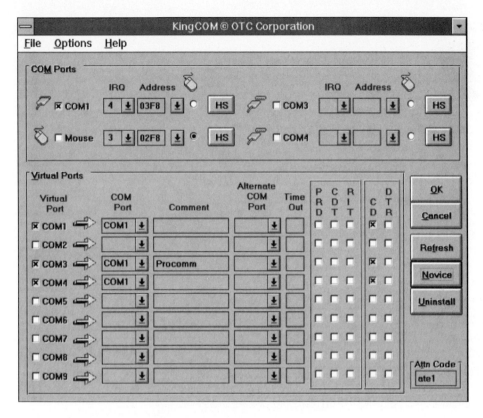

Figure 3-18: King Com's configuration dialog

Good Help Is Hard to Find

> Who ran to help me when I fell,
> And would some pretty story tell,
> Or kiss the place to make it well?
> My mother.

> — Ann Taylor, *Original Poems for Infant Minds*

Some of Windows components aren't just good, they are superb. The Windows Help engine is at the top of my list. Hard as it is to understand, there are a few programs out there that use proprietary help engines (often these are from companies that want to use the same help file on the Mac or in a DOS version of their product). But the overwhelming bulk of third-party Windows software ships with Windows help files and you have a common interface to help. And **winhelp.exe** is a wondrous hypertext engine.

You've probably already learned the basics but it's remarkable how many folks have never caught on to some of the more advanced features, so I'll give you a bunch of quick tips. You probably aren't used to thinking of help as a real application but it is, so do what you should do with any application you use a lot; explore its menus and buttons!

- Help files have the extension **hlp**. Windows installation should have added the line

  ```
  hlp=winhelp.exe ^.hlp
  ```

  to the **[extensions]** section of your **win.ini**. If it didn't, add it yourself using FileMan's **File/Associate**. You can double click on a help file and have **winhelp** loaded with it open. Any time you want to change help files, just use **File/Open** in the menus for help.

- I'm sure you know that **F1** brings up help in most applications, often context sensitive to the dialog that is currently up but did you know about **Shift+F1**? In many, but not all, applications it adds a question mark to the mouse pointer. Click on something and you get help on it. **Esc** gets you out if you hit **Shift+F1** in error.

- In help, the mouse pointer changes to a hand when it is over a hot spot, a point where clicking will do something. Usually, the hot spots are underlined words, with either dotted or solid underlines. The dotted underlines are called **glossary** items. Click on one and a brief explanation pops up. In some applications, there is a **Glossary** button on the help button bar which will call up a window of all the glossary terms.

- The solid underlines are called **jumpwords** or **hyperlinks**. They jump to a new help topic. You've probably learned to use the **Back** button to return to the last help screen. But don't forget about the **History** button. It will call up a list of all screens you've been to, even if opened several different **hlp** files. **History** is so useful that it is a good idea to get into the habit of hitting the minimize button after consulting Help rather than closing Help by **Double Clicking** on system menu. If you close Help, it forgets the history but if you minimize and later you invoke Help, you'll have access to the history list.

- I suspect that you use **Search** all the time because it has a button, but I bet you hardly use **Bookmarks** and **Annotations** and may not even know they are there because they are on the menus. The **Bookmark** menu lets you assign bookmark names to any screen you want with the bookmarks remembered from one session to the next. The bookmark information is stored in a common file called **winhelp.bmk** stored in your Windows directory. Despite the common bookmark file, only the bookmarks you made in the current file will appear on the **Bookmark** menu. If there are nine or fewer bookmarks for the current file, they all appear on the **Bookmark** menu. If there are ten or more, a **More..** entry appears.

- You can make text annotations to any item in any help file using the **Edit/Annotate** menu choice. It pops up a box to make notes in. Forever after, the topic header where you made that annotation will have a little paper clip icon next to it. **Click** on it and you get the annotation. Annotations for the file **foo.hlp** are stored in a file called **foo.ann** in your Windows directory. Once the file is made, it will not be deleted by winhelp even if you delete all annotations.

✄   ✄   ✄   ✄   ✄

Would you like to make your own help files, maybe to distribute company wide with a procedures handbook? To do so, you must make up a file in **RTF** format (something *Winword* can do) with all sorts of bizarre footnotes indicating jumpwords, glossaries and the like. Then you need to make a help project file and run it through the help compiler (a DOS program for gosh sakes!). This program, **hc.exe**, is distributed with the **SDK** and most languages that will compile Windows applications. If this sounds like the pits, that's because it is. But there is hope or rather, help. There are several tools to automate the production of help files. My favorite by far is Doc2Help (WexTech Systems, Voice: (212)949-4007, FAX: (212)949-9595). It even comes with the help compiler so you are ready to roll so long as you have Winword. Doc2Help provides families of Winword macros and lets you assign jumpwords, search items, etc to the logical objects — for example, jumpwords are Winword bookmarks and search items are index entries. Then you run a macro which does all the RTF conversions, makes the project file, and launches the help compiler. Watching this sucker run is almost as much fun as a video game.

No DOS Like an Ol' DOS

You Mean This Thing Runs on 88 Octane DOS?

This is not *the Mother of all DOS books* but there is no avoiding the fact that
Windows is running over DOS . Moreover, you likely still have one or more DOS
programs that you want to run so tricks to run them more smoothly and with as
much available DOS memory as possible become important. Settings in
`config.sys` and `autoexec.bat` become important. We begin with Mao's tips
for setting up DOS.

Be sure to include the line

`DOS=high`

or else

`DOS=high,UMB`

in your `config.sys` (requires DOS 5.0 or later). This command requires that you have
himem or another XMS manager loaded but you need that just to run Windows. This
command tells DOS to load a part of itself into the 64K of memory immediately above the 1
Meg boundary that DOS is normally restricted to. It frees up memory below the 640K line
giving you larger DOS sessions under Windows. If you are using a third-party memory
manager, use the version without the UMB since those are handled by the third-party
manager.

If you are using QEMM and need to set Last Drive (as you would with a network or
a CD or . . .), be sure to use QEMM's command to set the extra drives in UMB
space rather than below the 640K mark.

Similarly, use your memory manager's ability to load **Files=** tables high if it has
one. You should set **Files=30** or more. If you have a problem with insufficient
file handles in a DOS session, you'll need to look into the **PerVMFiles** variable in
`system.ini` (see Chapter 9 for discussion of this parameter).

Microsoft was an early proponent of CD-ROMs so it is surprising that the
DOS support for such drives has been so tepid. For DOS to access CDs,
you need a special driver in `config.sys` and you must load the MS CD
Extensions, called `MSCDEX.EXE`, in `autoexec.bat`. Until DOS 6,

MSCDEX required an awkward dance. The official line was that you had to get MSCDEX from your CDROM vendor which might not have been too unreasonable for an initial purchase but was crazy every time you upgraded DOS. And like other DOS components, MSCDEX checked version numbers so you really did need a new version.

Finally, in DOS 6.0, MSCDEX shipped on the DOS disks. Hooray, but . . . Smartdrv still ignores CD's (although there are rumors at the time of writing that this will change in DOS 6.2). And why should there be extensions. It's like having hard disk extensions. CDs are so important, they should link into the kernel. Oh, well, they'll get it right some time.

 It really burns me up that there are still programs that tell you to put them in your path as if you are only running one program. Every program can find out the directory that its executable is in so there is no excuse for it to need the path to locate extra libraries and other support files. Moreover winapps can set up an `ini` file in the Windows directory and store information on where their files are. Still a surprising number of programs want themselves put in your path. Particularly unforgivable are CD ROMs that put some files on your hard disk and want that directory placed in the path as if you ran that particular CD all the time.

The first defense against programs that insist being put on the path is to ignore them. Try removing them from the path and see if there is a problem. Often there won't be; the program is placing itself in your path due to force of habit on the part of the developers! But some really do require that they be put on the path. Your path starts growing long and you bump against the fact that DOS supports paths only up to 122 characters.

There are a few simple tricks to deal with a lengthy path:

- You can place the rude programs that really do need to be in the path in a subdirectory of the root to keep their total directory length as short as possible. You can even call their directory by a single letter name. Its crazy for the quirks of programs to force you to use directory names other than what you easily remember.

- If the rude program is a DOS program, do not place it in the global path, that is the path that you load before Windows. Rather start the program from a batch file that you start from Windows and increase the path only in that batch file.

- Use **subst**. This allows you to assign a single letter to any directory. So you could try

  `subst J: C:\rudeprogs\thisrude`

  and then add J:\ to your path. This one is controversial. The Windows documentation explicitly says not to use **subst**, **join**, **append** or **assign**. **Join**, **append** and **assign** are potentially dangerous but Mao runs **subst** all the time (both before and within Windows) and has never had any problem.

- Use the shareware program Batutil (Voice: 800-788-0787; the shareware version is on CD MOM). It allows paths up to 250 characters in length. Full disclosure: Barry is a coauthor of Batutil.

PIF, the Magic Drag On

Windows serves as a ring master, dispensing your systems resources to programs as needed. It has a good relationship with Winapps which know how to have frank discussions with Windows when resources are needed. But DOS apps are a different story. DOS applications were raised to think the computer is their oyster, that they literally controlled the machine and could do what they wanted with it. And they needn't ask — they could just take. Indeed, there are DOS programs that load and grab all available extended and EMS memory just in case they might be needed.

Early on, Windows architects realized that they needed a place to store the information that DOS programs didn't provide. So was born the **Program Information File** or **PIF** for short. Bear in mind that **PIF**s are *only* used for DOS programs and sessions and there is no point in setting one up for a Winapp; nice as it might be to setup hotkeys outside of ProgMan or to change the windows caption.

In the days of Windows 2.x, even in the early days of Windows 3.0, writing a mean **PIF** was a key part of being a Windows guru. But those days are past. Most DOS programs ship with **PIF**s that set most of the parameters for you so that adjusting **PIF**s is now most often for the users who like to spend so much time fooling around that what they really need is a *Personal* Information File that sets a maximum amount of resources they can commit to fooling around! Still `PIF`s can be useful to set simple program parameters and it can sometimes help to know some of the arcane parameters. But this section and the one called *Piffle Ball* are probably the least important of this chapter. If you get or have a DOS program without a PIF, Windows may have one ready made for you; I'll tell you more about that in *Do's for DOS* later in this chapter.

Whenever Windows starts a DOS program be it from ProgMan, FileMan, or a third-party shell, it looks for a `PIF` for that application. If the application is `george.exe`, Windows will look for `george.pif`. The sole exception is if you directly launch a `PIF` file; then Windows uses that `PIF` rather than one with the requisite name. For example, if `martha.pif` has an associated program name of `george.exe` and you double click on `martha.pif` in FileMan, `george.pif` isn't even looked for.

When looking for a `PIF` file, Windows looks at directories in the following order:

- the directory containing the application

- the current working directory (as you might set in a ProgMan item)

- the Windows directory

- the System directory of the Windows directory

- the directories on your path in the order they appear

- if all else fails it looks for **_default.pif** in the same order and uses it instead

I advise you to keep your `PIF`s in your Windows directory, much as I hate overloading that directory with too many files. I wish that Windows had a `pifdir=` line in `win.ini` but it doesn't and there are many advantages to having all your `PIF`s in one place. You could also place them in a directory in your path but you then risk confusion if somebody installs a PIF in your Windows directory. But be mindful of the above order if you make changes in a `PIF` in the windows directory and they don't seem to take. Most likely, the `PIF` being used is not the one you have changed but one in the application directory.

The *Windows User's Guide* and those books that copy, er, use it for inspiration, will lead you to believe that there is a second special PIF besides _default.pif, namely dosprmpt.pif and that this second PIF is used whenever you launch a DOS prompt rather than an application. Don't you believe it!

When Windows is installed, it sets up a group called **Main** which includes an item called **MS DOS Prompt** with the sexy DOS icon from **Progman.exe** rather than the ugly default DOS icon. If you look at the properties of this icon, you'll see that it runs the **PIF** file **dosprmpt.pif**. Windows itself gives no special status to this **PIF** file but if you launch it explicitly from a ProgMan item, by typing its name in **File/Run** or clicking on it in FileMan, it is used, of course. But if you set up a DOS prompt by running **command.com** directly in an item or by typing **command** in **File/Run**, then Windows will use **_default.pif** unless you set up a **command.pif**.

Because of the way that setup.inf is configured, if you tell *Windows Setup* to install command.com, it will also use dosprmpt.pif.

I'll talk about editing PIFs in *Piffle Ball* later but first a few detours on how DOS sessions work so the parameters in PIFs will be clearer.

Sometimes DOS is Full of It and Sometimes Not

Every time you run a DOS program or click the MS-DOS prompt icon in the Main group of ProgMan (which runs the DOS program command.com), you start a separate DOS session. Each such session can run full screen where it takes over the entire screen and looks as if Windows isn't there (although it is doing all sorts of stuff in the background). Or you can run it in a window. These are called Full Screen DOS sessions and Windowed DOS sessions respectively (not surprised, eh?).

A full screen session starts out in text mode (the screen mode that is typical for DOS without Windows) although a program can switch to a graphics mode as it is starting up or in the middle — for example, if you might ask Word Perfect for DOS to display a print preview. Even if the program thinks it is in text mode, when windowed it runs in graphics mode because that is the only way to show the rest of the Windows screen! Windows can run DOS programs that think they are in text mode in a window and also programs that run in the graphics modes used by the original CGA. But it can only run DOS programs that use the EGA or VGA graphics modes (and that is most of those DOS programs that use graphics) full screen. If you have a DOS program in text mode running windowed and it tries to switch to an EGA/VGA graphics mode, Windows will pop up an error message and suspend the session until you switch the session to full screen.

Which of full screen/windowed a DOS session starts in is determined by the `PIF` for that session (I'll describe editing `PIF`s in the section *Piffle Ball* later). Once started, you can toggle between modes by hitting the `Alt+Enter` hotkey while the session is active. In particular, if a windowed DOS session is suspended by Windows because it has gone into EGA/VGA graphics mode, you just hit `Alt+Ente`r to get it started again.

Should you run DOS sessions full screen or windowed? That's really a matter of taste. Even though graphics mode is usually slower than text, especially at scrolling, Windows has some tricks that speed up scrolling and display in windowed sessions so that the overhead of using graphics is not large, especially if you have an accelerated video driver. So it comes down if you like having windows to click on and quicker access to cut and paste or instead, you like the larger type size that you get with a full screen session.

The Amazing Time-o-matic — It Slices, Dices, Purees. . .

> No matter how thin you slice it, it's still baloney.
>
> — Alfred E. Smith, *Campaign speeches* [1936]

Windows is a multitasking environment. That means it gives the appearance of running several programs at once. It is only the appearance though since the CPU in your machine runs instructions sequentially. What Windows does is slice time into small chunks, called time slices, and run one program for a time slice, then switch to another for its time slice. If the slices are short enough, there will be the appearance that the programs are running at the same time.

The time slices are typically 20 milliseconds, a 1/50 of a second — short enough for you to have the impression of simultaneity but not a short time to your CPU. It's enough time for a 50 MHz 486 to run about a million instructions!

Windows is actually running two schedulers to control time slicing. The top level allocates time to different "virtual machines" (called VM for short) where Windows and all its Winapps are considered one virtual machine and each DOS session is considered a separate virtual machine. You can adjust how much time different virtual machines get as I'll explain.

In addition, there is a scheduler for the Winapps. When the Windows VM gets its time slices from the top level scheduler, it allocates time among the running Winapps. You have no control over this process. The theory is that DOS programs don't know they are being multitasked and can't help Windows out so you need the power to. But Winapps can and you shouldn't mess there.

Every DOS session has five special settings connected to time slices. There are three Yes/No settings — I'll postpone discussion of one of them and focus on two called **Exclusive** and **Background**. Their initial values are determined by the **PIF** for that session but you can change them by pulling down the system menu for the session, choosing the **Setting...** menu item and checking or unchecking those items in the resulting dialog.

 Your DOS session has to be windowed to access the system menu. If you are running a DOS session full screen, hitting **Alt+Space** is a shortcut for shifting to a windowed session and invoking the system menu at the same time. In the **Settings...** dialog, hit the radio button marked **Full Screen** in addition to changing **Exclusive** and/or **Background** and you'll switch back to where you started. Too bad Microsoft didn't allow you to change these settings with hotkeys.

Windows also has an **Exclusive** setting (but not a **Background** setting). You set it via a check box called **Exclusive in Foreground** in the **386Enhanced applet** of Control Panel, see Figure 3-19. I'll talk more about this is Chapter 7.

The Windows VM always gets its time slice no matter what the settings of the DOS sessions and an active DOS session always gets its time slice but a DOS session in the background will only get a time slice if two conditions hold:

- Its Background setting in On.

- The Exclusive Setting of the active DOS session (or Windows VM if a Winapp is active) is Off

Put differently, if the active application is set to Exclusive, then only it and the Windows VM get time and all other applications are suspended. If the active application has its Exclusive setting turned off than every DOS session that has its Background setting on will get some time.

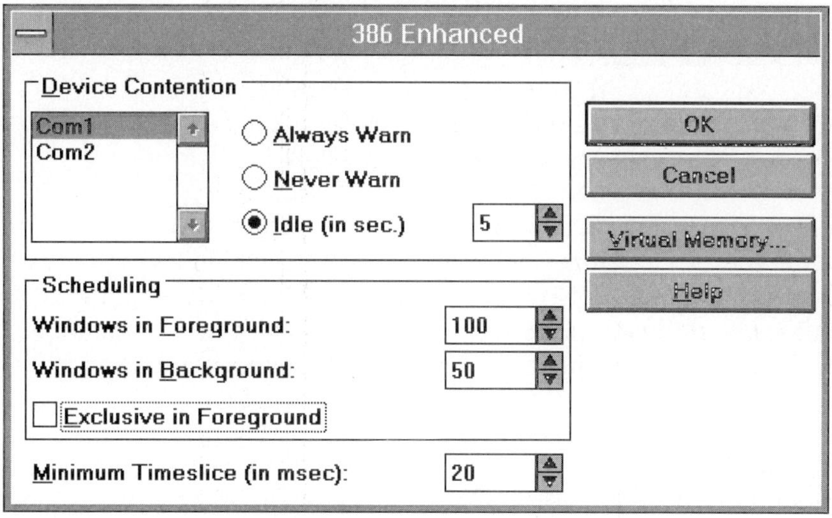

Figure 3-19: The 386Enhanced applet

How much time background applications get is determined by two numbers associated to each VM — for DOS sessions in the Advanced section of the `PIF` and for Windows in the `Scheduling` section of the `386Enhanced Applet` (Figure 3-19). One is called the **Foreground Priority** and the other the **Background Priority**. By default, they have the values 100 and 50 for any DOS session and for windows. I'll represent these numbers as `Foreground/Background` so the default is 100/50.

The priority numbers have to lie in the range 0–10,000. They do *not* represent absolute times but only relative priorities. If all applications have 1000/500 priority, you get the same behavior as with 100/50.

From the relative priorities, the scheduler computes what fraction of the time each VM should get. If you have five VMs with background turned on and background priority 50 and a sixth foreground VM which is not exclusive and foreground priority 100, one computes fractions by summing all priorities: 50+50+50+50+50+100=350 and dividing the sum into the priorities — so the background applications get 1/7 of the time and the foreground 2/7. That's not strictly true since there is time Windows needs for overhead so it is more accurate to say that the foreground gets 2/7 of the time that is not needed for overhead.

Up the foreground to 250 and the sum increases to 500 so the foreground gets 1/2 the time and each background 1/10.

Each DOS session also has a **Detect Idle Time** Yes/No setting as part of the Advanced **PIF**. When on, Windows tries to determine when a background application is idle and then doesn't give it its time slices. Basically, it looks for a program that is doing nothing more than waiting for keyboard input. But this is hardly exact. If a program is updating a ticking clock while waiting for keystrokes, Windows may not realize it is idle depending on how the program was written. Still, it does work much of the time and you'll want to leave that item checked unless you find that the program is not running in the background when it should be.

The last number that controls the scheduler is the Minimum Time Slice measured in milliseconds and set in the **386Enhanced applet**. The default is 20. Applications normally get time in multiples of this minimum time slice and most often, a single slice at a time. How often they get it is determined by the relative priorities. In the first example above, the foreground would get 2 out of every 7 slices, not successively but most likely with 2 or 3 background slices in between. In the second example, the foreground would get roughly every other slice.

Which of these parameters should you change from the default? Normally, not many! If you run many DOS sessions in background, consider upping the Windows VM priority to 200/100 since it needs to service multiple applications. If you have a PIF for a DOS communication program, set it with **Background** On but otherwise try to avoid background DOS application unless there is a positive need for it — unless Windows determines the application is inactive, a DOS app gets its full time slice even if it has nothing to do! If you occasionally need to run a DOS session in background, for example, a huge database with lengthy indexing or a finance package that can call to collect stock quotes, set the PIF with **Background** off and turn it on from the system menu at the point you need it. It is unfortunate that Windows doesn't let you turn **Background** On or Off with hotkeys or batch file commands. EDOS, which I'll discuss in Chapter 5, does let you do it with batch file commands.

For most systems, the 20 milliseconds background priority should be fine. If your applications seem to be a little jerky (possible on a slow machine), decrease that number but then things will run slower because more time will get sucked up in the overhead of switching.

Piffle Ball

PIFs are binary files which you access from a Winapp called **pifedit.exe**. It is installed as an icon in the **Main** group of ProgMan. The main screen of PIFEdit (Figure 3-20) gives you access to the parameters shown. The first four fields are roughly equivalent to the first three fields in a ProgMan item. In ProgMan, the field called **command line** combines the **Program Filename** and the **Optional Parameters**. The fourth field in a ProgMan item, to whit **ShortCut** key, is found on PIFEdit's **Advanced**.... screen.

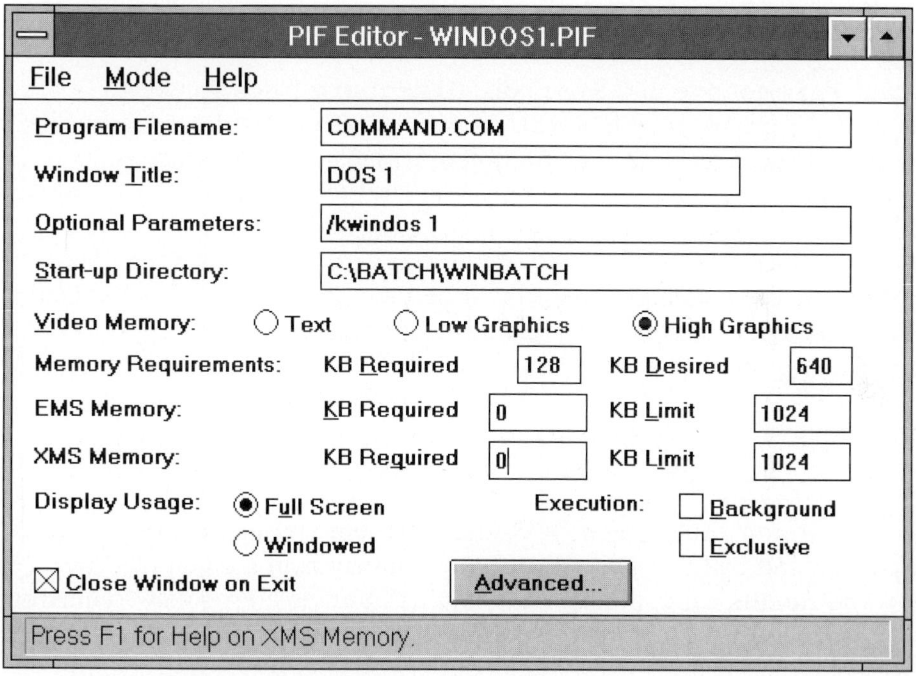

Figure 3-20: The main PIFEDIT screen

The thing to bear in mind is that if it has any excuse at all, Windows will override the information in these first four entries! If you have an executable **foobar.exe** and mistakenly type **fubar.exe** into PIFEdit's first field but call the **PIF** file **foobar.pif**, there will be no problem if you double click on **foobar.exe** — Windows launches the **exe** and ignores that field. Of course, if you should double click on foobar.pif itself, that field will get read.

Similarly, if you type in an optional parameter in the **File/Run** dialog of ProgMan, that parameter will get used and any parameter in the associated **PIF** field will be ignored. And all the fields in a ProgMan item — working directory, title (caption), command line and shortcut key take precedence over what's in the corresponding fields of the **PIF**.

If you make a question mark the first blank character in a **PIF**'s Optional Parameter field, the rest of the field is ignored and when you run the **PIF**, a box pops up asking you to type in optional parameters which are passed to the program. This is not true for question marks included in the command line for a ProgMan item.

The **Optional Parameters** and **Startup Directory** fields accept environment variables, items set with a **set** command before Windows loads. The syntax is the same as used to refer to environment variables in batch files — surround the variable name with % signs. So if you have
        foo=bar
in your **autoexec.bat** and place **%foo%** in the **Optional Parameter** field, when the **PIF** is run, the parameter passed will be **bar**. Because parameters need to be set before you load Windows, this feature is of limited value but might be useful to a network administrator setting up batch files to run from within Windows.

✖   ✖   ✖   ✖   ✖

Did you ever want to run a full screen DOS session where you first load some TSRs and set and prompt and path? If you just put the commands in a batch file, say **mybat.bat,** and run the batch file by using **mybat.bat** as a ProgMan command line, then the batch file loads the TSRs, sets the prompt, finishes running and the session ends — not what you wanted I'll bet. Under DOS versions up to 5.0, the best way out of this conundrum was to make **command** the last line of the batch file. This loads a new copy of command com and leaves you at a DOS prompt until you type **Exit**. Inelegant and somewhat wasteful of memory but it works. DOS 6 has a better way! It introduced a new switch to command.com — the /k switch —

which tells command to run the program following the switch and then remain resident until the user types **Exit**. So for the earlier batch file to work, you need only enter

```
command /k mybat.bat
```

to have the batch file run and leave you at a DOS prompt. (see Figure 3-20) The space after /k is optional.

⌘   ⌘   ⌘   ⌘   ⌘

The Video Memory radio buttons refer to how much memory Windows reserves to store the video image of the DOS session when you switch away from the session. If the **Text** button is chosen, it saves about 16K of RAM, if **Low Graphics** about 32K and if **High Graphics**, then about 128K. Low Graphics refers to CGA graphics modes and High graphics to Hercules, EGA and VGA modes.

 Unless you have an oldie but goodie game that you treasure, it is hard to imagine that have any program that uses CGA graphics — in fact, it is hard to believe you have a CGA game that you treasure. So the **Low Graphics** button is essentially useless, an artifact of history.

In any event, these radio buttons are not very important. Even if a button is set to Text, that session can still switch to Graphics if there is enough memory for Windows to allocate on the fly. So it seems that these buttons only determine what is initially allocated to the DOS session.

 It says "it seems" because the documentation is murky on this point but experimenting with switching modes even if **High Graphics** is not checked suggests it is possible.

The memory options are fairly straight forward. The **Required** boxes mean what they say. Windows will allocate the memory amounts required and will refuse to start a session if there is insufficient memory with a warning like the one in Figure 3-21. The **KB Desired** is the amount that Windows will allocate if available as main memory for the session. Note carefully that the extra number for XMS and EMS memory uses the term **Limit**. That memory is *not* allocated even if available until the program you are running asks for it. So there is no reason not to use at least the 1024/1024 numbers that **_default.pif** and **dosprmpt.pif** place there.

In four of the six memory fields (all but the XMS and EMS Required), you can use the number -1. This is interpreted by Windows to mean as much as available (up to 640K for the conventional memory settings).

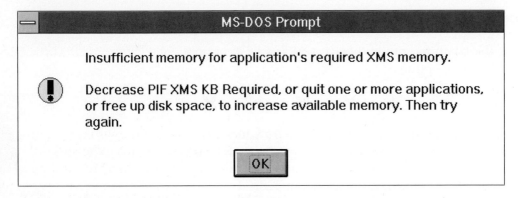

Figure 3-21: Windows warning if there is insufficient memory to meet requirements

The display usage Radio buttons determine if the application starts out initially running full screen or in a Window. You can always switch back and forth after the application starts using the **Alt+Enter** hotkey. Note that DOS applications cannot use high graphics modes when running in a window. If they try to switch to such a mode while in window, Windows will popup a message telling you that the application is suspended until it is switched to full screen.

I discussed the Exclusive and Background check boxes in the last section and the Display Usage radio button in the section before that. The **Close Window on Exit** check box involves an option intended to run DOS TSRs. For normal DOS programs and DOS prompt sessions, you'd want the check box checked. But if you load a TSR by hand (or batch file) and the box is not checked, at the point where the window would normally close, instead it says: "Your popup program is ready to run. When you have finished using it, press **Ctrl+C** to close this window and return to Windows." That allows you to popup the TSR and when you are done close the session with **Ctrl+C**.

If you run a DOS program with the **Close Window on Exit** check box unchecked but load no TSR, the "Your popup.." message will not appear but instead the session with switch to windowed and add "Inactive" to the window caption. To exit the session you need to **Double Click** on the system menu or hit **Alt+Space** followed by **C** (for the Close choice).

 You might think that Ctrl+C or the Alt+F4 close hotkey which is still marked on the menu would close such an inactive session but they do not.

✄   ✄   ✄   ✄   ✄

If you hit the Advanced. . . button in the PIF editor, you get to a second screen shown in Figure 3-22. I've already discussed the Multitasking options in the last section.

```
┌─────────────────────────── Advanced Options ───────────────────────────┐
│ ┌─Multitasking Options─────────────────────────┐   ┌──────────┐        │
│ │ Background Priority:  [50]   Foreground Priority: [100]  │   OK     │  │
│ │              ☒ Detect Idle Time                │   ├──────────┤        │
│ └──────────────────────────────────────────────┘   │  Cancel  │        │
│ ┌─Memory Options───────────────────────────────────────────┐          │
│ │  ☐ EMS Memory Locked          ☐ XMS Memory Locked        │          │
│ │  ☒ Uses High Memory Area      ☐ Lock Application Memory  │          │
│ └──────────────────────────────────────────────────────────┘          │
│ ┌─Display Options──────────────────────────────────────────┐          │
│ │ Monitor Ports:  ☐ Text   ☐ Low Graphics   ☐ High Graphics│          │
│ │           ☒ Emulate Text Mode    ☐ Retain Video Memory   │          │
│ └──────────────────────────────────────────────────────────┘          │
│ ┌─Other Options────────────────────────────────────────────┐          │
│ │ ☒ Allow Fast Paste            ☐ Allow Close When Active   │          │
│ │ Reserve Shortcut Keys:  ☐ Alt+Tab  ☐ Alt+Esc  ☐ Ctrl+Esc │          │
│ │                         ☐ PrtSc    ☐ Alt+PrtSc ☐ Alt+Space│         │
│ │                         ☐ Alt+Enter                       │          │
│ │ Application Shortcut Key: [                    ]          │          │
│ └──────────────────────────────────────────────────────────┘          │
│ Press F1 for Help on Uses High Memory Area.                            │
└─────────────────────────────────────────────────────────────────────────┘
```

Figure 3-22: The PIFEdit Advanced options screen

The three **Memory** options that mention **Locked** let you tell Windows *not* to swap the stated memory to disk using the swap file. Under normal circumstances you'd *not* want to check this. The Uses High Memory Area refers to the first 64K of memory above the 1 Meg boundary. If you took my advice and added DOS=high, that area is already used and DOS won't let anyone else use it whether that box is checked or not. So unless you are told by an application's tech support staff to change something in the **Memory** group, leave it alone — the defaults are what you want.

The **Display Options** group is also sufficiently specialized that you can normally leave it as the default (**Emulate Text Mode** checked). If most DOS applications display correctly but one has problems, try fooling with these options which are clearly described in the *User's Guide*.

Allow Fast Paste concerns the rate at which text is pasted from the clipboard into the DOS session. If not checked, it is pasted a single keystroke per DOS clock tick (roughly 1/18 of a second); if it is checked (the default), pasting is faster. Most applications can take Fast Paste but if you lose characters or get a lot of beeping while pasting, try unchecking this in the **PIF**.

Checking **Allow Close when Active** (*not* the default) is a dangerous way to avoid the great annoyance of trying to close Windows with a DOS session active and getting told that you can't do that because one or more DOS sessions are active. When Windows closes through normal channels, it sends a message to all Winapps, essentially saying "hey, guys, hasta la vista" and the Winapp can prompt you to save unsaved work. But DOS apps "ne hable Windows" so there is no way to allow them to warn you about unsaved work.

Two better ways to avoid the annoyance are Roger's Rapid Restart (on CD MOM) which lets you close all apps without warning but only at time you are sure and EDOS (discussed in Chapter 5) which will close a DOS session if it is at a DOS prompt (but not otherwise).

The **Reserve Shortcut Keys** doesn't say who they are reserved by! Normally, those are the keys that Windows uses from DOS sessions according to the following (see *Keys to the Kingdom* in Chapter 2 for more discussion of these keys):

Alt+Tab   Cool Switch key

Alt+Esc   Switches to the last application you used

Ctrl+Esc	Switches back to Windows and calls up TaskMan
PrtSc	Copies the entire screen to the clipboard, as text if the DOS session is in text mode and as graphics if you are in graphics mode
Alt+PtrSc	Same as PrtSc (for DOS sessions)
Alt+Space	Invokes the DOS session system menu, if necessary first switching to windowed DOS mode
Alt+Enter	Toggles DOS sessions between full screen and windowed

That's what happens if all the Shortcut key boxes are *not* checked. If one of your DOS applications uses one of these key combinations, just check the box by that combination and it will be reserved *for your application* and not available to Windows.

DOS fonts

This is a somewhat technical subsection about fonts used by Windows in DOS sessions intended more for your curiosity than for the usefulness of the information.

Windows uses very different font mechanisms in full screen vs. windowed DOS sessions. Full screen sessions essentially use DOS text mode. On most video adaptors, the text mode fonts are stored in ROM on the video board. On EGAs and VGAs, these in ROM fonts can be replaced by fonts stored in RAM. For example, the DOS TSR Ultravision (Personics, Voice: 508-897-1575) lets you use a variety of attractive fonts in DOS text mode and it works fine in full screen DOS sessions over Windows.

However, Windows does not use either the ROM based or EGA/VGA memory resident fonts when you switch to a windowed section. Instead it uses fixed pitch fonts stored in **FON** files on disk. What fonts are used are determined by five lines in **[386Enhanced]** section of **system.ini**. In a default installation (at least in the United States), they read

```
woafont=dosapp.fon
```

```
EGA80WOA.FON=EGA80WOA.FON
```

```
EGA40WOA.FON=EGA40WOA.FON
```

```
   CGA80WOA.FON=CGA80WOA.FON
```

```
   CGA40WOA.FON=CGA40WOA.FON
```

 Hey, wait a minute, didn't they leave the **h** out of whoa?

 No, grasshopper, WOA is short for Windows Old App, the quaint name that DOS programs have had at the internal level of Windows for some time. If you look in the `system` directory you'll find two files called `winoldap.mod` (for standard mode) and `winoa386.mod` (for enhanced mode). These are `dll`s that Windows uses to run DOS applications.

See Chapter 7 for details on the syntax of **ini** files. The left hand side of the equals are the lines that tell Windows that the right hand side are font files for DOS, er, WinOldApps. The right hand side are font resource files and could be third party files (for example, Manugistic's APL PLUS changes the right hand side of the woafont line to an **fon** file that it installs).

The Windows Resource Kit is crystal clear about those five lines. The fon file on the right side of **woafont=** is used for: "This entry specifies which font files are loaded into memory when running non-Windows applications." As for **CGA80WOA.FON=**, it says "This entry specifies the filename of the fixed-pitch display font used for non-Windows applications with a display of 80 columns and 25 or fewer lines" and similarly for the other three **WOA.FON** entries (EGA80 is 80 columns and more than 25 lines and the 40's are similar but for 40 column rather than 80).

 Whoa, er, woa, whatever. It seems to say that at the standard 80x25 screen size, `CGA80WOA.FON` is used but then why is `WOAFONT` loaded in memory? Separately, the description are clear but together, they are baffling, at least they appear so to me.

 Precisely grasshopper, but fear not, all will be made clear. But while you are contemplating the situation, listen to an aside on font sizes in a windowed DOS session.

As shown in Figure 3-23, you can pick one of 10 fonts sizes in a DOS session by choosing Fonts. . . from the System menu. Sizes are measured in pixels describing the dimensions of an imaginary box surrounding each fixed pitch character. The same menu of sizes appears in any screen resolution, although you'll probably want to choose a size depending on the resolution — picking a larger number of pixels at higher resolutions (since otherwise the apparent size on screen shrinks).

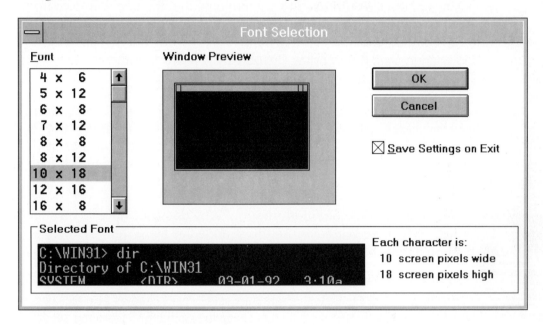

Figure 3-23: The DOS font dialog

Notice the careful layout of this dialog showing the way your current window size will resize under the new font and showing an actual sample.

 Notice that the 10 fonts sizes. Where are they stored? I found one expert who thought they were hard coded into winoa386.mod. But I looked at the five default fon files in Borland's *Resource Workshop* which let me see the actual fonts stored there and what I found was that **dosapp.fon** had six fonts and each of the other four had one each and here are the sizes of those fonts:

DOSAPP.FON   **4x6, 5x12, 6x8, 7x12, 10x18, 12x16**

CGA40WOA.FON   **16x8**

CGA80WOA.FON   **8x8**

EGA40WOA.FON   **16x12**

EGA80WOA.FON   **8x12**

So, all five of the files are used to get the fonts that the user can pick from and the one used depends on the user's choice. So, if one replaced `dosapp.fon` by another file then, some but not all of the font choices would change. And the Window Resource Kit is wrong with this stuff about `ega80woa.fon` only being used is columns=80 and rows>25.

Precisely. Manugistic's APL Plus includes a font file called `waplfont.fon` and their install replaces `dosapp.fon`. (by changing the `woafon=` line). It has 7 fonts in it but two duplicates sizes in the `c/ega40/80woa.fon` set. When their font file is installed, the font choice dialog shows 9 choices (5 from `waplfont.fon` and the four in the `c/ega40/80woa.fon` files).

Wow, Mao. Three questions though. Why does APL have its own font file? Why does Windows use this strange five file system? How should fonts be handled in DOS sessions?

The APL choice has to do with characters sets. Most Windows `fon` files use the ANSI set but the DOS session fonts have to use the IBM character set so there are the box drawing characters in the right place (character sets are discussed in Chapter 2 in the section called *Good Writing Needs Character Development* and shown in Appendix 3). Otherwise, the boxes DOS programs put up on screen wouldn't have the right borders. APL is a language which needs some special symbols. Long ago Manugistic (then called STSC) came up with a modified IBM character set that replaced some of the non box character symbols above code 128 by the APL symbols. They want those characters available in DOS sessions. Hebrew Windows include a fixed pitch `fon` file called `hebapps.fon` with the Hebrew characters in their standard places above 128.

Why five files? One can only guess, but I think the answer is historical. Old operating systems (and remember Windows is in version 3.1 following not only 3.0, but also 1.0, 2.03 and 2.1) are best studied by archaeologists. In Windows 3.0, where the font sizes used in DOS sessions were hard coded, there were the four `c/ega40/80woa.fon` files and they were used in the screen sizes specified in the current Windows Resource Kit, for example EGA80WOA.FON for 80 columns and more than 25 rows. I'd guess that because of some fears of backward incompatibilities, the Windows 3.1 designers left those files in place but added the fifth file. Alas, the authors of the Windows Resource Kit didn't change the descriptions of the c/ega40/80woa.fon form their 3.0 meanings.

As to what I'd like to see. First, DOS sessions should use True Type fonts and scale to keep the entire DOS screen in a window as it is stretched. This is precisely what `Desqview/X` does with PostScript outline fonts and it is most impressive. And the font file used should be part of the `PIF` so a product like APL can be accommodated without having to change all your DOS sessions.

Because the user can really confuse themselves if they use DOS fonts with the wrong character set, there should be a True Type header flag to tell Windows whether a True Type font is acceptable as a DOS session font. A system.ini entry should list a default font file to be used if the one in the PIF is invalid.

Giving DOS a Pasting

Transferring text between DOS apps via the clipboard is one of Windows most useful core features. While it is awkwardly implemented, such transfers can also be done to and from DOS sessions. You can paste from a Winapp to a DOS session, from a DOS session to a Winapp or between DOSapps.

One way to copy to the clipboard is to hit **PrtSc** in a DOS session, which, if the DOS session is running in text mode copies the entire screen as text to the clipboard. This is often not so useful because it is copied as 25 lines of 80 columns with spaces, graphics characters and all that.

For all other communications with the clipboard, you need to access the system menu for the DOS session which has to be done in windowed mode. **Alt+space** from a full screen session will switch modes and access that menu. On the system menu is a submenu called **Edit** ▶ which lets choose **Mark** and **Paste** starting from normal mode (the Scroll choice on that menu is for scrolling a DOS window which is not showing completely without needing a mouse — it has little to do with **Edit**ing). **Paste** will enter the contents of the clipboard through the keyboard to the current session.

Choosing **Mark** enters a special mode where you can pick a rectangular block and copy it to the clipboard. The **arrow** keys let you move a block cursor to pick the block anchor, that is the upper left corner of the block. **Shift+arrow** keys anchor the block and move the lower right corner to grow or shrink the block. Once you get the block you want, **Enter** or **Edit/Copy** from the system menu will copy the block to the clipboard and exit marking mode. Once you enter Marking mode, you can also set the block with a mouse by clicking to anchor the block and dragging to the size you want and then **Right Clicking**.

 If you enter marking mode and want to exit without copying anything to the clipboard, **Esc** will work. If you've anchored the block with **Shift+arrow** keys and want to start all over, hitting an arrow key at that point will return you to the initial marking mode state where you can rechoose the anchor point. You can use **Shift+arrow** to move the second corned above and/or to the left of the anchor point so that technically, the anchor can be any corner but you'll normally make it the upper left.

 I really think that Microsoft missed the boat on marking and pasting where a few small changes would have made life much easier. First of all, making **Edit** a submenu of the system menu rather than letting the **Edit** commands appear as a block on the system menu makes it harder than it should be to access what is an important feature. Moreover, they should have allowed hotkeys for both marking and pasting that among other benefits could work in full screen mode without the need to shift to windowed mode. There are even two natural hotkeys which aren't likely to be in use by DOS apps, namely **Ctrl+Ins** to enter marking mode and **Shift+Ins** to paste. Of course, with the shift to **Ctrl+C/Ctrl+V** (which aren't safe for DOS apps since they could be used there) for Windows cut/paste, the hotkeys could have been dropped out for political reasons.

Do's for DOS

Finally a miscellany of tips and tricks for running DOS applications with Windows:

Rather than try to make your own **PIF** for a DOS app or rely on **_default.pif**, you should see if it is a product that Microsoft has a **PIF** for. Run Windows SetUp and pick **Set Up Applications...** from the **Options** menu. The resulting dialog is shown in Figure 3-24. The default Search for Applications radio button will look for all DOS programs that Windows knows about and install them in ProgMan. If you have a specific one in mind, pick the **Ask you to specify an application** radio button as shown.

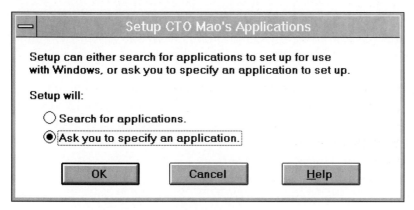

Figure 3-24: The Setup Applications dialog

 Hey Mao, how did you change the caption to include your name?

 Elementary, my dear Igor, I adjusted the `caption=` line in the file `apps.inf` found in the `system` directory. Remarkable, the fun you can have with Windows, isn't it?

You can then **Browse...** to locate the DOS program if you want. Windows looks in the file **apps.inf** to find the executable file's name and, if it does, uses the information there to make a **PIF**. If you want to check in advance, if the program is there, you can take a look at apps.inf — it lists the executables in alphabetical order. It's too big to load into **Notepad**, so you'll need to use **Write**.

- Some folks just want a DOS command line for a quick directory listing or a quick copy command. If that's all you use DOS for, there are several pseudo command lines — Winapps that give you what looks like a DOS command line but, for example, typically has direct cut and paste and the ability to launch Windows as well as DOS applications. Among the programs of this genre are Landmark DOS for Windows (Landmark, Voice: 800-683-6696) and a shareware programs that you'll find on CD MOM: WinCLI (Voice: 604-520-1543).

Mom's toolkit doesn't have any of these programs because EDOS (see Chapter 5) provides the extras that the pseudo DOS programs have and is real DOS after all but both are well done programs that may interest you.

- If you want to run a DOS program in full screen mode with a mouse, you'll need to load a mouse driver (typically **mouse.com** or **mouse.sys**) before you load Windows. It's normally put in **autoexec.bat** or **config.sys**. If you never run DOS programs with a mouse, you do *not* need these programs to get mouse support in Windows.

- If you get an "Unexpected Error #11" message from Windows as it terminates a DOS session, you almost certainly have a corrupted **winoa386.mod** or a corrupted 386 grabber. You can reinstall **winao386.mod** from the Windows install disks. System.ini will tell you the name of your 386 grabber file which should be on the disks your video driver came with.

- Be sure to check out chapter 9 for the **[NonWindowsApps]** section of system.ini.

- Some users like to run batch files from **PIF**s and would like double clicking a **bat** file to call it into Notepad. To do that, find the line in the **[Windows]** section of **win.ini** which almost surely reads
      Programs=com exe bat pif
  and remove **bat**. Then highlight a batch file in FileMan and use **File/Associate** to associate batch files to Notepad.

- If a DOS program should crash, try hitting **Ctrl+Alt+Del**. Windows will probably offer to close the application if you hit **Enter** (or offer to reboot if you hit **Ctrl+Alt+Del**) again. Enter should work to save the rest of your sessions. If that doesn't work, consider picking **Settings...** from the system menu (if the session is windowed) and choose the **Terminate...** button.

- There are a number of DOS commands you should not run under Windows. Basically, any program that directly manipulates the DOS File Application Table (aka **FAT**) shouldn't be run under Windows. That would include *Chkdsk* with the /f parameter, disk fix programs like *Norton Disk Doctor* and disk defraggers.

- There are two environmental variables related to DOS session you should be aware of. The first concerns the prompt. Normally, DOS looks for its prompt in the **prompt=** environmental variable which you can set up with **set prompt=** or with the **prompt** command. A special role is played by a variable called **winpmt** but only if you set it *before* starting Windows. When Windows starts a DOS session, it looks for this variable and if it find its interchanges the values of **winpmt** and **prompt** so that DOS sees what was **winpmt** as its new **prompt**. If you run Windows all the time, this is not so interesting since you can just set the prompt variable and be done with it. BUT, if you are sometimes in Windows and sometimes not and want to be reminded in a full screen DOS session that you are in Windows, you could try adding something like

```
set prompt=$p$g
```

```
set winpmt=We're not in DOS anymore, Toto$_$p$g
```

to your **autoexec.bat**.

- The other environmental variable is one that windows sets, typically as

```
windir=C:\WINDOWS
```

Normally DOS capitalizes all variable names but Windows uses **windir**, not **WINDIR**. This can be use to have a batch file test for whether is running or not. For example via

```
if %windir%="" goto skip
```

put here commands you don't want to run under Windows

```
:skip
```

CHAPTER 4
Windows Applets

Le mieux est l'enemi du bien.[1]

— Voltaire, "Dict. Philosophique," 1764

Good enough is the enemy of better.

— Jerry Pournelle, many places, 1980s

---

[1]"The better is the enemy of the good,"

In this chapter, Mom presents her version of the Windows Clock Manual, the discussion of the Windows small fry. It will be very different from what you'll find in the books that devote several hundred pages to the subject. First, I won't rewrite the *Windows User's Guide*, which considering the amount of material it needs to cover, is extraordinarily well-written. In fact, most of this chapter will follow a pattern you may get tired of — listing what is missing from the applets and briefly mentioning third party alternatives.

 You are probably thinking "Geez, these guys want me to spend a gazillion bucks replacing the Windows applets with better stuff." Oh, Con Trare, as Mao would say. Mind you, if you have a gazillion bucks, there are worse ways to spend them. But Pournelle had it right (and Voltaire wrong). Generally, the Windows applets are good enough but you should make an informed decision when to stick with what comes for free and when to get a replacement.

 You may be wondering how I decided what makes it into my toolbox in Chapter 5 and what only gets mentioned in passing here. Chapter 5 is the hall of fame, the creme de la creme, the great stuff. With a focus on the major components rather than little applets. So no Notepad replacement makes it (except that Norton has one) because they are useful but not quite essential. And, Chapter 5 focuses on Utilities so you won't find comprehensive reviews of word processors, comm programs or image editors there (or in this chapter) although Windows does ship with examples of those.

 This chapter is also a kind of Secrets of the Windows 3.1 Applets — features that, while sometimes even documented in the manual seem to be largely unknown. Did you know that you can set up a file so that Notepad time stamps it every time you open it? That Windows Write has a ruler? That Windows ships with a full fledged scientific calculator? Read on, grasshopper.

 Bear in mind that all the world's an applet. In Windows, you can load any Winapp with any other and the small applications that ship with the biggies, for example the WordPerfect file manager, will work with any other program that you want them to.

Could I Have a Word with You?

Once a word has been allowed to escape, it cannot be recalled.

— Horace, *Epistles, bk. I*

Your Pad or Mine? — Notepad and SYSEDIT

Take note, take note, O world!

— William Shakespeare, *Othello, Act: III, Scene: iii, Line: 378*

ASCII files are ones that store pure text together with characters that indicate the ends of lines. There is no formatting information stored. Examples of ASCII files are your basic configuration files (**win.ini**, etc.), **ini** files for most other programs and batch files.

 Any **ini** file that uses Windows inifile services is ASCII, but, for example, Word for Windows has a binary file it uses for **winword.ini**. As is so often the case, Winword marches to its own drummer.

 Language source code (except for many flavors of BASIC) is also ASCII. That means that the ASCII file editor market is broken into two parts — ones intended for mere mortals and the programmer's editors with macro languages to warm the heart of a true code aficionado, compile from within options and other goodies. I'll only talk about the editors for mere mortals.

So you need an ASCII editor to change your ASCII files. No problem if you have DOS 5.0 or earlier. You'll find a wonderful ASCII editor called Edlin. Hehe, I bet there are readers who have never seen Edlin since we don't have it to kick around any more (it was finally dropped from DOS 6). If not, you're in for a treat or at least a barrel of laughs and a lesson in how primitive computing was not so long ago.

But I digress with my joke about Edlin. Windows provides two programs to edit ASCII files — Notepad and Sysedit. You may not be aware of Sysedit since it is not documented in the *Windows User's Guide* (it is in the *Windows Resource Kit* and it is not preinstalled by Windows in ProgMan. But it is placed as **sysedit.exe** in your **system** directory. My advice is to add it as an item in ProgMan's main group.

Notepad will edit a single file at a time so long as the file isn't too large. Sysedit loads four files but those are hard coded as the four system files: **config.sys**, **autoexec.bat**, **win.ini** and **system.ini**. Sysedit also will only load these files if they aren't too large.

 How large can they be, you may ask? Your intrepid experimenter did some trials and learned that there aren't simple numbers. First, I found that while Notepad gives a clear **too large for Notepad** message, Sysedit only says **Unable to open config.sys** or whatever file is too large for it.

Secondly, for Notepad, things depend on the state of the program. It happened that I could get a `too large` message on a file, exit Notepad, restart it and find that the file loaded perfectly. Thirdly, one can't give a simple byte count limit — it is clearly a combination of lines and bytes that matters. While I could open files in `Notepad` of over 45K, if I tried a file with one character per line, I had problems about 10,000 lines (which meant about a 30K file since every line end in an ASCII file takes two bytes). General rule is that Notepad will refuse load files over 50K if they are typical and there is a smaller limit for files with lots of short lines. For Sysedit, there seemed to be problems as soon as the *total* for all four was over about 50K.

Most importantly, these programs acted flaky when the sizes were near the limits. Sysedit might load with `autoexec.bat` displayed as one long line and, in one case, it seemed to load a very large `config.sys` but it only loaded part of it, so that when I edited and saved it, I lost 90% of the file! My strong advice is to only use Sysedit if the total size of your four system files is under 40K and only use Notepad on files under 40K in size. If you have a lot of fonts, you may exceed this recommended limit for win.ini.

These files make automatic backups of an original file if you change and save it. For Notepad, the backup is given the extension **bak** and for Sysedit, the extension **syd** as in **win.syd**. Both programs will do simple searches backwards or forwards in the file, case sensitive or not as you choose. Both have single level undo.

Sysedit has no online help and its file menu has a **Print...** command — don't you believe the **...**; it prints the current file, no questions asked.

 Pity poor Microsoft. It seems quite clear that Sysedit was not intended for users but included as a tech support program — for Microsoft to have available if you called them for tech support. But all the books and magazines talk about it and this book complains about an incorrect dialog box indicator in the menu of this program that users weren't supposed to use in the first place.

Notepad's **Print** command lets you put in date/time and filename into headers and footers using the special codes shown below

&d	The current date
&p	Page numbers
&f	The current filename
&l	Text (following the code) to be aligned at the left margin
&r	Text (following the code) to be aligned at the right margin
&c	Text (following the code) to be centered between the margins
&t	The current time

so, for example, to have a header with the date at the left margin, filename centered in the middle and page number at the right, you would type **&l&d&c&f&rPage &p** in the header entry of the **File/Page Setup** menu dialog. These strings cannot be found in the Notepad online help but are in Calendar's help, so you can hit F1 and load Calendar's help to access the information if you need it.

Notepad lets you add the date and time to a file from **Time/Date** on the **Edit** menu. More interestingly, if you put **.LOG** on the first line of a file (it needs to be the only thing on the line, it must be the first line and it must start on the left), Notepad will append the date/time to the bottom of the file every time you open it.

On Notepad's **Edit** Menu is a toggle called **Word Wrap**. It wraps long lines at the word break closest to the right edge of the window, adjusting breaks as you resize the Notepad window. Use it with care because you can forget it is on and save a file missing line breaks. And don't print with it on because the **Print** does not wrap lines.

So what's missing? Here's a partial list:

- The ability to open several files at once. It sure would be nice to have the MDI interface found in *Sysedit* available in Notepad

- A most recently opened file list — for example have the file menu display the last three files that you opened and let you reopen by just picking

- Search and Replace as well as Search

- Ability to handle very large files — at least to 300K

- A Goto line number command and a status bar showing line numbers

- Multilevel undo

- The ability to insert a file

- A word count

- Memory via drop down lists of previous choices of print headers and previous search strings

Not such a long list but significant features. For many, Notepad will be good enough but if this list makes your mouth water, there are solutions. The Norton Desktop includes an editor with all these features except the word count. It's a lovely applet except for the fact that instead of the Windows common dialog for open/save, it uses its own non-standard and more awkward dialogs!

You'll find an impressive shareware editor on CD MOM — Wilson Windoware's Winedit in several levels of functionality.

One other function that Norton Desktop Editor has is the ability to compare two files, invaluable if an install program monkeyed around with your **system.ini** but you or it made a backup for you to compare. The Barry Press Utilities, a shareware product on CD MOM, has a simple Match program with similar functionality. Match (Figure 4-1) shows you two files side by side with differences highlighted and the ability to search for the next match or the next difference. You can even drag/drop the two files you want to compare from FileMan.

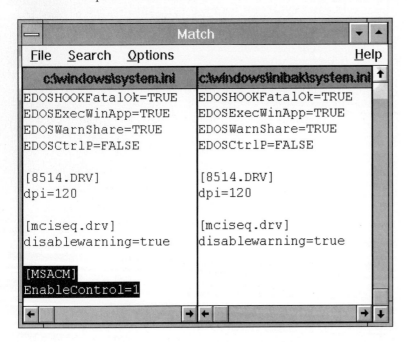

Figure 4-1: Match comparing two versions of system.ini

The Write Stuff

> I am not sorry for having wrought in common, crude material so much;
> that is the right American stuff
>
> — William Dean Howells, *Letter to Charles Elliot Norton*, 1903

Windows Write is a word processor included with Windows. If you use a word processor heavily, especially in a business setting, you can't afford not to have a major word processor, presumably one of the big three: Lotus' Ami Pro, Microsoft's Word for Windows or Word Perfect for Windows.

If you care about such things, the Ami Pro product manager claimed on CompuServe that the market shares were roughly 40% for Winword, 35% for Word Perfect and 20% for Ami Pro with the rest of the market getting a 5% share. At the time this is written, Mom's crew thinks that overall, Ami (version 3.0) is best, Winword (version 2.0) a close second and Word Perfect (version 5.2) not even close. But new versions of Winword and Word Perfect (both labeled version 6.0) are due out by the time this book appears and that could change. We actually use Winword in Mom's clubhouse because Ami isn't enough better to justify the switch and we have some dyn-o-mite macros that make up for its lacks.

But Write isn't half bad. For home use, say an occasionally letter to Mom, it is more than adequate. Heck, if you don't need tables, envelopes, frames, columns, and other high end stuff, it's plenty good. If word processors were still $300 on the street, Write would be an easy choice for a lot of folks; at $125 on the street for the top packages, it is less clear cut.

Even if you have a high-end word processor, don't remove Write from your disk. You'll need it for two purposes. First, since all Windows users have it, a lot of developers are will put their read me files in Write format and shareware authors, their online documentation in that format. Heck even most of the Windows read me files are in **wri** format.

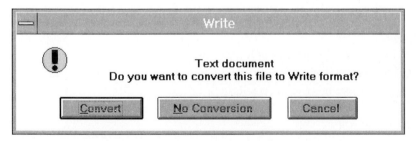

Figure 4-2: Write's Text Conversion dialog

Secondly, you can use Write to look at and even edit ASCII files that are too large for Notepad. Just be careful to pick **No Conversion** at the dialog (Figure 4-2) that pops up when you load a text file. In principle, any word processor can handle ASCII files but in my experience it is awfully easy to accidentally turn a text file into a native file for the word processor and all the binary junk that is added can confuse whatever program later tries to read the ASCII file.

Here are a few of the features that Write has that you might miss (some are shown in Figure 4-3).

- It has a ruler that you can turn on (via the Document menu). With the ruler, you can set margins by dragging the symbols below the marked line (dot for first line margin, arrow for other lines margin), set tabs by pointing to the ruler and choose the line spacing and justification with a simple point and click.

- As an OLE client, you can easily embed graphics so you can scan in a picture of the kids to include with your holiday greeting letter!

- It has decimal tabs (and the standard left tab) but neither a right nor a center tab.

- You can set up hanging indents.

- It has full TrueType font support, albeit somewhat awkward to reach since you must load the font Common Dialog each time you make a change and that can be slow if you have lots of fonts.

- Support for headers and footers including the page number.

In 1985, a lot of DOS users would have killed for such a wonderful word processing engine! It would take almost an entire book to list all the features that the current state-of-the-art word processors have but here's a list of some items they have missing in Write (I restricted my list to ten items):

- Paragraph styles, that is the ability to give a combination of font, justification, alignment, etc. a name.

- Templates, that is the ability to combine a set of styles and standard boiler plate (say a Memo header) in an easy to invoke package

- Table of Contents and Indexing

- Button Bar or Palette

- Macro language

- Drop down font list

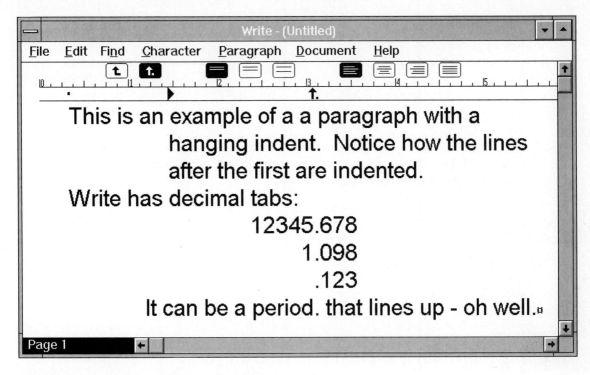

Figure 4-3: Windows Write's features

- Equation editor

- Frames or some other way to placement of graphics, drop caps, etc.

- Line drawing to make boxes, etc.

- Tables and Multiple column support

Yeah, I cheated and squeezed in twelve items, didn't I?

Toro! Toro! OLÉ!

> Truth, Sir, is a cow, which will yield skeptics no more milk;
> so they have gone to milk the bull.

> — Samuel Johnson

In this section, we present the bull behind OLE: the two applets Regedit and Object Packager. I'll assume that you've read the section of Chapter 2 entitled *OLÉ, Josó*. As a preliminary, you need to know that there are two players in each OLE transaction —

the program in which the object is linked or embedded, called the **OLE Client** and the program that is called to edit the object (most likely the program that created it but not necessarily), called the **OLE Server**. Not every program that supports OLE is both a server and a client; some are both but some are only configured to be one or the other. For example, Word Perfect for Windows 5.2 is an OLE Client but not a Server, while Winword and Ami are both. Sound Recorder is an OLE Server but not a Client.

 I am purposely not using the new Microsoft lingo which they recommend for OLE 2.0, to whit controller for client and object for server. I hope that terminology dies on the vine.

The Client calls on the services of the Server, so Client applications need a listing of OLE Servers, sort a phone book of whom they can call. That's part of the information put in the **Registration Database**. When you install an OLE Server, it registers itself in this database. Some programs, for example the Windows Media Player, check the registration database each time they are run and register themselves if they don't find themselves already there.

Probing the Hidden Recesses of Your Registration Database

"Sir Henry Baskerville is upstairs expecting you," said the clerk.
"He asked me to show you up at once when you came."
"Have you any objection to my looking at your register?" said Holmes.
"Not in the least."

— Sir Arthur Conan Doyle, *The Hound of the Baskervilles*

It's remarkable that Microsoft doesn't automatically install some of its neatest applets in ProgMan. But Sysedit and Regedit are secrets kept from the user apparently because there is a fear said user could shoot themselves in the foot. They are there for tech support purposes. But as long as you know what you are doing, and you will when I'm done, Regedit, formally called the **Registration Editor**, is an extremely valuable tool which lets you examine and edit the Registration Database. You normally will not need it to install Servers which should install themselves but you may need it as part of removing a program from your system and it can be useful for your own non OLE entries as we'll see. So you'll want to add **regedit.exe** as an item to your Accessories group. Regedit accesses what I'll call the surface parts of **reg.dat**.

If you're really brave, you may also want to install a second item with the command line **regedit /v**. I'll get back to that much later in this subsection but it's the tool that lets you really look into the guts of the Registration Database rather than the surface parts that plain **regedit** provides access to.

The registration database is a binary file, called **reg.dat** where applications can store information about themselves. At the surface level, reg.dat has a bunch of file types. Each file type has two mandatory properties and two optional ones (there can be additional properties hidden from Regedit without the **/v**). To the user, the most important of the required properties is the File Type, the name by which it appears on the main Regedit screen and in the FileMan Associations dialog. There is also a property called Identifier which much be unique for each item (you can have two file types with the same name as long as the identifiers are different; it is not recommended for you do this yourself but it can happen when a program installs its own information). These are the two required fields.

In addition, the optional fields are Action commands — the information to Open and to Print the File Type. Figures 4-4 and 4-5 show the command information that the *Ami Pro* installation program placed in **reg.dat** when it installed on Mao's machine. You can examine them for any File Type by highlighting the type in Regedit and picking **Modify File Type...** from the **Edit** menu (or **double clicking**). You pick which of the Actions is displayed with a radio button.

The action command can be a simple command line as is displayed for the Ami Print command (note that we scrolled the command line to display the end so the beginning of the path of the Ami Pro executable is not visible in Figure 4-5). The use of /p for Print is a Windows 3.1 standard and many Windows 3.1 specific applications will support it. In this simple command, the file name passed to the program by FileMan replaces the parameter %1. So, if Mao highlights a file in FileMan whose extension is associated to **Ami Pro Document** say **foobar.sam** and chooses the **File/Print** menu item in FileMan, FileMan tells Windows to run the command line **D:\words\ami\amipro.exe /p foobar.sam**.

If the application supports DDE, the Action can include DDE commands as is the case in the AmiPro Open command in Figure 4-4. The checkbox marked **Uses DDE** determines that. To see how you might exploit Regedit, let Mao tell you how he did:

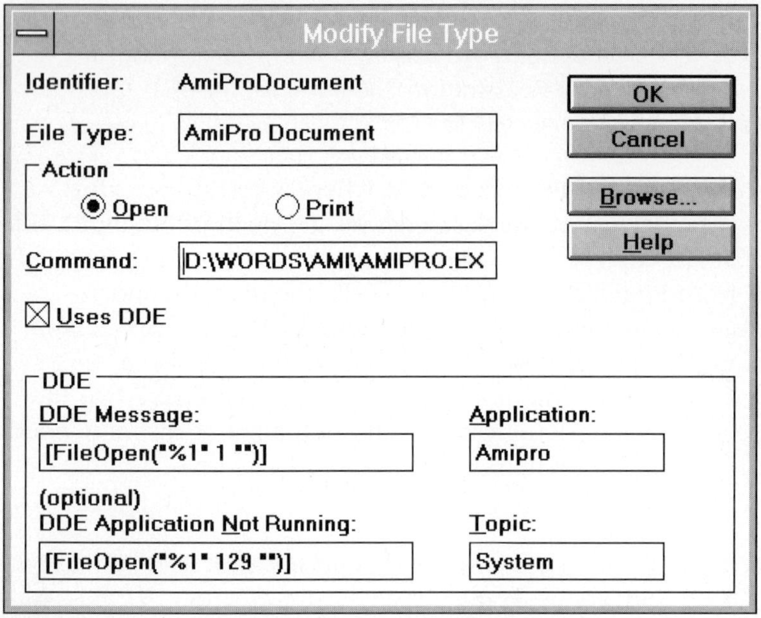

Figure 4-4: Ami Pro's Open information

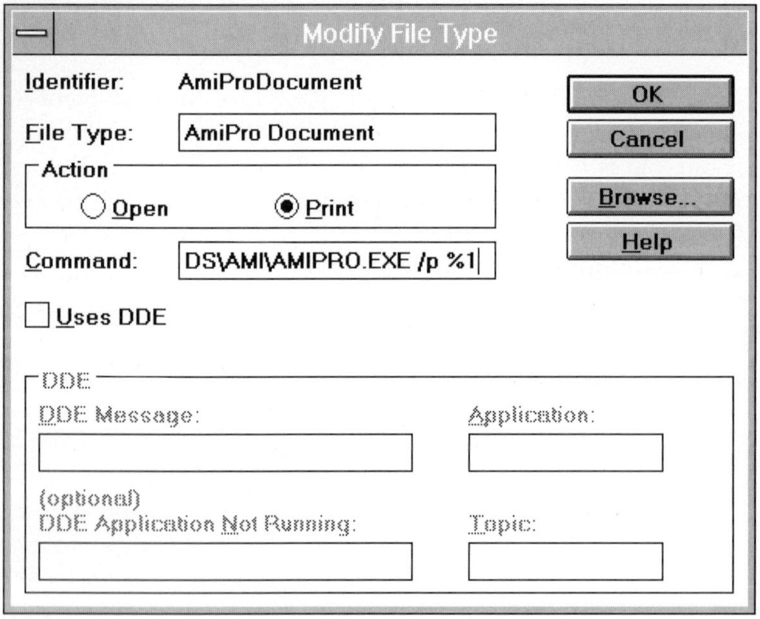

Figure 4-5: Ami Pro's Print Information

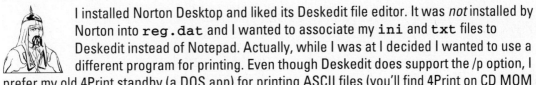 I installed Norton Desktop and liked its Deskedit file editor. It was *not* installed by Norton into `reg.dat` and I wanted to associate my `ini` and `txt` files to Deskedit instead of Notepad. Actually, while I was at I decided I wanted to use a different program for printing. Even though Deskedit does support the /p option, I prefer my old 4Print standby (a DOS app) for printing ASCII files (you'll find 4Print on CD MOM as well as 4Shell, a Windows interface for its many options). To print the file `foo.ini` with 4Print the way I like it (printed on one side of the paper, two pages side by side in landscape mode with no preliminary page count), the DOS command line would be `4print -s -q foo.ini`.

So I made a `pif` file `4p.pif` in my Windows directory with the full path name and other PIF options for *4print*. I then choose `Add File Type...` from the `Edit` menu in Regedit. In Figure 4-6, you'll see how I filled in the Print Action, Identifier (which can have no spaces) and File Type. The Open Action was similar but the command was `C:\winutil\norton\deskedit.exe %1`. I then choose `OK` and exited Regedit and loaded FileMan.

In FileMan, I invoked `File/Associate`, typed in ini in the top field and scrolled down in the bottom list to `Mao's File` as shown in Figure 4-7.

I hit `OK` and voilà, i had exactly what I wanted — `double clicking` an ini file launched Deskedit with it loaded and `File/Print` ran 4print for me. I used the same File Type for `txt` files.

Besides `Add File Type...` and `Modify File Type...`, the Edit Menu has `Delete File Type...` and `Copy File Type...`. Delete is the command you need to clean up File Types associated to programs you've removed from your system. If you change your programs around a lot, you need to periodically consider a clean up of `reg.dat` but be sure to keep a backup for several weeks!

The `File` Menu in Regedit has a sole item besides `Exit` and is called `Merge Registration File`. It has to do with the ways that third-party products are encouraged to change your Registration Database — via an ASCII file with extension `reg` that is merged into the Database. It is normally done in the background by the product's install so this is an item that you will not usually have to worry about.

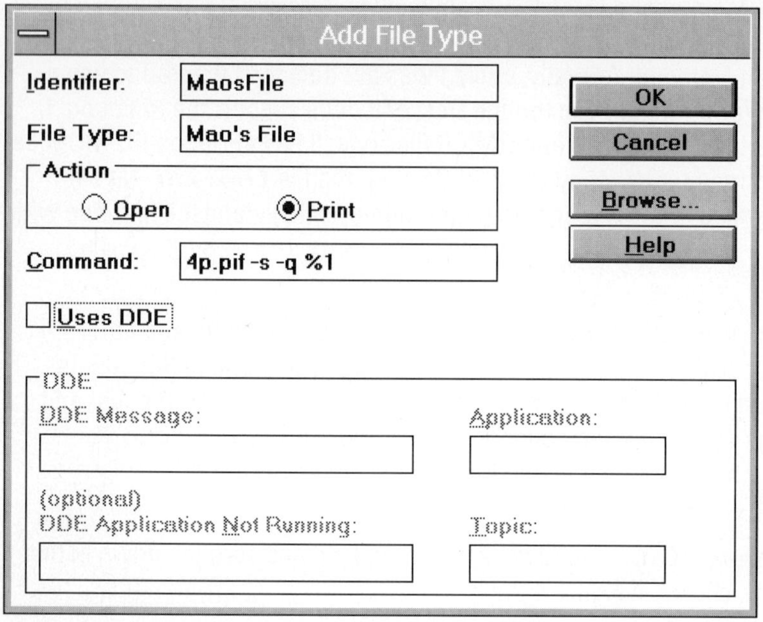

Add File Type

Identifier: MaosFile	**OK**
File Type: Mao's File	**Cancel**

Action
- ○ **Open**   ● **Print**

Browse...

Command: 4p.pif -s -q %1

Help

☐ **Uses DDE**

DDE

DDE Message: **Application:**

(optional)
DDE Application Not Running: **Topic:**

Figure 4-6: Mao's new File Type

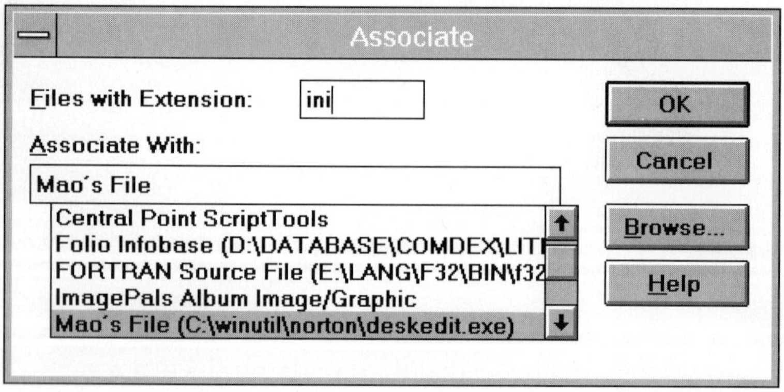

Associate

Files with Extension: ini

OK

Associate With:

Mao's File

Cancel

Central Point ScriptTools
Folio Infobase (D:\DATABASE\COMDEX\LITI
FORTRAN Source File (E:\LANG\F32\BIN\f32
ImagePals Album Image/Graphic
Mao's File (C:\winutil\norton\deskedit.exe)

Browse...

Help

Figure 4-7: Mao fixes the association in FileMan

The help file that comes with Regedit warns you that **Regedit /v** is something you should use only when directed by a third-party tech support staff. If that doesn't get your curiosity up ... but they are correct; you probably shouldn't use this mode for anything but looking, and if you do edit in this mode make sure to make a backup first. As an extra precaution, Regedit itself adds an extra level to editing in /v mode. In normal mode, it appears that changes are made to **reg.dat** when you close the dialogs for the various items on the **Edit** menu. In /v mode, you have to use explicit **File** menu commands to save your changes.

Figure 4-8 shows Regedit in /v mode showing all the data that AmiPro installs. The real way that the data is structured is as a tree like a directory tree and the line at the extreme left of the window is sneaking down from the root.

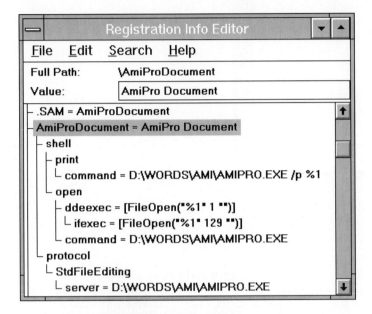

Figure 4-8: One view of Regedit /v

There are two types of top level nodes. One is the File Type we've already discussed above represented by the **AmiProDocument** entry. Figure 4-9 shows the MaosFile entry that I showed you how to make earlier.

The second type of entry are file extensions that appear starting with a period (and if you use the **Search** menu to look for a key you have to include the period if that is the key you are looking for). These can have the form of setting the entry to the identifier of a File Type as is true for the Ami's **.SAM** entry. Or they can take the form you see in Figure 4-9 for the **.bas** file of any explicit open command. When you choose **File\Associate** in FileMan, if you assign to a File Type, it places the extension in reg.dat in the File Type format. If you do the association by assigning to an executable it uses the **\shell\open\command** format; indeed, the entry you see was placed there by FileMan.

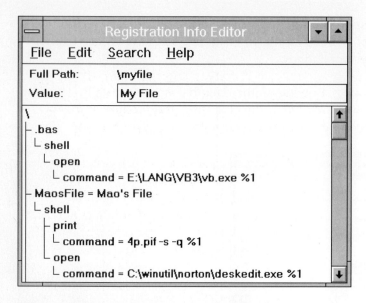

Figure 4-9: A second view of Regedit /v

Underneath the top level tree nodes can be two types of second level nodes called Shell and Protocol. The Shell node has below it the Open and Print command that we have already discussed and the Protocol has OLE server information.

This is true for every OLE 1.0 registration database that I've seen but with the introduction of OLE 2.0, there are some other kinds of top level nodes like Interface and nodes called Clsid at every level. These involve the technical guts of OLE 2.0 and are way beyond what end users need to worry about.

While Regedit displays File Types in alphabetical order, Regedit /v is like an archaeologist. It displays them in the order they were added with the newest additions on top. One tip is that it is easier to use Regedit /v with the applet maximized. I'd emphasize once again that Regedit /v is only for the fearless and should be used to look rather than edit, at least by most users.

Put that Package Over in the Corner

> When a man is wrapped up in himself, he makes a pretty small package.
>
> — John Ruskin

What if you want to access an program that is not an OLE server via OLE. Or how about if you like the way Sound Recorder encapsulates a sound with a Microphone icon you can double click and you'd like to do something similar with a picture but darned if it doesn't always insist on pasting in as a bitmap that shows.

Sounds like hopeless tasks but they are not thanks to Object Packager, one of the applets installed in the **Accessories** group of ProgMan. Packager lets set up packages which you can paste via the clipboard into any OLE client. You get to specify the contents of the package and what icon will be used to display the package.

The contents can be an OLE object pasted from the clipboard, a file associated to an OLE file type, a Windows **exe** file (winapps only) or a DOS command line. You can **Browse...** to pick the icon to use. Packager itself shows a split screen with the icon on the left and the contents on the right. Normally the contents are described by words but if the contents were pasted in and are a picture you can display the picture (in Object Packager; it is the icon that is always displayed in the OLE client).

You can use packages to set up Write documents of launch buttons by packaging Winapps and DOS command lines and pasting them into Write. This has got to be the world's weirdest Windows file launcher but it works and alas is competitive with some of the file launchers I've seen.

This is a program of limited use but when its services make sense, it delivers them in a neat package.

Windows Utility Toolkit

> Nothing can have value without being an object of utility.
>
> — Karl Marx, *Das Kapital*, 1885

Mao's Macro Musings

 While keyboard macros can be a wonderful productivity tool, no program is enough better than Windows *Recorder* to make Mom's toolbox, so Mao decided to preface the discussion of that applet with some general musings on macros.

 I don't understand what it is about macro programs. They were long a favored tool of DOS power users but the landscape is dotted with the carcasses of discarded DOS macro programs. The first macro program, SmartKey went through bankruptcy several times and seems to no longer be available. The first big success in the market, ProKey, disappeared from sight for some time; the company that made it — Rosesoft — was reborn with a Windows product but then sold to CE software, the makers of the leading

Mac macro program who will continue with the Windows product. Borland made a big splash with SuperKey but stopped development after a few years. And KeyWorks, which I felt was the best DOS macro program, was also dropped when its maker found the market just wasn't there.

I guess the death of general macro programs was that macros were built-in to the major applications, like word processors and spreadsheets, which could do more than just record keystrokes. But they don't really replace the simplicity of a record-on-the-spot recording tool that works anywhere. Perhaps the macro program marketers never made the point of how useful macro programs could be.

With Windows, macro programs can do more than record — for example, they can see the menu choices you make and call them without going through the keystrokes. So the borderline between macro programs and batch languages is blurred. Still, to me, what makes a macro program so useful for on the fly operation is that there are hot keys to start and stop recording. Even better was Keyworks special hotkey to start recording to a set key combination with no questions asked about which key (since it was set) or about overwriting what is there (because this hotkey was reserved for temporary macros only).

To me, you have to be able to edit macros and to record on the fly via a hotkey for the macro program to be serious. By these criteria, the only serious keyboard macro program for Windows is Prokey (CE Software; voice: 800-523-7638; 512-224-1995) and it is still falls short in terms of what and how it records to be something I can recommend (but version 2.0 may be much better). Power Launcher and PC Tools batch languages have wonderful record capability and allow considerable editing but do not allow you to start or stop recording from a hotkey so they aren't quite keyboard macro programs in the usual sense.

I'm still waiting for a decent option in the Windows keyboard macro scene.

The County Recorder

> Dr. Johnson can be thankful that God invented Boswell
> before science invented the pocket tape recorder.
>
> — Reviewer in *The Guardian*, 1986

Windows ships with a macro program, called Recorder, that lets you record actions for later playback. It's severely limited but useful at times.

Probably the most important tip I can give you about Recorder is to remember it is there and to use it occasionally. Fess up. Have you ever used it other than fooling around with it?

To record a macro, you to start Recorder, arrange the target application on top (if possible), **Alt+Tab** to Recorder and choose **Record...** from the **Macro** menu. The resulting dialog is shown in Figure 4-10. You'll want to choose a Shortcut key (of which more below). It is wise (although not required) to type in a Macro Name and Description. For the other items, the defaults are normally fine (if you set the defaults the way I'll recommend below!) so you can hit the Start Button.

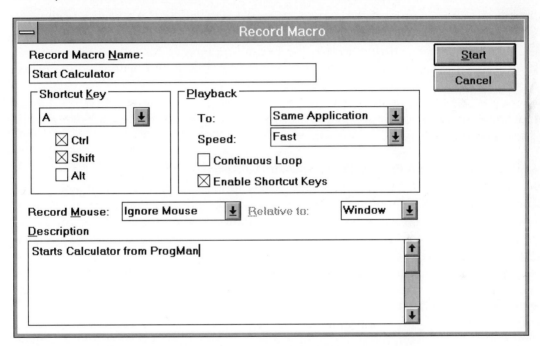

Figure 4-10: The `Macro/Record...` **dialog box in** *Recorder*

Recorder will minimize itself and you then do your action in the target application. Whenever possible use the keyboard rather than the mouse. So to move or resize a window, go through the system menu (which you should reach with **Alt+Spacebar**).

I recommend hitting **Ctrl+Break** to end the record operation. If your application is not running full screen, you can also stop by clicking on the flashing recorder icon. In either case a dialog pops up and you want to choose the **Save Macro** radio button.

You can later run the macro by hitting the hotkey or by double clicking on the macro list in Recorder. To reuse macros later, you'll need to save them in a file. I'll finish up my discussion of *Recorder* with a series of tips.

 Some of these tips use undocumented tricks that have found their way into numerous books and magazines and which seem to have been initially propagated on the BBS circuit. They go back to Windows 3.0. It amazes me that Microsoft didn't document them in Windows 3.1 given how common they were in discussions of Windows 3.0. Maybe they figured if they didn't document them, they wouldn't be as responsible for some of the silly quirks they have!

- Mouse recording is unreliable because it depends on size and/or position of the windows so it is best to only record keystrokes. I urge you to call up the Options/Preferences... dialog and set the Default preference for mouse **Record Mouse** to **Ignore Mouse**. You can always change that in the dialog shown in Figure 4-10 if you need to.

- Don't try to record keystrokes in a DOS session, either windowed or full screen. It doesn't work.

- You'll often want the Playback To choice to be **Same Application**. If it is, upon hitting the hotkey, Recorder will switch to that application and run the macro. The application has to be running for the macro to work and sometimes, the macro will not run properly if the target application is minimized when the macro is run.

- Ah, you may think, "I'll be clever and record a macro that calls up **Macro/Record...** in *Recorder* and so be able to set a hotkey that starts macro recording." Don't waste your time. It doesn't work. Any attempt to access Recorder while recording brings up the dialog to end recording!

- The hotkey drop down doesn't include letter keys, only function keys and keys like down arrow and backspace. However, you can assign macros to letter keys — just type them into the combo box associated with that drop down. Alas the default for hotkeys is to have **Ctrl** checked; I'd recommend using **Ctrl+Shift** or **Ctrl+Alt**.

- You can load a given file into Recorder by just using the syntax

    Recorder *filename*

An undocumented feature can be seen in Figure 4-11. I popped up the feature by entering recorder with a incorrect syntax, viz using –a as a parameter. It says the correct syntax for loading a macro file and running a given macro is to use

```
Recorder -h keyname filename
```

where –h is the parameter, keyname is the name of the key as specified in the next tip and filename is the macro file. For example

```
Recorder -h +^a my.rec
```

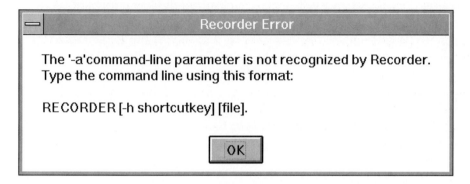

Figure 4-11: The only place the –h switch is documented

> Some books say that you have to use –H and not –h, but that is a Windows 3.0 quirk fixed in Windows 3.1. It sure is crazy to have a feature documented like this in an error message but not documented in the User's Guide!

- The keyname syntax is to use ^ for **Ctrl**, + for **Shift** and % for **Alt** and to follow by the name as it appears in Shortcut Key drop down. For a letter just use the letter. The above example shows the hot key **Ctrl+Shift+A**. (Don't confuse the + that I use in describing keystrokes and word to mean multiple keys and the + in the keyname syntax which means the **Shift** key).

- You can run a macro during Windows startup by placing an item your startup group which is recorder with the just mentioned command line.

- You can arrange to run a macro from an icon in ProgMan by using this syntax also but there is a weird gotcha that Recorder has. If it is not loaded, then the above syntax loads it with the specified filename and runs that macro. But if it is already loaded, the above syntax will restore Recorder's window, load the given macro file even if another file was previously loaded but it does not run the macro. Hey, it's an undocumented feature, so it doesn't have to work!

- If recorder can't figure out what to do during playback, for example if the target application isn't loaded, it will seem to freeze your system so that mouse movement doesn't have any effect. But fear not. After a minute or so (although it will seem an eternity if you aren't forewarned), it will popup an error box and let you go on your way. Or you can hit **Ctrl+Break** and abort any running macro including one in that state.

- If you want to launch a program via a macro, the easiest way is a macro recorded in ProgMan but you'll need to use the **File/Run...** command because clicking on icons is position dependent and won't play back properly if windows have moved or items reordered. There is an interesting gotcha here but it has a black magic work around! If you make ProgMan normal and record the **File/Run...** (or even if restore it during the recording), then the playback will work fine if ProgMan is not minimized when you try to replay the macro. But if ProgMan is minimized, the macro does not playback but instead you get the temporary freeze and error message. Some other applications are restored properly but not ProgMan in this case. But, if you use **Alt+Tab** to switch to ProgMan during the record operation, then the playback does work. Remarkably, it works even if the number of **Alt+Tab**s that you'd need is different than when you recorded the macros. Hey, don't ask me why it works. I only work here.

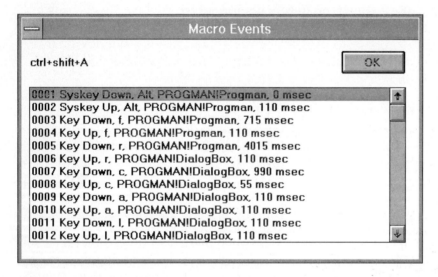

Figure 4-12: The Macro Events dialog

- You cannot edit macros but there is an undocumented way to at least see what was recorded, sort of. Highlight the macro you want, hold down the **Shift** key and choose **Properties** from the **Macro** menu. Without the shift you get a dialog much like the one in Figure 10 but with that **Shift**, you get the one shown in Figure 4-12. Each letter you type in appears in the list as separate key down and key up events. This listing is not complete; for example, the display is the same whether you do the **Alt+Tab** magic trick I just mentioned but the behavior is different.

- You can nest macros by having one macro call the hotkey for another. This lets you run a single macro that performs actions in multiple applications. Just have the main macro set to Same Application, record it as one of the applications you want and have it call a nested macro that was recorded in another application.

- I'll close the discussion of Recorder by repeating my admonition not to forget that it is there! It's sometimes exactly what you need.

Clip Joint

> The lights burn low in the barber-shop
> And the shades are drawn with care
> To hide the haughty barbers
> Cutting each other's hair.
>
> — Morris Bishop, *The Tales the Barbers Tell*

The Clipboard Viewer is simplicity itself. You've probably used it to look at what is on the clipboard but maybe you didn't even try the menus. The **File** menus let you save the state of the clipboard in a special binary format and later restore it. I'll have more to say about it in a moment. Don't think though that it is saved in a format that any other program can use directly. For example, taking a screen shot by hitting PrintScreen and saving the from the Clipboard Viewer does not save in PCX or TIFF or . . .— for that you'll need to paste into a paint program and save there.

The **Edit** menu has a single command but it is most important for some people! It is **Del** and it clears the clipboard after asking confirmation. Usually if you get **Out of Memory** messages, the messenger is talking about Free Resources but if you are running on a system without much RAM, it can happen that you run out of RAM. ProgMan's **About** box will tell you about the amount of Free RAM and Free Resources. If your RAM is low, the culprit may be the clipboard which can store megabytes if you paste a large enough item to it. Clearing the clipboard with **Edit/Del** should be your first recourse if you run low of RAM.

I've already talked about the third menu — **Display** in Chapter 2 in the Section called *The Delivery Van— Clipboard.*

It's gotten so that if I don't find any, er, anomaly in a Windows applet, I'm convinced I haven't tried it enough and have to keep looking. So I'm glad to say I found a doozy in looking at the Clipboard Viewer. Call up Winword, `Copy` some text from it and look at the formats listed on the `Display` menu of Clipboard Viewer. You'll find that nine are listed: `Owner Display`, three text, Picture and four that are connected to linking.

Now call up Excel and you'll be able to choose `Paste Link` from its `Edit` menu. Delete the link in Excel and now close Winword and look again at the Clipboard Viewer. It will only show four formats now that Winword has gone — owner display and the formats associated with links are gone. And if you try the `Edit` menu in Excel, you'll find that `Paste Link` is now greyed out.

So far, it seems not unreasonable behavior; it would be nice to be able to `Paste Link` after the application is closed but it is sort of understandable that it goes away when Winword closes. So I tried the following. Opened Winword, copied to the clipboard, and before closing Winword, I used `SaveAs..` on the Clipboard Viewer's `File` menu to save in a `clp` file. Then I closed Winword, cleared the clipboard (not necessary but I wanted to be certain that the `clp` was indeed loading) and `Open...` from the `File` menu in Clipboard Viewer. When the saved clipboard loaded, I looked at the Display menu and there were eight formats listed including the link formats.

I tried a Paste Link to Excel and it worked fine!! If it'll Paste Link fine without Winword open, why were those formats removed when Winword closed? That's crazy and the user loses functionality.

 I don't like your attitude Mao. Why are you only looking for one creepy crawly? Seems to me your job isn't done until you find at least two. So you haven't looked enough yet. Besides, the problem you found is in Winword, not the Clipboard Viewer. If you try with Ami, it leaves the links formats on the clipboard even after it closes (WordPerfect 5.2 isn't an OLE server so I couldn't check it out there). So back to clipboard old man. But do me a favor. Don't touch the computer with the minimized Mine Sweeper; I've a good game going.

Igor, do you think it wise to have Mao report on all the problems. After all, spurred by this book, Microsoft is sure to fix everything and we won't have anything left for the *Mother of All Windows 4.0 Books.*

 Fear not, Mom.

Do bear in mind that you can jiggle several different clips by saving to disk. Probably more trouble than it is worth unless you have a lot of boiler plate. If you have a saved clip and you can't remember the program that produced it, choosing `Picture` in the `Display` menu of *Clipboard Viewer* will usually display the icon of the program that produced it.

There are third-party clipboard enhancers available — the shareware Clipmate, the free Ultra Clip (both are on CD MOM) and Scrapbook+ (Central Point Software, Voice: 800-445-4208, 503-690-8090; FAX, (503)690-8083) come to mind. They'll store copies of what you had on the clipboard several cuts ago. But none has been so compelling and easy to use for the normal user that there is a clipboard enhancer in Mom's standard toolkit. Still, if you often find yourself wishing that you could save multiple clips, take a look at Ultra Clip.

Sound of One Applet Clapping

> And silence, like a poultice, comes
> To heal the blows of sound.
>
> — Oliver Wendell Holmes, *The Music Grinders*

The Sound Driver Microsoft Left Out on Purpose

> Actus non facit reum, nisi mens sit rea.[†]
>
> — Aristotle, *Rhetoric*, ca 322 BC

O.K., so you don't have a sound card yet. You're saving your shekels for a wave table beauty, so what do you do in the meantime? Beta testers of Windows 3.1 knew! During the beta test, Microsoft included a remarkable driver called **speaker.drv** that played **wav** files on ordinary PC speakers!! But it was pulled before the product shipped! Why? The beta test turned up some systems where it didn't work and there was the problem with interrupts that I'll discuss in a moment. So Microsoft decided it was likely to be a support headache and pulled it. Can't say that I blame them.

But in a brilliant example of letting you have the cake without MS having to eat it, the speaker driver is offered in the MS Driver Library and licensed to third parties to distribute with their applications. You can get it but only with the understanding that you have it AS IS and MS will not provide support if it doesn't work.

[†] The act is not criminal unless the intent is criminal.

You'll find it in the driver library of CD MOM and, if you have the diskette only version, as **speak.exe** one of the files on the disk.

Installation is easy. Put **speak.exe** on a diskette or in a directory other than your system or windows directories and run it. It will expand to five files — three boiler plate text files, the driver and an **oemsetup.inf** that the **Drivers applet** needs.

Now run that applet from Control Panel, choose **Add...** and pick **Unlisted or Updated Driver**. When it asks for the location, give the place where you ran **speak.exe**, and pick the choice **Sound Driver for PC-Speaker**. In the setup dialog, test the speaker and adjust the sliders.

It is remarkable how good the driver sounds on most systems considering that it is the silly old PC speaker. You can do wav audio only; no MIDI is included. And not all wav players will work. For example, Sound Recorder does but Media Player does not. In general, MCI wave sound will not work.

One other item to consider. By default, the speaker driver is configured to turn off interrupts when running (see *Port-Annoy's Complaint* in Chapter 3 for a discussion of interrupts.). If you change it not to do that it doesn't sound nearly as good but much tinnier. Turning interrupts off means when sounds are playing you can't move the mouse (try it while the hour glass is up in Sound Recorder!). And it means that you may have trouble when a comm program is running. So you need to change the configuration of the speaker driver before running a comm program. Highlight the speaker driver in the **Drivers applet** and hit **SetUp....** Check the box as shown in Figure 4-13.

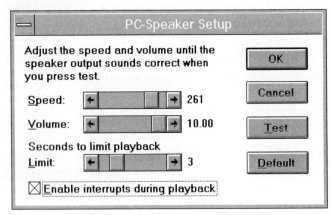

Figure 4-13: The Speaker Driver configuration box

Playing the Field — Media Player

> The media.
> It sounds like a convention of spiritualists.
>
> — Tom Stoppard, *Jumpers*, 1966

 Shortly after I installed my first CD that used the RunTime Video for Windows to display a multimedia video and it installed that RunTime, I noticed that it also installed a new version of Media Player, the applet that ships with Windows 3.1. After all, it had added `Video for Windows...` to its `Device` menu and it played `AVI` files without a hitch. Surprise! I had no new version of Media Player.

Media Player is both a very simple and a very smart application. It uses the MCI interface described in Chapter 2 in the section *Media Control Interface — Do You Mean David Gergen*. This is a standard API to any multimedia driver. Video for Windows installs the appropriate video drivers and adds them to the `[mci]` section of `system.ini`. It then adds `avi` to the `[mci extensions]` section of `win.ini`. When you ask Media Player to play an `avi` file, it looks in `win.ini`, sees their extension means that the AVIVideo driver should be used, it finds `AVIVideo=mciavi.drv` in `system.ini` and knows what driver to call. It doesn't need to know anything about the driver because as an MCI driver, it implements the standard play, stop, pause, resume command set that all MCI drivers have to obey.

 Actually, there *is* a new version of *Media Player* even though Mom doesn't have it. This new version ships with Video for Windows, was available on a Video for Windows demo disk and some CDs install it when they install the run time and some don't. So you may have the old version of `mplayer.exe` (dated 3–10–92) or you may have the new one (dated 10–28–92). You need to look at the file dates (or sizes); the About boxes for the applications are the same! Both CD MOM and the disks that come with the disk version of this book have the new Media Player. It's a lot better application so be sure to install it.

You'll see pictures of them in Figures 4-14 and 4-15. I'll call them the old Media Player and the new Media Player.

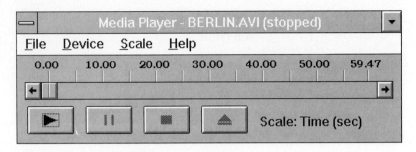

Figure 4-14: The old Media Player

Figure 4-15: The new Media Player

The new Media Player is more compact and elegant and has more features as you'd expect with a file which is 110K rather than 30K (the help has grown from 12K to almost 80K).

Both Media Players are simple shells to execute MCI commands from a VCR button type set. The old Media Player has four button. The first three buttons will play, pause/restart and stop (both play and pause/restart are used to resume). The fourth is an eject button and will work for suitable devices. For example, if you choose CD Audio from the Device menu, the eject button should become ungreyed and should eject your CD. This will be CD driver dependent — it worked on three the CDs around Mom's place and not on the fourth. The scroll bar acts like a conventional scroll bar, so, for example, clicking to the right or left of the slider moves the media by a "page" which typically means a sizable chunk. If you are using the old version, be sure to set the **Scales** menu item to indicate **Time**. The old version of Media Player does not support OLE.

The new version has eleven buttons in four sets. The set of three at the extreme left replace the four on the old version. The first is a play button that turns into a pause button when the media is playing! The middle set are movement buttons, to start, page back, page forward, and to the end (actually, not always, start and end as I'll explain). The third set of buttons below the slider are for making start and stop marks. You place them at two points in the media track to select what's in the middle for use by OLE. In addition, when one or both of these marks are present, the go to start/end buttons become go back one mark or forward one mark where there are also marks at the start and end as well as the places marked for selection. The final pair of buttons, to the right of the slider advance/go back by a single frame when `Scales` is set to `Frame`, a third choice added to the two in the old player (which had `Time` and `Track`).

Also added to the new version is support for OLE — the new Media Player acts as an OLE server. You can choose Copy Object from the Edit menu and it will copy a media clip to the clipboard to paste into OLE clients. The clip can include set marks, so for example you could paste in only a subsegment of a video file. Figure 4-16 shows Excel with an embedded video clip. The first frame is displayed. Double clicking will pop up a window in which the video plays out.

The new Media Player has two undocumented switches `/play` and `/close` when run from a command line. They must come before a file name. The switch `/play` starts Media Player and plays the file. When the play is finished, Media Player exits if `/close` is there. Media Player installs in the Registration database with these switchs so double clicking or using an OLE object will have both options in effect.

Igor experimented in embedding a video clip into six applications. All seemed to embed fine. Four of the six: Write, Winword (but you need version 2.0c or later; it failed in version 2.0a), WordPerfect and Excel played the video when he double clicked. Ami Pro and Quattro Pro failed to play the video.

The new player also supports configuring various playback devices. For example, you can configure the player to show video zoomed by a factor of two. If you are running with a video resolution of 800x600 or more, I recommend that you do precisely that.

Only three tips on using this useful little applet — the first two apply to both versions of Media Player and the last only to the new version. First, note that if you drag a multimedia file from FileMan to Media Player, it will load and start playing so that an ideal way to check out the `avi` files on a CD ROM or a bunch of `wav` files is load FileMan and Media Player side by side and drag the files over. If you drag over a file while another is playing, Media Player will stop the first and play the second.

Secondly, if you have a CD drive and would like to play audio CDs in the background, you can use Media Player to do precisely that so long as you've installed the CDAudio driver that comes with Windows (again subject to CD driver issues; the one CD around Mom's place that didn't eject also wouldn't play). So you do not need to go out and buy a separate program to play CDs.

Finally, if pasting a video clip as a full size picture as in Figure 4-16 seems a bit much, remember that you can use Object Packager to have it appear instead as an icon.

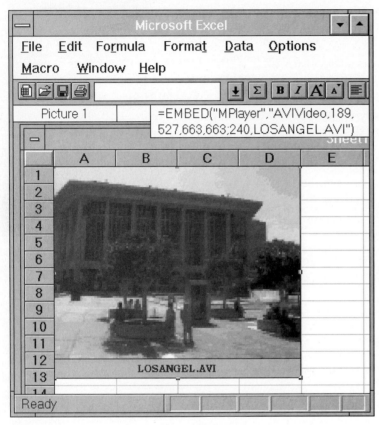

Figure 4-16: A embedded video clip!

Windows Sound Studio

> The sound of a kiss is not so loud as that of a cannon,
> but its echo lasts a great deal longer.
>
> — Oliver Wendell Holmes

Sound Recorder, as its name implies is an Applet that will record sound to a **wav** file. But it serves three other purposes.

* It provides information from the header of any **wav** file — the sample size, sample rate and number of channels (mono versus stereo). I described this header data in *Riding the Perfect Wav* in Chapter 2.

- It can be used as an OLE server for **wav** file. The new Media Player can also be an OLE server for **wav** files but the old version cannot.

- It is a rudimentary sound editor

Let's take them one at a time. You record sound by clicking the button with a mic on it; but there is no menu option and no way of using the keyboard except multiple **Tab** and **Enter**. Your sound card may have a mixer application which forces you to make one choice of input, typically among **CD**, **Mic**, and **Line In**. Be sure that **Mic** is chosen if you want to record.

The strangest one by far is the header information. To get the header information on a sound file, load it into Sound Recorder, and choose **Help/About** from the menu. The important part of that box is shown in Figure 4-17. Notice the fourth line which says **Mono 22.050kHz, 8-bit**. There it is, the header information.

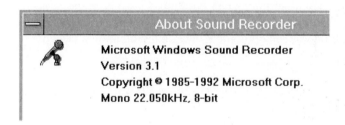

Microsoft Windows Sound Recorder
Version 3.1
Copyright © 1985-1992 Microsoft Corp.
Mono 22.050kHz, 8-bit

Figure 4-17: The Sound Recorder About Box

This has to rank as one of the weirdest tidbits in the Windows applets. Who had the idea of putting that information in the About box? Who'd normally expect to look there? Why isn't there an **Info...** choice on some menu? Crazy, isn't it?

To get OLE to work, just choose **Edit/Copy** from the Sound Recorder menus and paste into the client application. You'll see a microphone icon. Clicking on that will play the sound with no direct sign of Sound Recorder loading.

Sound editing is fairly limited. You can insert one **wav** file in another, mix two, increase/decrease volume and speed, reverse and add echo. It's amusing to play some sounds in reverse. What's missing from sound editing. The ability to deal with stereo channels, fade in and out, smoothing and noise filtering to name a few. Take a look at the working model of Sonic Foundry's Sound Forge (Voice: 608–256–3133) on CD Mom to get a feel for what a full fledged sound editor can entail.

What happens if you play `tada.wav` in reverse? Do you get a da–ta?

 No, adat, of course!

 Igor's right. It is data, after all!

La Scandale du WaveMapper

> I never give them hell. I just tell them the truth and they
> think it's hell.

— Harry Truman

 When Mom sent Igor and me out to make some sense of the Windows world, we knew that there would be some tough parts — things that aren't documented, or aren't documented correctly; things that go bump in the night. That's what we expected. That was part of our job description. Fair enough.

But something happened on our path to Windows enlightenment. We stumbled upon a dirty pool ... with carcasses floating belly up.

 Er, Mao, you misunderstood what Igor meant when he said that Microsoft was playing dirty pool.

Nevermind.

 Rooting out problems with Windows was in our job description; exploring nooks and crannies that had never been plumbed was in our job description, as was living to come back and write about it; finding neat and clever ways to solve your problems was in our job description.

But investigative journalism was not.

What the hell. We gave it a try anyway.

The next three sections describe what we saw, what we found, and why you might be very mad about certain things that are happening in the industry. Unfortunately, the whole story is mighty complicated — very technical, not the kind of thing you might want to read on a rainy afternoon, not the sort of thing you need to make Windows run better on your machine. And for that I apologize. Unfortunately, it's the nature of this beast.

You can skip the next three sections. I won't be offended. Neither will Mom. The technical stuff gets mighty thick. If you want an English translation of all the techy stuff, here's what it comes down to: Microsoft application folks got to ship and use a part of the operating system a full year before anyone else, thereby gaining an unfair competitive advantage. It's really that clear-cut, that black and white.

 This is a classic example of how Microsoft's operating system side sometimes only pays lip service to the "level playing field" idea — the idea that all applications developers, no matter what company they work for, should have equal access to information about the operating system. When the playing field isn't level, when Microsoft applications developers get the inside edge, Microsoft applications get an unfair leg up. As long as Microsoft enjoys a near-monopoly in the operating system business, it's important that they play fair in the application business.

 While testing out Sound Recorder, I came upon something very strange. When I loaded a **wav** file from the Microsoft Sound Bits packages in Sound Recorder, it would play fine but the wave form did not display and it could not be edited. Moreover, the About box claimed it was a 4-bit file which, because of the generally good quality of the sound, I was sure had to be wrong.

 Per Mom's orders, I checked out the details of what Mao had discovered. Checked with my buddies on CompuServe and in the industry. Some of this was hardly a huge secret since several issues were hotly discussed in the MDK section of CompuServe's WinSDK forum. But since La Scandale involves a small segment of the developer community, it hasn't received the attention it warrants — until now.

In part, the issue involves a line you may have in the **[drivers]** section of your **system.ini** file that reads

```
Wavemapper=msacm.drv
```

You may have it, but then again you may not: it depends on whether or not you've installed certain Microsoft products. You'll see how in a second.

The **ms** in MSACM stands for Microsoft *(rocket science, eh?)* and the **acm** stands for Audio Compression Manager. Got that? Good. There's another acronym you'll need: **adpcm**, for Adaptive Delta Pulse Code Modulation. (PCM is the technology used to encode the digital wave forms in **wav** files. Adaptive Delta adds a lossy compression scheme to the **wav** files.)

Compression is a way to try to squeeze down the size of files, so they take less space on disk. Compression comes in two types: lossless and lossy. The most celebrated lossless algorithm is Lempel–Ziv, the technology behind Pkzip, Stacker and DOS 6's Double Space. When you use lossless compression to squish a file, it can be reconstituted to an exact copy of the original. That's important if you're squishing programs or the data that's used to print your paycheck.

Sometimes, though, you don't need lossless compression — in some situations (like sound files) you can lose a little bit of data without really hurting anything. Sampled sound, pictures, and video compression schemes lose a little bit of data when they're squished: it's okay if, say, a few pixels have their shade changed or the amplitude of a high frequency sound changes by a little bit. Those kinds of losses are acceptable and have become very important as huge sound, picture, and video files are needed. Whereas lossless compression schemes typically squeeze files down to 25 to 50% of their original size, lossy compression schemes can squish files down to a very small fraction of their original size.

So you're saying that lossy compression can be used as a way to partially overcome the size disadvantage associated with digital sound versus MIDI?

Precisely! Someone using compressed **wav** files can squeeze more sound on a disk or on your hard disk.

In the Microsoft version of **adpcm**, the quality of the sound — the amount of "loss" — is adjusted so a 16-bit recording (CD-quality sound) is squished into a file one quarter its original size. The quality suffers a bit, but not much.

Microsoft has published the spec for **adpcm**, in a document called **riffnew.doc**. Folks who distribute **wav** files can thus produce their own compressed files. They can buy programs that compress the files, or they can write their own compression routines if they feel so possessed. That's cool. That's the way things should work.

The **msacm.drv** driver — it's called "The Wave Mapper" — will play **adpcm** compressed files. It actually reconstitutes the files on the fly, so the wave playing driver part of the operating system can play them.

In all of Microsoft's tons of documentation on Windows, I only found one cryptic reference to The Wave Mapper. The Windows Software Developer's Kit lists something called a WAVE_MAPPER parameter, and tells developers that they can use it. The documentation says that if a programmer calls a certain Windows function (**waveOutOpen**) with WAVE_MAPPER as a parameter, Windows checks to see if there is a **Wavemapper=** line in **system.ini**. (You can read about `SYSTEM.INI` in Chapter 10.) If there is such a line, whichever driver appears on the line — usually `MSACM.DRV` — is used to read the `.WAV` file. If there is no such line, Windows uses its own internal `.WAV` file reader.

That's how Windows hooks into **MSACM.DRV**, how it knows to use The Wave Mapper. In essence Microsoft's documents tell programmers how to use The Wave Mapper, but not how to write one.

 I confirmed that three components of Windows itself use The Wave Mapper, if it's installed — if that line appears in `SYSTEM.INI`. I know that The Wave Mapper is used in the Sound Events set in the Control Panel's Sound applet. I also know that it's used in the Sound Recorder and in the Media Player.

How did I find out? Good question. I relied on the `.WAV` files that ship with a Microsoft product called Sound Bits. It just so happens that those `.WAV` files play fine through The Wave Mapper, but they don't work at all with Windows' own internal `.WAV` file reader.

Here's an example. I used the Media Player to play the `.WAV` files that ship with Sound Bits. It worked fine. So I removed the `Wavemapper=` line from `SYSTEM.INI`, restarted Windows and guess what? The Sound Bits `.WAV` files wouldn't play at all. Sound of silence. When I restored the line they worked fine.

The Wave Mapper — this file called `MSACM.DRV` — does all sorts of things. In a moment I'll explain how you can make The Wave Mapper visible, but let me first continue the saga of my sordid discovery.

The Wave Mapper's "About" screen looks like Figure 4-18.

When I saw that screen, I deduced that The Wave Mapper must be smart enough to read these compressed `wav` files and automatically produce something the hardware can understand. If true, that would be an amazing capability. Among other things, it would mean that The Wave Mapper can read a 16-bit sound file, and immediately produce sound that will play on an 8-bit sound card.

 Whooooa! Time for an English translation, Mao. Sixteen-bit files produce CD quality sound, right? Eight-bit files are about like FM radio. You're saying that The Wave Mapper can take files created for CD quality sound, and play them on less expensive, older, more common 8-bit sound cards. Neat. I checked. You can't do that in Windows without The Wave Mapper: 8-bit sound will play on a 16-bit card, but 16-bit sound won't do diddly on an 8-bit card.

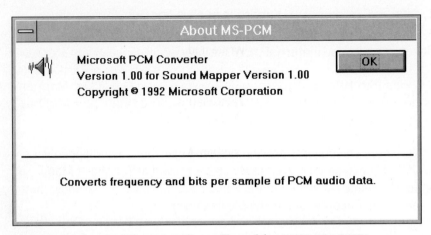

Figure 4-18: An other service offered by MSACM.DRV

You got it. When Microsoft products use The Wave Mapper, sounds in those products can be recorded at any bit-level — any "quality" level — and they'll play back on any hardware. That's a very nice capability; and in this case it's also an automatic one. The Wave Mapper is installed so easy for a programmer to use.

I checked this one out on Microsoft's EnCarta. The .WAV files in EnCarta were recorded at 16 bits. I double-checked that with Sound Recorder. Those files play just fine on an old 8-bit Sound Blaster Pro when The Wave Mapper is enabled. But when I tried to play them with The Wave Mapper turned off, I got an error message!

So you're saying that, with an 16/8 bit converter like The Wave Mapper, a vendor can ship 16-bit sound files, keep the owners of high end boards happy — after all, they spent big bucks to get all that sound fidelity — but still have the sound files play on 8-bit sound boards?

Yep. Without the converter, anybody who's selling applications with sound files has to ship the "lowest common denominator" — in this case, that means they have to ship 8-bit sound files. Folks who have 16-bit sound equipment but only 8-bit sound files aren't getting their money's worth.

It sounds like Microsoft is a white knight, with Windows providing a compression scheme and an easy way to translate sound files and other services to the world at large. No dirty pool; hooray for the Redmondians. Er.... uh.... where's the beef?

Here's the carcass ... er ... the kicker, Mom. I looked at the Wave Mapper program, the `msacm.drv` file, and what to my wondering eyes should appear... Up at the beginning of the file, the programmer who wrote it identifies it as `ProductName: Microsoft Windows`. Sure *sounds* like it's part of the operating system, no? And it *acts* like it's part of the operating system: the WAVE_MAPPER parameter shoots a programmer straight into The Wave Mapper. And The Wave Mapper hooks in Windows 3.1 have never been documented. It walks like a duck and it quacks like a duck.

But Microsoft didn't *treat* it like it's part of the operating system. Microsoft did *not* ship The Wave Mapper with Windows. It isn't available to Microsoft's competitors, developers who would like to distribute The Wave Mapper with their products.

I checked. The only way you can get The Wave Mapper is to buy one of Microsoft's products! You'll have to shell out the extra bucks for Sound Bits or one of various Microsoft CD products like EnCarta, Dinosaurs, and Musical Instruments. The Wave Mapper only ships with selected products from Microsoft's application division and has shipped that way since as early as the fall of 1992.

That's very different from the way Microsoft treats other extensions to the operating system: for example, the Video for Windows routines are available to any developer. Ditto for OLE 2.

Yup; I checked it out on CompuServe; even saved the messages where a developer was told in no uncertain terms that he could not get `msacm.drv` and if his users wanted the driver they'd have to go out and buy *Sound Bits*! So there is a piece of the Windows operating system which has not yet been released to (or documented for) the developer community at large but its services are available to Microsoft applications. So much for the idea of a level playing field — the "Chinese Wall" between applications and systems sides of the house that Microsoft management has talked about.

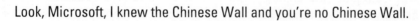

Look, Microsoft, I knew the Chinese Wall and you're no Chinese Wall.

Let me make one thing perfectly clear. No one is accusing Microsoft of plotting ways to hurt third-party developers. I'm convinced that Microsoft upper management didn't know all this was going on. But the folks who make decisions about what to keep internal and what to release to the world seem to have forgotten to think about the *ethics* of their policies. We'll leave the legalities to the FTC and Justice department.

While the infamous Chinese Wall language started with Microsoft, they now admit there is no total separation between apps and operating system. Programmers share the same lunchroom and often move from one group to another. But it behooves Microsoft because of this advantage of human interaction to lean over backwards — to give competing developers equal access to any technology that is in the operating system.

It's almost as if it never occurred to Microsoft that this kind of behavior is wrong. Plain and simple. <*Sigh.*> Sometimes, the mud slung at Microsoft only looks bad. Microsoft applications are caught using an undocumented whoosit or a hidden whatsit and after the dust settles it becomes clear that Microsoft didn't gain anything by playing dirty.

But in this case, Sound Bits certainly does gain unfairly, since it alone can distribute compressed `wav` files for users to play for events. And the Microsoft CDs which appear not to use compressed sound have the advantage of the Frequency/Bit conversion. I bet that Compton's and Grolier's wish their multimedia encyclopedias had the advantages that EnCarta had.

Another competitive advantage is that some competitors have been spending valuable resources trying to develop this technology over the past year where, by our reasoning, they should have had equal access to it.

The Saga Continues

After Mao discovered The Wave Mapper (he'll tell you how he did that at the end of the next section), I felt it important that he confront Microsoft with the information. We icons were hoping that upper management would realize there was a problem and rectify matters. I sent Mao as my personal emissary to Redmond to speak to a person high in the Windows/DOS system group but the response he got was most disturbing.

I learned of a group at Microsoft, both exciting to contemplate and disturbing in the way it straddles the Chinese Wall. It is called Advanced Computer Technology group, ACT for short. It is the current home of fonts and of multimedia technology but it is looking at other technological issues also.

While the multimedia group wrote the multimedia parts of Windows 3.1, they are not in the systems development part of Microsoft, but in ACT, so the argument of the official went, they could then turn around and provide services to the applications side. No problem, end of story.

We icons put our heads together and talked about this and decided the situation wasn't so clear cut. Microsoft has pursued what in many ways is an admirable strategy on multimedia, sponsoring conferences on CDs, including multimedia in the operating system and providing technology in Video for Windows that companies can license to redistribute by buying a single copy of the Video for Windows. Of course, Microsoft does this because they hope to do well by doing good. Multimedia is an area they plan to dominate — they have announced intentions to write hundreds of CD titles over the next two years. A thriving set of third-party products can only grow the market that they hope to dominate. But the point is that the underlying policy is a sound and attractive one and based on equal access to technology in products like Video for Windows.

 The 16/8 wave file conversion is a good example where the line is uncomfortably blurry. The technology could have been written by a third party for their own product and only used by their product. But it wasn't. Instead it used the undocumented Wave Mapper hooks that its authors, wearing their operating system hats, had put into Windows 3.1. So it seemed to me at best questionable. The use in Sound Bits which exploited the undocumented Wave Mapper hooks in a serious way was beyond questionable — it was wrong. In addition, the control panel applet and product name listing made it seem likely the module was really intended for the operating system at a later date. And one thing is clear to me: once something is earmarked for the operating system, there is a responsibility of equal access — if it is available to MS applications developers, it needs to be available to all comers.

 Just a week before we got galley proofs for the book here at Mom's place, Mao, with the help of my good friend Robin Raskin (Executive Editor of *PC Magazine*) made contact with yet another acronymic group at Microsoft called DRG for Developer Relations Group. As the name suggests, their charge is to deal with and help outside developers but it became clear they sometimes acted like the internal affairs guys on the cop shows trying to avoid problems like this one. It's too bad I didn't send out Igor because he is the bald one and what Mao learned is hair raising.

 I learned first of all that my surmise that this was intended for the operating system was correct. First MSACM.DRV will be part of the Video for Windows 1.1 runtime. Microsoft still insists that Video for Windows is not part of the operating system but no one outside Redmond believes that and if it isn't part of the operating system, why is it using undocumented operating systems calls? In addition a 32-bit version of MSACM.DRV ships in Windows NT!

I also confirmed that the wave mapper and its hooks are not documented. Microsoft claims that equivalent functionality is documented but upon pushing this point I learned that it wasn't fully equivalent (because of a technical issue called reentrancy) and the developer who wrote the Wave Mapper admitted that to figure out the equivalent with the documented calls would require "inspiration."

The reaction from Microsoft, once they decided this was a problem was rapid. Mao's first call with DRG was at 4 PM on a Friday. By Monday at 3, he had a second call in which he was assured that MSACM.DRV and a runtime license would be available to developers as soon as was possible. Moreover, Microsoft had scoured the CompuServe message traffic and calls to developer support and found 23 requests for information for licensing msacm.drv (from developers who had noticed it on the MS products) and promised to directly contact each of them to get them the driver when it became available. Sure sounds like a mea culpa to me!

Here's Mom's recap of the lessons we icons see that need to be drawn here. Microsoft is to be commended for agreeing to early release of the driver once the proper people were reached and it is clear that at least some people at Microsoft are worried about the problems, presumably due to a combination of a sense of a fair play and a concern for anti-trust laws! However, the decision to allow MSACM to ship with the Microsoft applications involved individuals at least at the product manager level and Microsoft has to do a lot — a whole lot — better job of sensitizing its employees to the anti-trust issue. Moreover, while the technology is now usable by third parties, Microsoft apps have had roughly a year head start, a year's use. Did this use give Microsoft a competitive advantage? At a minimum, some of their competitors were using valuable resources trying to reproduce technology that, by our reasoning, they should have had. It certainly didn't turn the playing field on its side but it did tilt it.

And unresolved is the disturbing implications of the ACT group within Microsoft that can write a part of the operating system one day and turn around and provide technology to the applications side the next.

So in summary, the use of The Wave Mapper is pure chutzpah on Microsoft's part.

I speak 23 dialects of Mandarin and at least one language associated to each Unicode alphabet but I have never seen this word hoots-bah.

Ah, Mao, the only dialects of Mandarin I speak are Duck and Orange, but I can tell you the word is pronounced with a guttural Ch at the start — chut-z-pa. It's Yiddish, one of my mother's native tongues since there used to be many natives in Rumania that spoke it. I learned it from her and when I was in, er, school I got to practice it with Meir Lansky. Anyhow, it is easy to translate Chutzpah, because it is one of those many Yiddish words that defies translation so the best translation of chutzpah is... chutzpah.

Windows Secret Sound Applet

> The secret of being a bore is to tell everything.
>
> — Voltaire, *Sept Discours*, 1738

If you have the version of the **msacm.drv** driver installed on your system, you have a hidden control panel applet called **Sound Mapper**. Check first if you have a line that starts **wavemapper** in your **system.ini;** if not you can install msacm.drv from CD MOM; see Chapter 11. Once you are sure you have the wavemapper installed, to make the hidden applet visible:

Add the following lines to the end of your **system.ini**:

[MSACM]

EnableControl=1

and restart Windows. When you do, the Sound Mapper applet shown in Figure 4-19 should appear when you run Control Panel.

Double click on it and you get the panel shown in Figure 4-20. This applet doesn't yet do much which buttresses the notion that the ACM that ships with the Microsoft products wasn't quite ready for general use yet.

You can disable the individual converters with the check box and you can access About boxes like the one shown back in Figure 4-18 which tell you what the modules do. But the greyed out **Config...** button and the potentially scrolling lists say a lot about the future. I note that the MSPCM Converter seems to be built into **msacm.drv** (at least the text of its About Box is there). The ADPCM CODEC (CODEC is short for COmpression/DECompression) seems to be in a file called **msadpcm.acm** also installed by the Microsoft program in system.ini. That suggests that third parties will eventually be able to add their own converters in **acm** files.

 At the risk of beating a dead horse, the scandal here is not hiding the Control Panel applet or the general scheme that seems to be under development. As with most of Windows Multimedia structures, it is well thought out and attractive. The problem is in allowing Microsoft application developers access to these features before other applications developers.

By the way, Mao, brilliant piece of detective work — but how did you find this applet and the About boxes?

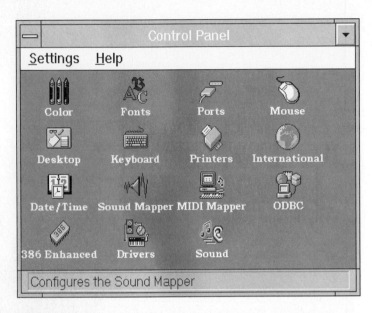

Figure 4-19: Control Panel with the Sound Mapper

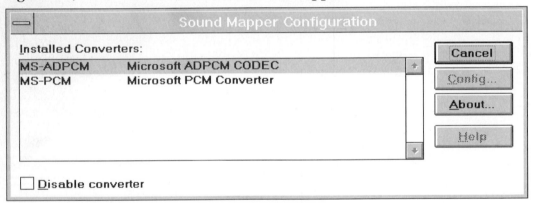

Figure 4-20: The Sound Mapper Applet running

Elementary, my dear Mom. When I found `msacm.drv`, I looked at the file first in the viewer in PC Tools File Manager. It shows you the exe header which is why I knew the module name was Microsoft Audio Compression Manager and that the product it was supposed to be part of was Windows! It also lists the C function calls in the driver and one was CPLAPPLET, which I knew from reading the SDK was the call that indicates that there is a Control Panel applet present. I also looked in the driver with a icon viewer and had my suspicions confirmed by seeing an icon that sure looked like it could be used in Control Panel (and indeed it was the icon that was used).

I knew such drivers applets were automatically installed in Control Panel so I wondered why it wasn't displaying. Such a puzzle was a challenge. So I looked at `msacm.drv` next in Magellan's default viewer which just displays text strings and I found the following bunch of strings in the middle:

```
EnableControl

MSACM

Disable%u

Record

system.ini
```

I pondered that for a while and decided to try the `system.ini` setting I gave you. Worked like a charm.

 While on the subject of Windows tilting the playing field, here's another interesting gotcha. On disk 1 of the Windows 3.1 diskettes, is a file called `win.src` (in compressed format). It's the initial `win.ini` used for new installs of Windows. It includes the lines

```
[Microsoft Word 2.0]
HPDSKJET=+1
```

And in the part of `setup.inf` on the same disk that updates an existing `win.ini` is the line:

```
win.ini , "Microsoft Word 2.0","HPDSKJET=","HPDSKJET=+1",

no clobber
```

Both serve the same purpose — to make sure that all users updating or installing Windows 3.1 will get those lines there. Their purpose is make the DeskJet work properly with the envelope printing feature in Winword 2.0. Service to their customers is the way those making this decision must have reasoned. Of course, it also saves the apps side of Microsoft some fair number of support calls.

The real point is that presumably, they didn't offer the same install-a-fix service to Ami Pro and Word Perfect or even to FlyByNight software's FooWord? Once again, Microsoft is using its quasi-monopoly in the Operating Environment to tilt the playing field, albeit in a minor way. And that's wrong.

As part of the reaction of DRG to Mao's talk with them, Microsoft gave me permission to put `msacm.drv` and installation code on CD MOM. You'll find directions on how to install it in Chapter 11. Before you do, call up the drivers applet in Control Panel and make sure that you do not have Microsoft Audio Compression Manager there because you could have a later version that some application installed for you.

The Windows Clock Manual

> When a man retires and time is no longer a matter of urgent importance,
> his colleagues generally present him with a clock.
>
> — R. C. Sherriff

Having made umpty-ump cracks about Windows Clock manuals, how much can we say about all the small stuff: clock, calendar, character map, calculator. Basically, don't read about it, just go out and *try* it! We'll say the most about the calculator, because if you just load it and use it in the obvious way, you'll not touch the menus and miss a large part of it!

Have You Got the Time?

> Since both its (Switzerland's) national products, snow and chocolate, melt,
> the cuckoo clock was invented solely in order
> to give tourists something solid to remember it by
>
> — Alan Coren, *The Sanity Inspector*

> In Switzerland they had brother love, five hundred years of democracy and peace,
> and what did they produce? The cuckoo clock!
>
> — Orson Welles

Oh, yeah, Windows Clock. I'd better not say much or I'll be in big trouble. But did you know you can configure the clock to give you a block to place in the lower corner of your screen or anywhere else you'd like without taking much real estate at all. It'll look like in Figure 4-21.

Figure 4-21: The Windows Clock

You can make it take even less height if you don't want the date shown (although you can't alter the width). The trick is to use the setting menu to be digital, turn off seconds, and to pick No Title. Then adjust the size to what you want it to be and the position. Consider if you'd like Clock to always float on top — if so, there is a choice on the System Menu for that (don't ask me why it isn't on the Settings menu; makes no sense to me either). Call up TaskMan, and choose **End Task**. It'll exit remembering all the settings including no title. Now just put clock in your **StartUp** group. Do not minimize it, which makes the time small but doesn't display the date.

Having said this, I should point out that there are better solutions. Mom's favorite is Almanac which I'll discuss in Chapter 5. You'll find several other clocks on CD MOM. Perhaps the cleverest is Bar Clock which places the time in the title bar of the active application. And I should mention All the Time which is free.

Let's Make It a Date

> A calendar, a calendar! look in the almanack; find out moonshine.
>
> — William Shakespeare, *A Midsummer-Night's Dream*, Act: III, Scene: i

Calendar breaks the mold that applets meet your needs if your needs are modest. It's really not very functional. You can't get a year at a glance for dates, or a week at a glance for appointments. You can't configure it to come up in month view (although bear in mind that double clicking the date written in English toggles between the two views). Appointments can only be at preset times and if you want an appointment at a quarter past, you'll need to display the entire day in 15-minute increments. I could go on and on complaining about this turkey, but I'll spare us both. You can save some disk space and delete `calendar.exe` and `calendar.hlp` from your disk.

If you need what Calendar is supposed to offer, you have some interesting options. For views of calendar with holidays, birthdays, etc. shown, Mom's Toolbox has Almanac which I'll discuss in Chapter 5. It has some support for appointments but is limited as a full fledged appointment manager. If you want appointment control, consider a full fledged PIM. The best options are Lotus' Organizer, Polaris' PackRat, Jensen-Jones' Commence, Abaresque's Ecco, and Okna's Desktop Set. You'll find part Desktop Set Jr, a free part of the Desktop Set (that includes a slick calendar) as a trial application on CD MOM.

How Much Is Two and Two?

Reeling and Writhing, of course, to begin with the Mock Turtle replied,
and the different branches of Arithmetic
Ambition, Distraction, Uglification, and Derision.

— Lewis Carroll, *Alice's Adventures in Wonderland*

Windows Calculator (Figure 4-22) is the Clark Kent of the Applets. Load it up as installed and it looks like an on screen version of the gizmos you can get at Kmart for under 10 bucks. Four arithmetic functions with a single element memory. Handy because you can copy numbers to the clipboard but hardly something to spend more than a sentence on.

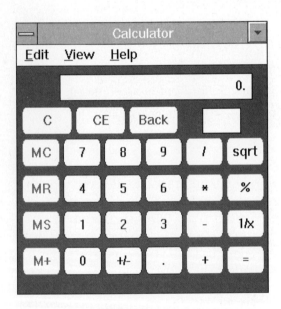

Figure 4-22: Mild mannered Calculator

Ah, but pull down the **View** menu and pick **Scientific** (Figure 4-23). Wow, this thing is on steroids! It is a scientific calculator, a programmer's calculator and statistics evaluator, all in one!

For programmers, it can compute in binary, hex and octal as well as decimal. The letters A-F at the bottom right are for entry of hex numbers. Many of the funny buttons on the right are for programmers only: And, Xor, Not, Or, and Lsh (left shift) are all binary operations that are needed by some programmers.

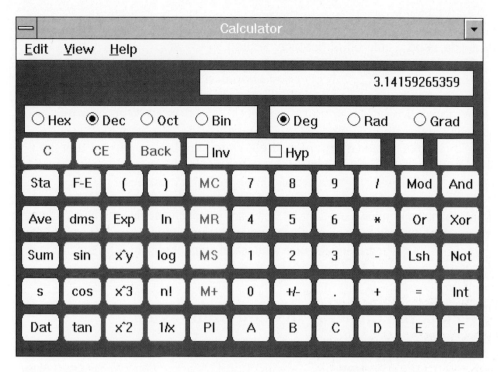

Figure 4-23: Calculator after stepping out of the phone booth

For scientists, there are trigonometric functions including hyperbolic and inverse functions and it even knows Pi to 12 places. It can display in scientific notation (the **F-E** button) and can convert to degree/minutes/seconds (the **dms** button).

The left hand column is the statistics module. Hitting the **Sta** button brings up a special statistic box. You can enter data by typing it into the calculator and hitting the **Dat** button. If you have a set of numbers in an ASCII file that you want to compute statistics on, there is an awkward way to enter them all into the statistic box: load the file into Notepad, add the character \ at the end of each line, select all lines, copy to the clipboard, activate the calculator (make sure that the statistics box is open but the calculator itself is active) and paste (the \ is interpreted as the **Dat** button but only during a paste operation!). While the statistics box is open, you can compute the average, the mean of the squares (check **Inv** and then the **Ave** button), the Sum, the Standard deviation with n-1 population weighting (Click the **s** button) or with n population weighting (check **Inv** and then click **s**).

 The calculator really is close to being a great applet but it has a few bizarre twists that keep it in its place. Why is the button labeled s rather than std? Why isn't there an easier way to load ASCII data? Why is the exponential function only available as the Inv ln? Why aren't accelerator keys underlined? Does hitting S do the `Sum` with a cap s or `sin` with a small s? (it's sin!). Close, but it coulda used a little bit of usability testing.

The calculator that ships with Windows is good enough that it is hard to imagine anyone going out to purchase another, unless they need a true high-end math package like MathCAD, Mathematica or Maple. But if you get the Norton Desktop, it comes with a three mode calculator — the plain calculator is enhanced by having a tape you can annotate with text, save and later recall. Alas, there is no simple way to save it as an ASCII file. The Scientific and Financial calculators are powerful but not easy to figure out unless you are familiar with the actual calculators on which they are modeled.

One final tip on Windows calculators. Folks are so used to seeing the numbers on screen, that they think they have to enter numbers with the mouse. Not so; you can enter from the keyboard. Indeed with a bunch of number to sum, hit NumLock and use the keypad.

What the Heck Is the Code for the Copyright Symbol?

> We need symbols to protect us from ourselves.
>
> — Edward Bond, *Narrow Road to the Deep North*

Character Map is a such a simple little utility that users often forget that it is there. It displays a font of your choice showing the character from ASCII code 32 up to 255 (see Figure 2-25 in Chapter 2). Press a character (click and hold) and it is shown blown up. Double click and it is copied to a holding area called `Characters to Copy`. Hit the `Copy` button and it is copied to the Clipboard.

By clicking in the `Characters to Copy` box, you can choose where the next character you double click gets put rather than just have them entered left to right. My friend the Rabbi used to use this trick to enter expressions right to left in a Hebrew font and then paste them into Winword. He's since gotten Hebrew Windows, available in the US from Glyph System (Voice: (508)470–1317).

That leaves one question open; when you copy from character map to the clipboard and then paste to an application, does the font information get pasted in also? Seemed simple enough so Mom asked Igor to do the tests. Here's his report:

Boy, oh, boy. Nothing is simple in Windows is it? I tried the paste test (hmm, sounds like a taste test doesn't it?) into the three main word processors in the version that I had at the time: Ami Pro 3.0, Word for Windows 2.0 and Word Perfect for Windows 5.2. Started out with the Wingding font. Pasted with the proper font into Ami and Winword — neato. Word Perfect, though ignored the font information, even if I used `Paste Special` with RTF format. Simple story I figured; Word Perfect flunked but Ami, Winword and Character Map passed.

Then since I had some time on my hands, I tried another font. Boy is Mom correct when she says that idle hands are the devil's work. What I found was nothing short of weird. There were some fonts that I could copy to the clipboard and have them display fine in the clipboard viewer, but when pasted into Winword, the Winword current font was used. Worse, both Ami and Word Perfect said they were unable to paste the sample (for example, Ami gave the error message `Unable to import all of .` although `Paste Special/Text` did paste in (without font information as is to be expected with a text only paste).

The TrueType fonts that ship with Windows and the fonts from Microsoft and Monotype all pasted properly as did a font that had been made from Font Monger starting with PostScript. But fonts from Bitstream, Cassedy & Greene, Davka and Kaballah all showed the strange `Unable to Paste` phenomenon. I'll never understand Windows!

 I ran this one past the font experts at Microsoft who found that the problem was that some TrueType fonts didn't quite follow the spec and left out a supposedly required field in the header (the PANTOSE number). Character Map did not react gracefully to this problem. In more recent releases of their fonts Bitstream has fixed this glitch.

One final remark; if you are using character map to enter non-standard symbols like © and ™, Mom's Toolbox has a better solution, the free Compose utility discussed in Chapter 5 and found on CD MOM and on the disks.

Applications on a Diet

> The best doctors in the world are Doctor Diet, Doctor Quiet
> and Doctor Merryman.
>
> — Jonathan Swift

Besides Write, Windows mini-word processor, the Windows box includes three other mini-applets: a communication program, a bitmap editor and a, what for lack of a better term, we'll call a flat file database. If you've recently used a real application in these categories, you know these mini-applications are toys. But the first two follow the pattern of being good enough for the needs of some — indeed, ten years ago, they'd have been competitive with some of the standard offerings of the time.

A Terminal Case

> Once there was an elephant
> Who tried to use the telephant
> No! No! I mean an elephone
> Who tried to use the telephone.
>
> — Laura Elizabeth Richards, *Eletelephony*

Windows Terminal, the communications program included with Windows would do poorly on all the Magazine's standard check lists. Its only terminal emulations are TTY, VT-52 and VT-100 and in particular it is missing ANSI-BBS. Its only binary transfer protocols are Xmodem/CRC and Kermit (it only has the Kermit transfers and is not a Kermit server) and, in particular, it is missing Zmodem which has become a requirement for inclusion in *PC Magazine* reviews. Its scripting language is primitive. It has no dialing directory and no provision for entering logon information (name and password).

Igor, when Mom gave you the assignment of reporting on *Terminal*, I figured you do a great job and you have but, you know, Terminal has no scripting language at all.

I know. How much more primitive can you get?

I'd better warn the comm aficionados to skip to the next section. Unlike any other area of software (other than operating systems) Communication seems to be like a religion to its users. Oh, sure you'll be able to get the worshipers of the Church of Word Perfect to complain if you say bad things about it, but if you say "but I don't care about printer settings", they'll shrug their shoulders. But say that Zmodem isn't that important or confuse baud and bps and you'll be threatened with hellfire or worse.

On the other hand, Terminal is far from a dog. It works with virtually any modem. It has no formal dialing directory but you can save settings including a phone number in a **trm** file and load those as needed. It lets you set up 40 buttons you can use to store password and logon name (and Igor was right after all, it has about five very primitive script command you'll find in online help under **Assigning Tasks to Function Keys**).

It really depends on your usage, style and budget. If you log on to a local BBS every day with a general purpose comm program, you definitely want to upgrade from Terminal. But if your access is like Mao's who uses dedicated programs to access

CompuServe and MCImail and only uses a comm program for an occasional call to a company BBS for their latest driver, you'll likely find Terminal more than adequate.

 Yeah, Terminal would likely suffice for my needs but I've been using ProComm so long that I remember when it was still shareware. ProComm for Windows is one slick puppy and I enjoy using it. I've also heard good things about Crosstalk for Windows and HyperAccess for Windows.

 But ya know, all those magazine reviews focus on stuff like the script language and if the program can do transfers at 10 gazillion baud or support 38 terminal emulations. They have to or the comm fanatics will burn them in effigy. But I never use a script or go over 9600 baud, so I go for *Microphone* which is the easiest Windows comm program to use.

I'll talk separately about CompuServe access programs in Chapter 6.

Painted into a Corner

> At one point I found myself standing before an oil of a horse
> that I figured was probably a self-portrait judging from the general execution...
>
> — Peter De Vries, *Let Me Count the Ways*, 1965

 I remember almost ten years ago, the first time that I saw a friend's Macintosh, then a black and white machine. Mostly I was unimpressed but MacPaint was another story. I have little artistic talent and the fact that I could draw straight lines and boxes easily, fill in grey patterns and edit my scribbles just blew me away. Windows Paintbrush is an impressive program by the standards of those days but it not close to the current generation of paint programs.

In many ways, the paint market has split into three pieces and Paintbrush does a little of each:

- Bitmap creation programs

- Bitmap edit programs

- Bitmap conversion programs

There are many programs that do more than one of these functions but most specialize in one of the areas. Bitmap creation is a specialized function and I'll say little about it except to mention that Fractal Painter and its greyscale cousin Fractal Sketcher (Fractal Design Corp., Voice: 408–688-5300) with their ability to mock a variety of media (from charcoal to waterpaint) are the tools to look at if your job involves any kind of artistic creation. But the other two functions are important utility areas and I'll talk about several programs in Chapter 5.

On bitmap creation, Paintbrush has a complete set of low end tools: freehand brush (with some choice of brush shape), airbrush, straight and curved line, flood fill, text, and four tools that deal with areas (rectangle, ellipse, curved corner rectangle, and polygon) in unfilled and filled versions. But real paint program let you put down color with a degree of opacity, can use anitaliased lines, distinguish between paint brush and pen (via soft edges on or hard as you paint).

And there are selection tools, important for both creation and editing. You want to select to be able to make a cutout, crop and most importantly mask, so, for example, when you flood fill, only the area within the mask is effected. Paintbrush has only two selection tools — straight rectangle and freehand — and even more seriously, the selection only works for cut or copy to the clipboard. No crop or mask; in fact, if you make a selection and pick any other tool, even call up help, the selection is lost. The best image editors will let you select based on color, add or subtract selections, even switch to a mode where you can paint on selection.

When it comes to image editing, Paintbrush is close to worthless. It does have a zoom mode where you can change individual pixels but that's it. You can't even change brightness or contrast, let alone the sharpen and other filters you find in real image editors.

Finally, on conversion, Paintbrush gets an F. It only supports BMP and PCX and its color conversion on saving a BMP as a PCX is very buggy.

So what's Paintbrush good for? If your only interest in bitmaps is to make some small changes in your wallpaper, it will suffice and it is a great program to unleash a seven year old on. But if you have any serious need for manipulating bitmaps, look at the programs in Mom's Toolbox.

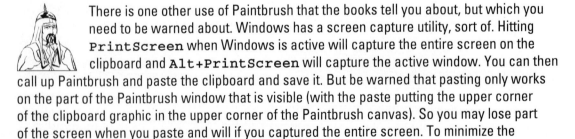 There is one other use of Paintbrush that the books tell you about, but which you need to be warned about. Windows has a screen capture utility, sort of. Hitting `PrintScreen` when Windows is active will capture the entire screen on the clipboard and `Alt+PrintScreen` will capture the active window. You can then call up Paintbrush and paste the clipboard and save it. But be warned that pasting only works on the part of the Paintbrush window that is visible (with the paste putting the upper corner of the clipboard graphic in the upper corner of the Paintbrush canvas). So you may lose part of the screen when you paste and will if you captured the entire screen. To minimize the

screen loss, maximize Paintbrush and uncheck `Tools and Linesize` and `Palette` on the `View` menu.

Pick a Card

> Trust everybody, but cut the cards.
>
> — Finley Peter Dunne

Cardfile, Windows primitive database, wins the Calendar memorial prize for poorness in the mini–application division. It acts like it hasn't been upgraded since Windows 2.0 except for adding OLE support in Windows 3.1.

Its cards have two fields — a one line index field that appears at the top of the card and the card body which can have text or "picture" but not both. "Picture" is actually an OLE container that will take one (and only one) OLE object.

I can't begin to describe all the limitations of this program but I'll at least mention the inability to search on anything in the card body, the inability to sort and the inability to shift from list to card view by any means other than the menus.

Cardfile isn't totally useless. If you want to store recipes on a computer, it isn't a terrible solution although you should consider one of the simple flat file databases instead. Cardfile will dial the first number that it finds on a card, so it is a primitive computer Rolodex but you'll get better use out of the free trial Desktop Set Jr. Phonebook/Dialer program instead — you'll find it on CD MOM — a really outstanding application (or get the full Desktop Set from Okna (voice: 201-909-8600)).

At one time, the fact that Cardfile was on every Windows user's disk made it an attractive way to distribute data and for that reason, it was advised to keep it around. But help authoring tools and other hypertext solutions have made such data less common. A search on the keywords **card**, **cardfile** and **crd** in the Microsoft's Windows forum on CompuServe turned up exactly one file and it was from 1990 with out of date information. The fact that it was still there says volumes about the forum management of Microsoft's CompuServe forums but that's a different story. So there is no reason not to just deep six Cardfile.

 Do you realize that we've only found two applets with their help files to delete saving a mere 200K. Either Microsoft is doing a good job or we aren't as tough as we should be.

Microsoft probably feels between a rock and hard place on Cardfile — I'll bet they'd like to dump it but they worry (rightfully!) about the users that have their own huge cardfiles to manipulate. But they should at least consider spending a couple of man weeks making it a touch more usable. I'd still complain it was a piece of junk if that all they did but it would still be useful for some.

I'm Game

> The game isn't over till it's over.
>
> — Yogi Berra

 Hey boss, you forgot da games.

 Games. Games! Games!! **Games!!!** You guys never get any work done around here you play Mine Sweeper so much. Get back to work. Or else.

 Psst, Mao. She's gone — break 'em out. Surely, you can tell me how to cheat!

 Well, just for a moment but I'll have to be brief because Mom could be back any minute. When playing Mine Sweeper, remember to use the right mouse button to mark what you are sure are mines. Once marked, you can't explode them by accident. And, if I must grasshopper, I do have a way to cheat, but I'll only tell you if you tell me what chutzpah means.

 You drive a very hard bargain CTO Mao. It looses in translation from the Yiddish but Chutzpah means nerve or gall — sort of. There is a Yiddish story about how to define the term. It tells the story of a young man who murdered his parents and then begged mercy from the court because he was an orphan. Now that's chutzpah. OK, I did my part of the bargain. Now it is your turn.

You can rack up high, I mean low, scores in Mine Sweeper by minimizing it and clicking again on the icon in ProgMan. That doesn't start a second copy but it stops the clock on the minimized game. Finish it and get fantastic scores to impress your friends.

 Gee, Mao. I fudged my best times by just editing `winmine.ini`. It was child's play.

 And besides, if you are going to play little games, put some variety in your life. There are some great game packs out there. The four Microsoft Entertainment Packs are superb — I'm especially fond of Pipe Dream from the third one and Jeez Ball from the fourth. And check out the shareware games on CD Mom. My favorite is Card Shark Hearts.

CHAPTER 5
Mom's Utility Toolbox

Every tool carries with it the spirit by which it has been created.

— Werner Heisenberg, *Physics and Philosophy*

All men know the utility of useful things; but they do not know the utility of futility.

— Chuang-tzu, *This Human World*

Mom's gang is a big fan of third-party utilities. If you are going to spend a lot of time interacting with a computer, every time saving device you have will save you time every day, day after day after day and that all adds up. Or if the utility adds a little spice to your life or makes computing more fun, that's important too.

 I heard of one MIS director who offered icon design classes to workers. When asked how he could possibly justify such a frill, this wise manager replied: "Computers tend to mystify people and feel foreign. But the first time that they design their own icon and slap it up there, suddenly the machine is their buddy and productivity soars." So, lighten up, Sonny and don't feel guilty at the frills you add to make your computer more livable.

Mom has a big advantage over the magazine reviews of utilities. They have to try to be comprehensive and include *all* products in a category, or at least a wide array of products. I can focus only on the utilities that I can recommend highly, a kind of Mom's honor role, the Icon's Choice winners. So I won't always rave below because it ain't necessary. Every product has an implicit rave just by being here.

The Virtual Desktop Shtick

A molehill man is a pseudo-busy executive who comes to work at 9 A.M. and finds a molehill on his desk. He has until 5 P.M. to make this molehill into a mountain. An accomplished molehill man will often have his mountain finished before lunch.

— Fred Allen

The underlying screen in Windows is called the desktop and that's a good name because it is a place to spread out your work.

But sonny, you keep it such a mess. Didn't your Mom teach you better than that? Windows and icons all over the place. It's a wonder you can find anything. Shape up and keep it neat — or else.

It's a hopeless task, isn't it? What you really need is a bigger desk. Say a stack of monitors so you could put Ami on that screen and Packrat on this one and Excel on the third. And a Rube Goldberg contraption to spin the monitor you wanted at any given moment into view. Guess what? You can do that, at least virtually speaking.

Virtual monitor programs, and there are literally dozens of them available, break up Windows into multiple virtual desktops and give you a method for switching from one desktop to another. Applications are normally assigned to a single desktop although some programs have a provision for you to assign an application as a tag along, appearing on each desktop. A tag along feature would be useful for a program like a clock that displays the current time in a bar.

So you could run Word full screen in on one virtual monitor, Organizer on another, and switch between screens without having to search for icons on a pile at the bottom of a screen.

 At a technical level, there are two general strategies used by virtual monitor programs. Often, how a program works technically is of no concern to end users but here the strategy effects how things function so they are of some concern. Moreover, in explaining how they work, I'll be discussing hidden programs, an issue of independent interest.

I'll call the two strategies the hidden program strategy and the big screen strategy. The former is used by only three programs that I'm aware of: Central Point's PC Tools for Windows, Fifth Generation's Direct Access Desktop and Xerox Rooms for Windows. The big screen strategy is used by many programs including hDC Power Launcher, Dashboard, Wintools, Wide Angle, the Amish Utilities and even as a utility bundled with the Windows Resource Kit.

Hidden program strategy is based on the notion of hidden windows. A program can run but mark some, or all, of its windows as being hidden. A hidden window sets up all the in–memory data structures that a visible window has but it marks them to not be displayed.

 Why would a program want to be hidden? There are basically two reasons. First, it takes time to set up the data structures for a complicated window, so a hidden window is quicker to display. So rather than unload a subwindow from memory, a program may choose to only hide it so it can blast it up when you next call it. As an example, Metz Task Manager, after its

initial load, hides itself rather than unloading, the faster to appear the next time
you double click on the desktop. The downside of this involves the problem of
limited System Resources that I discussed in Chapter 1. Hidden windows still take
resources and if they take a lot, the cost of the quicker reappearance may be too
high for you, the user.

The second reason concerns programs that only need to run in the background
without any visible window or icon. After Dark, a screen saver, runs as a hidden
program. If you try to load it a second time, it makes its window visible to allow
reconfiguration of the program. Try to minimize that window and the program
becomes hidden again. You'll need that configuration screen once in a blue
moon, so hiding it is good use of the hidden property that a window can have.

One warning if you use a task manager that shows hidden programs and
which you set to show hidden programs. Some hidden windows are not so
happy being unhidden and cannot be hidden again so if you decide to
experiment save your work first.

Hidden attributes are normally used by individual programs to control their own
destiny. Virtual monitor programs that use the hidden program strategy use the
attribute big time. Basically, *all* the programs on *all* the virtual screens are
running *all* the time. Those that are supposed to be on the virtual desktop that is
currently on screen, are run with their hidden attribute off, but those that are on other virtual
screens run hidden. When you tell the virtual desktop program to switch to another virtual
screen, it hides any programs currently visible that aren't supposed to be on that screen and
unhides any programs that are supposed to be on the new virtual screen.

So, with a virtual desktop using the hidden program strategy, your
desktop is as cluttered as it was before but a lot of the clutter is out of
sight. And with a wave of your magic wand, you can control which of
the clutter is out of sight. Don't you wish your real desk had this feature?

For controlling which desktop you are on, the hidden program strategy virtual
desktops will show them as linear or rectangular array, but that is a fiction
(convenient for remembering what is where) since they are totally separate
virtual screens. A 3x3 array and a 9x1 array are the same — just nine separate
screens laid out in different patterns for your convenience.

In distinction, the big screen strategy relies on getting Windows to use a larger logical screen size than is displayed and there is a significance to the layout of the screens. Suppose you are running an 800x600 video driver and use a program that sets up a 3x3 array of virtual screens. Then Windows thinks that it is running on a desktop that is 2400x1800 pixels. At any moment, you have an 800x600 viewport onto this larger desk. If a program is running full screen on the screen in the last column of row 2, its upper corner will be at pixel coordinates (1600,600) while if it is running in the upper left screen, the coordinates would be (0,0). Depending on where the viewport is, the program may be on or off screen.

 So a big screen is like going out and buying a bigger desk and spreading stuff out so it looks much neater. Your Mom would be proud of you.

The big screen approach has several gotchas that you need to be aware of. First, the various virtual screens really are next to one another. If you grab a window in normal state, move it so it is partly on the right side of the screen, and then move to a virtual screen located to the right of the current one, you'll find that you've moved the window partly onto the new virtual screen. This can be useful if you do it on purpose but a pain if done by accident.

Another gotcha can occur if you normally use a big screen desktop and run without it, say if the big screen program is in your startup group and you hold down `Shift` while Windows is loading. You load a program you use all the time and it is nowhere to be seen. Maybe even ProgMan is nowhere to be seen! The problem is that programs can store their location on screen and load in the same place the next time they are run. If they were on a virtual screen, other than the one in the upper left, they may restore themselves out of view! The solution is to call up TaskMan and Cascade Open Windows. That should bring the missing programs in from the cold.

The hidden program strategy has a number of advantages but one flaw that many will find fatal. The advantages include a clear separation of virtual screens and the possibility of assigning separate wallpaper or background colors to each virtual screen giving visual clues to where you are. The flaw? Because hidden programs are supposed to be hidden, the `Alt+Tab` cool switch which is controlled by Windows doesn't include them in the list of programs that it cycles through. So from a winapp, you can only `Alt+Tab` to a program on the current virtual screen.

Worse, if you are running DOS full screen, you can only **Alt+Tab** to programs which are on the virtual screen that you last visited.

Of course, a virtual desktop program has to provide ways to change which desktop you are on. Every one that we are aware of provides at least a special window that shows your virtual desks and lets you change by point and click (see Figures 5-6 and 5-20). But alternate approaches are a welcome addition — especially support for hotkey changes and/or a special Task Manager that shows programs on other virtual screens.

Mom's toolkit has three programs with virtual desktops: Dashboard, Power Launcher and PC Tools. Each is integrated with a complete launcher and shell to give you extra flexibility. If you have a different shell that you prefer, and just want a virtual desktop, consider Wide Angle, the Amish Utilities, the shareware Big Desk (on CD MOM), and the TopDesk program included with the Windows Resource Kit.

The Shell Game

> I do not know what I may appear to the world; but to myself I seem to have been only
> like a boy playing on the seashore, and diverting myself in now and then
> finding a smoother pebble or a prettier shell than ordinary,
> whilst the great ocean of truth lay all
> undiscovered before me.
>
> — Isaac Newton

Nothing effects the way you interact with Windows more than your program launcher and file manager. Which is probably why I've counted over three dozen available alternates, if you get tired of ProgMan and FileMan.

 We icons like to break shells into two categories — the Wagnerian shells, the ones that you know are always there — and the minimalist shells. Wagner must like it in the kitchen because the shells in the two kitchen sinks that I'll talk about in the next section both totally dominate the desktop. I'll start this section talking about two minimalist shells and end with replacements for TaskMan and FileMan. For those that like to stick with ProgMan, I'll talk about a pair of ProgMan enhancements in the next section.

Power Launcher

The product is called Power Launcher (from hDC, voice: 206-885-5550) and its components include Power Bar, Power Mouse, Power Keyboard, and Power Toolboxes. Are you getting a message? Yes, this is a Power User product. While that means that novices may not want it, it is a tinkerer's delight. No shell gives you quite so much. . ., why, so much power.

When you load Power Launcher, you can have (optionally) a Power Bar across the top of your screen. I've shown the Power Bar in Figure 5-1 split in three to fit on the page but you should picture it as one long strip. Reading across the strip we have:

- The hDC icon which gives access to its system menu. Power Launcher adds a great deal to any application's system menu: a user defined launch menu, a task list which shows hidden files (which you can unhide and switch to) ——and a Power Launcher submenu that includes a startup ecommand (more on ecommands below).

- An entry area where you can type in ecommands and execute with **Enter** or the check box.

- An arrow that calls up a ecommand builder (more on that below)

- The current directory that you can change with `cd...` commands in the command line. Press the directory name and FileMan is launched with that directory open!

- A visual resource panel showing free resources, memory, and disk space in a small size with a full panel accessible if you click.

- A box showing your virtual desktop set up with a highlight indicating which desktop you are on. Pressing the box will bring up a large desktop changer which allows you to drag from one desktop to another. The hDC task list will switch you to the desktop that an application is running on. You can also configure Power Launcher so that TaskMan causes a switch. You can also assign desktop changing to hot keys.

- Twenty teeny-tiny launch buttons (there are fewer at lower resolutions than
  1024x768). These are set to do things like launch Notepad but can be
  configured to do whatever you want!

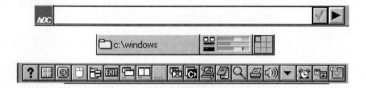

Figure 5-1: hDC's Power Bar

Central to much of what you can do with Power Launcher is what hDC calls
ecommands (short for enhanced command). Ecommands basically launch programs
or run built-in scripts. The program "launched" can be Power Launcher itself so you
can talk to Power Launcher from ecommands and, for example, tell it to switch
virtual desktops. The syntax of ecommands is a little obscure, so critical to the
working of the product is the ability to record ecommands and to build them with
the intelligent builder shown in Figure 5-2.

The command builder button bar, shown below the command window, lets you
browse to choose programs, choose from the special "microapps" that hDC supplies
(in Power Launcher and in a separate product called First Apps), choose a script
(which can make a noise or close an application or. . .), ask for user input
(including file browse to pick a file), call up fancy parameters (shown), and call up
a history of recent ecommands for recall and edit. The fancy parameters allow you
to hide an application (so a utility you want in the background need not show its
icon!), tell Power Launcher whether to launch a new version or use the existing one
and set size and position of the main application window. To decide on that, you
need not guess positions and sizes in pixels. You can call up the block shown in
Figure 5-3, place it and size it as you want, hit OK, and get the numbers sent to the
command builder.

You can change the icon and caption of Windows apps (hDC does not do that
successfully for DOS sessions the way that Dashboard, Norton Desktop, and PC
Tools can) and you can record keystrokes and menu commands to send to the
target application.

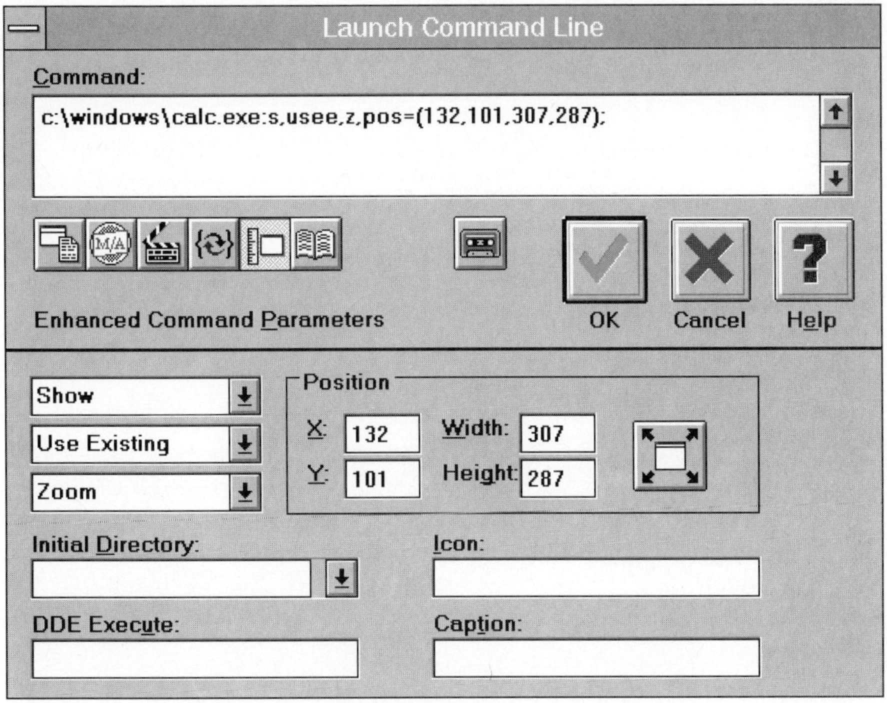

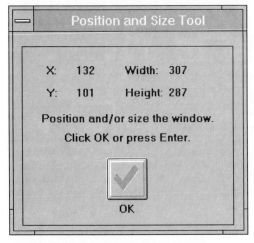

Figure 5-2: The Power Launcher Ecommand Builder

Figure 5-3: Position/Size Tool

Ecommands are not a real language since you cannot have branching or go tos, but you can string together multiple ecommands (separated by semicolons) into a single ecommand.

Part of the power in Power Launcher is the wide variety of ways you can start a launch command:

- You can type in an ecommand or build one from the Power Bar.

- You can include one in a startup ecommand.

- You can assign it to a keystroke (as shown in Figure 5-4). The stroke can be application dependent if you wish. You assign a hotkey to switch virtual screens by using the right ecommand and assigning it to the key that you want.

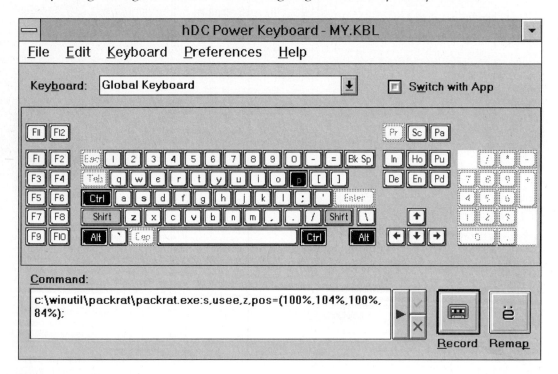

Figure 5-4: The Power Keyboard

- You can assign it to a mouse button.

- You can assign it to a toolbar. The toolbar is particularly useful because it can be application dependent. There is a separate set of toolbars sold for 40+ applications. The tool bar in Figure 5-5 is for ProgMan. The strip on the left shows for all applications and will, for example, launch FileMan, a DOS prompt, Sysedit, etc. and the strip on the right is ProgMan dependent including, from the top, New Group and New Item. The toolbar can be configured to always float on top and to travel along as you change virtual desktop.

- You could use the **power** command to launch an ecommand from a ProgMan icon thus assigning an icon to launch multiple programs.

- You can embed an ecommand in an OLE button so that any OLE server could have a button to launch the ecommand

Power Launcher is truly a power user's dream.

 By default, hDC shows its silly icon in place of the system menu of every application, just like PC Tools does. But unlike PC Tools, there is a way to return to the Windows standard. You need to add the following line to the [hDC Power Launcher] section of the hdc.ini file (which is kept in the Power Launcher directory, not the Windows directory):

```
System Menu Bitmap=0
```

Figure 5-5: Tool box

Dashboard

> Sweet Echo, sweetest nymph, that liv'st unseen
> Within thy airy shell
> By slow Meander's margent green,
> And in the violet-embroidered vale.

> — John Milton, *Comus*

Dashboard for Windows (Hewlett–Packard; Voice: 800-554-1305; 408-749-9500; FAX: 408-720-3574) is the king of the minimalist shells. It provides a tremendous wallop into the thin horizontal bar you see in Figure 5-6 (which you can configure to be vertical instead if you want). Below the title bar, you'll see some folders with tabs; those are ProgMan folders (or ones that you configure with Dashboard itself). Click on one and you get a menu listing of the group items. Double click and you get what looks like a ProgMan folder in a window.

Figure 5-6: Dashboard for Windows

Below that from left to right are

- A set of quick launch buttons for quick access to your favorite apps. One way of adding to these quick launch buttons is via drag and drop from the menu groups.

- A clock (not shown) and calendar. There is an alarm facility linked to the calendar.

- Three, 5, 7, or 9 virtual screens; you see on Dashboard the view of the screen and the buttons below which will switch screens. You can also switch with hotkeys. You can drag programs between screens on the screen panel.

- Resource information, including free memory (shown with the odometer), system resources (shown with the gas gauge) and free disk space (not shown).

You can pick a wav file to play every time resources drop below a user-specified level. Having the computer laugh sardonically at you at such a time has the ring of poetic justice.

- A panel of printer buttons, the chosen printer is indicated by a light next to the printer name. If you are running at high pixel density, you'll see several buttons here rather than one button and arrows.

- At the extreme right there are buttons to call help, a configure panel, and an about box.

Besides this, Dashboard has a pseudo-DOS command box as shown in Figure 5-7. You can enter commands at a pseudo prompt or in the Command line combo box. You can recall previous commands by using the **Up Arrow** at the prompt or with the command line drop down. You can launch both DOS and Windows applications from this prompt. It understands the basic DOS built-in commands like **dir** and **copy**. If you do a **dir**, you can take one of the filenames on the screen, highlight it, and drag it to any drag and drop target.

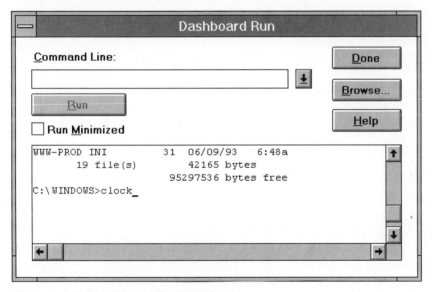

Figure 5-7: Dashboard's DOS box

The fake device **clp**, short for clipboard, can be used with the redirection commands > and <. This is the faster way to copy the contents of a file to the clipboard (use **type *filename* > clp**) or to get the contents of a directory there.

You can configure Dashboard so that there are hotkeys to invoke the main dashboard window and for the pseudo-DOS box.

Subjective About Objects

> An object in possession seldom retains the same charm that it had in pursuit.
>
> – Pliny the Younger, *Letters, bk. II, letter 15*

The term object oriented is one of the most overused and vague terms currently making the rounds in computerdom. Object Oriented Programming, OOP for short, is a well-defined paradigm for a kind of structured programming. Initially introduced in specialized languages like SmallTalk but is now part of Turbo Pascal and C++. But once one starts talking about Object Oriented Programs, and Object Oriented Operating Systems (OOOS), the precise meaning of object oriented becomes much less clear. You should be warned that an OOOS is likely to be in your future — Microsoft has its Cairo project, which will *not* be the basis of Windows 4.0, but could be the basis for the version after that. And Apple and IBM have teamed up to produce their own OOOS.

If the operating system is moving in that direction, why not get a Windows shell now that is Object Oriented? Several are available, notable WinTools and New Wave. But they leave me cold. They force you to think in a new way which may not be the one that Windows will take. New Wave tries to replace the DOS way of thinking of files. But since there are still DOS files underneath, the method is awkward, if, for example, you want to open several files in an MDI application. Both programs push the idea of acting on objects by tools. You may have to customize by dragging an object to a customize tool rather than choose customize from a menu.

None of the icons find this paradigm an attractive one, but even if we did, we wonder at the wisdom of using it in the face of the rather different paradigm used by virtually all other programs. So my advice is to pass on the object oriented shells.

Metz TaskMan

> But now my task is smoothly done:
> I can fly, or I can run.
>
> — John Milton, *Comus*

As its name implies, Metz Task Manager (Metz Software, Voice: 206-641-4524; FAX: 206-644-6026) is a replacement for Windows TaskMan. Since it is a powerful superset of TaskMan, and reasonably priced, getting it is almost a no brainer. Figure 5-8 shows how Metz TaskMan pops up if you have it installed as your Task Manager and you double click on the desktop, hit **Ctrl+Esc,** or choose **Switch To..** from a system menu. The key to what appears in the biggest subwindow is the drop down list that currently says **Accessories**. Hit the **Up Arrow** to its left and the main window changes to a task list or the **Down Arrow** on the right will display a list of group names. Change to a group, and it displays in the main window as shown here. You can display these lists as icon/text (as shown), icon only, or text only. There are a variety of sort options for these displays. Unlike the Windows Task Manager, Metz can be configured to show hidden programs in its task list.

Figure 5-8: Metz Task Manager

To the right of the main window are fifteen big buttons. The nine on the bottom in a 3x3 array are a quick launch pad — you get to put nine applications there (for example by dragging and dropping from the task list) and launch with a single click. I only wish there were more quick launch buttons.

The four buttons in the 2x2 block above the quick launch pad on the right are the equivalent of the three choices in TaskMan (to Cascade, Tile open windows, or Arrange minimized icons). There are four buttons because you can choose between two tiling strategies. The two buttons to the left of the arrangement buttons are equivalent to TaskMan's Switch To and End Task buttons. If you only want to tile or cascade a few tasks, you can select them in the task list and drag them to the appropriate button.

Below the main window and buttons is a **Run** box and below that is a status bar. You can type any command into the **Run** combo box or recall a recently run command from the drop down list. The status bar lists from left to right; date, time, free memory, and free resources.

To the right of the main drop down that says Accessories in Figure 5-8 are five small buttons. The first four are quick mini-file management buttons providing directory change, quick copy/move/delete, file search, and text search. These mini-file management popups are fairly simple without linked trees and are handy for quick operations.

The last of the small buttons brings up a small system report which will display: free disk space by drive, DOS and windows version, display driver information, and it will call any of the basic system files into Notepad.

The menus provide access to a wide variety of configuration options.

It's remarkable how much functionality Metz has squeezed into such a small space.

XTreeWin

> The tree is known by his fruit.
>
> — Matthew 12:33

Xtree (voice: (800)333-6561; (805)333-6561; FAX: (805)541-4762) was the dominant file manager in the DOS world and it has moved to Windows with a strong entry in the File Management category. Unique among the major players in the Windows file management market, it will display more than one drive in its tree window. Figure 5-9 shows such a window with just the drive names displayed. Hit the + next to one of the drives and the window shows the top level subdirectories, or hit one of the little numbers below the max/min buttons and all the trees will expand to that level (or to all levels if you hit the *). The flexibility of its tree windows extends beyond this to allow showing only a branch of a tree and extends to directory windows which can display multiple combined directories or drives.

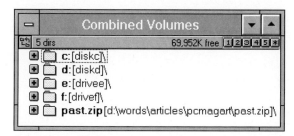

Figure 5-9: Xtree's drive/tree window showing a mounted zip

While there is a linked directory window for the active tree, you can also save a directory window as a separate MDI child providing an oft used directory at your fingertips. Xtree will remember your last window setup or can be configured to always load a given setup but alas you cannot store multiple setups and switch between them.

You can do the usual drag and drop between windows and, like File Manager, Xtree also serves as a drag and drop source. You can view files in a variety of graphics, word processor, and data formats and can print word processor and graphics files even if you don't have the creating program.

Xtree's handling of zips is noteworthy. It lets you treat them as if they were drives. You highlight a zip and use the **Mount Zip** command from the menus and that adds the zip to your drive list. Figure 5-9 shows a mounted zip in the tree window. Select the mounted zip as the current drive and the linked directory window shows the files in the zip. You can copy or move to and from the zip and view files in it as if it were just another directory, although the move/copy operations will zip or unzip along the way. I find this metaphor less natural than the zip as directory used by PC Tools, and Xtree is missing a few of the extra features of PC Tools zip handling. Still it is the second best zip maintenance available, and better than the specialized zip management programs you'll find on the shareware scene.

Rather than just supply a button bar (shown in Figure 5-10), Xtree provides an entire button bar maker which lets you make a button bar for any program. You attach scripts written to a BASIC-like language to each button. Alternatively, you can assign a run command to a button so that button bars can duplicate the functionality of ProgMan groups. Indeed, Xtree's Command Center will read your the contents of your ProgMan groups and make button bars for each. The script language can easily access menu commands and add functional button bars to any application. But you'll have to do that yourself since the only button bar that ships with the product is for Xtree itself.

Figure 5-10: Xtree's button bar

Mom's favorite File Manager for Windows is the one in PC Tools but Xtree is a close second.

Outside In

> Outside every fat man there is an even fatter man trying to close in.

> — Kingsley Amis

OutsideIn (System Compatibility Corp; Voice: 800-333-1395; 312-329-0700; FAX: 312-670-0820) is a Windows File Manager with some unique features revolving around file conversions, viewing, printing, and clipboard links. It's file management aspects are limited, but its viewer capabilities are outstanding.

The left part of its window has three viewing modes (controlled by the first three buttons on the button bar): A file finding mode and two much like what you see in Figure 5-11 with a file list below a directory list displayed either in list form (as shown) or as a tree. There are rudimentary file erase, copy and move but the key aspect of OutsideIn is the file viewer on the right side of the window. In Figure 5-11 the file viewer is showing a spreadsheet. It supports a vast variety of file types, being especially strong on obscure word processor types (e.g. MASS 11 or Sprint).

For many word processors, its viewers show formatting and even things like tables and OLE embedded objects.

It will print files it can view even if you do not have the underlying application on your disk. And you can copy a part of a viewed file to the clipboard, an invaluable feature. This copy to the clipboard should be standard in all file viewers but is not included in any of the other viewers that you'll find in Mom's toolbox. If you often need to look for files and then transfer data from them, OutsideIn is invaluable.

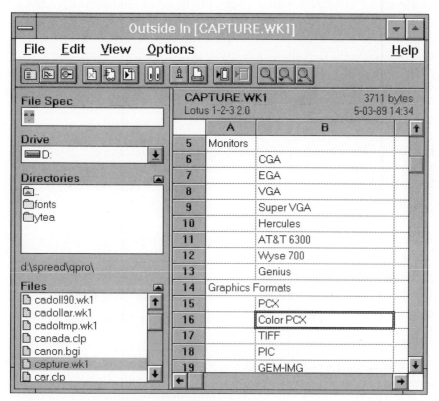

Figure 5-11: Outside In for Windows

The program has lots of intelligent extras to make life easier. The button bar is one of the few whose buttons really are intuitive and easy to remember. You can take any file you are viewing and tear it off from the program and leave it minimized on the desktop so long as OutsideIn is running.

OutsideIn will view a zip directory and let you view any file in it by double clicking. You can then cut and paste from the file inside the zip. It does this magic by unzipping the file to your temporary directory. The viewers are up to date including ones for Quattro Pro for Windows. You can control what clipboard formats are used when you do a copy.

OutsideIn has special integration for Windows' File Manager, for the big three word processors and for several major email programs. When you install it, it will optionally add an OI menu to FileMan with a View! menu item. Highlight a single file in FileMan and go to that menu and OutisideIn launches an appropriate viewer. For the word processing and mail applications, OutsideIn can be called from a menu item and can paste directly into the application doing the necessary file conversion along the way!

Windows on Steroids

"What's the big deal about alternate shells?" you think. You kinda like ProgMan and FileMan, although you wouldn't mind just a few little changes. Three shareware gems let you keep your friends but give them a face lift — two enhance ProgMan and one FileMan. All are found on CD MOM.

Plug-In for Program Manager

Plug-In for Program Manager (Plannet Crafters: Voice: (404)740-9821; FAX: (404)740-1914)) provides a variety of additional features to make ProgMan more attractive. At the top of most lists is the ability to assign icons to groups, as seen in Figure 5-12.

But that's just the start. Plug-In adds a top level menu to ProgMan and several menu items to the File and Options menus. It also displays the free memory and free resources in ProgMan's title bar, and it can display them in the minimized icon for ProgMan. You can also configure Plug-In to pop up a warning box whenever your free resources drops below a specified amount.

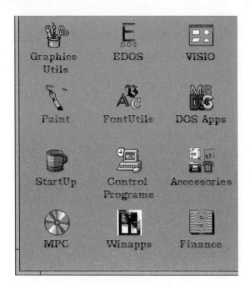

Figure 5-12: A section of Progman's Window when Plug-In is running

Having access to free resources on the ProgMan icon is very useful. If you don't use Plug-In, or one of the shells like Dashboard or Power Launcher, which displays free resources in their window, you may want to consider another program that displays free resources all the time or lets you see it easily. Two to consider, both found on CD MOM, are the shareware BarClock (which uses the title bar of the active program to display time but a simple click cycles to free resources) and the freeware Time after Time.

Two exceedingly useful items are added to ProgMan's `File` menu by Plug-In. One called `Install Application` checks your floppy drives searching for a program called `install.exe` or `setup.exe`. If found, it searches for `*.txt` or `*.wri` files and offers to let you read them (in Notepad of Write) before starting the installation.

> What an annoyance that Microsoft doesn't formally declare in the *Interface Guide* that the name for an installation program is `setup.exe`. As it stands, you have to type `A:\setup.exe` in the File/Run box when trying to install a program and, if that gives an error message, then try `A:\install.exe` (this problem is finessed if you have Plug-In). But some bozo programs feeling they have to assert their individuality call it `foosetup.exe` or something else with their name in it. Sigh.

The other new item on the **File** menu is a **Groups** submenu that lets you restore the groups to their startup positions, lets you specify an alternate startup group, copies groups, or most importantly, manages groups. The manage groups dialog lets you specify some groups as inactive; the group files are saved but no longer appear in ProgMan until you use the same menu item to reactivate them.

Added to the Options menu are commands to save configuration now (easier to remember then the trick of **Shift+Click** on the system menu), an elegant one panel SysInfo display and the configuration dialog shown in Figure 5-13. This shows the last few features — a separate quick launch menu that gets added to ProgMan, custom cursors for the main pointer and hourglass, and the ability to assign a shortcut key and icon to ProgMan itself. It is better to set a ProgMan hot key by the method we discussed earlier because it will work from DOS sessions.

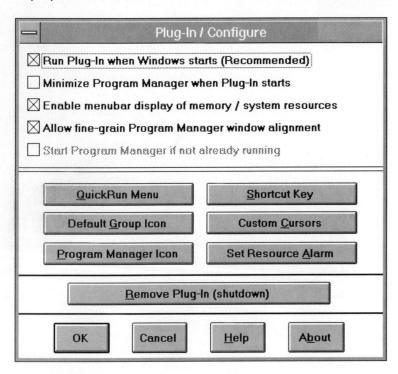

Figure 5-13: Plug-In's configuration menu

WindowMagic

WindowMagic (WinWear, Voice: 206-882-1530), a shareware ProgMan add-in that you'll find on CD MOM, provides a number of different services. First, you can assign your own icons to groups. WindowMagic goes beyond Plug-In in letting you use a drag and drop method to assign icons. Secondly, it provides what it calls Quick Access menus. When you right click on an icon, a text menu of the items in that group pops up (see Figure 5-14). You can choose one item in each group as a fast launch item and it gets automagically launched when you double right click on the group.

Third, like Plug-In, it provides an enhanced exit command which can restart Windows. This is useful if you find some programs have rudely eaten your system resources for lunch and you need to restart the process. Finally, WindowMagic lets you set up any group as a toolbar (see Figure 5-15) which you can minimize on screen and keep as a handy icon.

But that's just the start. Plug-In adds a top level menu to ProgMan and several menu items to the File and Options menus. It also displays the free memory and free resources in ProgMan's title bar, and it can display them in the minimized icon for ProgMan. You can also configure Plug-In to pop up a warning box whenever your free resources drops below a specified amount.

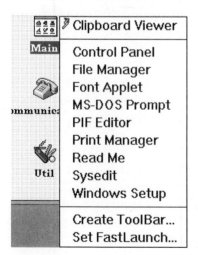

Figure 5-14: WindowMagic's Quick Access Menus

Figure 5-15: A WindowMagic Toolbar

WindowMagic and Plug-In have some services in common (group icons and enhanced exit) but they also have a number of useful distinct functions. They coexist quite happily so you can use them both, as Mao has for some time.

WizManager

WizManager, huh. I'm biting my tongue.

Want to give File Manager a shot in the arm at the risk of it failing a urine test? WizManager (Mijenix, voice: (608) 277-1971), a shareware program that you'll find on CD MOM adds a button bar and command line to FileMan and enhances it in numerous ways.

Figure 5-16 shows FileMan with WizManager installed (when it installs, it places itself as an add-on through FileMan's documented method of supporting add-ons). The two obvious changes are the button bar on the right, and the command line on the left. The button bar gives you access to every menu item in FileMan and to all the additions in WizManager itself. There are so many buttons that you need to be able to scroll them, which is what the pair of horizontal buttons next to the bar do. The user can customize the order of buttons. One nice touch is that when the cursor is over a button, it will show what the button does (in Figure 5-16, the cursor, though not shown, is over the first button, which, as indicated, sorts by name). This is handy when you are first learning the buttons and can be turned off if you wish).

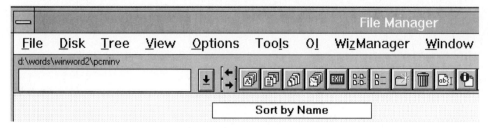

Figure 5-16: Wiz Manager's Button Bar and Command Line

The command line box will be welcome for those who prefer typing in commands to traversing menus. Shown above the box is the current directory for the command box which you can change with a **cd** command; just like in DOS except WizManager's command is clever enough to change drives if you preface the directory name by a drive letter different from the current one. The current directory in FileMan can be accessed from the command line with the symbol **;** so to copy all **doc** files in the current FileMan directory to A, you enter

```
copy ;\*.doc A:
```

in the Wiz Manager command box. The copy proceeds through FileMan with whatever confirmation settings you set there.

The command box understands almost 100 commands from internal WizManager commands (like **Mem** which displays free memory and resources) to FileMan menu commands to commands to invoke any of the standard Control Panel applets.

With WizManager installed, hitting the right mouse button anywhere in FileMan calls up a task list allowing you to switch to any running application (but the right button does not work outside FileMan). You can configure WizManager to show hidden tasks as well as normal ones.

WizManager also adds its own menu, shown in Figure 5-17, to FileMan. Most welcome are two Print Commands: **Print Tree** and **Print Directory**. **Print Tree** prints all directories on a drive with optional inclusion of all files and/or total file size per directory. **Print Directory** prints a standard directory listing with attribute information shown, either for the current directory or for the selected files.

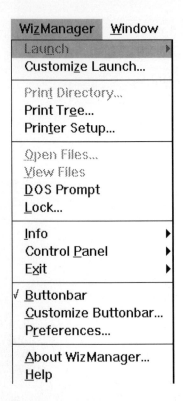

Figure 5-17: The extra menu that WizManager adds to FileMan

 I finally found a use for the `Generic/Text to File` Printer choice. WizManager's `Print Tree` command printed more or less properly to a file with that setting of printer. There was some extra garbage at the end of each page but I could easily remove that in Notepad if I wished. I could then print out in 4Print and get a compact listing.

The View Files menu entry does not mean that WizManager comes with a File Viewer. Rather it lets you link to a File Viewer of your choice. If you don't have anything better you can pick Notepad and even configure WizManager so that if multiple files are selected, it will run multiple copies of Notepad!

The **Lock** command is a password protection device. The **Info** command lets you get a readout on your system setup or on your disk drives. The Control Panel choice gives you access to the standard Control Panel applets and the **Exit** menu command lets you quickly exit or restart Windows or even reboot your machine (after a confirmation dialog box!).

You can also add a launch submenu of your favorite applications available from this menu or from the right mouse button menu.

Kitchen Sinks

The genesis of the utility category is very simple: in the beginning was Peter Norton and Peter said "let me unerase your files" and the public was amazed. Norton's magic trick was the start of a utilities empire. The Norton Utilities became synonymous with a well put together, elegant set of tools whose centerpiece was a byte level disk editor.

 Eventually, Norton sold his company to Symantec for megabucks, quite literally tens of millions of dollars, so that now all he lends to the products is his name and sometimes his folded arms in ads. He has become a patron of the arts and a retired programmer.

Then came a company whose initial big success was a product called Copy II PC whose purpose was to get around copy protection. These copy protection breakers were so effective and the attitude of the public and magazines towards copy protection was so negative that most software companies in the United States stopped using copy protection and the makers of Copy II PC had to find a new product area. They came out with a DOS shell which included a primitive disk editor. This first version of PC Tools sold for $19.95. Successive versions had price increases, added polish, and most importantly, more and more functionality. Eventually, PC Tools had everything including the kitchen sink — a shell, disk editor, file editor, calculator, cache, and defragger.

The makers of PC Tools, Central Point Software, gained considerable market share and Norton fought back adding a cache and a defragger, but not a shell. Norton was higher quality, but PC Tools for DOS was more of a kitchen sink. But a funny thing happened on the way to Windows. Norton and PC Tools switched roles!

Norton Desktop for Windows was there first — not long after Windows 3.0 shipped — and it captured a large part of the Windows utilities market, so much so that a lot of established Windows utilities languished. It was put together well, but with the inclusion of an icon editor, file editor, and calculator, it reeked of kitchen sink.

Central Point's strategy was shoved in their face. Central Point took its own sweet time responding, so much so that some began to wonder if it could fight back at all. Almost two years after Norton Desktop for Windows shipped, PC Tools for Windows was finally released. And guess what? While it had a lot, it was not as much a kitchen sink as Norton but instead, it went after quality!

NDW

Ready, take a really deep breath. Norton Desktop for Windows (Symantec; voice: 800-441-7234; 408-252-3570) includes Windows shell with program launching, file manager with built-in file viewers and a separate file viewer applet, virus protection and repair, backup to floppy disk or QIC 40/80 tape drives, erase protection and unerase, Norton Disk Doctor (including a DOS version for sensitive repairs that need to be done outside of Windows), File Search including search for files with a given text string, a full fledged batch language with a macro builder, a text editor, a system information utility, an icon editor and several supplied libraries of icons, a screen saver, three calculators (standard arithmetic with tape, scientific and financial), a scheduler, a shredder, and a character map type utility. Whew; makes me tired just listing them all.

The shell that comes with NDW takes over the entire desktop. A typical piece of it is shown in Figure 5-18. It shows your disk drives as separate icons. (F isn't a RAM drive but a regular hard disk partition on the machine where the screen shot was taken; all the buglets aren't in Windows, eh grasshopper?) Double click on a disk drive and you access the Norton File Manager as seen in Figure 5-19 which I'll discuss further in a moment.

NDW is distinguished by the raised icons that you see. These represent unopened, that is not running, programs. Double click on one and you start the corresponding program. You can place any program you want on the desktop but the three shown are NDW applications and have special features as drag and drop targets. One way of viewing a file is to drag it from an open disk window to the viewer icon. Similarly, providing the extension is registered to print in the registration database, you can drag to the printer icon to print. This is just like the way Windows File Manager cooperates with Print Manager except the printer icon in Norton isn't running; while Printer Manager needs to be running to act as a drag and drop target. As long as they will accept filenames as command line parameters, any unopened program can serve as a drag and drop target.

Figure 5-18: Norton Desktop for Windows Shell

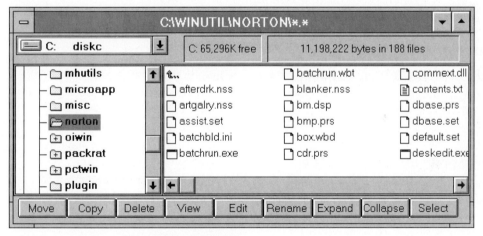

Figure 5-19: Norton's File Manager

Groups in Norton's Program Manager replacement, called Quick Access, can be placed outside its window and stay on the desktop. The groups in Quick Access can have their own icons and can have subgroups. Individual groups can be viewed not only in the standard ProgMan format but as buttons only or as a text list only.

Norton's File Manager is marked by several innovations. It has a button bar. One of the buttons is labeled **View** and opens (or closes) a view panel that is linked to display the file that is highlighted. The standard graphics, word processor and data types are supported but unlike PC Tools, Xtree or OutsideIn, you cannot view files inside zips (but OutsideIn can be configured to replace the Norton Viewers and then you can view inside zips because you are using OutsideIn!).

Another innovation is to go beyond the Windows paradigm of scrolling to the first file that starts with a *single* letter; instead you can type in several letters.

One limitation of NDW is that the file manager can only be accessed from the NDW desktop so you'll need to load the full desktop if you want to use the file manager.

Several of Norton's extra applications deserve special mention. The File Editor is wonderful. It supports multiple files, remembers recently used files and search strings, has a neat file compare feature, and a multiple level undo. The calculators are powerful but the scientific and financial calculators use reverse Polish notation so you have to be into hsiloP to really like them. The batch language is a licensed version of the Winbatch program that you'll find on CD MOM.

PC Tools

PC Tools for Windows (Central Point Software, Voice: 800-445-4208, 503-690-8090; FAX, (503)690-8083) is missing the calculators and file editor that you'll find in Norton, but it is no slouch in what it stuffs into the box. There's a desktop with virtual desk support including hotkey switching, ProgMan and FileMan replacements, file viewers including the ability to view files inside zips, backup including support for QIC and SCSI tapes, DiskFix and System Consultant (equivalents to Norton Disk Doctor and Norton's SysInfo), erase protection and unerase, virus detection and repair, icon editor, batch language with complete recorder facility, scheduler, and disk defragger.

Like Norton, PC Tool's desktop lets you place unopened icons on the desk and its program groups can have subgroups and alternate views such as the toolbox view seen in Figure 5-21. But it goes beyond Norton in several ways. First, having heard some of the complaints about Norton's omnipresence, PC Tools places its drive icons in a window which can be minimized or closed, so the non-Windows look of the desktop can be more effectively hidden from view. Secondly, its excellent file manager can be run independently of the desktop for those that want something lighter in a launcher.

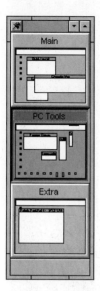

Figure 5-20: PC Tools for Windows' virtual desktop

But the biggest difference in the desktop is the virtual desktop feature in PC Tools. It uses the hidden program strategy and allows each virtual desktop to have its own wallpaper and/or background color. The desktop viewer shown in Figure 5-20 lets you view what's open on each desktop, drag applications from one desktop to another and switch desktops by clicking. Moreover, there is hotkey support for switching to any desktop.

One other thing to notice about the desktop with a loud Bronx cheer is what Central Point does to the system menu of every program running on the desktop if you run its desktop component. In Figure 5-21, look at the system menu button. No more familiar spacebar. Instead you have an ad for their company. Whose desktop is it anyway? When they are ready to pay me for the ad, I'll consider it as a possibility. Until then, I regard this as a major shortcoming (hDC plays a similar trick by default, but at least they have a way of turning it off for all windows but their own tool bar).

Figure 5-21: A PC Tools launch group set up as a toolbar

Noteworthy is the way that PC Tool's file manager handles zips and other archive files. It shows them in the tree as subdirectories although as a visual clue, another color is used for the folder icon placed next to them. When a zip is highlighted in the tree, the directory window shows the files in the zip and the viewer can display the files inside the zip. You can copy or move files to and from a zip as if they were files in a directory with the compression/decompression handled in the background.

If you double click on a document in a zip, PC Tools will offer to unzip the file and load it into the associated application. When you later close the application, PC Tools pops up with a box and offers to rezip the document. If you double click on an executable file in the zip, PC Tools will check what DLLs are called by the executable, and unzip both those and the application before starting it.

In almost all places where it competes, PC Tools aims to better Norton. Its icon editor is the best Mom has seen, with the ability to choose a rectangular region and move or flip the pixels only within that region. It's macro language is so powerful that Mao set up the PC Tools File Manager to have two button bars with buttons that switch between them by having the buttons run a script that drives the customization dialogs in File Manager. Its defragger really does seem to run safely under Windows. Its backup, unlike Norton, supports SCSI tapes.

Many utility fans own both NDW and PC Tools although at street prices over $100 each, I bet they have a boss paying for them rather than raiding the cookie jar. Certainly, each has enough superb tools to justify having both. For now (PC Tools 1.0 versus Norton 2.2), if you get only one, Mom's recommendation would be PC Tools. But both companies are fierce competitors and Mom has no doubt that the Nortonians are planning a version 3.0 that will try to put them back on the top. As usual, users benefit from a strong competition.

Picture This

Icon Edit It

If you care about icons, you'll likely want to touch them up a bit. There are many icon editors available but Mom's favorite by far is the one included in PC Tools for Windows (Figure 5-22). If you don't want to get that whole collection, the best shareware icon editor that Mom has seen is AZ Icon Edit (Figure 5-23), available on CD Mom.

Both let you edit on a pixel-by-pixel basis, have variable width line tools, flood fill, and tools to flip the icon horizontally and vertically. Both have a single level undo.

Both let you mark a rectangle, but here they part ways. AZ Icon Edit can only use that rectangle for cut, copy, and paste operations. PC Tools lets you do many things to it; move it, flip it, use it for cut, copy, or paste.

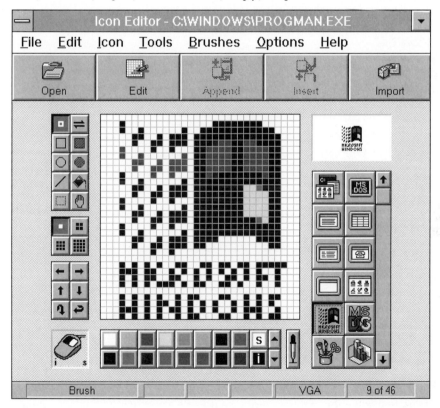

Figure 5-22: PC Tools' Icon Edit

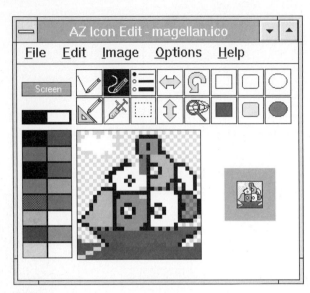

Figure 5-23: AZ Icon Edit

AZ Icon Edit has a capture utility that will let you pick a 32x32 pixel chunk off the screen while PC Tools has an eyedropper tool that lets you pick a color from the current icon.

Another place where AZ provides less flexibility than PC Tools is in support for icon libraries. AZ Icon Edit will only read and write individual icon files so you can't use it to directly read in icons from a library, **dll** or **exe** (but you could use the icon reading in ProgMan and AZ Icon Edit's capture tool) while PC Tools will read and write icon library files and read in icons from many sources, even **grp** files.

 One technical fact about icons which you should be aware of when using an icon editor. Standard icons are 32x32 pixels and 16 colors but each pixel can actually be one of 18 "colors" Huh? Why 18 and not sixteen? Simple — besides the 16 normal colors a pixel can be assigned the "colors" **screen** and **inverse**. **Screen** means transparent so that underlying background shows through. **Inverse** shows the underlying background but inverts the color (so bright red would become bright cyan for example). AZ Icon Edit only supports the **Screen** color and not **Inverse** but you'll rarely want inverse so that doesn't matter much. PC Tools supports both. Here support means allow you to paint, flood fill, etc. in these special "colors." Both use one of the 16 colors to display the special colors, so it can be confusing which, is which but they allow you to remap which color(s) are used for the `Screen` and `Inverse` so you can see what is going on by changing that mapping.

Icon Collect Some

O.K., you've gone wild about icons and gotten hundreds, even thousands of them (you'll find thousands of them on CD MOM!). Now what. How do you find that icon in a haystack? The key is Icon Manager (Impact Software; Voice: 909-590-8522), a wonderful shareware program (found on CD MOM) that lets you organize icons in its proprietary `ica` files or more standard icon libraries (`icl`'s). You can also read in `dll` or individual `ico` and can read and even replace the icons in `exe` files.

Icon Manager can load multiple libraries (and/or multiple ico files) into an MDI interface and you can move or copy icons between libraries with a simple drag and drop. Each icon can be given a name (as in Figure 5-24). You can sort the icons, alphabetically, in a library if you wish.

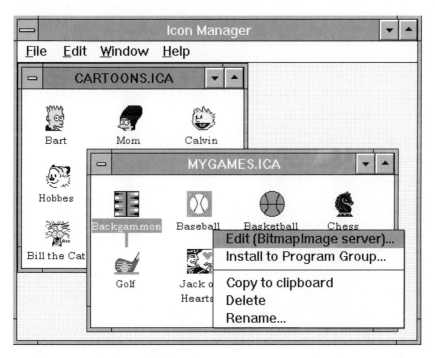

Figure 5-24: Icon Manager

A right button menu pops up as shown. In particular, you can use Paintbrush (or any other bmp OLE server) to edit icons with IconMan so you don't actually need an icon editor (alas, if you do have an icon editor, there is no way to get IconMan to directly load it although you can use the clipboard to transfer between that editor and IconMan). All in all, this is the tool of choice for the icon collector.

The Graphical Kitchen Sink

The rise of graphics for the masses in Windows has spawned a new software category of graphical kitchen sinks; where there are several products available with a remarkably similar set of basic modules, typically with street prices under $100. These are marked by:

- A program that catalogs graphics, generally both bitmapped and vector. The images in a catalog can be viewed as thumbnails on screen and assigned a name and/or keywords. Clicking on an image will let you see it full size. In the best cases, the thumbnails serve as drag and drop objects although many programs don't know how to deal with getting an image dragged to them! They show the image as a package rather than as the actual graphic. A typical catalog, an album in Image Pals, is shown in Figure 5-25

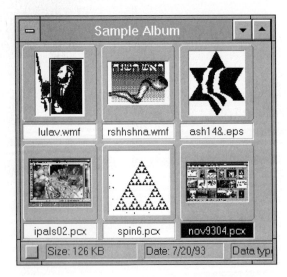

Figure 5-25: An Image Pals Album

- Some kind of screen capture utility

- A file conversion facility, at least from bitmap to bitmap but sometimes including vector conversion also

- Some kind of bitmap image processing that at least lets you adjust contrast and brightness, and sometimes a lot more. Typically this processor does not allow bit level editing or sophisticated selection tools.

Four general purpose graphical kitchen sinks are Collage Complete (Inner Media, Voice: 603-465-3216), Graphics Tools (Delta Point, voice: 408-648-4000; FAX 408-648-4020), Hijaak Pro for Windows (Inset Systems, Voice: 800-374-6738, 203-740-2400, FAX: 203-775-5634) and Image Pals (U-Lead Systems, voice: 800-858-5323; 310-523-9393). For general use, Mom puts Image Pals and Graphic Tools on top, although the other two have specialized strengths that make them stand out in certain situations.

Collage Complete (which does not have vector graphics support) has strong screen capture — roughly tied with Image Pals. It has the ability to capture the actual cursor and has the most powerful post-processing capability allowing even color remapping of an image captured in greyscale. You'll find a working model of Collage Complete on CD MOM.

Hijaak Pro is notable for the ability to read and convert virtually anything you throw at it, and the ability to convert to all sorts of variants of file formats tailor-made for your application.

 I've one particularly cranky EPS file without a TIFF header that prints properly on a PostScript printer but neither Adobe Illustrator nor Graphics Tools can read it. But Hijaak Pro can and will convert it to a form that the other can read. If you have a lot of conversion to do you can't afford to go without Hijaak Pro.

Image Pals' screen capture utility is especially strong. It can capture from a large variety of parts of the screen as shown in Figure 5-26. There is great visual feedback in choosing what part of the screen is picked in those items involving selections — you get a blown up pixel view in selecting an area and as you move the cursor around the screen in **Selected Object** mode, you see an outline of what will capture when you click. The destination can be one or more of a file, the printer, the clipboard or the capture workspace. And when you save to a file, you can arrange to have the capture placed into an album (Image Pals' name for their catalogs)! Activation can be by a hotkey or by a time delay. Post Processing includes conversion to grey scale.

Capture	
Source	Active Window Ctrl+W
Destination	Active Client
Cursor	Full Screen Ctrl+F
Activation...	Menu Under Cursor
Post Processing...	√ Selected Object
	Selected Area
	Clipboard
	Execution File...

Figure 5-26: ImagePals Capture Menu

Image Pals' album organizer has an MDI interface so you can move or copy thumbnails between albums by drag and drop. The thumbnail creation is especially speedy.

The weakest part of ImagePals is conversion which is limited to from bitmap to bitmap. It's image processor is a full fledged image editor. While not quite up to the strongest image editors, it is a solid program.

In distinction, Graphics Tools strong point is its image conversion which includes to and from bitmap and/or vector (it includes an autotrace module to "convert" from bitmap to vector). Its image processor is easy to use and, within the limitation that you can only act with filters on the whole image or a rectangular subpiece, quite powerful. Its albums and screen capture are not as flexible as Image Pals' and its conversion not as robust as Hijaak's but it is a close to these leaders in both areas.

If your conversion needs are limited to bitmaps, I'd recommend Image Pals. If you need other conversions, the best solution to is to get it and Hijaak but if the combined price seems steep, Graphics Tools is an excellent package and a good solution

Paint Shop Pro

Paint Shop Pro (see Figure 5-27) is a shareware graphics utility program that you'll find on CD MOM. It is more an image processor than an image editor in that you cannot change individual bits. But using its **Save** command, you can change between all the various supported formats: PCX, TIFF, GIF, BMP, TGA, and more. It's ideal for color reduction including change from color to grey scale. It can resize and I've already explained (see Wallpaper on the Rack in Chapter 2) how its **Resample** command can be used to stretch wallpaper.

If your graphical needs are relatively simple, this is the program that will win your heart. It is so quick and easy to use, yet so able to do its job, that when Mom asked the owner of a major shareware vendor to pick his favorite among all shareware programs, he picked this one saying he uses it extensively in preparation for a monthly newsletter.

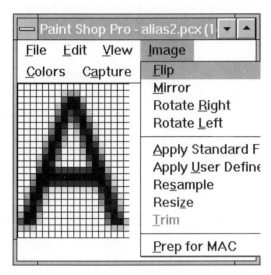

Figure 5-27: Paint Shop Pro

Image Editors Priced Like Utilities

Software prices in free fall and heavy competition have hit the image editing market in a big way so you are likely to be able to get a superb program for under $100, and a high-end one for as little as $150. What do image editors offer that you won't find in Paintbrush?

- They allow editing on the bit level with support for palettes with dozens of colors. An eye dropper tool lets you pick a color off the image. A magnification tool is available and some programs offer linked magnified/normal windows so you can point at the normal window to choose what section of the image appears in the magnified window.

- They allow intelligent creation of mask/selection areas. Once you've selected an area you can crop to it or copy it to another image. You can change colors only inside the selected area or apply a filter only to it. Or you can treat the selected area as a mask and have it protected while color changes and what not happen to the rest of the image. Selection tools often include a magic wand that picks nearby pixels with nearby colors as well as the more usual rectangle/ellipse/freehand tools. With high-end editors, you can often use paint tools to paint on a mask and Bezier curve techniques to modify the edges as curves. The high-end products are partly distinguished from the low-end products by how fancy their selection tools are.

- They have a variety of filters that let you transform the entire image or a selected part of it to make it brighter, enhance edges, or to produce special effects like blowing wind.

- They usually have some kind of scanner support, sometimes with a stitch command that lets you hand scan an image (too wide for the scanner) in several passes with the software intelligent enough to stick it all together.

While there are literally dozens of image editors out there, two stand out at the low end and three at the high end. At the low end (and except for the sophistication of their selection tools and some specialized things like handling of multimegabyte images and color separation, they aren't that low end!), you can't go wrong with Micrografx's Photo Magic (voice: 800-733-3729; 214-234-1789; FAX: 214-234-2410) or Zsoft's Photo Finish (voice: 404-428-0008; FAX: 404-427-1150). Corel Draw has a version of Photo Finish bundled with it.

At the higher end, there is Adobe's Photo Shop (voice: 415-961-4400), Aldus' Photo Styler (voice: (619) 695-6956) and Micrografx's Picture Publisher.

The list prices for these products is in the $500–$800 range and normally only for the serious photographer, artist, or desktop publisher; but don't forget the competitive upgrade price. Micrografx has an aggressive program of competitive upgrades. Who knows, maybe they'll consider a competitive upgrade from Windows Paintbrush! You'll also find that brand name full page scanners come with a high-end image editor.

CD MOM has working models of the following image editors: Aldus Photostyler and Micrografx Picture Publisher. Check 'em out, dude.

What's Cooking in the Pot Pourri

Almanac

Almanac, a shareware calendar program that you'll find on CD MOM is the calendar program to end all calendar programs! You can configure it to normally sit on your screen showing the date and time like so:

`9:04 AM | Jul. 21 | Wed.`

That time can be placed anywhere on the screen with the position remembered from one running to the next. (Mao puts it in his StartUp group). But double click on that time bar and you'll get a full-fledged calendar and more.

Figure 5-28 shows the monthly view which can include the Jewish and English dates, shows the phases of the moon, and can display (color coded if you want) holidays, family birthday's, and the like. Click on a button and get the sunrise and sunset time. Click on a date and you can see notes you've made for the day or a schedule. While not a full-fledged PIM, it does support scheduling and a simple to do list. Almanac is the best desktop clock/calendar around.

What the Hack Is Going On
Here: Winsleuth Gold and Skylight

If you are a sophisticated user, you'll occasionally want to know about technical details of memory usage, disk partitions, video driver aspects and other parts of your system. Among the various system reporting utilities for Windows, two stand out — Winsleuth Gold Plus (Dariana, Voice: (714)236-1380; FAX: (714)236-1390) and Skylight (RenaSonce Group, Voice: (619)287-3348; FAX (619)287-3554). The graphics in Winsleuth Gold Plus shown in Figure 5-29 are spectacular.

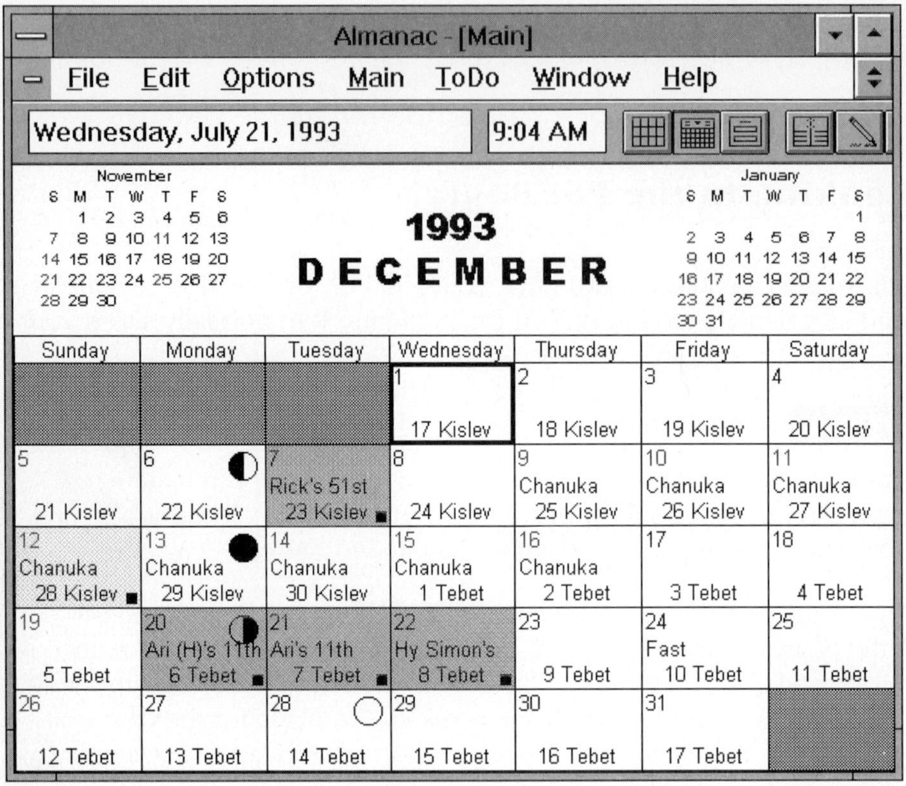

Figure 5-28: Almanac's Calendar

One nice aspect of Skylight is that it gives a top level of information without overwhelming detail while allowing you to drill down to the detail if you want.

Both programs report on I/O port usage and IRQs, two items that can be useful when you need to install new boards. Winsleuth Gold Plus also reports on DMA channel usage. Both make recommendation on changes you might make to your system files to improve performance.

You'll find a fully functional copy of Winsleuth Gold, a precursor to Winsleuth Gold Plus, on CD MOM and you'll find an upgrade coupon in the book.

Figure 5-29: Winsleuth Gold Plus

DOS on Steroids: EDOS

If you only run Winapps and don't even use DOS for file management, skip this subsection. EDOS (Firefly Software Systems Corp; Voice: 1-800-248-0809; 1-503-694-2282) is short for Enhanced DOS and as it's name implies only effects your DOS sessions. EDOS provides these DOS services without taking any memory from the DOS sessions themselves. It does this with the magic of a VxD — a Windows virtual device driver. These DLLs which only work in 386 enhanced mode can provide services in DOS sessions without using any DOS memory because they run in protect mode. For now the most notable VxDs are EDOS, the WinJet software (which provides PostScript emulation in DOS sessions without taking any memory from the DOS sessions) and the various sound drivers that run sound cards in DOS sessions over Windows. But VxDs figure to play a big role in Windows 4.0/DOS 7.0. But I digress.

The most obvious change that EDOS provides is shown in Figure 5-30 — it gives DOS menus, many of them the usual DOS session system menu moved to a more logical place. But the particular menus shown illustrates two other services that

EDOS provides: it will run winapps from DOS sessions and it gives DOS drag and drop target capabilities.

When EDOS is running (unless you turn off the option!), if you type in the name of a winapp at the DOS command line in either a full screen or windowed DOS sessions, EDOS will switch back to the Windows screen and run the winapp!

If you are running in a windowed DOS sessions and you drag a file from FileMan (or other drag and drop source) to the windowed session, the full pathname of the file is entered through the keyboard. This is useful at the DOS prompt but also works inside DOS applications.

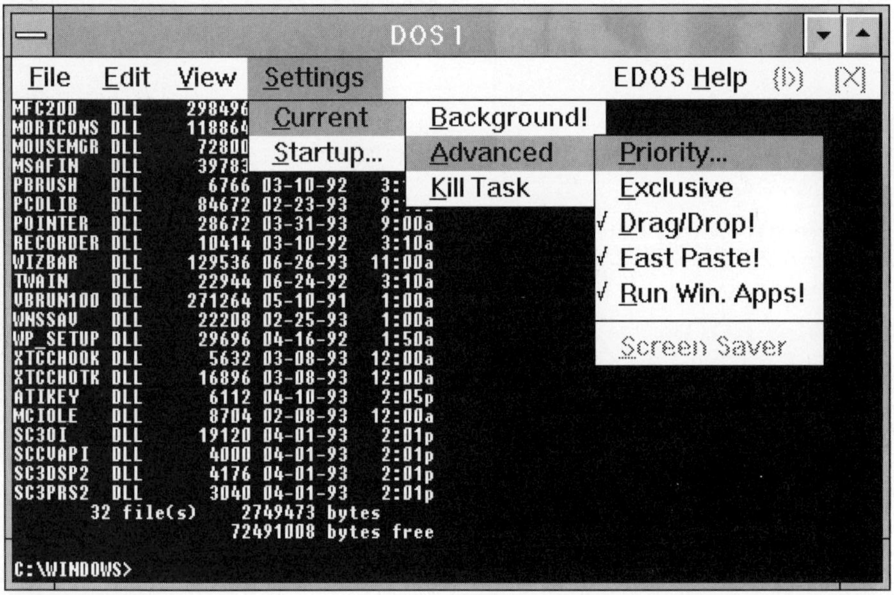

Figure 5-30: EDOS gives menus to DOS

Other EDOS enhancements include:

•   Visual indicators of whether a windowed session has background and/or exclusive turned on

•   The ability to change the background and exclusive parameters of a DOS session in a batch file (or from the command line)

- The ability to view the clipboard contents from a DOS session and redirect them to a file or the printer

- A browse command to pick a filename to be entered through the keyboard to the DOS session

You'll find a shareware version of EDOS on CD MOM.

Installing Is Such Sweet Sorrow

 My **system.ini** has been mugged so often by some thuggish install that I've lost count of which scars came from which encounter.

No general aspect of interaction with software is as annoying and fraught with later havoc as the modern install procedure. How do I hate thee? Let me count the ways:

- The worst thing is that changes in my system are made without telling me what they are. At one point in the DOS world, install programs changed **autoexec.bat** and **config.sys** without permission. A hue and cry from users, led by the press, put a stop to that. Most installs ask you if they can make changes in these two files and may even let you review the changes and/or make backups for you. But, it seems like **win.ini** and **system.ini** are fair game. The industry seem to have decided that they are so complicated that no one can track them.

- Some programs go so far as to change a value that you already have in your **ini** files without asking you. In fact, they are probably written in a way that they didn't even realize that you had such a value there!

- Some installs take forever. The worst are installs done with the setup kits provided with Microsoft languages. You spot them because they come up with a screen showing a decent blue to black color gradient instead of the ugly bands that some other install programs use. But you pay for that pretty gradient. The culprit is the compression technology that Microsoft uses. Unwilling to license from PKZIP or ARJ, and perhaps concerned by possible implication of a Unisys patent, Microsoft has its home grown compression stuff which is fairly efficient at compression size but SLOOOOW at decompressing.

- Software piracy is a problem for vendors so I sympathize with their desire to have you enter your name and company during install. Since I can't see where it gives them much protection, I have less sympathy for requiring you to type in a serial number like A2$&8dop12LkJcRaZy23lkop, all case sensitive of course. But the piracy problem is so serious, I can even forgive them that. But how about some thought and consideration.

How ridiculous to have you input a serial number when you run install from disk 1 and the number is only *on* disk 1's label? Put the serial number on disk 2. In any event, Mr. or Ms. vendor, please, please, PLEASE put a clear note on the screen as to where the heck the user is to find said serial number. My favorite is vendors that hide it on a sticker on page 3 of the manual.

- Some installs make you do unnecessary disk shuffles, reinserting disk 1 late in the process.

- Some installs make you sit there for the whole process even if you have lots of disk space. I'd like to see programs check how much space is free on your hard disk. If there is room, they should let you copy all the install disks to the hard disk and do the uncompressing from there. It would be faster and you need not stick around. Of course, they'd need to delete the compressed files when the process is over.

- If installs use a DLL, even if it is private DLL, they could just as well store it in their program directory. Too often they feel they can place that DLL in the Windows or in the System directory. And those directories grow and grow and grow and grow. Arrgghh.

- Some programs will change a DLL even if a later one is on your system. Or they'll blindly put a DLL into your Windows directory overriding a DLL by the same name in your System directory (since Windows looks in the Windows directory before the System directory). Or they'll copy a standard Windows 3.1 DLL (needed if you are still running Windows 3.0) into their private directory without checking that you already have it in your Windows or System directory.

- Too often installs insist on their own ProgMan group, not bothering to give you a choice of using an existing group. And if you are using an alternate shell, forget about getting help on adding the program to its groups.

- Less common, but not unheard of, installs insist on being on drive C, or insist that they have to be in a subdirectory of the root, or to bomb if your Windows directory isn't on drive C, or isn't named **windows**. Whose system is it anyway?

 Mom's recommendations for installers is obvious — avoid these problems! Always check with a GetProfile API call before using a SetProfile and ask if a value is already there. Always, always, always offer an uninstall program and consider partial uninstall options (e.g. a shell should have a way to keep it on the system but replace it as the formal Windows shell).

 Herewith a modest proposal from CTO Mao. Every Winapp should make a file called **install.dta** in their home directory with a clear statement of what files got added where and what changes in public ini files were made. If a DLL is used but was not installed because it was already present. **install.dta** should tell you that. What I'd really like is to have Microsoft set up a standard for storing this information and keep it in a single common file so that you could instantly identify all the programs that use a given DLL.

 If you are brave, you might consider with a large enough install copying all the disks to your hard disk and installing from there. That works fine with the Windows disks themselves. Place the files in a subdirectory of your hard disks route called **\DISK1**. Believe it or not that will allow install of some programs that otherwise would refuse to find the files.

Uninstaller

If you want to remove a program that doesn't have its own built-in uninstall routine, you'll love Uninstaller — shown in Figure 5-31 (Microhelp; Voice: 404-516-0898). It goes through your ProgMan items and lets you pick one. It can then, at your option, delete all files in the corresponding directory, look for **dlls** called by the **exes** in that directory, remove the program and its accompanying entourage. The package also includes an **ini** file editor.

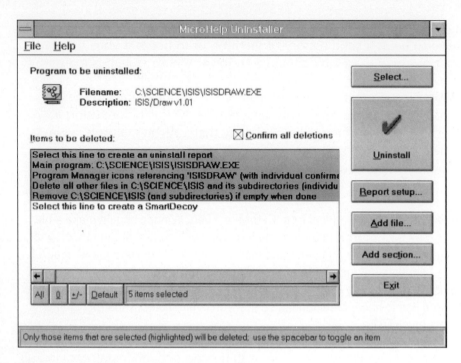

Figure 5-31: Microhelp's Uninstaller

Making Windows Look Good

In this section, we talk about programs that make Windows look better. Most, but not all, serve no useful purpose except making your interaction with Windows more pleasant.

Who Turned Out the Lights: After Dark

> Put out the light, and then put out the light:
> If I quench thee, thou flaming minister,
> I can again thy former light restore
>
> — William Shakespeare, *Othello Act: V, Scene: ii*

They still tell you to get screen blankers to avoid phosphor burn in. That's a great urban legend. Monochrome monitors could be victims of burn in but it is virtually unheard of with the analog monitors used for VGA. But, hey, if you were selling screen blankers, wouldn't you still use fear too? There is only one reason anyone at Mom's place uses a screen blanker — the same reason you do. It's fun.

 It may be a problem to convince your boss to get the screen blanker because its fun but don't try the phosphor line on her. Because she's likely to reply "If you're worried about phosphor burn in, why not use the screen blankers that come with Windows." And she'd be right (see Chapters 8 and 9 for a discussion of Windows screen blankers) but the screen blankers in Windows aren't quite as fun as the ones you want to get.

If you are going to get a blanker, may as well go with the standard — After Dark (Berkeley Systems; Voice: 800-344-5541). You'll need one of two basic packages: the original After Dark or Star Trek, the Screen Saver. Unless your a real trekkie, I'd recommend the original which will work from full screen DOS sessions and which comes with the famous flying toasters (Figure 5-32) and the world's best fish (Figure 5-33). There is also a More After Dark product with extra razor blades, er, blankers for the After Dark engine included in the basic packages.

Figure 5-32: Half a Toasted Bunny Mark

Figure 5-33: Catch dem fish

One neat feature of After Dark is that you can set up a randomizer which will cycle through a selection of blankers. After Dark has sound support (which you can turn off) so you can hear the wings on those toaster flapping and. . .

Wow — That Window Is Sure Stacked: Makeover

It's remarkable that while Windows 3.0 introduced the 3-D look that had people go gaga, the 3-D effect was not used on title bars and borders. The top half of Figure 5-34 shows dull old Windows while the bottom half shows the effect of running OSFrame, part of Makeover (PlayRoom, Voice: 704-536-3093). Every item that Makeover enhances is user-configurable so if, for example, you don't like the stripes in the title bar, you can turn them off.

The passage from screen to paper and the shift to greyscale has made some of the effects less dramatic and in particular washed out the raise text look of the word **Active** in the active title bar.

Among the effects that you can get with OSFrame are 3-D title bars with the ability to set different degrees for the active and inactive window as in Figure 5-34. You can also raise the menu bar and make borders 3-D. The interface is an extension of the familiar **Color** applet in Control Panel; you can save schemes including the state of raised border and bars and you can adjust many more colors than in the applet including what OSFrame uses for shadows and lighted areas. You get to choose if you want the effects to also appear in dialog box title bars and borders.

If you look at what OSFrame does, what's missing is button customization. Fear not, that is in Makeover via a program called ButtonMaker. It lets you change the buttons that Windows uses to one of several built in sets including what you see in Figure 5-35 or you can draw your own!

ButtonMaker does its magic by replacing the bitmaps that store the buttons that are stored in your screen driver.

 Oy, it changes my screen driver? Call me superstitious but screen drivers are so darned buggy, I'd not consider changing one, even if only to replace the buttons.

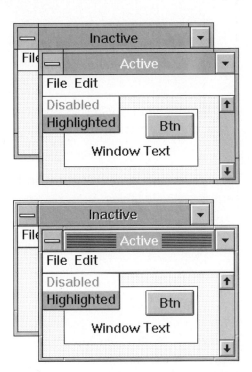

Figure 5-34: Makeover's 3D look

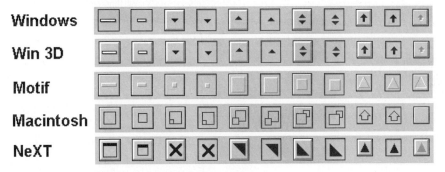

Figure 5-35: Makeover's Button Sets

 Real silly, Mao, old man. The buttons are just resources in the screen driver, dumb sets of pixels that get loaded en masse. It is totally, completely safe to change them. If you enjoy the new look, by golly, you should use ButtonMaker.

You speak the truth grasshopper. Still. . .

In addition to its core components of OSFrame and ButtonMaker, Makeover includes a calculator, an icon editor, a program to change the behavior of your **CapsLock** key and a music game.

It's strange. If you get used to using OSFrame on your computer and move to another one, Windows seems positively lifeless.

The New Microsoft Mouse Driver

The new Microsoft Mouse 2 ships with a new set of mouse drivers, the Mouse 9.0 drivers. If you own an older Microsoft Mouse, you can purchase the upgrade and you should seriously consider doing so because of the Windows driver's features.

To upgrade, you have to own a Microsoft Mouse but even if you own an old Microsoft Mouse and are using someone else's mouse now, you can upgrade and it is likely that your mouse will work with the Microsoft drivers. To be sure, run Windows setup and switch to the built-in Microsoft Mouse driver; if that works, so should the 9.0 drivers.

Here are the features in the 9.0 driver:

•   You can choose three sizes of cursor (see Figure 5-36), a godsend not only for laptop users but for those of us with tired old eyes. Not only does the pointer change, but all mouse cursors from the hour glass to windows resize cursors.

•   You can choose to have the cursor start small and only grow when you move it rapidly and then decrease to small after a specified time.

•   You can turn on a feature that lets the mouse cursor wrap around to the other side when you move the cursor to an edge.

- You can have the cursor jump to the default button choice whenever a dialog pops up, a wonderful feature when your mouse starts out clear across the screen.

- You can have a hotkey move the cursor to center screen, a useful feature on a laptop where the mouse can get lost.

- You can pop up a magnifier (see Figure 5-37) that blows up a part of the screen to allow precise placement for something like a selection box in an image editor.

- You can turn on mouse trails — a feature that causes a ghosting effect to help you better locate the mouse on laptop. This feature seems to only work with the Windows-supplied screen drivers.

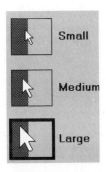

Figure 5-36: A sizable mouse cursor

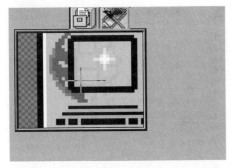

Figure 5-37: The mouse magnifier

The Case of the Mommy's Cursor

The last of the utilities that Mom recommends for customizing the look of Windows is a custom cursor utility. You may already have some customization in the Mouse 9.0 driver which only changes size but that is enough for the less common cursors like the window size cursor. The cursors that you'll most want to change are the pointer and hourglass.

If you use Plug-In for Program Manager, it lets you change the pointer or hourglass or both choosing from its built-in choices or from any CUR file you might have lying around. But if you want to jazz your cursor even more, there are some interesting possibilities.

Moon Valley Software (voice: 602-375-9502) has products that include extensive collections of icons, cursors, wallpapers, screen savers, sounds and animated icons and cursors together with programs to use them in Windows. The core package is IconHearIt although there is also a CD-ROM version, RoMaterial (which installs 7.5 MB of files on your desktop) and a version, IconDoIt without sound stuff. (They also have editors for the file types in IconMakeIt).

The cursor support in these products allows you to change your pointer and hourglass to one of dozens of possible cursor choices (hundreds in the CD ROM version). Besides the cursor support, they let you place animated icons in ProgMan and assign **wav** files to a huge variety of windows events, even at the level of individual dialog boxes.

Magic Cursor II (Fanfare Software, voice: 310-828-8448) concentrates almost entirely on cursors (although there is a program included in the package to define the right mouse button) and delivers more in that area. To get the full benefit of the package, you need to use their VGA or superVGA driver in which case you can have color cursors and also a full screen crosshair cursor. If you use another driver (which you'll need to take advantage of a graphics accelerator), you at least get the ability to assign nine cursors including the resize, pointer, hourglass, text (I beam), four headed arrow and crosshair. Included in the package are over one hundred cursors to choose from.

Most spectacular by far is Color Cursor (Artisoft; voice: 510-426-5355) which I only saw in beta. It claims to work with a wide variety of video drivers and worked with the notoriously cranky ATI video drivers. As the name implies, the cursors are in color but even more so, they can be quite a bit larger than the largest cursors I've seen in any other program. It allows change of eight cursors in all (the nine mentioned above except for the four headed cursor). There is something wonderful about replacing the I beam cursor with a big bold pencil with a sharp point; I found it much easier to mark text while writing. And a horizontal resize cursor that has a face putting the window edge in her mouth and biting is a hoot. Animated cursors work especially well as replacements for the hourglass.

 If the idea of custom cursors appeals to you, keep you eye on Color Cursors. Once it appears, it looks to be the program of choice for solving the case of the mommy's cursor.

The Gold Fin in the Porphyry Font

> Now sleeps the crimson petal, now the white;
> Nor waves the cypress in the palace walk;
> Nor winks the gold fin in the porphyry font

— Alfred, Lord Tennyson, *The Princess*, 1847

The final tool collection in Mom's cupboard involve fonts and characters. Saving the best for the last, Compose is something that should be on every Windows user's machine. The other font utilities are of interest if you have and use lots of fonts, typically a dozen or more. Printer's Apprentice will display intelligently laid out specimens of your fonts on screen or paper and Font Assistant is typical of a family of Windows applications that let you organize your fonts into groups. Font Monger is everyman's font editor, an admittedly specialized program brought to the masses.

One class of utilities that are too specialized to make into the Mother of All Toolboxes are the font effects programs that let you wrap and warp type to make eye catching headlines for fliers and presentations. Without a doubt the leading font effects utility is Corel Draw (Corel; voice: 800-836-3729) which not only captured the drawing market, but expanded it way beyond its normal audience with an array of features lead by its font tricks. More specialized programs that focus on font effects include MakeUp (Bitstream; voice: 800-522-3668; 617-497-6222; FAX: 617-868-4732). For home use, fonts can be transmuted in making greeting cards, posters and fliers with Instant Artist (Autodesk; voice: 800-228-3601) and PrintShop Deluxe for Windows (Broderbund; voice: 800-521-6263).

Wasn't Mickey Mouse the Printer's Apprentice in Fontasia?

In the old days, professional printers had font specimen books, catalogs of fonts by name that let them see sample output at varying font sizes and weights and let them look at the character sets for symbol fonts. Printer's Apprentice, a shareware program that you'll find on CD MOM, is an ideal tool for producing such font catalogs of your own fonts and to look at the font on screen in various ways.

The main screen (seen in Figure 5-38) displays a font in a large point size one character at a time — you can dial up the character and size with sliders and pick the font from a drop down list. For further on-screen exploration, Printer's Apprentice provides three optional windows that let you view the font on screen:

- One displays a graphical keyboard with the characters displayed on the keys changing as you hit the shift. Like Character Map, you can enter characters this way and paste to the keyboard. But unlike Character Map, no font information goes along.

- One displays the alphabet, numbers, symbols or one of four user designated quotes in a user set point size.

- One displays the characters in ASCII order.

As for font individual printouts, there are six different sheets that can be printed out:

- An uncrowded specimen sheet with the alphabet in 24 point and point size samples in 8, 10, 12, 14, 18, 24, 30, 36, and 48 point

- A crowded specimen sheet with point sample in normal and bold at 6, 8, 9, 10, 11, 12, 14, 18, 24, and 30 point, a sample alphabet and a print sample

- A keyboard map and map of the characters above ANSI code 128

- A character set in ANSI order

- An ANSI chart — the character set with larger numbers but smaller sized characters

- A spec sheet for a single character showing it in 12 sizes and four weight/styles

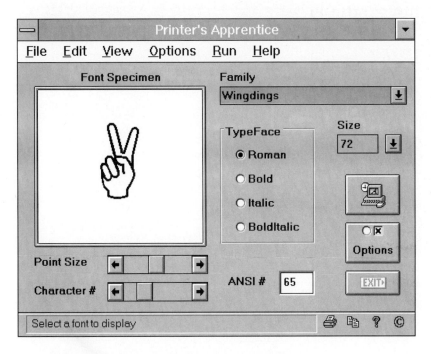

Figure 5-38: Printer's Apprentice main screen

Finally, you can print out font catalogs as seen in Figure 5-39. There are three choices of output:

- 42 fonts per page in two columns at 18 point, in AaBbCc. . . format where, for a typical font, you get to the letter M or N

- 17 fonts per page in a single column at 24 point, in AaBbCc. . . format where, for a typical font, you get to the letter S or T

- 3 fonts per page with complete alphabets in 6, 8, 10, 12 and 14 points, sample bold, italics and bold italics and AaBbCcXxYyZz in 60 point

Printer's Apprentice is a wondrous tool for cataloging your fonts.

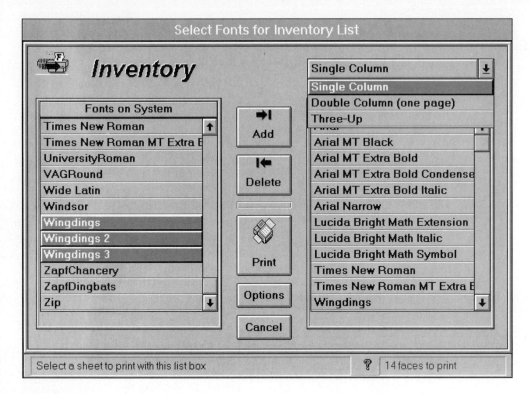

Figure 5-39: Printer's Apprentice Font Printing dialog

Igor, I Font You for My Assistant!

If you lose control and get several font packs or, against my advice, get one of the 250 fonts font packages, you'll want a way to organize your fonts. So you don't have to go on a coffee break every time the font common dialog loads, you'll want to keep the number of fonts installed at any given moment to no more than 50 or 100. But different projects may require different sets of fonts.

What you want is a tool that lets you set up distinct sets of fonts and lets you easily load change which of the sets is currently loaded into Windows. Microsoft Font Assistant is one of several tools that does precisely that. It is included in any True Type Font Pack except the original. If you're into lots of fonts, it is worth getting one of the Microsoft font packs for Font Assistant alone! But note that the initial release breaks when its ini file reaches 64K which is about 500 fonts.

Rube Goldberg's Fontasmagoric Machine: Font Monger

If you are a font designer, you'll want to use Fontgrapher (Altsys Corp., Voice: 800-477-2131; 214-680-2060; FAX: 214-680-0537), a high end font editor with a high end price tag, great power and a, er, challenging interface. Mere mortals can't beat Font Monger (Ares Software, voice: 800-783-2737; 415-578-9090; FAX: 415-378-8999), an easy to use full-featured font editor which is priced like a utility.

When you load a font, it can appear in a keyboard map (as shown in Figure 5-40) or in character order. Double click on a character and the edit box shown in Figure 5-41 appears on which you can edit curves making up the font if you are particularly brave, foolhardy or both. What civilians will most want from Font Monger's character level modification is to make fraction fonts (see Figure 41), small cap fonts and to move characters positions.

Font Monger also lets you change the font header. Finally, the service Font Monger offers of most interest to some users is font conversion between TrueType and Post Script, Type 1. Since hand hinting is not carried over, this is only useful for specialty fonts which haven't been hand tuned.

Figure 5-40: The Font Monger Keyboard

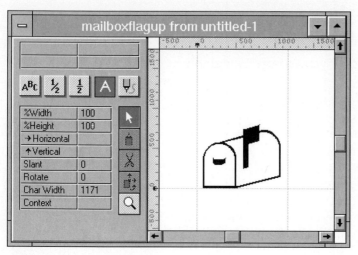

Figure 5-41: Font Monger's Edit box

For an ANSI Headache, Take Compose

It's the pits to have to enter characters that don't have keyboard equivalents like the cents and pound sign, accented characters (on an American keyboard), copyright symbol, publishers quotes and em/en dashes. In Winword, you have to press down **Numlock** and use the **Alt+keypad**, if you can remember the numeric codes. Or you have to use Character Map or a special character entry code.

Well, it need not be the pits if you use the free program on CD MOM from DEC called Compose. With it, you pick a special "compose" key, by default the right **Ctrl** key (since you have the left **Ctrl** key to use for **Ctrl**, that's a good choice!). When Compose is loaded and you hit the compose key, the word Compose appears in a box on your lower right screen and the next key or few keys serve as a shortcut. The idea is to use mnemonics for the shortcuts. For example, the default sequences include c/ to enter the cents sign, L= for the pound sign, a^ for â, and co for the copyright sign.

 I've added my own natural single character signs for the special publisher's symbols. For example after the compose key, ' become ', - becomes the en dash (–), = the em dash (—) and I use [and] for the open/close publisher's quotes (" and ").

Multiple shortcuts can lead to the same sequence if you want, and any sequence can be defined so that order doesn't matter. Thus you needn't remember if it is co or oc that lead to © — both work.

Figure 5-42 shows part of the define sequence dialog and indicates special built in codes for date, time, date/time and the popup of a dialog that lets you choose characters for a symbol font. Use your initials to enter your name or some abbreviation to enter your name and address — the possibilities are limitless.

Given that the program is free and takes little memory or resources, it is no brainer to use Compose.

Define Compose Sequences			
Sequence	Case Sens.	Any Order	Resulting String
D\<sp\>		x	*** Date
T\<sp\>		x	*** Time
DT		x	*** Date & Time
\<sp\>\<sp\>			*** Choose
c|		x	¢
c/		x	¢
L-		x	£
L=		x	£
Y-		x	¥

Figure 5-42: The Compose Define Sequence dialog

CHAPTER 6

Staying Current

What I am really trying to do is bring birth to clarity, which is really a half-assedly thought-out pictorial semi-vision thing.

I would see the jiggle-jiggle-jiggle or the wiggle of the path. Even now when I talk about the influence functional, I see the coupling and I take this turn — like as if there was a big bag of stuff — and try to collect it away and to push it.

It's all visual.

It's hard to explain.

— Richard Feynman, quoted in James Gleick's *Genius,* 1992

Chameleon

"Why can't computers be an appliance like a car or a VCR?" "Why do I have to spend so much time keeping up?" If you don't ask those questions, I'll bet your significant other does. There are many reasons.

Sure you can do lots with a car: go to the local store, ride the open road, impress your girl friend. But think what you can do on a PC: format a newsletter with pictures and font effects, project your company's sales by region for the next year, track your customers and orders, design a house, analyze a CAT scan, even do your taxes! That should impress your girl friend *and* her Mom.

But with the ability to wow your clients with nearly typeset quality business correspondence comes the necessity to learn something about fonts. As computers bring a vast array of technologies to your fingertips, you need to learn some of the basics of those technologies to keep up. So the first reason you need information and to invest time, is just to absorb the power at your command.

The second reason is the newness of the technology and the inherent instability associated with that newness. The DOS user clinging to his 1985 program suite smugly giggling at your occasional crashes in Windows forgets, or chooses to forget, that from 1985 to 1987, he/she had horrendous crashes due to TSR conflicts until the vendor community learned to make TSRs that worked together and the users learned to avoid those that didn't. If you are staying at the bleeding edge to get the advantages of the latest wonderful features, you need to keep your ear to the ground about what the pitfalls are.

The third reason is the complexity of the technology. Vendors spend enormous efforts, with varying degrees of success, trying to make their products more accessible, but the fact remains that there are often multiple ways to skin a cockroach and you can often pick up time-saving tips for everyday use.

But the most important reason that you have to keep up is that the technology is changing so rapidly. Windows is continually being reinvented. New media like video and sound are introduced. Fonts technique is pushed in new directions with multiple masters and portable documents. OLE 2 changes the landscape of interoperability between applications. And that's just some of the hot topics in the last half of 1993.

I've ordered Igor and Mao to help me tell you about the variety of places you can find help and information to keep up because keep up you must.

And now a word from our sponsor. The authors of this book have both written articles for several magazines and so approach the subject with a certain expertise but also a built in bias. Moreover, the bulk of their writing overall has been for Ziff-Davis publications (*PC Magazine, PC/Computing, Windows Sources, PC Week, Computer Shopper,* and the Cobb Group newsletters are Ziff-Davis publications that will be mentioned in this chapter). Bias doesn't necessarily mean prejudice but candor requires that we add this full disclosure.

Sources of Information

Sukha matteyyata loke[†]

— Dhammapada, Canto XXIII, ca 500 B.C.

Magazines

Why can your cable company include so many channels in its basic fee? Because those channels have ads — it's that simple. They pay for the bulk of the costs/profits just as they pay for all of it on free TV. It's the same story for magazines. I estimate that a typical computer magazine has ad income which is 3-10 times its subscription income, so they are a highly subsidized medium which makes them a particularly sensible buy.

Does that mean that advertisers are favored in the magazines because of a fear they will pull the ads if the magazine writes bad things? You will certainly see some hotheads on BBSs claiming this is the case. But the authors of this book tell me that in their magazine writing, they hàve seen no evidence of this and they have sometimes panned products from advertisers.

[†] To be a mother in this world is bliss.

Magazines are the single best, fastest, least expensive way to keep up to date. If you subscribe, a magazine will cost $1.50-$2 an issue; figure $20 a year for a monthly and $35/year for *PC Magazine* with 22 issues a year.

 New subscribers often get special deals. If you care about saving a few bucks, when you get a renewal notice, call up the 800 number on the card or that you'll find in the magazine and first ask their best rate for new subscribers (you may or may not get quoted what is their bast rate really is!) and then (but not before) tell them you want to renew and assume you can get the same rate. Usually, you can. If you don't, do not yell and scream. You have three options — hang up and decide if you want to resubscribe later, accept their quoted rate on the spot, or ask to speak to a supervisor. It's likely to be only a few bucks difference and only you can decide if it is worth the hassle.

 What magazines? At the top of the list has to *PC Magazine* with its 10,000+ pages a year of comprehensive coverage. It has it all: first look reviews, opinion columns, programming tools reviews, blockbuster features, programming columns, tips, and reviews of home software. And we claim to say that without undue bias.

PC Magazine definitely has a technical outlook, something that some readers find disconcerting — but most want. It is somewhat surprising that such a technoid publication has over one million subscribers; the only magazines with more readers are ones like *TV Guide, Reader's Digest,* and *Time.*

Don't plan on reading *PC Magazine* cover to cover. The features are so comprehensive (trying to review every product that meets a well-defined and fairly broad filter) that unless you are currently in the market for what's under review, you'll probably want to skim or skip it. A good strategy is to skim them, at least reading the introduction and storing away the subject so when you are in the market six months from now, you'll know where to look.

 After *PC Magazine*, the next on my list of recommendations would be one or both of the two main general Windows focused publications: *Windows* magazine and *Windows Sources. Windows Sources* is somewhat more technically oriented so the apt analogy might be that *Windows Sources* is to *Windows* magazine as *PC Magazine* is to *PC World* or *PC/Computing.*

After the Windows specialized magazines come the other general purpose computing magazines — notably *PC/Computing* and *PC World* which have a less technical and usually lighter focus than *PC Magazine*. In recent months, *PC/Computing* in particular has made great efforts to appeal to Windows users. There are still some folks that swear by *Byte* but no one at Mom's place has read it regularly for five years and towards the end only Pournelle was worth reading. You can pick up all of those magazines at any corner drug store.

Then depending on your interests there are lots of very specialized magazines on subjects like multimedia or desktop publishing or home offices or mobile computing. Often if you can qualify these publications are free so at least ask if there is a process to qualify for a free subscription.

 Finally, the techies will revel in magazines that share their angst: *PC Techniques* (voice 602-483-0192, FAX 602-483-0193) and *Windows Tech Journal* (voice 800-234-0386, FAX 503-746-0071) — two of our favorites — cover the broad range; *Visual Basic Programmer's Journal* (formerly *BasicPro*, voice 800-848-5523 or 303-541-0610) and its ilk specialize; and if you're into disk-based magazines or disk/printed combos, Jonathan Zuck's Visual Basic series (CompuServe 76702,1605), Pinnacle's *Smart Access* (voice 800-788-1900 or 206-251-1900) for the data debased, *Windows OnLine* (available from most BBSs; it's a multimedia Help document), and others deserve special recognition — as does the Cobb Group, which has launched its own series of disks, too.

The Weaklies

Then we come to the computer weeklies. While there are other computer related weeklies, to most savvy PC users, "weeklies" means *PC Week* and *Infoworld*. Both have similar mixes of coverage — news features about what's happening in the industry including reviews of beta versions of especially hot software, columns, some in-depth reviews, gossip on the back page.

Infoworld is definitely better — its reviews are more thorough and are often among the best you'll find in any computer literature, the columns of Livingston and Gibson (when he isn't tied up with SpinRite) are noteworthy and while Spencer Katt, *PC Week*'s gossip monger is good, Cringley (the one in *Infoworld*) is great. But both mags are worth getting, if you can, since you can't beat the price.

The overwhelming majority of subscribers to *Infoworld* and *PC Week* are free ones to qualified readers. You need to fill out a form and periodically resubmit it to determine if you qualify. Qualification depends on how many machines your employer has and the number for which you recommend purchases. The more computers you control, the larger the number of computers and computer users under your influence, the greater your chances for receiving a free subscription. And *you* get to say how many people you influence.

 Lot's of folks lie on their qualification forms, but you wouldn't lie, now would you sonny? You know what we Moms think about lying. But Moms do encourage you to put yourself forward in the best possible light. So if that manager down the hall with 40 machines in his group periodically asks what you think about Norton Desktop — guess what? You are making recommendations for those 40 machines, even if it isn't part of your formal job description. Be sure to count stuff like that.

Some unscrupulous people count the number of computers in their cars, in their refrigerators, in their VCRs. They even count digital thermometers that happen to be in their medicine cabinets.

 Don't forget all of your relatives who occasionally ask you technical questions and the people you talk to at computer user meetings. Some folks also count anybody who's hooked directly into their ESP/channeling experiments. Gorp the Great, heavenly patriarch of the Phoenician Gorp'ia sect — whom you, personally, channel into the present — certainly needs a couple dozen 486s.

Oh. And, if you talk to Elvis, remind him that he still needs a LAN. I keep telling him that, but he never listens to *moi*.

You can probably get qualification forms from friends who get the publication but you can phone 708-647-7925 to get a qualification form for *Infoworld* and 609-461-2100 to get one for PC Week.

The Only Other Windows Books You'll Ever Need

[1] ויתר מהמה בני הזהר עשות ספרים הרבה אין קץ ולהג הרבה יגעת בשר

— **קהלת** (a.k.a. *Ecclesiastes*), 12:12

Andrew Tobias wrote a blockbuster financial advice book some years ago and called it *The Only Investment Book You'll Ever Need*. But some years after, he wanted to write another one. What to do? He called it *The Only Other Investment Book You'll Ever Need*. Now that's class.

Of course, *The Mother of All Windows Books* is the only Windows book you'll ever need. But what if you are a junkie? I looked at a lot of books about Windows in the course of writing this one and two stood out: Fred Davis' *Windows 3.1 Bible* (Peachpit Press) and *2001 Windows Tips* by Mike Edelhart and the folks at *PC/Computing* (Ziff-Davis Press). If you're diving into the guts of the Windows `.INI` files and need a second opinion, I also recommend *Tuning Windows 3.1* by Neuman, et. al. (Que).

For many products, the online help is so good, it may suffice but if you use a product a lot, it may pay to get a product specific book. Pay attention to authors rather than titles. Maybe you thought *DOS for Dummies* was the greatest thing since sliced bread, but that doesn't mean that *Weird Imperfect for Dummies* will be any good if it has a different author. Find authors you like, authors you trust, and stick with them. And read the reviews. They will at least give you some information about the books.

Bear in mind that not every review is written by a reviewer who has read the book cover to cover! Book reviews are the Rodney Dangerfield of computer journalism. Here's a test — let's call it the IghorStone. Hey, you, Mr. Book Reviewer! Yoooo-hooooo! Are you watching? Let us know if you read this section. If you did, just say in your review, "I passed the IghorStone." Mom's minions will be waiting with bated breath, to see if you took the hook. *Heh heh heh.*

---

[1]And furthermore, my son, be admonished; of making books there is no end; and much study is a weariness of the flesh.

Newsletters

Newsletters have several things in common. They rarely have many ads and they cost mucho dinero — not unrelated issues. Prices of $150, $250, or even $500 per year are not uncommon.

Some newsletters are of interest to computer industry executives — often filled with useful information on trends in costs of support or media or other developments of specialized interest. They are rarely of interest to end users.

The Cobb Group (voice 800-223-8720, FAX 502-491-8050) offers a panoply of pricey ($80/year) newsletters, each tailored to a specific Windows topic or application. Quality of the Cobb "Inside...." newsletters ranges all over the lot: some are very well done, some do little but rehash the user manual. Be sure you take a look at a sample issue or two before you shell out the bucks. You may find Cobb's "Software Connection" monthly disks particularly useful, if you don't have — or don't take — the time to ferret out excellent shareware.

Mom isn't high on the tips type newsletters because she has rarely found one with really useful stuff and, other than some of the Cobb Group newsletters, the ones that she's seen aren't much more than you can find on the CompuServe forums.

Not exactly a newsletter but priced like one is *The Windows Shopper Guide* from WhiteFox Communications (Voice 503-629-5612, FAX 503-645-8642). It has product listings with detailed information for over a thousand Windows products. Since vendors have to pay for the listing (just like in the Yellow Pages), the lists sometimes have gaps. There are missing categories (for example, MPC titles) and categorization is often bizarre but, in spite of that, it is an exceedingly useful product for someone doing a lot of purchases. There is also an on disk version of the *Guide* in Toolbook format called *The Windows Source Book*.

User Groups

If you have the time to invest in the monthly meeting, local user's groups are often a great source of information and help. The really large ones will get speakers like Bill Gates and Philippe Kahn, so you can also get to meet industry leaders which can be fun.

To find the name of your local users group, you can call APCUG (a.k.a. Association of PC Users' Groups) User Group Locator at 914-876-6678 or write them at 1730 M St. NW Suite 700, Washington, DC 20036.

Trade shows

If you've never been to a major computer trade show, you'll be overwhelmed when you go to your first one. There are usually costly seminars on specialized areas but they can wait until you really learn about what's what in computers (and even then your time may be better spent at the exhibits).

The reason most folks go to shows is to attend the exhibits. There are literally hundreds of exhibits at the big shows, which can have thousands of attendees and make the New York subway at rush hour seem like a stroll in the park. Other than using the actual product or a working model, there is no better way to get a quick feel for a product than to see the vendor demo it. Sure, they'll emphasize the strong points but who knows the product better?

What are the shows you want to try to go to? The Mother of All Computer Shows is Fall Comdex, held in Las Vegas each Fall, normally in mid-November. 130,000+ computer users descend on Vegas straining its hotel capacity! Las Vegas' two biggest industries — gambling and prostitution — have a lousy week but the taxis and hotels make out like bandits.

Fall Comdex is so information rich that, if you can afford the time, it is worth making the trek. Ask your travel agent about gambling junkets — you may be able to get good airfare and hotel prices that way.

For most end users, Fall Comdex is the only show worth considering traveling to but if you live near any of the three other really big shows, try to spend a day or two there. The three:

- Spring Comdex, often held towards the end of May (but it varies and has been as early as the beginning of April) in Atlanta or Chicago

- PC Expo — New York, held at the end of June

- PC Expo — Chicago, held in September or October

There may be other local shows and specialized ones of interest to you like NetWorld or Seybold's Desktop Publishing shows.

 Two tips. First you can usually get free admission tickets for the exhibits if you do it in advance. Find a vendor who you think will be there and call them and ask if they have an application for free tickets. If you are on CompuServe, drop by the vendors forums, or drop by the shareware forum, and ask the organization there if they have tickets (the Association of Shareware Professionals often has a booth at the big trade shows).

My second tip is to not be shy. Vendors will often have group demos without a real chance to ask questions but there are usually separate work stations with people who can show the product one on one. While they are cruising for press and big corporate buyers, if you ask to see a demo and/or ask some questions that weren't addressed in the group demo, you'll usually find someone glad to oblige.

Tune In, Turn On, Take Off

What is often your best source of information is sitting at the end of your serial port. Bulletin Boards generally fit into four categories:

- The national services of which the best known are CompuServe, Prodigy, America Online and GEnie. They are marked by being accessible via local phone calls and having monthly charges that cover some services and hourly charges for the others.

- The large local BBS. These have many lines and hundreds of users. Two of the better known are Exce-PC in Chicago and Channel One in Boston. They often have yearly membership fees.

- The smaller local BBS (in reality, there is a continuum of public access BBS but perhaps the dividing line is whether they are run as a business or a hobby). These typically have one or two lines in and not that many users, but they are good sources of shareware/freeware and often have interesting discussions, especially via one of the networks that have network-wide discussion threads.

- Support BBS for various vendors, especially hardware vendors. This is one place to ask questions and get the latest drivers. But you may need to demon dial or try at 2 A.M. to get on. If there is support on CompuServe or one of the other services, you may find it easier to use that.

 I regard CompuServe as such an essential source of information and support that I devote an entire section to it; it's coming up next. But the other services have their strengths. Prodigy is well set up for families, especially with preteen kids. CompuServe is weak there. GEnie's pricing structure is such that it has been popular as a hang out for teenagers and young adults who just want to chat about the world. But its pricing has recently changed and that may effect this position.

Mom's gang spends so much time on CompuServe, that they haven't seriously explored the large and small BBS. If the idea appeals to you, pick up a BBS specific magazine like *BoardWatch* to get more information.

The Mother of all Information Services

> It is the same if one contemplates one's own true nature
> or the Buddha.
>
> — *Sermon on Sudden Awakening*, Shen Hui, ca 500 B.C.

CompuServe is an information cornucopia. It is a wonderful way to make contacts. Indeed, the authors of this book "met" on CompuServe and have only seen each other face to face one time. Among CompuServe's many information sources are:

- Electronic Mail
- Support forums
- General Computer Forums
- Non Computer Forums
- News and Weather
- Stocks
- Travel
- . . . and much, much more

CompuServe is really called the CompuServe Information Service (CIS for short) but we icons hate fuNny cAps and couldn't handle quite so many in one chapter, so we've spared you and us. It started as a time sharing service in 1969 and became an online service in 1979, so it is the Grandfather of all Information Services as well as the Mother. In 1980, the company was bought by H&R Block so it's not surprising that some folks find CompuServe taxing.

CompuServe shows its antiquity by running on ancient DEC machines. While these are finally being replaced, their legacy continues in two ways. CompuServe filenames are limited to 6+3 characters (even less than DOS' 8+3) because the DEC operating system used that convention. And CompuServe PPN (the ID number that the system uses) are octal, that is, base 8. Of course, any octal number looks like a decimal number but you'll never find an 8 and or 9 in a PPN (because it is octal after all).

Pricing

> What is a cynic? A man who knows the price of everything, and the value of nothing.
>
> — Oscar Wilde, *Lady Windermere's Fan*

It may seem strange to start out a discussion of CompuServe by talking about pricing but new users have been known to rack up $200+ bills their first month so the costs can't be ignored. Costs have dropped since the time that some wags talked of CI$ or Compu$erve, but they can still mount up. I'll only discuss pricing in the United States which is complicated enough. There are extra costs for many places outside the United States.

Most users will want CompuServe's so called Standard Pricing Plan (rather than the Alternate Pricing Plan I'll discuss in a bit). For an $8.95 monthly fee, you get unlimited free access to more than 30 Basic Services and to CompuServe support area plus a $9.00 allowance towards that month's private email charges. Computer related forums are *not* included in the Basic Services and have an hourly surcharge.

With Standard Pricing, there is no charge for reading private mail except for mail coming from Internet. The cost of messages sent or for reading Internet messages is 15 cents for the first 7,500 characters and 5 cents for each additional 2,500 characters. So, if you send messages that aren't overly long and don't use Internet, your $9 allowance is good for sending 60 messages per month, roughly two messages a day.

Internet is a collection of nodes which can receive mail and which also have discussion groups, file repositories, and other services. It grew out of ARPANET, the Army's Research network. I'll say more about it when I discuss mail in detail below.

Mail can be sent to multiple recipients but the charges are multiplied by the number of recipients. If you send binary files via mail, the byte count is as if they were characters. So sending a 300K binary file to six people will cost a whopping $36 ($.20 per 10Kx30x6).

On top of the monthly fee, there may be network or phone charges if you aren't located in a large urban area. CompuServe has many nodes in big metropolitan areas but away from them you may need to make a toll call. As an alternate, there is an 800 number you can dial with a surcharge of $8.70/hour or you can use LATA Networks, Sprintnet, TYMNET, or AlaskaNet with varying hourly charges.

Here are two tips if you go on the road with a laptop and modem. Before you go, log on to CompuServe and GO PHONES (a Basic Service) and get the local numbers for the places you'll be visiting. If the hotel you are staying in has a large surcharge for local calls but none for 800 numbers, it may be cheaper to use CompuServe's 800 number than pay the hotel surcharge.

You need a Ph.D. to understand all the pricing options if you use services beyond the basic ones included in the monthly fee. Mercifully simple are what CompuServe calls Extended Services which have simple hourly surcharges (charged in minute increments, rounded upwards): $8/hour for 2400 baud and $16/hour for 9600 baud. Fortunately, the computer forums are in the Extended category and many users don't access much else.

Next there are CompuServe's Premium Services. These have the Extended Services hourly charge plus an additional hourly surcharge that depends on the service — most often $15 /hour but much higher on some of the IQuest services where CompuServe is serving as a gateway to high priced third party databases. They may also have per item surcharges, for example per stock quote.

Lastly, as far as CompuServe Standard Pricing is concerned, there is Executive Service. If you agree to a monthly minimum $10 charge (towards which the $8.95

monthly charge counts), then there are some additional services available to you which typically also have surcharges.

 Executive Service is an absurdity. It's a holdover from the old days before there was Standard Pricing. Why complicate people's lives for a promise to spend at least $1.05/month beyond the standard pricing. Executive Service should have been included in the Standard Pricing Option.

Affiliated to CompuServe is Ziffnet, the online service associated to the Ziff-Davis publications with separate forums for *Windows Sources*, *PC/Computing* and several for *PC Magazine*. These forums are accessible from CompuServe if you are a Ziffnet member. There is a monthly fee of $2.50 once you join Ziffnet (until you explicitly resign) whether you use Ziffnet that month or not.

That's it for Standard Pricing. There is also Alternate Pricing which has a $2.50 per month fee and hourly charges of $12.80 for 2400 baud and $22.80 for 9600 baud. Nothing is free with standard pricing except for a few CompuServe support forums – everything is based on connect time (premium services still have a surcharge). There is a 10 cent surcharge for email sent to multiple recipients after the first.

 Generally, you'll want a Standard Pricing account but there are some special situations where you may want to use Alternate Pricing. One involves someone who has a CompuServe account and their employer gives them another one to use. If they want to keep their old account active, in case they should lose the company account, it may be wise to keep that account as an alternate pricing account.

 Even more to the point is the case of someone who sends a lot of binary files by email. Remember that 300K binary file by email to 6 people that costs $36 to send with Standard Pricing. With Alternate pricing, you can send the file to all six as a single message (there will be a 50 cent surcharge for sending to six recipients under alternate pricing) with a single upload. At 9600 baud, you can expect the upload to take about 5 minutes which means a cost of $22.80/12=$1.90. So instead of $36, that binary file costs $2.40. If you send a lot of binary email, but use CompuServe for other purposes, it may be worth your while to have two accounts: one used only for binary email and set to Alternate Pricing and another under Standard Pricing.

Access Software

You can access CompuServe with a general purpose communications program like ProComm or CrossTalk, but that's a mistake. If you use CompuServe enough to justify the monthly fee, you'll want a specialized product to help in your access. CompuServe Information Manager (CIM for short, often called WinCIM and DOSCIM for its two versions) is essentially free. You'll find a totally free copy on CD MOM but if you haven't a CD or access to one, you can usually find WinCIM in a deal from CompuServe that includes a usage credit equal to the cost of the program!

WinCIM is a remarkably good product, especially if you've suffered through the first DOS version. Those sections of CompuServe that have been given special hooks to CIM, for example Executive News Service or EAASY SABRE travel service, are a pleasure to use. In some other sections, you have to use a dumb terminal mode, but even there WinCIM puts you in a window where saving the session to a file is as easy as clicking on the part of the frame that says **Off** next to the words **File Capture**.

For sending and receiving email, you have access to an Address Book which you can add names to by merely clicking a button next to the sender's name or next to the sender or recipient of any forum message that you read. There is special support for sending binary files with a simple browse mode for picking the file. You can make a menu choice to log on to CompuServe and pick up your messages and log off (useful if you are on Alternate Pricing where time in email is charged by the minute; less important with Standard Pricing where it is not). And you have a filing cabinet with folders so you can organize your correspondence.

The one place that WinCIM is weak is in access to the forums more because it encourages you to spend more time on line (with the meter ticking even with Standard Pricing) than because its feature sets is weak. Compare CIM's approach where you enter a forum and search for messages or files online with that in the DOS program TapCIS (Support Group, voice: 800-872-4768) where you can fill out a dialog and have the program log on and download a catalog of matching files for you to browse offline. Or, for messages, where you can log on, download names of message threads, log off, pick the threads you want using a program that remembers which threads you've been following previously and then log on to collect the messages. With TapCIS, you can access multiple forums and have the program log off automatically so you can get a copy of coffee while forum messages are being collected.

The bad news is that while there were several Windows based forum access programs in beta when this was written, none were ready. It is also possible that CompuServe will move its Navigator program from the Mac to Windows giving you a better choice from them for forum access than WinCIM. While waiting for the Windows options to clarify, Mom's gang is using TapCIS, more from force of habit than a positive decision that it is the best alternative out there. My advice is to go with TapCIS or else log on to a forum with WinCIM and ask for suggestions on forum access program and then stand back while the firefight progresses — users tend to get emotionally attached to their forum access programs!

You'll find TapCIS and a TapCIS addon called ReCon in the shareware part of CD MOM.

Mail

CompuServe Mail is very flexible. You can send messages to multiple recipients and ask for return receipts if you want (both are extra cost items). You can send a FAX of a text message or a CongressGram to a CongressCritter. You can send a binary file, although not as an attachment to a message, but as a separate message — which can be confusing for the recipient. Be wary of the fact that binary messages can be expensive since the cost is roughly 2 cents per 1000 bytes per person receiving the message.

CompuServe Mail is linked to other commercial email services, most notably MCIMail and Internet. Internet is a collection of UNIX machines that includes virtually every major academic institution in the world (even in the former Soviet Union!), most government entities and a fair number of businesses. And users on some services like America Online and Fidonet can be reached from CompuServe through Internet addresses.

To send a message to someone on Internet whose Internet address is

`jdoe@somewhere.edu`,

you'd use the CompuServe mail address

`Internet:jdoe@somewhere.edu`

and if your CompuServe PPN is **12345,701** they would use the Internet address

```
12345.701@CompuServe.com
```

(note that the comma has become a period).

Forums

> What is called eloquence in the forum is
> commonly found to be rhetoric in the study.
>
> — Henry David Thoreau, *Walden*

 There is nothing quite like the forums on CompuServe. But be warned that their true cost isn't the connect time (and since forums are not included in the Basic Services, there will be connect time charges), it's the time you spend on the reading and replying to messages (presumably offline). And the forums are addictive; many who develop the habit, spend hours daily on it. Don't say I didn't warn you.

Imagine a mixture of the smartest gurus in an area of computing, with a few loud mouths thrown in for seasoning, and you describe almost any of the computer forums on CompuServe; whether its a specialized area like Visual Basic or MIDI music or a general area like IBM PC compatible software.

The caliber of advice you can get on the forums both from the support personnel on company run fora and from other users is generally superb.

 How come folks that would charge consulting fees running into hundreds of dollars a day — or wouldn't spend their valuable time consulting at all — do it for free on the forums? Sometimes, it is the opportunity to show your stuff in what is a crowded room. More often, though, gurus give their help freely because they've gotten into the spirit of the forum. It's a bit hard to explain, kind of a semi-vision thing, a throwback to the ethic of the '60s. The gurus teach and help, and in so doing, learn. Even the best of gurus learn enormous amounts from the forums by watching the other experts and confronting problems they might not have thought of. Many gurus feel a duty to pay the system back, by helping others. In the best fora, computers become fun again. The group of regulars become a source of information and camaraderie and *gemütlichkeit*, something you have to experience to understand.

At any given time, any given forum has a general tone. Sometimes it is downright nasty as users gang up on some company that has released a buggy new version of software and the company reps lose their cool in return. And during the great operating system wars right after the Microsoft/IBM divorce, the tone of some general interest forums was venomous. But that's the exception. There is most often a friendly, joking, light tone. Sometimes there are ingroups and ongoing lines that give a forum a special taste. At one point a group of users that called themselves the WinWord Gadflies gave a special flavor to the Word for Windows forum, for example, but a generally hostile attitude from the WinWord management pretty much killed the Gadflies; the demise chronicled in James Gleick's classic "Chasing Bugs in the Electronic Village" (*New York Times Magazine*, June 14, 1992, pp 38-42). And so it goes.

CompuServe is text based so you'll find heavy use of ASCII artifacts, called emoticons to try to leaven the conversation. The most famous is the sidewise smile shown as `:-)`. Turn the page on its side; you'll see it. In a similar vein, is the `<grin>` written with the < and >. They play an important role. Electronic forums can be a hot medium with users sometimes logging on hourly to take part in an ongoing argument. While `<grin>`s are sometimes used in a message that essentially starts with "Excuse me, while I shove this knife in your back and twist it," they also are used in the middle in a genuine attempt to add some humor that could be misinterpreted without the body English you get with face to face conversation.

Besides the special emoticons, there is heavy use of **TLA**s. **TLA** stands for Three Letter Acronym and is one itself. Here's a brief summary of some of CompuServe's most popular emoticons and acronyms:

BTW   By The Way

IMHO   In My Humble Opinion (never humble, BTW)

IANAL   I am not a lawyer (normally followed by an amateur's legal opinion)

TANSTAAFL   There ain't no such thing as a free lunch

BRS   Big Red Switch (computer on/off switch)

gdr   grinning, ducking and running

gdrvvvvf	gdr very, very, very, very fast
OIC	oh, I see
PMJI	pardon my for jumping in
ROFL	rolling on floor, laughing
:-(	sad face
@>--->---	a rose
_.|..	the Fudpucker emoticon; named for Orville Fudpucker, a sysop on Ziffnet. (Hint: the _ is a thumb).

You'll find a file on CD MOM called **wink.txt** that contains a larger listing.

If you want to find a company on line, just try GO followed by the company name. That works for Microsoft, Borland, and Lotus, as well as smaller companies like Mathsoft or Polaris. Besides the company forums, there are Multimedia forums (GO MULTIMEDIA), MIDI forums (GO MIDI), IBMNET (no connection with IBM; go IBMSW or GO IBMHW or ...), the Ziff-Davis magazine forums on Ziffnet (GO ZNT:WinSoruces, GO ZNT:Editorial for PC Magazine) and the ASP forum (GO SHARE). And more, and more and more.

If you want to talk about politics, diseases, human sexuality, investments, or even yell at Rush Limbaugh, you'll find them all on CompuServe.

The Best of the Rest (Basic Services)

Virtually none of the CompuServe services with a direct relation to computers are included in Basic Services (although you can buy computer gear in the Mall) but there is some really neat stuff that you get unlimited access to with your monthly fee including:

- Accuweather Maps — WinCIM will even download a map as a GIF for you (GO MAPS)

- EAASY SABRE — American Airlines managed flight listings. You can make reservations if you have "joined" but you can always browse to get information even if you prefer to use your local travel agent in the end. (GO SABRECIM with WinCIM or GO SABRE)

- Roger Ebert's Movie Reviews (GO EBERT)

- Stock, option, etc. quotes delayed at least 15 minutes (i.e. the data is not what is current at the exchanges, not that you have to wait 15 minutes to get it!). (GO BASICQUOTES)

- Zagat Restaurant Surveys (GO ZAGAT)

- Department of State Advisories — information on unrest, hotel shortages, currency restrictions, etc (GO STATE)

- The Electronic Mall — Mail order by modem (GO MALL)

- The practice forum. A great place to learn about how forums work at no cost. (GO PRACTICE)

These are mainly accessible on WinCIM's menus or the default favorite places but in case you can't locate the them, you can use the GO menu choice and use the item name that we give.

The Best of the Rest (Extended and Premium Services)

There are literally hundred of databases available but I'll mention two available of direct computer interest. CompLib consists of Computer Directory, a listing of thousands of products and vendors (with phone numbers, list prices, etc. included), and Computer Database Plus, a listing of thousands of reviews of products in the major computer publications. Even though this service is provide by Ziffnet, it is available, even if you don't belong to Ziffnet by using GO COMPLIB. It is a premium charge service; expect to spend about $2–$5 per listing in Computer Directory and $2–$15 per product in Computer Database Plus. That's on top of connection charges and coping with a terrible terminal mode interface.

You can set Executive News Service (ENS) to look for a set of keywords you define in press releases from AP and several other services. By picking Microsoft and a few other keywords, you can scan for computer-related news. The WinCIM interface to ENS is slick. You can easily scan headlines and decide which releases to download in full. You can then read them offline. ENS requires that you have the Executive Service Option and has a surcharge over standard hourly charges.

Mom and CompuServe

On MOM's companion CD, you'll find a full, "legit" copy of WinCIM. When you install WinCIM, you'll have an opportunity to sign up for CompuServe — the program even dials the phone for you! — and get started. To make this great deal even better, CompuServe is offering MOM readers their first month of basic services free.

It's an amazing deal, worth two or three times the price of the CD. You should take advantage of it.

How to Read a Review

 The letter to *OB Magazine* was irate: "How dare your Premier View of SuperDuperPaint say that the program could edit ico files. After using the product for eight hours a day for six weeks, I discovered if you load a 64x64 pixel icon instead of the normal 32x32, SDPaint crashes. You guys are incompetent." It happens all the time.

The problem isn't with the review. It's with the reader. The author of that letter hasn't a clue of how to read reviews. That's an important skill, one you need to learn.

When reading a software or hardware review, you should keep a few factors in mind:

- There are different types of reviews — warmed over press releases, beta reviews, first looks, comparative reviews, detailed tips articles. You need to realize which you are reading, and adjust your expectations accordingly.

- Realize that you are paying for the reviewer's expertise and general experience rather than extensive use of the program itself. That's a tough nut to swallow, but you have to understand that reviews are often written quickly, with deadlines looming. Invariably, if you use the program daily, you'll log more time on the program — after a few months, even weeks, you'll know more about the product than the reviewer.

- Pay attention to bylines. While Igor and Mao may trash a product with relative impunity — and great relish! — many reviewers bend over backwards to say at least one good thing about a product, even if they have to look long and hard to find something worthy of praise. Some reviewers aren't so kind. Thus it would behoove you to keep in mind who's writing the review. Don't mis-read a polite reviewer's diplomatic phrasing as an endorsement.

- Bear in mind the review is aimed towards a general audience. If you have special needs, the review may not even discuss them and if it does, the factor that may be crucial to you may not be a factor in the reviewers overall rating of the product.

- If the review downgrades a product, try to understand why. A database may be regarded as close to totally unsuitable if it won't read SQL, but if you don't know the difference between a SQL and a trilogy, you may want to upgrade the reviewer's rating.

- As a corollary of the last two items, it is usually a mistake to automatically go with the Editor's Choice (or equivalent name) without understanding the reasoning behind that choice.

Categories of Reviews

Reviews can really be categorized into four categories. At the bottom of the food chain is the warmed over press release. These are usually short, less than a quarter page, and marked with a New Product headline or something similar. In the weeklies, they may appear as news stories.

New Products pieces should not be confused with hands-on types of reviews, "real" reviews that sit higher up in the reviewing food chain. Sometimes the writer of a New Products piece has not even run — and may not even have — the product. Other times the New Products author has run the product and added his or her own insights, but you shouldn't depend on it. If this New Products kind of review says the product does X, Y, and Z, that is the vendors claim, and most likely has not been verified.

As long as you know what they are, these New Products reviews can be invaluable — unless you just happen to get press releases from the manufacturer. Use New Products reviews to get an idea of what has just come out. You may even learn about upgrades to products earlier than if you wait for the vendor to do the mailing.

Next up the food chain is the review of a beta product, and that requires a little explanation.

Programs are tested in stages. Initially, there may be an early internal test called an alpha test. Then various users and other outsiders will be asked to test a version, or versions and this is called a beta test. A few vendors have taken to sending out the final release candidate when it is sent to be duplicated calling it a gamma test. If a horrendous bug is found, the vendor can stop the duplication and fix it, although this is rare.

 What exactly is a beta tester and how can you become one? Beta testers are normally users of a previous version of the product or potential users of a new product. Typically they are not paid except for a free product or upgrade. Some vendors provide such a free product to all testers, but a few track how much feedback they get from you and only provide a free product if you've sent in all or most of the reports that they want.

How do tests work? It varies — most often the vendor will send you beta disks and documentation, but sometimes they expect you to download from their BBS or CompuServe. Depending on the vendor, feedback may be on a closed CompuServe forum, BBS, written report or even phone interview. Beta tests can run from two weeks to a year although 3-6 months is average.

Beta testers are usually required to sign an NDA (non-disclosure agreement) pledging to keep the test and its details secret unless the vendor gives permission to do otherwise.

Why beta test? Sometimes its for the thrill of using buggy code that destroys your data so beta testers should back up often and save their work often. But some beta tests are remarkably smooth and then you will get an advanced peek at the code and often a direct line to the developers so your requests for improvements are taken very seriously for the beta and future versions.

In the end, beta testing makes enough demands on your time, that the only reason to beta test is that you enjoy it and your boss will let you (if it is on company time).

If you want to beta test a product, call up tech support or, if you can locate a tech support rep on CompuServe, send them email. You'll likely have to complete a form and wait to see if you are accepted. If you frequent the general interest CompuServe forums, you will sometimes see a call for beta test volunteers.

 Despite the NDAs, beta tests of hot products from main stream vendors have a way of leaking out. Its a dog-eat-dog industry and competitors often learn of a product and all its new features at the beta stage. And publications often get unauthorized beta copies which they feel they can review without permission or the vendor allows them to review a beta obtained under NDA. So was born the beta review.

Most beta reviews are worth more than the paper they are written on — barely! First, it is important that you know if the review you are reading is a beta review and alas that is not always so easy. In particular, *Windows* magazine is notorious for publishing reviews of beta products without clearly stating the product is in beta.

Reviews of early betas are the worst. Often not all features are implemented so the review either skips what can turn out to be important features or fakes it talking about how features are supposed to work according to a spec. Even late beta reviews are suspect because of the treatment of bugs. Some reviewers feel it inappropriate to talk about bugs because, after all, they could disappear by the time the product ships. Other reviewers complain about bugs which actually do disappear before the product ships.

Alas, the public seems to eat up reviews of beta products, giving publications extra points for being the first to review a product, even if it isn't really the product!! So in accordance with Gresham's Law, non–beta reviews are driven out and more and more beta reviews appear. Only *PC Magazine* has more or less resisted the pressures and even it has slipped occasionally, although its beta reviews are clearly marked as Preview or Beta Review. It's an unfortunate trend that only the public can break.

Next up the chain and the first "real" review is the First Look or equivalent. These are hands-on reviews of new products, usually a page or less, although occasionally 1 1/2 or 2 pages. That means anywhere from 300 to 1,500 words, most often in the 500-800 range. Not a heck of a lot but enough for an experienced First Looker to really catch the main points. But remember the name. Because of scheduling pressure, the author is likely to have had the shipping version for only a week or two. He or she may have had a beta for some time before that and so not come into the review cold, but some products have betas that don't really work until very late in the process. So First Looks can be invaluable to find out what's in an upgrade, what a new product does, and if it lives up to its advanced billing, but they can't represent the insight someone might have after using a product for months.

The top of the food chain is the full fledged comparative review. These often have detailed scripts for a reviewer to follow during the test procedure and can have 100+ item feature tables (check lists). Depending on the magazine, these can involve 20 products run against one another.

What Reviewers Bring to the Party

An outside reviewer (and that means anyone not on the masthead and folks with the title of Contributing Editor which is a name for a glorified freelancer) is paid anywhere from $150 to $1500 for a review with the low end for the marginal publications we haven't even listed and the high end for several page reviews of complex products. Typically the range is $300 to $700. How many hours can a reviewer afford to fool with a product keeping in mind that there is time involved in writing, taking screen shots, etc.? How many days/weeks/months before you are likely to log more time in the application?

And internal editors usually have many, many other responsibilities so their time is likely to be less than a freelancer, not more.

The point is that you are not reading the review because the reviewer is spending enormous time in the application checking out every minor feature in dozens of ways. A conscientious reviewer of a graphics program, say, is likely to load a GIF graphics file or two to confirm that a program's claim of support for a GIFs is accurate but he/she is not likely to try a dozen of them and so unlikely to turn up problems that occur under unusual circumstances.

So what does the reviewer bring to the party? Most of all, expertise and experience. The reviewer is likely to have seen several other programs in the same genre or ones that at least have something in common. That means the reviewer will have a mental list of features he/she expects to be there. Moreover, if technical expertise is an issue, the reviewer should have whatever is required to understand the technical issues.

By the Byline

If you are reading reviewers because of the authors' expertise, well then the author counts, right? If you are interested in a particular area, learn the names of the folks who review products in that area and learn which ones have the goods when it comes to expertise. For example, Mom's gang knows that any thing written on fonts by Ed Mendelson or on graphics by Luisa Simone is going to be golden. They eat, sleep, live, and breathe that stuff; they're the ones the gurus turn to.

Can't you rely on the magazines to be sure their reviewers are competent. Most of the time, yes. But everyone has to have a first review in an area and occasionally they have huge lacks. For example, one magazine published a review in the spring of 1993 which spent a quarter of the review complaining about how unnatural and awkward the color picker was — describing the color dialog and all its shortcomings in loving detail. In fact, the dialog being complained about was the Windows common dialog for color. Oy! Obviously, this reviewer of a graphics product did not recognize the common dialog!

Beyond the Bottom Line

It's tremendously tempting for a category, especially one with lots of products to just buy the Editor's Choice. After all, they've looked at the category and if you have a boss looking over your shoulder, it's sure the safest thing to do. If disaster strikes, you can blame it on *OB Magazine*, but if you pick another product and there is a disaster what are you going to say when your boss says "You jerk, why didn't you go with the recommendation of *OB Magazine?*"

In many cases, that is not a bad strategy. The magazines are aware how seriously users take these picks so a tremendous effort goes into making these picks.

But the choice is made for the bulk of users. You may have special needs or some advanced needs so you can't take the easy way out. You actually need to read some reviews! For example, a magazine may feel support for some file type is critical and downgrade a product that is missing it, thereby knocking out of the editor's choice box. If that file type is of no interest to you, you may want to consider the product even though it is not editor's choice.

On the other side, consider the example of backup software. At this point in time, the majority of tape drives out there are QIC drives so it is possible a backup program without SCSI support could garner Editor's Choice honors. But if you have a SCSI drive, it is a non-starter for you!

The moral is to read a comparative review in an area you are considering making a purchase by first making a list of those features that are central to you. Then look at the 3-5 leading products. You may be able to figure them out by looking at the Editor's Choice box if there are honorable mention entries. Otherwise, you may need to skim all the reviews. Then read the reviews of the leading products using your weighting in terms of the products you think important. You may be surprised that your choice is sometimes not the one the Editors made.

If you have a boss to mollify, make a memo to the file (or to your boss!) explaining your reasoning. I bet it'll gain you stature in the boss's eyes.

Keep Your Eye on The Price

> Only Bulgarians pay retail.
>
> — *Igor's Book of Fractured Yiddish Quotes*

The Legend of the SRP

One of the difficulties of figuring out what to buy is that price is likely to be a significant factor. Finding out the price of a piece of computer hardware or software is not as easy as you might think; the prices you'll see in the magazines often bear no resemblance to reality.

The set of prices that you can believe most of the time are those listed by direct mail OEM advertisers. For example, if Gateway lists a computer system as being $2399, that's likely to be what it will cost. But you can't be sure. If you are making a big purchase, you may want to look at several recent ads by the company because the prices may vary (more often in the included extras) and most companies will honor the best ad if you know to ask and there isn't some unusual price change.

Similarly, the prices listed by direct mail sellers of software are reliable in that this is what you'll pay them. Again it may pay to look at several ads, not from the same advertiser, but from different ones to get an idea of how you might do elsewhere.

One direct mail seller I've only had good experience with is PC Connection (voice: 800-800-0004). Their prices aren't bad but you can possibly do a few bucks better on many items. What makes them so great is the service. Typical example was a case where Mao ordered a VGA card that had just added 24-bit support without changing the price but they didn't change the boxes (you could only tell the difference by looking at one of the chips on the board!) and in error, PC Connection sent out the older non-24 bit board. When Mao discovered the problem, not only was a new board sent out overnight at PC Connection's expense but they arranged for Airborne to come and pick up the return again at their expense.

But once you get away from prices quoted by direct mail advertisers, you can't believe what you read. The worst are the prices listed in magazine reviews which are the manufacturer's suggested retail price — SRP for short. These were never very meaningful but have become less so.

Most software and some hardware is sold by the manufacturer to a distributor like Merisel who then supplies them to end retailer. It used to be that manufacturers could get 45 – 60% of their SRP from the distributor with the rest going for the distributor's markup and retail markup. That meant that the street price figured to be about 65% of SRP, give or take a few shekels. But the price competition of the last year has changed that.

One extreme case I can think of was the initial release of WinMaster, a Windows utility pack form the makers of the SuperPCQwik disk cache. The SRP was $129 but you could get it as low as $19 with $29 typical. But its more complicated. Some packages had the disk cache thrown in "for free" although the actual price was typically closer to $55 — so what "for free" meant was that the SRP, which was meaningless, was unchanged. This is not to knock the makers of WinMaster. That's what the marketing game has become and they played it that way. But it does mean you have learn that the SRP is often meaningless.

Another vendor, Broderbund has decided that the SRP is meaningless so it no longer sets any! Rather it lists what it calls "an expected price range." That's a reasonable stance by itself but if the magazines just list "price" you are likely to be comparing apples and oranges if you see prices listed by Broderbund and a competitor in a single review. Add to this that some vendors offer competitive upgrades and will sometimes give that price to all comers if you buy directly from them and you have chaos.

So, the moral of all this is that prices listed in magazine reviews are often of no significance and you'll need to make some phone calls to get pricing information. Don't forget to include the vendor on the list of folks you call. Since they can avoid the middleman, they may have some kind of attractive special offer if you go directly through them.

Where to Buy

There are good reasons for buying from a local supplier. If you need one-on-one support (yeah, some folks call that "hand holding"), or feel more comfortable working with somebody you can see, there aren't many alternatives. Occasionally a local yokel will bundle classes with their hardware or software — and a hands-on class can be enormously useful, if the instructor knows the topic and communicates it well. That can be a mighty persuasive reason for buying local.

Some local suppliers, particularly those in large cities, take special pride in matching or beating the best prices you'll find in the magazines.

But an ever-increasing majority of computer folk opt to buy mail order. If you don't need the hand-holding, if you don't want to take a class, if you couldn't care less about talking to somebody face-to-face, if you want to get the latest stuff, cheap, mail order is probably your best bet.

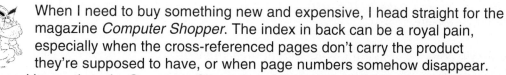
When I need to buy something new and expensive, I head straight for the magazine *Computer Shopper*. The index in back can be a royal pain, especially when the cross-referenced pages don't carry the product they're supposed to have, or when page numbers somehow disappear. By and large, though, *Computer Shopper* consistently has the broadest selection of advertisers, carrying a bewildering array of products, often with the lowest prices.

When I need to buy something new and cheap, I don't bother scanning the ads. I call PC Connection, and they get it to me right away. Why sweat the small stuff?

On the expensive stuff, ɫ go for price. An HP LaserJet 4 from Joe's Lobotomy and Laser Supply is the same as a LaserJet 4 from The Official Hoity-Toity HP Store. You might consider paying more to buy "service." That's fine, if that's your thing — go ahead and spend a few hundred bucks to get a fancy receipt. But the most "service" I've ever needed from a mail order supplier is to replace something that's missing or broken, and most (but not all) mail order firms do that quite well.

Repairs are another story, of course, and a particularly vexing one at that. But if the Official Hoity-Toity HP Store will repair LaserJet 4s (and they may ship 'em out!), it rarely makes any difference if you bought the LaserJet 4 from them or from Joe's. They fix 'em all just the same.

 Buying a whole computer system presents a real problem. You'll see my biases in Chapter 7 — I deal with mail order firms, and only a handful of them, mostly obscure. You may find it better to buy a computer from a local dealer, simply because there's so much that can go wrong in the first few days: screwed up software, dead hardware components, programs that won't talk to each other, or to you. Any way you shake it, though, problems in the first few days can be most time consuming.

Some people think it's better to buy a whole computer from a local company because it's easier and faster to get repairs locally. I haven't found that to be true. A good mail order firm will often ship a replacement part by overnight courier. Sometimes the local yokels won't even *look* at a dead machine until it sat in their shop for a day or two. If you need to take in your whole system — if it's really and truly dead — the local shop will take several days (maybe several weeks) to get it working again. On whole systems, most mail order firms include a year of on site service — don't buy a system without it. The exception is laptops which normally need to be sent back to the manufacturer for repair whether you buy them mail order or locally.

When it comes to buying a whole computer, there are no easy answers, pilgrim.

A Buyer's Black Belt

 No matter where you buy, no matter what you buy, use a credit card.

That's so important, I'm going to say it again: *no matter where you buy, no matter what you buy, use a credit card.*

You should never, ever, ever write a check or *<shudder!>* pay cash for any piece of hardware or software. It's that simple.

Computer companies go in and out of business with alarming frequency. Even the big guys can go belly-up, sometimes in a matter of weeks, or even days. Millions of dollars of shoddy equipment — even completely bogus software! — gets foisted on unsuspecting users every day, and rip-offs in the computer industry abound. The only rock-solid guarantee you have is your credit card, and your ability to "dispute" a charge.

Usually you have less than a month to dispute a charge, so it pays to move quickly. But almost all show-stopping lemons will make themselves known to you within a few days.

 You have a lot of leverage with a charge. If you order something and it doesn't arrive when the vendor promised it would, call your credit card company and cancel the charge. (Always follow up the phone call with a registered letter, return receipt; the credit card company rep on the phone will give you the address.) If you order something and it doesn't work right, call the vendor and try to work things out. If they stiffed you with a pile of compucrap, ship it back, call your credit card company, and cancel the charge. Tell 'em Mom sent ya.

Some vendors have a nasty habit of posting your charge the day they receive your order, instead of the day they ship. Not only does that put your money in the vendor's pockets before it should, it starts your "disputed charge" clock ticking earlier. (They'd never get away with it in court, but it can cause you undue headache.) Watch out for companies that charge before the product ships, and keep your eyes open in the trade press for reports of companies that do so. Refuse to do business with them.

There are several shopping tips of secondary importance. Always ask for a discount. You might be surprised. Be flexible in what you need and what you want; some vendors may be able to swap out nearly identical components at considerable savings. If you're looking for a vendor, post a message on CompuServe — it's the ultimate grapevine, a place where you can talk to those who both praise and damn a vendor. The longer you can wait for any particular technology, with rare exceptions, the cheaper it will become. Watch out for re-packaged software: almost every software retailer has access to shrinkwrap machines; look for books with broken spines, or disks with greasy fingerprints; if you find something that's been re-packaged, don't install it (the risks of viri are too great!), return it to the place you bought it, and complain. Loudly.

And, of course, read Chapter 7 before you buy hardware.

But all of these pale in comparison to the cardinal rule, the *sine qua non* of blackbelt computer purchases: no matter where you buy, no matter what you buy, use a credit card!

Sign Posts in the Software Jungle

> Now these are the Laws of the Jungle, and many and mighty are they;
> But the head and the hoof of the Law and the haunch and the hump is — Obey!
>
> — Rudyard Kipling, *The Second Jungle Book*, 1895

The Software Family Tree

In trying to keep track of the varying types of software, it is useful to think of a hierarchical structure with software broken into application and utility with further subdivisions below that. Of course, this breakup and the others that I'll discuss, aren't always clean. For some an image editor is a utility while for others it is an application. But the categorization is still useful.

Figure 6-1 shows a schematic software family tree. Since I discussed utilities extensively in Chapter 5, I've focused on the application side. At the top level, there are the big three: word processing, spreadsheets, and databases (which I'll discuss in some further detail). Then there are the two junior partners: graphics and communications which I won't detail except to note that you probably want to stick to simple presentation programs for now. Multimedia and animated presentations are a time sink that all but specialists should avoid. The coming category in communications is email programs that collect from all the services you access — say MCI mail and CompuServe — and give you a single place to read, answer, and send messages.

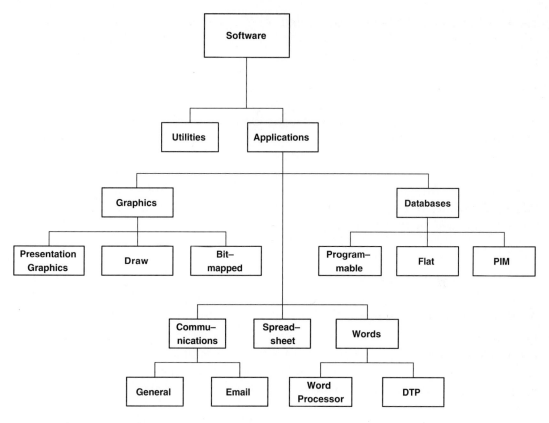

Figure 6-1: The Software Family Tree

As complicated as Figure 6-1 looks, it's only the tip of the iceberg. I haven't listed truly vertical software (for example, that you use to manage a medical office) or even specialized products that are of interest to several different groups but not broadly used — for example, CAD, accounting or statistics. I've left out all programming languages and tools since they too are specialized. My goal is to list those categories of application that I think most users will want to have in their stable of products, and even there I fudged in two ways.

First, there are two categories, DTP and programmable databases that you'll see. Although most users don't need them; they are there because if you read the press, you might think they do — this is not to say that no one needs them, only that they are specialized products like accounting.

Hey Boss, you left out da games.

And I left out the broad array of home products — not just games, but personal finance, taxes, educational and, if you'll pardon the use of an awful buzzword, edutainment. The criteria are just different for the home so it wouldn't make sense to combine everything in one even more complicated diagram. Still, the remarkable thing is that you'll want to have most items in Figure 6-1, on a home as well as an office machine. About the only exception is Presentation Graphics unless you think that your kids are more likely to accept a lower allowance when your arguments are accompanied by bullet charts.

In the Beginning Was the Word

You want one of the three main word processors for Windows — Ami Pro, Microsoft Word or Word Perfect. It's that simple. As long as you print any words on paper, you can't afford not to have the tools to print them with good effect and these products are both powerful and easy to use. About the only exceptions are if your needs are simple and you rely on one of the Works packages that include lower end word processing (but still functional with most of the basics).

The need for desktop publishing programs is much less clear. Their day in the sun *as general purpose products* has passed. Don't get me wrong. If you are producing monster technical books you'll likely want FrameMaker and if you are digitally typesetting books written by someone else for a commercial publisher, or producing newsletters to go to a service bureau, you'll want one or more of PageMaker, Quark, or Ventura. But those are for specialists. Most folks don't need these products and certainly don't need the various low-end DTP programs that once filled a significant niche. Because word processing programs have absorbed the feature sets that once made DTP a separate category. For example, the big three have the ability to embed graphics and flow text around it, support multiple columns, and have powerful table capabilities.

You should be aware that there are specialized word processing products of many different types. If you are into foreign languages with special alphabets, consider UniVerse (Gamma Productions, voice: 310-394-8622; FAX: 310-395-4214) or for Hebrew/English word processing one of several products with names like Dagesh

(Davka; voice: 800-621-8227, FAX: 312-262-9298) and HaKotev (voice: 801-377-2045). For a few equations in a document, you'll be able to use the equation editors included in the major word processors (but be aware that the one in Word Perfect is pretty poor). For full fledged scientific word processing, you may want to look at Scientific Word (TCI, voice: 505-522-4600; FAX: 505-522-0116).

Spread 'em

If you've ever seriously used a spreadsheet, you understand what a wonderful tool they can be and should skip this section. But if you haven't and you need to manipulate sets of numbers for anything from grading a course to tracking your kid's Little League team's batting averages, you simply must have a spreadsheet.

If your needs are serious (hey, you were supposed to skip this section, remember) you'll want to look at the high-end features, compare reviews and consider new approaches like Lotus' Improv. But most users need only a very small fraction of the features and can happily use virtually any spreadsheet from the ones included in the Works packages to the big three: 1-2-3, Excel, and Quattro Pro.

Dealing with Personal Data

When it comes to databases, the lunatics are running the asylum. From the earliest days of computing, a major use has been for businesses and other organizations to track specialized data, and for that it paid to have custom applications written by consultants who used programmable databases. That is still true for those needs but those are the wrong tools for users trying to track personal data or even data that doesn't warrant a consultant writing a custom application. Yet, to the magazines, too often database is synonymous with the high-end programmable products. Even the non-programmable products (sometimes called Flat File although they can be relational) are reviewed with criteria that make sense if they are being used for similar purposes to the programmable products.

 Most users have no need for Access, dBase, FoxPro, or Paradox. There I said it, and no doubt Philippe and Bill will take me off their Xmas card lists. But its true.

For access to organized data, most users are best served by the non-programmable products. The main candidates include Lotus' Approach, Symantec's Q&A/Win, and Claris FileMaker Pro.

And for tracking appointments, to do lists, and telephone appointments, don't forget the PIMs, short for Personal Information Manager. Too many users haven't gotten into the PIM habit but those who have find they use them as much or more than any other application. The category is much less standardized than say, Word Processors, where the approach and basic structure is the same across the category. So you'll need to look closely at the reviews, talk to friends, ask advice on CompuServe and see demos at trade shows to decide which is the best fit for you. Major contenders include Symatec's ACT, Jensen–Jones' Commence, Arabesque's ECCO, Lotus Organizer, Polaris Packrat. Some of these are billed as contact managers but PIM and Contact Manager have essentially merged into a single category.

How Suite It Is

Microsoft says that as of Spring 1993 over half the new sales of Winword are as part of Microsoft Office, its suite of applications. There are three main suites available — the one from Microsoft (with Access, Excel, Mail, PowerPoint and Word), one from Lotus (with 1–2–3, Ami, cc:Mail, Freelance, Organizer, and presumably, soon also Approach), and a one offered jointly by Borland and Word Perfect (Paradox, Quattro, and Word Perfect).

It is interesting that market pressure in favor of these products was so strong that Borland and WordPerfect were forced to join forces. Of course, with the Borland product, you lose the advantage of a common interface at a detailed level. Still, there are those who would argue that uniformity is not one of the strong points in any of the suites.

There are real advantages to suites. There is noise, slowly being realized, of adding common macro components across applications so that the ones in a suite will act together more smoothly. There is an advantage of a similarity of interface so that, for example, the programs in the suite use similar button bar layouts and you only have to learn one set of inscrutable icons. But so far the advantages aren't so great that they are totally compelling. If you are currently using Ami and Excel, for example, there is no special reason for you to jump ship to one suite or the other.

There's at least one suite disadvantage that may not be all that apparent. When you buy a suite, you're buying one single license for all the products: you can't break 'em up. A company that shells out money for Microsoft Office, for example, has the right to run Word, Excel, PowerPoint, Mail, and Access *on one machine*. You can't break out Word for one employee, Excel for another, and Access for a third. Most people don't realize it, but the suites are sold as single-user bundles, all for one and one for. . . uh. . . one.

 In 1985, Lotus tried to repeat is huge 1–2–3 success with Symphony, an integrated package but it, and its competitors, never captured the imagination of the market, in part because of the decathlon effect — the products typically had at least one weak component and usually none that was as outstanding as the very best in the product category. It is interesting that almost ten years later, the strategy in a somewhat different guise has become a huge success!

 I see several reasons for this. In one sense, there was no need to create a new market. The names of the suite components were already well known. There is no stigma of using less than the best since the suite consists of stand alone products. The integration is now provided by Windows which users are familiar with. And the components are all world class products.

 In a nutshell: you won't go wrong with any of the three big suites. Yes, there are advantages and disadvantages to particular components of each suite. I, personally, prefer Microsoft Office, but there are good reasons for picking either of the other two.

Not long ago, several of the major Windows applications didn't *feel* like Windows applications. Software manufacturers, in their haste to port DOS products over to Windows, didn't seem to "get" it; their products acted like ported DOS products, not new Windows apps. That's changing with the latest versions of the big packages: by the time you read this, I don't think it will be much of a consideration.

Even the differences among the major applications are fading — new, compelling, capabilities in any product will soon appear in all its competitors. More and more, it becomes a question of usability (ach! I *hate* that word!) and how much the disparate products appear and act as a unit, a cohesive whole.

If the current price trends continue — if Microsoft, Lotus and Borland/WP keep shaving their prices, selling suites for barely more than the price of two of the components — you'll soon have little reason *not* to choose a suite. It's the wave of the future, and a welcome one at that. Suites hold enormous potential for reducing training times, shaving down the learning curve, and tying together applications in strange and exotic ways. Just imagine how different the world will look five years from now if the software vendors succeed in developing a uniform macro language, a consistent user interface, and applications that take advantage of the best characteristics of each app. We've come a long way since the days of writing memos with a spreadsheet. The suite future looks stunningly bright.

The Mother of All Easter Eggs

Wanna see who wrote Windows? Do the following. Call up your favorite program that comes with Windows from ProgMan to Calendar. Throughout the following exercise kept the **Control** and **Shift** both held down. Choose **About...** from the **Help** menu and double click on the icon in the box and hit **OK**. Nothing will happen but you didn't expect something really important like this to be easy, did you? Now (keeping the silly shifts depressed) do the **Help/About...** click on the icon routine yet again and you'll get the message shown in Figure 6-2.

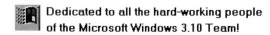 Dedicated to all the hard-working people of the Microsoft Windows 3.10 Team!

Figure 6-2: Start of the Egg

Big deal! All that work for a little message. Ah, but don't stop now. Keeping those shifts down, do the menu plus click routine yet one more time and whatya know, you start getting rolling credits of the folks who worked on Windows 3.1. And there's a little character pointing out these folks. One of the four shown in Figure 6-3 will appear.

 Bill Gates   Steve Balmer   Brad Silverberg   the bear

Figure 6-3: Egg all over your face!

You know who Bill Gates is. Steve Ballmer was the senior VP for systems during the development of Win 3.1. He's one of the early Microsoft employees and one of the three billionaires that Microsoft made. Brad Silverberg is the VP for DOS and Windows. The bear prefers to remain anonymous.

This kinda thing is called an Easter Egg after the concoctions that Faberge made for the Russian Czar. Those were jeweled boxes with a secret button or other gizmo that displayed a little secret compartment or other goodie. Just like Windows.

 I'm so excited; Mom is about to break new ground with the first book Easter Egg. In fact, it is so good I've applied to the IEEE for their approval as an IEEE Easter Egg, otherwise known as an IEEEEE. OK — ready. Lie down on the floor, lift your feet in the air, close your eyes and rub your tummy making *ommm-ommmm* noises. Now get up, walk in a circle, and do it again. You'll see mental pictures of the authors float before your eyes.

 What? It didn't work? You didn't do it right, sonny. Go and try it again and don't you dare show up here again until it does work.

See — I told you it would work.

 I find it remarkable how popular Easter Eggs are. They are in all sorts of programs with all sorts of weird callups. I really don't see the point except that folks feel special knowing something that no one else does I guess. Credit is nice but I don't like the secret handshake stuff. I'd like to see an Easter Egg entry on the Help menu instead of the stuff and nonsense. Oh, well, IEEEEE, *IEEEEE, IEEEEE.* Primal scream therapy.

 And don't forget what happened to that Czar.

How to Make a Mom

 You guys better be careful what you do with a section with this title or we could lose our PG 13 rating.

If you want to see what really goes on behind the scenes, you should take a look at what people use, day to day — not necessarily what they write about, what they say might work best in a hypothetical situation.

Mom is one of the few PC books to be conceived, developed, written, edited and ultimately printed from a PC, and we used Windows exclusively. Most PC books, believe it or not, are still typeset on a Mac!

We're particularly proud of the fact that this book was all done with a word processor; there's no publishing package or DTP system lurking in the background. Except for the quality of the final printed masters — which would be expensive, but not difficult, to duplicate — *you* could produce a book just like this in the comfort of your home or office. The publishing industry has come a long, long way, and *Mom* is riding the crest of the wave.

All the icons used Word for Windows 2.0 to prepare the manuscript. It was great to be able to place the screen shots into the manuscript as well as placing the icons themselves. We even had a macro that Igor wrote that popped up a box (shown in Figure 6-4) to make placement of the icons and figures easier. The icons needed to be put into what Winword calls a frame in order to have them appear with text wrapped to their left. All that could be automated in macros. The macro also used the {seq} field to label figures and allow renumber after new figures were inserted out of sequence.

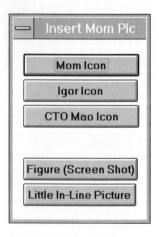

Figure 6-4: Mom's macro

We also made use of the table feature and Mao liked the ability to place lots of bullets. The one place that Winword got stressed was in making the Mother of all Font catalogs which really stressed the system because Winword 2.0 goes bananas with more than 255 fonts in the system.

The Winword spell checker gets credit for one of the puns. There was a section in Chapter 5 which was called *What the heck is going on here* but the spell checker didn't like *heck* and suggested *hack*. That fit the subject so we let the speller checker's pun stand. Talk about artificial intelligence!

That spell checker sure is intelligent. If it finds ODBC, it suggests ODDBALL as the correct spelling. You don't suppose it's Philippe in disguise, do you?

The other tools critical for manuscript preparation involved preparation of the many screen shots you see here. We'll let Igor and Mao tell you what software tools they used; they spill the beans on hardware in Chapter 7.

I used Collage to take all my screen shots. Paint Shop Pro came in handy several times for sizing. HiJaak Pro was invaluable for translating Chapter 14's .ICO files to something WinWord could understand. The icons, the pictures, come from CorelDRAW!'s fine clipart library, with a special nod to the folks at Metro Image Base. Several times I popped into Visio to make a quick schematic drawing. Great stuff.

I used Excel to do all the spreadsheets and number crunching, and to keep track of the progress of the book. PackRat held the crucial contact information. I created the CD MOM master by using PC Tools' backup program, to a Colorado Memory Systems Jumbo 250 tape. Mastering a CD is much easier than it appears. Ah well. Maybe I'll cover that in another book.

We communicated constantly via CompuServe, sending files and ideas and barbs back and forth, gathering software for CD MOM, seeing what problems confound people the most. I used — and don't know how I could live without! — TapCIS, RECON, and TurboCom for communication and WinZIP and PKZip for file compression.

I used Image Pals for almost all the shots I took. It's ability to take a single object was invaluable. I like to see how the screen shot will look so I post processed shots to convert to grey scale, color correct,. . . and for that I most often used Picture Publisher 4.0 whose color shield and smart fill are great. For some simple picture processing I used the shareware Paint Shop Pro which loads fast and does what it does very well. A very few times, I used Photoshop (for example to get the arrows you see in some of Chapter 2's figures) and I used Paintbrush to get the grid you see (Paintbrush doesn't draw grids but it shows a grid when you magnify and I took screen shot of that!). For some flow charts, I used Visio. I also tracked contacts in PackRat (like, Igor, I stuck with version 4.1).

To help in making the *Mother of All Icon Catalogs*, I had to place all the icons from `progman.exe` and `moricons.dll` into individual ico files where a Winword macro could suck them into the manuscript. Icon Manager made quick work of that. And for CompuServe, I used TapCIS.

MOM wouldn't be nearly as much fun without all those corny, crazy, sometimes cogent quotes. You'd be surprised how many people wonder where they came from — "What possessed you to think of that?" may be the question I hear most often. Many of the quotes come from the WinWord CD — "Word for Windows and Bookshelf Edition" they call it. Most of the quotes, though, just come from the fuzzy recesses of my abscessed brain, and a very eclectic library that has been my constant companion over the years.

SECTION 2

A Win TuneUp

Sat cito si sat bene[†]

— Latin Proverb

 In Section 2, you'll find everything you need to know to make Windows dance on its ear. While you might want to read Chapter 7 from beginning to end, the other three chapters are strictly for reference.

[†] It is done quickly enough if it is done well.

CHAPTER 7
Killer Hardware

In the discovery of secret things and in the investigation of hidden causes, stronger reasons are obtained from sure experiments and demonstrated arguments than from probable conjectures and the opinions of philosophical speculators. . .

— William Gilbert, *De Magnete*, 1600

In this chapter, Mao (with a bit o' help from the other Icon-o-Clasts) lectures on the hard windows facts of life: what you need; what to buy; what works; what doesn't. Mom summarizes it all in the next to last section — so even if you skip the details, check out *Mom's Red Book* at the end of this chapter.

Dirty Laundry

Pssssst. Want to know the computer industry's second-dirtiest little secret?

 Those hardware testing benchmarks you rely on — the ones in all the major magazines and papers? — the ones that tell you and millions of other computer jocks how to spend gazillions of bucks? Well, I say they don't hardly mean diddly. They don't do a good job of figuring out how the hardware will work with your setup; and even if they did, there's a whole lotta cheatin' goin' on.

The joke's on you. Read on, read on.

Oh. The dirtiest secret? Heh heh heh. That's easy. Every program over 2K or so in size — Windows, DOS, UNIX, CP/M, COBOL, C++, FORTRAN, PL/I, Basic, IMS, CICS or otherwise — has bunches and gobs of creepy-crawly bugs. True fact.

Mom's Board

This chapter assumes a nodding acquaintance with PCs and their innards — if you can point out a motherboard, you'll be okay.

But if you're hardware illiterate, not to worry: there's a book available that will walk you through the basics, over, under, around, and through the essential workings of any PC. It's *PC/Computing — How Computers Work*, by Ron White and illustrator extraordinaire Timothy Edward Downs (ZD Press, 1993). Or, if your machine has a CD-ROM drive and you'd rather learn about your beast from the beast itself, get a copy of ComputerWorks from Software Marketing Corp. Both the book and the program are simply gorgeous, exquisitely done.

Keep Your Eyes on the Prize

I'm forever amazed at people who admit they bought a Brand X SuperFlummoxer over the Brand Y FlummoxerPro because X ran 10% faster than Y in a big magazine's speed test. Or folks who won't buy a particular brand of computer because it doesn't run cache write-backs in the way the experts say is optimal. Or those who only consider MCA (*M*is*C*reant *A*rchitecture) bus systems because they know all the little cars inside their computer need MCA so they can run at 55 miles per hour — *that's what IBM's TV ad says, isn't it?*

What a crock.

CTO Mao on Hardware

 Here's the true fact of Windows hardware upgrades: a speed gain of 25% — maybe even 50% — on any single component of your computer won't matter much. You may not even notice the difference. Speed your *whole computer* up by 25% and you'll notice it for a week or two. Maybe. But upgrading an individual component on your computer with something that runs 25% faster is an exercise in futility. You'll lose more time installing the upgrade than you'll ever recoup with improved hardware performance.

There are some extenuating circumstances, of course: if you have a number-crunching Windows program that takes over your computer for hours at a stretch, a 25% improvement in CPU speed may be noticeable. If your machine is running real-time stock quote updates, where every millisecond counts, you may see some gains. If you're on a network with a file server, it has to be jacked up to get data in to and out of the machine quickly. Fair enough. DOS is another story entirely. But for the vast majority of Windows users, 25% is an undistinguished drop in the bucket.

Video rates as a very special case because Windows is so dependent on slapping pixels on the screen. Sometimes you *will* be able to feel a 25% increase in video speed, but the thrill won't last for long; you'll be begging for more within a month. I'll talk about video in depth later on in this chapter — and introduce my seminal video rating, the ToastedBunnyMark.

The simple fact is that when you're running typical Windows applications, your computer spends 80 to 90% or more of its time twiddling its thumbs, waiting for something to happen. Speed up one component of your system by 25% and your computer *still* spends 80 to 90% or more of its time twiddling its thumbs, albeit a bit faster.

Save your money, pilgrim. Go for the big improvements: 50% speed gain on a single component at a minimum; 25% or more on the whole system — and preferably twice that. Ignore the ads. You won't be missing as much as you think.

Besides, no matter what you buy, two years from now it won't be good enough.

They're the Bench; You're the Mark

What's a benchmark. . .and who cares? Good questions!

> **benchmark** [techspeak] n. An inaccurate measure of computer performance. "In the computer industry, there are three kinds of lies: lies, damn lies, and benchmarks." Well-known ones include Whetstone, Dhrystone, Rhealstone. . .
>
> — *The New Hacker's Dictionary*

A hardware benchmark is a timed test that tells you how well a particular piece of hardware performs. A benchmark is supposed to have some predictive power: a good benchmark score (e.g., more floozles per second, or fewer seconds per googlefloozle) is supposed to tell you something innate about the hardware — a better benchmark score should tell you which piece of hardware will perform better on your setup, running your programs.

Like all such tests, hardware, human, or otherwise — and we won't mention the SAT test by name — a benchmark only measures the ability to perform a certain set of necessarily narrowly-defined (usually replicable) actions, under a very limited set of circumstances.

Read anything more into a benchmark, and you'll do so at your own peril. Buy hardware based solely on benchmarks, and you'll get what you deserve.

Back in the old days (say, five years ago) when life was much easier, you could look at the number of the processor inside a computer and come up with an educated guess about performance: an 80286-based computer running at 12 MHz (i.e., 12 million cycles per second, commonly called a 286/12), ran about 50% faster than an 80286 at 8 MHz. With the 386 chips, you could fudge a bit: a 386SX/16 was maybe twice as fast as a 286/12, give or take a nudge.

Things are much, much more complex nowadays. Processors have all sorts of strange numbers. Worse, you have to look at the performance of individual components of a computer — simple processor statistics no longer suffice. Benchmarks evolved to test those individual pieces of a computer, and bottom-line results (medians, modes, harmonic means, subharmonic ways) grew from the pieces. While the bottom-line numbers are certainly easy to use, they belie enormously complex, and valid, questions about statistical sampling, weighting, and replicability. Is processor speed more important than video speed? Is a slightly slower disk more of a drag on system performance than marginally inferior memory access speed? Those questions have no facile answers.

 My approach to benchmarks is simple. If you can't *feel* the difference, it ain't worth the effort. Forget the numbers. In a sufficiently advanced civilization, 12,187,346 video WinMarks™ is indistinguishable from 10,319,426 video WinMarks... they measure 'em that way, by the way, with eight significant digits. No joke!

Humbug. A piece of hardware should be so fast, compared to what you currently use, that it'll have you grabbing the seat of your pants, begging for mercy. Anything less, and you're wasting your money.

It's not an academic question. Hundreds of millions of dollars ride on benchmark results. People spending their own hard-earned bucks want the best they can afford. Corporate buyers often feel they have to recommend the hardware that shows up as number one or number two on the benchmark charts.

It's scary. Hardware companies have been made and broken by their relative locations on a meaningless benchmark list. The benchmark results look so official, replete with eight-places-of-accuracy ratings, scientific sounding mumbo-jumbo, red lines, queue lines, and bottom lines, all culminating in putative winners and losers. The numbers speak for themselves, eh?

Not so. The numbers. They lie.

The MhomStone

> Quis custodiet ipsos custodes?[†]
>
> — Decimus Junius Juvenalis, *Satires*, ca. 100 A.D.

I can hear the screams all the way up here: those big computer magazines and newspapers have millions of dollars invested in benchmarks. They've been tested

---

[†] *Who will guard the guards themselves?* In Juvenal's time, hired guards protected the reputation — if not the fidelity — of women whose husbands made war.

and calibrated and Ph.D. certified and debated and debauched and detonated. . . how *dare* Mom take their tests to task in such a cavalier way?

Let's see if those big-time publishers will put their mouths where their money is. Mom would like to issue a little challenge; we'll call it the MhomStone.

Next time one of those big magazines publishes a test of. . . let's say video cards. . . Mom would like to see the publisher gather the professional benchmarkers together in a room. Yeah. The guys and gals who created and ran the tests. The experts.

Nawwwww. . .we don't want to line 'em up and shoot 'em. They're not the enemy: they have an impossible task, and do their level best to create benchmarks that help you. As Pogo knew well, the enemy is us — and our insane insistence on quantifying everything. . .

We'd fill that room with identical computers: identical except for video cards, natch. Then, running just the Windows applications normal people use — WordPerfect, WinWord, or Excel, CorelDRAW, or QuarkXPress — on real files, real data, Mom would like to see those pro benchmarkers rank the machines by how fast they run: top to bottom, fastest to slowest. No pre-fab test suites. No do-nothing macros. No abstractions about "typical" users and "profile" activities. No hundredths-of-a-second stopwatches. Just the pro benchmarkers and some real work. . . *mano y mano*, against their own benchmarks.

Whaddya want to bet that, 80% of the time, the pros can't line the machines up in the right performance pecking order, can't replicate their benchmarks in the real world? Even on video cards, which should show enormous fluctuations in Windows performance. And whaddya want to bet that most of the other 20% of the time they'll really identify a board by its quirks, bugs, or problems they've already encountered with the driver?

Hey, if one of those fancy schmancy publishers has the guts, Mom herself might even be persuaded to make a personal appearance. Who knows? Maybe she could ply the workers in the trenches with cookies and ice cream. It'd sure beat slaving over a hot keyboard all day.

Now *there's* a benchmark.

The Lonely Voice of Youth

> Le scandale du monde est ce qui fait l'offense,
> Et ce n'est pas pécher que pécher en silence.[†]

> — Jean-Baptiste Poquelin

The computer industry seems to spawn a scandal every few months. Trade secrets and hiring practices. Unfair advantage from undocumented calls. Nocturnal habits of high level executives. You know the tune.

When the computer historians write about The Big Scandal of 1993-4, no doubt they'll focus on video benchmarks. Accusations and cover-ups, charges and counter-charges abound. If it weren't so laughable, it'd be prime grist for a daytime soap. At the heart of the matter: do video board or chip manufacturers "cook" their boards, building routines into their boards that do nothing but detect big-time benchmarks and spew out surreptitiously inflated results? And do the video driver folks cook their programs, too?

 Simple fact is that many, perhaps most, video boards or drivers (or both), at one point or another, were cooked. Many, perhaps most, still are; the manufacturers have simply become more clever, or learned to use a somewhat fancier cookbook, one more palatable to the computer press.

The initial uproar over manufacturers' intransigence took several amusing turns. At one point, a board peddler convinced a major national magazine that their particular method of cooking was legitimate because, in addition to giving artificially inflated results on the magazine's benchmark, this particular form of "bitmap cache" cooking also sped up Windows programs, in certain circumstances, from time to time.

The bitmap cache debacle isn't harmful in itself; it merely shows that there are many, many ways to cook a cat. . . er. . . cockroach; many ruses that sound plausible enough, many arguments board manufacturers can put forward, none of which help the normal garden-variety Windows user, unless you happen to cut and paste stuff between windows all day long.

[†] *Public scandal is the one that causes offense; those who sin in silence have not sinned at all.* French playwright Jean-Baptiste Poquelin, a.k.a Molière, was no stranger to vice.

There's one born every minute, eh?

I viewed the brouhaha with a certain sense of deja vu. Why? Because hardware and software manufacturers have been cooking their products — devoting enormous amounts of time and effort to boosting benchmark ratings solely for the sake of boosting benchmark ratings — *for as long as there have been benchmarks!*

In the computer industry the practice dates back at least 30 years. Unconfirmed rumors say that hardware benchmark cooking may go back as far as Hollerith cards, used in the 1890 U.S. Census.

If you were a manufacturer, wouldn't you streamline your product so it looked good? If everybody else in the game devotes a big part of their budget to coming up with better cooks, can you afford to sit by and play the game straight? For that matter, what is "straight"? The question is far from black-and-white.

Bangs 'n Bucks

We'll beat up on benchmarks one more time, then move on to more important stuff.

There's a particularly insidious form of benchmarking that's usually described as "Bang for the Buck." Yes, one of the big PC magazines uses that precise terminology; but nearly all the mags and rags rely on this sort of analysis in one way or another. A typical situation might be where a newspaper reviews all 486SX systems with 4 MB memory and 120 MB disk, with a list price under $2,000. That's a bang for the buck comparison, whether it's explicitly identified that way or not.

I know all about bangs for bucks. They run in the family. Learned long ago that there's only two minor problems with 'em: the bangs. . . and the bucks!

On the bang side: no matter how you slice it, "bang" is a very relative term. For example, as Windows users we're very concerned with video performance (it's the tail that wags the WinDog); but disk access times, especially with a properly installed SMARTDrive, usually doesn't matter much. DOS users aren't nearly as dependent on video times. Net result: a Windows bang isn't even close to a DOS bang. Close only counts in hand grenades and benchmarks.

Compounding the problem: there are thousands of possible "bang" variables, millions of variations. You couldn't even begin to list the major ones, much less the niggling little ones.

Under Windows, for example, a 386DX/33 with 8 MB memory and a good video card can run rings around a 486SX/25 with 2 MB and an old-fashioned video card. Yet if you compare the two configurations running DOS programs, you'll probably find precisely the opposite to be true. The relative "bang" of the two systems is entirely dependent on how they're used.

It's not just DOS. Even under Windows, there can be huge variations. A 486SX/25 system that runs WinWord like a bat out of hell may be slow, slow, slow recalculating compute-intensive floating point Excel spreadsheets; popping a 486DX/25 into the same machine may make Excel hum, but have virtually no effect on WinWord.

If you commonly keep, say, WordPerfect/Win and 1-2-3/Win open simultaneously, pasting stuff back and forth, you may find that boosting your system's memory from 4 MB to 8 MB creates more "bang" than upgrading your disk drive, video board, and processor, all at once!

What's a bang to you may well be a whimper to Igor.

On the buck side: these comparisons almost always rely on the machine vendor to supply the configuration that they think will do best in the mag or rag's comparisons. And the vendors are in the same quandary we're in.

Say your name is Miguel O'Dell and you're asked to provide a machine for *OB Magazine*'s front-cover review of 486DX2/66 blazers. Landing an Editorialist's Choice Award could mean a hundred million dollars in business over the next year (not an exaggeration). What do you send 'em? Your souped-up but slightly more expensive WinScreamer? Or your more modestly priced, but still highly respectable, DOSTurtle? Do you create a whole new machine, geared to the *OB Magazine* benchmark suite? Probably. But does that machine lean more toward DOS or Windows, quality graphics or a big disk, larger memory or an exotic bus?

Do you cook the sucker? For that matter, do you know for sure that the video card you're using isn't cooked?

The simple fact is that even the vendor can't pick a single machine (or even a small handful of machines) that's best for you and your problems, not to mention one that'll satisfy every review, maximize every benchmark. No matter what the vendor does, the "buck" side of the equation is largely a matter of the vendor putting all their eggs in one basket, and hoping that one basket wins the beauty contest.

 So tell me, sonny. If you can't trust the bang or the buck, how can you trust the two together?

Consider this. Back in March 1993 *PC Week* took a look at a Cyrix 486DLC/40 based notebook computer, and came to the conclusion that this particular notebook isn't as powerful as an i486DX/33 based Compaq ProLinea. Whooooo! *Cyrix hit the fan!* The Director of PR at Cyrix fired off a letter to *PC Week* — and it sounded like a legal shot across the bow: "an inaccuracy resulting from a partial disclosure of facts," the letter decries. "Based on internal documents obtained from *PC Week* by Cyrix..." he continues, steeped in neo-legalese, "what failed to be disclosed were DOSmark scores. . . the 486DLC/40 with a DOSmark of 38 clearly outperforms the Compaq ProLinea 4/33 with a DOSmark of 27."

PC Week shot back: "the Compaq system performed three times faster in Ziff Davis Labs' video benchmark..." and on and on. Cyrix claims that, for the money a user saved buying their product, they could opt for a faster disk, which would narrow the benchmark differences: bangs and bucks incarnate. *PC Week* countered with complaints about a missing video driver. It would take several pages here to follow the major themes of *l'contest pissant. . .*

A gross miscarriage of journalistic justice? Or a vendor's sour grapes over an inadequate machine? You might think all this sturm und drang hinged on major differences between the notebook and the Compaq, a mud-slinging blight on the face of Cyrix's marketing strategy. Here's the punch line: the *PC Week* analysis pegged this particular notebook 6% slower than the ProLinea in processor operations per second, and 9% slower in conventional memory reads and writes. Two big companies at each others' throats over a reported performance difference that is *totally imperceptible!*

 But that's the name of this high-stakes bangs and bucks game. If you measure DOSmarks you'll get one set of numbers. Measure WinMarks and you'll get another. Try a SPECint92 and you'll see yet a third, and who knows what SpitzerMarks might bring. Shave $100 off the processor price, and you may make the speed back on a more expensive, faster disk cache.

Incredibly, people still buy computers based on 9% conventional memory read/write performance differences; when they, and their programs, wouldn't know a conventional read from an unconventional plight.

There's only one constant in this boiling morass of claims and counter-claims, the alphabet soup of processor types and court cases and fear, uncertainty and bangs for doubting Toms' bucks: no matter what the benchmark, no matter what the score, you can bet your sweet bippy the little differences in benchmark numbers won't tell you a whole lot about how *your* Windows programs are going to run.

A Solution Exists

> For all men strive to grasp what they do not know,
> while none strive to grasp what they already know;
> and all strive to discredit what they do not excel in,
> while none strive to discredit what they do excel in.
> This is why there is chaos.
>
> — Chuang-tzu, *A Protest Against Civilization*, ca 300 B.C.

So much for benchmark bashing. If you can't rely on the numbers, you rightfully ask, what's left?

First, you can use the benchmark numbers in the publications to evaluate individual pieces of hardware, but take them with a grain of salt. Realize from the get-go that no benchmark is going to tell you much about how a particular piece of hardware will run on your machine, doing your work. With very few exceptions, performance differences of 25% won't be noticeable. And beware of cooked results!

Second, you can use the benchmarks to pin down performance differences among entire classes of hardware: does EISA really run faster than ISA? Will I get off work earlier if I upgrade from a 486SX/25 to a 486DX2/50? Is local bus disk access really faster than plain vanilla? Are accelerated video cards that much better than dumb cards? The answers to these questions can be gleaned from many benchmark reports, but you may have to do a bit of your own scouting. Benchmark results are often pegged to individual products; you'll have to identify the technology behind the products yourself.

For example, a magazine may report the relative processing speed of various brands of 486DX/33 computers. You may be struggling with a decision about SCSI disk drives; are they fast enough to warrant the extra price? If you scan the reviews and see which computers use SCSI, then compare the disk benchmark numbers for SCSI-based computers versus all the others, you may get a good feel for what SCSI disks can, and can't do.

That's an interesting example, by the way. Da Boss has seen some hard disk benchmarks intentionally run with SMARTDrive turned off. Why? Because if you leave SMARTDrive running (as most people do, especially with Windows) there's often very little performance difference among the different drives! Watch the fine print to see if the benchmark you're using tweaks things to produce differentiation at any price.

Third, and probably most important: the best way to evaluate hardware performance is to do it yourself, with your own applications, using your own "typical" day's work. It's easier than you may think.

If you're buying a new computer and considering Video Board X versus Video Board Y, call the people who want to sell you the computer and tell them you want to buy both boards — with a 30-day option to return one or the other. Be up-front about the whole transaction. Most computer vendors have a 30-day return policy. Use it!

While you're waiting for the boards to arrive, keep track of the things that take forever to run on your current machine: is there a big Amì Pro document that scrolls like molasses, or a Micrografx graphic that loads like it's on Phenobarbital? Good. Those are the ones you want to watch.

Now hop down to your local KMart and pick up a $5 stopwatch. Put it on the expense account. Tell your boss that Mao said it was OK.

Then, one by one, time those slow activities on your current machine. Does it take three minutes to scroll through that Amì Pro document? Write down both the name of the file, and the time it took. Keep identifying, tracking, and timing those slow activities until you have a dozen of 'em or so. It's important that you identify the problems, and time your old system *before* the new system arrives, because once it's in, you're going to automatically assume that the new system is ten times faster than your current one and you'll lose sight of what used to drive you nuts. It's human nature.

When the boards arrive, give yourself a day to *feel* each one. Use them on real work. Run through your personal benchmarks; see if the document scroll really improves all that much, or if the graphic really loads significantly faster. You may be surprised.

Which brings me to the fourth alternative to slavishly following published benchmarks.

You gotta look at the big picture. *Listen up, sonny!*

In the grand scheme of things, shaving a few seconds here or there isn't going to matter nearly as much as running a solid, dependable system. You will lose much, much more time on a bad video driver, say, than you'll ever gain by improved scroll times or faster graphic redraws. That's why it's so important that you batter new hardware in your environment, with your setup, before you commit to it. Even a mind boggling 100% redraw speed gain won't pay you back for a couple days lost due to a buggy driver.

If you can't talk a vendor into sending you several different pieces of hardware, there's still hope. Log on to CompuServe (see *The Mother of All Information Services* in Chapter 6) and ask! A short message posted on the CIS:IBMHW (IBM-compatible hardware) forum or any of a dozen other fora will no doubt trigger a long string of responses from people who have tried the hardware you're considering. There's no finer source of real, down-to-earth information, from real, down-to-earth people.

Process or Force?

So much for generalities. Now that you're suitably skeptical about benchmarks, let's get down to specifics. I'll take a look at things to consider when buying a new machine. Along the way, I'll mention various upgrade possibilities, and take a look at how well the upgrade options compare to buying new.

Microsoft will tell you that Windows 3.1 will run on any computer that hasn't spent more than a month as a totally submerged boat anchor, South China Sea barnacles notwithstanding. Some power users will tell you that running Windows on anything less than a 486DX2/66 with 64 MB of memory is criminal. The truth lies somewhere between.

We're going to concentrate on hardware for Windows and Windows alone. If you spend a significant portion of your working day outside of Windows, this is only part of the picture. What's good to goose DOS is not necessarily good for a Windows gander.

Da Brains — A Brief History of Tines

> Know thy ass well, for it bears thee.
>
> — Anonymous

There are so many different kinds of PC chips available that it would take a book — a *thick* book — to list their similarities and differences. We'll have Igor skip lightly through the major in(tel)-breeds, and try to put the history into some perspective.

 In da beginning there was the PC. Well, no, that isn't really true: the Altair 8800 actually appeared on the cover of *Popular Electronics* in 1975 — the PC hardly sprang forth fully formed in 1981 from the Boca Raton DNA pool — but it's a good enough starting point. The original $3,005 IBM PC ran on an Intel 8088, and shipped with 64K (count 'em, 65,536 characters) of main memory and a single 5¼-inch one-side-only disk drive.

 $3,005? Not $2,995?

Sounds like some clerk added five bucks when he should've subtracted....

Not coincidentally, about the time IBM started shipping PCs, the folks at Xerox's Palo Alto Research Center were churning out a pace setter of a different color: the Alto — an amazing machine, never sold commercially, that included a mouse, built-in Ethernet communications, and the Smalltalk object oriented programming language.

For many, many years Intel would insist that its newer generations of chips mimic the old ones; so-called backward compatibility. Somehow the 8088/8086 method of operation became known as "real mode" (begging the question, "which reel?"). Adherence to real mode operation ultimately proved a millstone around Windows' neck.

Users needing fast floating-point calculations (typically for hard-core scientific math problems, but also occasionally for spreadsheets and other number crunching) could buy a second chip, a math co-processor, and stick it next to the 8088. The math co-processor was known as an 8087.

Verily, in 1983 the PC begat the PC-XT. This $4,995 screamer shipped with a huge 10 MB hard disk; that's 10,485,760 characters!

At about the same time, *PC Magazine* was sold off, and much of the staff left to form *PC World*. Microsoft shipped *Word Version 1.0*. And IBM dumped millions of bucks down a deep black hole called PCjr. Most importantly to me, in 1983 Microsoft announced Windows, its fancy new multitasking windowing environment. Windows didn't quite ship on time, but what the hay. . .

The XT in turn begat the PC-AT, an 80286-based machine that ran ten or twenty times faster than the original PC. At $5469 in 1984 dollars, the AT offered 256K of main memory, and a 1.2 MB floppy disk drive.

The AT marked the end of an era: it was the last IBM machine with a 16-bit processor, i.e., it handled data *two* eight-bit characters at a time. In addition to the 8088-aping real mode, the 80286 could run in so-called "protected mode;" an important new way of policing running programs. In protected mode, the computer itself stood as traffic cop, regulating which programs ran as well as and when and where, protecting programs from each other. In real mode, by contrast, programs could (and often did) clobber each other with impunity: run more than one program at a time, and they could trounce all over each other.

While the advent of protected mode made possible program-switching systems like Windows, the 80286 was designed before the PC shipped. Its designers didn't foresee any reason why an operating system would want to switch from protected to real mode and back again; and they failed to provide for that eventuality in the 80286's native instructions. Switching modes could only be accomplished by an odd series of time-consuming machinations, something perilously akin to restarting the computer.

When Windows, or any other multi-tasking operating system for that matter, came along, the ability to switch back and forth between modes became paramount: there was no other way to switch into and out of old DOS programs. The 80286 would ultimately receive the well-deserved appellation "brain dead" for this shortcoming and a couple others.

Also in 1984 Steve Jobs unleashed the first Macintosh; IBM shipped TopView, its fancy new multitasking windowing environment; and Satellite Software International delivered WordPerfect for the IBM PC.

In 1985 Microsoft finally shipped Windows 1.0, its fancy new multitasking windowing environment, two years late and at least two cards short of a full deck.

Although Intel announced the 80386DX chip in 1985, it took a while for manufacturers to catch on. Advanced Logic Research, at the time virtually unknown in the industry, is credited with being the first to introduce a PC based on the 386 chip. Compaq came a bit later. IBM lollygagged around, not introducing a 386-based machine until 1987.

 The first 386 machines led to the first iteration of what we icons call the great "it's only good for a server" crock. Every significant improvement of processor speed since then has been accompanied by pundits who declare knowingly, "of course, such power is only needed for a network server." Within two years — at most — these machines "only needed for servers" become the new desktop standard. It is to laugh but the pundits love to recycle that line.

 The pundits need to learn Igorson's Law: Software expands to overwhelm any available hardware — and then some.

The 386 broke significant new technical ground, introducing a new "virtual mode" — establishing something that appears, to programs, to be real mode, yet maintaining the benefits of protected mode — expanding the chip's instruction set, driving a golden nail into the 286's coffin. The 386 was a major improvement on almost all fronts, yet the industry at first failed to give it the respect it deserved.

Citing a huge installed based of 286 machines, most software companies, including Microsoft and IBM, just missed the boat, hobbling their products to accommodate the quirks of the 286. Instead of breaking cleanly with the past and running with the vastly improved 386 architecture, users were treated to such garbage as OS/2

1.0 and Windows/286; two of the worst pieces of software ever unleashed on an unsuspecting public.

Significantly, though, Microsoft shipped Excel 1.0 for the PC, the first *real* Windows application, in 1987.

In 1988 Intel announced the 80386SX, a stripped-down version of the 80386DX. While the 80386SX runs internally at a full-bore 32 bits (four characters at a time), it communicates with the outside world 16 bits at a time. This distinction allowed computer system designers to make much less expensive machines, retaining much of the performance and architectural capability of the DX. Like the 8088 and 80286, the 80386DX and 80386SX could also accommodate math co-processors.

Then all hell broke loose in 1989. Intel announced the i486DX (dropping the "80" prefix), and the computer companies fell all over themselves getting hot new machines to market.

While the i486 ran in much the same way as the 80386, the i486DX offered two key enhancements for current-day Windows users: it could run most instructions in one clock cycle (thus beating the pants off the 80386, which takes nearly two cycles on average); and it came with a built-in 8K memory cache.

 In my opinion, there are only two important differences between an 80386 and an i486 for Windows users: the ability to run most instructions in one cycle, and the on-board cache. The i486DX also has a built-in math co-processor, but most Windows users will rarely need it.

Windows 3.0 hit the streets in May of 1990, and the computer industry will never be the same.

By 1991 some smart marketing folks at Intel discovered that they could take broken i486DX chips, ones that came off the assembly lines with faulty math co-processors, and create (or, more importantly, sell) a whole new line of processor: the i486SX. Since an i486SX didn't have a math co-processor, it sold for much less than the i486DX. By positioning the chips this way, Intel managed to woo much of the old 80386 market up to an i486SX, without chewing into its own (monopolized) i486DX market — putting a severe crimp on the margins of the 80386 clone chip manufacturers.

The i486SX sold so well that Intel started taking perfectly good i486DX chips off the assembly line, disabling the co-processor, and selling the resulting neutered chips as the i486SX.

Although it may be hard to believe, there's no other difference between the i486DX and i486SX chips. That's why you'll find no noticeable performance spread between an i486DX/25 and an i486SX/25 under Windows, unless you're doing lots of spreadsheet recalculations. It's all marketing smoke and mirrors.

It's also a great example of how, in the computer business, manufacturing costs often have no bearing on final retail price: it costs more for Intel to make an i486SX — Intel has to go through an additional, neutering step in manufacture — yet the chip sells for much less than a comparable i486DX. And they're selling zillions of them.

In 1992 computer manufacturers started building many of their i486 machines with a spot for an extra chip; not a math co-processor, mind you, but something known as an OverDrive chip. This so-called "clock doubler" chip is designed to run at twice the speed internally as it does in its interactions with the outside world. It's a brilliant concept. You might have a machine with an i486DX/25 running at 25 MHz. Pop in an OverDrive "clock doubler" and all of a sudden the heart of your machine starts marching to the double-time beat of a different drummer, running at 50 MHz. The rest of your computer doesn't know the difference and couldn't care less because the OverDrive chip talks to the outside world at 25 MHz. As of this writing there are 50 MHz and 66 MHz OverDrive chips available, and a 99 MHz "clock tripler" chip will no doubt be available by the time this book hits the stands.

Perhaps the ultimate chip irony: when you plug an OverDrive chip into its socket, the old chip is completely disabled. It doesn't do a thing. Put out to silicon pasture.

This is where things start getting really complicated. Many i486SX computers were built with a ready-made slot, presumably for an i487SX math co-processor. (The i487SX is really a full-fledged i486 that takes over the machine and puts the i486SX out to pasture; Intel sure likes to re-use successful marketing strategies.) The OverDrive chip will (generally) work in that slot. In fact, OverDrive chips may well work in your i486SX, even if you don't have a ready-made slot: you may be able to pop out the old chip and pop a new one in. And you shouldn't have any problem at all sliding an OverDrive chip into any i486DX machine. Check with your dealer for exact chip part numbers.

So where's the DX2 fit in, that fancy chip at the heart of the systems everybody's salivating over? Well, mostly the DX2 rates as another bit of obfuscation. The DX2 is identical to the OverDrive, except we mere mortals can only buy a DX2 as part of a new computer. Intel only sells OverDrives to "the consumer channel" (read: real people), while DX2s only go to computer manufacturers. That's it.

A 50 MHz OverDrive chip plugged into an old i486SX/25 works precisely the same way as a brand-spanking new i486DX2/50. There will be performance differences between the two, no doubt, simply because DX2/50 systems are usually built with more fancy stuff than i486SXs. But as far as the 486 chip is concerned, they're like two peas in a pod.

Many companies, over many years, have promised upgradeable computers; ones that fight the ravages of age with slots that can be filled, or boards that can be replaced, with the latest and greatest. While a few manufacturers have managed to produce and sell upgrades, in almost every case it was as expensive to upgrade an old computer as to buy a whole new one! OverDrive technology changed that. The Intel engineers developed a genuinely useful, economical alternative to trashing old machines; if you have a 486DX or SX machine, OverDrive merits your attention.

In April 1993 Intel announced the next generation of chips. Dubbed the Pentium, in deference to marketing types and lawyers, this breed promises outstanding performance (perhaps double that of the 486DX2/66) at outlandish prices — at least for the near term. You've probably been following the progress of the Pentium in the trade press.

Mimicking the success of the OverDrive approach, more and more 486 machines are being built with a "Pentium slot." You can tell whether you have a real Pentium slot on your motherboard by counting the holes in the slot where the new chip will go: if there are 238 holes, you got it.

While details aren't yet completely clear, it looks like the Pentium slot will ultimately accommodate a chip that's something like the Pentium. Sorta. Code-named the P24T (the OverDrive's code name was P23T), it should give the high-end 486 business a mid-life kicker, while those of us with finite means wait for Pentium prices to descend from the stratosphere.

That's the history. Let's look at today's reality.

Thanks for the Memories

Given a choice between Windows on a 286 in CGA
and a poke in the eye with a sharp stick,
Take the stick.

— An early Windows developer

 I've run Windows successfully on a 286/12 with 2.5 MB of RAM. Got some real work out of it, too — my first WinWord machine. If you're only running one Windows application at a time, don't mind working in monochrome, and tend to have a laid-back-cum-comatose disposition, you *can* run Windows on a 286 with just a couple of megs memory. It isn't easy, mind you, but it can be done.

Perhaps "run" is an overstatement. Let's say Windows "saunters" on a 286.

If you aren't quite so laid-back, or if you're in a situation where there's pressure to get things out on time, you'll need at least a middle-of-the-road 386 (say a 386DX/25) with 4 MB of memory. That setup will let you run two Windows apps simultaneously, and still not put you to sleep waiting for screen updates. But if you get stuck running Windows on a 386, don't ever, ever, ever let anybody talk you into test-driving Windows on a 486, not even for a minute. You'll be spoiled for life.

If you're in the market for a new computer and want to run Windows on it, there's no reason in the world why you should settle for less than a 486SX with 4 MB of memory and an accelerated local bus video card. Buy anything less than that; finking out with a 386, fewer than 4 MB of memory, or non-local-bus video — and you'll be hobbling your new system unnecessarily. Moving up will cost no more than a few hundred bucks, and that is money well spent. Perhaps surprisingly, if you have a few shekels left, your best investment on this kind of system will be four more MB of memory, to come up to 8 MB.

I have one important piece of advice. Buy a good, powerful, system even if you have to stretch the budget a bit. It'll last longer. I've found over and over again that it doesn't pay to go for the bottom of the market; you'll be frustrated and fuming and ready to trash your beast in less than a year, losing time and money along the way. Far better to overshoot a bit and get yourself a system that will last a couple years. Even if you end up replacing a few key components, swap out the video board or upgrade to a bigger hard drive, the advantages to keeping your base system are enormous, if only to reduce the hassle factor inevitable in any system replacement.

Or you can do what I do. Learn how to find solid, fast systems cheap, cheaper than the big chain stores, and plan on upgrading every six months, selling off the previously-owned systems to family or friends. You'll get six months' use of a top-of-the-line system, and by the time you're ready to trade up, your friends will be delighted to pick up a system that's at least as good as anything they'll find in the chain stores, at a very competitive price.

Those are the insider's tricks of the trade-up. But it begs the 64-KiloBuck question: which brand of computer should you buy? Alas, there's no simple answer to this, the most basic of hardware questions. But a few insights may prove useful.

First, PCs have become a commodity, and they're getting more commodity-like with every passing month. Aaron Goldberg in the May 10, 1993 issue of *PC Week* said, "It is essential that customers remember the movement toward the feature orientation of products. The disturbing counterpoint to this is the assumption by many unknowledgeable users that PCs are commodities; they clearly aren't and will become even less so."

Oh yeah? I don't know what a "movement toward feature orientation of products" might be, but I'll tell you this, bucko, even the big boys use generic parts. Sheeesh, one of the major developments in computer retailing this decade is IBM's decision to sell a totally generic, totally off-the-wall. . . er. . . shelf machine. If that's "feature orientation," well, everybody's doing it.

Years ago IBM was the Mercedes Benz/Rolls Royce of the computer industry. Then Compaq came along, following ALR's lead, and brought the 80386 to market before Big Blue had time to scratch its butt. Ever since then, far too many industry pundits behave as if IBM and Compaq make better, more solid, more advanced computers than the "second tier." Ha! They know better than that.

Many of the big trends rolling over the market right now had their beginnings with second, third, fourth, and no-tier companies: local bus, SCSI-2, accelerated video, CD-ROM, sound, full motion video. Neither IBM nor Compaq was first to market with any of those products. Feature orientation, you say? Unknowledgeable? Pig pucky. Er, cockroach pucky. Now don't get me wrong: IBM and Compaq make good machines. But they're no longer way out ahead of the pack; no longer the *de facto* leaders by which all others are measured. You shouldn't have to pay a premium for a name these days. And that's what commodities are all about.

Whew.

Second, service (especially during the first few days while you're setting up your machine) may be more important than the machine itself. PCs often have their worst problems in the first few days or weeks; service immediately after the sale is crucial.

Third, don't overlook the value, or lack thereof, of pre-installed software. Providing you get original disks and manuals, pre-installed software can save you tons of money, time, and frustration.

Finally, don't believe everything you read about the tenuous future of small PC companies. There's no guarantee that any PC manufacturer you buy from today will be in business tomorrow. Heavily capitalized companies with very deep pockets can make your machine an orphan just as fast as the Tricky Disk's PC Emporium in your home town. Just ask folks who bought a NeXT.

Mao to the Rescue

> When you tip the ketchup bottle,
> First will come a little, then a lot'll.
>
> — Anonymous (from *Poem Stew*, 1981)

Yeah, yeah, yeah. You need benchmark numbers. Something to show the boss. Or the spouse. We know, we know.

Fair enough. I came up with some performance numbers, and a way to interpret them that makes some modicum of sense. I scoured the major magazines and books, wrote away to manufacturers, tested scores of machines, pleaded, cajoled, threatened, and swore, and came up with a set of numbers that make some sense. Then I calculated a few ratios, stuck 'em in Mao's CPU Chart (see Figure 7-1) and threw the original numbers away. Inscrutable, eh?

My CPU chart should tell you a bit about the relative performance of various kinds of chips, when they're embedded in "typical" systems. Given a specific chip, the Chart won't tell you diddly about performance differences between individual machines or vendors. There's a reason for that. No matter what the magazines would have you believe, performance differences among various brands are minuscule, much more dependent on other components than on the processor chip itself. With one waffle: there's an initial period of time, immediately after the announcement of a new chip and lasting perhaps a few months, where there may be significant differences among brands. Those differences always disappear as vendors zero-in on the best way to connect the new chip to the rest of the machine. If you're trying to choose among brands, fix on a chip then look at the rest of the machine. To paraphrase Gertrude Stein, a 486/33 is a 486/33 is a 486/33.

Here's how you read Figure 7-1. Say you're considering giving the old 386SX/16 to the kids, and replacing it with a 486SX/25. Look down the left column. See the 386SX/16 listed on the left? Good.

Now read across to the column marked 486SX/25. CTO Mao estimates that your Windows programs will run about 6 times faster on the 486, roughly a 500% speed increase. That's a *real* speed improvement, one you'll feel day after day after day.

See the caveats that follow.

	386SX 16	386DX 25	386DX 33	486SX 25	486DX 25	486DX 33	486DX 50	486DX2 50	486DX2 66	Pentium 66
80286	2 X	5 X	11 X	16 X	17 X					
80386SX/16		2 X	4 X	6 X	7 X	9 X	15 X			
80386DX/25			40%	2 X	2 X	3 X	5 X	4 X	6 X	
80386DX/33				50%	60%	2 X	3 X	3 X	4 X	7 X
486SX/25					NETPA	50%	2 X	2 X	3 X	5 X
486DX/25						40%	2 X	90%	3 X	5 X
486DX/33							60%	40%	90%	4 X
486DX/50								NETPA	NETPA	2 X
486DX2/50									40%	3 X
486DX2/66										80%

Figure 7-1: Mao's CPU Speed Chart

NETPA = Not Enough To Spit At: after a week, you couldn't tell the difference

Thinking of upgrading your 486DX/25 to a 486DX2/50, using an OverDrive? Look at Mao's Speed Chart. It says that your Windows programs will run about 90% faster after the upgrade: call it twice as fast, give or take a hiccup.

That's a significant improvement. . . but the real question is whether it's worth the expense. Only you know for sure. A 90% speed boost is nice, but it won't cure your acne or keep you from prematurely graying.

The missing numbers in the upper-right corner were simply off the scale; indeed, it's hard to think of a scale that would make any sense whatsoever. Gauging performance of a Pentium/66 versus a 80286/12 is like weighing the souls of Mahatma Gandhi versus Rush Limbaugh.

Caveat #1: Hey, comparing Windows performance across different kinds of computers is SWAG time. Anybody who claims otherwise is sellin' you a bill of goods. There are a zillion different variables.

Mao tried to pick on "typical" systems, but in reality there's no such thing: add a little memory here, drop a lousy video board there, and the numbers can change wildly. *This is not gospel.*

Caveat #2: Mao's Speed Chart only deals with Intel processors. You cannot assume that Cyrix or AMD or IBM chips with similar names perform at the same level as their Intel sound-alikes.

 For example, I put both the AMD 386DXL/40 and the Cyrix 486DLC/33 right around the Intel 486SX/25 in terms of Windows ooooomph. The IBM 486/SLC2 seems to run just a tad faster than a 486DX/25. In spite of the *PC Week* article quoted earlier, and in spite of published Norton SysInfo ratings (Norton SI is a YAB — Yet Another Benchmark, we found the Cyrix 486DLC/40 runs about the same as an Intel 486DX/33, as does the AMD Am486DX/33.

 Some chip manufacturers have taken great liberties with Intel's original numbering system. As a result, pandemonium reigns. You can expect any chip with a "386" in its name will be compatible with the Intel 80386 — that is, they will all run the 386 machine instructions.

Similarly, variants with "486" in their names will usually run the 486 instruction set — which is nothing but the 80386 instruction set with a couple of rarely-used odds 'n ends tossed in for good measure. But that's where the similarities end. For example, Figure 7-2 shows how Intel stacks up against the Cyrix sound-alikes:

		Processor Bits	Data Path Bits	Math Coprocessor	On Chip Memory Cache
Intel	80386 SX	32	16	No	None
	80386 DX	32	32	No	None
	80486 SX	32	32	No	8K
	80486 DX	32	32	Yes	8K
	Pentium	64	64	Yes	8K + 8K
Cyrix	386DXL	32	32	No	None
	486SLC	32	16	No	1K
	486DLC	32	32	Integer Mult	1K

Figure 7-2: Igor's HomoPhonolyzer

 As you can see, not all 486 chips are created equal. Mao says the only big differences between a 80386 and an i486 are the one instruction per cycle speed up and the on-board cache. But *how much* cache? See how Cyrix fudged things with a 1K cache? Is 512 bytes enough? Two bytes? In the final analysis, just about anybody can make anything and call it a 486. I'm surprised no vendors have tried re-packaging an 8008 calling it a 486/80.

Caveat #3: Many, many different tests masquerade with the same name, and tests with the same name often won't give the same results! There must be a dozen different programs that claim to measure MIPS; yet they all produce different results on any given machine.

Version numbers matter. On many, many machines, for example, there's a huge difference between version 3.1 and version 3.11 ZD Labs WinMark scores; and much of the difference is attributable to "cooked" video drivers. That's not the only one. The Norton SysInfo number has often been manipulated to fit vendors' fancies or fantasies: manufacturers have been known to publish performance numbers from SysInfo versions that are years out of date, simply because an older version of SysInfo might show their hardware to better advantage. Be careful when comparing numbers. If you don't know the version number of a benchmark, you don't know anything!

Caveat #4: Finally, should you take it upon yourself to run a benchmark program on various machines, make sure that you always boot the tested machine with a "clean" (or at least a uniform) **CONFIG.SYS** and **AUTOEXEC.BAT**. Make sure you set up SMARTDrive reasonably. One slight software difference between two tested machines, an errant TSR, say, or a driver loaded in high memory, can completely invalidate your test results. Don't try to compare your results with published test results (and by all means do *not* compare them with Mao's CPU Chart!) unless you boot "clean".

Reality check: Intel published some interesting statistics comparing the 486DX2/66 with the Pentium 66, running real-world applications, albeit on one-of-a-kind hardware. Intel says Quattro Pro 1.0 for Windows runs 30% faster on the Pentium, Excel 4.0 is about 50% faster, and WinWord 2.0 seem to run about 65% faster on Pentium. Those are the speed gains with original versions of the software; once they're re-compiled to take advantage of the Pentium, they may well run a bit faster. Mao's Speed Chart says you can expect about an 80% speed boost, going from a DX2/66 to a Pentium 66. Looks pretty close, but this should emphasize the most important point of benchmark charts: take 'em with a grain of salt!

Roll Yer Own

 Heh heh heh. Mao thought he threw away the original benchmark numbers, but I found them in an old, deleted Excel spreadsheet file. Who among us can fathom the ways of Tao — or DOS 6 undelete? Here are the numbers Mao used. If you don't like 'em, change 'em, bucko, and calculate your own ratios. Don't be bashful. There's nothing sacred about 'em.

The numbers in Figure 7-3 aren't particularly exciting, really, and you should view them with the same skepticism any benchmark numbers deserve. Far as we know, the only thing that's noteworthy about this collection is that it seems to be the first time all these different benchmarks have been put together in one table.

The numbers came from all sorts of different places. It's important to understand the pedigree 'fore you buy the dog. . .

MIPS (Millions of Instructions per Second) is an abstract measure, and the numbers are thus immediately suspect. There is no reliable, universally accepted definition of an "instruction", much less millions of 'em, so beware! For the DX/25 and slower machines we relied on published ratings that are generally accepted in the industry.

The faster machines reflect Dhrystone ratings. Many third-party performance monitoring programs claim to rate systems on the basis of MIPS, but such tests must be run with care and interpreted *cum grano salis.* Your results will vary. Bottom line: any relation MIPS ratings have to actual performance is strictly coincidental.

Caveat Benchmarkor!

	Chip			Mom		Mom1		Mom2		Mom3		Mom4
					MIPS		PCBench		iCOMP		SPECint	
Intel	8088		4.7	0.02	0.3	0.02						
Intel	80286		8	0.06	1.2	0.06						
Intel	80386	SX	16	0.15	2.5	0.13			22	0.18	2	0.15
Intel	80386	DX	16	0.30	6	0.30						
Intel	80386	DX	25	0.46			3634	0.53	49	0.40	6	0.45
Intel	80386	DX	33	0.63			5011	0.73	68	0.56	8	0.60
AMD	386	DX	40	0.85			5901	0.85				
Cyrix	486	DLC	33	0.92			6338	0.92				
Intel	i486	SX	20	0.76	17	0.83	5286	0.77	78	0.64	11	0.83
Intel	i486	SX	25	0.94			6486	0.94	100	0.82	14	1.05
Intel	i486	DX	25	1.01	20	1.00	6902	1.00	122	1.00	14	1.05
Intel	i486	DX	33	1.38			8753	1.27	166	1.36	20	1.50
Intel	i486	DX	50	2.20	55	2.75	12541	1.82	249	2.04	29	2.18
Intel	i486	DX2	50	1.87	40	2.00	11390	1.65	231	1.89	26	1.95
Intel	i486	DX2	66	2.61	65	3.25	16176	2.34	297	2.43	32	2.41
Intel	Pentium		66	4.77	112	5.60	27266	3.95	567	4.65	65	4.89
DEC	Alpha		150	6.78	160	8.00					74	5.56
MIPS	R4000		100	4.66							62	4.66
MIPS	R4400		150	6.17							82	6.17
HP	PA-RISC		99	6.02							80	6.02
Sun	SPARC		40	3.98							53	3.98
IBM	PowerPC	601	50	3.01							40	3.01
IBM	PowerPC	601	66	4.51							60	4.51

Figure 7-3: Mao's Scorecard

PCBench (Ziff Labs PC Benchmark) ratings came from a seminal article in *PC Magazine* (April 27, 1993). They're composite numbers, "Operations per Second," averaging the PCBench numbers for five different systems in each processor category: they don't measure the performance of any particular machine. Kinda phantom numbers, not unlike Mao's scorecard in general. Later in this chapter when we talk about video benchmarking we'll give you all the trademark notices, legal disclaimers, and why's and wherefore's on the ZD Labs tests.

That *PC Magazine* article rates four stars, and if you're looking further into CPU comparisons, it's a good place to start.

The iCOMP number appears as a handy fiction developed and promulgated by Intel.

Watch out: these are the same people who advertise the Pentium chip as having extra-sensory powers. "We programmed the chip to be clairvoyant," the ad copy attests. No kidding! Gotta get that sucker hooked into the stock market. . .

iCOMP is supposed to take into account the inherent capabilities of each processor; these numbers came from official Intel publications. You can get your own copy of those publications by calling Intel at 800-633-6335. If you scan down the numbers in Mao's scorecard and compare the iCOMP ratings to what you've felt with various machines, you might come away convinced that the iCOMP number reflects Windows performance surprisingly well. The iCOMP is a composite benchmark; components include PCBench numbers ('tho they're different from the more recent ones Mao used), Whetstones (from PowerMeter version 1.7), SPECint92 numbers (which Mao used in his averages), and SPECfp92 results (which Mao ignored).

Finally, the SPECint92 number is yet another generally accepted measure of integer performance, thus immediately suspect. Mao ignored the SPEC floating point performance numbers, the SPECfp92, simply because so few Windows programs benefit from hot floating point capabilities. SPECint92 benchmarking takes into account performance in real-world application areas like circuit theory, the LISP interpreter, logic design, text compression algorithms, spreadsheet, and programming.

So if you're using C++ to produce a LISP program which compresses a discourse on circuit theory, this is the benchmark you need. Sheesh. Who do they think they're kidding?

The SPECint92 numbers for the DX2/66 and lesser endowed machines are from Intel; the others came primarily from chip manufacturers' press releases, which may be the singularly least reliable source of any data, anywhere.

The Mom1, Mom2, Mom3, and Mom4 numbers are based on those raw benchmarks. All CTO Mao did was "normalize" the numbers: divide by whatever it takes to make a 486DX/25 come up with a value of 1.0. There's no magic in that. To arrive at a final number, Mao averaged the Mom1, Mom2, Mom3, and Mom4 values. You could do it yourself, with any moderately sentient spreadsheet.

 So much for the main processor and the memory attached to it. Now we'll take a look at ways to get stuff into and out of memory — the bus.

Greyhound

> But that's all shove be'ind me — long ago an' fur away,
> An' there ain' no 'buses runnin' from the Bank to Mandalay;
> An' I'm learnin' 'ere in London wot the ten-year soldier tells:
> 'If you've 'eard the East a-callin' you won't never 'eed naught else.'

> — Rudyard Kipling, *Mandalay*, 1892

ISA Taking the Bus — ISA Versus EISA Versus MCA

Having decided on a processor, the next problem confronting you is the choice of an architecture. "Architecture" is just a fancy word for "plumbing": computer manufacturers have several different means of attaching the guts of the machine — the processor — to all the things that hang on the periphery — the peripherals. If you're a little sketchy on the details, look at *PC/Computing How Computers Work*, mentioned at the beginning of this chapter. The three fundamental architectures are called ISA (pronounced "eye-suh"), EISA ("suh" or, rarely, "suh"; sometimes, confusingly, "eye-suh"), and MCA ("eye-bee-em").

There's an enormous amount of heat generated on this subject. . . and not much light. Put ISA, EISA, and MCA bigots in a room and you could heat Brooklyn for a winter. Or start a riot. It's a question of the PC's bus: the bus controls everything going into or out of the main part of the computer. Expansion cards plug into the bus. In theory, the bus can be a major bottleneck in your new system's performance. Practice is another story.

 ISA "Industry Standard Architecture" machines are built around the old-fashioned IBM PC/AT style bus. It's an unremarkable, Neanderthal, low cost alternative to the two upstarts. Boards for ISA machines are cheap and readily available. I use an ISA system and recommend that most Windows users with semi-finite funds do the same, particularly with the advent of local bus.

ISA boards take their data a paltry 16 bits at a time. They're limited to a now-unfashionable theoretical maximum of 8 MHz (8 million cycles per second), while processors chug along at 25 or 33 MHz or faster. A good ISA connection can pump up to 5 million bits (5 Mb) of data per second into your computer's innards.

There are problems with ISA, to be sure; I would never claim otherwise. That 8 MHz speed limitation can be very frustrating if you are trying to shuffle large quantities of data on a hard disk. And the method for installing and configuring new ISA boards, involving wonderful arcane inanities with names like IRQ and I/O Base Address, can drive even the most hardened PC pro over the brink.

 Think it's easy? Oy! Try whispering the letters "IRQ" into the ear of anybody who's tried to install a scanner or an Ethernet card on a PC with four COM ports...

 You could be nice and offer to loosen their restraints — but only momentarily — while you're at it.

Just as DOS keeps on defying the Grim Reaper through various tricks and twists, outdistancing its putative useful life over and over again, the ISA bus too manages to keep on going and going and going. Most recently, the advent of local bus has given ISA a new lease on life, primarily because speed-sensitive peripherals in local bus machines can now bypass the ISA bus entirely. Other tricks abound: many machines now have a SCSI port built onto the motherboard itself; caching software makes hay while ISA's sun shines; and on and on. While it's true that ISA isn't the fastest kid on the block, it still has lots of life left.

 There are efforts underway to simplify board installation, dragging that ancient problem kicking and screaming into the 20th century, trying to make sure the user isn't left holding the IRQ. While the proof will be in products implementing the spec, the most important computer development of 1993 may well be the

Plug 'n Play spec promulgated by Intel and Microsoft. his specification is supposed to make the computer figure out how to handle your boards: IRQ conflicts may go the way of the dodo. Before long, it seems likely that you will want to be sure that new computers have a Plug 'n Play BIOS and that any peripheral you buy supports the spec also.

But don't feel that you've got to run out and buy the first computer that comes along trumpeting Plug 'n Play capability. Like so much earlier progress in the industry, the first iterations of a spec are likely to have rough spots.

EISA machines (Extended Industry Standard Architecture, yeah, the name doesn't mean anything to me either), are theoretically capable of slinging data to and from the main part of the computer faster than ISA machines. The EISA bus is 32 bits wide, and in many cases can run much faster than the ISA's 8 MHz. Theoretically, you can get up to 32 Mb per second through an EISA connection. There are several EISA standards floating around: the so-called EMB-66 and EMB-133 try to turbocharge EISA by teaching all boards to stand back while one of them launches into burst mode.

In my experience, the only time you'll see a big improvement in Windows performance with an EISA machine — not benchmark numbers, mind you, but real, live SMARTDrive enabled performance — comes when you're dealing with huge databases. Even then, it's entirely possible that you'll get better performance out of an ISA machine with a fast SCSI or local bus hard disk controller (we'll talk about those in a minute).

I don't know of any situation where I'd recommend EISA for a Windows user, particularly when you factor in the extra cost of EISA cards.

ISA cards plug into an EISA machine just fine, they just sit a bit higher in the slot. Which is nice, because special purpose EISA cards can be very hard to find. An ISA card in an EISA machine won't buy you anything over a plain-Jane ISA machine, but at least you won't be left out in the cold with a card that won't work.

While the EISA bus can run faster than 8 MHz, mixing ISA and EISA cards in the same machine will often result in incompatibilities: ultimately, you may be forced to throttle the EISA cards back to 8 MHz, to keep them from stepping on the ISA cards. It's a jungle out there.

Which brings us to MCA.

Didn't Firesign Theater say they're all bozos on that bus?

 Now, now. If you can't say anything nice, don't say anything at all.

MCA (Micro Channel Architecture) machines were born in 1987 of an unholy alliance between IBM techies and marketing types. While there are no doubt learnéd studies somewhere demonstrating the obvious superiority of this technology, in my experience it hasn't done squat. Bus mastering (where the card takes the bus into its own hands) is good, but even ISA has learned the bus master boogie. Fast direct memory access might shave off a second or two here or there. By and large, though, on a good day MCA and EISA will run neck-and-neck; and in almost all real-world cases they're indistinguishable from ISA.

That said, there are several other considerations in the ISA vs EISA vs MCA wars. If you absolutely love a machine that only comes in EISA or MCA flavors, you may be stuck. EISA and MCA add-in boards are significantly more expensive than their ISA counterparts (less demand, higher manufacturing costs, "stuck" customers). And they're often harder to find. On the other hand, many people find it less complex to install boards on MCA systems; there have been some significant advances made on that front, although ISA may be on its way to catching up.

Bottom line for Windows users: unless you have big databases, or you have money to burn (and burn and burn), stick with ISA architecture. Spend your money on something sexier.

Local Bus — ISA's Ticket to Reid

 There's a very simple rule of thumb when it comes to local bus: if you're buying a new computer for Windows, always, always, always buy one with local bus slots. The additional cost is minimal; the benefits enormous. It's really that easy, that absolute.

Don't let the buzz words scare you. The "local bus" has been around for a long time. You just haven't been able to get on it.

The bus controls everything going into or out of the main part of the computer; when you stick new things into your computer, they hang off the bus. Hook a new board inside your computer and it physically plugs into the bus: those prong thingies on the bottom of the board more-or-less slide into a slot, and the slot is soldered onto the bus.

Now for the confusion. Buses come in two different flavors, "local" and "expansion"; they differ in how they physically hook up to the main processor, and how fast they can talk to the main processor (see Figure 7-4):

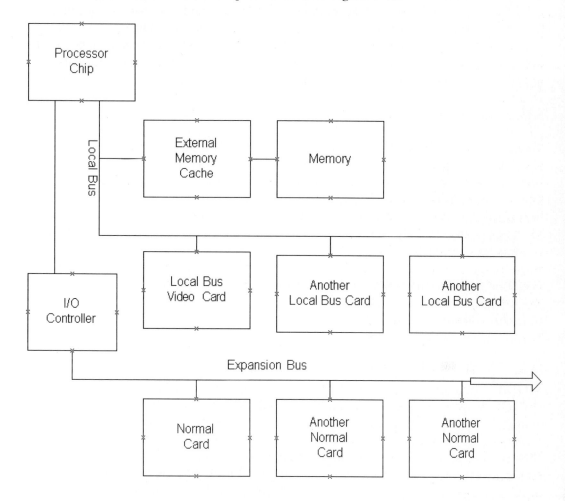

Figure 7-4: Local versus Expansion Bus

We've already talked about the expansion bus. The three different expansion bus architectures, ISA, EISA, and MCA, determine how the guts of the machine connect to the outside world. The old-fashioned expansion bus, connected to the inside of the machine via an input/output controller, takes a leisurely view: at best, ISA cards talk to the main processor at about 5 MB per second; EISA can run up closer to 32 MB.

 The local bus, by contrast, hooks *inside* the main part of the computer: it's way down inside, next to the bundle of wires (actually etched circuits, but you get the idea) that connect your computer's processor to its memory. By getting in closer to the heart of the beast, local bus boards can run at more than 100 MB per second — a speed increase that'll rattle your jowls. Instead of artificially limiting speeds to 8 MHz, as required by the expansion bus, local bus can get away with running as fast as your processor, up to a maximum (as of this writing) of about 33MHz.

Sound complicated? It isn't.

Think of your hometown library. Michael Crichton and Madonna have just teamed up to write *Jurassic, an Illustrated Autobiography,* and you want to read it so bad your toes itch. You walk into the library and check the shelves. If the book is there, you can grab it and with a few formalities the book is yours. When your time's up, you drop the book in the collection box and that's that: the book is checked back in, sorted, placed on the shelves, and the next reader gets his chance.

If the book isn't in the stacks, you'll have to ask the librarian. More than likely you'll be asked to add your name to a waiting list, and queue up with the rest of the unwashed masses seeking a shot of *Jurassic* enlightenment. Sooner or later the librarian will call, and at that point you can schlep back to the library, pick up the book, and go on your merry way.

Now look at the same situation from the librarian's point of view. *Jurassic* comes in, you, the librarian, see it and you check it out. Boom. Boom. Boom. When you're done, you bring it back. That's all. No special trip to the library: like, *you're already there.* No adding your name to a list; no queues; no phone call when the book comes in; no deposit box. If the book's there, you got it. If it isn't, you have first dibs on it as soon as it arrives, unless there's another librarian around who happens to see it first. Moreover, if the librarians involved in this inside track are fast readers and conscientious about turning around *Jurassic* quickly, the unwashed masses will hardly notice.

That's the essence of local bus.

While most people check out library books the normal way, a select few in the *sanctum sanctorum* may be able to circumvent the normal procedures, with little or no detriment to the system at large, if the folks on the fast track keep things moving.

Similarly computer buses. Most work goes through the normal (expansion) bus, be it ISA, EISA, or MCA. But if your computer is so equipped, a very small number of "librarians" sitting on the local bus can zoom and zip around, running on the inside track, operating at amazing speed, while the more pedestrian peripherals wait their turn.

Four types of cards rank as major contenders for local bus slots: accelerated video cards, which handle huge amounts of data constantly; hard drive controllers, which handle even larger amounts of data, but usually only in short bursts; SCSI cards, which can be hard drive controllers, too; and network cards, which may sit idle for ages before suddenly switching into hyperactivity.

Manufacturers started building local bus machines in 1982; the Tower of Babel had nothing on this run. Each manufacturer, left to its own devices, constructed completely unique and incompatible local bus systems. Not a moment too soon, the Video Electronics Standards Association (VESA) jumped into the fray and brought some sanity to the process.

The original standard developed in August 1992 by VESA and its member organizations is called VESA VL-Bus or, more commonly, VL-B. Although some vendors have found ways to jigger the standard a bit, the "classic" VL-B connection is 32 bits wide, can handle a maximum of three cards, and runs at the system's speed, up to a maximum of 33 MHz. By the time you read this, the second VESA local bus standard should be a reality. VL-64 is expected to run at 64 bits, at a faster bus speed, and permit more than three cards.

Not satisfied with merely blazing speed, Intel developed a second local bus standard, called PCI (for Peripheral Connect Interface). PCI runs 64 bits at a pop, can handle a handful of cards, and runs as fast as the machine will bear.

As of this writing, it's a horse. . . er. . . cockroach race. Neither VL-B nor PCI has emerged as a clear-cut winner. Not surprisingly, we users are left in the lurch. It's entirely possible that one or the other local bus standards (or one of its descendants) will fade into the sunset. Technological superiority is no assurance of longevity — look at what happened to Betamax video tapes. So while the market decides which standard to follow, rest assured of one thing: either kind of local bus is vastly preferable to no local bus at all.

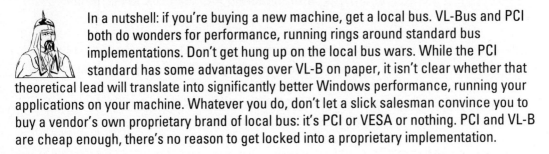 In a nutshell: if you're buying a new machine, get a local bus. VL-Bus and PCI both do wonders for performance, running rings around standard bus implementations. Don't get hung up on the local bus wars. While the PCI standard has some advantages over VL-B on paper, it isn't clear whether that theoretical lead will translate into significantly better Windows performance, running your applications on your machine. Whatever you do, don't let a slick salesman convince you to buy a vendor's own proprietary brand of local bus: it's PCI or VESA or nothing. PCI and VL-B are cheap enough, there's no reason to get locked into a proprietary implementation.

If you're upgrading your current computer's motherboard, look hard and long at local bus. Few upgrades offer so much for so little. You may regret missing out on this opportunity.

Take It And Run

> Nouveau is better than no riche at all
>
> — Monsieur Marc, *Autobiography*, 1983

Caching In

It must be an Immutable Law of Science: some things are faster than others. In the computer age Maslow's Hierarchy of Speeds, the processor chip usually resides at the top of the speed pyramid, with the befuddled human sitting at the bottom. It's easy to see why. A 486DX2/66 chip running full-bore at 66 MHz flips and flops 66,000,000 times a second. A world class Kelly Speed Typist running full-tilt-boogie hits the keys maybe 10 times per second. Maybe.

Your computer only operates — oh, let's be charitable — say, five million times faster than you do.

Buried inside your computer are components that operate at vastly different speeds. While none of the speed variations are as gross as the difference between human and processor, they're still quite significant. One part of the machine may work 100 times faster than another. Keeping the tortoise and hare working together can be quite challenging.

The fundamental dichotomy? Money versus capacity. Computer components that hold large amounts of data tend to be slow and cheap: make them faster and they cost more; enlarge the capacity and they get slower.

Enter the buffer.

A buffer is just a temporary storage area in memory. In its simplest form, it's usually a piece of high-speed real estate used to store pieces of data from slower, cheaper, and typically more capacious media, making it ready for faster, more expensive, and usually less ample parts of the computer. Or vice-versa.

Oh Buffer, My Buffer

The most common variant on the buffering schtick is the sequential buffer: something that grabs data, sequentially, from one part of your computer, and delivers it — typically at a much faster or much slower rate — to another part of your computer.

Sequential buffers appear in your communication ports (to mediate between a slow modem and fast memory), the keyboard's input buffer (to come between you, the turtle, and your *oh!* so much faster programs), maybe in your hard drive (to pull off all the data that fits in one turn of the disk), or in a print spooler like Print Manager (to accept output from a program, storing it up for spoon-feeding to your printer).

There are actually two different types of buffers at work here. The disk cache and print spooler take from a fast component and store stuff so a slower component can use it. The hare hands stuff off to the buffer so that the hare won't have to wait for the tortoise.

But the other two examples seem puzzling. If your computer is so much faster than you, why the heck does it need a buffer to store the keys you type? Simple! The computer is sometimes too busy to bother looking at what the user is typing — so a buffer is used to store stuff from the slowpoke. The torotise hands off to the buffer so it doesn't have to wait until the hare deigns to look at the data, until the hare is no longer busy with something else.

Consider a *Student Prince Gedanken* experiment. . . beer chugging. There's a keg of beer sitting on a counter, and a thirsty undergrad foaming at the bit. The undergrad needs his thirst quenched; several alternatives present themselves. You (the detached designated driver)

could pop open the keg, hand the undergrad a straw, and tell him to start sucking. Depending on the undergrad's IQ, auditory acuity, and several hereditary factors, this approach could keep him occupied for minutes or days. Regardless of the duration of the experiment, the quantity of brew consumed per second would not set any records.

On the other hand, you could instruct the undergrad to lie on the floor and open his mouth. With the aid of a couple of burly friends, you might then jump up, pop the keg, drag it over to the undergrad, aim, and pour — in no particular order. In the computer biz, this is called "bus mastering". While the floor may emerge somewhat the worse for wear and the risk of drowning is considerably increased, the undergrad's gallons-per-minute benchmark rating should improve substantially vis-a-vis the single straw methodology.

Perhaps the highest benchmark scores, though, might emerge from a combination of the two approaches. Attach a funnel to the end of a hose. Let the undergrad lie on the floor again, but this time have him hold the funnel up where you can pour beer into it. Tell him to control the flow rate by crimping the hose. You and your burly friends need only concentrate on keeping the funnel from going dry. If you can do that, you'll know that the undergrad is chugging just as fast as he can. If the undergrad needs to interrupt the flow, perhaps to recycle the golden brew, he can crimp the hose, allowing the beer to back up in the funnel.

Aside from a few minor implementation details, that's how a sequential buffer works.

An example. Windows' Print Manager is a rather fancy sequential buffer. Why do you need Print Manager? Often word processors (and other apps) can spit out pages several times faster than printers can print. If the word processor is hooked up directly to the printer, your system will get all backed up, waiting for the pokey printer to do its thing. The speed of the printer controls the overall speed of your system: you'll just sit there watching pages go by in slo-mo.

Aha! A funnel opportunity exists!

Print Manager comes between your word processor and your printer. Like a big funnel, Print Manager grabs pages just as quickly as your word processor pours them out. The printer, sitting at the end of a serial port hose, accepts those pages as fast as it can. By placing the funnel in the middle, both your word processor and your printer can chunk along at their own pace. In most cases, that's exactly what you want: the word processor "lets go" faster; you don't have to wait for the printer. The speed of the word processor controls the overall speed of your system.

That's what a sequential buffer does.

There are other kinds of sequential buffers floating around in most systems. Most video cards store screen images in a kind of video buffer. Plug-in fax cards may have their own internal storage, to hold onto faxes received while the computer has turned casters-up: that's a kind of buffer, too. The undergrad's bladder is a buffer. And on and on.

Other Cache

Caches are like buffers in that they offer a repository — a place to put stuff — that sits between faster and slower storage.

To first approximation, caches differ from buffers in that buffer contents get used exactly once, while the cache's contents can be used more than once — or may not be used at all.

No, it isn't that complicated. I mean, if Igor can do it...... C'mon Igor, tell them what you know about cache. The bank job. Remember?

Wuh? Oh. Yeah. I know what you mean. I got a job as a bank clerk — this uncle of mine asked me to do it, see, said something about an "inside job", and I figured it was better than an outside one. Anyway, every morning this greasy kid back in the vault gave me this drawer with a whole bunch of. . .er. . . cash in it. I'd take it out to my teller. . . er. . . window.

People would come up to me and hand over deposits. Didn't need to rough 'em up or nothing. Real polite like. I'd take their money. Maybe pay a little bit out now and then, especially when these gorillas came in with business suits. From the government, they said.

Every time I ran out of twenty dollar bills, say, I'd lock up the drawer and go back to the vault. The greasy kid back there would hand me a wad and I'd sign this paper, see, saying that I got a bunch of twenties. If I got too many fives in the till, say, I'd take 'em back to the same greasy kid, and he'd sign this paper saying I brought in fives. At the end of the day I'd take the till back to that kid; he'd grab the money, count it and stick it back in the vault.

Then one day my uncle came by. He was wearing this hat... well, it looked more like a ski mask, really, kinda pulled down over his face so's I wasn't really sure if it was him at first, ya know. He walks up to me real nonchalant like and winks at me and. . .

Thanks, Igor. Mao can take it from here.

But it was real strange. I mean, he handed me this piece of paper and I looked at it and it said "This is a shtick up." And I thought. . . mnnnfff..

Anyway, Igor's bank teller's till acts a lot like a cache. If a teller had to run to the vault every time a customer came by seeking money, work at the bank would quickly grind to a halt. Instead, tellers get a little stash of high-speed cache. . . er. . . money. Most of the time the teller can handle things simply by working with what they have in the till (that's called a "cache hit," no doubt in deference to Igor's family). In unusual situations the teller may have to take the long walk to the vault, but in the best of all possible worlds the till holds enough high-speed money to handle most eventualities.

Caches make your system quicker if they manage to hold everything that's going to be needed in the near future. More often than not, what the computer will want in the future is very close to what it's been working on in the past. So caches are usually constructed so they hang on to old stuff for as long as they can (i.e., until something has to be thrown out to make way for the new stuff). They often go out and suck up stuff close to what's currently being used, just in case it'll be needed in the near future. The technical terms for those two methods are "Least Recently Used Cache Management" and "Look-Ahead Buffering," but don't let the fancy words confuse you. The concepts are really quite simple — and effective.

An example. A processor chip running at 66MHz needs feeding every 15 nanoseconds, i.e., 15×10^{-9} or 15 billionths of a second. The main memory chips you have inside your computer, the 4 MB or 8 MB of "RAM" random access memory, can typically regurgitate their contents every 60 or 70 nanoseconds. That factor of four-or-five speed difference, repeated every time the processor needs something, can really cripple Windows. So computer designers stick a high-speed bank teller's till between main memory and the processor.

i486 chips have 8K of cache already built in to the chip, but nearly all 486 computers sold nowadays go an extra mile, with even more cache out beyond the chip itself. Termed a "memory cache", the comparatively small (typically 64 K bytes to 512 K) and rather expensive ($50 to $200) chunk of memory chugs away at 20 or so nanoseconds.

Another example. Take your hard disk. Getting at data on a hard disk consumes 10 to 20 milliseconds — 10 or 20 thousandths of a second — to get the heads lined up, wait for the platters to spin around to the correct location, then read and transfer the numbers. That's *several hundred thousand* times slower than your main memory can handle.

Once the correct initial location on the disk has been reached, it takes very little time to scarf up subsequent blocks of data, because the heads only have to bring in whatever happens to be spinning under them at the moment. Actually, clever computer folk have created three very different kinds of cache for hard drives. First, the disk drive itself may contain a cache of plain RAM memory, typically 64K to 256K in size. This on-board cache adds little to the cost of the drive, and can help performance, particularly if your programs go out to the disk infrequently.

Second, the controller, the card that attaches your hard drive to the computer's bus, may contain plain RAM. These caching controllers may be as small as 256K, or as large as 16 MB, with 512K to 4 MB being typical. The extra RAM and the circuitry necessary to handle it, can add considerably to the cost of a controller, and at least under Windows the comparative benefit is negligible, or worse. I'll talk about caching controllers later.

Finally, the most common and least expensive kind of disk cache is a "software cache." You already own an excellent software cache: it's called SmartDrive, and it ships with both Windows and DOS. SmartDrive carves out a chunk of main memory inside your machine and reserves it for shuffling data to and from your hard drive. With very rare exceptions, Microsoft's SmartDrive works well and deserves to be on your system.

Floppy disk drives and CD-ROM drives have access times measured in large fractions of a second.

Those rare times you need to access a floppy you'll be glad that SmartDrive is there. Some CD-ROM drives, like their hard kin, have on board caches. Most, though, spin around oblivious to their drag on system performance.

So what's the difference between a cache and a buffer? Not much. It's mostly a question of semantics, and the distinction gets more cloudy all the time. A buffer is a place to stick stuff temporarily, to make sure nothing gets lost in transit between the slower parts and faster parts of your machine and, if you're lucky, speed up your computer in the process. Fair enough. A cache takes on many characteristics of a buffer, but adds the abilities to reuse data and to scarf up data that is easy to get and which might be used.

While we're on a semantic track, there's one more term that pops up all the time: a "spooler." IBM supposedly coined the phrase "Simultaneous Peripheral Operation Off-Line" back in the '60s, thus the SPOOL acronym.

Print Manager is a spooler; it exhibits all the characteristics of a good spooler. First and foremost it's a sequential buffer. But there are some higher-level capabilities tacked on such as setting output priority, or removing entire blocks ("print jobs") from the buffer.

Caches, buffers, and spoolers. Three names for set-aside chunks of real estate. I'll be talking about them a lot through the rest of this chapter.

Memory Cache

> Those who follow different roads
> Cannot take counsel in each other.
>
> — Confucious, ca 500 B.C.

The Intel 486DX chip comes with a small 8K built-in memory cache. Pentium has two 8K caches built-in. Most computers sold these days have an additional, sometimes called an "external," memory cache. One that's used in conjunction with the chip's built-in memory cache: 64K is not unusual, and some machines go as high as 512K of additional memory cache. The extra fast memory helps speed up your system overall, although by how much and under what circumstances is entirely open to debate.

 People who analyze cache stuff over afternoon drinks — Cachers in the Rye, so to speak — talk about a "hit rate". The concept is pretty easy: when that blazingly fast processor chip needs feeding, every 15 billionths of a second or so, it should be able to pull what it needs from the memory cache. When the data the processor needs is ready and waiting in fast 20 nanosecond memory cache, there's a "hit." But if the processor has to go rummage through slow 70 nanosecond memory, everything bogs down. A 90% hit rate can really speed things up. A hit rate of 100% probably reflects a cooked benchmark run. As with any other benchmark, the hit rate is a handy fiction that can vary all over the place, for all sorts of reasons, and you shouldn't read too much into the numbers.

That said, I generally find that an 8K cache on a Windows machine running one application will garner a 75 to 80% hit rate. Boost the cache to 64K, and the hit rate jumps to 90%, 128K could take you as high as 92 or 93%, but any more than 128K and the point of diminishing returns is well within sight.

If you run more than one major Windows app at a time, though, all bets are off. And as Windows evolves into a 32-bit environment, with more programs bumping into each other, cache should become more and more important.

There are all sorts of different kinds of memory caches, in many different sizes, and they use all sorts of different tricks to do their thing. Experts in the field will talk about banking and two-way set associative write backs and direct mapped write throughs and working sets and benchmarks and LRU algortithms until they're blue in the face. While the intellectual exercise is interesting, it's precisely that — an exercise.

In my experience, any memory cache is better than no memory cache. A 64K cache can improve performance on your Windows system noticeably. Anything beyond that is probably wasted money, at least for now. If you're buying a new machine, you might want to consider getting 128K or even 256K of memory cache if the price is right. But if you do so, recognize it as an investment in the future: 'tis a rare Windows user indeed who could tell the difference between 64K and 128K cache. And the performance difference attributable to all those arcane considerations the intelligentsia argue about is effectively negligible.

Yes, the design of the cache can make a difference if your machine hiccups on a power surge. That's why we recommend a cheap UPS (see later discussion in this chapter). Yes, there are pro's and con's all over the place. And the debates will rage on.

Spinners

> One good turne asketh another.
>
> — John Heywood, *Proverbes*, 1546

It's Been a Hard Drive's Night

The Windows disk challenge is twofold: how big and what type of controller?

The easy question is, which brand? The answer: any brand you like. All of the major hard disk manufacturers make solid, relatively worry-free products. Real-life performance (i.e., with SMARTDrive on) is virtually identical within a given size of disk — all the 120 MB run about the same speed; as do the 200 MB and the 500 MB. I've found almost no difference in quality, lifetime, reliability, support or performance among all the major brands.

That should tick off a few disk manufacturers. Sorry, folks, but Mom's made up her mind.

The question of disk capacity is not so simple. Is 80 MB enough? 500 MB too much? I can just about guarantee that you'll regret buying an 80 MB hard drive. A few months of sincere Windows use will blow away the lion's share of an 80 MB disk; if you play around with complex drawings or large documents, it won't even take a few months.

I'm convinced it takes at least 120 MB to give Windows a little breathing room. And if you plan to use three or more Windows applications, you should seriously consider starting with 200 MB. Windows eats hard drive space for lunch. If you're the adventurous type, you could use DOS 6.0 (or one of the competing programs) to compress your disk on-the-fly: so-called DoubleSpace or Stacked Disk or whatever.

I don't use DoubleSpace, but I tend to be very superstitious about such things. There's no technical reason to avoid it, aside from the rare horror story; I'm just not comfortable with the concept as yet. One of these days, though, my hard drive will get really crowded and I'll probably succumb to the DoubleTemptation. On-the-fly compression has only been around for a few years, and is in daily use on many millions of systems. Still. . . old habits die hard.

Even if you do compress your disk, go for 120 MB minimum (240 MB compressed). The price increment from 80 MB to 120 MB is small enough for the piece of mind.

Partitioning is another question altogether. DOS gives you the ability to carve your disk into chunks, called "partitions," and assign different drive letters to each partition: different parts of one hard disk could be accessed as **C:**, **D:**, and **E:**, for example. Again, there are technical pro's and con's, but in the end it's mostly a matter of how you organize things best. If you like to see all your options at once, forget about partitioning. If you work better with things tightly compartmentalized, partitioning is probably for you. When in doubt, use one partition and forget about it. You have bigger fish to fry.

On-board cache, the kind that comes built-in to the drive itself, may help performance just a touch. It's difficult to test in real-world conditions. Don't put too much stock in it. By and large, though, you get it whether you want it or not, so why not splurge on 64K? It ought to be worth $10 anyway.

You'll often see ads for disks quote other numbers: seek time, transfer rate, MTBF (mean time between failure), whatnot. The seek time is a fairly well-defined number that gives a theoretical average time necessary to position things so your hard drive can start reading data. While drives with a lower seek time find the first batch of data more quickly than those with higher seek times, a difference of a few milliseconds means nothing. The transfer rate measures, theoretically, how fast data can be shot from the disk to your computer's memory; in practice, there are many other factors that cloud the picture. MTBF ratings can be safely ignored: they won't tell you anything, really, about the drive.

By far the most important thing a vendor can give you when you buy a hard drive is a copy of the pages in the manufacturer's repair manual that pertain to the drive. Sooner or later you'll want to know the number of cylinders, heads, landing zone, and similar inanities. More important, some day you'll need to know which jumpers on the drive control master and slave settings: you'll need those to hook up a second drive to your computer. While you're at it, get the manufacturer's tech support telephone number. And make sure you get the warranty in writing.

Cached Writes Versus DoubleSpace

There's an important, if subtle, problem combining DoubleSpace, or any other disk compressor, with SMARTDrive, or any other disk cache. It isn't really a bug; think of it as a subtle gotcha.

The focus of this problem: cached writes.

Cached writes help speed up disk access in a very simple way. Programs constantly write new data out to disk. Computer jocks discovered long ago that those writes can go much faster if they're bundled up and done all at once. Without write caching, your computer gets a write instruction, waits for the spinning disk platters to line up just right, and writes one blob of data. When the next write comes through (possibly while the first one was still in progress), your computer then waits for the platters to line up again, and writes again. Since the platters rotate much slower than the write instructions can come down the pike, uncached disk writes can really bog down your system.

A disk write caching routine, on the other hand, saves up the writes and performs them in bunches, waiting for the optimal time.

All of the popular disk caching programs have a setting that allows cached writes. When this setting gets turned on, the caching program holds onto disk writes, waiting to see if your program makes further changes to a chunk of data before it's written out to that slow, slow disk. Cached writes can really speed up performance, especially if you're running a program that makes a lot of changes to a little bit of data.

Typically, disk writes only get held up for a maximum of five seconds. That's not much to you and me, but it's an eternity in computer time. Unless you change it manually, SMARTDrive sets itself up for 5-second cached writes. Don't bother looking it up in Microsoft's DOS 6 manual: the manual hardly mentions SMARTDrive, and doesn't say squat about cached writes (Microsoft sometimes calls them "lazy writes"). To find out more about SMARTDrive, you have to find and read a file called **SMARTMON.HLP** that DOS 6 installs in your DOS directory, or type **HELP SMARTDRV** at the DOS prompt.

Here's the problem: if your machine croaks while disk writes remain in the cache, you could scramble a file or two. I've seen it happen many, many times.

 Don't think it's dangerous? Ask the editors at *InfoWorld* what happened in their DOS 6.0 testing when they forgot about SMARTDrive cached writes, clobbered a whole bunch of data, and blamed the resulting mess on nonexistent bugs in DOS 6. Front page headlines, no less. And front page retractions.

If your computer dies while SMARTDrive is holding onto a handful of cached disk writes, you are in deep, deep doo-doo. The same conclusion holds true for other types of caches; whatever you're working on at the time can really get trashed, and you may never be able to recover your work. It's particularly insidious working with DoubleSpace or other compressed drives, because of the way data is compressed: a couple of scrambled bits can really do major damage to a file.

 Yet another one they don't tell you about in the manuals, eh?

You must be very, very careful. I've established a few iron-clad rules for combining SMARTDrive and DoubleSpace:

1)   Avoid unexpected outages: always use an Uninterruptable Power Supply.

2)   Always exit Windows before turning off your computer. Leaving Windows flushes the cached SMARTDrive writes — makes sure all of them get written out to disk.

3)   Always disable cached writes on portables, especially portables running DoubleSpace. It's easy. Find the **SMARTDRV** line in your **AUTOEXEC.BAT** file. Then simply put the letter of the drive that should have write cache disabled, after the command. Something like this:

```
C:\DOS\SMARTDRV C
```

You can check if you have write caching on by typing **SMARTDRV** at a DOS prompt and looking in the column labelled Write Cache.

4)   Before you turn off a machine that's running DOS, wait at least fifteen seconds after the hard drive activity light goes out, or run this command:

```
SMARTDRV /C
```

The **/C** parameter flushes the cached writes. If you have just exited Windows, it is enough to wait for the C:> DOS prompt after which it is safe to turn off the machine.

Disk Controllers

> You can't make a silk purse out of a sow's ear.
>
> — Jonathan Swift, *Polite Conversation*, 1738

Hard drives come in many different flavors, from the ancient (i.e., more than three years old) MFM and RLL to ESDI to the whippersnapper IDE and the schizophrenic

SCSI. When you talk about Windows machines and their disks, you'll invariably come down to the final two: IDE (pronounced "Eye Dee Eee") and SCSI ("scuzzy"). The latest incarnation of SCSI is called SCSI-2. There are lots of technical things behind the alphabet soup, most of which don't mean much to normal Windows folk: IDE (Integrated Drive Electronics) refers to a method of sticking most of the electronics on the disk itself, as opposed to the controller card. SCSI (Small Computer System Interface) refers to a long-standing method of attaching many different kinds of devices to a computer.

Choosing among the different flavors of hard drives isn't as difficult as it once was. Nobody, it seems, makes MFM or RLL drives any more, and almost everybody agrees that ESDI costs more than it's worth: at one point it was the only game in town for large disks, but now it's a technology whose time has passed. IDE is the rave at the moment, and for good reason. It's reliable, cheap, and powerful. A tough combination to beat.

The SCSI "standard" has, until very recently, been subject to varying interpretation. Far from a standard, it was more like a loose collection of vaguely related methods for hooking things into a computer. In theory, one SCSI controller should let you attach up to seven SCSI devices to your computer: hard drives, scanners, CD ROM drives, tape drives, removable drives, WORM drives, drive drives. In practice, some controllers work with some hardware, others don't, and nobody seems to know from day-to-day what will work and what won't.

HP scanners, in particular, are notorious for being difficult to match with any controller other than the one that ships with the scanner. HP scanners call themselves SCSI (at least they did at one time) but for all intents and purposes they aren't. Or at least they're a different kind of SCSI, which is just as bad.

If you buy a drive, scanner, or whatever, with a cheap no-name SCSI controller, you may be in for a rude surprise. On the other hand, if you stick to the big name SCSI controller manufacturers — preferably a manufacturer who touts ASPI compatibility, you're much more likely to land a controller that will work with more than one SCSI device.

As a general rule of thumb, a blazing SCSI-2 controller on an ISA machine can slap data around significantly faster than an IDE controller on an ISA machine. If you use an IDE controller in an ISA local bus slot (see the earlier discussion on local bus), the speed will fall roughly half way between normal IDE and SCSI-2. But even with all the measurable performance differences down at the disk level, SMARTDrive can be a huge equalizer; 'tis a rare Windows user indeed who can *feel* the difference between IDE and SCSI-2, or local bus and non-local bus disk access.

Part of the problem here is in the inherent design of disk drives. They were made to work on the old PC/AT bus, running at 8 MHz, and there's been very little impetus thus far to crank up the data transfer speed, except on enormously expensive, huge disks. Sticking a pokey hard drive on the back of a methedrine-influenced controller card might sound good in theory, but in practice it doesn't seem to do much. IDE drives, in fact, mirror the electrical connections of the ISA bus: look for no silk purse of this sow's ear.

 I recommend plain vanilla (and cheap!) IDE drives, in most situations. If you have outrageously heavy data requirements, the move to SCSI-2 may prove worthwhile: there *is* a noticeable improvement in data access speeds with a fast SCSI-2 implementation, but most folks don't spend enough time slapping big files around to worry about it.

If you decide to go with SCSI, consider getting the CorelSCSI software package. These folks are serious about making SCSI work on PCs; the software (about $79 on the streets) could save you days of headache. Voice: 800-836-SCSI or 613-728-8200 FAX: 613-761-9176.

There's another extenuating circumstance. If you plan on buying a SCSI controller anyway, to run a CD-ROM drive, or maybe a fancy tape backup unit, using SCSI disk drives instead of IDE drives may eliminate the need for an IDE controller card, and thus leave an extra slot inside your machine free. Check with the vendor before making any assumptions, but if the number of free slots has been a bone of contention for you, SCSI may save you a lot of headache.

 One thing you don't need is a caching IDE controller, a fancy, expensive controller card that takes its own memory and uses that memory to shuffle data between the disk and your computer's main memory. Save your money. If you use SMARTDrive, it's much ... uh ... smarter to forget the caching controller (which duplicates and, in some cases, *negates* the benefits of SMARTDrive!) and put those extra bucks in main memory.

I know. Mom bought one.

On a Clear Day

> The difference between
> Men and boys
> Is in the resolution
> Of their toys
>
> — Mangled

Monitors and Merry Macs

Ah, for the good old days, when a color monitor meant you could see amber on black instead of green on green. Or perhaps run in CGA mode, boon of the PC game player, where fuzzy crawling bugs looked like fuzzy crawling bugs. When power users felt lucky to get more than 25 lines of 80 characters each. When plugging the wrong monitor into a perfectly good video card could result in a full-fledged fire, set off smoke alarms, forcing everyone on your floor to immediately debate the wisdom of pouring water on a french-fried monitor.

Recent history has taken its toll on video. Windows stretches the old DOS weirding video ways far beyond the breaking point. And it's taken quite a few Windows users along with it.

Let's start by looking at standard monitors: you may call 'em CRTs or TV tubes or boob tubes or something similar. The panels on portable computers work differently; let's save them for last.

 Three R's drive Windows video: Refresh rate, Resolution, and coloR. Well, two R's and a C if you lack imagination. Whenever you consider buying a new monitor, replacing an old one, or changing out video boards, this is the place to start — even before you start looking at performance or price.

Refresh Rate: The Eyes Have It

Computer monitors, just like TVs, create images by scanning an electronic beam across the inside of your screen, zapping little dots, and making them light up. In a color monitor there are three beams, one each for red, green, and blue dots, but you get the idea. Each time the beam scans over the entire screen it's called a "refresh". When the beam hits the lower-right-hand corner of the screen it jumps back to the upper-left-hand corner and starts again, refreshing the screen once more.

Each little dot only gets zapped once during a single refresh: the dot has to keep on glowing until it gets refreshed again. If the dot doesn't glow long enough, or if the refresh happens too slowly, your monitor will flicker: the pulsing dots glow brighter and darker very quickly, and your eyes see that as flicker. It'll drive you nuts.

Refresh rates are measured in cycles — refreshes — per second, or Hz. A 60 Hz refresh rate means that the screen gets redrawn 60 times per second. The tricky part: both your monitor and your video card have to run at the same rate.

No two pairs of eyes see flicker the same way. It seems to get worse when the background color is light or white. And since Windows often uses light backgrounds, flicker that's barely noticeable in DOS programs may overwhelm you in Windows. Flicker also often gets worse when fluorescent lights shine directly on the screen, or when glare forces you to turn up the screen's contrast. Larger, higher resolution monitors can enhance flickering. Finally, some programs add to the flicker effect by not drawing or redrawing characters quickly enough.

 Not sure if your monitor is flickering enough to bother you? It isn't a black-and-white question. Flicker may not be immediately apparent; you may not feel its effects until you get a pounding headache after working at a monitor for an hour. Here's a quick test: turn your head, and look at the monitor out of the corner of your eye. If you can feel a pulsing coming from the direction of the monitor, you probably need to boost the refresh rate.

Without a doubt, the higher the refresh rate you can maintain the less your chances for flicker. Some people do just fine at 60 Hz. Most people need a higher refresh rate. Just about everybody will feel comfortable at 72 Hz, providing there are no fluorescent lights shining directly on the screen.

Most monitor user's manuals, if you can find yours buried under that ton of junk, will list Vertical Scan Frequencies (another name for refresh rate). That's the number you need. You might also find a notation that looks like this: fV/73.486Hz. That's engineering shorthand for "Vertical frequency 73.486 Hz." Often the refresh rate will vary depending on resolution (see the following section). In any case, if you have a fairly modern monitor, it will usually, within the limits mentioned in your user manual, latch onto the fastest refresh rate your video card can support.

The manual for your video card will usually list specific, discrete refresh rate values. For example, you might see "Vertical Refresh Rate 43, 60, and 72 Hz". Providing your monitor is up to it, the card will normally drive your monitor at the highest possible rate.

There's one little gotcha in the refresh game: interlacing. Some video cards and monitors will only refresh every-other line. On the first pass, they hit the odd numbered lines, on the second pass only the even numbered lines, and so on. Interlacing is a sleight of hand invented to fool you into believing that a monitor or card can do more than it should. Televisions interlace. You don't want interlacing. Fortunately, interlacing is dying a well-deserved death.

So now you know that you need 70 Hz refresh or better, in a non-interlaced setup, right? Good. That's really all you need to know.

Peaceful Resolution

> Eyes and ears are bad witnesses to men
> if they have souls that understand not their language.
>
> — Heraclitus, *The World*, ca 500 B.C.

Resolution refers to the number of dots and lines displayed on your screen. If you have Windows running at 1024 x 768, your monitor will display 1024 dots across the screen by 768 lines up and down.

Various manufacturers support many different resolutions. By far the most common are "Standard" VGA (640 dots x 480 lines), "Super" VGA (800 dots x 600 lines), and a mode called "8514" (1024 dots x 768 lines). Actually, "8514" refers to the way the software talks to your monitor, and "Super VGA" often includes 1024 x 768, but those subtleties tend to get lost in everyday parlance.

The bizarre names stem from accidents of history: "VGA" means "Video Graphics Array", an early name for a now-obsolete video card; "8514" comes from the name of a *then*-obsolete monitor, and that was in 1987. Don't get hung up on the names. They don't matter much.

What matters is the number of dots and lines, and how they translate into better or worse pictures on your monitor. Once you've decided on the resolution you like, it becomes a question of digging up the money for a sufficiently spacious monitor. At very high resolutions, you might also need to look into getting a beefier video card.

Going for a higher resolution doesn't give you more detail; it merely lets you see more. Say you scanned a picture of Mom, and the scanned image is 320 x 240 dots, in 256 colors. If you run your video card in Standard VGA mode, that picture will take up a quarter of the screen. If you then flip your video card into Super VGA mode (many cards let you do that rather easily), Mom's picture suddenly takes but 16% of the screen. It *looks* smaller, you may have to stick your nose right up to the monitor to see Mom's beaming visage, but the detail doesn't change one whit.

Moving any particular picture from VGA to Super VGA won't make that particular picture sharper; instead, the higher resolution will let you see more pictures, side-by-side; or, if you have a large picture, more *of* the picture.

Take a look at the three screen shots in Figure 7-5. They show precisely how Mom's desktop looks in Program Manager, at the three most common screen resolutions.

Don't get hung up on how I do my icons, sonny. *De gustibus non est disputandum*[†], eh? That FOX in the Comm group is for Fidelity On-Line Express, not the database. And DOS Edit appears twice intentionally, so I can find it easier. No, Sysedit2 in the WinWord group wasn't supposed to be there: this little kid shanghaied my system, and he moved some stuff around. And just because I have ATM doesn't mean I use it. Some service bureaus are still in the dark ages. OK? Sheesh.

Now, now. Don't you worry that pretty little head of yours. Nobody is *that* nosey.

At the highest resolution shown here, 1024 x 768, Mom's desktop can hold about 14 plain vanilla Program Manager icons across and about 10 icons up-and-down. When the resolution goes down to 800 x 600, though, the desktop shrinks: it will only hold 11 icons or so across by maybe 8 top-to-bottom. At standard VGA, 640 x

[†] *There is no disputing tastes*. Hey, it ain't none of your business.

480 resolution, the desktop is so small it will only hold 8 or so across, and 6 up-and-down.

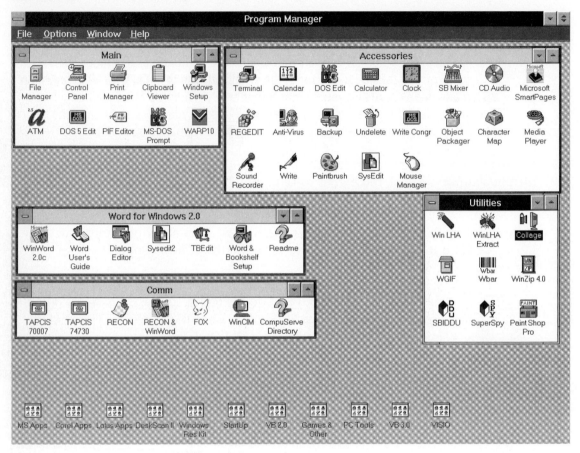

Figure 7-5: Mom's Desktop, at 1024 x 768 Resolution

Higher resolutions require more data from your computer. If you run a 16-color (4-bit) image at 640 x 480 resolution, one screen full of information takes 640 x 480 x 4 or 1,228,800 bits. If you run a 256 color (8-bit) image at 1024 x 768 resolution, your computer has to generate 1024 x 768 x 8 or 6,291,456 bits.

That's a whole lotta bits to blast.

There's a reason for the resolution differences and, as you might guess, the crux of the matter is money. On a cheap 14-inch monitor, 640 x 480 may be all you can handle: trying to run at 800 x 600 will turn icons and text so small, you'll need a magnifying glass to see anything. A good flat-screen 15-inch monitor, though, may be big enough to step up to 800 x 600. The differences are subtle and perceptions vary greatly from person to person. Unfortunately, the only way you'll know for sure if you can stand a given resolution on a specific monitor is by spending hours, possibly days, with the combination.

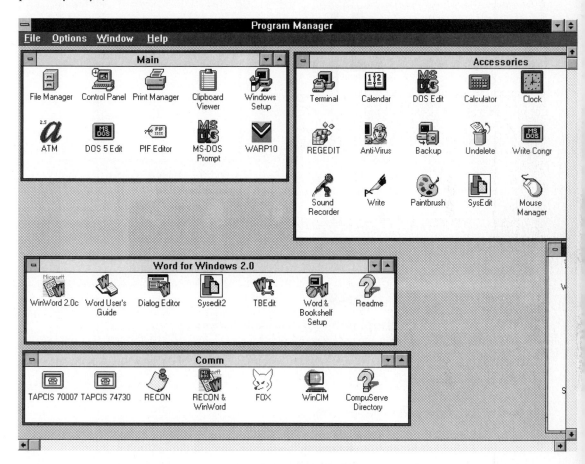

Figure 7-6: Mom's Desktop, at 800 x 600 Resolution

Yeah, yeah, yeah. You need numbers. Okay, okay.

Figure 7-8 shows how I figure things stack up at the various commonly available resolutions.

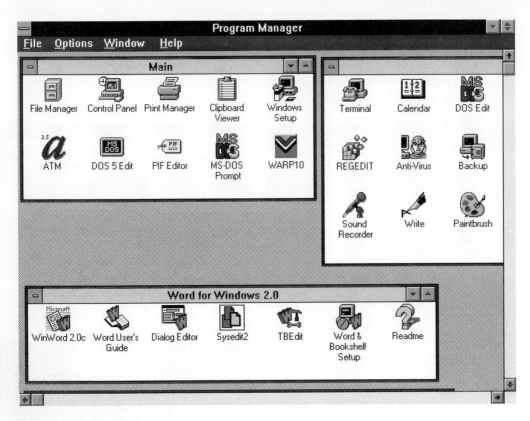

Figure 7-7: Mom's Desktop, at 640 x 480 Resolution

Resolution	Dots (Pixels)	Size vs 640 x 480	ProgMan Icons	Minimum Screen Size	
				Teenagers	Old Farts
640 x 480	307,200	-	48	any	any
800 x 600	480,000	56% Larger	88	15 "	17 "
1024 x 768	786,432	2.6 X Larger	140	17 "	19 "
1152 x 900	1,036,800	3.4 X Larger	180	19 "	21 "
1280 x 1024	1,310,720	4.3 X Larger	238	21 "	Ha!

Figure 7-8: Reaching Resolution

The Size column merely recounts the differences in the number of dots on the screen: 800 x 600 resolution, for example, shows 56% more dots than 640 x 480; 1024 x 768 shows 2.6 times as many. The ProgMan Icons column gives a rough estimate of how many "normal" Program Manager icons might fit on the screen.

That number varies depending on average description lengths, and a whole bunch of other factors, so don't take it as gospel.

I had to break the Minimum Recommended Screen Size column into two categories, dependent on how sharp your vision is. If you're 65 years old, can still see a cow pie at 75 yards, *and* you can read stock listings at six inches, go ahead and use the teenager column. If you're 12 years old but couldn't tell Bill Gates from Norman Schwartzkopf, better to run with the Old Farts.

Screen size is the nominal size advertised by monitor manufacturers. It has very little to do with the actual diagonal screen size, which can be a couple of inches less than the nominal size, and a lot to do with how the particular monitor is placed in a vendor's line-up. Still, most nominal 17-inch monitors will be sufficient for teenagers running 1024 x 768 or old farts running 800 x 600.

If you have a limited amount of desk space — not disk space, *desk* space — make sure you've checked the dimensions of the monitor and its weight before ordering it. Monitors over 17 inches or so can take enormous amounts of desk real estate. Perhaps surprisingly, the major constraint will often be front-to-back, not side-to-side. If you can scoot your desk around, away from walls, so the pointy end of the monitor can hang over the edge, like Igor's beer belly, you'll gain considerable flexibility in positioning your monitor.

 I resemble that remark.

One final note on resolution. Dot pitch used to be a very important consideration when acquiring a monitor, and it still is worth considering if you're buying a monitor without looking at it (a risky proposition by any measure).

Dot Pitch measures the distance between adjacent dots on the screen. The technical definition is more complex and gets tied up in shadow masks and the like, but to a first approximation this should do. The smaller the dot pitch, the closer together the dots, and the finer the picture.

 In practice, you should always stick to monitors with a dot pitch at, or under, 0.28 mm. Little monitors, say 14 inches or smaller, better come in under 0.26 mm, or you'll spend more money on opthamologists than you saved on the monitor.

Once upon a time, 14-inch monitors with 0.31 mm dot pitch came bundled with really cheap systems. You can spot the folks who bought those systems: they're still running around with Coke-bottle glasses and migraine headaches. Fortunately, manufacturers have caught on; almost all monitors sold today meet my minimal criteria. Monitors based on the Sony Trinitron tube are different. Because of the way they're made, their dot pitch isn't directly comparable to other monitors'.

The Cry and Hue

> One fish, two fish,
> Red fish, blue fish
>
> — Dr. Seuss

Video refresh rate emerges as a compromise between your video card and monitor. Resolution, while driven by the video card, plays second fiddle to your monitor's quality. In both cases the monitor defines and (usually) limits video performance.

The third R, coloR, is a little different. While the quality of colors that you see, brighter reds, deeper blues, more accurately burnt umbers, are largely a function of the monitor, the burden of providing large numbers of colors (called a "palette") lies squarely on the shoulders of the video card.

Many video cards these days can provide you with as many colors as you like, at least at lower resolutions, if you're willing to buy enough memory to keep the card happy.

 I could have CTO Mao go back and forth on the pro's and con's, and let Igor tell you about the *real* con's, but I'm going to cut to the Franklin. You have three basic choices in Windows: run at 16 colors, 256 colors, or 24-bit (so-called "true" or "real" or "full") color. Yeah, there are all sorts of deviant color schemes, but for most people, it all boils down to those three. And here's my simple advice: you should plan on running 256 colors, and buy a video card that supports 256 colors at your chosen resolution.

Some people can get away with just 16 colors. If you do nothing but calculate spreadsheets or type memos all day, every day, and never see a picture on screen, you might be able to survive with 16 colors. But there's little, if any, extra cost in moving up to 256 colors, and the old performance penalty isn't anywhere near as bad as it once was, so why hassle it?

Other people really do need full 24-bit color: anybody editing photographs or pasting up four-color publications qualifies. If you need full color, you already know it, and no matter what I tell you, you'll get it. Fair enough. Admittedly, it's nice to have true color available on the off chance a more-than-256-color picture comes across your desk. But do you really need it?

I Hate It When You Squeeze the Tube in the Middle

Bottom line for buying a monitor: pick a resolution you can live with. Look at the Old Fart Chart to see how big a monitor you need. Then dig into the magazine reviews and see which monitors come out on top.

Personally, I've always had good luck with Nanao and NEC monitors, and recommend them vociferously. Over the years Nanao has repeatedly produced the finest monitors available. Not coincidentally, they tend to be just about the most expensive, as well. NEC monitors are also well known for their exceptional quality and reliability. But they, too, tend toward the expensive.

If you have a sizable budget, look at the Nanao and NEC, shop around for a highly discounted price, and feel good about choosing either one. If you have a finite budget, Nanao and NEC may not be your best buys; you'll have to start shopping around.

You can generally trust the magazine reviews of monitors, particularly when reviewers start talking about their subjective *feel* of how things appear on the monitor. That's because major monitor reviews usually involve lining up the monitors in one big line, and having the reviewers take a good, hard look at the pictures. Remember the last time you bought a TV set? Did you look at a row of TVs, and settle on one that had great picture quality, even if it cost a few bucks more? Well, that's what the reviewers do, and it works.

Ideally you'd like to be able to pick a computer monitor by eye-balling the competitors, the same way you pick a TV set, but it never works that way. Walk into a computer store and you'll be lucky to find two monitors side-by-side hooked up to the same video board, much less a dozen of 'em. This is one situation where you have to trust reviewers.

Don't be swayed by the reviewers' description of minutia, by the way: if you don't understand what they're talking about, ignore it. Many of the monitor measuring tools out there right now are so picky you can't see the differences they report; only a properly calibrated, expensive machine can pick 'em up. So don't let the numbers fool you.

Windows Sources Magazine and *Windows User Magazine* (before its untimely demise) in particular have done an excellent job of avoiding the numbers crap trap and telling it straight.

I guarantee you won't notice 0.1% of pincushioning or half a barrel of keystones once you start working with a monitor, day in and day out. Assuming you can even *see* the subtleties that drive so many reviews, most folks find their eyes adjust to tiny anomalies (say, a little bit of barrel distortion) after a day or two.

While you will notice major defects in a monitor—it's hard to ignore a picture that's rotated 45°, or a screen that flip-flip-flips out of synch—manufacturers have by and large eliminated the big problems; chances are good the gross stuff can be traced to a shipper who dropped a box.

Of Whistles and Bells

> Keeping time, time, time,
> In a sort of Runic rhyme,
> To the tintinnabulation that so musically wells
>
> — Edgar Allen Poe, *The Bells*, 1849

Monitor vendors seem hell-bent on selling little niceties, proffering bells and whistles in an attempt to separate you from your bucks. Most vendors would be better off spending their R&D budgets on delivering a better picture, but if they did something so unnatural, they might fall behind in the featuritis race.

 I just love it when reviewers fuss over the position of a monitor's control panel, even downgrading their analyses of monitors with control panels that are a bit hard to get at. The True Fact is that most normal Windows users fix their monitor settings maybe once or twice, getting the picture centered and extended out to the edges of the screen, then they never set it again. Many monitors go for years without twiddling the dials. Tell the truth, when's the last time you adjusted your monitor? Yeah, I thought so.

There's a reason why reviewers get concerned about placement of control panels; they have to adjust 'em all the time! The sins of the fathers are vested on their readers.

Color adjustment on a monitor is very important if precise calibration of color output is part of your job description. For the vast majority of Windows users, though, a fancy color matching scheme amounts to a huge time and money sink. You'll probably never get it right anyway. Color calibration on systems only used for black-and-white printing may rate as the ultimate conceit.

Auto power-down "green" monitors are all the rage. The good ones detect when you aren't using your monitor, reduce its power consumption in steps, then spring back to life in five or ten seconds when you need the monitor again. While that feature can help those who leave their monitor unexpectedly unused a dozen times a day, for most of us there's a simpler solution. It's called a power switch. Power-up time may be twenty seconds, twice that of the green monitors, but electricity consumption while in the "off" position tends to be fairly minimal.

Keep it in perspective, sonny. Your monitor uses about as much power as a light bulb. Well, maybe a big light bulb. Your computer itself might use another light bulb's worth. Folks who see their electric bills soar when they install a new computer often discover the source of their inflated bill isn't the new computer — it's all the lights that they use to illuminate the computer room!

One final topic. Radiation.

That's a tough one. While there's no proof radiation from monitors carries any sort of medical consequence, there's no proof that it doesn't, and therein lies the difficulty. Yes, one study discovered a correlation between CRT use and miscarriages in pregnant CRT operators. No, that study didn't show the CRTs *caused* the miscarriages; something else might have caused them; the whole thing could've been a statistical aberration.

The only solid fact floating around in this scientific cesspool: radiation falls off dramatically as you increase the distance between the monitor and the person. You can always decrease your exposure by taking a clue from Yosemite Sam and backing off.

I'm superstitious about things I don't understand, and low-level electromagnetic emission places high in that category. Personally, I would only consider a low-EMF monitor, one that conforms to the Swedish MRP-2 guidelines. Will it help? Who knows. . . but more to the point, what can it hurt?

LCD Displays

LCD screens — usually, but not exclusively, found on laptops — are a cockroach of a different color. Resolution takes a back seat to the LCD technology itself, and dot pitch isn't really a consideration at all.

If you can live with Windows in black-and-white, make sure you get a screen that supports 256 levels of gray. If you need color in a laptop, get active matrix. "Active matrix" refers to a method of putting one transistor behind every dot on the screen; what it means for you is sharper, deeper colors that won't wash out under normal office lights, good to excellent scrolling speed, and a fair-to-middlin' chance you'll be able to see your cursor every now and then.

How Much is Too Much?

You won't hear me making this kind of impassioned recommendation very often, so pay attention. If you spend a fair amount of time every day in front of a computer, the choice of monitor is crucial. Buy as much monitor as you can afford. No, buy *more*.

You can skimp on all sorts of things, but don't skimp on this one. Get a good, solid, big monitor, with a card that will drive it at 70 Hz or better. Even if you have to move down a notch in processor speed, or disk capacity, or hold off on that sound card for another six months. It really is that important.

Few things in the computer realm will treat you as well, or mean as much, as a little relief for your eyes. A good monitor reduces fatigue and lets you do your best work. A great monitor rates as a nonpareil blessing, a gift you'll relish over and over and over again, every single day.

Seers

> Yatha bubbulakam passe yathat passe maricikam[†]

— Gautama Buddha, *Dhammapada*, ca 600 B.C.

Acceleration Versus Co-Processing

 So much for monitors. It's time to dive into video cards — the brains behind those big, beautiful pictures.

While several manufacturers still ship "dumb" video cards, they're usually intended for "dumb" DOS machines. You'll find those machines on the super-discount table at your local Joe's PC and Suds Emporium.

Dumb video cards, also called frame buffered cards, ruled the video roost for many years. As the name aptly indicates, dumb cards take pictures generated by your main processor and slap them up on the screen; they don't try to help the processor. They're the Stoop N. Fetchit of the video industry. And they're the death of Windows.

Accelerated and co-processed video cards, by contrast, contain some native intelligence. Instead of stoop 'n fetching every single bit of data, these cards receive commands from the main processor. The commands tell the video card what to do: draw circles, connect lines, form rectangles, move bits, that sort of thing. By putting intelligence in the video card, the amount of data being shuffled across that *oh!* so terribly slow bus decreases, sometimes by an order of magnitude.

Think of it this way. I have two friends, one of whom uses Windows all the time; the other only runs DOS. Both want to print a .PCX picture on their printer. The Windows friend calls me and asks how to do it. "Easy!" I say, "crank up Paintbrush, click on File Open, pick up the file, and click on File Print." My Windows friend, demonstrating considerable native intelligence, understands my abbreviated commands and has the picture printed in ten seconds. Then my DOS friend calls. "Well," I say, "do you have the C prompt in front of you?" My DOS friend hems and haws and says, "I can see a cee colon slash dee oh ess greater than. Is that what you mean?" I say,

---

[†] *Look upon the world as a bubble, regard it as a mirage*

444 • Chapter 7: Killer Hardware

"Good. Type cee dee space period enter." Click click click. "Uh," my friend says, "do you spell 'enter' with a capital eee?" And so it goes. With no native intelligence on the other end, I have to shove an enormous amount of information over the phone line. Printing the .PCX file takes ten times as long.

Accelerated video cards speak in the commands Windows uses. They're intelligent, although the intelligence is burned into the card: they're smart, but they won't get any smarter.

Co-processed video cards, usually based on the Texas Instruments 340x0 series processors, have the smarts now, and can also be programmed to gain new smarts in the future. They're computers in and of themselves, with more than 80 instructions at their disposal. Co-processed video cards, not unexpectedly, also cost more than the accelerated kind, by a factor of five or so.

 The folks who sell co-processed video cards, naturally, see all sorts of advantages. "Buy an accelerated card and you're doomed to obsolescence!", they say, citing magazine articles and so-called experts. Horse. . . er. . . Cockroachpucky. You could buy the greatest accelerated card now, and then buy another greatest card a year from now, and another the year after that, and one more the year after that, and you still wouldn't pay as much as you would for a co-processed card today.

There *are* cases where a 340x0 co-processed card makes sense, though. But I'm getting ahead of the story.

Local Bus Video Cards

 If you're going to buy a new computer, you're going to get a local bus machine with an accelerated video card. It's that simple.

The particular brand of video card isn't nearly as important as the presumption of local bus; almost any accelerated card on a local bus will run rings around the alternative. At this moment the Weitek P9000 chip on a local bus card (as in the Diamond Viper) seems to be in first place for video performance, but the standard bearer changes week-to-week. By the time you read this, no matter what accelerated local bus card you buy, it will be fast enough for normal Windows use:

once you go over 20 or 30 million WinMarks (or 10 ToastedBunnies; see next section), video no longer rates as Windows' great nemesis. The game changes completely.

Put this in perspective. Windows is the first widely used program in the history of the PC that taxed everyday users' hardware to the breaking point. Prior to Windows, there were the odd (and I *do* mean odd) CAD users or Humungo Database users or desktop publishers who needed every ounce of hardware they could get, just to make their applications work. But with the advent of Windows, *everybody* suddenly finds themselves in that position: the hardware simply hasn't kept up with the software.

Accelerated local bus video is finally getting fast enough that video may no longer be the major bottleneck in new Windows machines. That's an incredible development, actually. It's why I automatically assume that if you buy a new machine you'll get accelerated local bus video, and why I won't bother you with performance comparisons of local bus video cards: they're all fast enough for normal Windows work. Besides, details on individual boards change so fast that anything I might say now will be obsolete by the time this book hits the stands.

The next watershed differentiation in video card performance will come when full-motion video becomes commonplace — and that's at least a year or two away.

Non-LB Video and the ToastedBunnyMark

If you're trying to wring the maximum Windows performance out of your existing non-local-bus machine, the very first thing you should consider (after bumping up to 8 MB memory) is upgrading your video card. No other single upgrade will do so much for your machine, or your disposition, day after day after day.

That's why Mom figured it was so important to take an in-depth look at some of the non-local-bus video cards out there, realizing full well that the model numbers and exact performance numbers will change by the time you read this. Not to worry. You're going to learn about the story behind the numbers, something much more important than numbers themselves.

You won't find many reviews of individual pieces of hardware in computer books. Why? Because the lead times inherent in producing a good-sized computer book rival those of launching a minor war. By the time any book hits the stands, at least one, and possibly two, generations of hardware changes and improvement stand between the review and the products available on dealers' shelves.

Perhaps surprisingly, the reviews you see in the major magazines often lag product availability by three months or more: lead times in the magazine industry hover around two to three months; if publishers try to cheat the deadlines, typically by reviewing pre-release beta test versions, they'll end up reviewing products that never make it to market! It happens all the time.

 I spent months looking at all the video benchmarking routines, reading the reviews, pounding the boards, seeing how video board manufacturers were cooking their scores, how publications were lambasting some of the vendors and letting others squeeze by on technicalities, trying to come up with a measurement that somehow reflected the *feel* of speed in a dozen different video boards.

 Then I called Mao one day and remarked how much faster the toasters flew across my screen with this new video card.

 The rest, as they say, is history.

Or at least road kill.

I found, over and over again, that the After Dark flying toaster screen saver would send toasters whizzing by faster with video boards that *felt* faster, and slower on the laggards. And I could quantify the difference.

The Toasters held all sorts of advantages. In a time when so many video manufacturers exhibit the moral sensitivity and tact of alley cats, it was refreshing to find a significant nook where no cheater had trod before. After all, no video board manufacturer in their right mind would cook, much less toast, performance on a screen saver, fer heaven's sake. Anybody with After Dark (Berkeley Systems, 2095 Rose St, Berkeley CA 94709 Voice: 510-540-5535) and a stopwatch could run their own tests at home or in the office.

Besides, how often can you write off a screen saver as a fully legitimate business expense? Or contribute to the livelihood of people who begin their user's manual with an entreaty from four centuries ago:

> Sweet Phosphor bring the day;
> Light will repay
> The wrongs of night;
> Sweet Phosphor, bring the day
>
> — Francis Quarles (1592-1644)

I thought I had the problem licked: a cook-free benchmark, cheap, easily replicated, with a high correlation to perceived performance.

And then the Bunny dropped in. Literally. *Deus ex Rabbita. . .*

Where After Dark is a Class Act, the Energizer Bunny (PC Dynamics, 31332 Via Colinas, Suite 102, Westlake Village, CA 91362) descends on your screen in a crass display of commercialism, bangs his drum slowly, and keeps on going. . . and going. . . and going. . .(a phrase, the documentation asserts, is trademarked by the Eveready Battery Company).

More to the point, this Bunny really hauls butt with faster video boards, and moonwalks when the board is slow. Ba-da-boom ba-da-bing, we got ourselves a benchmark.

Such was the genesis of the ToastedBunnyMark — CTO Mao's seminal contribution to the field of scientific measurement and statistical analysis, the Cook-Free Benchmark of the Nineties, the Standard by Which All Future Standards Shall Be Standardized... *we now refer to Mao as the Vicar of Video Vivisectionists. Don't tell anybody but he's turned into such a snob he won't toast with anything less than a DualIt. This benchmark stuff can certainly turn your head.*

Instead of concentrating on numbers, the fictitious and all-too-often misleading bottom line, I'm going to take you through the steps I took in evaluating boards (see Figure 7-9) in the hopes that you might find a few good tricks to employ to find a good video board for you. In the process of battering these boards, I'll fill you in on a few tricks I've learned over the years. I want you to see what you might look for before the 30-day evaluation is over, stuff that'll drive you batty if you have to live with it for any length of time.

Some of these board manufacturers are going to get mad at me, so let me clearly explain how I ran all of these tests. All the following non-local bus cards were on my standard (non-local bus) ISA system: a Comtrade 486/50 (AMI BIOS UM486 v 1.4 dated 3/24/92), 20MB memory, with 2 serial ports (COM1 mouse and COM2 modem); one parallel port (attached to a LaserJet); a SoundBlaster Pro set up on IRQ7 with a 220h base address; a CD Technology CD-ROM running the latest MSCDEX with a Future Domain SCSI card; and an Intel Ether Express running on IRQ10 and address 300h. I was using DOS 6.0, Windows 3.1, and an 8 MB SMARTDrive. I explicitly excluded A000 to DFFF in EMM386 and the same region in the [386Enh] section of **SYSTEM.INI**. I took all the significant drivers out of upper memory, and double-checked everything with Microsoft's MSD and the DOS 6 MEM command.

Then I ran the video boards straight out of the box, with the drivers supplied by the manufacturers, just like you would on your machine. I didn't ask for any special help from the board manufacturers. I took their product at its word, no special fixes, no patches, no nothing.

This test setup is about as plain-vanilla as one would normally find on a networked, multimedia Windows machine (except for the CPU and memory, perhaps), and by excluding all that memory you might think that the drivers had all the room in the world. Any thorough testing by the manufacturer should've uncovered conflicts with the SoundBlaster Pro or the Ether Express, the two top-selling cards in their class.

Shoulda.

Let's take a look at the columns.

It's very important that you understand what those numbers mean before you start shootin' off your mouth.

So listen up, sonny!

	Chip	Driver Rank	Toasted Bunny Mark	Hacker Scroll Rate	WinMark v. 3.11	Toasters per Second	Bunnies per Minute
Old-Fashioned VGA board	ET4000	B	1.0	10	1.8	0.8	0.2
Orchid Fahr 1280 "Classic"	86C911	B	1.9	17	4.1	1.4	0.5
NDI Volante AT2000	34020	B	2.8	21	5.8	1.9	0.9
NDI Volante Warp10Plus	86C801	A	4.5	25	10.6	3.0	1.5
ATI Graphics Ultra Pro	Mach32	F					
BMP caching on, Crystal fonts off			*	22	12.2	6.0	*
BMP on, Crystal fonts on			*	12	9.7	6.0	*
BMP off, Crystal fonts off			2.1	24	6.3	0.4	1.7
BMP off, Crystal fonts on			2.1	10	3.7	0.4	1.7

* Completely crapped out; the bunny wouldn't appear (who could blame it?)

	Chip	Driver Rank	Toasted Bunny Mark	Hacker Scroll Rate	WinMark v. 3.11	Toasters per Second	Bunnies per Minute
Hercules Graphite HG420	AGX014	D	2.5	25	8.2	1.6	0.9
Diamond Stealth 24	86C801	D	4.5	25	9.3	3.3	1.2
Video 7 WinPro	86C801	C	5.7	26	12.8	4.0	1.7
Number Nine #9GXE	86C928	B	4.3	23	9.0	3.0	1.3
Matrox Impression 1024	86C911	A	2.0	18	4.1	1.5	0.5
Western Digital Paradise	90C31	C	2.9	20	3.0	2.1	0.8

Figure 7-9: Video Road Kill

Rank Drivers

> I bought my wife a new car.
> She called me and said there was water in the carburetor.
> I said where's the car?
> She said in the lake.
>
> — Henny Youngman

 The Driver Rank column points out the totally rank drivers. Each video board has a certain personality, and most suffer from poor drivers. It's almost as if some manufacturers concentrate more on good benchmark scores, and couldn't care less about whether their boards actually *work*. Scary. The rank I've assigned is utterly subjective, but in general an "A" indicates the driver proved itself stable and easy to use over a very wide range of conditions, and an "F" connotes a driver that's buggy as a springtime picnic in the woods, hard to use and/or install. Grading is on the curve, so a "C" is not necessarily a bad rating.

Just to make sure the test was rigorous, I put the boards through Mao's Hell: a full work week for each one, using all sorts of software, under all sorts of conditions. Most magazine and newspaper reviewers don't have the luxury of spending that much time with each board. I wanted to know these boards as well as their Moms know 'em. For better or worse.

Many of the drivers offer utility packages that let you do some interesting things with Windows video. "Zoom" routines let you instantaneously double (or halve) the size of the image on the screen, not unlike the Microsoft Mouse driver version 9.0. Some board vendors have programs that expand the size of the desktop, perhaps by a factor of nine; they let you slide around the gargantuan desktop by bumping your mouse against the side of the screen. Still other packages have video data compression routines built-in. And on and on. Number Nine, in particular, has assembled a particularly compelling collection of such routines.

 Personally, I don't use any of those utilities, so I didn't consider them when evaluating the drivers. (One exception: ATI's Crystal Fonts, which proved a real eye-opener, but didn't really change my opinion of their driver; see the discussion below.) You may need one of the utilities, though, particularly if you're stuck with a little 14-inch screen, so your evaluation of drivers may well vary from mine!

Anyway, here's what I found:

The old-fashioned ET4000-based Super VGA driver worked just fine, but it was s-l-o-w. I'd give it a good, solid B.

The "classic" Orchid Fahrenheit 1280 came through with flying colors, once I found the latest (August 1992) driver. Earlier drivers — including the one that shipped in late 1992 with the board — had all sorts of odd problems: specs and blotches would form on the screen; sometimes pictures had odd bands of off-centered stripes; large characters in odd fonts would suddenly acquire dots and paisley patterns; dialog boxes wouldn't clear completely from the screen; and every so often, my machine would just die with a General Protection Fault. 'Tho the symptoms would vary, ultimately it was the fault of the old driver.

I worked with the older Fahrenheit 1280, the one without the microphone jack, by the way: as far as I'm concerned a video board needs a mike like a fish needs a bicycle.

Orchid installs an icon that appears in your Windows Control Panel. Double-click on the icon, and all the Fahrenheit options spring immediately to life. One problem: there's no easy way to get rid of the icon! Overall score: a gentleman's B, heavily influenced by the bad Orchid drivers that floated around for so long.

The NDI Volante boards stood out for their stable drivers and easy setup. While the AT2000 seems terribly overpriced and of dubious value to any but professional photo retouchers (see the later discussion of 34020-based boards), the Warp10Plus board finally won me over. I spent *two* weeks trying to make the driver go belly-up; no luck. In the end I liked it so much, I bought one. And it's still running day-in and day-out with nary a hiccup. Score: a well-deserved A.

ATI drivers are not noted for their reliability; the Ultra Pro driver version we tested, numbered 1.5.59, is no exception. While the ATI Ultra Pro has several benefits, e.g., it comes with a mouse port and a $19 mouse, the touted Crystal Fonts aren't among them. Crystal Fonts sure look pretty on small screens, but they'll make your menus flicker like a firefly on Quaaludes. I had repeated devastating General Protection Faults, from a dozen different programs, under many different circumstances. I wouldn't recommend this driver to my worst enemy. Score: an abject F.

 Late Development: Just as we went to press, ATI shipped version 2.0 of their drivers, touted as a vast improvement. Version 2.0 *is* a vast improvement: only about half as many applications flat out refuse to run. Software vendors are beginning to catch on. At least half a dozen ship their products with read-me files saying they can't help it if their programs had problems with ATI. I'd say ATI went from an F to a solid F-. The rest of the industry should thank ATI for setting a standard. Several drivers that probably deserved an F got a D because they looked so good in comparison to ATI.

The Hercules Graphite also had extensive driver problems: they were rather reminiscent of the difficulties I described earlier with the old Fahrenheit drivers. Word for Windows, in particular, came up with page streaks and strange artifacts; several times, simple operations in WinWord (such as adjusting the width of a column in a table) would trigger GPFs. Excel dialog boxes sometimes refused to clear away completely; click OK in a dialog box, and the gray background part of the OK button would remain on the screen.

In the first four months of the Graphite's life, Hercules officially released five different drivers — giving a new dimension to the phrase "driver of the month club". You should read between the lines. Score: a charitable D.

The Diamond Stealth 24 (in its ISA, not VLB incarnation) gave us fits and starts. Merely getting Windows to *run* with the driver took half an hour. Strange, recurring GPFs popped up all over the place. I'd be hard pressed to say precisely how this driver is better than the ATI driver, although the board is less than half the price of the ATI. That's worth some small consideration. Score: another charitable D.

The Video 7 Win.Pro driver worked pretty well, but it had a hard time displaying italic characters in WinWord and Excel: they would overlap and generally get twisted around, reappearing magically when the cursor approached incorrectly hidden characters. Very disconcerting. I also got several GPFs while running in 1024 x 768 x 256 mode, but they were irreproducible, and didn't seem to occur in 800 x 600 x 256 mode. That's about par for the course; it's a good enough driver. Score: C.

Number Nine's drivers are well known for their versatility and robustness. The #9 GXe driver we tested lived up to the manufacturer's reputation. It goes in easy and keeps on rockin'. We had occasional problems with Visio icons appearing in the wrong place, but in the grand scheme of things that's a nit. Score: a strong B; if you can use the GXe utilities, make it an A.

The Matrox Impression 1024 driver ran wonderfully. While the Impression board is comparatively slow and technically on its last legs (superseded by the MAG), it was a pleasure to use and was solid and reliable as every other Matrox driver we've used. Score: A.

Finally, our Western Digital Paradise board also ran in the middle of the road. Occasional unexplained GPFs, but nothing drastic. Screen artifacts now and again, but nothing that couldn't be cured by minimizing the application and restoring it. Score: C.

 Da boss has had lots of problems with drivers from Orchid, Diamond and ATI. Not just once or twice, mind you, but over the course of months, even years. That's often enough to wonder if the difficulties aren't congenital. Conversely, the drivers from NDI (Volante), Matrox and Number Nine have always gone in well, gone in right the first time and. . . *Mirable dictu.* . . worked!

That's no guarantee all future drivers from those companies will suffer or shine like their progenitors (in particular, we've heard recent disconcerting talk of a buggy Number Nine driver — just one) but it's something to think about.

Not all the blame for buggy drivers can be laid at the foot of the chip and board manufacturers. I've found that some of the bugs you'll see in these drivers appeared, at least in pupal stage, in the demo drivers supplied by Microsoft. The folks who write drivers often start with Microsoft's prototypes, and build on them. Sample drivers ship with Microsoft's DDK, the developer's kit for device drivers. If there's a bug in the prototype, it will often propagate to a vendor's final product. Bugs have a way of reproducing uncontrollably. These are some of the worst.

Performance

Looking back at Figure 7-9 the ToastedBunnyMark column in the Video Road Kill chart is just the sum of Toasters per Second and Bunnies per Minute, both of which are farther over to the right. Note how a dumb VGA card, the kind you're probably using right now, if you're worried about upgrading your video, comes in at 1.0.

 Dumb luck.

 Luck is in the eye of the beholder, grasshopper. I prefer to think of it as divine perspiration.

The next column in the Video Road Kill chart measures a real-world text scrolling rating. I spend a lot of time with Word for Windows, so I wanted to know how fast these boards will respond to scrolling. You may find that you grow gray hair as Windows recalculates a spreadsheet, redraws a particularly nasty graph, or imports a complex graphic. I turn old watching WinWord scroll. Whatever your particular poison, it would behoove you to grab a stopwatch and check it out. No pre-fab benchmark will tell you better than you can tell yourself.

Here's how I timed the scrolling: I cranked up Word for Windows version 2.0c - CD, the latest version as of this writing. I opened a monster document: Section 4 of the *Hacker's Guide to Word for Windows.* You can look at that file if you have the book at hand. It's a gargantuan 7.4 MB of snarly WinWord stew: mixed fonts, headers and footers, paragraph shading, narrow margins, pictures and flotsam, with virtually no white space. I scroll through that document almost every day. It's an ideal test for me; and I'll bet you can think of an ideal test for you, right off the top of your head.

Testing came easy. I checked to make sure WinWord was in Page View, at 100% Zoom — that's the way I like to work with my files. Then, stopwatch in hand, I put the mouse over the scroll-down arrow and hit the mouse button and stopwatch button simultaneously. With a keen eye on the watch, a minute later I let go of the mouse button, waited for the screen to stabilize, and read off the page number. That's the number you see in the Video Road Kill table. The test really was that simple.

Note in particular what I didn't do. I most emphatically did not use a self-timing WinWord macro to perform the scroll. Why? Because there is no way to replicate what I do most often — scroll the screen without moving the cursor — in a WinWord macro! Every screen scrolling benchmark I've seen relies on a macro to do the dirty work: it's easier and far more accurate to let the computer do the timing. *You'd have a hard time getting eight digits of accuracy with a K-Mart stopwatch, eh?* But no macro, at least in this case, could possibly do what I do, so the published benchmark results aren't valid for me. They might be valid for you, of course.

The next column shows my results running the Ziff Labs Video WinMark version 3.11 (in millions) 800 x 600, 256 colors, 70 Hz refresh rate.

 These numbers weren't generated by Ziff-Davis, of course, and anybody who says otherwise has me to answer to. There's a standard disclaimer I need to throw in here. Lemme dig it out. Ahem. . .

. . .you may also publish the test results obtained by you from use of the Software, provided with each such result you: A. Identify ZD Labs, the name and version number of the benchmark Software used (i.e., ZD Labs' WinBench(tm) Ver. 3.11). B. Identify the exact name, processor speed and type (Comtrade 486/50), amount of RAM (20 MB), amount of secondary RAM cache, if any (256K), hard disk size (520 MB), type of hard disk controller (Paradise), and size of hardware hard disk cache, if any (2.5 MB), of the PC used for the test. C. Identify the exact video adapter name, amount and type of RAM on it, video driver name and date, and monitor refresh rate that produced the result (noted above). D. Identify the operating system version (MS-DOS 6.0), size and type of software disk cache, if any (SMARTDRV 8MB cache), video resolution and color depth (800 by 600 pixels with 256 colors), and any other special conditions used to achieve the result (I swore and kicked a lot). E. State that all products used in the test were shipping versions available to the general public.

Don't you just love this neo-legalese garbage? All the ZD lawyers require is that you *say* that the products are shipping versions. Doesn't matter if they really *are* shipping versions. Makes me glad I didn't raise no fools. Or lawyers (sorry, George). Anyway, in Mao's case, I can readily attest that these products — boards, drivers, the works — are the ones you can buy off the shelf, anywhere, any time.

F. State that the test was performed without independent verification by ZIFF. G. Follow proper trademark usage and acknowledge ZIFF's trademark rights (e.g., "[ ] achieved a 4.5 million Graphics WinMark(tm) test score. WinBench(tm) and WinMark(tm) are trademarks of Ziff Communications Company").

Whew!

Now we get to the fun part: Toasters per Second. Those are IEEE Standard After Dark 2.0 Flying Toasters we're talking about, by the way — best of breed in Toaster Taste Tests; accept no substitutes. I set up After Dark to display flying toasters, 7 flying things, no sound, medium toast. I then clicked the Demo button and my stopwatch at the same time. I counted toasters only, not toast. (Nobody's gonna be able to say this test was cooked, no way, no how.) Any partial toaster soaring across an edge of the screen counted as a full toaster; there was no discrimination against partially formed toasters. After 15 seconds, I stopped counting. I then divided the number of toasters by 15. The result is the number you see.

Energizer Bunnies per Minute proved a touch more elusive, primarily because there aren't many standards in this emerging area. After consultation with several experts on the topic, I decided to standardize on the Energizer Bunny 1.0 screen called "E.B. in the Old West". That screen clearly stands out as the most interesting of the bunch.

Since there is no IEEE standard yet defined in the fast-changing E.B. field, and North American standards organizations appear to have little interest in furry critter quality standards — they threw out my request for an ISO 9600.0001 rating — I've contacted the European authorities and proposed E.B. in the Old West for official CCITT V.33bis ("bunny interface standard") status. As of this writing, the application was pending. I'm going for a Malcolm Baldridge on this'n.

I set up E.B. in the Old West to run with no sound, then clicked the "Demo" button and the stopwatch at the same time. I waited until the bunny completed his march across the screen, and clicked off the stopwatch at the precise moment the right edge of his big bass drum touched the right edge of my screen. I then divided the number of seconds so acquired into 60 and the result is the number you see in the Video Road Kill chart.

And that's it for video performance numbers. I hope you've come to the conclusion that you can construct and perform benchmarks yourself — and come up with numbers that are much more indicative of your own Windows usage than anything Mao or the big magazines could concoct. Roll out the Bunny. Catch a Flying Toaster. Ride the wave. And do it yerself.

 I talked to Igor's lawyer to make sure we got this right; you can never be too careful about such officious things. (Igor says his lawyer's name is Con C. Gliere, but I may have misunderstood. Those Rumanian names always confuse me.) Here's the legalese that applies if you want to test video boards and publish the resulting ToastedBunnyMark score:

. . .you may also publish the test results obtained by you from use of the ToastedBunnyMark, provided with each such result you: A. Do it right; and B. Tell the truth, so help you Mom.

Non-LB Redux

Where does that leave us, really? Good question.

The video market churns like a rattler pinned by the tail: if you grab straight for the head, by the time you reach down there the sidewinder will have moved, and you'll be damn lucky to get your hand back intact. If you try to anticipate where things are going, you stand a very good chance of missing the snake entirely. One bad move and you'll be treated to a venomous, hissing vision of viper hell, fangs planted firmly in your neck, blood gushing in 24-bit colors.

Yeah, a bad video board can be that bad.

On the other hand, if you're a heavy Windows user, a good video board can save you ten or twenty minutes every day. That's an amazing productivity boost you can't afford to ignore.

So which of the rated boards, you ask, is best? And why? Tough questions.

After trying just one accelerated board, of any type, you will never willingly go back to your old, un-accelerated board. Guaranteed.

A quick glance at the Video Road Kill chart will show you that there are performance clusters: video boards based on the same processor chip tend to bunch together. Video board chips have notoriously short lives: performance levels leapfrog when new technology enters the market. Top dog this month may well become dog food next month, and lawn fertilizer the month after that. No other segment of the PC industry changes so rapidly.

There are a few rules of thumb you may find useful. First, the co-processed video cards, the expensive hummers typically based on TI 34010 or 34020 processors, offer no advantage to garden-variety Windows users. If you do a lot of work retouching 24-bit full-color photographs, the $1,000-plus boards may be useful, but for ordinary 800 x 600 x 256 applications, they're not only too expensive, they're actually slower than many accelerated cards. And as Mom mentioned earlier you could buy a whole bunch of nimble accelerated cards for the price of one co-processed behemoth.

 My nephew found a "true color" video card that seems to be bucking the trend. It's called a Spectrum/24 board, and it's from SuperMac. (Yeah, it speaks Windows.) Initial reports are very promising: it's fast; at under $1,000 it's comparatively cheap; it comes in ISA, EISA, and VL-Bus versions; and the driver worked straight out of the box. You'll need a standard VGA card to get started, but if your tastes run to 24-bit color, this is a card to check.

Second, if you spend a sizable part of your life in DOS (for example, running AutoCAD in DOS), you can't rely on *any* Windows performance figures. There seems to be almost no correlation between Windows video performance and DOS video performance, except that local bus helps both.

Third, you may actually find it easier to narrow in on a particular chip — for example, focus on boards that use the 86C801 chip from S3 — thus choosing a basic performance level, and then pare away vendors based on price, the quality of their drivers, and support.

 After spending several months with these boards, there's no doubt in my mind which ones I would buy for normal Windows work: the NDI Volante Warp10, one of the least expensive of the bunch, comes out tops, followed (in alphabetical order) by the Matrox Impression 1024, Number Nine #9GXe, and the Orchid Fahrenheit 1280 "Classic," any of which would be excellent choices.

No, that isn't how the performance numbers stacked up: the fastest boards threw temper tantrums worse than any two-year-old. No, it has nothing to do with price: if you pay more for a particular video board, the only thing you're guaranteed is that. . . you paid more for the board.

My choices have everything to do with usability, something that never shows up in the benchmarks, something you couldn't quantify if you had to.

It continues to amaze me how a board manufacturer can rack a few top benchmark scores in the major magazines, ratchet up their prices, cut back on the little things (such as drivers that work or telephone support), and sell the boards like there's no tomorrow.

 Don't you get caught in that trap, sonny. If you buy a video board and suddenly start getting General Protection Faults or weird streaks on your screen, send the sucker back! Scream loud, preferably in a public place like CompuServe. Repeat after me: *I'm mad as hell, and I won't take it any more. Mom told me so. . . you video guys take it back. . . pretty please.*

 It doesn't matter a bit if the board won *Editio Princeps*† Choice in *OB Mag* three months running, or if it scores billions and billions of SaganMarks, if your best friend swears she has absolutely no problem running it, or if His Hirsuteness Hisself recommends it. Any sudden change in Windows' stability immediately following installation of a new video board must be regarded as bug spoor. The vendor will try to talk you out of it. Take my word: you aren't crazy. They're wrong. Get your money back and look elsewhere.

Truly Peripheral

> There is no jesting with edge tools.
>
> — John Fletcher, *The Little French Lawyer,* 1647

Printers

 I won't presume to tell you which printer to buy, except to note that Hewlett Packard LaserJet printers generally have the largest follow-on market, and are thus usually first endowed with interesting add-ons.

To be sure, lasers aren't necessarily the alpha and omega of the industry. There are excellent alternatives to lasers; for many people a bubble printer will suffice. How to tell if you're one of those people? Easy. Look around your office or drop by your

---

† *First edition.* Usually, first printed edition, if you're into splitting hairlines.

local computer store, pick up a page of output from a good laser and a good bubble printer, and hold them side-by-side. Now see if you can tell the difference. Many people won't see much difference at all; and if you're one of those people, you're a good candidate for a bubble printer.

Before you plunk down that American Express Platinum card you save for times just like this, though, consider one more expense: consumables. You might be surprised how the price of toner can level the playing field. Much depends on whether you trust recycled laser toner cartridges (I don't!), and/or whether you will take the time to inject refill ink into those little bubble printer heads (I won't!).

 Figure 7-10 is rather startling, eh? The cheapest option in this admittedly stylized comparison comes from a combination of bubble printer and refilled cartridge; the most expensive by far is *the same printer* using one-off original cartridges.

Over the lifetime of a printer, the original purchase price is just a small part of the total amount you'll end up spending. You can, and should, re-calculate these numbers before buying a printer, modifying them for your situation. Some folks have had nothing but headaches using recycled laser toner cartridges. I, personally, have yet to find one that produces output anywhere near as nice as an original cartridge. And those bubble cartridge refill packages can be awfully messy, at least until you get used to them. You may project fewer than 100,000 copies over the lifetime of your printer; then again, you may need more.

One tip: when looking at the total number of pages printed by a single cartridge, ignore the "draft" ratings, unless you're conscientious enough to flip into draft mode for most of your printing.

Most Windows users opt for a moderate resolution (300 or 600 dots per inch) laser printer, and that's a fine choice for normal office work. If you need a high resolution printer (800 dpi or more), probably to produce camera ready copy, you already know it. Be sure you check out the add-on board options mentioned later before spending big bucks on a typesetter.

Color printers at this point can be divided into two types: (1) very expensive, very slow, and good; or (2) cheap, fairly fast, and not very good. Serious color printing requires a serious color printer. No matter what the sales clerk says, you won't get photo quality from a color dot matrix or bubble printer. Dye-sublimation and other high-quality color printers can produce lovely prints, but they don't come cheap.

Dot matrix and bubble color printers don't cost much more than black-and-white, but the output all too often looks like it came from the Crayola School of Fine Art. And the consumable costs will drive you to the poor farm: figure on spending 35 cents per page for good quality color output, maybe much more.

	Cartridge Cost	Pages	Cost per 1000 pages	Printer Cost	Printer + 100,000 Pages
Lasers					
LaserJet III, HP cartridge	$75	4000	$18.75	900	$2,775
LaserJet III, refilled cartridge	$60	4000	$15.00	900	$2,400
LaserJet 4, HP cartridge	$100	6000	$16.67	1400	$3,067
Bubble Printers					
Original cartridge	$17	500	$34.00	400	$3,800
High Capacity cartridge	$25	1000	$25.00	400	$2,900
Original cart + two refills	$26	1500	$17.33	400	$2,133

Figure 7-10: Consider Lifetime Costs

Before you buy a low-end color printer, do two things, sonny. First, get a copy of a printout from the printer and take a good hard look at it. See those jagged lines, how the colors don't quite line up right, how the whole thing looks like it's been through the spin cycle a couple of times? Yeah. That's par for the course.

Second, force yourself to think for a few minutes: how often do you really need color? How often do you really need color of this quality? Wouldn't it be smarter to get a black and white printer, and take the odd color job down to your local computer shop?

All too often Windows folks get absorbed in how much more they think they can do with a color printer, when they may actually be getting less. Is the color worth the cost? The print time? With some exceptions, probably not.

One thing you don't need: a PostScript printer. I talked about the pro's and con's (mostly con's) of PostScript fonts back in Chapter 2. For the same reasons, the vast majority of Windows users don't need a PostScript printer. Yes, there are exceptions: if a big part of your life involves producing low resolution previews of PostScript files — presumably prior to typesetting on a fancy machine — you want a PostScript printer. Some offices need PS to swap files back and forth between PCs, Macs, and workstations. If you need exceptional picture print quality, PS presents a reasonable alternative, although the WinJet series boards (discussed later) may do better. By and large, though, the typical Windows user needs a PS printer like a moose needs a Rocky rack.

 Was that a Bullwinkle joke?   I dunno about the "winkle" part.

The best source of up-to-date printer information, bar none, is the annual *PC Magazine* issue devoted to printers. It usually appears in late November. At 600+ pages, it's usually the thickest, most popular, and most often swiped issue *PC Magazine* produces. Rightfully so.

Print Accelerators

> Waiting is, until fullness.
>
> — Robert Heinlein, *Stranger in a Strange Land*, 1961

One of the best reasons for buying an HP brand laser printer is the burgeoning add-on market. Microsoft itself makes an add-on called the Windows Printing System. LaserMaster has long produced something called a WinJet. They're both good products.

So good, in fact, that I decided to put 'em head-to-head and toe-to-toe, to see which one flinched.

As of this writing, Microsoft's Windows Printing System (WPS) only works on LaserJet II and III series. The LaserMaster WinJet 800 works on LJ II and III; the WinJet 1200 works on LJ 4. Got that? Naw, it isn't important. It's just a boring technical explanation of why we ran these tests on a LaserJet III, not a LaserJet 4, so we could get comparable numbers.

The WinJet contains a card that plugs into your computer, another card that slides into the printer, and a cable to connect the two. WPS only needs a card in the printer; it's real easy to set up. Both work only in Windows. The WinJet works in DOS sessions running under Windows, even giving you the capability of printing

PostScript jobs from DOS applications. WinJet mainly uses the special cable it comes with but also uses the old printer cable, which you'll need to keep attached. The WPS and WinJet take very different roads to Windows print speed nirvana.

WPS relies on the native Windows graphic-cum-printer language (called "GDI"). It teaches your LaserJet how to speak that language, taking control of the printer's internal processor chip and memory to work its magic. GDI commands flow down the cable. It replaces the Windows Print Manager with a noisy, flashy huckster (which, fortunately, can be silenced from the Control Panel!) that tells you when to feed the printer paper, when it's jammed, and the like.

WinJet, in great contrast, speaks the printer's most fundamental language, a language of dots. It commandeers your computer's processor chip and memory to wreak its havoc, rasterizing your pages (i.e., translating them to dots) and shipping the dots down that cable. It, too, replaces the Windows Print Manager with a WinJet Print Manager that isn't nearly as flashy as WPS's, it doesn't talk or show animated sequences, but it does more.

In an extraordinary feat of smoke and mirrors, WinJet also lets you print in a super high resolution mode, extracting amazing print quality from your plain-Jane printer. The WinJet 800 actually coaxes 800 dots per inch (horizontally) on a 300 dot per inch LaserJet. That virtuosity comes at a price: running in high resolution mode can take twice as much time as standard 300 dpi mode.

When WPS first shipped it wouldn't print PostScript Type 1 fonts, even if you had Adobe Type Manager installed. I'm happy to say that problem was resolved quickly, and Type 1 fonts now work fine with WPS. The WPS fails to recognize embedded printer commands, a real pain in the posterior for advanced WinWord users who have come to rely on so-called {print} fields. Helen Feddema, Mom's stitch-n-bitch partner, swears WPS won't work with HP's LaserJet Fax: they stomp all over each other.

On the positive side, both WPS and WinJet can print odd-and-even pages, so you can print on both sides of each sheet of paper and still keep the pages in order (called duplex printing). The WinJet also prints thumbnails (many pages on a single sheet of paper), sideways two-up (two pages on a single sheet of paper), and booklet sequence (you need only staple in the middle and fold — a booklet). And both will let you print pictures that might otherwise trigger "out of memory" errors on a LaserJet with 512K or 1 MB.

Speed on the WinJet depends directly on the speed of your main computer; it does the rasterizing. The WPS works differently: it analyzes your main computer's speed and "pre-chews" the data stream in the main computer, to try to balance the work done by your main computer and your printer. The goal is to provide eight page-per-minute performance on 8-page-per-minute printers, 4 ppm on 4 ppm printers, and so on, once the actual printing starts.

Theoretically at least, you can thus speed up the WinJet by upgrading your computer, although we've found available memory to be the major controlling factor (4 MB extra memory is nice; 8 MB even better; 16 MB doesn't hurt one bit).

 Yeah, yeah, yeah. You want numbers. So here you go. This time I borrowed Vince Chen's computer, hooked it to a LaserJet III with 5 MB of memory, using Microsoft's print driver (HPPCL5MS.DRV, version 2.0); WPS (driver version 1.0); and the WinJet in standard (300 dpi) and high resolution (800 dpi) modes (driver version 1.70). The test system: a Gateway 486/33, 24 MB of memory (WinJet likes a lot!), WinWord 2.0c, Excel 4.0, and CorelDRAW 3.0b.

I printed four different test documents: a ten-page WinWord document with 1 TrueType font; a ten-page WinWord document with 9 TrueType fonts; a one-page WinWord document with 2 TrueType fonts and an embedded Excel chart; and the CorelDRAW! figure that ships with the product called CADILLAC.CDR. Those aren't scientifically selected; I don't hold them out to be typical. They're just interesting.

I recorded three times: when the Print dialog box disappeared, i.e., when the application (WinWord or CorelDRAW!) got control; when printing started; and when printing ended.

Personally, I care more about when I get control back. But if you sit next to your printer and often find yourself twiddling your thumbs waiting for the printer to finish, the end printing time will concern you more.

Figure 7-11 shows what happened.

For raw text printing, WPS and the WinJet in 300 dpi mode ran neck-and-neck for the best overall printing time. The major difference: WPS uses Print Manager to give control back to WinWord much faster; the WinJet in 300 does not use a spooler. The normal LaserJet III printer and the WinJet 800 mode were roughly equal and took about 20 to 30 percent longer than the speed demons.

Graphics printing times shocked me. The WPS (using the default graphics setup) was by far the slowest of the bunch in printing that CorelDRAW! Caddy, while the WinJet in 300 mode turned in by far the fastest time — one third the time of the WPS. And, wonder of wonders, the normal LaserJet III turned in the second fastest time!

	Bone Stock LaserJet III	WPS	WinJet 300 dpi	WinJet 800 dpi
10 pages / 1 font				
Regain Control	6.5	6	77	10.5
Start Printing	32	12	3.5	17
Finish Printing	116	92	92	115
10 pages / 9 fonts				
Regain Control	17	8	77	15
Start Printing	38	12	3.5	29
Finish Printing	121	92	92	127
1 page w Excel chart				
Regain Control	2.5	2.5	3.5	2.5
Start Printing	11	6	6	10
Finish Printing	29	23	22	27
CADILLAC.CDR				
Regain Control	152	277	83	16
Start Printing	205	284	85	245
Finish Printing	220	320	102	264

Figure 7-11: Print Speed

How about print quality? There's no question that the WinJet in 800 mode produced the best output. It's gorgeous. Although WinJet in 300 was fast, it doesn't take advantage of the LaserJet III's Resolution Enhancement Technology; consequently, it produced the worst output, with very visible "jaggies" that is typical of standard 300 dpi printers, including the older LaserJet II series. WPS uses Resolution Enhancement, so its outputs were essentially indistinguishable from normal LaserJet III output.

 Which one is best? Alas, there's no easy answer. It all depends on how you work, and how much money you want to spend — the WPS is considerably less expensive.

If you like stunning printouts, the WinJet in 800 dpi mode can't be beat. Surprisingly, the WinJet magic comes with little, if any, performance penalty on text, compared to a bone-stock LaserJet III. And it races around the LJ III when releasing CorelDRAW! from printing a complex picture.

If you're most concerned with getting back to your word processor quickly, WPS emerges on the top of the heap. That's a significant accomplishment, because many Windows users fall squarely into this category. But heaven help ya if you need to print a CorelDRAW! graphic!

On the other hand, if you tend to sit and wait for the printer to finish, and aren't too picky about print quality, the WinJet in 300 dpi mode comes out first. While WPS keeps up with the WinJet in timed text tests, there's no comparison with graphics: WinJet in 300 wins hands-down. Contrariwise, the WinJet in 300 dpi mode locks up your computer for just about as long as it take to print.

Finally, if you're sitting on a LaserJet II, without the LJ III's Resolution Enhancement, WPS probably drives the best bargain between high-quality print and speedy times. But if quality reigns supreme in your neck of the woods, the WinJet 800 at 800 dpi has no peer.

If you're thinking of buying more printer memory, seriously consider either the WinJet or the WPS, and forget the memory. You'll get a lot of bangs for your bucks — and extra printer memory won't help (or hinder) either.

What do *I* use, you ask? Ah, perceptive inquiry, grasshopper. Read on, read on. . .

CD-ROM

Not long ago CD-ROMs only popped up on machines featured in *Lifestyles of the Rich and Malodorous.* Lately, though, it's reached the point where you're missing much of what makes computing fun, or at least bearable, if you don't splurge on a CD player.

 I took the plunge when CorelDRAW came out with that gigantic clip art collection on CD-ROM. All the fonts didn't hurt, either.

 Word for Windows on CD-ROM changed my life. That hummer — officially known as Microsoft Word for Windows & Bookshelf Multimedia Edition — has certainly saved hours of browsing and paper cuts up the wazoo.

You boys don't get around much, do you? Have you seen the Oxford English Dictionary on CD? Played King's Quest or Sherlock Holmes Consulting Detective? More to the point, have you ever tried to keep a four-year-old occupied on a rainy winter afternoon without Mixed-Up Mom Goose? Sheesh. There's an entire generation of kids who won't grow up hating or fearing computers, simply because of the likes of PuttPutt and Just Grandma and Me. Talk about enabling technologies.

CD-ROM drive prices fell like a rock in 1993. If you're still sitting on the dime, now's the time to get off it. Even the cheapest CD-ROM drive, one that runs no faster than a floppy disk drive, opens horizons that qualified as pipe dreams just a few years ago.

While it's nice to get a Multi-Session Kodak Photo-CD compliant, double-dip screamer CD-ROM drive with internal cache, low access time, and huge transfer rate, you can bring home a decent CD-ROM drive for a couple hundred bucks. If you've never heard about the Multi-Session Kodak Photo-CD standard, don't worry about it. The other stuff is nice, but when software based CD-ROM caching becomes more commonplace, it will look just like hard drive read caching, the performance numbers won't be so important.

Besides, no matter how you cut it, CD-ROM runs like a slug.

Take care in selecting the SCSI adapter that will connect the CD-ROM to your system. Make sure you get one that can work easily and work well with other pieces of hardware, should you ever decide to chain more stuff onto the adapter.

Sound

> . . .it is a tale
> Told by an idiot. . .
>
> — Shakespeare, *Macbeth*, 1605

No, you don't need it. Yes, you do want it. 'Nuff said.

You aren't really reading this section because you want to learn technical details about sound, now, are you? What you really want to know is how to justify buying a nice sound system, how to sell it to yourself or the boss or the spouse, right? Yeah. I thought so. Who you think you're fooling?

While the first half of the traditional multi-media equation — the CD-ROM — represents enormous opportunity for the typical Windows user, in most cases the second half — sound — lacks a compelling *raison d'être. . .* until you need to learn how to pronounce *raison d'être,* of course. CD-ROM is one of those rare computer developments that you can't live without. Sound is one of those common computer developments that doesn't really live up to its advance billing, although it does have its uses. With that bit of warning out of the way, let's dig in and have a little fun.

 Yes, there are legit business applications of sound. Having a sound program read off a list of numbers from a spreadsheet, while you double-check the numbers (presumably on a printout) manually, qualifies as an application, at least in some circles. The ability to add sound annotations to documents can be fun. Speaking dictionaries can be a boon to people unfamiliar with the pronunciation of a particular word, or folks trying to learn a new language. Sound clips in an encyclopedia bring a subject to life: there's a world of difference between reading and hearing *Ich bin ein Berliner.*

Two acronyms pop up in the video world over and over again. MIDI refers to a standard that lets you efficiently record and playback sounds that mimic musical instruments. MIDI files can be one-one thousandth the size of Windows sound (.WAV) files. MIDI can be used to provide a musical background for presentations, but its constraints severely limit MIDI's use for most Windows folks.

Then there's the MPC sticker. MPC (Multimedia PC Council) sound boards have to meet several requirements: they must play MIDI music; have a joystick port; sample and play audio at 22 kHz or better sample rate; and control a CD-ROM drive, including the ability to take audio directly off the CD-ROM.

Microsoft, one of the pioneers of the MPC spec, abandoned it for their own product, the Microsoft Sound System. It is not MPC compliant, no way, no how; the box says the Sound System "supports all MPC titles," which is quite true, in our experience, but the board lacks that all-important CD-ROM control gizmo.

 Far as I'm concerned, the MPC is dead, long live the MPC. And for good reason: the market has passed it by. MIDI recording capabilities, once thought to be an important component of multimedia (whatever *that* is), aren't all that useful in the business world. While it doesn't hurt to have an official MPC sticker on your sound board (and CD-ROM, for that matter), you needn't feel inadequate if your board lacks a joystick-cum-MIDI-interface port.

The Windows sound food chain contains several links. Your PC's internal speaker scavenges as the bottom-feeder: it can squeak and squawk a bit, and particularly well designed sound files play pretty well on the speaker, but by and large the internal speaker fails miserably. Still, if you want to try the internal speaker, take a look at SPEAK.EXE, available on CD MOM or *MOM's* companion disk.

Just above the scavengers you'll find cards that can play but not record sounds. Many of the old-fashioned sound cards fit on this strata: they can play a pretty tune, but they won't listen to you. Right now the most popular variant on this theme is the Disney Sound Source. Don't laugh. For a very modest price, the Disney Sound Source offers decent quality sound and a virtually bullet-proof installation, without opening your machine — something that cannot be said of the hoity-toity boards.

The next notch on the food chain holds those mainstream boards that can both play and record. They use a technique called digital sampling, where incoming sound waves are converted to numbers. The numbers get stored away until needed, at which point they're converted back into sound. (That's the guts of DAC, Digital-to-Analog Conversion.) It's the same process used to create and play back audio CDs, although the quality of the sound often fails to live up to audio CD standards. Almost all of these cards play sounds quite well; they vary mostly in their ability to record.

At the top link lurk professional sound recording and playback cards, the kind of stuff that took a multi-million dollar recording studio just a few years ago. Turtle Beach and Roland frolic in these waters. They're very nice, very expensive, and more than most normal Windows users will want.

The next wave of sound boards will distinguish themselves by their ability to play exquisite MIDI sounds. Look for something called a "wave table lookup" function; that's a fancy way of saying that the card comes with a database of pre-recorded sounds, used to replicate natural sounds with stunning accuracy. Most Windows-based sound is in the so-called **.WAV** format. Wave table cards don't do anything with **.WAV** files — they only work on MIDIs — but as this wave table technology spreads, you're bound to see more MIDIs.

I had a chance to hear the Sound Galaxy NX Pro 16 from Aztech Labs, and it blew me away. It's like the difference between dot matrix and laser print. Phenomenal. The only glitch, of course, is that wave table magic only works on MIDI files — other files play fine, but MIDI really shines.

Dive into Chapter 2 before buying a sound board. There are lots of considerations, lots of gotchas.

Fury

> I like the silent church before the service begins,
> better than any preaching.
>
> — Ralph Waldo Emerson, *Self-Reliance*, 1844

I took a look at four very different approaches to giving your PC a voice: the Creative Labs SoundBlaster Pro Basic, Media Vision's Pro Audio Studio 16, the Microsoft Windows Sound System, and the Disney Sound Source. There's a world of difference among them: not unexpected, because each targets a different audience.

SoundBlaster from Creative Labs took over the standard-bearer slot from the old Ad Lib card and spawned an entire industry. In the world of games and educational software, SoundBlaster sets the norm; virtually every sound-enabled program supports SoundBlaster. Even the Microsoft Sound System claims SoundBlaster compatibility — albeit with a hokey configuration program that must be run before SoundBlaster compatibility is assured. That's a nod you can't ignore.

Unfortunately, the SoundBlaster can be the most cantankerous piece of hardware you've ever installed. I've put in three of them, on very different systems, and each installation took hours. The software isn't smart enough to recognize conflicts (the nefarious IRQ and I/O base address problems I mentioned earlier in this chapter). When the SoundBlaster hits a situation it can't quite handle, it slaps up a message — but the messages are utterly inscrutable, if not downright misleading!

Offsetting this frustration, though, is solid tech support, over the phone. If you resign yourself to the fact that you'll need to call tech support at least once to install the board — and plan for the price of the call when looking at competitors' prices — you'll be in good shape.

The SoundBlaster Pro supports 8-bit stereo 44 kHz recording. It pumps out four watts per channel into four ohms, more than enough to drive a cheap pair of speakers, and includes a headset and a bunch of software, some of which is useful. All in all it's a good setup, if you can get the bloody thing installed.

 The Media Vision Pro Audio Studio 16 blew me away. Not just because of the capabilities of the board — at 16-bit stereo 44 kHz it's no slouch — but because of the easy, easy, easy installation, high quality toll-free tech support, and extraordinary help on CompuServe.

The QuickStart installation system took over, transforming what I've come to expect as a three-hour trip through IRQ hell into a smooth, simple, painless no-brainer. While the microphone is nothing to write home about (it sticks on your monitor), and the software still shakes in a few places, the wondrous installation and easy operation of this product may actually give sound boards a good name. And the software suite that comes packed with the board, including a program for embedding sounds in documents and spreadsheets, will keep you involved for days.

I liked it. Could you tell?

If you need to do what it does, the Microsoft Windows Sound System (WSS) hits the spot; for most business users, and many game players, MSS fits the bill. Perhaps the best way to understand what WSS *is*, is to first figure out what it isn't.

WSS won't work with your DOS games, or any other DOS programs, for that matter, unless you run a special program to set the board up; there's a reason why "Windows" is part of WSS's name. You'll find the board setup routine klunky and a pain in the neck if you frequently switch to DOS to play games.

Also, as I noted earlier, WSS isn't MPC compliant: it doesn't have a MIDI (or joystick) port, and it won't connect to a CD-ROM. You'll need another port to run a joystick, there's no reason to use MIDI with the WSS, and if you get a CD-ROM you'll have to attach it to something else. Consider that most Windows folk don't need or use the extra ports, you'll probably want a separate industrial-strength SCSI card to run your CD, and there are few games or other products that require a joy stick.

If you can live with those limitations, WSS sports remarkably easy installation — on a par with the Studio 16, thus light years ahead of much of the industry — and software that's virtually guaranteed, by dint of Microsoft's standing in the computer biz, to work with anything.

Sound quality is outstanding, for both recording and playback: 16-bit stereo at 44 kHz helps. The microphone won't win any prizes, but it's certainly capable of recording voice, and doing so quite well. Quick Recorder does yeoman work for fancy manipulation of .WAV files. ProofReader will read off a list of spreadsheet numbers (hey! a *real* business application!) in Excel or 1-2-3/Win. And there's a set of headphones in the box.

The Disney Sound Source, unlike the three boards here, was made for people like me who don't want to go through the hassle of pushing cards into sockets and running inscrutable setup routines. It's a little box on a dongle — pull the printer cable off your computer, push on this dongle thing, then stick the cable back on the end. If you want to get real fancy, you can tighten down all the screws with a screwdriver, but that's about it.

Ya know those speakers they have in drive-in movie theaters? Well, the Disney Sound Source looks, and sounds, like a little drive-in speaker. The cord plugs in where the printer goes. It takes a nine-volt battery. The speaker isn't CD quality hi fi or anything like that, but it works great for kids' games, and it's about one-tenth the price of all those fancy-schmancy boards. While it's true that you can run any .WAV file through the Disney Sound Source (with the DSS.EXE driver), you'll probably find the sound quality wanting.

While the names and brands will change, with one board coming out on top in the ratings this month and another next month, this quick look at four approaches to sound should leave you with a few impressions.

First, while sound was once the *bête noir* of the add-on card business, deservedly so, given the atrocious installation problems, things are getting better. Media Vision and Microsoft, in particular, deserve much praise for pioneering easy installation and outstanding phone and CompuServe customer support.

Second, the MPC label doesn't mean much any more. If you can do without DOS sound support (or I should say kludgey DOS sound support), the non-MPC Microsoft Windows Sound Source is an excellent choice, particularly for business use.

Third, if your needs are limited to kids' games, there's no reason to avoid sound because of high costs or soldering iron gymnastics. The Disney Sound Source installs in minutes, and works without you having to lift a finger.

Fourth, you gotta listen to the difference a wave table can make. That Aztech board is somethin' else.

 A final note on speakers. You can spend a *lot* on speakers, and not get much for your money. I've found a few approaches that work pretty well. Games with gonzo stereo sound work best with headphones. The stereo channel separation on phones runs rings around almost anything you can set up on a desk, unless you want to invest many hundreds of bucks in a steroid-pumped 100 watt per channel stereo system.

Voice and other sounds that are essentially mono (whether they're recorded that way or not!) or weakly separated stereo work best with little speakers placed right next to your monitor. That way the sound seems to emanate from the computer itself. Corny, but true. I've had great luck with a cheap pair of amplified speakers (about $25), designed to plug into portable radios and tape players. I use double-back tape to stick them on my monitor, at ear level.

If you go that route, make sure you get speakers that will plug into the wall: batteries get mighty expensive.

'Course you might drop a hint the next time your birthday rolls around. Those $200 a pair ASMCEZ (Amplified Stereo Multimedia Computer El-Zappo) speakers sure do *look* sexy. Mom might spring for 'em. *Hey, it could happen. . .*

Backup

 Repeat after me: no system is complete without some sort of usable backup. No system is complete without some sort of usable backup. No system is complete without some sort of usable backup. No system is complete without some sort of usable backup. . . *you are getting sleepy. . .*

I know. Backup is boring. Backup is for C:\> prompt weenies. Backup is something the pro's tell beginners they have to do — *do as I say, not as I do,* — but when is the last time your favorite local pro ran a full backup? Weeks? Months?

Over the lifetime of your PC, you will lose more time to botched data than to any other cause. Whether you delete a file of your own volition (and stupidity), or your system scrambles a few bits for breakfast, or your hard drive decides to take early retirement, some day lack of a good backup will bite you in the butt, and bite you good. It's as inevitable as death and increasing taxes.

If you don't have a lot of data you might be able to back up to disks. If you're on a network, or have two hard disk drives and a lot of extra space, you can back up your data by copying it onto a different drive. But for almost all Windows users, backup means getting a good tape drive and using it.

I've seen no good reason to buy one brand of tape drive over another: they all work reasonably well; they're all reliable; they all come with software that you'll probably throw away immediately in favor of one of the big packages' backup programs (e.g., Norton or PC Tools).

The primary differences in tape drives lie in capacity and speed. Since most folks perform backups at night, speed usually doesn't matter much, unless you happen to have so much data it can't be backed up in twelve hours or so, or you prefer to backup while doing your normal Windows work (which isn't a bad idea). Speed also comes into play when you retrieve data from the tape.

Most of all it boils down to a question of capacity. If you can't fit all of your data on one tape, somebody, somehow, has to swap out tapes in the middle of a backup, and that can be a monumental pain. There are two solutions to the capacity problem: either buy a tape drive with large enough capacity to start with, or space out your backups over several days (actually, nights) so no single backup needs more than one tape.

If you can live with 120 MB or 250 MB of backup at a pop, a cheap QIC (pronounced "quick") tape drive will work just fine. QIC tapes fit into the palm of your hand or a shirt pocket. (Actually, QIC refers to the recording method, but most folks call 'em QIC drives and QIC tapes.) QIC tape drives can be installed several different ways, but the simplest is to use a "Y" cable to split it off one of your floppies. Colorado Memory Systems, for one, has a nearly idiot-proof installation sequence.

If you need more capacity, you'll be looking at Digital Audio Tape (DAT), which can hit 4 GB — 4,096 MB, six or seven times as much as a CD — in size. DAT tapes look a lot like regular audio cassette tapes; their appetite for data, voracious. You'll probably need a SCSI adapter to hook the tape into your computer, but if you can afford the DAT drive, a SCSI adapter rates as small change.

Other Stuff

> I have found the best way to give advice to your children
> is to find out what they want and then advise them to do it.
>
> — Harry Truman, 1955

Several other pieces of hardware need special attention in the Windows environment.

UPS: If you use SMARTDrive, or any other disk cache with disk write caching enabled, you need an Uninterruptable Power Supply (UPS). Something else they didn't tell you when you bought that machine, eh? Certain kinds of external memory cache can sure get scrambled, too, when the power heads south.

That's why every Windows user needs a UPS, a little box that keeps the power going to your computer, even when the power to your office goes *glop*. You don't need a fancy UPS; most folks can save everything and power down in just a few minutes, even in the middle of something very complicated. But those few minutes can be crucial.

 I always go for cheap UPSs: I don't need thirty minutes — or even ten minutes — of backup power; all I want is a couple of minutes to get the hell out and shut down. The smallest UPS you can buy, 250 volt-amp (VA), suffices for all but the largest desktop computers, and should cost less than $100. A 400 VA unit at less than twice the price will cover the most power-hungry PC you've ever seen.

Think of it as insurance.

If you don't get a UPS, fer heaven's sake, get a simple surge protector. It's the least you can do to protect your friend and ally. For a very thorough review of surge protection and protectors, see the August 29, 1993 issue of *PC Magazine*.

Modem and fax: Using Windows without a modem is like landing a 747 without a control tower. Yes, you can do it, but chances are you'll crash and burn. Repeatedly. The single best source of Windows support is CompuServe (see Chapter 6), and you can't get to CompuServe without a modem.

Modems come in two flavors: internal and external. Internal modems install just like any other card; plug in the board, connect the phone line and you're off. External modems get their power by plugging into the wall. They sit outside your computer. Most come with lights that flash and, if you can figure out the obscure codes, tell you something about how the computers' conversation is going. It's almost always easier to install an external modem.

Modems are rated by their speed. While the terms "baud" and "bits per second" aren't synonymous, they're pretty close, so don't get heartburn if a sales clerk first says you need a 9600 bps ("bee pee ess") modem, then says you need 9600 baud ("bawd"). You're most likely to encounter 2400, 9600 and 14,400 bps modems. The 2400 bps modem has become rather passé: while 2400 may be sufficient for a free, local-call bulletin board, it will suck up expensive time on pay-by-the-minute boards. If you're buying a new modem, 9600 bps is your best bet, with 14,400 an attractive alternative.

The hardest part of buying a modem has to be wading through the obscure terminology, but if you limit your search to 9600 and 14,400 bps modems, it isn't all that bad. Any real 9600 bps modem will have "V.32" somewhere on the box or in the product literature. Any real 14,400 bps modem will say "V.32bis". That's all you need to look for, really.

Beware of boards that claim an "effective 9600 bps throughput" or some such, but fail to identify themselves as V.32. Unscrupulous vendors inflate throughput claims: "effective 9600 bps" could well mean 2400 bps with a standard, everyday data compression scheme factored into the equation. It's like claiming a new car has an "effective throughput" of 320 miles per hour because it can carry four people at 80 mph each.

If you want fax capability with your modem, look for the term "Group 3" on the box or in the product literature. While a fax modem can be handy, you'll probably find that you need a fax machine anyway.

 Most of my fax traffic involves sending copies of hard-copy pages already lying around the office. I sign a contract, say, and fax it to a company. Or I have a newspaper clipping that needs to go out. Sometimes it's product literature or a pre-printed form. My cookie recipe makes great fax.

A fax modem won't handle that sort of stuff unless you have a scanner and don't mind laboriously scanning each page into your machine, assembling the scanned images somehow, and shipping them off to the proper party. While a fax modem does great work with pages that originate on your computer, and good fax software can make that kind of faxing much simpler than the manual variety, most folks need to work with hard copy.

On the other hand, a fax modem makes scanning incoming faxes much faster and simpler: a significant consideration if you get lots of junk fax. On the third hand, you'll usually have to keep your computer on 24 hours a day to receive faxes, and handling an incoming fax can slow down the rest of your computer. So think about your fax situation before spending bucks on a fax modem.

There's one little trick in the modem biz that you would be wise to consider. Windows has a nasty habit of stomping over modem communication. Your communication program must monitor the phone line every few milliseconds; otherwise, the program might drop a byte here or there — which can be disastrous. Unfortunately, Windows has been known to tie up computers for more than a few milliseconds at a crack. Thus, it's possible for Windows comm programs to drop the ball, and drop a few characters. It's by no means normal, particularly if you avoid running other programs while your comm program is underway, but it does happen.

The solution? A little chip that stores — buffers — data from the phone line as it comes in. There's enough room on the chip to hold a fair amount of data, waiting for Windows to get its act together and come and retrieve the incoming bits. This magical chip goes by the name of 16550AFN UART, but friends just call it 16550. If you're buying an internal modem, make sure "16550" appears somewhere on the box or in the product literature. If you're getting an external modem, you'll have to find a way to attach a 16550 to your COMM port. That can be as easy as pulling one chip and slipping in another; it can be as tough as replacing your I/O board or adding a new one. Check with your computer's manufacturer to see what they recommend.

Floppy disk: Don't skimp. Windows software finds its way into marketing channels on both 1.2 MB 5¼-inch and 1.44 MB 3½-inch disks. Periodic shortages of one size or the other can swing the market around, so a company that only distributed 3½-inch disks may find it exorbitantly expensive, and suddenly switch to 5¼.

Why sweat the small stuff? Get both size drives.

Mouse: Perhaps the most personal of all peripherals, the only right mouse is the one you like best. Try a bunch of them, and pick one you can live with.

 They'll have to pry my Microsoft Mouse 2.0 from my cold, dead fingers.

 Hmmmm...

That can be arranged.

 Have you boys seen the belly button mouse, the one in the IBM ThinkPad? It's the only mouse I'd consider using while on the road. Best thing to come out of Armonk in years. Especially because it didn't come out of Armonk. . .

Keyboards: Some Windows applications do strange things to F11, F12, and any higher-numbered F keys. You may not be able to use them, so don't buy a keyboard just because it has F keys above F10.

 If you like "clicky" keyboards, make sure you look at the Northgate OmniKey series (under $100; call 800-453-0095 or 612-943-8181). The relocatable `Alt` and `Ctrl` keys can make a big difference to some Windows users, although the extra-large backspace key is unnecessary because Windows users never make mistakes.

Ergonomics: Saving the most important topic for last, the way you lay out your computer, furniture and office can have enormous impact on your work.

The single most important interface in the Windows Land of Interfaces is the one between you and your computer — where your hands and eyes meet the machine, where rubber meets the road. That small step between your computer and your senses can be a giant leap for your physical, if not psychological, well being.

I've already waxed poetic about the benefits of a great monitor.

Two other very important, and not very expensive, products that can be crucial in your effective use of a computer are the keyboard and the mouse. It doesn't pay to get a cheap keyboard or mouse. Your hands deserve the best.

Repetitive motion disorders sound like some sort of ruse an ambulance chasing shyster invented to milk big companies out of insurance dollars. But I can testify, first. . . uh. . . hand, that carpal tunneling and tendonitis can be excruciating, debilitating problems. Numbness in the fingers. Shooting pains in the wrist and forearm, like somebody jabbed you with a knife, then dunked the knife in salt and jabbed and twisted again. It gets so bad you slam your hand on a table, just to see if you can feel something, *anything*..... Oh yeah, I've been there. Folks who think you're faking it are lucky: they've never been through that sort of hell.

If you've experienced problems like that, if you're prone to tendonitis, repetitive motion syndrome, or any of those excruciatingly painful side effects of touch typing, try a wrist rest. A rest hasn't cured my problem, but it does help.

Most of all, if you have shooting pain in your forearms or wrists, or if your fingers get numb from time to time, find a doctor who understands — a doctor who knows the disease, who knows what they're talking about. No matter what the company nurse or doctor says, it is not your imagination, not stress induced, and it will not get better if you take a day or two off.

You need a good chair. A desk that can hold that 100-pound monitor. Lighting from almost any direction except the glare position just above and behind your head. A phone you can reach without pulling a Rosemary Wood. And on and on.

Adjusting all that stuff can be problematic. The top of your monitor should be even with your forehead. When you plant your feet firmly on the floor, your thighs should just clear the chair. When you type at the keyboard, your elbows should bend down just slightly, so your wrists come out straight — a position that's virtually impossible to attain with the keyboard sitting on a desk.

Sit up straight! Jaw foreward! Feet flat on the floor. Suck in that gut. You hear me, sonny?

I'll Show You Mine If. . .

> and his heart was going like mad
> and yes I said yes I will Yes.

> — James Joyce, *Ulysses*, 1922

Here's the acid test.

Writing about computers is one thing. Spending hard-earned bucks on real, day-in and day-out working hardware can be quite another. If you want to know what a computer guru really thinks, take a look at what they use, not what they review. How? *Windows User Magazine* used to publish writers' configurations along with every article — an admirable, if subtle, insight into the real world. (*Windows User Mag* went belly-up not long ago.) In many other magazines you can often read between the lines; occasionally the author will let a tantalizing tip drop.

Well, Mom lined the icons up and threatened to whop 'em upside the head if they didn't spill the beans and tell you precisely what they bought and why. Mom's particularly interested in the mistakes the icons made — *hey, these talking heads are spewing out recommendations; they should be immune from mistakes!* — in the hope that you'll learn from them.

We humans and icons used three different computers to write this book: one bought brand new while the project was under way; one upgraded just before the wordslinging started; and one that mutated only slightly during the course of the project.

The Mom Machine

 My computer, the one that came through with minimal changes, is a Comtrade 486DX/50. (Comtrade, 15314 East Valley Blvd, City of Industry CA, 800-969-2123, 818-961-6688, FAX 818-369-1479.) It's a plain-vanilla ISA setup; dates back to pre-local-bus times. I put 20 MB of memory into it.

When I bought the machine, it appeared as if the 486DX/50 would have an upgrade path, with the possibility of a clock doubling chip. Now the prospects of a 486DX2/100 OverDrive seem remote; there haven't been a whole lot of 486DX/50s sold. Rumor has it Intel decided to drop 486/100 plans because of the relatively small market, potential heat problems, and the possibility a 486/100 would eat into sales of the Pentium. Are any of those rumors true? Who knows?

The 486DX/50 came with 256K of external memory cache. The standard machine came with 64K of cache; I figured an extra $100 was a reasonable investment in the future. If I had to do it over again, I don't think I would spend the money.

For video, I have a Nanao T560i. That's the 17-inch version of the finest monitor ever made — and you'll read about the T560i's big brother here in a minute. You'll find that all of us icons run Nanaos. Why? They're simply the finest monitors available. I'm no teenager; my eyes can use all the help they can get. It wasn't easy *finding* a T560i, but the folks at Comtrade managed to rustle one up for me. They aren't cheap. But, oh, are they sweet.

When I started working on my book, I was using an Orchid Fahrenheit 1280 "Classic" video card. You can read about my travails with the video driver, earlier in this chapter. Then I started testing video cards, fell in love with the Volante Warp10, and bought one. Bye-bye Orchid, hello NDI.

For printing, I use an HP DeskJet 500. Pretty soon now I'll get the 486/50 networked to Igor's machine, so I can use his LaserJet 4.

The 486/50 has a 520 MB Conner IDE hard disk, two Toshiba floppies, a big tower case (Igor is all thumbs, and he does my hardware upgrades), a Colorado Memory Systems Jumbo 250 for tape backup, American Power Conversion Back-UPS 250 power supply, Northgate OmniKey 102 keyboard, and Microsoft Mouse, version 1.0. My CD-ROM drive is a CD Technology 3301; it plugs into the 486/50 with a cheap Future Domain SCSI card. Those all work great. I'd recommend them to anyone.

Now for the mistakes. I bought a caching IDE disk controller, and put 2.5 MB of memory on it. (The brand doesn't matter: the controller works fine; I'm the one who screwed up.) If I had only read Mao's admonitions before blowing the bucks on that controller! I bought it based on DOS benchmarks that showed much faster disk accesses. Well, maybe some DOS user somewhere could take advantage of this'n, but it would've been a whole lot smarter for me to set aside more main memory for SMARTDrive, and forget about the caching controller.

I also put a SoundBlaster Pro in the 486/50. You can read about the installation fun and games earlier in this chapter. It wasn't a pretty sight. If I had it to do over again, I'd go with a Pro Audio Studio 16. The SBPro connects to an old $10 stereo system I bought at a garage sale. I set the bookshelf speakers next to the monitor; crank it up and the sound will blow you away.

Igor's Installation

 My machine came in as we started working on the fourth chapter of Mom's book. I won't let Mom touch it because she'd never let go. It's a Comtrade (yeah, we icons have a thing about Comtrade) 486 DX2/66, VL-B local bus, ISA screamer. I maxed it out with 32 MB of memory; memory was cheap back then, and I figured that much memory would take me through Windows NT and who-knows-what-all. The 486 processor chip comes in a ZIF (Zero Insertion Force) base, so it should be relatively easy to upgrade the machine to a Pentium OverDrive when the time comes. My only real concern is cooling: the P24T chip is said to run very hot; I don't know if there's enough air flow in this tower to handle it.

The machine comes with 128K of external memory cache, and I figured that was good enough.

My monitor is the *monitoro di tutti monitori*, the Nanao T660i, a 100-pound behemoth, 20 (some would say 21) inches of stunning beauty. It's so flat that the first time I sat down to use it, I truly thought the screen was concave. A work of art. They're very hard to find, and outrageously expensive, but if you shop around you should be able to find a good price.... if you can find one at all. Just like Mom's T560i, the folks at Comtrade rustled up this one. I liked it so much I sat down and wrote an unsolicited fan letter to the Nanao USA distributor. True fact.

The Diamond Viper VL-B video board comes with this hummer, and I'm developing a real love-hate relationship with it. This P9000 chip based board, as of this writing anyway, wins every benchmark test by a large margin. You have to witness the speed to believe it.

But, dammit, the driver stinks! I've had no end of problems with Diamond's software, and each iteration of the driver seems to introduce new problems. I'm keeping on top of the new versions of the drivers, via CompuServe, to see if they finally get it right. If they don't, I may well return the board and get something that's slower but works. The jury's still out, even as we went to print. I'd only recommend this card to people who are willing to endure a significant amount of pain — and waste all sorts of time — waiting for Diamond to get its act together.

Even we icons get the driver blues.

Printing on this DX2/66 rates as a religious experience. I have an HP LaserJet 4, and it's lovely. But the icing on the cake is the LaserMaster WinJet 1200. Like the WinJet 800, discussed earlier in this chapter, the WinJet 1200 consists of two boards — one for the computer, one for the printer — a cable, and software. Run it in high-speed mode (nobody in their right mind would call it "draft") and my WinWord documents pop out the printer about 25% faster than they do with PrintManager; CorelDRAW! graphics come out in half the time.

What you have to see, though, is the 1200 dpi typeset-quality printing the WinJet 1200 produces, in about the same time as standard Print Manager output. Admittedly, the difference in plain text is hard to see: the LaserJet 4 prints text wondrously. But pictures ... ah, pictures! ... truly appear typeset. Even lowly screen shots and clip art practically pop off the page. Want to see what I'm talking about? Call LaserMaster (800-365-4646 or 612-944-9330) and ask them to send you a sample printed page.

I did make a mistake with the printer, though. Before I put in the WinJet 1200 I kept getting "Overflow" errors on my LJ 4 when printing CorelDRAW! graphics. So I went out and bought an additional 8 MB of memory. Big mistake. The Overflow errors didn't stop. Ends up the Overflow errors are due to a bug in the LJ 4 driver. (Neither HP nor Corel will call it a bug, but it squeaks like a bug and it squashes like a bug.) The latest LJ 4 driver was supposed to correct the problem, but now I'm getting Overflows on WinWord documents. Oy! Meanwhile, I'm out three hundred bucks on memory that I'll never use; the WinJet doesn't touch any of it, and I'm using the WinJet exclusively these days.

This 486DX2/66 came with a Conner 520 MB IDE hard disk, two floppies, and a mini tower case (Mom's got a big nose and she's always poking it where it doesn't belong). I use a Colorado Memory Systems Jumbo 250 for backup, and an American Power Conversion Back-UPS 400 power supply, the 400 volt-amp rating I figure is better with such a big monitor. I use a Practical Peripherals PM14400 FXMT modem, Northgate OmniKey 102 keyboard, a classic, and a Microsoft Mouse version 2.0.

I splurged on the CD-ROM drive, picked up a fast Toshiba XM-3401. And I love it. The drive attaches to the 486 with an Adaptec 1540 SCSI adapter, a real workhorse. I plan to daisy chain my HP ScanJet IIc off that adapter, as soon as I get the software ironed out. For fax, I use an HP LaserJet Fax: it plugs into the LJ 4, turning the printer into a plain paper fax machine. The LJ Fax doubles as a handy, fast single-sheet copier.

After thinking about it quite a while, I put Microsoft's Windows Sound System into the 486. It was tough choosing the WSS, but I'm going to need it for hardware and software evaluations. If you run games there are better choices. The WSS is connected to a pair of cheap powered Seiko speakers, originally bundled with a little tape recorder, which I stuck to the sides of my T660i with some double-stick tape.

Did I make any other mistakes? I don't think so. It would've been nice to get a local bus SCSI adapter, but at the time I bought the machine I wasn't really comfortable mixing the technologies. The Diamond video driver and the extra LJ 4 memory were pretty big mistakes in the first place. Check back in six months, though. I may have changed my mind.

Mao's Mate

 I made a few mistakes too, but by and large I feel really good about my new system. Like Igor, I have an ISA 486DX2/66 VL-B local bus system. Unlike Igor, I had it assembled by a local hardware guru. It's based on an AMI VLB 486/66 motherboard with 32 MB. I expect that during the lifetime of this machine, I'll max the memory out to the 64 MB allowed. I have 256K of external cache memory, and I'm convinced that it's a good investment.

I liked the tower case on my old system (a 386/25 I'd had for 5 years), so I kept it and some other stuff from that old system: the CD ROM, scanner, and a 600 MB hard driver. Then the power supply died on that old case and a new one seemed hard to get so I got a new tower case from PC Power & Cooling (voice: 800-722-6555). It is a work of art. Six half height external drive bays, one full height internal bay, incredibly sturdy design and powered by their famous power supply which is so quiet you don't even know the machine is on.

Igor convinced me to spend the bucks and get a Nanao T660i. I hate the bloody thing. Every day I look at that monitor and think, "I'll never be able to use another monitor again." It's a pity. There should be a law.

I use an ATI Graphics Ultra Pro Plus VL-B video card. It's a nice, fast card, but oy! the problems I've had with drivers. I've already told about the fact that version 2.0 of the drivers are only a marginal improvement. I just love it when vendors use their customers as beta testers. I'll probably stick with the card, but I don't have to like it.

I also have a mono card and monitor attached to the system, so I can spy on myself. That way my right head will know what my left head is doing.

I print with my trusty HP LaserJet III, a printer that's seen me through all sorts of tough situations. I've hooked up the WinJet 800 and use it all the time. Great piece of hardware. And I use a JetFax, which plugs into the LJ III, for faxing.

This 486 came with 1.8 GB of disk space, using a fast SCSI controller. It's a good, reliable, fast alternative to IDE. I intentionally chose SCSI drives because I knew I would need a SCSI controller anyway. And what a SCSI controller: it's from Ultrastor, and it fits in the VL-B local bus slot. Quick.

I have two floppies, a tower case (between Igor's thumbs and Mom's nose, I needed the space), an OmniKey keyboard, and a Microsoft Mouse version 2.0. My CD-ROM is a Toshiba; it connects to the 486 through the SCSI controller. I have an HP ScanJet Plus, but it uses its own "SCSI" card. And I use a SoundBlaster Plus. Installation on this one wasn't as tough as Igor's Pro.

To back up that big drive, I picked a tremendous tape drive, an Archive Viper DAT drive with a capacity of 4 GB. I take backup seriously.

 So there you have it, warts and all. I hope you've found this chapter useful, if not particularly reassuring. Hardware can be enormously frustrating, even to those who should know better. Nobody gets it right the first time. Or the second or third.

The best we can all do is to keep chipping away at the vendors, in the hope that. . . some day. . .they'll treat us customers with more respect.

Mom's Red Book

 Hey, if Mao can put his most important wisdom in a Red Book, so can I. Here's the quick summary distilling the advice sprinkled throughout this chapter.

- When you get a new machine, stretch. Push the budget and the envelope some. You'll buy machines less often and be happier with you get. A double win.

- Processor? For a new machine, get a 486. That'll probably be the right choice until some time in late 1994 when Pentium pricing may become accessible to the mass market. If you have a 286 but use Windows much, upgrade (to a 486). With a 386, there isn't the same compelling reason to upgrade, so its a question of speed versus time versus money that only you can balance.

- Video? With a new machine, get a local bus for the video and get an accelerated (not coprocessed) card to go in the local bus. With an old machine, if you don't have an accelerated video card, it will be your most sensible upgrade to speed up Windows. Plan on running 800x600x256 colors or higher. Get the best/biggest monitor your budget can afford. Your eyes will thank you.

- RAM? Get at least 4 MB for Windows. Upping that to 8 or even 16 MB is the most important upgrade you can make after accelerated video.

- Disk space? You can't be too thin, too rich, or have too much disk space. Get at least 120 MB. More if you can. The extra cost for a larger hard disk when you make an initial purchase is not usually that much so that's the best time to stretch.

- Cache? With a 486, getting 64K of external processor cache is a good idea. More is a toss up. Don't think about dedicated hard disk cache on a controller — instead give some of your precious RAM over to SMARTDrive.

- Printer? Get a LaserJet or an InkJet. HP dominates the market for cause; you can't go wrong with an HP printer.

- What else? No question that the most important other thing you must consider is a tape backup because you have too much to wind up bothering to do floppy backups. After that, I suggest a modem, a CD ROM drive and then a sound card.

CHAPTER 8

WIN.INI, Windows' Heart

They call it elusive, and say
That one looks
But it never appears.
They say that indeed it is rare,
Since one listens,
But never a sound.
Subtle, they call it, and say
That one grasps it
But never gets hold.
These three complaints amount
To only one, which is
Beyond all resolution.

Describe it as form yet unformed;
As shape that is still without shape;
Or say it is vagueness confused:
One meets it and it has no front;
One follows and there is no rear.

If you hold ever fast
To that most ancient Way,
You may govern today.
Call truly that knowledge
Of primal beginnings
The clue to the Way.

— Lao Tzu, *Tao Tê Ching*, ca 350 B.C.

In this chapter CTO Mao steps you through the **WIN.INI** Way. Those great little tweaks that work will make Windows scream. The ones that don't will make *you* scream.

Et Tu, INI

> I find no reason which I can offer without immodesty
> except the rather poor one that I should like to see a Uniform Edition myself.
> It is nothing; a cat could say it about her kittens.
> Still, I believe I will stand upon that.
>
> — Samuel Clemens, *The Innocents Abroad*, 1869

 Unlike most of the rest of *MOM*, the next three chapters aren't really designed to be read straight through. Rather, this is a place to hop around, let your mind wander a bit, absorb all that's buzzing about. For this *is* Windows — or at least the part you can get to; it's all right here in the `.INI` files. There's a mini-index at the beginning of each chapter that will point you to particular places you may find useful.

 The other icons and I have tried to make these chapters exhaustive, simply because none of us could find any single reliable source of information about Windows' `.INI` files.

Hey, you might not need a definitive reference, a Uniform Edition, but I sure do. So I wrote this chapter for myself. There. That's the truth, straight out. I'm tired of flipping through a dozen books and getting all sorts of different and conflicting info, only to find that most of it is copied practically verbatim from the official documentation — and that a whole bunch of it is, simply, dead wrong.

The `.INI` files — the heart and soul of Windows — are, in places, undocumented, inadequately documented, incompletely documented, or (worst of all) incorrectly documented. I think of it as the three *i*'s of Windows docs: inadequate, incomplete, incorrect. You'll see it over and over again: the official documentation is wrong, wrong, wrong. I would guesstimate that half to two-thirds — *maybe more* — of the `.INI` settings you're likely to use are botched in the official docs.

Here in these three chapters you're going to get the straight scoop, the results of months of exhaustive testing, banging, kicking, and knocking around Windows: battering it and stomping on its heart, jumping on it 'til it yelled uncle.

I'm not going to tell you how Windows' designers thought it should work or how Windows 2.x or 3.0 worked. All too often, that's exactly what made it into Microsoft's Windows Resource Kit, and has been parroted in dozens of Windows

Resource Kit re-writes. Nope. I'm going for the jugular, grasshopper, and I don't give a damn what the official party line might be. I want to be able to tell you what *really* happens, how, when, why.

Why such fanaticism over such an obscure corner of Windows? Because none of the `.INI` settings are interesting or important. . . until the very second you need them. Microsoft doesn't give them the credit they're due. Almost all of the existing documentation is sloppy, obtuse, inconsistent, riddled with jargon randomly applied.

If you put this discourse on `.INI`s side-by-side almost any other listing of `.INI` settings — official, unofficial, or otherwise — you'll start wondering whether those authors actually tried to use the settings before they wrote about 'em. It's scary.

Sooner or later just about every Windows user ends up wallowing in the `.INI`s. The least you can expect — the least you should *demand* — is an accurate guidebook.

Sometimes it helps to have a second opinion. If you find yourself buried deep in a *MOM* discourse and you're still scratching your head, you might want to consult another source. Although we differ on quite a few points, I've found the discussions of `.INI`s in *The Windows 3.1 Bible*, by Fred Davis (Peachpit Press, 1993), *Tuning Windows 3.1*, by Sally Neuman *et al* (Que, 1992), and *2001 Windows Tips*, by Mike Edelhart *et al* (Ziff-Davis Press, 1993) to be enlightening and often very helpful, and would recommend any of those three books should you require a different point of view. For an overall survey of Windows and comprehensive (albeit quite technical) discussions of how the pieces of Windows fit together, I find myself constantly turning to the ultimate authority on Windows' wierding ways, *Windows Internals* by Matt Pietrek (Addison-Wesley, 1992).

In Chapters 8, 9, and 10 you'll find dozens of previously undocumented topics and hundreds of corrections to the official documentation, any one of which could save you hours of frustration. These chapters alone should pay for *MOM* over and over again.

I've avoided the temptation to point out a dozen or two dozen hypothetically concocted "tips." There is so much to **WIN.INI** and **SYSTEM.INI** and the others, and each Windows setup is so different, that it would be unfair to rate one group of tips, one list of suggestions, over another. All three chapters are non-stop recitations of tips, tricks and hints, gotchas, warnings, commiserations.

 I will give you one tip, though, and this should keep the twiddler in you occupied: if you want to tinker with your Windows setup, particularly to improve its performance, simply open any one of these chapters to any random page and start reading. I'll bet you find something (or *many* somethings!) you'll be able to use, right off the bat.

Just make sure you back up often, and back up well.

 When I couldn't test something independently, but had to rely on the official documentation, I'll let you know. In the few cases where all of us tried to figure out what Windows was doing, but we couldn't make heads from tails of it — because the official documentation doesn't explain things well enough for a mere mortal to understand, or simply because *nobody knows* — I'll tell you exactly that.

And I'll try to cut through the crap and explain this stuff in plain English.

My goal? To make *MOM* the first real-world, down-and-dirty, reliable reference on Windows' .INI files.

Did we make it?

I dunno. You tell me.

INI Gadda da Vida

> "The novel is dead."
>
> — Gore Vidal, Interview, 1993

> "Gore should curl up with a good computer book."
>
> — *Pensées Pinecliffius*

It's a common problem, dating back to The Dawn of Computers: programs need to store and retrieve settings. A game program might store away the highest player scores. An envelope printing program will certainly store your name and address. A drawing program might want to keep track of your favorite color palette. And on and on.

Windows itself stores away an enormous amount of information, retrieving the bits every time it starts: what kind of wallpaper do you like? Which color should appear as the background on active windows? Where are your printers connected?

Back in the days of DOS, those settings were usually consigned to small files with weird names. **BARFBLST.CFG**. **HISCORE.SAV**. **SUPERBUZ.SET**. **DIFF.DEF**. **LEN.NON**. **OH.NO**. You know the tune. Open any of those old DOS files, and there's no telling what you might find: simple text, compressed bit patterns, even elaborate encoding schemes, all too often designed to minimize your chances of copying the program to a different machine. Truly inscrutable.

INI Anatomy

Windows introduced some semblance of order to this polyglot world. In Windows parlance, these files are called Initialization Files (pronounced "innie files"); their names almost always end in **.INI**; they usually reside in your Windows directory (e.g., **C:\WINDOWS**); they're almost always plain, simple, text files; and they almost always follow a very rigid pattern (Microsoft's own **WINWORD.INI** in WinWord versions 1 and 2 being very notable exceptions — in spite of the name they aren't **.INI** files, and I will ignore them for the rest of this chapter).

Windows itself is governed by two **.INI** files, **SYSTEM.INI** and **WIN.INI**. Every major, and most minor, Windows applications have their own **.INI** files. In many cases there is a program that lets you change **.INI** file settings, although in some cases you'll find that you need to dig into the **.INI** file itself, taking your system's destiny into your own hands.

Changing settings in an **.INI** file is as simple as using a text editor like Windows' own Notepad, opening up the file, and typing away. *Clobbering* an **.INI** file can be just as easy, and involves the same steps, so a big part of learning about **.INI** files involves learning what *not* to do.

CD MOM, our companion CD, contains two programs that will help prevent you from spontaneous INI self-immolation. Both INI Manager and INI ProFiler, outstanding shareware programs, are important additions to your Windows arsenal: although they don't handle every eventuality, chances are awfully good that anything you need to do to an INI will be easier and safer with either of these programs. You can read about them in the GENERAL\ section of Chapter 12.

.INI files are different from other simple text files in two important respects: Windows provides tools for programmers to get at values in .INI files; and, more importantly, almost all Windows programs use those tools. That's good news for us Windows users, because it brings some uniformity to an old morass.

At least the bugs are easier to identify.

This chapter will talk about many ways to improve Windows' performance by tweaking your software. Part and parcel of tweaking software in the Windows world is a understanding of — and respect for — the .INI file.

Windows may rule the world, but .INIs control Windows: they're the hands that rock 'n roll the Windows cradle. If you are to master your Windows destiny, you must dig into your .INI files.

It's important that you understand the structure of .INI files to keep from shooting yourself and your system in the foot, so bear with me a minute while we go through the details. This may start to look like *<shudder!>* programming, but it isn't, really. You'll be able to understand it, even if the idea of writing a program gives you the willies.

Let's start by looking at a real-life example. Igor's **WIN.INI**. Many parts of **WIN.INI** are controlled by the Windows application called the Control Panel, which I've already discussed in Chapter 3 in the section *Beam Me Up, Scotty — Control Panel*. It's probably in the MAIN section of your Windows desktop right now. Take a gander at Figure 8-1, which shows Igor's setting in the "Printer" section of his Control Panel, and compare it with the **[PrinterPorts]** section of Igor's **WIN.INI**.

See how each of the entries in the **[PrinterPorts]** section of the Control Panel has one corresponding entry in **WIN.INI**? It's not always quite that simple, not by a long shot, as you'll soon see, but you get the idea.

Here are some of the **WIN.INI** lines surrounding Igor's **[PrinterPorts]** section:

```
[MS Proofing Tools]
Spelling 1033,0=C:\WINDOWS\MSAPPS\PROOF\MSSPELL.DLL
Custom Dict 1=C:\WINDOWS\MSAPPS\PROOF\CUSTOM.DIC

[PrinterPorts]
Generic / Text Only=TTY,FILE:,15,100
HP LaserJet 4/4M=HPPCL5E,LPT1:,15,45
HP LaserJet III=hppcl5a,LPT1:,15,45,LPT2:,30,60
LM WinJet 1200 PS=LMPS,WinSpool:,15,45
```

```
LM WinPrint Direct=WinPrint,Direct:,15,45

[devices]
Generic / Text Only=TTY,FILE:
HP LaserJet 4/4M=HPPCL5E,LPT1:
HP LaserJet III=hppc15a,LPT1:,LPT2:
LM WinJet 1200 PS=LMPS,WinSpool:
LM WinPrint Direct=WinPrint,Direct:
```

See the pattern there? That's how `.INI` files in general are structured. They're simple text files broken into sections, with variables and values in each section. Like this:

```
[Section Name]
Variable=Value
AnotherVariable=SomeOtherValue
```

An `.INI` file can have just one section name, or it may have hundreds. Each section might have one variable/value pair, or none at all, or hundreds, even thousands.

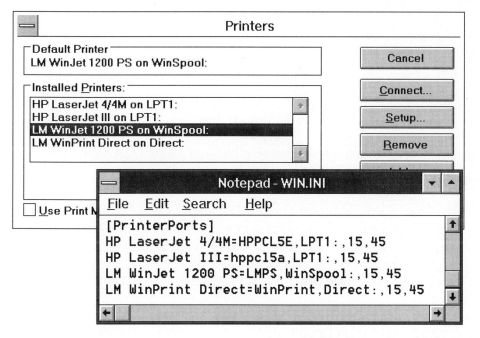

Figure 8-1: Igor Can Print

Windows programs get at `.INI` file values by saying, "Okay, Windows. Go out to this particular `.INI` file, look in such-and-so section, and give me the value of this here variable." For example, an `.INI` file called **ANATOM.INI** might contain these lines:

```
[Belly Buttons]
Mine=Innie
Yours=Outie

[IQ]
Bill=150
```

Any Windows program that says, "Yo! Windows! Go get me the value of **Yours** in the **Belly Buttons** section of **ANATOM.INI**" will receive a value of **Outie**.

Conversely, Windows programs can and often do change `.INI` file values. If you run a program that tells Windows to change the value of **Bill** in the **IQ** section of **ANATOM.INI** to 140, the file will suddenly look like this:

```
[Belly Buttons]
Mine=Innie
Yours=Outie

[IQ]
Bill=140
```

Which is precisely what you would expect, eh?

INI Rules

 Since Windows has a lot of control over these `.INI` files, and since almost all Windows programs rely on the values stored in the `.INI` files, you might imagine that it's important to carefully follow Windows' rules when changing `.INI` files — otherwise your programs may respond to your futzing with the Wrath of Khan.

Here are my rules for dealing with `.INI` files. Ignore them at your own peril!

Rule 0: Always, always, always, make a backup copy of any `.INI` file before changing it. Then write down the name of the backup file, just in case you forget it.

Even if you're extremely careful, a wayward comma or mis-typed number can freeze Windows tight. In rare cases, particularly if you're extraordinarily talented at zapping your machine, all you need to do is make one simple typing mistake and you may not even be able to re-start Windows. So keep a good backup copy, and if you're forced to resort to the three-finger salute, use DOS to replace the mangled `.INI` file with the good one before re-starting Windows.

I, personally, clobbered **WIN.INI** more than once while writing this chapter. And the first time I didn't have a recent backup. Do as I say, not as I do. . .

Rule 1: Don't duplicate section names. If you have a section called **[Fahrquahrt]** at the beginning of an `.INI` file, and another called **[Fahrquahrt]** located at the end, Windows won't mind a bit: Windows is smart enough to know that any time a program goes looking for **[Fahrquahrt]**, it wants the first one. But you aren't so smart! You may well find yourself changing the section at the end — and those changes don't mean diddly to Windows.

 Rule 2: This is my rule. Don't delete any lines from an `.INI` file, sonny. Some day you might wonder what used to be there. Windows has a convention for "comment" fields in `.INI` files: simply put a semi-colon at the beginning of the line. (It's not unlike putting a REM at the beginning of a line in a DOS batch file.) When you want to get rid of a line in an `.INI` file, put a semi-colon at the beginning — maybe write a note to yourself to remind you why you made the change — but don't delete the line. You can even make the note on a separate line so long as you start the line with a semi-colon.

Rule 3: Always use a text editor or INI file editor on `.INI` files. SYSEDIT (described in Chapter 4) works fine on **WIN.INI** and **SYSTEM.INI**, and Notepad does a bang-up job on any `.INI` file. But avoid using Windows Write — or any other word processor for that matter — unless you're careful to keep from converting the file to the word processor's format. Word processors have a nasty habit of changing the file all around, making it conform to the word processor's concept of what a file should look like; Windows demands a plain text file.

Rule 4: Use blank lines to make things more legible. Windows ignores blank lines, but your eyes don't. You can always tell when somebody is trying to scan an `.INI` file with all the sections bunged together. Their eyeballs go WHUP-WHUP-WHUP so loud you can hear 'em across a room.

Rule 5: Don't get fancy. While it's true that you can put spaces and tabs and other effluvia in strange places (variable names, for instance, may be preceded by any number of tabs; values may be preceded or followed by spaces), you'll only confuse yourself in the long run. Keep it simple.

Section Tricks

Windows makes a few demands on section names. (Some Windows documentation insists on using the term "application" instead of "section", a throwback to the Windows 2.x days when most section names were, in fact, the names of applications. Times have changed.)

All section names begin with a [left bracket and end with a] right bracket. Microsoft's documentation (c.f., `WININI.WRI`, which ships with Windows, or the Windows Resource Kit) says the left bracket must appear in the first column of the `.INI` file, but that isn't true: Windows will find any section name that appears on its own line, preceded or followed by any number of spaces or tabs.

Section names may consist of letters or numbers, spaces, weird things like the _underscore character or the $ dollar sign, and a whole bunch of other things. Windows isn't very picky about the characters that go into section names.

Capitalization doesn't matter. You can call that "case insensitive" if you want; far be it from me to declare any Windows thing "insensitive."

All three of these section names are treated identically:

```
[Belly Buttons]
    [Belly Buttons]
[bellY buttonS]
```

Contrariwise, spaces between the [brackets] do make a difference. These four section names are all treated differently; as far as Windows is concerned, they are completely different sections:

```
[Belly Buttons]
[BellyButtons]
[Belly Buttons ]
[ Belly Buttons]
```

A section name should precede the very first variable=value line in every `.INI` file. Since Windows only gets at `.INI` file values by using section names, variables should be tied to sections; putting a variable=value line before the first section name ensures that Windows programs won't be able to get at either the variable or the value!

Sections may appear in any order; Windows doesn't care. Similarly, variable=value pairs may appear in any order, within a particular section.

 Why are these nit-picking details important? Because they can make or break your Windows setup! If you start playing with your `WIN.INI` and accidentally put an extra space in the `[PrinterPorts]` section name — turn it into `[Printer Ports]`, say — all your printer settings will suddenly go haywire, for no apparent reason.

Be careful. Back up often. Back up well.

Variable Tricks

As with section names, variable names enjoy a wide latitude. Windows will find any variable name that appears on a line, preceded or followed by any number of spaces or tabs, and followed by an equals sign.

Variable names, like section names, may consist of letters or numbers, spaces, and oddball characters like the underscore or dollar sign, but avoid using [brackets]! They are case insensitive: capitalization doesn't matter.

All four of these variable names are treated identically, and as you'll see in a minute, they all have identical values:

```
Mine=Innie
Mine = Innie
    Mine        =Innie
Mine    =       Innie
```

As with section names, spaces within the variable name *do make a difference*. These three variable names are all treated differently; as far as Windows is concerned, they refer to completely different variables:

```
Mine = Innie
M ine = Innie
   M i ne= Innie
```

If you've ever accidentally, mysteriously lost an `.INI` variable value, chances are mighty good you inadvertently stuck an extra space in the middle of the variable name. That turns it into an entirely different variable, and nothing short of a very sharp eye will ever catch the problem.

Family Values

 Windows bigots would have you believe that the values stored in `.INI` files are unwavering; the interpretation of `.INI` values immutable. That's simply not true. Windows 3.0, for example, would interpret a value of -1 very differently from how Windows 3.1 would interpret it. If Windows itself can't get it straight, you're to be forgiven if you have to look things up from time to time.

Programs can ask Windows for `.INI` data in one of two flavors: as integers (i.e., a positive or negative whole number, or zero) or strings (i.e., a bunch of characters). While you're usually insulated from the inner machinations of all this, occasionally the distinction will drive you nuts. For example, if you set an `.INI` variable's value to 1.5 and the Windows program that uses that value reads it as an integer, the program will only pick up a 1: the fractional part never even makes it into the program. (If the same program asks for the same value, only this time as a string, it will get 1.5.) So if the values you type into an `.INI` file don't seem to make it into the program intact, remember that Windows itself may be discarding fractions.

 Let's start with string values. A very large percentage of all `.INI` values are strings; the `[Belly Button]` section I showed you earlier dealt entirely with strings. In a rather strange twist of events, Windows programs that change `.INI` values can only change them to strings. But that's a bit esoteric.

When Windows goes looking for a string, it massages the value it finds before returning it to the program. Let's look at an example while we're discussing the precise steps involved.

```
[Belly Buttons]
Mine=     "Innie"
```

Step 1: Windows grabs everything to the right of the (first) equals sign. In this example, that's four spaces, followed by a double-quote, followed by the characters `Innie`, and finally another double-quote.

Step 2: Windows trims all the spaces and tabs off the front and the back of the string. In the example here, the four spaces at the front get the heave-ho.

Step 3: If the first and last characters are both single quotes (character number 39), or if the first and last characters are both double quotes (character number 34), both the first and the last character are removed. In the example, both quotes disappear, and the value returned to the Windows program is `Innie`. What the program does with it is another story entirely, of course.

 Windows seems to have a tough time with Step 3 when there are tabs between a pair of quotes: it appears that everything following the tab (including the final quote) is stripped, while the initial quote remains. Whatever the rationale, it looks like a bug to me. Word to the wise: avoid mixing quotes and tabs in an `.INI` value. And I'll be tarred and feathered if I can figure out what happens to [brackets] in values. Avoid them, too.

These rules are followed very literally. Consider what happens if a program asks Windows for the values in the **[Belly Buttons]** section given below:

```
[Belly Buttons]
Mine= "Innie "
Yours = ""Outie"
Ours = ""Hairy
Theirs='Kinky'
```

Mine comes back with six characters, **Innie** and a trailing space. **Yours** has a value of one double-quote followed by **Outie**. **Ours** comes back with seven characters: two double quotes and **Hairy**. **Theirs** is simply **Kinky**.

I'm referring to the San Antonio **Theirs**, of course. No relation to the Des Moines **Theirs**. They... uh... already have theirs.

Now consider numbers. They're a bit more complex.

Step 1: Once again, Windows grabs everything to the right of the (first) equals sign.

Step 2: Once again, Windows trims all the spaces and tabs off the front and the back of the value.

Step 3: Windows takes a look at the first character. If it's a minus sign (what some people would call a hyphen), Windows makes note of the fact that it is looking at a negative number, skips to the character following the minus sign, and continues with Step 4. If the first character is not a minus sign, Windows goes on to Step 4.

Step 4: Windows takes a look at the current character. If it's a digit (i.e., a number between 0 and 9), it accumulates the digit just as you would expect, moves on to the next character, and repeats Step 4. If it isn't a digit, Windows skips to Step 5.

Step 5: If Windows hasn't accumulated any digits, it returns a zero. If it has accumulated digits, the number is calculated just as you would expect, and that number is returned to the program.

These steps are followed slavishly, and the results can be quite surprising, they can jump out and bite you when you're least expecting it. Consider this **[IQ]** section:

```
[IQ]
BillG = 200
Mao = 180.1
Woody= +150
Mom =98.6
Igor = -25XYZ
Garth = - 100
```

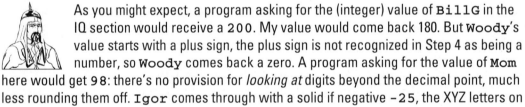

As you might expect, a program asking for the (integer) value of `BillG` in the IQ section would receive a `200`. My value would come back 180. But `Woody`'s value starts with a plus sign, the plus sign is not recognized in Step 4 as being a number, so `Woody` comes back a zero. A program asking for the value of `Mom` here would get `98`: there's no provision for *looking at* digits beyond the decimal point, much less rounding them off. `Igor` comes through with a solid if negative `-25`, the XYZ letters on the end being ignored.

Hey, you think *I* got it bad. Look at `Garth`. There's a space after the minus sign. According to Step 4, Windows stops looking when it hits that space. `Garth` comes back a big, fat zero. You read that right. A `-100` comes out `-100`. But a `- 100` (with a space between the minus and the `100`) comes out zero. I think that's a bug, and I'll bet you do, too.

Anyway, as you can see, when it comes to evaluating `.INI` values, there's a hell of a lot of drip 'twixt lip and sip.

That's why, when you have a choice, you should use a program to change `.INI` file settings. Like Control Panel. Or INI ProFiler or INI Manager. Or even Windows Setup. Little gotchas like the space-after-minus-sign bug should make you feel very insecure, and for good reason. At least in theory, one small typo can put a whole file out of whack.

'Course a buggy program can do the same thing.

Maxi and Mini .INIs

If you look in your Windows directory (e.g., `C:\WINDOWS`), you'll find all sorts of `.INI` files. The tips, warnings and gotchas I've just described apply to all of those `.INI` files, whether they were created by Windows or some other program.

Next, I'm going to take a look at a handful of `.INI` files that are particularly important to the proper care and feeding of Windows itself.

`SYSTEM.INI` (see Figure 8-2) is the file that sets up Windows; it's the one Windows digests every time it springs to life, the one that controls Windows' persona. If you screw up **SYSTEM.INI**, and don't have a handy backup, you could spend hours — even days — trying to unscrew it. As a general rule of thumb, the **SYSTEM.INI** settings are directly tied to your hardware; some of them can be changed by running the Windows Setup program.

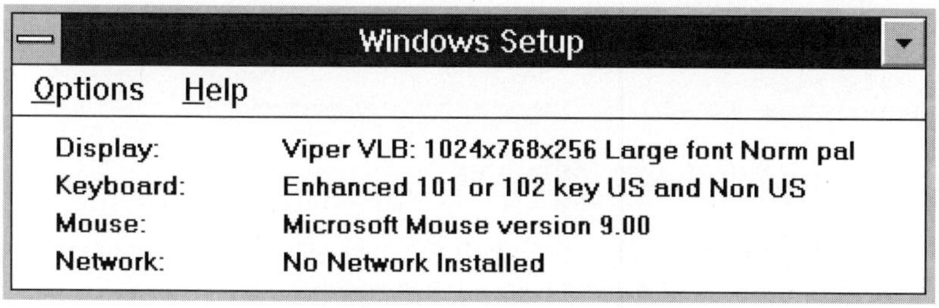

Windows Setup	
Options Help	
Display:	Viper VLB: 1024x768x256 Large font Norm pal
Keyboard:	Enhanced 101 or 102 key US and Non US
Mouse:	Microsoft Mouse version 9.00
Network:	No Network Installed

Figure 8-2: Setup, a SYSTEM.INI Front-End

Most **SYSTEM.INI** settings not accessible through Windows Setup are quite esoteric. Changes to those settings have to be made by hand, and should be approached with appropriate fear and trepidation. Changes to **SYSTEM.INI**, once made, will not "take" until you re-start Windows.

The Mother of all **.INI** files, **WIN.INI**, controls the Windows desktop, fonts, ports, and devices connected to your computer. No, the distinction between **SYSTEM.INI** and **WIN.INI** is not clear-cut; you may find yourself looking in both files when attempting to unravel a particularly sticky question. Many **WIN.INI** settings are accessible through the Windows Control Panel.

Often, changes made to **WIN.INI** take effect immediately. When you modify something in **WIN.INI**, using a Control Panel applet (see Figure 8-3), Windows sends out a little message to all running applications that says, in effect, "Hey, App Turkey! **WIN.INI** just changed. Go take a look at it." Unfortunately, not all Windows programs are bright enough to respond to that particular Windows message so sometimes you'll have to re-start Windows to make sure all your applications get the idea.

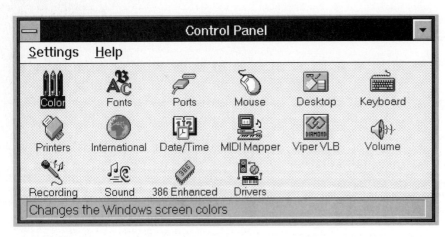

Figure 8-3: Control Panel, the Window to WIN.INI

Many Windows applications will pick up changes if they're made with the Control Panel applets, but won't even know anything has happened if you change **WIN.INI** with SYSEDIT, or some other text editor.

To further complicate things a bit, the Control Panel has its own `.INI` file, called **CONTROL.INI**, that stores settings germane to the Control Panel alone. There are similar files for Program Manager (**PROGMAN.INI**) and Windows Help (**WINHELP.INI**).

I'm going to discuss **WIN.INI** first, simply because it's the most likely target of your affections. *Or is that affectations?* Then I'll boggle you down with **SYSTEM.INI**. And finally I'll atone for my sins by digging into **CONTROL**, **PROGMAN** and **WINHELP**.

Some of the stuff here duplicates what you'll find in Chapter 3 on the Control Panel. In most cases the overlap is minor and intentional, simply so you don't have to flip back and forth in the book.

I had to make a decision about how to structure the rest of this chapter, and it wasn't easy. I finally decided to list [Section]s within each file in alphabetical order. Why? Because *no* order makes any sense. The official manuals would have you believe that there's a real difference between any two sections, that all is logical in the `.INI` jungle. Not so. Sections are all jingled-jangled, with lots of overlap and little coherence. Confusion rules.

So we put our iconic heads together and decided that, instead of making you think there is some order where truly none exists, it's best to forget the artificial distinctions and just make things easier for you to look up. The technical term for this is "punting".

Oh. The official documentation says that you can often use Yes, True, On, and 1 interchangeably to mean "yup"; and No, False, Off or 0 to signify "nope." I've found that many settings correctly interpret any of those values, but some do not. To avoid extreme confusion, I've tried to limit my descriptions here to a simple On or Off. If you want to experiment with Yes, True, 1, Da, Affirmative, or whatever, be my guest. But be forewarned that the official docs are wrong in many places: the values are *not* interchangeable in all situations.

Icon's Choice Awards

> Get a life.
>
> — William Shatner, on *Saturday Night Live*

You've probably read a hundred different magazine articles, and more than a few chapters in books, that claim to present the best Windows tuning tips: how to set **WIN.INI** to make your Barfoblaster Supra bypass the bandersnatch and run 3% faster; where to put a line in **SYSTEM.INI** so when your mother-in-law tries to bring up Windows, the monitor starts smoking; how many furbishers to allocate to SmartDrive so it's all it can be.

 As you might have noticed, these chapters are rather. . .large. No, ponderous. There's the word. If the boys and I started listing our favorite **WIN.INI** settings and **SYSTEM.INI** tweaks, you'd still be reading this when Windows 5.0 hit the streets. That's why Igor promised we wouldn't hit you with lists of tips, extolling the virtues of one bunch of settings over another, or expounding on relatively trivial settings at the expense of the more difficult ones.

But both of the boys wanted to point out one very, very special setting — something you're unlikely to have seen before, something you can use every day. Something to make these chapters worth slogging through. It almost came to mutiny. So here goes.

 My favorite is the **TASKMAN.EXE** setting in **SYSTEM.INI**'s **[boot]** section. If you set it to any program — *any* program at all — that program will pop up whenever you double-click on the bare Desktop, or hit **Ctrl+Esc**. It's fast, too. Few Windows programs have the guts to re-map **Ctrl+Esc**, so it's almost always available. Mom thinks I set it to **COLLAGE.EXE**, so I can take screen shots faster. But I really turned it to MS Golf.

 My favorite setting is terribly obscure. It changes the color of the screen that you see when you hit **Ctrl+Alt+Del**. That white-on-blue screen is OK *<yaaawn>*, but if I'm about to reboot my computer I want to be warned, big time. By adding two lines, **MessageBackColor=C** and **MessageTextColor=D**, to the **[386Enh]** section of **SYSTEM.INI**, I'm jolted to attention whenever the three-finger salute is about to kill my machine.

Sections

To know a thing well, know its limits.
Only when pushed beyond its tolerance will true nature be seen.

— Frank Herbert, *Dune*, 1965

Here, in alphabetical order, are the [section]s Windows puts in `WIN.INI`, along with a more or less accurate description of what each [section] controls. Remember that the order of [section]s within `WIN.INI` isn't important, and that capitalization is optional; I've merely duplicated the names precisely as they appear after Windows installs itself.

Section Name	What it affects
[colors]	Controls every color you can imagine, except for Help. When you install Windows, this section is *not* created automatically, so it may be missing on your machine.
[Compatibility]	Fudge bits that help applications maintain compatibility across different versions of Windows.
[Desktop]	Wallpaper, background pattern, what icons look like.
[devices]	A holdover from Windows 2.0. Useless.
[embedding]	Supposed to be the repository for OLE objects. Replaced by the Registration database. Largely useless except as a crude backup.
[Extensions]	Associates file names with applications. For example, **.DOC** files might be associated with WinWord, **.PCX** files with Paintbrush. Overruled by the Registration database.
[fonts]	Lists available TrueType fonts and the location of their associated **.FOT** files. The **.FOT** files, you may recall from Chapter 2, do not contain the font itself, but "resource" information about the font, and something that points to the location of the **.TTF** font file.
[FontSubstitutes]	If Windows can't find a font, it looks here to see if you have a preference for which font should be used to fake it.
[intl]	Time, date, and currency formats, units of measurement (e.g., inches versus cm), language. Supposedly "international" settings, but that's a bit of a stretch.

[mci extensions]	Like **[Extensions]**, except this only deals with audio and video file names. For the multimedia player. Oddly, not superseded by the Registration database.
[Microsoft Word 2.0]	Yeah, you're going to think I'm nuts. But I swear that every time you install a recent copy of Windows, this section is placed in **WIN.INI**, along with the line **HPDESKJET = +1**. That line is a kludge that's necessary to make WinWord's built-in envelope printing routine work on DeskJet printers. We 'cons call this the Justice Department Special 'cuz right here Microsoft used its operating system monopoly to cover up a glitch in one of their applications.
[network]	Network info. I won't go into a whole lot of detail, simply because networking Windows would take a book to itself. Windows does not put this section in **WIN.INI** until you try to hook up a network.
[ports]	Lists parallel ports, serial ports (with baud rate and comm info), and dummy file "ports," which are useful for printing to files.
[PrinterPorts]	Lists available printer drivers, which port (if any) they are attached to, and the time-out values for the port. Windows does not put this section in **WIN.INI** until you connect a printer: it may be missing on your machine.
[programs]	A kludge that helps Windows find applications if you move them and don't update the Registration database like you should. Windows doesn't create this section in **WIN.INI** until you start asking it to run moved apps.
[RegEdit]	The Registration database editor stores inconsequential information here.
[Sounds]	Lists system "events," and the sounds (if any) that go with them.

`[TrueType]`	Controls the use of outline versus bitmap fonts on the screen; also controls how/when/if TrueType fonts are to be used.
`[Windows Help]`	Lets you change colors used by Help. Also tracks location of the Windows Help window. Windows does not put this section in `WIN.INI` until you start using Help.
`[windows]`	Miscellaneous. Stuff that doesn't fit anywhere else.

If you look at your `WIN.INI`, you'll see all sorts of extraneous garbage: every Windows application and its brother sticks stuff in `WIN.INI`. If you're lucky most of that stuff has a [section] name that makes some sense, so at least you can identify the culprits. By and large, though, your `WIN.INI` will get cluttered with the remnants of long-dead and better-dead programs, and the onus is on you to keep it clean.

Cross Reference

Hey, these settings are spread out all over the place. Abbott and Costello could've created a whole new "Who's On First" routine, based solely on `WIN.INI` settings. Anyway, to make your life easier, I've cross-referenced the settings, according to what they effect. If only a few settings in a section are involved, I've listed the settings. If the whole section revolves around a particular topic, I just mention the section.

Cursor
> `[windows]` CursorBlinkRate=, MouseSpeed=, MouseThreshold1=, MouseThreshold2=, MouseTrails=

File Manager
> `[Extensions]`; `[network]` DriveLetter:=; `[programs]`; `[windows]` Documents=, Programs=

Fonts
> `[fonts]`; `[FontSubstitutes]`; `[TrueType]`

Help
> `[Windows Help]`

Icons
> **[Desktop]** IconSpacing=, IconVerticalSpacing=, IconTitleFaceName=, IconTitleSize=, IconTitleStyle=, IconTitleWrap=

Keyboard
> **[windows]** KeyboardDelay=, KeyboardSpeed=

Menus
> **[windows]** MenuDropAlignment=, MenuShowDelay=

Mouse
> **[windows]** DoubleClickHeight=, DoubleClickWidth=, DoubleClickSpeed=, MouseSpeed=, MouseThreshold1=, MouseThreshold2=, MouseTrails=, SwapMouseButtons=

Networks
> **[network]**; **[windows]** NetWarn=

Operation
> **[Extensions]**; **[intl]**; **[programs]**; **[TrueType]** OutlineThreshold=;**[windows]** CoolSwitch= (Fast Alt+Tab Switching), DefaultQueueSize=, DosPrint=, Load=, Run=, NetWarn=, Programs=

Printers, Print Manager
> **[ports]**; **[network]** port:=, port-OPTIONS=; **[windows]** Device=, DeviceNotSelectedTimeout=, DosPrint=, NullPort=, Spooler=, TransmissionRetryTimeout=

Program Manager
> **[Extensions]**; **[programs]**; **[windows]** Load=, Run=, Programs=, IconSpacing=, IconVerticalSpacing=, IconTitleFaceName=, IconTitleSize=, IconTitleStyle=, IconTitleWrap=

Registration database
> **[Extensions]**; **[mci extensions]**; **[programs]**; **[RegEdit]**

Screen
> **[Desktop]** GridGranularity=; Pattern=, TileWallpaper=, Wallpaper=, WallpaperOriginX=, WallpaperOriginY=;**[windows]** BorderWidth=,

ScreenSaveActive=, ScreenSaveTimeout; also see the **scrnsave.exe=** setting in the **[boot]** section of **SYSTEM.INI**.

Sound

> **[windows]** Beep=; **[mci extensions]**; **[Sounds]**

Remember that the following list of [Section]s is arranged alphabetically, and that settings within the sections are alphabetized, too, according to the variable name. You aren't supposed to read this straight through — if you do, I sincerely hope it doesn't put you to sleep.

[colors]

The easiest way to change **[colors]** settings is by using the Color applet in the Control Panel. If you crank it up and click on the Color Palette>> button to reveal its full glory, you'll see the dialog box shown in Figure 8-4.:

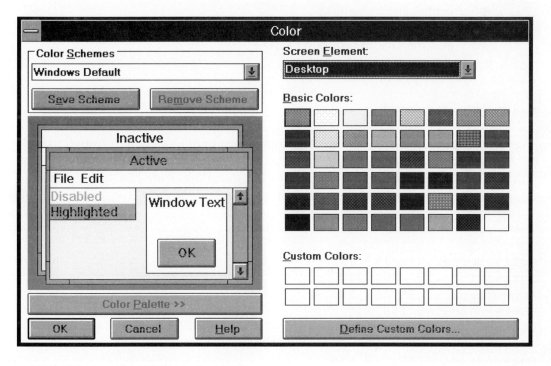

Figure 8-4 Color Command Central

The Color Schemes you see mentioned in the dialog box are just a handy shorthand: they stand in for a whole bunch of individual color settings, identifying them for human consumption with an easy-to-remember name. They're stored in the **[color schemes]** section of **CONTROL.INI**: see the discussion of **CONTROL.INI** in Chapter 10 if you're interested.

Some third-party add-ons (e.g., MakeOver which is discussed in Chapter 5) give you quite a bit of control over colors — far greater control than Windows itself. If you're really into color schemes, be sure you check out the alternatives before spending a whole lot of time with the Windows settings.

The **[colors]** section of **WIN.INI** concerns itself with the Desktop Elements list you can see in the Colors dialog box. It exhaustively lists each thing on the desktop that can have a color, and assigns a color to each of the 21 Desktop Elements.

 The Windows Resource Kit and almost every Windows reference book I've seen only list 20 Desktop Elements. The missing link is the **ButtonHilight=** setting.

Why was the Hilight dropped? Who knows?

Settings in the **[colors]** section look like this:

```
DesktopElement=red green blue
```

where **red**, **green** and **blue** are color intensities, numbers ranging from 0 to 255: a 0 0 0 is black as night; 255 255 255 white. For a more detailed discussion of color numbers, and a far-ranging discussion of color, including some fascinating bugs in the Color applet, be sure to take a look at *Winning on the First Palette* in Chapter 2.

The Windows Default color scheme looks like this:

```
ActiveBorder=192 192 192
ActiveTitle=164 200 240
AppWorkspace=255 251 240
Background=160 160 164
ButtonFace=192 192 192
ButtonHilight=255 255 255
ButtonShadow=128 128 128
ButtonText=0 0 0
```

```
GrayText=192 192 192
Hilight=164 200 240
HilightText=0 0 0
InactiveBorder=192 192 192
InactiveTitle=255 255 255
InactiveTitleText=0 0 0
Menu=255 255 255
MenuText=0 0 0
Scrollbar=192 192 192
TitleText=0 0 0
Window=255 255 255
WindowFrame=0 0 0
WindowText=0 0 0
```

Those names are a bit confusing — much more confusing than they need to be, simply because no care was taken to make them consistent — so let's go through them slowly.

When Windows is running, exactly one window has "focus." To a first approximation, the window that has focus is the one that will receive input if you push a key on the keyboard; it's often the window that's highlighted, visually made different from the other windows.

The **ActiveBorder=**, **ActiveTitle=** and **TitleText=** settings accomplish that highlighting. If the window that has focus is not iconized, its border will be painted with the **ActiveBorder=** color, its title bar up at the top will display in the **ActiveTitle=** color, and the text that appears in the title bar of the window will be painted with the **TitleText=** color. If the window that has focus is reduced to an icon, there is no border or title bar to paint, but the caption beneath the icon will appear in the **TitleText=** color.

Contrariwise, all the windows that do not have focus bear the **InactiveBorder=** color in their borders and **InactiveTitle=** color in their title bars (if they are not iconized), and the **InactiveTitleText=** color for the title (or icon caption) text.

 There are a few little oddities I found: they've confused me in the past; I'm happy to report that Windows is crazy, not me. Some applications, like Program Manager, have windows within their main window — in ProgMan these sub-windows are called "Groups." Usually, whenever one of those sub-windows is active, both it and the main application get the "Active" colors. If a dialog box pops up, though, it gets the "Active" colors, and its owner turns to the "Inactive" colors.

The **ActiveBorder=** and **InactiveBorder=** colors are only used on the borders of *resizable* windows. Fixed-size windows' borders take on the **ActiveTitle=** and **InactiveTitle=** colors. That's pretty strange. Finally, some programs that should know better — including Microsoft's Mouse version 9.0 control program — ignore the border color settings entirely.

The **AppWorkspace=** setting controls the background color in many applications: it's the color you'll see behind a page in a word processor or spreadsheet, say, or underneath the Program Manager's groups, or behind the Control Panel's icons. Generally, it's used for the background color for applications that conform to Microsoft's Multiple Document Interface spec.

The **Background=** setting is for the color of the desktop. If you have both a **Background=** color and a **Pattern=** setting in the **[Desktop]** section of **WIN.INI** — accessible from the Desktop applet in the Control Panel — the **Background=** color is blended with the **WindowText=** color, more or less; see the discussion of **Pattern=** below for an exact description.

If you have both a **Background=** color and a **Wallpaper=** setting in **[Desktop]**, the Wallpaper takes over the desktop: you'll only see the **Background=** color peeking out from behind the caption of minimized icons on the desktop.

The **ButtonFace=, ButtonHilight=, ButtonShadow=,** and **ButtonText=** settings control the color of pushbuttons. See Figure 8-5.

Figure 8-5: Who's Got The Button?

The **ButtonFace=** color is painted on the top of the button; in the above figure it's gray.

The **ButtonHilight=** is the color of the thin line to the top and left of the button; in the above figure it's white. The **ButtonShadow=** number controls the color of the thin line to the right and below the button; in the above figure, it's a dark gray. When you push a button, the **ButtonShadow=** color is painted on the top and left of a button, while the **ButtonHilight=** color disappears.

The **ButtonText=** color is the color of the text on top of the button; above, it's black. Windows uses the solid color closest to the color you've chosen. (See the discussion of **pattern=** under **[Desktop]** for details.)

 That's all pretty much what you would expect, eh? But there are a few quirks lurking; and there's nothing worse than a lurking quirk. For example, the solid line drawn around the button, thin for an unselected button, thicker for a selected one, is drawn in the **WindowFrame=** color. That's not what I would expect.

The **ButtonFace=** color is used for the scrollbar "thumb," the little floating block that moves as you scroll through a scrollbar. It's also used as the background color for the status bar in many places; including the File Manager, the PIF editor, Character Map and Control Panel, for example, but not Windows Write, along with the **ButtonText=** color for text on the status bar. It's even used as the application's background color in the Windows Clock and Multimedia player. Quite a mixed bag.

Various applications pick up on these colors in often surprising ways. EXCEL 4.0 uses the **ButtonFace=** and **ButtonText=** settings for the font selection arrow, but nothing else, not even the status bar. WinWord 2.0 uses the **ButtonFace=** color for the background on the Toolbar, the status bar, and the background and button faces on the Ribbon, but not the button faces on the Toolbar; WinWord also uses the **ButtonText=** color for the Ribbon and the status bar, but nothing else. And on and on.

Bottom line: don't be too surprised if your **Buttonxxx=** settings start knocking colors in your applications completely out of whack, in mysterious and bizarre ways.

The **GrayText=** color controls how to display grayed-out (or "dimmed" or "disabled," if you prefer) options. Grayed-out text can appear in all sorts of places: on menus, lists, radio buttons, check boxes. Windows uses the solid color closest to the color you specify. Surprisingly, **GrayText=** also controls the color on the outermost bottom and right edge of the box around dropped-down menus, 'tho I suspect this is just another attempt to seed difficult Computer Bowl trivia questions into the mainstream Windows community.

The **Hilight=** and **HilightText=** settings only concern Windows internal stuff: they have nothing to do with highlighted text in your documents, spreadsheets, or anything else. In many Windows programs, when you pass the cursor over an item in a menu, or select it with keyboard accelerator keys, say, the text suddenly takes on the **HilightText=** color (more accurately, the solid color closest to that color; see the **pattern=** setting in **[Desktop]** for more information), and the stripe immediately underneath that item takes on the **Hilight=** color. Items in list boxes take on these colors when selected. Empty drop-down list boxes get the **Hilight=** color when they're selected. Files and directories in File Manager do too, as do the boxes around the pictures of selected drives. These colors pop up all over.

The **Menu=** setting controls the color of the menu bar itself and the background in any dropped-down menus. (Except for at most one stripe, behind the currently highlighted menu item, which is in the **Hilight=** color.) The **MenuText=** setting is the color used to display text on the menu bar and in the drop-down menus, except the grayed-out text (which appears in the **GrayText=** color) and at most one currently selected item (which shows up in the **HilightText=** color).

The **Scrollbar=** setting is used to paint the body of the scroll bar itself, not the floating "thumb", or the arrow buttons at the top and bottom. The thumb's color is controlled by the **ButtonFace=** setting. But those up and down arrows are another story: in fact, I haven't found *any* way to change the color of those little hummers.

When you click inside a scrollbar and it takes a while to catch up with you, the part of the scrollbar you clicked turns a different color. I've been trying to figure out what Windows is doing, but it isn't obvious. My guess is that it Windows uses a photographic negative (for lack of a better term) of the **Scrollbar=** setting, i.e., subtracting each of the three color values from 255, for that "wait while I'm trying to catch up" color.

The **Window=** color is the one used as the background inside most applications' windows. For example, it's the color of the paper in a word processor or the color of the sheet in a spreadsheet. Many applications use this color for the background in dialog boxes and list boxes. It's also the background color Program Manager uses insides all of its groups.

The **WindowFrame=** color is the color of the outer line of virtually every element on the screen: buttons, boxes, scroll bars, lists, menus, title bars, you name it.

And `WindowText=` is the color of text inside almost any application you can name. (Actually, once again, Windows uses the solid color closest to the color you've chosen; see the `pattern=` setting under `[Desktop]` for a discussion of solid colors.)

[Compatibility]

This section includes a bunch of kludge bits, designed to help applications cope with changing versions of Windows. When Windows installs itself, it adds more than 20 lines to this section, and other applications may add more lines as they are installed. A typical entry looks like this:

`VB=0x0200`

Windows 3.1 looks at the module names to the left of the equals sign and, based on the hex number to the right of the equals sign, mimics Windows 3.0 behavior in very specific ways, even to the point of replicating bugs in Windows 3.0!

At least in theory, a Windows 3.0-compliant application listed in the `[Compatibility]` section should behave precisely the same way under Windows 3.1 as it did under Windows 3.0.

If you're curious about all the gory details, pick up a copy of *Undocumented Windows* by Andrew Schulman, David Maxey, and Matt Pietrek (Addison-Wesley, 1992). It's a fascinating, if highly technical, read.

Don't touch the `[Compatibility]` section. Let the apps, and Windows, do it themselves.

[Desktop]

This section controls some, but by no means all, of the settings associated with the appearance of your Windows desktop.

`GridGranularity=`_SnapNumber_

Grids are handy little creatures that, properly used, let you position things precisely without going blind. If you are using Program Manager, most Windows windows on your desktop (except, notably, Group windows in Program Manager, and many child windows in other Multiple Document

Interface-compliant programs) can be forced to "snap to" an invisible grid that's superimposed on your desktop. The actual method for establishing the grid and making the windows snap to it are a touch complicated (and previously undocumented, I believe), so let's take a stab at it.

With **GridGranularity=0**, as in Figure 8-6, Windows doesn't snap anything, and permits windows to be resized to any oddball dimensions (in units of one pixel, of course!).

If you set the **GridGranularity=1**, say, the Windows Grid Police hop into action. First, they draw an invisible grid over your desktop, with the horizontal and vertical lines spaced 8 pixels apart (more about that in a minute). Then the GridCops "snap" each resizable window to the grid, by moving the window around so its center falls dead-square on one of the grid points. Finally, whenever you try to re-size a window, the GridCops take over and only let you shrink or grow the window on grid lines, i.e., eight pixels at a time; in addition, whenever you move a window, it's re-sized to conform.

If you set **GridGranularity=2**, the Windows GridCops force everything to align to an imaginary grid with horizontal and vertical lines spaced 16 pixels apart. At **3**, the grid is 24 pixels. And so on, up to **49** — a spacing of 392 pixels — which is, for all intents, utterly useless.

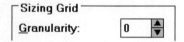

Figure 8-6: Grid Granularity in the Desktop Applet

You can set the **GridGranularity=** by changing the number in the Desktop applet in the Control Panel. If you go into **WIN.INI** and change it manually, though (using a text editor), don't expect your changes to "take" until you restart Windows. Even the Desktop applet will ignore any changes you've made manually.

When Windows installs itself, it puts a **GridGranularity=0** line in your **[Desktop]** section.

Oh. If you're looking for the **BorderWidth=** parameter — the little box that appears directly below the Granularity setting in the Desktop applet? — you're in the wrong place. For some inscrutable reason, that setting is in the **[windows]** section.

IconSpacing=*NumberOfPixels*

IconVerticalSpacing=*NumberOfPixels*

 These settings affect the way PROGMAN moves around the icons on your desktop. Program Manager will attempt to line up your icons in two cases. First, if "Auto Arrange" is checked under the Options menu, Program Manager automatically re-arranges icons whenever PROGMAN is opened up (including at startup), and it re-arranges any icon as soon as you move it. Second, if you click on "Arrange Icons" under the Window menu, PROGMAN will re-arrange all icons in the currently active group (unless it's minimized) or, if the selected group is minimized , PROGMAN re-arranges all the minimized group file folder icons.

Windows itself also uses these settings whenever you minimize a program on your desktop. The spacing is used to figure out where to put the icon for the program you've just minimized: there's no "auto arrange" for Windows in general. Finally, truly MDI (Multiple Document Interface) compliant programs will use this spacing for displaying icon-size documents within the parent application — iconized spreadsheets within EXCEL, for example.

The method for placing the icons is a touch complex. Like the GridGranularity setting discussed above, Windows constructs an invisible grid, calculates which grid points have been occupied (even if there's no icon precisely positioned on the grid point), then attaches the middle of the icon being re-arranged to one of the grid points. The precise definition of "middle" is hard to pin down, but Windows seems to take into account the size of the icon's caption. Demonstrably, the algorithm Windows uses isn't perfect (overlapping icon captions look terrible!), but all in all it isn't bad.

Windows sets up the grid lines with side-to-side spacing ("horizontal" spacing) based on the **IconSpacing=** value, in pixels. If there is no such setting, Windows uses a value of 75 pixels. Windows sets up the top-to-bottom spacing ("vertical" spacing) based on the **IconVerticalSpacing=** value, in pixels. If there is no such line in **[Desktop]**, Windows uses some weird formula that I never could figure out — based (as best I can tell) on the size of the caption's font — that more-or-less allows for three lines of caption.

IconSpacing= can be set at any value between 32 (too scrunched together to be of much use and 512 (way too far apart). The easiest way to set the **IconSpacing=** setting is in the Control Panel's Desktop applet (see Figure 8-7). The value sits down near the bottom on the right-hand side.

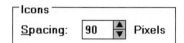

Figure 8-7: Spaced Icons

On the contrary, the only way to change **IconVerticalSpacing=** is to jimmy open **WIN.INI** itself and do it manually. Chances are good you won't find a line in there; you'll have to add a new one yourself. If you change the settings manually, you'll have to restart Windows for them to take effect: even Desktop ignores manual changes.

 These settings would be a whole lot more useful if there were separate numbers for Program Manager (where you might want to crank the setting way down and strip off icon captions, to create an Icon Box effect), the Windows desktop itself (where you usually want to expand the spacing because so many applications include a loooooooong file name in the caption), and the MDI windows (where, for various reasons, you may want icons packed more densely or more sparsely than in either Progman or the Windows desktop).

Personally, I set IconSpacing=90 (see Figure 8-8). That's a lousy compromise between Progman, where the icons should be packed closer together, so I could get more on-screen, and Windows, where the icon captions (particularly with applications like WinWord that insist on displaying a file name with the full path in front of it) still bang into each other.

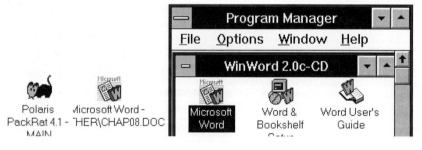

Figure 8-8: IconSpacing=90 at 1024 x 768

See how a setting of **90** is too close together for the icons on the left, the ones on the Windows desktop? Their captions clobber each other. But it's just fine for the icons on the right, the ones in Program Manager. That's the kind of compromise you face.

You'll see many WinGuri recommend that you monkey with this setting, turning it down to get more icons into Progman. Go ahead and try, if you like. But make sure you take a look at the spacing on the Windows desktop, and in MDI compliant applications like SYSEDIT, before you commit yourself to a lifetime of overstruck captions. Progman isn't the only player in this game.

 When you install a fresh copy of Windows, `IconSpacing=` and `IconVerticalSpacing=` lines are not inserted in your `[Desktop]` section. And, in spite of what you may read in the official (and all the unofficial) documentation, if there is no `IconSpacing=` line in your `[Desktop]` section, Windows uses a value of 75 — *not* 77.

`IconTitleFaceName=`*FontName*

`IconTitleSize=`*PointSize*

`IconTitleStyle=`*1forBold*

 Font Snobs of the World Unite! Stand up and take notice, folks. You have nothing to lose but your descenders. . . This is one of very, very few places in the entire Microsoft universe where you'll find a mention of "Face" (as in "Typeface"), as opposed to the ubiquitous and inaccurately applied term "Font." Somebody, somewhere, sitting in a cubicle in Redmond, is still chortling at the way they slipped `IconTitleFaceName` past the design review teams. Bravo, bravo! Author! Author!

Hey, lay off the font snobs. Some of my best friends are font snobs, and I won't have their name maligned. Besides, they're usually typeface snobs. Call a spade a spade, Mao. When's the last time you heard a snob declaring the obvious superiority of ITC Cheltenham Light Condensed Italic 8 point? Sheeeesh. ITC Cheltenham Light Condensed Roman, maybe. But that's a typeface, not a font. See the difference?

These three settings control the appearance of icon captions. Strangely, the `IconTitleFaceName` is used by Print Manager to list available printers and pending print jobs, down in the body of Print Manager's dialog box, but the `IconTitleSize` setting is not. The three settings don't control the font used for menus, the font inside File Manager, or anything else, far as I can tell.

You have to watch out for some renegade video drivers: you may make changes using the driver — say, switching from "large" (so-called "8514") fonts to "small" (so-called "VGA") fonts — and discover that the video driver changed the `IconTitleFaceName=` setting.

Windows straight out of the can doesn't place any of these three lines in `[Desktop]`.

The `IconTitleFaceName=`, as you might expect, is the name of the font that you want Windows to use for icon captions. Whatever name you pick should be on the left side of an equals sign in the `[fonts]` section of **WIN.INI**. The name has to be spelled precisely as it appears in `[fonts]`. If there is no value specified, or if the line is missing, Windows assumes

`IconTitleFaceName=MS Sans Serif`

`IconTitleSize=` picks the point size for icon captions. If there is no value given or if the line is missing, Windows chooses **8** points, except for **Small Fonts**, which seems to set itself at 7 points.

You should use **IconTitleStyle=1** if you want the captions to appear in bold; anything else and they'll be "normal," i.e., not bold. For some reason, `IconTitleStyle=` isn't even mentioned in the official documentation.

To change any of these settings, you'll have to go into **WIN.INI** and edit it manually.

While you can use any TrueType font for icon captions, you probably won't like TrueType fonts as much as the hand-tuned bitmap fonts that ship with Windows — sometimes the TrueType fonts don't look as good on the screen; and they're always slower to redraw. The custom crafted fonts you might want to consider for icon captions are these:

`MS Sans Serif` in 8, 10, 12, 14, 18, and 24 point

`MS Serif` in 8, 10, 12, 14, 18, and 24 point

`Courier` in 10, 12, and 15 point

`Small Fonts` in 7 point and smaller

 Go ahead and try several combinations. There's no one "right" or "best" setting; it all hinges on what your monitor can handle and what is pleasing to your eyes. I, personally, prefer the default: `MS Sans Serif`, 8 point.

`Small Fonts` (Figure 8-9) is a good alternative, but only if you can stand what it does to Print Manager — or, better, if you don't use Print Manager at all. Ever. This is one font that goes to pieces at 10 point; since you can't change the size of the font used in Print Manager (which has all the hallmarks of a first-class bug), you're totally SOL.

 Stuff and nonsense about not using TrueType for IconTitles. On a fast machine, the speed penalty is so small I defy you to notice it. And so long as you use a bold face font, they look really very good. I use `IconTitleFaceName= Bookman Old Style` and `IconTitleStyle=1` and really like it. Bookman Old Style is a font in the Microsoft Font Pack One and the Monotype True Type Font Pack.

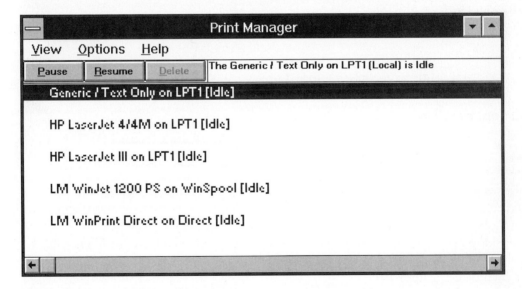

Figure 8-9: Small Fonts Go Boom

You can also change the font Windows uses for window titles and menus. See **SystemFont=** in the **[Windows]** section.

IconTitleWrap=*0ForNo*

This setting controls whether Windows will try to break up icon captions, fitting long captions onto two or (at most) three lines. The break always occurs at a space; thus, if the caption contains no spaces, it won't be broken up, no way, no how. (You can see several examples of icon caption wrapping in the earlier discussion of **IconSpacing=**.)

If you give this setting a value of **0**, Windows turns off icon caption wrapping. Anything else turns it on; and if the line is missing entirely, caption wrapping is assumed to be on. When you install Windows, it doesn't put an **IconTitleWrap=** line in **[Desktop]**, so unless you change something, Windows will always wrap icon captions. Which is as it should be.

 The official documentation (and all the unofficial documentation I can find) says turning caption wrapping on adds to the **IconVerticalSpacing=**, enough to allow three lines of caption. That's crap. Automatic top-to-bottom spacing of icons is not affected in any way by the **IconTitleWrap=** setting.

Try it. You'll see.

IconVerticalSpacing=*NumberOfPixels*

See **IconSpacing=**.

Pattern=*n1 n2 n3 n4 n5 n6 n7 n8*

Windows lets you pick a background pattern, a bit of fabric that underlies everything on the Windows desktop. This is the setting that controls the pattern, an array 8 pixels tall by 8 pixels wide, which is duplicated all over the screen. Using the Desktop applet in the Control Panel, you may either select one of Microsoft's built-in patterns, or by clicking on the Edit Pattern button, you can build one of your own (see Figure 8-10).

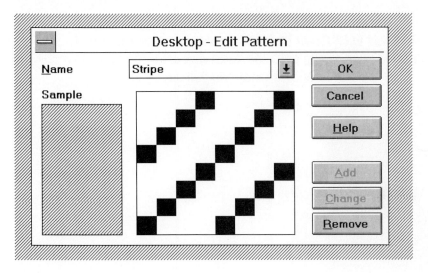

Figure 8-10: Custom Pinstripes

If you're familiar with binary notation, it won't surprise you to find that this
particular custom pattern is stored away as shown in Figure 8-11.

```
0  0  0  1  0  0  0  1
0  0  1  0  0  0  1  0
0  1  0  0  0  1  0  0
1  0  0  0  1  0  0  0
0  0  0  1  0  0  0  1
0  0  1  0  0  0  1  0
0  1  0  0  0  1  0  0
1  0  0  0  1  0  0  0
```

Figure 8-11: Pinstripe Bit Pattern

Windows builds the pattern by interspersing pixels of two different colors. Both of
the colors come from the **[colors]** section of **WIN.INI**; most users set them with
the Colors applet in the Control Panel. According to the official documentation, the
spots represented by 0s get the **Background=** color; and the spots with 1s get the
WindowText= color.

 Alas, that isn't quite true. In fact, if you have a **Pattern=**, Windows uses
the solid color closest to the **Background=** and **WindowText=** colors (if
you have no pattern, Windows dithers). There's an extensive discussion
of dithering and solid colors in Chapter 2, but if you want to grab a quick

peek at the solid color closest to your `Background=` color, say, fire up the Colors applet in the Control Panel, click Color Palette>, make sure the Desktop is selected (that's what the Color applet calls the `Background=` setting), then click Define Custom Colors. Figure 8-12 shows what you will see.

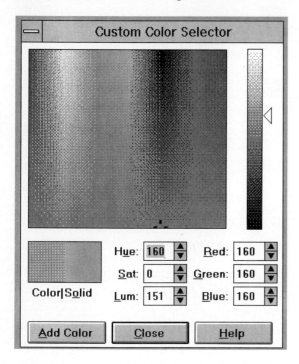

Figure 8-12: The Solid Color

See the Color | Solid picture in the lower left corner? That's where you'll be able to find the solid color closest to your chosen `Background=` color. I think the closest color is calculated by selecting the smallest distance in RGB color space (i.e., by summing the squares of the differences in the red, green and blue color numbers), at least that's how *I* would do it, but none of this appears to be documented anywhere, so it's anybody's guess.

If you've ever wondered how to change the desktop pattern's color, well, now you know the rest of the story.

In general, the `Pattern=` setting consists of eight numbers, each of which corresponds to one line, one row, in the bit pattern. Here's the weird part: the numbers in the `Pattern=` setting are the decimal representation of each line in the bit pattern, interpreted in binary!

If you're rusty on binary, not to worry. Since we're working with 8-bit numbers, the first bit is worth 128, the second 64, third 32, fourth 16, fifth 8, sixth 4, seventh 2, and eighth 1. Tally off the 1s and total the result. In the Stripe pattern shown above, for example, the first line reads 00010001. That's 0 + 0 + 0 + 16 + 0 + 0 + 0 + 1, or a total of 17. The fourth line is 10001000, or 128 + 0 + 0 + 0 + 8 + 0 + 0 + 0, or a total of 136.

Calculate the other lines (you won't even need to take off your shoes) and you'll see why the Stripe pattern is represented this way in **[Desktop]**:

`Pattern=17 34 68 136 17 34 68 136`

Don't get confused. Names of patterns, the things you can select when you click on the Name part of the Desktop applet's dialog box, are stored away in `CONTROL.INI`. They don't appear anywhere in `WIN.INI`.

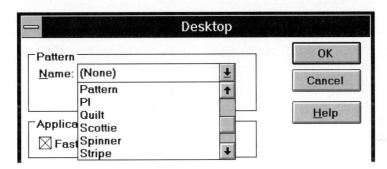

Figure 8-13: Pattern Choices in the Desktop Applet

When you choose a name from the Desktop applet this way, Windows looks up the set of eight bit pattern numbers stored (see Figure 8-13) with the name in **CONTROL.INI**, and alters the **Pattern=** line to reflect those new numbers. The **Pattern=** setting takes only eight numbers at a crack, not names. Except. . . except. . .

. . . except *no pattern at all* is represented by a line in the **[Desktop]** section that looks like this:

Pattern=(None)

which just happens to be the line Windows puts in **[Desktop]** when it's installed. Because of the difference between solid colors and dithering, **Pattern=(None)** which uses the possible dithered Background Color is different from **Pattern=0 0 0 0 0 0 0 0** which uses the solid color closest to the Background Color. Got that? Good.

TileWallpaper=*1ForYes*

Wallpaper=*File*

WallpaperOriginX=*Pixels*

WallpaperOriginY=*Pixels*

Once Windows has covered the screen with whatever tiny 8 by 8 pixel pattern is stored in **Pattern=**, it then looks to see if you have chosen to display wallpaper. The wallpaper is placed on top of the pattern according to the dictates of the **TileWallpaper=**, **WallpaperOriginX=** and **WallpaperOriginY=** settings.

 Oddly, any icons subsequently placed on top of the Windows wallpaper let the pattern "leak through" the wallpaper, at points immediately surrounding the icons' captions. There's probably some excuse for this kind of behavior, but it sure feels like a bug to me — let the background color show through, sure; but why cram the pattern into such a little space?

Figure 8-14 shows an actual screen shot, showing how the "Diamonds" pattern leaks through the "Egypt" wallpaper, in two icons' caption areas. The net result can be very confusing. Combine wallpaper and patterns with caution.

Figure 8-14: Diamonds in Egypt

Personally, I avoid using a pattern and wallpaper, simply because of the performance hit. Windows spends too bloody much of its time drawing and re-drawing and re-re-drawing those fancy pictures; every time you turn around, Windows is off in a corner slapping pretty picture pixels on the screen. Mao can't wake up in the morning without his Yoda wallpaper, though, so I guess you gotta make some allowances.

You can use any bitmap (`.BMP`) or run-length encoded (`.RLE`) file as wallpaper. When you pop open the Desktop applet in the Control Panel, you'll be presented with a drop-down box containing entries for all `.BMP` files in the Windows and Windows system directory (e.g., `C:\WINDOWS` and `C:\WINDOWS\SYSTEM`), although none of the `.RLE` files — not even the Windows 3.1 logo file, `VGALOGO.RLE` — will be listed.

You can pick one of the files in the list, or just go ahead and type in the file name (with full path information!) of any `.BMP` or `.RLE` file on your disk. Equivalently, you can edit `WIN.INI` with a text editor, and change the setting manually (see Figure 8-15).

`Wallpaper=256color.bmp`

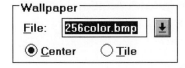

Figure 8-15: Desktop Applet's Wallpaper Setting

When Windows installs itself, it adds a `Wallpaper=(None)` line to `[Desktop]`.

This is a real underachiever of a setting. Yes, you can use `.RLE` files as wallpaper, although that fact doesn't appear anywhere in the official documentation, and the names of `.RLE` files never appear in the drop-down box choices. No, the Desktop applet isn't smart enough to give you a Browse button, a *stunning* underachievement. Yes, you must type in the extension: `256color.bmp` is okay, but `256color` doesn't make it. And, in spite of what the official documentation says, Windows uses the normal file-searching rigmarole: if you don't put the full path on the file name, it looks first in the

Windows directory, then in the Windows System Directory, and then it follows the DOS path. Far as I know, that's never been documented before. Amazing, eh?

The **TileWallpaper=** setting corresponds to the Center/Tile radio buttons in the Desktop applet. A value of **1** (i.e., the "Tile" button selected) makes Windows fill the entire desktop with rubber-stamped copies of the wallpaper. Any other value (or if the line is missing entirely) forces Windows to put one single copy of the wallpaper file on the screen.

When Windows installs itself, it does not put a **TileWallpaper=** line in **[Desktop]**. Thus, you'll get "Centered" wallpaper unless you change things.

The location of the wallpaper is controlled by the **WallpaperOriginX=** and **WallpaperOriginY=** settings, neither of which appear in the official documentation.

For "Centered" wallpaper (see Figure 8-16a), **WallpaperOriginX=** is the distance, in pixels, from the left edge of the desktop to the left edge of the wallpaper; **WallpaperOriginY=** is the distance from the top of the desktop to the top edge of the wallpaper.

When the "Tiled" option is selected (see Figure 8-16b), Windows positions one copy of the wallpaper at the **WallpaperOriginX=** and **WallpaperOriginY=** coordinates, then fills in the rest of the screen.

Figure 8-16a: Egypt Centered

Figure 8-16b: Egypt Tiled

Negative values are treated as zero. Missing entries are treated differently, depending on the **TileWallpaper=** setting. For "Centered" wallpaper, a missing coordinate is calculated so the wallpaper is, indeed, centered: if neither **WallpaperOriginX=** nor **WallpaperOriginY=** lines appear in **[Desktop]**, the wallpaper pops up in the middle of the screen. For "Tiled" wallpaper, missing coordinates are treated as zero.

Windows fresh out of the package does not place `WallpaperOriginX=` or `WallpaperOriginY=` lines in `[Desktop]`. Worse, there's no easy way to change either setting. If you want to change 'em, you have to go into `WIN.INI` with a text editor and do it manually.

Watch out if you start editing `WIN.INI` manually. Your changes generally won't "take" until you re-start Windows. And for some reason the Desktop applet sometimes picks up the wrong settings, refusing to re-read `WIN.INI` every time it's launched.

[devices]

> Seek an understanding of faith. It will do you good.
>
> — Rory Nugent, *The Search for the Pink-Headed Duck*, 1990

This section is a throwback to Windows 2.0: if you're working with ancient programs, you might possibly hit one that needs to look up something in `[devices]`. At least in theory, the entries in this section should match those in `[PrinterPorts]` precisely, without the final two values, the timeouts. Look at `[PrinterPorts]` for details.

Yes, you may have more than one port associated with a printer, e.g.,

```
Generic / Text Only=TTY,FILE:,LPT3:
```

but whether any old Windows 2.0 apps will pick up on the subtlety is anybody's guess.

Use the Control Panel's Printer applet to update your printer connections, and you'll never have to worry about this section: the Printer applet automatically maintains it as a mirror image of **[PrinterPorts]**.

Anyway, if you're playing with apps that date back before Windows 3.0, you're going to need a lot more help than **[devices]** can render. Forget about it.

[embedding]

This section should've been called "[dead as a dodo]."

Many Windows applications can embed OLE "objects": put a Paintbrush picture in a WordPerfect document, say, or stick a `.WAV` audio file in an EXCEL spreadsheet. That's plain-vanilla OLE, and most Windows apps are smart enough to use it. Once upon a time, this section was used to list all the things, all the objects, that could be stuffed into other applications.

I hate to use the word "object" because it has acquired so many meanings in so many different contexts, but it has become the standard terminology. Though Microsoft marketing types might argue differently, these OLE "objects" have essentially nothing in common with what most computer jocks identify as "objects" or "object oriented".

Paintbrush puts an entry in here, as did the sound recorder. But as Windows grew more sentient, it became apparent that this kind of information needed a home of its own. Such was the genesis of the Registration database. And, as the Registration database came in and took over, the importance — indeed the very use — of the **[embedding]** and **[Extensions]** sections waned.

When Windows installs itself, it sticks three lines in **[embedding]**:

```
SoundRec=Sound,Sound,SoundRec.exe,picture
Package=Package,Package,packager.exe,picture
PBrush=Paintbrush Picture,Paintbrush Picture,pbrush.exe,picture
```

The name on the left side of the equals sign is used internally by Windows to keep track of all the different objects. Windows applications may refer to this as the Object Class Name. The first entry to the right of the equals sign is often picked up by Windows applications as a short description of the object; it's usually what you'll see in a dialog box, when you try to insert an object in a Windows application. The second entry is a longer version of the first; the official documentation says that this is the name used by the Registration database editor. (In practice, the first and second values to the right of the equal sign are almost always identical.) The next entry points to the program that does the work; the one that controls the embedable object. And the final entry is supposed to give the data type of the embedded object: **picture** being the most common, signifying a Windows metafile. In practice, we couldn't find anything but **picture**s: even the sound recorder embeds a **picture**. Go figger.

In spite of what you read in the official documentation (and all its derivatives), the [embedding] section of WIN.INI is used in exactly two ways. First, some old applications (usually Windows 3.0 apps) may take a look in this section for information about embedable objects. "Old" is relative, of course. Word for Windows 2.0 and 2.0a, for example, apparently looked in this section. Word for Windows 2.0b and all subsequent versions got smart enough to deal directly with the Registration database; they don't even look at the [embedding] section; couldn't care less whether it exists or not, whether it conflicts with the Registration database or not.

Second, Windows may use this section to construct a minimal Registration database if the real one gets screwed up. Every time you start Windows, it looks to see if the database — a file called **REG.DAT** — is alive and well. If the file is missing or clobbered somehow, Windows scans the entries in **[embedding]** and uses them to create a new **REG.DAT**. The **[embedding]** entries have only a small part of all the information normally stored in **REG.DAT**, but it's the best Windows can do.

Once Windows has found or created **REG.DAT**, it holds onto its copy, feeding settings to any application that asks. Changing **REG.DAT** via the **RegEdit** program will update that copy, but not much else does. So, for example, if you start up Windows and immediately delete **REG.DAT**, any Windows application that relies on **REG.DAT** for data will get the data it seeks: Windows provides the data from the copy of **REG.DAT** still stored in memory.

[Extensions]

 This section, largely a throwback to earlier versions, helps Windows keep track of which file name extension is associated with which application. This is where you can log the fact that .WRI files are Windows Write files, .CALs are Calendars, .HLP files are for Windows Help, and so on.

Associating file name extensions with programs is important. It helps all of us work faster: by double-clicking on an appropriately pegged file in File Manager, the associated program springs to life, with the file loaded and ready for bear. In Program Manger, you can click on File, then Run, type in the name of a file and, if it has an associated extension, get the right program running with the file started. Inside Program Manager, you can create an icon with a file name in place of the usual command line; if the extension is properly logged, Progman is smart enough to find the right program and get it going. All in all, association is a great idea. It's just that **[Extensions]** isn't the best place to put an association.

The Registration Database (see Chapter 3), Windows' repository of application specific information, has largely taken over the function of the **[Extensions]** section. If there is a conflict between the info stored in the Registration Database and the info stored in the **[Extensions]** section of **WIN.INI**, [Extensions] is simply and unceremoniously ignored.

When Windows installs itself, it creates a simple **[Extensions]** section that logs the file names used by the standard Windows apps. It looks like this:

```
[Extensions]
cal=calendar.exe ^.cal
crd=cardfile.exe ^.crd
trm=terminal.exe ^.trm
txt=notepad.exe ^.txt
ini=notepad.exe ^.ini
pcx=pbrush.exe ^.pcx
bmp=pbrush.exe ^.bmp
wri=write.exe ^.wri
rec=recorder.exe ^.rec
hlp=winhelp.exe ^.hlp
```

The first entry there tells File Manager, simply, that if you double-click on a file with a name that ends in **.CAL**, you want File Manager to launch the program **CALENDAR.EXE**, which happens to be the Windows Calendar applet, with the selected file loaded. (The caret in **^.CAL** jazz means "take the original file name, strip off the extension, and put it where the caret is.")

Compared to the Registration Database, which includes automatic printing and Dynamic Data Exchange and OLE information, that's pretty ho-hum stuff.

While you can change the **[Extensions]** section manually, using a text editor, you should work through File Manager's File/Associate menu item: File Associate (Figure 8-17) changes both the Registration Database and the **[Extensions]** section, simultaneously, so it'll keep you from shooting yourself in the foot.

```
┌─────────────────────────────────────────────────────────┐
│ ─                    Associate                            │
├───────────────────────────────────────────────┬─────────┤
│  Files with Extension:    │ doc     │          │   OK    │
│  Associate With:                                         │
│  ┌────────────────────────────────────────┐   ┌─────────┐│
│  │ Word Document                          │   │ Cancel  ││
│  │ Sound Finder (C:\UTILITY\SNDSYS\SNDFIN ↑│            │
│  │ Terminal Settings (terminal.exe)        │  ┌─────────┐│
│  │ Text File (notepad.exe)                 │  │ Browse..││
│  │ Word Document (C:\WINWORD\winword.exe)  │  ┌─────────┐│
│  │ Write Document (write.exe)            ↓ │  │  Help   ││
│  └────────────────────────────────────────┘            │
└─────────────────────────────────────────────────────────┘
```

Figure 8-17: Guilt By Association

From inside File Manager, simply select a file with the extension you want to log —
say, **CONTROL.INF** in your Windows system directory — click on File, then
Associate, scroll down to "Text File (notepad.exe)" and click on it, then click OK.
Next time you double-click on **CONTROL.INF** (or any other file name that ends in
.INF), File Manager will crank up Notepad, with your chosen file ready to roll.

You can associate an extension with just about anything that Windows can run:
.EXE or **.COM** files, of course — even dumb DOS programs — but also **.PIF** and
.BAT files.

Any file name extension that appears in the **[Extensions]** section is
automatically considered to be a "document", at least to File Manager. Take a look
at the **Documents=** setting in the **[windows]** section and the **[programs]**
section, both later in this chapter, for a thorough discussion. *(Yawn!)*

Psssst. Want to see what's really going on when you associate stuff? Go
into Program Manager, click on File then Run, and type in **REGEDIT /V**.
That runs the Registration Database program with all its internals
exposed. Great stuff. Just don't muck with it without reading the nostrums
in Chapter 4, unless you would like to become accustomed to tongue-tied
applications and monstrous crashes at unexpected times.

All is not sweetness and light in the realm of registration. I've hit some problems
trying to register an extension that already exists in the **[Extensions]** section. In
particular, TaxCut 92 puts this entry in **[Extensions]**:

```
T92=d:\taxcut\tcwin.exe -f^ -d^.T92
```

In File Manager, if I click once on a `.T92` file and try to associate it with Taxcut, I trigger an inscrutable error: apparently RegEdit (via File Manager) has trouble associating a complicated multi-switch run line with an extension. I'm not sure exactly what is causing the problem, but it sure smells like a bug.

[fonts]

 If you're thinking of messing around with the `[fonts]` section, stop right now and read the extensive discussions of fonts in Chapters 2 and 3. It's a very complex topic; as you'll see, making untoward changes in this section can really throw things off.

Now that the caveat is out of the way, there are two things you need to know about the `[fonts]` section. First, if you don't know what you're doing, don't touch the section's entries; use the Fonts applet in the Control Panel to add and remove fonts. Second, if you *do* know what you're doing, ask yourself this: *are you sure?* Adding directory information to a `.FOT` file entry is pretty straightforward. But major surgery is. . . major surgery.

All right. You're forewarned. You've read the other chapters, so you know that a `.FOT` file is a TrueType font resource file, little more than a tiny pointer file created by Windows when you install a "real" TrueType `.TTF` file; and you know that a `.FON` file is a bitmapped or vector file; and you know the difference between a `.FOT` and a `.FON`, right?

Okay.

The Fonts applet pops up like Figure 8-18.

Clicking on the Add button lets you pick out a directory. Windows scans the directory for fonts files, and lets you pick which fonts you want to install. Clicking on any single font's name, then clicking on Remove will remove the font from the `[fonts]` section, and optionally wipe the font file off the disk. Clicking on TrueType brings up options that go into **WIN.INI**'s **[TrueType]** section. I'll talk about them later.

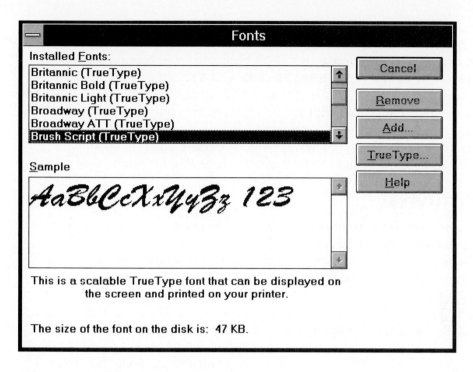

Figure 8-18: Why Brush My Script

The entry in the **[fonts]** section of **WIN.INI** that corresponds to the Brush Script font in the figure looks like this:

```
Brush Script (TrueType)=BS_____.FOT
```

The text to the left of the equals sign describes the font. That precise text is used in the Fonts applet, and (often with the "(TrueType)" stripped) in most Windows applications.

The file name to the right of the equals sign points to the location of the **.FOT** or **.FON** file associated with that description. In spite of what all the official and unofficial documentation says, Windows uses the usual file searching routine to find the file: if you don't have a full path typed in, Windows first looks at your Windows directory, then your Windows system directory, and finally along your DOS path.

When Windows installs itself you get a pot full of TrueType fonts: Arial, Courier New, Times New Roman, WingDings, and Symbol. You'll also get a handful of virtually useless plotter fonts: Roman, Script, and Modern.

In addition you'll get several nice hand-tuned fixed pitch fonts: MS Sans Serif, Courier, MS Serif, and another Symbol. If you installed onto a VGA system, those fonts will be marked (VGA res), and the **.FON** file names will contain the letter **E**, i.e., **SSERIFE.FON**, **COURE.FON**, **SERIFE.FON** and **SYMBOLE.FON**, respectively. If you installed onto a Super VGA system, they'll be marked (8514/a res) and all the **E**s in the file names are replaced with **F**s. If you were unfortunate enough to install an EGA system, they're marked (EGA res) and the **E**s are replaced with **B**s, but you probably won't be able to see 'em anyway: if you've spent any time at all with Windows at EGA, your eyes ought to be ready for recycling by now.

[FontSubstitutes]

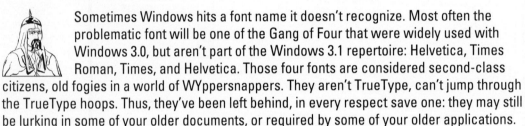 Sometimes Windows hits a font name it doesn't recognize. Most often the problematic font will be one of the Gang of Four that were widely used with Windows 3.0, but aren't part of the Windows 3.1 repertoire: Helvetica, Times Roman, Times, and Helvetica. Those four fonts are considered second-class citizens, old fogies in a world of WYppersnappers. They aren't TrueType, can't jump through the TrueType hoops. Thus, they've been left behind, in every respect save one: they may still be lurking in some of your older documents, or required by some of your older applications.

When Windows encounters a font name that it can't identify; a name that isn't in the **[fonts]** section, a name that some other rasterizing program like Adobe Type Manager won't lay claim to, it has no choice but to punt. This is where you teach Windows *how* to punt.

Entries in this section look like this:

MissingFontName=TheFontWindowsShouldUse

where the font on the left side of the equals sign is one that you think Windows might come looking for, and the font on the right side of the equals sign is the one you want Windows to use, should it come looking.

When Windows installs itself, it puts four lines in the **[FontSubstitutes]** section:

```
Helv=MS Sans Serif
Tms Rmn=MS Serif
Times=Times New Roman
Helvetica=Arial
```

Not surprisingly, these lines tell Windows how to punt if it should encounter those four common Windows 3.0 fonts. The fonts on the right side of the equals signs are all installed by Windows 3.1, so they're pretty much guaranteed to be around.

There are a couple of lines you might want to put in **[FontSubstitutes]**, now while you're thinking about it. Try these:

```
Courier=Courier New
MT Symbol=Symbol
```

The first line traps old references to the Courier font and re-routes them to Courier New. You might not have the Courier font installed on your computer, but everybody gets Courier New. The second line tells Windows how to punt if it comes looking for the MT Symbol font. The MT Symbol font was distributed during the Windows 3.1 beta test; by the time the final product hit the stands, this font was re-incarnated as plain ol' Symbol. Some applications (and documents) created during the Windows 3.1 beta still look for MT Symbol.

Remember, it never hurts to put a line in **[FontSubstitutes]**. Windows only goes looking here if it can't find a font.

[intl]

All of these settings are related to the International applet in the Control Panel (see Figure 8-19). Many of these settings stretch the idea of "international" beyond the breaking point, so don't take the section's title too seriously. (Sorry, but the format of dates and times has little to do with anything "international," in spite of what Microsoft might think. . . though the choice of *calendars,* which Windows can't handle, might be.)

All of the settings are prefixed with either an "i" or an "s," the former representing integer values, the latter text strings. You'll see how that works in a second.

Those of you of the programming persuasion may be astonished to see some vestige of Hungarian Notation (where the first few letters of a variable's name describe its format) here in `.INI` land. Relish it while you can, Simonyiites: here in the real world there are precious few places where prefixes rule.

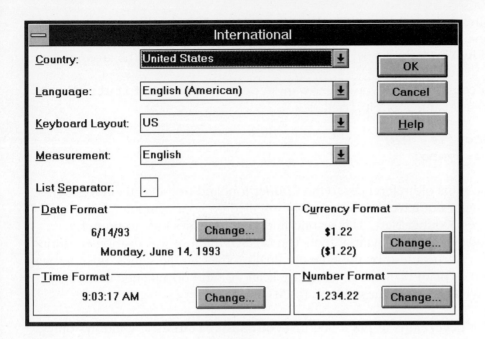

Figure 8-19: It's A Small World, After All

When alphabetizing things here in this section, I'll drop the "i" and "s", so like settings will appear together.

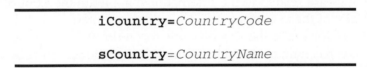

iCountry=*CountryCode*

sCountry=*CountryName*

 The **iCountry=** setting is supposed to nail down the resident country of the person using Windows. The **sCountry=** setting is supposed to be a text string naming that country. In practice, these settings are usually established when Windows is installed, and rarely intentionally changed.

Don't read too much into the settings. For example, just because the **[intl]** section of **WIN.INI** has **iCountry=49** (the country code for Germany), it does *not* necessarily follow that the user is running the German version of Windows: menus may not be in the German language; the keyboard may not be the German version; and on and on.

In spite of what all the official and unofficial documentation may say, the mother lode list of country codes is not in `WININI.WRI` or `CONTROL.INI`. Instead, it's in a little-known file called `CONTROL.INF` (note the `F`). With a little bit of massaging, this is what you'll find there:

sCountry	iCountry	sLanguage	Language
Australia	61	ENG	"International" English
Austria	43	DEU	German
Belgium (Dutch)	32	NLD	Dutch
Belgium (French)	32	FRA	French
Brazil	55	PTG	Portuguese
Canada (English)	2	ENG	"International" English
Canada (French)	2	FRC	Canadian French
Denmark	45	DAN	Danish
Finland	358	FIN	Finnish
France	33	FRA	French
Germany	49	DEU	German
Iceland	354	ISL	Icelandic
Ireland	353	ENG	"International" English
Italy	39	ITA	Italian
Mexico	52	ESP	Spanish
Netherlands	31	NLD	Dutch
New Zealand	64	ENG	"International" English
Norway	47	NOR	Norwegian
Portugal	351	PTG	Portuguese
South Korea	82	KOR	Korean
Spain	34	ESP	Spanish
Sweden	46	SVE	Swedish
Switzerland (French)	41	FRA	French
Switzerland (German)	41	DEU	German
Switzerland (Italian)	41	ITA	Italian
Taiwan	886	ENG	"International" English
United Kingdom	44	ENG	"International" English
United States	1	ENU	U.S. English
Other Country	1	ENU	U.S. English

In the normal course of things, a Windows user will crank up the International applet and pick out a Country (corresponding to **sCountry=**) from the proffered list. As soon as a Country is chosen, Windows fills in all the other entries in the dialog box with reasonable guesses, based solely on the Country. Some of those additional entries are relatively obvious: for example, the currency format is often (but not always) straightforward. Others, though, such as the choice of a date and time format, can't be taken so lightly.

If you click OK in the International dialog bog, the **iCountry=** code will be changed to match the chosen country text string. The only other way to change the **iCountry=** is to go into **WIN.INI** with a text editor and do it yourself.

You cannot type a country name into the International dialog box: you must choose a country from the established list. If you go into **WIN.INI** and change the **sCountry=** entry manually, and your choice does not conform to the precise spelling of one of the countries in **CONTROL.INF**, the International applet will interpret your choice as "Other Country".

---

iCurrDigits=*NumberOfFractionalDigits*

iCurrency=*CurrencySymbolPositionCode*

sCurrency=*CurrencySymbol*

iNegCurr=*NegativeCurrencyFormatCode*

Windows has amazingly well-thought-out and well-implemented facilities for currency. *Hey, if you're selling product in 100 different countries, you better know how to print the invoices!* Not all Windows applications take their clue in formatting currencies from the default Windows settings. But they really should.

If you click on the Change button in the International applet's Currency Format box, here's what you'll find lurking (see Figure 8-20).

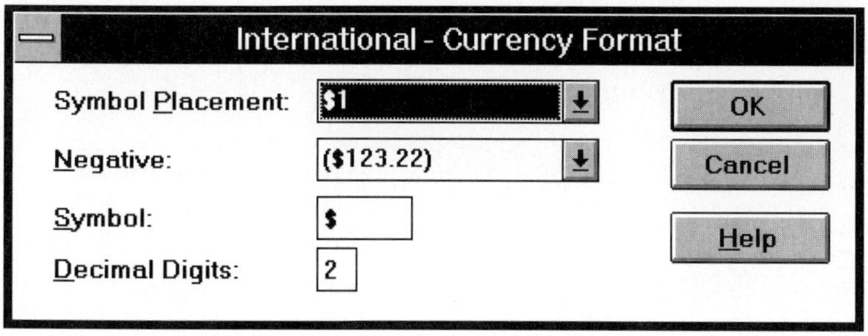

Figure 8-20: Makes the World Go Round

The **iCurrency=** setting corresponds to the Symbol Placement list. A value of **0** puts the currency symbol immediately in front of the number, e.g., $123.45. A value of **1** turns it around, e.g., 12RMB. A value of **2** adds a space to the front, e.g., £ 123.45. Finally, a value of **3** adds a space on the end, e.g., 12345 ¥. When the USA version of Windows installs itself, it puts a **iCurrency=0** line in **[intl]**.

You specify the currency symbol with **sCurrency=**. The USA version of Windows, straight out of the can, sets **sCurrency=$**.

The **iNegCurr=** setting tells Windows how to handle negative currencies. With a $ for the **sCurrency=** setting, and **iNegCurr=0** (how the USA version installs), negative currencies appear as ($123.45). An **iNegCurr=1** gives -$123.45. **2** shows as $-123.45. **3** comes out $123.45-. **4** is (123.45$). **5** indicates -123.45$. **6** is 123.45-$. **7** is 123.45$-. **8** yields -123.45 $ (with an extra space before the $). **9** shows up -$ 123.45. And **10** finishes it out with 123.45 $-. Yeah, the official documentation is wrong again.

Finally, the **iDigits=** setting tells Windows how many significant monetary digits should normally be printed or displayed. Not surprisingly, the USA version of Windows installs with **iDigits=2**.

All of these settings can be adjusted equally well by manually editing **WIN.INI**, or by using the International applet in the Control Panel.

iDate=*Gibberish*

Windows 3.1 doesn't even use this setting, a holdover from Windows 2.x —
although when Windows installs itself, it does add an **iDate=0** line to the **[intl]**
section, presumably in case any old Windows 2.x apps are still looking for it.

If you're still running Windows 2.x apps, believe me, you've got much
bigger problems.

Forget about **iDate=**. Look at **sLongDate=** and **sShortDate=**.

---

sDecimal=*DecimalPunctuationMark*

iDigits=*NumberOfDecimalDigits*

iLzero=*ZeroOrOne*

sThousand=*ThousandsSeparator*

If you click the Change button in the Number Format part of the International
applet's dialog box, here's what you will find (see Figure 8-21).

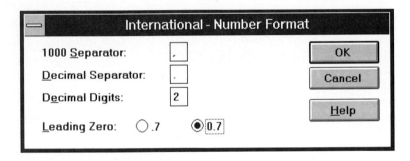

Figure 8-21: Numb Format

These settings all relate to those number formatting choices. Many applications will
pick up these settings, but a large percentage of those applications also let you
change them, within the application. Sometimes the settings can come in handy. If
you're trying to use a Windows app that has fractional numbers represented with a
comma (e.g., "0,25 cm" for a quarter-centimeter), for example, you may have some
luck getting that app to work by switching the Decimal Separator to a comma.

Then again, you may not.

sThousand= keeps track of the thousands separator, e.g., the "," in 100,000,000. (For some reason, many Americans don't realize that the "." period is used throughout much of the world as a thousands separator.) When the USA version of Windows installs itself, it puts a **sThousand=,** line in **[intl]**. I would be very interested in learning how (if!) Windows handles the Indian subcontinent's method of separating crore and lakh with spaces.

sDecimal= behaves similarly for the decimal point, e.g., the "." in 123.45. (Again, many Americans don't realize that the comma is used all over the world as a decimal point. Spock would call that a parochial attitude.) The USA version of Windows installs with **sDecimal=.**, as you would expect.

iDigits= tells Windows how many digits to display when confronted with a fractional number. (The **iCurrDigits=** settings is analogous, but for currency.) The USA version of Windows installs with **iDigits=2**.

Finally, **iLzero=** tells Windows whether it should put a zero in front of fractional numbers, i.e., numbers between -1 and +1, exclusive. **iLzero=0** says no, **iLzero=1** says yes. In spite of what all the documentation says, when the USA version of Windows goes in, it puts a **iLzero=1** line in **[intl]**.

---

sLanguage=*ThreeCharacterCode*

This setting is supposed to tell Windows the native language of the user. Like the **iCountry=** and **sCountry=** settings discussed above, this setting should be taken with a grain of salt. Just because **sLanguage=DEU**, for example, does not necessarily imply that the user is running the German language version of Windows, that they're using the German standard keyboard, or anything else for that matter.

Here's a list of all the valid three-character language codes I've been able to find that are actually *used* in Windows itself. Upper/lower case makes no difference.

sLanguage	Language	sLanguage	Language
DAN	Danish	ISL	Icelandic
DEU	German	ITA	Italian
ENG	"International" English	KOR	Korean

ENU	U.S. English	NLD	Dutch
ESP	Spanish	NOR	Norwegian
FIN	Finnish	PTG	Portuguese
FRA	French	SVE	Swedish
FRC	Canadian French		

The official documentation draws a distinction between ESN "Modern Spanish" (which I couldn't actually find *used* anywhere), and ESP "Castillan Spanish." Yet the International applet only offers "Spanish" and "Spanish (Modern)": it doesn't even mention Castillian. As both Spain and Mexico are associated with ESP (Castillian Spanish) by default and ESN appears nowhere in `CONTROL.INF`, it's a sure bet that something got totally screwed up, and at least some of the folks involved in implementing this part of Windows don't know Español from Cathtillano.

There are other oddities. While Word for Windows (and most of the English-speaking world) would draw a distinction between Strine. . . er. . . Australian English and UK English, fair dinkum, Windows doesn't seem to know. Or care. Ditto for the flavors of Portuguese in Brazil and Portugal — WinWord can tell them apart, but Windows can't. And would somebody tell me why it's **DAN** for *Dansk* (Danish), and **DEU** for *Deutsch*, etc., but **FIN** for *Suomi?*

The name of the language, as displayed in the applet's dialog box, is controlled by the **language.dll=** entry in the **[boot.description]** section of **SYSTEM.INI**. Yeah. You read that right.

---

sList=*ListSeparatorCharacter*

So call me cynical. Every book on Windows that I've seen, every bit of documentation, official, unofficial, or otherwise, says this is "the list separator." What's that, you ask? Why, the thing that separates items in lists, of course. Says so right here in this book. And this one. And this one. And this one.

All right. So what happens if you change the list separator? Good question. I changed it. And I ran Windows for a whole day, with the list separator changed from a comma to a semicolon. Banged on it hard. Tried all the Control Panel applets, over and over again. Ran through multimedia and CD stuff and modem stuff and a bunch of applications and all sorts of things that should go bonkers if they couldn't decipher the lists Windows stores away. Guess what? Nothing happened.

Not a bloody thing.

Maybe there's some Windows program somewhere that uses this setting. But I'll be drawn and quartered in the Building 7 parking lot if I can find it.

Oh. When Windows installs itself, it puts a **sList=,** line in your **[intl]** section. Ain't you the lucky one.

sLongDate=*LongDateFormatCode*

sShortDate=*ShortDateFormatCode*

These settings, on the other hand, are used by all sorts of different Windows applications, including the Windows Clock (although, surprisingly, ~~note~~ not the Windows Calendar). Most often they're the default "format" in which the applications display dates, and they can run the gamut from a terse "20-Oct-93," say, to a verbose "Saturday, April 16, 1994".

If you click on the Change button inside the Date Format part of the International applet's dialog box, here's what you will see (Figure 8-22).

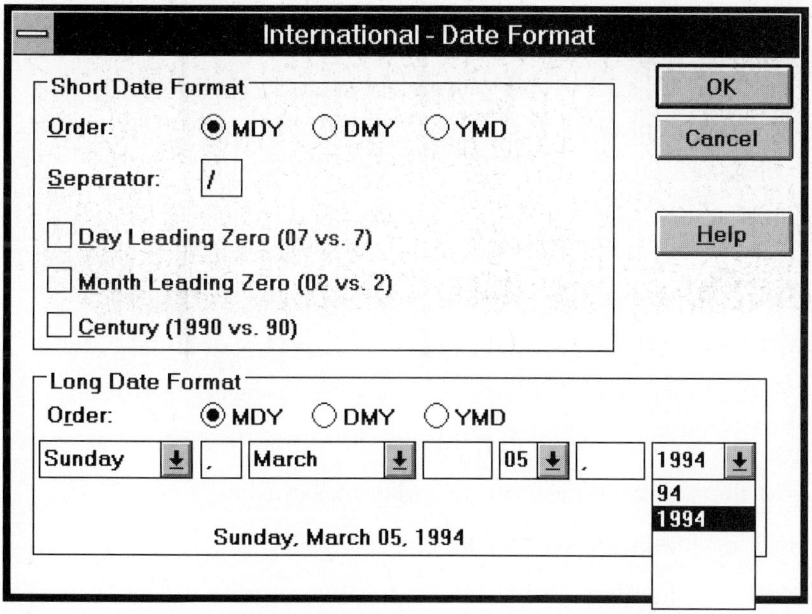

Figure 8-22: Long Date Format

Many people find it extremely annoying that the current day and time are set in the Control Panel's Date/Time applet, while the format of the day and time are set in something called "International."

Windows in general, and many Windows apps in particular, support two different formats for dates; but, surprisingly, only one for times. The "short" format is intended to be the kind of thing you'd jot down if you were in a hurry, or if you were filling out a form. The "long" format is more like the kind of date you'd put at the top of a letter or on a report. You can do whatever you like, of course, but you'll find things are more consistent in Windows applications if you keep the short format very short, and the long format fairly short, too. Not many businesses start out their letters with "Today's date is: Saturday, April 16, 1994."

The best way to set the date formats is from this dialog box. Those of you who like to tinker can try to cobble something together yourself. The rules for doing so are a bit complex, but two examples may help. When the USA version of Windows installs itself, it adds two lines to the [intl] section:

```
sShortDate=M/d/yy
sLongDate=dddd, MMMM dd, yyyy
```

and a typical short date comes up "10/20/93"; a typical long date "Saturday, April 16, 1994". See how that works? Good. Now here are the rules:

Windows lets you pick up any of the following ten key items:

Code	Meaning
d	Current day of the month, no leading zeroes (1 to 31)
dd	Current day of the month with leading zeroes on single-digit days (01 to 31)
ddd	Current day of the week, three letter abbreviation (Sun to Sat)
dddd	Current day of the week, spelled out (Sunday to Saturday)
M	Current month, no leading zeroes (1 to 12)
MM	Current month, with leading zeroes on single-digit months (01 to 12)
MMM	Current month, three letter abbreviation (Jan to Dec)

MMMM   Current month, spelled out (January to December)

yy   Last two digits of the year (00 to 99)

yyyy   Four digit year

Note in particular that those **M**s are capitalized — Windows reserves the lower-case **m** for minutes.

You may intersperse a few other characters between those key items. This is a valid setting:

`sLongDate=dddd,, MMMM dd, yyyy`

Single quotes can go around certain characters, although the precise way they're interpreted is open to question. By and large, you can't get too fancy. Even the International applet will croak on anything mildly interesting.

---

iLzero=*ZeroOrOne*

See **sDecimal=**.

---

iMeasure=*UnitsCode*

As they say on the right side of the big puddle, this one's a hoot. Windows can work in metric, or it can work in inches/feet/miles/furlongs/cubits/ bushels/fathoms/ pecks/pounds/ounces /acres/gallons/quarts/pints/grains/ hectares/rods/tons/yards/ barrels/board-feet/teaspoons/tablespoons/ cups. Quick. What's the difference between a fluid ounce, avoirdupois ounce, apothecary ounce, and a troy ounce? How many board-feet in 10 eight-foot 2 X 4s?

You might call the former "SI Units" or "MKSA System" or just plain "metric." But no matter how hard you rationalize, you cannot call the latter "English": the English haven't used that bastard system in nearly half a century. The USA is the only country remaining on the face of the earth that subjects its citizenry to such barbarism. These are US measurements, whether we Gringos like it or not.

Windows has a slightly disjoint world view. Click on the Measurement down-arrow in the International applet, and here are your choices (Figure 8-23).

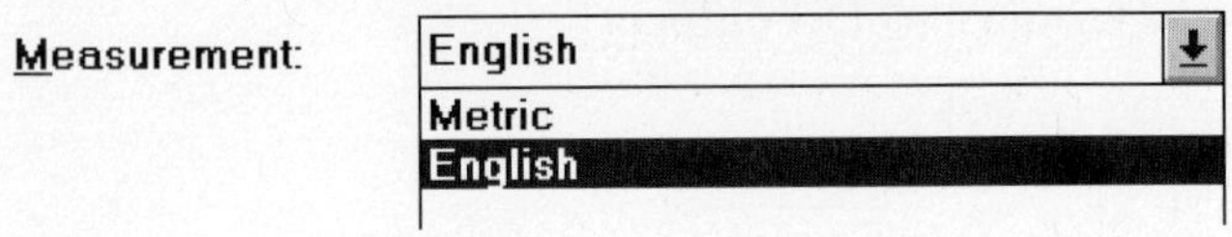

Measurement:	English ▼
	Metric
	English

Figure 8-23: Eh, Wot?

Some choice, eh?

A setting of **iMeasure=0** means that Windows (and most applications) will interpret measurements in metric. A setting of **iMeasure=1** runs to the US "system" of measurements. When the USA version of Windows installs, naturally, it puts **iMeasure=1** in **[intl]**.

---

iNegCurr=*NegativeCurrencyFormatCode*

See **iCurrDigits=**.

---

sShortDate=*ShortDateFormatCode*

See **sLongDate=**.

---

sThousand=*ThousandsSeparator*

See **sDecimal=**.

---

iTime=*ZeroOrOne*

sTime=*TimeSeparator*

iTLZero=*ZeroOrOne*

s1159=*AMCharaterString*

s2359=*PMCharaterString*

When you click on the Change button in the International applet's Time Format box, here's what you will see (Figure 8-24).

```
┌─────────────────────────────────────────────────────────┐
│ ▭         International - Time Format                     │
├─────────────────────────────────────────────────────────┤
│  ◉ [1_2 hour]   00:00-11:59    ┌──────────┐    ┌────────┐ │
│                                │ AM       │    │   OK   │ │
│  ○ 2_4 hour     12:00-23:59    ┌──────────┐    └────────┐ │
│                                │ PM       │    │ Cancel │ │
│  S_eparator:    ┌───┐          └──────────┘    └────────┘ │
│                 │ : │                          ┌────────┐ │
│                 └───┘                          │  Help  │ │
│  L_eading Zero:   ◉ 9:15    ○ 09:15            └────────┘ │
└─────────────────────────────────────────────────────────┘
```

Figure 8-24: Time Format

 It's amazing to me that Windows doesn't have the flexibility in formatting times that it does in formatting dates. Some folks would like to see minutes and seconds — or minutes and decimal fractions of minutes — but that isn't possible. It would be nice if I could flip from a 12-hour clock formatting to a 24-hour formatting with the ease of a Short/Long date format. Or specify fixed text: sometimes I want the AM to follow the number immediately, with no intervening space. And so on.

That Time Format dialog box defines the alpha and omega of Windows' time formatting capabilities. You can edit this stuff manually, but doing so won't give you any more options than the drab dialog box.

When **iTime=0**, Windows uses a 12-hour clock. **iTime=1** specifies a 24-hour (some would say "military" or "European") clock. The USA version of Windows installs with **iTime=0**.

sTime= is the time formatting separator, e.g., the ":" in 12:34. The USA version of Windows installs with **sTime=:**.

iTLZero= controls whether a leading zero appears on single-digit hours. An **iTLZero=0** means no leading zero; **iTLZero=1** means there is a leading zero. The USA version comes in with **iTLZero=0**.

 Hey, is this boring or what? Sheeesh. Here's a bit of trivia, for that burned-out brain of yours. When Windows installs itself the **iLzero=** setting doesn't capitalize the **z**, whereas **iTLZero=** does. Doesn't make any difference, but it might keep you awake. Pick your head up. Take a few deep breaths. Whooooooaa. . .

The **s1159=** string tells Windows what text string to stick on the end of the time when **iTime=0** (i.e., 12-hour clock) and the time is between 0:00 AM and 11:59 PM. Similarly, the **s2359=** string is the suffix for times from 12:00 noon to 11:59 PM. (When **iTime=1**, you're on a 24-hour clock and the **s1159=** and **s2359=** settings don't matter.) When Windows installs, it puts **s1159=AM** and **s2359=PM** lines in **[intl]**. While you can use more than two characters for these settings, there's no guarantee Windows or Windows applications will pick them up: the Windows clock, for example, only grabs the first six characters in the setting.

How's that for trivia?

[mci extensions]

 Given all the fun and games with incorrect official documentation of the [Extensions] section, I approached [mci extensions] with great fear and loathing. Turns out I wasn't disappointed.

The section has settings that look like this:

```
EXT=MCIDeviceType
```

and the MCIDeviceType values correspond to settings in the **[mci]** section of **SYSTEM.INI**.

When Windows installs itself, it puts three entries in **[mci extensions]**, to-wit:

```
wav=waveaudio
mid=sequencer
rmi=sequencer
```

The MCIDeviceTypes (i.e., the stuff on the right side of the equals signs) correspond with what Windows, on installation, automatically sticks in the **[mci]** section of **SYSTEM.INI**:

```
WaveAudio=mciwave.drv
Sequencer=mciseq.drv
CDAudio=mcicda.drv
```

and those entries, in turn, point to multimedia drivers.

When Windows installs itself, it associates the **.WAV** extension with **SOUNDREC.EXE**, the sound recorder; **.MID** and **.RMI** are associated with **MPLAYER.EXE**, the Windows Media Player. Which is all pretty much what you might expect: in File Manager, if you double-click on an **.RMI** file, say, you'll get the Multimedia Player going, playing the selected file.

How are the **[mci extensions]** entries used? As best I can tell they're only used by the Windows Media Player, **MPLAYER.EXE**, and only when you open a new file. **MPLAYER** looks up the extension of the newly opened file in **[mci extensions]**, takes the MCIDeviceType and bangs it against the **[mci]** section of **SYSTEM.INI**, then picks up the correct **.DRV** device driver to use when playing the newly opened file.

 Circuitous, eh? It's strange that **MPLAYER**, one of the most recent of all the Windows applets, has to rely on old-fashioned **WIN.INI** settings to do its thing; you'd think this stuff would be in the Registration database.

Other applications may use **[mci extensions]**, so you don't want to mess around with the entries too much. Unlike **[Extensions]** entries, which are pretty innocuous and overridden by the Registration database anyway, you really *can* clobber stuff royal by playing around with **[mci extensions]**. Some applications (e.g., CorelDRAW 4.0) put their own extensions in here; they also automatically handle the associated entries in **SYSTEM.INI**'s **[mci]** section.

[network]

Like Einstein's universe, most networks are finite but unbounded.

— Clifford Stoll, *The Cuckoo's Egg*, 1991

 As I've explained before, I'll touch on network settings, but don't expect any amazing insight or between-the-eyes analysis. Networking Windows is a topic unto itself, and would require a book at least the size of *MOM* to do it justice. Besides, if you're networking Windows, you're probably already into -Windows NT, and — as much as Microsoft Marketing would have you believe otherwise — those beasts have quirks of their own, quite different from the mother of all Windows. Windows for Warehous...er... Workgroups is regular ol' Windows with networking tacked on, almost as an afterthought, and the networking part is pretty much an exercise unto its own, not unlike LANtastic or Novell.

Windows only bothers to put the **[network]** section in **WIN.INI** if and/or when it detects a network card. If you installed Windows at some point in time when you didn't have a network card, or if the network card wasn't working at that moment, there will be no **[network]** section in your **WIN.INI**. Indeed, you won't get a **[network]** section unless and until Windows suddenly realizes you're connected to a network, and it needs some settings.

There's little uniformity in network connection dialog boxes, terminology, even in the format of **WIN.INI** settings, so let's hold our noses and go wading.

DriveLetter:=*NetworkDrive*

Entries that follow this tune point to networked drive connections that should be restarted whenever you crank up Windows. You'll want to set these connections from File Manager, by clicking on Drive, and then Network Connections. If you then pick a drive and click the "Permanent" box, it'll be added to the **[network]** section of **WIN.INI**.

The entries might look like this:

```
N:=[KUNG/FOO:] PUBLIC
O:=[KUNG/FOO:] NETLIB
```

mapping **N:** to the **PUBLIC** directory and **O:** to **NETLIB**. But the actual appearance of the entries (not to mention the dialog box you use to connect them) could be entirely different. Best to get at the setting through File Manager, and leave the bit twiddling to Windows.

InRestoreNetConnect=*ZeroOrOne*

The official documentation says this setting controls whether or not Windows tries to reconnect you to the network every time Windows is started: a 1 indicates you want to be reconnected automatically; a 0 says no. If the line is missing, Windows assumes you meant 1.

Supposedly, the setting works for MS-Net, LAN Manager Basic, and LAN Manager 2.0. You may want to play with it if you are (or are not) getting reconnected at startup, and want to change the behavior — but don't be too surprised if it doesn't work on your system.

The best way to change the number is with Control Panel's Network applet, if it has the setting available and you can figure out which one it is.

---

port:=_NetworkPath_

port-OPTIONS=_OptionList_

Windows itself supports the **port:=** setting; you may find you also have **port-OPTIONS=** lines, too. They'll look something like this:

```
LPT1:=KUNG/FOO
LPT1-OPTIONS= ......
```

The **port:=** settings are established via the Printers applet in the Control Panel. If you crank it up, select a driver, and hit the Connect button, you'll probably find the "Network" button is active. Push on it to jump into the Printer Connection dialog box. Find the print server you want. Make sure you check the "Permanent" box, and a **port:=** line will (probably) be added to the **[network]** section.

The **port-OPTIONS=** settings are usually accessible through the "Options" button in that same Printer Connection dialog box. Typically **port-OPTIONS=** contains a hodgepodge of information: whether you should be notified when the print job is done; whether your print job should start on a fresh piece of paper; how long you want to the printer to wait for your job to get transmitted; whether you want a banner to print at the beginning of your print job and, if so, what the banner should say; and on and on.

Also make sure you look at the **NetWarn=** setting in the **[windows]** section of **WIN.INI**.

[ports]

Your computer has two different kinds of ports: serial ports spit out and take in one bit at a time; parallel ports send and receive eight bits at a time. This section of **WIN.INI** (as you might imagine!) contains settings relevant to parallel and serial ports, but it also contains settings for "Print to File" files — files that behave as surrogate printers, accepting data as if they were printers — and a couple of other squirrely things. So sit back and relax while the boys traipse through the details.

Let me start with one big documentation bug. The official docs, and all the unofficial ones I've seen, insist that you can't have more than ten entries in this section: if you do, supposedly, the extra ones are ignored. That's hogwash. I have 14 entries in `[ports]`, and they all work fine. *Windows itself installs with 11 entries.* How anybody came up with a limit of ten is beyond me.

Igor, my guess is that at some point in the past — Windows 3.0, maybe Windows 2.11, whatever — there really was a limit of ten. The documentation in the Windows Resource Kit and the read-me files never got updated. Thus, dozens of Windows books have repeated and perpetuated the insanity.

I'm going to start by stepping through the settings for serial ports. Keep in mind that the `[ports]` entries may appear in any order, and that there are four different kinds of "ports" (serial, parallel, finking out to DOS, and "file") — I'm just peeling them off one at a time, to make the going a little easier. And you may find it useful to refer to the more detailed discussion of ports in's and out's in Chapter 3.

Serial port settings look like this:

```
COM1:=9600,n,8,1,x
```

You'll usually find four serial port entries just like this in **[ports]**, one each for **COM1:**, **COM2:**, **COM3:**, and **COM4:**.

The easiest way to get at these settings is through the Ports applet of the Control Panel. Double-click on the Ports applet, pick a port, click Settings, and Figure 8-25 will be your result.

You can get to the same Settings dialog box by double-clicking on the Control Panel's Printers applet, clicking Connect, picking a **COMn:** serial port, and clicking on Settings. If you're saddled with a printer connected to a serial port, you might find it more logical to approach things through the Printer applet. Most folks, though — the ones who hang their printers off parallel ports, where the WinDeity intended — would only get confused by this little detour.

In general, the serial port settings in **[ports]** look like this:

```
COMn:=speed, parity, data, stop[, handshake]
```

where **n** can be 1, 2, 3, or 4, signifying the number of the port involved.

speed is the bits-per-second rate. Windows has pre-set values of 110, 300, 600, 1200, 2400, 4800, 9600, or 19200. You can adjust the rate manually, type in the highest value your modem or comm software will allow, but watch out for flaky results if you goose it too much.

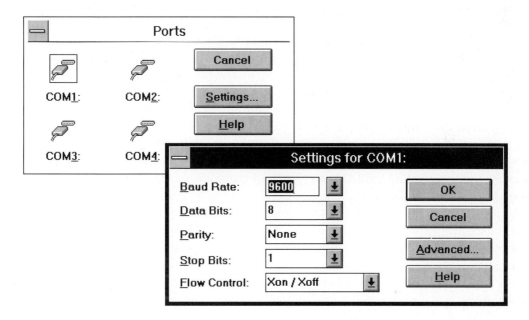

Figure 8-25: Pick-A-Port

The **parity** setting reflects the parity checking in effect. Single-bit parity checking is a rudimentary method of making sure that bits don't get scrambled during transmission. It doesn't always work, but it does catch some errors. **parity** can have one of five values. **n** means none; that the device on the other end of the line doesn't use any parity checking. That's most common by far. **e**, for even parity checking, means that the receiving device expects an even parity bit, an extra bit tacked on the end of each 8-bit byte, to make the number of 1 bits in the 9-bit pack even. (Yeah, stuff can be transmitted in smaller packs; hang on a second.) **o**, for odd parity checking, is similar except the ninth bit is set to make the total number of 1 bits in the 9-bit pack odd. **m**, mark parity, always sets the ninth bit to 1; it's a lot like a stop bit (see below). **s**, space parity, is similar to mark parity, except it always sets the ninth bit to 0.

The **data** number specifies the number of bits in each packet, before the parity bit (if any) is tacked on the end. It's almost always 8, although occasionally you'll hit a BBS that runs on 4 bits, or a peripheral that only takes 7.

The **stop** bit is a method of synchronizing things, a pulse that's sent along immediately after each data pack, used to keep the sending and receiving computers in synch. They're measured in terms of how long they last, compared to a "typical" bit in the data pack. A value of **1** means the synch pulse, the stop bit, is as long as a regular bit. A value of **1.5** means the synch pulse goes 50% longer than a regular bit, and a **2** indicates pulse synchs last twice as long as a regular bit.

And the **handshake** setting just tells your computer how to figure out when it should shut up. An **x** stands for something called X-On/X-Off Handshaking: in this case, the receiving computer sends a special code down the line when it's ready to receive stuff, and it sends a different code to your computer when it wants your computer to stop sending stuff. That's the most common method for bulletin boards (BBSs). Alternatively, if the receiving device is set up for it, you can specify **p** for hardware control: for hardware control to work, both your computer and whatever you're talking to must agree to delegate a couple of wires in the connecting cable to controlling the flow of information. At the risk of over-generalizing, modems never use **p**, but serial printers and directly connected computers may. Finally, if there is no handshake entry, *yenta* mode, where both the letter and the comma are missing, there is no provision established for the receiving computer to tell your computer to knock it off. It'll keep on yakking and yakking and yakking.

So when do you want to play with the settings? Good question.

If you have a mouse attached to one of your serial ports (most often it's **COM1:**), there's no reason to play with its settings.

If you have a printer attached to one of your serial ports, it should've been set up properly during the print driver installation procedure. HP plotters, for example, set themselves up to run at seven data bits, no parity, and one stop bit. Don't monkey around with printer settings directly: if you have problems, just re-install the driver.

If you have a modem attached to one of your serial ports (most often it's **COM2:**, but it could be any of the four), you'll have to look several places to get these settings right. The "Baud Rate" is just the bits-per-second speed rating of your modem; you can find that in your modem's manual. The Data Bits, Parity, and Stop settings depend on the system you're calling: you'll have to contact the (BBS) operator or modem owner on the other side of the connection to get it right. Almost all BBSs use X-On/X-Off handshaking. Most good communication software can adjust all these parameters on the fly and make you set them in their parameter screens, so normally you don't need to sweat this setting much.

 A good first try — by far the most common setting for modems — is "8N1", i.e., eight data bits, no parity, one stop. But don't take these settings too seriously: almost every moderately capable communications program can reach in and change things around. You're just setting up defaults.

And if you're serious about modem communication, you already own a 16550 UART chip and the TurboCom or KingComm program, like I discussed in Chapter 37, right? Good.

If you have another computer attached directly to one of your serial ports (typically through something called a null modem cable), you can usually crank the speed up to 19200. Just make sure all the settings are identical on both machines.

When Windows installs itself, it puts four **COMn:** lines in **[ports]**, i.e.:

```
COM1:=9600,n,8,1,x
COM2:=9600,n,8,1,x
COM3:=9600,n,8,1,x
COM4:=9600,n,8,1,x
```

So much for serial ports. Now let's look at the easy one, parallel.

After Windows installs itself, you'll find four lines in **[ports]** that relate to parallel ports:

```
LPT1:=
LPT2:=
LPT3:=
EPT:=
```

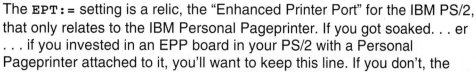 The **EPT:=** setting is a relic, the "Enhanced Printer Port" for the IBM PS/2, that only relates to the IBM Personal Pageprinter. If you got soaked. . . er . . . if you invested in an EPP board in your PS/2 with a Personal Pageprinter attached to it, you'll want to keep this line. If you don't, the line is totally dispensable. Go ahead and nuke it with impunity.

The other three lines tell Windows that you have three ports: called **LPT1:**, **LPT2:**, and **LPT3:,** to which you might, at some indeterminate point in the future, attach printers. That's all. For details, look up the **device=** setting in the **[windows]** section of **WIN.INI**.

Those **LPTn:=** lines don't have any parameters. They just kinda sit there, for the benefit of the Control Panel's Printer applet Connect button.

In a very clever bit of insight, the folks who created Windows realized that "printing" to a file should be handled analogously to "printing" to anything else. Thus, the **[ports]** section lets you specify "ports" that aren't really printer ports at all, but are, in fact, files. If you "print" to one of these files, all the stuff that would normally be sent to the printer: formatting codes, printer reset strings, bounce-off-the-wall commands, the whole shootin' match gets shoved into a file.

 There are three common (and many uncommon!) reasons why you might want to print to a file, instead of a printer.

First, you might want to keep an exact image of the printed output around, particularly if there's a chance you'll want to print your document sometime in the future, or if you want to print to an identical printer attached to a different computer. Yes, you can keep the document file itself, but by keeping a print-to-file ("print image") file around you're going to save yourself formatting time (i.e., however long it takes for your application to generate something printable); you'll be able to print on systems that don't have the application hanging around; you might be able to set up your computer to schedule a massive print job late at night; you'll also be keeping an exact record of how the printout appeared, your application can change around, but the print-to-file file won't.

To copy your print-to-file file (say, **C:\PATH\MYFILE.XXX**) to a printer (say, on **LPT1:**), get to the DOS prompt, and type:

```
COPY C:\PATH\MYFILE.XXX LPT1
```

Second, you may hit some weird bug somewhere that can only be resolved by looking at the commands the Windows print driver is sending to your printer. While you yourself may not get involved in reading such inscrutable drivel, your printer manufacturer may bless the very ground upon which you stand if you can trap a tough bug this way.

Third, and most important to me, is using print-to-file to make absolutely, totally, 100% sure that you have what you think you have. Let me explain.

Many people create documents on their computers, print drafts on their local printer, then when all is well, print to file and send the file off to a service bureau or expensive in-house typesetter for final printing and distribution. Once in a very blue moon, the typeset PostScript copy won't look the same as what came off the draft printer: a line will break differently, or a picture location jogs a touch. Just enough to drive you nuts; possibly enough to cause an expensive re-run. I don't know why, but it does happen.

The solution? Print your very final draft to file, then copy the file to the printer. That's the only way you can be absolutely, positively sure that the application isn't doing something funny to the output, that the service bureau (if it has the fonts installed properly, anyway) will get a clean version.

Try it. It works.

Windows lets you specify print-to-file file names in two ways. First, you can just put a file name in the **[ports]** section. Like this:

`MYPRINT.FIL=`

where, in spite of the documentation, any valid file name, including full path information, to the left of the **=** equals sign will work. Here's the catch: no matter what path information you do (or do not) include, Windows always writes the file to the currently active directory. So if you put this line in the **[ports]** section:

`c:\winword\mother\test.tmp=`

then use File Print Setup in any sufficiently endowed application (or the Printer applet in the Control Panel) to connect a printer to that ersatz "port", just as you would connect to a real port. Finally, print with the newly assigned printer. You'll get a file called **TEST.TMP** that contains the print-to-file information, but the file will be deposited in whichever directory was active at the time you ran the print. It most assuredly will not end up in the directory you've specified in the **[ports]** section (unless that just happens to be where you were when the print came down).

And if there's already a file called **TEST.TMP** in the current directory, it's unceremoniously overwritten; you don't even get a chance to tell Windows to wait.

Note that, unlike all the other **[ports]** settings, there is no colon at the end of the file name in this kind of setting.

The second way to specify a print-to-file file name is to stick a line in **[ports]** that looks like this:

FILE:=

As in the previous case, Windows will let you connect any printer to something called "**FILE:**", just as you would connect to any real port. If you subsequently try to print with the printer connected to "**FILE:**", Windows is smart enough to intercept the printing and ask you which file you'd like to print to (see Figure 8-26).

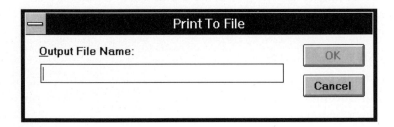

Figure 8-26: Printing to FILE:=

You may specify any valid file name, and this time Windows is smart enough to stick the print-to-file file in whatever directory you specify. It's even smart enough to warn you if you're trying to over-write an existing file.

 Now for the fourth and final kind of entry in the **[ports]** section. It's actually a file entry, just like the files I've been talking about, but there's a little trick that makes these "finking out to DOS" files different.

Dear ol' DOS has several reserved names, names that can't be used for any files. **NUL** is one of them. So are **LPT1**, **LPT2**, and **LPT3**. In DOS, if you try to copy a file to **LPT1.ZIG**, say, poor ol' DOS only runs through the command as far as the **LPT1.**, and then it gets all confused. Since **LPT1** is a reserved name, DOS figures

that you must've mis-spelled something, and instead of copying your file to
LPT1.ZIG, it copies the file to the **LPT1:** parallel port, typically your printer.

Don't believe it? Try it. Just bop over to the DOS Command Prompt right now and
try running a straight DOS copy to any file name that starts with **LPT1.**, say

COPY SYSTEM.INI LPT1.YEP

There. Did you get a copy of **SYSTEM.INI** to print on your printer? (Assuming
your printer is on **LPT1:**, of course.) How 'bout that.

Windows takes advantage of that little loophole in DOS to implement what I call a
"finking out to DOS" print. Most of the time Windows takes over your printer ports
and works directly with your printer. (See the description of the **DosPrint=**
setting in the **[windows]** section of **WIN.INI** for the one exception, the so-
called "Fast Print Direct To Port" option.) When Windows takes over, it bypasses
DOS entirely, and all of the centuries-old DOS printing capabilities stand back as
Windows does its thing.

Occasionally, though, you may want to use DOS to do your printing. You might
have some strange DOS MODE command that you want to take over the printer
port. Or maybe you have a printer that works fine printing from DOS but goes
berserk under Windows. Sometimes network printers prefer the rubdown DOS
delivers. In any case, finking out to DOS is quite simple. Look for entries in
[ports] that look like this:

LPT1.DOS=
LPT2.DOS=

or just add one, using the port name as the first four characters, and any old
extension you like (the extension is ignored completely).

LPT1.XX=

Now pop into the Control Panel's Printers applet and Connect the desired printer to
one of these finking out ports.

When you print to a printer connected that way, Windows thinks you're printing to
a file: Windows doesn't know an **LPT1...** file name from shinola. But when
DOS gets that file, the light goes on: *AHA!* That's not a valid file name, it's a printer
port name! And, lo and behold, the file is shuffled to the printer port, same as a
DOS copy.

When Windows installs itself, it'll put three **LPTn:=** lines in **[ports]**, four
COMn:= lines, an **EPT:=** line, a **FILE:=** line, and two **LPTn.DOS=** lines. That's a
total of eleven ports, and as far as I know, notwithstanding the official
documentation, you can add as many as you like.

[PrinterPorts]

 For an overview of this section and its meaning in the general Windows
scheme of things, take a look at the **Device=** setting in the **[windows]**
section.

This section has but three reasons for existence: it supplies the list of printers for
the Printer applet's dialog box; it stores the two time-out settings Windows needs in
the Printer applet's Connect box, the **DeviceNotSelectedTimeout=** and
TransmissionRetryTimeout=, both discussed in the **[windows]** section, and
they keep track of the name of the print driver used by the particular printer, so the
correct name can be stuck in the **devices=** entry in the **[windows]** section.

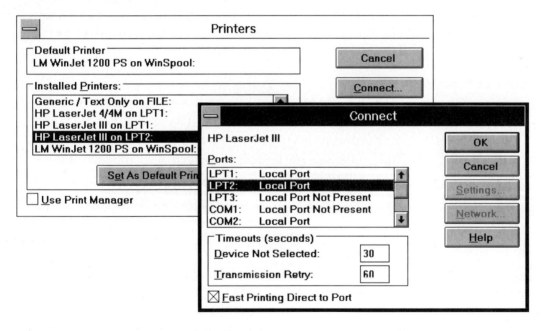

Figure 8-27: The Printer Applet Connects

The only thing in this section that directly affects the current status of printing is the time-out values. Everything else just floats around, keeping track of the options that let you choose among various printers and ports, should you be so inclined.

The **[PrinterPorts]** entries that give rise to Figure 8-27 look like this:

```
Generic / Text Only=TTY,FILE:,15,45

HP LaserJet 4/4M=HPPCL5E,LPT1:,15,45

HP LaserJet III=hppcl5a,LPT1:,15,45,LPT2:,30,60

LM WinJet 1200 PS=LMPS,WinSpool:,15,45
```

The stuff to the left of the equals sign is the printer name. Take great care, should you decide to edit the name by hand: it must be spelled quite precisely. Immediately following the equals sign is the driver name associated with the printer, minus the **.DRV** extension. As usual, Windows looks for the driver first in the Windows directory, then in the system directory, and finally along the DOS path. If you don't put the driver somewhere in one of those subdirectories, make sure you qualify it with a full path.

Next come a set of three values, which can be repeated as many times as you like. The first of the three is the port name; it must match an entry in the **[ports]** section precisely. Second is the **DeviceNotSelectedTimeOut=** value that is to be associated with this printer on the indicated port. And finally there's the **TransmissionRetryTimeout=** value.

The official documentation says that if there is no port on the right side of the equals sign, that the **NullPort=** entry from **[windows]** will be used, but that isn't true. If there's absolutely nothing on the right side of the equals sign, Windows gets rid of the line as soon as it notices. If there are some settings, but the port is missing (e.g., **TTY,,15,45**), Windows comes up with a blank for a port name. Finally, if there is a driver specified but nothing else, Windows seems to glom onto **LPT1:**. What's happening? I dunno.

Windows does not put a **[PrinterPorts]** section in **WIN.INI** until you install a printer.

[programs]

Gallia est omnis divisa in partes tres.[†]

— Julius Cæsar, ca 50 B.C.

 Windows puts all files into one of three categories, based on the extension in the file name: there are "programs," "documents," and "other." That part is pretty easy. The rest of it gets mighty complicated. Let's have Mao take a look at each of those three categories, and fill you in on what's really going on behind the scenes.

None of this is documented anywhere else, so listen up!

 First the "programs." As far as Windows is concerned, at least as far as I can tell, a program must have a file name that ends in `.BAT`, `.COM`, `.EXE`, `.SCR` or `.PIF`, although you can tell Windows if you don't want one (or more) of those extensions to be treated as a program's extension. (See the `programs=` entry in the `[windows]` section later in this chapter for a more complete description. A `.SCR` file is just a renamed `.EXE` file.) Once Windows has an extension defined as a program, you can use File Manager to double-click on a file with that extension and it will run. You can use Program Manager's `File / Run` menu to run it (or, equivalently, set it up as an icon on the desktop). Or you can use File Manager's drag 'n drop capability to drop a "document" on the file, and have it run with the indicated "document" loaded.

 Which, naturally, begs the question: what's a "document"? Although I go into greater detail when discussing the `documents=` line in the `[windows]` section in `WIN.INI` (again, later in this chapter), there are three ways to tell Windows which file name extensions correspond to documents.

First, you can use File Manager or the Registration database editor to associate a file name extension with a program: tell Windows that all `.DOC` files are WinWord documents, say, or that all `.PCX` files are Paintbrush documents. (Note how a "document" needn't be a document, in the classic sense: it's just the file name extension of a type of file that can be fed to a program. Most folks wouldn't think of a `.WAV` sound file as a document, for example, but that's exactly what Windows

---

[†] All Gaul is divided into three parts.

thinks of them.) Those associations are logged in the Registration database. And that's the best place to store them. All good Windows programs log their associated documents in the Registration database upon installation.

Second, you can use the **[Extensions]** section of **WIN.INI** to associate documents with programs. I covered the **[Extensions]** section earlier in this chapter: look there for details.

Third, you can use the **documents=** line in the **[windows]** section of **WIN.INI** to identify documents, but in this one case you can't tel Windows which program is associated with the document. That makes the **documents=** line virtually useless.

The first two types of documents hold a special place in Windows' heart. You can use File Manager to double-click on them, and they'll spring to life: Windows looks in the Registration database or, failing that, the **[Extensions]** section of **WIN.INI** to find the associated program, then Windows will get the program running, and feed it the document. You can use File Manager's **File / Run** to do much the same. You can even set the document up as an icon, double-click on it, and have it take off.

Finally, any extension that isn't a "program" or a "document" is, by definition, "other." Windows doesn't do anything fancy with "other" files.

 Phew. Now I can tackle the **[programs]** section of **WIN.INI**.

It's all a question of how Windows looks for programs associated with the first two kinds of documents.

When Windows hits a document extension associated with a program, it has to find the program, right? Usually that's pretty easy: the Registration database or the **[Extensions]** section will often contain the full path of the program — **.DOC** files will point to **C:\winword\winword.exe**, say. Sometimes the Registration database or the **[Extensions]** section will drop the path qualification — for example, **.LOG** files might be associated, simply, with **write.exe**.

If Windows hits a bad or non-existent path, it runs through the traditional Windows file location rigmarole: first it looks in the **windows** directory, then in the **system** directory. If the program isn't found there, it looks along the DOS path (which is set by the **PATH** statement, typically in **AUTOEXEC.BAT**).

Here's the kicker: if Windows doesn't find the associated program anywhere in its normal search routine, it looks in the **[programs]** section of **WIN.INI** to see if there is an entry listing the program. If **.LOG** files were associated with **write.exe**, say, and Windows couldn't find **write.exe** using the normal search routine, it would look in **[programs]** for a line like this:

```
write.exe=C:\oldwin\write.exe
```

If Windows encountered such a line, it would look in **c:\oldwin** to see if **write.exe** was there. Note how this is the very, very last place Windows looks. And it will only use this entry if the program name matches the one it's looking for. Precisely.

In the normal course of things, **[programs]** entries are built by Windows: if it can't find a program, it will ask you where you stuck it. See Figure 8-28.

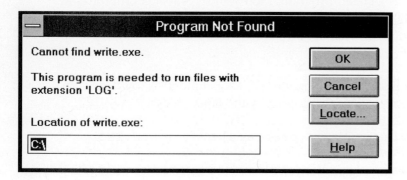

Figure 8-28: Pgm, Pgm, Who's Got Da Pgm?

If you find (using the Locate button) or type in a valid program, Windows automatically generates a **[programs]** entry, pointing the way for future reference.

 Amazingly, though, Windows does *not* update the Registration database with this new information. In order to do that — and you really should, so all Windows applications can find your program — you'll have to go into File Manager or the Registration database editor and make the association manually.

That's a strange oversight. And a disconcerting one, too.

[RegEdit]

 I don't believe this section is documented anywhere. If you start up the Registration database editor (`REGEDIT.EXE`), change the size of the window, then leave RegEdit normally, it'll keep track of its size in this section. Surprisingly, unlike Windows Help, there is no attempt to save the maximized/restored state of RegEdit.

A typical entry looks like this:

```
width=308
height=416
```

where both settings are in pixels.

[Sounds]

These settings go hand-in-hand with the Control Panel's Sound applet's "Events". The dialog box for Windows' bone-stock Sound applet looks like Figure 8-29:

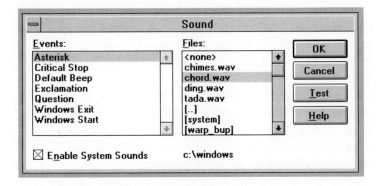

Figure 8-29: One Hand Clapping

If you've installed the Windows Sound System, or any of several other sound packages, your Sound applet won't look like that. Not to worry. If you stick to using the Sound applet, regardless of its pedigree or appearance, you should be in good shape.

See that "Enable System Sounds" box at the bottom of the dialog box? It's tricky. For a description of the "Enable System Sounds" mystery, see the **[windows]** section's **Beep=** setting. In a nutshell, some sound drivers look for the **Beep=** setting, some don't, and your particular Sound applet's dialog may not even have a box to mute the mother!

If Windows detects a sound card on your system during installation, it creates a **[Sounds]** section and fills it with these lines:

```
SystemDefault=ding.wav, Default Beep
SystemExclamation=chord.wav, Exclamation
SystemStart=tada.wav, Windows Start
SystemExit=chimes.wav, Windows Exit
SystemHand=chord.wav, Critical Stop
SystemQuestion=chord.wav, Question
SystemAsterisk=chord.wav, Asterisk
```

Not surprisingly, those are precisely the events listed in the standard Sound dialog box.

If you've installed a fancy sound package, you may well have more lines than these. In general, though, they all follow the same pattern. To the left of the equals sign is an "Event," something Windows tracks. Immediately to the right of the equals sign is the **.WAV** sound file that's supposed to be played when the event occurs. And at the tail end there's a place to put a simple description of what the event means; it's strictly for show, a text string to toss out at human beings, for them to tell heads from tails.

Note how Mao glossed over the "Event" concept, the thing that drives these settings. Windows has a pot full of standard events, and makes allowances for new ones. At least in theory, whenever a Windows application encounters one of these events, it's supposed to send Windows a message saying what has happened: "Yo! Windows! I just had an asterisk event!" Like that.

When Windows gets a message along those lines, it's supposed to look up the sound associated with the event, and, if **Beep=yes** in **[windows]**, or if a Beep-unaware sound driver has taken over, play the sound. That actually works, far as I can tell. The Achilles heel here is with the applications: they're given free reign in determining when an event has occurred; they're even allowed to figure out what kind of event has happened.

There's very little uniformity between applications. So don't be too surprised if a situation in one application gives a ding ding, while the same situation in a different application gives rise to a boink boink. Indeed, in most applications events make no sounds at all because the programmers didn't bother to put the hooks in the application.

You may well find sound settings in other files. The Windows Sound System, for example, stores its settings in a file called **SNDSYS.INI**. The file holds a dozen or so sections, with hundreds of settings. One line that's bound to build confidence in the Sound System: the first line in the **[Drivers]** section of **SNDSYS.INI** looks like this:

Patches=C:\WINDOWS\SYSTEM\SNDSYS.PAT

You might assume that "Patches" is not the name of a song.

Actually, Grasshopper, I'll bet it isn't the bug kind of patch either. In the *Wasn't General MIDI in the Battle of the Choral C?* section of Chapter 2, I discussed patch maps. I'm sure that's the kind of patch intended here.

[TrueType]

This section contains two settings that control how TrueType operates behind the scenes. It also contains settings that correspond to the TrueType box in the Control Panel's Fonts applet.

When Windows installs itself, it creates this section, but doesn't put any lines in it.

OutlineThreshold=*PixelsPerEm*

As far as I know, this setting has never been correctly documented. The Windows Resource Kit and every book I could find is way off base — it's almost as if the folks who wrote the official documentation couldn't figure it out either, so they kinda made things up as they went along. I'd like to thank the *MOM* beta testers, including the phont pholks at Microsoft, for their help in finally setting the record straight.

If you read Chapter 2, you know how fonts can be stored as bitmaps (actual dot patterns) or as outlines (mathematical formulae which can later be turned into dot patterns, for use on a screen or on the printer). Windows has to convert outlines to bitmaps, so characters can be shown on the screen. That's the job of the TrueType rasterizer: it converts outlines to dots, and tries to have the dots ready just in time for Windows to use them.

Windows has two different TrueType rasterizers: a small one (16-bit) and a big one (32-bit). If Windows feeds a small character to the small rasterizer, it works like greased lightning. If Windows sends a small character to the big rasterizer, things go much slower — there's lots of overhead in the big rasterizer, overhead that just isn't necessary to handle a tiny character. Sending a big character to the big rasterizer won't set any speed records, but big characters just take longer to convert into dots. More dots take more time. The worst possible situation arises when Windows sends a big character to the small rasterizer: the rasterizer overflows and recalculates and chugs and re-chugs, and generally runs like a slug.

 Believe me, once you've seen a Redmond slug, you know what a real slug can be. Yeah, snail slugs. The. . . gooey. . . kind. All through the forests surrounding Redmond. Come out in droves when it rains. Six, eight, ten inches long. They don't squish when you step on 'em: they explode.

How does Windows know when to flip from the small rasterizer to the big one? Good question. It uses the **OutlineThreshold=** setting, right here in the **[TrueType]** section.

When you type a character, Windows quickly looks to see what font and what point size you're using. Based on the font and point size, it looks up the "em width." Then, Windows looks at your screen resolution, and calculates how many pixels (dots on the screen) it takes to span the em width, for the font and point size you're using.

If that number is less than the **OutlineThreshold=** value, Windows goes to the speedy small TrueType rasterizer to pick up the corresponding bitmap and slap it on the screen. If that number is more than the **OutlineThreshold=** value, Windows goes to the slug big rasterizer to put the character on the screen.

If there is no **OutlineThreshold=** line in **[TrueType]**, Windows gives it a value of 256. That's a reasonable value: on a plain 1024 x 768 screen, it has Windows use the small TrueType rasterizer for fonts up to 80-100 points. (The actual point cutoff is determined by the em-width of the font you're using, of course.) If you are working with fonts larger than the 80-100 points, Windows slows down and bangs against the big rasterizer.

And it isn't just on the screen. Windows does the same thing when printing, using the TrueType rasterizer on smaller fonts, and GDI calls on larger fonts.

 Why would you want to change the setting? Well, you probably wouldn't. The official Windows documentation says that if you are running out of memory, you might lower the value. I couldn't see any significant reduction in memory usage, even with `OutlineThreshold=50`, and with a properly functioning swap file it's hard to imagine how there might be *any* real benefit. I've come to the conclusion that everything in the official documentation about this setting is a crock. Period.

Microsoft does warn folks not to set this entry higher than 300. They sat you may have problems displaying or printing larger size fonts if the number gets too high.

If you want to change the setting, you'll have to do it manually, with a text editor.

TTEnable=*ZeroOrOne*

TTOnly=*ZeroOrOne*

These two settings correspond to the box you'll see if you crank up the Control Panel's Font applet, and click on the TrueType button (see Figure 8-29).

TrueType can be turned on and off. You'll almost always want it on, but if you turn it off, only non-TrueType fonts appear in all your Windows applications. **TrueType=1** means TrueType is turned on, and the "Enable TrueType Fonts" box is checked; **TrueType=0** means TrueType and the box are off. If there is no **TrueType=** setting in the **[TrueType]** section, Windows assumes you mean 1. And you probably do.

 Why would you want to turn TrueType off? Some folks may find that capability useful if they're creating documents destined to a PostScript-only service bureau. By turning TrueType off, you're more or less guaranteed that a non-Type 1 font will stick out like a sore thumb. (But beware of your **[FontSubstitute]** settings!) You might also want to turn TrueType off if you fed Windows a few thousand TrueType fonts and you're tired of scrolling through all of them, but you don't want to remove them. (In that case, you really should use a font manager; see Chapter 5.)

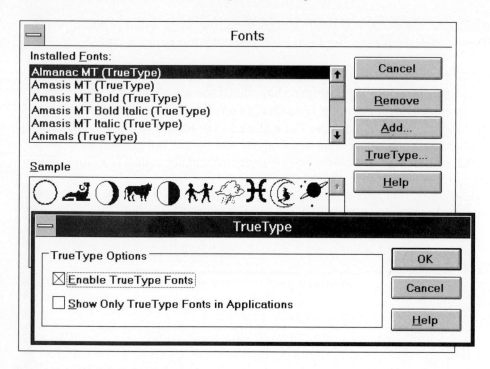

Figure 8-29: TrueType Box

In a spectacular show of hubris, Windows also lets you turn off all fonts other than TrueType fonts. (Microsoft thinks of it as a design feature; you can make up your own mind.) **TTOnly=1** corresponds to the "Show Only TrueType Fonts in Applications" box being checked; **TTOnly=0** means it isn't checked. Thankfully, if the **TTOnly=** setting is missing from **[TrueType]**, Windows assumes you mean 0.

You might want to use the **TTOnly=1** setting if you want to make non-TrueType fonts stick out like a sore thumb, for example, if you're worried a couple of Type 1 fonts might've snuck into a document you're sending to someone else. It could also come in handy if you accidentally installed a thousand Type 1 fonts, and an application that goes bananas when confronted with more than a couple hundred fonts (e.g., Word for Windows) starts jumping up and down like a banana-stuffed monkey. . . . er. . . . cockroach on a hot tin roof.

Windows only looks at the **TTOnly=** setting if **TrueType=1**. If you somehow get the two settings crossed, with **TrueType=0** and **TTOnly=1**, the latter setting is ignored.

TTIfCollisions=*ZeroOrOne*

For over a thousand generations the Jedi knights
were the guardians of peace and justice in the old Republic.
Before the dark times. Before the Empire.

— Obe-Wan Kenobe, *Star Wars*

I can kinda buy the idea of Microsoft as the Evil Empire. Bill looks like Luke Skywalker, even though Luke never succumbed to the Dark Side. Maples could certainly play Darth ("Destroy them!") Vader and Ballmer works as The ("You'll beg me!") Emporer. There's just one little problem. I know Jedi knights. I worked with Jedi knights. And, Adobe, you're no Jedi knight.

Sometimes Windows hits a situation where it has two different fonts, both with the same name. If one of those fonts is a TrueType font, and the other is not, this setting tells Windows how to resolve the conflict.

A setting of **TTIfCollisions=1** tells Windows that, if it encounters a situation where two different fonts have the same name, where one is TrueType and the other is not, it should always pick the TrueType font. Conversely, **TTIfCollisions=0** says Windows should always defer to the non-TrueType font.

In spite of what the official documentation says, if there is no **TTIfCollisions=** line in your **[TrueType]** section, Windows assumes a value of 1.

To change the setting, you'll have to go into **WIN.INI** with a text editor and do it by hand.

You may find reference to a setting called NonTTCaps= in some documentation. It's a throwback to the Windows 3.1 beta test, when it looked like Microsoft might actually capitalize all non-TrueType font names (e.g., the resolutely TrueType Courier New would be Courier New, but a Type 1 Courier would show up on all applications' font lists as COURIER). Thanks to a loud chorus of boos and more than a few brickbats, Microsoft decided to change that behavior before Windows 3.1 shipped (kudos!), opting instead for those cute icons in front of font names to identify their pedigree. The upshot: the **NonTTCaps=** setting has no effect, at least none I can discern.

[windows]

> Many that are first shall be last; and the last shall be first.
>
> — Matthew 19:30

Alphabetically last (well, almost last), geographically and temporally first (Windows puts this section at the beginning of **WIN.INI**), and least in the hearts of its countrymen, the **[windows]** section can accurately be called "all other". Here you will find all the news that doesn't — and probably shouldn't — fit.

Beep=*YesOrNo*

Yes, **True**, **On**, and **1** are all valid values in the affirmative; **No**, **False**, **Off** and **0** (zero) all work to tell Windows no.

 This one is a little strange because it doesn't work on some machines — in spite of what all the documentation says. Far as I can tell, if you have almost any kind of sound extension to Windows installed, the **Beep=** setting has absolutely no effect on anything.

If you're still using the PC's internal speaker, though, setting **Beep=No** will keep Windows from beeping at you when it normally would (i.e., the Asterisk, Critical Stop, Default Beep, Exclamation and Question events — and, since every application gets to decide *when* each of those events occurs, there's no uniformity). See the **[Sounds]** section for more details.

If you're on the speaker, there's no need to edit **WIN.INI** to change the **Beep=** setting. Simply crank up Control Panel, start the Sound applet, and clear out the check box marked "Enable System Sounds." This is shown in Figure 8-30.

If you've installed any of several Microsoft sound-related applications (like one of the Sound Bits packages or the Windows Sound System), your Sound applet dialog box won't even look like this one: among other things, the Enable System Sounds checkbox isn't there. Don't worry about it. In place of the checkbox, up at the top you'll find a list of "Sound Schemes". To turn the **Beep=** off — that is, to mute Windows — just pick the Sound Scheme called **<none>**.

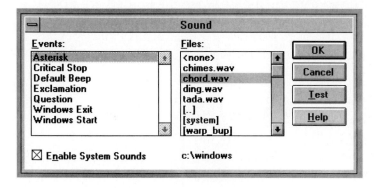

Figure 8-30: Go Dink, Dink, My Darlink

When Windows installs itself, it adds the line **Beep=yes** to the **[windows]** section.

BorderWidth=*NumberOfPixels*

 Resizable windows (i.e., windows that can be stretched) have borders, and the thickness of those borders can be adjusted. This setting counts the number of pixels — dots on the screen — that Windows uses as the thickness of resizable window borders. Windows straight out of the box sets this number to 3, which is a usable number for screens at almost any resolution.

Why would you want to change the **BorderWidth=**? Good question. If you're running in VGA 640 x 480 mode and want to finagle a (very!) little more screen space, you could set **BorderWidth=** to 2. At 1024 x 768, a setting of 4 might make it easier to grab the edges of a window. Maybe. At 1152 x 900 and greater, we've found a setting of 5 to be useful. But if your mousing skills are well-honed and your hand doesn't waver too much, 3 will probably work just fine at any resolution.

Windows will let you get away with settings of 1 to 50 pixels — the latter possibly of benefit to those with vision impairments.

If you want to change the **BorderWidth=**, don't edit **WIN.INI** manually. Look at the bottom of the Desktop applet in the Control Panel (see Figure 8-31).

I use a `BorderWidth=5` at 1024 x 768 resolution and better. It uses up a little extra space on my Windows desktop, but there's a little more room to manipulate the mouse when the borders are a bit wider.

When Windows is installed, a `BorderWidth=3` line gets inserted into the `[windows]` section of `WIN.INI`.

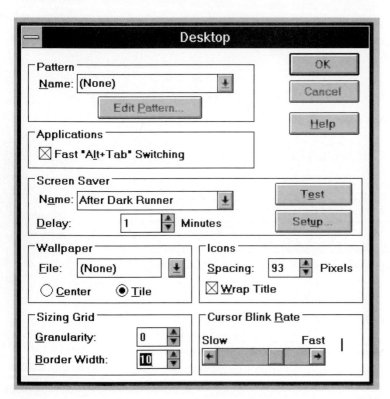

Figure 8-31: The Desktop Window with a Border Width of 10

If you're looking for the `GridGranularity=` setting, which sits just above the `BorderWidth=` entry in the dialog box, you're in the wrong place. That one is in the `[desktop]` section.

`CoolSwitch=`*0ForNo*

No, **False**, **Off** and **0** (zero) all work to tell Windows no. If you have **Yes**, **True**, **On**, or **1**, or the line is missing entirely, Windows uses yes.

 As described in Chapter 2, Microsoft's idea of a "cool" switch is the ability to hit **Alt+Tab** and cycle through little pictures of all the running programs. **Alt+Shift+Tab** does the same thing, but in reverse order. No doubt the next Windows release will have an **UltraCoolSwitch**.

If you turn **CoolSwitch=** off, hitting **Alt+Tab** brings up each running application, in its current size, at its current location, showing the window border but nothing inside the window. Iconized applications only show the title. It's visually distracting because the windows hop all over the screen, depending on where each application currently resides on the screen. It's also slow with some applications.

With **CoolSwitch=** on, **Alt+Tab** ing will show nice, neat synopses of the running applications, all smack dab in the middle of the screen like Figure 8-32.

Figure 8-32: CoolSwitch Picture

It's hard to imagine why you would want to turn **CoolSwitch=** off, but if you do, bring up the Desktop applet in the Control Panel, and clear out the checkbox that says "Fast Alt+Tab Switching".

There is no **CoolSwitch=** line inserted in the **[windows]** section when you install Windows. Thus, if you do nothing to change things, **CoolSwitch=** is on.

CursorBlinkRate=*Milliseconds*

Windows' text cursor — the "insertion point" — blinks on and off. This setting controls how fast.

Didja notice how, when you dig into the belly of the beast, the politically correct terminology, "insertion point" and "caret" and all that fancy-schmancy crap, melts away like a tax-and-spend Democrat at a Ross Perot rally? Down here where the rubber meets the road, it's a "cursor," just like the WinDeity Herself intended. Does my heart good. Kinda gives me hope that sanity prevails somewhere.

The number here represents the number of thousandths of a second the cursor will blink on, then the thousandths of a second the cursor will disappear. According to the documentation, a value of 1000, for example, is supposed to set the cursor blinking on for a full second, then off for a full second, then back on for a second, and so on.

In my tests, though, a setting of 1000 produced a blink on for 1.2 seconds, and a blink off for 1.2 seconds. Surprisingly, a setting of 5000 put the blink at about 5 seconds.

Sometimes Windows "forgets" to blink. I've seen that happen repeatedly when Word for Windows is trying to update its status bar, or save a file. So if precise timing is important (and I can imagine a few situations where it might be), be sure you double-check the machine you'll be using, and don't rely on the blink timing at all when some real work is going on.

Windows straight out of the can sets **CursorBlinkRate=530**. Why? Who knows? Some Redmond usability lab probably determined that a 0.53 second blink rate would increase sales. You can adjust the timing with the scroll bar at the bottom of the Control Panel's Desktop applet: the fastest setting is 200, the slowest 1200. If you dig into **WIN.INI** and set the number manually, it appears as if any number less than 200 is treated as being 200.

DefaultQueueSize=*Messages*

Windows establishes message queues — little sequential buffers — for each Windows program. That's where Windows sticks things it wants to send to the application: "The user just clicked the mouse over here" or "Your window has been resized; handle it", things like that.

This number tells Windows how many messages each applications' message queue should be able to handle before consigning additional messages to the bit bucket. Unless you change it manually (or someone else has changed it for you), the value is 8 — and if the `DefaultQueueSize=` entry is completely missing from `WIN.INI`, the value is also 8.

 If you're smart, you won't play with this setting. There are certain strange circumstances where your applications may start blowing the queue size, but every situation I've seen involves a complex time-intensive application that gets inundated with (often bogus) messages. The folks responsible for applications like that should've already adjusted your `DefaultQueueSize=`, if it'll help any, probably without you knowing about it. So if you find an entry here, don't touch it.

Device=_Printer,Driver,Port_

This entry tells Windows which printer is currently active, which driver Windows should use to talk to that printer, and to which port the printer is currently attached. If you printed something in Windows right now, it would go to this printer. For example, if you are running a LaserJet III on your first serial port, using the standard HP driver, you'll have an entry like this:

```
device=HP LaserJet III,hppcl5a,LPT1:
```

In theory, the name of the printer should match one of the entries in the `[PrinterPorts]` section of `WIN.INI` precisely, no extra spaces, the exact capitalization, and so on.

The driver here is the name of a `.DRV` file in your Windows or System directory, or along the DOS path. At least in theory, it's the `.DRV` file that Windows should use to print on the chosen printer. And it ought to match this particular printer's driver entry in the `[PrinterPorts]` section.

The port must be one of the entries in the `[ports]` section; it can be a file (see `[ports]`). It, too, ought to match this particular printer's port entry in the `[PrinterPorts]` section.

 So how do all of these interact, you ask? Good question, grasshopper. This line, the `device=` line in the `[windows]` section of `WIN.INI`, is the one that actually controls printing; when Windows wants to print something, it looks here. The `[ports]` entries are used when you're in the middle of the Printers applet, trying to attach a printer to a port with the Connect button. The lines in the `[PrinterPorts]` section of `WIN.INI` provide the choices you'll see if you choose

File/Print Setup from most applications; they're also in the first list you'll see if you crank up the Printers applet in the Control Panel. The [PrinterPorts] section also provides time out information for each printer: how long Print Manager should wait for a printer to report that it's alive (the DeviceNotSelectedTimeout=); and how long Print Manager should wait for the printer to respond to any particular attempt to communicate before complaining to the boss (the TransmissionRetryTimeout=). You're the boss.

 While you might think there would be some sort of mysterious interconnection between the three sections, I didn't find any. device= does the work; [PrinterPorts] keeps track of the options for Print Setup and the Printer applet and holds the timeouts, and [ports] keeps track of the Printer applet connect options. [devices] doesn't seem to do anything. The section names aren't very illuminating; there's an enormous duplication of information among the four sections; and all that duplication and obfuscation leads to any number of different ways you could shoot yourself in the foot, if you're not careful. Even if you are careful.

The **device=** entry is usually established when you install Windows; that's why Windows steps you through a printer setup during installation. While it's possible to bypass the printer setup on installation, few people do, so this entry is almost always filled out.

 If you decide to change the device= line manually, be very cautious of the spelling of the printer name. In general, you'd be crazy to try to coordinate all of these settings manually: it's much smarter to use the File/Print Setup option of most applications, or the Control Panel's Printer applet, to finagle this line. *Don't say I didn't warn you.*

DeviceNotSelectedTimeout=*Seconds*

TransmissionRetryTimeout=*Seconds*

 Talk about confusing. No, this is *not* the current "Device Not Selected Timeout" setting. It's the *default* "Device Not Selected Timeout" value, the value that would be used if, at this very moment, you went into the Control Panel's Printer applet, tried to set up a printer, and pushed the Connect button. (See the previous discussion for a definition of "Device Not Selected Timeout".)

Similarly, *mutatis mutandis,* the `TransmissionRetryTimeout=` number you specify here is *not* the current "Transmission Retry Timeout" value. It's the default "Transmission Retry Timeout" value that would be used if you went into the Control Panel's Printer applet, tried to set up a printer, and pushed the Connect button.

The exception being when you click on Connect to connect a PostScript printer. If Windows discovers you're trying to connect a PostScript printer, it peeks into **WIN.INI**, looks at the `TransmissionRetryTimeout=` value, doubles it, and uses that number as the default "Transmission Retry Timeout" value in the dialog box. (Yeah, the official documentation is wrong again.)

 To find the current "Device Not Selected Timeout" and "Transmission Retry Timeout" values, you'll have to look at the `[PrinterPorts]` setting for the printer currently specified in the `device=` line of this section. Got that? Yeah. Now get this: sometimes Print Manager *doesn't even wait* for the "Device Not Selected Timeout" time to pass. Sometimes you get the elevator; sometimes the shaft, eh?

Windows right out of the box sets `DeviceNotSelectedTimeout=15` and `TransmissionRetryTimeout=45` seconds. You may want to change them if you have decided that all new printers you connect to your system should be given a bit more (or less) time to identify themselves to Print Manager as alive and breathing; or if you think all the new printers should have more time to come up for air.

If you want to change them, you'll have to do it manually. And remember, you're changing the default value for the Connect box in the Printer applet, not the `...Timeout=` setting for the currently active printer, or any other printer, for that matter. Many Print Manager alternatives (notably the WinJet print spoolers) don't even look at this number.

`Documents=`*Ext Ext Ext ...*

Chances are very good that this entry is *not* what you're looking for. Read on, read on.

The `Documents=` line takes a list of three-character file name extensions, separated by spaces (not commas). For example, this line:

```
Documents=doc wrt foo bar dd
```

will tell File Manager that all files with names that end in `.DOC`, `.WRT`, `.FOO`, `.BAR`, and `.DD` are to be treated as "documents." This line only applies to File Manager, and only in a very peculiar sense. When File Manager thinks it has a "document", it does two things. First, it puts a little "document" icon next to the file name in its listings as in Figure 8-33.

📄 fonts.doc	4044
📄 frontm.doc	331395
📄 galley.doc	6107
📄 moremoms.doc	71484
📄 proposal.doc	34840

Figure 8-33: File Manager's Document Icon

Second, if you use the View by File Type option in File Manager — one of the more obscure settings, for sure — you can tell File Manager to display (or ignore) all "documents." That's *everything* File Manager does with "documents" — a different icon and an obscure View option. Thus, **Documents=** is definitely a minor league setting, one you can almost always safely ignore.

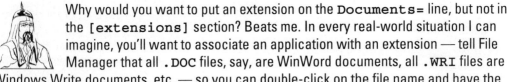 Here's another good reason to ignore it. Regardless of what you'll read in the official documentation or any other book, File Manager looks in three places to pin down file name extensions that should be considered "documents." First, it looks in the Registration database to see if there's an application associated with files with the given extension. Second is this **Documents=** line in the **[windows]** section. Third is the list of every extension in the **[extensions]** section.

In fact the **Documents=** line and the **[extensions]** section only differ in one important respect: extensions listed in the **[extensions]** section have applications associated with them, so you can use File Manager to double-click on a file name and have the application launch with the file loaded.

Why would you want to put an extension on the **Documents=** line, but not in the **[extensions]** section? Beats me. In every real-world situation I can imagine, you'll want to associate an application with an extension — tell File Manager that all `.DOC` files, say, are WinWord documents, all `.WRI` files are Windows Write documents, etc. — so you can double-click on the file name and have the associated application spring to life with the document loaded. That kind of association is done with the **[extensions]** section. It is not done with the **Documents=** line.

Hey, why sweat the small stuff? Ferget about this setting. If you want to designate an extension as a document, go ahead and use File Manager to associate it with an application — even something as innocuous as Notepad. You'll get all the benefits of a `Documents=` like entry; the only disadvantage being that, if you double-click on the file's name while in File Manager, Notepad will launch with that document loaded. Big deal.

When Windows installs itself, you get a **Documents=** line with no extensions listed. If you insist upon changing it, you'll have to go in with a text editor and do it manually.

Serves you right.

Oh. Look in the **[programs]** section of **WIN.INI** for some interesting related facts. It ain't as easy as it seems!

DosPrint=_YesOrNo_

Yes, **True**, **On**, and **1** are all valid values in the affirmative; **No**, **False**, **Off** and **0** (zero) all work to tell Windows no.

This **[windows]** setting is the one that reflects the checkedness of the "Fast Printing Direct to Port" option in Control Panel's Printers applet, Connect box — see Figure 8-34.

When **DosPrint=No**, Windows writes directly to the printer port. That's the fast setting; it corresponds to the "Fast Printing Direct to Port" box being checked. (**No** means it _is_ checked — confusing, eh?)

 When **DosPrint=Yes**, Windows takes a little side-trip on its way to the printer port. It uses the DOS routines, the same ones that DOS uses to write to the printer. (**Yes** means the "Fast Printing Direct to Port" box is _not_ checked.) If you're among the cognoscenti — the kind of person who calculates baseball batting averages in hex — the DOS routine in question is the file handling service at Interrupt 21h; but if you know what Interrupt 21h is, you probably didn't need me to tell you that it's the appropriate DOS routine!

Windows installs itself with **DosPrint=No**. That's the faster option, and it works in the vast majority of cases. If Windows refuses to print, no way, no how, and your print driver is installed right, and you can print just fine from DOS outside of

Windows, you should: 1) change this setting to **Yes**; 2) restart Windows and see if it'll print; and, if you're successful, 3) get on the phone and raise bloody hell with the printer manufacturer. There's absolutely no excuse in this day and age for a printer to be incompatible with Windows.

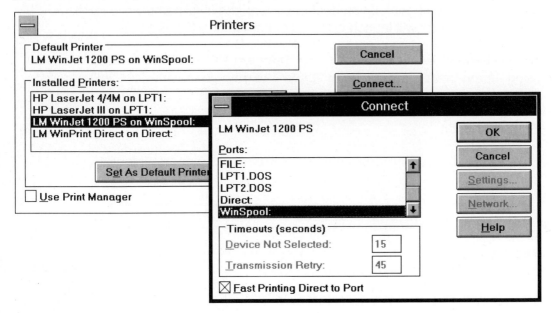

Figure 8-34: Direct to Starboard

One little-known fact: printing to one of the phantom "ports" (e.g., **LPT1.OS2** or **LPT2.DOS**) forces Windows to use the DOS BIOS routines, ignoring the **DosPrint=** setting. That sounds like the answer to a trivia question, but it can be useful if you want to check out whether a printer is dying because of the "Fast Printing Direct to Port" option.

DoubleClickHeight=*Pixels*

DoubleClickWidth=*Pixels*

DoubleClickSpeed=*Millisecond*

Ever wonder how Windows tells a double-click from two single-clicks? It's all controlled by these three settings. In short, you must click twice within the allotted **DoubleClickSpeed=** time, and the **DoubleClickHeight=** and

`DoubleClickWidth=` space. If you're too slow, the clicks are spaced more than the set number of milliseconds apart, or if you move the mouse too much, more than the calculated number of dots on the screen, Windows will interpret your hot double click mouse action as two lame single clicks.

 Actually, that "calculated number of dots" is a little more complicated than you might imagine. Windows takes your `DoubleClickHeight=` (respectively, `DoubleClickWidth=`), divides by two, rounds up to the nearest integer, and lets your mouse move that many pixels up or down (respectively, left or right) before calling the whole double-click off. In effect, and despite what you might read elsewhere, the `DoubleClickHeight=` and `DoubleClickWidth=` define the height and width of a rectangle, centered at the point of the first click, that must contain the location of the second click.

Windows right out of the box does not place either `DoubleClickHeight=` or `DoubleClickWidth=` lines in `[windows]`. If Windows looks for a `DoubleClickHeight=` or `DoubleClickWidth=` and doesn't find one, it assumes a value of 4.

Thus, unless you've changed things, to effectively execute a double-click you must click once, move at most two pixels up, down, left or right, and then click the mouse again. And you have to get the two clicks down within the `DoubleClickSpeed=` amount of time.

Young hands and shaky hands often have trouble holding the mouse perfectly steady for the duration of a double-click. Folks who run on high resolution monitors, jack up the acceleration setting for their mouse, or refuse to clean their mice more than once a month may also benefit from changing this value. To do so, you'll have to open up **WIN.INI** manually and add a couple new lines or, if the lines are already there, type in a new value.

Microsoft says the `DoubleClickSpeed=` setting is in milliseconds, but I couldn't figure out a reliable way to test it. I did find that a setting of 100 (presumably one-tenth of a second) was so fast that I physically *couldn't click the mouse fast enough* to trigger a double-click.

The `DoubleClickSpeed=` is much easier to change than the `DoubleClickHeight=` and `DoubleClickWidth=`: use the Mouse applet in the Control Panel. If you are running Windows with the original mouse driver, the

Double Click Speed setting is in the applet's primary dialog (look under **MouseSpeed=** in Figure 8-35. If you're using the Microsoft Mouse 9.0 Driver, you'll have to click on the "Sensitivity" button in the main dialog to adjust the Double Click Speed.

When Windows installs itself, it sets the **DoubleClickSpeed=452** milliseconds. Why? Who knows? Some genius in the Redmond Usability Labs probably averaged results from 226 different experiments, then multiplied by two. The scroll bar in the applet will let you adjust the DoubleClickSpeed to any value from 100 to 900, a range that should suffice for just about anybody.

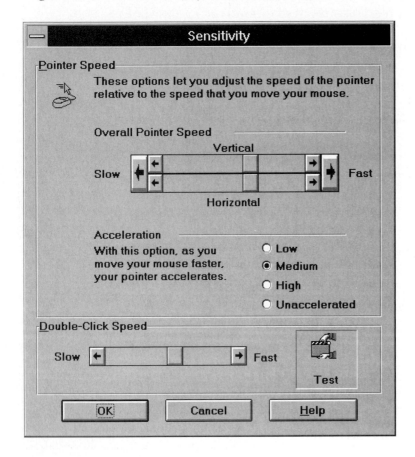

Figure 8-35: One Sensitive Mouse

You may find a much larger `DoubleClickHeight=` and `DoubleClickWidth=`, and a somewhat shorter `DoubleClickSpeed=`, to be to your liking. Personally, I prefer a `DoubleClickHeight=10` and `DoubleClickWidth=10` with a `DoubleClickSpeed=300`: that way I have more room to move, but my scaling back on the repeat speed reduces the chance of a misfire.

`KeyboardDelay=`*QuarterSecondsMoreOrLess*

`KeyboardSpeed=`*CharactersPerSecond*

 Windows provides key repeating, hold down a key on the keyboard for long enough and it repeats itselffffffffffffff, even for those without a repeater feature on their keyboards. Nice feature. These two settings control the two factors in key repeating: how long you have to hold down the key before it starts repeating; and, once repeating starts, how quickly the ersatz key presses are generated.

 All the documentation I've found, official, unofficial, or otherwise, says the `KeyboardDelay=` and `KeyboardSpeed=` settings are in milliseconds. That simply isn't true: try it yourself and you'll see. My guess is that the `KeyboardDelay=` setting is roughly quarters of a second, and the `KeyboardSpeed=` is roughly the number of ersatz characters generated per second. Microsoft's documentation is only off by a factor of several hundred or so on `KeyboardDelay=`; and it's completely, demonstrably bass-ackwards on `KeyboardSpeed=`.

 Now, now, boys. If Microsoft got the documentation right, it would leave most users with nothing to do most workday evenings, and on Saturdays and weekends, too. Not to mention put a whole bunch of very nice writers out of business. And bookstores. No need to carp. As Monty says, "Always look on the bright side of life. . ."

Not surprisingly, a **0** value for **`KeyboardDelay=`** does *not* mean that the repeat action is instantaneous: there's a built-in lag of a fraction of a second before the repeater kicks in. That's expectable and reasonable. A value of **1** on my bone-stock Northgate Omnikey keyboard introduces a small but very noticeable hesitation in the repeat: I'd guess about a tenth to a quarter of a second. A value of **2**, subjectively, doubles the time lag, to perhaps half a second. **3** goes up again;

maybe it's at three-quarters of a second. Settings higher than **3** don't seem to do much: they all behave as if the value were **3**.

Go figger.

The easiest way to set the **KeyboardDelay=** is by popping into the Keyboard applet of the Control Panel. There you'll see a dialog that looks like Figure 8-36.

The "Delay Before First Repeat" scrollbar only stops in four places: the far left gives rise to a **KeyboardDelay** value of **3**; all the way over to the right produces a **0**; and the two intermediate spots, left to right, are **2** and **1**. When Windows installs itself, it includes a line in **[windows]** that says **KeyboardDelay=2**.

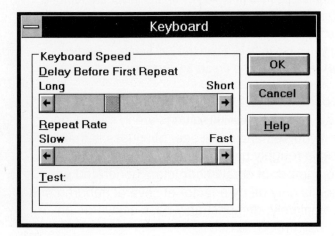

Figure 8-36: Over and Over and Over and Over

The **KeyboardSpeed=** setting can have a value from **0** to **31**. In the Keyboard applet above, **0** corresponds to the far left position of the scrollbar, **31** to the far right. Keep in mind that, if your keyboard supports key repeating (and most do), a setting of **0** in Windows will *not* disable your keyboard's native repeating ability. Thus setting **KeyboardSpeed** to **0**, in general, will not turn off key repeating. For some strange reason Windows, upon installation, cranks this setting up as high as it will go, a righteous (and blinding!) **KeyboardSpeed=31**.

Watch Out! If you're mucking around with editing these entries in `WIN.INI`, then flipping into the Keyboard applet in the Control Panel to test your settings, you may be astonished to discover that the Keyboard applet often picks up the *wrong values* for `KeyboardDelay=` and `KeyboardSpeed=`. It's a bug, pure and simple, and it hit me over and over again. To be absolutely sure you have the setting you want, you should rely on the text in `WIN.INI`, not the scrollbar position in the Keyboard applet.

 I, personally, prefer a `KeyboardDelay=3` and `KeyboardSpeed=15` or so. A teenager might find the delay much too long, but sometimes I let my pinkies rest on the keys a bit longer than they should: the added delay lets me lollygag around a bit. My `KeyboardSpeed=` setting represents a compromise between two competing problems: I'd like the cursor to move faster when I'm using the arrow keys; I'd like it to move slower when I'm deleting or backspacing.

 The old, dumb IBM 3278 terminals used to have an accelerator key on 'em: push the accelerator key and an arrow key at the same time, and the arrow flew (relatively speaking, of course; we *are* talking big iron here). It's a pity that design never found its way to the PC.

`load=`*Program Program Program ...*

`run=`*Program Program Program ...*

When Windows starts, it checks a couple of things, then loads Program Manager (or whichever Windows shell is active; see the **shell=** setting in the **[boot]** section of **SYSTEM.INI** detailed later in this chapter). The **load=** and **run=** settings give you an opportunity to tell Program Manager which programs you want to get started before Program Manager finishes. If you want to crank up programs after Program Manager finishes — or if you have no particular preference one way or another — put those programs in Program Manager's Startup group: it's a whole lot easier to drag programs in a group than to futz with these lousy lines in **WIN.INI**. And, as explained in Chapter 3, the Startup group is a whole lot easier to bypass.

 If you don't use Program Manager — preferring the likes of shells such as Norton Desktop, say, or Central Point's PC Tools Desktop — the **load=** and **run=** lines may be ignored completely, or interpreted in a different way. If you have a shell other than Program Manager, you'll have to consult the shell's documentation to see what (if anything) is done with **load=** and **run=**. You can also ignore the rest of this discussion.

Each program on the **load=** line is "loaded": set running, in iconized form, at about the same time that Program Manager comes alive. The **run=** line is quite similar to **load=**. The only difference is that **run=** programs get started in their restored (i.e., partial screen, not iconized, not full screen) state.

Although it's a bit hard to tell because there's a lag time between starting a Windows program and it actually appearing on the screen, it looks to me like the **load=** programs are run, in the order they appear in **WIN.INI**; then the **run=** programs get going immediately after the **load=** programs; then the Program Manager itself finishes loading; finally programs in the Startup group are started, one by one, beginning with the first icon in the group, running from left to right, top to bottom.

 In spite of what Microsoft's documentation says, the only way to add programs to the **load=** line is to type 'em in yourself, using a text editor on **WIN.INI**. Putting a program in Program Manager's Startup group most assuredly does *not* add it to the **load=** or **run=** line.

According to Microsoft's Knowledge Base, the order of execution of programs in the Startup group is actually a bit more complex. Windows apparently looks at all the programs in the Startup group, left to right, top to bottom, but the order of execution depends on whether the programs are Windows apps or not. It starts the first Windows program, the second Windows program, and so on, until it hits the end of the list. Next, it loops up to the beginning and runs the *second* DOS program, the third, and so on, finally running the first DOS program last.

Wait. It gets worse. According to Microsoft, if you have an icon in the Startup group that completely covers another, the one underneath won't be run at all.

You might also want to experiment with *removing* programs from the **load=** and **run=** lines: some over-zealous installation programs stick themselves on those lines simply because it's easier than adding themselves to your Startup group.

Names on the **load=** line should be separated by single spaces. "Program" names on this line follow the usual Windows routine: if you don't tell Windows where to find the program, it first looks in the Windows directory (e.g., **C:\WINDOWS**), then the Windows System directory, and finally along the DOS PATH. If the file you specify isn't a program, Windows looks in the Registration Database and **[extensions]** to see if there's a program associated with the particular extension and, if so, cranks up the program with the indicated file loaded.

Sound complicated? It isn't. Consider this load line:

```
load=c:\winword\mother\chap08.doc pointer
```

Windows first looks at **c:\winword\mother\chap08.doc**. It doesn't even look for the file; instead it checks to see if **.DOC** is a valid extension for a program (see **Programs=** down below). It isn't. But the Registration Database tells Windows that **.DOC** files are associated with a program called **c:\winword\winword.exe**. So Windows fires up **winword.exe**, feeding it **chap08.doc**, and WinWord suddenly appears as an icon on my desktop, **chap08.doc** already trapped in its maw.

Then Windows looks at **pointer.exe**. Yep, Windows decides (looking quickly at the **Programs=** entry), that's the name of a valid program. So Windows tries to find it, first in the Windows directory (not there), then in the **windows\system** directory (not there either), then it marches down all the directories on my DOS path. It just so happens that **pointer.exe** is in my **c:\utility\mouse** directory, which is on the path, so Windows runs **pointer.exe** as an icon.

While all of this is going on, Windows is also initializing Program Manager. Once Progman is ready, it steps through the Startup group. And it all happens in a few seconds. Not exactly the Big Bang, but whaddya expect for less than a hundred bucks?

load= and **run=** lines are limited to 127 characters each. If you need to trim the lines down, remember that Windows is smart enough to look along your DOS path for programs that don't sit in your Windows or System directories. Also keep in mind that **.EXE** extensions are optional: **pointer.exe** and just plain **pointer** will crank up the same program.

MenuDropAlignment=*1ForYes*

Usually when you click on a menu, all the menu choices appear directly below the top menu item, left-aligned. Perhaps in deference to those cultures that read right-to-left, Microsoft built in the capability of right-aligning the drop on menus. For example in Windows Write, a right aligned File menu drop looks like Figure 8-37.

A **MenuDropAlignment=0** triggers left-aligned drop menus, as does the absence of the entry entirely; a value of **1** makes them right aligned. The only way to change the value is to edit **WIN.INI** with a text editor — and you'll probably have to add the whole line, as Windows doesn't put one in **[windows]** when it installs.

 Note that this setting does *not* right-align the top level menu names; nor does it right-align the entries within the dropped down menu. Because of that simple fact, setting menus to right alignment makes a general mish-mash of the screen; it's certainly of little use to those who read right-to-left. It's hard to imagine a real-world situation where right aligning menus will do anything more than frustrate you.

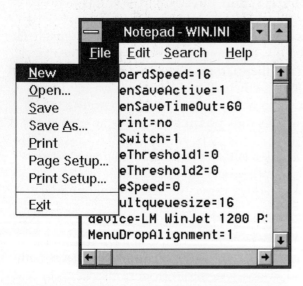

Figure 8-37: Notepad Right Drop Align

MenuShowDelay=_Milliseconds_

Don't tell Mao, but I call this one "Emperor Has No Clothes Delay." The official documentation talks about it; every Windows reference I've looked at parrots the official documentation; but I'll be hog-tied and festooned in sheep dip if I can get it to work on *any* 386 or 486 system.

Here's the theory. If you hold down your left mouse button and run the mouse across a menu, each menu list drops down, one at a time. No surprise there. On a fast system, swiping your mouse quickly along the menu bar can trigger quite a light show as each menu falls, then rolls back up, the next one drops, and so on.

On a slow system, though, swiping your mouse quickly along the menu bar can get real confusing: Windows can't clear out one menu before the next drops down, and the dropped lists fumble all over each other like hardware vendors at a Cringely COMDEX party.

The **MenuShowDelay=** setting is supposed to improve Windows on a slow system by slowing it down even more. Get that?

In theory, again, Windows is supposed to look at the **MenuShowDelay=** setting before dropping a menu list, and wait for the specified number of milliseconds before it actually drops. That's supposed to keep the menus from falling all over each other. The default setting for 286 systems is supposed to be **400** milliseconds; for 386 and 486 systems, it's supposed to be **0**. But, again, no matter what setting we used, we didn't see *any* effect on 386 or 486 systems.

MouseSpeed=*SpeedSetting*

MouseThreshold1=*Pixels*

MouseThreshold2=*Pixels*

Windows has a mouse turbocharger. The basic idea is pretty simple. Like a car engine turbocharger, the Windows mouse turbo sits around twiddling its thumbs when you're moving slowly: when you're going slow, the turbo kicks out and lets you get maximum maneuverability at low speed. But when you finally take off, when your mouse starts moving quickly, the turbocharger kicks in and screams, letting you cover vast amounts of screen real estate with relatively short, quick moves.

The uncanny part of mouse turbocharging (Windows calls it "acceleration"): for quite a few mousers, it feels so natural. Many people don't even realize it's happening.

 Don't be confused if these three settings don't work: different mice stick their settings in different places. The Microsoft Mouse 2.0, with its MS Mouse Driver 9.0, for example, bypasses the **WIN.INI** settings entirely. You'll find MS Mouse Driver 9.0 settings in the **MOUSE.INI** file, located in the **\mouse** subdirectory. The format of these other mouse settings can be completely different from the ones in **WIN.INI**. My **MOUSE.INI**, for example, starts out like this:

```
[mouse]
Memory=HighMem
MouseType=SERIAL1
Device=Mouse
PhysicalButtons=2
HorizontalSensitivity=65
VerticalSensitivity=65
ActiveAccelerationProfile=2
RotationAngle=0
PrimaryButton=1
SecondaryButton=3
ClickLock=0
```

which doesn't look anything at all like the three settings in **WIN.INI**. So before you start playing around with these three mouse lines in **WIN.INI**, make sure your mouse driver uses them!

MouseSpeed= can have three values. A **0** indicates that you don't want turbocharging; the pointer on the screen should move at the same rate as the mouse itself. Without acceleration, most people will bite their nails off waiting for Windows to move the pointer around.

 Setting **MouseSpeed=1** activates standard turbocharging. Here's how it works. Periodically, your mouse taps your computer on the shoulder and says, "I'm here now." That's how your computer keeps track of where the mouse is located. (Actually, the mouse says "I moved *this* far in *that* direction," but I digress. . .) Every time the mouse taps your computer on the shoulder, it's called an "interrupt," because, quite literally, it interrupts the machine. The mouse driver keeps track of these interrupts, feeding Windows the current location of the pointer on the screen.

With **MouseSpeed=1**, the mouse driver looks to see if the mouse has moved more than **MouseThreshold1=** pixels between any pair of interrupts. For example, if **MouseThreshold1=5**, the mouse driver looks to see if the pointer has moved five or more pixels between interrupts. If so, the turbocharging kicks in: the driver *doubles* the number of pixels' movement it feeds to Windows. If the mouse moved 8 pixels, Windows is told that it moved 16. And so on.

With **MouseSpeed=2**, the mouse driver jumps into hyperspace. Not only does it double the number of pixels it reports to Windows if **MouseThreshold1=** is exceeded, it quadruples the number of pixels if **MouseThreshold2=** is exceeded. Fast, indeed.

Say you have things set up so **MouseSpeed=2**, **MouseThreshold1=5**, and **MouseThreshold2=10**. If you move the mouse eight pixels between interrupts, exceeding **MouseThreshold1=,** the mouse driver will tell Windows that you moved 16 pixels. If you move the mouse 12 pixels, more than **MouseThreshold2=,** the driver fibs and says you moved 48.

 If you think that sounds a lot more complicated than it should be, well, I'd have to agree with you. The MS Mouse Driver 9 uses a sensitivity rating that hides some of the details, but still gives you a lot of control: for most people, it's much more intuitive and usable than the standard Windows driver.

If you're looking to change these settings, the best place to start is the mouse applet in the Control Panel (see Figure 8-38). It cranks up a box that looks like this (the MS Mouse Driver Version 9 replaces this box with the one I described under **DoubleClickSpeed=** earlier):

The Mouse Tracking Speed scrollbar has seven positions. If you click on each one, from left to right, 1 to 7, here are the settings you will see in the **[windows]** section:

@ Scrollbar Position	1	2	3	4	5	6	7	Default
MouseSpeed	0	1	1	1	2	2	2	1
MouseThreshold1	0	10	7	4	4	4	4	5
MouseThreshold2	0	0	0	0	12	9	6	10

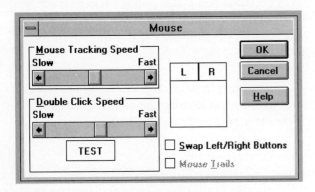

Figure 8-38: Standard Mouse Dialog

When Windows installs itself, it doesn't put any of these three lines in **[windows]**. In the face of no reliable way to clock these small settings, I have to rely on Microsoft when it tells me what the default values might be: Microsoft says it's **MouseSpeed=1**, **MouseThreshhold1=5**, and **MouseThreshhold2=10**. If you've waded this far into the book, you know damn good and well how reliable the official documentation can be, so don't take those published default values (i.e., **1**, **5**, and **10**) as gospel!

 Does it seem odd to you, too, that there is no way to change the settings back to the default 1, 5, and 10 from the Control Panel? Doesn't it seem even odder that the default **MouseSpeed=** setting would ignore **MouseThreshhold2=**, yet assign a value to the **MouseThreshhold2=** setting — a value that you can't retrieve, can't use, in any way whatsoever?

I remain skeptical.

MouseTrails=*NumberOfGhosts*

If you're running Windows on a laptop, you've no doubt discovered that the mouse pointer can be terribly hard to *see*. This setting tells Windows to track movement of the pointer with hazy ghost-like images, accentuating the arrow and making it easier to follow.

The number of ghosts can range from **0** to **7**. If there's no **MouseTrails=** line in the **[windows]** section, and there won't be one if you don't put it in there, or click on the checkbox, Windows assumes a value of **0**.

 There are several oddities lurking with this setting. For starters, it only works for sure with the standard, dumb Windows EGA, VGA and SuperVGA video drivers — the ones that ship with Windows. I'm not sure exactly how Windows determines whether the standard bone-stock video drivers are installed (or, more to the point, how you might fake Windows out and make it *believe* it has the stock drivers installed), but I have yet to see the **MouseTrails** setting work with any other video drivers.

If you look at Figure 8-38 you'll see that "Mouse Trails" is a check box. If you are using any video driver except the bone-stock EGA, VGA, or SuperVGA drivers, the text next to that box will be grayed out, precisely as shown in the picture.

 That's strange. This is bizarre. From the Control Panel, *there's no provision for entering a number, no way to set the number of ghosts that will track the mouse pointer.* Windows has created a crafty kludge to reconcile the dialog box's check box with the **WIN.INI** file's numeric setting: it turns the **MouseTrails=** number negative!

If you check that Mouse Trails box immediately after installation, Windows sets **MouseTrails=7**. Fair enough. If you then clear the checkbox, Windows sets **MouseTrails=-7**. Yeah. You read that right. Apparently negative numbers are treated the same as zero, i.e., they turn off mouse droppi. . . er. . . trailings. (And here's yet another reason for getting the treatment of negative numbers in **INI** files documented correctly.)

When you subsequently check the Mouse trails box, Windows turns it to a positive **7**. If you manually set the Mouse Trails number to **2**, say, and then *un*check the Mouse Trails box, Windows turns the value to **-2**. Et cetera, et cetera. . . and so forth.

Oh, Mao. Your Yul Brynner impression is so. . . virile.

NetWarn=*0ForNo*

Every time you start Windows, it looks to see if you've set it up to be on a network and, if so, tries to re-establish communication with the network. If Windows can't get on the network, it normally pops up a message warning you of that fact, and then bypasses all the fun network setup stuff.

A **NetWarn** of **0** tells Windows to forget about the warning message. A value of **1** makes Windows display the message, should one be warranted. (That's also what happens if there is no line in the **[windows]** section.) The easiest way to change the setting is to go into the network applet in the Control Panel. There will be a checkbox saying "Disable warning when network not running" or "Network warnings" or some such: precise wording varies depending on which network you have installed. Check or clear that box to change **NetWarn**. Doesn't it strike you as strange that this one is in **[windows]** and not **[network]**. Yeah, me too.

NullPort=*PortName*

I am not an ass; only the saddle of an ass.

— Samuel Clemens, *Recent Carnival of Crime*, 1877

If you can find even one use for this setting, you're a better organism than I, Gunga Din. The official documentation says it's in **[windows]** to fill in the name of a port when a printer is installed but not connected to any port; supposed to be behind the Connect button in the Control Panel's printer applet. Kind of a default default, if you know what I mean.

Hogwash. I've connected plenty of printers and I've never seen anything assigned to the **NullPort** "port". Try it yourself. Even on a freshly installed copy of Windows, there's no **None** in the Connect box. Windows *does* install with a line in **[windows]** that says **NullPort=None**, which is all well and good, if it were of any use. Maybe you can find a use for **None** or **NullPort** someplace, but I sure can't.

Lemme give you a tip, kid. Avoid this line in **WIN.INI**. It doesn't seem to hurt anything, but it doesn't seem to do anything, either. Kinda like several Congressional Committees I could mention. But don't get me started. Take a look at the **[PrinterPorts]** section for yet another description of how and when **NullPort=** doesn't work.

Programs=_Ext Ext Ext ..._

 This one really sent me on a wild goose chase. The official documentation says that the **Programs=** setting tells Windows the extensions of files that are to be treated as programs. As far as I can tell, Windows only uses this setting in three ways: (1) File Manager puts a "program" icon (see Figure 8-39) in front of all files with an extension listed in the **Programs=** line, and treats 'em as programs in the "View by File Type" option (c.f. the **Documents=** line in the **[windows]** section); (2) File Manager tries to run something when you double-click on a file name with one of the listed extensions, or drag a document onto one; and (3) Program Manager tries to run something when you click on File, then Run, then choose a file with one of the listed extensions.

```
test.bat         20
wlhatemp.bat    127
lha.exe       34283
ohmon.exe      9555
```

Figure 8-39: File Manager's "Program" Icon

Windows right out of the box puts this line in the **[windows]** section of **WIN.INI**:

```
Programs=com exe bat pif
```

and the official (and unofficial!) documentation says that you need to list the three-letter extension of all files that Windows should consider as applications, no periods, separated by spaces not commas. The default setting says that **.COM** files, **.EXE** files, **.BAT** files, and **.PIF** files are all programs, all executable by double-clicking on the file name in File Manager, or doing a File Run from Program Manager. Fair enough.

That's the theory, interpreted as best I can see. Implementation is a bit different.

 I tried adding a three-letter extension, TST, to the Programs= list. Then I re-named all sorts of executable files — .COMS, .EXES, .BATS, and .PIFS — so they had a file name of TEST.TST. That .TST extension should tell Windows that the programs are runnable, right? .NOT!

While File Manager properly identified TEST.TST with a program icon, neither File Manager nor Program Manager could execute the file. I kept getting this dialog box seen in Figure 8-40.

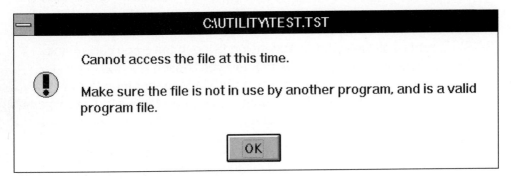

Figure 8-40: Outta Luck, Turkey

To make matters worse, the dialog box was system-modal; in other words, it sat up on the screen and I couldn't get anything to run until I clicked OK.

Bummer. Experiments with other extensions proved equally fruitless. . . and frustrating. I'm forced to conclude that the only valid entries on the Programs= line are the defaults, COM, EXE, BAT and PIF plus the SCR which is just a synonym for EXE.

For some interesting related information, take a look at the [programs] section of WIN.INI.

If you don't want Windows to run one of these four types of files (some people want to associate the PIF editor with double-clicking on a .PIF file, for example;

other folks might want to associate a text editor with a `.BAT` file), remove the offending extension.

`run=`*Program Program Program ...*

See `load=`.

`ScreenSaveActive=`*ZeroOrOne*

`ScreenSaveTimeOut=`*Seconds*

 These settings sent me off on another romp down the Windows hole. And I'm still not sure I understand all I saw. But in a nutshell, these settings do *not* necessarily reflect reality; the only way I found to get the straight scoop is to bring up the Desktop applet from the Control Panel.

The `ScreenSaveActive=` setting is supposedly put at **0** when Windows' screen saver is off. It's supposedly set to **1** when Windows' screen saver is on. (If you use another screen saver, such as After Dark, this setting still seems to make the screen saver active. I think.

Unfortunately, it doesn't work the way it's documented. Try it yourself. Use the Desktop applet to turn Windows' screen saver off. Then go into `WIN.INI` with a text editor, and change `ScreenSaveActive=` to **1**. Guess what? The screen saver does not spring back to life. In fact, you can save `WIN.INI`, exit and restart Windows, and it *still* won't be re-activated.

The inconsistency stems from a failure to update the `scrnsave.exe=` setting in the `[boot]` section of `SYSTEM.INI`, and you should look up that setting if you're messing around with the screen saver.

`ScreenSaveTimeout=` gives Windows' screen saver time delay, in seconds. Oddly, the Desktop applet only lets you specify this setting in minutes. Any number you choose in the applet is multiplied by 60 and stuck in the setting: the smallest number you can type in the box is 1, the largest 99. Manually setting `ScreenSaveTimeout=0` seems to turn off the screen saver.

Windows' screen saver will not jump into action if a DOS window occupies the full screen. Commercial screen savers generally have ways to work around the problem.

When Windows installs itself, it sets **ScreenSaveActive=0** (off) and **ScreenSaveTimeout=120** (two minutes).

 The bottom line: don't muck with these settings manually. I don't care what the documentation says. Even if you can change things (and you probably can't!), it's hard telling what might happen if the settings get crossed with an add-on screen saver. Use the Desktop applet — or, better (and certainly more fun!) get a replacement screen saver and forget the one that comes with Windows.

Besides, screen savers don't really do much. Back in the old days of CGA and Mono video, screen burn-in was a real problem: leave the same image on the screen long enough (where "long" is measured in months) and sooner or later the phosphors would become permanently altered. Nowadays, it's very, very hard to burn in a decent monitor. And there's always the off switch.

Oh. If you're searching for the method to bypass the Windows screen saver password, you're in the wrong file: look at the **PWProtected=** settings in **CONTROL.INI**.

---

spooler=_YesOrNo_

 While Print Manager may not be the very best print spooler on the market, it's certainly among the best. (If you're unfamiliar with the concept of a print spooler, look in Chapter 7, under the section *Oh Buffer, My Buffer.*) The **spooler=** setting lets you turn Print Manager on and off.

If you set **spooler=yes**, Print Manager will be enabled for the next Windows print job. If you set it to anything else (e.g., **no**), Print Manager probably won't be used on the next print job.

 "Probably" is the operative word here. If Print Manager is still running on an old print job when you set **spooler=no**, and while that old job is still going you print something new, the new print job probably will be spooled to Print Manager. Sometimes it seems Windows gets confused, though, and tosses this dialog box (see Figure 8-41) up on the screen.

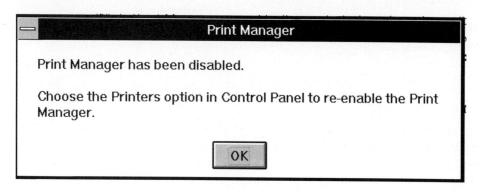

Figure 8-41: Stumbled

It seems to be timing dependent, which is to say, it may jump up and bite you some day. If you're careful to let all your print jobs come out of Print Manager before you turn it off, you should be in good shape.

Why would you want to turn off Print Manager? Good question. There's a more complete explanation in Chapter 3, but in a nutshell: with Print Manager on, your application will "come back" quicker, so you can do something more important while the computer is printing; with Print Manager off, you'll lose control of the computer for a bit longer, but the paper will come out the printer faster.

When you install Windows it turns Print Manager on, i.e., it sets **spooler=yes**.

 Most people find it better to use the Print Manager (or some other spooler) most of the time, but if you're printing a long report and the boss needed it, like, yesterday, turn off the Print Manager and you'll be in the boss's office sooner.

The easiest way to change this setting is with the "Use Print Manager" box in the Printer applet's dialog box. Look under the **DosPrint=** setting above for a picture of that dialog box.

SwapMouseButtons=_YesOrNo_

 Here's yet another one of those mouse settings that doesn't seem to work right. In theory, Windows has the ability to switch the operation of the left and right mouse buttons: if the user so chooses, the "left" (sometimes called "primary") button can be activated by physically clicking the right mouse button; the "right" ("secondary") button can be activated by physically clicking the left mouse button. Some — but by no means all — southpaws find the arrangement useful.

The official documentation is wrong. **SwapMouseButtons=yes** will swap the function of the left and right buttons; any other setting (including **1**!) makes the mouse behave normally.

Windows applications don't seem to pick up on the setting if you change it manually (i.e., change the line to **SwapMouseButtons=yes** with a text editor). The mouse applet in the Control Panel doesn't even pick up the current setting: it only works with the one in effect when Windows was started. So if you go in and change the setting manually, you'll have to exit and re-start Windows to make sure the change "took."

SystemFont=*FONFileName*

This one doesn't appear in the official docs. If you'd like to change the font Windows uses for window titles and menus, simply set **SystemFont=** to any **.FON** file. Windows goes through the usual search: if you don't qualify the file name, it first searches in the Windows directory, then the System directory, then along the DOS path.

Not terribly exciting, but it may come in useful sometime. For a few little tips, see **IconTitleFaceName=.**

TransmissionRetryTimeout=*Seconds*

See **DeviceNotSelectedTimeout=.**

[Windows Help]

> Chu ma nyok na dang
> Sem ma chöna dé.[†]
>
> — Traditional Tibetan saying

[†] If you don't stir the water, it will clear by itself.

The magnificent Windows Help engine stores its settings here: location, size, colors, the works. As I explained in the section *Good Help Is Hard to Find* in Chapter 3, Windows Help is a tremendous tool, one of the best reasons to buy and use Windows. A pity it isn't better documented, and that the documentation that exists is all too often incomplete or utterly, demonstrably incorrect.

And it wouldn't hurt a bit if Microsoft's own applications used `[Windows Help]` the way it's supposed to be used. I just love to point out how all the `.HLP` files that ship with Word for Windows 2.x cavalierly reset the main window size. There doesn't appear to be anything you can do about it. Cowboy Help, I call it: WinWord assumes it knows more about how you want your help than you do.

When Windows installs itself, it doesn't even create this section. But when you use Windows Help, change the size of the Main, History, Copy or Annotate dialog boxes, and exit Help normally, this section is created, the current settings stored away for future use.

Typical settings might look like this:

```
M_WindowPosition=[0,0,800,759,1]
H_WindowPosition=[8,559,983,147,0]
C_WindowPosition=[7,474,988,279,0]
A_WindowPosition=[8,324,895,294,0]
```

Those settings correspond to the size of the Main, History, Copy and Annotate windows, respectively. You can manually delete those [brackets] and Help doesn't seem to mind, your settings will still be picked up and interpreted correctly, although Help does replace the brackets whenever you exit Help normally.

The official documentation and almost all the unofficial documentation I've seen doesn't even mention the brackets, and the books that do mention the brackets don't tell you they're optional. If you've been trying to figure out why your lines in `[Windows Help]` don't look like the ones in the books, well, now you know the rest of the story.

The settings in general look like this:

```
x_WindowPosition=[top,left,width,height,maximized]
```

Where **top** is the distance from the top of the dialog box to the top of the screen, in pixels; **left** is the distance from the left edge of the dialog box to the left side of the screen, in pixels; and **width** and **height** are the width and height of the box in pixels.

Windows Help only looks at the **maximized** value for the main window: if it's **1**, the main window is maximized; if it's **0**, the main window is "restored," i.e., it takes on the size specified by **top**, **left**, **width** and **height**. The other three windows, History, Edit, and Annotations, don't even have maximize or minimize buttons!

This section also has five settings that you might want to monkey with, if you enjoy changing colors and can't stand to let Windows Help off the hook.

Unless you do something to change it, Help emphasizes Popups, Jumps, and Help Macros by setting them off in a moderate-green type. A Popup tells the Help user that there's a little box hiding underneath. The box typically contains a short explanation or a definition. Here's a Popup (Figure 8-42) associated with the phrase "title bar" in Program Manager's help:

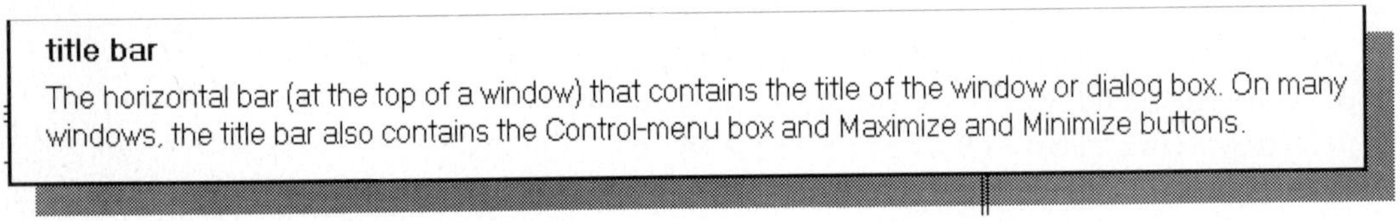

title bar

The horizontal bar (at the top of a window) that contains the title of the window or dialog box. On many windows, the title bar also contains the Control-menu box and Maximize and Minimize buttons.

Figure 8-42: A Popup for title bar

Note how "title bar" has a dotted underline. You can't change the underline. "title bar" appears on-screen in green, or whichever color you specify in this section.

Here's a couple of Jumps, associated with "Arrange Windows and Icons" and "Change and Icon," again from Program Manager (see Figure 8-43).

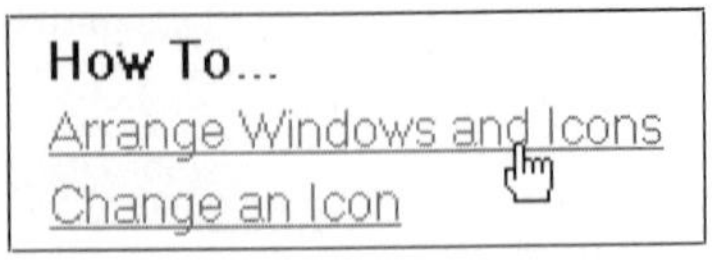

How To...
Arrange Windows and Icons
Change an Icon

Figure 8-43: The Underscored Lines Are Jumps

When you push a Jump, Windows Help jumps: if you're unfamiliar with the action, just crank up Program Manager and click on Help, then Contents. The Jump is underlined with a solid underscore (which you can't change), and usually appears in green (which you can change).

Finally, folks who are very adept at creating Windows Help files may also use macros — programs embedded within the help file. You'll know when a macro lurks beneath the text you see on the screen: they're double-underlined (which you can't change) and usually display in green (which you can).

The **[Windows Help]** section lets you set colors for Popups, If Popups (which are just like Popups, except they spin out to another Help file to pick up the information), Jumps, IfJumps (just like Jumps, except they move to another file), and Macros. The lines look like this:

```
PopupColor= 0 128 0
IfPopupColor= 0 128 0
JumpColor= 0 128 0
IfJumpColor= 0 128 0
MacroColor= 0 128 0
```

The three numbers to the right of the equal sign are the red, green, and blue values, respectively. (See Chapter 2 for a discussion of color numbers.) They can fall between **0** and **255**. Windows won't dither the colors, of course: it will use the closest solid color. And if you try a setting that doesn't follow the rules (e.g., **256 0 255**), Windows just finks out to black.

When Windows installs itself, it doesn't put any of these lines in **WIN.INI**. (Hey, it doesn't even create a **[Windows Help]** section; whaddya expect?) If any particular setting does not appear in **[Windows Help]**, Windows assumes you wanted a setting of **0 128 0**. That's the standard Windows Help green.

CHAPTER 9

SYSTEM.INI, Windows' Soul

Each new experience, each new situation of life, widens our mental outlook and brings about a subtle transformation within ourselves. Thus our nature changes continually, not only on account of the conditions of life, but — even if these would remain static — because by the constant addition of new impressions, the structure of our mind becomes ever more diverse and complex. Whether we call it "progress" or "degeneration," we have to admit the fact that it is the law of all life, in which differentiation and co-ordination balance each other.

Thus each generation has its own problems and must find its own solutions. The problems, as well as the means to solve them, grow out of the conditions of the past and are therefore related to them, but they can never be identical with them. They are neither completely identical nor completely different. They are just the result of a continuous process of adjustment.

Great religions and deep-rooted philosophical attitudes are not individual creations, though they may have been given their first impetus by great individuals. They grow from the germs of creative ideas, great experiences and profound visions. They grow through many generations according to their own inherent law, just like a tree or any other living organism. They are what we might call "natural events of the spirit." But their growth, their unfoldment and maturity need time. Though the whole tree is potentially contained in the seed, it requires time to transform itself into a visible shape.

— Lama Anagarika Govinda, *Foundations of Tibetan Mysticism*, 1960

Sections

I still believe that every human being stands for something.
You stand for something, I stand for something. Just being on this planet,
wearing the clothes we wear, doing the work we do, we each stand for something.
And in this little corner of the world, we stand for cutting the crap.

— Michael Crichton, *Rising Sun, 1993*

Following, in alphabetical order, are the [section]s that Windows puts in **SYSTEM.INI**, along with a description of what each [section] controls. Just as in **WIN.INI**, the order of [section]s within **SYSTEM.INI** isn't important; capitalization is optional; I've merely duplicated the names precisely as they appear after Windows installs itself.

Section Name	What it affects
[386Enh]	Primarily (but not exclusively!) settings that apply when Windows is running in Enhanced mode. That covers quite a bit of ground, including time slicing, virtual memory management, and much more.
[boot]	Specifies drivers, the Windows shell (e.g., Program Manager), much more that is fundamental to your configuration.
[boot.description]	Mostly text strings used in Windows Setup.
[drivers]	A central list of multimedia drivers. Most of the action is in the **driver=** lines of **[boot]**, not here.
[keyboard]	Handles different kinds of keyboards. *\<yawwwwn>*
[mci]	Windows Media Control Interface drivers list. Mostly points back to the **[mci extensions]** section of **WIN.INI**.
[NonWindowsApp]	A hodgepodge of settings that control how Windows treats DOS programs running in a window.
[standard]	Primarily (but, again, not exclusively!) concerns how Windows behaves when run in Standard mode. You probably run in Enhanced mode, so few of these settings will make any difference to you.

Some Windows applications make changes to `SYSTEM.INI` settings, but on the whole it isn't anywhere near the nuclear dumping ground `WIN.INI` has become.

Backup Alert! With `SYSTEM.INI`, more than any other single file on your computer, you *must* make reliable backups. You shouldn't even consider making one single change to `SYSTEM.INI` without squirreling away a backup — and two backups is not unreasonable. If you can, use the built-in applets to make changes to `SYSTEM.INI`. Modifying it by hand is playing with fire.

Most changes to `SYSTEM.INI` (particularly the most basic operational parameters, e.g., in `[boot]`, `[keyboard]`, and `[386Enh]`) won't "take" until you exit and re-start Windows.

The following list of [Section]s is arranged alphabetically; settings within the sections are alphabetized, too, according to the variable name. Enjoy!

[386Enh]

Lha gya lo!†

— Tibetan saying

These settings control how Windows works in Enhanced mode. Since you're running in Enhanced mode (else Mom would be very, very disappointed, true?), this particular section is of paramount importance to you. This section's enhanced mode settings are also incredibly convoluted, unnecessarily technical, and at times utterly inscrutable. But they're all we've got.

If you are not running in Enhanced mode (in particular if you're still struggling with a 286 class machine), you can ignore most of this section, `COMxBase=` being a notable exception.

In case you were wondering, "Enhanced mode," "386 Enhanced," and "386 Enhanced mode" all refer to the same thing — Windows' method of operation that avoids restrictions of the brain-dead 80286 chip, taking advantage of virtual memory and all sorts of other

---

† May the gods be victorious.

goodies. Don't get caught up in the terminology: there will be terms flying all over the place in this section that have little relationship to similar terms in other contexts. Put your Windows techno-speak filters on, and hitch up the hip waders. This will be thick going.

32BitDiskAccess=*OffOrOn*

Speaking of lousy terminology. This one takes the cake. Contrary to what any normally intelligent person might think, "32 bit disk access" has nothing to do with the width of the data bus connecting your disk to the main part of your computer: indeed, as of this writing anyway, 32-bit disk controllers are rare as pteradon teeth. The term "32 bit" refers to a specific kind of 80386/80486 instruction that is used when these more advanced machines are trying to pretend that they're archaic 8086/80286s.

If you double-click on Control Panel's 386 Enhanced Applet, then click Virtual Memory, and Change, you'll get a dialog box that is mostly concerned with virtual memory settings (more about that later). You may or may not have this check box at the bottom (see Figure 9-1).

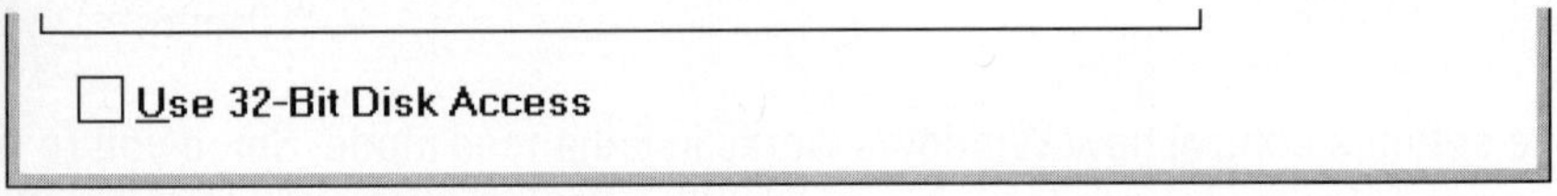

☐ U̲se 32-Bit Disk Access

Figure 9-1: More Bits, I Say!

That checkbox should really say something like "Use Windows FastDisk for disk access" or some such: the question is whether or not Windows should use its own routines, commonly called, collectively, "FastDisk," instead of DOS' regular method (including your computer's BIOS) to get at your hard drives. It has nothing to do with whether your machine is capable of supporting a 32-bit data path to your disk.

When Windows uses DOS' routines, things slow down a bit. The extent of the slowdown may not be as great as you think, simply because DOS/BIOS disk access has been honed to something of a fine art. Switching over to FastDisk will speed things up; it may also let you keep more DOS boxes open at once. The why and how are a bit complex.

Windows runs in protected mode, the mode that lets several programs run simultaneously without stepping all over each other. (For a more thorough discussion, see Chapter 7.) DOS and your computer's built-in BIOS run in real mode, the mode that opens the computer up, so any program can clobber any other program, at whim. When Windows uses the DOS routines to get at your disk, the interaction goes like this:

First, Windows pops into real mode and shoots the disk command to DOS. Then DOS takes a look at the command and creates one or more BIOS calls (INT 13h). Windows flips back to protected mode and tells DOS everything is OK.

If there are BIOS calls, Windows intercepts them, sees that they're for the BIOS, flops back into real mode, and hands the calls to the BIOS. The BIOS does whatever is required, working with your hard disk's controller, then hands its results back to Windows, which passes the data back to the program that wanted it, and keeps on truckin'.

All that flip-flopping around can take a lot of time.

When Windows uses FastDisk, it intercepts those calls to the BIOS and works directly with your hard disk's controller. That's all. The BIOS middlemen, and all their flipping overhead, disappear.

 FastDisk also lets you load more DOS programs into memory than would otherwise fit. With FastDisk disabled, Windows won't even try to swap DOS programs running in the background out to the disk. It's a result of how DOS works: poor DOS can only handle one request for disk data at a time.

Why? Well, say you had a DOS program running under Windows, and you let Windows swap the program's disk buffer out to disk. (The disk buffer is the place DOS puts disk data when it's retrieved, storing it before feeding it to the program.) Now say that program tries to read some data from the disk. The program knocks on DOS's door and says, "Hey, go get this disk data and stick it in my buffer." DOS looks around: the disk buffer isn't there, so without really knowing that it's doing so (this virtual memory stuff is loaded with smoke and mirrors), DOS knocks on Windows' door and says, "Hey, bring back the disk buffer."

Windows looks in its tables, finds where the disk buffer has been swapped out to disk — even though Windows has no idea it's retrieving a disk buffer; far as

Windows is concerned it's just another block of memory swapped to disk — and says, "Yo, DOS! Go get me this little bit of stuff from the hard disk."

Catch-22.

If you could do all that, DOS would just sit there. Unable to serve two masters at once, it would freeze: it can't obey the program's wishes, because it can't bring the data in from the disk, when the buffer is out to lunch, there's no place to put the data. At the same time, it can't obey Windows' wishes, to bring back the buffer, in fact, it doesn't even know about Windows' wishes, because DOS can only run one instruction at a time.

That, in a nutshell, is why Windows won't swap active DOS programs out to disk while the usual DOS disk access is in effect (i.e., when FastDisk is disabled). Windows fills up memory, but if you keep launching DOS programs sooner or later Windows won't have enough room to stick the last DOS program into memory. When that happens, Windows will die with one of my favorite error messages: "This application has violated system integrity." Then there's something about bending over and kissing your butt good-bye, while Windows comes crashing down around your ears. (It isn't quite that bad — *you* get to turn Windows off and back on again — but that's small comfort when you're trying to get some work done.)

When Windows uses FastDisk, though, it bypasses DOS entirely, talking directly to the hard disk controller. The DOS program can request away, and DOS (through Windows and FastDisk) can bring back the data, while Windows in its end-run way retrieves the disk buffer while nobody is looking and makes everything hunky-dory.

Sounds great in theory, eh?

There's one little problem: Windows can't speak to just any hard disk controller. In fact, it only speaks *one* hard disk controller's language: the Western Digital WD-1003 language. DOS, via BIOS calls, can talk to any hard disk. (Well, any hard disk that can connect to your computer, anyway.) When Windows uses DOS, it can talk to anything, too: DOS and the BIOS provide all necessary translations. But if you try to force Windows to talk directly to the hard disk controller, using this `32BitDiskAccess=` setting, that hard disk controller better speak-it-a WD-1003. If the hard disk controller is WD-1003 impaired, and you tell Windows to talk to it anyway, your whole system can go to hell in a handbasket with scrambled files and irretrievably lost data.

Microsoft claims that 90% of all hard disk controllers speak the WD-1003 language. That may have been true once upon a time, but I doubt it holds true today. Personally, I've been blessed with three different controllers, on my three most recent machines, that don't know WD-1003 from an African "click" language. The controller gods must be crazy.

While a fair percentage of IDE drives will speak WD-1003, very few SCSI or ESDI drives will. And hooking up a fancy caching controller to an IDE drive may make the combination of the two WD-1003 illiterate.

Actually, there's a second little problem. If you are trying to run FastDisk on a computer (usually a portable) that automatically powers down the hard drive, you may get all sorts of strange results. The power-down technology puts the drive to sleep: disk access through the normal DOS route will wake up the drive before instructing the computer to read or write data. If FastDisk is enabled, though, Windows will start talking to the hard drive controller no matter what state the drive is in, oblivious to whether the disk is trying to sleep. If it blasts data at the drive, the data could end up looking like a chicken trying to cross an interstate.

When Windows installs itself, it runs a rather complicated series of tests to see if your hard disk controller speaks the WD-1003 language. If it finds the hard disk to be all tongue-tied, incapable of understanding its commands, the Windows installer doesn't do anything: no lines related to FastDisk will appear in **[386Enh]**.

On the other hand, if your hard disk controller passes muster, Windows puts these three lines in **[386Enh]**:

```
32BitDiskAccess=OFF
device=*int13
device=*WDCtrl
```

The latter two lines tell Windows to use internal routines (identified with a *****; see **device=** later) to capture calls to the DOS disk routines, also known as Interrupt 13h, and to take over access to a Western Digital-conversant hard disk controller.

Note in particular that Windows does *not* turn FastDisk on — you have to do that yourself.

There are all sorts of gotchas, of course. In rare cases, Windows has been accused of identifying a controller as being WD-1003 conversant when in fact it isn't. Had you been plagued with this problem, you should've noticed it immediately the first time you tried to start Windows: it would've locked up tighter than a junk bond dealer under oath. Sometimes Windows fails to recognize disk controllers as being WD-1003 savvy, when in fact they are. In that case, you'll have to do some experimenting, out on the bleeding edge — and you'll be working without a net. You may install a new hard drive, or added a new hard disk controller, and wonder if it does (or does not) speak WD-1003.

Anyway, for whatever reason, some day you will probably find yourself wondering if you can or should turn on FastDisk. Even if your hard disk controller talks every known dialect of WD-1003, you'll still have to turn on FastDisk manually: Microsoft made it that way. It's a potentially dangerous leap of faith. Here's my advice.

Step 0: back up your entire disk. The whole thing. In fact, it wouldn't hurt to back it up twice, so if the first backup fails you can retrieve your data from the second.

Step 1: Go into Control Panel, double-click on the 386 Enhanced icon, click Virtual Memory, and click Change. If you can see the checkbox at the bottom marked "Use 32-Bit Disk Access" (there's a picture of it at the beginning of the discussion for this setting), go on to Step 3.

Step 2: If you cannot see that checkbox, Windows, upon installation, determined that the hard disk controller you were using at the time is not WD-1003 compliant. Think real hard: do you *really* want to mess with Mother Nature? It's one thing to turn on FastDisk after installing a brand new disk — Windows may not know about your new disk, or its WD-1003 capabilities — but if Windows' installation routines have already taken a look at your disk and Windows turned up its nose, by disabling the "Use 32-Bit Disk Access" checkbox, you better know an awful lot about that disk before you enable FastDisk.

If you decide to proceed, grab your lucky rabbit's foot and start rubbing like hell. Cancel all the way out of the Control Panel, then using SYSEDIT go into **SYSTEM.INI**'s **[386Enh]** section and add this one line:

32BitDiskAccess=OFF

That isn't a typo: you want to turn it **OFF**. Now go back into Control Panel (no need to reboot Windows), the 386 Enhanced icon, Virtual Memory, Change. Now you should see the "Use 32-Bit Disk Access" check box. (If you don't, you probably mis-spelled the **32BitDiskAccess=OFF** entry.)

Step 3: Click the "Use 32-Bit Access Box," and click OK. You will first be asked the question shown in Figure 9-2.

Figure 9-2: It's the First Thing To Go

If you respond Yes, you'll be confronted with a second chance to change your mind. It's a rather dire — and well-considered! — warning that looks like the one in Figure 9-3.

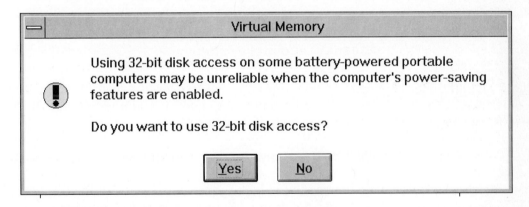

Figure 9-3: Spin Doctor

Remember that enabling FastDisk on a portable with a spin-down power saving capability is playing Russian Roulette with your data. Click Yes, if you dare, and Windows will let you re-start with FastDisk in place. Leave Windows and come back.

Step 4: Run the least important DOS applications you own. If they start behaving oddly, can't find data, if they come up with screwed settings, if they don't exit or start correctly, whatever, get out of Windows immediately. Your rabbit's foot should be smoking. When you're back in DOS, start Windows with this line:

WIN /D:F

That tells Windows to start, but disable (D) the FastDisk (F) option. Immediately pop over to the Control Panel, remove the check box from the "Use 32-Bit Disk Access" and click OK all the way back, exiting Windows to DOS. Then immediately run whatever disk fix-up routines you may own: Central Point, Norton, whatever. Probably wouldn't hurt to run two or three of 'em. And forget about FastDisk. It's good, but it isn't that good.

Step 5: Even if you passed the "unimportant DOS app test" with flying colors, keep an eagle eye on your machine, and only use your least important Windows apps for a while. At the first sign of trouble, and trouble can come in many guises, bail out, fast, using the technique in Step 4.

That's it. Most disks will work with FastDisk. But not all, pilgrim, not all. If you want to twiddle with FastDisk, take a look at the **PageBuffers=** setting in [386Enh].

A20EnableCount=*OffOrOn*

According to the official documentation, this entry has to do with what Windows feeds **HIMEM.SYS** for the "enable count on the A20 line." If you understand that, great. If, like me, you don't, don't mess with this setting.

Okay, okay. That didn't scare you away, huh? Too bad. Here's the scoop.

The A20 line controls access to the high memory area; an A20 handler controls the A20 line. There are many different kinds of A20 handlers. Usually **HIMEM.SYS** can tell which A20 handler is being used, but sometimes it needs help. As far as I can tell (and the official documentation doesn't help much — the terminology in the DOS world and the Windows world is completely different), this "enable count" is actually the A20 handler code number you would normally specify in the **/machine:** parameter of the **HIMEM.SYS** command line. For a list of those code numbers, look up **HIMEM.SYS** in the

DOS *Technical Reference*. The *Tech Ref* says that a few machines, including the Acer 1100, Wyse, and IBM 7552, require this parameter. If you have one of those machines, you shouldn't be doing this brain surgery alone: call the manufacturer or the folks who sold you the machine and gripe. Loud.

If you're bumping into this setting and using a memory manager other than **HIMEM.SYS**, check the vendor's documentation, or consider moving. Pulling up stakes and moving to another state may be cheaper, and less hassle, than making all those long distance calls to the vendor's tech support group.

Windows doesn't put this line in **[386Enh]** when it installs: instead, the number is calculated dynamically, each time Windows loads.

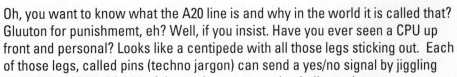 Oh, you want to know what the A20 line is and why in the world it is called that? Gluuton for punishmemt, eh? Well, if you insist. Have you ever seen a CPU up front and personal? Looks like a centipede with all those legs sticking out. Each of those legs, called pins (techno jargon) can send a yes/no signal by jiggling voltages. On the original 8086 chip, 20 of those pins were used to indicate the memory address that the CPU was sending data to (and other pins were used for the data itself). Since computer people like to start counting with 0, the pins were called A0, A1, A2,. . . A19 with the A for address. The number of addresses was 2 to the power 20 which is exactly 1024x1024 — one megabyte. This is the origin of the famous one megabyte limit. The CPU could only address 2 to the power twenty addresses.

The 80286 had 24 pins (for 16 meg of addresses) and the 386/486 has 32 pins (for a cool 4 Giga of physical addresses) since 2 to the 32 power is 4x1024x1024x1024. The A20 line is just the 20th address line, the one that determines the part of an address just over 1 megabyte. Because of the way that memory is managed in the modes that emulate an 8086, controling the area just above one megabyte requires a memory manager to jiggle the A20 line. Sorry you asked?

By the way, if you've read how deleting the **WINA20.386** file in your root directory will clobber Windows, you're running a full version behind. Windows 3.1 doesn't require that file. You can delete it with impunity. While it's true that Windows 3.0 would die a thousand deaths with the file absent, Windows 3.1 actually has code in it that disables all the old Windows 3.0 warnings! Go ahead. Make my day. Zap it.

AllEMSLocked=*OffOrOn*

AllVMSLocked=*OffOrOn*

SysVMEMSLocked=*OffOrOn*

Back in Chapter 3, in the part called Piffle Ball, I told you about the PIF editor and several of its settings. These three lines let you override the PIF "EMS Memory Locked" and "XMS Memory Locked" entries. They concern DOS applications that (mis-)use expanded/EMS (or extended/XMS) memory. You may need to lock EMS or XMS memory for ill-behaved DOS applications that assume the location of data stored in EMS or XMS memory doesn't change.

Don't know the difference between EMS and XMS? Don't worry about it. They're just two different ways of using memory with physical addresses above 1 MB. XMS is the newer technology, the stuff Windows likes to use EMS is only around because some DOS apps require it. There's lots of technical mumbo-jumbo that wafts through most discussions of EMS vs. XMS — memory banks and switching and smoke and mirrors, doncha know — but none of it makes much difference. If you have a moderately modern machine and are running Windows, everything beyond the first meg is almost undoubtedly pegged as XMS. ('Tho, just to complicate matters, EMS memory on 80386/486 machines is actually XMS memory being forced to behave like EMS memory *Wheels within wheels within wheels.*)

Setting **AllEMSLocked=ON** tells Windows that you want EMS memory used by any DOS applications to be "locked," i.e., you don't want Windows to swap the contents of any DOS program's EMS memory to disk. Ever.

This setting overrides the PIF's "EMS Memory Locked" value. If you turn this setting ON, it's the same as checking the "EMS Memory Locked" checkbox in the PIF editor's Advanced dialog, for every application being run.

SysVMEMSLocked=ON is quite similar, except it permits EMS data to be swapped out to disk when a Windows app is active. The contents of EMS memory is restored before any DOS program takes over, and locked during the execution of the DOS program.

AllXMSLocked=ON behaves much as **AllEMSLocked=**, except it locks up XMS memory per the "XMS Memory Locked" checkbox in the PIF editor.

Should you change these settings? Highly unlikely. It's much smarter to identify the dumb DOS programs you own that don't use old-fashioned EMS memory correctly, and use the PIF editor to lock EMS memory for the offenders.

`AllVMsExclusive=`*OffOrOn*

With `AllVMsExclusive=ON`, Windows runs each DOS session full-screen and exclusive. It's that simple.

This setting overrides the "Full Screen" radio button in the Display Usage: part, and the "Exclusive" checkbox in the Execution: part, of the PIF editor.

Some DOS applications go bananas when run at less than full screen, or non-exclusive. If you can identify those apps, change the PIF and don't worry about it. The official docs, though, say that you may encounter some Windows-bashing network drivers or insensitive TSRs that crash Windows more readily with this setting turned off.

I've never seen it happen, but you may.

`AltKeyDelay=`*seconds*

`AltPasteDelay=`*seconds*

The `Alt` key holds a special place in the hearts, minds and curses of Windows users: it's the magic key that unlocks the menu. But if you're running a DOS program under Windows, and that program needs `Alt` key combinations, `Alt` is the key Windows is most likely to gobble. These settings lessen the likelihood that Windows will swallow an `Alt` key pressed while you're running a DOS program.

In spite of what the official documentation says, the `AltKeyDelay=` setting tells Windows how long to wait between the time the `Alt` key is pressed on the keyboard and the time that key is fed to the active program. All the docs I've seen say `AltKeyDelay=` is the delay between the time the `Alt` key is fed to the active program and the time the *next* key-press is processed, but that isn't true: set `AltKeyDelay=1`, say, and see for yourself. Hit the `Alt` key, and it will take Windows a full second to pass the `Alt` key-press on to the active program. Hit `Alt+F` and it will take the same amount of time to pass the `Alt+F` key-press to the active program.

For some reason I don't understand, this setting does *not* seem to affect the time Windows spends processing so-called SendKeys commands — those commands in macro and programming languages that simulate the pressing of keys at a keyboard. That's unfortunate, because timing problems using SendKeys with **Alt** keys can shaft a program.

If you can't get your DOS program to recognize **Alt+** key combinations typed at the keyboard, try bumping up this value. According to the official docs, no **AltKeyDelay=** value leads to a delay of 0.005 seconds, which has to be very nearly the amount of time Windows needs to process any key-press.

When Windows pastes **Alt+** key combinations into a running DOS program, it pauses immediately after the **Alt** key, to give the DOS program time to catch up. The **AltPasteDelay=** number tells Windows how many seconds to wait. If there's no entry, Windows uses a value of 0.025 seconds. You may want to increase this number if you are pasting **Alt+** key combinations into a DOS program, and the **Alt**s get swallowed.

`AutoRestoreScreen=`*OffOrOn*

When you switch to a DOS program running under Windows, somebody has to paint the DOS screen. Otherwise you couldn't see it, eh?

Some DOS programs are smart enough to paint their own screens, when so instructed by Windows. Many are not. When **AutoRestoreScreen=ON**, or the line is missing, and you're using a VGA monitor, or so the official documents say, Windows takes over: it stores away a snapshot of the screen when you switch away from a DOS app, then restores that snapshot when you switch back to the DOS app. When **AutoRestoreScreen=OFF**, Windows doesn't take the time or memory necessary to tuck away a snapshot of the screen; instead, it lets the DOS program repaint itself when you switch back to it. If there's no entry, Windows assumes you mean ON, i.e., that Windows should handle the screen restoration.

Turning **AutoRestoreScreen=OFF** may save you a little bit of memory. It'll also slow things down: a redraw from a DOS app is inevitably slower than slapping up a snapshot of the old screen. Why bother?

BkGndNotifyAtPFault=_OffOrOn_

You know how some kids, no matter what you say to them, don't listen. You may was well be talking to yourself. Well a DOS session is like that to ole mother Windows. Ain't no way that Mom Windows can talk to that little DOS session and get it to pay no mind. DOS sessions can't be talked to by anybody — that's the way they work.

The official docs for **BkGndNotifyAtPFault=** are unadulterated TechnoBabble, a model of what the writers of the _Windows Resource Kit_ should never ever do — punting but in the wrong direction. Makes no sense and whatever sense you can make of them is wrong. They talk about this detemining whether Windows notifies DOS sessions to avoid accessing the display at certain times but there ain't no way Windows can notify DOS sessions of anything at any time. And the docs say there is a different default depending on adapter but I couldn't get Windows to put this line into **system.ini** under any circumstances.

If I make the bold assumption that the authors of this part of the doc at least had a vague idea of what the command was about, I can make some guesses of what this is good for. It has something to do with how Windows handles screen switches. If you find switching between DOS sessions produces partially corrupted displays after the switch, try adding

BkGndNotifyAtPFault=On

to your **[386Enh]** section. It may help, but more likely you're the victim of a buggy screen driver and nothing will help.

CGA40WOA.FON=_FonFileName_

CGA80WOA.FON=_FonFileName_

EGA40WOA.FON=_FonFileName_

EGA80WOA.FON=_FonFileName_

woafont=_FonFileName_

I covered these in Chapter 3, in the DOS fonts section. In essence, they specify the names of .FON font files that are used when you dig into the Fonts setting, the one accessible from the little hyphen-thingy in the upper left corner of a DOS box.

All the existing documentation I've seen on these settings, official, unofficial or otherwise, is dead wrong. In particular, all the stuff you may read about 25-line screens and 40-column lines and all that other crap has nothing to do with reality. Look in Chapter 3 for the straight scoop.

When Windows installs itself, it puts these five lines in **[386Enh]**:

```
EGA80WOA.FON=EGA80WOA.FON
EGA40WOA.FON=EGA40WOA.FON
CGA80WOA.FON=CGA80WOA.FON
CGA40WOA.FON=CGA40WOA.FON
woafont=dosapp.fon
```

To change them, you'll have to go into **SYSTEM.INI** with a text editor.

CGANoSnow=*OffOrOn*

If you're trying to run Windows on a CGA system, you deserve all the snow you can get. Put it right between yer ears....

Set **CGANoSnow=ON** if you must run on a CGA monitor and the best picture you can get looks like the TV reception in Myanmar.

 Hey, was that a Rangoon joke?

Nuthin' wrong with Burma that a good revolution couldn't cure.

Com1AutoAssign=*-1to999*

Com2AutoAssign=*-1to999*

Com3AutoAssign=*-1to999*

Com4AutoAssign=-*1to999*

These settings correspond to the top part of the Control Panel's 386 Enhanced dialog box, shown in Figure 9-4.

```
┌────────────────────────────────────────────────────────────────┐
│ ─                        386 Enhanced                            │
├──────────────────────────────────────────────────────────────  │
│  ┌─Device Contention──────────────────┐    ┌──────────────────┐ │
│  │ Com1                                │    │       OK         │ │
│  │ Com2      ○ Always Warn             │    └──────────────────┘ │
│  │                                     │    ┌──────────────────┐ │
│  │           ○ Never Warn              │    │     Cancel       │ │
│  │                                     │    └──────────────────┘ │
│  │           ● Idle (in sec.)   [ 2 ]▲▼│    ┌──────────────────┐ │
│  │                                     │    │  Virtual Memory… │ │
│  └─────────────────────────────────────┘   └──────────────────┘ │
└──────────────────────────────────────────────────────────────────┘
```

Figure 9-4: Com AutoAssign

A value of -1 is the same as "Always Warn"; a 0 is "Never Warn"; and any other number, between 1 and 999, specifies the number of seconds of "Idle."

DOS programs working with Com ports under Windows can be most cantankerous. That's expectable: many DOS comm routines were written back in the good old one app, one port days — when one application got control of the machine and didn't let go until it was bloody well good and ready. Windows changed all that. Now more than one DOS program (or a DOS program and a Windows program) can try to get at a single Com port simultaneously. It's a jungle out there.

 I tend to think in terms of a sow with a dozen piglets, all trying to get at mom's milk simultaneously. If there are only ten spigots working, the twelve piglets must jostle each other aside, competing for their meals... sort of a porcine serial sibling rivalry.

Windows, as the ultimate arbiter in such things, must decide which app takes precedence over others that may be contending for the same port: Windows must figure out which piglet gets priority, which has to suck hind teat. This **Com**n**AutoAssign=** setting defines the method of arbitration.

Say one DOS program is using Com3 and Windows detects two different DOS programs that want to use the Com3 port. If **Com3AutoAssign=-1**, "Always Warn," Windows pops up a dialog box, asking the user which of the two programs should take priority. If **Com3AutoAssign=0**, "Never Warn," Windows tells the second program that the port is unavailable and the first program continues undisturbed. If the value of **Com3AutoAssign=** is between 1 and 999, Windows tracks when a program is actually using a com port. If the first program has the port open but hasn't used it for the indicated number of seconds, then Windows lets the second program take the port away from the first. My advice is to set the number to 2 or 3.

If there is no **Com***n***AutoAssign=** entry for a particular port, a value of 2 is used: Windows times out the port and passes it to the next program after 2 seconds of idle time.

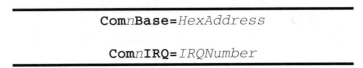

What these settings are doing in **[386Enh]** escapes me. The first bunch consists of four entries, specifying the base addresses of Com1, Com2, Com3, and Com4, in hex. The second bunch consists of four more entries, specifying the IRQ lines used by Com1, Com2, Com3 and Com4. These entries are used by Windows, regardless of the mode it's running (i.e., either Enhanced or Standard).

The official docs say that if the **Com***n***Base=** lines are missing, Windows scans your BIOS to find the base addresses for Com1, Com2, and Com4, and assigns **Com3Base=03E8h**. You can assign different values for any or all of the Com ports' base addresses by cranking up Control Panel, clicking on Ports, then Settings, then Advanced (see Figure 9-5).

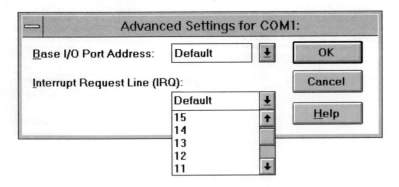

Figure 9-5: Comm Base, IRQ Settings

Most Windows users will discover that Com1 is based at 03F8h, Com2 at 02F8h, and Com4 at 02E8h. You can find the base addresses on your machine by running any of the "sleuth" programs, or (after exiting Windows) Microsoft's Diagnostic program, **MSD.EXE**.

The **Com***n***IRQ=** settings tell Windows which IRQ lines are used by which ports. The docs say that Windows uses a **Com1IRQ=4**, **Com2IRQ=3**, **Com3IRQ=4** (or **3** on MCA machines), and **Com4IRQ=3**, which is the most common setup. Again you can nail down the IRQs on your machine by running a "sleuth" program, or **MSD.EXE**. If you want to turn a port off entirely, set its **Com***n***IRQ=-1**.

Note that changing these settings does not change the Com port's base address, or its IRQ! You're merely informing Windows of the address/IRQ reality. Changing base addresses or IRQs all too often involves moving jumpers on an I/O card, or on your computer's motherboard.

 If you're at this point in MOM looking for advice on resolving IRQ conflicts, the best I can do is direct you to Chapter 3 and its brief discussion of IRQ hunting, and strongly suggest that you contact the vendor who sold you your latest piece of IRQ-using hardware, and bitch! I've lost hours, no, days, maybe weeks, trying to trace down IRQ/base address conflicts, and know well how frustrating it can be.

The only truly effective method I've found for resolving those conflicts is to call the manufacturer and ride them until they get things ironed out. You can threaten to return the hardware, if necessary — and follow through with the threat!

Com*n***Buffer=***Bytes*

Com*n***Protocol=***XOFF*

If you're dropping characters in a DOS communication program running under Windows, these settings may prove key, although I'd first recommend that you get either TurboCom-, KingComm (see Chapter 3), or any other program that replaces Windows' arcane serial port handlers. The only thing worse than the Windows 3.1 serial handlers are the Windows 3.0 serial handlers!

If you're only transferring text over your modem (that is, if you don't send or receive entire files, but limit yourself to plain ol' text), and the modem seems to be dropping characters randomly, try setting

`Com2Protocol=XOFF`

(use your modem's Com port number, if it isn't on Com2). The docs say that this setting tells Windows to "stop simulating characters in a virtual machine" after the comm program sends an XOFF. Fair enough.

If, like most folks, you're transferring files as well as plain ol' text and run into problems with dropped characters, you could be experiencing all sorts of mean, nasty, ugly comm glitches that may not appear, at first blush, to be "dropped character" problems: frequent bad packets on file transfers; high retransmission numbers; abysmally slow response times; spontaneous disconnects; as well as random missing characters in text.

Should you be plagued with those kinds of problems, you should first look to TurboCom and KingComm, and think hard about installing a 16550 UART (see Chapter 3). But if you're a masochist at heart, leave **Com*n*Protocol=** alone and try jacking up **Com*n*Buffer=**.

Windows normally allocates a 128 byte buffer for communication; try setting

`Com2Buffer=256`

and see if that makes any difference. (Again, use your modem's Com port number, if it isn't on Com2.) You don't want to set the number too high, because it may slow down communication overall.

If this doesn't solve your dropped character problems, also look at **ComBoostTime=**. Consider installing 16550 UARTs. Try running the Comm program exclusive (look at the PIF setting in Chapter 3). And keep in mind that this is a black art: Windows is designed to block off access to the buffers unless and until your Comm program is running.

Com*n*FIFO=*0Or1*

These four settings tell Windows if the 16550 UART's buffer should be used. For more details on the 16550, and its limited implementation in Windows 3.1, see Chapter 3.

If your modem is on Com2, and it has a 16550 UART, put this line in **[386Enh]**:

`Com2FIFO=1`

Note that the value must be 1: Windows doesn't recognize anything else, including, e.g., True, On, Yes, Javol, +1, or any other value that may make sense to you. Any value other than 1 is treated the same as a 0.

These are four more settings that don't belong in **[386Enh]**, because they are used regardless of the mode which Windows is running (enhanced or standard). They're also ignored unless the Com port in question has a 16550-style UART, with a buffer.

Com*n*IRQ=*IRQNumber*

See **Com*n*Base=**.

Com*n*Protocol=*XOFF*

See **Com*n*Buffer=**.

ComBoostTime=*milliseconds*

When a DOS communication program running under Windows gets a character on a Com port, Windows has to give the DOS program enough time to grab the character. Otherwise, characters will get dropped during transmission, and your DOS comm program will receive a garbled mess.

This setting tells Windows the minimum amount of time it should allot for your DOS comm program to retrieve a single character. If there is no such entry in the **[386Enh]** section, Windows assumes **ComBoostTime=2**.

 The official documentation says you should increase this value if you "lose keyboard characters on the screen" while running a DOS comm program. I'm not sure what that means, although it doesn't sound to me like a **ComBoostTime=** related problem.

Instead, you might want to play around with this number in conjunction with increasing **Com*n*Buffer=**, if you're dropping characters and don't want to spring for a copy of TurboCom or KingComm.

ComDrv30=*OffOrOn*

Hey, you can forget about this one. You should only set `ComDrv30=On` if you're running with the Windows 3.0 Comm drivers. And if you're running the Windows 3.0 Comm drivers, you're probably drooling all over this book, mumbling to yourself, snatching spiders from Nosferatu's floor and sucking the life out of them.

Don't worry. I hear they loosen the strait jackets every other Thursday, for two minutes at a stretch. The rats are only figments of your imagination. Oh. They're lying to you. The cell padding will wear thin if you beat your head against it often enough.

ComIRQSharing=*OffOrOn*

This entry tells Windows is you're machine is smart enough to share an IRQ line among more than one Com port. (See Chapter 3 for a discussion of IRQs.) If you have a plain vanilla ISA system, or don't know ISA from EISA from MCA, don't monkey with this setting.

ISA and EISA systems typically assign both Com1 and Com3 to IRQ 4, and they assign both Com2 and Com4 to IRQ 3. MCA systems typically assign Com1 to IRQ 4, and Com2, Com3, and Com4 to IRQ 3. On most ISA systems, you can't run more than one Com port at a time from the same IRQ: for example, if both Com1 and Com3 are assigned to IRQ 4, you won't be able to use Com1 and Com3 at the same time; attempting to do so will probably lock up your machine.

EISA and MCA systems often aren't so constrained, and you can buy I/O boards for ISA machines that will jimmy around the IRQ limitations. Your computer's (or I/O board's) users manual should tell you if your system will let you run more than one Com port from a given IRQ simultaneously.

If you have an ISA system, and your computer can handle more than one Com port on a given IRQ, and if you actually want to run more than one Com port simultaneously from a single IRQ, you need to turn **ComIRQSharing=On**.

If you have an EISA or MCA machine and you want to prohibit Windows from using more than one Com port on a particular IRQ line, you should set `ComIRQSharing=Off`.

Those are the only two situations when you would want to change this setting.

---

device=*FileOrDevicename*

display=*FileOrDevicename*

ebios=*FileOrDevicename*

keyboard=*FileOrDevicename*

mouse=*FileOrDevicename*

network=*FileOrDevicename*

 This is the heart and soul of **[386Enh]**. The **device=** lines and their brethren (listed above) tell Windows which virtual device drivers (known as "VxD"s) to load at startup-. When Windows runs in Enhanced mode, any number of DOS programs and Windows itself may need to get at your hardware, and they may all want to do it at the same time. Virtual device drivers let Windows run in Enhanced mode by arbitrating among multiple DOS programs ("virtual machines") and Windows itself. They're traffic cops that keep Windows and those DOS programs from bumping into each other.

When Windows installs itself, it lists all the virtual device drivers it thinks it will need. A typical installation on a Super VGA setup might yield these lines in **[386Enh]**:

```
display=VDD8514.386
ebios=*ebios
keyboard=*vkd
mouse=*VMD
network=*dosnet,*vnetbios
device=vtdapi.386
device=*vpicd
device=*vtd
device=*reboot
device=*vdmad
device=*vsd
device=*v86mmgr
device=*pageswap
```

```
device=*dosmgr
device=*vmpoll
device=*wshell
device=*BLOCKDEV
device=*PAGEFILE
device=*vfd
device=*parity
device=*biosxlat
device=*vcd
device=*vmcpd
device=*combuff
device=*cdpscsi
device=lanman10.386
```

As you can see, **device=** entries come in one of two flavors: they can either point to a file, with a (possibly qualified) file name; or they can use one of Windows' built-in virtual device drivers, indicated by a ***** at the beginning of the name. Those built-in virtual device drivers reside in **WIN386.EXE**.

The **display=** entry points to Windows' virtual display driver: **display=*vddvga** tells Windows to use the standard VGA driver located in **WIN386.EXE**, when in Enhanced mode. The **ebios=** line points to Windows' extended BIOS support routines. **keyboard=** points to the virtual keyboard device driver. **mouse=** points to the virtual mouse device driver. **network=** points to one or more network routines.

In general, you have no reason to go mucking about with these settings. If you feel you need to change something, it's much, much safer to go into Windows setup and let Windows make the changes for you, or to run the setup routines for, e.g., your network.

If you're puzzling over the **device=*int13** and **device=*WDCtrl** entries, take a look at the **32BitDiskAccess=** setting in **[386Enh]**. These two devices are the drivers Windows needs to run FastDisk. You'll find it much easier to leave these **device=** lines in **[386Enh]**, and manipulate FastDisk via the check box described under **32BitDiskAccess=**. (The **device=*BLOCKDEV** and **device=*PAGEFILE** lines are also necessary for FastDisk, but these virtual device drivers are always installed, and you shouldn't play around with them.)

A number of third-party programs inclduing EDOS and Norton Desktop add their own **device=** lines to **system.ini**. Alas, too often uninstall programs do not remove these devices. There is no easy way to detect such extraneous devices unless you try to track changes in **system.ini** after each install.

DMABufferIn1MB=*OffOrOn*

DMABufferSize=*KB*

HardDiskDMABuffer=*KB*

EISADMA=*OffOrChannel,Width*

MaxDMAPgAddress=*AddressInHex*

MCADMA=*OffOrOn*

 Direct Memory Access, DMA, refers to a controllers' ability to stick data in memory directly, without going through the main processor. By bypassing the main processor, data can be moved around inside your computer much more quickly. But since all of this happens without Windows' direct involvement (in effect, behind Windows' back) all sorts of things can go wrong.

The DMA buffer is that hunk of memory set aside to hold incoming DMA data, storing it until Windows is ready to scarf it up. The location and the size of the DMA buffer can cause headaches. Usually Windows sticks the DMA buffer wherever it can find the space; more often than not, that's someplace way up in the higher regions of memory.

 If you have an old-fashioned 8 bit DMA-savvy controller, it may not work if the DMA buffer is placed above the 1 MB line. (The card's documentation should tell you. . . if you can find it.) A **DMABufferIn1MB=On** setting forces Windows to clear out room in the lower 1 MB of memory to hold the DMA buffer. You shouldn't need this line unless you have an 8 bit card that cannot handle DMA buffers located above 1 MB.

Windows starts with a DMA buffer size of 16K. That appears to work for some types of cards, but it just isn't adequate for many CDs, backup devices, or sound cards. If your application starts telling you it's hitting a DMA buffer overflow, try setting **DMABufferSize=64** and see if that solves the problem. There's very little overhead in cranking this setting up to 64, so don't be bashful. (Hey, if Windows can't find an extra 48K in upper memory, you're in all sorts of trouble anyway.)

I'm not aware of any currently available controllers that need more than 64K, but it's conceivable; check the manufacturer's documentation to see if a **DMABufferSize=** larger than 64 might be beneficial.

If you're running a network, be sure to look at the **NetDMASize=** entry in **[386Enh]**.

The **HardDiskDMABufferSize=** setting makes no difference if you are running SmartDrive with double buffering. Double buffering is a way to implement DMA in Windows using bus mastering controllers accustomed to a DOS world; if you have double buffering enabled, your **CONFIG.SYS** will include a line that looks like this:

```
device=smartdrv.exe /double_buffer
```

See Chapter 10 for details.

If you're running SmartDrive without double buffering, or if you aren't running SmartDrive at all, the **HardDiskDMABufferSize=** setting tells Windows how large a DMA buffer you want for your hard drive(s). The official docs say that the default value is **HardDiskDMABufferSize=0** for ISA systems, and **64** for MCA computers or EISA computers that use DMA channel 3.

You might want to jigger this setting around if you have a bus mastering hard disk controller card, but you don't want to run SmartDrive with double buffering. There seems to be little, if any, overhead, so if you think Windows incorrectly identified the bus mastering capabilities of your hard drive controller (or if you've installed a new controller), go ahead and try a **HardDiskDMABufferSize=64** and see if it speeds things up.

EISADMA= and **MCADMA=** settings only apply to EISA and MCA machines, respectively. In their simplest form, they let you turn off Windows DMA access for (respectively) EISA and MCA machines. If you suspect that DMA transfers are killing your MCA system, for example, try setting **MCADMA=Off** and crank up Windows in Enhanced mode. Similarly, **EISADMA=Off** will turn off DMA transfers on an EISA machine.

In addition, the **EISADMA=** setting lets you override Windows pre-determined DMA transfer width settings. Recognized values are 8 (8-bit transfers), 16w (16-bit word aligned), 16b (16-bit byte aligned), and 32 (32-bit). The official documentation says that the defaults for a standard EISA system are:

```
EISADMA=0,8
EISADMA=1,8
EISADMA=2,8
EISADMA=3,8
EISADMA=5,16w
EISADMA=6,16w
EISADMA=7,16w
```

If you know your system well enough to figure out if any of those settings are in error — or you can ferret the information out of your user's manual or with snooping software — by all means go ahead and change them.

The **MaxDMAPgAddress=** entry lets you tell Windows how high in memory it can put a DMA page. According to the official documentation, the default value for this setting is 0FFFh (i.e., 1 MB) for ISA machines and 0FFFFh for EISA machines (the docs don't mention MCA machines).

 This **MaxDMAPgAddress=** line finally left me scratching my head... and other parts of my anatomy. I'll be hanged if I can figure out how this setting relates to **DMABufferIn1MB=**. Or why Windows defaults to **DMABufferIn1MB=Off**, on an ISA machine, yet sets **MaxDMAPgAddress=0FFFh** (per the official documentation, anyway). Curious.

DOSPromptExitInstruc=*OffOrOn*

 This one's my candidate for the Phineas T. Fahrquahrt Weird Name Award. You'd think that, having taken twenty characters for the DOS Prompt Exit Instruc... variable name, Microsoft would've added the missing "tion."

When you shell out to DOS, you're greeted with the message in Figure 9-6.

```
  ▌ Type EXIT and press ENTER to quit this MS-DOS prompt and
    return to Windows.
  ▌ Press ALT+TAB to switch to Windows or another application.
  ▌ Press ALT+ENTER to switch this MS-DOS Prompt between a
    window and full screen.


Microsoft(R) MS-DOS(R) Version 6
        (C)Copyright Microsoft Corp 1981-1993.

C:\WINDOWS>_
```

Figure 9-6: Nag, Nag, Nag

Unless you set **DOSPromptExitInstruc=Off**, in which case Windows doesn't provide you with all those verbose instructions.

My problem with the exit screen you see in the Figure above is twofold: at the same time, it is both too little and too much. Too much, in that I never read it, I've popped into DOS enough times that I know how to type Exit, or **Alt+Tab** or **Alt+Enter**. Too little, in that the screen scrolls off quickly, and I will occasionally forget that I'm in a DOS box, and try to run things that shouldn't be run from Windows, like disk defraggers.

The solution: a little-known DOS environment variable called Winpmt. If you put this line in your **AUTOEXEC.BAT**:

```
Set Winpmt=EXIT to Win * $p$g
```

Windows will use Winpmt as the DOS prompt whenever you're running Windows.

 Actually, it's a little more complicated than that: Windows, on startup, looks to see if there's a Winpmt variable in your DOS environment string; if it finds such a string, it swaps the Winpmt and the Prompt strings before starting Windows, then swaps them back when you leave Windows. Kinda strange, but that's how it works.

If you combine this new Winpmt prompt with a **DOSPromptExitInstruc=Off**, you'll get a very compact initial DOS screen, and the DOS prompt from inside Windows will look like this:

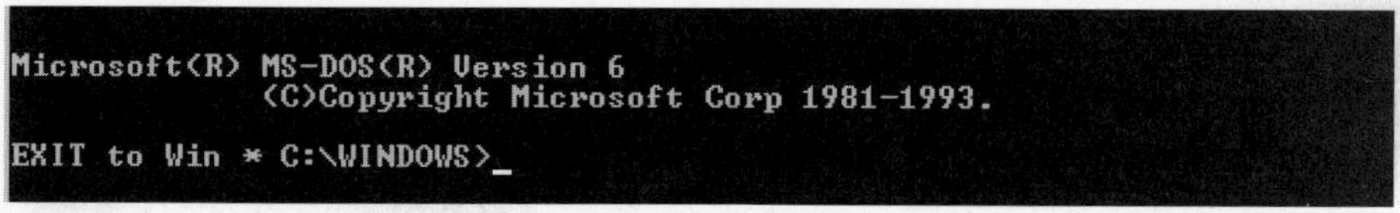

```
Microsoft(R) MS-DOS(R) Version 6
           (C)Copyright Microsoft Corp 1981-1993.
EXIT to Win * C:\WINDOWS>_
```

Figure 9-7: Pithy

That's a handy little trick, eh?

DualDisplay=*OffOrOn*

 Hey, maybe I'm losing my mind. But the documentation I've found on this setting seems to talk in circles. In particular, the official stuff in the Windows Resource Kit and in `SYSINI.WRI` appears to be self-contradictory, full of pseudo-technical gobbledygook signifying nothing.

Here's what I *think* is happening.

Some people install both a color card and a monochrome card on their systems: usually these two-headed systems are for programmers who program on one monitor and watch the results of their programming on the other. Good work if you can get it.

The section of memory known as B000 to B7FF is used for the monochrome card, or the mono mode of a VGA card. If you aren't going to use that chunk of memory, it would be nice to give it back to Windows. That, I believe, is where this setting comes in.

If you are (1) using Microsoft's EMM386 as a memory manager, and (2) have an EGA card but (3) no mono card, you could try to reclaim the B000 to B7FF section of memory by putting this line in **[386Enh]**:

DualDisplay=Off

and by putting this line (or one like it) in **CONFIG.SYS**:

device=EMM386.EXE i=B000-B7FF

Presumably, you could also use both of those settings if you (1) use EMM386, (2) use a VGA or Super VGA card, (3) know for an absolute dead-certain fact that your video card will never, ever flip into mono mode, and (4) need the extra chunk of free memory... desperately enough to risk crashing your system if you somehow inadvertently jump into mono mode.

That isn't what the official documentation says. But it's the only thing I could figure out that makes any sense. Presumably, you could do the same sort of thing with a memory manager other than EMM386.

There's only one other situation I can see where you might want to use **DualDisplay=**. You could try to force Windows to keep its hands off the B000 to B7FF area by setting

DualDisplay=On

But it makes a whole lot more sense to use the **EMMExclude=** setting in **[386Enh]** to banish Windows from specific blocks of memory — and it makes a whole lot more sense to exclude the area from the get-go in **CONFIG.SYS**, using EMM386 or whatever memory manager you may have.

John Oellrich at AT&T suggests that you might want to turn **DualDisplay=On** to keep Windows' stinkin' fingers off that area, period. **EMMExclude=** only says that part of memory shouldn't be used for EMS services. And he's also found this setting useful for network adaptors. Go figger.

---

ebios=_FileOrDevicename_

See **device=** in **[386Enh]**.

EGA40WOA.FON=_FonFileName_

EGA80WOA.FON=_FonFileName_

See **CGA40WOA.FON=** in **[386Enh]**.

EISADMA=_OffOrChannel,Width_

See **DMABufferIn1MB=** in **[386Enh]**.

EMMExclude=*StartAddress-EndAddress*

EMMInclude=*StartAddress-EndAddress*

 Sometimes Windows steps all over itself, sometimes it steps all over display adapter memory, sometimes it steps all over memory occupied by another program, sometimes it just steps in *it*. Squish.

The **EMMExclude=** setting keeps Windows from treading in places it doesn't belong. More often than not, you'll use one or more **EMMExclude=** lines in conjunction with **EMMInclude=** lines to figure out where Windows is stepping, why it's crashing. And you'll probably have a tech support type on the phone while you're doing it.

The basic drill goes like this: create one or more **EMMExclude=** statements, to tell Windows where to avoid. Then add one or more **EMMInclude=** statements to see if you're excluding too much. The addresses are in hex, of course. For example, you may want to see if your machine can survive Windows sticking its nose into the area B200 to B2FF, but not B000-B1FF or B300-B7FF or D000-DFFF. You'd use these lines:

```
EMMExclude=B000-BFFF
EMMExclude=D000-DFFF
EMMInclude=B200-B2FF
```

The official docs say Windows rounds the starting address down to the nearest 16K, and the ending address up to the nearest multiple of 16K. (If you need to lop off a smaller part of memory, look at **ReservedHighArea=** and **UseableHighArea=** in **[386Enh]**.) The addresses are case insensitive: cfff and CFFF are treated the same.

See how that can get real crazy, real quick? Every time you change the **EMMExclude=** and **EMMInclude=** statements, you'll have to re-start Windows and see if it crashes.

You can work with memory in the range A000 to EFFF — the span between 640K and 1 MB, the memory most commonly clobbered. Lockups with old-fashioned

Windows impaired video boards can often be circumvented by an
EMMExclude=C000-CFFF.

No matter how hard you try, though, you can't **EMMInclude=** any memory that's
been excluded by EMM386, or any other memory manager you may use.

When you're done working through all the permutations and
combinations over the phone, go ahead and yell at the tech support
person. Tell 'em Mom would beat them over the head with a rolling
pin, if they were in range. Their cards (applications, whatever) should
be Windows aware, and smart enough to keep Windows out of places it doesn't
belong. A couple years ago they would've had an excuse. Not these days.

EMMPageFrame=*StartAddress*

Epanded memory management requires a contiguous 64K chunk of memory, called
a "page frame", to hold blocks of data. Think of the page frame as the mirror part
of EMM's smoke and mirrors.

Windows usually goes out and finds a 64K block of unused memory and sticks the
page frame there. The official docs say that, if Windows can't find an unused 64K
block, it looks to this setting for the location of a pristine chunk of 64K. You
provide the starting location, in hex, e.g.,

EMMPageFrame=C400

The docs don't say how this setting interacts with the **frame=** parameter
of your **CONFIG.SYS**'s **device=EMM386.EXE** statement, or the
ReservePageFrame= setting in **[386Enh]**. I have no idea which (if any)
takes precedence, or why you would specify the page frame's location in
this obscure Windows backwater, and not in **CONFIG.SYS**.

EMMSize=*bytes*

According to the official docs, if **EMMSize=65536** or the lines is missing,
Windows treats all available memory as extended. That can cause problems if
you run a DOS program that allocates all available memory as extended, and
then run another DOS program that requires any extended memory: the first

If you ever run a DOS program that gloms onto all available expanded memory, and (while the first program is running) run a second DOS program that needs expanded memory, the docs say, you'll have to change this setting, to something like

`EMMSize=32768`

If you want to have the Enhanced mode extended memory manager load itself, but not dole out any extended memory to any DOS program (heaven knows why), you're supposed to use this line:

`EMMSize=0`

If you don't want the extended memory manager to load at all, use

`NoEMMDriver=On`

Why you would use any of this stuff and not the EMS size limit in the application's PIF file is a mystery to me.

`FileSysChange=OffOrOn`

When Windows changes a file — creates a new one, deletes a file, copies or moves a file, or writes to one — Windows notifies File Manager of the change. If File Manager learns that there's been a change in a file that affects the contents of the current screen, it will often update the screen, or possibly hit you with a message that looks like Figure 9-8.

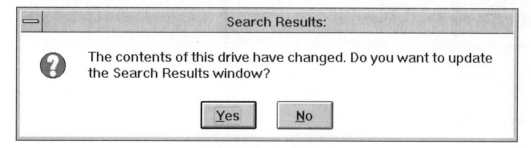

Figure 9-8: How Much Is That Window In the Doggie?

Thus, when File Manager is running, it's kept abreast of the latest status of all files changed by Windows and passes the latest info on to you. That's great.

Life in the DOS lane isn't so simple. Unless you do something to this **FileSysChange=** setting, changes to files done by a DOS program running under Windows won't "take" in File Manager. Poor File Manager is doomed to living in the past, only showing file info that is current as of the last time the disk was scanned.

That isn't necessarily bad. If you know that DOS is chugging away in the background, changing files, you can always tell File Manager to retrieve the latest list by clicking on Window, then Refresh, or hitting F5. If you *don't* realize that there's a DOS program out there wreaking havoc, though, you may not realize that the stuff you see in File Manager doesn't reflect reality.

If **FileSysChange=On**, any changes to files made by DOS programs are reported to File Manager, the same way that Windows changes are reported. But if **FileSysChange=Off**, or if the line is missing (or if you're running in Standard mode, regardless of any settings), DOS programs' changes to files are not reported to File Manager.

When Windows installs itself, it puts this line in [386Enh]:

FileSysChange=off

Why Windows does that is anybody's guess: the Off setting is the same as not having the line in there at all.

The docs warn you that setting **FileSysChange=On** will slow down system performance significantly. On my machines, DOS programs that change just a few files slow things down, but not by enough to spit at. All bets are off, of course, if you have a DOS program that changes dozens or hundreds of files.

Here's something more important than a tiny performance hit: **FileSys-Change=On** locked up my machines, repeatedly. Windows seems to croak with the setting On, if you run a DOS program Exclusive and that program does anything, anywhere, to change any file. Try it and you'll see: a three-finger salute will kill off the offending DOS program, but the file changed by the DOS program floats around in a never-never land. Far as I can tell, nothing short of rebooting your the offending DOS program, but the file changed by the DOS program floats around in a never-never land. Far as I can tell, nothing short of rebooting your machine (or running SHARE) will let you get at the file that's been changed by the DOS program.

Global=*DeviceDriver*

Local=*DeviceDriver*

 These settings refer to the device drivers you load in `device=` lines in `CONFIG.SYS`. When Windows starts, it takes a look at all those devices, and has to decide whether to make each one global or local. It's a question of what Windows does with the memory area taken by the driver each time a it loads a new DOS session or program. If the driver is "Global," the memory region taken by the original driver is mapped into each DOS session and is used in common. If the driver is "Local," Windows instead makes a copy of the original driver in a different part of physical memory for each session and remaps that copy so it resides at the proper location in the sessions' virtual memory addressing. Basically, if the driver is global, all sessions share a common code and common data while if it is local, each session has its own data and code.

Most DOS device drivers are loaded Global, and work fine that way. The consistent exception is CON, the "console" keyboard/video driver, which needs to be loaded Local so each DOS window can put stuff in the keyboard buffer or on the screen without stepping on the other DOS windows. CON isn't smart enough to handle more than one DOS program at a time, so you need copies of it in with each DOS window. *No CON can serve two masters. . .* Thus Windows, when it installs itself, adds this line to **[386Enh]**:

`Local=CON`

Details on other exceptions to the Global rule are sketchy. Apparently some Windows virtual device drivers can jump in here and insist that certain DOS device drivers be Local, the official docs mention the **MS$MOUSE** driver, which is bumped to Local by the *vmd virtual mouse driver.

If you wanted to force the **MS$MOUSE** driver to be Global (heaven knows why!), you would use a line like this:

`Global=MS$MOUSE`

and, conversely, use **Local=** to force a device driver to Local. All the docs warn that these values are case-dependent — **MS$MOUSE** is not the same as **ms$mouse,** and that DOS device names are almost always all-caps.

HardDiskDMABuffer=_KB_

See **DMABufferIn1MB=** in **[386Enh]**.

IdleVMWakeupTime=_Seconds_

Some DOS programs running under Windows, or so I'm told, will go to sleep and slumber forever unless stimulated by timer interrupts; specifically INT 08h and INT 1Ch timer interrupts. Think of them as a kind of DOS alarm clock.

If you set **IdleVMWakeUpTime=**4, for example, Windows will force a timer interrupt on all DOS programs every four seconds, even if they're sleeping, inactive, in the background.

The value is rounded to the next lower power of 2, **IdleVMWakeUpTime=20** only "ticks" every 16 seconds. If the line is missing, Windows assumes a value of 8 seconds.

IgnoreInstalledEMM=_OffOrOn_

When Windows starts in Enhanced mode, it looks around to see if there are any extended memory managers running. If Windows detects an extended memory manager but doesn't recognize which one is in action, Windows should refuse to load; in some cases it may just completely clobber the active EMS manager.

By setting **IgnoreInstalledEMM=On**, Windows will continue to load, regardless of what extended memory manager may be at the helm. That can be dangerous if you try to start Windows when there are any programs running that use EMS: Windows will step all over them.

If this line is missing, Windows assumes you want it Off.

InDOSPolling=_OffOrOn_

Some DOS TSRs set a flag called the InDOS flag. (It's supposed to be set while a DOS program is in a critical section with an INT 21h call, if that makes any sense to you. A "critical section" is a short bit of code that shouldn't be interrupted by anything else, lest your entire system lock up.) Anyway, if `InDOSPolling=On`, Windows checks to see if the InDOS flag is set before giving time to another program.

It's extremely unlikely that you'll have to change this setting, but if you learn that your DOS program is crashing sporadically because Windows is stepping into the middle of an INT 21h critical section (I can just imagine a techie telling you that over the phone, in the middle of the night, and can only guess at your reaction!) you'll have to set `InDOSPolling=On`.

If you turn `InDOSPolling=On`, Windows will not interleave input/output requests among DOS programs. See `OverlappedIO=` in `[386Enh]` for details.

If the line is missing in `[386Enh]`, Windows assumes you want it Off. And you probably do, you probably do....

Int28Critical=*OffOrOn*

The official description of this setting is all screwed up. When you are looking at a DOS prompt, DOS is sitting in a loop waiting for keyboard input and doing all sorts of housekeeping. If a TSR should pop up and ask DOS to do some of the same housekeeping, DOS can get very confused and the system can go bananas. To indicate safe times for a TSR to pop up, DOS periodically inssues an INT 28h to tell TSRs that they can run code that makes critical calls to DOS. When a TSR is doing that, it could be dangerous for Windows to switch away from the DOS sesion depending on the TSR and how it was written. The `Int28Critical=` setting tells Windows whther it should avoid switching in the middle of an INT 28h because some TSR could become unhappy if it did.

Some network software uses INT 28h interrupt for task switching, and they have "critical sections" (see previous setting) in the INT 28h handler.

If this line is missing, or set to `Int28Critical=On`, Windows assumes that you are running software with critical sections in the INT 28h handler, and won't switch away from a DOS session in the middle of an INT 28h.

If you're absolutely sure that you don't have any software with a critical section in the INT 28h handler, you might set `Int28Critical=Off` and see if you can feel the speed-up, the wind rushing through your hair as you liberate Windows from its INT 28h critical section handling burden.

One hint, pilgrim. You won't be able to tell the difference. You just lost more time trying to figure out what an INT 28h critical section *is* than you'll ever save by changing the setting.

IRQ9Global=*OffOrOn*

According to the official docs, this setting may help you convince your ancient floppy disk drive controller to work with Windows. It all has to do with the way Windows handles the IRQ 9 line. In a nutshell, if you can't get your floppy drives to work while you're running in Enhanced mode, you're supposed to stick this:

IRQ9Global=On

in **[386Enh]**.

The only problem is that the diskette controller uses IRQ6, not IRQ9. IRQ9 is used by the second PIC to talk to the first (see the discussion of PICs in *Port-Annoy's Complaint* in Chapter 3). So either the person who named this setting or the person who wrote up the Windows Resource Kit docs was a mite confused.

Or both.

---

keyboard=*FileOrDevicename*

See **device=** in **[386Enh]**.

KeyBoostTime=*Seconds*

When running a DOS program under Windows, every time you punch a key on the keyboard, Windows gives the DOS program a little juice, and little extra priority for processing the keystroke. Without this "boost time," some DOS programs can have trouble bringing in keystrokes and processing them properly.

This line tells Windows how long to apply the juice, every time a key is pressed. If there's no such line in **[386Enh]**, Windows assumes a value of 0.001 second — one millisecond.

If you find yourself running several DOS programs in the background, and your keyboard starts acting flaky — dropped characters, or significant delays in characters appearing on the screen — try setting **KeyBoostTime=0.010** and see if that helps.

KeyBufferDelay=*Seconds*

 In spite of what you may read, this setting doesn't have anything to do with the keyboard. It only comes into play when Windows is pasting stuff from the clipboard into a DOS window.

Windows pastes stuff into the DOS window in one of two ways, depending on how the DOS program is expecting to get keyboard input. "Fast paste" works when the DOS program sits in a loop saying, "Feed me a key. Feed me a key. Feed me a key." and Windows obliges, notifying the DOS program that a key is available, simultaneously sticking it in the keyboard buffer. (Techies will recognize this as the INT 16h approach.) "Slow paste" involves Windows stuffing characters directly into the keyboard buffer, in essence, plodding away, faking out the DOS program, making it think that somebody is typing, when in fact Windows is pulling the strings. (This is the so-called INT 9h approach.) Windows will try fast paste first, then revert to slow paste if the fast kind doesn't seem to be working — see **KeyPasteTimeout=** below.

A problem arises when the keyboard buffer gets full. Just as a very fast typist (or slow program) can fill up the keyboard buffer and start the machine beeping like a pager on steroids, Windows may try to over-stuff characters into the DOS window, too many, too fast. When Windows detects that it's pumping out characters faster than the DOS program can take them, it fills up the keyboard buffer, then pauses for **KeyBufferDelay=** seconds, before trying to cram more characters into the buffer.

If there is no such line in **[386Enh]**, Windows assumes **KeyBufferDelay=0.2**.

If your machine starts beeping every time you copy stuff into a DOS window, and characters don't get copied properly, first look at **KeyPasteDelay=**, **KeyPasteSkipCount=** and **KeyPasteCRSkipCount=**. If that doesn't seem to clear up the problem, try setting **KeyBufferDelay=0.5** and see if that helps.

KeyIdleDelay=Seconds

 When a DOS program running under Windows is waiting for the user to type something on the keyboard, it just sits there, waiting to be fed. "I'm idle." "Hey, anybody out there looking? "Yoooo-hooooo. I'm not doing anything." "I'm gonna sit here with my mouth open until you feed me a key." Kinda like a five-year-old during Summer vacation.

When Windows sees that the DOS program is idle, it may jump in and give the time slice to another application, a program that can use the time. Usually, that's a good idea.

As soon as the user types something at the keyboard, Windows gathers the key and shoots it to the DOS program. Since it takes a little while to whop the DOS program upside the head and tell it there's a key waiting, the sequence goes like this: DOS program says "Feed me. Feed me. Feed me." Windows sends the key. DOS program keeps saying, "Feed me. Feed me. Feed me. Gulp. Blast. There's a key. I'm busy. I'm busy. I'm busy." Once the DOS program finishes processing the key, it goes back to "Feed me. Feed me. Feed me."

Here's the problem. There's a delay between the time Windows shoots the key to that DOS program, and when the DOS program stops whining "Feed me. Feed me." You don't want Windows to switch to another DOS program during that little bit of time, the span necessary to whop the DOS program upside the head.

The **KeyIdleDelay=** time is the amount of time Windows should ignore those "Feed me. Feed me." signals, after it sends a key to the DOS program. If there is no such line in **[386Enh]**, Windows assumes **KeyIdleDelay=0.5**, a half second, which seems reasonable enough. Supposedly you can speed up DOS program execution time by decreasing this value, but I couldn't tell any difference. And the official docs warn that setting the value to 0 may actually slow down your DOS programs — Windows can switch away at the wrong time and bog down everything.

KeyPasteCRSkipCount=*NumberToSkip*

KeyPasteSkipCount=*NumberToSkip*

These settings have nothing to do with the keyboard. They control the way Windows pastes characters from the clipboard into DOS programs.

DOS applications running under Windows spend a lot of time waiting for keystrokes. They will often sit for ages saying, in effect, "Feed me a key." "Hey, you out there, give me a key." "I'm waiting for a key in here." "Anybody got a key?" "Key, please."

Some DOS programs are smart enough to do work while waiting for a key stroke. They'll start the "Feed me a key. Feed me a key. Feed me a key." routine. Then they'll get a key, and start digesting it, but continue to ask for more keys while the work progresses. It goes something like this: "Feed me a key. Feed me a key. Gulp. OOPS. I better start working on this one. Feed me a key. Work. Work. Feed me a key. Work. Work. Feed me a key. Done. Feed me a key. Feed me a key...."

As long as a human is punching away on the keyboard, the DOS program generally has more than enough time to finish its work while the human is lollygagging around, typing at 100 words a minute, glacially slow by PC standards.

The problem arises when Windows, using the fast paste method, starts pasting characters into the DOS program's keyboard buffer (see **KeyBufferDelay=** above). Windows can paste characters much, much faster than any mere human can type. The resulting deluge may overwhelm the DOS program, causing skipped or missed characters, or even locking up your machine entirely.

KeyPasteSkipCount= tells Windows how many "Feed me a key" entreaties it should ignore after stuffing one character in the keyboard buffer, before stuffing in the next.

KeyPasteCRSkipCount= does the same thing, except it controls how many "Feed me a key" requests are ignored after a *carriage return* is pasted into the keyboard buffer. Some DOS programs — DOS Edit, for example — do a significant amount of processing whenever they encounter a carriage return; they need a whole lot more time to digest a carriage return than any other character.

If these lines don't appear in **[386Enh]**, Windows assumes **KeyPasteSkip-Count=2** and **KeyPasteCRSkipCount=10**. Those work fine for me, but if you have a weird DOS application that bytes off more than it can chew, dropping characters pasted into the app from Windows, you might try boosting either or both of these numbers. If doubling or tripling the numbers doesn't work, look at **KeyBufferDelay=**.

***

KeyPasteDelay=*Seconds*

***

This setting has nothing to do with the keyboard. It controls the way in which Windows pastes stuff from the clipboard into a DOS program.

When Windows uses the slow paste method (see **KeyBufferDelay=** above), it pauses between each pasted character. This setting controls the length of the pause.

If this line is missing in **[386Enh]**, Windows assumes a **KeyPasteDelay=0.003**, or 3 milliseconds. If you lose a lot of characters when pasting stuff into a DOS window, try setting **KeyPasteDelay=0.010**, or even higher.

***

KeyPasteTimeout=*Seconds*

***

Again, this setting has nothing to do with the keyboard. It determines how long Windows tries the fast paste method (see **KeyBufferDelay=** above) before reverting to the slow paste method.

Put another way, it's the length of time Windows waits for the DOS application to say "Feed me a key." before it reverts to stuffing keystrokes brute-force into the keyboard buffer. (Equivalently, it's the amount of time Windows waits for an INT 16h call before finking out with INT 9h keystroke processing.)

If there is no entry in **[386Enh]**, Windows assumes **KeyPasteTimeout=1**, or one second's delay. If you find that most of your DOS apps rely on slow paste, you might want to decrease this number, but you probably won't notice much improvement in performance. Setting it too low may force Windows to use slow paste when it could've used fast paste.

KybdPasswd=*OffOrOn*

 Yeah, that's how this setting is spelled. If u cn rd ths u cn prgrm wndws.

If you own an IBM PS/2 (cross yourself twice and grab some garlic), you may have a keyboard with the 8042 controller, the one that lets you password-protect access to your computer. Lucky you.

If you have such a keyboard, Windows should've detected it on installation, and put this line in **[386Enh]**:

KybdPasswd=On

That instructs Windows to work with 8042-style keyboard password protection.

I suppose it's conceivable that Windows didn't detect your 8042 keyboard controller when it installed, or (shudder!) you may have swapped out a decent keyboard for an 8042 and need to inform Windows of the change. In either case, you can add the line manually.

KybdReboot=*OffOrOn*

If a Windows program goes belly-up, you can press **Ctrl+Alt+Del** and get the standard Windows screen that lets you kill off the offending application. When you're in that screen, if you press **Ctrl+Alt+Del** again, Windows will reboot your system. You knew that, right?

Well, there's one little problem. When you hit **Ctrl+Alt+Del** that second time, Windows uses a keyboard controller call to force the system to reboot — it's a PC's politically correct way to force a "warm boot." Alas, some keyboard controllers don't respond to that call properly. They lock the machine up, so you have to push the Reset button on your machine, force a "cold boot," to get things going again.

Bummer.

If you put **KybdReboot=Off** in the **[386Enh]** section, that second **Ctrl+Alt+Del** does something rather strange. Instead of trying to reboot the computer, Windows pops out to some black never-never land (nope, you aren't in DOS any more, Toto) and sticks this message up at the top of the screen:

Press Ctrl-Alt-Del again to reboot your machine

At that point your machine is frozen solid. The keys don't respond. The mouse is dead. You can't do anything but reboot. Hitting `Ctrl+Alt+Del` at this point is supposed to reboot your machine, but.... believe it or not, on one of my machines, things are so locked up at this point that `Ctrl+Alt+Del` doesn't work; I have to hit the Reboot button or turn the computer off, then back on again!

So the **KybdReboot=Off** setting bypasses the keyboard controller and, if all works well, forces you to hit **Ctrl+Alt+Del** *three* times to reboot.

Local=*DeviceDriver*

See **Global=** in **[386Enh]**.

LocalLoadHigh=*OffOrOn*

Windows usually gloms onto all the upper memory blocks (UMBs; the chunks of memory between 640K and 1 MB) it can find. According to the official docs, if you are using DOS 5.0 or later, you can tell Windows to be a little less stingy, and leave some of the UMBs around for use by DOS programs running under Windows.

Setting **LocalLoadHigh=On** tells Windows to leave some of the UMBs free. If the line is missing, or **LocalLoadHigh=Off**, Windows sucks up all the available UMBs.

The official docs are not clear about how Windows decides which UMBs to take, and which to pass. I tried poking around a bit and couldn't find a simple formula.

LocalReboot=*OffOrOn*

If a Windows program or DOS program under Windows gets carried away, you can push `Ctrl+Alt+Del` and Windows will let you (1) hit Escape to go back to the runaway program; (2) hit Enter and end the aberrant program, or (3) hit `Ctrl+Alt+Del` again to reboot the system. That's Windows' normal behavior; it's called Local Reboot.

But sometimes, a program clearly crashes; for example its hour glass comes up and stays up. You hit Ctrl+Alt+Del and Windows informs you sweetly that "Although you can use CTRL+ALT+DEL to quit an application that has stopped responding to the system, there is no application in this state." And you want to scream at the screen: "Mr. Know–It–All Windows — you are wrong. Just kill the active program, will ya and don't lecture me." Alas, yelling doesn't help. I sure hope the next version of Windows lets me kill a program if I want to.

If you set `LocalReboot=Off`, a `Ctrl+Atl+Del` does not trap the running program; it shuts down Windows entirely (possibly with the hang-up described under `KybdReboot=` above) and completely reboots the machine. In effect, `LocalReboot=Off` makes a Windows `Ctrl+Alt+Del` act much like DOS.

A `Ctrl+Alt+Del` in Windows immediately flushes the SmartDrive write buffer. (See Chapter 7 for a discussion of why that's important, especially with disk compression software.) A `Ctrl+Alt+Del` in DOS does ~~not~~ flush the buffer. I couldn't find any information one way or the other about Windows' behavior with `LocalReboot=Off`.

If this line is missing, Windows assumes `LocalReboot=On`. It's hard to imagine why you would want to make Windows mimic DOS, but you can change this line manually if you must.

LPTnAutoAssign=Seconds

If you have any lines like this in **[386Enh]**, go ahead and delete 'em. They're throwbacks from Windows 3.0.

LRULowRateMult=*Multiplier*

LRURateChngTime=*Milliseconds*

LRUSweepFreq=*Milliseconds*

LRUSweepLen=*NumberOf4KPages*

LRUSweepLowWater=*NumberOf4KPages*

LRUSweepReset=*Milliseconds*

Ah, the joys of garbage collection. Chances are very good you've read about these settings, at one time or another, in some magazine or book: it seems to be something of a tinker's delight, prime grist for "make the most of Windows" columns and lengthy discourses in Windows books. That's reasonable. There's a lot of arcane stuff floating around in these parts. If you're the tinkering kind, you may not be able to resist the temptation to go in and "tune" how Windows swaps your virtual memory onto and off of disk.

 But if you are running in Enhanced mode, with either a permanent or temporary swap file, you're in for a big surprise. Make sure you read the last two paragraphs of this discussion first, before you get all tongue-tied with high rate Sweeps and LRU bits.

What you find may surprise you.

 Windows keeps track of memory in 4K-byte blocks called "pages." It doles out memory to demanding applications by the page, keeps track of which blocks of memory have been used ("Accessed") by the page, keeps track of which blocks of memory have changed (or made "Dirty") by the page, shuffles memory out to disk (the "virtual" in "virtual memory") in pages, and so on. The memory inside your machine starts looking like a patchwork quilt after a while: this page belongs to that program, the page sitting next door belongs to somebody else, that page has swapped out to disk until it's needed.

When a program asks for memory, Windows takes a look around to see if there's any unused memory sitting in the machine (in 4K-byte chunks, of course). If there isn't enough memory to satisfy the program's request, Windows has to shuffle pages out to disk, to make room. The obvious question: which pages stay in memory, and which get shipped to Siberia?

Windows uses a simplistic scheme, one that's been shown to work very well, called "Least Recently Used," or LRU, to determine which pages stay inside the computer and which get the heave-ho. Very simply, Windows holds onto the pages that have been used most recently, and shuffles the ones that haven't been used in quite a while out to disk, or just overwrites the pages if they don't have anything new in them.

Each time a program requests an allocation of memory, Windows first looks to see if there are any pages that have not been used at all. If there aren't enough virgin pages available, Windows looks to see which pages have not been accessed since they last came in from disk; any such pages are fair game for tossing.

When Windows *running in Standard mode* figures out that it doesn't have enough memory to satisfy a program's request, or it's running mighty low on available pages, it initiates something called a "Sweep." (There are much more descriptive terms for this process, not all of them suitable for a family publication, so we'll bow to Redmond's sensibilities here and stick with their terminology.) The purpose of a Sweep is to keep the most recently used pages in memory, while shuffling the least recently used ones out to disk, where they can wait until they're needed. Windows gives preference to swapping out pages that have been Accessed (i.e., read), but are not Dirty (i.e., written to, or changed). The Dirty ones are left for last.

The Sweep starts out running at a "high rate," shoving all other programs to the side as it tries to do a bit of cleaning. If the Sweep bogs down, with few pages being shuffled to disk, Windows drops the priority and reverts the Sweep to a "low rate." That lets you take back control of the system, so you can get some work done in spite of Windows' overhead.

Windows keeps track of how often pages are used by flipping one bit. Let's call it the LRU bit. (Actually, the bit is in the page descriptor, and it's set by the processor itself; see *Windows Internals* by Matt Pietrek (Addison-Wesley, 1992) for details.) Every so often Windows roams through all the pages in memory and resets the LRU bit to 0. Then, as pages are used, their LRU bits are turned to 1. When Windows initiates a sweep it looks at the LRU bit: any that are turned to 1 have been used recently, and their pages should remain in memory; any that are still 0 have not, and are likely candidates to be shuffled to disk.

The actual implementation involves a couple of different lists; the details aren't particularly important for our purposes.

 According to the documentation (as best I can interpret it, anyway; the official description of this setting is abysmal!), the `LRUSweepReset=` time tells Windows how much time it should take to reset all the LRU bits in 4 MB of memory. If `LRUSweepReset=500`, and you're running on a 4 MB system, Windows should pace itself to reset all the LRU bits every half-second. Presumably the same value on an 8 MB system would lead to a reset every second.

If there is no such line in **[386Enh]**, Windows assumes **LRUSweepReset=500**. And the docs say the minimum value is 100.

The **LRUSweepLowWater=** setting tells Windows how many available pages it should have before initiating a Sweep. If the line is missing from **[386Enh]**, Windows assumes **LRUSweepLowWater=24**, i.e., it starts a Sweep any time it discovers there are fewer than 24 free pages left in memory.

Windows continues its "high rate" Sweep for **LRURateChngTime=** milliseconds. If the Sweep has identified no pages that can be shuffled to disk in that amount of time, Windows drops back to the "low rate" Sweep. Then it keeps trying, for **LRURateChngTime=** milliseconds, to shake loose a page at the "low rate." If Windows doesn't manage to shuffle a page to disk during that stretch of time, it calls off the Sweep. If there is no value in **[386Enh]**, Windows assumes an **LRURateChngTime=10000**, i.e., ten seconds.

 Again it's hard to tell from the abysmal documentation, but the **LRUSweepFreq=** setting appears to be the minimum amount of time Windows allows between "high rate" Sweeps. If there is no such line in **[386Enh]**, Windows assumes **LRUSweepFreq=250**, a quarter-second. And apparently Windows multiplies the **LRUSweepFreq=** number by the **LRULowRateMult=** number to come up with the minimum amount of time it allows between "low rate" sweeps. If there is no line in **[386Enh]**, Windows assumes a value of **LRULowRateMult=10**, constraining "low rate" sweeps to every 2.5 seconds.

Finally, the official docs are completely self-contradictory when discussing the setting **LRUSweepLen=**. As best I can tell, it specifies the number of 4K-byte pages Windows should examine on each Sweep, and it defaults to 1024 (i.e., a Sweep of 4 MB). That isn't what the documentation *says*, mind you, but it seems reasonable.

 The 'Softie who wrote the LRU documentation should be strung up by the. . .well, let's say by the tongue. It's frustrating — almost criminal — that Microsoft would leave these settings out where you can get at them, but couch the explanation in such convoluted, self-contradictory, obfuscating verbiage that a fancy $350-an-hour New Yawk Computer Lawyer couldn't divine its meaning.

 Here's the punch line. As best I can tell, all the official and unofficial `.INI` documentation is wrong. Windows running in Enhanced mode with either a permanent or a temporary swap file in place — what the techies would call "Enhanced mode with paging enabled" — doesn't use this LRU Sweep mish-mash at all. When Windows is running Enhanced and paging, I'm told, it takes care of all of this stuff as part of its normal paging routines: it's part and parcel of the pageswap routine buried in `WIN386.EXE` and specified in the `device=*pageswap` line in `[386Enh]`.

Unless I'm terribly mistaken (and it wouldn't be the first time!), all of the sound and fury and hundreds of column-inches and dozens of book pages about adjusting sweeps and the optimal settings for these six entries doesn't mean a thing if you're running Enhanced with a swap file. And chances are very, very good you're doing precisely that.

Go figger.

I think — *think!* — that the packages which claim to "compact" memory launch one of these LRU sweeps. Again, though, that would seem to have no effect if you're running in Enchanced mode.

MapPhysAddress=*MB*

Some old DOS device drivers must have large blocks of contiguous memory. This entry lets you set aside big blocks of linear memory for their use. There's no need to use this setting unless you need to set aside a big chunk of memory for an old-fashioned extended memory gobbling disk cache or RAM drive. If you're saddled with such a beast, take a look at DOS's alternatives.

MaxBPs=*NumberOfBreakPoints*

Some old-fashioned memory managers set large numbers of break points, the docs say, all the better to speed switching between real and protected mode. If this line is missing in `[386Enh]`, Windows sets aside 200 breakpoints, which is more than adequate for Windows use. If you have an old third-party memory manager, you may have to change this setting, but you're undoubtedly better off upgrading to a memory manager that's Windows aware.

Also see **SetROMBreakpoint=** in **[386Enh]**.

MaxComPort=_NumberOfComPorts_

If you have more than four Com ports, use this setting to tell Windows about them. The largest number you can use is MaxComPort=9.

Replacement Windows Comm programs (e.g., TurboCom and KingComm) keep track of their own ports; if you're using one of the replacements, there's no need to change this setting.

MaxDMAPgAddress=_AddressInHex_

See **DMABufferIn1MB=** in **[386Enh]**.

MaxPagingFileSize=_KB_

This is the size of the largest temporary swap file Windows will put on the swap disk. The setting makes no difference unless you are using a temporary swap file.

The value is recalculated every time you pull up the 386 Enhanced applet from the Control Panel, and click Virtual Memory, then Change. Windows will set the variable to half the available space on the swap disk.

 Much of the time, especially if you are just starting out with a rather clean disk, that's an outrageously large amount of space. Scale it back by playing around with the 386 Enhanced applet. If you have a substantial amount of real memory, 16 MB or more, don' t be bashful about turning the whole thing off; see **Paging=** in **[386Enh]** for some hints.

Also see the **MinUserDiskSpace=** setting.

MaxPhysPage=_HexPageNumber_

According to the official docs, this setting tells Windows the maximum physical page number that Windows' virtual memory manager can address.

If you set it below the actual physical memory size (say, 6 MB on an 8 MB machine), Windows is supposed to ignore any memory above the indicated location (in this example, the top 2 MB). If you set it above the actual physical memory size (say, 10 MB on an 8 MB machine), you "allow pages to be added at a physical address above" the physical memory. Whatever that means.

I played around with this setting for a bit; there don't appear to be any examples of its use in any of the Windows books. I found that, on a 32 MB machine, setting

MaxPhysPage=1000

does, indeed, limit Windows to the lower 16 MB of memory. (If you're wondering about the math: 1000 hex = 4096 decimal; 4096 pages at 4K per page is 16 MB.)

MCADMA=*OffOrOn*

See **DMABufferIn1MB=** in **[386Enh]**.

MessageTextColor=*ColorNumber*

MessageBackColor=*ColorNumber*

Ah, my favorite secret settings. Who woulda thought that a couple of screen color settings would be buried here, in the **[386Enh]** section of **SYSTEM.INI**?

When you hit **Ctrl+Alt+Del**, Windows brings up that big screen saying you can push Esc to go back to the program you were working with, Enter to kill the program (if one is hung up), or **Ctrl+Alt+Del** again to reboot your machine.

It's a nice screen. Lots of info, well presented. The white characters on electric blue looks pretty good. There's just one problem: if I'm about to reboot my machine, I want the be hit over the head with the fact, shot right between the eyes. If I'm fumbling for a cup of coffee in the wee hours of the morning, I want that screen to jump out and grab me, shake me by the collar till I yell "uncle". . . In short, I want the screen to be RED and PINK! (Well, it isn't exactly pink. There's a touch of blue in there. Whatever.)

The official documentation says that Windows is looking for a "VGA Color Attribute." Best I could tell is that Windows is looking for a single number, in hex. Although there is some variation (not all numbers produce the same color when used as background colors as they do as text colors), here's a starting point: 0=black; 1=blue; 2=green; 3=cyan; 4=red; 5=magenta; 6=brown; 7=light gray; 8=dark gray; 9=bright blue; A=bright green; B=bright cyan; C= bright red; D=bright magenta; E=yellow; F=white.

My favorite settings:

MessageBackColor=C
MessageTextColor=D

and I'll never, ever, ever ignore the **Ctrl+Alt+Del** screen again.

MinTimeSlice=_Milliseconds_

This setting corresponds to the "Minimum Time Slice" number in the Control Panel's 386 Enhanced applet, down at the bottom of the dialog box in Figure 9-9.

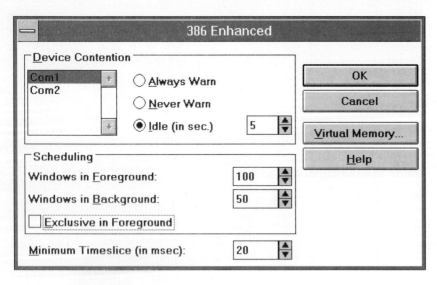

Figure 9-9: It Slices, It Dices. . .

This is the minimum amount of time Windows will give to a DOS program before switching over to another DOS program, or to Windows itself. The setting has no effect on time slicing among Windows programs; it only controls the minimum slice for DOS programs, and the length of the slice that all Windows programs together receive.

If Windows doesn't find this line in **[386Enh]**, it assumes **MinTimeSlice=20**, i.e., Windows should dole out a minimum of 20 milliseconds to each DOS program before switching to the next one.

If you increase this number, you'll reduce Windows' overhead and thus speed things up in general, but you'll also increase the possibility that one of the DOS programs won't pop up frequently enough to do what it needs to do (e.g., retrieve a byte from the modem) and make the foreground program appear jerkier.

If you decrease this number, you'll add to Windows' overhead, potentially slowing things down.

 I haven't found any perceptible difference between settings of 5, 10, 20, and 30 milliseconds, on a fast 486. Unless you have compelling reasons to the contrary, leave this number at 20. If you must change it, perhaps to test and see if you can get a monster DOS program in the background to speed up a bit, use the Control Panel's 386 Enhanced applet, and rely on your stopwatch.

MinUnlockMem=*KB*

According to the official documentation, when Windows resumes execution of a DOS program, and there are two or more DOS programs running, Windows first checks to make sure there's some small amount of memory left "unlocked," i.e., unclaimed by other programs. If there isn't at least **MinUnlockMem=** kilobytes still available, apparently, Windows croaks.

If the line is missing, Windows assumes **MinUnlockMem=40**.

MinUserDiskSpace=*KB*

When Windows creates a temporary swap file, it leaves a bit of room on the disk: after all, if the temporary swap file swallowed up the whole disk, you wouldn't have any room to do any real work!

If this line is missing, Windows assumes **MinUserDiskSpace=2000**, i.e., when Windows makes a temporary swap file, it will always leave a minimum of 2 MB free on the swap disk. (The official docs are wrong.)

This setting is ignored completely if you have a permanent swap file, or have chosen to run without any swap file at all. Also see **MaxPagingFileSize=**.

---

mouse=*FileOrDevicename*

See **device=** in **[386Enh]**.

MouseSoftInit=*OffOrOn*

DOS programs have a specific method for talking to the mouse. Function call 0 of INT 33h resets the mouse. Normally INT 33h function 0 resets the software and sends a reset command out the mouse port to the hardware. But to fool the mouse into working in a windowed DOS session, Windows needs to avoid this hardware reset and instead handle it all in software. So while the default for this setting is called **MouseSoftInit=On**, it would be more accurate to call it **MouseHardInit=Off**.

> If you can't get your mouse to work right in a DOS window, and want to turn it off completely in all DOS windows, you can set **MouseSoftInit= Off**. Personally, I've never hit the problem, and would recommend that you first try to install a good mouse driver, like the Microsoft Mouse Driver version 9.0 or later, to see if that will clear up your problems.

NetAsynchFallback=*OffOrOn*

NetAsynchTimeout=*Seconds*

Windows sets aside space in its global network buffer to receive responses to application's asynch NetBIOS calls. If there isn't enough room in the global network buffer, Windows looks to see if there's a **NetAsynchFallback=** line in

[386Enh]. If there is no such line, or it's set to Off, Windows fails the NetBIOS call.

On the other hand, if there isn't enough room in the global network buffer, and **NetAsynchFallback=On**, Windows sets up space in local memory for the NetBIOS response. Windows prohibits all other DOS programs from running until it receives the NetBIOS response, or **NetAsynchTimeout=** seconds have passed.

If there is no time-out entry, Windows assumes **NetAsynchTimeout=5.0**.

NetDMASize=*KB*

When Windows starts, it looks to see if there is a network installed. If so, it then looks at this entry and at the **DMABufferSize=** setting, and creates a DMA buffer as big as the larger of the two settings.

If this line is missing, Windows uses a **NetDMASize=32** for MicroChannel machines (i.e., the smallest DMA buffer used on a network-connected MCA machine is 32 KB), 0 for non-MCA machines.

NetDMASize=*KB*

When Windows is running in Enhanced mode and it discovers it needs a network buffer down in lower memory, it looks to this setting to see how large the buffer should be.

If this entry is missing, Windows assumes **NetHeapSize=12**, i.e., Windows allocates 12 KB of lower memory for a network buffer.

For the analogous setting in Standard mode (which defaults to 8 KB), see the **NetHeapSize=** setting in the **[Standard]** section.

---

network=*FileOrDevicename*

See **device=** in **[386Enh]**.

NMIReboot=*OffOrOn*

The Non Maskable Interrupt — NMI — is the "Jeeeeeez. What do we do now, Ollie?" command of the PC biz. Among other things, you'll get an NMI if your system discovers a memory parity error. Often NMIs represent trouble, big time.

Usually Windows punts when it hits an NMI: sometimes it'll put up a screen that tells you you're in deep doo-doo; sometimes it just freezes. By setting **NMIReboot=On**, you can have Windows automatically reboot every time it encounters an NMI. (If the line is missing in **[386Enh]**, Windows assumes **NMIReboot=Off**.)

If you have repeated NMIs, you need to find out what might be causing them. Turning **NMIReboot=On** will virtually guarantee that you'll never find out — if the machine doesn't stop dead in its tracks, you'll have little chance of finding out what triggered the NMI. I can't imagine any circumstance where you would want this to be on.

NoEMMDriver=*OffOrOn*

If you set **NoEMMDriver=On**, Windows will not load its virtual expanded memory driver on startup. If this line is missing, or it's set Off, the Windows Enhanced mode EMS driver is used.

For an alternate approach, also see **EMMSize=**.

If you think there might be a conflict with your hardware or software expanded memory manager, you could try setting **NoEMMDriver=On** and see what happens. Also, if you know that you will never run a DOS program under Windows that requires expanded memory, you could set **NoEMMDriver=On** and see if that frees up any appreciable quantity of conventional memory.

NoWaitNetIO=*OffOrOn*

Windows normally converts synchronous NetBIOS calls to asynch calls. If you set **NoWaitNetIO=Off**, though, Windows keeps them synchronous. That can slow things down, but may help ensure the calls behave properly.

If you're having synch problems with NetBIOS calls, take a look at the **[386Enh]** setting for **NetAsynchFallback=**.

OverlappedIO=*OffOrOn*

Windows tries to interleave input/output requests from all your active programs: that's one of the major time-saving benefits of Windows. Still, sometimes DOS programs have a hard time if their I/O work is interrupted by another programs'. In such a case, you can set **OverlappedIO=Off**, and Windows will revert to one-I/O-call-at-a-time operation.

If **InDOSPolling=On** (see the explanation of **InDOSPolling=** earlier in the **[386Enh]** section), Windows won't interleave I/O requests: in effect, if you have set **InDOSPolling=On**, Windows is forced to **OverlappedIO=Off**. In all other cases, though, Windows assumes **OverlappedIO=On** unless you explicitly turn it off with this setting.

You probably shouldn't touch this setting unless a tech support guru tells you it's necessary. And if a techie should tell you to do it, scream and moan: by setting **OverlappedIO=Off**, you're losing one of the big performance enhancements you paid for when you bought Windows.

PageBuffers=*NumberOf4KPages*

If Windows is using FastDisk (see the discussion of **32BitDiskAccess=** in **[386Enh]**) with a permanent swap file, it sets aside a small buffer area, to speed up FastDisk access. The buffer shuffles pages (i.e., 4K byte blocks of memory) to and from the hard disk, via Windows' FastDisk routines.

This setting lets you tell Windows how many 4K byte hunks you want to set aside for the FastDisk buffer; it only takes effect is FastDisk is running (i.e., "32 Bit Access" is in effect, and you have a permanent swap file). If the line is missing, Windows assumes **PageBuffers=4**, i.e., it should set aside 16K of memory for FastDisk buffering.

The official docs say you can pick any number between 0 and 32. If you spend a lot of time swapping programs in and out of memory, it may be worth the effort to set **PageBuffers=16** or even 32. Personally, I couldn't tell any difference.

PageOverCommit=*Multiplier*

The official docs say Windows has to decide how large a virtual address space it should support, how many bytes it should map onto your physical memory and the swap file on your disk. When Windows starts, it checks to see how much real memory is installed on your system. Windows then rounds that number up to the nearest 4MB, and multiplies that number by this `PageOverCommit=` value.

If there is no such line in **[386Enh]**, Windows assumes `PageOverCommit=4`.

An example: say you have 10 MB on your system, you're running in Enhanced mode, and you haven't done anything to turn off virtual memory. As Windows cranks itself up, it looks at the 10 MB, rounds it up to 12~~16~~ MB, then multiplies by 4: you'll get a virtual memory of 48 MB.

 And that's where I run into problems. Virtual memory isn't abstract: virtual addresses can't be mapped over the top of each other. What happens if the documentation is right, Windows determines it'll support 48 MB, and there's a puny 5 MB swap file, with no 48 MB to be found? What happens if Windows determines it'll support 48 MB, but there's a 50 MB permanent swap file? Alas, the docs don't say, and I don't have any way to find out. Haven't a clue.

Paging=_OffOrOn_

PagingDrive=_DriveLetter_

PagingFile=_path_

 These three settings are infernally difficult: the official documentation is wrong over and over again; it's not at all obvious how the Control Panel settings affect the **[386Enh]** entries; and it's not obvious (at least to me) how the **[386Enh]** settings are interpreted when Windows builds a temporary paging file.

The **Paging=** setting can be controlled by the 386 Enhanced applet in the Control Panel. If you bring it up, click Virtual Memory, then click Advanced, and Change, you will see something like Figure 9-10.

```
┌──────────────────────────────────────────────────────────────┐
│ [─]                    Virtual Memory                          │
│ ┌─Current Settings────────────────────────┐   ┌────────────┐  │
│ │ Drive:    C:                             │   │     OK     │  │
│ │ Size:     4,095 KB                       │   └────────────┘  │
│ │ Type:     Permanent (using BIOS)         │   ┌────────────┐  │
│ └──────────────────────────────────────────┘   │   Cancel   │  │
│                                                 └────────────┘  │
│                                                 ┌────────────┐  │
│                                                 │ Change>>   │  │
│                                                 └────────────┘  │
│                                                 ┌────────────┐  │
│ ┌─New Settings────────────────────────────┐   │   Help     │  │
│ │                                          │   └────────────┘  │
│ │ Drive:   [▤ c: [woody1]        ] [▼]     │                   │
│ │                                          │                   │
│ │ Type:    [Temporary            ] [▼]     │                   │
│ │          ┌───────────────────────┐      │                   │
│ │ Space Av │Permanent              │      │                   │
│ │          │Temporary              │      │                   │
│ │ Recomme  │None                   │      │                   │
│ │          └───────────────────────┘      │                   │
│ │ New Size:            [    79571 ] KB     │                   │
│ └──────────────────────────────────────────┘                  │
└──────────────────────────────────────────────────────────────┘
```

Figure 9-10: Better 'n No Memory At All

First, some general advice about temporary swap files in general.

 If your machine is endowed with 16MB or more of memory — or if you have 8 MB and don't often run more than one big application at a time — you should seriously think about turning paging off, i.e., setting the Control Panel's 386 Enhanced Applet Virtual Memory to "None." That's considered blasphemy in some quarters, but I don't see any particular reason to run virtual memory unless you're going to need it.

Alas, Igor, there are some applications that refuse to run if you don't have a permanent swap file. The most famous is Adobe Photo Shop. You could have 128 MB of real memory and without a sawp file, this program won't load. Makes no sense but that's the way this and some other programs are written. If such a program refuses to load, it will give you a clear message explaining why it refused and you can add a swap file but you should be aware you might try a new program and find this problem.

There's one simple rule of thumb with paging files and paging drives: you should never, ever, ever point the temporary paging file to a RAM drive! The point of paging is to get this stuff out of memory: if you swap it to a RAM drive, it stays stuck in memory, and all you do is make Windows run around chasing its own tail.

It's surprising how many people point the temporary swap file to a RAM drive. Don't you join the fray.

 Now to the mechanics of how the **Paging=**, **PagingDrive=** and **PagingFile=** settings are set and what they really do. There are lots of permutations in these three entries. The interaction is very complex, and I don't claim to understand it all, but here's what I've been able to discern.

If you choose "Temporary" from the drop-down list, Windows puts a **Paging=On** line in **[386Enh]**. If you choose "None" from the list, you'll receive a **Paging=Off**. If you choose "Permanent," the line is completely removed from **[386Enh]**.

PagingFile= isn't nearly so simple. In theory, it should point to a place Windows can stick its temporary paging file, commonly called **WIN386.SWP**. All I know for certain is that all the current documentation is demonstrably wrong: the Windows Resource Kit says that Windows defaults to a value of **\WINDOWS\WIN386.SWP**, if no name is given, but that isn't true; as a quick glance at any **SYSTEM.INI** set up for a temporary swap file will show.

If you go into the Control Panel and switch to "Temporary," and the Drive you choose is the one from which Windows was started, Windows seems to put a line like this in **[386Enh]**:

PagingFile=D:\WINDOWS\WIN386.SWP

where, in spite of what you may read, the drive letter and the path point to the location from which Windows was started. If you switch to "Temporary," but the Drive you choose is not the one used to start Windows, you'll get a line like this in **[386Enh]**:

PagingFile=E:\WIN386.SWP

pointing to the root directory of whichever drive you choose.

I couldn't, under any circumstances, get Windows to put a **PagingDrive=** line in **[386Enh]**. And no matter what I did, I always got a drive letter at the beginning of the **PagingFile=** line. All the documentation is wrong, far as I can tell.

 That's how Windows seems to establish the **[386Enh]** entries. Now let's look at the other side of the equation: how Windows interprets those settings on startup.

Apparently, if Windows sees **Paging=On**, it knows that you want a temporary swap file. The method it uses to locate that file reads like a Groucho Marx routine. First, Windows looks in **[386Enh]** for the **PagingFile=** line. If it's there, and it points to a valid subdirectory, that's the file Windows uses.

If the **PagingFile=** line isn't there, or it doesn't point anyplace Windows can understand, Windows next looks for the **PagingDrive=** line. If it encounters a valid entry, e.g.,

PagingDrive=d

Windows places the **WIN386.SWP** file in the root directory of the **PagingDrive=** drive.

Finally, if all that fails, Windows puts **WIN386.SWP** in the directory from which Windows was started (typically **c:\windows**). The official docs warn that, if there isn't enough room on the disk for the temp swap file, Windows starts without any swap file.

If you manually insert a **PagingDrive=** line in **[386Enh]**, and subsequently go into the Control Panel's 386 Enhanced Applet, you'll be greeted by the warning in Figure 9-11.

Oddly, neither the official documentation nor any of the myriad of Windows books on the market I've seen have picked up on this strange dialog box. Don't be fooled by it: the dialog box is wrong. **PagingDrive=** *does* work, in a very limited sense, as noted above.

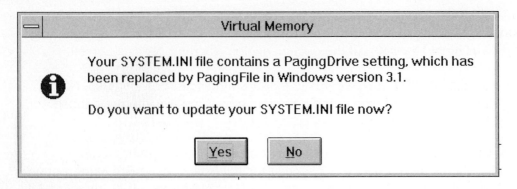

Figure 9-11: In Pax Vobiscum

 I tried hundreds of different combinations to see if Windows could be tricked into using a permanent swap file instead of a temporary, or vice-versa. As best I can tell (and you'll have to test this on your own setup, should these bugs start biting you), Windows interprets a `Paging=Off` as saying there is no temporary or permanent paging file. (In fact, setting `Paging=Off` completely disables the Virtual Memory Manager in `WIN386.EXE`.) Windows interprets a `Paging=On` or the presence of a valid `PagingFile=` setting as saying there is a temporary (not permanent) paging file. And in all other cases it appears to try to build a permanent swap file.

Again as best I can tell, Windows does not always clean up its swap file, especially if you're changing from temporary to permanent, and don't reboot immediately when you're supposed to: old temp swap files can clutter up your disk until you remove them manually. From time to time you should probably fall back into DOS and scan your disks for old `WIN386.SWP` files (i.e., ones pre-dating the start of the current Windows session; if you re-start Windows every day, look for `WIN386.SWP` files dated yesterday or earlier), and delete them.

`PerformBackfill=`*OffOrOn*

 "Backfilling" memory is a method of taking extended memory and treating it as if it were conventional memory, i.e., as if it were down below 640K. If you are running Windows with 512K conventional memory and 1MB of extended memory, you should first consider seeing an analyst, and then figure out whether you want Windows to take 128K of that extended memory, and "backfill" it, so Windows thinks you have a full 640K of conventional memory. Running Windows without a full complement of 640K conventional memory is like running an XJ-12 with the plug wires pulled on 11 cylinders.

If you want Windows to backfill (you do, you do!), or don't know extended from expanded and couldn't care less, you needn't do a thing: Windows backfills automatically. If you get a techie on the phone who says you're crashing Windows because it's backfilling memory incorrectly, you may have to add

PerformBackfill=No

to the **[386Enh]** section.

PermSwapDOSDrive=*DriveLetter*

PermSwapSizeK=*KB*

Here are two more **[386Enh]** settings with confounding behavior. The only thing I know for sure is that all existing documentation, at least all the documentation I've seen, official, unofficial or otherwise, is wrong, wrong, wrong.

The Windows Resource Kit would have you believe that **PermSwapDOSDrive=** points to the drive containing a permanent swap file (it's the file called **386SPART.PAR**, marked hidden, located in the root directory), and that **PermSwapSizeK=** is its size. That's simply not the truth; try changing the settings yourself with a text editor, restart Windows, and you'll see it in a second.

I spent hours trying to figure out exactly what the hell is going on. This is the best I could piece together.

When Windows creates a permanent swap file, or when you use the 386 Enhanced applet in Control Panel to switch over to a permanent swap file, Windows also creates a tiny file called **SPART.PAR**, and puts it in the Windows directory. That file, **SPART.PAR**, not these two settings in **SYSTEM.INI**, tells Windows on startup how big the permanent swap file should be, and where to put it.

If you switch to a permanent swap file via the Control Panel, Windows updates both **SYSTEM.INI** and **SPART.PAR** with the new location and size. But if you go in and monkey around with the **SYSTEM.INI** settings manually, Windows ignores your changes entirely, with one exception.

If there is no **SPART.PAR** on startup (e.g., if it was deleted while you were out working in DOS), Windows re-creates the file using these two settings. That's the only situation I've found where the **PermSwapDOSDrive=** and **PermSwapSizeK=** settings do anything at all.

 I also believe that, if you go into the 386 Enhanced applet in the Control Panel and the applet discovers that settings in **SPART.PAR** conflict with the **PermSwapDOSDrive=** and **PermSwapSizeK=** entries, you'll get a dialog box like the following. (There may be other circumstances under which you get this dialog box (see Figure 9-12); but mixed **SPART.PAR** and **SYSTEM.INI** settings seems to guarantee it.)

Figure 9-12: Got 'em Crossed

So if you want to know the real story behind your permanent swap file, forget about the **[386Enh]** settings. Grab a hex editor and look at **SPART.PAR** in your Windows directory.

 If you want to change the location or size of your permanent swap file, make sure you do it via the Control Panel's 386 Enhanced applet. Manual changes don't make it. (With one exception: you can tell Windows to forget about using a permanent swap file by removing both of these lines from **[386Enh]** and deleting **SPART.PAR** from the Windows subdirectory. If you do that, you should delete the permanent swap file, too.)

If you change the location of the permanent swap file, make sure you use your fastest hard drive: the swap file is one of the very few files that benefit greatly from faster disk access.

Finally, as I noted in the temporary swap file settings, if your machine has 16MB or more of memory, or if you have 8 MB and don't often run more than one application at a time, consider turning paging off by setting the Control Panel's 386 Enhanced Applet Virtual Memory to "None." Why run virtual memory if you don't need it?

PerVMFiles=*NumberOfHandles*

Have you ever played with the **FILES=** line in **CONFIG.SYS**? If so, this setting should seem mighty familiar.

Whenever DOS starts, inside Windows or outside, doesn't matter, it sets aside a fixed amount of memory to keep track of all open files. (Technoids call 'em "file handles." 10-4 Good Buddy.) Since you're running Windows, you probably learned long ago to set **FILES=30** or more in your **CONFIG.SYS**.

If you're running DOS SHARE, the **PerVMFiles=** setting doesn't matter; all file handles are managed in one big pool. But if you don't run SHARE (and you aren't alone!), each new DOS window, as it's started, has to set aside enough room for file handles. This setting tells Windows how many file handles to set up for each new DOS window.

If the line is missing in **[386Enh]**, Windows assumes **PerVMFiles=10**, and each new DOS window gets 10 new handles. If you have a DOS program that opens a lot of files, that may not be adequate: the program will probably start whining about insufficient file handles, or tell you to bump up **FILES=** in **CONFIG.SYS**, or it may just crash and burn unexpectedly when it tries to open or create a new file. If you encounter any of those symptoms, you should increase **PerVMFiles=** until the DOS program works right.

Nope, you can't specify a different number for each DOS window. You only get one value, and it applies to each and every DOS window.

DOS has this nifty limitation: it can. . . uh. . . handle at most 255 file handles. So if you multiply the number of open DOS windows by this **PerVMFiles=** number, and add to that the number in the **FILES=** statement in **CONFIG.SYS**, you better stay under 255. If you try to open up too many DOS windows, and blow the 255 limit, Windows simply doesn't allocate any more room for file handles, and your DOS programs may bomb out.

PSPIncrement=*NumberOf16ByteBlocks*

See **UniqueDosPSP=** in **[386Enh]**.

ReflectDosInt2A=*OffOrOn*

Some network software uses a DOS interrupt called INT 2Ah. Normally Windows absorbs all INT 2Ah calls; your programs will never see them. But if you set **ReflectDosInt2A=On**, Windows will pass those interrupts on. Setting it On is said to reduce performance.

ReservedHighArea=*StartAddress-EndAddres*

UseableHighArea=*StartAddress-EndAddress*

Far as I can tell, these settings behave precisely the same way as **EMMExclude=** and **EMMInclude=**, except they give you greater control over the start and ending addresses. While **EMMExclude=** and **EMMInclude=** round to the nearest multiple of 16K, these settings only round to the nearest 4K. I can't find any other documented differences.

ReservePageFrame=*OffOrOn*

When Windows starts, it looks for an unused chunk of upper memory (between 640K and 1 MB) to hold DOS data transfer buffers — a spot to transfer data between Windows and DOS.

If Windows can't find a large enough block in upper memory, it looks to this setting to see what it should do. If **ReservePageFrame=On**, or the line is missing, Windows puts the DOS transfer buffers down in lower memory (below 640K).

If you turn **ReservePageFrame=Off**, Windows will clobber the EMS page frame area, the chunk of 64K in upper memory used to implement old-fashioned expanded/EMS memory access, and stick the DOS transfer buffers in there.

If you're absolutely sure none of your DOS programs running under Windows will ever use EMS memory, and you're worried about Windows swallowing up conventional memory for its DOS transfer buffers, you can try setting **ReservePageFrame=Off**.

Also see **EMMPageFrame=** in **[386Enh]**.

ReserveVideoROM=*OffOrOn*

According to the official docs, setting **ReserveVideoROM=On** tells Windows that pages C6 and C7 contain video ROM; thus Windows should avoid that area.

This entry seems to duplicate many others. I have no idea, for example, why you would use this setting instead of **EMMExclue=C600-C7FF**.

Windows is usually smart enough to avoid places it doesn't belong. If you find that your video is flaky on startup, though, you might try setting **ReserveVideoROM=On** and see if it makes any difference.

ROMScanThreshhold=*NumberOfChanges*

When Windows starts up, it scans the area between 640K and 1 MB looking for unused blocks of memory. Some of that memory is mapped as read-only (ROM); Windows can't use ROM, of course. Most video adapters and other cards that use that upper memory are nice enough to identify themselves — with something called a ROM header. Unfortunately, not all cards are so polite.

According to the *Windows Resource Kit* docs, the `ROMScanThreshhold=` setting tells Windows "how many transitions (value changes)" memory has to go through before it's identified as ROM... "If the number of transitions is greater than the value for this entry, Windows recognizes the memory as ROM."

Apparently this all has to do with blocks of phony memory that may be confused as ROM. Normally, these pieces of memory have the same value repeated over and over — say FF FF FF or 00 00 00. The transitions referenced here are the byte-by-byte changes from one value to another that Windows encounters as it marches up this part of memory. Unfortunately, the docs don't say how large an address area is involved, so this setting is pretty puzzling.

The only useful tidbit I could find was a suggestion that, if you want Windows to avoid glomming onto any of this memory (and it isn't clear what memory; the docs say it's "usually between C000-EFFF"!), you should set **ROMScanThreshhold=0**.

There's not a hint of reasoning that I could find anywhere that might explain why you would use this setting and not **EMMExclude=**.

ScrollFrequency=*NumberOfLines*

 DOS screens scroll. *Profound, eh?* When a DOS program decides to write a new line at the bottom of the screen, the old stuff on the top line scrolls off, making way for the new stuff at the bottom.

DOS programs running under Windows are managed a little differently. Windows tries to reduce the number of screen updates, to speed things up a bit. One way you can reduce the number of screen updates is to delay scrolling of DOS screens: instead of scrolling one line, say, Windows can save up the new lines and only scroll when two lines, or three or four, have changed.

This setting is supposed to tell Windows how many new lines have to come out of a DOS program before it scrolls the screen. If there is no such line in **[386Enh]**, Windows assumes **ScrollFrequency=2**, i.e., Windows only scrolls the screen when it has two lines of new data waiting.

There's some degree of futzing involved in all of this: demonstrably, Windows will scroll down one line at a time, you can see it yourself if you run a DOS program in a window; the lines appear one at a time, just like they should, regardless of this setting.

Still, if you have a program that really scrolls through a lot of lines; a communication program, perhaps, or a file listing program that races through the lines like mad, changing this setting to **ScrollFrequency=6** or more will make the screen update jerky. It appears as though Windows saves some time by scrolling less frequently. Whether that scrolling boost translates into appreciably reduced time on-line, say, is questionable.

Also see **WindowUpdateTime=** in **[386Enh]**.

SGrabLPT=*PortNumber*

This setting redirects printer interrupts from the DOS session to the Windows screen: **SGrabLPT=1**, for example, tells Windows to redirect all DOS programs' LPT1 printer interrupts to the Windows screen. It's mostly useful, I'm told, for debugging.

SyncTime=*OffOrOn*

TrapTimerPorts=*OffOrOn*

Windows marches to the beat of a diffident drummer.

— Pensées Pinecliffius

As with so many Einsteinian *gedanken* experiments, there are two different clocks floating around. The first clock is your computer's hardware clock, the so-called CMOS clock: it's supposed to keep track of the time of day. The second clock is Windows' own internal clock: it keeps track of the elapsed time since Windows was started. If you're steeped in the lore of relativity, you know how difficult it can be to synchronize clocks. Well, Windows has the same problem, albeit on a somewhat less profound scale.

Some programs, games and comm programs are offered as examples, can change the timer interrupt interval (the time between "ticks" of the clock) and thus speed up or slow down the computer's CMOS clock. Thus, at any given moment, the

Windows clock may be out of synch with the computer's CMOS clock: Windows marches to the beat of a different drummer.

These two settings give you several different ways to handle the problem.

If **SyncTime=On** and **TrapTimerPorts=On,** which is the default situation, the one that applies if you do nothing, if these lines are missing from **[386Enh]**, Windows checks periodically and synchronizes its clock with the computer's CMOS clock. Windows also intercepts reads and writes to the computer's CMOS clock, keeping it informed of any changes in the timer interrupt interval.

If **SyncTime=On** and **TrapTimerPorts=Off**, Windows still synchronizes watches with the computer's CMOS clock, but it doesn't bother intercepting reads and writes to the CMOS clock. That has two effects: the Windows clock can get way out of whack with the CMOS clock (although it's frequently brought back into synch); and programs that read from or write to the computer's CMOS clock, unencumbered by the Windows interrupt trapping, can run faster.

If **SyncTime=Off** and **TrapTimerPorts=On**, Windows tries to keep its clock in synch with the CMOS clock by looking at changes in the timer interrupt interval, but it does not explicitly synchronize the Windows clock with the CMOS clock. If you're critically dependent on accurate elapsed time readings from Windows, this is the combination to use: the clocks may drift out of synch slowly, but since there's never a time-check, there will be no abrupt changes in the Windows clock.

Finally, if **SyncTime=Off** and **TrapTimerPorts=Off**, you can kiss the Windows clock good-bye. It will neither synch nor monitor changes to the timer interrupt interval.

SetROMBreakpoint=*OffOrOn*

When Windows starts it looks at the area immediately before the 1 MB line to see if there is a special error-reporting breakpoint set there. If you're using a third party memory manager (e.g., QEMM or 386^MAX), the area just before 1 MB may have been moved somewhere else — it may be remapped — and Windows can go nuts sifting through the garbage.

If you are using a memory manager that can move around the memory just before 1 MB, set **SystemROMBreakpoint=Off**.

Also see **MaxBPs=** in **[386Enh]**.

SysVMEMSLimit=_KB_

SysVMEMSRequired=_KB_

Every man has his own _mishegoss._

— Leo Rosten, _The Joys of Yinglish_, 1990

 According to the official docs, the **SysVMEMSLimit=** setting tells Windows how much expanded (EMS) memory it is permitted to use. I'm not sure what that's supposed to mean, or what this setting really does, but I can tell you for an absolute fact that the docs got this one wrong. Repeatedly. Try a little experiment and you'll see for yourself.

Create a little do-nothing **.BAT** file, say **TEMP.BAT**, that consists of the single DOS command **Pause**. Then use the PIF editor to create a **TEMP.PIF** that Requires a minimum of 1024 KB of expanded memory. Now try running that little **.BAT** file a few times, leaving the program hanging each time, so the expanded memory is allocated and not released. On my system, the fourth time I try to run **TEMP.BAT**, Windows pops up and says it can't run the program because there isn't enough expanded/EMS memory. Fair enough.

The docs say that, if this line is missing in **[386Enh]**, Windows assumes a value of **SysVMEMSLimit=2048**. Okay. So try setting **SysVMEMSLimit=4096**, restart Windows, and try the little **TEMP.BAT** experiment. See that? As far as I can tell anyway, **SysVMEMSLimit=4096** behaves the same way as no **SysVMEMSLimit=** at all. It does not seem to limit the total amount of EMS memory Windows can use.

Alright. Maybe **SysVMEMSLimit=** limits the amount of old-fashioned EMS memory any single DOS program can get. (That isn't what the docs say, but it seems to be a reasonable guess, especially because a value of 0 is supposed to seal off EMS, and a value of -1 is supposed to open up all EMS.) So try setting **SysVMEMSLimit=512**, restart Windows, and try the **TEMP.BAT** test. See how **TEMP.BAT** runs, even though it requires 1024 KB of EMS? I couldn't tell any difference between **SysVMEMSLimit=512**, 2048 or 4096: they all seem to work the same.

In spite of what all the official and unofficial documentation says, I don't think `SysVMEMSLimit=` *does anything at all.*

So I turned my attention to the description of the **SysVMEMSRequired=** setting, the next one in line. Guess what? It doesn't make any sense! The docs say that when Windows starts it's supposed to look at the **SysVMEMSRequired=** value and refuse to start if there isn't at least that many KB of old-fashioned expanded/EMS memory available. More than that, the official docs say this defaults to zero, and to leave it there if no DOS programs are going to require EMS memory. (That's *meshugge.* The default doesn't allow for any EMS memory for DOS programs?)

So I set **SysVMEMSRequired=262144,** telling Windows that it shouldn't start unless there's 256 *mega*bytes of EMS memory available. Guess what? Windows didn't care; it started anyway.

I have no idea if either setting does anything. My guess is they don't.

SysVMEMSLocked=*OffOrOn*

See **AllEMSLocked=** in **[386Enh]**.

SysVMV86Locked=*OffOrOn*

As best I can tell, setting **SysVMV86Locked=On** causes all Windows programs' (as opposed to DOS programs') virtual memory to be "locked," i.e., prevented from being swapped out to disk — which, of course, means that it isn't virtual memory at all.

SysVMXMSLimit=*KB*

SysVMXMSRequired=*KB*

These settings appeared to be just as screwed up (or, more accurately, useless) as **SysVMEMSLimit=** and **SysVMEMSRequired=**, which see.

TimerCriticalSection=*milliseconds*

Some DOS programs rely on timer interrupts to do their thing: they hook into "ticks" of the clock, and use the "ticks" to wake themselves up. Some of those DOS programs get cranky if they are interrupted while processing a clock "tick." This setting is used to put those cranky DOS programs at ease: it tells Windows to wait a little while after each "tick," to let the DOS program do its thing.

If this line is missing or **TimerCriticalSection=0**, Windows doesn't wait after a clock "tick": it keeps doing what it normally does, possibly taking control away from a DOS program immediately after a "tick." If you set **TimerCriticalSection=10**, for example, Windows will always wait 10 milliseconds after a "tick" before horning in on the DOS program.

If you have a network program or DOS TSR that's behaving oddly, your problem may be solved by setting **TimerCriticalSection=10** or 20 or more. By all means, give it a try. Just realize that any value other than 0 will eat into processing time.

TokenRingSearch=*OffOrOn*

According to the documentation, when Windows starts on an ISA machine, it looks in the section of memory between 640K and 1 MB for a Token Ring Adapter, a particular type of network card. Sometimes Windows gets fooled by other kinds of cards: it thinks you have a Token Ring Adapter when in fact you don't.

If Windows can't find one of your add-in cards, and you know for sure that you do not own a Token Ring Adapter (you probably don't!), set **TokenRingSearch=Off**.

TranslateScans=*OffOrOn*

 The Windows Resource Kit says that this setting only applies to non-standard keyboards, and only affects the "Switcher Screen and full-screen message boxes." Alas, the only full-screen message boxes I know about are the one that controls **Ctrl+Alt+Del** restarting, the **Alt+Tab** box you get when you're running DOS windows full-screen, and a few really nasty messages that say, in effect, that Windows blew up, push Enter to continue.

If you own a really bizarre keyboard and Windows doesn't recognize your responses to those message boxes, I guess you could try setting

TranslateScans=On. Better, go out and get a good keyboard. They're cheap. Other than that, I have no idea what this setting does.

TrapTimerPorts=*OffOrOn*

See **SyncTime=** in **[386Enh]**.

UniqueDosPSP=*OffOrOn*

PSPIncrement=*NumberOf16ByteBlocks*

 Some networks identify different applications by their location in memory — often called a load address or a Program Starting Point (the "PSP" in these settings). Back in the not-so-good-old days, every DOS program would load at a different location, and the PSP was a good unique identifier. Not so with Windows and virtual memory: far as Windows is concerned *all* DOS programs could "start" at the same address.

Windows has to trick these networks (they're listed in the file **NETWORKS.WRI** in your Windows directory), by assigning different PSPs every time Windows starts up a new DOS window.

The method for pulling off this sleight of hand is pretty simple: the first DOS window starts at some address, call it x. When Windows starts its second DOS window, it sticks 32 bytes of zeros at address x, then loads the second program at location x + 32. The next DOS window gets 64 bytes of zeros, and the DOS program starts at x + 64. The fourth DOS program starts at x + 96. Each DOS program gets a unique starting point, and the network is happy.

If this line is missing, or **UniqueDosPSP=No**, Windows doesn't bother trying this sleight of hand. If you manually put the line **UniqueDosPSP=On** in **[386Enh]**, Windows shuffles each DOS program to get unique start points.

The **PSPIncrement=** setting tells Windows how many 16-byte blocks to jump when starting each subsequent DOS window. If the line is missing, Windows assumes **PSPIncrement=2**, which gives rise to the 32-byte jump described earlier. Since 32 bytes is as good as any — any number other than zero will give you unique PSPs — I don't know of any reason to change this setting.

UseableHighArea=*StartAddress-*
EndAddress

See **ReservedHighArea=** in **[386Enh].**

UseInstFile=*OffOrOn*

This is a setting used by Windows 3.0 to ensure Windows 2.x backward compatibility. It has no effect on Windows 3.1. The official docs are wrong.

UseROMFont=*OffOrOn*

Your video card has a font stored away in ROM; it's the font you'll see when you reboot your machine, or run DOS programs outside Windows.

If this line is missing, or **UseROMFont=On**, Windows uses that font for any full-screen DOS windows.

If you're getting a lot of garbage on the screen when running DOS windows full-screen, try putting **UseROMFont=Off** in **[386Enh]** and see if that helps.

VGAMonoText=*OffOrOn*

VGA adapter cards commonly use the memory area B000-B7FF for monochrome text, and Windows usually skips that region of memory when it's looking for places to stick stuff.

If you know for an absolute fact that your adapter card does not use B000-B7FF, or that you will never, ever, ever, flip into a video mode that requires that chunk of memory, you could try setting **VGAMonoText=Off**, to give that memory over to Windows.

VideoBackgroundMsg=*OffOrOn*

When a DOS program running under Windows gets suspended or can't update the display because of insufficient video memory, Windows flashes a message on your screen warning you about the problem.

This is an ostrich setting. By using **VideoBackgroundMsg=Off**, you'll prevent Windows from showing you that message — so things will go to hell in a handbasket, and you'll never know why.

VirtualHDIRQ=*OffOrOn*

In my experience, of all the **SYSTEM.INI [386Enh]** settings, this is the one you're most likely to encounter. While the latest versions of most types of hardware and software have (finally) made their peace with this setting, earlier versions of PC-Kwik, some Broderbund games, memory cards, and ESDI hard drives, to mention just a few, ran afoul of **VirtualHDIRQ=**.

Your hard disk controller uses an IRQ line (IRQ14) to tell your computer when data is ready to be transferred. When Windows runs in Enhanced mode, it tries to take control of that line, bypassing the BIOS routines that normally handle interrupts on IRQ14. If Windows can get away with bypassing the usual BIOS routines, your system will run faster. Unfortunately, some programs and some hardware go berserk if IRQ14 interrupts aren't handled through the usual BIOS routines.

If you are using an ISA machine and this line is missing, or **VirtualHDIRQ=On**, Windows takes over the hard disk IRQ line. If you are using an EISA or MCA machine, or if **VirtualHDIRQ=Off**, Windows backs off and lets the BIOS interrupt handler take care of hard disk interrupts.

More often than not, you'll find yourself futzing with this setting when a techie on the phone tells you it's necessary to make your program or hardware work. In such a situation, you should swear loudly at the techie: the product's setup program should've made the changes for you, and you're going to sacrifice Windows performance to accommodate that product.

You might also try setting **VirtualHDIRQ=Off** if you can't get Windows to recognize your hard disk. You'll know Windows is having trouble recognizing your hard drive when you've just changed disks (e.g., switched over to a SCSI disk), and Windows locks up immediately when you try to start it.

WindowKBRequired=*KB*

This is the kind of setting that drives me nuts. I'm mad as hell and I'm not going to take it any more. There. I got that off my chest. Let's go on. . .

The official documentation and every book and magazine article I could find says that this is the minimum amount of conventional memory required for Windows to start. That is, before Windows loads itself, it's supposed to look at this setting and sees if there is at least **WindowKBRequired=** KB of memory below the 640K mark available. If there isn't enough memory, Windows isn't supposed to start. (And if the line is missing, Windows assumes **WindowKBRequired=256**, i.e., you must have at least 256K of conventional memory free for Windows to load itself.)

Guess what? It's crap. At least on my machine. Windows always loaded itself, and started running in Enhanced mode, no matter what value I used for **WindowKBRequired=**, no matter how much conventional memory was available. I even tried adding an "s" to the setting, **WindowsKBRequired=1024**, on the off chance that the entry was mis-spelled in the official docs. No luck. Windows started right up.

I don't think this line does anything.

WindowMemSize=*KB*

According to the official documentation, this setting tells Windows how much conventional memory it can use when running in Enhanced mode. If the line is missing from **[386Enh]** or **WindowMemSize=-1**, Windows grabs all the memory it can find below 640K. If you manually set it to a different value, e.g., **WindowMemSize=500**, Windows only takes the indicated amount of conventional memory (i.e., in the first 640K) when it starts; in this case, 500KB.

I couldn't get this setting to do anything worthwhile.

WindowUpdateTime=*Milliseconds*

This entry controls how often Windows updates the screen for DOS programs running under Windows. If the line is missing, or **WindowUpdateTime=50**, Windows updates DOS screens at 50 millisecond intervals; a minimum of 50 milliseconds will pass between each screen update.

Setting this entry higher decreases the frequency of screen updates, and that may speed up your DOS programs — particularly ones that scroll data so fast your eyes go whup-whup-whup like a runaway window shade trying to keep up. Setting this entry lower increases the frequency of DOS screen updates, so graphics will scroll more smoothly, but your programs probably won't run as fast.

Also see **ScrollFrequency=** in **[386Enh]**.

WinExclusive=*OffOrOn*

This setting corresponds to the "Exclusive in Foreground" check box in the Control Panel's 386 Enhanced applet (see Figure 9-13).

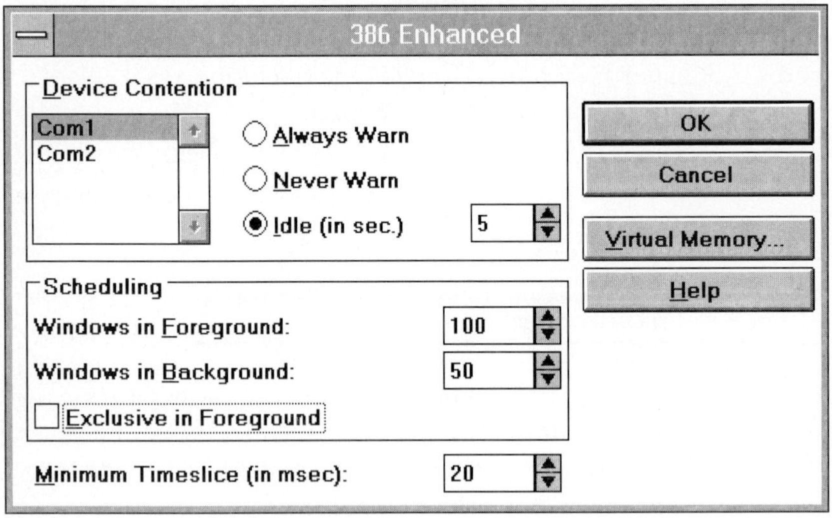

Figure 9-13: Very Exclusive

If this line is missing in **[386Enh]**, or **WinExclusive=Off** (which corresponds to the "Exclusive in Foreground" box not being checked), Windows allocates time normally, allowing all Windows programs and DOS programs running under Windows their due time (see **WinTimeSlice=** next).

If **WinExclusive=On**, Windows cheats the DOS programs: no DOS program is allowed to run while any Windows program is active. In effect, this value gives Windows programs complete priority over all DOS programs.

You might want to think about turning this setting On if you have unimportant
monster DOS programs that run in the background and make your Windows
programs run like Redmond slugs. With the setting On, Windows will get all the
time slices until you switch over to any DOS program, at which point the normal
time-slicing kicks in.

Speaking of normal time-slicing. . .

WinTimeSlice=_Foreground, Background_

Windows in Enhanced mode can run several programs — both DOS programs
and Windows programs — simultaneously. Well, they don't _really_ run
simultaneously: you knew that. Windows juggles things around so each
program gets a little slice of time before passing control of the computer over
to the next program. Since the time slices are mighty small, the net effect, far as you're
concerned, is that the programs are all running at the same time.

This **WinTimeSlice=** setting, along with the DOS time slice priority numbers in
DOS programs' **.PIF** files, control how much time Windows allots to each running
program.

Let's start with a basic premise. Windows calculates and re-calculates and
re-re-calculates these priority numbers all the time. Lots of things — say, a
disk access, or an interrupt — can cause Windows to cut a program's time
slice short. So no matter what you do, no matter how finely you craft these
priority numbers, you're never going to have complete control over the relative
priorities of various programs, and Windows is never going to apportion time
precisely as you specify. You're doomed to failure from the get-go.

Each running program has a priority number. The numbers mean nothing in and of
themselves: only the ratios count. For example, if two programs are running, one
with a priority of 2 and the other with a priority of 1, the former program should
get twice as much computer time as the latter; contrariwise, if the first program has
a priority of 5000 and the second a priority of 2500, the first program will, again,
get twice as much computer time as the latter. Values _machs nichts_. Ratios rule.

Say there are three programs running, each with a priority of 50. You would expect
each of the three programs to get the same amount of time, right? They each have
the same number of priority "points," for lack of a better term. Easy.

Now say there are three programs running, the first with a priority number of 100, the second with a priority number of 50, and the third with a priority number of 50. You would expect the first program to get half the computer time, since the first program has half of all the priority points — because 100/(100+50+50) is ½ — wouldn't you? And you would expect the other two programs would get a quarter apiece, because they each have a quarter of the priority points, i.e., 50/(100+50+50) is ¼, right? Think about it for a second. It's the only thing that makes sense.

Well, I'm happy to say, that's exactly how it works with Windows.

 You're saying
Windows makes
sense?

 Nawww. . . I wouldn't
go *that* far.

The actual method used by Windows is only a shade more complicated. There are two tricks.

First, all Windows programs are tossed into the same bucket. Time slices are allotted among (1) each DOS program running under Windows, and (2) *all* Windows programs taken together. (Windows has a second time slicer — one you can't get at — to allocate slices among Windows applications. See Chapter 3 for details.) If you have seven Windows programs running and two DOS programs running at the same time, say, Windows only divvies out time slices three ways: the first DOS program, the second DOS program, and *all* Windows programs taken together.

Windows gives a time slice to the first DOS program, then it gives a time slice to the second DOS program, and then it gives time to itself; and all the Windows programs together get to fight for time, within that Windows time slice. Then it's back to the first DOS program, the second DOS program, *all* the Windows programs, and so on.

The second complication lies in the fact that each program has two priority numbers, not one.

At any given moment, exactly one program is running in the foreground: it's the active program, the program that has focus, the one that will receive keystrokes if you type at the keyboard. Every other program running is said to be in the *background*. Windows maintains separate foreground priority numbers and background priority numbers. (It's a little more complicated than that, because each DOS program may be marked to run exclusively, or to not run at all in the background; see Chapter 3 for details.)

So when Windows decides it's time to re-calculate the relative priorities of the DOS windows and the Windows window, it first determines who is running in the foreground. Windows uses the foreground priority number for that application; all other applications get their background priority number tossed into the calculation hopper.

If you don't change the priority numbers in your .PIFs, your DOS programs will pick up the numbers from **_DEFAULT.PIF**, and those numbers are 100 in foreground, 50 in background (see Figure 9-14).

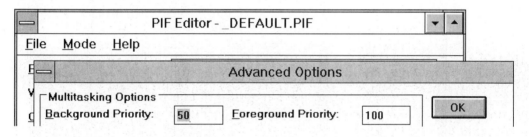

Figure 9-14: The _Default PIF

If the **WinTimeSlice=** line is missing in **[386Enh]**, Windows assumes that **WinTimeSlice=100,50**, i.e., all the Windows programs have a foreground priority of 100 and a background priority of 50.

An example: say you have seven Windows programs running and two DOS programs running. You haven't monkeyed around with either the DOS programs' **.PIF** or the **WinTimeSlice=** entry, so everybody is set at 100 foreground, 50 background. One of the DOS programs is on top: it's running foreground, it has focus, it's the active window, whatever terminology you prefer.

The next time Windows recalculates priorities, it will look at the DOS program running in the foreground and give it a priority number of 100. It'll look at the second DOS program and give it a 50, the background priority number. Finally, it'll look at the Windows background priority setting and assign it a 50. Thus, the first DOS program will get about half of all available time — 100/(100+50+50) = ½. The second DOS programs will get about a quarter of all available time because

50/(100+50+50) = ¼. And all the Windows programs together will get about a quarter of all available time since, as before, 50/(100+50+50) = ¼.

Priority numbers, whether in the DOS **.PIF** or in this **WinTimeSlice=** setting, can run from 1 to 10000.

So much for how it works. Now, why would you change the foreground and background priorities? Good question.

If you rarely run DOS programs, there's no reason to change any of the settings. With no DOS programs running under Windows, the priorities don't mean diddly: Windows gets all the time slices, and that's that.

If you run a DOS communication program from time to time, or any other DOS program that needs pretty high priority, you might consider jacking up the foreground and background priorities of the program, in its **.PIF** file. Personally, when I run DOS comm programs under Windows I don't want anything else to interfere, so I've checked the "Exclusive" box in the comm programs' **.PIF**. With the comm program running exclusive, these priorities don't mean anything, so I don't bother changing them.

If you often run a DOS program or two in the background, leave them sitting there, so they're easy to switch to, and spend most of your time with Windows in the foreground, you should consider raising the foreground **WinTimeSlice=** number. By boosting the number to, oh, **WinTimeSlice=1000,50**, you'll minimize the amount of time Windows spends swapping out to the nascent DOS programs.

Er. . . uh. . . Why not just turn background processing off for those programs, via their PIF files? Look at Chapter 3 for details.

If you commonly ping-pong back and forth between a couple of DOS programs, consider reducing Windows' background priority: a **WinTimeSlice=100,10** may give your DOS programs a little more zing by reducing the amount of time allocated to Windows while it's in the background.

Go ahead and play with the numbers a bit. I bet you'll be impressed by how *little* they effect your day-to-day work, how in most circumstances you can barely tell the difference from one set of values to the next.

---

woafont=*FonFileName*

See **CGA40WOA.FON=** in **[386Enh]**.

XlatBufferSize=*KB*

Normally Windows can only write data to disk and read data from disk if it works through conventional memory, i.e., that part of memory below 640K: the data has to be stuck down there in the lower 640 before it's written, or it will be stuck down there when read. That's a limitation of the ancient PC architecture.

It's an old-fashioned time vs. space tradeoff. The lower 640 can get crowded, so Windows doesn't want to take up too much space for disk reads and writes. Conversely, the more space you can carve out for the disk I/O demons, the faster that I/O will run.

Values are rounded up to the nearest multiple of four. If this line is missing, or **XlatBufferSize=8**, Windows sets aside 8 KB of conventional memory for these "translate buffers."

If disk throughput is important for you, and you have room between 640K and 1 MB, consider setting **XlatBufferSize=16** or more. It may speed up disk access.

The official docs warn that, if you use a network that operates with "named pipes" (a fancy way of letting programs talk to each other), you may have to adjust this setting so **XlatBufferSize=4**.

XMSUMBInitCalls=*OffOrOn*

If this line is missing or **XMSUMBInitCalls=On**, Windows uses your extended memory manager's upper memory block (i.e., 640K to 1 MB) handling routines. If you've installed a third party extended memory manager, the installation may have turned **XMSUMBInitCalls=Off**.

[boot]

 This is it, Windows' *sanctum sanctorum*, the place where you specify the most basic of all of Windows' settings. Treat it carefully and with great respect: else, Windows may die. Horribly. Unexpectedly. Whenever possible, use the Windows Setup applet (probably in your MAIN) group to make changes — at least that will keep you from making simple mistakes. And one mis-typed file name is a simple, deadly mistake.

The [boot] section is a masterpiece of Microsoft ingenuity. Truly. It's the place where utility programs — everything from Norton Desktop to TurboCom — can hook into Windows, replacing standard components of Windows with ones that *you* choose. Think of it as Dr. Frankenstein's Lab, where you can pull a head from one corpse, a heart from another, patch the whole together with baling wire and chewing gum, shoot it with a zillion watts, and watch the monster emerge. It may not be pretty, but it's *your* monster.

Most of the settings in this section are established at setup, and vary depending on what kind of monitor, keyboard, mouse, etc., you have installed. A very rudimentary setup on a VGA system yielded these settings:

```
[boot]
shell=progman.exe
mouse.drv=mouse.drv
network.drv=
language.dll=
sound.drv=mmsound.drv
comm.drv=comm.drv
keyboard.drv=keyboard.drv
system.drv=system.drv
386grabber=vga.3gr
oemfonts.fon=vgaoem.fon
286grabber=vgacolor.2gr
fixedfon.fon=vgafix.fon
fonts.fon=vgasys.fon
display.drv=vga.drv
drivers=mmsystem.dll
```

I'm going to step through those slowly, in alphabetical order. Walk this way.... no, this way. . .

```
286grabber=DriverName

386grabber=DriverName
```

 What's a grabber? Good question. I had to call Brother Mike, my revered teacher, and confer. Brother Mike knows more about running DOS under Windows than any organism alive. He's now a Trappist Monk, which may explain why he only answers direct phone calls from major deities and old friends. Old codger friends, that is.

When a DOS program runs under Windows, it writes to the screen the same way it always did, with one little twist. Windows tricks DOS into thinking that it's writing to the screen area, the "display space," when in fact DOS is writing to a chunk of regular old memory.

The duty of the grabber is to take whatever DOS sticks in this ersatz screen area and do whatever is necessary to paste it up in the correct Windows window. That's called rendering.

When DOS puts a new character in the screen area, Windows taps the grabber on the shoulder and says, "OK. You know what the DOS screen is supposed to look like. You know what kind of window you have to work with. Now suck up the DOS screen and regurgitate it in the Windows window, so the user can see it."

The grabber also works with the Windows clipboard: it shuffles stuff in and out of the clipboard; makes the "Mark for copying" work in the DOS box; and it handles the PrtScr copy-to-clipboard function.

Windows uses two different grabbers, and picks between them when you start Windows, using one or the other depending on whether you're running in Standard mode (without a resizable DOS window, thus comparatively simple) or in Enhanced mode (where the DOS windows can flip-flop all over the place, fonts can change around, and so on). In a brilliant bit of naming obfuscation, Windows calls the former kind of grabber — the one for Standard mode — a 286grabber; and it calls the latter kind of grabber, for Enhanced mode, a 386grabber. Don't be confused by the names.

Both the Standard mode grabber and the Enhanced mode grabber are Windows Dynamic Link Libraries, plain ol' DLLs. In yet another bit of naming nonsense,

Windows refuses to use the normal **.DLL** file name extension for these DLLs, opting for the illuminating suffixes **.2gr** and **.3gr**. The result is a bit of gobbledygook that looks like this:

```
286grabber=vgacolor.2gr
386grabber=vga.3gr
```

Windows ships with seven Standard mode grabbers: **CGA.2GR** for CGA; **EGACOLOR.2GR** and **EGAMONO.2GR** for EGA; **HERCULES.2GR** for the old mono Hercules card; something called **OLIGRAB.2GR** for the old AT&T card; and **VGACOLOR.2GR** and **VGAMON.2GR** for VGA.

Windows also ships with seven Enhanced mode grabbers: **EGA.3GR** for EGA; **HERC.3GR** for the old Hercules cards; **PLASMA.3GR** primarily for Compaq portables; **V7VGA.3GR** for the original Video 7 VGA; **VGA.3GR** for VGA; and **VGA30.3GR** which is supposed to work for folks who are still laboring with Windows 3.0 video drivers — all two of you.

Every video board manufacturer comes up with a new Enhanced mode grabber. That .3GR file should install when you go through the video board's installation procedure, and the **386grabber=** setting probably points to it. There isn't much effort put into Standard mode grabbers, though, so you may well have the original Windows-installed grabber still sitting around, should you be tempted to try Standard mode.

CachedFileHandles=*Number*

 The official documentation says this is the number of most-recently used **.EXE** and **.DLL** files Windows can leave open at one time. It goes on to say that you can specify a number from 2 to 12 for the value, with 12 as the default.

Clearly that isn't the case. It's easy to have more than 12 **.EXE**s and **.DLL**s running at once: you probably do it every day, without thinking, most recently used or not.

What does the setting really represent? And why is it in the **[boot]** section? Who knows? The official documentation says that some networks won't let their servers keep too many files open; I found one reference to a maximum of 255 files on the servers of one type of network. Supposedly, if you have problems with too many

`.EXE` and `.DLL` files open on a network server, you can reduce the value of this setting to throttle back Windows. And you'll have to manually edit this line (probably have to add it) with a text editor. You're on your own, pilgrim.

---
comm.drv=*DriverFile*

This entry points to Windows' communication driver, the one that handles the serial ports. Windows only has one comm driver, so the uninitiated will probably have a line that looks like this:

comm.drv=comm.drv

Not you, of course. You're smart. You got TurboCom or KingComm a long time ago. When you installed it, the installer magically changed this line around to point at the new driver. Good thinking. You don't have to deal with the Windows plain-vanilla driver.

Don't mess around with this line manually. If it looks like it got screwed up, re-install your comm driver, or if you absolutely must, use a text editor to change it back to look like the line above.

---
display.drv=*DriverFile*

This line points to your %$^$#@! video driver, the piece of software singularly most likely to crash and burn Windows.

Normally, you'll select a driver by choosing from the English-language descriptions offered in the Windows Setup program. Double-click on Setup (which is probably in your MAIN group), then click on Options to Change System Settings, and you'll see Figure 9-15.

Often, but not always, the driver choices offered to you include some indication of the resolution (1024 x 768 here) and the color depth (256 colors or 65K colors here).

Higher resolution entries often let you choose between "Large" (sometimes called "8514") and "Small" (sometimes called "VGA") system fonts. That controls whether a larger or smaller font should be used for icon text, window titles, menu text, and much more. In addition to changing the **display.drv=** setting, those choices will control the **oemfonts.fon=**, **fixedfon.fon=** and **fonts.fon=** settings described later.

When Windows installs itself, it will add this line to **[boot]**, using one of the video drivers that ship with Windows, to-wit: **8514.drv** (IBM 8514); **ega.drv** (EGA); **egahibw.drv** (EGA with 128K); **egamono.drv** (EGA mono); **hercules.drv** (old-fashioned Herc); **olibw.drv** (AT&T mono); **plasma.drv** (Compaq portable with plasma screen); **supervga.drv** (800 x 600 x 16 colors only); **tiga.drv** (TIGA video); **v7vga.drv** (Video 7 VGA or Super VGA); **vga.drv** (VGA); **vgamono.drv** (VGA mono); or **xga.drv** (IBM XGA).

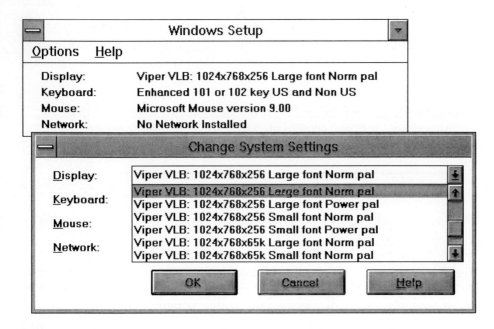

Figure 9-15: Video Setup

When you install a new video board, the **display.drv=** line in **[boot]** will undoubtedly get changed; the two grabber lines, the Windows startup routine **WIN.COM**, and the three font lines will be changed as well. Changes won't "take" until you exit and restart Windows.

In case you're curious, here's what selecting some of the standard Windows setup video modes will trigger:

Driver Description	display.drv=	286grabber=	386grabber=	WIN.COM logo	WIN.COM rle
8514/a	8514.drv	vgacolor.2gr	vgadib.3gr	vgalogo.lgo	vgalogo.rle
8514/a (Small fonts)	8514.drv	vgacolor.2gr	vgadib.3gr	vgalogo.lgo	vgalogo.rle
Compaq Portable Plasma	plasma.drv	cga.2gr	plasma.3gr	cgalogo.lgo	cgalogo.rle
EGA	ega.drv	egacolor.2gr	ega.3gr	egalogo.lgo	egalogo.rle
EGA black and white (286 only)	egahibw.drv	egacolor.2gr,	ega.SYS	cgalogo.lgo	cgalogo.rle
EGA Monochrome (286 only)	egamono.drv	egamono.2gr	ega.SYS	egamono.lgo	egamono.rle
Hercules Monochrome	hercules.drv	hercules.2gr	herc.3gr	herclogo.lgo	herclogo.rle
IBM MCGA (286 only)	vgamono.drv	vgacolor.2gr	vgadib.3gr	cgalogo.lgo	cgalogo.rle
Olivetti/AT&T Monochrome or PVC Display	olibw.drv	oligrab.2gr	plasma.3gr	cgalogo.lgo	cgalogo.rle
QuadVGA, ATI VIP VGA, 82C441 VGAs	vga.drv	vgacolor.2gr	vga30.3gr	vgalogo.lgo	vgalogo.rle
TIGA (Small fonts)	tiga.drv	vgacolor.2gr	vgadib.3gr	vgalogo.lgo	vgalogo.rle
TIGA (Large fonts)	tiga.drv	vgacolor.2gr	vgadib.3gr	vgalogo.lgo	vgalogo.rle
VGA	vga.drv	vgacolor.2gr	vga.3gr	vgalogo.lgo	vgalogo.rle
VGA (Version 3.0)	vga.drv	vgacolor.2gr	vga30.3gr	vgalogo.lgo	vgalogo.rle
VGA with Monochrome display	vgamono.drv	vgamono.2gr	vgadib.3gr	egamono.lgo	egamono.rle
Super VGA (800x600, 16 colors)	supervga.drv	vgacolor.2gr	vga.3gr	vgalogo.lgo	vgalogo.rle
XGA (640x480, 16 colors)	vga.drv	vgacolor.2gr	vga30.3gr	vgalogo.lgo	vgalogo.rle
XGA (Small fonts)	xga.drv	vgacolor.2gr	v7vga.3gr	vgalogo.lgo	vgalogo.rle
XGA (Large fonts)	xga.drv	vgacolor.2gr	v7vga.3gr	vgalogo.lgo	vgalogo.rle
XGA (640x480, 256 colors)	xga.drv	vgacolor.2gr	v7vga.3gr	vgalogo.lgo	vgalogo.rle

It would be exceedingly poor form (indeed, it would be courting disaster) to monkey around with the **display.drv=** line manually. Either use Setup's Display options or your video board manufacturer's routines to change the entry. If you think this setting may be zapped, back up the current **SYSTEM.INI**, exit Windows, hop into the **\windows** directory, run setup, and see if you can recover by choosing the video driver that's supposed to be controlling your machine. If all else fails, you can fall back on one of the standard Windows drivers listed earlier: **vga.drv** works, sorta, on just about any modern system.

In spite of what the official documentation says, the default for this entry is *not* blank. A blank **display.drv=** will lock up your system. Tight.

---

drivers=_DriverFile_

The **drivers=** setting lists the drivers that are to be loaded as Windows boots. Not many drivers get that kind of treatment, Windows itself kicks in the MultiMedia driver **MMSYSTEM.DLL**, and some sound packages add their event handlers to the stew, but by and large, drivers aren't loaded until they're needed.

Entries on this line look like this:

drivers=mmsystem.dll sndevent.dll alias

where the driver's file names appear in the list, as do **alias** entries which refer to lines in the **[drivers]** section (see the discussion in the **[drivers]** section).

One oddity: there's no provision on this line to feed programs command-line switches or other parameters, so if you have a driver that needs to be fed such effluvia, it will be listed here as an alias, and the alias listing down in **[drivers]** will contain all the parameters.

It's highly unlikely that you'll ever play with this line. Programs that need to kick-start drivers will put them in here; you won't need to do it manually. If you think the line got screwed up, simply replace it with the default:

drivers=mmsystem.dll

and re-boot.

In spite of what the official documentation says, the default is *not* (blank): Windows installs itself with the **drivers=mmsystem.dll** line in **[boot]**.

---

fixedfon.fon=*FONFileName*

fonts.fon=*FONFileName*

oemfonts.fon=*FONFileName*

Let's start with the easy one, **fixedfon.fon=**. That entry usually applies to Windows 2.x programs running under Windows 3.1; in general, it's not something you're likely to be concerned about. The "fixed" does not refer to the reproductive state of this dog — presumably that would involve a setting like **neutered.fon=**, and raise immediate questions about serifs. Rather, "fixed" here means "monospaced," i.e., the **.FON** file referenced in this setting is not a proportionally spaced font.

In spite of what the official documentation says, when you install Windows on a VGA system, you'll get the line

`fixedfon.fon=vgafix.fon`

in your **[boot]** section. Windows also ships with **egafix.fon** and **8514fix.fon**.

 Ah, but there's an oddity lurking here, something not covered in the official documentation. The `fixedfon.fon=` font is used for text in the Windows 3.1 Notepad and Card File, and it has some effect (I'm not sure what!) on the font used in Terminal.

If you want Notepad and Card File to use a proportional font, instead of that boxy monstrosity it usually employs, or if you have a Windows 2.x application still hanging around that insists on using monospaced fonts when you'd prefer proportional — try switching this line around. Instead of `fixedfon.fon=8514fix.fon`, say, you might use `fixedfon.fon=8514sys.fon`. Or try **vgasys.fon**. You may find the change very useful, if you can stand what it does to Terminal!

Should you decide to play with this entry, you'll have to edit **SYSTEM.INI** manually.

Unlike the fun with an innocuous **fixedfon.fon=** setting, the **fonts.fon=** setting is crucial to running Windows: it sets the font to be used for a whole bunch of things. Alas and alack, your video driver might actually go in and take over some of those "things," so my list may not be accurate on your machine.

On every system I've tried, the **fonts.fon=** setting controls the font in windows titles, menus, some dialog boxes, most applications' status bars, Calendar, and SysEdit.

 Surprisingly, though, the `fonts.fon=` setting does *not* control the font used for Notepad text or Card File (see `fixedfon.fon=`), Terminal, the PIF Editor, or some other dialog boxes. On some systems you'll see the two different dialog box fonts if you go into Terminal, click on Phone, then Dial (for one kind of box font), then click on File Exit (for the other kind).

Almost all of the `fonts.fon=` fonts that appear on the screen appear to me to be done in bold. The only consistent exception to that rule seems to be in the status bar, where the `fonts.fon=` fonts appear to be "straight."

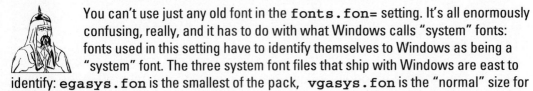 You can't use just any old font in the `fonts.fon=` setting. It's all enormously confusing, really, and it has to do with what Windows calls "system" fonts: fonts used in this setting have to identify themselves to Windows as being a "system" font. The three system font files that ship with Windows are east to identify: `egasys.fon` is the smallest of the pack, `vgasys.fon` is the "normal" size for VGA users and `8514sys.fon` fonts are the largest, the ones most commonly used at high resolution.

Those three files define the extent of Windows' repertoire. Other `.FON` files on the `fonts.fon=` line lock up the system: Windows won't even start, and you'll be stuck fumbling with backups or editing **SYSTEM.INI** from DOS.

If you've ever wondered what the "small fonts" and "large fonts" options in many Windows video setup selections mean, well, they simply control whether `fonts.fon=` is set to `vgasys.fon` (the "small") or `8514sys.fon` (the "large").

You can swap the `.FON` files around manually, if you like, although it's much easier to use your video board manufacturer's routines, or the Windows Setup applet.

 There's one case where a manual swap is certainly called for. If you're stuck using the standard Windows Super VGA driver (i.e., if you have the line `display=svga.drv` in the `[boot]` section of **SYSTEM.INI**), you may be pleasantly surprised by how much nicer the larger fonts look. To install them, first make sure the file `8514SYS.FON` is in your Windows system directory (if it isn't, see Appendix 2 for detailed instructions on retrieving it), then using SysEdit or some other text editor, change the `fonts.fon=` line in the `[boot]` section to look like this:

```
fonts.fon=8514sys.fon
```

Then reboot Windows. Your eyes will start applauding.

The `oemfonts.fon=` setting is a bit obscure: among other things, the official documentation is dead wrong. The basic concept is pretty simple, though. It all has to do with the IBM character set — some folks call it the PC-8 character set — the one you used in DOS for so many years. The old IBM character set includes lines and corners and such

> ╔══════════════════════════════════════╗
> ║ that will let you draw boxes like this. ║
> ╚══════════════════════════════════════╝

No doubt you've struggled with the character set. It also has some weird characters like Ω and ≡ and √. None of those are in the standard Windows character set. (See Appendix 3.)

 In Microsoft Lingo, anything called "oem" really means "ibm." It's almost a speech impediment. And I'll bet the neologism took root back when the Boys in Blue fell out of favor with the Redmond brass. Whaddya want to bet it went something like this. . .

There's a nervous Microsoft font techie in front of a Windows design review meeting, trying to explain how Windows is going to handle the IBM character set.

The timorous techie looks at the assembled brass and starts talking about the old DOS character set, "We're going to use a different font to handle most of the i. . . i. . . i. . .," he starts to stutter, beads of sweat forming on his forehead. He backs up a step and tries again. "The Symbol font will have many of the i. . . i. . . i. . . i. . .". The Gaze of Bill descends upon him. He can't spit out the words. Starts rocking back and forth, the chant turning to a scream, "i. . . I. . . AYYYYYYYY." He collapses to the floor, shaking violently, froth visible on his lips.

From the back of the room a lone voice with a Texas drawl adroitly parts the silence. "Let's just say OEM." A double-beat pause, with a low moan coming from the front of the room. All eyes are drawn to Tex. "Stands for Obsolete Equipment Manufacturer, 'course."

Tex is now a vice president, with stock options worth several million.

 Anyway, the `oemfonts.fon=` setting points to a `.FON` font file that the system can use to get at the old IBM character set. The IBM character set is identical to the Windows character set in the lower 128 characters. Differences only appear with the higher characters.

There's only one Windows applet that uses **oemfonts.fon=** directly: the Clipboard Viewer. It offers a great opportunity to show you exactly what's up with OEM character sets.

Every character has a number. You know that. The capital "A" for example is character number 65. The lower case "b" is character number 98. And so on. In the Windows character set, character number 212 is a trademark symbol, a ™. But in the IBM character set, it's something else.

Now say you go into a Windows application and copy a ™ character onto the clipboard. Pop up the Clipboard Viewer and you'll see precisely what you copied into the clipboard, ™ and all. But if you then click on Display, then OEM text, the Clipboard Viewer flips over to using the **oemfonts.fon=** font, and the ™ suddenly turns into something else — in this case, an odd asterisk (see Figure 9-15).

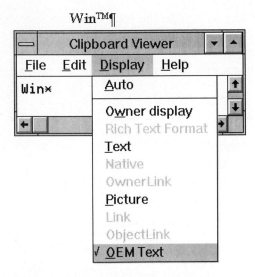

Figure 9-15: An OEM Trademark

Windows programs occasionally need to display text in the IBM character set. When that's the goal, **oemfonts.fon=** provides the mechanism.

The three **oemfonts.fon=** files that ship with the U.S. version of Windows, **egaoem.fon**, **vgaoem.fon** and **8514oem.fon,** are all old Bitstream ("Copyright Bitstream 1984") terminal fonts.

In spite of what the documentation says, when Windows installs itself, it puts all three lines font lines in **SYSTEM.INI**. A typical VGA installation will yield these three lines in **[boot]**:

```
fixedfon.fon=vgafix.fon
fonts.fon=vgasys.fon
oemfonts.fon=vgaoem.fon
```

If you screw up any of those lines, Windows will refuse to start, typically with a "Cannot load **GDI.EXE**" message. Should that happen to you, go into the Windows directory and run Setup from DOS. Pick a stable video configuration: bone stock VGA is a good starting point. That should get you up and going long enough to re-install your video card's drivers.

If you're struggling with non-US versions of Windows, make sure that the code page associated with the **oemfonts.fon=** setting matches the one in the **oemansi.bin=** setting in the **[keyboard]** section of **SYSTEM.INI**.

---

keyboard.drv=*KeyboardDriverFile*

Windows comes with three keyboard drivers: **keyboard.drv**, the normal one; **kbdhp.drv**, a driver that's supposed to be for old HP computers; and **kbdmouse.drv**, supposedly for ancient AT&T keyboards, the ones with the attached mouse — or so I'm told.

There's just one little problem. No matter how hard I try, I can't get Windows to put anything but **keyboard.drv=keyboard.drv** in the **[boot]** section. You might think you could change the **keyboard.drv=** in the Windows Setup applet, by clicking on Options, then Change Settings, and pulling down the Keyboard list. refer to Figure 9-16.

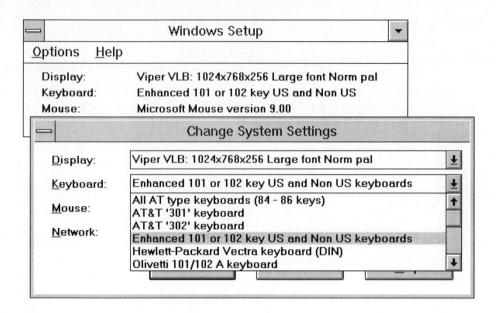

Figure 9-16: Keyboard Setup

But no matter what I tried, I couldn't get the driver to change. I'm firmly convinced that the documentation is all wrong, and that the **[keyboard]** section of **SYSTEM.INI** is doing all the work.

---

language.dll=_LanguageFile_

Windows relies on certain programs — certain **.DLL**s — to provide support for non-USA versions. This entry, if left blank, tells Windows to use the built-in USA English support. If there is a **.DLL** specified, Windows will use that **.DLL** for language services.

It's easiest to change this setting from Control Panel, in the International applet. If you pick a new Language in the second drop-down list box, Windows will change this line. According to the official documentation, values include **langdut.dll** (Dutch), **langfrn.dll** (French), **langger.dll** (German), **landsca.dll** (Finnish, Icelandic, Norwegian, Swedish), **langspa.dll** (Spanish) and **langeng.dll** (all other).

When the U.S. version of Windows installs itself, it places a

language.dll=

line in the **[boot]** section.

---

mouse.drv=*MouseDriverFile*

> As I was walking up the stair
> I met a mouse who wasn't there.
> He wasn't there again today;
> I wish to hell he'd go away.
>
> — *Pensées Pinecliffius*

This entry points to the location of the active mouse driver. When Windows installs itself, it sticks a mouse driver in the \system directory and puts in a line appropriate for your mouse, for example,

mouse.drv=mouse.drv

into the **[boot]** section. That line says, "Use the file on the right side of the equals side, the file **mouse.drv,** as the mouse driver."

Windows ships with seven mouse drivers: the standard (version 8.2) Microsoft **mouse.drv**; **hpmouse.drv** for the HP HIL mouse (whatever that is); **kbdmouse.drv** for the AT&T mouse attached to the keyboard (which, again, I've never seen); **lmouse.drv** for Logitech 3-button mice; **msc3bc2.drv** for the Mouse Systems 3-button mouse on COM2 (hey, where did they find these things?); **mscmouse.drv** for the Mouse Systems serial bus mouse; and my favorite, **nomouse.drv**, the no mouse mouse driver.

If you get a new mouse, or a new driver, the installation routine should be smart enough to either point this entry at the new driver, or copy the new driver into your \system directory. Installing the (slick!) Microsoft Mouse 9.0 driver to the \mouse subdirectory, for example, changed this line around to

mouse.drv=c:\mouse\mouse.drv

If you're having problems with Windows recognizing a new mouse driver, I suggest that you seriously consider re-installing the driver. Every installation routine I've seen is smart enough to update this setting, providing (in some cases) that you point the installer to your Windows subdirectory.

You may need to make a detour through the Windows Setup routine to pick up all the pieces.

If you have to edit this setting by hand, make sure you point this entry at your latest mouse driver — usually the mouse-related **.DRV** file with the latest date stamp. You might want to double-check your **AUTOEXEC.BAT** or **CONFIG.SYS** to gather some (contrarian?) opinions about where your latest driver might reside.

---

network.drv=*NetworkDriverFile*

If you're seriously looking at this entry, put down *MOM* and get to your computer. In your Windows directory, you'll find a file called **NETWORKS.WRI**. Read it. Memorize it. Take it to bed at night. Because, if you really do need to change **network.drv=**, that file will become your constant companion for the next couple of days. Or weeks. Or months.

 Yeah, this is the line that tells Windows which network driver to use. Change it manually at your own peril — and expect to knock your machine out for an extended period of time, should you attempt such a foolish action. Use your network's Windows setup routines to make this setting right; if all else fails, go into the Windows setup applet.

If, in the face of all my warnings, you change this setting, you *must* also look at 22 other settings in **SYSTEM.INI**: the **Int28Filter=** and **NetHeapSize=** lines in **[standard]**, **NetAsyncSwitching=** in **[NonWindowsApp]**, and the **AllVMsExclusive=**, **CachedFileHandles=**, **EMMExclude=**, **ExcludeHighRegion=**, **FileSysChange=**, **InDOSPolling=**, **Int28Critical=**, **NetAsyncFallback=**, **NetAsyncTimeout=**, **NetDMASize=**, **NetHeapSize=**, **Network=**, **PerVMFiles=**, **PSPIncrement=**, **ReflectDOSInt2A=**, **ReservedHighArea=**, **TimerCriticalSection=**, **TokenRingSearch=**, and **UniqueDOSPSP=** settings in **[386Enh]**.

Now you know why I tell you to use the setup routines. And why it would take a whole new book to do justice to the networking topic.

---

oemfonts.fon=*FONFileName*

See **fixedfon.fon=**.

---
shell=*ShellFileName*

 This **shell=** program is the *only* program that Windows launches when it starts. Conversely, the **shell=** program is the program that, if exited, will cause Windows itself to terminate. (Exceptions: the programs that make up Windows itself are launched when Windows starts, of course; as is any program mentioned on the DOS command line.)

Aside from those two characteristics, though, the Windows shell is just another program. That's a remarkable design feature, by the way — plug 'n play interfaces — an amazing bit of functionality delivered to us by the designers of Windows.

When you install Windows, it chooses Program Manager as your shell and puts this line in the **[boot]** section of **SYSTEM.INI**:

```
shell=progman.exe
```

You can change that line to point to just about anything you like. One fashionable replacement, once upon a time, was to change over to use File Manager as your Windows shell. That's easy: you just change the line here to say **shell=winfile.exe**. I don't recommend that you do it, FileMan is a lousy shell. Besides, if you're advanced enough to replace your shell manually, you'll probably want PC Tools or Norton or a similar industrial-strength shell, if not a garden-variety YAWS (Yet Another Windows Shell).

If you want to get rid of a renegade shell, try editing **SYSTEM.INI** and changing this line back so it points to **progman.exe**. The industrial-strength shells have options that let you flip back to program manager without getting your text editor going, but the lesser ones may not.

In spite of what the official documentation says, the default is *not* (none), and if you blank out the shell file's name, or delete this line, Windows flounders like a dead duck in a Redmond cesspool: it won't start at all. If you put in a Windows program that isn't designed to be a Windows shell, Windows will usually start up and the indicated program will run, but the startup sequence won't do the "normal" things, like launching the **load=** and **run=** programs listed in the **[windows]** section of **WIN.INI**.

The file name in this entry follows the usual Windows conventions: if you don't put a full path on this line and the file isn't in your Windows or system subdirectory, Windows looks along the DOS path.

The only way for you to change this line is by editing **SYSTEM.INI** manually.

---

sound.drv=*SoundDriverFileName*

This entry points to the Windows sound driver, usually **MMSOUND.DRV**. If Windows detects a multimedia sound capability on your system when it installs, it puts the line

```
sound.drv=mmsound.drv
```

into the **[boot]** section. Do not confuse this sound driver with the drivers that come with your sound card. They are almost always separate drivers in the **[drivers]** section of **system.ini** with names like **AUX**, **MIDI**, **Wave**, and **MIDI1** and perhaps a VxD added as a **device=** in **[386Enh]**.

---

system.drv=*SystemDriverFileName*

This is the mother of all drivers: it lies at the core of Windows. When Windows installs itself, it usually places this line in the **[boot]** section:

```
system.drv=system.drv
```

 Windows also ships with a file called **HPSYSTEM.DRV** that's supposed to work for HP Vectra computers, but I've never used it. If you install Windows on an HP Vectra computer, you'll probably get a line that looks like **system.drv=hpsystem.drv** in **[boot]**. Talk about trivia.

Ever wonder how Adobe Type Manager gets its hooks into your system? This is the place. When Adobe Type Manager installs itself, it changes this single line to a pair:

```
system.drv=atmsys.drv
atm.system.drv=system.drv
```

With `ATMSYS.DRV` running as the system driver, Adobe Type Manager handles all system driver calls. Whenever a program asks the system driver for font-related help, `ATMSYS.DRV` looks at the request and checks to see if it's related to one of the ATM fonts. If so, `ATMSYS.DRV` handles the request. If not, the request is passed on to the `atm.system.drv=` driver — which is usually the old-fashioned Windows system driver, `system.drv`. It's all very reminiscent of the old TSR interrupt chaining follies. . .

If you're trying to manually remove ATM, you need to remove those two lines and stick back the original. Other programs may circumvent your **system.drv=** setting in a similar way.

Taskman.exe=_WindowsEXEFileName_

This entry specifies which Windows application is to be started when you double-click on the Desktop, or hit **Ctrl+Esc**. Unless you (or a program you install) explicitly change it, that program is the Windows Task Manager (see Figure 9-17).

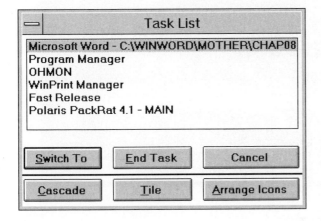

Figure 9-17: Task, Man!

When Windows installs itself, it doesn't put this line in **[boot]**. If the line is missing, or if there is nothing to the right of the equal sign, Windows assumes you meant **TASKMAN.EXE** and runs it on a **Ctrl+Esc**.

But there's no reason in the world why you can't change it! You can pop up a frequently-used program. Or a phone dialer. Or a game. While working on this book, I set it to `COLLAGE.EXE`, the program I use to do screen shots. Zip-zap-zooop. Couple of clicks and I have the shots in the bag. Couldn't be simpler.

[boot.description]

This is a weird section that keys the Windows Setup applet and the DOS command-line setup to long, Byzantine text strings. Apparently Windows Setup looks at these strings and feeds them to you when you go into the applet, or when you try to run setup from DOS (see Figure 9-18).

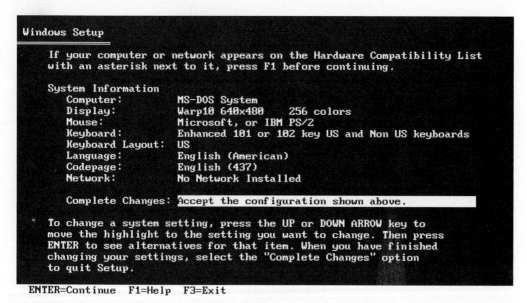

Figure 9-18: Windows Setup From DOS

A plain-vanilla installation of Windows like that above produced these entries:

```
[boot.description]
system.drv=MS-DOS System
display.drv=Warp10 640x480       256 colors
mouse.drv=Microsoft, or IBM PS/2
keyboard.typ=Enhanced 101 or 102 key US and Non US keyboards
```

```
language.dll=English (American)
codepage=437
network.drv=No Network Installed
displayinf=OEM_WARP.INF
woafont.fon=English (437)
aspect=100,96,96
```

 The official documentation contains dire warnings about not changing the strings: else, so the story goes, "you cannot use Windows Setup to update drivers to newer versions." Hogwash. I changed around several of the descriptions and had no trouble at all installing new drivers, or retrieving old ones. When I changed the text in the `system.drv=`, `display.drv=`, `mouse.drv=`, `keyboard.typ=`, or `network.drv=` entries, the only effect I saw was a change in the text that Windows Setup displays. A change in `keyboard.typ=` for example, led to Figure 9-19.

⊟	Windows Setup	▼
Options **H**elp		
Display:	Viper VLB: 1024x768x256 Large font Norm pal	
Keyboard:	Igor Was Here. Hi, Mom!	
Mouse:	Microsoft Mouse version 9.00	
Network:	No Network Installed	

Figure 9-19: Hi, Mom!

with no real effect on anything. If there's something lurking beneath the surface, I never found it. Switching back to show the name of the original drivers takes a couple of clicks: just pick Options, Change System Settings, and pick your original setting. Big deal.

The `language.dll=` setting seems to change the "Language" text in the Control Panel's International applet. As far as I could tell, most any non-standard setting (see the `sLanguage=` setting in the `[intl]` section of `WIN.INI`) flipped the chosen language to Danish. Again, picking my original language in the applet reset the line in `[boot.description]`. No biggie.

The **codepage=** setting may seem inscrutable until you understand that "code page" is archaic (read: DOS) terminology for what most Windows initiates would call a character set.

For example, the old-fashioned DOS character set — the one with box characters and all that — is called "Code page 437." You probably call it the old-fashioned DOS character set, or if you've been reading too many HP printer manuals, you might call it the PC-8 character set or if you are looking for a job at Microsoft you might call it the OEM character set.

Another way to look at it: the **codepage=** setting helps DOS show the same character on screen as the user thought they typed on the keyboard. When DOS runs under Windows, it needs a **codepage=**.

The 850 code page contains all the fancy characters necessary to display most European languages, some places it's called Multilingual (Latin I), other places it's just called Multilingual. For no apparent reason, the 852 code page, Slavic (Latin II), ships with DOS, but not with Windows. The 861 code page, Icelandic, ships with Windows, but not DOS. Go figger.

I couldn't find an easy way to change the **codepage=** setting, or any documentation about it. You might assume that switching to Icelandic (code page 861) in the International applet would reset the **codepage=** setting, but that isn't the case. I assume it's buried in the routines that control the language setting in the **[intl]** section of **WIN.INI**, but don't know for sure.

Similarly, I had no luck finding any information on the **aspect=** setting: I would guess it concerns an aspect ratio (of the display? of DOS fonts in a Windows DOS box?), but beyond that you're on your own. The **woafont.fon=** setting presumably concerns DOS fonts, but I could find nothing definitive. It does not point to a valid font file. And the **displayinf=** setting, which does not appear in all systems, appears to be a reminder stuck in **SYSTEM.INI** by some video driver manufacturers.

[drivers]

This section is tied to the Drivers applet in the Control Panel. Double-click on the Drivers icon and you'll see something like Figure 9-20.

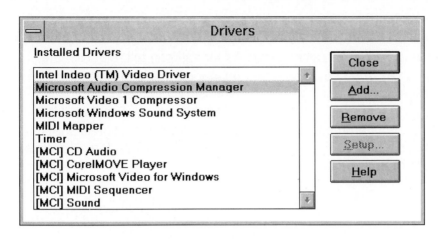

Figure 9-20: The MS Audio Compression Manager

The six drivers at the top of the list correspond to these entries in the **[drivers]** section:

```
VIDC.RT21=indeo.drv
WaveMapper=MSACM.DRV
VIDC.MSVC=msvidc.drv
wave=SNDSYS.DRV
aux=SNDSYS.DRV
midi=SNDSYS.DRV
midimapper=midimap.drv
timer=timer.drv
```

Descriptions of the drivers — the text you can see displayed in the dialog box — are drawn from the **CONTROL.INI** file, where they are stored in the **[drivers.desc]** section and indexed by the driver name. Like this:

```
indeo.drv=Intel Indeo (TM) Video Driver
MSACM.DRV=Microsoft Audio Compression Manager
msvidc.drv=Microsoft Video 1 Compressor
SNDSYS.DRV=Microsoft Windows Sound System
midimap.drv=MIDI Mapper
timer.drv=Timer
```

The official documentation (and all the other documentation I've seen for that matter) says that this section sets up aliases for the **drivers=** line of the **[boot]** section of **SYSTEM.INI**. As far as I can tell, that isn't the case: while a few of these drivers may be loaded at startup by inclusion on the **drivers=** line — and aliasing may be necessary if the driver needs command-line parameters (see the discussion of the **drivers=** line; I couldn't *find* any drivers that need parameters) — it sure looks like this section is primarily maintained for the care and feeding of the Control Panel's Drivers applet, and as a central list of available multimedia drivers.

The Windows Software Development Kit does mention one other use for these entries. Basically, a program can call a Windows driver by an alias. When that happens, Windows looks here to find which driver should really be loaded. For example, a MIDI file player may ask Windows to load the MIDI driver; Windows would look here to find out what file to load. It's a convenient way to load standard driver types, and at the same time let third-party software developers get at their drivers using generic names.

If you're trying to figure out what's going on with the WaveMapper **MSACM.DRV** driver, see the discussion in Chapter 34.

[keyboard]

Keyboards come in all shapes and sizes. More importantly for the discussion at hand, keyboards come with their keys stuck in different places. The {curly bracket keys}, for example, may be next to the P on your keyboard, but a standard German keyboard might have different keys there, as would an Arabic or Thai keyboard.

Windows interacts with the keyboard in two separate steps. First comes the keyboard driver, the driver specified in the **keyboard.drv=** line in the **[boot]** section of **SYSTEM.INI**. That driver talks directly with the keyboard, although (as you'll note in the discussion of **keyboard.drv=**) apparently not the way it's described in the official documentation.

If you are using a standard IBM compatible U.S. keyboard (or, the official documentation says, an AT&T 301 or 302, or an Olivetti 83-key), that one driver is all you need. It talks straight to Windows. And when Windows installs itself, you'll get lines like these in the **[keyboard]** section of **SYSTEM.INI**:

```
subtype=0
type=4
keyboard.dll=
oemansi.bin=
```

On the other hand, if you have a non-standard or non-US keyboard, the
keyboard.drv= driver needs help; that's where this section comes in.

---

keyboard.dll=*KeyboardTranslatorFileNam
e*

This entry corresponds to the Keyboard Layout list in the Control Panel's
International applet, or the Keyboard Layout list from Windows Setup run from
DOS — but, oddly, the settings are not accessible from the Windows Setup applet.
Fire up the International applet and here's what you'll see (see Figure 9-21).

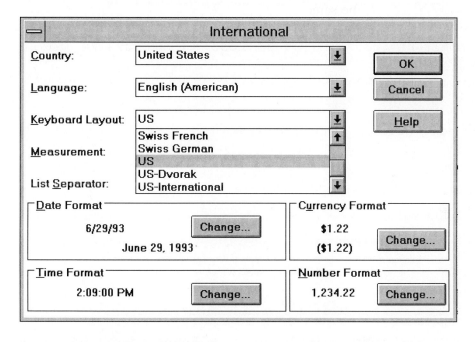

Figure 9-21: Keyboard Choices

Choosing a different Keyboard Layout will adjust the **keyboard.dll=** setting. The
standard choices in the list box and their associated settings are:

Choice in List	Setting	Choice in List	Setting
Belgian	kbde.dll	Italian	kbdit.dll
British	kbduk.dll	Latin American	kbdla.dll
Canadian Multilingual	kbdfc.dll	Norwegian	kbdno.dll
Danish	kbdda.dll	Portuguese	kbdpo.dll
Dutch	kbdne.dll	Spanish	kbdsp.dll
Finnish	kbdfi.dll	Swedish	kbdsw.dll
French	kbdfr.dll	Swiss French	kbdsf.dll
French Canadian	kbdca.dll	Swiss German	kbdsg.dll
German	kbdgr.dll	US	kbdus.dll
Icelandic	kbdic.dll	US-Dvorak	kbddv.dll
		US-International	kbdusx.dll

---

oemansi.bin=_KeyboardTranslatorFileName_

This number should match the code page — the DOS character set number — contained in **oemfonts.fon=** setting of the **[boot]** section of **SYSTEM.INI**.

See the discussion of the **codepage=** setting in **[boot.description]** for an explanation of code pages. (They're just character sets; not to worry.)

If there's no **oemansi.bin=** setting here, Windows assumes a code page 437, which is for the IBM PC-8 character set. Other valid values include 850 (general European), 860 (Portuguese), 861 (Icelandic), 863 (French Canadian) and 865 (Norwegian/Danish).

This value is supposed to be set whenever you use the Windows Setup applet or the International applet in the Control Panel.

---

type=_Number_

---

subtype=_Number_

These values tell the standard keyboard driver, **keyboard.drv**, what kind of keyboard is being used. Ignore any other printed list you've ever seen, including the one in the Windows Resource Kit; far as I know, this is the first time the correct values have appeared in print:

Choice in the Windows Setup Applet	Type	SubType
All AT type keyboards (84 - 86 keys)	3	(blank)
AT&T '301' keyboard	1	2
AT&T '302' keyboard	1	4
Enhanced 101 or 102 key US and Non US keyboards	4	(blank)
Hewlett-Packard Vectra keyboard (DIN)	3	(blank)
Olivetti 101/102 A keyboard	4	40
Olivetti 83 key keyboard	1	(blank)
Olivetti 86 Key keyboard	3	10
Olivetti M24 102 key keyboard	2	1
PC-XT 83 key keyboard	1	42
PC/XT - Type keyboard (84 keys)	1	(blank)

A blank setting is the same as a zero.

Yes, it's true. Choosing either "All AT type keyboards (84-86 keys)" or "Hewlett-Packard Vectra keyboard (DIN)" will give rise to identical settings for `type=` and `subtype=`. Apparently `keyboard.drv` isn't concerned about the differences (if any) between the two keyboards.

[mci]

The balance of the multimedia drivers — the ones that don't go into the `[drivers]` section of `SYSTEM.INI` — live here. These drivers are all associated with Windows' Media Control Interface, which is covered in excruciating detail in Chapter 3.

If you look at the screen shot in the `[drivers]` section a few pages back, you'll see five drivers in Control Panel's Drivers applet that aren't listed in the `[drivers]` section. In the dialog box they're all prefixed with the characters [MCI] — that's a dead giveaway that they reside here, in the `[mci]` section of `SYSTEM.INI`.

Those five drivers come from the following five lines in my `[mci]` section:

```
WaveAudio=mciwave.drv
Sequencer=mciseq.drv
CDAudio=mcicda.drv
```

```
AVIVideo=mciavi.drv
CorelMOVE=C:\COREL40\PROGRAMS\mcicmv40.drv
```

the first three of which are added automatically to **[mci]** when Windows installs itself.

So what do they *do*, you ask?

They link back into the entries in the **[mci extensions]** section of **WIN.INI**! *Wheels within wheels within wheels, eh?* Check out the description under **[mci extensions]** for a bird's-eye view of what's happening. It all has to do with the care and feeding of **MPLAYER.EXE**, the Windows media player.

The safest way to edit settings in this section is with the Control Panel's Drivers applet.

[NonWindowsApp]

A NonWindowsApp is just a DOS application. Actually, if you work with 'em long enough, you'll come to think of 'em as *ANTI*WindowsApps, but that's a different story. When you get right down to it, the **[NonWindowsApp]** section of **SYSTEM.INI** has nothing to do with non-Windows applications.

This section controls the behavior of DOS when run in a window. It doesn't provide any settings for DOS or Non-Windows applications, *per se.* For those, you should be looking at the PIF editor.

There's lots of talk in the official documentation about the effect these settings have on DOS 3.2 and earlier. If you're still running DOS 3.2 or earlier, heaven only knows why, you'll have to refer to the Windows Resource Kit. If you're laboring under a 3.2 delusion, seriously consider donning a strand of garlic before digging into the **[NonWindowsApp]** settings; and don't forget to carry a mirror and wooden stake.

CommandEnvSize=*Number*

You control DOS through something called a command interpreter. Typically, it's the program called **COMMAND.COM**.

When DOS gets the command interpreter going, it allocates a specific amount of space for something called the "Environment Area." That's where the command interpreter sticks the names and values of its variables — the so-called Environment String. If you don't tell DOS to set aside enough space, all hell breaks loose. On the other hand, that space is carved out of the lower part of memory, so you don't want to tell DOS to set aside too much.

Hard to believe anything so archaic has survived into the 1990s, eh?

When Windows kick-starts a DOS session, or runs a **.BAT** file (which, in turn, kick-starts a DOS session), it has to tell DOS how much memory to set aside for the Environment String. There are three ways to tell Windows (and DOS) how much space to allocate.

First, the normal way. In your **CONFIG.SYS** file there's probably an entry that looks like this:

```
SHELL=C:\DOS\COMMAND.COM C:\DOS\  /p /e:512
```

That little **/e:** switch tells DOS how much room it should allocate for the Environment String: in this case, it's 512 bytes. The **/p** switch ("make permanent") tells DOS that this is the primary copy of **COMMAND.COM**, the one that runs when the computer boots. (As a Windows user, you will often run several copies of **COMMAND.COM**.) Thus, if you have a line like that in your **CONFIG.SYS**, DOS will always start out with 512 bytes for the Environment String.

Second, you can set the size of the Environment String by monkeying around with the PIF file that launches **COMMAND.COM**. If you look at the **DOSPRMPT.PIF** file, the file Windows runs when you ask to get to the DOS prompt, typically by using the icon in the MAIN group, it probably looks like Figure 9-22.

PIF Editor - DOSPRMPT.PIF	▼ ▲
File **M**ode **H**elp	
Program Filename:	COMMAND.COM
Window **T**itle:	MS-DOS Prompt
Optional Parameters:	
Start-up Directory:	

Figure 9-22: Command!

See the Optional Parameters box? You could put an **/e:1024** in there, say, to get the DOS command line going with 1024 bytes reserved for the Environment String. (DOS copies over the old Environment String when you fire up a new copy of **COMMAND.COM**; see the DOS Technical Reference for details.) If you don't specify an **/e:** value, DOS gives the new copy of **COMMAND.COM** an **/e:** setting of the maximum of: (1) the current **/e:** size, rounded up to the nearest multiple of 16; or (2) 256 bytes.

Third, you can use this line, the **CommandEnvSize=** setting, in the **[NonWindowsApp]** section of **SYSTEM.INI**.

Of course, with three possible sources of **/e:** values, the fundamental question is, which one takes over?

 As far as I can tell, it works like this: In no case will DOS let the **/e:** size go below 160 bytes or above 32768 bytes. That's a DOS limitation, and it appears to be observed scrupulously even out here in the Windows world.

If there is no **/e:** value in the original **command** or **shell=** line, DOS uses 256. Again, that's a DOS fetish.

If there is an **/e:** value specified in the PIF file, and its value is greater than the **/e:** value in effect when the PIF file is run (the multiple-of-16 or 256 byte default assigned by DOS, as described earlier), the PIF file's **/e:** is used.

If there is a **CommandEnvSize=** specified, there is *no* **/e:** value in the PIF file, *and* the **CommandEnvSize=** value is greater than the **/e:** value in effect when **COMMAND.COM** is run, the **CommandEnvSize=** value is used.

At least, that's sure how it seems to work on my system, and I don't care what the official documentation says. (I couldn't make heads from tails out of the *Resource Kit*. So sue me.) If you want to change the **CommandEnvSize=** value, you'll have to hack at **SYSTEM.INI** with a text editor.

DisablePositionSave=*YesOrNo*

I must've started and re-started Windows a hundred times, trying to track this one down. Here's what I found: in spite of what it says in the official documentation, and in every single book and article I could find that discusses this setting, with one very minor exception, `Disable-PositionSave=` doesn't do a thing!

Yeah. You read that right. Not one bloody thing.

When Windows runs a DOS app, it can keep track of the font dot-size and the position of the DOS window. In fact, it can keep track of the dot-size and position for each DOS application you run, with different settings for each app. It stores those numbers in a file called **DOSAPP.INI**.

You set those numbers by clicking on the little hyphen-thingy in the upper left corner of a DOS box, then clicking on Fonts. . . Up pops the DOS fonts box (like in Figure 9-22).

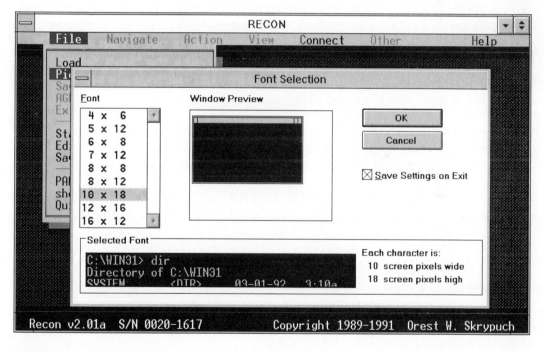

Figure 9-22: DOS Fonts

If you check that box over on the right, the one that says "Save Settings on Exit,"—then Windows will do precisely that: it will save both the dot-size setting and the current window position, the next time it leaves this DOS program. It stores those settings in **DOSAPP.INI** in a form like this (see Chapter 10 if you're curious about the numbers):

```
C:\TAPCIS\TAPCIS.EXE=1 10 18 808 486 22 0 1 65535 65535 60 60 7 65531 815 480
C:\TAPCIS\RECON.EXE=1 10 18 808 486 22 2 3 65535 65535 16 39 1 2 809 487
```

If you clear out that "Save Settings on Exit" box, Windows doesn't save the new settings, the next time you start that particular DOS application, none of the changes you may have made will "take." **DOSAPP.INI** isn't modified. The world is as it once was. That's all well and good: it's what I would expect Windows to do.

 Supposedly, depending on what you read and whom you believe, the **DisablePositionSave=** parameter is supposed to keep Windows from updating these **DOSAPP.INI** settings. But I'll be hog-tied and dipped in sheep shingles if I can get **DisablePositionSave=** to *do* anything useful. If I set it to 1, On, Yes, or True, the "Save Settings On Exit" checkbox determines whether **DOSAPP.INI** settings are saved or not. If I set it to 0, Off, No, False, leave it blank, or remove the line entirely, why, the "Save Settings On Exit" checkbox *still* determines whether **DOSAPP.INI** settings are saved or not. For the life of me, I don't see any difference.

Contrary to what you may read in the *Windows Resource Kit* or **SYSINI.WRI**, or any of dozens of books, the **DisablePositionSave=** setting does not (at least as far as I can tell) control whether the position of a DOS window is saved; it does not control whether the dot-size of the font in the DOS window is saved; it does not disable saving of "new" settings (i.e., for DOS programs not already in **DOSAPP.INI**); it doesn't even control whether the "Save Settings On Exit" check box comes up checked or not.

 The one teensy, tiny exception: if **DisablePositionSave=0**, or if it's missing, *and* you clear the "Save Position on Exit" checkbox, the first number in the application's entry in **DOSAPP.INI** is changed to reflect the "Save Position on Exit". (See Chapter 10 for a more thorough description of **DOSAPP.INI**.) Far as I can tell, that's it.

Sheesh.

FontChangeEnable=*YesOrNo*

If you are using ancient Windows 3.0 screen grabbers (look for a **.GR3** instead of the Windows 3.1 grabber's **.3GR** in the **[boot]** section's **386grabber=** line), you need to set this to 0. But Windows should've already done that for you.

If you change this setting, you're begging for trouble: dropped characters, flip-flopping cursors, premature psoriasis, wandering mice, and elephantine nose warts, — the kind that grow inward. Don't touch **FontChangeEnable=**.

GlobalHeapSize=*KB*

When Windows is running in Standard mode and it starts a DOS application, it can set aside some memory to share information among the DOS applications. This is the amount of memory, in K bytes. If there is no setting, Windows assumes a value of 0.

You may have an application that jimmies around this setting. You shouldn't.

---
localtsrs=*TSR,TSR, ...*

In the world of DOS, Terminate and Stay Resident programs (TSRs) sit around waiting for you to push the right keys, to make them spring to life. A very carefully constructed TSR may be smart enough to work in a Windows DOS box without stomping all over everything. And an utterly brilliant TSR may be smart enough to work in *all* Windows DOS boxes, concurrently, without crashing your whole system.

When Windows installs itself, it puts just one line in **[NonWindowsApp]**:

localtsrs=dosedit,ced

Note how this entry is different from so many others in that the values are separated by commas, not spaces.

MouseInDOSBox=*YesOrNo*

When the mouse passes over a DOS window (assuming the mouse driver isn't archaic and you're running with a Windows 3.1 grabber, both of which are highly likely), the cursor can react in one of two ways: it can let the DOS application take over, so the mouse behaves the same as it would if you were just running the DOS application, without Windows, or it can go into this weird text marking mode, where you can mark DOS text for copying by dragging the mouse over it.

The text marking mode is the same one you'd enter if you clicked on the hyphen-thingy in the upper left corner of the DOS box, clicked Edit, then Mark.

Some folks, for some reason, prefer to put their mouse in the marking mode, bypassing the native mouse handling of the DOS application. Those folks should dig into **SYSTEM.INI** and put this line in **[NonWindowsApp}**:

MouseInDOSBox=0

MouseInDOSBox=1 sets the mouse up so the DOS application reacts to mouse movement. When Windows installs itself, it looks to see if there's a reasonably sentient mouse driver loaded (the docs say it looks for one with a .COM or .SYS extension, that supports mouse activity in a DOS box). If one is available, it doesn't put this entry in **[NonWindowsApp]**. If the line does not appear in **[NonWindowsApp]**, Windows assumes you meant a value of 1. And that's precisely as it should be.

 But, in spite of what the official documentation says, *any other value* turns the setting off, and the mouse reverts to its marking ways.

Among other things, using **MouseInDOSBox=False** is the same as **MouseInDOSBox=True**, which is the same as **MouseInDOSBox=On**, and **MouseInDOSBox=Yes**, which in turn are all the same as **MouseInDOSBox=0**. Don't believe anything you read to the contrary.

NetAsynchSwitching=*YesOrNo*

This is another one of those settings that only applies if you are running in Standard mode. `NetAsynchSwitching=0` makes Windows "lock in" a DOS window once it's made an asynchronous network BIOS call. In plain English: if you're working with a DOS box that calls up the network, you won't be able to switch out of that DOS box. You'll have to kill off the DOS window (e.g., by exiting the program) before you can do anything else.

It isn't nice to call the network and then walk away.

 If you're absolutely certain that it's OK for your DOS programs to make asynch NetBIOS calls, and then not be available when the network comes calling back, you could try to set `NetAsynchSwitching=1`. But don't blame me if Windows suddenly starts suffering from the black death: screen comes up slate black, with at most a little blinking cursor, and nothing, not even the Vulcan nerve pinch, can bring it back.

ScreenLines=*Number*

 Here's yet another `SYSTEM.INI` setting that's incorrectly documented everywhere I've seen: official docs, unofficial docs, they all have it wrong. I'm not going to swear I've got it right, but this is what seems to happen, at least on my system. You can try it on yours.

Back in the good old days, all DOS programs supported 25 lines of text. (Well, not really, but that's a convenient fiction.) Then all of a sudden some programs learned how to display more lines, 50 spreadsheet lines on a decent EGA monitor wasn't out of the question. This **ScreenLines=** setting may have an effect on how many lines your DOS programs will display on the screen.

Note how I said "may." The number of lines can be set in four different ways. First, some DOS applications themselves can be pre-set to a particular number of lines. You'll have to look in your app's documentation to see how that is done. Second, Windows keeps track of the number of lines in effect in DOS when Windows starts; change the number of lines in DOS prior to starting Windows, and that can change the number of lines in a DOS box. Third, Windows stores the number of lines associated with any specific DOS application in **DOSAPP.INI**. Finally, there's this setting, the **ScreenLines=** number in the **[NonWindowsApp]** section of **SYSTEM.INI**.

If there's anything I've learned traipsing through the .INIs, it's this: when there are n different sources of Windows settings, there are a minimum 2^n different, independent sources of confusion. And the chances of any random source of information getting the details correct are, at best, 2^{-2n}.

Here's how it seems to go.

If the DOS application has been set to a specific number of lines, that's the setting that takes over. Simple enough. The application has control, just as it does in DOS.

If the DOS app is not set for anything in particular, and there is an entry in **DOSAPP.INI** for that application, the setting in **DOSAPP.INI** goes into effect. If you don't like it and want to wipe out the **DOSAPP.INI** setting, just go into the file and delete the line associated with the program.

If the DOS app is not internally set, and there is no entry in **DOSAPP.INI**, the **ScreenLines=** setting takes over.

Finally, if the DOS app doesn't have a preference, there is no entry in **DOSAPP.INI**, and there is no **ScreenLines=** setting, I do believe that Windows uses the number of lines that were in effect in DOS when Windows was started.

At least that *seems* to be how it works, on my system.

SwapDisk=*d:\directory*

If you are running in Standard mode, and if you do not have the **TEMP** variable set (more about that in a second), this entry tells Windows where to swap out DOS applications when they get too big to fit into memory, or when you switch from one to another.

If you have a **TEMP** variable set, it takes precedence. If you have no **TEMP** variable and the **SwapDisk=** setting is missing or incorrect, the official documentation says that Windows swaps out to the root directory of your first hard disk (typically **c:**).

If you're running in Enhanced mode — like you *should* be! — this setting doesn't do diddly.

Don't even consider adding this setting to **[NonWindowsApp]**. Use the DOS environment variable called **TEMP**. Most often you'll stick a line like this in **AUTOEXEC.BAT**:

```
Set temp=c:\temp
```

telling Windows where to put its temporary files. Some folks recommend that you point **TEMP** to a RAM disk, but that can lock up a lot of memory, and the performance gains over shuffling to SmartDrive are questionable. I've had the most luck, with SmartDrive enabled, pointing **TEMP** to my fastest hard disk.

[standard]

While there are settings that only apply to Windows running in Standard mode scattered throughout **WIN.INI**, the highest concentration is right here.

 Once again, for the last time, sonny! you should be running in Enhanced mode. Yes, Standard mode can be a touch faster if you only run one DOS app at a time. No, you won't be able to feel the difference. None of the settings in the **[standard]** section should mean anything to you. So forget this section: go read something enlightening and intellectually stimulating. . .like a Mad Magazine. Even Alfred Neuman runs in Enhanced mode. There. Now it's out. Alfred has to go somewhere for computer commiseration. I mean, it's *tough* staring into a screen and seeing a gap-tooth reflection. With Gaines gone, Alfred may as well talk to another icon, so he talks to me. I'm not ashamed. You made me admit it. Are you proud of yourself?

When Windows installs itself, it doesn't put anything in this section.

FasterModeSwitch=*YesOrNo*

This setting only applies to 286 computers, running in standard mode. It partially compensates for the "brain dead" way 286s switch between real and protected mode. If you have a 286 try setting **FasterModeSwitch=1** and see if it crashes your system, or if you suddenly start losing characters, particularly when running a communication program.

If this line is missing (and it will be unless you put it in **[standard]**), Windows assumes a value of 0, i.e., to run slow.

Int28Filter=*HowManyToThrowAway*

DOS interrupt 28 (in hex), more commonly known as INT 28h, is an idle loop, the keyboard busy loop; it's called from the routine in DOS that looks for keyboard input; it's the hook that TSRs scan. Windows throws away most INT 28h interrupts, only passing a small fraction of them on to any DOS TSRs (including, for example, network routines) that were running before Windows started.

According to the official documentation, the number in this setting tells Windows how many INT 28hs to throw away: an **Int28Filter=10** (the value Windows uses if you haven't set it to anything else) tells Windows to only pass through one out of every ten INT 28h interrupts. A 2 says pass through half of them; 1 means pass through all of them; 0 says don't pass any through.

Setting the number higher than 10 may make Windows run faster. Then again, it may screw up some time-sensitive TSRs, like network software. Using a number lower than 10 will make Windows run slower.

MouseSyncTime=*Milliseconds*

Again according to the official docs, this setting only applies to PS/2 machines running in Standard mode. It tells Windows how long to wait for a data packet from the mouse before giving up and just using whatever data it has at hand. If you don't add this line manually, Windows assumes a value of 500 milliseconds — half a second; an eternity in computer time.

NetHeapSize=*KB*

Okay. You tell me why this is in **[standard]**, while **GlobalHeapSize=** is in **[NonWindowsApp]**. Both of those settings only apply to Windows in Standard mode; both set aside lower memory for buffers, both for DOS apps. The only difference is that this setting applies to network buffers; the other to copy buffers.

If Windows needs a network buffer, it looks here to see how big the buffers should be. If there's no entry, it uses 8K. If you aren't yet sufficiently confused, also look at the **NetHeapSize=** setting in **[386Enh]**.

PadCodeSegments=*YesOrNo*

Hey, you know about code segments and data segments, right? And C2 stepping with 80286 chips? Sure you do....

What? You don't know? You don't *care*? Welcome to the club.

Here's the story, best I can tell. Some very old 80286 chips step through memory in a weird way called "C2." If you are using one of those very old chips, and you have code segments (chunks of memory containing programs) too close to data segments (other chunks of memory containing data), *and* you are running in Standard mode, the chip may get all confused and your system won't even run.

So here's what you need to do. If you're using a computer with an old 80286 chip, and it crashes every time you try to run Windows in Standard mode, pop into **SYSTEM.INI** with a text editor, and add one line to the **[standard]** section:

PadCodeSegments=1

then try to crank up Windows in Standard mode. Windows will re-align data segments so they fall on 16 byte boundaries (I believe that's what the official documentation is trying to say), thus allowing your old 80286 to C2 tiptoe through the Standard tulips.

Stacks=*HowMany*

StackSize=*KB*

The official *Windows Resource Kit* documentation says that these numbers relate to "interrupt reflector stacks used by the standard mode MS-DOS Extender (DOSX) to map an MS-DOS or BIOS API from real mode to protected mode." That has to be the most mind-warping bit of techno-crap obfuscation I've seen in recent history. It sets new standards, even for **.INI** file documentation.

Now, now, Mao. Calm down. You're almost done with this chapter. Just sit back and breathe slowly. There, there. *Illegitimus non carborundum*, eh? No reason to have a heart attack, even if the official documentation *is* buried ten layers deep in dog doo-doo. I guess it's telling when every Windows book parrots the official techno-babble, almost without translation, simply because *nobody* can figure out what Microsoft means.

Here's my best guess as to what this setting really entails: when Windows is running in Standard mode, it's forever flip-flopping between the 80286 real and protected modes (see Chapter 7 for a description of the brain dead flip). While the flipping is going on, Windows has to keep track of DOS interrupts, and my guess is that it keeps track of those interrupts in "interrupt reflector stacks."

The first setting, **Stacks=**, tells Windows the maximum number of interrupt reflector stacks it can use. Unless you come in and add this line to the **[standard]** section, Windows assumes a max of 12. The official documentation says you can specify a number between 8 and 64. If you get an error message (which I've never seen) that says

Standard Mode: Stack Overflow

you're instructed to increase the value of **Stacks=** and try again.

The **StackSize=** argument is supposed to tell Windows how big each of these interrupt reflector stacks should be. Unless you put a line in **[standard]** with a different number, Windows uses 384. Do yourself a favor. Don't touch this setting.

Yours was not, in the beginning, a criminal nature, but circumstances changed it.

At the age of nine you stole sugar.

At the age of fifteen you stole money.

At twenty you stole horses.

At twenty-five you committed arson.

At thirty, hardened in crime, you became an editor.

You are now a public lecturer.

Worse things are in store for you. . .

— Samuel Clemens, *Lionizing Murderers*, 1872

PROGMAN.INI

Windows' Program Manager ("Progman" for short) maintains its settings in a separate file called **PROGMAN.INI**.

A couple of these settings can be very useful. They're arranged in three sections. Just as in **WIN.INI**, the order of [section]s within **PROGMAN.INI** isn't important; capitalization is optional; I've merely duplicated the names precisely as they appear after Windows installs itself.

Section Name	What it affects
[Groups]	Lists the "groups" (Program Manager's collections of programs, the stuff in one file folder), and points to the **.GRP** files Program Manager uses to keep track of them.
[Restrictions]	Limits Progman functions. Can be very useful, especially if you're setting up Windows for a novice with a propensity toward shooting him/her/itself in the foot.
[Settings]	All the miscellaneous stuff.

When you make changes to **PROGMAN.INI**, you'll have to re-start Windows for them to take effect.

[Groups]

Progman keeps track of its groups in this section.

Groupn=*FileName*

The entries in **[Groups]** look like this:

```
[Groups]
Group1=C:\WINDOWS\MAIN.GRP
```

```
Group2=C:\WINDOWS\ACCESSOR.GRP
Group3=C:\WINDOWS\GAMES.GRP
Group4=C:\WINDOWS\STARTUP.GRP
```

Each of those `.GRP` files corresponds to one Progman "group," one bunch of programs stored in an erstwhile file folder on the Program Manager desktop. The `.GRP` files need not reside in your `\windows` directory; you can put them anywhere you like, providing you point Progman in the right direction with a `Groupn=` entry. If there is no directory information, Windows uses the usual search method by first looking in the Windows directory, then in the System directory, then along the DOS path, for a file with a matching name.

The numbers needn't run consecutively. If you delete a group a gap will appear in the number sequence. The numbers don't have to be in order either; the line for Group2 can appear after the line for Group4. No biggie.

Normally you'll add new groups to Progman by clicking on File, then New, clicking the Group button, and typing in a group name. It's very rare that you'll futz around with these lines manually.

In the course of preparing this book, I ran across an interesting limitation. It looks like Progman has a maximum of 40 groups. That's rather surprising, and a bit of a pain if you're an advanced user. Watch out.

There are several reasons why you might want to edit the `Groupn=` lines. First, you may want to have Windows start from time to time with different groups. If you write a `.BAT` file that swaps out one copy of `PROGMAN.INI` for another before launching Windows, you can control groups (or any other `PROGMAN.INI` settings, for that matter) by copying over `PROGMAN.INI` and then starting Windows.

Second, if your desktop gets clobbered and some groups disappear (which happens to me with alarming frequency!), you can bring the groups back onto the desktop by adding a `Groupn=` line, using the next larger number for **n**, and pointing to the missing `.GRP` file. You can do the same thing from inside Progman by clicking on File, then New, then Group, and typing in the name of the `.GRP` file like in Figure 10-1.

Program Group Properties		
Description: [　　　　　　　　　　　　]		OK
Group File: [c:\windows\mygroup.grp│]		Cancel
		Help

Figure 10-1: Arise, My Group!

and clicking OK. You'll probably find the latter method much simpler and certainly less error-prone; details are in Chapter 3.

When Windows installs itself, it adds these lines to **[Groups]**:

```
Group1=C:\WINDOWS\MAIN.GRP
Group2=C:\WINDOWS\ACCESSOR.GRP
Group3=C:\WINDOWS\GAMES.GRP
Group4=C:\WINDOWS\STARTUP.GRP
```

where the entries point to your **\windows** directory. If Windows recognizes any applications already residing on your hard disk during installation, it may also add a **Group5=C:\WINDOWS\APPLICAT.GRP** line to **[Groups]**.

***

Order=*Bogus Bogus Bogus*

***

 The official docs and almost every book I could find talk about the **Order=** entry in the **[Groups]** section. There's just one teensy-tiny problem. The **Order=** line is in the **[Settings]** section; a quick glance at your own **PROGMAN.INI** will convince you.

If you want to change the order in which groups' windows are painted on the screen (to control the way they overlap), look at **Order=** in the **[Settings]** section below. And ignore anything you might read to the contrary.

[Restrictions]

While the [Groups] section doesn't do much of anything — doesn't even do what little the docs say it will do — the [Restrictions] section works like a champ.

If you want to change anything in the [Restrictions] section, indeed, if you even want to add the section to **PROGMAN.INI,** you'll have to dive in with a text editor: when Windows installs itself, it doesn't even put in a [Restrictions] section. I think Microsoft intentionally made access to this section difficult, to keep beginners from accidentally shutting something off and to let more advanced users set things up in an obscure outpost of Windows civilization, to help keep novices from shooting themselves, self-inflicted wounds being the major cause of Windows trauma.

Everything in here can be overridden, of course. All it takes is a text editor and DOS; a couple of snips in **PROGMAN.INI** will change things back. These settings don't rate as an ultra-secure way to control Progman or Windows. Still, it's enough of a backwater that many users won't even think to look here when Progman locks them out.

Unless they've read MOM, of course, in which case you're SOL — this chapter not only tells you how to lock people out, it also tells you how to bypass the lockout settings quickly and easily.

EditLevel=_CodeNumber_

The **EditLevel=** setting gives you a lot of control over what can and cannot be done in Program Manager. It's a robust, well implemented entry. Too bad the other Windows applets don't have this kind of flexibility.

If the **EditLevel=** line is missing, or **EditLevel=0**, Program Manager will let you do all the usual things: (1) create, delete or rename groups; (2) create, delete, rename or move programs within the groups; (3) change the command lines (in the Program Item Properties box seen in Figure 10-2) of those programs; and (4) change the starting directories, icons, and descriptions of those programs.

```
┌─────────────────────────────────────────────────────────┐
│  ─          Program Item Properties                       │
├─────────────────────────────────────────────────────────┤
│  Description:      ┌──────────────────────┐  ┌──────────┐ │
│                    │ PackRat              │  │    OK    │ │
│  Command Line:     ├──────────────────────┤  └──────────┘ │
│                    │ C:\WINUTIL\PACKRAT\PACKRA│ ┌──────────┐│
│  Working Directory:├──────────────────────┤  │  Cancel  │ │
│                    │ C:\WINUTIL\PACKRAT   │  └──────────┘ │
│  Shortcut Key:     ├──────────────────────┤  ┌──────────┐ │
│                    │ Ctrl + Shift + P     │  │ Browse.. │ │
│                    └──────────────────────┘  └──────────┘ │
│      (icon)          □ Run Minimized         ┌──────────┐ │
│                                              │Change Icon..│
│                                              └──────────┘ │
│                                              ┌──────────┐ │
│                                              │   Help   │ │
│                                              └──────────┘ │
└─────────────────────────────────────────────────────────┘
```

Figure 10-2: Program Item Properties

If **EditLevel=1** (see Figure 10-3), Progman keeps you from creating, deleting, or renaming groups. It also keeps you from changing the **.GRP** file name associated with the group. With **EditLevel=1**, the Program Group Properties dialog box is grayed out:

```
┌─────────────────────────────────────────────────────────┐
│  ─          Program Group Properties                      │
├─────────────────────────────────────────────────────────┤
│  Description:   ┌──────────────────────────┐ ┌─────────┐ │
│                 │ HiJaak PRO               │ │   OK    │ │
│                 └──────────────────────────┘ └─────────┘ │
│  Group File:    ┌──────────────────────────┐ ┌─────────┐ │
│                 │ C:\WINDOWS\HIJAAKPR.GRP  │ │ Cancel  │ │
│                 └──────────────────────────┘ └─────────┘ │
│                                              ┌─────────┐ │
│                                              │  Help   │ │
│                                              └─────────┘ │
└─────────────────────────────────────────────────────────┘
```

Figure 10-3: EditLevel 1 Group Properties

 The official docs, and all the unofficial ones, say that setting **EditLevel=1** also grays out the Move and Copy choices in the File menu, when a group is selected. But Move and Copy are *always* grayed out when a group is selected. Sheesh. What're ya gonna move or copy a group *to*? The Move and Copy commands are there so you can move or copy programs, little icons, from one group to another. They don't work on groups; never have, never will.

Here's how Program Manager keeps you from creating new groups: if you select a group but not a program and click File, the New menu is grayed out. (You can only select a group without selecting a program by minimizing the group and clicking on it once.) If you select a program, though, and click File, then New, Progman jumps directly to the Program Item Properties dialog box, thus forcing you to create a new program item, keeping you from creating a new group. Slick.

This isn't a terribly restrictive setting. With **EditLevel=1**, Progman will still let you move or copy programs from one group to another, or add or delete programs from any group. It'll also let you maximize, move, resize or minimize any group. You're only prohibited from creating, deleting, or renaming a group.

With **EditLevel=2**, things crack down a bit harder. As with **EditLevel=1**, Progman keeps you from creating, deleting, or renaming groups. In addition, Progman keeps you from creating, deleting, moving or copying program items. You can't drag an icon from one group to another. In fact, you can't even *move* an icon around inside its group! The only way you can get an icon to budge is by turning on Auto Arrange in the Options menu, and resizing a group's window.

There's a loophole, though. When **EditLevel=2**, Progman will let you change anything in the Program Item Properties box. So, even though you can't create new icons or delete existing icons in a group, you can monkey with the Program Item Properties and change the program assigned to an icon, change its description, change its default directory, even *change the icon itself*.

At **EditLevel=3**, Progman does everything it does with **EditLevel=2**, and it grays out the Command Line entry in the Program Item Properties dialog box (see above). That's it. You're still free to change the description of the program, its starting directory, and its icon, you just can't change the command that invokes it.

With **EditLevel=4**, you get all the restrictions of **EditLevel=3**, plus Progman grays out everything else in the Program Item Properties dialog box. You can't change the description (i.e. the title that appears under the icon), starting directory or the icon itself. In effect, Progman lets you use everything, but change nothing.

Well, that's not quite accurate: you can still control the size of the groups, and you can minimize or maximize them, and fiddle with the menu settings. With Auto Arrange on, Progman will move around icons within a group. But that's it.

If you are setting up a user's system with EditLevel set to 1 or higher, consider making **progman.ini** read only as an extra level of protection.

NoClose=_1ForOn_

There are five "normal" ways to exit Windows from Progman. "Normal" in this case means "without shutting off the power or putting a .38 slug through the case." Go ahead, CyberPunk. Make my day.

Most folks click on File, then Exit, or they double-click on the hyphen thingy in the upper left corner of the Progman window. Those two are pretty normal. Some incorrigibles might click once on the hyphen thingy, then click Close. That's a nerd exit. Others know that pressing **Alt+F4** will kill Windows. And some just go for the all-purpose **Ctrl+Alt+Del** Vulcan nerve pinch.

Hehe, Mao, I've got a sixth way which I'll let you in on at the end of this section after the readers have had a chance to think on it.

If **NoClose=1**, Progman disables all of its available means of exit except the Vulcan nerve pinch. (If you have a program that restarts Windows, like Roger's Rapid Restart or OH, Mon! — both of which are on CD MOM — they aren't affected. This is strictly a Progman setting.)

This is a cruel setting, one that should only be used if you must absolutely ensure that Windows is always running on the afflicted machine. Sometimes you can't hold it any more: your Free System Resources run out, and you have to get out of Windows. Setting **NoClose=1** makes exiting and restarting Windows a painful, drawn-out process, requiring a re-boot along the way.

NoFileMenu=_1ForOn_

If **NoFileMenu=1**, Progman completely removes the File menu from its menu bar (see Figure 10-4).

You won't see it at all.

File	Options	Window	Help

New...	
Open	Enter
Move...	F7
Copy...	F8
Delete	Del
Properties...	Alt+Enter
Run...	
Exit Windows...	

Figure 10-4: Program Manager's File Menu

The commands that are normally available from the File menu are no longer accessible from the menu (hey, the menu isn't even there!), and most of the shortcut keys are disabled too. **F7**, **F8**, **Del**, and **Alt+Enter** won't work with **NoFileMenu=1**.

Enter still cranks up the highlighted program, though. You can still exit by double-clicking on the hyphen thingy, clicking once on the hyphen and clicking Close, or hitting **Alt+F4**. And you can still run programs through the File Manager.

NoRun=*1ForOn*

Setting **NoRun=1** in **[Restrictions]** tells Progman that it should gray out the "Run" command on the File menu. Anybody who's savvy enough to use File/Run, though, is probably capable of working around this setting; it isn't difficult.

Let's see. With File/Run grayed out, what's left?

Well, you can still run programs by double-clicking on them in File Manager. And any of the Windows batch (or macro) languages will still run. If worse comes to worst, you could always click on any convenient program icon, click File then Properties, and change the icon to crank up whichever program you like. There are many, many ways to skin this cat.

NoSaveSettings=*1ForOn*

This is one of the most useful settings in any of Windows' `.INI` files. It's particularly useful if you are setting up Windows for a novice; it may keep them from shooting themselves in the foot.

The Program Manager Options menu has three on/off choices. The one we're concerned with here is the "Save Settings on Exit" choice: it controls whether changes made to the size and location of groups and icons under Progman are saved from one Windows session to the next.

If **NoSaveSettings=1**, Progman completely disables the "Save Settings on Exit" choice: it turns gray, and there's no way you can click on it. More, Progman disables all the other tricky ways it has to save settings: even the venerable **Shift+** double-click on the hyphen thingy trick, which usually saves the current state of the desktop, won't work. With **NoSaveSettings=1**, nothing you do short of adding or deleting a group will change the appearance of the desktop.

(The way Progman figures out which settings are worth saving is a bit complex; see **SaveSettings=** below for a detailed explanation.)

If you want to set up Windows for a novice so it's harder to clobber, consider putting this line in **[Restrictions]**. It won't prevent the user from deleting groups or icons — and won't rescue them if they do. It has a lousy way of displaying newly created groups. Still, the **NoSaveSettings=1** entry will go a long way toward assuring the user that Windows will restart in some semblance of an earlier state. That can be mighty comforting in an overwhelming new world.

[Settings]

This section contains miscellaneous settings that concern Progman. Three of them fall under Progman's Options menu (see Figure 10-5).

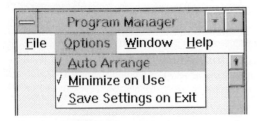

Figure 10-5: Program Manager's Options

AutoArrange=*1ForOn*

If the "Auto Arrange" menu item is checked, Progman will rearrange all icons so they're evenly spaced (see the **IconSpacing=** entry in the **[Desktop]** section of **WIN.INI**). Whenever you check Auto Arrange, or if Auto Arrange is on and you change the size of a group, or do anything to an icon — move one, add or delete one — Progman scans all the visible groups and rearranges icons.

If you change the check mark on Auto Arrange, Progman immediately re-writes **PROGMAN.INI** to reflect the change: **AutoArrange=0** means that Auto Arrange is currently off, **1** means it's on.

When Windows installs itself, it doesn't put this line in **[Settings]**, which is the same as **AutoArrange=0**.

---

display.drv=*FileName*

I have no idea why this entry is here. It makes absolutely no sense. It better be the same as the **display.drv=** setting in the **[boot]** section of **SYSTEM.INI**, or your machine is well on its way to crashing. The official docs don't even mention the setting, but when Windows installs itself it puts a line like this:

```
display.drv=vga.drv
```

in **[Settings]**. If you're tempted to change it, be sure you look at **[boot]** before diving off the deep end.

MinOnRun=*1ForOn*

If the "Minimize On Use" menu item is checked, Progman will minimize itself immediately before running a program. That can be very handy if you run programs that don't fill up the whole screen (e.g., Visual Basic), and you don't want to see the Program Manager desktop leak through.

When you change the check mark on "Minimize On Use," Progman immediately re-writes **PROGMAN.INI** to reflect the change: **MinOnRun=0** means that Minimize on Use is currently off, **1** means it's on.

When Windows installs itself, it doesn't put this line in **[Settings]**. No entry at all is the same as **MinOnRun=0**.

Order=*WindowNumber WindowNumber* ...

I've only seen one book (*Tuning Windows 3.1*, Neuman *et al*) that got this entry right. According to the official docs, this line should go in **[Groups]**. But if you put it there, it won't do anything. Try it yourself. You'll see.

 To work, **Order=** must be in **[Settings]**. Don't believe anything else you might read.

The line looks like this:

Order=8 17 3 1 2 4 9 10

where the numbers correspond to the group numbers *n* in the **Group*n*=** lines of the **[Groups]** section. The numbers establish the order in which groups are drawn on the desktop, the first-numbered group drawn first, then the second, and so on. The last group in the list gets drawn over the top of everybody. That lets you paint one group on top of another, or overlap the groups' windows any which-way you like. Nice.

If you have **SaveSettings=1** (see next), Program Manager resets this line every time you exit Windows. If **SaveSettings=0**, the painting order of the groups is unchanged. There's some fancy footwork with newly created and deleted groups (which might not appear in the **Order=** line). The last drawn group, typically the last group in the **Order=** list, is the one that is highlighted, the one that receives focus, when Progman starts. See **SaveSettings=** for details.

SaveSettings=*1ForOn*

If the "Save Settings On Exit" menu item is checked, Progman will save the configuration of the desktop when you leave Windows, and restore the desktop when you come back to Progman.

When you change the check mark on "Save Settings on Exit", Progman immediately re-writes **PROGMAN.INI** to reflect the change: **SaveSettings=0** means that Save Settings on Exit is currently off, **1** means it's on.

If you have a **NoSaveSettings=1** line in the **[Restrictions]** section of **PROGMAN.INI** when Program Manager is first cranked up (generally, when you start Windows), the value of the **SaveSettings=** line is ignored, Progman behaves as if **SaveSettings=0**, and the "Save Settings On Exit" choice in the Options menu is grayed out so it can't be changed.

So much for the mechanics. Now to the heart of the matter...

Which Settings are Saved? Surprisingly, that isn't a simple question at all. The answer... well, it depends.

If **SaveSettings=1**, Program Manager saves the current location of every icon, and the size, location, and maximized/minimized status of each group. In short, Progman remembers everything, and brings it all back the next time it's started.

If **SaveSettings=0**, though, the situation is a bit more complex. Say you start Windows, delete a group, leave **SaveSettings=0**, and restart Windows. You wouldn't expect Windows to show the deleted group when it's restarted — and in fact it doesn't. Whatever used to lie below the deleted group shows through; the deleted group is gone. That's great.

If you start Windows, add a group, leave **SaveSettings=0**, and restart Windows, you might expect Progman to remember the last size and location of the new group, but it doesn't. Instead, when restarted, Progman redraws the new group in the precise location that it originally appeared when you created it. So if you start Windows, go into Progman and add a group, then minimize the new group, say, and restart Windows, that new group will not be minimized within Progman. The new group shows up in precisely the location it originally occupied, back when you created it.

Strange, eh?

Wait. It gets stranger.

With **SaveSettings=0**, if you move an icon within a group, then restart Windows, Progman moves the icon back whence it came. That's reasonable. If you create a new program item icon and restart Windows, it shows up in the location it originally occupied, back when you created it. That's reasonable too.

But deleting icons gets screwy. If you start Windows with **SaveSettings=0**, delete an icon in the middle of a group, and restart Windows, Progman's behavior seems to depend on the AutoArrange setting! If **AutoArrange=0**, Progman leaves a hole where the old icon once stood. But if **AutoArrange=1**, the icons are re-spaced, the hole filled.

The status of the three Options menu items — Auto Arrange, Minimize on Use, and Save Settings on Exit — is always saved, whether **SaveSettings=0** or **1**. Contrariwise, the location and size of the Progman window is only saved if **SaveSettings=1**.

When Windows installs itself, it doesn't put this entry in **[Settings]**. No entry at all is the same as **SaveSettings=0**.

Startup=*GroupName*

When Program Manager starts, it can automatically launch all the applications in a pre-determined group. This line tells Progman which group contains the apps that should be launched when Progman starts.

If there is no such entry, or if **Startup=Startup**, Progman launches all the applications in the group called Startup. When Windows installs itself, it doesn't put this line in **[Settings]**, so unless you change it manually, Progman will always launch all the apps in the group called Startup.

Progman is looking for the group name, not a file name. The group name appears in the group's window title, or as the icon text when the group is minimized. If you have a group called "Misc Stuff" connected to the file **c:\windows\glop.grp** (to see the associated **.GRP** file, click once on the minimized group icon, click File, then Properties), you want a line that looks like this:

Startup=Misc Stuff

Capitalization isn't important, but spaces are very important. No need to put quotes around the name.

If Progman hits a group name it doesn't understand or if you have a line that looks like

Startup=

with no group name, Progman doesn't launch any apps when it starts.

If you want to bypass the running of apps in this Startup group, hold down the **Shift** key while Windows is starting — I always do it when Windows starts flashing its "Flying Window" screen. Progman comes to life, along with the **run=** and **load=** programs from the **[windows]** section of **WIN.INI**, but none of the Startup group's programs are run.

Window=*Left Top Width Height MaxOrMin*

This line tells Progman about the size and location of its window, along with an indication about whether it was last maximized, minimized, or floating.

Measurements are in pixels.

When MaxOrMin is 0, Progman uses the other four numbers to determine the size and location of the screen. When MaxOrMin is 1, Progman maximizes the screen. And when MaxOrMin is 2, Progman minimizes its window — turns itself into an icon. These settings only affect how Progman appears when Windows is started, and can be overridden by the **MinOnRun=** value. (Progman minimizes itself when it first runs if **MinOnRun=1**.) Anything you do to the window after it first appears will override these settings.

On a 1024 x 768 Super VGA screen, for example, I like to use this:

Window=0 0 1024 768 0

That tells Progman to start itself out floating (i.e., not maximized or minimized), but to take up the whole screen.

Progman may or may not change this line automatically, depending on the **SaveSettings=** entry.

OK, grasshopper, what's the sixth way to end ProgMan?

Call up TaskMan, highlight Program Manager and hit the **End Task** button.

CONTROL.INI

Windows' Control Panel can jump through quite a few hoops. This **.INI** file keeps it in line.

You can run any Control Panel applet by clicking on File, then Run, and typing in CONTROL followed by the applet's name. You can also assign any Control Panel applet to the Program Manager's desktop by creating a new icon, just as you would for any program, and typing CONTROL followed by the applet's name in the Command Line box. For example

```
control international
```

when used from File Run, or in a program item's Command Line, would crank up the Control Panel's International applet.

The Control Panel re-reads **CONTROL.INI** every time it's started. Thus, you shouldn't have to re-start Windows each time you make a change to **CONTROL.INI**; changes you make should take effect with the next time you start Control Panel.

[color schemes]

Here live all the pre-defined and custom Windows color schemes available to you: these are the names that appear in the Color Schemes box of the Control Panel's Color applet. Each color scheme is a collection of 21 colors, expressed as a hex string. They look like this:

```
Mine062293=FFFFFF,80FFFF,FFFFFF,0,FFFFFF,0,F0C8A4,FFFFFF,0,C
0C0C0,C0C0C0,0,C0C0C0,C0C0C0,808080,0,C0C0C0,F0C8A4,0,0,FFFF
FF
```

In this example, the color scheme called **Mine062293** consists of the indicated 21 colors, one for each of the 21 lines in the **[colors]** section of **WIN.INI**. (Those are for Background, AppWorkspace, Window, WindowText, Menu, MenuText, ActiveTitle, InactiveTitle, TitleText, ActiveBorder, InactiveBorder, WindowFrame, Scrollbar, ButtonFace, ButtonShadow, ButtonText, GrayText, Hilight, HilightText, InactiveTitleText, and ButtonHilight.)

If you create your own custom color scheme using the Control Panel's Colors applet, and give it a name, the scheme will appear here along with all the others.

 If you've ever wondered how to copy a custom color scheme from one computer to another, here it is. Simply take the appropriate entry from one system's **[color schemes]** section of **CONTROL.INI**, and put it in the other. Magically, the transferred color scheme will appear as an option in the Colors applet on the new machine, and the identical color setup will be available.

Windows ships with 22 predefined color schemes: Arizona, Black Leather Jacket, Bordeaux, Cinnamon, Designer, Emerald City, Fluorescent, Hotdog Stand, LCD Default Screen Settings, LCD Reversed - Dark, LCD Reversed - Light, Mahogany, Monochrome, Ocean, Pastel, Patchwork, Plasma Power Saver, Rugby, The Blues, Tweed, Valentine, and Wingtips.

The translation between hex color numbers here in **CONTROL.INI** and the decimal color number triplets in the **[color]** section of **WIN.INI** is just another bit of obfuscation. For more details about colors, see **[color]** in **WIN.INI**.

[current]

This section has but one entry, and its only use is as a reminder to the Color applet in the Control Panel about which color scheme is the one currently in use. When Windows installs itself it puts this line in **[current]**:

```
color schemes=Windows Default
```

Note that changing this value in **[current]** will not change the colors on the desktop! It will just change the name of the color scheme shown in the Color applet's dialog box.

[Custom Colors]

In addition to Windows' standard palette, you may use the Color applet's custom color routine to build and store away your own colors, to a maximum of 21 custom colors. If you create a custom color, it is stored here in **CONTROL.INI**. You may move custom colors between machines by copying **[Custom Colors]** entries, in much the same way as described earlier for color schemes — see Figure 10-6.

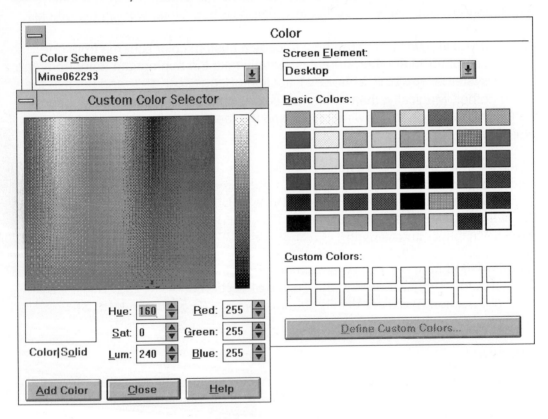

Figure 10-6: Define Custom Colors

The individual colors are only identified in **[Custom Colors]** by a letter, from A to P. When Windows installs itself it adds 21 custom colors, all white, with these entries:

```
ColorA=FFFFFF
ColorB=FFFFFF
ColorC=FFFFFF
ColorD=FFFFFF
ColorE=FFFFFF
ColorF=FFFFFF
ColorG=FFFFFF
ColorH=FFFFFF
ColorI=FFFFFF
ColorJ=FFFFFF
ColorK=FFFFFF
ColorL=FFFFFF
ColorM=FFFFFF
ColorN=FFFFFF
ColorO=FFFFFF
ColorP=FFFFFF
```

Yawwwwwwwwwwn.

[don't load]

Here's one to perk you up. I haven't seen any mention of it in the official docs.

You can tell Control Panel, in effect, "Yo! Next time you start, don't show the Colors applet or the 386 Enhanced applet." Pretty neat, eh?

If you create a **[don't load]** section (yeah, with the apostrophe and the space, just like that), put the name of any applet on the left of the equals sign, and put any value at all to the right of the equals sign, that applet won't appear in the Control Panel, next time it starts! This section:

```
[don't load]
Fonts=1
Ports=0
Desktop=zap
```

in **CONTROL.INI** will force Control Panel to completely forget about the applets called Fonts, Ports, and Desktop, the next time it starts. Just use the applet name — the name that appears below the icon in the Control Panel — to the left of the equals sign, and anything but a blank to the right.

[drivers.desc]

This section ties a text description of multimedia drivers to the entries in the **[drivers]** section of **SYSTEM.INI**. It's entirely cosmetic: Control Panel uses the text to the right of the equals sign so it can present something intelligible to the user.

Your **[drivers.desc]** might look like this:

```
mciwave.drv=[MCI] Sound
mciseq.drv=[MCI] MIDI Sequencer
timer.drv=Timer
midimap.drv=MIDI Mapper
```

Each **.DRV** file listed to the left of the equals sign is probably in the **[drivers]** section of **SYSTEM.INI**, too.

[installed]

This is a handy catch-all place Windows uses to list which drivers (primarily printer drivers) are currently installed. Control Panel makes use of the list to splash this kind of dialog box up on your screen (see Figure 10-7).

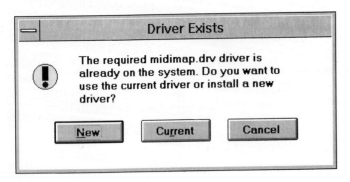

Figure 10-7: Got Yer Driver

The entries are particularly unenlightening as every entry always seems to have yes as a value. Here's a typical list:

```
3.1=yes
HPPCL5A.DRV=yes
HPPCL5A.HLP=yes
HPPCL5OP.HLP=yes
TTY.DRV=yes
TTY.HLP=yes
HPDSKJET.DRV=yes
UNIDRV.DLL=yes
UNIDRV.HLP=yes
FINSTALL.HLP=yes
FINSTALL.DLL=yes
PSCRIPT.DRV=yes
PSCRIPT.HLP=yes
TESTPS.TXT=yes
LANGENG.DLL=yes
LANGSCA.DLL=yes
LANGFRN.DLL=yes
```

[MMCPL]

 Don't let the "MM" throw you. These are settings that apply to the care and feeding of the Control Panel dialog box itself. "MM" must stand for "Multimedia," but I'll be hornswaggled if I can figure out why. The Control Panel controls all sorts of things, not just multimedia.

You'll see references to "Multimedia Control Panel" in many books, including all the official docs. Don't worry. They're just using a funny name for our good ol' everyday Control Panel.

A typical **[MMCPL]** section might look like this:

```
NumApps=12
X=0
Y=0
W=430
H=240
```

NumApps= is the number of applets that last appeared in the Control Panel (see Chapter 4 for a lengthy discussion of how and when and why applets appear and disappear). **X=** is the distance from the left side of the Control Panel dialog box to the left side of the screen. **Y=** is the distance from the top of the dialog box to the top of the screen. **W=** is the width and **H=** is the height. All measurements are in pixels.

This section can also have the names of Dynamic Link Libraries, DLLs, that have Control Panel applets hidden in them. For example

ODBC=C:\WINDOWS\SYSTEM\ODBCINST.DLL

This line tells Control Panel to search the indicated DLL for applets; if any are found, they're added to the Control Panel display. The actual name and icon are taken from the DLL so the key to the left of the = has no meaning to Control Panel and is for your aid only (I changed ODBC= to Igor= and the applet still appeared with the name ODBC).

[Patterns]

This is a repository for pattern settings, a handy way to store away patterns for the Desktop applet in the Control Panel. When the Desktop applet hands you a list of Pattern Names, those names come from here.

The numbers are rather strange. See the **[Desktop]** section under **WIN.INI** for a complete description. Here's my first few entries:

```
(None)=(None)
Boxes=127 65 65 65 65 65 127 0
Paisley=2 7 7 2 32 80 80 32
Weave=136 84 34 69 136 21 34 81
```

As with the Color Scheme and Custom Color settings, you can create and copy patterns by simply moving the appropriate line from one Windows setup to another.

[Screen Saver] and the Like

If you use the Desktop applet to run Windows' screen saver, several sections may be created, each keyed to a different screen saver (see Figure 10-8). Windows does not create this section when it is installed.

Other screen saver programs (e.g., After Dark, Intermission) also stick settings in **CONTROL.INI**. You'll have to ask the manufacturer for details about their entries.

There is one important setting in this section: **PWProtect=**. (Some of the Windows screen savers call it **PWProtected=**.) It controls password protection with the standard Windows screen saver. If **PWProtect=1**, Windows requires you to enter a password before it will clear off the screen saver. If the line is missing or **PWProtect=0**, the built-in Windows screen saver does not require a password. It's the same thing as selecting a Screen Saver name in the Desktop applet, clicking the Setup button, and checking the Password box.

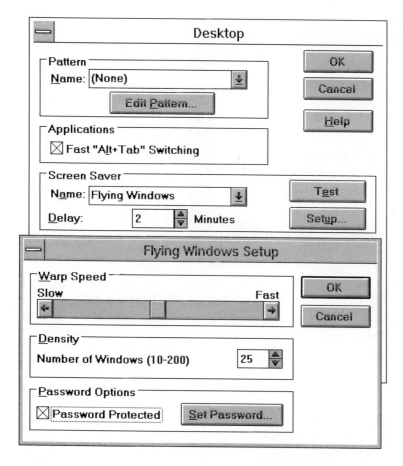

Figure 10-8: Screen Saver Settings in the Desktop Applet

If you're poking around this setting, chances are good you're the victim of some turkey who thought they'd be funny and turn on password protection with one of the Windows screen savers. Then again, it is possible you turned on password protection yourself and forgot (or mis-typed) the password.

If you want to bypass the standard Windows screen saver password "protection", just hit **Ctrl+Alt+Del** and restart Windows. As soon as Windows restarts, go into the Desktop applet in the Control Panel, click Setup, and clear out the "Password Protected" checkbox and click OK all the way back out. That's all it takes; that's how much "protection" this setting provides (see Figure 10-9)

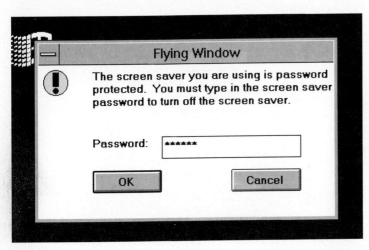

Figure 10-9: Feed Me

 Oh. The standard Windows screen saver's password itself is stored in this section, in the entry called **Password=**. If you try setting a password and then look at **CONTROL.INI**, you'll see that the **Password=** value is encrypted: the password **justin**, for example, turns into

```
Password=4TgxO2
```

Windows scrambles the password you typed and stores the scrambled password in **CONTROL.INI**. Whenever Windows asks you for a password, it takes whatever you type and scrambles it the same way, then compares the resulting nonsense with the **Password=** setting. I only mention that to assure you that you're not going nuts: the password you type into the screen saver's dialog box is not the same as the value you'll see for `Password=`.

Bypassing Windows' password "protection" is so simple, there's not much sense in monkeying around with the `Password=` setting.

[Userinstallable.drivers]

I'm not sure *what* this section does. I have a line that looks like this:

```
CDAudio=mcicda.drv
```

and it doesn't seem to do anything but sit there. Mao has seven entries in his. The Windows Resource Kit talks about it, but only in its usual obfuscatory chain of nonstop nonsense syllables.

DOSAPP.INI

Windows stores information about locations and options for DOS sessions in a file called **dosapp.ini** which is stored in the Windows directory. It tracks your preferences on a program by program basis. The file should be updated automatically by Windows whenever you exit a DOS program or session and does not seem to be documented anywhere. To satisfy your curiosity about what the long string of numbers means, I'll describe what my spelunking in the file has turned up.

There is a single section entitled **[DOS Applications]**. The variables in the section are the filenames of pif or exe files. Normally they have full pathnames, for example

```
C:\WINDOWS\DOSPRMPT.PIF=1 8 12 652 390 22 0 1 65535 65535
123 19 123 19 775 435
```

(the line wraps in this book but it is a single line in the file).

Occasionally, an entry appears without a path before the exe or pif name but I've not been able to figure out when that happens.

To the right of the = sign appears either 1 or 17 positive numbers between 0 and 65535 (64K minus 1). One number rather than 17 appears if and only if you have always run the program full screen. Hit **Alt+Enter** twice to momentarily run in a DOS windowed session and exit the session and you'll get 17 numbers instead of 1. If there is only one number, its value is 1.

When there are 17 numbers, I'll call them n1, n2,. . ., n17. Here is their values and meaning briefly with more details below:

Number	Values	Meaning
n1	0 or 1	State of **Save Setting on Exit** check box in the **Font Selection** dialog box for the session. 1=checked; 0=not checked. Determines whether all 17 numbers are saved on exit. This is used when you make a session at a later date.
n2,n3	4-18	The size in pixels of the font used in the DOS session (can be other than 4-18 if you are using a third party variant of one of the five font files discussed in the **DOS fonts** section of Chapter 3). n2 is the width; n3 is the height. In the above example, the font is 8x12, i.e. 8 pixels wide and 12 high. This is used when you make a session at a later date.
n4,n5	varies	Idealized size (n4 pixels wide; n5 high) of maximized window. Determined by n2,n3 and the Border Width set in the desktop applet. Discussed below.
n6	22	Discussed below.
n7	0 or 2	Determines whether the last state of the session when neither minimized nor full screen was normal (n7=0) or maximized (n7=2). This is used when you make a session at a later date if and only if you start the session windowed. If you start it full screen and hit **Alt+Enter**, the window will be normal even if n7 is 2. Discussed below.
n8	1,2 or 3	Determines the state when you last exited the session. 1=normal, 2=full screen or iconized, 3=maximized. You'll only exit with the session iconized if you use the Terminate button in settings. This is **not** used when you make a session at a later date. Discussed below

n9, n10	65,535	Discussed below.
n11,n12	varies	Location in pixels of upper left corner of window when last in a maximized state. If you've never run maximized or the maximized state is identical to the normal state, both numbers are 65,535 although sometime it appears as 65,530 (bug alert!). This is used when you make a session at a later date.
n13,n14	varies	Location in pixels of upper left corner of the window when last in a normal state. This is used when you make a session at a later date.
n15,n16	varies	Location in pixels of lower right corner of the window when last in a normal state. This is used when you make a session at a later date.

It may seem strange that the three fixed values n6, n9 and n10 are stored but there is a reason. The last eleven numbers form a structure described in the SDK called a WindowPlacement structure. Its first number is the number of bytes in the structure which is 11x2=22 (2 bytes for each unsigned integer) which is why n6=22. Values that are always the same like n11,n12 are carried over to have the whole structure in place to pass to Windows.

n4 and n5 seem to be determined by the formulae:

n4 = cols*n2 + borwid*2 + 2

n5 = rows*n3 + borwid*2 + 30

where cols and rows are the number of columns and rows in the last text mode used (usually 80 and 25) and borwid is the border width as set in the Desktop applet of Control Panel. The 30 extra pixels in the n5 are for the height of the title bar.

In the sample line above, borwid=5, rows=25 and cols=80.

These are idealized numbers. If the normal session is stretched to be as large as possible, you'd expect that

n15 = n13 + n4

and that

n16 = n14 + n5

but in the sample line above only the n15 formulae is valid and that the n16 number seems to be saying that the height of the window is 26 pixels more than the maximum window size would allow. That's because on Mao's machine *EDOS* was running and it adds a menu bar to windowed DOS sessions so there were an extra 26 pixels in the actual window size which is what n15,n16 measure. But n4,n5 seem to be idealized numbers and I don't see any place that they are used by the session.

 The n9,n10 numbers correspond (in the WindowPlacement structure) to the location of the icon when minimized. It appears that the values 65,535 65,535 tell Windows to place the icon where it wishes. Even if you change these numbers by hand, Windows changes them back to 65,535 65,535 and ignores the numbers you put in.

Possible values for the pair (n7,n8) are (0,1) and (2,3) if you exited normally from a windowed session and (0,2) or (2,2) if you exited from a full screen mode.

And now you know the rest of the story. . .

WINFILE.INI

File Manager stores its settings in this file — in a section called, disingenuously, `[Settings]`.

Everything in `[Settings]` can be controlled by making the appropriate (and obvious!) choices in File Manager. No need to bother with **WINFILE.INI** at all — File Manager will take care of it for you.

There can also be an **[AddOns]** section of **winfile.ini**; see the discussion in Chapter 3.

WIN.COM

> The deed disappears when the doer is annihilated.
> The deed has no function apart from the doer;
> The doer has no function apart from the deed.
>
> — *Seng Ts'an's Poem on Trust in the Heart*, ca 600 A.D.

It's hard to believe, but the main program that gets Windows started is a Lilliputian, a little 5K-or-less file called `WIN.COM`. When you type `win` at the DOS prompt, you're invoking the diminutive `WIN.COM`.

Small things come in good packages, eh?

`WIN.COM` is a loader. Its sole purpose in life is to slap something on the screen — *fast!* — to tell you that Windows is coming, and then crank up Windows itself. It's a psychological thing: Microsoft discovered long ago that you will feel better if the computer seems to be doing something immediately, in response to your commands. Thus, `WIN.COM` was designed to give you a bit of instant gratification, to make you feel like Windows is getting started quickly. Figure 10-10 shows the Windows startup screen.

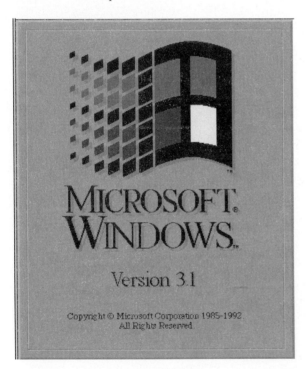

Figure 10-10: The Windows Startup Screen

Most of `WIN.COM` is just the picture that goes on the screen.

Chances are very good that the reason you're reading this right now is that you want to get rid of Microsoft's screen and replace it with one of your own. Your wish is Mom's command. . .

Windows Startup Screen

 Yes, you can change the screen that Windows uses on startup. It's much simpler than you might think. All you need is an .RLE file, a run-length-encoded picture. (See Chapter 3 for a discussion of graphic file types.) Here's all you need to do. Note that this won't work if you're using CGA or EGA graphics.

1. Get your **.RLE** file going. Several graphics viewer/converter programs will change any file you might have into an **.RLE** file. I wanted Windows to start with Mom's smiling face, so I used Hijaak Pro to change Mom's picture from a **MOM.WMF** to **MOM.RLE**. You might want to start with a **.PCX** or a **.BMP**. No sweat.

2. Back up **WIN.COM** in your Windows directory, typically **c:\windows,** and **VGALOGO.RLE** in your system directory, typically **c:\windows\system**. You won't be needing either of them any more, but it doesn't hurt to keep extra copies should something go awry.

3. Move your **.RLE** file into the system directory, and rename it **VGALOGO.RLE**.

4. Now we're going to trick Windows into re-creating **WIN.COM**. Double-click on the Windows Setup icon. Unless you've moved it, it's sitting in Program Manager's MAIN group.

5. Click Options, then Change System Settings. Make a note of which video driver you're currently using, then change the driver. Doesn't matter which one you pick, although it'll be easier if you pick one that has the files already installed, otherwise you'll have to break out the original Windows diskettes.

    Personally, I always switch over to the standard Windows VGA driver, because I know the files are already on my hard disk. They probably are on your system, too.

    If you're asked, click YES, you do want to use the currently installed driver.

6. Click OK. You'll be asked if you want to restart Windows. You don't. Click Continue. You might hear your hard disk whir a bit. That's good. Windows is rebuilding **WIN.COM**. See Figure 10-11.

Figure 10-11: Continue, Continue

7. Now, *immediately go back and pick your original video driver!* YES, you do want to use the currently installed driver. Click OK. You'll be asked once again if you want to restart Windows. There's no need to, really, so click Continue.

That's all it takes. Next time you start Windows, you'll get your own **.RLE** file up on the screen, instead of the Microsoft ad.

Neat, huh?

Windows Startup Parameters

 WIN.COM will take a few startup switches and other parameters that force Windows to start in a particular way. If you type **win /s** at the DOS prompt, for example, Windows will be forced to start in standard mode.

Here are the ones we know about. For step-by-step instructions on using the /switches, be sure you look at the troubleshooting advice in Appendix 4.

You can tell Windows to start with a specific program loaded and ready for bear. For example, the DOS command line

```
win winword
```

will start Windows with Word for Windows up and going, assuming Windows can find the program called **winword** in the Windows or system directories, or along the DOS path.

In fact, anything that you could type into Program Manager's File/Run menu will work here. The Registration database is in full effect; file name extensions are recognized. If Windows is smart enough to know that all **.DOC** files are WinWord files, for example, this line

```
win mom.doc
```

starts Windows with Word for Windows running, and the file **mom.doc** already loaded. The easiest way to teach Windows which file extensions belong to which programs is via File Manager; see the discussion of **WIN.INI**'s **[Extensions]** section in Chapter 8.

The **/2** and **/s** switches both force Windows to start in Standard mode. They can be mixed with startup file names, providing you put the file name after the switch. Both of these commands will get Windows going in Standard mode:

```
win /s
win /2 mom.doc
```

the second line also starts WinWord with **mom.doc** loaded.

 You might find yourself starting Windows in standard mode if it locks up when started in Enhanced mode: on very rare occasions memory conflicts will allow Windows to start Standard but not Enhanced — and those kinds of conflicts are becoming more rare every day. See Appendix 4, Mom's HAAAALP discourse, if you can't get Windows to start.

The /e and **/3** switches forces Windows to start in Enhanced mode.

If you have an 80386, 80486, or Pentium-based PC with at least 1 MB of extended memory (in addition to the usual 640K of lower memory), Windows normally starts in Enhanced mode. It only reverts to Standard mode if determines that it can't start in Enhanced, typically because it isn't finding enough memory.

You would only use this switch if you want to override Windows' auto sensing. You may well end up crashing Windows, too, in the process.

The **/b** switch tells Windows to write out a log of every action it's taking as it boots. That can be useful if Windows freezes on startup. The log is written to a regular text file called **BOOTLOG.TXT**.

Windows has four **/d** switches, each of which disables a particular feature of Enhanced mode. If Windows will run in Enhanced mode with any of these switches set, there's a corresponding entry in **SYSTEM.INI**'s **[386Enh]** section that will make the change permanent..

win /d:f disables FastDisk. It's tied to the **32BitAccess=** setting.

win /d:s disables ROM breakpoints in upper memory. Look at the entry for **SystemROMBreakPoint=**.

win /d:v disables Windows' attempts at handling hard disks. See **VirtualHDIRQ=**.

win /d:x keeps Windows from looking at upper memory. See **EMMExclude=**.

Finally, you can force **WIN.COM** to skip the display of the startup screen entirely by typing this at the DOS prompt:

win :

Yeah, that's a space and a colon. Some folks have reported bizarre behavior when the colon option is used; personally, I've never hit a problem with it. If you time Windows startup with and without the startup screen, though, you'll find that showing the screen adds no perceptible overhead. So why turn it off? If you don't like the Microsoft ad flashing on the screen, use the instructions above to create your own.

Autoexec.Bat, Config.Sys Windows Style

While there are a few troubleshooting hints that require changes to **AUTOEXEC.BAT** and **CONFIG.SYS**, the basic rules are pretty simple. **CONFIG.SYS** should have **FILES=60**, **BUFFERS=20**, and **STACKS=9,256**. Be sure to have **DOS=HIGH** or **DOS=HIGH,UMB**.

If you are running SMARTDrive and don't have a tape backup or CD, you can decrease BUFFERS to 8 — but it won't save anything because if DOS=HIGH, buffers are also stored in the HMA region.

Lots of books — even Microsoft itself — will tell you to add the Windows directory to your **PATH**. Don't you believe it. Once Windows starts, the standard Windows search routine looks in the Windows directory before it even thinks about your path. So the only reason why you might want it in your path is to be able to start Windows from anyplace you'd like. If you run Windows all the time and start it from your **AUTOEXEC.BAT**, there's no reason at all to put the Windows directory in your path statement.

I finally found a reason to include the Windows directory in my path but that was because I use EDOS. EDOS lets you type the name of a Windows application at the command line in a DOS session under Windows. When you do that EDOS will switch to the Windows screen and start the Winapp. EDOS gets the program name from DOS, and DOS is only smart enough to look in its PATH; it will ignore the Windows directory unless you put it in explicitly.

You can change the prompt DOS uses while it's running under Windows by modifying **AUTOEXEC.BAT**. See the discussion of **DOSPromptExitInstruc=** in **SYSTEM.INI**'s **[386Enh]** section, Chapter 9.

Samples

Here's a very simple, effective starting point for Windows, should you ever reach the point where you've thrown up your hands and want to start over with a clean boot. I'll show you the commands valid for DOS 5.0 or later, where Windows is in **c:\windows** and DOS is in **c:\dos**; if you keep Windows or DOS in different subdirectories, you'll have to change these lines to point to them.

For **AUTOEXEC.BAT**:

```
PROMPT $p$g
PATH C:\DOS
C:\DOS\SMARTDRV.EXE
SET TEMP=C:\windows\temp
cd c:\windows
WIN
```

For **CONFIG.SYS**:

```
BUFFERS=15,0
FILES=60
STACKS=9,256
DEVICE=C:\DOS\SETVER.EXE
DEVICE=C:\DOS\HIMEM.SYS
SHELL=C:\DOS\COMMAND.COM C:\DOS\   /p
```

If everything works well with those lines, try adding these at the end, in this order:

```
DEVICE=C:\DOS\EMM386.EXE
DOS=HIGH,UMB
```

Almost every modern system I've seen will work — and work well! — with those settings. If you have DOS 6 or later and want to use MEMMAKER, or any other memory squisher, start with an **AUTOEXEC** and **CONFIG** like these, and then let the squisher take its licks.

SMARTDrive

SMARTDrive is now up to version 4.2 (at least!). Chances are good you're still running version 4.0 or 4.1. *MOM* to the rescue. To see what SMARTDrive is up to, hop over to the DOS prompt and type **smartdrv** (see Figure 10-12).

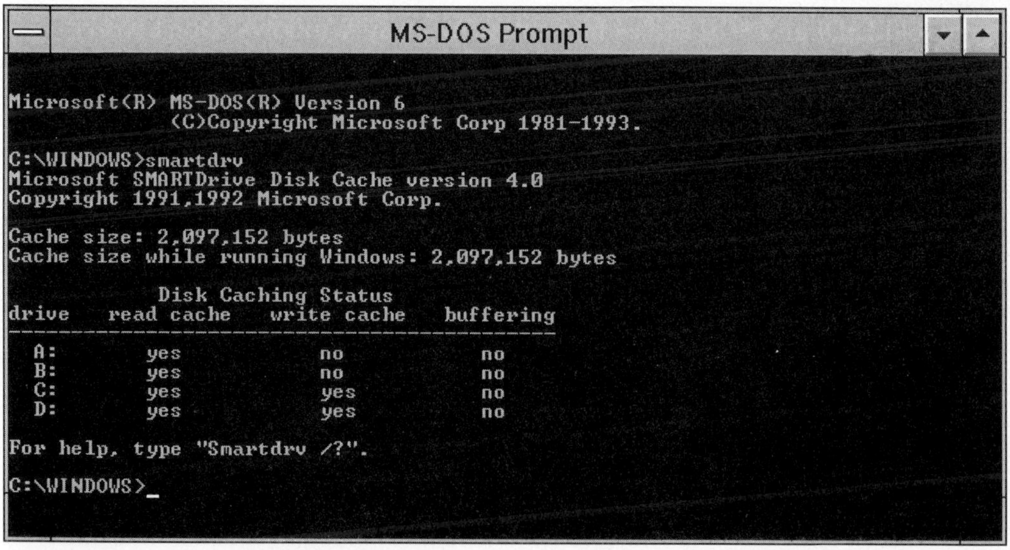

```
                            MS-DOS Prompt                          ▼  ▲

Microsoft(R) MS-DOS(R) Version 6
          (C)Copyright Microsoft Corp 1981-1993.

C:\WINDOWS>smartdrv
Microsoft SMARTDrive Disk Cache version 4.0
Copyright 1991,1992 Microsoft Corp.

Cache size: 2,097,152 bytes
Cache size while running Windows: 2,097,152 bytes

              Disk Caching Status
drive    read cache    write cache    buffering
-----------------------------------------------
  A:         yes           no            no
  B:         yes           no            no
  C:         yes           yes           no
  D:         yes           yes           no

For help, type "Smartdrv /?".

C:\WINDOWS>_
```

Figure 10-12: That's Smart

The version number is displayed immediately after the **smartdrv** command. Be sure to check out CD MOM or the MOM companion disk for SMARTDrive 4.2 if you don't have it already, check Chapter 11 to see if you should install it.

See that column marked "buffering"? If you see a "yes" in that column, SMARTDrive has determined that you need something called double-buffering, and has started it for you. In Windows lingo, a double buffer is a second buffer Windows must stick down in lower memory to accommodate a few naughty, old ESDI and SCSI bus mastering controllers. (See Chapter 7 for a discussion of bus mastering.)

 Here's the strange part: double-buffering is independent of SMARTDrive's normal caching functions; it is loaded separately.

That leads to all sorts of confusion.

Double-buffering is specified in **CONFIG.SYS**, with a line that looks like this:

```
device=smartdrv.exe /double_buffer
```

If you have that line in your **CONFIG.SYS**, keep one thing in mind: it does *not* invoke SMARTDrive! It merely sets aside some lower memory to keep those naughty, old ESDI and SCSI drives from blowing away Windows. Don't worry about it. Double-buffering won't hurt anything; it just uses some memory that could be used for other things.

Should there be a "yes" or a "-" (which means "don't know") entry in the buffering column of the SMARTDrive report, you will probably find that there is a **device=** line like the one above in **CONFIG.SYS**. If there are "no"s all the way down the buffering column, and there's a **device=** line like that in **CONFIG.SYS**, you can safely delete it.

Even if you have one of those naughty, old bus mastering controllers, they may be tamed by a third-party product: EZ-SCSI does it, as do others, and they don't need SMARTDrive's help. So if it ain't broke, if your disk is working just fine, don't try to fix it with a **device=** line.

Now that you know that any mention of `smartdrv` in `CONFIG.SYS` doesn't really pertain to SMARTDrive, you might reasonably ask, "What the hell does?" It ends up that SMARTDrive — the real SMARTDrive, the disk caching utility — is invoked in `AUTOEXEC.BAT`.

Your SMARTDrive line in **AUTOEXEC.BAT** probably looks something like this:

`C:\DOS\SMARTDRV.EXE 2048 1024`

If it's pointing at your Windows directory (`c:\windows\smartdrv.exe ...`), don't worry about it. Chances are good it's pointing at whatever you installed last, a DOS upgrade, or Windows.

There are a couple of switches on **SMARTDRV.EXE** that are important. Surprisingly, they don't appear to be documented in either the Windows Resource Kit or in the DOS 5 User's Guide, but they do appear in what Microsoft now seems to think is the "real" documentation: at the DOS prompt, type SMARTDRV /?. If you include a drive letter after the command, e.g.,

`c:\windows\smartdrv.exe b c`

SMARTDrive will enable read caching, but disable write caching, for that drive; the above example disables write caching on **b:** and **c:** and enables both read and write caching on all other drives. If you stick a drive letter on the line, but put a minus sign after it, all caching for that drive is disabled. This:

`c:\windows\smartdrv.exe a- d`

disables all caching on **a:**, and write caching on **d:**, but enables read and write caching on all other drives.

If there are numbers on the tail end of the line, they specify (respectively) the size in KB of SMARTDrive's cache while Windows is not running, and while Windows is running. SMARTDrive has the ability to whittle itself down when Windows gets going, to give Windows more room. So this line:

`c:\windows\smartdrv.exe e- 2048 1024`

says, "SMARTDrive, read and write cache all drives except **e:**, start out with a size of 2 MB, and if Windows gets going, shrink down to 1 MB."

If you don't pick out a pre-Windows and post-Windows size for SMARTDrive, it takes a look at how much extended memory you have on your machine, and makes the following guesses:

Extended Memory	sans-Windows cache	with-Windows cache
Up to 1 MB	all extended memory	no cache
>= 1 MB, < 2 MB	1 MB	256K
>=2 MB, < 4 MB	1 MB	512K
>=4 MB, < 6 MB	2 MB	1 MB
>= 6 MB	2 MB	2 MB

Those are decent guesses: you may want to add to the numbers if you have 8 MB or more.

SMARTDrive has all sorts of additional neat features. **SMARTDRV /S**, for example, will give you a great snapshot of how cache hits are going; **SMARTDRV /C** flushes the write buffers; and so on. **SMARTDRV /?** tells all.

Also see **HardDiskDMABufferSize=** in **SYSTEM.INI**'s **[386Enh]** section.

RAM Drives

 I don't use RAM drives under Windows any more. I used to point the TEMP variable to a RAM drive (see the **SET TEMP=** command in **AUTOEXEC.BAT** above), but found that simply pointing TEMP to any cached hard drive worked just as well.

There's one distinct advantage to pointing TEMP at a cached hard drive: it won't run out of space as easily as a TEMP pointing to a RAM drive (which, by its very nature, tends to be just a few MB). Print Manager, for one, sometimes behaves very strangely when it runs out of TEMP space. By pointing TEMP to a real drive, I can print larger files and go a lot longer between Print Manager crashes.

I doubt that you'll find any significant performance differences between RAM drives and cached hard drives, at least under normal circumstances.

To SHARE or Not to SHARE?

 Ah, nothing like finishing our little discussion with a philosophical debate.

The DOS SHARE command lets more than one program access a file simultaneously. A few years ago, running SHARE was one of the surest ways to crash your system. The term "unstable" gave SHARE the benefit of the doubt.

Like so many other parts of DOS (and Windows!), SHARE has improved with age. In its current incarnation, SHARE seems to have learned a few house manners: it no longer sits in the corner, belching, ogling unsuspecting and naive programs.

Which is not to say that SHARE isn't without its problems, some of which are by design. With SHARE running, for example, Windows won't warn you if you try to start a second copy of Excel, or if two different programs are both going after a text file simultaneously.

 True confessions time: I used to avoid SHARE like the plague. Now, because of some new software that requires SHARE, I run it all the time. It hasn't bothered me enough to cut it off at the knees.

Yet.

Disposable Files

 Windows itself will help you get rid of up to about 2.4 MB of marginally useful files. From inside Program Manager, run Windows Setup (it's probably in the MAIN group). Click on Options, then "Add/Remove Windows Components." You'll be presented with a chance to take out large quantities of Windows files with a click or two (see Figure 10-13).

Click on the Files button(s) to narrow down your pruning. Using the built-in Setup applet's add/delete routines is far superior to deleting things manually: among other things, it's relatively safe, and restoring anything wrongly deleted is much easier.

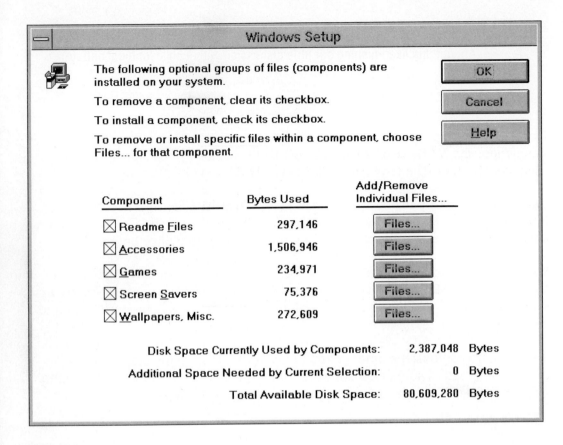

Figure 10-13: Away! Fie!

If that doesn't free up enough space for you, there are two other easy sources of space. First, the fonts applet in the Control Panel will let you delete any unused fonts. By clicking on the font's name you can see the size of the file, down at the bottom of the dialog box — see Figure 10-14.

Should you decide to delete the font, click Remove, and make sure the "Delete Font File From Disk" box is checked before clicking Yes. At 50 to 100K per font file, you can reclaim a fair amount of room this way.

Second, you can delete print drivers — the LaserJet III driver, for example, takes up about 400K. There's a right way to delete print drivers: you need to use the Control Panel's Printer applet to disconnect the driver first (click on the printer, click Remove); then *and only then* you can remove the driver from your hard disk.

Sometimes it's hard figuring out which file is associated with which printer —
HPPCL5A for the LaserJet III and HPPCL5E for the LaserJet IV, for example — so
you may have to check around, typically by posting a message on CompuServe.
When you delete the `.DRV` file associated with the printer, make sure you also zap
out the `.HLP` file; if the driver isn't installed, you won't need help for it!

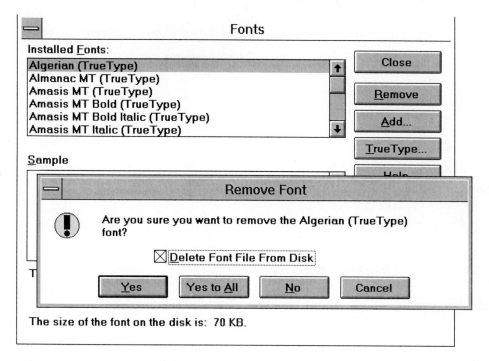

Figure 10-14: Away! Font!

Other files can get the heave-ho. Take a look at **AUTOEXEC.BAT** and
CONFIG.SYS to see where they're going to find SMARTDRV, EMM386, and
HIMEM. If you're only using the versions in your DOS subdirectory, there's no harm
in deleting them from your Windows subdirectory. If you don't use Windows Write,
get rid of **WRITE.EXE** and **WRITE.HLP**. If you don't need Print Manager (and
you probably don't if you're only printing a few pages at a pop), get rid of
PRINTMAN.EXE.

Finally, if you're running in Enhanced mode exclusively (and you should!), you can
delete **DOSX.EXE, DSWAP.EXE, KRNL286.EXE, WINOLDAP.MOD, WSWAP.EXE**,
and any file ending in **.2GR**.

WINMINE.INI

 Hey, Boss, you forgot da games.

 Righto, Igor, the boys left out the most important Windows `.INI` file.

It's **WINMINE.INI**, and you wouldn't believe what setting

```
Sound=10
```

does to the Minesweeper's sound. That's my choice for a favorite setting. You guys can have all that technical mumbo-jumbo. This one makes a real difference in my everyday working life.

 <sniff> Ah, but Minesweeper only uses the PC's speaker — even if you have a fancy, expensive sound card installed.

Mom, how could you recommend something so. . . *retro?*

 Well, of course it uses the PC speaker, oh Igornominious one. It's from the Microsoft Entertainment Pack I. . . which was available before the multimedia sound extensions were available.

I think it's a rather interesting setting, personally.

SECTION 3
The CD and More

The invention of printing, though ingenious, compared with the invention of letters is no great matter.

— Thomas Hobbes, *Leviathan*, 1651

 Section 3 runs through the contents of the CD — shareware in Chapter 12, everything else in Chapter 11 — and presents the most complete font cataloge assembled to date. It ends with a cross-reference that actually makes the huge icon collection on the CD usable.

CHAPTER 11
What's on the CD?

Your bait of falsehood takes this carp of truth:
And thus do we of wisdom and of reach,
With windlasses and with assays of bias,
By indirections find directions out.

They have a plentiful lack of wit.

Though this be madness, yet there is method in 't.

These tedious old fools!

— Shakespeare (att.), *Hamlet*, Act II

The subdirectories on CD MOM are presented here, in alphabetical order. Utility programs as well as add-ons for Windows applications — denizens of the \utility subdirectory — are listed and described in Chapter 12. We'll also describe the files on *MOM's* companion diskettes, those little floppies. Fonts, some of which are on CD MOM, reside in Chapter 13. The giant icon collection is catalogued in Chapter 14.

Special thanks to Ed Hoffmann for all the help pulling this gargantuan project together.

IMPORTANT — YO! TAKE NOTE!

Although I tried very, very hard to ensure that all these programs would install and run properly from the CD, it's possible something slipped by. (In any collection this huge, there's bound to be a few bugs. It's Murphy's Mom's Law.)

If you start getting weird error messages when trying to install a program, you might try one little trick: first copy the files from the CD to a hard drive — or even a diskette! — and try to install from there.

Did Murphy have a mother?

Mom's Revolution

I'm so proud! CD MOM is not only one of the first CDs in a computer book and the first that we know of in a general purpose book, but it's the first book CD to contain working models. And this is going to radically change how careful buyers purchase software. Why, it's revolutionary — and you know how I like revolutions.

Oh, don't puff out your chest so much boys. CDs in books are an inevitable combination and with CDs becoming a standard offering on some computer companies' high-end machines, their time is ripe. So you are more riding a wave than making one. Still there is a revolution under way.

When I started to put together the suite of working models on CD MOM with some help from the staff at Addison Wesley *(thanks Claire!)*, I was surprised what a variety of responses there were. Some companies had all their products in working models, some a few and some none. That's bound to change.

There are three concerns that a vendor needs to address when making a working model.

- The code for the product needs to be crippled without effecting your ability to try it out, for example by disabling a Save command. This is a small amount of work for the programmers.

- The new version needs to be tested. The changes are normally so minor that this is usually no big deal.

- The vendor has to figure out how to distribute the working model — and there is the rub. If a product nets a vendor $80 after the middlemen get their cuts, spending $10 on the working model (not unusual given the cost of diskettes, postage and handling) is not sensible. Besides to be effective the working model has to be there when the user is interested not a week later after phoning and shipping.

The revolution is that the third factor — which used to be the hard one — is, beginning with this book, now easy. The cost of delivering the working model has become zero for the vendor because it's going to start appearing on the CD that will *soon be a standard part of every computer book*. In fact, it will get to the point that vendors can't afford to not have working models since if they don't their competitors will have a real advantage.

This should mean that a lot of the products which didn't have working models when I was putting CD MOM together will have them soon. What we have now is an amazing, unprecedented collection; by the time the next version of *The Mother of All Windows Books* hits the stands, you can expect to see even more new goodies.

 CD MOM contains almost 9,000 files, over 250,000,000 bytes. That's about 100 *times* as much as information as the typical two-diskette book can hold. And it's why I constantly harp on the fact that, if you didn't get the CD with the book, you better order it right now, even if you don't own a CD-ROM drive. It's no exaggeration to say that this is the finest, most important, *most useful* collection of Windows software ever assembled. And for those who don't have CD drives but can beg, borrow, or steal one for a few minutes, moving the files to diskette is easy.

In a nutshell, here's what CD MOM gives you:

- A full "legit" working copy of WinSleuth Gold (retail value: $189)

- A full "legit" working copy of WinCIM, the CompuServe program, plus a free sign-up to CompuServe, and the first month of basic services free (retail value: over $25)

- 20 working models of major Windows applications, including Ami Pro, Claris Works, Freelance Graphics, Picture Publisher, Quark XPress, Visio, and much more.

- All of the latest Windows drivers. If you haven't updated your printer or video card driver since you installed Windows, you *must* get these onto your system. In many cases, they'll keep your computer from freezing, and make it run better.

- The top 100 Windows shareware products, chosen by folks who know shareware. Utilities. Games. Enhancements. Add-ons. Replacements. Complete applications. Info Managers. DOS extensions. Much more, from the world's best shareware authors.

- Dozens of newsletters. General interest. Reviews. Visual Basic. Access. Programming.

- Thousands of icons, indexed in Chapter 13.

- A hundred fonts. Good ones, not the cheap crap, not rip-offs.

- More than 100 megabytes of video clips, sounds, pictures and more.

- The latest version of SmartDrive 4.2, the "safe" version; and the entire Video for Windows runtime library, including the latest Multimedia player, the thing you need to play video clips on your computer.

 It took me months to assemble this collection. If you tried to do it yourself, you'd spend hundreds of dollars, dozens of hours on-line, many more hours on the phone. . . and you'd probably go nuts in the process.

I did.

Mom's Disk and What to Do with It

The contents of CD MOM can be roughly divided into two parts: the shareware (which is in the **UTILITY** subdirectory), and everything else.

The trick, of course, is to figure out what stuff you want, figure out where it is, and then get that stuff off the CD and onto your computer. It isn't as difficult as you may think.

If You Don't Have a CD-ROM Drive

 Pulling files off the CD is as simple as cranking up File Manager and copying away. I've included the number of files and file sizes along with each listing, just so you have a good idea of how many floppies it'll take.

Here are step-by-step instructions, designed to help you pull the most off CD MOM with a minimum of delay: yeah, I know, you're doing this while the network guy is breathing down your back, trying to take his CD-ROM drive back, or while the commissioned clerk at the local computer store thinks you're taking the Furmisher Bandersnatch Blastoids game for a test run. Just make little squeaky "Putt-Putt" noises while you're borrowing the CD-ROM drive and he'll never know the difference.

Heaven help ya if you have to copy these files using DOS. It's possible, but calling it "tedious" is to understate the case. Try to find a CD-ROM drive attached to a Windows machine, and use File Manager.

Step 0: Plan ahead. Leaf through the listings in this and the following chapters. Make sure you know which programs you want, and which subdirectories contain them. Write it all down on a piece of paper. If any of the programs need **VBRUN100.DLL**, **VBRUN200.DLL,** or **VBRUN300.DLL** — the files that make Visual Basic programs work — make a note of that, and plan on grabbing the appropriate **VBRUNxxx** files from CD MOM's root (base) directory. Count up how many bytes are involved, estimate how many diskettes you'll need, then add 50%. Get enough clean diskettes to handle all the files. *Yo!* Make sure they're already formatted and ready to go, OK? Put shiny new sticky labels on them, and mark them with big numbers: 1, 2, 3,. . . like that. Take off or flip out the write-protect tabs. Grab the paper, and head for the CD-ROM drive.

Step 1: The clock starts ticking. Make your apologies and grab a chair. Slip CD MOM into the CD-ROM — if you've never done that before, you may need help the first time, but you'll catch on real quick. *Tick tick tick.* Stick the first diskette (the one marked 1, eh?) in the floppy drive. Crank up File Manager, and double-click on the drive thingy that corresponds to the CD-ROM. It's easy finding the CD-ROM drive: File Manager gives it a picture that looks like a hard drive with its tongue hanging out. *Pant. Pant.*

Step 2: Start the copying. Find the CD MOM subdirectory that you want, and grab it — click once on the subdirectory name itself, way over on the left hand side — grab it and drag the subdirectory file-folder thing onto the symbol for the floppy drive that contains disk 1. You'll hear some whirring.

Step 3: Quick. Get that sheet of paper (*you remembered it, didn't you? Jeeeeez. . . I thought this was going to be quick!*) and jot down which subdirectory is going on Disk 1. Don't worry about listing anything else, just the name of the subdirectory. Good. You're getting better at this.

Step 4: Sooner or later you're going to run out of room on the floppy. File Manager will pop up, tell you which file it's trying to copy across, and put something like the messagge in Figure 11-1 on the screen.

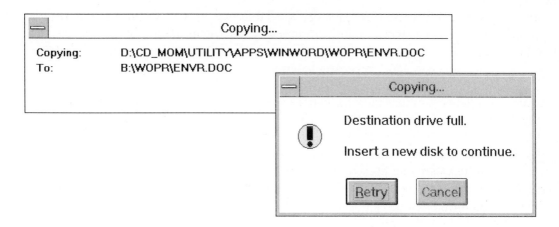

Figure 11-1: Too Big, Too Bad

Step 5: Here's the real speed demon part. You want to do all of this quickly, with a minimum of motion. First, stick the next diskette in the drive. Then, using that piece of paper with the log of which subdirectories are on which disk, write down the number of the diskette and name of the file that was too big. In this case, it would be **ENVR.DOC**. Click RETRY. There. That's it.

Step 6: When you have the first subdirectory copied over to a floppy (or floppies), and File Manager calms down, pick up the next program's subdirectory, drag the file folder over to the diskette, and jot down which subdirectory is piling on next. Keep going just like that: if you run out of room, start a new diskette, and note the name of the next file.

Step 7: Assuming you put the diskettes into the floppy drive in the correct order (uh, you *did*, didn't you?), you should finish with a rather short list of subdirectory and file names and a stack of diskettes. Breathe easy. You're almost done. Thank the folks who lent you their CD-ROM drive, make a note of how nice it is to have so much information at your bloody fingertips, and go back to your regular machine.

Step 8: When you get back to your regular machine, get File Manager going again. Create a fresh, clean subdirectory on your hard drive. Call it, oh, **MOM**. Then stick the first diskette in the floppy drive. Double-click on the picture of the floppy drive, and arrange the windows inside File Manager so you can see both the files on the floppy and the **MOM** subdirectory at the same time. Finally, taking the disks one at a time, re-create the precise directory structure that was on CD MOM. Your notes will show you how. Click once on any subdirectory file folders that appear over on the left side, and drag them under MOM. Then gather up any stray files that are sitting in the "root" directory, and, referring to your notes, stick 'em where they belong.

That's all it takes. You're ready to install everything, the same as if you were installing directly from CD MOM herself.

Well, with one little exception. I tried hard to have all the CD MOM contributors limit their files to a maximum of 1.2 MB, so you could copy any file directly onto any (high density) floppy. In very rare circumstances you may encounter a file that's too long to fit on any diskette, no way, no how. In such a situation, the best I can do is point you at PKZIP, the program that "squishes" files down, and reconstitutes them. There are options to have single files span multiple diskettes, and much more. You'll find PKZIP in the `UTILITY\ZIP\PKZIP\` subdirectory on CD MOM.

Whether You Have a CD or Not

Directions for installing each program are here in *MOM*. The procedure varies slightly depending on the program, but in general all you have to do is go into File Manager, find the subdirectory you want, and double-click on **SETUP.EXE** or **INSTALL.BAT.** When it works, it works very well indeed.

There are a few oddities that I should warn you about.

Many of the **UTILITY** programs require **VBRUN100.DLL**, **VBRUN200.DLL**, or **VBRUN300.DLL**. The description of the program here in the book will tell you very explicitly if you need one of those files. They're "run time libraries" necessary to run Visual Basic programs, so if the program you're interested in was created with Visual Basic, you'll need one of those three files.

Chances are very good you already have one, two, or all three of those files on your system. Take a minute — use File Manager's File/Search command, if you aren't sure — and see if they're already on board. If not, you can copy any or all of them from the "root" directory of CD MOM to your Windows directory. (**VBRUN100.DLL** is 271,264 bytes; **VBRUN200.DLL** is 356,992 bytes; and **VBRUN300.DLL** is 394,384 bytes.) Note that the files aren't interchangeable: if you need VBRUN200, you need *it*, and not VBRUN100 or VBRUN300.

That said, I strongly recommend you bite the bullet and move all three files into your Windows directory. Unless you live the life of a vestal virgin, sooner or later you'll need one or all of them. Yeah, they're big. Yeah, it's a pain. But it's easiest to just do it once and be done with it.

Some of these subdirectories have a weird **DISK1** hanging off of them, and the files are all jumbled under **DISK1**. Why, you ask? Because that's the only way they'll work!

It ends up that certain setup routines tend to blithely assume you'll be installing off a diskette — they are CD-impaired, so to speak. When I found a program that's so impaired, I avoided the temptation to go in and change the setup routine — lots of shareware authors would be mad at me if I did that! — but instead gave the setup routine what it wanted: I hung the whole she-bang off a **DISK1**. Don't ask me why it works, but it does. I think.

Stuff You Shouldn't Overlook

If you have a speaker on your PC (and you do!), you should use the Windows Speaker driver, known as **SPEAKER.DRV**. Bop over to the **DRIVERS\AUDIO\SPEAK** subdirectory on CD MOM, or extract the ZIPped **SPEAKER.ZIP** file from the companion diskette and look at **SPEAKER.TXT** for information on how to install it.

If you don't already have the Windows Multimedia player, **MPLAYER.EXE**, you should install it, too. Take a look at the **VIDEO** section of this chapter for details.

The latest version of SmartDRIVE, known as 4.2, is also on the companion disks. You might want to use it; then again, you may not. See the **SMARTDRV** section of this chapter for more details.

The Stuff on Diskette

You really, really need the CD. OK? I mean it. Even if you don't have a CD-ROM drive, it's very easy to borrow one, slap the files onto diskette, and copy them to the hard drive on your machine.

Everything that is on the diskettes is also on the CD. You won't miss a thing if you got the CD version of *MOM* — in fact, you'll find that using the diskettes is a big pain because all the diskette stuff is compressed, and you're stuck with going through an additional decompressing step. Blecch.

Here's what's on the diskettes.

Diskette #1

UNZIP5.EXE — it's an unZIPer. Copy the file to your hard disk, then run it, just like you would a program. See the description of UnZip in the **ZIP** section of Chapter 12.

All of the other files on the *MOM* diskette are Zipped — they've been squished down, concentrated, all the juice has been sucked out of them. You'll need UnZip or another Zip program of your choice (e.g., PKZip), to reconstitute all of them before you can actually use them. You can read the docs about UnZip, if you like, but here's a quick introduction. If the companion disk is in the b: drive, say, and UnZip is on your DOS path, you would unZip Bar Clock (file **BARCLK22.ZIP**) to your **c:\\test** directory by using this command:

UNZIP B:\\BARCLK22.ZIP C:\\TEST

Once you've unZipped the file, pop over to the **c:\\test** directory, and follow the instructions later in this chapter to install the program.

ALM30H.ZIP — The Almanac version 3.0H is a calendar, scheduler, and personal information manager, all rolled into one. See the **PIMDATA** section of Chapter 12 for details.

BARCLK22.ZIP — Bar Clock version 2.2 puts the time and date and much more on every Windows window title bar. Igor uses the alarm clock every day. See the description in the **GENERAL** section of Chapter 12.

CMPOSE.ZIP — Compose, a free utility to make it easier to put odd symbols, like ©, ½, ™, ¢, and ¥, into your documents. See the **GENERAL** section of Chapter 12.

CSHEARTS.ZIP — CardShark Hearts, one of the finest Windows games ever made. You've never played hearts like this. See **GAMES** in Chapter 12.

EDOS.ZIP — EDOS version 3.65D is the only way to run DOS under Windows. See the **DOS** section of Chapter 12.

ICM33.ZIP — Icon Manager version 3.3 is everything you ever wanted in an icon manager. Finally, there's a way to organize your thousands of icons. See **ICONS** in Chapter 12.

IGOR.ZIP — Yeah, he's one ugly mother, but he's one of our own. UnZIP it and it will turn into a 40K **.AVI** video clip. Play it with **MPLAYER.EXE**, see next. Ars Gratia Artis.

MPLAYER.ZIP — This is Microsoft's latest multimedia player. (To get the full Video for Windows runtime, which includes the player, you'll need CD MOM: see the **VIDEO** section later in this chapter.) After you unZip it, run **MPLAYER.EXE**, and check out the **.HLP** file. You'll catch on quickly.

SMARTDRV.ZIP — SmartDrive 4.2, the "safe" version. You may or may not want to install it. UnZIP into a clean, new directory, then read the explanation about **SMARTDRV** later in this chapter.

SPEAKER.ZIP — The Windows speaker driver. Microsoft didn't distribute it because it doesn't work with every system. But it *does* work with every system I've encountered lately. UnZIP it into a new, empty directory, then follow the instructions in **SPEAKER.TXT**.

WINK.ZIP — UnZips into a text file containing a hodge-podge of terms and "emoticons" commonly used on-line. Fun stuff.

WINZIP.ZIP — WinZip version 4.1a, an outstanding program for managing .ZIP files and archives. Works best if you also have PKZip, which is on CD MOM, but you can rig it up to work with UnZip, here on the diskette. See **ZIP** in Chapter 12.

Diskette #2

AZICED.ZIP — A-Z Icon Editor version 1.8 lets you create, modify, and otherwise scrunch around icons. Amazingly powerful. See **ICONS** in Chapter 12.

DAVYFONT.ZIP — Davy's Dingbats and Davy's Other Dingbats, two of the neatest fonts (actually, miniature art collections!) you'll ever encounter. TrueType. UnZip them and install using the Control Panel's Fonts applet. See **FONTS** in Chapter 12.

STICKIES.ZIP — Stickies! Version 2.1 lets you "stick" yellow sticky-notes on your screen, and much more. See **GENERAL** in Chapter 12.

WINMAGIC.ZIP — WinMagic lets you assign icons to groups, sets up an accelerated icon box, and does so many other things it'll make you wonder why Microsoft couldn't have built Program Manager this way. See **PROGMAN** in Chapter 12.

WINPAK1.ZIP — WinPack #1 is about as much fun as you can have in Windows with your clothes on. Four animated screen savers, two TrueType fonts, and over 100 icons. See **SCREEN** in Chapter 12.

WIZMGR.ZIP — WizManager makes File Manager usable, and does so with great style. You'll be amazed at how it'll make your life easier. See **FILEMAN** in Chapter 12 for details.

WNSLEUTH.ZIP — and finally, WinSleuth Gold. This is a full, "legit," working version of the award-winning product, the kind you could buy in stores for $189. The folks who make WinSleuth want you to take a look, and if you like it, consider buying WinSleuth Gold Pro. A great snooper. See **WNSLEUTH** later in this chapter for details.

Sound Files: AUDIO\

There's quite a collection of audio files on CD MOM. The "serious" music — the stuff that will push your audio equpment to the limit — is in the **MIDI** subdirectory (21 files; 473,527 bytes); the "unstuffed shirt" stuff is in **WAV** (16 files; 1,095,927 bytes). And there's even a fun, fun program, called Spooky, in **WAV\SPOOKY** (11 files; 1,086,305 bytes).

MIDI\

These files all originated on the CompuServe MIDI forum (GO MIDIFORUM), where many talented composers and performers congregate.

The first three files, **BACHA1.MID**, **2**, and **3** are the three movements of J.S. Bach's violin concerto in A minor. Extraordinary. They're part of a two-disk set called *The Violin Music of J.S. Bach*, which contains all the Bach violin works except the trio sonatas and the concerto for violin, oboe, and orchestra. The *Violin Music of J.S. Bach* and the Brahms D minor violin sonata is offered by Dietrich Gewissler, 92 Smith St., Howell, NJ 07731 (phone 908-364-8719) for $29.95 + $2.50 s/h.

BEE5MV1.MID is the first movement of Beethoven's Fifth. From Jonathan Chalaturnyk. **EKNM.MID**, the allegro from Mozart's *Eine Kleine NachtMusik*. Perfect for your favorite little night. From Geoffery King. **ENTRTNR2.MID**, Joplin's *Entertainer*, natch. Played in real time by Ken Gilliland using Voyetra's SP Pro. **GLDBRG.MID** contains the aria and first three variations from J.S. Bach's *Goldberg Variations*. From Ryan Neaveill. Wagner's *Lohengrin* is in **LOHENGRI.MID**. From Jim Clemens. Paul King brings you Joplin's *Maple Leaf Rag* in **MAPLE.MID**. **MARS.MID** is Holst's *Mars*, compliments of Jack Hines. Prokofiev reigns in **PROK05.MID** and **PROK06.MID**, the Largehetto and Gavotte movements from his *Classical Symphony, Op. 75*, arranged for strings. From Larry Roberts. **RITSPRNG.MID** is the first movement from Stravinsky's *Rite of Spring*. From Edwin R. Fischer. **SYNC.MID** is Leroy Anderson's *The Syncopated Clock*, arranged for strings, from John Carretta. J.S. Bach strikes again with the *Tocatta in D Minor*, **TOCAT.MID**, from Robert Urschel. **VALSE07.MID**, **14**, and **15** are Chopin's #7, #14, and #15 waltzes, recorded in real time by Ken Gilliland. **WEDDING.MID** has Mendelssohn's *Wedding March*. From Jim Clemens. Bach's *Invention in B Minor* for Windows is in **WINVNB.MID**, from Richard J. Fennimore. Finally, **WTC5.MID** contains J.S. Bach's Prelude and Fugue #5 in D Minor, from the *Well Tempered Clavier*. From Andrew J. Crabtree.

SPOOKY\

Magnifique!

This is the way Gomer Addam's computer would talk, if he had a sufficiently capable PC. Hand ain't got nuthin' on this dude.

Ooooooh, Igor, I just love it when you speak French.

What to do with the kids on a rainy day? Set 'em up with Spooky. . . and turn out the lights. *Heh heh heh.* Spooky isn't your run-of-the-mill shareware (which is why we put it here, not in the utilities section). It's a wonderful bit o' hacking from a handful of wondrously talented young hacks. Donations accepted: Erik Fink, 7652 Hampshire Ave. N., Brooklyn Park, MN 55428-1457.

WAV\

Here's a bunch of whizzes and bangs and audio gew-gaws you can assign to events, using the Control Panel's Sound applet.

Windows Driver Library: DRIVERS\

 This subdirectory contains the latest versions of all the Windows drivers we could find. (1,972 files in 177 libraries, total 39,601,492 bytes). It is the mother lode of driver libraries. If something in Windows has been screwing up on you, chances are good that a driver from this collection will make your life much simpler.

In particular, if you have not updated your video or printer driver since the day you installed Windows, you *must* look at these files.

There are separate subdirectories for audio drivers, video rivers, network card adapters, and printers. In addition there's a "miscellaneous" subdirectory that covers everything from Novell drivers to Reversi upgrades to a new version of the **TADA.WAV** sound file and a new **MARBLE.BMP** pattern.

There are certain licensing requirements, which you will find repeated over and over in the **LICENSE.TXT** files that exist in nearly every subdirectory. Each driver has attached to it (at the ankles and wrists) a general license restriction, disclaimer, "you're on your own turkey — our lawyers won't let us take responsibility for this stuff" warning, that looks like this:

1. GRANT OF LICENSE. Microsoft grants to you the right to use and to reproduce and distribute all or a portion of the Windows Driver, Schedule + and Microsoft Mail Help File Library ("Software") provided that (i) the Software is not distributed for profit; (ii) the Software is used only in conjunction with licensed copies of Microsoft Windows 3.xx products, including Windows for Workgroups; (iii) the Software may not be modified; (iv) all copyright notices are maintained on the Software; and (v) the licensee/end user agrees to be bound by the terms of this Agreement.

2. COPYRIGHT. The Software is owned by Microsoft or its suppliers and is protected by United States copyright laws and international treaty provisions. You may not remove the copyright notice from any copy of the Software or any copy of the written materials, if any, accompanying the Software.

3. OTHER RESTRICTIONS. This Microsoft License Agreement is your proof of license to exercise the rights granted herein and must be retained by you. You may not rent or lease the Software. You may not reverse engineer, decompile or disassemble the Software.

NO WARRANTY. ANY USE BY YOU OF THE SOFTWARE IS AT YOUR OWN RISK. THE SOFTWARE IS PROVIDED FOR USE ONLY WITH MICROSOFT WINDOWS 3.XX PRODUCTS AND RELATED APPLICATION SOFTWARE. THE SOFTWARE IS PROVIDED FOR USE "AS IS" WITHOUT WARRANTY OF ANY KIND. TO THE MAXIMUM EXTENT PERMITTED BY LAW, MICROSOFT AND ITS SUPPLIERS DISCLAIM ALL WARRANTIES OF ANY KIND, EITHER EXPRESS OR IMPLIED, INCLUDING, WITHOUT LIMITATION, IMPLIED WARRANTIES OF MERCHANTABILITY AND FITNESS FOR A PARTICULAR PURPOSE. MICROSOFT IS NOT OBLIGATED TO PROVIDE ANY UPDATES TO THE SOFTWARE.

NO LIABILITY FOR CONSEQUENTIAL DAMAGES. In no event shall Microsoft or its suppliers be liable for any damages whatsoever (including, without limitation, incidental, direct, indirect special and consequential damages, damages for loss of business profits, business interruption, loss of business information, or other pecuniary loss) arising out of the use or inability to use this Microsoft product, even if Microsoft has been advised of the possibility of such damages. Because some states/countries do not allow the exclusion or limitation of liability for consequential or incidental damages, the above limitation may not apply to you.

INDEMNIFICATION BY YOU. If you distribute the Software in violation of this Agreement, you agree to indemnify, hold harmless and defend Microsoft and its suppliers from and against any claims or lawsuits, including attorney's fees that arise or result from the use or distribution of the Software in violation of this Agreement.

There's an additional section that applies to U.S. government rights; see the file **LICENSE.TXT**, in almost any of the subdirectories.

So much for the legalese. Let's get down to the nitty-gritty.

You won't need all of these drivers. Not by a long shot. The trick is finding, then installing, the correct driver for your hardware (and, in some cases, software). It would be a good idea to browse through this part of the CD as soon as you have a chance, to see if any new drivers are available for stuff you're using right now.

Start by looking at **WDL.TXT** (you can open it up with Windows Write, or any other handy word processor). Print out the file. See if any hardware you're using is on the list at the end of the file, and mark it so you can come back to it.

Now comes the hard part. The list at the end of **WDL.TXT** points to **.EXE** files: for example, the latest Chitz Wallpaper, per **WDL.TXT**, is in a file called **CHITZ.EXE**. You want to look at the part of the file name before the ".**EXE**". In this case, **CHITZ** is important; **.EXE** is not.

Take the name (without the **.EXE**) and browse through CD MOM's **DRIVERS** subdirectory. You're looking for a subdirectory of the same name. In the case of **CHITZ.EXE**, you would figure out, sooner or later, that wallpaper files are in the **DRIVERS\MISC** subdirectory, and you'd finally find the **DRIVERS\MISC\CHITZ** subdirectory. That's the one you want. Write it down.

Next, if you don't have a CD-ROM drive attached to your machine and you're sweating while the fat guy at the computer store is looking over your shoulder *(hey! don't worry; it could be me!)* — or the MIS types are ticked that you're tying up the only $179 CD drive on your multi-million-buck mission critical network — grab a diskette, and copy everything in that subdirectory onto the diskette.

Great. You're almost done.

Somewhere in that subdirectory (if you're working with the CD), or on that diskette (if you had to copy the files over) there will be two **.TXT** files. One of them, **LICENSE.TXT**, will look just like the legal mumbo-jumbo you saw earlier. The other one will contain setup instructions for that particular driver.

While the exact method for installing different drivers can vary widely, the instructions are pretty easy as long as you know where the files are located. Follow the instructions to the letter, and you should have your new driver installed in no time.

Windows drivers change like leaves in September: it would be wise to frequently double-check and see if there are new drivers for your hardware. Personally, I try to do it once a month.

If you're on CompuServe, it's easy (although, for some reason, Microsoft forces you to go in and do all this stuff manually). Simply GO MSL. Pick choice 4 — Download a File. Then download **WDL.TXT**. Log off quickly. Scan this latest version of **WDL.TXT** for your hardware, as described earlier. If there's a new driver that has your name written on it, get back on CompuServe, GO MSL, choice 4, and download the **.EXE** file you need. Once again, log off quickly.

 Now — this is important — stick that .EXE file in a brand-spanking new directory. Whatever you do, do *not* put it in your Windows or System directory. From File Manager, run the .EXE file. It will decompress itself into several files, one of which is a .TXT file that contains further installation instructions. The rest of the installation is similar to what I described previously.

Icon files: ICONS\

This directory holds 4,185 files — 4,185 icons — all 3,353,493 bytes of 'em. The brute-force way to use these icons (that is, if you don't have a good icon manager utility), is by looking up the icon you want in Chapter 14, clicking once on the Program Manager icon you want to replace, clicking File, then Properties, then Change Icon, then Browse, and popping on over to CD MOM.

Most — but not all — of these files are standard 766 byte `.ICO` files.

`ALLICONS.DOC` — contains Howard Friedman's explanation of how he assembled this gigantic collection of icons. Icons are grouped into more-or-less related subdirectories, and catalogued in *MOM*'s Chapter 14.

`ICONS\APPSICON` (147 files, 113,724 bytes) — icons for general Windows applications, databases and integrated programs

`ICONS\CHARICON` (182 files, 138,480 bytes) — cartoon characters

`ICONS\COMHDWIC` (84 files, 62,432 bytes) — communications hardware

`ICONS\COMMICON` (175 files, 130,756 bytes) — general communication icons

`ICONS\COMPICON` (127 files, 95,886 bytes) — computer hardware

`ICONS\DESKICON` (169 files, 133,614 bytes) — things you might find on a desktop

`ICONS\DOSICON` (172 files, 155,776 bytes) — DOS utilities

`ICONS\FILEICON` (75 files, 56,494 bytes) — files and folders

`ICONS\FINICON` (81 files, 61,478 bytes) — financial stuff

`ICONS\FLAGICON` (116 files, 88,856 bytes) — flags

`ICONS\GAMEICON` (216 files, 165,004 bytes) — computer and non-computer games

`ICONS\GRAFICON` (256 files, 224,376 bytes) — graphics, scanners

`ICONS\IMAGICON` (471 files, 359,762 bytes) — "images"

ICONS\LANGICON (68 files, 52,088 bytes) — icons for computer languages

ICONS\MISCICO1 (277 files, 237,106 bytes) — miscellaneous icons, A thru N

ICONS\MISCICO2 (287 files, 244,190 bytes) — miscellaneous icons, O thru Z

ICONS\PLAYICON (181 files, 138,472 bytes) — mostly non-computer games

ICONS\SIGNICON (136 files, 104,176 bytes) — traffic and other signs

ICONS\SPRDICON (154 files, 143,490 bytes) — icons for spreadsheets

ICONS\SYMBICON (107 files, 80,536 bytes) — symbols

ICONS\UTILICON (195 files, 149,384 bytes) — Windows and DOS utilities

ICONS\WINICON (165 files, 127,102 bytes) — Windows accessories and add-ins

ICONS\WORDICON (151 files, 115,340 bytes) — word processing and printing

ICONS\WRITICON (147 files, 134,104 bytes) — books; writing implements

ICONS\ZIPICON (45 files, 33,514 bytes) — icons for zip/compression programs

Newsletters: NEWSLETR\

We've brought together sample copies of the best on-line newsletters. These journals are electronic, and proud of it. They're widely available on bulletin boards or by subscription; see the individual issues for details.

There are four big advantages to electronic newsletters. First, the distribution time is minimal — often you'll see the latest developments in the field reflected in these journals within days, not months. Second, distribution costs are nominal. While it may take $1 million or more to launch a new printed magazine, electronic newsletters needn't leap that huge capital hurdle. Third, the writers can include real, working files along with the journal: you can get the programs and the words at the same time. Finally — perhaps most importantly — electronic writers aren't constrained by the printed medium: anything you can do on a computer, you can do in an electronic journal.

Many journal writers and editors have taken advantage of the Windows Help engine: the journals are giant `.HLP` help files, complete with pop-up definitions, hot keys, hypertext links — the whole nine yards. And since every Windows user has the Help engine built-in, folks who write newsletters directed at the Windows community have a huge leg up.

When you look through these files, you'll note that most of the newsletters have `.HLP` extensions. For most Windows users that means you can start reading the newsletter by simply starting up File Manager and double-clicking on the `.HLP` file. (A few earlier issues are in `.TXT` text format; you can look at those with Windows Write.)

`NEWSLETER\VBZ` (178 files in 6 subdirectories, 1,156,859 bytes) — Jonathan Zuck's Electronic Journal on Visual Basic has reached cult status in just a short time. If you want to get the straight scoop on VB, check out these files; CD MOM has the full contents of Zuck's first four issues, complete with sample files, running applications, things you can use immediately. The issues themselves are in Windows Help format: start File Manager and double-click on the `.HLP` files.

Subscriptions to *VBZ* run $73 a year: call 202-387-1949, fax 202-785-1949, or drop a line on CompuServe to 76702,1605. You'll get your copies sooner if you request delivery to your CompuServe i.d.. Failing that, *VBZ* can be mailed to you, with sample files on diskette. If you want to get the most out of Visual Basic, you need *VBZ*. Personally, I don't know what I'd do without it.

`NEWSLETR\WINONLIN` (12 files, 13,052,830 bytes) — *Windows OnLine Review*, issues 67 (December, 1992) to 76 (August, 1993). This is a first-class on-line general Windows newsletter, the grandaddy of them all, edited by Frank J. Mahaney. From File Manager, simply double-click on the `WOLRnn.HLP` file (nn=issue number).

`NEWSLETR\WINONSHA` (12 files, 4,744,939 bytes) — *Windows OnLine Review / Shareware*, issues 12 (June, 1993) to 21 (August, 1993). From the operators of the Windows OnLine bulletin board and editors of *Windows Online Review*. Another classic, well worth your perusal. Double-click on the `WOLRSnn.HLP` files.

`NEWSLETR\WINONIDX` (10 files, 8,843,058 bytes) — Windows OnLine Index, text files that you can search for information on Windows, DOS and OS/2 news and reviews in *Windows OnLine Review*. Five years' worth: it's quite a collection.

Windows OnLine is an on-line service dedicated to supporting Windows users and Windows network professionals. They have 17 phone lines running 24 hours a day, 365 days a year. It has more than 10,000 Windows programs and files available — quite possibly the most extensive collection ever assembled. Call their BBS at 510-736-8343 for sign-up details, and tell 'em Mom sent ya.

NEWSLETR\WINPROGJ (146 files in 8 subdirectories, 1,620,512 bytes) — contains the first seven issues of the *Windows Programming Journal,* along with dozens of ancillary sample files to help get you started. The *Windows Programming Journal* covers a lot of ground in the Windows arena: starting with issue 6 there's even a series of beginner's columns.

As *MOM* was going to press, the editors of *Windows Programming Journal* were about to take their publication "legit," turn it into a regular printed magazine: prices had not yet been set. For subscription inquiries, call 703-503-3165 or drop a line to CompuServe 71141,2071.

Starting with issue number 5, *Windows Programming Journal* converted to Help File format.

Pictures: PICTURES\

Mom assembled a collection of her favorite computer-based art (12 files, 802,562 bytes). The pictures are in .GIF format — the format developed by CompuServe. You can use Paint Shop Pro (described in the next chapter) or the working model of Micrografx Picture Publisher (described later in this chapter) to look at them.

The kind of art that you can produce with a computer is mind boggling and the best place to learn more about the what and how is on CompuServe's Computer Graphics forums (counting graphics vendor support forums, there are 13 of 'em!). The center for computer art *per se* is the Computer Art Forum (GO COMART) and CD MOM has a selection of 12 files from the forum all Hall of Fame winners or honable mentions.

The art you'll see is all 256 color; once 24-bit color is more common, it will be even more spectacular. Some observers think that when Color LCD panels become inexpensive enough, folks will hang large panels on thier walls and display a fine art reproduction of the week. In preparation, a fellow named Bill Gates has been buying electronic rights to all sorts of paintings from the museums that own them. Yeah, that Bill Gates.

 If your net worth is seven thousand dollars, doubling it isn't that hard but when its seven billion dollars, you gotta hustle to keep up. Hmm, I guess what's really easy is doubling your net worth if it is minus seven thousand dollars.

Oh. Even if you don't have 256 colors, take a look at **BUNNY.GIF**. It's a marvelous example of what can be done with just two colors. **WARBLE.GIF** is Mom's favorite. **CHASE1.GIF** is Mao's favorite — and one of the few with an identified artist, Jim Burton. Ty Halderman created **CCHESS.GIF**. Bruce Ordway made **RACCOO.GIF**.

SMARTDrive: SMARTDRV\

There are three versions of SmartDRIVE floating around. Each has different requirements, different restrictions, different advantages.

 Chances are very good you either have SmartDRIVE 4.0 (for that version the file **SMARTDRV.EXE**, probably located in your Windows subdirectory, is 43,609 bytes long and dated 3/2/92), or SmartDRIVE 4.1 (in that version, **SMARTDRV.EXE** is probably in your DOS directory, is 42,073 bytes long, and is dated 3/10/93). In fact, there's a very good chance you have *both* versions on your hard drive. If you have both, you should figure out which one you're using.

There are two ways to see which version your machine is currently using. The easy way is to look later in this chapter for instructions on installing WinSleuth, which is on the companion disk. Simply clicking on WinSleuth's Environ button will show you everything you wanted to know about SmartDRIVE. If you don't have WinSleuth installed yet, pop into **AUTOEXEC.BAT** and see if you have a line that looks something like this:

```
C:\WINDOWS\SMARTDRV.EXE
```

possibly with **LH** or **LOADHIGH** in front of the line. Look at the size and date of the file referenced on this line. (If there is no directory information — if you just have **SMARTDRV.EXE** — you're probably using the version in your DOS subdirectory.)

SmartDRIVE 4.0 ships with Windows 3.1. It works fine, as long as you don't have a double-spaced ("stacked") hard disk. If you do have a squished disk and decide to stick with SmartDRIVE 4.0, make sure you read about SmartDRIVE in Chapter 7 and follow the instructions there precisely.

SmartDRIVE 4.1 ships with DOS 6. If you installed DOS 6 while Windows 3.1 is on your machine, DOS 6 makes sure you run SmartDRIVE 4.1. Everything I just said about SmartDRIVE 4.0 and how it works with squished disks also applies to SmartDRIVE 4.1. Actually, on my machine it's called SmartDRIVE 4.16, but that's close enough for government work.

SmartDRIVE 4.2 (42,585 bytes, dated 6/9/93) is a new version of SmartDRIVE that's on MOM's companion disk. It's a Microsoft replacement for SmartDRIVE, but *you may not want it!* SmartDRIVE 4.2 is particularly useful for people who are using DOS 6.x (it won't work on earlier versions of DOS) and who have double-spaced/stacked their hard disk.

With the old versions of SmartDRIVE (i.e., anything before 4.2), it's very easy to shoot yourself in the foot by turning off your machine at the wrong time. If you trip the power switch — or your utility company trips it for you — in the few seconds after the **C:** prompt appears, but before all your changes are written out to your hard disk, you can turn the whole disk into brain salad surgery.

SmartDRIVE 4.2 makes sure that the disk buffers are flushed before DOS returns to the **C:** prompt. In other words, SmartDRIVE 4.2 keeps you from shooting yourself in the foot. It isn't clear precisely how SmartDRIVE 4.2 flushes the buffers while working with Windows, but if you're careful to exit Windows and wait for the **C:** prompt before turning off your machine — as I recommend repeatedly in this book — you'll be safe. Flushing details are in the file **SMARTDRV.TXT**.

So how to use SmartDRIVE 4.2? Good question. Personally, I stuck SMARTDRV.EXE 4.2 in a subdirectory all by itself — I call it **C:\DOS\SMARTDRV** — and then I alter that one line in my **AUTOEXEC.BAT** to point to the new subdirectory.

The authors and icons are equally divided on upgrading to SmartDRIVE 4.2.

 I always remember to exit Windows, wait for the **C:** prompt, and then wait another 15 seconds before turning off my machine. I use SmartDRIVE 4.1, prefer getting my **C:** prompt back faster, and don't see any reason to switch.

I would probably do the same thing, except I have problems with five-year-old Igor Jr. occasionally borrowing my machine. He sometimes turns it off at inopportune times — he figures the fat lady's over when Little Critter sings. I don't really care if it takes a few extra seconds to get my `c:` prompt back. So I'm hooked on SmartDRIVE 4.2.

 MOM has the full Microsoft Video for Windows runtime — everything you'll need to run videos (`.AVI` files) on your computer. Just hop into the `VIDEO\VIDWIN` subdirectory (30 files; 529,279 bytes). Check out `VFW.WRI`, if you're into reading documentation, and then run `SETUP.EXE`. You'll get the new media player, and a whole bunch of ancillary stuff installed on your hard drive. That's the first step in running Windows video.

There. Now you've got the player. Time to get some videos! And, oh, do we have a selection.

 Starlite Software Company and Pegasus Development have graciously given MOM readers a real treat: a complete array of video viewing software, along with a handful of video clips that will tickle your funny bone, guaranteed. They're doing that to introduce their new collection of astounding video software on CD.

We've arranged a very special deal for MOM readers: for just $29.95 you can get Starlite's Classic Clips Trailers Sampler (regularly $39.95); in addition, and only on your first order, you may choose either Classic Clips Vicious Vixens — campy, cuddly, and strictly PG rated! — or Classic Clips Science Fiction, or Classic Clips Horror Trailers for an additional $19.95 (they're regularly $29.95). Starlite is doing that because they know that once you've seen these CDs, you'll be clamoring for more. And you will, you will.

Was that confusing enough? Okay. Here it is again, speaking slowly and in English. $29.95 will get you the Classic Clips Trailer CD. $49.90 will get you Classic Clips Trailer plus one of the other three CDs.

 Call Starlite at 800-767-9611 (outside the USA 314-965-5630) and say "I want the MOM special!" Oh. And the folks at Starlite asked me to add this: The sample data files from Starlite Software is licensed for unadvertised, private home use only. All other rights are retained by the copyright proprietor. All other use is prohibited.

So I guess that means we can't open up a movie theater, advertise, and charge to show 100-by-100 pixel movies?

Sheesh. Here I thought we had a toe-hold on a whole new industry.

Classic Clips

Starlite let us put one clip from each of their four CDs on CD MOM. Use Clip Director (see next) to take a peek.

VIDEO\CLASSICS\AFRICA.AVI (1 file, 22,704,456 bytes) — is a clip from "The African Queen." Marvelous stuff. Bogart. Houston's wizardry. Hear Katherine Hepburn exclaim, "I never dreamed that any mere physical experience could be so stimulating!" This is just one of the clips from Starlite's "Trailers Samplers" collection.

VIDEO\CLASSICS\BERSERK.AVI (1 file, 17,642,888 bytes) — And who could forget "Berserk"? Make sure you watch the end of the clip; test your shock limit: "I get dizzy watching a garroted body swinging." Classy stuff here, one of the clips from Starlite's "Horror Trailers" *(is that a Winnebago joke?)* collection.

VIDEO\CLASSICS\TEENDOLL.AVI (1 file, 13,712,536 bytes) — "Teenage Doll is not a pretty picture. It can't be pretty and still be true. . . hell cats in tight pants. . . we gotta get you out of town — way out!" Another classic, this one from Starlite's "Vicious Vixens" collection.

VIDEO\CLASSICS\GORGO.AVI (1 file, 22,786,712 bytes) — ". . . from the depths of prehistoric mystery comes. . . towering over the cities of the world as millions flee in awesome terror!. . . GORGO!" This clip puts the "B" back in "B-movies". It's a sample clip from Starlite's "Science Fiction" collection.

Clip Director

VIDEO\CLIPDIR (40 files, 651,233 bytes) — Clip Director Demo version 1.00 is a *great* video clip viewer that you can use to view the Starlite clips on CD MOM — or any other **.AVI** files, for that matter, including Igor's magnificent snarl. Starlite Software and Pegasus are giving demo versions of this first release of Clip Director to *MOM* readers. Free. You can get the "real" version with the Classic Clips Trailer Sampler CD.

That was mighty nice of them.

Well, Mom, it ain't *all* unbridled altruism. They know that if they make it easy and fun for you to look at `.AVI` files, you'll consider picking up the CDs. It's a, uh, win-win Win situation. These guys are on the cutting edge of video technology. And they're strutting some mighty fine stuff.

You can run **CLIPDEMO.EXE** directly (see Figure 11-2), or copy the files over to a hard disk and run from there. *This* is the way to look at **.AVI** files.

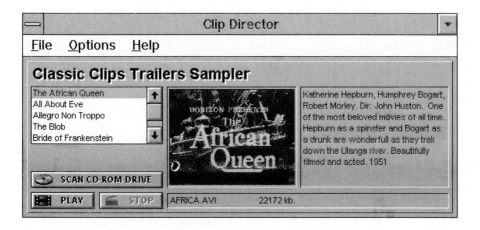

Figure 11-2: Lights! Camera! AVIction!

Mom's AVIs

Microsoft has kindly given Mom permission to distribute a really cool video clip; one that involves fantastic cartooning around, Roger Rabbit style, ending with BillG hisself executing his signature spectacle-ular push-up, and announcing "Cool." Not surprisingly the clip is called **COOL.AVI** (4,944,338 bytes). And it's neat: where else can you see the country's richest man — depending on the current state of MSFT on NASDAQ, a 7 billion dollar man, plus or minus a pittance — give such an endorsement!

Actually, all joking aside, the whole lot of us are tickled. . . uh. . . Pink that Bill's minions let us use his image in the book.

Next, from the wizardry of Ron Wodaski and PhotoMorph from North Coast Software, and Ron's book *PC Video Madness*, **FRG2CHK2.AVI** (167,298 bytes) is a neat "morph" — a frog that changes into a chick. To see what's going on, start up Media Player (**MPLAYER.EXE**), open **FRG2CHK2.AVI**, pull down the Scale menu and pick Frames. Then use the two little buttons at the middle right to see how the morph. . . morphs. Fascinating stuff.

Oh. And while you're at it, take a look at **IGOR.AVI**. (A measly 43,196 bytes!) It's a little bit of inspirational instruction I put together when writer's block and programmer's block gripped me simultaneously. You may distribute it freely, providing that on a Tuesday morning (of your choosing) between 4:00 and 4:01 A.M. local time you face Colorado, rub your belly, pat your head, and repeat the Mom Mantra three times: "Igor. Igor. Igor." Try to get the full intonation: eeeeeegooorrrrrr. It works better if you inhale, in spite of what Mr. Rodham says.

Mom has tough licensing restrictions.

WinCIM: WINCIM\

If you've ever thought of trying out CompuServe, here's your chance. CD MOM includes a fully functional copy of WinCIM — the CompuServe Information Manager for Windows, version 1.0.5, from the folks at CompuServe itself (25 files, 2,298,727 bytes).

If you have a modem, in a matter of minutes you can install the WinCIM software, sign up for CompuServe, get on-line immediately, and receive your first month of basic services *FREE!* It's quite a deal, and I'm proud to be able to give it to you.

Take a gander at **WINCIM.WRI** for all the details, then install WinCIM from File Manager by clicking on **SETUP.EXE**. (Yeah, yeah, the instructions say you need to put the diskette in drive A:, but you can install just as well off the CD.) You'll have a couple of options — YES, if you aren't currently a CompuServe subscriber, you probably do want to sign up — and you'll be up and running in no time. A standard WinCIM installation will take less than 3 megabytes of hard disk space.

Doesn't matter how you get on CompuServe, but you're really missing out on an extraordinary opportunity if you don't get off your duff right now and sign up. This is the best chance you'll ever have: you have all the software you'll need, free, right here on CD MOM, the sign-up is free and automatic, and your first month is free, for basic services.

I'm on CompuServe, as are the flesh-and-blood authors.

 Me too.

 Me three.

So *do* it.

WinSleuth Gold Plus: WNSLEUTH\

 Yeah, you read it right. This edition of *MOM* contains a free, complete, "legit" copy of the award-winning WinSleuth Gold version 3.05 (4 files, 1,165,104 bytes). And, yep, it retails for $189.

 Hey, Dariana Software isn't going stir-crazy. They're betting that, once you see how well WinSleuth Gold works, you'll run right out and pick up a copy of their enhanced version, WinSleuth Gold Plus. Matter of fact, that's exactly what I did: I called their order line (714-236-1380) and bought it right on the spot. True fact. But you be the judge.

WinSleuth is a top-notch Windows "snoop" program. It'll show you which device drivers are running, where your IRQs are stomping on each other, test your system's memory, and much more.

I could rattle on about it, but the best thing for you to do right now is install the program, and go spelunking. You can start the CD MOM version by going into File Manager and double-clicking on **WNSLEUTH.EXE**, or by extracting **WNSLEUTH.ZIP** on the diskette.

Take advantage of the tuning tips. Look at some of the 400 screens of online help. Poke around in the nooks and crannies, and see what's really going on behind the scenes. You'll see why it's won so many awards and drawn such praise in the press.

Working Models: WORKMODL\

 My friends in the industry — *and before this book hit the stands there were a few of them left!* — gave us permission to distribute these working models. Some were even constructed specially for you MOM-o-philes. The overwhelmingly positive response to CD MOM's unique, new distribution method really bowled us over.

 A working model is not a demo. We won't waste our time or yours with cheapo demos that tease but don't tell. These are versions of the real, working product, that have been "crippled" in some way: word processors may save only a couple of pages; draw programs may only give you access to a subset of the usual tools, and on and on.

 None of these models are flipping mind-numbing slide shows. They're the Real McCoy, with a few wing feathers clipped. You should be able to install any of these working models and give the product a real workout — on *your* computer, with *your* setup.

So have at it, pilgrim. There's never been a finer collection.

Access Data Password "Crackers"

WORKMODL\PASSWORD (17 files, 304,472 bytes) — This may be the most astounding demo on CD MOM. My jaw dropped when I saw it. Have you ever password protected a WinWord, Excel, WordPerfect, 1-2-3, Quattro Pro, Paradox, or Novell Netware file, and *forgotten the bloody password?* I sure have. Access Data's programs can crack many passwords on those kinds of files — and this demo will prove it to you. The demo is limited to 10-character passwords, surely enough to prove to yourself that it works. Start up **DEMO.EXE** and select from there.

Aldus IntelliDraw

WORKMODL\INTLIDRW (16 files, 3,451,497 bytes) — The fancy new drawing program from Aldus. Take it for a test spin by starting up **IDRAW.EXE**. (To make it run faster, copy the whole thing to your hard drive first.) See for yourself why other folks are talking.

Aldus PhotoStyler

WORKMODL\PHOTOSTY (111 files, 2,569,379 bytes) — A spectacular "trial version" working model, complete with a handful of photos guaranteed to knock your socks off. Try the Aldus method of editing images, touch-up, and enhancement. Scanning. Masking. The whole nine yards. Install the working model by running **TVSETUP.EXE**. Version 1.1a.

Avantos ManagePro

WORKMODL\MPRO (72 files, 7,623,069 bytes in 3 directories; but if you're copying to diskette, just copy the **DISK1** and **DISK2** subdirectories) — ManagePro takes a unique approach to "smart" software: its sole purpose in life is to help managers manage better. There are tools to help plan, delegate, and track projects. Different and interesting. For installation instructions, see the text file called **READ.ME**.

Claris Works

WORKMODL\CLARISWK (37 files, 2,860,839 bytes) — Meet Claris Works, a very impressive all-in-one program for Windows. Take a look at the **README.WRI** file, then get the model running by starting **CWDEMO.EXE** — or, to make it run faster, copy the whole subdirectory to your hard disk, and crank 'er up from there.

Farallon Replica

WORKMODL\REPLICA (1 file, 671,694 bytes) — A giant leap along the road to the paperless office, Replica lets you exchange documents with other users, whether they have your word processor installed or not, whether they have your fonts installed or not. The copy prints, displays, and acts much like the original. Even the fonts are transported, albeit in slightly modified form. Run **SETUP.EXE**; it'll install Replica in a directory of your choosing, consuming about 1.4 MB.

Foresight — Drafix Windows CAD

WORKMODL\DRAFIX (26 files, 1,021,076 bytes) — Ever wonder what CAD (computer aided design) would be like with a real Windows CAD program? Here's your chance to take a look. Drafix Windows CAD packs the punch of an industrial-strength CAD package with the simplicity of a well-designed Windows interface. Try it for yourself. Start by running **WINSTALL.EXE** (that's the Windows installation routine). If you like what you see, call the Drafix folks for a getting started card — or, better, play with it a bit.

Inner Media Collage Complete

WORKMODL\COLLAGEC (20 files, 943,694 bytes) — This is the package *MOM*'s authors and icons used to capture many of the screen shots you'll see right here in the book: it's a real workhorse. Collage Complete 1.0 offers fancy screen capturing, image management, format conversions, drag and drop, and a whole bunch more. This working model lets you install Collage Complete (run **INSTALL.EXE**; it'll take about 2 MB of hard disk space), and run Collage 20 times.

Lotus Ami Pro

WORKMODL\AMIPRO (39 files, 2,367,884 bytes) — I'll confess to being a long-time Word for Windows user. In the same breath, though, I'll have to admit that this working model turned my head. It's very well put together, runs wonderfully, and shows Ami Pro to very good advantage. Lotus says, "Ami Pro is the only word processor that was designed from the ground up for Windows," and it shows, even in the working model. To install it, just run **INSTALL.EXE**; it'll take about 5 MB of hard disk space.

 Which word processor is right for you? Well, take this working model for a ride and compare it to the word processor you use right now. See how it works on *your* machine, doing *your* work. The result may surprise you.

Lotus cc:Mail

WORKMODL\CCMAIL (40 files, 1,115,739 bytes) — If you've never seen cc:Mail in action, you owe it to yourself to check it out. This working model will only let one person at a time get into the "post office," and there are a few missing filters, but it certainly will give you a very thorough overview of Lotus' hot mail product. As a little icing on the cake, the working model installs and runs like a champ. Start **SETUP.EXE** and cc:Mail will do the rest. Modifies **WIN.INI**, so you may want to make a backup, but it's worth the hassle. Takes about 2 MB on your hard disk.

Lotus Freelance Graphics

WORKMODL\FREELANC (86 files, 4,330,953 bytes) — In direct contrast to the superb implementation of the cc:Mail and Ami Pro working models, the Freelance Graphics working model is a bear to install.

You'll have to format three 1.44 MB 3½-inch diskettes, then copy the contents of each of the three subdirectories (I called 'em **DISK1**, **DISK2**, and **DISK3** — *ingenious, eh?*) onto each of the diskettes. Note that, in File Manager, you can't just drag the **DISK1** folder over to the **B:** drive — you have to double-click on the **DISK1** folder, then select everything inside the subdirectory (click the first file, hold down Shift, click the last file on the list), and drag the selected stuff to the diskette.

To install the working model, run **INSTALL.EXE** on the first diskette. To install the Adobe Type Manager working model, run **INSTALL.EXE** on the third diskette.

We wouldn't put you through all this bother, except the working model, if and/or when you get it installed, is quite spectacular: you get almost everything except the ability to save your work, and the help files. Be sure to start with the QuickStart automated tutorial. Takes about 6 MB on your hard disk. To de-install the working model, delete the files (probably in **C:\FLW**), delete **FLW2.INI** from your Windows directory, zap out the icons in Program Manager, and take out the **pre=**, **prs=**, **sym=**, and **mas=** lines from **WIN.INI**'s **[Extensions]** section.

MathSoft — Mathcad

WORKMODL\MATHCAD (144 files, 1,951,344 bytes) — The award-winning math package that puts a GUI light and a "document" feel to equations, symbolic math, and much more. Crank up **MCAD.EXE**, then click on Help, then Getting Started. This working model, too, will run faster if you copy all the files to a hard disk.

Micrografx Picture Publisher

WORKMODL\PICPUBLI (5 files, 2,291,667 bytes) — A top notch demo of the top rated program, this Picture Publisher working model will take your breath away. Two limitations: you can't print or save your work. Other than that, you have the full program, right here at your beck and call. Give it a shot. You won't be disappointed. Run **INSTALL.EXE** and take it away; use the **.GIF** files in CD MOM's **PICTURES** subdirectory for starters. Installation takes about 3.6 MB on your hard drive.

Okna Desktop Set Jr.

WORKMODL\DESKTOP (31 files, 1,603,258 bytes) — A very impressive personal information manager, with phone book, calendar, phone dialer, and much more. Okna's creator Konstantin Monastyrsky has taken a unique approach to distributing Dekstop Set: one version, Desktop Set Jr., contains a subset of the full Desktop Set capabilities; it's distributed freely. The other version, the full-blown Desktop Set, costs $89 and is available from Okna Corp. Give it a try by running **INSTALL.EXE**; you'll need about 2 MB free on your hard disk.

QuarkXPress

WORKMODL\QUARKXP (36 files, 3,169,066 bytes) — Is a word processor enough for you, or do you need industrial-strength page layout? Only you know for sure — and now you can check it out on your machine. Run **INSTALL.EXE** and take this legendary program for a test drive. Files you save with this demo version won't be usable by other versions of QuarkXPress; printouts are limited to five pages; and all output contains the words "QuarkXPress Demo." Other than that, though, this working model of QuarkXPress is fully functional.

Shapeware Visio

WORKMODL\VISIO (7 files, 1,183,029 bytes) — This template-based drawing program revolutionized the way Windows users look at "draw" programs. Just run **SETUP.EXE**, and the Visio Sampler Working Model will be installed: it takes about 2 MB on your hard disk.

Sonic Foundry — Sound Forge

WORKMODL\SNDFORGE (22 files, 484,795 bytes) — Digital sound editor extraordinaire Sound Forge. This working model will let you do everything the commercial version does, except save your work. Run **SETUP.EXE** and enjoy! It'll take about 880K on your hard disk.

TAL Enterprises B-Coder

WORKMODL\BCODER (10 files, 574,583 bytes) — B-Coder Professional is a bar code graphics generator that is used in conjunction with other Windows applications. B-Coder bar code graphics can be pasted into other Windows apps via the clipboard; it also supports DDE. To get it going, crank up **BCODER.EXE**.

CHAPTER 12

Mom's Utilities

It is plain that the state is not determined merely by community of place and by the exchange of mutual protection from harm and of good offices. These things must, indeed, exist, if there is to be a city, yet the existence of all of them does not at once constitute a state; there must be, both in households and families, a sharing of the good life, in a form at once complete and self-sufficient.

— Aristotle, *Politics*, ca 350 B.C.

 I've grouped all the shareware and freeware on the CD into the `utility\` subdirectory. There's some astounding shareware available for Windows, with newer and better products being hatched every day. This isn't "shovelware": each product has been lovingly selected and examined at length, by a couple of hard-nosed Windows users who have seen thousands — truly *thousands* — of shareware programs.

They're the same hard-nosed Windows users who wrote this book!

We only included our favorites on CD MOM — and hope that you find a handful of real nuggets in this collection.

If you have a specific problem to solve, shareware may be your best bet.

 You register the shareware you use, doncha? All three icons — not to mention the two authors and many of their friends — derive a (sometimes modest) income from shareware registrations. If you use it, pay for it, *capice*?

 Registered users are what keep the shareware phenomenon alive. Every single registration counts. Individuals. Companies. Organizations.

That means *you*, too!

Shareware, Freeware, and More

Everything in the UTILITY\ subdirectory is either shareware or freeware. There are lots of nuances and copyright concerns and all that, but here's the basic idea.

Shareware: Try Before You Buy

The basic concept behind shareware is pretty simple: the program's creators let you try the program for a period of time. If you use it, you're expected to pay for it. That's all.

Imagine trying to buy a car that way. General Ford Corp, if run as a shareware company, would simply hand you the keys to the car of your choosing and let you drive it for a while. If you drove it more than a few days, they would ask you to pay for it; if you tried it for a while and didn't like it, you could just leave it somewhere. Pretty bizarre, eh?

Well, I'm happy to say that the shareware concept works, and it works because a significant percentage of the people who use shareware pay for it. It's all based on trust, honesty, and the kind of attitude that largely went out of fashion about twenty years ago.

Shareware authors put specific restrictions on their products: if you use it beyond X number of days, say, you're expected to pay for it. Some will let you freely distribute their programs far and wide; others don't want you to distribute their programs via certain channels. There's no overriding rule, so you have to check the documentation to see if you're playing by the rules.

There's a reason why shareware is so popular: money. Launching a commercial software product can easily consume $1 million in capital. Easily. Full-page ads in the big computer magazines cost $10,000 or more. *Each*. You know those fancy, glossy magazines from the big mail order companies? Well, software vendors *pay for space* in the magazines — those things that look like product listings are actually ads! — at thousands of bucks for a little corner of a page. The big software distribution companies won't talk to you unless you have an advertising budget the size of a third world country's gross national product. And even then, the software vendor *pays the distributor* for the privilege of carrying their product. Don't even think about the chain stores: it's impossible to get your foot in the door without big sales histories, spending megabucks on lousy cardboard packaging that does nothing but bloat landfills. . . and even then, you're lucky if the cash flow can keep your business alive.

I know. I've been there.

For many talented, innovative computer jocks — the ones with a vision, a problem to solve, and a neat solution — the only thing that makes sense is shareware. A software vendor can launch a solid shareware product with tens of thousands of dollars, not hundreds of thousands. They can sell the product directly, without the hassle of satisfying huge corporate conglomerates. The vendor can concentrate on plowing money into more and better products, not glossier and glitzier ads. The customer often finds shareware companies are more responsive to their problems, incorporating their real-world suggestions in new versions of the product. It's a win-win Win situation.

The media like to talk about "virtual corporations" and their benefits: low overhead, folks who care, suppliers close to their customers, employees who live where they want and work all they can. The shareware industry has thrived on "virtual corporations" for many years.

A Different World

When you enter the world of shareware it's much like stepping back in time, to an era when computers were viewed more as a means to change the world, and less as a method to generate obscene revenue streams. Most shareware is still written by small firms: groups of two or three or ten or twelve hacks with a vision, and the know-how and moxie to bring that vision to market. Shareware is the first — and last! — refuge of computer jocks with dreams and hard-core experience, who don't happen to have a $5 million advertising budget in their back pockets. Not surprisingly, shareware is a hotbed of creativity, new ideas, better approaches, and solutions to specific problems that work, and work right.

All of us — icons and authors, ink and blood alike — are quite proud to be associated with the shareware industry. It's how we got started; our "roots." Many of our friends are shareware authors, and proud of it.

Shareware authors are notorious for being individualistic, opinionated, and highly motivated. Some compare them to old-world craftspeople, laboring away for weeks, months, years, polishing and refining and improving, often primarily for the joy of creating something unique, something to instill pride.

That's why you'll often find outstanding support from shareware authors and companies. You can almost see the fire in one author's eyes, for example, when he writes on the front page of his program's manual:

> If (our product) ever fails to live up to your expectations
> — doesn't matter what you expected, or why —
> simply return the package to us, tell us how much you paid,
> and we'll refund your money immediately.
> Period.

Imagine getting that kind of guarantee from one of the Titans of the software industry! Not every shareware author has a guarantee that iron-clad, of course, but by and large you'll find shareware folks are fiercely interested in making top quality products that work for you.

Sometimes it's hard to understand what motivates shareware authors to such a frenzy. Most often it's the pride that comes with crafting a work of art. And it's hard to argue with someone who can make a living doing something they love.

Registration fees are at the heart of shareware. Shareware fees usually keep shareware authors alive, keep their kids fed and gas in the car — although some shareware authors, admittedly, have other motives. The fees for Davy's shareware fonts, for example, go directly to a Columbia University program that sponsors concerts by the University's budding composers; another shareware company gives a large percentage of its annual income to help refugees; and on and on.

La Creme de La Creme

There's a flip side to all of this. The shareware industry — by its nature highly egalitarian — isn't regulated in any way; thus, there is no guarantee that the shareware you may find on a garden-variety bulletin board (or, indeed, on a gold-plated one!) will even work. That's why it pays to find and follow shareware reviewers you trust. It's also a good reason to avoid shovelware: indiscriminate collections of shareware accumulate like stacks of straw, and it can be abysmally difficult to find a golden system needle in all the gigantic haystacks.

 We've brought together here, on CD MOM, what I believe to be the finest collection of Windows shareware assembled. It took months of hard work, but I think you'll find the effort was worth it. While we've probably missed a few top-notch Windows programs — it's inevitable, given the thousands of Windows shareware packages on the market — the ones you'll find here are outstanding samples of their genre.

We could've duplicated each shareware's documentation right here in the book, but if we did that there would only be room for a handful of packages. Instead, we've decided to present you with a one-paragraph synopsis of the program, and let you decide for yourself if the package sounds interesting. If it does, you're better off reading the real docs anyway, straight from the vendor's fertile mind, instead of some hashed-over mishmash.

The vendors of all these products have bent over backwards to give you the latest, best, most usable versions of their software. All they ask is that you give 'em a try — and if you find yourself using the product, pay for it.

Freeware and Public Domain

Freeware is copyrighted software, with no registration fee. Occasionally software authors will advertise their products as "freeware." Often, they'll do that in an attempt to solicit suggestions and opinions from potential customers. As its name implies, freeware is free — you aren't obligated to pay anything, should you continue to use the product — but it is still the property of the author. If a particular product is widely distributed (e.g., posted on a major bulletin board), but contains no notice about registration fees or procedures, or copying restrictions, you can generally assume it's freeware.

Public Domain software, on the other hand, is not copyright. You may do with it what you will. Public Domain software contains specific wording to that effect, "This is committed to the public domain." The author(s) must explicitly declare it to be public domain; if they don't, it's still copyright, and thus the property of the author.

Demoware, Crippleware, BuyerBeware

These terms are all a matter of degree. In essence, they indicate that the author has removed, curtailed, or otherwise lopped off significant parts of the program before distributing it widely. While there's nothing inherently wrong with crippleware, it can be a real pain to spend $10 downloading a program that doesn't do anything but wink at you.

ASP

 And that leads us to the Association of Shareware Professionals, the ASP. The ASP is not a trade group. It's a self-policing organization of folks who produce and distribute shareware. If you see the name "ASP" attached to a piece of shareware, you know that the author has been through a thorough vetting process, and that if you find the shareware to be significantly crippled, you can — and should! — gripe to the ASP Ombudsman.

Every piece of ASP shareware is required to contain a full statement of why and when and how to contact the ASP, should you find the program in question to be crippled, or if you have a dispute with a shareware author that cannot be resolved. Similarly, ASP approved shareware disk dealers and bulletin boards are required to follow a very strict set of rules about the sale and distribution of shareware.

Note that this isn't a blanket endorsement: you'll find some stinkers marked "ASP", and you'll find many outstanding programs that do not come from ASP authors. What it does give you is some recourse: if you blow $10 on a download of a piece of ASP shareware, and that shareware is so badly crippled you can't properly evaluate it, you can complain and potentially force the author to remove the "ASP" designation.

The intent is to make "ASP" something you can rely on: any shareware marked with those three letters should be pretty darned good, and functional enough that you can tell what it does — whether it's worth buying — without jumping through hoops.

I've tried hard to mark ASP shareware on the CD. No doubt I missed a few, and for those I apologize.

Applications: APPS\

In this subdirectory you'll find various full-fledged applications, plus a handful of add-ons for two big commercial applications — Access and Word for Windows. These are products that will make your Windows apps run better, faster, smarter.

4Shell

UTILITY\APPS\4SHELL (3 files, 636,770 bytes) — A Windows front-end for two of the most popular shareware products ever made, 4Print and 4Book, the routines that let you "squish" more than one page on a single sheet of paper. Includes full evaluation copies of 4Print and 4Book, from Korenthal Associates. Run **INSTALL.EXE**. ASP Shareware from Paul Mayer and ZPAY Payroll Systems. Registration: $25 for 4Shell; $69.96 for 4Print and 4Book for Windows.

Access Add-Ons: ACCESS\

These are add-ons for Access 1.x, compliments of Helen Feddema, Paul Litwin, Stan Leszynski, and the editors of *Smart Access* magazine. If you program Access, you should check out the magazine: call 800-788-1900 or 206-251-1900 for a free sample. Subscriptions run $139 for a full year, and each issue includes a diskette crammed with goodies.

UTILITY\APPS\ACCESS\ADDBOOK (21 files; 2,153,510 bytes) — At last! A dynamite, easily used, full-featured address book for Access. Lots of bells and whistles. Merge to WinWord. Much, much more. See **ADREADME.DOC**. Shareware from Helen Feddema. Registration: $25.

UTILITY\APPS\ACCESS\DDETEST (6 files; 336,218 bytes) — If you've ever tried Dynamic Data Exchange between Access and WinWord, you're probably two shakes shy of blithering. This shows you how it's done. Programs and examples, not for the novice. Freeware from Helen Feddema. Originally published in *Smart Access*.

UTILITY\APPS\ACCESS\PERSADD (8 files; 221,194 bytes) — Detailed demo shows you how to select an address in Access and paste it into a letter in WinWord, using only macros and the clipboard. Freeware from Helen Feddema. See **WINAPIUT.TXT**. Originally published in *Smart Access*.

UTILITY\APPS\ACCESS\SYSLOG (2 files; 99,560 bytes) — A method of keeping a log of activities within an Access database. See **README.TXT**. Freeware from Stan Leszynski and Helen Feddema. Originally published in *Smart Access*.

UTILITY\APPS\ACCESS\TASKLIST (2 files; 230,416 bytes) — A simple Access task list application. Daily, Near Future, Ongoing tasks. Requires Super VGA monitor. Quite suitable for novices, or anyone who wants a personal information manager that isn't overwhelming. See **TASKLIST.TXT**. Shareware from Helen Feddema. Registration: $10.

UTILITY\APPS\ACCESS\TBAR (3 files; 593,962 bytes) — Custom Toolbars in VGA and Super VGA. The buttons Microsoft forgot — little things, like Save and Print. Freeware from Helen Feddema. Originally published in *Smart Access*.

UTILITY\APPS\ACCESS\UPLOAD (8 files; 368,660 bytes) — Here's another Access add-in that takes a bit of know-how. It generates CompuServe upload scripts using Norton Desktop and Batch Runner. Could save you a *lot* of time, if you're doing a bunch of uploads. Freeware from Helen Feddema.

Hi, Finance!

UTILITY\APPS\HIFINANC (26 files, 711,099 bytes) — Hi, Finance! version 2.18 is a financial planning and calculation package. Financial calculator, loan and amortization calculation, financial planning, investment analysis. Run **SETUP.EXE**. ASP Shareware from Roger Hoover and Brightridge Solutions. Registration: $64.

Homeworks

UTILITY\APPS\HOMEWRKS (23 files, 505,697 bytes) — The ultimate home inventory package, Homeworks 1.0 makes it easy: a must for keeping track of things around the house. Excellent on-line Help, dynamite interface. The creation of this program is detailed in *Writing Windows Applications From Start To Finish* by Dave Edson. Run **SETUP.EXE** from the **DISK1** subdirectory. Shareware from Dave Edson and Edson Software. Registration: $49.95.

Money Smith

UTILITY\APPS\MONEYSMT (14 files, 778,331 bytes) — MoneySmith version 2.0 is a complete double-entry accounting system. Investment tracking, fancy financial calculator, much, much more. ASP Shareware from Bradley J. Smith and Money Smith Systems. Run **SETUP.EXE**. Registration: $33.95.

Time-Speed-Distance

UTILITY\APPS\TIMESPD (3 files, 371,926 bytes) — Ahoy! Here's a nautical calculator that will calculate time, speed, and distance for those of you who are navigationally challenged. Version 1.0. Run **INSTALL.EXE**: it'll take about 500K of hard disk space. ASP Shareware from ZPAY Payroll Systems. Registration: $20.

WinCheck

UTILITY\APPS\WINCHECK (47 files, 1,021,514 bytes) — The personal finance manager for windows, WinCheck 3.0p lets you manage checking, savings, cash, and credit card accounts. Excellent interface, easy to use, with very flexible reports. Supports DDE. Run **SETUP.EXE** to get started. ASP Shareware from Wilson WindowWare. Registration: $69.99.

Word for Windows Add-Ons: WINWORD\

These are add-ons for Word for Windows 2.x, compliments of the denizens of CompuServe's PROGRAMS forum.

UTILITY\APPS\WINWORD\DOCUPOWR (21 files, 920,740 bytes) — Total System Solutions' DocuPower Pro 2.0. Gives WinWord files long names, up to 45 characters long. Documents can be grouped into folder. File Find, Text Search, Merge, Print, FAX, LAN support, and much more. Open up **INSTALL.DOC** and follow the instructions. Shareware. Registration: $59.95.

UTILITY\APPS\WINWORD\FILEWARE (11 files; 384,247 bytes) — Also from Total System Solutions, Fileware version 2.4 lets you control files from inside WinWord: create directories, delete files, rename, move, copy, all of those file management problems that can be so frustrating in WinWord. From WinWord, open **FILEWARE.DOC**. Shareware. Registration: $39.95.

UTILITY\APPS\WINWORD\GLJMRK (1 file; 41,168 bytes) — Plants a "watermark" — a gray "Confidential" or "Office Copy" or whatever — on your WinWord documents. Far and away the best way to watermark a doc, if you're using a LaserJet. From WinWord, open **GLJMRK.DOC** and follow the instructions. Version 2.03. Shareware from WinWord guru and Gadfly Guy Gallo. Registration: $10, or register all of GToolbox for $49.95.

UTILITY\APPS\WINWORD\GTOOLBOX (4 files; 688,004 bytes) — A classic collection of WinWord extensions, macros, all sorts of goodies. From WinWord, open **GTOOLBOX.DOC**. Shareware from Guy Gallo. Registration: $49.95.

UTILITY\APPS\WINWORD\GSCRIPT (8 files; 541,961 bytes) — The most advanced script-writing suite in existence. If you write scripts, screenplays, and the like, you need GSCRIPT (version 2.9b). To get started, open **GSFDEMO.DOC** from WinWord. Shareware/ demoware from Guy Gallo. Registration: $99.95.

UTILITY\APPS\WINWORD\MASTERS (4 files; 237,394 bytes) — MasterMind Software's MasterSeries version 2.02. All sorts of goodies from Shawn Wallack, WinWord Master. MasterPrint, MasterFAX, MasterDial and Open and Close, much more. From WinWord, open **MSTRMIND.DOC**. Shareware. Registration: $20.

UTILITY\APPS\WINWORD\MEGAWORD (5 files; 1,533,820 bytes) — An outstanding collection of WinWord hacks, tips, tricks, utilities, and much more. This is the "Standard Edition," what some would call demoware, with lots and lots of useful stuff. Open **MEGAWORD.DOC** and follow the instructions. Registration, which brings the "Professional Edition," including full source code, is $54.

UTILITY\APPS\WINWORD\WOPR (37 files, 1,538,670 bytes) — Woody's Office POWER Pack, the number one add-on to Word for Windows. Yeah, *that* Woody is *this* Woody. So we're biased. Don't take our. . . uh. . . word for it: if you use WinWord, open up **README.DOC** and take WOPR for a test drive. This is the Windows Magazine Win100 Award Winner, critically acclaimed, used by thousands worldwide every day. ASP Shareware. Registration: $49.95 + $4.50 s/h.

World Time

UTILITY\APPS\WRLDTIME (5 files, 183,877 bytes) — World Time version 2.10d is more than just another clock. It will instantly show you the current time (and date) in six different locales, around the world. You can choose from World Time's 170 built-in locations, or add your own. It even keeps track of daylight savings time and those fun "plus or minus a half-hour" time zones like the ones in India (no, it won't handle Nepal's +10 minute time zone). Just run **WTIME21.EXE**. Shareware from Matthew Smith and Pegasus Development. Registration: $16.

ZK-Shell

UTILITY\APPS\ZKSHELL (3 files, 528,762 bytes) — At last, a Windows front-end for ZipKey, the ZIP code look-up routine. Includes a full evaluation copy of ZipKey, from Eric Isaacson. Run **INSTALL.EXE**. ASP Shareware from Paul Mayer and ZPAY Payroll Systems.

Audio: AUDIO\

Wave Editor

UTILITY\AUDIO\WAVEDIT (5 files, 443,874 bytes) — Wave Editor 2.0 is a powerful 16-bit **.WAV** file stereo sound editor. Includes Fourier Transforms and other effects. Just run **WAVEDIT.EXE**. Shareware from Starlite Software. Registration: $24.95.

Whoop It Up!

UTILITY\AUDIO\WHOOPIT (14 files, 146,816 bytes) — This is the one you've seen with the Star Trek screen savers. Whoop It Up! 3.0 lets you assign sounds or **.AVI** files to system events — even certain events within specific applications. Check out **DRUM.WAV** and the other **.WAV** and **.MID** files in this directory. Slick. Run **WHOOP.EXE**. Shareware from Starlite Software. Registration: $29.95, which brings you more than a megabyte of additional sounds.

Calculator, Clock, Clipboard: CLOCKETC\

All The Time

UTILITY\CLOCKETC\ATT (33 files; 645,707 bytes) — All the Time for Windows version 3.0 is a customizable clock that not only shows the current time and date, but also memory, disk, and free system resources. On a coolhood scale from one to ten, this is an eleven. Stopwatch and all. Look at **AREADME.WRI** for instructions. Freeware, in the public domain, from Wilson Smith. Requires **VBRUN300.DLL**, which is in the root directory of CD MOM.

ClipMate

UTILITY\CLOCKETC\CLIPMATE (14 files; 451,483 bytes) — ClipMate 2.07 from Thornton Software Solutions remembers everything you copy to the Clipboard. You can view, edit, combine, and print clipboard data, and data gets saved to disk between Windows sessions. New thumbnail view. Run **SETUP.EXE** to get going. Great stuff. ASP Shareware. Registration: $25.

Power Button Notepad

UTILITY\CLOCKETC\PBNOTEPD (2 files; 93,984 bytes) — Turns the standard Windows Notepad into something usable — which is no mean feat! Simply copy **PBNOTE.EXE** to a convenient directory, and set up an icon to run it instead of Notepad. You'll need **VBRUN100.DLL** somewhere on your DOS path (there's a copy in the root directory of CD-MOM). Shareware from David Stewart at Argyle Softstuff. Registration: $15, $22 for a customized version (such a deal!).

Power Button Write

UTILITY\CLOCKETC\PBWRITE (4 files; 113,704 bytes) –– I never would've believed it till I saw it. Yes, you *can* use Windows Write, and actually produce decent files. Every Windows programmer who needs to create .WRI files should get PBWrite. Version 5.0a includes a ruler, icons for centering and other formatting, and much more. Copy **PBWRITE.EXE** to a convenient directory, and set up an icon to run it instead of Windows Write. You'll need **VBRUN200.DLL** somewhere on your DOS path (there's a copy in the root directory of CD-MOM). More excellent shareware from David Stewart at Argyle Softstuff. Registration: $17; cheap at twice the price.

UltraClip

UTILITY\CLOCKETC\ULTRCLIP (4 files; 369,102 bytes) — Ultra Clip version 1.7 gives you extreme control over the clipboard — or should I say any number of clipboards? To install, follow the instructions in **UC.WRI**. Freeware from Doug Overmyer.

Yakkity Clock

UTILITY\CLOCKETC\YAKCLOCK (11 files, 495,301 bytes) — If you like your clocks normal, this ain't yer cup o' tea. But if you like 'em sassy, with lots of personality and customizing, you gotta look at Yakkity Clock 1.04. No, it won't change the world. But it will bark like a dog — or chime, or speak in a good-as-Barrett female voice — whenever you tell it to. Just run **YAKCLOCK.EXE**. Shareware from Matthew Smith and Pegasus Development. Registration: $15.

Communications: COM\

RateClock

UTILITY\COM\RATECLOK (3 files; 84,758 bytes) — An absolutely brilliant, simple solution to a vexing problem: how to keep track of how much you're spending while you're connected on-line? Here it is. Watch the bills pile up in real time. Read **RCDOC.WRI** to get started. Requires **VBRUN200.DLL**, which is in CD MOM's root directory. Shareware from Andy LeMay. Registration: $5. It'll pay for itself the first week — maybe, if you're like me, the first *day*.

RECON

 UTILITY\COM\RECON (14 files; 918.613 bytes) — You will find very, very few DOS programs on CD MOM. I've only included DOS programs when there is absolutely no alternative, and when the DOS program is so good I can't imagine living without it. Such is RECON version 2.20. It's used with TAPCIS (see next) to organize messages, and generally keep you from going crazy. *Important: copy all files in this subdirectory to your hard drive before trying to run RECON.* See **RECON201.DOC** for important setup instructions. Quite literally, I couldn't have written this book without it. See Chapter 4, The Mother Of All Information Services. ASP Shareware from Orest Skrypuch. Registration: $45.

TAPCIS

UTILITY\COM\TAPCIS (44 files; 853,712 bytes) — If you use CompuServe and spend a fair amount of time on the fora, this is the program you need. Yes, it's tough to learn: you're better off learning the CompuServe ropes with WinCIM. But after you've WinCIMmed for a month or two, you (and your pocketbook!) will be ready for TAPCIS. This is the program that logs on and off just as quickly as it can, saving you connect time charges, allowing you to produce and consume many times as many messages as you do now. Start by reading **README.DOC**. ASP Shareware from Support Group. Registration: $79. This is the key to unlock CompuServe.

Wink

UTILITY\COM\WINK.TXT (1 file; 19,294 bytes) — A list of on-line abbreviations, emoticons, and more. The electronic underground has a language unto itself. This text file will help you crack some of the more arcane three-letter acronyms, and see the ill logic behind the shorthand pictures. adTHANKSvance to Josh Mandel, James Bach, Joan Friedman, Sal Neuman, Neil Rubenking, Orville Fudpucker, Dave Konkel, Axel Roschinski, and anyone else who participated but may have gone unmentioned.

DOS Assist: DOS\
EDOS

UTILITY\DOS\EDOS (42 files, 453,467 bytes in 2 subdirectories) — EDOS version 3.65-D gives dramatic improvement in running DOS under Windows. Can run up to 736K, menu bar, edit/append, drag/drop, diagnostics, much, much more. Outstanding, award-winning shareware from Mike Maurice and FireFly Software. Registration: $45 with discounts. Late news: Mom scrambled a bit in EDOS; the CD MOM master got screwed up and we couldn't fix it by press time. Sorry! For the latest version, log onto FireFly's bulletin board at 503-694-2220 and ask Brother Mike. Well worth the effort. Tell him Mom sent ya.

Stamper

UTILITY\DOS\STAMPER (3 files, 45,790 bytes) — Have you ever wanted to change a file's date and time stamp? This'll do it — with panache. Tell Stamper which date and time to use (you can set up to five at a time), minimize Stamper, then drag files to the Stamper icon. Poof. Just run **STAMPER.EXE** from CD-MOM, or to make it run faster, copy all the files to a hard disk. Shareware. Registration: $10.

WinCLI

UTILITY\DOS\WINCLI (10 files, 141,072 bytes) — The Windows Command Line Interface, version 3.02. Like the DOS prompt, only better: copy, rename, move bunches of files, do anything you could do in DOS quickly and easily. Command history. Editing. Simply run **WINCLI.EXE**. Put it on your hard disk to run faster. Shareware from Robert Salesas and Eschalon Development Inc. Registration: $35.

Editor: EDIT\
WinEdit

UTILITY\EDIT\WINEDIT (33 files, 1,090,208 bytes) — WinEdit version 2.0n is a fast, powerful Windows programmer's text editor; one of the best. Run **WSETUP.EXE** to get started. ASP Shareware from Wilson WindowWare.

Registration: Lite $29.95; Std (compile direct, view output) $59.95; Pro (scripting language) $89.95.

File Manager Add-Ons: FILEMAN\

Drag and View

UTILITY\FILEMAN\DRAGNVU (37 files, 996,510 bytes) — From Canyon Software, Drag and View version 2.0 lets you see the contents of files from inside File Manager by simply dragging and dropping. View ASCII, Hex and many popular spreadsheet, database, word processing and graphic formats. Search and goto functions. Open multiple windows and compare files. Run **DVSETUP.EXE** to get started. ASP Shareware: $25 registration.

File Commander

UTILITY\FILEMAN\FILECOMM (39 files, 622,552 bytes) — File Commander 2.0k attaches itself to File Manager and adds up to 4 new menus, each with three levels of submenus and 99 items. Improved dialog boxes. Run **WSETUP.EXE** to get started. ASP Shareware from Wilson WindowWare. Registration: $49.95.

WizManager

UTILITY\FILEMAN\WIZMGR (17 files, 609,588 bytes) — This one will leave you wondering why Microsoft couldn't build a better File Manager in the first place. Excellent button bar, DOS command line box, print directory list, much more. The kind of product that gives shareware a good name. Just run **INSTALL.EXE**. From Mijenix. ASP Shareware: $39.95 registration.

Fonts: FONTS\

MOM has two collections of shareware fonts — about 100 fonts in total — from two of the most talented font artists in the world, plus an important font that somehow didn't make it into the standard Windows collection.

Davy's Fonts: DAVY\

This part of CD MOM contains 83 subdirectories, each with one or more different Davy's fonts, in TrueType format. These are outstanding, often exquisite examples of primarily decorative fonts, done with the kind of care and attention to detail rarely seen these days. All of the Davy's fonts on CD-MOM are shareware (some are free); registration terms are detailed in text files included in the subdirectory. Yeah, you'll see: registration fees — often outrageously determined, but always amazingly inexpensive — go to Columbia University, as cash for concerts for Columbia's composers. David calls it shareware with a difference. (Note that all of these fonts are copyright by David Rakowski.)

To install the fonts, simply pop into the Control Panel's Fonts applet, click "Add", and point Windows over to the correct subdirectory.

Many of David Rakowski's fonts are now commercially available. Rakowski, a well-known composer and Assistant Professor of Music at Columbia University, has (with great prodding from his many fans and friends) recently released an extraordinary collection of commercial fonts: contact him on CompuServe at 73240,3060 for details.

As always, a percentage of the proceeds from the sale of his fonts goes to help support young composers. It's a great deal, no matter how you slice it.

AARCOVER (2 files, 27,986 bytes) Aarcover, a font that looks like static electricity or limp lightning. All caps, numbers, punctuation. Shareware. Registration: $1.

ADINEK (2 files, 35,048 bytes) Adine Kirnberg script font with rounded caps and relatively small lower-case characters. German Art Nouveau, similar to Romana. Shareware. Registration: $7.49.

AMSLAN (2 files, 54,961 bytes) Gallaudet, the American Sign Language font. Free.

ANNSTONE (2 files, 57,165 bytes) AnnStone is a late 19th century German drop cap woodcut font. Companion to JeffNicholls (see below). Free.

BEFFLE (2 files, 26,842 bytes) Beffle, a drop cap similar to Fry's Ornamental. Caps, some punctuation, no numbers. Shareware. Registration: $3.00.

BENJAMIN (2 files, 20,605 bytes) Benjamin display capitals. Shareware. Registration: $2.99.

BIZARRO (2 files, 42,787 bytes) Bizarro is a caps only font with bizarre silhouetted characters in the shape of people, animals, sprite, harlequins, and daemons. 17th/18th century style. Shareware. Registration: $3.00.

BRAILLE (1 file, 14128 bytes) A font in Braille. Free.

CARRICK (2 files, 43,068 bytes) Carrick display capitals, a black Gothic style font on top of a stained glass window pattern. Shareware. Registration: $2.99.

CHINA (2 files, 20,516 bytes) NixonInChina, a sort of chopstick-style font, much as you might expect to see on menus in Chinese restaurants. Upper/lower case, plus punctuation, no numbers or diacritics. Free.

DAVDING (2 files, 194,738 bytes) Davy's Dingbats, quite possibly the most eclectic "font" ever created: 200 pictorial characters, Art Nouveau images, cats, animals, ballerinas, moons, floral patterns. Breathtaking. Shareware. Registration: $12.

DAVODING (2 files, 103,337 bytes) Davy's Other Dingbats. An extraordinary, classic collection. Symbols, ornaments, musicians. Free.

DINER (5 files, 52,382 bytes) A family of tall, thin, rounded Art Deco fonts similar to Huxley Vertical. Regular, Skinny, Fatt, and Obese weights. Caps, numbers and punctuation. Extra alternate shapes on lower-case a, k, m, w, y. Shareware. Registration: $9.50.

DOBKIN** (2 files, 32,731 bytes) Dobkin Script is an Art Nouveau script font similar to Bizarro. Includes numerals and punctuation. Frilly but readable. Shareware, but to understand the registration fee, you'll have to fully *grok* **DOBKIN.TXT.

DRAGONWI (2 files, 25,558 bytes) Dragonwick, an interesting calligraphic font. Shareware. Registration: $4.99.

DUBRIEL (3 files, 80,480 bytes) Dubriel and Dubriel Italic. Similar to Torino. Shareware. Registration: $14.99.

DUPUY (4 files, 74,072 bytes) Set of Dupuy fonts, like cartoon lettering in the comics of the 1940's and 50's. Regular, heavy and light. Kerned alphabet, numbers and punctuation. Upper and lower case identical. Shareware. Registration: $5.

EILEEN (3 files, 111,712 bytes) Eileen Caps and Eileen Caps Black. Complete alphabet of elegant Art Nouveau drop caps. Uncial decorated with vines and leaves. Similar to Elzevier-Initialen. Eileen Caps is white on a black box. In Eileen Caps Black the box is cut out and the letters are black. Shareware. Registration: $7.50.

ELIZANN (2 files, 37,635 bytes) Elizabeth-Ann, a serif display font with thinly etched white lines drawn through the characters. Punctuation and numbers. Shareware. Registration: $3.00.

ERASERDT (2 files, 127,335 bytes) Eraser Dust, a font that looks like thick chalked letters on a blackboard. Free.

FIRE (2 files, 34,086 bytes) Crackling Fire, the font that looks like a torched Dom Casual. Arthur Brown would love it. Free.

GARTON (2 files, 38,315 bytes) Garton is a semi-script serif display font. All characters, numbers, punctuation, a few ligatures, and a few upper and lower case swash characters. Shareware. Registration: $6.00.

GESSELE (2 files, 33,158 bytes) Gessele-Script, based on the rare Art Nouveau font Rondes-Ancienne. Elegant unslanted script, as if done with a quill pen. Full alphabet, numbers and punctuation, no diacritics. Shareware. Registration: $6.49.

GREENCAP (2 files, 33,242 bytes) GreenCaps, a display caps font, hollow top, filled lower. Shareware. Registration: $2.99.

GRIFFIN (2 files, 212,651 bytes) Griffin Dingbats, about 155 picture characters and an ornate Gothic drop cap font. Pictures range from Art Nouveau, Renaissance and woodcut printer ornatments to smiling, walking vegetables. Drop caps similar to Celebration. Shareware. Registration: $12.

HANDWRIT (2 files, 40,806 bytes) Davy's Crappy Writing font, which — as its name implies — is just Davy's handwriting when he's having a bad penmanship day. Use it to sign checks or threats to your favorite personalities. Use at 24-point. Free. Which is more than it's worth.

HARTING** (2 files, 104,063 bytes) Harting2, a font that mimics a typewriter which has a ribbon that is running out of ink. Monospaced. Looks better at higher resolutions. Shareware. And you gotta read **HARTING2.TXT (wherein the innovative shareware fee structure is explained), even if you never *look* at the font. If this font is too weird for you, look at McGarey Fractured.

HEADHNTR (2 files, 43,169 bytes) A Head Hunter font *dem bones dem bones dem dryyyyy bones.* Perfect for employment agency letterhead. Some punctuation, no numbers. Shareware. Registration: $2.99.

HOLTZSCH (2 files, 54,206 bytes) Hotzschue is a caps and numerals only font, white on top stepping down to black, with a sprig of greenery. Shareware. Registration: $3.00.

HORST (2 files, 21,965 bytes) Horst Caps. Full alphabet of Art Nouveau script capitals with fairly substantial curlicues. Shareware. Registration: $2.99.

IANBENT (2 files, 57,201 bytes) Ian-Bent, full alphabet of Art Nouveau script capitals surrounded by stained-glass patterns. Similar to a German Art Nouveau font drawn by Otto Eckmann. Free.

JEFFNICH (2 files, 52,362 bytes) Jeff-Nichols, an ornate, detailed, late 19th century Art Nouveau font. All caps. Free.

KEYBOARD (2 files, 63,977 bytes) Davy's Big Key Kaps font reproduces the look of keys on the IBM and Mac extended keyboards. Shareware. Registration: $10 for commercial use, free otherwise.

KINIGSTN (2 files, 40,831 bytes) Kinigstein Kaps, a decorative Art Nouveau caps font, drawn in black as if pressed onto a square of foil. No Q, X, or Y. Shareware. Registration: $2.99.

KONANUR (2 files, 34,401 bytes) Konanur Kaps, cloudy caps. Shareware. Registration: $2.99.

KOSHGARN (2 files, 28,529 bytes) Koshgarian-Light, a square, sans-serif font, similar to Handel Gothic Light, more rounded than Eurostile. A "Pepsi"-like font. Full set, punctuation and numbers, no diacriticals. Shareware. Registration: $10.

KRAMER (2 files, 41,243 bytes) Kramer is an Art Nouveau drop cap font. The letter outlines themselves are cut out to form the lower case letters. Free.

LEECAPS (2 files, 37,563 bytes) LeeCaps, 3-D block capitals with shadows. Shareware. Registration: $2.99.

826 • Chapter 12: Mom's Utilities

LEMIESZ (2 files, 46,187 bytes) Lemiesz, similar to Mesozoic. Free.

LILITHHV (2 files, 27,537 bytes) Lilith Heavy, a corpulent adjunct to Lilith Light (see below). Shareware. Registration: $3.01 (or $4.01 if your last name is hyphenated).

LILITHIN (2 files, 45,075 bytes) Lilith Initials, a flowery drop cap font. Companion to Lilith Light (see next). Caps only. Free.

LILITHLT (2 files, 27,398 bytes) Lilith Light, a semi-calligraphic display font with long vertical strokes thicker at the top. Short x-height. Shareware. Registration: $3.00.

LOGGER (2 files, 58,460 bytes) Logger. Logs, all the logs, and nothing but the logs. Caps and punctuation. Free.

LOWEREST (2 files, 56,494 bytes) Lower East Side, a nailed-plank font with. . . uh . . . woody overtones. Shareware. Registration: $4.99.

LOWERWST (2 files, 40,283 bytes) Lower West Side, a vibrating, earthquake kind of font. Shareware. Registration: $4.99.

MCGAREY (2 files, 54,162 bytes) The McGarey Fractured font is a typewriter-like font with mild contusions on the characters. See "Harting" font for a really "bunged up" old typewriter/bad ribbon/cheap mimeograph look; the McGarey font looks much more normal, but still broken up, a little crooked, and rather cheap. The difference is, it prints *much* more quickly than Harting. Use it for the "I typed it myself, I don't own a computer" look. Free.

MULTIFRM (2 files, 28,100 bytes) Multiform, a hand-drawn Art Nouveau font. Free.

NAUERT** (2 files, 51,301 bytes) Nauert is a chiseled, mid-19th century style font. Generously kerned. Looks best at 48 points and above. Shareware. Registration is detailed in **NAUERT.TXT. *And you better have a size 7 shoe or smaller, otherwise it's a rip.*

PARISMET (2 files, 19,822 bytes) Paris-Metro, caps only. Shareware. Registration: $4.99.

PHONETIC (2 files, 25,369 bytes) The International Phonetic Alphabet (IPA). Free.

PIXI (2 files, 31,606 bytes) PixiFont. Shareware. Registration: $4.99.

POINTAGE (2 files, 39,336 bytes) Pointage, an all caps font resembling Torino. Each letter is grasped in a hand with a Victorian-style pointing finger, pointed right. Shareware. Registration: $3.03.

POLOSEMI (2 files, 30,495 bytes) Polo SemiScript. Shareware. Registration: $4.99.

 RABBIT (2 files, 22,434 bytes) Rabbit Ears, kinda like Cooper Black with lower case identical to upper case, but the B, H, F, K, and L are much taller than the rest — ergo, "rabbit ears." I woulda called it a SpockFont, but *de gustibus. . .* It's a 1940's style advertising font. Shareware. Registration: $4.49 (or $3.49 if your name is hyphenated).

RECHTMAN** (2 files, 39,096 bytes) Rechtman Script, a chiseled script font. Includes numbers and punctuation. Shareware. Fee is ... uh ... detailed in **RECHTMAN.TXT.

RELIEF (4 files, 88,378 bytes) Relief Pak, a collection of three special purpose sans serif relief fonts, known as WhatARelief, ReliefInReverse, and RoundedRelief. Shareware. Registration: $4.99.

REYNOLDS (2 files, 10,536 bytes) Reynolds Caps. Shareware. Registration: $2.99.

RIBBONS (2 files, 80,773 bytes) Davy's Ribbons, banner display caps with fancy ends. Shareware. Registration: $7.49.

ROCKMAKR (2 files, 38,994 bytes) Rockmaker, a rough, broad paintbrush-stroke font. Similar to Trading Post. Caps, numbers, and punctuation. Free.

ROTHMAN (2 files, 16,797 bytes) Rothman, an Art Deco font based on Empire. Full set of alpha and numeric characters, plus punctuation. Free.

RUDELSB (2 files, 38,551 bytes) Rudelsburg. Shareware. Registration: $4.99.

SALTER (2 files, 28,319 bytes) Salter, a fun 3-D font. Free.

SHOHFLD (2 files, 36,248 bytes) Shohl-Fold novelty fanfold font. Some letters face left, others right. Shareware. Registration: $3.

SHOWBOAT (2 files, 99,793 bytes) Showboat decorative drop caps. Shareware. Registration: $4.99.

 SMELLY (1 file, 187,728 bytes) No, this isn't a font. It was too complex to make it as a font, so David Rakowski created a .TIF file, chock full of letters made of old body parts and innards. Eh, what else? Think of a Sesame Street alphabet routine peppered with the sounds of AK-47s. *OHHHHH a serial murderer is a person in your neighborhood, in your neighborhood, in your neigh-bor-hood. . .* Definitely *not* for the faint of heart. Free. Which is just as well.

STARBRST (2 files, 43,228 bytes) Starburst, all caps with radial starburst pattern. Shareware. Registration: $9.99.

STENCIL (2 files, 30,960 bytes) Lintsec, a stencil-style font. All caps, numbers and punctuation. Free.

TEJARAT (2 files, 23,858 bytes) Tejaratchi Caps is a caps only, raised, quasi-metallic font. Free.

TENDRLF (2 files, 45,581 bytes) TenderLeaf, a display font of rough capital letters that look like twisted branches with leaves growing out of them. Caps and some punctuation. Free.

TONE_DEB (2 files, 45,949 bytes) ToneAndDebs, a black sans serif font topped with a layer of snow. Shareware. Registration: $3.

TRIBECA (2 files, 36,712 bytes) Tribeca, an elegant font. Shareware. Registration: $4.99.

UECHIGOT (2 files, 71,520 bytes) Uechi Gothic, a full display font with fantastic ornate capitals. Shareware. Registration: $3.02.

UPPEREST (2 files, 32,641 bytes) Upper East Side, similar to Parisian. Shareware. Registration: $9.95.

UPPERWST (2 files, 92,713 bytes) Upper West Side, similar to the New Yorker font, including the famous fantabulous fop. Shareware. Registration: $6.41.

VARAH (2 files, 56,268 bytes) Varah Caps, an illuminated Art Nouveau font. Shareware. Registration: $4.99.

VICTORIA (2 files, 29,015 bytes) Victoria's Secret. No, it isn't what you think. It's a script font that looks a lot like handwriting. Free.

WEDGIE (2 files, 36,328 bytes) Wedgies, a delightful 3-D font. Free.

WHARMBY (2 files, 30,773 bytes) Wharmby, a shadowed font with caps and numbers only. Shadow falls in front, as if lit from behind. Named after the gracious and magnanimous CompuServe denizen Eileen Wharmby. Free.

WILLHAR (2 files, 57,420 bytes) Will-Harris font. Looks like a downtown skyline seen through Venetian blinds. Free.

ZALESKI (2 files, 18,264 bytes) Zaleski Caps, a bold, brash art deco face based on Ashley Crawford. Shareware. Registration: $4.99.

ZALLMAN (2 files, 55,019 bytes) Zallman Caps, an ornate drop cap. Filled serif surrounded by vines, leaves, blossoms. No X or Y, punctuation or numbers. Free.

ZODIAC (1 file, 30,080 bytes) Eileen's Medium Zodiac: all 12 signs of the zodiac. Free.

 Font maven and scion of the shareware industry Gary Elfring has included a shareware sampler of his fonts on CD MOM. You'll find many of his most popular TrueType fonts here on the CD, plus a special price on a big bonus pack. Gary's been in the font biz for years: he did fonts before fonts were cool.

UTILITY\FONTS\ELFRING (22 files, 459,050 bytes) — A sampler of Elfring's critically acclaimed and widely requested TrueType fonts, including Aapex, Century, Century Bold, Cursive Elegant, Fritz Quad, Fritz Quad Bold, MicroStile, MicroStile Bold, Old English, and Zap Chance.

For samples of the fonts, take a look at **SAMPLE.WRI**. To get going, run **INSTALL.EXE**. ASP Shareware. When you register Elfring's Soft Fonts ($25), you'll get 15 more fonts. And for a great tutorial on fonts in general, see **SOFTFONT.WRI**.

Fonter

UTILITY\FONTS\FONTER (4 files, 113,972 bytes) — George Campbell's legendary font lister/cataloger/printer. View fonts on screen at three different zoom levels; print font lists with your own sample text; complete font books. TrueType, ATM, FaceLift are all supported. Shareware from OSOSoft. Registration: $15.

Font Namer

UTILITY\FONTS\FONTNAMR (2 files, 39,838 bytes) — Reaches into the bowels of your TrueType and ATM font files and extracts their names. Prints complete lists, and lets you safely delete the files themselves. Freeware from OSOSoft and George Campbell.

Printer's Apprentice

UTILITY\FONTS\PRINTAPPR (19 files, 791,980 bytes) — Okay. So now you have a thousand fonts. What do you *do* with 'em? Good question. Printer's Apprentice version 5.61 prints font specimens, ANSI charts, just about everything you need to catalog and keep track of all those phonts. To get going, just run **INSTALL.EXE**. Shareware from Bryan Kinkel at LYM (Lose Your Mind!) Development. Registration: $25.

Video Terminal Font

I've heard more requests for this font than any other. It's a straightforward, dot-based font that recreates characters precisely as you see them on a DOS screen. (For the technically inclined, it's a pixel-based rendering of the PC-8 character set.) If you're trying to print something that looks just like a DOS computer screen, this is the font you need.

UTILITY\FONTS\VTSR (6 files, 66,686 bytes) — Ed Behl's Video Terminal Screenl font, version 3.1. This is the classic, the one you've probably been looking for. Follow the instructions in **VTS.TXT** to install the font. **VTSNOTES.TXT** steps you through a DOS screen capture — what you need to do to copy a DOS screen into your Windows document. Shareware. Registration: $10. Behl Technologies has several other eminently useful fonts available; see **ORDERFRM.TXT** for details.

Games, Education: GAMES\

Atoms

UTILITY\GAMES\ATOMS (6 files, 68,346 bytes) — *Hey, it's fun!* Atoms version 2.1 has you uncover an invisible pattern by "firing" atoms into it. Run **ATOMS.EXE**. Shareware from Mike McNamee and MP Software. Registration: $5.

Blackout

UTILITY\GAMES\BLACKOUT (4 files, 215,616 bytes) — Mouse Shootout *(Mouse Out?)* at the OK Corral. Blackout 3.0 is a fun game that little kids can master in a minute, but keep adults going for hours. Hone your clicking skills. Betcha any ten-year-old can beat anybody over 30! Requires that both **VBRUN300.DLL** (which is in CD-MOM's root directory) and **THREED.VBX** (which is in this subdirectory) be along your DOS path. Just run **BLACKOUT.EXE** or check the installation instructions in **READMECD.TXT**. Shareware from Patrick Mills and Zarkware. Registration: $15, which brings you more buttons, sounds, and a 3-D look.

Card Shark Hearts

UTILITY\GAMES\CSHEARTS (22 files, 741,175 bytes) — This isn't so much a card game as a way of life. You may *think* you know how to play Hearts, but I guarantee you've never played it like this. The opponents — and you can choose who to play against, even their aggressiveness — wisecrack as you make mistakes, and The Shark makes an occasional guest appearance <gulp>. Full of sound and fury; a grand ride. Just copy the files to your hard disk and run **CSHEARTS.EXE**. ASP Shareware from Nelson Ford at PsL. Registration: $25.

Flash-21

UTILITY\GAMES\FLASH-21 (11 files, 296,953 bytes) — No, this isn't another dumb flashcard program. It's more like a flashcard authoring system, where you can create your own flashcards. Lots of neat options, including a unique front-to-back and back-to-front flipper — just what you need if you're learning how to translate languages back and forth. From Dick Bryant at Open Windows. Run **OWSETUP.EXE** and you're off. ASP Shareware. Registration: $18.

Super Video Poker

UTILITY\GAMES\SVPOKER (5 files, 332,050 bytes) — Even if you don't play cards. Even if you don't play computer games. You gotta check this one out. Super Video Poker 1.0 matches the best video poker machines Vegas has to offer — and it even gives you "hints" about the best choices. Face cards have real faces. You'll see. Shareware from Elton Inada. Registration: $15.

General Utilities: GENERAL\

Barry Press Utilities

UTILITY\GENERAL\BPUTIL (28 files, 466,534 bytes) — A giant grab-bag of things that Microsoft forgot: launch buttons, command line icons, monthly calendar, compare files, printer orientation, clock, print text files, and much more, all with a drag and drop interface. Shareware from the fertile mind of Barry Press himself. Registration: $20.

Bar Clock

UTILITY\GENERAL\BARCLOCK (5 files, 65,311 bytes) — You'll wonder how you ever lived without it. BarClock version 2.2 puts the current date in the left corner of every window, and the current time in the right. Ingenious and slick. You can also show free memory, system resources, and available disk space up on the bar, *and* a whole bunch more. For installation instructions, see **BARCLOCK.WRI**. Shareware from Patrick Breen. Registration: $5 — one of the greatest bargains in Windowdom.

ChangeIt

UTILITY\GENERAL\CHANGEIT (2 files, 18,180 bytes) — If you've just moved Windows from one drive to another — or installed a new drive, or let Stacker or DoubleSpace get at your Windows drive — you have a lot of changes to make! All your Windows stuff has to point to the new drive. While ChangeIt won't automatically pick up every nuance, you'll find it invaluable in getting things re-arranged. Read about it in **CHANGEIT.TXT**, then just run **CHANGEIT.EXE**. Freeware from the legendary Thom Foulks.

Chooser

UTILITY\GENERAL\CHOOSER (5 files, 128,653 bytes) — A fantastic, quick utility that lets you change the printer and the page orientation with just a click. For installation, see **CHOOSER.WRI**. Requires that **VBRUN100.DLL** be in the Windows directory, or along the DOS path (**VBRUN100.DLL** is in the CD-MOM root directory). Shareware from Derek Cohen. If you like Chooser, you're asked to make a donation to Gay Men Fighting AIDS (GMFA), P.O. Box 99, London SW2 1EL.

Compose

UTILITY\GENERAL\COMPOSE (7 files, 154,967 bytes) — One of the most useful utilities you'll ever see. And it's free. Compose version 1.67 lets you get at oddball characters with simple keystrokes — "1 2", say, for ½ — look at characters, insert the time, and see font samples. Discussed extensively in Chapter 5. Run **COMPOSE.EXE** and take a look. Most excellent freeware from Jerry Cummings at Digital Equipment Corp. (Note that DEC doesn't support it!)

Filer

UTILITY\GENERAL\FILER (4 files, 231,667 bytes) — A free file finder and viewer. Text. PCX, GIF, BMP, WMF. Even listen to WAV files. Sophisticated search capabilities. Look at **FILER.WRI**. Requires **VBRUN200.DLL**, which is on CD-MOM's root directory. Freeware. But if you try it and like it as much as I do, would you do me a favor? Write to George and ask him why in the blue blazes he's giving something this good away for free? Thanks.

Foreigner

UTILITY\GENERAL\FOREIGNR (3 files, 109,051 bytes) — Foreigner version 3.10 from Gordon Goldsborough sticks all those oddball characters into most Windows applications. You can choose from any of the 256 characters in a font, zoom the picking window, and much more. Just run **FOREIGN.EXE**. Shareware. Registration a paltry $6.50 — and for that you also get a TrueType fraction font.

INI Manager

UTILITY\GENERAL\INIMAN (5 files, 139,221 bytes) — A top-notch utility for managing INI files, INI Manager version 2.00.02 lets you create and delete files, edit sections, print, search, show, sort keys, and much more. Follow the instructions in **README.TXT**. Requires **VBRUN300.DLL**, which is in CD MOM's root directory. Shareware from Martinsen's Software. Registration: $30.

INI ProFiler

`UTILITY\GENERAL\INIPRO` (6 files, 249,388 bytes) — Here's another great INI editor, with an outstanding interface and easy backup. Now there's no excuse for shooting your INI files in the foot! Run `INIPRO.EXE`. Shareware from Matthew Smith and Pegasus Development. Registration: $16.

MultiLabel

`UTILITY\GENERAL\MULTLABL` (8 files, 341,456 bytes) — Create any type of label — use Avery labels or use your own layout. Clip art. Line drawing tools. Address Book module. Mail merge. Much more. To start, look at `MLTLBL.WRI`. Shareware from OSOSoft and George Campbell. Registration: $20.

ProMenu

`UTILITY\GENERAL\PROMENU` (5 files, 88,816 bytes) — It takes a while to get used to it, but once your hand-eye co-ordination groks it, ProMenu /S version 1.0 can be a big time saver. Click your right mouse button, and your application's menu (in full 3-D attire) appears at the cursor location. ZAP! This "/S" version is the shareware incarnation of the commerical product ProMenu: several capabilities of the commercial product are not implemented. Run `PROMENUS.EXE`, and click your right mouse button. You'll catch on right away. From Christopher Cain and Cain International Corp. Registration: $25.

Rockford

`UTILITY\GENERAL\ROCKFORD` (7 files, 332,851 bytes) — George Campbell has done it again! If you need special business cards, this is your solution. Fast. Versatile. Supports clip art, any printer, three major pre-cut card sizes. To start, look at `ROCKFORD.WRI`. Requires `VBRUN200.DLL`, which is on CD-MOM's root directory. Shareware from OSOSoft. Registration: $20.

Stickies!

`UTILITY\GENERAL\STICKIES` (15 files, 754,362 bytes) — At last! Fast, easy, "stick-on" notes for your applications. Want to make a note, but don't want to change the file? Stick on a stickie. Most impressive. Stickies 2.1 is from Looking

Glass Technologies. Run **INSTALL.EXE**; it'll take about 1 MB of hard disk space. There are several file conversion utilities in the **\FREEBIES** subdirectory. Shareware. Registration: $30.

Sysback

UTILITY\GENERAL\SYSBACK (3 files, 317,744 bytes) — A poor man's (organism's?) backup, done in style. Windows System Backup Version 2.30a gives you one-click backups of **AUTOEXEC.BAT** and **CONFIG.SYS**, plus .**INI**, .**PIF**, and .**GRP** files — and any other extensions you care to list. Copy **SYSBACK.EXE** and **BWCC.DLL** to any handy directory and run the former. Nicely done. Shareware from Nick Hodges. Registration: $2 (no, that isn't a typo!).

UN4Win

UTILITY\GENERAL\UN4WIN (6 files, 102,966 bytes) — Installing ain't easy. Un-installing — removing all the vestiges of software you no longer wish to support in the manner to which it has become accustomed — can be murder. Uninstall For Windows Version 1.5 isn't going to solve all of your uninstall problems, but it'll help a lot. Copy all the files over to your hard drive, then follow the instructions in **UN4WIN.DOC**. Shareware from It's Your Money Inc. Registration: $19 (or $28 with printed docs and a three-issue trial subscription to *IYM Software Review*).

WinGRAB

UTILITY\GENERAL\WINGRAB (3 files, 614,717 bytes) — Grabs addresses from any Windows program, prints envelopes and much more. Built-in address book, with lots of bells and whistles. Version 1.7. Run **INSTALL.EXE**: it'll take about 800K of hard disk space. ASP Shareware from ZPAY Payroll Systems. Registration: $44.95.

WinKey

UTILITY\GENERAL\WINKEY (10 files, 147,138 bytes) — WinKey version 1.0 turns your keyboard every which way but loose. Well, maybe loose, too. You control how Shift Lock works, whether NumLock or Scroll Lock start out on or off, the location of the Ctrl and Caps Lock keys, and more. Look at **WINKEY.WRI** for installation instructions; it'll take about 200K on your hard drive. Shareware from Terry Lindeman and DataGem. Registration: $15.

WinLabel

UTILITY\GENERAL\WINLABEL (22 files, 1,153,778 bytes) — Need to print a diskette label, like, fast? This is what you need. WinLabel version 3.01. It'll also print directory listings and a whole bunch more, but for diskette labels, this is the cat's meow. Run **SETUP.EXE**. Shareware from Robert Amans and Practice Marketing Services. Registration: $35.

WinUpD8R

UTILITY\GENERAL\WINUPD8R (10 files, 369,696 bytes) — If you need to synch files on two or more machines, this utility from Open Windows is a godsend. It's yet another example of a fine shareware program that solves a specific problem, and solves it well, at one-tenth the price of commercial software. Synchs and re-synchs files, directories, groups of subdirectories, and more. Run **OWSETUP.EXE** and you're off. ASP Shareware. Registration: $18.

Graphics: GRAPHICS\

PaintShopPro

UTILITY\GRAPHICS\PSPRO (10 files, 369,696 bytes) — The polyglot graphics package, PaintShop Pro supports BMP, CLP, CUT, DIB, EPS, GIF, IFF, IMG, JAS, JIF, JPG, LBM, MAC, MSP, PCD, PIC, PCX, RAS, RLE, TGA, TIF, WMF, and WPG file formats. You can display, convert, alter, scan and print images. Oh, did I mention it also does screen captures? ASP Shareware from Bob Voit and JASC Inc. Registration: $74.

PaintShop

UTILITY\GRAPHICS\PS (5 files, 277,842 bytes) — No, you aren't seeing double. double. JASC still distributes its older, somewhat less endowed (but still mighty powerful!) version of PaintShop, should you find PaintShop Pro overwhelming. ASP Shareware from JASC Inc. Registration: $44.

PixFolio

UTILITY\GRAPHICS\PIXFOLIO (52 files; 874,252 bytes) — PixFolio version 2.0.87 is a great way to keep track of your picture files, catalog them, slide shows, all sorts of neat stuff, including several sophisticated features. Run **SETUP.EXE**; it's down in the **DISK1** subdirectory. Shareware from Allen Kempe and ACK Software. Registration: $39.

WinClip

UTILITY\GRAPHICS\WINCLIP (10 files, 141,072 bytes) — A single-purpose, dynamite utility that lets you view and catalog BMP and PCX files. Zoom, scroll, print, copy, move, delete, and more. Requires **VBRUN200.DLL**, which is in CD MOM's root directory. To start, look at **WINCLI.WRI**. Shareware from OSOSoft and George Campbell. Registration: $20.

Icons: ICON\

A-Z Icon Edit

UTILITY\ICON\AZICONED (5 files, 114,279 bytes) — An Icon Editor's Icon Editor. AZ Icon Edit version 1.8 does it all: cut, paste, capture, shift, fill, nine different drawing tools, and on and on. Just copy the files to your hard drive and run the executable file to get started. Shareware from AZ Computer Innovations. Registration: $20.

Icon Manager

UTILITY\ICON\ICONMGR (12 files, 170,356 bytes) — So now you have thousands of icons. How do you keep track of 'em? Good question. Icon Manager version 3.3 will help you manage icons in Program Manager or Norton Desktop: just drag & drop to move, copy, or organize icon files within Icon Manager. This Icon Manager is designed to manage the icons you have on your disk; look at Icon Manager in the **SCREEN** section for a program to manage icons on the desk. They're very different programs! Run **SETUP.EXE**; it'll take about 200K of space on your hard drive. Shareware from Leonard Gray and Impact Software. Registration: $29.95.

Languages, Macros: LANG\

Stackey/Batutil

UTILITY\LANG\BATUTIL (37 files in 3 subdirectories, 945,390 bytes) — This one is a bit difficult to categorize. Stackey and Batutil version 4.0 have evolved to the point that they're full-fledged languages. Think of them as fancy macro languages for DOS **.BAT** files — and sometimes the easiest way to get something done in Windows is to do it in DOS. Written by Barry Simon and Rick Wilson. It's great, but we're biased: *that* Barry is *this* Barry. So run **BUDEMO.BAT** and **SHOWDEMO.BAT**

and all those other xx**DEMO.BAT**s. Bet you'll be impressed. To install, run
INSTALL.BAT. ASP Shareware from CtrlAlt Associates. Registration: $49.

WinBatch

UTILITY\LANG\WINBATCH (49 files, 622,836 bytes) — WinBatch 4.0k, the
original batch programming language for Windows. Enormously powerful. Nearly
200 different commands: this is the easy way to start industrial strength Windows
programming. Semantec liked it so much, they bundled an older version of it as the
"macro language" in Norton Desktop for Windows! Run **WSETUP.EXE** to get
started. ASP Shareware from Wilson WindowWare. Registration: $69.95.

Personal Info / DataBase: PIMDATA\

 Yeah, yeah, yeah. I couldn't decide if this section should be called "Personal
Information Managers" or "Databases" or "Calendars and Phone Books" or
"Keeping Your Life Straight" or whatever. So let's just leave it at **PIMDATA**,
OK? I won't tell Mom if you don't.

Oh. Make sure you take a look at Helen Feddema's Access applications, over in the
APPS\ACCESS section. She has two Access databases that may do everything you
need.

2Do

UTILITY\PIMDATA\2DO (16 files, 1,144,834 bytes) — 2Do Version 1.1 is a
task/contact manager with a twist: it revolves around tasks, not times. Play with it a
bit and you'll see what I mean. Run **SETUP.EXE**. ASP Shareware from Bill
Anderson. Registration: $30.

Address Manager

UTILITY\PIMDATA\ADDRMGR (45 files, 889,769 bytes) — Names, addresses,
phone numbers. Print lists, envelopes, labels. Autodialer. Data import/export via
DDE. If you don't need all the fancy-schmancy commercial PIM bells and whistles
— and wouldn't mind saving a few hundred bucks in the process — you need to

look at Address Manager 2.1c. Run **WSETUP.EXE** to get started. ASP Shareware from Wilson WindowWare. Registration: $39.95.

Almanac

UTILITY\PIMDATA\ALMANAC (28 files, 407,826 bytes) — Almanac version 3.0H is a powerful calendar/scheduling/personal information manager that combines a traditional calendar with windows for your daily schedule, notes, and to-do list. Alarm clock. Lots of goodies. Run **SETUP.EXE**; it'll take about 400K of space on your hard drive. Shareware from Leonard Gray and Impact Software. Registration: Basic, $49.95; Premium (retail version with upgrades and notification), $79.95.

Reminder

UTILITY\PIMDATA\REMINDER (19 files, 366,077 bytes) — Another standout from Wilson WindowWare. Reminder 1.3d is a time management tool: it keeps track of to-do lists, sets alarms (which can launch apps), prints reports, much more. Supports DDE. Run **WSETUP.EXE** to get started. ASP Shareware. Registration: $59.95.

Time & Chaos Pro

UTILITY\PIMDATA\TCHAOS (12 files, 681,874 bytes) — Time & Chaos 4.01 is a great calendar, diary, to-do list, autodialer, and much more. Requires **VBRUN200.DLL**, which is in CD-MOM's root directory. To get started, copy the files to your hard drive and run **INSTALL.EXE**. Shareware from iSBiSTER International. Registration: $59.95.

Program Manager Add-Ons: PROGMAN\

Command Post

UTILITY\PROGMAN\COMMANDP (38 files, 820,339 bytes) — Command Post 8.0h replaces Program Manager entirely with a fast, small, and easily customizable text-based shell. You can create your own menus, use the built-in batch language and file viewer. Run **WSETUP.EXE** to get started. ASP Shareware from Wilson WindowWare. Registration: $49.95.

Detour

UTILITY\PROGMAN\DETOUR (3 files, 23,961 bytes) — Detour version 1.4 from Christopher Bolin bypasses the normal File Manager and Program Manager extension associations. You may have **.DOC** files set up so that when you File/Run them, or double-click on them in File Manager, WinWord pops up with the **.DOC** file loaded. Sometimes, though, you'd like to be able to bypass that usual association and just quickly shuffle the file to Windows Write. Detour lets you double-click on the file, but then get a chance to route the file to a different app. There's a very neat hack described in **DETOUR.WRI** that shows you how to set up **.BAT** files so you can either run them, or edit them, with one click. Copy **DETOUR.EXE** and **DETOUR.INI** to your hard drive, and follow the instructions in **DETOUR.WRI**. Freeware.

Plug-Ins for Program Manager

UTILITY\PROGMAN\PLUGIN (31 files, 463,862 bytes) — Plug-Ins for Program Manager version 1.3 adds extensive group management, run command history, different icons for groups, custom cursors, and much more that Microsoft forgot. Check **README.DOC** to get started. ASP Shareware from David Mandell and Plannet Crafters. Registration: $20.

Salvation

UTILITY\PROGMAN\SALVTION (14 files, 576,144 bytes) — This one is a bit hard to categorize. Salvation version 1.15 replaces both the Windows File Manager and Program Manager, with an integrated set of disk, file, text, and other utilities. Give it a shot. Check out the instructions in **README.TXT**. Shareware from Vitesse, Inc. Registration: $20.

WindowMagic

UTILITY\PROGMAN\WINMAGIC (19 files, 522,836 bytes) — Icons to the max. WindowMagic lets you assign icons to Program Manager groups, applications, and the lot. Great drag and drop interface. Quick launch. Fancy icon bar. Look at **INSTALL.TXT** and give it a shot. Shareware from Troy Werelius and WinWear. Registration: $49.95.

Resources, Restart: RESOURCE\

Bailout

UTILITY\RESOURCE\BAILOUT (5 files, 116,874 bytes) — Bails out of Windows, lickety-split. Set up as a "Click and Die" icon. From Dick Bryant at Open Windows. Run **OWSETUP.EXE** to install. Freeware.

Beyond Windows Exit

UTILITY\RESOURCE\BWE (4 files, 29,182 bytes) — Beyond Windows Exit, version 1.11 exits Windows, but with a twist: it can exit and re-start Windows, and run any DOS program you like in between. Neat drag & drop interface. Take a look at **README.TXT** for installation instructions. Shareware from Martinsen's Software. Registration: $5.

Roger's Rapid Restart

UTILITY\RESOURCE\RRRESTRT (8 files, 104,039 bytes) — Roger's Rapid Restart gets you in and out of Windows quickly, optionally running a DOS program before restarting. Check **README.DOC** to get started. ASP Shareware from David Mandell and Plannet Crafters. Registration: $10.

Screen, Desktop Work: SCREEN\

Big Desk and BackMenu

UTILITY\SCREEN\BIGDESK (17 files, 483,345 bytes) — Big Desk version 2.40 gives you a huge virtual desktop — up to 64 times bigger than the regular one — that you can use to organize things, yet keep it all accessible. Included is BackMenu, a routine that lets you double-click on the desktop and get an immediate menu. Look at **BIGDESK.WRI** and **BACKMENU.WRI** for instructions. Shareware from SP Services. Registration: £25.

Icon Manager

UTILITY\SCREEN\ICOMAN (5 files, 561,991 bytes) — Icon management meets drag 'n drop. This program actually changes the way Windows handles iconized apps: they're put in a single window, and you choose among them with text buttons. If you're looking for something that manages icons on your disk, look at the Icon Manager in the **ICONS** section. This Icon Manager manages icons on your desk; that other Icon Manager manages icons on your disk. They're very different: give 'em a try and you'll see. Copy all the files to a new subdirectory on your hard drive. Then copy BWCC.DLL from CD MOM's \utility\system\sysback to the new subdirectory. Run ICONMAN.EXE to get started. Shareware from Scott Bender and Harmony Data Systems. Registration: $20.

Movie Time Screen Saver

UTILITY\SCREEN\MOVIETM (5 files, 81,573 bytes) — The next generation in screen savers. Movie Time actually plays movies when the screen falls idle. Any **.AVI** file. Look at **MVTIME.TXT** for installation instructions: it works just like Windows' native screen savers. Shareware from Starlight Software. Registration: $19.95.

Wallpaper Manager

UTILITY\SCREEN\WALLPMAN (4 files, 34,197 bytes) — Wallpaper Manager version 1.50 is the last word in wallpaper management: pick 'em, change 'em, preview 'em. Follow the instructions in **README.TXT**. Requires **VBRUN300.DLL**, which is in CD-MOM's root directory. Shareware from Martinsen's Software. Registration: $30.

WinPak #1

UTILITY\SCREEN\WINPAK (21 files, 269,456 bytes) — From Rhode Island Soft Systems, WinPak#1 has a bunch of fun stuff: four original Windows 3.1 animated Screen Savers, two TrueType fonts, and over 100 icons! Comes complete with a quick and easy setup program. From inside file manager, simply run **SETUP.EXE** and then activate these Win3.1 screen saver add-ons and Fonts via the Windows Control Panel. (WinPak#1 installs itself in your Windows **\SYSTEM** directory.) The Window Washer screen saver is so ultra-cool, it's replaced my enfatuation with the Energizer Bunny and the After Dark Flying Toasters. ASP Shareware, $19 registration, with more WinPaks to come.

ZipStuff: ZIP\

CCIZIP

UTILITY\ZIP\CCIZIP (9 files, 690,099 bytes) — CCIZip version 2.0, an archive management program with a neat interface. Good hooks into virus scanners. Follow the instructions in **CCIZIP.WRI** to install. Shareware from The Creative Consortium. Registration: $33.

LHA

UTILITY\ZIP\LHA (4 files, 81,935 bytes) — Classic file compression from the inimitable Yoshi. In general, LHA produces files just slightly larger than those from PKZip 2.04 (see below), but the price is right. Freeware — but copyrighted! — from Yoshi.

PKZip

UTILITY\ZIP\PKZIP (17 files, 571,976 bytes) — Phil Katz' monumental achievement, PKZip version 2.04 wrings every last bit out of your files. The industry standard, and for good reason. Start by reading the **README.DOC** file. ASP Shareware. Registration: $47. It'll pay for itself over and over again.

UnZip

UTILITY\ZIP\UNZIP (17 files, 571,976 bytes) — Hey, it's quick, it's tiny, and it's free. Who could ask for more? Well, no, it won't zip files up. It only exists to reconstitute **.ZIP** files back to their original state. Still. . .

 This un-zipper declares that you can distribute it as long as you make it clear that it is "not being sold, that the source code is freely available, and that there are no extra or hidden charges resulting from its use by or inclusion with the commercial product." Well, it isn't, it is (in the CompuServe IBMPRO forum), and there aren't. There. The authors claim that they don't give a rat's posterior about legalities and all that mumbo-jumbo. My kind of folks.

UnZip is a collaborative effort from (I think this is in chronological order): Samuel H. Smith, Carl Mascott, David P. Kirschbaum, Greg R. Roelofs, Mark Adler, Kai Uwe Rommel, Igor Mandrichenko, Johnny Lee, Jean-loup Gailly; Glenn Andrews, Joel Aycock, Allan Bjorklund, James Birdsall, Wim Bonner, John Cowan, Frank da Cruz, Bill Davidsen, Arjan de Vet, James Dugal, Jim Dumser, Mark Edwards, David Feinleib, Mike Freeman, Hunter Goatley, Robert Heath, Dave Heiland, Larry Jones, Kjetil J(o)rgenson, Bob Kemp, J. Kercheval, Alvin Koh, Bo Kullmar, Johnny Lee, Warner Losh, Fulvio Marino, Gene McManus, Joe Meadows, Mike O'Carroll, Humberto Ortiz-Zuazaga, Piet W. Plomp, Antonio Querubin Jr., Steve Salisbury, Georg Sassen, Jon Saxton, Hugh Schmidt, Martin Schulz, Charles Scripter, Chris Seaman, Richard Seay, Alex Sergejew, Cliff Stanford, Onno van der Linden, Jim Van Zandt, Antoine Verheijen, Paul Wells.

It's a neat thing to distribute with diskettes that contain .**ZIP** files. No need to worry about licensing or fees or whatnot, as long as you follow the instructions in the file called **COPYING**. Freeware. I've been using it for a couple of months now, on all sorts of **.ZIP** files, and haven't hit a problem.

WinZIP

UTILITY\ZIP\WINZIP (12 files, 316,806 bytes) — This my favorite Windows unZIPper. Must've used it a thousand times in the course of putting the book together. A full, robust Windows interface with PKZip (which must be registered separately). A real workhorse. ASP Shareware from Nico Mak. Registration: $29.

CHAPTER 13
Mom's Font Catalog

Here are samples of bread and butter fonts from the three big vendors and from Casady & Greene. You'll also find a large selection of doo-hickey fonts.

Doo-hickey fonts are mainly dingbat and pictograph fonts — purely symbolic, but there are some text faces which clearly fall into this category.

Bread and Butter Fonts

Monotype TrueType Value Pack

Arial Narrow (in four weights)

ABCDEFGHIJKLM nopqrstuvwxyz **ABCD**EFGH**IJKLM** nopq*rstuv***wxyz**

Book Antiqua (in four weights; aka Palatino)

ABCDEFGHIJKLM nopqrstuvwxyz **ABCD**EFGH**IJKLM** nopq*rstuv***wxyz**

Bookman Old Weight (in four weights; aka Bookman)

ABCDEFGHIJKLM nopqrstuvwxyz **ABCD**EFGH**IJKLM** nopq*rstuv***wxyz**

Century Schoolbook (in four weights; aka New Century Schoolbook)

ABCDEFGHIJKLM nopqrstuvwxyz **ABCD**EFGH**IJKLM** nopq*rstuv***wxyz**

Century Gothic (in four weights; aka Avant Garde)

ABCDEFGHIJKLM nopqrstuvwxyz **ABCD**EFGH**IJKLM** nopq*rstuv***wxyz**

Monotype Corsiva (in two weights; aka Zapf Chancery)

ABCDEFGHIJKLM nopqrstuvwxyz ABCDEFGHIJKLM nopqrstuvwxyz

Monotype Sorts (samples in 18 point; aka Zapf Dingbats)

Baskerville MT (in four weights)

ABCDEFGHIJKLM nopqrstuvwxyz **ABCD**EFGH**IJKLM** nopq*rstuv***wxyz**

Calisto MT (in four weights)

ABCDEFGHIJKLM nopqrstuvwxyz **ABCD**EFGH**IJKLM** nopq*rstuv***wxyz**

Arial Extra Bold (in three weights)

ABCDEFGHIJKLM nopqrstuvwxyz ABCDEF*GHIJKLM* nopqrst*uvwxyz*

Arial Black (in two weights)

ABCDEFGHIJKLM nopqrstuvwxyz *ABCDEFGHIJKLM nopqrstuvwxyz*

Times New Roman MT Extra Bold (in two weights)

ABCDEFGHIJKLM nopqrstuvwxyz *ABCDEFGHIJKLM nopqrstuvwxyz*

Eight Script Fonts

Biffo Script: ABCDEFGHIJKLM nopqrstuvwxyz

Forte: ABCDEFGHIJKLM nopqrstuvwxyz

Klang: ABCDEFGHIJKLM nopqrstuvwxyz

Mercurius Script: ABCDEFGH ijklmnopqrs

Monoline Script: ABCDEFGHIJ klmnopqrstuvw

Monotype Script: ABCDEFGHIJ klmnopqrstuvw

New Berolina: ABCDEFGHIJK lmnopqrstuvwxyz

Pepita: ABCDEFGHIJKLM nopqrstuvwxyz

Twelve Display Typefaces

Bodini Bold Condensed: ABCDEFGHIJKLM nopqrstuvwxyz

Bodini Ultra Bold: ABC*DEFGH* ijk*lmno*

Braggadocio: ABCDEFG hijklmn

CASTELLAR: ABCDEFGHIJKLMNOPQRS

Clearface Gothic: ABCDEFGHIJKLM nopqrstuvwx

Headline: ABCDEFGHIJKLM nopqrstuvwxyz

Ellington Extra Bold: ABCDEFG hijklmnopq

MONOTYPE ENGRAVERS: ABCD

Old Style Bold Outline: ABCDEF ghijkl

Photina Ultra Bold: ABCDEFG hijklmno

Placard Bold Condensed: ABCDEFGHIJKLM nopqrstuvwxyz

Rockwell Bold Condensed: ABCDEFGHIJ klmnopqrstuv

Rockwell Extra Bold: ABCDE fghijk

Microsoft Font Pack I (*TrueType Font Pack for Windows*)

Includes the Arial Narrow, Book Antiqua, Bookman Old Style, Century Gothic, Century Schoolbook, Monotype Corsiva, and Monotype Sorts identical to the ones in the Monotype TrueType Value Pack (Microsoft licensed them from Monotype).

Lucida Family

Blackletter: ABCDEFGHIJKLM nopqrstuvwxyz

Bright: ABCDEFGHIJKLM nopqrstuvwxyz

Calligraphy: ABCDEFGH ijklmnopqrst

Fax: ABCDEFGHIJKLM nopqrstuvwxyz

Handwriting: ABCDEFGH ijklmnopqrs

Sans: ABCDEFGHIJKLM nopqrstuvwxyz

Typewriter: ABCDEFGHIJ klmnopqrstuv

Lucida Math Fonts (three families)

$$()[]\|\lceil\{\}\langle\rangle/ \bullet \bullet \otimes \otimes \Sigma \Pi \int \cup \cap \uplus \wedge \vee \Sigma \Pi$$

$$\chi \psi \omega \varepsilon \vartheta \varpi \varrho \varsigma \varphi \leftarrow \leftarrow \rightarrow \rightarrow \beta \chi \Pi < \Upsilon \Phi / \Omega \phi \Theta$$

$$< > \leftarrow \rightarrow \uparrow \downarrow \leftrightarrow \nearrow \searrow \simeq \Leftarrow \Rightarrow \Uparrow \quad \otimes \mathfrak{R} \div \exists \circ \diamond \pm - \cdot \varnothing * +$$

Microsoft Font Pack 2

New Caledonia (in four weights)

ABCDEFGHIJKLM nopqrstuvwxyz **ABCDEFGH*IJKLM* nopq*rstuv* wxyz**

Baskerville Old Face (in one weight)

ABCDEFGHIJKLM nopqrstuvwxyz ABCDEFGHIJKLM nopqrstuvwxyz

Centaur (in one weight)

ABCDEFGHIJKLM nopqrstuvwxyz ABCDEFGHIJKLM nopqrstuvwxyz

Eurostyle (in two weights)

ABCDEFGHIJKLM nopqrstuvwxyz **ABCDEFGHIJKLM nopqrstuvwxyz**

Futura (in three weights)

ABCDEFGHIJKLM nopqrstuvwxyz **ABCDEFG**HIJKLM **nopqrst**uvwxyz

Fourteen Headline Fonts

Braggadocio: ABCDEFG hijklmn

Britannic Bold: ABCDEFGHIJKLM nopqrstuvwxyz

CASTELLAR: ABCDEFGHIJKLMNOPQRS

Contemporary Brush: ABCDEFGHIJKLM nopqrstuvwxyz
(also in Bold)

DESDEMONA: ABCDEFGHIJKLM NOPQRSTUVWXYZ

Elephant: ABCDEFGHIJ klmnopqrstuv
(also in Italic)

Gill Sans Ultra Bold: ABCDE fghij

Impact: ABCDEFGHIJKLM nopqrstuvwxyz

Onyx: ABCDEFGHIJKLM nopqrstuvwxyz ABCDEFGHIJKLM nopqrstuvwxyz

Playbill: ABCDEFGHIJKLM nopqrstuvwxyz ABCDEFGHIJKLM nopqrstuvwxyz

Ransom: ABCDEFGHIJKLM nopqrstuvwxyz
(also in Bold, Italic, and Bold Italic)

STENCIL: ABCDEFGHIJKLMNOPQRSTUV

STOP: ABCDEFGHIJKLM NOPQRSTUVWXYZ

Wide Latin: ABCD efghij

Ten Decorative Fonts and Two Symbol Fonts

AUGSBURGER INITIALS • ABCDEFGHIJKL

BriemScript: ABCDEFGHIJKLM nopqrstuvwxyz

Eckmann: ABCDEFGHIJKLM nopqrstuvwxyz

EddA: ABCDEFGHIJKLM NOPQRSTU

Gradl: ABCDEFGHIJKLM nopqrstuvwxyz ABCDEFGHIJKLM nopqrstuvwxyz

Harrington: ABCDEFGHIJKLM nopqrstuvwxyz

Mistral: ABCDEFGHIJKLM nopqrstuvwxyz

Old English Text MT: ABCDEFG hijklmnopqrst

Parade: ABCDEFGHIJKLM nopqrstuvwxyz

Peignot Medium: ABCDEFGHIJKLM nopqrstuvwxyz

(Wingdings 2)

(Wingdings 3)

Bitstream TrueType Font Pack

Geometric (in four weights)

ABCDEFGHIJKLM nopqrstuvwxyz ABCDEFG**HIJKLM** nopqrstuvwxyz

Humanist 521 Condensed (in two weights)

ABCDEFGHIJKLM nopqrstuvwxyz **ABCDEFGHIJKLM nopqrstuvwxyz**

Humanist 777 (in four weights)

ABCDEFGHIJKLM nopqrstuvwxyz **ABCD**EFGHIJKLM **nopq**rstuv**wxyz**

Humanist 970 (in two weights)

ABCDEFGHIJKLM nopqrstuvwxyz **ABCDEFGH ijklmnopq**

Imperial (in three weights)

ABCDEFGHIJKLM nopqrstuvwxyz **ABCDEF**GHIJKLM **nopqrst**uvwxyz

Revival 565 (in four weights)

ABCDEFGHIJKLM nopqrstuvwxyz ABCD*EFGHIJKLM* nopq*rstuvwxyz*

Square Slabserif 711 (in three weights)

ABCDEFGHIJKLM nopqrstuvwxyz **ABCDEFGHIJKLM nopqrstuvwxyz**

Fifteen Decorative Faces

Bitstream Oz Handicraft: ABCDEFGHIJKLM nopqrstuvwxyz

Clarendon Bold Condensed: ABCDEFGH hijklmnopqrs

English 157: ABCDEFGHIJKLM nopqrstuvwxyz

𝔉𝔯𝔞𝔠𝔱𝔲𝔯: ABCDEFGHIJKLM nopqrstuvwxyz

Freehand 575: ABCDEFGHIJKLM nopqrstuvwxyz

Freehand 591: ABCDEFGHIJKLM nopqrstuvwxyz

HUXLEY VERTICAL: ABCDEFGHIJKLM NOPQRSTUVWXYZ

Impress: ABCDEFGHIJKLM nopqrstuvwxyz

Incised 901 Nord: ABCD efg
(also in Italic)

INFORMAL 011: ABCDEFGHIJKLMNOPQRS
(also in Black)

Nuptial: ABCDEFGHIJKLM nopqrstuvwxyz

Poster Bodini: ABCDEFG hijklmnopqr
(also in Italic)

Staccato 555: ABCDEFGHIJKLM nopqrstuvwxyz

UMBRA: ABCDEFGHIJKLMNOPQRSTUVWXYZ

Vineta: ABCDEFG hijklmno

Bitstream TrueType Font Pack 2

Geometric 415 (in four weights)

ABCDEFGHIJKLM nopqrstuvwxyz ABCD*EFGHIJKLM* nopq*rstuvwxyz*

Square 721 Condensed (in one weight)

ABCDEFGHIJKLM nopqrstuvwxyz ABCDEFGHIJKLM nopqrstuvwxyz

Zapf Elliptical (in four weights)

ABCDEFGHIJKLM nopqrstuvwxyz **ABCD***EFGHIJKLM* nopq*rstuv***wxyz**

Eleven Decorative Faces

American Text: ABCDEFGHIJKLM nopqrstuvwxyz

Broadway: ABCDEFGH ijklmnopqrst

Cooper Black: ABCDEFGH ijklmnopqr

Brush 738: ABCDEFGHIJKLM nopqrstuvwxyz

DAVIDA BOLD: ABCDEFGHIJKLMNOPQRSTUVWX

Embassy: ABCDEFGHIJKLM nopqrstuvwxyz

Exotic 350: ABCDEFGHIJKLM NOPQRSTUVWXYZ

Handel Gothic: ABCDEFGH ijklmnnopqrst

Hobo: ABCDEFGHIJKLM nopqrstuvwxyz

VAG Rounded: ABCDEFGHIJKL mnopqrstuvwx

Zurich Bold Extra Condensed: ABCDEFGHIHK lmnopqrstuvwx

Casady & Greene Fluent Laser Fonts

Alexandria (in four weights)

ABCDEFGHIJKLM nopqrstuvwxyz ABCDEFGHIJKLM nopqrstuvwxyz

Bodoni (in four weights)

ABCDEFGHIJKLM nopqrstuvwxyz ABCDEFGHIJKLM nopqrstuvwxyz

Bodoni Ultra (in two weights)

ABCDEFGHIJKLM nopqrstuvwxyz ABCDEFGHI jklmnopqrstuv

Bodoni Ultra Condensed (in two weights)

ABCDEFGHIJKLM nopqrstuvwxyz ABCDEFGHIJKLM nopqrstuvwxyz

Galileo (in four weights)

ABCDEFGHIJKLM nopqrstuvwxyz ABCDEFGHIJKLM nopqrstuvwxyz

Highland Gothic (in three weights)

ABCDEFGHIJKLM nopqrstuvwxyz ABCDEFGH nopqrstu

Kasse (in three weights)

ABCDEFGHIJKLM nopqrstuvwxyz ABCDEFGH nopqrstu

LaPeruta (in three weights)

ABCDEFGHIJKLM nopqrstuvwxyz ABCDEFGHIJKLM nopqrstuvwxyz

Micro (in four weights)

ABCDEFGHIJKLM nopqrstuvwxyz ABCDEFGHIJKLM nopqrstuvwxyz

Micro Extended (in four weights)

ABCDEFGHIJKLM nopqrstuvwxyz ABCDEFGHI nopqrstuv

Monterey (in five weights)

ABCDEFGHIJKLM NOPQRSTUVWXYZ ABCDEFGHIJKLM NOPQRSTUVWXYZ

SansSerif (in four weights)

ABCDEFGHIJKLM nopqrstuvwxyz **ABCD**EFGHI*JKLM* **nopq**rstuv**wxyz**

SanSerif Bold (in two weights)

ABCDEFGHIJKLM nopqrstuvwxyz *ABCDEFGHIJKLM nopqrstuvwxyz*

SanSerif Book (in two weights)

ABCDEFGHIJKLM nopqrstuvwxyz ABCDEFGHIJKLM nopqrstuvwxyz

SanSerif Extra Bold, Bold Condensed, and Extra Bold Condensed

ABCDEFGHIJKLM nopqrstuvwxyz ABCDEFGHIJKLM nopqrstuvwxyz

Thirteen Script Faces

Blackknight: ABCDEFGHIJKLM nopqrstuvwxyz

Bonnard: ABCDEFGHIJKLM nopqrstuvwxyz

Calligraphy: ABCDEFGHIJKLM nopqrstuvwxyz

Coventry Script: ABCDEFGHIJKLM nopqrstuvwxyz

Dorovar: ABCDEFGHIJKLM nopqrstuvwxyz

Gregorian: ABCDEFGHIJKLM nopqrstuvwxyz

Paladin: ABCDEFGHIJKLM nopqrstuvwxy

Phoenix Script: ABCDEFGHIJKLM nopqrstuvwxy

Prelude: ABCDEFGHIJKLM nopqrstuvwxyz

Regency Script: ABCDEFGHIJKLM nopqrstuvwxyz

Sedona Script: *ABCDEFGHIJKLM nopqrstuvwxyz*

Slendar Gold: *ABCDE FGHI JKLM nopqrstuvwxyz*

Zephyr Script: ABCDEFGHIJKLM nopqrstuvwxyz

Twenty-five Decorative Faces

ABILENE: ABCDEFGHIJKLMNOPQRSTU

Campanile: ABCDEFGHIJKLM nopqrstuvwxyz ABCDEFGHIJKLM nopqrstuvwxyz

Chicago: ABCDEFGHIJKLM nopqrstuvwx

COLLEGIATE REGULAR: ABCDEFG HIJKLMNO

COLLEGIATE OUTLINE: ABCDEFG HIJKLMNO

COLLEGIATE INSIDE: ABCDEFGH IJKLMNOPQ

COLLEGIATE BORDER: ABCDEFGH IJKLMNOP

COLLEGIATE BLACK: ABCDEFGH IJKLMNOPQ

Cutouts: ABCDEFGHIJKLM nopqrstuvwxyz

DESPERADO: ABCDEFGHIJKLMNOPQRS

DRY GULCH: ABCDEFGHIJKLMNOPQRST

Epoque: ABCDEFGHIJKLM nopqrstuvwxyz

FATTIPATTI: ABCDEFGHIJKLMNOP

FATTIPATTI BOLD: ABCDEFGHIJKL

Fletcher Gothic: ABCDEF GHIJKLM nopqrstuvwxyz

Gatsby: ABCDEFGHIJKLM nopqrstuvwxyz
(also in Bold and Italic)

Gazelle: ABCDEFGHIJKLM nopqrstuvwxyz

Giotto: ABCDEFGHIJKLM nopqrstuvwxyz ABCDEFGHIJKLM nopqrstuvwxyz
(also in Bold)

Harlequin: ABCDEFGHIJKLM nopqrstuvwxyz
(also in Extra Bold)

Jott: ABCDEFGHIJKLM nopqrstuvwxyz
(in four weights)

Kells: ABCDEFGHIJKLM nopqrstuvwxyz

Meath: ABCDEFGHIJKLM nopqrstuvwxyz

MICHELLE: ABCDEFGHIJK

MICHELLE BOLD: ABCDEF

Moulin Rouge: ABCDEFGHIJ klmnopqrstuv

Nouveau: ABCDEFGHIJKLM nopqrstuvwxy

Pendragon: ABCDEFGHIJKLM nopqrstuvwxyz

Right Bank: ABCDEFGHIJKLM NOPQRSTUVWXYZ

Ritz: ABCDEFGHIJKLM nopqrstuvwx

Ritz Condensed: ABCDEFGHIJKLM nopqrstuvwxyz

Rocko: ABCDEFGHIJKLM nopqrstuvwxyz

Vertigo: ABCDEFGHIJKLM nopqrstuvwxyz ABCDEFGHIJKLM nopqrstuvwxyz

Four Symbol Fonts

BUTTON PLAIN button plain
(Button Plain)

BUTTON PLAIN button plain
(Button Highlight)

ABCDEFGHIJKLM nopqrstuv
(Check Box)

A B C D E f g h i + F8 @ # $
(Key Caps)

Fun Fonts

Agfa Discovery TrueType Pack

Garth Graphic (in four weights)

ABCDEFGHIJKLM nopqrstuvwxyz **ABCD***EFGHIJKLM* **nopq***rstuvwxyz*

Garth Graphic Condensed (in two weights)

ABCDEFGHIJKLM nopqrstuvwxyz **ABCDEFGHIJKLM nopqrstuvwxyz**

Nadianne (in three weights)

ABCDEFGHIJKLM nopqrstuvwxyz **ABCDEFGHIJKLM nopqrstuvwxyz**

Shannon (in four weights)

ABCDEFGHIJKLM nopqrstuvwxyz **ABCDEFGH***IJKLM* **nopqrstuv***wxyz*

Wile (in four weights)

ABCDEFGHIJKLM nopqrstuvwxyz **ABCD***EFGHIJKLM* **nopq***rstuv**wxyz*

Fourteen Headline Fonts

Artistik: ABCDEFGHIJKLM nopqrstuvwxyz

Bernhard Fashion: ABCDEFGHIJKLM nopqrstuvwxyz

Bernhard Modern: ABCDEFGHIJKLM nopqrstuvwxyz

Broadway: ABCDEFGHIJ klmnopqr

Carmine Tango: ABCDEFGHIJKLM nopqrstuvwxyz

CG Poster Bodoni: ABCDEFGHIJKLM nopqrstuvwxyz ABCDEFGHIJKLM

Cooper Black: ABCDEFG hijklmno

DELPHIAN: ABCDEFGHIJKLMNOPQRSTUVWXYZ

Dom Casual: ABCDEFGHIJKLM nopqrstuvwxyz ABCDEFGHIJKLM

ECCENTRIC: ABCDEFGHIJKLMNOPQRSTUVWXYZ

Goudy Handtooled: ABCDEFGH ijklmnopq

Old English: ABCDEFGHIJ klmnopqrstuvwxyz

Revue Shadow: ABCDEFG hijklmnopq

Signet Roundhand: ABCDEFGHI jklmnopqrstuvwxy

Fifteen Clip Art Typefaces

(Borders and Ornaments 1)

(Borders and Ornaments 4)

(Borders and Ornaments 5)

(Communications 1)

🏠 ✉ ... ⛺ ... ... 🏠 ... 🔥 🏠 ... ... 🚐 WC ... 🚗 🚐 ... ...

(Communications 2)

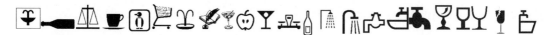

(Communications 3)

(Communications 6)

(Games and Sports 1)

(Games and Sports 3)

(Games and Sports 4)

(Holiday)

(Industry and Engineering 1)

(Industry and Engineering 2)

(Transportation 1)

(Transportation 2)

Monotype FunFonts

<u>Amasis (in four weights)</u>

ABCDEFGHIJKLM nopqrstuvwxyz **ABCD**EFGHIJKLM **nopq**rstuv**wxyz**

<u>Headline Faces</u>

Bembo: ABCDEFGHIJKLM nopqrstuvwxyz

Blado: ABCDEFGHIJKLM nopqrstuvwxyz

Clarendon: ABCDEFGHIJKLM nopqrstuvwxyz

FELIX TITLING: ABCDEFGHIJKLMNOPQRSTU

Figaro: ABCDEFGHIJKLM nopqrstuvwxyz

Gil Sans: ABCDEFGHIJKLM nopqrstuvwxyz

Goudy: ABCDEFGHIJ klmnopqrstuv

Old English Text: ABCDEFGHI jklmnopqrstuv

Palace Script: ABCDEFGHIJKLM nopqrstuvwxyz

20th Century: ABCDEFGHIJ klmnopqrstuv

<u>Clip Art Faces</u>

(Almanac)

(Botanical)

(Circle Frame)

(Circle Frame Negative)

(Directions)

(Sports One)

(Sports Two)

(Square Frame)

ABCDEFGHIJKLMNOPQRSTUVWX
YZ01234567890123456 7890

(Square Frame Negative)

(Transport)

(Vacation)

Bitstream Li'L Bits Font Packs

The Jetsons

(Jetsons)

ABCDEFGHIJKLMNOPQRSTUVW

(Jets Original)

ABCDEFGHIJKLMNOPQRSTUVWXY

(Jets Black)

ABCDEFGHIJKLM nopqrstuvwxyz

(Amerigo)

ABCDEFGHIJKLM nopqrstuvwxyz

(Geometric 231)

ABCDEFGHIJKLM nopqrstuvwxyz

(Egyptian 505 Light)

The Flintstones

(Flintstones)

ABCDEFGHIJKLMNOPQRSTUVWXYZ

(Bedrock)

ABCDEFGHIJKLMN nopqrstuvwxyz

(Impress)

ABCDEFGHIJKLM nopqrstuvwxyz

(Cooper Light)

ABCDEFGHIJKLM nopqrstuvwxyz

(Swiss 721)

Looney Tunes 1

(Looney Tunes)

ABCDEFGHIJKLMNOPQRS

(Looney Tunes Tilt)

ABCDEFGHIJKLM nopqrstuvwxyz

(Aachen)

ABCDEFGHIJKLMN nopqrstuvwxyz

(Freehand 471)

ABCDEFGHIJKLM nopqrstuvwxyz

(Incised 901 Bold)

ABCDEFGHIJKLMNOPQRSTUVWXYZ

(Stencil)

Star Trek

ABCDEFGHIJKLM nopqrstuvwxyz

(Star Trek)

ABCDEFGHIJKLM nopqrstuvwxyz

(Star Trek Film)

(Star Trek PI)

ABCDEFGHIJK

(Starfleet Extended Bold)

ABCDEFGHIJKLM nopqrstuvwxyz

(Square 721 Condensed)

ABCDEFGHIJKLM nopqrstuvwxyz

(Venetian 301)

Star Trek: The Next Generation

ABCDEFGHIJKLMNOPQRSTUVWX

(Star Trek Next)

(Star Trek Next PI)

ABCDEFGHIJKLM nopqrstuvwxyz

(Swiss 911 Ultra Compressed)

ABCDEFGHIJKLM nopqrstuvwxyz

(Crillee Italic)

ABCDEFGHIJKLM nopqrstuvwxyz

(Transitional 521)

Winter Holiday

ABCDEFGHIJKLM nopqrstuvwxyz

(Snowcap)

(Holiday PI)

𝔄𝔅𝕮𝔇𝔈𝔉𝔊𝔥𝔍𝔍𝔎𝔏𝔐 nopqrstuvwxyz

(Cloister Black)

ABCDEFGHIJKLM nopqrstuvwxyz

(Freeform 721)

A B C D E F G H I J K L M nopqrstuvwxyz

(Shelley Allegro)

DavkaBats

CHAPTER 14

Icon See Clearly Now

Pare ca na vijananti mayamettha yamamase
Ye ca tattha vijananti tato sammanti medhaga†

— Dhammapada, ca 500 BC

Mom's Companion Disk contains a gigantic subdirectory, crammed with thousands of icons. There's one problem with huge icon collections, though: how in the infernal tarnation can you find the picture you want, without clicking and clicking and clicking through the whole collection?

 Well, I've tried to simplify things a bit by reproducing all of those icons right here, where you can get at 'em quickly and easily. Regrettably, the pictures aren't in color, but even so I think you'll find it much easier thumbing through these pages than hopping through all those `.ICO` files.

---

† Most people never realize that all of us here shall one day perish. But those who do realize that truth settle their quarrels peacefully.

The Built-In Icons

Windows comes with two rather meager sets of icons; one bunch is stored in
PROGMAN.EXE; the other is stored in **MORICONS.DLL**. They're easy to use: from
inside Program Manager click once on the icon you'd like to change, click File, then
Properties, then Change Icon, and type in **PROGMAN.EXE** or **MORICONS.DLL**.

Here are the 46 icons you'll find inside **PROGMAN.EXE**:

PMAN01	PMAN02	PMAN03	PMAN04	PMAN05
PMAN06	PMAN07	PMAN08	PMAN09	PMAN10
PMAN11	PMAN12	PMAN13	PMAN14	PMAN15
PMAN16	PMAN17	PMAN18	PMAN19	PMAN20
PMAN21	PMAN22	PMAN23	PMAN24	PMAN25
PMAN26	PMAN27	PMAN28	PMAN29	PMAN30
PMAN31	PMAN32	PMAN33	PMAN34	PMAN35
PMAN36	PMAN37	PMAN38	PMAN39	PMAN40
PMAN41	PMAN42	PMAN43	PMAN44	PMAN45
PMAN46				

And these are the 106 icons stored inside **MORICONS.DLL**:

MORI001	MORI002	MORI003	MORI004	MORI005
MORI006	MORI007	MORI008	MORI009	MORI010
MORI011	MORI012	MORI013	MORI014	MORI015
MORI016	MORI017	MORI018	MORI019	MORI020
MORI021	MORI022	MORI023	MORI024	MORI025
MORI026	MORI027	MORI028	MORI029	MORI030
MORI031	MORI032	MORI033	MORI034	MORI035
MORI036	MORI037	MORI038	MORI039	MORI040
MORI041	MORI042	MORI043	MORI044	MORI045
MORI046	MORI047	MORI048	MORI049	MORI050
MORI051	MORI052	MORI053	MORI054	MORI055
MORI056	MORI057	MORI058	MORI059	MORI060
MORI061	MORI062	MORI063	MORI064	MORI065

MORI066	MORI067	MORI068	MORI069	MORI070
MORI071	MORI072	MORI073	MORI074	MORI075
MORI076	MORI077	MORI078	MORI079	MORI080
MORI081	MORI082	MORI083	MORI084	MORI085
MORI086	MORI087	MORI088	MORI089	MORI090
MORI091	MORI092	MORI093	MORI094	MORI095
MORI096	MORI097	MORI098	MORI099	MORI100
MORI101	MORI102	MORI103	MORI104	MORI105
MORI106				

AllIcons

Howard Friedman assembled a massive collection of nearly 5,000 icons, gathered from dozens of bulletin boards and on-line services all over the world, and put them in a big file called **ALLICONS.ZIP**. CD MOM contains all of Howard's wondrous collection, arranged by topic area, underneath the ALLICONS subdirectory.

These icons run quite a gamut, from rather crude to utterly stunning — some of them, in my mind, qualify as classic miniature works of art. It's incredible what a talented artist can do with 32 by 32 points of color.

Unfortunately, the identity of the artists has been lost over time. That's a real pity in many cases because the pictures are so extraordinary. I sincerely hope the anonymous folks who created these tiny works of art will accept my "Thank You" on behalf of the hundreds of thousands of people, all around the world, who use these pointillistic masterpieces every day.

Applications

These are primarily icons for databases and other programs, including "integrated" programs that don't have a category of their own. Somehow Amí Pro snuck into this subdirectory.

`.ICO` files located in **ALLICONS\APPSICON:**

AGENDA	AGENDA1	AGENDA2	AGENDA3	ALPHA
ALPHA4	ALPHA4A	ALPHA4B	ALPHA5	AMI
AMI1	AMI2	AMI3	AMIPRO	AMIPRO2
AMIPRO3	CLARION	CLARION1	CLARION2	CLIPPER
CLIPPER1	CLIPPER2	CLIPPER3	CODEBASE	DATA
DATA01	DATA02	DATA1	DATA2	DATABS2
DATAEX	DATAEX1	DATEASE1	DATEASE2	DB01
DB03	DB1	DB4	DB5	DB6
DB7	DB8	DB9	DBASE-A	DBASE-C

DBASE	DBASE01	DBASE03	DBASE05	DBASE1
DBASE2	DBASE3	DBASE4	DBASE5	DBASE6
DBASE7	DBASEI	DBASEIII	DBASEIVC	DBIIIA
DBIV	DBXL	DBXL1	DBXL2	DBXL3
FOX	FOX1	FOX2	FOX3	FOXBASE
FOXPLUS	FOXPLUS2	FOXPRO	FOXPRO01	FOXPRO2
FOXPRO3	FOXPRO4	FOXPRO5	FOXPRO6	JAV
JAV1	MAG	MAG1	MAG2	MAGELL
MAGELLAN	PARADX01	PARADX02	PARADX03	PARADX04
PARADX05	PARADX06	PARADX07	PARADX08	PARADX09
PARADX10	PARADX11	PARADX12	PARADX13	PARADX14
PARADX15	PARADX16	PARADX17	PARADX18	PC-FIL
PCFILE	PROJ	PROJ01	PROJ02	PROJ04
PROJ06	PROJ07	PROJ08	QA	QA03

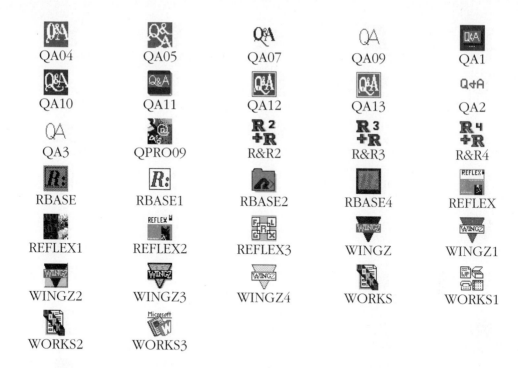

Characters

Most of these icons are cartoon characters and pictures of the denizens of several classics. There are a couple of pictures of. . . uh. . . questionable taste. They've been included for the sake of completeness. Just don't tell Mom, okay?

`.ICO` files located in `ALLICONS\CHARICON`:

BAT

BAT1

BAT2

BATMAN

BATMAN1

BATMAN2

BATT

BATXL

BEAR

BELLBOY

BELLBOY1

BIGBIRD

BIKINI

BIMBO

BIRD11

BOOP

BOOP1

BRUTE

BUG

BUG11

BUG12

BUG13

BUG2

BUG21

BUG23

BUG3

BUG32

BUGLOC

BULLDOG

BUMBLBEE

BUNNY

CALVIN

CALVIN1

CALVIN2

CALVIN3

CALVIN4

CARMEN1

CAT

CAT1

CHESTER

CHIPMUNK

COMIC

COMIC1

COMIC2

COOKIE

COOPER

CROC

CYBERG

CYBERMAN

DAD

DALEK

DAVROS

DICK

DOG

DOG1

DONALD

DONALD1

DONATELO

DOPEY

DRAGON

DRAGON1

DRAGON2

DRAGON3

DTHWLDR

ELVIS

FRED

FRED2

FUNFACE

GARFLD

GEISHA

GIPET2	GOOFY	GREMLIN	GROVER	GUMBY
GUMBY1	GUMBY2	HAGAR	HARE	HILDA
HOBBES	HOLMESWT	HOMER	HOMER1	HOOK
HOOK2	HOYLE1	HUMPTY	HUNTER	JANE-J
JESICA	JESSICA	JISEL	JULIA	KAA
KERMIT	KERMIT2	LAURA	LEONARDO	LOBSTER
LSL2	LURCH	MAGGIE	MAGGIE1	MARGE
MARGE1	MICHELO	MICKEY	MICKEY3	MINNIE
MOWGLEE	NOID	OSCAR	PALADIN	PANGO
PASCAL	PECOS	PEPPER	PIG	PLAYBOY
PLUTO	PLUTO1	PONY	POPEYE	R2D2
RABBIT	RAISIN1	RAPHEAL	RIBBIT	ROGER2
RUBRDUCK	SADGUY	SCROOGE	SHEREKAN	SKULL
SNOOPY	SPIDER	SPOCK	SQRL1	SQRL2

SQRL3	STARGOOS	STRIPPER	SUNSMILE	THUMPER
TICTOC	TWEETIE	TWEETY	VILLAN	WALLY
WHO1	WHO2	WILMA	WIZARD	WIZARDES
WOM-FACE	ZUG	ZUG1	ZUG2	ZUG3

Communications Hardware

These icons cover telephones, LANs, networks, modems, terminals and the like. If you don't see what you want here, look in the next section.

.ICO files located in **ALLICONS\COMHDWIC:**

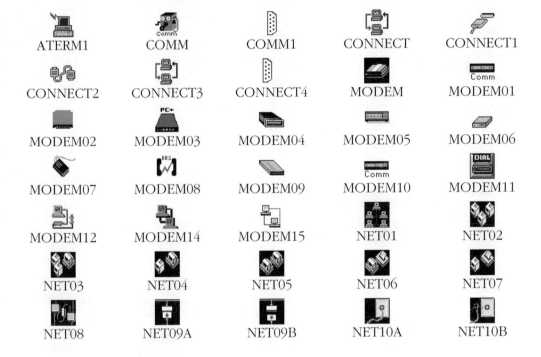

ATERM1	COMM	COMM1	CONNECT	CONNECT1
CONNECT2	CONNECT3	CONNECT4	MODEM	MODEM01
MODEM02	MODEM03	MODEM04	MODEM05	MODEM06
MODEM07	MODEM08	MODEM09	MODEM10	MODEM11
MODEM12	MODEM14	MODEM15	NET01	NET02
NET03	NET04	NET05	NET06	NET07
NET08	NET09A	NET09B	NET10A	NET10B

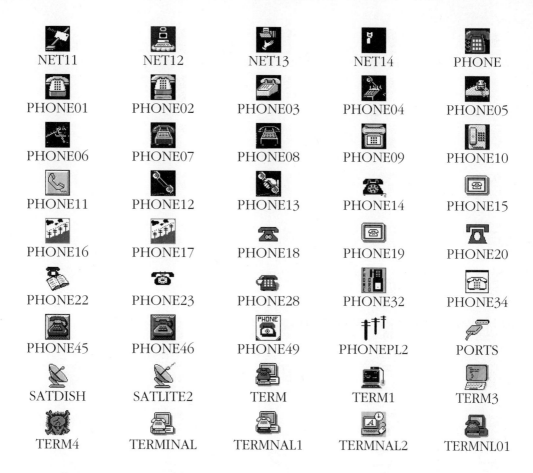

Communications

Most of these pictures refer to software or companies involved in the communications game, but there are a few oddballs. If you don't see what you want here, look in the previous section.

`.ICO` files located in **ALLICONS\COMMICON**:

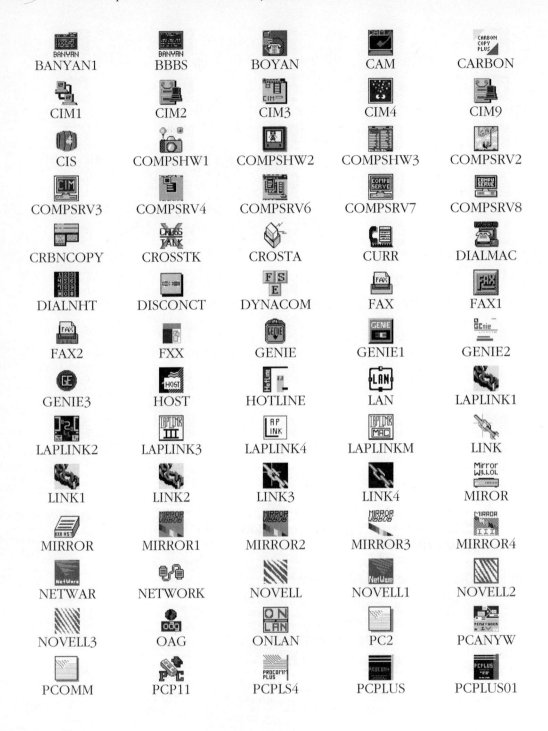

BANYAN1   BBBS   BOYAN   CAM   CARBON

CIM1   CIM2   CIM3   CIM4   CIM9

CIS   COMPSHW1   COMPSHW2   COMPSHW3   COMPSRV2

COMPSRV3   COMPSRV4   COMPSRV6   COMPSRV7   COMPSRV8

CRBNCOPY   CROSSTK   CROSTA   CURR   DIALMAC

DIALNHT   DISCONCT   DYNACOM   FAX   FAX1

FAX2   FXX   GENIE   GENIE1   GENIE2

GENIE3   HOST   HOTLINE   LAN   LAPLINK1

LAPLINK2   LAPLINK3   LAPLINK4   LAPLINKM   LINK

LINK1   LINK2   LINK3   LINK4   MIROR

MIRROR   MIRROR1   MIRROR2   MIRROR3   MIRROR4

NETWAR   NETWORK   NOVELL   NOVELL1   NOVELL2

NOVELL3   OAG   ONLAN   PC2   PCANYW

PCOMM   PCP11   PCPLS4   PCPLUS   PCPLUS01

PCPLUS02	PCPLUS03	PCPLUS04	PCPLUS06	PCPLUS07
PCPLUS08	PCPLUS09	PCPLUS11	PCPLUS12	PCPLUS14
PCPLUS15	PCPLUS24	PCPLUS3	PCPLUS4	PCPLUS5
PCPLUS6	PHONBOOK	PHONE#S	PROCOM12	PROCOM14
PROCOM18	PROCOM19	PROCOMM	PRODGY1	PRODGY2
PRODGY3	PRODGY4	PRODGY5	PRODIGY	PRODIGY2
PRODIGY3	PRODIGY4	PRODIGY5	PRODIGY8	PRODIGY9
PRODY3	QM	QMOD	QMODE	QMODE01
QMODE02	QMODE03	QMODE06	QMODE12	QMODEM
QMODEM1	QMODEM2	QMODEM3	QMODEM6	RBBSPC
RBBSPC1	SCOM3	SPRINT	SPRLOGO	TAP53
TAPCIS	TAPCIS1	TELE	TELECOM	TELECOM1
TELECOM2	TELELINE	TELESCPT	TELEX	TELIX
TELIX1	TELIX2	TELIX3	TELIX4	TELIX5

TELIX6   TELIX9   UNICOM   USROBOT1   USROBOT2

VT100   VT52   WIZARD2   X10   XCOM1

XTALK   XTALK01   XTALK1   XTALK2   XTALK4

XTALK8   XTALK9

Computer Hardware

Most of these pictures cover hardware: chips, computers, every kind of disk drive you've ever seen. Some are generic computer icons. If you need a picture of a diskette, make sure you also look at the DOS section.

.**ICO** files located in **ALLICONS\COMPICON**:

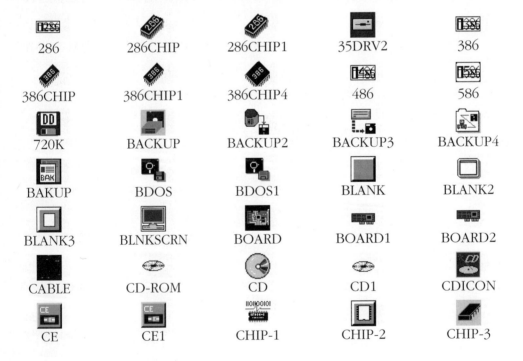

286   286CHIP   286CHIP1   35DRV2   386

386CHIP   386CHIP1   386CHIP4   486   586

720K   BACKUP   BACKUP2   BACKUP3   BACKUP4

BAKUP   BDOS   BDOS1   BLANK   BLANK2

BLANK3   BLNKSCRN   BOARD   BOARD1   BOARD2

CABLE   CD-ROM   CD   CD1   CDICON

CE   CE1   CHIP-1   CHIP-2   CHIP-3

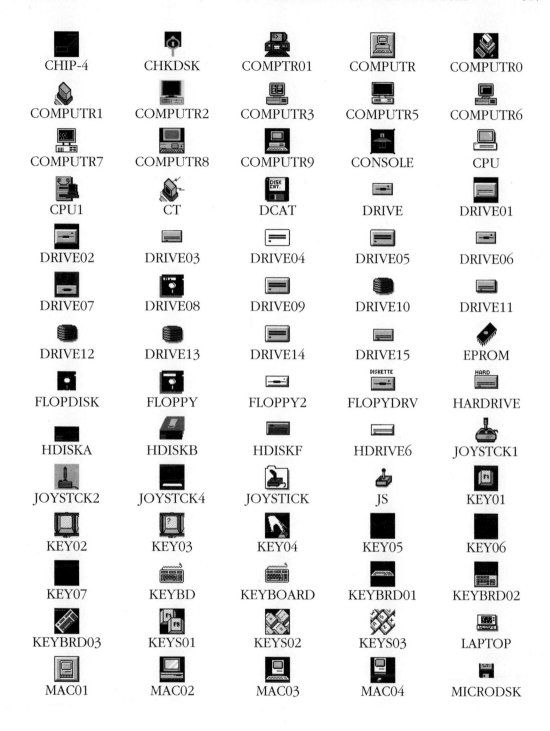

CHIP-4	CHKDSK	COMPTR01	COMPUTR	COMPUTR0
COMPUTR1	COMPUTR2	COMPUTR3	COMPUTR5	COMPUTR6
COMPUTR7	COMPUTR8	COMPUTR9	CONSOLE	CPU
CPU1	CT	DCAT	DRIVE	DRIVE01
DRIVE02	DRIVE03	DRIVE04	DRIVE05	DRIVE06
DRIVE07	DRIVE08	DRIVE09	DRIVE10	DRIVE11
DRIVE12	DRIVE13	DRIVE14	DRIVE15	EPROM
FLOPDISK	FLOPPY	FLOPPY2	FLOPYDRV	HARDRIVE
HDISKA	HDISKB	HDISKF	HDRIVE6	JOYSTCK1
JOYSTCK2	JOYSTCK4	JOYSTICK	JS	KEY01
KEY02	KEY03	KEY04	KEY05	KEY06
KEY07	KEYBD	KEYBOARD	KEYBRD01	KEYBRD02
KEYBRD03	KEYS01	KEYS02	KEYS03	LAPTOP
MAC01	MAC02	MAC03	MAC04	MICRODSK

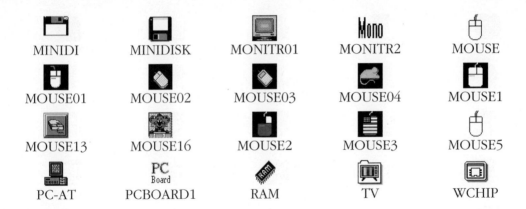

MINIDI	MINIDISK	MONITR01	MONITR2	MOUSE
MOUSE01	MOUSE02	MOUSE03	MOUSE04	MOUSE1
MOUSE13	MOUSE16	MOUSE2	MOUSE3	MOUSE5
PC-AT	PCBOARD1	RAM	TV	WCHIP

Desk

Most of these pictures concern office equipment and tasks, charts, labels, pens and pencils, paper clips, and applications related to the Windows desktop.

.ICO files located in **ALLICONS\DESKICON:**

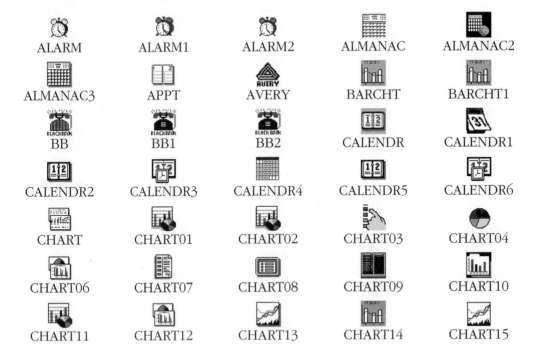

ALARM	ALARM1	ALARM2	ALMANAC	ALMANAC2
ALMANAC3	APPT	AVERY	BARCHT	BARCHT1
BB	BB1	BB2	CALENDR	CALENDR1
CALENDR2	CALENDR3	CALENDR4	CALENDR5	CALENDR6
CHART	CHART01	CHART02	CHART03	CHART04
CHART06	CHART07	CHART08	CHART09	CHART10
CHART11	CHART12	CHART13	CHART14	CHART15

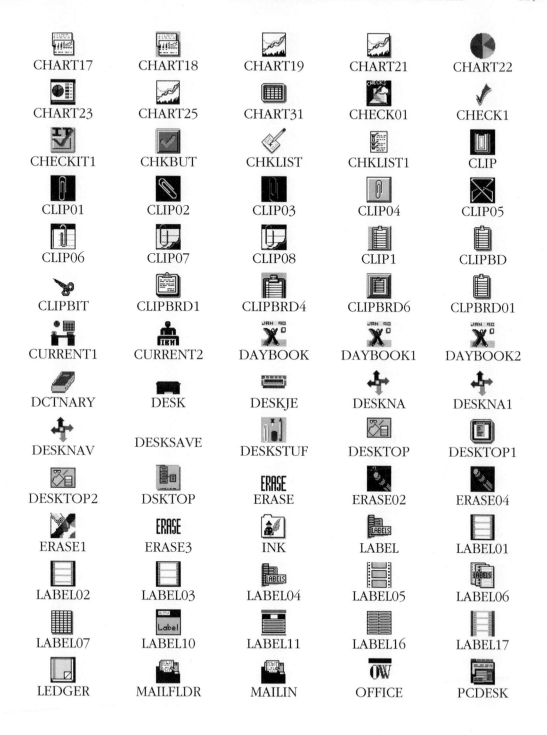

CHART17	CHART18	CHART19	CHART21	CHART22
CHART23	CHART25	CHART31	CHECK01	CHECK1
CHECKIT1	CHKBUT	CHKLIST	CHKLIST1	CLIP
CLIP01	CLIP02	CLIP03	CLIP04	CLIP05
CLIP06	CLIP07	CLIP08	CLIP1	CLIPBD
CLIPBIT	CLIPBRD1	CLIPBRD4	CLIPBRD6	CLPBRD01
CURRENT1	CURRENT2	DAYBOOK	DAYBOOK1	DAYBOOK2
DCTNARY	DESK	DESKJE	DESKNA	DESKNA1
DESKNAV	DESKSAVE	DESKSTUF	DESKTOP	DESKTOP1
DESKTOP2	DSKTOP	ERASE	ERASE02	ERASE04
ERASE1	ERASE3	INK	LABEL	LABEL01
LABEL02	LABEL03	LABEL04	LABEL05	LABEL06
LABEL07	LABEL10	LABEL11	LABEL16	LABEL17
LEDGER	MAILFLDR	MAILIN	OFFICE	PCDESK

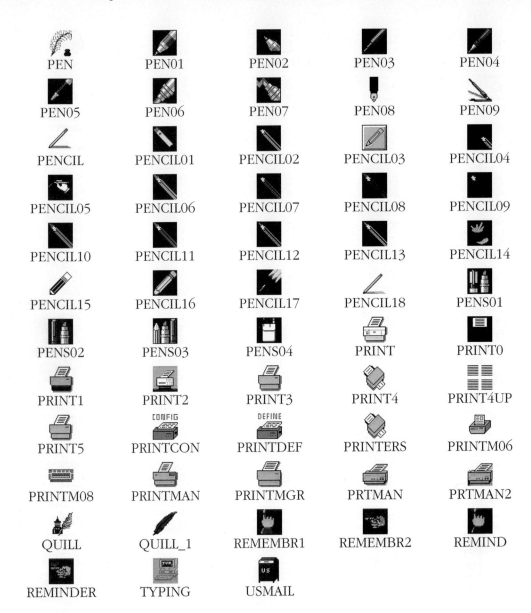

DOS

These icons concern basic DOS commands, file handling, the `C:>` prompt, diskettes, and the like. If you're looking for diskettes and drives, make sure you also look at the Computers section.

.ICO files located in **ALLICONS\DOSICON**:

COPY2PC	COPYA	COPYB	CPRMPT	CPRMPT01
CPRMPT02	CPRMPT03	CPRMPT04	CPRMPT05	CPRMPT06
CPRMPT07	CPRMPT08	CPRMPT09	CPRMPT10	CPRMPT11
CPRMPT12	CPRMPT13	CPRMPT14	CPRMPT15	CPRMPT16
CPRMPT17	CPRMPT18	CPRMPT19	CPRMPT20	CPRMPT21
CPRMPT22	CPRMPT23	CPRMPT24	CPRMPT25	CPRMPT26
CPRMPT28	CPRMPT29	CPRMPT31	CPRMPT32	CPRMPT33
CPRMPT39	CPRMPT41	CPRMPT47	CPRMPT48	CPRMPT49
CPRMPT50	CPRMPT51	CPRMPT52	CPRMPT53	CPRMPT54
DIRTREE	DISK-3B	DISK-3R	DISK-3Y	DISK-5B
DISK-5R	DISK-5W	DISK-5Y	DISK002	DISK01
DISK012	DISK013	DISK015	DISK02	DISK03
DISK04	DISK05	DISK06	DISK07	DISK08

DISK09

DISK10

DISK11

DISK12

DISK12M

DISK12M1

DISK12M2

DISK13

DISK14

DISK144

DISK144A

DISK144B

DISK144C

DISK15

DISK16

DISK17

DISK18

DISK19

DISK20

DISK25

DISK27

DISK28

DISK29

DISK30

DISK30A

DISK31

DISK32

DISK33

DISK34

DISK35

DISK35B

DISK36

DISK37

DISK38

DISK39

DISK40

DISK41

DISK42

DISK48

DISK50

DISK51

DISK525A

DISK60

DISK67

DISK73

DISK81

DISK82

DISK83

DISK84

DISK85

DISK86

DISK87

DISK88

DISK89

DISK90

DISK95

DISK97

DISK98

DISK99

DISKBU

DISKCPY1

DISKCPY2

DISKCPY4

DISKDUPE

DISKOVER

DOS01

DOS02

DOS03

DOS04

DOS12

DOS13   DOS14   DOS15   DOS16   DOS17

DOS28   DOS31   DOS6   DOSPRO   DOSPRO1

DOSPRO2   DOSPRO4   DOSPRO5   DOSPRO6   DOSPRO7

FMATS101   FMTMAS   FORMA   FORMAT   FORMAT1

FORMATA   FORMATAB   FORMATB   FORMB   FREEMEM

FREEMEM1   PARK   PARK1   PARK3   UNFORMAT

XCOPY

Files

Most of these pictures are of files and folders.

`.ICO` files located in **ALLICONS\FILEICON:**

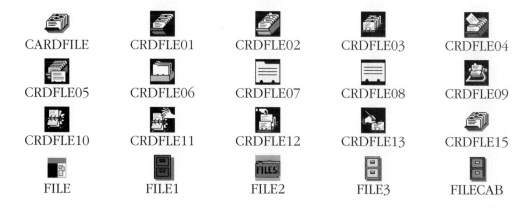

CARDFILE   CRDFLE01   CRDFLE02   CRDFLE03   CRDFLE04

CRDFLE05   CRDFLE06   CRDFLE07   CRDFLE08   CRDFLE09

CRDFLE10   CRDFLE11   CRDFLE12   CRDFLE13   CRDFLE15

FILE   FILE1   FILE2   FILE3   FILECAB

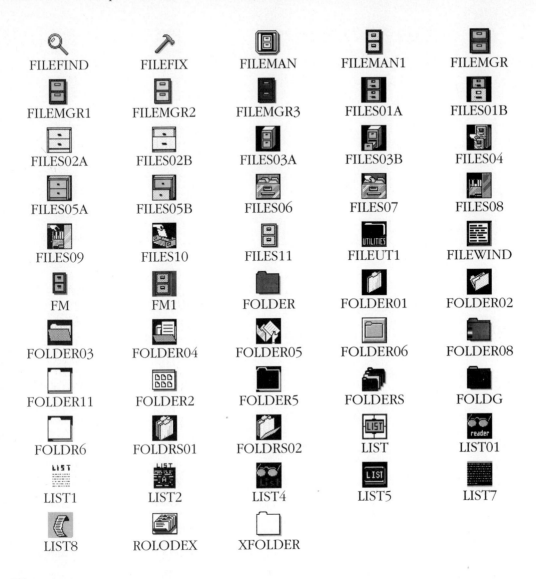

FILEFIND	FILEFIX	FILEMAN	FILEMAN1	FILEMGR
FILEMGR1	FILEMGR2	FILEMGR3	FILES01A	FILES01B
FILES02A	FILES02B	FILES03A	FILES03B	FILES04
FILES05A	FILES05B	FILES06	FILES07	FILES08
FILES09	FILES10	FILES11	FILEUT1	FILEWIND
FM	FM1	FOLDER	FOLDER01	FOLDER02
FOLDER03	FOLDER04	FOLDER05	FOLDER06	FOLDER08
FOLDER11	FOLDER2	FOLDER5	FOLDERS	FOLDG
FOLDR6	FOLDRS01	FOLDRS02	LIST	LIST01
LIST1	LIST2	LIST4	LIST5	LIST7
LIST8	ROLODEX	XFOLDER		

Finance

These are the money pictures: financial software, dough on the hoof, stacks and piles of greenbacks. You know the tune.

.**ICO** files located in **ALLICONS\FINICON:**

ACCEXCEL	ACCPAC	ACCPAC2	BUDGET	CASHREG
CASHREG1	CCARD	CGA	CHECK11	CHECK2
CHECK3	CHECK4	CHECK5	CHECK6	CHECKBK5
CHECKFR1	CHECKFR2	CHECKFR3	CHECKFR4	CHECKS01
CHK	CREDIT	CW	D40	DAC1
DAC7	DACEZ	DACEZ1	DOLLAR$	DOLLAR
DOLLAR02	DOLLAR03	DOLLAR07	DOLLAR1	DOLLAR10
DOLLAR3	DOLLAR4	DOLLAR5	FINCALC	FY
HP12C	HP16C	HPCALC	INVOICE	INVOICE1
LEDGER	MC6_0	MONEY	MONEY1	MONEY2
MONEY3	MONEY4	MONEYL	MORTGAGE	MORTPLAN
MORTPLN	MYM	MYM1	MYM2	PEACH
PEACH4	PRO$TOCK	QUICKC4	QUICKE	QUICKEN

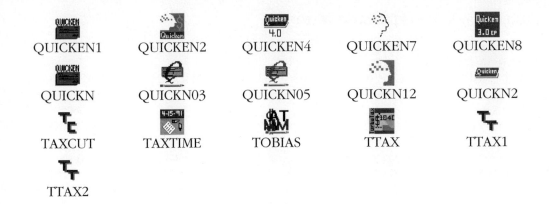

QUICKEN1   QUICKEN2   QUICKEN4   QUICKEN7   QUICKEN8

QUICKN   QUICKN03   QUICKN05   QUICKN12   QUICKN2

TAXCUT   TAXTIME   TOBIAS   TTAX   TTAX1

TTAX2

Flags

Flags from all around the world.

.ICO files located in ALLICONS\FLAGICON:

FLAG   FLAG1   FLAGANDO   FLGADDIS   FLGAFGHA

FLGAMBIA   FLGARGEN   FLGASTRL   FLGAUSTA   FLGAUSTR

FLGAZUAY   FLGBAHR   FLGBANGL   FLGBELG   FLGBELG1

FLGBISSA   FLGBOLIV   FLGBOTS1   FLGBOTSW   FLGBRAZL

FLGCAMER   FLGCAN   FLGCANAD   FLGCHAD   FLGCHAD1

FLGCHILE   FLGCHINA   FLGCOLOM   FLGCONGO   FLGCSA

FLGCZEC1   FLGCZECH   FLGDEN   FLGDENMA   FLGDENMK

FLGDJIBO	FLGEGYPT	FLGETHIO	FLGFIN	FLGFINLA
FLGFRAN	FLGFRANC	FLGGABON	FLGGERM	FLGGERMA
FLGGHANA	FLGGREEC	FLGGRNLD	FLGGUINE	FLGHUNG
FLGHUNG1	FLGICEL	FLGICEL1	FLGINDIA	FLGINDON
FLGIRAN	FLGIRAQ	FLGIREL	FLGIREL1	FLGIREL2
FLGISRAE	FLGITAL1	FLGITALY	FLGIVOR1	FLGIVORY
FLGJAPA1	FLGJAPAN	FLGLEONE	FLGLIBER	FLGLIECH
FLGLUXE1	FLGLUXEM	FLGMALAW	FLGMALI	FLGMALI1
FLGMAURI	FLGMEX	FLGMEXIC	FLGMONAC	FLGMONGO
FLGMOROC	FLGNETH	FLGNIGE1	FLGNIGER	FLGNIGRI
FLGNORW	FLGNZ	FLGPERU	FLGRUSS	FLGRUSS1
FLGSALVA	FLGSENEG	FLGSKORE	FLGSPAI1	FLGSPAIN
FLGSWED	FLGSWED1	FLGSWED2	FLGSWISS	FLGSWITZ
FLGSYRIA	FLGTAIWA	FLGTOGO	FLGTURK	FLGTURKE

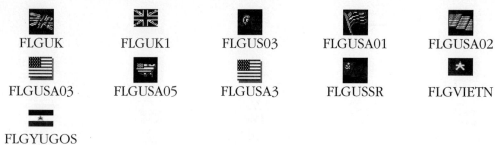

FLGUK	FLGUK1	FLGUS03	FLGUSA01	FLGUSA02
FLGUSA03	FLGUSA05	FLGUSA3	FLGUSSR	FLGVIETN

FLGYUGOS

Games

Icons for computer and non-computer games. There are more game-related icons in the Play section.

.ICO files located in ALLICONS\GAMEICON:

007A	3D-BLOCK	3DPOOL2	688	688A
688B	688C	688D	688E	688F
ACE	ARKANO	BIG2	CADDIE	CARMEN
CLUB	CRIMEWVE	CRIMWAVE	CYBERMAN	DRAGCITY
DSTRIK	DSTRIKE	EMPIR	EMPIRE	EMPIRE1
EMPIRE2	FACETRIS	FL-LOTTO	FL	FLTSIM02
FLTSIM03	FLTSIM04	FLTSIM05	FLTSIM06	FS
FS4	FS40B	FSA	HARPOON	HARPOON1

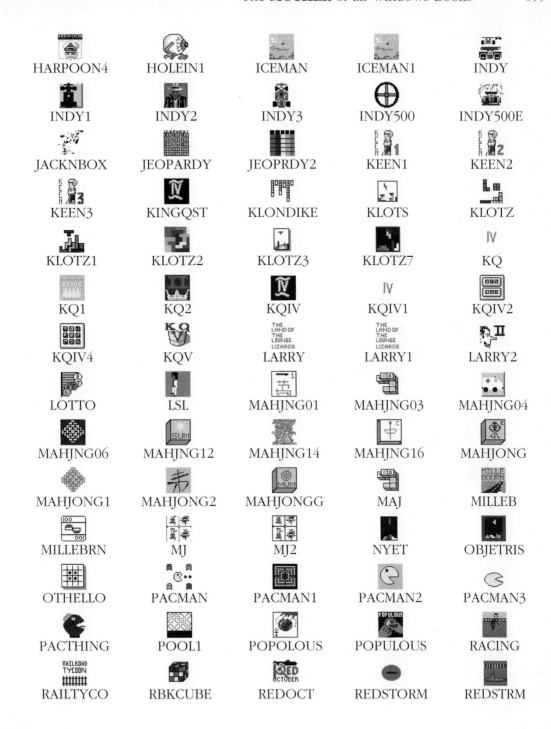

HARPOON4	HOLEIN1	ICEMAN	ICEMAN1	INDY
INDY1	INDY2	INDY3	INDY500	INDY500E
JACKNBOX	JEOPARDY	JEOPRDY2	KEEN1	KEEN2
KEEN3	KINGQST	KLONDIKE	KLOTS	KLOTZ
KLOTZ1	KLOTZ2	KLOTZ3	KLOTZ7	KQ
KQ1	KQ2	KQIV	KQIV1	KQIV2
KQIV4	KQV	LARRY	LARRY1	LARRY2
LOTTO	LSL	MAHJNG01	MAHJNG03	MAHJNG04
MAHJNG06	MAHJNG12	MAHJNG14	MAHJNG16	MAHJONG
MAHJONG1	MAHJONG2	MAHJONGG	MAJ	MILLEB
MILLEBRN	MJ	MJ2	NYET	OBJETRIS
OTHELLO	PACMAN	PACMAN1	PACMAN2	PACMAN3
PACTHING	POOL1	POPOLOUS	POPULOUS	RACING
RAILTYCO	RBKCUBE	REDOCT	REDSTORM	REDSTRM

REDSTRM1	REDSTRM4	REVERSI	REVERSI1	REVERSI2
RRTYCN	SCRABBL1	SCRABBLE	SCRABLE	SIERRA
SIERRA1	SIERRA3	SIERRAME	SIMCIT	SIMCITY
SIMCITY1	SIMCITY2	SIMCITY3	SIMCITY4	SIMCITY5
SIMCITY7	SINVADER	SPACEQST	SPACEWAR	SPACINV1
SPVADER	SR	SROYALE	STARFL	STARFLT
STARTR	STARTREK	STARTRK1	STARTRK2	STARTRK3
STARTRK7	STELCRUS	STRATEGO	STRATGO	TAIPAI
TAIPE1	TAIPEI	TAIPEI1	TAIPEI2	TENNIS
TET	TET2	TET3	TET4	TETRIS
TETRIS01	TETRIS02	TETRIS03	TETRIS07	TETRIS08
TETRIS09	TETRIS1	TETRIS14	TETRIS15	TETRIS16
TETRIS19	TETRIS2	TETRIS20	TETRIS21	TETRIS25
TETRIS28	TETRIS29	TETRIS3	TETRIS31	TETRIS32

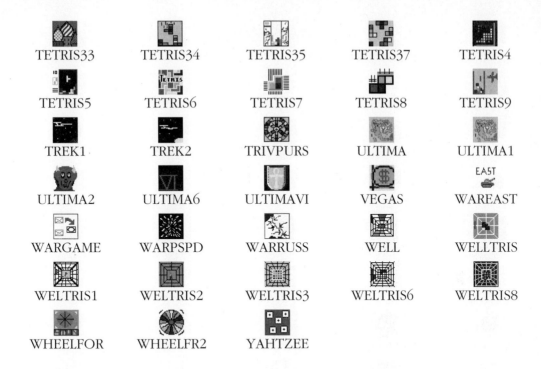

TETRIS33	TETRIS34	TETRIS35	TETRIS37	TETRIS4
TETRIS5	TETRIS6	TETRIS7	TETRIS8	TETRIS9
TREK1	TREK2	TRIVPURS	ULTIMA	ULTIMA1
ULTIMA2	ULTIMA6	ULTIMAVI	VEGAS	WAREAST
WARGAME	WARPSPD	WARRUSS	WELL	WELLTRIS
WELTRIS1	WELTRIS2	WELTRIS3	WELTRIS6	WELTRIS8
WHEELFOR	WHEELFR2	YAHTZEE		

Graphics

Icons for graphics software, draw programs, scanners, and the like.

.ICO files located in **ALLICONS\GRAFICON**:

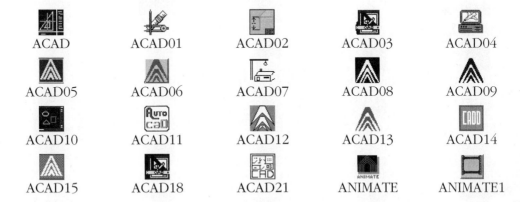

ACAD	ACAD01	ACAD02	ACAD03	ACAD04
ACAD05	ACAD06	ACAD07	ACAD08	ACAD09
ACAD10	ACAD11	ACAD12	ACAD13	ACAD14
ACAD15	ACAD18	ACAD21	ANIMATE	ANIMATE1

ANIMATOR APPLAUS1 APPLAUS2 APPLAUSE ARTLET

ARTLET1 ARTLET2 ARTLET3 ARTLINE AXUM

BRUSH CAMERA CAMERA1 CAMERA2 CAMERA3

CAMERA8 CHARISM CHARISM1 CHARISM2 CHARISM3

CIRCLSQU CRAYON CRAYON1 CSHOW2 CWBUT

CWICONZ1 CWICONZ2 DESIGN DESIGN1 DESIGN2

DESIGN3 DESIGN4 DESIGN5 DESIGN6 DESIGN8

DP DPAINT DRAFIX DRAW DRAW1

DRAW2 DRAW5 DRAWAP DRHALO DRHALO1

DRHALO2 DSKART EASEL2 EASYCAD ECAD

FILLCIRC FILLRECT FLOODFIL FLRPLAN1 FLRPLN

FREEL GALLERY GCADD GEM1

GF GIF GIF2 GIF2BMP GIF2PCX

GIFBUT GIFV GRAFKSWS GRAFNBOX GRAPH

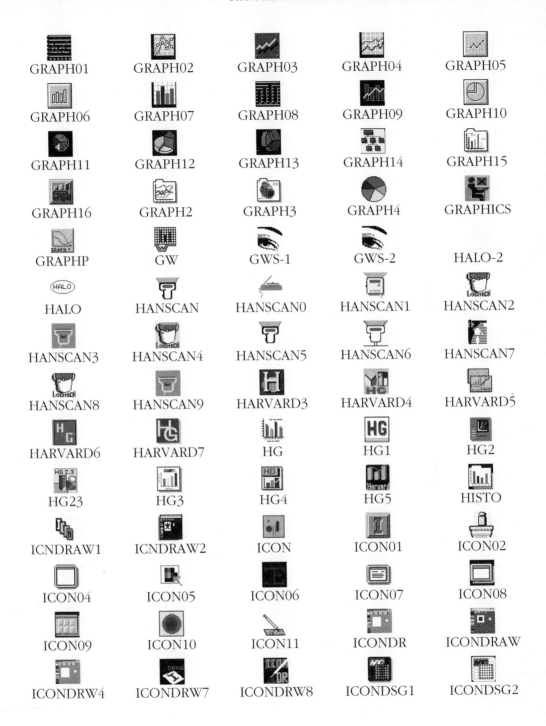

GRAPH01	GRAPH02	GRAPH03	GRAPH04	GRAPH05
GRAPH06	GRAPH07	GRAPH08	GRAPH09	GRAPH10
GRAPH11	GRAPH12	GRAPH13	GRAPH14	GRAPH15
GRAPH16	GRAPH2	GRAPH3	GRAPH4	GRAPHICS
GRAPHP	GW	GWS-1	GWS-2	HALO-2
HALO	HANSCAN	HANSCAN0	HANSCAN1	HANSCAN2
HANSCAN3	HANSCAN4	HANSCAN5	HANSCAN6	HANSCAN7
HANSCAN8	HANSCAN9	HARVARD3	HARVARD4	HARVARD5
HARVARD6	HARVARD7	HG	HG1	HG2
HG23	HG3	HG4	HG5	HISTO
ICNDRAW1	ICNDRAW2	ICON	ICON01	ICON02
ICON04	ICON05	ICON06	ICON07	ICON08
ICON09	ICON10	ICON11	ICONDR	ICONDRAW
ICONDRW4	ICONDRW7	ICONDRW8	ICONDSG1	ICONDSG2

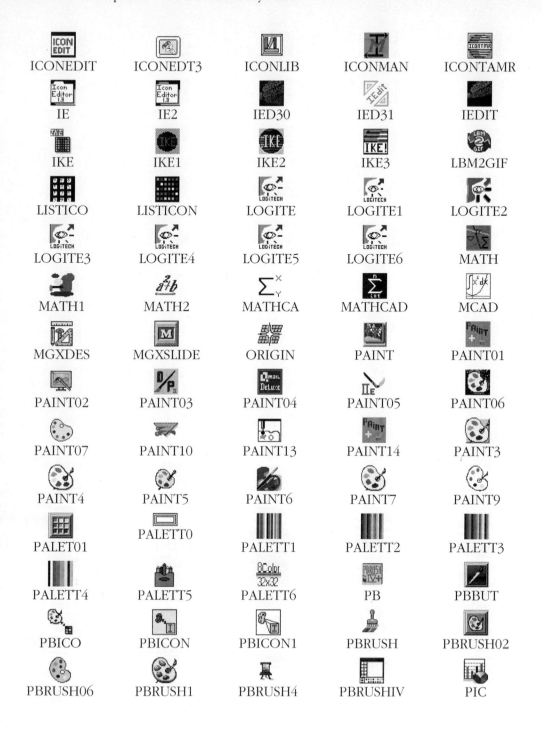

ICONEDIT	ICONEDT3	ICONLIB	ICONMAN	ICONTAMR
IE	IE2	IED30	IED31	IEDIT
IKE	IKE1	IKE2	IKE3	LBM2GIF
LISTICO	LISTICON	LOGITE	LOGITE1	LOGITE2
LOGITE3	LOGITE4	LOGITE5	LOGITE6	MATH
MATH1	MATH2	MATHCA	MATHCAD	MCAD
MGXDES	MGXSLIDE	ORIGIN	PAINT	PAINT01
PAINT02	PAINT03	PAINT04	PAINT05	PAINT06
PAINT07	PAINT10	PAINT13	PAINT14	PAINT3
PAINT4	PAINT5	PAINT6	PAINT7	PAINT9
PALET01	PALETT0	PALETT1	PALETT2	PALETT3
PALETT4	PALETT5	PALETT6	PB	PBBUT
PBICO	PBICON	PBICON1	PBRUSH	PBRUSH02
PBRUSH06	PBRUSH1	PBRUSH4	PBRUSHIV	PIC

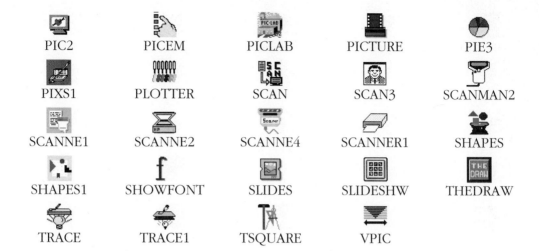

Images

These are just raw, random pictures.

`.ICO` files located in **ALLICONS\IMAGICON:**

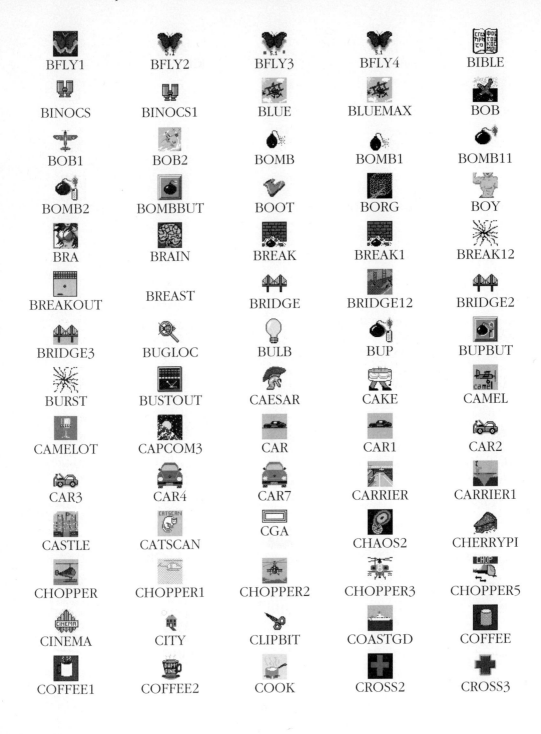

BFLY1	BFLY2	BFLY3	BFLY4	BIBLE
BINOCS	BINOCS1	BLUE	BLUEMAX	BOB
BOB1	BOB2	BOMB	BOMB1	BOMB11
BOMB2	BOMBBUT	BOOT	BORG	BOY
BRA	BRAIN	BREAK	BREAK1	BREAK12
BREAKOUT	BREAST	BRIDGE	BRIDGE12	BRIDGE2
BRIDGE3	BUGLOC	BULB	BUP	BUPBUT
BURST	BUSTOUT	CAESAR	CAKE	CAMEL
CAMELOT	CAPCOM3	CAR	CAR1	CAR2
CAR3	CAR4	CAR7	CARRIER	CARRIER1
CASTLE	CATSCAN	CGA	CHAOS2	CHERRYPI
CHOPPER	CHOPPER1	CHOPPER2	CHOPPER3	CHOPPER5
CINEMA	CITY	CLIPBIT	COASTGD	COFFEE
COFFEE1	COFFEE2	COOK	CROSS2	CROSS3

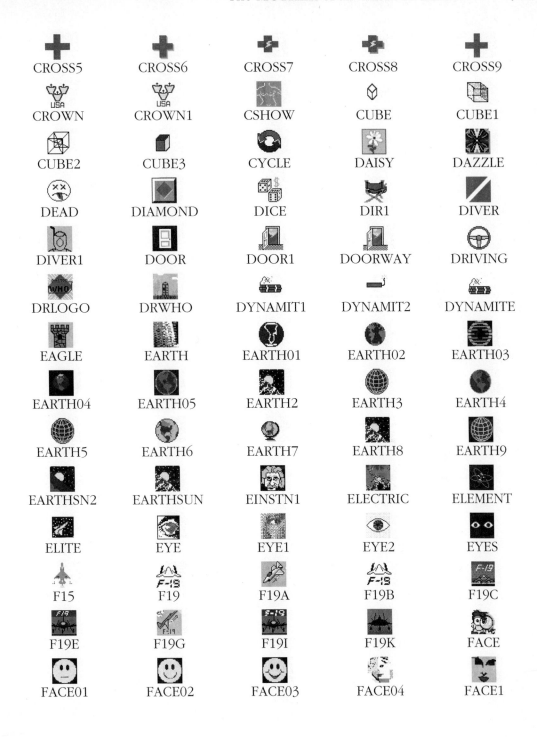

CROSS5	CROSS6	CROSS7	CROSS8	CROSS9
CROWN	CROWN1	CSHOW	CUBE	CUBE1
CUBE2	CUBE3	CYCLE	DAISY	DAZZLE
DEAD	DIAMOND	DICE	DIR1	DIVER
DIVER1	DOOR	DOOR1	DOORWAY	DRIVING
DRLOGO	DRWHO	DYNAMIT1	DYNAMIT2	DYNAMITE
EAGLE	EARTH	EARTH01	EARTH02	EARTH03
EARTH04	EARTH05	EARTH2	EARTH3	EARTH4
EARTH5	EARTH6	EARTH7	EARTH8	EARTH9
EARTHSN2	EARTHSUN	EINSTN1	ELECTRIC	ELEMENT
ELITE	EYE	EYE1	EYE2	EYES
F15	F19	F19A	F19B	F19C
F19E	F19G	F19I	F19K	FACE
FACE01	FACE02	FACE03	FACE04	FACE1

FACE2	FACE3	FACE5	FACE6	FACE7
FADE	FALCON	FAMILY	FIRE	FIRE1
FIREWKS	FIREWO	FIREWORK	FIS4	FISH
FISH1	FISH2	FISH2A	FISH3A	FISH3B
FISH3C	FISH3D	FISH4	FISH4A	FISH5
FISH6	FLARE	FLIGHT	FLIGHT2	FLIGHT4
FLIGHT6	FLOWER	FLOWER1	FLOWER3	FLOWER5
FRAC	FRAC1	FRACTINT	GALAXY	GALAXY1
HAMB	HAND	HEART	HEARTS	HELLO
HERO	HIKER	HIKER1	HIWAY	HORN
HORSE	HORSE1	HOUSE	HOUSE1	HOVER
HURRICAN	HURRICN1	HURRICN3	ILOVENY	ILOVEY
ISHIDO	ISHIDO1	ISLAND	ISLAND2	ISLAND3
JAGAROTH	JET	JETFGHT2	JIGSAW	JOUST

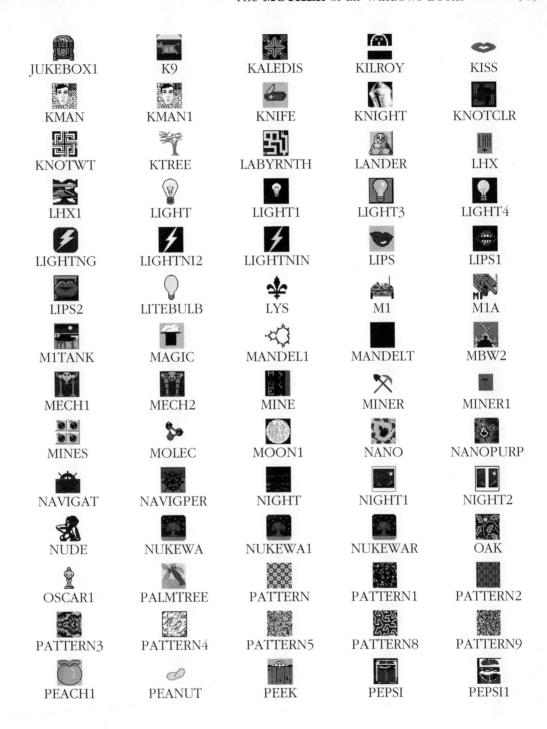

JUKEBOX1	K9	KALEDIS	KILROY	KISS
KMAN	KMAN1	KNIFE	KNIGHT	KNOTCLR
KNOTWT	KTREE	LABYRNTH	LANDER	LHX
LHX1	LIGHT	LIGHT1	LIGHT3	LIGHT4
LIGHTNG	LIGHTNI2	LIGHTNIN	LIPS	LIPS1
LIPS2	LITEBULB	LYS	M1	M1A
M1TANK	MAGIC	MANDEL1	MANDELT	MBW2
MECH1	MECH2	MINE	MINER	MINER1
MINES	MOLEC	MOON1	NANO	NANOPURP
NAVIGAT	NAVIGPER	NIGHT	NIGHT1	NIGHT2
NUDE	NUKEWA	NUKEWA1	NUKEWAR	OAK
OSCAR1	PALMTREE	PATTERN	PATTERN1	PATTERN2
PATTERN3	PATTERN4	PATTERN5	PATTERN8	PATTERN9
PEACH1	PEANUT	PEEK	PEPSI	PEPSI1

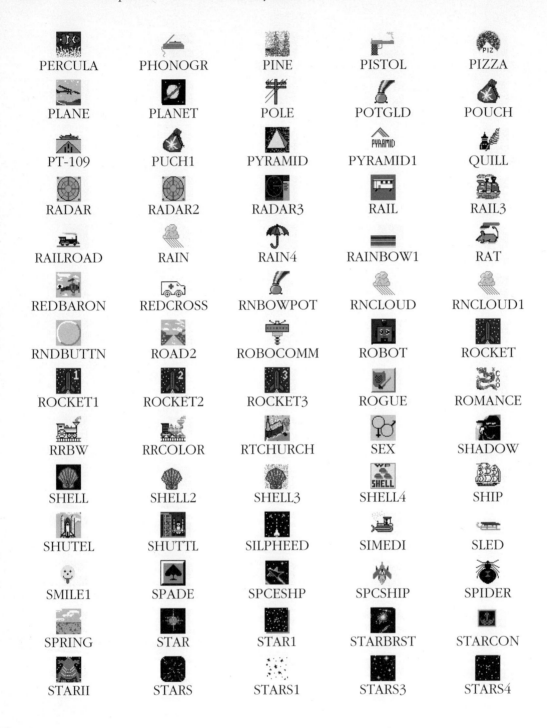

PERCULA	PHONOGR	PINE	PISTOL	PIZZA
PLANE	PLANET	POLE	POTGLD	POUCH
PT-109	PUCH1	PYRAMID	PYRAMID1	QUILL
RADAR	RADAR2	RADAR3	RAIL	RAIL3
RAILROAD	RAIN	RAIN4	RAINBOW1	RAT
REDBARON	REDCROSS	RNBOWPOT	RNCLOUD	RNCLOUD1
RNDBUTTN	ROAD2	ROBOCOMM	ROBOT	ROCKET
ROCKET1	ROCKET2	ROCKET3	ROGUE	ROMANCE
RRBW	RRCOLOR	RTCHURCH	SEX	SHADOW
SHELL	SHELL2	SHELL3	SHELL4	SHIP
SHUTEL	SHUTTL	SILPHEED	SIMEDI	SLED
SMILE1	SPADE	SPCESHP	SPCSHIP	SPIDER
SPRING	STAR	STAR1	STARBRST	STARCON
STARII	STARS	STARS1	STARS3	STARS4

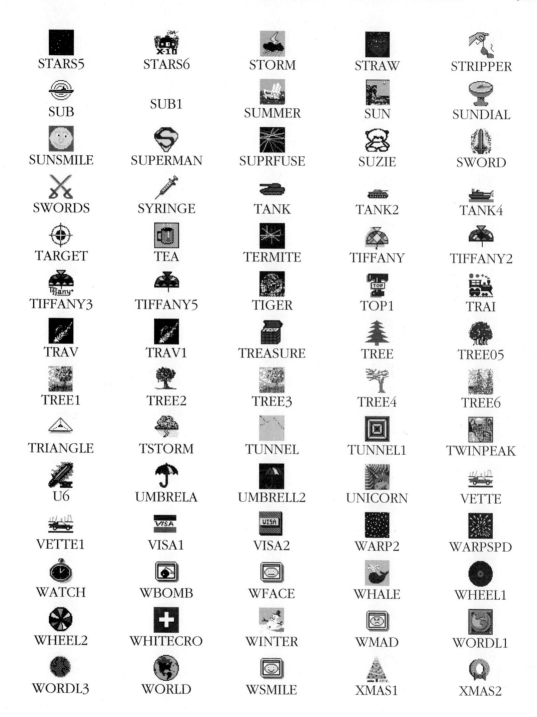

STARS5	STARS6	STORM	STRAW	STRIPPER
SUB	SUB1	SUMMER	SUN	SUNDIAL
SUNSMILE	SUPERMAN	SUPRFUSE	SUZIE	SWORD
SWORDS	SYRINGE	TANK	TANK2	TANK4
TARGET	TEA	TERMITE	TIFFANY	TIFFANY2
TIFFANY3	TIFFANY5	TIGER	TOP1	TRAI
TRAV	TRAV1	TREASURE	TREE	TREE05
TREE1	TREE2	TREE3	TREE4	TREE6
TRIANGLE	TSTORM	TUNNEL	TUNNEL1	TWINPEAK
U6	UMBRELA	UMBRELL2	UNICORN	VETTE
VETTE1	VISA1	VISA2	WARP2	WARPSPD
WATCH	WBOMB	WFACE	WHALE	WHEEL1
WHEEL2	WHITECRO	WINTER	WMAD	WORDL1
WORDL3	WORLD	WSMILE	XMAS1	XMAS2

XMAS3

XWING

YELBUD

Languages

Here's a handful of pretty little pictures for your favorite computer languages and programming-related topics.

`.ICO` files located in **ALLICONS\LANGICON:**

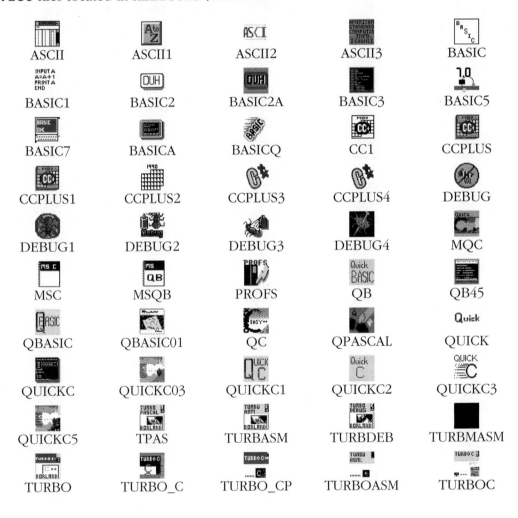

ASCII	ASCII1	ASCII2	ASCII3	BASIC
BASIC1	BASIC2	BASIC2A	BASIC3	BASIC5
BASIC7	BASICA	BASICQ	CC1	CCPLUS
CCPLUS1	CCPLUS2	CCPLUS3	CCPLUS4	DEBUG
DEBUG1	DEBUG2	DEBUG3	DEBUG4	MQC
MSC	MSQB	PROFS	QB	QB45
QBASIC	QBASIC01	QC	QPASCAL	QUICK
QUICKC	QUICKC03	QUICKC1	QUICKC2	QUICKC3
QUICKC5	TPAS	TURBASM	TURBDEB	TURBMASM
TURBO	TURBO_C	TURBO_CP	TURBOASM	TURBOC

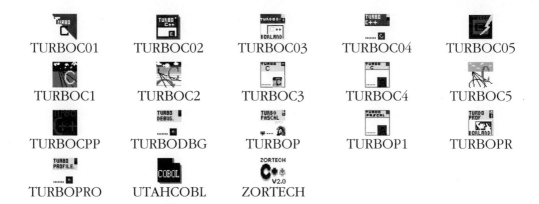

TURBOC01	TURBOC02	TURBOC03	TURBOC04	TURBOC05
TURBOC1	TURBOC2	TURBOC3	TURBOC4	TURBOC5
TURBOCPP	TURBODBG	TURBOP	TURBOP1	TURBOPR
TURBOPRO	UTAHCOBL	ZORTECH		

Miscellaneous #1

All the views what's fit to print. There are lots of icons here that were created for specific applications. Also make sure you look at the Miscellaneous #2 and Images sections.

`.ICO` files located in **ALLICONS\MISCICO1**:

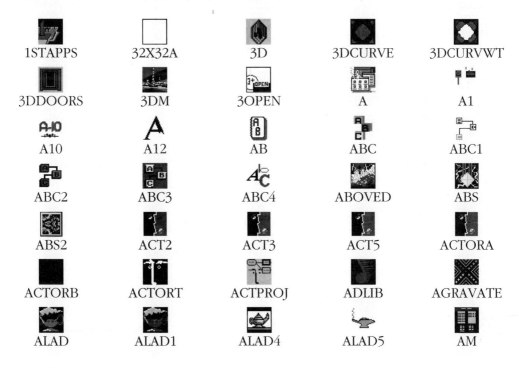

1STAPPS	32X32A	3D	3DCURVE	3DCURVWT
3DDOORS	3DM	3OPEN	A	A1
A10	A12	AB	ABC	ABC1
ABC2	ABC3	ABC4	ABOVED	ABS
ABS2	ACT2	ACT3	ACT5	ACTORA
ACTORB	ACTORT	ACTPROJ	ADLIB	AGRAVATE
ALAD	ALAD1	ALAD4	ALAD5	AM

AQ	AUTOMA	AVAGIO	B	BANNER
BANNER1	BEAST	BH1942	BILL	BILLTC
BIO	BIO2	BITCOM	BITS	BLCKOUT1
BLOCKOUT	BLOCKS	BMP	BON	BOOT2
BOX11	BOX12	BOX13	BOX2	BOXES
BOXES1	BOXLABL	BRIEF	BRIEF1	BRIEF2
BRIEF3	BRIEF4	BRIEF5	BRIGHTWR	BROKEEP
BUTTON	C	CAPCOM	CASSETT1	CASSETT2
CASSETT3	CATCHEM	CATDISK	CATSCA	CBT
CENT	CEO	CEO04	CEO1	CEO2
CEO3	CEO4	CEO5	CEO6	CIPHER
CLEAN	CLEAN2	CLEAN3	CLEAN5	CLEAR
CLEF	CLEF1	COLNQST	COLONQST	COMP
COMPILE	COMPILER	CONVERT	CONVERT1	CONVERT2

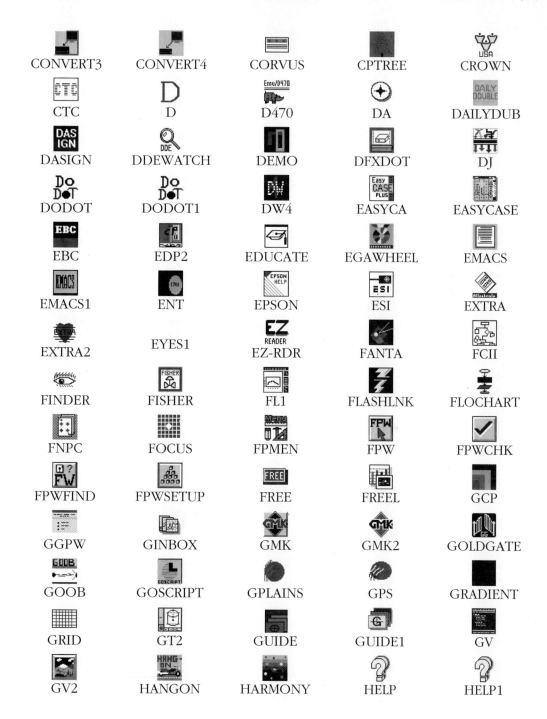

CONVERT3	CONVERT4	CORVUS	CPTREE	CROWN
CTC	D	D470	DA	DAILYDUB
DASIGN	DDEWATCH	DEMO	DFXDOT	DJ
DODOT	DODOT1	DW4	EASYCA	EASYCASE
EBC	EDP2	EDUCATE	EGAWHEEL	EMACS
EMACS1	ENT	EPSON	ESI	EXTRA
EXTRA2	EYES1	EZ-RDR	FANTA	FCII
FINDER	FISHER	FL1	FLASHLNK	FLOCHART
FNPC	FOCUS	FPMEN	FPW	FPWCHK
FPWFIND	FPWSETUP	FREE	FREEL	GCP
GGPW	GINBOX	GMK	GMK2	GOLDGATE
GOOB	GOSCRIPT	GPLAINS	GPS	GRADIENT
GRID	GT2	GUIDE	GUIDE1	GV
GV2	HANGON	HARMONY	HELP	HELP1

HR2	HR2A	HUD	I	I2
I3	IDEA1	IDEA2	IN1	IN2
INSPECT	INTEROUT	INTERVAL	IRMA	ITI
J	JB	JF	JF2	JUNK
KEEPOUT	KFREE	KFREE1	KFREE2	KIVIAT
KOCH	KPWIN	LASER	LASER1	LASER3
LAST	LAST1	LATEX	LCN	LEWP
LEXIS	LEXIS1	LEXIS2	LINER	LOGO
LOOM	LOOM1	LORENZ	LS	MACOLA
MACRO	MACRO1	MAGNIFY	MAGNIFY2	MANIFE
MANIFEST	MAPMEM	MASTRKEY	MATH	MATH1
MATRIX	MATRIX1	ME	ME1	MECH
MEM	MEMORY	MENU	MENU1	MENU2
MENU3	MENU7	MESSY	MIDI	MIPS

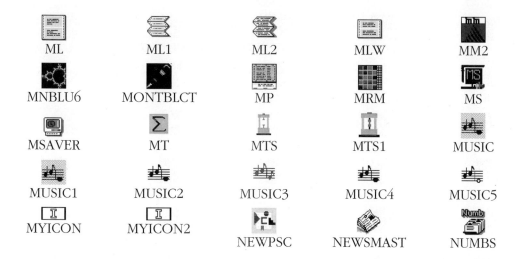

ML	ML1	ML2	MLW	MM2
MNBLU6	MONTBLCT	MP	MRM	MS
MSAVER	MT	MTS	MTS1	MUSIC
MUSIC1	MUSIC2	MUSIC3	MUSIC4	MUSIC5
MYICON	MYICON2	NEWPSC	NEWSMAST	NUMBS

Miscellaneous #2

Miscellaneous, continued. Also make sure you look at the Miscellaneous #1 and Images sections.

.ICO files located in ALLICONS\MISCICO2:

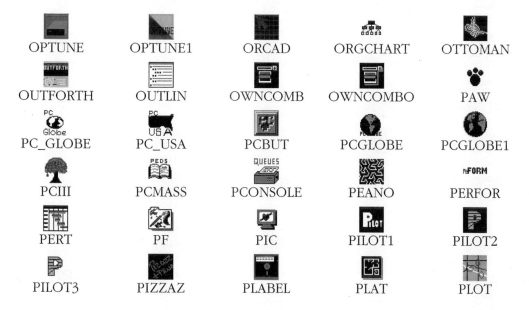

OPTUNE	OPTUNE1	ORCAD	ORGCHART	OTTOMAN
OUTFORTH	OUTLIN	OWNCOMB	OWNCOMBO	PAW
PC_GLOBE	PC_USA	PCBUT	PCGLOBE	PCGLOBE1
PCIII	PCMASS	PCONSOLE	PEANO	PERFOR
PERT	PF	PIC	PILOT1	PILOT2
PILOT3	PIZZAZ	PLABEL	PLAT	PLOT

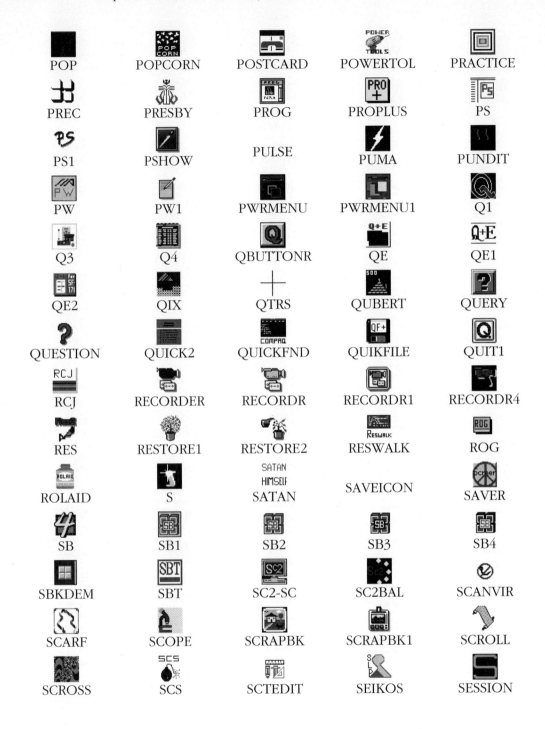

POP	POPCORN	POSTCARD	POWERTOL	PRACTICE
PREC	PRESBY	PROG	PROPLUS	PS
PS1	PSHOW	PULSE	PUMA	PUNDIT
PW	PW1	PWRMENU	PWRMENU1	Q1
Q3	Q4	QBUTTONR	QE	QE1
QE2	QIX	QTRS	QUBERT	QUERY
QUESTION	QUICK2	QUICKFND	QUIKFILE	QUIT1
RCJ	RECORDER	RECORDR	RECORDR1	RECORDR4
RES	RESTORE1	RESTORE2	RESWALK	ROG
ROLAID	S	SATAN	SAVEICON	SAVER
SB	SB1	SB2	SB3	SB4
SBKDEM	SBT	SC2-SC	SC2BAL	SCANVIR
SCARF	SCOPE	SCRAPBK	SCRAPBK1	SCROLL
SCROSS	SCS	SCTEDIT	SEIKOS	SESSION

SESSUTIL	SETPRN	SETTIME	SFX	SHELF
SHOWDIB	SIDEKICK	SIDEWA	SK	SK1
SK2	SK3	SLBBS	SMTNEW	SNAP
SNOOPER	SOL2	SOLLOGO	SOUND	SOUND2
SPEAKER	SPEED	SPEED1	SPINFONT	SPIRAL
SPLASH	SPOTS	SPY1	SQ3	SQSPIRL
SS	SS1	SS2	SS3	STARDOS
STAT	STATS	STOCK	STORY	STORYBD
SUCCESS	SUPRSTAR	SW	SWP	SWP3
SYSCON	SYSEX	SYSGRAPH	T	T1
T3	TABLE	TABLE1	TAMER	TAP
TAPE	TAPE1	TAPE2	TAPE4	TAPELIB
TASK	TBANDIT	TCONTENT	TD	TE
TEST	TEST1	TEX	TEXT2PCX	THENC

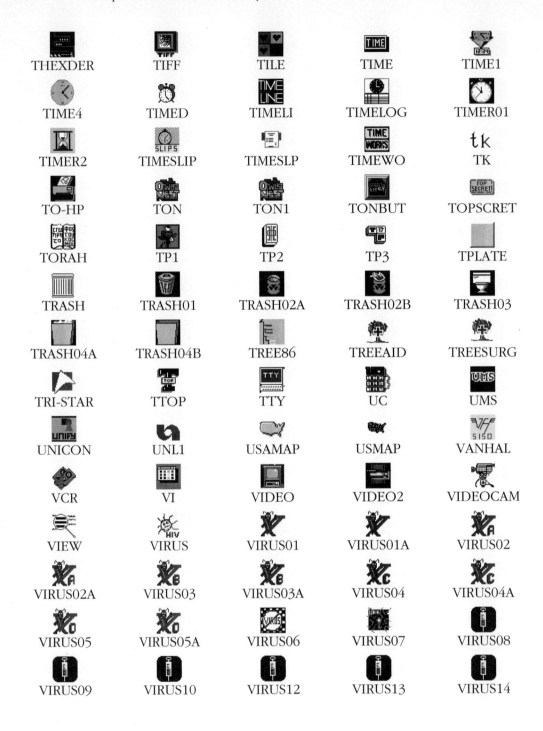

THEXDER	TIFF	TILE	TIME	TIME1
TIME4	TIMED	TIMELI	TIMELOG	TIMER01
TIMER2	TIMESLIP	TIMESLP	TIMEWO	TK
TO-HP	TON	TON1	TONBUT	TOPSCRET
TORAH	TP1	TP2	TP3	TPLATE
TRASH	TRASH01	TRASH02A	TRASH02B	TRASH03
TRASH04A	TRASH04B	TREE86	TREEAID	TREESURG
TRI-STAR	TTOP	TTY	UC	UMS
UNICON	UNL1	USAMAP	USMAP	VANHAL
VCR	VI	VIDEO	VIDEO2	VIDEOCAM
VIEW	VIRUS	VIRUS01	VIRUS01A	VIRUS02
VIRUS02A	VIRUS03	VIRUS03A	VIRUS04	VIRUS04A
VIRUS05	VIRUS05A	VIRUS06	VIRUS07	VIRUS08
VIRUS09	VIRUS10	VIRUS12	VIRUS13	VIRUS14

VIRUS15	VIRUS16	VIRUS17	VIRUS18	VIRUS19
VIRUS20	VIRUS21	VIRUS23	VIRUS24	VIRUS25
VIRUS30	VIRUS37	VIRUS39	VIRUS40	VP
VPCAM	VPCOLOR	VPDEF	VPWIN	VUIMAG
W	WESTLAW	WFNBOSS	WFNCONV	WGRID
WHERE	WILL	WLDTIME	WORK	WSMOOTH
XBUT	XPORT	XRTD1	XRTD2	XRTD3
ZM				

Play

Pictures of your favorite — primarily non-computer — games and teams. If you don't find what you're looking for here, make sure you check out the Games section.

.**ICO** files located in **ALLICONS\PLAYICON**:

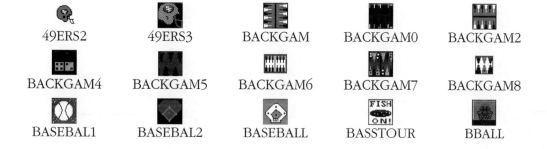

49ERS2	49ERS3	BACKGAM	BACKGAM0	BACKGAM2
BACKGAM4	BACKGAM5	BACKGAM6	BACKGAM7	BACKGAM8
BASEBAL1	BASEBAL2	BASEBALL	BASSTOUR	BBALL

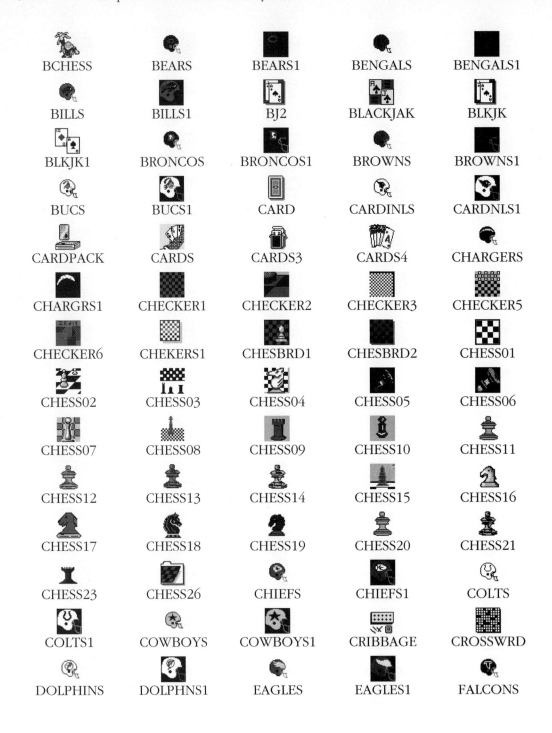

BCHESS	BEARS	BEARS1	BENGALS	BENGALS1
BILLS	BILLS1	BJ2	BLACKJAK	BLKJK
BLKJK1	BRONCOS	BRONCOS1	BROWNS	BROWNS1
BUCS	BUCS1	CARD	CARDINLS	CARDNLS1
CARDPACK	CARDS	CARDS3	CARDS4	CHARGERS
CHARGRS1	CHECKER1	CHECKER2	CHECKER3	CHECKER5
CHECKER6	CHEKERS1	CHESBRD1	CHESBRD2	CHESS01
CHESS02	CHESS03	CHESS04	CHESS05	CHESS06
CHESS07	CHESS08	CHESS09	CHESS10	CHESS11
CHESS12	CHESS13	CHESS14	CHESS15	CHESS16
CHESS17	CHESS18	CHESS19	CHESS20	CHESS21
CHESS23	CHESS26	CHIEFS	CHIEFS1	COLTS
COLTS1	COWBOYS	COWBOYS1	CRIBBAGE	CROSSWRD
DOLPHINS	DOLPHNS1	EAGLES	EAGLES1	FALCONS

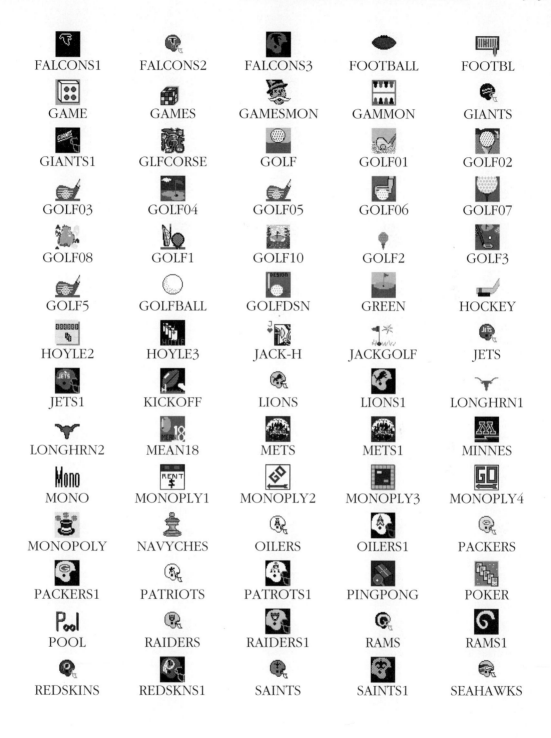

FALCONS1	FALCONS2	FALCONS3	FOOTBALL	FOOTBL
GAME	GAMES	GAMESMON	GAMMON	GIANTS
GIANTS1	GLFCORSE	GOLF	GOLF01	GOLF02
GOLF03	GOLF04	GOLF05	GOLF06	GOLF07
GOLF08	GOLF1	GOLF10	GOLF2	GOLF3
GOLF5	GOLFBALL	GOLFDSN	GREEN	HOCKEY
HOYLE2	HOYLE3	JACK-H	JACKGOLF	JETS
JETS1	KICKOFF	LIONS	LIONS1	LONGHRN1
LONGHRN2	MEAN18	METS	METS1	MINNES
MONO	MONOPLY1	MONOPLY2	MONOPLY3	MONOPLY4
MONOPOLY	NAVYCHES	OILERS	OILERS1	PACKERS
PACKERS1	PATRIOTS	PATROTS1	PINGPONG	POKER
POOL	RAIDERS	RAIDERS1	RAMS	RAMS1
REDSKINS	REDSKNS1	SAINTS	SAINTS1	SEAHAWKS

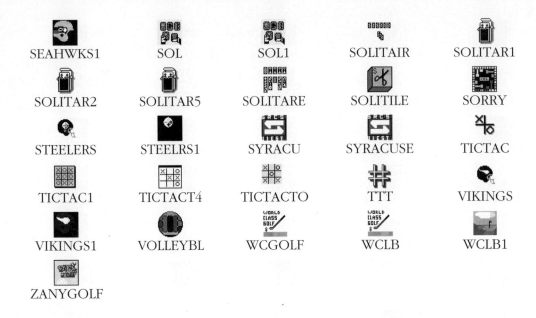

SEAHWKS1	SOL	SOL1	SOLITAIR	SOLITAR1
SOLITAR2	SOLITAR5	SOLITARE	SOLITILE	SORRY
STEELERS	STEELRS1	SYRACU	SYRACUSE	TICTAC
TICTAC1	TICTACT4	TICTACTO	TTT	VIKINGS
VIKINGS1	VOLLEYBL	WCGOLF	WCLB	WCLB1
ZANYGOLF				

Signs

These are mostly traffic and directional signs.

.**ICO** files located in **ALLICONS\SIGNICON:**

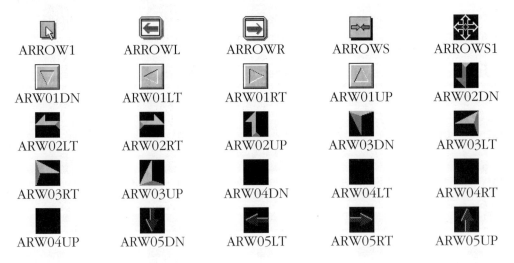

ARROW1	ARROWL	ARROWR	ARROWS	ARROWS1
ARW01DN	ARW01LT	ARW01RT	ARW01UP	ARW02DN
ARW02LT	ARW02RT	ARW02UP	ARW03DN	ARW03LT
ARW03RT	ARW03UP	ARW04DN	ARW04LT	ARW04RT
ARW04UP	ARW05DN	ARW05LT	ARW05RT	ARW05UP

ARW06DN	ARW06LT	ARW06RT	ARW06UP	ARW07DN
ARW07LT	ARW07RT	ARW07UP	ARW08DN	ARW08LT
ARW08RT	ARW08UP	ARW09DN	ARW09LT	ARW09RT
ARW10NE	ARW10NW	ARW10SE	ARW10SW	ARW11NE
ARW11NW	ARW11SE	ARW11SW	ARWUP	MISC01
MISC02	MISC03	MISC04	MISC05	MISC06
MISC07	MISC08	MISC09	MISC10	MISC11
MISC12	MISC13	MISC14	MISC15	MISC16A
MISC16B	MISC17A	MISC17B	MISC18	MISC19
MISC20	MISC21	MISC22	MISC23	MISC24
MISC25	MISC26	MISC27	MISC28	MISC29
MISC30	MISC31	MISC32	MISC33	MISC34
MISC35	MISC36	MISC37	MISC38	MISC39A
MISC39B	MISC40	MISC41	MISC42	MISC43

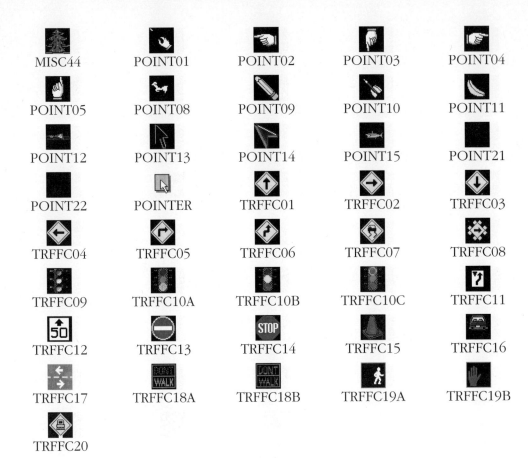

MISC44	POINT01	POINT02	POINT03	POINT04
POINT05	POINT08	POINT09	POINT10	POINT11
POINT12	POINT13	POINT14	POINT15	POINT21
POINT22	POINTER	TRFFC01	TRFFC02	TRFFC03
TRFFC04	TRFFC05	TRFFC06	TRFFC07	TRFFC08
TRFFC09	TRFFC10A	TRFFC10B	TRFFC10C	TRFFC11
TRFFC12	TRFFC13	TRFFC14	TRFFC15	TRFFC16
TRFFC17	TRFFC18A	TRFFC18B	TRFFC19A	TRFFC19B
TRFFC20				

Spreadsheets

Pictures to attach to your favorite rows 'n columns.

.ICO files located in **ALLICONS\SPRDICON:**

123-A	123-AB	123-AC	123-AD	123-AE

123-AF	123-AG	123-AH	123-AI	123-AJ
123-AK	123-AL	123-AM	123-AN	123-AO
123-AP	123-AQ	123-AR	123-AS	123-AT
123-AU	123-AV	123-AV1	123-AW	123-AX
123-AY	123-AZ	123-B	123-BA	123-BB
123-BC	123-BD	123-BE	123-BF	123-BG
123-BH	123-BI	123-BJ	123-BK	123-BL
123-BM	123-BN	123-BO	123-BP	123-BQ
123-BR	123-BS	123-BT	123	123W
123WINS1	123WINS2	123WINS3	123WINST	EXCEL
EXCEL00	EXCEL01	EXCEL02	EXCEL03	EXCEL04
EXCEL05	EXCEL06	EXCEL07	EXCEL08	EXCEL09
EXCEL10	EXCEL11	EXCEL12	EXCEL13	EXCEL14
EXCEL15	EXCEL16	EXCEL17	EXCEL18	EXCEL19

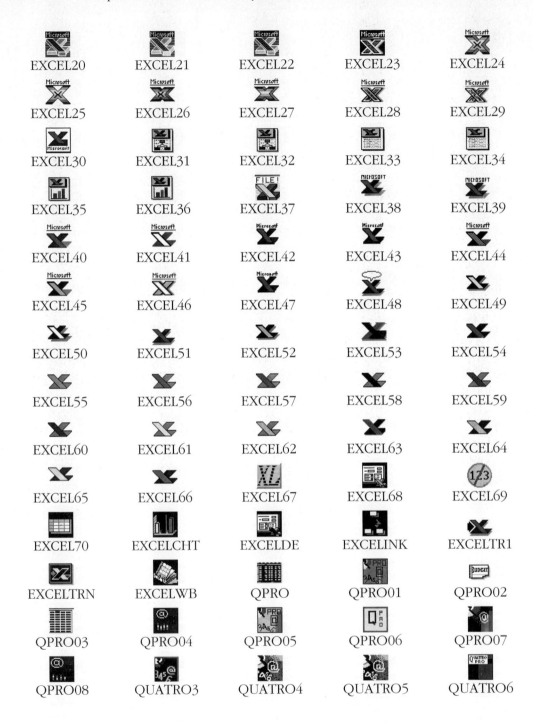

EXCEL20	EXCEL21	EXCEL22	EXCEL23	EXCEL24
EXCEL25	EXCEL26	EXCEL27	EXCEL28	EXCEL29
EXCEL30	EXCEL31	EXCEL32	EXCEL33	EXCEL34
EXCEL35	EXCEL36	EXCEL37	EXCEL38	EXCEL39
EXCEL40	EXCEL41	EXCEL42	EXCEL43	EXCEL44
EXCEL45	EXCEL46	EXCEL47	EXCEL48	EXCEL49
EXCEL50	EXCEL51	EXCEL52	EXCEL53	EXCEL54
EXCEL55	EXCEL56	EXCEL57	EXCEL58	EXCEL59
EXCEL60	EXCEL61	EXCEL62	EXCEL63	EXCEL64
EXCEL65	EXCEL66	EXCEL67	EXCEL68	EXCEL69
EXCEL70	EXCELCHT	EXCELDE	EXCELINK	EXCELTR1
EXCELTRN	EXCELWB	QPRO	QPRO01	QPRO02
QPRO03	QPRO04	QPRO05	QPRO06	QPRO07
QPRO08	QUATRO3	QUATRO4	QUATRO5	QUATRO6

QUATTRO QUATTRO1 QUATTRO2 QUATTRO3 SPREAD

SPREAD1

Utilities

Emphasis here is on file and disk utilities and general Windows utilities. If you're looking for pictures of disks, check out the Computer and DOS sections.

`.ICO` files located in **ALLICONS\UTILICON:**

386MAX	4DOS	4DOS1	4DOS2	4DOS3
4DOS4	4DOSM	4DOSM2	CORETEST	DISKEDIT
DISKREET	DSKTOOLS	FAST	FAST1	FAST2
FAST3	FASTBA	FB	FB1	FB2
FB3	FB4	FB5	FIFTHG	FILEFIND
FILEFIX	FIVE	MACE	MACE1	MFT
MFT1	MFT2	MFT3	NC	NC1
NC2	NC3	NC6	NC7	NCD
NDD	NDD1	NDD2	NDDW	NDDW1

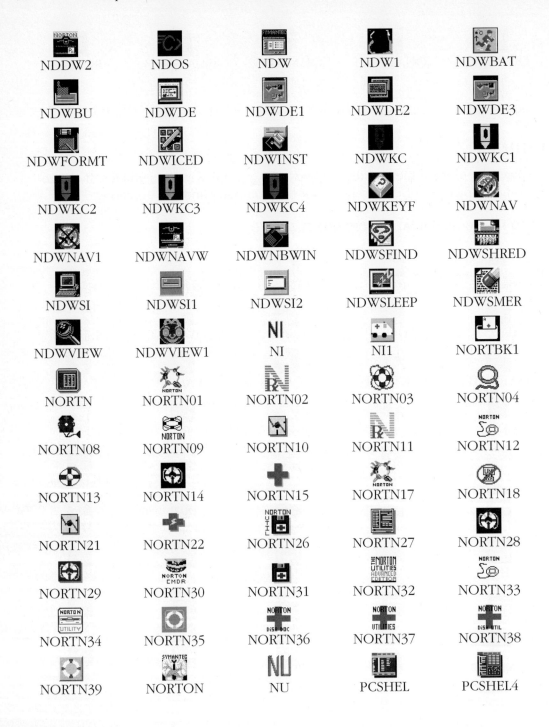

NDDW2	NDOS	NDW	NDW1	NDWBAT
NDWBU	NDWDE	NDWDE1	NDWDE2	NDWDE3
NDWFORMT	NDWICED	NDWINST	NDWKC	NDWKC1
NDWKC2	NDWKC3	NDWKC4	NDWKEYF	NDWNAV
NDWNAV1	NDWNAVW	NDWNBWIN	NDWSFIND	NDWSHRED
NDWSI	NDWSI1	NDWSI2	NDWSLEEP	NDWSMER
NDWVIEW	NDWVIEW1	NI	NI1	NORTBK1
NORTN	NORTN01	NORTN02	NORTN03	NORTN04
NORTN08	NORTN09	NORTN10	NORTN11	NORTN12
NORTN13	NORTN14	NORTN15	NORTN17	NORTN18
NORTN21	NORTN22	NORTN26	NORTN27	NORTN28
NORTN29	NORTN30	NORTN31	NORTN32	NORTN33
NORTN34	NORTN35	NORTN36	NORTN37	NORTN38
NORTN39	NORTON	NU	PCSHEL	PCSHEL4

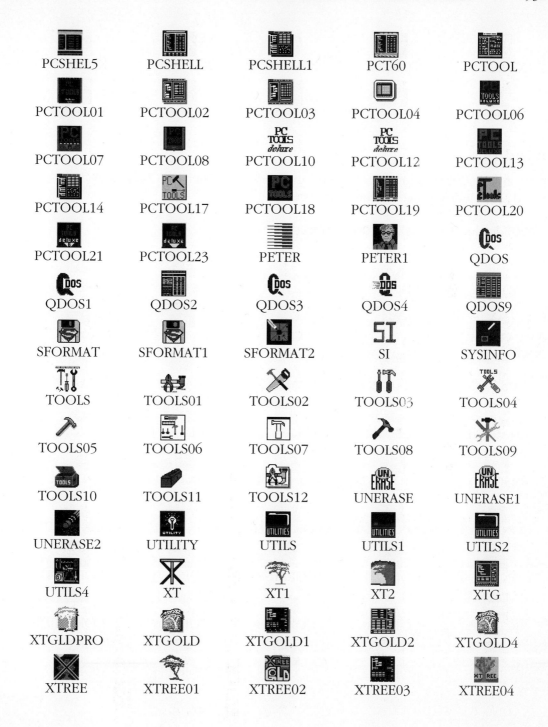

PCSHEL5	PCSHELL	PCSHELL1	PCT60	PCTOOL
PCTOOL01	PCTOOL02	PCTOOL03	PCTOOL04	PCTOOL06
PCTOOL07	PCTOOL08	PCTOOL10	PCTOOL12	PCTOOL13
PCTOOL14	PCTOOL17	PCTOOL18	PCTOOL19	PCTOOL20
PCTOOL21	PCTOOL23	PETER	PETER1	QDOS
QDOS1	QDOS2	QDOS3	QDOS4	QDOS9
SFORMAT	SFORMAT1	SFORMAT2	SI	SYSINFO
TOOLS	TOOLS01	TOOLS02	TOOLS03	TOOLS04
TOOLS05	TOOLS06	TOOLS07	TOOLS08	TOOLS09
TOOLS10	TOOLS11	TOOLS12	UNERASE	UNERASE1
UNERASE2	UTILITY	UTILS	UTILS1	UTILS2
UTILS4	XT	XT1	XT2	XTG
XTGLDPRO	XTGOLD	XTGOLD1	XTGOLD2	XTGOLD4
XTREE	XTREE01	XTREE02	XTREE03	XTREE04

XTREE05	XTREE06	XTREE07	XTREE08	XTREE09
XTREE10	XTREE11	XTREE12	XTREE13	XTREE14

Windows

Lots of icons for Windows accessories and add-ins. Somehow CorelDRAW and Word for Windows made it into this section.

.ICO files located in ALLICONS\WINICON:

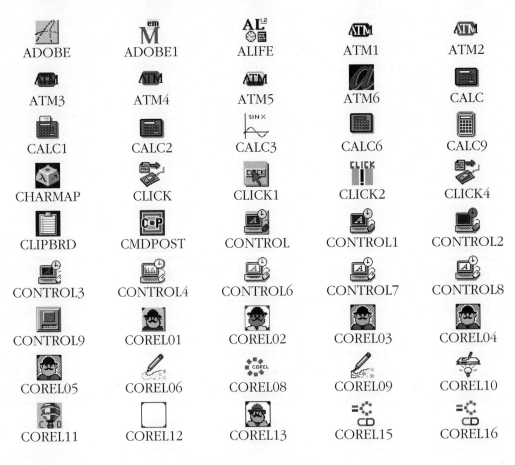

ADOBE	ADOBE1	ALIFE	ATM1	ATM2
ATM3	ATM4	ATM5	ATM6	CALC
CALC1	CALC2	CALC3	CALC6	CALC9
CHARMAP	CLICK	CLICK1	CLICK2	CLICK4
CLIPBRD	CMDPOST	CONTROL	CONTROL1	CONTROL2
CONTROL3	CONTROL4	CONTROL6	CONTROL7	CONTROL8
CONTROL9	COREL01	COREL02	COREL03	COREL04
COREL05	COREL06	COREL08	COREL09	COREL10
COREL11	COREL12	COREL13	COREL15	COREL16

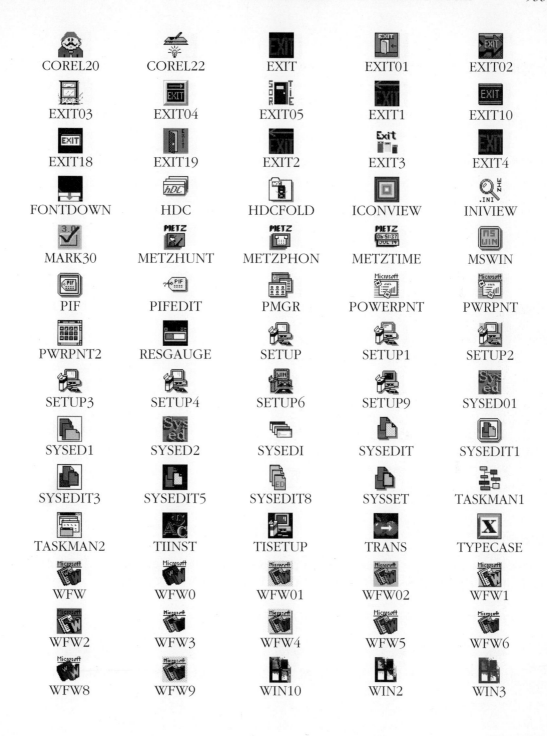

COREL20	COREL22	EXIT	EXIT01	EXIT02
EXIT03	EXIT04	EXIT05	EXIT1	EXIT10
EXIT18	EXIT19	EXIT2	EXIT3	EXIT4
FONTDOWN	HDC	HDCFOLD	ICONVIEW	INIVIEW
MARK30	METZHUNT	METZPHON	METZTIME	MSWIN
PIF	PIFEDIT	PMGR	POWERPNT	PWRPNT
PWRPNT2	RESGAUGE	SETUP	SETUP1	SETUP2
SETUP3	SETUP4	SETUP6	SETUP9	SYSED01
SYSED1	SYSED2	SYSEDI	SYSEDIT	SYSEDIT1
SYSEDIT3	SYSEDIT5	SYSEDIT8	SYSSET	TASKMAN1
TASKMAN2	TIINST	TISETUP	TRANS	TYPECASE
WFW	WFW0	WFW01	WFW02	WFW1
WFW2	WFW3	WFW4	WFW5	WFW6
WFW8	WFW9	WIN10	WIN2	WIN3

WIN3REAL WIN4 WIN5 WIN6 WIN7

WIN8 WIN9 WINBEGIN WINCAP WINCHAR

WINCOLOR WINCRD WINDOW01 WINDOW02 WINDOW07

WINDOW08 WINDOW09 WINDOW11 WINDOW15 WINDOW3

WINDOW4 WINDOW5 WINDOW6 WINDOW7 WINDOW8

WINDOW9 WINDOWS WINEXIT WINEYES WINICO

WININI WINJACK WINMAIL WINNAV WINPARK

WINPARK1 WINPIE WINSETUP WINSTUP1 WINVER

WINWHER1 WINWHER2 WINWHER3 WINWHER4 WINWHERE

WINWORD WNDW-VGA WTREE

Word

These icons are mainly related to word processing and printing. For Amí Pro icons, look at the Applications section; for WinWord icons, look at Windows.

`.ICO` files located in **ALLICONS\WORDICON**:

ALDUS ALDUS1 ALDUS2 ALDUS3 ALDUS4

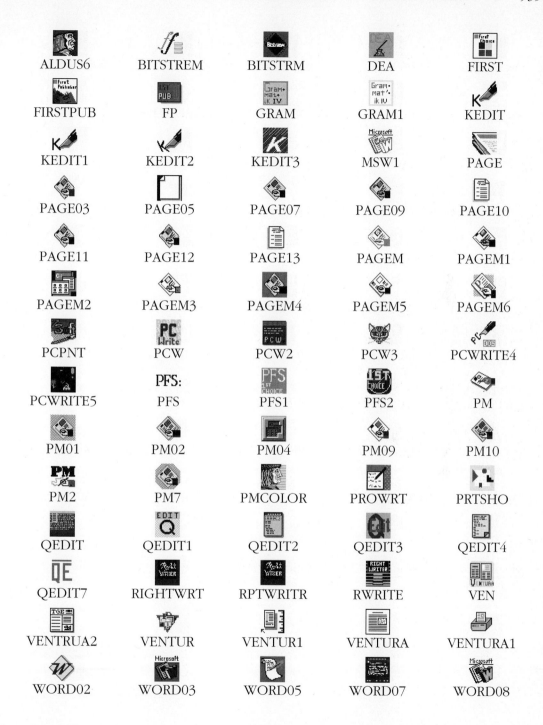

ALDUS6	BITSTREM	BITSTRM	DEA	FIRST
FIRSTPUB	FP	GRAM	GRAM1	KEDIT
KEDIT1	KEDIT2	KEDIT3	MSW1	PAGE
PAGE03	PAGE05	PAGE07	PAGE09	PAGE10
PAGE11	PAGE12	PAGE13	PAGEM	PAGEM1
PAGEM2	PAGEM3	PAGEM4	PAGEM5	PAGEM6
PCPNT	PCW	PCW2	PCW3	PCWRITE4
PCWRITE5	PFS	PFS1	PFS2	PM
PM01	PM02	PM04	PM09	PM10
PM2	PM7	PMCOLOR	PROWRT	PRTSHO
QEDIT	QEDIT1	QEDIT2	QEDIT3	QEDIT4
QEDIT7	RIGHTWRT	RPTWRITR	RWRITE	VEN
VENTRUA2	VENTUR	VENTUR1	VENTURA	VENTURA1
WORD02	WORD03	WORD05	WORD07	WORD08

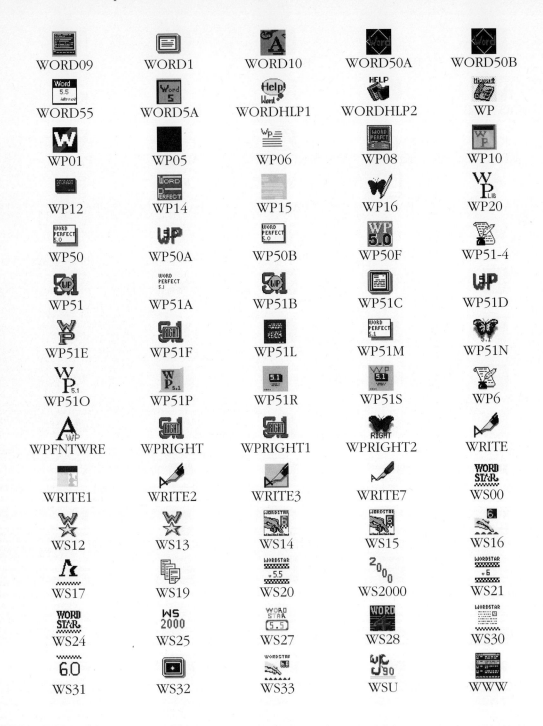

WORD09	WORD1	WORD10	WORD50A	WORD50B
WORD55	WORD5A	WORDHLP1	WORDHLP2	WP
WP01	WP05	WP06	WP08	WP10
WP12	WP14	WP15	WP16	WP20
WP50	WP50A	WP50B	WP50F	WP51-4
WP51	WP51A	WP51B	WP51C	WP51D
WP51E	WP51F	WP51L	WP51M	WP51N
WP51O	WP51P	WP51R	WP51S	WP6
WPFNTWRE	WPRIGHT	WPRIGHT1	WPRIGHT2	WRITE
WRITE1	WRITE2	WRITE3	WRITE7	WS00
WS12	WS13	WS14	WS15	WS16
WS17	WS19	WS20	WS2000	WS21
WS24	WS25	WS27	WS28	WS30
WS31	WS32	WS33	WSU	WWW

XYWRIT

ZSOFT1

ZSOFT2

ZSOFT3

Writing

Pictures for the wordsmythe.

.ICO files located in **ALLICONS\WRITICON:**

BOOK	BOOK01	BOOK02	BOOK03	BOOK04
BOOK05	BOOK06	BOOK07	BOOK08	BOOK09
BOOK10	BOOK11	BOOK12	BOOK13	BOOK14
BOOK15	BOOK16	BOOK17	BOOK18	BOOK19
BOOK20	BOOK21	BOOK22	BOOK27	BOOK34
BROWSER	BS	CCMAIL	DCTNARY	DOC
DOC1	DOC3	DOC4	DTPUB1	DTPUB2
EDIT	EDIT1	EDIT2	EDIT3	EDITOR
EMAIL	EMAIL08	EMAIL1	EMAIL2	EMAIL3
EMAIL4	EMAIL5	EMAIL6	EMAIL7	EMAIL8

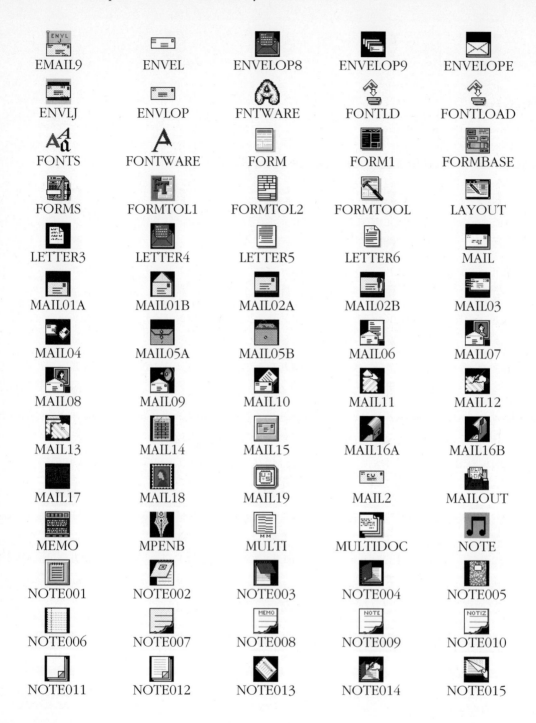

EMAIL9	ENVEL	ENVELOP8	ENVELOP9	ENVELOPE
ENVLJ	ENVLOP	FNTWARE	FONTLD	FONTLOAD
FONTS	FONTWARE	FORM	FORM1	FORMBASE
FORMS	FORMTOL1	FORMTOL2	FORMTOOL	LAYOUT
LETTER3	LETTER4	LETTER5	LETTER6	MAIL
MAIL01A	MAIL01B	MAIL02A	MAIL02B	MAIL03
MAIL04	MAIL05A	MAIL05B	MAIL06	MAIL07
MAIL08	MAIL09	MAIL10	MAIL11	MAIL12
MAIL13	MAIL14	MAIL15	MAIL16A	MAIL16B
MAIL17	MAIL18	MAIL19	MAIL2	MAILOUT
MEMO	MPENB	MULTI	MULTIDOC	NOTE
NOTE001	NOTE002	NOTE003	NOTE004	NOTE005
NOTE006	NOTE007	NOTE008	NOTE009	NOTE010
NOTE011	NOTE012	NOTE013	NOTE014	NOTE015

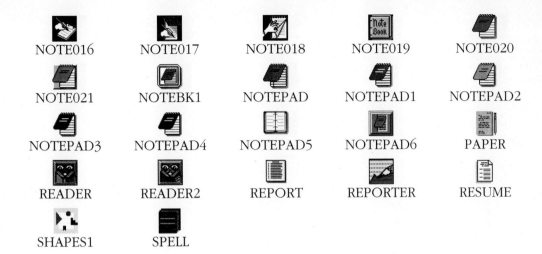

NOTE016	NOTE017	NOTE018	NOTE019	NOTE020
NOTE021	NOTEBK1	NOTEPAD	NOTEPAD1	NOTEPAD2
NOTEPAD3	NOTEPAD4	NOTEPAD5	NOTEPAD6	PAPER
READER	READER2	REPORT	REPORTER	RESUME
SHAPES1	SPELL			

Zip

The final section, these are pictures to attach to your file compression programs.

.ICO files located in **ALLICONS\ZIPICON:**

ARCMASTR	ARCMSTR1	ARCTOOL	ARCTOOL1	COMPRESS
LHARC	LZH	PAK	PAK2	PK-ZIP
PKUNZIP	PKWARE	PKWARE1	PKXARC	PKXARC1
PKZIP01	PKZIP2	PKZIP3	PKZIP4	PKZIP5
PKZIP6	PKZIP7	SHEZ	SHEZ1	SHEZ2
SHEZ6	UNARC	UNPAK	UNZIP	UNZIP1

UNZIP2

UNZIP3

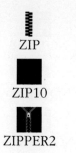
ZIP

ZIP01

ZIP03

ZIP04

ZIP09

ZIP10

ZIP14

ZIPMAN1

ZIPMAN2

ZIPPER

ZIPPER2

SECTION 4
More Nitty Gritty

Section 4 holds some of the final pieces to the Windows puzzle. Appendix A pulls together all of Mom's votes for some of the most innovative products for Windows.

APPENDIX A

Mom's Little Black Book

Boy:

And everything in the South changed, Papa, when Eli Whitney invented the cotton gin.

Father:

The what?

Boy:

The cotton gin.

Father:

Gevalt! In the South they drink *cotton?*

— Leo Rosten, *The Joys of Yinglish*

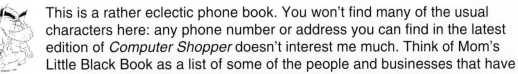 This is a rather eclectic phone book. You won't find many of the usual characters here: any phone number or address you can find in the latest edition of *Computer Shopper* doesn't interest me much. Think of Mom's Little Black Book as a list of some of the people and businesses that have brought really innovative things to the Windows arena: phone numbers, addresses, and CompuServe ids for many of the folks who don't spend millions of dollars a year on advertising, and contact information for companies that don't have retail operations. They're an elusive group. And, hard as we tried, the list could never be complete. At least I hope you'll find it accurate and useful. Apologies in advance to everyone I missed. Drop me a line on CompuServe and I'll try to get you in the next edition.

Thanks to Linda Sharp, Pinecliffe International, for her help in compiling this list. Linda is The Loving Wife of Woody™ , Mother of Justin and Sass, who has been putting up with Woody and Barry trying to finish WinMom for the past nine months. Woody tried unsuccessfully to get out of writing WinMom by breaking his leg. Linda, being the loving and thoughtful wife she is (Ed Note: she wrote this), always put through Barry's encouraging phone calls, to keep this madness going. Finishing WinMom was important to Barry, to keep his kids in bagels. Speaking of bagels. . . Barry and Woody owe Linda two dozen of NYC's finest bagels — BIG TIME!

Ace Software Corporation
1740 Technology Drive, Suite 680
San Jose, CA 95110
AceFile
Sales: 408-451-0100
Fax: 408-437-1018

Acer America Corporation
2641 Orchard Parkway
San Jose, CA 95134
Computers
Sales: 408-432-6200

Access Data
87 East 600 South
Orem, UT 84058
*Password Crackers for WinWord, XL,
WordPerfect, Lotus 1-2-3, Quattro Pro, Paradox,
and Novell*
Sales: 801-224-6970
Fax: 801-224-6009

ACK Software
298 W. Audubon Drive
Shepherdsville, KY 40165-8836
PixFolio
CompuServe: 71220,23

Adaptec
691 South Milpitas Boulevard
Milpitas, CA 95035
SCSI Controllers

Sales: 408-945-8600
Tech Support: 408-945-2250
BBS: 408-945-7747

Addison-Wesley
One Jacob Way
Reading, MA 01867
*Publishers of great intestinal fortitude.
Hey, they took a chance on MOM
and the gang. Thanks, y'all. . .*

Adobe Systems, Inc.
1585 Charleston Road, P.O. Box 7900
Mountain View, CA 94039-7900
Adobe Illustrator, Type Library, Type Manager
Sales: 415-961-4400, 800-344-8335
Tech Support: 800-292-3623
Upgrades: 800-383-FONTS
Fax: 415-961-3769
CompuServe: GO ADOBE

Agfa
90 Industrial Way
Wilmington, MA 01887-3495
Discover TrueType Packs
Sales: 508-658-5600
Fax: 508-657-8268

Aldus Corporation
411 First Avenue South
Seattle, WA 98104-2871
PageMaker, IntelliDraw, PhotoStyler
Main #: 800-243-3173
Sales: 206-622-5500, 800-333-2538
Fax: 206-343-3360
CompuServe: GO ALDUSFOR

ALKI Software Corporation
219 First Ave N, Suite 410
Seattle, WA 98109
Word Add-Ons
Sales: 206-286-2600
Fax: 206-286-2785

Altsys Corporation
269 W. Renner Parkway
Richardson, TX 75080
Fontographer
Sales: 214-680-2060
CompuServe: GO MACBVEN

Amdox Co, Ltd
217 Terrace Hill Street
Brantford, Ontario, Canada N3R 1G8
RECON — CompuServe/TAPCIS add-on
CompuServe: 76672,1273

American Megatrends, Inc.
6145-F Northbelt Parkway
Norcross, GA 30071
Home of the AMI BIOS
Sales: 404-263-8181

American Power Conversion
132 Fairgrounds Road
P.O. Box 278
West Kingston, Rhode Island 02892
Uninterruptable Power Supplies
Sales: 800-800-4272
Tech Support: 401-789-5735

William Anderson
13020 N. E. 71st Court
Kirkland, WA 98033-8317
2Do
CompuServe: 71662,545

AniCom
2551 Owens Court
Chapel Hill, NC 27514
3D Choreographer, for 3D animation
Sales: 919-469-5436

Argyle Softstuff
2087 Edgewood
Berkley, MI 48072
PBNotepad, PBWrite
CompuServe: >AOL:Doc Yeah

Artisoft, Inc.
691 East River Road
Tucson, AZ 85704
LANtastic peer-to-peer network
Sales: 800-846-9726, 602-670-7000
Tech Support: 602-293-6363
BBS: 602-293-8065
CompuServe: GO ARTISOFT

Artist Graphics
2675 Patton Road
St. Paul, MN 55113
WinSprint Video boaRoads
Sales: 612-631-7800, 800-627-8478
Fax: 612-631-7802

askSam Systems
119 S. Washington Street
Perry, FL 32347
askSAM info management
Sales: 904-584-6590

Association of PC User Groups
To find a PC user group near you, call. . .
Locator Service: 914-876-6678
CompuServe: 72241,1233

Association of Shareware Professionals
545 Grover Road
Muskegon, MI 49442-9427
The original shareware organization
CompuServe: GO ASP

Asymetrix Corporation
110 110th Avenue NE, Suite 700
Bellevue, WA 98004
Multimedia ToolBook
Sales: 206-462-0501
CompuServe: GO MULTIVEN, GO ULTIATOOL,
GO WINAPA

Atech
5964 La Place Court, Suite 100
Carlsbad, CA 92008
AllType, AllFonts, FastFonts
Sales: 619-438-6883, 800-786-3668
Fax: 619-438-6898

ATI Technologies
3761 Victoria Park Ave
Scarborough, Ontario M1W 3S2
Video boaRoads
Sales: 416-756-0718
Fax: 416-756-0720
Tech Support: 416-756-0711
BBS: 416-756-4591
CompuServe: GO GRAPHAVEN

Autodesk
11911 North Creek Parkway
South Bothell, WA 98011
AutoCAD, Animator, Multimedia Explorer
Sales: 206-487-2233
Tech Support: 800-228-3601
CompuServe: GO ARETAIL

Automap, Inc.
9831 S. 51st Street, Suite A-131
Phoenix, AZ 85044
Bodyworks, Chemistry Works, Orbits
Sales: 602-893-2400

Avantos Performance Systems
5900 Hollis Street, Suite C
Emeryville, CA 94608
ManagePro
Sales: 800-282-6867
Fax: 510-654-1725

Avery International
777 East Foothill Boulevard
Azusz, CA 91702
Labels, Windows Label Print
Sales: 800-252-8379, 818-792-1724
CompuServe: GO PCVENF

AZ Computer Innovations
P.O. Box 10514
Glendale, Arizona 85318
A-Z Icon Editor
CompuServe: 72607,1633

Banyan Systems Inc.
120 Flanders Road
Westboro, MA 01581
Banyan Vines
Sales: 508-898-1000
Fax: 508-898-3604
CompuServe: GO BANFORUM

Barry Press Utilities *Look under "P," That's his name.*

Bear Rock Technologies
4140 Mother Lode Drive, Suite 100
Shingle Springs, Ca 95682-8038
Bear Rock Labeler
Sales: 916-672-0244, 800-232-7625
Fax: 916-672-1103
Tech Support: 916-6720450

E A Behl Technologies
Tech/Type Typeface Products
2663 Red Oak Court
Clearwater, Florida 34621-2319
Fonts, including VTSR
Fax: 813-787-9414
CompuServe: 70413,1073

Berkeley Systems
2095 Rose Street
Berkeley, CA 94709
After Dark screen saver
Sales: 510-540-5535, 800-877-5535
Fax: 510-540-5115
Tech Support: 510-540-5335
CompuServe: GO WINAPC

BERL
180 Beacon Hill Lane
Ashland, OR 97520
TurboCom — Windows comm driver
CompuServe: 71521,760

Binar Graphics
30 Mitchell Boulevard
San Rafael, CA 94903-2034
AnyView, Recall
Sales: 415-491-1565
Fax: 415-491-1164

Bitstream, Inc.
215 First Street
Cambridge, MA 02142
FaceLift, TrueType Font Packs
Sales: 800-522-FONT, 800-223-3176, 800-873-
2480, 617-497-6222
Fax: 617-868-4732
Tech Support: 617-497-7514
CompuServe: GO DTPVEN

Blue Sky Software Corporation
7486 La Jolla Boulevard, Suite 3
La Jolla, CA 92037
RoboHELP, BugMAN, QuickMENU, Magic Fields,
WindowsMaker
Sales: 800-677-4WIN, 619-459-6365
Fax: 619-459-6366
Tech Support: 619-551-5680

Boca Research Inc.
6413 Congress Ave
Boca Raton, FL 33487-2841
boards
Sales: 407-997-6227
Tech Support: 407-241 8088

Borland International, Inc.
1800 Green Hills Road
Scotts Valley, CA 95066
Quattro Pro, Paradox, etc.
Sales: 800-331-0877, 408-438-8400
Tech Support: 800-524-8420
Fax: 408-438-9119

CompuServe: GO BORLAND
BBS: 408-438-5780

Patrick Breen
3920 Mystic Valley Parkway #1119
MedfoRoad, MA 02155
BarClock
Sales: 617-396-2673
CompuServe: 70312,743

Brightridge Solutions, Inc.
1534 Brightridge Drive
Kingsport, TN 37664
Hi, Finance!
Sales: 800-241-7203, 615-246-3337
Fax: 615-246-6385
CompuServe: 74676,235

Brother International Corporation
8 Corporate Place
Piscataway, NJ 08855-0159
Printers
Sales: 800-284-4357, 210-981-0300
Parent Office: Brother Industries Ltd.
46-15, Ohsu, 3-chome
Naka-Ku
Nagoya 460, Japan

Brown-Wagh
160 Knowles Drive
Los Gatos, CA 95030
Studio Magic video production system
Sales: 408-378-3838

Button Ware, Inc.
See McAffee Associates
CompuServe: GO PCVENA

Caere Corporation
100 Cooper Court
Los Gatos, CA 95030
OmniPage, Typist, FaxMaster
Sales: 800-535-7226, 408-395-7000

Cont.
Fax: 408-354-2743
Tech Support: 408-395-7000

Cables To Go
1501 Webster Street
Dayton, OH 45404
Mom's favorite source of oddball cables
Sales: 800-826-7904

Calera Recognition Systems, Inc.
475 Potrero Avenue
Sunnyvale, CA 94086
WoRoadScan, TopScan
Sales: 408-720-8200, 800-544-7051
Fax: 408-720-1330
Tech Support: 408-720-0999

Cain International Corporation
ProSoft Division
8675 Ballantrae Drive
Colorado Springs, CO 80920
ProMenu
Sales: 800-793-2246
CompuServe: 73757,3135

Canon USA, Inc.
1 Canon Plaza
Lake Success, NY 11042
Printers, computers
Sales: 800-441-1313, 516-488-6700
Parent Office: Canon, Inc.
7-1, Nishi-Shinjuku, 2-chome
Shinjuku-Ku
Tokyo 163, Japan

Canyon Software
1537 Fourth Street, Suite 131
San Rafael, CA 94901
Drag And View
Sales: 415-382-7999
Fax: 415-382-7998

Cardiff Software, Inc.
531 Stevens Avenue, Bldg. B
Solana Beach, CA 92075

Teleform fax-to-PC date capture
Sales: 619-259-6444

Central Point Software
15220 NW Greenbrier Parkway
Beaverton, OR 97006
Central Point Backup, PC Tools
Sales: 503-690-8090
Fax: 503-690-8083
Tech Support: 503-690-8080
CompuServe: GO CPSWINMAC

Clarion Software
150 E. Sample Road
Pompano Beach, FL 33064
Clarion database software
Sales: 305-785-4555

Claris Corporation
5201 Patrick Henry Drive, Box 58168
Santa Clara, CA 95052-8618
Claris Works, Hollywood, FileMaker
Sales: 800-544-8554, 408-987-7000
Tech Support: 408-727-9054
CompuServe: GO CLARIS

Compton's NewMedia, Inc.
2320 Camino Vida Roble
Carlsbad, CA 92009
Lots of CD titles
Sales: 619-929-2500

The Cobb Group, Inc.
9420 Bunsen Parkway, Suite 300
Louisville, Kentucky 40220
Newsletters
Sales: 800-223-8720, 502-491-1900
Fax: 502-491-4200

Colorado Memory Systems
800 S. Taft Ave
Loveland, CO 80537
Tape Backup
Sales: 800-845-7905, 303-669-6500
Fax: 303-667-0997
Tech Support: 800-845-7906

Cont.
BBS: 303-679-0650
CompuServe: 71621,3022

CompuServe
5000 Arlington Centre Boulevard
Post Office Box 20212
Columbus, Ohio 43220
The Mother Of All Information Services
Sales/Support: 800-848-8990, 614-457-8600
CompuServe: GO FEEDBACK, GO WINCIM

Computer Associates International, Inc.
One Computer Associates Plaza
Islandia, New York 11788-7000
CA-all sorts of stuff
Sales: 800-225-2554, 516-342-5224
Tech Support: 800-531-5236, 516-342-5734
Fax: 516-432-0614
CompuServe: GO CAIPRO

COMTRADE
15314 East Valley Boulevard
City of Industry, CA 91746
Igor's favorite computers
Sales: 800-969-2123, 818-961-6688
Fax: 818-369-1479
Tech Support: 800-899-4508
BBS: 818-961-6098

Conner
36 Skyline Drive
Lake Mary, FL 32746
hard drives, backup software
Sales: 407-262-800

Corel Systems Corporation
1600 Carling Avenue
Ottawa, Ontario, Canada K1Z 8R7
CorelDRAW, CorelSCSI
Sales: 800-836-DRAW, 613-728-8200
Fax: 613-761-9176
Tech Support: 613-728-1990
CompuServe: GO COREL

The Creative Consortium
P.O. Box 47745
Oak Park, MI 48237
CCIZip
Sales: 313-589-8247

Creative Labs, Inc.
131 South Maples Ave #6
South San Francisco, CA 94080
SoundBlaster, Video Spigot
Sales: 408-4286622
Tech Support: 415-742-6107

CtrlAlt Associates
Advanced Support Group
11900 Grant Place
Des Peres, MO 63131
Stackey, BATUTIL
Sales: 314-965-5630; 800-788-0787
Fax: 314-966-1833
CompuServe: GO ASG

CTX South, Inc.
6090-F Northbelt Parkway
Norcross, GA 30071
Monitors
Sales: 404-729-8909, 714-595-6146

DAK Industries
8200 Remmet Ave
Canoga Park, CA 91304
Hardware, software at a discount
Sales: 800-DAK-0800, 818-888-8220
Fax: 818-888-2837
BBS: 818-715-7153

Dariana, Inc.
5241 Lincoln Ave Suite B5
Cypress, CA 90630
WinSleuth
Sales: 800-892-9950, 714-236-1380
Fax: 800-892-9951

DataGem Corporation
1420 NW Gilman # 2859
Issaquah, WA 98027, USA
WinKey
Sales: 206-391-4415
CompuServe: 75540,762

DataEase International, Inc.
7 Cambridge Drive
Trumbull, CT 06611
DataEase databases
Sales: 800-243-5123

Datastorm Technologies, Inc.
P.O. Box 1471
Columbia, MO 65205
ProComm
Sales: 800-326-4999
Fax: 314-443-3282
CompuServe: GO DATASTORM

DCA
1000 Alderman Drive
Alpharetta, GA 30202
Crosstalk, IRMA Workstation
Sales: 404-442-4000
CompuServe: GO XTALK

Dell Computer Corporation
9505 Arboretum Boulevard
Austin, TX 78759
Computers
Sales: 800-289-3355

Delrina Technology, Inc.
6830 Via Del Oro, Suite 240
San Jose, CA 95119
WinFax, PerForm
Sales: 800-268-6082, 408-363-2345
Fax: 408-363-2340
Tech Support: 416-441-0921
CompuServe: GO DELRINA

DeltaPoint
2 Harris Court, Suite. B-1
Monterey, CA 93940

Graphics Tools, DeltaGraph
Sales: 408-648-4000

Design Science, Inc.
4028 Broadway
Long Beach, CA 90803
MathType
Sales: 800-827-0685

Diamond Computer Systems, Inc.
532 Mercury Drive
Sunnyvale, CA 94086
Video cards
Sales/Tech Support: 408-736-2000
Fax: 408-730-5750
BBS: 408-730-1100
CompuServe: GO GRAPHBVEN

Digital Communications Associates
1000 Alderman Drive
Alpharetta, Georgia 30202
Crosstalk, IRMA
Sales: 404-442-4000
Fax: 404-442-4399

DPMA — Data Processing
Management Association
505 Busse Hwy.
Park Ridge, IL 60068-3191
Training, certification
Inquiries: 708-825-8124

Elfring Soft Fonts
PO Box 61
Wasco, IL 60183
Elfring's Fonts
Sales: 708-377-3520
Fax: 708-377-6402
CompuServe: 72417,3437

Epson America, Inc.
Computer Products Division
2780 Lomita Boulevard

Cont.
Torrance, CA 90505
Printers, computers
Sales: 800-421-5426, 213-539-9140
Parent Office: Epson Corporation
80 Hirooka, Shiojiri-shi
Nagano 399-07, Japan

Eschalon Development Inc.
110-2 Renaissance Square
New Westminster, BC
V3M 6K3 Canada
WinCLI
Sales: 604-520-1543
CompuServe: 76625,1320

F

Farallon Computing, Inc.
2470 Mariner Square Loop
Alameda, CA 94501
Replica
Sales: 510-814-5000
Fax: 510-814-5020

Fawcett Technical Publications
280 Second Street, Suite 200
Los Altos, CA 94022-3603
Visual Basic Programmer's Journal
Sales: 303-541-0610
Fax: 415-948-7332

Helen Feddema
R.D. 1, Box SS2
Kerhonkson, NY 12446
Address Book, Access guru
Sales: 914-626-3750
Fax: 914-626-2331
CompuServe: 70700,1561

Fifth Generations Systems Inc.
10049 N. Reiger Road
Baton Rouge, LA 70809
FastBack, Direct Access
Sales: 800-873-4384, 504-291-7221

Tech Support: 800-766-7283, 504-295-3344
BBS: 504-966-3400
CompuServe: GO FIFTH

Erik Fink
7652 Hampshire Avenue N.
Brooklyn Park, MN 55428-1457
Spooky

FireFly Software
P.O. Box 5035
Oregon City, OR
EDOS
Sales: 800-248-0809, 503-694-2282
Fax: 503-665-9876
BBS: 503-643-8396
CompuServe: 71171,47

Foresight Resources Corporation
10725 Ambassador Drive
Kansas City, MO 64153
Drafix Windows CAD, Office Planner
Sales: 816-891-1040
Fax: 816-891-8018
CompuServe: GO PCVENA

Fractal Design Corporation
335 Spreckels Drive, Suite F
Aptos, CA 95003
Fractal Design Painter
Sales: 408-688-8800
CompuServe: GO ULTIATOOL

Frame Technology
Frame Maker
Sales: 408-433-3311
CompuServe: GO DTPVEN

Fujitsu America, Inc.
3055 Orchard Drive
San Jose, CA 95134-2017
Printers, keyboards, disks
Sales: 408-432-1300
Parent Office: Fujitsu, Ltd.
6-1, Marunouchi, 1-chome

Cont.
Chiyoda-Ku
Tokyo 100, Japan

Future Domain Corporation
2801 McGaw Ave
Irvine, CA 92714
SCSI Boards
Sales: 714-253-0400
Fax: 714-253-0913

Future Soft Engineering, Inc.
1001 S. Dairy Ashford, Suite 203
Houston, TX 77077
DynaComm
Sales: 713-496-9400
Fax: 713-496-1090
CompuServe: GO WINAPA

William H. Gates III
CompuServe: >INTERNET:billg@microsoft.com

Genoa Systems Corporation
75 E. Trimble Road
San Jose, CA 95131
Video cards
Main #: 408-432-9090
Fax: 408-434-0997

Dietrich Gewissler
92 Smith Street
Howell, NJ 07731
Violin Music of J.S. Bach
Sales: 908-364-8719

Gordon Goldsborough
Brandon University
Brandon, Manitoba, Canada R7A 6A9
Foreigner
Sales: 204-727-9786
Fax: 204-726-4573
CompuServe:
    >INTERNET: goldsborough@brandonu.ca

Gryphon Software Corporation
7220 Trade Street, Suite 120
San Diego, CA 92121
Application Morph
Sales: 619-536-8815

Halcyon Software, Inc.
1590 La Pradera Drive
Campbell, CA 95008
DoDOT graphics utilities
Sales: 408-378-9898

Hayes Microcomputer Products
5835 Peachtree Corners E
Norcross, GA 30092
Modems
Sales: 404-840-9200
Tech Support: 404-441-1617
BBS: 800-874-2937
CompuServe: GO HAYFORUM

hDC Computer Corporation
6742 185th Avenue NE
Redmond, WA 98052
hDC First Apps, Power Launcher, etc.
Sales: 800-321-4606
Fax: 206-881-9770
Tech Support: 206-885-5550
CompuServe: GO WINAPA

Heizer Software
P.O. Box 232019
Pleasant Hill, CA 94523
EXCEL Add-Ins
Sales: 800-888-7667
Fax: 510-943-6882
Tech Support: 510-943-7667

Hercules
3839 Spinnaker Court
Fremont, CA 94538
Video boaRoads
Sales: 800-532-0600, 510-540-6000

Cont.
Fax: 510-623-1112
Tech Support: 510-623-6050
BBS: 510-540-0621
CompuServe: GO GRAPHBVEN

Hewlett-Packard
974 East Arquez Avenue
Sunnyvale, CA 95086
Printers, Scanners, New Wave
Sales: 408-720-3441, 800-554-1305, 800-752-0900
Fax: 408-720-4033
Tech Support: 408-720-4040
CompuServe: GO HP

Hitachi America, Ltd.
19530 Cabot Boulevard
Hayward, CA 94545
Sales: 415-785-9770
CD-ROM drives, memory
Parent Office: Hitachi Engineering Co., Ltd.
6 Kandu-Shurgadai, 4-chome
Chiyoda-Ku
Tokyo 101, Japan

Home Automation Laboratories
5500 Highlands Parkway, Suite 450
Smyrna, GA 30082
Dynasty house control systems
Sales: 404-319-6000

IBM
Old Orchard Road
Armonk, NY. 10504
Blue Three Piece Suits
Sales: 800-336-5430, 800-426-333
Tech Support: 800-992-4777

IBM Personal Software Products
11400 Burnet Road
Austin, TX 78758
OS/2

Sales: 512-823-0000
CompuServe: GO IBMDESK

ICCP — Institute for Certification
of Computer Professionals
2200 E. Devon Avenue, Suite. 268
Des Plaines, IL 60018-4503
CPP, CDP, CSP certification
Inquiries: 708-299-4227

Impact Software
12140 Central Avenue, Suite 133
Chino, CA 91710
Icon Manager
Sales: 909-590-8522
CompuServe: 71630,1703

IMSI
1938 Fourth Street
San Rafael, CA 94901
TurboCAD
Sales: 415-454-7101

Elton Inada
117 Smart Court
Encinitas, CA 92024
Super Video Poker
CompuServe: 72233,3451

Infoworld Publishing Company
155 Bouvet Road, Suite 800
San Mateo, CA 94402
Infoworld
Offices: 415-572-7341
Subscriptions: 708-647-7925

Ingres
1080 Marina Village Parkway
Alameda, CA 94501
INGRES databases
Sales: 800-4-INGRES

Inner Media, Inc.
60 Plain Road
Hollis, NH 03049
Collage Complete

Cont.
Sales: 603-465-3216, 800-962-2949
Fax: 603-465-7195
Tech Support: 603-465-2696
CompuServe: 70444, 31

Inset Systems
71 Commerce Drive
Brookfield, CT 06804
Hijaak
Sales: 800-374-6738, 203-740-2400
Fax: 203-775-5634
CompuServe: GO INSET

Intel Corporation
5200 N.E. Elam Young Parkway
Hillsboro, Oregon 97124
Chips, cards
Sales: 800-538-3373
Fax: 800-458-6231
CompuServe: GO INTELFORUM

Intergraph Corporation
Huntsville, AL 35894
CAD hardware and software
Sales: 800-826-3515

International Campaign for Tibet
1511 K Street NW
Washington, DC 20005
To help those in great need. . .
Inquiries: 202-628-4123
Fax: 202-347-6825

Iomega Corporation
1821 W. 4000 S
Roy, UT 84067
Bernoulli removable drives
Sales: 801-778-1000
CompuServe: GO PCVENE

iSBiSTER International
1314 Cardigan Street
Garland, Texas 75040
Time & Chaos
BBS: 214-530-2762
CompuServe: 74017,3424

Iterated Systems Inc.
5550-A Peachtree Parkway, Suite. 650
Norcross, GA 30092
Images Inc. III fractal compression
Sales: 404-840-0310

It's Your Money Inc.
3 Floyd Drive
Mount Arlington, NJ 07856
Uninstall For Windows
Sales: 201-663-4577
CompuServe: GO GENCOM

JASC Inc.
10901 Red Circle Drive, Suite 340
Minnetonka, MN 55343
PaintShop Pro
Sales: 612-930-9171
Fax: 612-930-9172
CompuServe: 72557,256

Jensen-Jones, Inc.
328 Newman Springs Road
Redbank, NJ 07701
Commence
Sales: 800-289-1548, 908-530-4666
Fax: 908-530-9827
CompuServe: GO WINAPA

JetForm
800 South Street, Suite 305
Waltham, MA 02154
JetForm forms design
Sales: 617-647-7700, 800-267-9976

Knowledge Garden, Inc.
12-8 Technology Drive
Setauket, NY 11733
KnowlegdePro
Sales: 516-246-5400
Fax: 516-246-5452
CompuServe: GO WINAPB

Korenthal Associates
511 Ave of the Americas #400
New York, NY 10011
4Print, 4Book print squishers
Sales: 212-242-1790, 800-KA-PROGS
Fax: 212-242-2599
CompuServe: 76004,2605

Kyocera Electronics, Inc.
100 Randolph Road
Somerset, NJ 08875
"Green" printers
Sales: 908-560-3400

LaserMaster
6900 Shady Oak Road
Eden Prairie, MN 55344
WinJet LJ enhancers, Printers
Sales: 612-944-9457, 800-950-6868
Fax: 612-944-9519

Laser Printer Accessories Corporation
10865 Rancho Bernardo Road
San Diego, CA 92127
doubleRES for LaserJets
Sales: 619-485-8411

Andy LeMay
P.O. Box 131841
Street Paul, MN 55113
RateClock
CompuServe: 71554,2425

Woody Leonhard
Hack
CompuServe: GO WOPR

Logitech, Inc.
6505 Kaiser Drive
Fremont, CA 94555
SoundMan, ScanMan, MouseMan, mice
Sales: 510-795-8500
CompuServe: GO LOGITECH

Looking Glass Technologies
P.O. Box 8636
Endwell, NY 13762-8636
Stickies!
CompuServe: 71055,1240

Lose Your Mind Development
506 Wilder Square
Norristown, PA 19401-2643
Printer's Apprentice
Sales: 215-275-7034
CompuServe: 70564,2372

Lotus Development Corporation
55 Cambridge Parkway
Cambridge, MA 02142
*1-2-3, Ami Pro, Notes, cc:Mail, Freelance
Graphics, Improv*
Sales: 800-553-4270, 617-577-8500
Tech Support: 800-223-1662
CompuServe: GO LOTUS

Macmillan New Media
124 Mt. Auburn Street
Cambridge, MA 02138
Multimedia CD-ROMs
Sales: 617-661-2955

Mag Innovision
4392 Corporate Center Drive
Los Alamitos, CA 90720
Monitors

Cont.
Sales: 800-827-3998, 714-827-3998
Fax: 714-827-5522

Nico Mak
P.O. Box 919
Bristol, CT 06011-0919
WinZip
CompuServe: 70056,241

Manzanita Software Systems
2130 Professional Drive, Suite. 150
Roseville, CA 95661
BusinessWorks accounting
Sales: 916-781-3880

Mao, Chief Technical Officer   *See Salvatorre,*
Igor Guido

Martinsen's Software
5501 Tullis Drive
Building 2, Suite 304
New Orleans, LA 70131-8864
INI Mgr, Wallpaper Mgr, Beyond Windows Exit
Sales: 504-394-6045
CompuServe: 71202,1750

MasterMind Software
601 Pennsylvania Avenue NW
Box 1402 North
Washington, DC 20004
MasterSeries for WinWord
CompuServe: 72630,555

MathSoft
201 Broadway
Cambridge, MA 02139
Mathcad
Sales: 800-MATHCAD, 617-577-1017
Fax: 617-577-8829

Matrox
1055 Street Regis Boulevard
Dorval, Quebec, Canada H9P 2T4
Video boaRoads

Sales: 514-685-2630, 514-685-2630
Fax: 514-685-2853

Maxis
2 Theater Square, Suite 230
Orinda, CA 94563
SimCity, SimEarth, RoboSport
Sales: 510-254-9700, 800-336-2947
Fax: 510-253-3736
Tech Support: 510-253-3755
CompuServe: GO GAMBPUB

Media Cybernetics, Inc.
8484 Georgia Avenue
Silver Spring, MD 20910
HALO imaging software
Sales: 301-495-3305

Media Vision Inc.
3185 Laurelview Court
Fremont, CA 94538
Audio and Video Boards
Sales: 800-845-5870, 800-638-2807, 510-770-8600
Fax: 510-770-9592
Tech Support: 510-770-9905
CompuServe: GO MULTIVEN

MEI Micro Center
110 Steelwood Road
Columbus, OH 43212
High quality, cheap diskettes and QIC tapes
Sales: 800-634-3478
Fax: 614-486-6417

Metz Software
P.O. Box 6699
Bellevue, WA 98008-0699
Task Manager, File F/X
Sales: 800-447-1712
Fax: 206-644-6026
Tech Support: 206-641-4525
CompuServe: GO WINAPC; 75300, 1627

Microcom
500 River Ridge Drive

Cont.
Norwood, MA 02062-5028
Carbon Copy, Virex
Sales: 617-551-1000, 800-822-8224
Fax: 617-551-1968

Micrografx, Inc.
1303 Arapaho
Richardson, TX 75081-2444
Draw, Designer, Picture Publisher, etc.
Sales: 214-234-1769, 800-733-3729
Fax: 214-994-6475
Tech Support: 214-234-2694
CompuServe: GO WINAPA

Microsoft Corporation
One Microsoft Way
Redmond, WA 98052-6399
Mutant Ninjas
Sales: 800-426-9400, 206-882-8080
Fax: 206-93-MS-FAX
Tech Support: 206-454-2030, 206-637-7098
BBS: 206-637-9009, 206-936-6735
CompuServe: GO MICROSOFT
*Microsoft has many excellent fora on
CompuServe; they change from time to time, so
the smartest way to see what's where is to GO
MICROSOFT*

Miller Freeman Inc
411 Borel Ave Suite 100
San Mateo, CA 94402
Microsoft System Journal, Dr. Dobb's, many more
Sales: 800-666-1084, 303-447-9330
Fax: 415-358-9732
CompuServe: GO

Mom *Phone Home, Sonny*

Money Smith Systems
P.O. Box 333
Converse, TX 78109
Money Smith
Sales: 800-242-4775
CompuServe: 70324,1077

Moon Valley Software
21608 N. 20th Ave
Phoenix, AZ 85027
Icon Tamer, Icon Do-It
Sales: 602-375-9502, 800-473-5509
Fax: 602-993-4950
CompuServe: 71054, 3425

**Claudette Moore, Moore Literary
Agency** *World's Greatest Agent*

MP Software
18511 SE 207th Street
Renton, WA 98058
Atoms
CompuServe: 76260,306

Nanao USA Corporation
23535 Telo Ave
Torrance, CA 90503
Monitors that are works of art
Sales: 310-325-5202
Fax: 310-530-1679

National Computer Security Association (NCSA)
10 S. Courthouse Avenue
Carlisle, PA 17013
Who You Gonna Call?
Inquiries: 717-258-1816

National Cristina Foundation
42 Hillcrest Drive
Pelham Manor, NY 10803
Distributes used computers to the needy
Sales: 914-738-7494

National Design, Inc (NDI)
1515 Capital of Texas Highway S
Fifth Floor
Austin, TX 78746
Volante video boaRoads
Sales: 800-827-8799, 512-329-5055

Cont.
Fax: 512-329-6326
Tech Support: 800-253-8831

NEC Information Systems, Inc.
155 Swanson Road
Boxborough, MA 01719
Monitors, computers, CD-ROM drives
Sales: 617-635-4400, 800-343-4418
Personal Computer Division
1255 Michael Drive
Wood Dale, IL 60191-1094
Sales: 800-323-1728

Northgate Computer Systems
7075 Flying Cloud Drive
Eden Prairie, MN 55344
Computers
Sales: 800-548-1993, 612-943-8181
BBS: 612-943-8341

Novell, Inc.
122 East 1700 South
Provo, Utah 84606
NetWare, DR-DOS
Sales: 800-453-1267, 800-NET-WARE, 801-429-
7000
Fax: 801-429-3951
CompuServe: GO NOVLIB

Number Nine Computer Corporation
18 Hartwell Ave
Lexington, MA 02173
Video boaRoads
Sales: 617-674-0009
Fax: 617-674-2919

Odyssey Development Inc.
650 S. Cherry Street, Suite. 220
Denver, CO 80222
ISYS info retrieval package
Sales: 303-394-0091

Okna Corporation
P.O. Box 522
Lyndhurst, NJ 07071
Desktop Set
Sales: 201-909-8600
Fax: 201-909-0688
CompuServe: GO WINAPD; 71420,3445

Open Windows
P.O. Box 49746
Colorado Springs, CO 80949-9746
WinUpD8R, Bailout, Flash-21
Sales: 719-531-0403
CompuServe: 75236,3243

Orchid Technology
45365 Northport Loop, West
Fremont, CA 94538
Video Cards
Sales: 800-7OR-CHID, 510-683-0300
Fax: 510-490-9312
Tech Support: 510-683-0323
BBS: 510-683-0327

OsoSoft
1472 Sixth Street
Los Osos, CA 93402
Fonter, Rockford, Filer, WinClip, MultiLabel
CompuServe: 71571,222
BBS: 805-528-3753

OTC Corporation
17300 17th Street, Suite J-117
Tustin, CA 92680
KingCom comm drivers
Sales: 714-832-4833
Fax: 714-832-4563

Pacific Data Products, Inc.
9125 Rehco Road
San Diego, CA 92024
PacPage, 25-in-One, Printer stuff
Sales: 619-597-4632, 619-552-0880

Cont.
Fax: 619-552-0889
BBS: 619-452-6329

Panacea, Inc.
24 Orchard View Drive
Londonderry, NH 03053
WinSpeed
Sales: 800-729-7920
Fax: 603-434-2461

Panasonic Industrial Co.
2 Panasonic Way
P.O. Box 1503
Secaucus, NJ 07094
Printers, computers
Sales: 201-348-7000
Parent Office: Matsushita Electric Co., Ltd.
1006, Kadona-City
Osaka 571, Japan

Paradise/Western Digital Imaging
800E. Middlefield Road
Mountain View, CA 94043
Paradise video cards
Sales: 415-960-3360, 800-356-5787

PC/Computing
Ziff-Davis Publishing Co.
950 Tower Lane
20th Floor
Foster City, CA 94404
PC/Computing, the #1 monthly computer mag
Subscriptions: 800-365-2770, 303-447-9330
Offices: 415-578-7000
CompuServe: GO ZNT:PCCONTACT

PC Connection
6 Mill Street
Marlow, NH 03456
Mao's favorite source of computer supplies
Subscriptions: 800-800-0004, 603-446-0004
Fax: 603-446-7791

PC-Kwik Corporation
15100 S.W. Koll Parkway, Suite L

Beaverton, OR 97006
Super PC-Kwik, Power Pack
Sales: 503-644-5644, 800-395-5945
Fax: 503-646-8267
Tech Support: 503-627-0905
CompuServe: GO PCVENA

PC Magazine
Ziff-Davis Publishing Co.
One Park Avenue
New York, NY 10016
PC Magazine, the #1 computer mag
Subscriptions: 800-289-0429
Offices: 212-503-5446
CompuServe: GO ZNT:EDITORIAL
Ziff-Davis has an entire section of CompuServe called ZiffNet. For help in getting around, try GO ZNT:TIPS and ask.

PC Techniques
7721 E. Gray Road, Suite 204
Scottsdale, AZ 85260
PC Techniques
Subscriptions: 602-483-0192
CompuServe: 76711,470

PC Week
Ziff-Davis Publishing Co.
10 Presidents Landing
MedfoRoad, MA 02155
PC Week
Subscriptions: 609-461-2100
CompuServe: GO ZIFFNET

PC World
IDG Communications
501 Second Street
San Francisco, CA 94107
PC World magazine
Offices: 415-243-0500
Subscriptions: 800-234-3498, 303-447-9330
CompuServe: 74055,412

Peachtree Software
1505C Pavilion Place
Norcross, GA 30093

Cont.
Accounting software
Sales: 800-247-3224, 404-564-5800
Tech Support: 404-564-5700
CompuServe: GO PCVENF, GO WINAPD

Pegasus Development
Advanced Support Group
11900 Grant Place
Des Peres, MO 63131
INI ProFiler, Yakkity Clock, World Time
Sales: 800-788-0787, 314-965-5630
Fax: 314-966-1833
Tech Support: 314-965-5630
CompuServe: GO ASG

Persoft, Inc.
465 Science Drive, P.O. Box 44953
Madison, WI 53744-4953
SmartTerm communications emulators
Sales: 608-273-6000

Pinecliffe International
Advanced Support Group
11900 Grant Place
Des Peres, MO 63131
WOPR — Woody's Office POWER Pack
Sales: 800-OK-WINWORD, 314-965-5630
Fax: 314-966-1833
Tech Support: 314-965-5630
CompuServe: GO WOPR

PKWare, Inc
9025 N. Deerwood Drive
Brown Deer, WI 53223
PKZip
Sales: 414-354-8699
Fax: 414-354-8559
CompuServe: 75300,730

Plannet Crafters, Inc.
2580 Runic Way
Alpharetta, Georgia 30202-5078
Plug-In for Program Manager, Roger's Rapid Restart
Sales: 404-740-9821

Fax: 404-740-1914
BBS: 404-740-8583
CompuServe: 73040,334

Platinum Software Corporation
15615 Alton Parkway, Suite. 300
Irvine, CA 92718
Accounting software
Sales: 800-999-1809

Polaris Software
17150 del Campo, Suite 307
San Diego, CA 92127
PackRat
Sales: 619-674-6500, 800-PACKRAT
Fax: 619-674-7315
CompuServe: GO WINAPA

Practice Marketing Services
3242 Salem Drive
Rochester Hills, MI 48306
WinLabel
Sales: 313-373-7904
CompuServe: 72716,1522

Barry Press
1571 E. Locksley Circle
Sandy, UT 84092
Barry Press Utilities
CompuServe: 72467,2353

Primavera Systems, Inc.
Two Bala Plaza
Bala Cynwyd, PA 19004
Project Planner
Sales: 215-667-8600

PRIME Development Group
2629 Manhattan Ave, Suite 273
Hermosa Beach, CA 90254-2447
PRIME — PackRat Info Management (for WinWord)
Sales: 310-318-5212
Fax: 310-798-2360
CompuServe: 76655,1140

Public Brand Software
P.O. Box 51315
Indianapolis, IN 46251
Shareware disks
Sales: 800-426-3475, 317-856-7571
Fax: 317-856-2086
CompuServe: GO ZNT:PBSAPPS

Public (software) Library — PsL
Nelson Ford
P.O. Box 35705
Houston, TX 77235-5705
Shareware disks
CardShark Hearts
Sales: 800-242-4775, 713-524-6394
Fax: 713-524-6398
CompuServe: 71355,470

Q+E Software
(formerly Pioneer Software)
5540 Center view Drive, Suite 324
Raleigh, North Carolina 27606
Q+E database software
Sales: 919-8592220, 800-876-3101
Support: 919-851-1152
Fax: 919-859-9334
CompuServe: GO WINAPD

Qualitas
7101 Wisconsin Avenue, Suite 1386
Bethesda, MD 20814
386^Max memory manager
Sales: 800-733-1377, 301-907-6700
Tech Support: 301-907-7400

Quark Inc.
1800 Grant Street
Denver, CO 80203
Quark XPress publishing software
Sales: 303-894-3365
Tech Support: 303-934-0784

Quarterdeck Office Systems
150 Pico Boulevard
Santa Monica, CA 90405
QEMM memory manager
Sales: 310-392-9851

David Rakowski
Davy's Fonts
CompuServe: 73240,3060

Recognita Corporation of America
1156 Aster Avenue, Suite. F
Sunnyvale, CA 94086
Recognita Plus, optical character recognition
Sales: 408-241-5772

Rhode Island Soft Systems, Inc
P.O. Box 748
Woonsocket, RI 02895
WinPak
Sales: 401-658-4632
CompuServe: 73770,1633

Igor Guido Salvatorre
CompuServe: GO WOPR

Sampo Corporation of America
5550 Peachtree Industrial Boulevard
Norcross, GA 30071
Monitors
Sales: 404-449-6220

Samsung Electronics America/
Samsung Electronics Co., Ltd.
18600 Broadwick Street
Rancho Dominguez, CA 90220-5030
Sales: 213-537-6791
Computers, printers, drives, monitors
Parent Office: Samsung Electronics Co., Ltd.

Cont.
Joong-Ang Daily News Bldg., 7th Fl.
7 Soonwha-Dong, Chung-Ku
Seoul, Korea

Saros Corporation
10900 N.E. Eighth Street, Suite. 700
Bellevue, WA 98004
Mezzanine document management
Sales: 206-646-1066
CompuServe: GO WINAPC

Seagate Technologies
920 Disc Drive
Scotts Valley, CA 95066
Disc Drives — probably 920 of 'em by now
Sales: 408-438-6550
Tech Support: 408-439-3244

Shapeware Corporation
1601 Fifth Ave, Suite 800
Seattle, WA 98101-1625
Visio
Sales: 206-467-6723
Fax: 206-467-7227
Tech Support: 206-467-6727
CompuServe: GO VISIO

Sharp Electronics Corporation
Sharp Plaza
P.O. Box 650
Mahwah, NJ 07430
Computers, Projection panels
Sales: 201-529-9500
Parent Office: Sharp Electronics Corporation
22-22, Nagaikecho
Abenoku Osaka 545, Japan

Barry Simon
CompuServe: 76004,1664

Smart Access
P.O. Box 888
Kent, WA 98035-0888
Smart Access newsletter

Sales: 800-788-1900, 206-251-1900
CompuServe: 72600,140

Softbridge, Inc.
125 Cambridge Park Drive
Cambridge, MA 02140
Bridge Batch, Bridge Toolkit, Auto Test Facility
Sales: 617-576-2257, 800-955-9190
Fax: 617-864-7747
CompuServe: GO WINAPB

Software Labs
100 Corporate Pointe, Suite 195
Culver City, CA 90231
Shareware disks
Sales: 800-569-7900, 310-410-2030

Software Publishers Association
1730 M Street NW, Suite 700
Washington, DC 20036-4510
Software Anti-Piracy
Voice: 800-388-7478, 202-452-1600

Software Publishing Corporation
3165 Kifer Road
P.O. Box 54983
Santa Clara, CA 95056
Superbase, Harvard Graphics, Pro Write
Sales: 408-988-7518, 408-986-8000
Tech Support: 408-988-4005
CompuServe: GO SPCFORUM

Romke Soldaat
1, Chemin des Moulines
34230 Street Bauzille de la Sylve
FRANCE
MegaWord
CompuServe: 1000273,32

Sony Corporation of America
Business Products Division
1 Sony Drive
Park Ridge, NJ 07656
Monitors, disk drives, computers
Sales: 201-930-1000, 800-222-SONY
Parent Office: Sony Corporation

Cont.
6-7-35, Kitashinagawa
Shiagawa-Ku
Tokyo 141, Japan

SP Services
PO Box 456
Southampton,
United Kingdom SO9 7XG
BigDesk, BackMenu
CompuServe: 100016,1625

SPSS
444 North Michigan Avenue
Chicago, IL 60611
Statistical software
Sales: 800-521-1337, 312-329-2400
Tech Support: 312-329-3410

Stac Electronics
5993 Avenida Encinas
Carlsbad, CA 92008
Stacker disk squisher
Sales: 619-431-7474
Tech Support: 800-522-5335
BBS: 619-431-5956
CompuServe: GO STACKER

Starlite Software
Advanced Support Group
11900 Grant Place
Des Peres, MO 63131
Classic Clips, Whoop It Up!, Movie Time Screen Saver
Sales: 800-767-9611, 314-965-5630
Fax: 314-966-1833
Tech Support: 314-965-5630
BBS: 206=437-0116
CompuServe: 70304,3642; 71431,1571

Sonic Foundry
1110 E. Gorham
Madison, WI 53703
Sound Forge
Sales: 608-256-3133
Fax: 608=256-7300

Support Group, Inc
Lake Technology Park
P.O. Box 130
McHenry, MD 21541
TAPCIS — CompuServe access program
Sales: 800-USA-GROUP, 301-387-4500
Fax: 301-387-7322
CompuServe: GO TAPCIS

Symantec
10201 Torre Avenue
Cupertino, CA 95014
Norton Desktop, Backup, AntiVirus, Actor, Q&A
Sales: 800-441-7234, 408-253-9600
Tech Support: 800-441-7234
CompuServe: GO SYMAPPS

T

TAL Enterprises
2022 Wallace Street
Philadelphia, PA 19130
B-Coder
Sales: 800-SCAN-004, 215-763-2620
Fax: 215-763-9711

Tatung Co. of America, Inc.
2850 El Presidio Street
Long Beach, CA 90810
Monitors, computers
Sales: 800-827-2850, 213-637-2105
Parent Office: Tatung Company
22 Chung Shan North Road
Sec. 3 Taipei, Taiwan, R.O.C.

Tektronix, Inc.
P.O. Box 1000, MS 63-630
Wilsonville, OR 97070
Phaser IISD color printer
Sales: 800-835-6100

Thornton Software Solutions
PO Box 26263
Rochester, NY 14626
ClipMate

Cont.
Sales: 716-227-6505
Fax: 716-227-1145
CompuServe: 70743,2546

Toshiba Computer Systems
9740 Irvine Boulevard
Irvine CA 92718
Computers, printers, drives
Sales: 714-583-3000
Parent Office: Toshiba Corporation
1-1, Shibaura, 1-chome
Minato-Ku
Tokyo 105, Japan

Total System Solutions, Inc.
1530 East 18th Street, Suite 6H
Brooklyn, NY 11230
DocuPower, Fileware
Sales: 800-814-2300, 718-375-2997
Fax: 718-375-6261

Tseng Laboratories Inc.
6 Terry Drive
Newtown, PA 18940
Video chips
Sales: 215-968-0502
CompuServe: GO GRAPHBVEN

Turtle Beach Systems
P.O. Box 5074
York, Pennsylvania 17405
Sound boaRoads, software
Sales: 717-843-6916
Fax: 717-854-8391
CompuServe: GO MIDIAVEN, GO MULTIVEN

U-Lead Systems, Inc.
970 W. 190th Street, Suite. 520
Torrance, CA 90502
ImagePals imaging and graphic tools
Sales: 310-523-9393

U.S. Robotics, Inc.
8100 N. McCormick Boulevard
Skokie, IL 60076
Modems
Sales: 708-982-5010

VBZ
User Friendly, Inc
1718 M Street, NW, Suite 291
Washington, DC 20036
VBZ Visual Basic newsletter
Sales: 202-387-1949
Fax: 202-785-3607
CompuServe: 76702,1605

Ventura Software Inc.
15175 Innovation Drive
San Diego, CA 92128
Ventura Publisher
Sales: 800-822-8221, 619-673-0172
Tech Support: 619-673-6000
Fax: 619-673-7777
CompuServe: GO VENTURA

Video Seven/Headland Technology
Video boaRoads
Video Seven went out of business in July 1993

ViewSonic
20480 Business Pkwy.
Walnut, CA 91789
Monitors
Sales: 800-888-8583

Vitesse, Inc.
P.O. Box 929
La Puente, CA 91747-0929
Salvation
Sales: 800-777-7344 or 818-813-1270
Fax: 818-813-1273
CompuServe: 73130,1213

Voyetra Technologies
333 Fifth Avenue
Pelham, NY 10803
Sequencer Plus sound recorders/editors
Sales: 914-738-4500

Weitek Corporation
1060 E. Arques Ave
Sunnyvale, CA 94086
Graphics and co-processor chips
Sales: 408-738-8400

Western Digital
Hard drives
Sales: 800-228-6488
Tech Support: 714-932-0952
BBS: 714-753-1068

WexTech Systems
310 Madison Ave
Suite 905
New York, NY 10017
Doc-to-Help, Quicture for Word for Windows
Sales: 212-949-9595
Fax: 212-949-4007
CompuServe: GO WINAPD

Wilson WindowWare
2701 California Ave SW
Seattle, WA 98116
WinEdit, Address Manager, WinBatch, File Commander, Command Post, Reminder, WinCheck
Sales: 800-762-8383, 206-938-1740
Fax: 206-935-7129
Tech Support: 206-937-9335
CompuServe: GO WILSON; 76702,1072

Windows Magazine
CMP Publications
600 Community Drive
Manhasset, NY 11030
Windows Magazine

Offices: 516-562-5000
Subscriptions: 800-284-3584, 303-447-9330
CompuServe: 76520,2513

Windows Online Review
Box 1614
Danville, CA 94526-6614
Windows Online Review
Sales: 520-736-4376
BBS: 510-736-8343

Windows Programmer's Journal
9436 Mirror Pond Drive
Fairfax, VA 22032
Windows Programmer's Journal
Sales: 703-503-3165
Fax: 703-503-3021
CompuServe: 71141,2071

Windows Sources
Ziff-Davis Publishing Co.
One Park Avenue
New York, NY 10016
Windows Sources magazine
Offices: 212-503-3500
Subscriptions: 800-365-3414, 303-447-9330
CompuServe: GO ZNT:WINSOURCES

Windows Tech Journal
Oakley Publishing
P.O. Box 70167
Eugene, OR 97401-0110
WinTech Journal
Subscriptions: 800-234-0386, 503-747-0800
Fax: 503-746-0071
CompuServe: GO CLMFORUM

WinWear
P.O. Box 346
14150 NE 20th Street
Bellevue, WA 98007
WindowMagic
Sales: 206-882-1530
Fax: 206-557-8324
CompuServe: 70743,1132

Wolfram Research, Inc.
100 Trade Center Drive
Champaign, IL 61821
Mathematica
Sales: 217-398-0700
CompuServe: GO WOLFRAM

WordPerfect Corporation
1555 North Technology Way
Orem, UT 84057-2399
WordPerfect, Presentations
Sales: 801-225-5000
Tech Support: 800-451-5151
Fax: 801-222-5077
BBS: 801-225-4444
CompuServe: GO WPUSERS

WordStar & ZSoft Corporation
P.O. Box 6113
Novato, CA 94948
Publishers PaintBrush, Type Foundry, PhotoFinish
Sales: 415-382-8000, 800-227-5609
Tech Support: 404-428-0008
Fax: 415-883-1629
CompuServe: GO WORDSTAR

Z

Zarkware
2243 E. Thompson
Springfield, MO 65804
Blackout
CompuServe: 71211,1250

Zoom Telephonics
207 South Street
Boston, MA 02111
Modems
Sales: 617-423-1072

ZyLAB Corporation
100 Lexington Drive
Buffalo Grove, IL 60089
ZyINDEX, ZyIMAGE retrieval software
Sales: 708-459-8000

> Writing is easy.
> All you do is sit staring at a blank sheet of paper
> until the drops of blood form on your forehead.
>
> — Gene Fowler

The Windows Resource Kit contains a list of all Windows files, along with a description and the location of each file — "location" means which disk, in the distribution disk set that came in the box when you bought Windows, contains the compressed version of the file.

That list is in the Resource Kit file called **`LAYOUTS.WRI`**. It's an important list. So important that I decided to run it again, backwards. Truth be told, I went back to the original disk sets, just in case there are any errors in **`LAYOUTS.WRI`**. This short appendix contains a list of each distribution disk — both 1.44 MB and 1.2 MB versions — and which files are on each disk. It also tells you how to retrieve individual files from those disks, using Microsoft's EXPAND program.

For a description of the files, and their expanded sizes, look at **`LAYOUTS.WRI`**.

The Distribution Disks

Ever wonder what file is on which Windows disk? Ever accidentally delete a Windows file and wonder how to get it back? Well, here's a handy little cross-reference and a few reconstitution instructions that'll save your tail some day.

Almost all files on the Windows 3.1 disks are compressed; you'll need a program to uncompress the appropriate file and shuffle it to your hard disk. Fortunately there's a utility called **EXPAND.EXE** that does precisely this; it should be in your Windows directory.

There's only one problem with EXPAND: it doesn't have a graphical interface! It's a klunky old DOS throwback.

To use EXPAND, first use the following lists (or the list in the Windows Resource Kit's **LAYOUTS.WRI** file) to find the disk containing the file you want to expand. Compressed files on the Windows disks have an underscore for the last character of the file name: if you're looking for **8514SYS.FON** you'll actually need a file called **8514SYS.FO_**. It just happens to be on the disk marked Disk #1 in the six-disk, 1.44 MB (3½-inch) Windows distribution set, or Disk #2 in the seven-disk, 1.2 MB 5¼-inch distribution set.

Flip through the distribution disks — the disks you got in the box when you bought Windows. Stick the right disk in a floppy drive. Now go into Program Manager. Click on File, then Run. Type in something like this and click OK:

```
expand -r b:8514sys.fo_ c:\windows\system
```

The **-r** tells EXPAND to rename the file as it's expanded: EXPAND is smart enough to know that files ending in **.fo_** are really **.FON** files. The next entry points to the compressed file, presumably on **a:** or **b:**. The final entry tells EXPAND where to put the expanded file.

So now all you need is a cross-reference of files and disks, right? Here ya go. . .

3½-Inch 1.44 MB Distribution Disks

1.44 MB — Disk 1

8514.DR_	8514SYS.FO_	APP850.FO_	COMM.DR_
CPWIN386.CP_	DISK1	EGA.3G_	EGA.DR_
EGACOLOR.2G_	EGAFIX.FO_	EGALOGO.LG_	EGALOGO.RL_
EGAOEM.FO_	EGASYS.FO_	GDI.EX_	HERCLOGO.RL_
HERCULES.2G_	HPEBIOS.38_	KBDHP.DR_	MMSOUND.DR_
MSCVMD.38_	MSNET.DR_	OLIGRAB.2G_	PMSPL20.DL_
SETUP.EXE	SETUP.HL_	SETUP.INF	SETUP.SHH
SETUP.TXT	SYSTEM.DR_	SYSTEM.SR_	TIGA.DR_
V7VDD.38_	VDD8514.38_	VDDCT441.38_	VDDEGA.38_
VDDTIGA.38_	VDDVGA30.38_	VDDXGA.38_	VGA.3G_
VGASYS.FO_	WIN.CN_	WIN.SR_	WINHELP.EX_
XGA.DR_	XMSMMGR.EXE		

1.44 MB — Disk 2

386MAX.VX_	8514FIX.FO_	8514OEM.FO_	BANINST.38_
BLUEMAX.VX_	CGA.2G_	CGA40850.FO_	CGA40WOA.FO_
CGA80850.FO_	CGA80WOA.FO_	CGALOGO.LG_	CGALOGO.RL_
CONTROL.HL_	DECNB.38_	DECNET.38_	DISK2
DOSAPP.FO_	DOSX.EX_	EGA.SY_	EGA40850.FO_
EGA40WOA.FO_	EGA80850.FO_	EGA80WOA.FO_	EGAHIBW.DR_
EGAMONO.2G_	EGAMONO.DR_	EGAMONO.LG_	EGAMONO.RL_
HERC.3G_	HERC850.FO_	HERCLOGO.LG_	HERCWOA.FO_
HPMOUSE.DR_	HPSYSTEM.DR_	IPX.OB_	IPXODI.CO_
KBDBE.DL_	KBDCA.DL_	KBDDA.DL_	KBDDV.DL_
KBDFC.DL_	KBDFI.DL_	KBDFR.DL_	KBDGR.DL_
KBDIC.DL_	KBDIT.DL_	KBDLA.DL_	KBDMOUSE.DR_
KBDNE.DL_	KBDNO.DL_	KBDPO.DL_	KBDSF.DL_
KBDSG.DL_	KBDSP.DL_	KBDSW.DL_	KBDUK.DL_
KBDUS.DL_	KBDUSX.DL_	KEYBOARD.DR_	KRNL286.EX_
KRNL386.EX_	LANGDUT.DL_	LANGENG.DL_	LANGFRN.DL_
LANGGER.DL_	LANGSCA.DL_	LANGSPA.DL_	LANMAN.DR_
LANMAN.HL_	LANMAN10.38_	LMOUSE.CO_	LMOUSE.DR_
LSL.CO_	LVMD.38_	LZEXPAND.DL_	MOUSE.DR_
MSC3BC2.DR_	MSCMOUSE.DR_	NETAPI20.DL_	NETWARE.DR_
NETWARE.HL_	NETX.CO_	NOMOUSE.DR_	NWPOPUP.EX_
OLIBW.DR_	PCSA.DR_	PLASMA.3G_	PLASMA.DR_
POWER.DR_	POWER.HL_	SL.DL_	SL.HL_
SUPERVGA.DR_	TBMI2.CO_	TIGAWIN.RL_	USER.EX_

V7VGA.3G_	V7VGA.DR_	VDDCGA.38_	VDDHERC.38_
VER.DL_	VGA.DR_	VGA30.3G_	VGA850.FO_
VGA860.FO_	VGA861.FO_	VGA863.FO_	VGA865.FO_
VGACOLOR.2G_	VGADIB.3G_	VGAFIX.FO_	VGALOGO.LG_
VGALOGO.RL_	VGAMONO.2G_	VGAMONO.DR_	VGAOEM.FO_
VIPX.38_	VNETWARE.38_	VPOWERD.38_	WINDOWS.LO_
WINPOPUP.EX_	WINPOPUP.HL_	XLAT850.BI_	XLAT860.BI_
XLAT861.BI_	XLAT863.BI_	XLAT865.BI_	

1.44 MB — Disk 3

256COLOR.BM_	APPS.HL_	ARGYLE.BM_	CALC.EX_
CALC.HL_	CALENDAR.EX_	CALENDAR.HL_	CANYON.MI_
CARDFILE.EX_	CHARMAP.EX_	CHIMES.WA_	CHORD.WA_
CLOCK.EX_	DISK3	EGYPT.BM_	EXPAND.EXE
FLOCK.BM_	GLOSSARY.HL_	HERCULES.DR_	MORICONS.DL_
MPLAYER.EX_	MPLAYER.HL_	MSADLIB.DR_	NETWORKS.WR_
NOTEPAD.EX_	PACKAGER.EX_	PACKAGER.HL_	PBRUSH.DL_
PBRUSH.EX_	PBRUSH.HL_	PIFEDIT.HL_	PRINTERS.WR_
PRINTMAN.HL_	README.WR_	RECORDER.DL_	RECORDER.EX_
SCRNSAVE.SC_	SETUP.INI	SNDBLST.DR_	SNDBLST2.DR_
SOL.EX_	SOL.HL_	SOUNDREC.EX_	SOUNDREC.HL_
SSFLYWIN.SC_	SSMARQUE.SC_	SSMYST.SC_	SYSINI.WR_
TADA.WA_	TERMINAL.HL_	THATCH.BM_	TIMER.DR_
VADLIBD.38_	VSBD.38_	VTDAPI.38_	WINFILE.EX_
WINHELP.HL_	WININI.WR_	WINMINE.EX_	WINTUTOR.DA_
WINTUTOR.EX_	WRITE.EX_	WRITE.HL_	

1.44 MB — Disk 4

APPS.IN_	ARCADE.BM_	ARCHES.BM_	CARDFILE.HL_
CARS.BM_	CASTLE.BM_	CHARMAP.HL_	CHITZ.BM_
CLIPBRD.HL_	COMMDLG.DL_	DDEML.DL_	DISK4
DRIVERS.CP_	DRWATSON.EX_	DSWAP.EX_	EMM386.EX_
HONEY.BM_	LEAVES.BM_	MAIN.CP_	MARBLE.BM_
MCICDA.DR_	MCISEQ.DR_	MCIWAVE.DR_	MIDIMAP.CF_
MIDIMAP.DR_	MMSYSTEM.DL_	MONOUMB2.38_	MOUSE.CO_
MOUSE.SY_	MOUSEHP.CO_	MOUSEHP.SY_	MPU401.DR_
MSD.EXE	NOTEPAD.HL_	OLESVR.DL_	PRINTMAN.EX_
PROGMAN.EX_	RAMDRIVE.SY_	RECORDER.HL_	REDBRICK.BM_
REGEDIT.EX_	REGEDIT.HL_	RIVETS.BM_	SHELL.DL_
SMARTDRV.EX_	SND.CP_	SQUARES.BM_	SSSTARS.SC_
TARTAN.BM_	TERMINAL.EX_	WIN386.EX_	WIN87EM.DL_

WINFILE.HL_	WINLOGO.BM_	WINMINE.HL_	WINOA386.MO_
ZIGZAG.BM_			

1.44 MB — Disk 5

ARIAL.FO_	ARIAL.TT_	ARIALB.FO_	ARIALBD.FO_
ARIALBD.TT_	ARIALBI.FO_	ARIALBI.TT_	ARIALI.FO_
ARIALI.TT_	CLIPBRD.EX_	CONTROL.EX_	CONTROL.INF
CONTROL.SR_	COUR.FO_	COUR.TT_	COURB.FO_
COURBD.FO_	COURBD.TT_	COURBI.TT_	COURE.FO_
COURF.FO_	COURI.FO_	COURI.TT_	DING.WA_
DISK5	HIMEM.SY_	MMTASK.TS_	MODERN.FO_
MSD.IN_	OLECLI.DL_	PIFEDIT.EX_	PROGMAN.HL_
REGEDITV.HL_	ROMAN.FO_	SCRIPT.FO_	SERIFB.FO_
SERIFE.FO_	SERIFF.FO_	SETUP.RE_	SMALLB.FO_
SMALLE.FO_	SMALLF.FO_	SSERIFB.FO_	SSERIFE.FO_
SSERIFF.FO_	SYMBOLB.FO_	SYMBOLE.FO_	SYMBOLF.FO_
SYSEDIT.EX_	TASKMAN.EX_	TIMES.FO_	TIMES.TT_
TIMESB.FO_	TIMESBD.FO_	TIMESBD.TT_	TIMESBI.FO_
TIMESBI.TT_	TIMESI.FO_	TIMESI.TT_	TOOLHELP.DL_
WIN386.PS_	WINOLDAP.MO_	WINVER._	WSWAP.EX_

1.44 MB — Disk 6

40291730.WP_	40293930.WP_	CANON10E.DR_	CANON130.DR_
CANON330.DR_	CAN_ADF.EX_	CIT24US.DR_	CIT9US.DR_
CITOH.DR_	COURBI.FO_	DEC1150.WP_	DEC2150.WP_
DEC2250.WP_	DEC3250.WP_	DECCOLOR.WP_	DECLPS20.WP_
DICONIX.DR_	DISK6	DM309.DR_	DMCOLOR.DL_
EPL75523.WP_	EPSON24.DR_	EPSON9.DR_	ESCP2.DR_
EXECJET.DR_	FINSTALL.DL_	FINSTALL.HL_	FUJI24.DR_
FUJI9.DR_	GENDRV.DL_	HERMES_1.WP_	HERMES_2.WP_
HPDSKJET.DR_	HPELI523.WP_	HPIID522.WP_	HPIII522.WP_
HPIIP522.WP_	HPPCL.DR_	HPPCL5A.DR_	HPPCL5A.HL_
HPPCL5OP.HL_	HPPLOT.DR_	HP_3D522.WP_	HP_3P522.WP_
IBM17521.WP_	IBM39521.WP_	IBM4019.DR_	IBM5204.DR_
IBMCOLOR.DR_	L200230&.WP_	L330_52&.WP_	L530_52&.WP_
L630_52&.WP_	LBPII.DR_	LBPIII.DR_	MT_TI101.WP_
N2090522.WP_	N2290520.WP_	N2990523.WP_	N890X505.WP_
N890_470.WP_	NCM40519.WP_	NCM80519.WP_	NEC24PIN.DR_
O5241503.WP_	O5242503.WP_	OKI24.DR_	OKI9.DR_
OKI9IBM.DR_	OL840518.WP_	OLIVETI1.WP_	OLIVETI2.WP_
P4455514.WP_	PAINTJET.DR_	PANSON24.DR_	PANSON9.DR_

PG306.DR_	PHIIPX.WP_	PROPRINT.DR_	PROPRN24.DR_
PRTUPD.INF	PS1.DR_	PSCRIPT.DR_	PSCRIPT.HL_
Q2200510.WP_	Q820_517.WP_	QWIII.DR_	SEIKO_04.WP_
SEIKO_14.WP_	SF4019.EX_	SFINST.EX_	SYMBOL.FO_
SYMBOL.TT_	TESTPS.TX_	THINKJET.DR_	TI850.DR_
TIM17521.WP_	TIM35521.WP_	TKPHZR21.WP_	TKPHZR31.WP_
TOSHIBA.DR_	TRIUMPH1.WP_	TRIUMPH2.WP_	TTY.DR_
TTY.HL_	U9415470.WP_	UNIDRV.DL_	UNIDRV.HL_
WINGDING.FO_	WINGDING.TT_		

5¼Inch 1.2 MB Distribution Disks

1.2 MB — Disk 1

8514.DR_	APP850.FO_	CPWIN386.CP_	DISK1
EGA.3G_	EGAFIX.FO_	GDI.EX_	KBDHP.DR_
LZEXPAND.DL_	SETUP.EXE	SETUP.HL_	SETUP.INF
SETUP.SHH	SETUP.TXT	VDDCT441.38_	VDDTIGA.38_
VDDVGA30.38_	VGA.3G_	WIN.CN_	WIN.SR_
WINHELP.EX_	XGA.DR_	XLAT850.BI_	XLAT863.BI_
XMSMMGR.EXE			

1.2 MB — Disk 2

386MAX.VX_	8514FIX.FO_	8514OEM.FO_	8514SYS.FO_
BANINST.38_	BLUEMAX.VX_	CGA.2G_	CGA40850.FO_
CGA40WOA.FO_	CGA80850.FO_	CGA80WOA.FO_	COMM.DR_
DECNB.38_	DECNET.38_	DISK2	DOSX.EX_
EGA.DR_	EGA.SY_	EGA40850.FO_	EGA40WOA.FO_
EGA80850.FO_	EGA80WOA.FO_	EGACOLOR.2G_	EGAHIBW.DR_
EGALOGO.LG_	EGALOGO.RL_	EGAMONO.2G_	EGAMONO.DR_
EGAMONO.LG_	EGAOEM.FO_	EGASYS.FO_	HERC.3G_
HERC850.FO_	HERCLOGO.LG_	HERCLOGO.RL_	HERCULES.2G_
HERCULES.DR_	HERCWOA.FO_	HPMOUSE.DR_	HPSYSTEM.DR_
IPX.OB_	KBDBE.DL_	KBDCA.DL_	KBDDA.DL_
KBDFC.DL_	KBDFI.DL_	KBDFR.DL_	KBDGR.DL_
KBDIC.DL_	KBDIT.DL_	KBDLA.DL_	KBDNE.DL_
KBDNO.DL_	KBDPO.DL_	KBDSF.DL_	KBDSG.DL_
KBDUK.DL_	KBDUSX.DL_	KEYBOARD.DR_	KRNL286.EX_
KRNL386.EX_	LANGDUT.DL_	LANGENG.DL_	LANGGER.DL_
LANGSCA.DL_	LANGSPA.DL_	LANMAN.DR_	LANMAN10.38_
LMOUSE.CO_	LMOUSE.DR_	LSL.CO_	LVMD.38_
MMSOUND.DR_	MOUSE.DR_	MSCMOUSE.DR_	MSCVMD.38_

MSNET.DR_	NETAPI20.DL_	NETWARE.DR_	NOMOUSE.DR_
OLIBW.DR_	OLIGRAB.2G_	PCSA.DR_	PLASMA.3G_
PLASMA.DR_	PMSPL20.DL_	POWER.HL_	SL.DL_
SL.HL_	SUPERVGA.DR_	SYSTEM.DR_	SYSTEM.SR_
TIGA.DR_	TIGAWIN.RL_	V7VDD.38_	V7VGA.3G_
V7VGA.DR_	VDD8514.38_	VDDCGA.38_	VDDEGA.38_
VDDHERC.38_	VDDXGA.38_	VER.DL_	VGA850.FO_
VGA860.FO_	VGA861.FO_	VGACOLOR.2G_	VGADIB.3G_
VGAFIX.FO_	VGALOGO.LG_	VGAMONO.2G_	VGAMONO.DR_
VGAOEM.FO_	VGASYS.FO_	VIPX.38_	VNETWARE.38_
WINPOPUP.EX_	XLAT860.BI_	XLAT861.BI_	

1.2 MB — Disk 3

APPS.HL_	ARGYLE.BM_	CARS.BM_	CGALOGO.LG_
CGALOGO.RL_	CHARMAP.EX_	CHORD.WA_	CONTROL.HL_
DISK3	DOSAPP.FO_	EGAMONO.RL_	EXPAND.EXE
FLOCK.BM_	GLOSSARY.HL_	HPEBIOS.38_	IPXODI.CO_
KBDDV.DL_	KBDMOUSE.DR_	KBDSP.DL_	KBDSW.DL_
KBDUS.DL_	LANGFRN.DL_	LANMAN.HL_	MPLAYER.HL_
MSADLIB.DR_	MSC3BC2.DR_	NETWARE.HL_	NETWORKS.WR_
NETX.CO_	NOTEPAD.EX_	NWPOPUP.EX_	PACKAGER.HL_
POWER.DR_	PRINTERS.WR_	README.WR_	RECORDER.DL_
RECORDER.EX_	RECORDER.HL_	REDBRICK.BM_	REGEDIT.EX_
SETUP.INI	SNDBLST.DR_	SNDBLST2.DR_	SOUNDREC.HL_
SSFLYWIN.SC_	SYMBOLF.FO_	SYSINI.WR_	TBMI2.CO_
TIMER.DR_	USER.EX_	VADLIBD.38_	VGA.DR_
VGA30.3G_	VGA863.FO_	VGA865.FO_	VGALOGO.RL_
VPOWERD.38_	VSBD.38_	VTDAPI.38_	WINDOWS.LO_
WINFILE.HL_	WINHELP.HL_	WININI.WR_	WINPOPUP.HL_
WINTUTOR.EX_	WRITE.EX_	XLAT865.BI_	ZIGZAG.BM_

1.2 MB — Disk 4

256COLOR.BM_	ARCHES.BM_	CALENDAR.EX_	CARDFILE.EX_
CARDFILE.HL_	CHARMAP.HL_	CHIMES.WA_	CLIPBRD.EX_
CLOCK.EX_	COMMDLG.DL_	CONTROL.EX_	DISK4
DRWATSON.EX_	EMM386.EX_	HIMEM.SY_	HONEY.BM_
MARBLE.BM_	MIDIMAP.DR_	MONOUMB2.38_	MORICONS.DL_
MOUSE.CO_	MOUSEHP.CO_	MPU401.DR_	NOTEPAD.HL_
OLECLI.DL_	PACKAGER.EX_	PBRUSH.DL_	PBRUSH.HL_
PRINTMAN.EX_	PRINTMAN.HL_	PROGMAN.EX_	RIVETS.BM_
SCRNSAVE.SC_	SOL.EX_	SOUNDREC.EX_	SSMARQUE.SC_
SSMYST.SC_	SSSTARS.SC	TADA.WA_	TARTAN.BM_

TERMINAL.EX_	TERMINAL.HL_	THATCH.BM_	WIN87EM.DL_
WINFILE.EX_	WINLOGO.BM_	WINMINE.EX_	WINMINE.HL_
WINOA386.MO_	WINTUTOR.DA_	WRITE.HL_	

1.2 MB — Disk 5

CALC.EX_	CALC.HL_	CALENDAR.HL_	CANYON.MI_
CHITZ.BM_	DDEML.DL_	DING.WA_	DISK5
DRIVERS.CP_	DSWAP.EX_	EGYPT.BM_	MAIN.CP_
MCICDA.DR_	MCISEQ.DR_	MMSYSTEM.DL_	MOUSE.SY_
MOUSEHP.SY_	MPLAYER.EX_	MSD.EXE	OLESVR.DL_
PBRUSH.EX_	PIFEDIT.EX_	PIFEDIT.HL_	PROGMAN.HL_
RAMDRIVE.SY_	REGEDITV.HL_	SERIFF.FO_	SHELL.DL_
SMARTDRV.EX_	SOL.HL_	SSERIFE.FO_	SSERIFF.FO_
SYSEDIT.EX_	TOOLHELP.DL_	WIN386.EX_	WINOLDAP.MO_
WINVER._	WSWAP.EX_		

1.2 MB — Disk 6

40291730.WP_	APPS.IN_	ARCADE.BM_	ARIAL.FO_
ARIAL.TT_	ARIALB.FO_	ARIALBD.FO_	ARIALBD.TT_
ARIALBI.FO_	ARIALBI.TT_	ARIALI.FO_	ARIALI.TT_
CASTLE.BM_	CLIPBRD.HL_	CONTROL.INF	CONTROL.SR_
COUR.FO_	COUR.TT_	COURB.FO_	COURBD.FO_
COURBD.TT_	COURBI.FO_	COURBI.TT_	COURE.FO_
COURF.FO_	COURI.FO_	COURI.TT_	DISK6
HERMES_1.WP_	HERMES_2.WP_	HPELI523.WP_	HPIID522.WP_
HPIII522.WP_	HPIIP522.WP_	HPPLOT.DR_	HP_3D522.WP_
IBM17521.WP_	LEAVES.BM_	MCIWAVE.DR_	MIDIMAP.CF_
MMTASK.TS_	MODERN.FO_	MSD.IN_	NEC24PIN.DR_
PRTUPD.INF	REGEDIT.HL_	ROMAN.FO_	SCRIPT.FO_
SERIFB.FO_	SERIFE.FO_	SETUP.RE_	SMALLB.FO_
SMALLE.FO_	SMALLF.FO_	SND.CP_	SQUARES.BM_
SSERIFB.FO_	SYMBOL.FO_	SYMBOL.TT_	SYMBOLB.FO_
SYMBOLE.FO_	TASKMAN.EX_	TIMES.FO_	TIMES.TT_
TIMESB.FO_	TIMESBD.FO_	TIMESBD.TT_	TIMESBI.FO_
TIMESBI.TT_	TIMESI.FO_	TIMESI.TT_	WIN386.PS_
WINGDING.FO_	WINGDING.TT_		

1.2 MB — Disk 7

40293930.WP_	CANON10E.DR_	CANON130.DR_	CANON330.DR_
CAN_ADF.EX_	CIT24US.DR_	CIT9US.DR_	CITOH.DR_
DEC1150.WP_	DEC2150.WP_	DEC2250.WP_	DEC3250.WP_

DECCOLOR.WP_	DECLPS20.WP_	DICONIX.DR_	DISK7
DM309.DR_	DMCOLOR.DL_	EPL75523.WP_	EPSON24.DR_
EPSON9.DR_	ESCP2.DR_	EXECJET.DR_	FINSTALL.DL_
FINSTALL.HL_	FUJI24.DR_	FUJI9.DR_	GENDRV.DL_
HPDSKJET.DR_	HPPCL.DR_	HPPCL5A.DR_	HPPCL5A.HL_
HPPCL5OP.HL_	HP_3P522.WP_	IBM39521.WP_	IBM4019.DR_
IBM5204.DR_	IBMCOLOR.DR_	L200230&.WP_	L330_52&.WP_
L530_52&.WP_	L630_52&.WP_	LBPII.DR_	LBPIII.DR_
MT_TI101.WP_	N2090522.WP_	N2290520.WP_	N2990523.WP_
N890X505.WP_	N890_470.WP_	NCM40519.WP_	NCM80519.WP_
O5241503.WP_	O5242503.WP_	OKI24.DR_	OKI9.DR_
OKI9IBM.DR_	OL840518.WP_	OLIVETI1.WP_	OLIVETI2.WP_
P4455514.WP_	PAINTJET.DR_	PANSON24.DR_	PANSON9.DR_
PG306.DR_	PHIIPX.WP_	PROPRINT.DR_	PROPRN24.DR_
PS1.DR_	PSCRIPT.DR_	PSCRIPT.HL_	Q2200510.WP_
Q820_517.WP_	QWIII.DR_	SEIKO_04.WP_	SEIKO_14.WP_
SF4019.EX_	SFINST.EX_	TESTPS.TX_	THINKJET.DR_
TI850.DR_	TIM17521.WP_	TIM35521.WP_	TKPHZR21.WP_
TKPHZR31.WP_	TOSHIBA.DR_	TRIUMPH1.WP_	TRIUMPH2.WP_
TTY.DR_	TTY.HL_	U9415470.WP_	UNIDRV.DL_
UNIDRV.HL_			

Es bildet ein Talent sich in der Stille,
Sich ein Charakter in dem Strom der Welt.†

— Goethe, *Torquato Tasso*, 1790

 Windows has its characters. Man, is that an understatement.

Here they are, in all their shining glory, along with an indication of how things sort in the Windows *Strom der Welt*.

---

† Talent is formed in stillness, character in life's torrents.

Windows Character Set

Here are all of the printable ANSI Windows characters, in the TrueType Garamond font, from number 33 (!) to number 255 (ÿ) — character number 39 is in the upper-right corner:

	0	1	2	3	4	5	6	7	8	9
30				!	"	#	$	%	&	'
40	(	)	*	+	,	-	.	/	0	1
50	2	3	4	5	6	7	8	9	:	;
60	<	=	>	?	@	A	B	C	D	E
70	F	G	H	I	J	K	L	M	N	O
80	P	Q	R	S	T	U	V	W	X	Y
90	Z	[	\	]	^	_	`	a	b	c
100	d	e	f	g	h	i	j	k	l	m
110	n	o	p	q	r	s	t	u	v	w
120	x	y	z	{	|	}	~	•	•	•
130	‚	ƒ	„	…	†	‡	•	‰	Š	‹
140	Œ	•	•	•	•	'	'	"	"	•
150	–	—	•	™	š	›	œ	•	•	Ÿ
160		¡	¢	£	¤	¥	¦	§	¨	©
170	ª	«	¬	-	®	¯	°	±	²	³
180	´	µ	¶	·	¸	¹	º	»	¼	½
190	¾	¿	À	Á	Â	Ã	Ä	Å	Æ	Ç
200	È	É	Ê	Ë	Ì	Í	Î	Ï	Ð	Ñ
210	Ò	Ó	Ô	Õ	Ö	×	Ø	Ù	Ú	Û
220	Ü	Ý	Þ	ß	à	á	â	ã	ä	å
230	æ	ç	è	é	ê	ë	ì	í	î	ï
240	ð	ñ	ò	ó	ô	õ	ö	÷	ø	ù
250	ú	û	ü	ý	þ	ÿ				

DOS ("OEM") Character Set

Here are all of the printable DOS characters, in the TrueType MS Line Draw font, from number 33 (!) to number 255 (□) — character number 39 is in the upper-right corner:

	0	1	2	3	4	5	6	7	8	9
30				!	ö	#	$	%	&	'
40	(	)	*	+	,	–	.	/	0	1
50	2	3	4	5	6	7	8	9	:	;
60	<	=	>	?	@	A	B	C	D	E
70	F	G	H	I	J	K	L	M	N	O
80	P	Q	R	S	T	U	V	W	X	Y
90	Z	[	\	]	^	_	`	a	b	c
100	d	e	f	g	h	i	j	k	l	m
110	n	o	p	q	r	s	t	u	v	w
120	x	y	z	{	|	}	~	□	Ç	ü
130	é	â	ä	à	å	ç	ê	ë	è	ï
140	î	ì	Ä	Å	É	æ	Æ	ô	ö	ò
150	û	ù	ÿ	Ö	Ü	¢	£	¥	₧	ƒ
160		í	ó	ú	ñ	Ñ	ª	º	¿	⌐
170	¬	½	¼	¡	«	»	░	▒	▓	│
180	┤	╡	╢	╖	╕	╣	║	╗	╝	╜
190	╛	┐	└	┴	┬	├	─	┼	╞	╟
200	╚	╔	╩	╦	╠	═	╬	╧	╨	╤
210	╥	╙	╘	╒	╓	╫	╪	┘	┌	█
220	▄	▌	▐	▀	α	ß	Γ	π	Σ	σ
230	µ	τ	Φ	Θ	Ω	δ	∞	ø	ε	∩
240	≡	±	≥	≤	⌠	⌡	÷	≈	°	•
250	·	√	ⁿ	²	■	□				

Sort Sequences

The USA version of Windows always sorts characters between number 32 (space) and 255 (ÿ) in the following (ascending) order:

Sequence Number	The Character	Character Number
1		32
2	,	44
3		160
4	•	128
5	•	129
6	,	130
7	ƒ	131
8	„	132
9	…	133
10	†	134
11	‡	135
12	•	136
13	‰	137
14	‹	139
15	•	141
16	•	142
17	•	143
18	•	144
19	'	145
20	'	146
21	"	147
22	"	148
23	•	149
24	–	150
25	—	151
26	•	152
27	™	153
28	›	155
29	•	157
30	•	158
31	!	33

32	"	34
33	#	35
34	$	36
35	%	37
36	&	38
37	'	39
38	(	40
39	)	41
40	*	42
41	+	43
42	–	45
43	.	46
44	/	47
45	:	58
46	;	59
47	<	60
48	=	61
49	>	62
50	?	63
51	@	64
52	[	91
53	\	92
54	]	93
55	^	94
56	_	95
57	`	96
58	{	123
59	|	124
60	}	125
61	~	126
62	•	127
63	¡	161
64	¢	162

65	£	163		105	À	192
66	¤	164		106	Á	193
67	¥	165		107	Â	194
68	¦	166		108	Ã	195
69	§	167		109	Ä	196
70	¨	168		110	Å	197
71	©	169		111	Æ	198
72	ª	170		112	a	97
73	«	171		113	à	224
74	¬	172		114	á	225
75	-	173		115	â	226
76	®	174		116	ã	227
77	¯	175		117	ä	228
78	°	176		118	å	229
79	±	177		119	æ	230
80	²	178		120	B	66
81	³	179		121	b	98
82	´	180		122	C	67
83	µ	181		123	Ç	199
84	¶	182		124	c	99
85	·	183		125	ç	231
86	¸	184		126	D	68
87	¹	185		127	Ð	208
88	º	186		128	d	100
89	»	187		129	ð	240
90	¼	188		130	E	69
91	½	189		131	È	200
92	¾	190		132	É	201
93	¿	191		133	Ê	202
94	0	48		134	Ë	203
95	1	49		135	e	101
96	2	50		136	è	232
97	3	51		137	é	233
98	4	52		138	ê	234
99	5	53		139	ë	235
100	6	54		140	F	70
101	7	55		141	f	102
102	8	56		142	G	71
103	9	57		143	g	103
104	A	65		144	H	72

145	h	104		185	ø	248
146	I	73		186	P	80
147	Ì	204		187	p	112
148	Í	205		188	Q	81
149	Î	206		189	q	113
150	Ï	207		190	R	82
151	i	105		191	r	114
152	ì	236		192	S	83
153	í	237		193	Š	138
154	î	238		194	s	115
155	ï	239		195	š	154
156	J	74		196	ß	223
157	j	106		197	T	84
158	K	75		198	t	116
159	k	107		199	U	85
160	L	76		200	Ù	217
161	l	108		201	Ú	218
162	M	77		202	Û	219
163	m	109		203	Ü	220
164	N	78		204	u	117
165	n	110		205	ù	249
166	Ñ	209		206	ú	250
167	ñ	241		207	û	251
168	O	79		208	ü	252
169	Œ	140		209	V	86
170	Ò	210		210	v	118
171	Ó	211		211	W	87
172	Ô	212		212	w	119
173	Õ	213		213	X	88
174	Ö	214		214	x	120
175	×	215		215	Y	89
176	Ø	216		216	Ÿ	159
177	o	111		217	Ý	221
178	œ	156		218	y	121
179	ò	242		219	ý	253
180	ó	243		220	ÿ	255
181	ô	244		221	Z	90
182	õ	245		222	z	122
183	ö	246		223	þ	254
184	÷	247		224	Þ	222

No one is so rich that he does not need another's help; no one so poor as not to be useful in some way to his fellow man; and the disposition to ask assistance from others with confidence, and to grant it with kindness, is part of our very nature.

— Pope Leo XIII, *Graves de communi*, 1901

This is where you should look when you're ready to buy a shotgun and put your computer out of its misery.

Windows Won't Start

Well begun is half done.

— Horace, *Epistles*, ca 5 B.C.

Windows Is DOA

If Windows doesn't start — and never has started — on your machine, you're in for some interesting times.

 First, pick up the phone. You should contact the people who sold you the computer and scream bloody murder. They may have a solution, although it's far more likely they'll blame somebody else. Tell 'em you expect your machine to run Windows straight out of the box, and you have a friend named Igor who thinks the same way.

If you're running any version of DOS prior to 5.0, it's time to spring for the upgrade. If you have DOS 5.0, the need to upgrade to 6.x isn't burning but with earlier than 5.0, pick up the current version (likely to be 6.2 by the time you read this).

Make sure you have the latest Windows drivers for your video card. But put it aside and at least make sure that you can run Windows with the standard VGA driver. If you're running a SCSI hard drive, contact the SCSI adapter manufacturer. If you have some weird piece of hardware, call the manufacturer and ask if they have any suggestions for running Windows.

Next, see if Windows will start in Standard mode, by typing **win /s** at the DOS prompt. If Windows runs in Standard mode but not in Enhanced mode, you're in luck; see "Windows Won't Run Enhanced" below.

If Windows won't even run in Standard mode, make sure your **CONFIG.SYS** file has a **HIMEM.SYS** line, **FILES=60**, **BUFFERS=20**, and **STACKS=9,256**. (You can almost always look at and change **CONFIG.SYS** by simply typing **edit c:\config.sys** at the DOS prompt.) Try **Ctrl+Alt+Del** rebooting your computer and running Windows again.

If that doesn't work, you probably have a memory conflict. Before you try anything else, you want to "disable RAM shadowing." Yeah, yeah, yeah, it's another buzzword, so don't sweat it. Check your computer's user manual and turn the sucker off; if you can't find the user manual, call the folks who sold you the machine and find out how to do it.

If Windows still won't run, banish it (and almost everything else!) from upper memory by adding the switch **x=a000-ffff** to EMM386. You do that by looking in **CONFIG.SYS** (again) for the EMM386 line and tacking the switch on the end. You'll end up with something that looks like this, more or less:

```
device=c:\dos\emm386.exe x=a000-ffff
```

Just stick the **x=** thing on the end of the line; don't change anything else. (If there's already an **x=** switch on the line, change it to say **x=a000-ffff**.) Reboot your computer and see if Windows will run now.

If that doesn't work, it's time to clean up your **AUTOEXEC**. Go into **AUTOEXEC.BAT** (with, e.g., **edit c:\autoexec.bat**) and put **REM** in front of every line except the one that says **PATH**. You'll end up with lines that may look as complicated as this:

```
REM LH /L:0;1,43920;2,16400 /S C:\WINDOWS\SMARTDRV.EXE
```

Now reboot your computer and try running Windows again. If that works, go back into **AUTOEXEC.BAT** and take out the **REM**s, one by one, rebooting your computer each time, until you identify the offending line. Trace down the company that put that line in your **AUTOEXEC.BAT** (I know, it ain't easy!) and see if they have anything Windows friendly available.

Finally, if all else fails, try running Windows with this line:

```
win /d:b
```

then grab the file called **BOOTLOG.TXT** and call Microsoft — or, better, get online with CompuServe and post the contents of **BOOTLOG.TXT**, **CONFIG.SYS** and **AUOTEXEC.BAT** in the **GO WINDOWS** forum.

If that doesn't work, sell your old PC and buy a new one, with Windows already installed. I'm serious. It'll cost you more in the long run to iron out these momentous problems than it will to swap out your old machine for a newer and better one.

Besides, you always wanted an excuse to do that anyway, didn't you? Yeah. I thought so.

Windows Won't Start Today

If Windows has been running just fine, and one morning you wake up and it won't start at all, chances are good you clobbered a file. Sometimes the clobberable files are pretty obvious (e.g., **WIN.INI**), but others have weird names.

Check that your **win.ini** and **system.ini** aren't clobbered: both files should be in you Windows system directory, typically **c:\windows\system**. Load them into DOS edit and see if they look like ASCII files without garbage. If either looks suspicious, restore from backups, if you have them. Then run setup from DOS and switch to a simple screen driver like the standard VGA driver to see if that helps. At that point drop back ten yards and punt — reinstall.

If you re-install you'll probably find that DOS is running older versions of key programs — an older version of **HIMEM.SYS**, or **SMARTDRV** — but that's rarely fatal.

Here's the safest way to re-install Windows. Make backup copies of your key Windows customizing files — **REG.DAT** and all **.GRP**, **.INI** and **.PIF** files in your Windows directory — and stick them some place safe. Install Windows from the original disks, but put it in a brand new directory, *not* the one you're currently using. Let's call it **c:\newwin**. When the installation is over, change over to the **newwin** directory, and type **win**.

Windows should run, although it won't have any of your customizing. Now copy the old, backed up **REG.DAT**, and all the **.GRP**, **.INI** and **.PIF** files to **c:\newwin**. Will Windows start? If so, you should be in pretty good shape: delete your old Windows directory after a week or two of glitch-free operation in the new directory. If not, you're up the old creek. Your best bet is to re-install Windows once again, and go through the laborious process of re-installing and re-customizing all your applications. Blecch.

Sometimes Startup programs can lock up Windows. It's easy to check. Simply type **win** at the DOS prompt, and hold down the **Shift** key. If Windows runs that way, but chokes when you don't hold down the **Shift** key, you have a bad startup program. Pull all of the programs out of Program Manager's Startup group and add them back one-by-one. (It's also possible that you have a bad program on the **run=** or **load=** lines of **WIN.INI**'s **[windows]** section. See Chapter 8 for details. Note that the **run=** and **load=** programs run whether you hold down **Shift** or not.)

Windows Won't Run Enhanced

 If you have to type **win /s** to get Windows to run, or if you type **win** but click on Program Manager's Help/About screen and discover that you're running in Standard mode, there are a few tricks that may help you figure out why Windows won't run Enhanced.

If you have an 80286 or earlier machine, forget it. Windows can't run Enhanced with the brain dead. If you have less than 1 MB of extended memory, Windows won't run Enhanced either.

In my experience, the most likely cause of Windows Enhanced antipathy is an upper memory conflict, so let's hit that one first. Try typing this at the DOS prompt:

win /d:x

That tells Windows to start, but to avoid upper memory. If using this setting turns Windows into Enhanced mode, you'll have to figure out what's causing the memory problems — and that can take forever. Some insight may be gained by running **win /b** and looking at the file **bootlog.txt**, but then again you might not learn anything at all. To keep Windows from looking at the upper memory area, permanently, look at the **EMMExclude=** setting in **SYSTEM.INI**'s **[386Enh]** section, chapter 9.

Sometimes you'll hit problems with your disk drive: you might accidentally turn "32 Bit Disk Access" on, or Windows will do it for you, or maybe you've just installed a new hard drive and can't get things to work. Try to start Windows with

win /d:f

Should you find yourself magically transported into Enhanced mode, take a look at the **32BitDiskAccess=** setting in **SYSTEM.INI**'s **[386Enh]** section, chapter 9. Also try this switch:

```
win /d:v
```

and see if that helps. If it does, look at the **VirtualHDIRQ=** setting in **SYSTEM.INI**'s **[386Enh]** section, Chapter 9. (Hint: you want to turn it OFF.)

Finally, if all else fails, try

```
win /d:s
```

and if that works, take a look at the **SystemROMBreakPoint=** setting in **SYSTEM.INI**'s **[386Enh]** section. (You want to turn it OFF.)

Resources

> Superior, and alone, Confucius stood,
> Who taught that useful science — to be good.
>
> Alexander Pope, *The Temple of Fame*, 1714

What's the Best Way to Learn Windows?

Take the tutorial: from Program Manager, click on Help, then Windows Tutorial. That's the best way to learn Windows from scratch. You should also take the tutorial again after you've been using Windows for a few weeks.

Other than that, just use it! *MOM* will help you through the sticky parts, but there's nothing that will bring you up to speed faster than banging against Windows day in and day out. It's like learning a foreign language — use it, use it, use it!

What's the Best Way to Get Help?

CompuServe. See *The Mother of All Information Services* in Chapter 6. Don't bother with the phone: you'll only end up frustrated, it'll cost a fortune, and you may not get the right answer anyway. Go on-line.

How Do I Keep Up?

You don't. Windows is changing so fast, with so many new products introduced every day, that you haven't a snowball's chance in hell of keeping up. The best you can hope for is to know where to go for answers. MOM will help there, of course, as will all those back issues of *PC Magazine*, *Windows Magazine*, *Windows Sources*, *PC/Computing*, and the like. If you can't find what you're looking for, get on CompuServe and ask.

Shopping

> To gain teacheth how to spend
>
> George Herbert, *Outlandish Proverbs*, 1640

Which Computer Should I Buy?

 This is the question I hear most often. If you need an answer in one hundred words or less — and don't mind a very opinionated answer — this is what I recommend to my friends for a *minimal* Windows machine: 486 (SX or DX) IDE with local bus video, 4 MB memory, 120 MB hard drive, two floppies, 15 inch monitor (0.28 dot pitch or smaller), 2400 baud modem, Microsoft or Logitech mouse, and a Northgate OmniKey if you like "clicky" keyboards.

Don't pay any extra money for a "brand" name computer.

If you have extra bucks, go for (in this order) 8 MB memory; 200+ MB hard drive; DX/33 or DX2, DX3, or Pentium processor; CD-ROM; 64K cache memory; QIC-80 tape; 9600 baud modem; larger/better monitor.

 I dunno. I learned in er, school, to always look behind me for trouble. Backup with floppies is a no go with 100+ MB of disk space (even with compression, you'll need over 50 floppies). So I put the tape drive much higher on *my* list. Probably something that is essential with the computer.

As for printers: look at the output from an HP DeskJet. If you can stand it, get one; otherwise go for an HP LaserJet.

If you're going to need help, try to buy from a local company with a tech guru who will hold your hand. If you're willing to go it alone, buy mail order.

Which Major Applications Should I Buy?

That's the second-most-frequently asked question. Here's what I recommend to my friends: if your needs are not very great, get Microsoft Works for Windows. If you want industrial-strength applications, jump directly to Microsoft Office. Three exceptions: if you're on a network, go with what everybody else is using; if you're hung up on 1-2-3, get Lotus SmartSuite; if you have lots of WordPerfect files that must be duplicated precisely in Windows, or if you simply *must* have dBase IV, get Borland's application suite.

Weird Stuff

> No one can give you better advice than yourself.
>
> — Cicero, *Ad Atticum*, ca 50 B.C.

"Insufficient Memory" or "Not Enough Memory"

Chances are very good that you have plenty of memory, and buying more RAM isn't going to solve your problem. You probably ran out of "Free Resources". In Program Manager, click on Help, then About, and see: if you're under 30% Free Resources or so, you're begging for trouble. Exit and re-start Windows, and don't open up so many programs at once. If that doesn't work, get on CompuServe and ask.

Files "Disappeared"

This one's for my mother-in-law. Sometimes, when you're dragging files around in File Manager, your files will disappear. Chances are very good you dragged them some place out of the way, that they're still around, but you have to look through your directories to find them. Click on File/Search in File Manager to look for them (a "*" is the wild card for file names). To make it more difficult to screw yourself up in the future, click on Options, Confirmation, and make sure the Mouse Actions button is checked.

Files *Really* Disappeared

If you think you deleted a file accidentally, and you're using DOS 6.x, leave Windows immediately. At the DOS prompt type **UNDELETE**, followed by the subdirectory that held the lost file (e.g., **UNDELETE C:\WIWNORD**). Follow the instructions.

Runaway Printer

If you discover that the file you just sent to your laser or jet printer is the wrong one, pull out the paper tray. Quick. Go into Print Manager, click on the job, and click Cancel. Then reset the printer by pushing the appropriate buttons on the front of your printer.

Fonts Go Screwy

Some Windows apps have trouble handling more than 255 fonts. If you're using Adobe Type Manager, go into its control panel and turn it off. If that doesn't work, you'll have to start removing your fonts, one by one, from the Control Panel's Font applet.

Password Lockout on the Screen Saver

If Windows comes up with a screen that says you have to enter a password, tell it to buzz off. Hit **Ctrl+Atl+Del** twice; re-start Windows (typically by typing **WIN**); go into the Main group, Control Panel, Desktop applet, and clear out the Password check box.

CD-ROM Drive Works Sporadically

Chances are good you have a bad terminator or a cable that isn't seated right. Get out a clean, new, rubber eraser. Pull the cables and/or terminator from the back of the drive. Erase all the contacts. Blow off the gunk and stick 'em back where they belong.

Parity Error; System Halted

Tough luck. You got a bad chip — and locating it can be nigh on impossible. If you just bought a handful of chips, take them out and return them to the vendor. If you've had the memory for a while, you're in for some interesting times.

Some people have luck getting things working again by using a hair dryer to warm up the memory chips, but don't get them too hot. Generally you'll have to run some sort of memory diagnostic routine, and even that won't often find the problem.

General Admonitions

Save often. Save well.

Back up everything. Every day.

When you change something inside your computer, write all the new settings down on a permanent-stick label, and plaster it to the case.

Keep your receipts and warranty slips in one place.

Get it in writing.

Use a credit card. Always.

A Literary Salute

We'll Be Back

For the late Richard Brautigan, one of the geniuses of the 20th century: *mayonnaise.*

SETTINGS INDEX

Note: WINPAK1.ZIP on Disk 2 (not on the CD) may show a bad CRC. Just install it anyway, it works fine.

—*Woody*